Practice makes perfect in accounting.

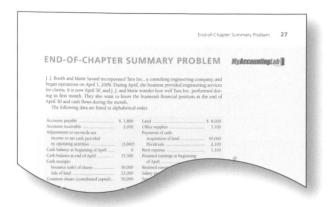

The algorithmic engine that drives MyAccountingLab means you can practise questions any number of times and actually master the content, not just memorize it!

88% of students surveyed found the algorithmic practice to be either very helpful (33%) or extremely helpful (55%)

You will have more "I get it" moments in and out of the classroom!

MyAccountingLab doesn't just provide opportunities for limitless practice – it recreates the "I get it" moments of the classroom by providing clear guidance when you need it most.

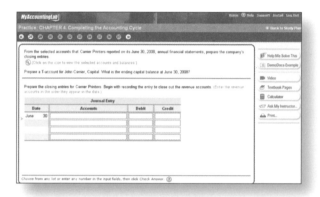

Having difficulty solving a question?

Click the *Help Me Solve This* button anytime and a pop-up window will appear with tips to help you solve the specific part of the problem you are working on. It's just like having a friend standing over your shoulder helping you—right in the middle of the problem— so that you can get through it and understand how to solve it.

Want to view the textbook while you work?

MyAccountingLab contains an *online version of the textbook.* By clicking on the ebook link, you are immediately taken right to the section of the textbook related to the problem you are working to solve. You can even take notes and highlight key passages in the ebook.

www.myaccountinglab.com

WALTER T. HARRISON, JR. Baylor University

CHARLES T. HORNGREN Stanford University

W. MORLEY LEMON University of Waterloo

SANDRA ROBERTSON LEMON Consultant

RAY F. CARROLL Late Professor, Dalhousie University

THIRD CANADIAN EDITION FINANCIAL ACCOUNTING

Pearson Canada
Toronto

Library and Archives Canada Cataloguing in Publication

   Financial accounting / Walter T. Harrison Jr. .. [et al.]. — 3rd Canadian ed.
Includes index.

ISBN 978-0-13-208468-0
   1. Accounting—Textbooks.   I. Harrison, Walter T.   II. Title.

HF5635.F43095 2010   657'.044   C2009-901524-2

978-0-13-208468-0

Vice President, Editorial Director: Gary Bennett
Executive Editor: Nicole Lukach
Sponsoring Editor: Carolin Sweig
Executive Marketing Manager: Cas Shields
Senior Developmental Editor: John Polanszky
Production Editor: Mary Ann Blair
Copy Editor: Deborah Cooper-Bullock
Production Coordinator: Deborah Starks
Layout: Hermia Chung
Photo and Permissions Research: Sandy Cooke
Art Director: Julia Hall
Interior and Cover Design: Anthony Leung
Cover Image: Veer Inc.

5   13 12 11 10

Printed and bound in the United States.

Photo Credits

1 Courtesy of Sun-Rype; 50 Courtesy of Research In Motion; 103 CP PHOTO/Don Denton; 167 Keith Brofsky/Getty Image/Photodisc; 215 Shutterstock; 261 Courtesy of Leon's; 314 CP PHOTO/Andrew Vaughan; 366 CP PHOTO/Larry MacDougal; 422 CP PHOTO/Don Denton; 479 CP PHOTO/Larry MacDougal; 523 CP PHOTO/Mario Beauregard; 561 Courtesy of PotashCorp; 620 Carlos Osorio/Toronto Star

To Jake, Max, Meg, Ben and Tessa

—W.M.L. and S.R.L.

Brief Contents

Contents

Chapter 8
Liabilities   366

Chapter 9
Shareholders' Equity   422

Chapter 10
Long-Term Investments and International Operations 479

Chapter 11
The Income Statement and the Statement of Shareholders' Equity 523

About the Authors

Walter T. Harrison, Jr. is Professor of Accounting at the Hankamer School of Business, Baylor University. He received his B.B.A. degree from Baylor University, his M.S. from Oklahoma State University, and his Ph.D. from Michigan State University.

Professor Harrison, recipient of numerous teaching awards from student groups as well as from university administrators, has also taught at Cleveland State Community College, Michigan State University, the University of Texas, and Stanford University.

A member of the American Accounting Association and the American Institute of Certified Public Accountants, Professor Harrison has served as Chairman of the Financial Accounting Standards Committee of the American Accounting Association, on the Teaching/Curriculum Development Award Committee, on the Program Advisory Committee for Accounting Education and Teaching, and on the Notable Contributions to Accounting Literature Committee.

Professor Harrison has lectured in several foreign countries and published articles in numerous journals, including *The Accounting Review*, *Journal of Accounting Research*, *Journal of Accountancy*, *Journal of Accounting and Public Policy*, *Economic Consequences of Financial Accounting Standards*, *Accounting Horizons*, *Issues in Accounting Education*, and *Journal of Law and Commerce*. He is coauthor of *Financial Accounting*, Seventh Edition, 2006 (with Charles T. Horngren) and *Accounting*, Eighth Edition (with Charles T. Horngren and Linda S. Bamber) published by Pearson Prentice Hall. Professor Harrison has received scholarships, fellowships, research grants, or awards from Price Waterhouse & Co., Deloitte & Touche, the Ernst & Young Foundation, and the KPMG Peat Marwick Foundation.

Charles T. Horngren is the Edmund W. Littlefield Professor of Accounting, Emeritus, at Stanford University. A graduate of Marquette University, he received his MBA from Harvard University and his Ph.D. from the University of Chicago. He is also the recipient of honourary doctorates from Marquette University and DePaul University.

A Certified Public Accountant, Horngren served on the Accounting Principles Board for six years, the Financial Accounting Standards Board Advisory Council for five years, and the Council of the American Institute of Certified Public Accountants for three years. For six years, he served as a trustee of the Financial Accounting Foundation, which oversees the Financial Accounting Standards Board and the Government Accounting Standards Board.

Horngren is a member of the Accounting Hall of Fame.

A member of the American Accounting Association, Horngren has been its President and its Director of Research. He received its first annual Outstanding Accounting Educator Award.

The California Certified Public Accountants Foundation gave Horngren its Faculty Excellence Award and its Distinguished Professor Award. He is the first person to have received both awards.

Horngren was named Accountant of the Year, Education, by the national professional accounting fraternity, Beta Alpha Psi.

Horngren is also a member of the Institute of Management Accountants, where he has received its Distinguished Service Award. He was a member of the Institute's Board of Regents, which administers the Certified Management Accountant examinations.

Horngren is the author of other accounting books published by Pearson Prentice Hall and Pearson Education Canada Inc.: *Cost Accounting: A Managerial Emphasis*, Fifth Canadian Edition, 2010 (with George Foster, Srikant Datar, and Maureen Gowing) and *Accounting*, Canadian Eighth Edition, 2010 (with Walter T. Harrison, Linda S. Bamber, W. Morley Lemon, Peter R. Norwood, and Jo-Ann Johnston).

Horngren is the Consulting Editor of the Charles T. Horngren Series in Accounting.

W. Morley Lemon is Professor Emeritus, University of Waterloo, where he was a faculty member for 24 years. He served as Director of the School of Accountancy in 1987-1988 and 1998-2002. He obtained his BA from the University of Western Ontario, his MBA from the University if Toronto, and his PhD from the University of Texas at Austin. Professor Lemon obtained his CA in Ontario. In 1985, he was honoured by that Institute, which elected him a Fellow; in 2003 he received that Institute's ICAO Award of Outstanding Merit. Professor Lemon received his CPA in Texas.

Professor Lemon was awarded the University of Waterloo Distinguished Teacher Award at the 1998 University of Waterloo convocation. In 2004 he was awarded the L.S. Rosen Outstanding Educator award by the Canadian Academic Accounting Association. Professor Lemon recently has spent five semesters as a Visiting Professor at the University of Texas in Austin and two semesters at the University of Auckland, New Zealand.

Professor Lemon was co-author, with Arens, Loebbeke, and Splettstoesser, of *Auditing and Other Assurance Services,* Canadian Ninth Edition, published by Pearson Education Canada, and co-authored five previous Canadian editions of that text. He is also co-author, with Horngren, Harrison, Bamber, and Norwood, of *Accounting,* Canadian Sixth Edition, published by Pearson Education Canada. He coauthored the five previous Canadian editions of that text. Professor Lemon was co-author, with Harrison, Horngren, and Lemon of *Financial Accounting,* Canadian Edition, published by Pearson Education Canada.

He was a member of the Canadian Institute of Chartered Accountants' Assurance Standards Board. He has also served on the Institute of Chartered Accountants of Ontario Council, as well as a number of committees for both bodies. He has chaired and served on a number of committees of the Canadian Academic Accounting Association. Professor Lemon has served on Council and chaired and served on a number of committees of the American Accounting Association.

Professor Lemon has presented lectures and papers at a number of universities and academic and professional conferences and symposia in Canada, the United States and China. He has chaired and organized six audit symposia held at the University of Waterloo. He has served on the editorial board of and reviewed papers for a number of academic journals, including *The Accounting Review, Contemporary Accounting Research, Journal of Business Ethics, Issues in Accounting Education, Auditing: A Journal of Practice and Theory, Advances in Accounting, Journal of Accounting and Public Policy,* and *CA Magazine.* Professor Lemon has coauthored two monographs and has had papers published in *Contemporary Accounting Research, Research on Accounting Ethics, Journal of Accounting, Auditing and Finance, The Chartered Accountant in Australia* and *CA Magazine.* He has had a chapter published in *Research Opportunities in Internal* Auditing and papers published in the following collections: *Educating the*

Profession of Accountancy in the Twenty-First Century, Comparative International Accounting Education Standards, Comparative International Auditing Standards, and *The Impact of Inflation on Accounting: A Global View.* Professor Lemon served as a judge for *CA Magazine*'s Walter J. Macdonald Award.

Professor Lemon has received a number of research grants and has served as the Director of the Centre for Accounting Ethics, School of Accountancy, University of Waterloo. He has written a number of ethics cases published by the Centre.

Sandra Robertson Lemon presently is a consultant providing accounting and financial services to owner-managed businesses. A graduate of McGill University, she also obtained a Diploma in Accounting from Wilfrid Laurier University. Her experience provides her with a knowledge of the requirements and responsibilities of external reporting as well as an understanding of the value of accounting in providing relevant and reliable information to management.

Ms. Lemon was a staff accountant for an international public accounting firm. In this capacity, she was involved in the conduct of review engagements and audits of financial statements. Following that, she assumed the position of Chief Financial Officer for a Canadian owner-managed business through its growth phase and subsequent merger with an international company. Her responsibilities as a member of the management team included all the accounting systems and reporting, the tax and legal issues, and the treasury function.

Ms. Lemon has served on the board of a number of community organizations; some of this service included executive responsibility.

Ms. Lemon was co-author, with Harrison, Horngren, and Lemon of *Financial Accounting,* Canadian Edition and Second Canadian Edition, published by Pearson Education Canada.

Preface

TO THE STUDENT

Welcome to accounting! You will apply your knowledge of accounting in many diverse ways in your personal and business life.

Our goal in preparing the third Canadian edition of *Financial Accounting* is to explain the fundamentals of accounting and provide opportunities for you to apply your learning in different situations. We have focused on your success in learning the accounting fundamentals. Your success and performance go hand in hand. Many opportunities are provided for you with your instructors to practise accounting fundamentals and their application throughout the course.

Good luck. Your success is our measure of performance.

Walter T. Harrison, Jr.
Charles T. Horngren
W. Morley Lemon
Sandra Robertson Lemon

How Do We Do This?

- We focus on accounting fundamentals and the accounting cycle in the first 3 chapters.
- We build on these first 3 chapters throughout the rest of the text.
- We start with basic procedures and concepts, then place them in a business context.
- We emphasize decisions and how to use accounting information to make those decisions.
- We use examples of real businesses you know, such as Sun-Rype Products, to show you accounting issues in the context of these companies.
- We provide access to the Accounting Cycle Tutorial and MyAccounting Lab, which enables you to explore online the concepts in each chapter and then test your understanding.
- We provide you (and your professor) with the most complete supplements package available.

Features in *Financial Accounting*

Learning accounting can be overwhelming, especially if you have little business or accounting experience. *Financial Accounting* has unique features designed to enhance your learning experience. These features are introduced and described on the following pages.

Learning Objectives are listed on the first page of each chapter. This "roadmap" shows you what will be covered and what is especially important. Each learning objective is repeated in the side margin where the material is first covered in the chapter.

Chapter-Opening Vignettes immerse you in the real world of accounting, where business decisions affect the future of actual organizations. These stories show why the chapter topics are important to real companies. Some of the companies you'll read about include Canadian companies such as RIM, Mullen Group, Leon's Furniture, and Air Canada.

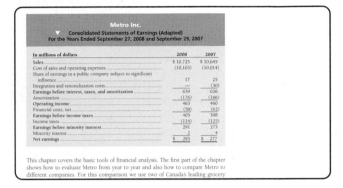

Objectives in the margins signal the beginning of the section that covers the learning objective topic. Look for this feature when you are studying and want to review a particular topic.

Accounting Vocabulary key terms are highlighted in boldface within the text and their full definitions are given at the end of each chapter. These terms are collected in the glossary at the end of the text.

Horizontal Analysis

Objective

1 **Perform** a horizontal analysis of comparative financial statements

Many decisions hinge on the trend of the numbers in sales expense so on. Has the sales figure risen from last year? If so, by how m sales have increased by $200,000. Considered alone this fact is no but the *percentage change* in sales over time helps a lot. It is better have increased by 20% than to know only that the increase is $20

The study of percentage changes from year to year is called **h** Computing a percentage change requires two steps:

NEW IFRS Alert boxes and **IFRS icons** found throughout the text integrate and explain the impact of the International Financial Reporting Standards on accounting practices in Canada and internationally.

IFRS ALERT

The International Accounting Standards Board (IASB) (www.iasb.org) is charged with setting International Financial Reporting Standards (IFRSs). At time of writing, IFRSs are required, or their use is permitted, in more than 100 countries around the world. IFRSs have been adopted by the European Union and the Financial Accounting Standards Board (FASB), the American standard setting body; the United States is working toward convergence of U.S. GAAP with IFRSs.

CICA's (www.cica.ca) Accounting Standards Board (AcSB) made the decision in January 2006 to converge Canadian GAAP for Canadian publicly accountable enterprises (PAEs) with IFRSs. The last year for reporting under Canadian GAAP will be the year ending December 31, 2010. The first year for reporting under IFRS-based standards will be 2011. The changeover date is January 1,

NEW MyAccountingLab icons in the first three chapters direct readers to an online **Accounting Cycle Tutorial** that can be found through the MyAccountingLab site at **www.myaccountinglab.com**. These icons appear whenever a topic is covered in a tutorial or application. When readers enter the tutorial, they'll find 3 buttons on the opening page of each module: Tutorial provides a review of the major concepts, Application provides practice exercises, and Glossary reviews important terms.

Owners' Equity

MyAccountingLab
Accounting Cycle Tutorial
Balance Sheet Accounts and
Transactions Tutorial

The owners' equity of any business is the assets of the business minus its lia We can write the accounting equation to show that the owners' claim to ass residual—what is left over after subtracting liabilities from assets.

Assets − Liabilities = Owners' Equity

The owners' equity of a corporation—called **shareholders' equity**, or *equity*—is divided into two main subparts: contributed capital and retained ea

Decision topics are highlighted throughout the chapter to show how accountants use accounting information to make decisions that affect the rest of the business.

DECISION   How Do We Compare One Company to Another?

The percentages in Exhibits 13-4 and 13-5 can be presented as a separate statemen that reports only percentages (no dollar amounts). Such a statement is called **common-size statement**

On a common-size income statement, each item is expressed as a percentage the net sales amount. Net sales is the *common size* to which we relate the othe amounts. In the balance sheet, the common size is total assets. A common-size state

NEW User Alerts in each chapter focus on issues that can affect accounting decisions or on pitfalls to watch out for.

Stop & Think boxes are inserted at critical junctures in each chapter. Students are asked to "Stop and Think" about what they have just learned.

Mid-Chapter and **End-of-Chapter Summary Problems** give you the opportunity to pause and assess your understanding of chapter concepts at two locations within each chapter—midway and at the end of the chapter. Full solutions appear with the problems for immediate feedback. Each probem has been enhanced with annotations to guide you through the thought processes involved in each step.

NEW Each of the summary problems can also be found on the MyAccountingLab that accompanies the text. MyAccountingLab provides students with the opportunity to practise these problems over and over with new values and data until they've mastered the underlying concepts.

Decision Guidelines, found towards the end of each chapter, show when, why, and how business people use accounting information to make business decisions—why accounting principles and concepts are important in a broader business context, not just to accountants. The Decision Guidelines also serve as an excellent summary of the chapter topics.

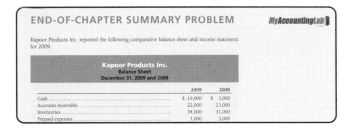

Review the Chapter with These Features

Quick Check provides multiple-choice questions with answers included for quick self-assessment.

Accounting Vocabulary lists and defines the special accounting terms introduced in boldface in the text. Page numbers are given for your reference. These terms are also defined in the Glossary at the end of the book.

Assess Your Progress with These Features

NEW Each of the exercises and problems marked in red can be found at **www.myaccountinglab.com**. Students can practise them as often as they want, and they feature step by step guided solutions to help them find the right answer.

Short Exercises are single-concept exercises designed to serve as warm-ups for homework assignments. The topic of the short exercise and the learning objectives covered are given in the margin.

Exercises on a single or a small number of topics require you to "do the accounting." The topic of the exercise and the learning objectives covered are given in the margin. The pencil icon in the margin indicates a writing exercise or problem.

NEW Some chapters also include **Serial Exercises** that involve an accounting cycle that spans several chapters.

Challenge Exercises provide a challenge for those students who have mastered the Exercises.

A multiple choice **Quiz** follows the exercises in each chapter. This quiz asks students to think back to some of the key concepts from the chapter before moving on to solve some more complicated problems.

Problems are presented in two groups that mirror each other, "A" and "B." Many instructors work through problems from Group A in class to demonstrate accounting concepts, then assign problems from Group B for homework or extra practice. The topic of the problem and the learning objectives covered are provided in the margin.

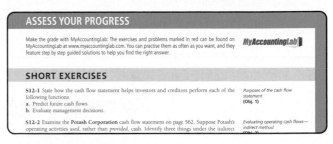

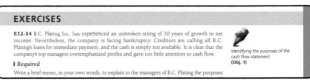

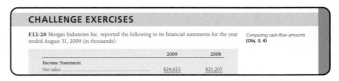

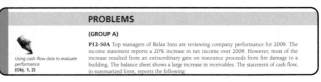

Apply Your Knowledge with These Features

Decision Cases put you in business situations where you need to apply your accounting knowledge to make recommendations.

Ethical Issues are thought-provoking situations that help you recognize when ethics should affect an accounting decision.

Focus on Financials and **Focus on Analysis** cases give readers the opportunity to explore sections of the Sun-Rype Products Ltd. and Mullen Group 2007 Annual Reports, which are included as Appendices at the back of the book. As students work with Sun-Rype and Mullen throughout the course, they will develop the ability to analyze actual financial statements. By using these annual reports, students can compare how different companies present financial information.

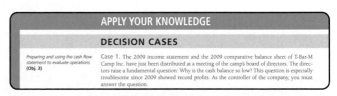

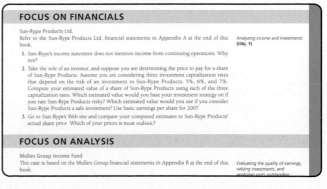

GROUP PROJECT

Select a company and research its business. Search the business press for articles about this company. Obtain its annual report by requesting it directly from the company or from the company's Web site.

Required

1. Based on your group's analysis, come to class prepared to instruct the class on six interesting facts about the company that can be found in its financial statements and the related

MyAccountingLab

NEW Group Projects at the end of each chapter provide both in-class and homework assignments that require collaboration and cooperation among students.

Student Resources

MyAccountingLab is a powerful online learning tool that not only provides opportunities for limitless practice, but recreates the "I get it" moments from the classroom. MyAccountingLab provides a rich suite of learning tools including

- static and algorithmic versions of exercises and problems from the textbook
- an online, interactive Accounting Cycle Tutorial
- IFRS summaries and questions
- Mini-Cases
- Help Me Solve It question-specific interactive coaching
- a dynamic ebook with links to a multimedia library
- Excel application problems
- Access to StudyLife, a social networking site designed to help students find their ideal study partner
- Multiple Pathways to Learning Assessments to help students discover their personal learning style

A **Study Guide** is available for purchase. This chapter-by-chapter learning aid systematically and effectively helps you study financial accounting and get the maximum benefit from your study time. Each chapter provides a Chapter Overview and a Chapter Review, a Featured Exercise that covers in a single exercise all of the most important material from the chapter, and Review Questions and Exercises, with solutions, that test your understanding of the material.

TO THE INSTRUCTOR

Welcome to *Financial Accounting*, Third Canadian Edition. *Financial Accounting* provides full introductory coverage of financial information from both preparer and user perspectives. The clear writing style, logical and well-structured examples, and colourful presentation in *Financial Accounting* are designed to provide students with the opportunity to learn accounting in a business context—to prepare, interpret, and make decisions based on financial information. The text is presented so that all students, no matter what their levels of business and accounting background are or what their future accounting goals are, will be encouraged to develop their knowledge of accounting.

Accounting concepts and procedures in *Financial Accounting* are illustrated using examples from real Canadian companies and some well-known international companies, as well as carefully developed prototypes of real-world business situations throughout the chapters and assignment material. Students are able to see how the accounting concepts they are learning are applied in the world of business to companies and in situations with which they are familiar. This form of presentation in *Financial Accounting* enlivens accounting concepts, provides relevant examples, and makes difficult concepts easier to grasp. As always, interested students, an enthusiastic instructor, and a good text are the essentials for an accounting course's success.

A significant addition in this edition of *Financial Accounting* are the references to International Financial Reporting Standards (IFRS). Chapters, where it is appropriate, have one or more IFRS Alerts that explain the convergence of the *CICA Handbook* with the relevant International Accounting Standards (IAS) as the convergence pertains to the material in the chapter. The IFRS icon appears in the margin whenever the text includes reference to or mention of IFRS.

The students are introduced to Sun-Rype Products Ltd. and Mullen Group Income Fund in Chapter 1 of *Financial Accounting*. Relevant information from the annual reports of the two companies is provided in Appendices A and B, respectively. Subsequent chapters include references to and questions based on the financial statements of these two companies. This approach allows students to apply the material they learn from chapter to chapter to real companies. By the time they have completed the book, students will have seen how what they are learning relates to a real company's public financial face—its annual report.

The first three chapters of *Financial Accounting* introduce students to the process of recording, summarizing, and reporting financial information, the fundamentals of the financial statements, and the acceptable alternative ways of accounting for transactions. While "how to prepare" financial statements is clearly illustrated, the importance of understanding and interpreting the information in the financial statements is emphasized. These three chapters are the foundation for the remaining in-depth discussion of financial information by specific topic. Students will understand the relationship among financial statements by the end of Chapter 1 and the elements of the accounting cycle by the end of Chapter 3. Elements like accounts receivable, debt, and the cash flow statement are introduced in the first three chapters and explored in depth later in the text.

Internal Control and its role in corporate governance is introduced and discussed in Chapter 4 with illustrations of effective systems, appropriate application of controls, and real-world examples of effective and non-effective controls. Chapters 5 through 10 provide coverage of the components of a balance sheet and an income statement. While Chapter 10 focuses on long-term investments, it also reflects the increasingly global nature of commerce in Canada with a section on international operations. Cash flow statements, introduced and discussed briefly in Chapter 1 and included in the discussion of the balance sheet and income statement components in the following chapters, are discussed in depth in Chapter 12.

While the focus of *Financial Accounting* is good accounting, there is discussion of how accounting can be inappropriate, with examples such as Enron. In that way, students learn that accounting is not always the straightforward application of rules. Thoughtful judgment is required.

The topic of Chapter 13, the final chapter of *Financial Accounting*, is financial statement analysis. This chapter, which focuses on analyzing the information in financial statements, pulls together the accounting concepts introduced in the preceding chapters and shows how the wide variety of users analyze financial statements of real companies to make business and investment decisions. These are skills and concepts that students will remember and use in business and investment decisions no matter what their vocation.

Instructor Supplements

Instructor's Resource CD-ROM: This resource CD includes the following instructor supplements:

- **Instructor's Solutions Manual:** This manual contains full solutions for all end-of-chapter material.

- **Instructor's Resource Manual:** This manual contains valuable resources including chapter outlines, teaching tips, and assignment grids.

- **Pearson TestGen:** Over 1500 test questions, including multiple-choice, true/false, and essay questions, are provided in TestGen format. TestGen is a testing software that enables instructors to view and edit the existing questions, add questions, generate tests, and distribute the tests in a variety of formats. Powerful search and sort functions make it easy to locate questions and arrange them in any order desired. TestGen also enables instructors to administer tests on a local area network, have the tests graded electronically and have the results prepared in electronic or printed reports. TestGen is compatible with Windows and Macintosh operating systems, and can be downloaded from the TestGen website located at www.pearsoned.com/testgen. Contact your local sales representative for details and access.

- **PowerPoints:** PowerPoint presentations offer an outline of the key points for each chapter.

- **Personal Response System**: These multiple-choice questions are created in PowerPoint for use in Personal Response Systems. Also known as "clickers," these systems allow instructors to poll students in class and to display aggregated results of answers.

These instructor supplements are also available for download from a password-protected section of Pearson Education Canada's online catalogue (www.pearsoned.ca). Navigate to your book's catalogue page to view a list of those supplements that are available. See your local sales representative for details and access.

Pearson Advantage: For qualified adopters, Pearson Education is proud to introduce the **Pearson Advantage**. The Pearson Advantage is the first integrated Canadian service program committed to meeting the customization, training, and support needs for your course. Our commitments are made in writing and in consultation with faculty. Your local Pearson Education sales representative can provide you with more details on this service program.

Innovative Solutions Team: Pearson's Innovative Solutions Team works with faculty and campus course designers to ensure that Pearson technology products, assessment tools, and online course materials are tailored to meet your specific needs. This highly qualified team is dedicated to helping schools take full advantage of a wide range of educational technology, by assisting in the integration of a variety of instructional materials and media formats.

ACKNOWLEDGMENTS

The authors would like to pay tribute to Ray Carroll, whose contributions to the second edition of *Financial Accounting* continue to be reflected in the updated current edition. We would also like to thank Tom Harrison and Chuck Horngren for their encouragement and support.

Particular thanks are due to the following instructors for reviewing the manuscript for the third Canadian edition and offering many useful suggestions:

Clair Batty, Red Deer College

Dr. Liang Hsuan Chen, University of Toronto at Scarborough

Robert Collier, University of Ottawa

Jeremy Jarvis, Kwantlen University College

Marg Johnson, Thompson Rivers University

Howard Leaman, University of Guelph

Jennifer Li, Brock University

Carol Meissner, Georgian College

Elisa Zuliani, University of Toronto

Thanks are extended to Sun-Rype Products Ltd. and Mullen Group Income Fund for permission to include portions of their annual reports in Appendix A and Appendix B of this text. Appreciation is also expressed to the following sources of material for this text: the Canadian Institute of Chartered Accountants, Deloitte LLP, SEDAR (the website operated by the Canadian Securities Administrators (CSA) and the Canadian Depository for Securities (CDS)), *The Globe and Mail Report on Business,* the *Financial Post, Canadian Business,* The Bank of Montreal, and the annual reports of a large number of public companies.

The authors acknowledge with gratitude the professional support received from Pearson Education Canada. In particular we thank Carolin Sweig, Sponsoring Editor; John Polanszky, Senior Developmental Editor; Jennifer Parks, Media Content Developer; Mary Ann Blair, Manager Production/Editorial; and Cas Shields, Executive Marketing Manager.

The authors would like to thank those colleagues at the University of Waterloo and in the accounting profession for their willingness to help us get it right.

We acknowledge the students and business colleagues who have contributed to our knowledge and experience enabling us to write *Financial Accounting,* Third Canadian Edition.

Prologue: Accounting Much More Than Counting Things

Accounting literacy is the skill and judgement to

- Record financial information
- Report financial information
- Interpret/analyze financial information
- Use financial information in decision making

An in-depth understanding of accounting fundamentals and the accounting cycle is fundamental to accounting literacy.

Accounting literacy can lead to many diverse opportunities. Look at what these accountants do:

Douglas W. Dodds, FCMA, is Chief Strategy Officer of Maple Leaf Foods Inc. Mr. Dodds assumed his current role in 2005 after playing an integral role as Chair, Merger Leadership Council, in the merger of Schneider Foods with Maple Leaf Consumer Foods. As Chief Strategy Officer, Mr. Dodds has the vital role of supporting the overall strategy and value generation across the Maple Leaf businesses and guiding the Company's global growth through strategic acquisitions.

Mr. Dodds' career with Schneider Foods spanned more than three decades. During his tenure he held senior management positions of increasing responsibility including: Division Superintendent, Distribution; Western Controller; Treasurer; Vice President, Finance and Administration; President of Link Services, a distribution subsidiary of Schneider Foods; and President and Chief Executive Officer. Under his leadership, Mr. Dodds established Schneider Foods as a leader in the branded packaged and specialty meats and grocery products in the Canadian market with a strong commitment to product innovation and consumer responsiveness.

Alison Knight, FCA, is the Chief Administrative Officer for the Anglican Diocese of Toronto. As such, she reports to the Archbishop of Toronto. Her background is in financial accounting and reporting, and previous positions in industry have required her to use her accounting training to measure success. Success in those instances was defined as increasing shareholder value. Ms. Knight uses similar tools in her new position in the not-for-profit area of church financial matters, but now performance is measured in terms of the good provided by each dollar of input and each hour of volunteer time, a difficult task. Success is not measured only in financial terms. The Diocese must consider the contribution a parish is making to its members and community as well as the parish's financial viability.

Vern Krishna, FCGA, LLB, LLM, serves as Tax Counsel in the Ottawa office of Borden, Ladener, Gervais, a national law firm, as well as being a Professor of Law and Executive Director of the Tax Research Centre, University of Ottawa. Professional Krishna has served society as a member of the Ontario Securities Commission and as a member of both federal and provincial committees and commissions. He has served his two professions of accounting and law in a variety of leadership roles including as President of the Law Society of Upper Canada and of the Certified General Accountants of Ontario. In 2004, Professor Krishna was made a member of Order of Canada.

Karen Maidment, FCA, was the Chief Financial and Administrative Officer of the Bank of Montreal Financial Group. Ms. Maidment was responsible for BMO Financial Group's financial strategy, accounting and corporate financial information, as well as the taxation, treasury, investor relations, legal, economics, and corporate communication functions. She was responsible for corporate governance, and was accountable for the accuracy and transparency of financial reports to management, regulators and shareholders alike. Ms. Maidment was named Canada's CFO of the Year in May 2006.

Every organization has a mission. Hospitals provide health care. Law firms advise clients. Auto dealers sell cars. All these organizations use *accounting* because no one can physically observe all the aspects of a business. Accounting helps managers view the organization as a whole without drowning in the details. Let's see how people use accounting to make decisions.

Suppose you own a software consulting firm. How will you decide on office rent, employee salaries, and computer software? You will be limited by your cash balance, which you can access from accounting records. After the business becomes a success, how will you decide whether to expand?

Good contacts and intelligence are important, but they are not enough for wise decision making. You must "run the numbers" to determine how much you will earn from the business. Your banker will be more impressed with a detailed plan than with a few vague ideas. Accounting will help you develop a business plan.

Good managers plan for the future. They develop a *budget*, which is a formal plan stated in monetary terms. For example, a product manager for Future Shop will have an annual sales budget. If she makes more than the budgeted level of sales, she will receive a bonus. You need to know how a budget works because a budget will be used to evaluate your own performance.

Accounting helps banks decide to whom they will lend money. Bankers can study customers' financial statements to predict their ability to repay the loan. And they monitor borrowers' progress by examining their financial reports.

Accounting provides information that helps investors pick shares of stock. An investor may not be able to check every detail of a company before buying its shares. But he can examine the company's financial reports and figure out whether the company is profitable and well managed. Why are investors willing to spend their money this way? Because accounting statements and other reports provide data that people trust.

What can you expect if you enter accounting? Exhibit 1 shows the positions within public accounting firms and other organizations. An accounting background opens doors in many lines of business because accounting deals with all facets of an organization. This is why accounting provides such an excellent basis for gaining business experience. After all, accounting is the language of business.

EXHIBIT 1   **Accounting Positions within Organizations**

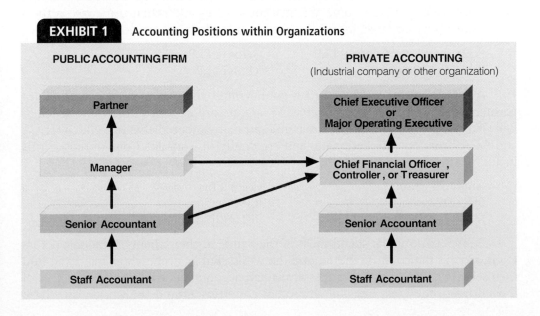

Where Accountants Work

Where can you work as an accountant? There are four kinds of employers.

Public Practice

Public accountants serve the general public and collect professional fees, as do doctors and lawyers. Public accountants are only a small fraction of all accountants. Many of the accountants who are in public practice in Canada have met the educational and experience requirements in accounting, auditing, and tax of their respective professional bodies. Most are CAs or CGAs, although some CMAs are in public practice.

Like private accountants, public accountants provide valuable services:

- *Assurance services* include auditing. In conducting an audit, CAs or CGAs from outside a business examine its financial statements. The CAs or CGAs give a professional opinion stating whether the firm's financial statements agree with generally accepted accounting principles (GAAP). Shareholders and creditors need assurance that the financial picture of a potential investment is complete and accurate.

- *Tax accounting* has two aims: complying with the tax laws and minimizing taxes to be paid. Because combined federal and provincial income tax rates range as high as 53 percent for individuals and 46 percent for corporations, reducing income tax is an important management consideration. Tax work by accountants consists of preparing tax returns and planning business transactions to minimize taxes. In addition, since the imposition of the Goods and Services Tax (GST), public accountants have been involved in advising their clients how to properly collect and account for GST. Public accountants advise individuals on what types of investments to make, and on how to structure their transactions. Accountants in corporations provide tax planning and preparation services as well.

- *Consulting* describes the wide scope of advice CAs, CGAs, or CMAs provide to help managers run a business. CAs, CGAs, or CMAs look deep into a business's operations. With the insights they gain, they make suggestions for improvements in the business's structure.

- *Financial planning* helps individuals map out their investments to save for retirement and children's education expenses.

Most professional employees of the larger accounting firms are CAs. Accounting firms vary greatly in size. Some are small businesses and others are large partnerships. There are four large, international accounting firms:

PricewaterhouseCoopers LLP	Deloitte LLP
Ernst & Young LLP	KPMG LLP

All of these firms are organized as partnerships, and they each have hundreds of partners worldwide. These firms serve the largest corporations in the world (such as Bell Canada, Sony, and British Petroleum) and many other clients as well. Other CA and CGA firms operate nationally and regionally in Canada. Some of these firms include

Grant Thornton LLP	Collins Barrow
BDO Dunwoody LLP	RSM Richter
Myers Norris Penny LLP	PKF Hill LLP

Public accountants spend most of their time at their clients' locations: across town, around the country, and around the world. Public accountants may even find themselves in some unlikely places. Canadian accountants have served in offices of their firms in the U.S., England, and other countries around the world. They have completed forensic accounting assignments and testified in court as expert witnesses, and performed a wide range of services for the firms' clients.

Managerial Accounting

Instead of working for a wide variety of clients, you can work within one corporation or nonprofit enterprise such as a hospital. Your role within the organization is to analyze financial information and communicate that information to managers, who use it to plot strategy and make decisions. You may be called upon to make recommendations on how best to allocate corporate resources or improve financial performance. For example, you might do a cost-benefit analysis to help management decide whether to acquire a company or build a factory; or you might describe the financial implications of choosing one strategy over another. You might work in areas such as internal auditing, financial management, financial reporting, treasury management, and tax planning. The highest position in management accounting is the CFO position, with some CFOs rising all the way to the top to become CEOs.

Government

You can also work as an accountant for the government, be it at the federal, provincial, or local level. Like your counterparts in public accounting and business, your role as an accountant in government includes responsibilities in the areas of auditing, financial reporting, and management accounting. You'll evaluate how government agencies are being run and advise decision makers in allocating resources to promote efficiency. You might find yourself working for the Auditor General at the federal or provincial level, Canada Revenue Agency, a provincial securities commision or the federal or a provincial or municipal government.

Education

Finally, you can work at a college or university or a professional school of accountancy, advancing the thought and theory of accounting and teaching future generations of new accountants. On the research side of education, you might study how companies use or misuse accounting to further their goals, or you might develop new ways of categorizing financial flows, or study accounting practices in different countries. You then publish your ideas in journal articles and books and present them to your colleagues at meetings around the world. On the education side, you can help others learn about accounting and give them the tools they need to be their best.

CA, CGA, CMA: Letters That Speak Volumes

When employers see a professional designation such as CA, CGA, or CMA, they know what to expect about your education, knowledge, abilities, and personal attributes. They value your analytic skills and extensive training. Your credential gives you a distinct advantage in the job market and instant credibility and respect in the workplace. It's a plus when dealing with other professionals such as bankers, attorneys, auditors, and federal regulators. In addition, your colleagues in private industry tend to defer to you when dealing with complex business matters, particularly those involving financial management.

The Hottest Growth Areas in Accounting

Recent legislation, such as the Sarbanes-Oxley Act of 2002 in the U.S. and similar legislation in Canada has brought rising demand for accountants of all kinds. In addition to strong overall demand, certain areas of accounting are especially hot.

Sustainability Reporting

Sustainability reporting involves reporting on an organization's performance with respect to health, safety, and environmental (HSE) issues. As businesses take a greater interest in environmental issues, professional accountants are getting involved in reporting on such matters as employee health, on-the-job accident rates, emissions of certain pollutants, spills, volumes of waste generated, and initiatives to reduce and minimize such incidents and releases. Utilities, manufacturers, and chemical companies are particularly affected by environmental issues. As a result, they turn to professional accountants to set up a preventive system to ensure compliance and avoid future claims or disputes or to provide assistance once legal implications have arisen.

Corporate social responsibility reporting is similar to HSE reporting but with a broadened emphasis on social matters such as ethical labour practices, training, education, and diversity of workforce and corporate philanthropic initiatives.

Assurance Services

Assurance services are services provided by public accountants that improve the quality of information, or its context, for decision makers. Such information can be financial or nonfinancial; it can be about past events or about ongoing processes or systems. This broad concept includes audit and attestation services and is distinct from consulting because it focuses primarily on improving information rather than on providing advice or installing systems. You can use your analytical and information-processing expertise by providing assurance services in areas ranging from electronic commerce to elder care, comprehensive risk assessment, business valuations, entity performance measurement, and information systems quality assessment.

Information Technology Services

Companies can't compete effectively if their information technology systems don't have the power or flexibility to perform essential functions. Companies need accountants with strong computer skills who can design and implement advanced systems to fit a company's specific needs and to find ways to protect and insulate data. Public accountants skilled in software research and development (including multimedia technology) are also highly valued.

International Trade

Globalization means that cross-border transactions are becoming commonplace. Countries that previously had closed economies are opening up and doing business with new trading partners. The passage of the North American Free Trade Agreement (NAFTA) and the General Agreement on Tariffs and Trade (GATT) facilitates trade, and the economic growth in areas such as the Pacific Rim further brings greater volumes of trade and financial flows. Organizations need accountants who understand international accounting and financial reporting, international trade rules, accords, and laws; cross-border merger and acquisition issues; and foreign business customs, languages, cultures, and procedures.

Forensic Accounting

Forensic accounting is in growing demand after scandals such as the collapse of Enron. Forensic accountants look at a company's financial records for evidence of criminal activity. This could be anything from securities fraud to overvaluation of inventory to money laundering and improper capitalization of expenses. Their work is becoming so well known that forensic accountants are appearing in mainstream novels. In *The Devil's Banker* by best-selling author Christopher Reich, a spy teams up with a forensic accountant to chase down a terrorist ring.

So, whether you seek

- a steady career or a life of international adventure
- a home in a single organization or exposure to the needs of an ever-changing mix of clients
- the personal satisfaction of work for a nonprofit or the financial success in a hot new company

Accounting has a career for you. Every organization, from the smallest mom-and-pop music retailer to the biggest government in the world, needs accountants to help manage its resources. Global trade demands accountability, and ever-more complex tax laws mean an ever-increasing need for the skills and services of accountants.

The Financial Statements

Learning Objectives

1. **Use** accounting vocabulary

2. **Learn** accounting concepts and principles

3. **Apply** the accounting equation to business organizations

4. **Evaluate** business operations

5. **Use** financial statements

SPOTLIGHT

What is your favourite Sun-Rype product? Is it one of the apple juice blends, a fruit snack, or Fruit-to-Go™? Sun-Rype has a wide range of delicious, healthy fruit-based products.

As you can see, Sun-Rype sells lots of juice, fruit snacks, and other fruit products: $135.13 million in 2007 (line 1 of Sun-Rype's income statement). On these revenues, Sun-Rype earned net income of $4.64 million in 2007.

These terms—revenues and net income—may be foreign to you now. But after you study this chapter, you'll be able to use these and other business terms. Welcome to the world of accounting!

Sun-Rype Products Ltd.		
▼ **Statements of Operations and Retained Earnings** **For the Years Ended December 31**		
	(in millions of dollars)	
	2007	**2006**
Net sales	$135.14	$130.62
Cost of sales	93.30	85.31
Gross profit	41.84	45.31
Expenses		
Selling, general, and administrative	28.54	30.48
Amortization	4.18	3.86
Interest	0.15	0.04
Loss on disposal of property, plant, and equipment	0.21	0.13
Foreign exchange loss	1.98	0.11
	35.06	34.62
Earnings before income taxes	6.78	10.69
Income taxes	2.14	3.42
Net earnings and comprehensive income	4.64	7.27
Retained earnings, beginning of year	19.31	29.58
Dividends paid	(1.62)	(17.54)
Retained earnings, end of year	$ 22.33	$ 19.31

Each chapter of this book begins with an actual financial statement. In this chapter, it's the income statement of Sun-Rype Products Ltd. The core of financial accounting revolves around the basic financial statements:

- Income statement (the statement of operations)
- Statement of retained earnings
- Balance sheet (the statement of financial position)
- Cash flow statement

Financial statements are the business documents that companies use to represent their finances to the public. In this chapter we explain all the items that appear in each statement. To learn accounting, focus on decisions. Decisions require information, and accounting provides much of the information for people's decisions, as illustrated in the following diagram:

You take actions every day that require accounting information. For example, the decision to go skiing depends on whether you can afford it. The same is true for big companies such as Google and Petro-Canada. They must weigh what they want to accomplish against what they can afford.

We begin with an overview of how accounting is practised.

Business Decisions

Sun-Rype managers make lots of decisions. Which juices and fruit products are selling best? Is Sun-Rype Vita Burst™ bringing in profits? Should Sun-Rype expand? Accounting helps managers make these decisions.

Take a look at Sun-Rype Products Ltd.'s income statement on page 2. Focus on net income (line 12). Net income is profit, the excess of revenues over expenses. You can see that Sun-Rype earned a $4.64 million profit in 2007. That's good news because it means that Sun-Rype had $4.64 million more revenue than expenses for the year.

Sun-Rype's income statement conveys more good news. Sales for 2007 exceeded sales for 2006. Companies want sales to grow because increasing sales signal that the company is growing, and investors buy the shares of growing companies.

Suppose you have $5,000 to invest. What information would you need before investing in Sun-Rype Products Ltd.? Let's see how accounting works.

Accounting Is the Language of Business

Accounting is the information system that measures business activities, processes data into reports, and communicates results to decision makers. Accounting is "the language of business." The better you understand the language, the better you can manage your own finances.

Accounting produces financial statements that report information about a business entity. The financial statements measure performance and tell us where a business stands in financial terms. In this chapter we focus on Sun-Rype Products Ltd.

Don't mistake bookkeeping for accounting. Bookkeeping is a mechanical part of accounting, just as arithmetic is a part of mathematics. Exhibit 1-1 illustrates accounting's role in business. The process starts and ends with people making decisions.

EXHIBIT 1-1   **The Flow of Accounting Information**

1. People make decisions.

2. Business transactions occur.

3. Businesses report their results.

  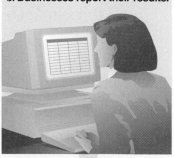

Who Uses Accounting Information?

Decision makers need information. A banker decides who gets a loan. Sun-Rype decides whether to add a new juice flavour. Let's see how some others use accounting information.

Individuals. People such as you manage bank accounts and decide whether to rent an apartment or buy a house. Accounting provides the information you need.

Investors and Creditors. Investors and creditors provide the money to finance Sun-Rype. People want to know how much income they can expect to earn on an investment. This requires accounting data.

Government and Regulatory Agencies. Most organizations face government regulation. For example, the Ontario Securities Commission (OSC), a provincial agency, requires public companies to report to the investing public. Sun-Rype Products Ltd., Magna International Inc., and other companies publish annual reports.

Taxing Authorities. There are all kinds of taxes. Sun-Rype pays property tax on its assets and income tax on profits. Retailers collect sales tax and goods and services tax from customers. Most taxes are based on accounting data. Taxing authorities use the accounting information provided to them to determine if companies are paying the correct amount of taxes.

Not-for-profit Organizations. Not-for-profit organizations—churches, hospitals, and charities, such as Habitat for Humanity and the Canadian Red Cross—base their decisions on accounting data.

Two Kinds of Accounting: Financial Accounting and Management Accounting

There are both *external users* and *internal users* of accounting information. We can therefore classify accounting into two branches.

Financial accounting provides information for people outside the firm, such as investors, creditors, government agencies, and the public. This information must meet standards of relevance, reliability, and disclosure.

Management accounting generates inside information for the managers of Sun-Rype Products Ltd. Management information is tailored to the needs of managers and must also meet high standards of reliability.

Ethics in Accounting and Business

Ethical considerations are important to accounting. Companies need money to operate. To attract investors and obtain loans, companies must provide information to the public. Without that information, people won't invest. The Canadian and provincial governments have laws that require companies to report relevant, reliable information to outsiders. Relevant means the information has predictive value or feedback value and is timely and thus can influence a decision. Reliable means the information is verifiable and is free from bias.

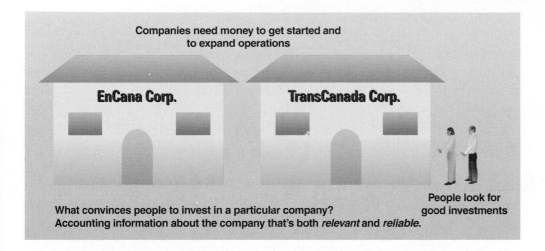

Companies need money to get started and to expand operations

EnCana Corp.   **TransCanada Corp.**

People look for good investments

What convinces people to invest in a particular company? Accounting information about the company that's both *relevant* and *reliable*.

Occasionally, a company will report biased information. It may overstate profits or understate the company's debts. In recent years, Livent Inc., the theatrical production company, allegedly kept two sets of books and falsified its financial reports. Several well-known U.S. companies were charged with reporting misleading information. Enron Corporation, at the time one of the largest companies in the United States, admitted understating its liabilities (debts). Xerox and WorldCom were accused of overstating profits. If these accusations were true, the published financial data of these companies were not reliable and thus failed the basic test of good ethics. The result? People invested in them, lost money, and filed lawsuits to recover their losses. Reporting relevant, reliable information to the public is the ethical course of action.

Standards of Professional Conduct for Accountants. What are the criteria for ethical judgments in accounting? The three professional accounting bodies discussed below, other professional organizations, and large companies have codes of conduct that require high levels of ethical conduct. There is a need for high standards of ethical behaviour by accountants if people are going to rely on information for decision making produced by or audited by those accountants.

The position of accounting in today's business world has created the need for control over the professional, educational, and ethical standards of accountants. Through statutes passed by provincial legislatures, the three accounting organizations in Canada have received the authority to set educational requirements and professional standards for their members and to discipline members who fail to adhere to their codes of conduct. The acts make them self-regulating bodies, just as provincial associations of doctors and lawyers are.

The *Canadian Institute of Chartered Accountants (CICA)*, whose members are chartered accountants or CAs, is the oldest accounting organization in Canada. CAs belong to a provincial institute (*ordre* in Quebec) and through that body to the CICA. The provincial institutes and ordre grant the right to use the professional designation CA and have the responsibility for developing and enforcing the code of professional conduct that guides the actions of the CAs in that province.

Members of the *Certified General Accountants Association of Canada (CGAAC)* are allowed to use the designation Certified General Accountant or CGA. They belong to provincial associations (*ordre* in Quebec) and, in turn, to the CGAAC. The provincial associations and ordre grant the right to use the professional designation CGA and are responsible for developing and administering the code of professional conduct that guides the actions of the CGAs in that province.

Members of the *Society of Management Accountants of Canada (SMAC)* are permitted to use the designation Certified Management Accountant or CMA. They belong to provincial societies (*ordre* in Quebec) and, in turn, to the SMAC. The provincial societies and ordre grant the right to use the professional designation CMA and are responsible for developing and administering the code of professional conduct that guides the actions of CMAs in that province.

The recent corporate failures have driven home the need for good ethics among accountants as never before.

DECISION **We Need an Audit to Validate the Financial Statements**

Each chapter of this book begins with an actual financial statement. Chapter 1 has the income statement of Sun-Rype Products Ltd. Throughout this book we use actual examples to show how accounting relates to your daily activities. For example, when you are thirsty do you choose Sun-Rype Apple Juice, Orange Juice, or Strawberry-Kiwi Juice? All these brands are Sun-Rype products.

Sun-Rype Products Ltd. reports that it's profitable. But did the company really sell that much juice and that many fruit snacks? Were profits really $4.64 million? Who reports these figures?

Sun-Rype's top management is responsible for both (a) company operations—how well the company *really* performs—and (b) the information Sun-Rype *reports* to the public. Can you see the conflict of interest here? A company's real performance may differ from what gets reported to the public. Company management has a built-in motivation to make the company look good—especially when times are tough. Most managers are high-principled men and women, but a few managers have "cooked the books" to overstate their companies' *reported* profits.

How does society deal with this conflict of interest? Canadian and provincial regulation and securities acts require all companies that sell shares to the public to have an annual audit by independent accountants. Audits are intended to protect the public by ensuring that accounting data are relevant and reliable. It turns out that Sun-Rype Products Ltd. passed the audit test. The accounting firm of Deloitte & Touche LLP audited the financial statements of Sun-Rype Products Ltd. and stated that in its opinion, "The financial statements present fairly the financial position of the company and the results of its operations and its cash flows."

The take-away lesson is this: Avoid a company if its auditor does not state that the company's financial statements "present fairly...."

Organizing a Business

A business takes one of three forms of organization, and the accounting can depend on which form the organization takes. Therefore, you need to understand the differences among the three types: proprietorships, partnerships, and corporations. Exhibit 1-2 compares the three types.

Proprietorships. A **proprietorship** has a single owner, called the proprietor. Proprietorships tend to be small businesses or individual professional organizations, such as physicians, lawyers, and accountants. From a legal perspective, the business *is* the proprietor, and the proprietor is personally liable for all business debts. But for accounting, a proprietorship is distinct from its proprietor. Thus, the business records do not include the proprietor's personal finances.

Partnerships. A **partnership** joins two or more persons as co-owners, and each owner is a partner. Many retail establishments and some professional organizations of physicians, lawyers, and accountants are partnerships. Most partnerships are small or medium-sized, but some are gigantic, with several hundred partners. Accounting treats the partnership as a separate organization, distinct from the personal affairs of each partner. But the law views a partnership as the partners: Normally, each partner is personally liable for all the partnership's debts. For this reason, partnerships can be quite risky. Recently, professional partnerships such as public accounting firms and law firms have become *limited liability partnerships* (LLP), which limits claims against the partners to the partnership assets.

Corporations. A **corporation** is an incorporated business owned by **shareholders**. These people own shares of **stock**, which represent shares of ownership in a corporation. Corporations dominate business activity in Canada even though proprietorships and partnerships are more numerous. Corporations transact much more business and are larger in terms of total assets, income, and number of employees. Most well-known companies—such as Intrawest, Petro-Canada, Air Canada, and one of the two companies we will examine in depth throughout this text, Sun-Rype Products Ltd.—are corporations. Corporation names (in their entirety) include *Limited*, *Incorporated*, or *Corporation* (abbreviated *Ltd.*, *Inc.*, and *Corp.*, respectively) to indicate that they are corporations—for example, The Forzani Group Ltd., Danier Leather Inc., and Lions Gate Entertainment Corp. Some bear the name "Company," such as Hudson's Bay Company. A proprietorship and a partnership can also bear the name "Company."

A corporation is a business entity formed under federal or provincial law. From a legal perspective, unlike proprietorships and partnerships, a corporation is distinct from its owners. The corporation is like an artificial person and possesses many of the rights that a person has. Unlike proprietors and partners, the shareholders who own a corporation have no personal obligation for its debts. So we say shareholders have limited liability, as do partners in an LLP. Also unlike the other forms of organization, a corporation pays income taxes. In the other two cases, income tax is paid personally by the proprietor or partners.

A corporation's ownership is divided into shares of stock. One becomes a shareholder by purchasing the corporation's shares. Sun-Rype Products Ltd., for example, has issued more than 10,000,000 shares of stock. Any investor can become a co-owner by buying 1, 30, 100, 5,000, or any number of shares of its stock through the Toronto Stock Exchange (TSX), a national stock exchange.

Ultimate control of a corporation rests with the shareholders. They normally get one vote for each common share they own. Shareholders elect the members of the

EXHIBIT 1-2	The Various Forms of Business Organization		
	Proprietorship	*Partnership*	*Corporation*
Owner(s)	Proprietor—one owner	Partners—two or more owners	Shareholders—generally many owners
Life of entity	Limited by owner's choice or death	Limited by owners' choices or death	Indefinite
Personal liability of owner(s) for business debts	Proprietor is personally liable	Partners are usually personally liable	Shareholders are not personally liable
Accounting status	Accounting entity is separate from proprietor	Accounting entity is separate from partners	Accounting entity is separate from shareholders

board of directors, which sets policy for the corporation and appoints officers. The board elects a chairperson, who is the most powerful person in the corporation and may also carry the title chief executive officer (CEO), the top management position. Most corporations also have vice-presidents in charge of sales, manufacturing, accounting and finance, and other key areas.

Over the past years, a number of Canadian companies converted their shares into units and became income trusts. An *income trust* is an entity that holds an underlying asset or group of assets such as a company. Income trusts have unitholders instead of shareholders. Most of the income these assets generate is distributed to the unitholders. In contrast, shareholder-owned companies usually retain and re-invest their earnings, and sometimes pay out a small portion of earnings to their shareholders as dividends. Income trust distributions are not assured, however, and depend entirely on the financial performance of the underlying entity or entities.

An income trust structure is formed when, instead of offering its securities directly to the public, an operating entity creates a trust. The trust offers units to the public and uses the proceeds to purchase the common shares and high-yield debt of the operating entity. The *Income Tax Act* changed the tax status of income trusts in 2006 (to be effective in 2011 for existing trusts and in 2007 for trusts created after the announcement), and their popularity has declined.

An example of a company that has become an income trust is Mullen Transportation Inc., which was a publicly listed company for a number of years, including the fiscal year ended December 31, 2004. In July 2005, an income trust, Mullen Group Income Fund, was formed, and it acquired all the assets of Mullen Transportation Inc. The shareholders of Mullen Transportation became unitholders of Mullen Group Income Fund. Mullen Group Income Fund is one of the two companies that will be examined in depth throughout this text.

How to Do Accounting: Principles and Concepts

Accountants follow professional guidelines called **GAAP**, which stands for **generally accepted accounting principles**. In Canada, the CICA has the responsibility for issuing accounting standards that form the basis of Canadian GAAP. GAAP are like the laws of accounting: rules for conducting behaviour in a way acceptable to the majority of people. The rules that govern how accountants measure, process, and communicate financial information fall under the heading GAAP.

The Canadian Securities Administrators, a body composed of officials appointed by the provincial and territorial governments with securities exchanges to set securities law, issued National Policy Statement 27 (NP 27) designating the *CICA Handbook* as generally accepted accounting principles. The *Canada Business Corporations Act* also designated the *CICA Handbook* as GAAP, and the *Ontario Securities Act* followed suit. In these ways, the CICA became the official promulgator of generally accepted accounting principles. Exhibit 1-3 illustrates how the authority for setting GAAP is delegated to the CICA by the federal and provincial and territorial governments and the Securities Administrators.

GAAP is in a state of flux as new issues arise. In 1988, the CICA set up the Emerging Issues Committee (EIC) to develop appropriate accounting standards for emerging accounting issues on a timely basis. The abstracts of issues published by the EIC are considered to be an authoritative source of GAAP in the absence of an accounting Recommendation. GAAP is summarized in Appendix E.

EXHIBIT 1-3   Flow of Authority for Developing GAAP

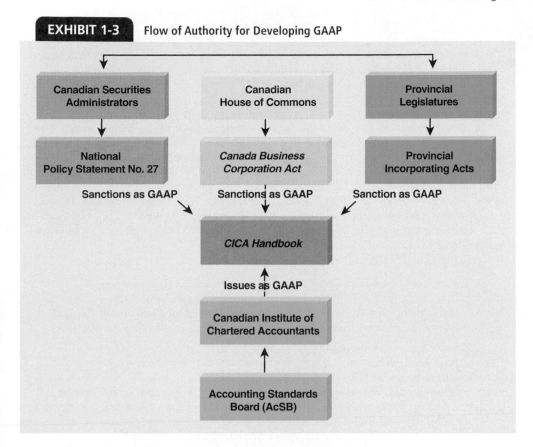

The world of commerce is becoming more global, and the global accounting profession recognized that there was a need for international accounting standards (see Exhibit 1-4). The International Accounting Standards Board was set up to meet that need.

GAAP rest on a conceptual framework (see Exhibit 1-5). To be useful, information must be understandable, relevant, reliable, and comparable. This course will expose you to the generally accepted methods of accounting. We will discuss these as they become relevant in each chapter. We also summarize them in Appendix E. First, however, you need to understand several basic concepts that provide the foundation for accounting practice.

EXHIBIT 1-4   Creation and Convergence of International Financial Reporting Standards

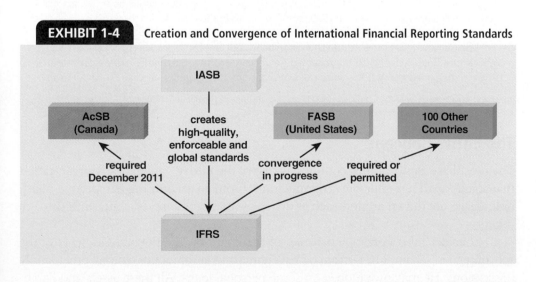

IFRS ALERT

The International Accounting Standards Board (IASB) (www.iasb.org) is charged with setting International Financial Reporting Standards (IFRSs). At time of writing, IFRSs are required, or their use is permitted, in more than 100 countries around the world. IFRSs have been adopted by the European Union and the Financial Accounting Standards Board (FASB), the American standard setting body; the United States is working toward convergence of U.S. GAAP with IFRSs.

CICA's (www.cica.ca) Accounting Standards Board (AcSB) made the decision in January 2006 to converge Canadian GAAP for Canadian publicly accountable enterprises (PAEs) with IFRSs. The last year for reporting under Canadian GAAP will be the year ending December 31, 2010. The first year for reporting under IFRS-based standards will be 2011. The changeover date is January 1, 2011, for annual periods beginning on or after January 1, 2011, when IFRSs will replace Canadian GAAP for PAEs. Note: The converged standards will apply to PAEs and not to private companies, not-for-profits, and government entities. Those organizations will use the *CICA Handbook— Accounting* in the short run. The IASB is working on developing IFRSs for small and medium enterprises (SMEs).

The CICA states in *IFRS in Canada* that

> IFRSs are generally similar to Canadian GAAP. They are based on a similar conceptual framework with similar style and form, and generally reach similar conclusions. This fundamental similarity, combined with the orderly, five-year transition period adopted by the AcSB, should ensure a relatively smooth transition for Canada's publicly accountable enterprises.

> IFRSs are based on a conceptual framework that is substantially the same as that on which Canadian standards are based. IFRSs cover many of the same topics and reach similar conclusions on many issues. The style and form of IFRSs are generally quite similar to Canadian standards and considerably more similar than U.S. standards (although there is some variation within all three sets of standards). IFRSs are laid out in the same way as the *CICA Handbook—Accounting* (Handbook) Sections, highlight the principles and use similar language. Individual IFRSs and Handbook Sections are of similar length and depth of detail. The complete sets of standards are also similar in length.

> The following examples from *IFRS in Canada* are useful illustrations of the work in process:

- IASB and FASB have commenced a project to develop a converged conceptual framework. Canada is participating. The IASB/FASB project is a long-term project—parts of which might not be complete until after the required convergence in 2011.
- AcSB has approved amendments to Section 1400 that converge with the going-concern paragraphs of IAS 1.
- AcSB has issued an Exposure Draft on internally developed intangible assets, the proposals of which would require changes to Section 1000. If adopted, the changes would clarify the role of "matching" in financial reporting and make Section 1000 more similar to the framework in this regard.

The AcSB recognizes that many Canadian companies are cross-listed in the U.S. and that, despite the fact that FASB is also working towards convergence, there could be situations where there is divergence between certain IFRS and U.S. GAAP. In those situations the AcSB will consider the impact of adopting the particular IFRS before the differences are reconciled.

The Canadian Securities Administrators issued CSA Concept Paper 52-402 "Possible Changes to Securities Rules Relating To International Financial Reporting Standards," which considers the issues relating to adopting IFRSs since existent securities laws require Canadian GAAP for PAEs.

Source: *The CICA's Guide to IFRS in Canada* (2008 Canadian Institute of Chartered Accountants: Toronto).

The Entity Concept

Objective

2 **Learn** accounting concepts and principles

The most basic concept in accounting is that of the **entity**, which is any organization that stands apart as a separate economic unit. From an accounting perspective, sharp boundaries are drawn around each entity so as not to confuse its affairs with those of others.

Consider John Forzani, chairman of the board of The Forzani Group Ltd., the sporting goods chain. Mr. Forzani owns a home and automobiles, among other family possessions. He may owe money on some personal loans. All these assets and liabili-

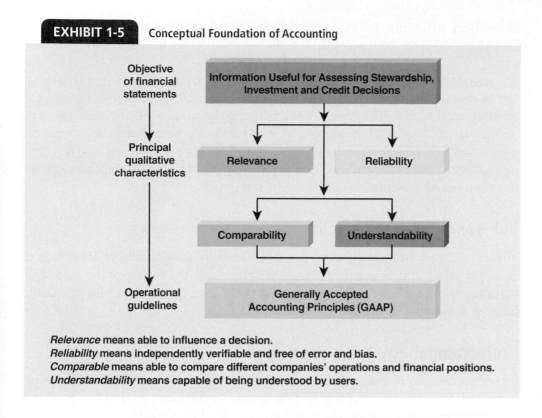

EXHIBIT 1-5   Conceptual Foundation of Accounting

Objective of financial statements → Information Useful for Assessing Stewardship, Investment and Credit Decisions

Principal qualitative characteristics → Relevance   Reliability

Comparability   Understandability

Operational guidelines → Generally Accepted Accounting Principles (GAAP)

Relevance means able to influence a decision.
Reliability means independently verifiable and free of error and bias.
Comparable means able to compare different companies' operations and financial positions.
Understandability means capable of being understood by users.

ties belong to John Forzani and have nothing to do with The Forzani Group Ltd. Likewise, The Forzani Group Ltd.'s cash, computers, and store equipment belong to the company, not to John Forzani. Why? Because the entity concept draws a sharp boundary around each entity. In this case The Forzani Group Ltd. is one entity and John Forzani is a separate entity.

Let's consider Toyota, which has several divisions. Toyota management evaluates each division as a separate entity. If Lexus sales are dropping, Toyota can identify the reason. But if sales figures from all divisions of the company are combined, then management cannot tell how many Lexuses the company is selling. To correct the problem, managers need data for each division of the company. The transactions of different entities should not be accounted for together. Each entity should be evaluated separately.

Relevance Characteristic

Relevance is usually defined in terms of the predictive value or feedback value of the information. If the information in the financial statements is to be useful for users, it must be appropriate to the decision the user wishes to make. If information is to be useful for decision making, it must be received by the decision maker before the information loses its capacity to influence a decision. Information becomes less useful for decision making as time passes. For example, if the user is a bank loan officer and the company is requesting a loan, the information must be such that the loan officer can reasonably assess whether or not the company has the ability to pay the carrying costs (interest) on the loan and repay the principal when it comes due.

The Reliability Principle

To ensure that they are reliable, accounting records and statements are based on the most objective data available. This is the **reliability principle**, also called the

objectivity principle. Ideally, accounting records are based on information supported by objective evidence. Without the reliability principle, accounting records would be based on opinions and subject to dispute.

Suppose you want to open a stereo shop and are trying to buy a small building. You believe the building is worth $155,000. Two real estate professionals appraise the building at $147,000. The owner of the building demands $160,000. Suppose you pay that price. Your belief about the building's value and the real-estate appraisals are merely opinions. The accounting value of the building is $160,000 because it is supported by the objective evidence of a completed transaction. The business should therefore record the building at its cost of $160,000.

Relevance versus Reliability

There is a tension between the two concepts of relevance and reliability. For example, an appraisal of undeveloped land may be relevant to the owner of the land who wishes to sell it; however, the historical cost of the land is more objective or reliable from an accounting perspective.

Understandability Characteristic

If the information in financial statements is to be useful for users of the financial statements, the users must be able to understand the information. The users need not be experts but should have a reasonable knowledge of accounting.

Comparability Characteristic

Users of financial statements should be able to compare different companies in terms of their operations and financial position.

The Cost Principle

The **cost principle** states that acquired assets and services should be recorded at their actual *historical cost*.[2] Suppose your stereo shop purchases stereo equipment from a supplier who is going out of business. Assume that you get a good deal on this purchase and pay only $2,000 for merchandise that would have cost you $3,000 elsewhere. The cost principle requires you to record this merchandise at its actual cost of $2,000, not the $3,000 that you believe it is worth.

The Going-Concern Concept

The **going-concern concept** assumes that the entity will remain in operation long enough to use existing assets—land, buildings, supplies—for their intended purposes. Consider the alternative to the going-concern concept: going out of business.

A store holding a going-out-of-business sale is trying to sell all its assets. In that case, the relevant measure of the assets is their current market or liquidation value.

---

[2]The cost principle may not be as powerful as it once was. Accounting is moving in the direction of reporting assets and liabilities at their fair value. **Fair value** is the amount that the business could sell the asset for, or the amount that the business could pay to settle the liability. The impact of IFRS on reporting the values of financial assets and liabilities in discussed in subsequent chapters where those assets and liabilities are discussed.

But going out of business is the exception rather than the rule, and for this reason, accounting lists a going-concern's assets at their historical cost.

The Stable-Monetary-Unit Concept

In Canada, we record transactions in Canadian dollars, the medium of exchange. British accountants record transactions in pounds sterling, and Japanese accountants in yen. Europeans who belong to the European Union price goods and services in euros.

Unlike a litre or a kilometre, the value of a Canadian dollar or a Mexican peso changes over time. A rise in the general price level is called *inflation*. During inflation, a dollar will purchase less milk, less toothpaste, and less of other goods. When prices are stable—when there is little inflation—a dollar's purchasing power is also stable.

Accountants assume that the dollar's purchasing power is relatively stable under the **stable-monetary-unit concept**. We ignore inflation, and this allows us to add and subtract dollar amounts as though each dollar has the same purchasing power.

STOP & THINK

You are considering the purchase of land for future expansion. The seller is asking $50,000 for land that cost the seller $35,000. An appraisal shows a value of $47,000. You first offer $44,000, the seller makes a counter-offer of $48,000, and you agree on $46,000. What dollar value is reported for the land on your financial statements?

Answer:
Report the land at $46,000, which is its historical cost.

Limitations of GAAP

In Section 1000, the *CICA Handbook* points out that GAAP are usually the criteria against which the disclosures on financial statements are measured. However, there may be situations when GAAP are not appropriate, such as

1. When GAAP do not lead to fair presentation
2. When the financial statements are prepared in accordance with regulatory legislation
3. When the financial statements are prepared in accordance with contractual requirements

In each of those three cases, the preparers must use their judgment in deciding the appropriate basis of accounting and must ensure that the basis is fully disclosed in the notes to the financial statements. An accountant who determines the *Handbook* is not appropriate and selects some other basis of accounting must be prepared to defend that decision.

Objective

③ **Apply** the accounting equation to business organizations

The Accounting Equation

As you will see for Sun-Rype Products Ltd. and Mullen Group Income Fund, the two companies we will be examining in depth throughout this text, the financial statements tell us how a business is performing and where it stands. They are the final product of financial accounting. But how do we arrive at the financial statements? Let's see their building blocks.

Assets and Liabilities

The financial statements are based on the **accounting equation**. This equation presents the resources of the business and the claims to those resources.

- **Assets** are the economic resources of a business that are expected to produce a benefit in the future. Sun-Rype Products' cash, accounts receivable, inventory, and property, plant and equipment are examples of assets. Claims on assets come from two sources.
- **Liabilities** are "outsider claims." They are debts payable to outsiders, called *creditors*. For example, a creditor who has loaned money to Sun-Rype has a claim—a legal right—to a part of Sun-Rype's assets until Sun-Rype repays the debt.
- **Owners' equity** (also called **shareholders' equity** or **capital**) represents the "insider claims" of a business. Equity means ownership, so shareholders' equity is the owners' interest in the assets of a corporation. Also called **net assets**.

The accounting equation shows the relationship among assets, liabilities, and owners' equity. Assets appear on the left side of the equation. The legal and economic claims against the assets—the liabilities and owners' equity—appear on the right side. As Exhibit 1-6 shows, the two sides must be equal.

Consider the assets and the liabilities of Sun-Rype Products Ltd. What are some of Sun-Rype's assets? The first asset listed for all businesses is **cash**, the liquid (cash) asset that is the medium of exchange. Another important Sun-Rype asset is **accounts receivable**, which primarily represents amounts due from customers who have purchased Sun-Rype products on account (credit). **Inventory** is another major asset; it includes the raw materials that go into Sun-Rype products. Sun-Rype also has assets in the form of **property, plant, and equipment** (often abbreviated as *PPE*). These are the long-lived assets that Sun-Rype uses to manufacture its products, as well as buildings, computers, and so on. Land, buildings, and equipment are also called **tangible capital assets**, **fixed assets**, or **plant assets**.

Sun-Rype's liabilities include a number of payables, such as accounts payable and accrued liabilities. The word *payable* always signifies a liability. An **account payable** is a liability for goods or services purchased on credit and supported only by the credit standing of the purchaser. A **note payable** is a written promise to pay on a certain date. **Long-term debt** is a liability that falls due beyond one year from the date of the financial statements.

Owners' Equity

Accounting Cycle Tutorial
Balance Sheet Accounts and
Transactions Tutorial

The owners' equity of any business is the assets of the business minus its liabilities. We can write the accounting equation to show that the owners' claim to assets is a residual—what is left over after subtracting liabilities from assets.

$$\text{Assets} - \text{Liabilities} = \text{Owners' Equity}$$

The owners' equity of a corporation—called **shareholders' equity**, or simply *equity*—is divided into two main subparts: contributed capital and retained earnings. The accounting equation can be written as

$$\text{Assets} = \text{Liabilities} + \text{Shareholders' Equity}$$
$$\text{Assets} = \text{Liabilities} + \text{Contributed Capital} + \text{Retained Earnings}$$

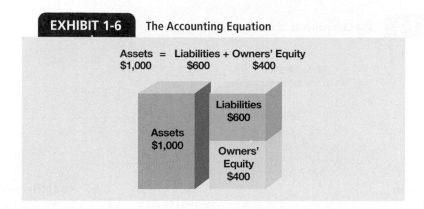

EXHIBIT 1-6 The Accounting Equation

Contributed capital is the amount the shareholders have invested in the corporation. The basic component of contributed capital is **common shares**, which the corporation issues to shareholders as evidence of ownership.

Retained earnings is the amount earned by income-producing activities and kept for use in the business.

Two types of transactions affect retained earnings:

- **Revenues** are increases in retained earnings from delivering goods or services to customers. For example, Sun-Rype's sale of a case of apple juice brings in revenue and increases Sun-Rype's retained earnings.

- **Expenses** are decreases in retained earnings that result from operations. For example, the wages that Sun-Rype pays its production people constitute an expense and decrease retained earnings. Expenses are the cost of doing business and are thus the opposite of revenues. Expenses include office supplies, salaries, and utility payments. Expenses also include amortization of property, plant and equipment such as computers and buildings.

Businesses strive for profits, the excess of revenues over expenses.

- When total revenues exceed total expenses, the result is called **net income**, or **net earnings** or **net profit**.

- When expenses exceed revenues, the result is a **net loss**.

- Net income or net loss is the "bottom line" on an income statement. Sun-Rype's bottom line reports 2007 net income of $4.64 million, as shown on page 2.

A successful business may pay dividends. **Dividends** are distributions to shareholders of assets (usually cash) generated by net income. Remember: *Dividends are not expenses. Dividends never affect net income.* Exhibit 1-7 shows the relationships among

- Retained earnings
- Revenues − Expenses = Net income (or Net loss)
- Dividends

Some companies have more net losses than net profits, making retained earnings negative. In that situation, the resultant balance is called a deficit and the amount is deducted from contributed capital.

The owners' equity of proprietorships and partnerships is different. These types of businesses make no distinction between contributed capital and retained earnings. Instead, they use a single heading—Capital—for example, Walker, Capital, for a proprietorship, and Chin, Capital, and Muesli, Capital, for a partnership.

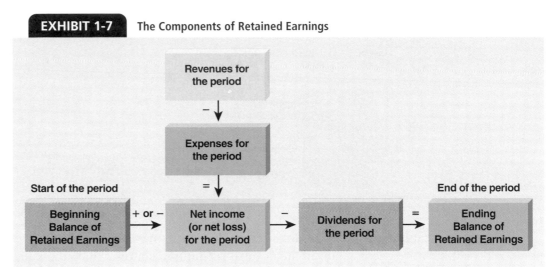

EXHIBIT 1-7   The Components of Retained Earnings

STOP & THINK

1. If the assets of a business are $174,000, and the liabilities are $82,000, how much is the owners' equity?
2. If the owners' equity in a business is $60,000, and the liabilities are $36,000, how much are the assets?
3. A company reported monthly revenues of $80,000 and expenses of $84,000. What is the result of operations for the month?

Answers:

1. $92,000 ($174,000 − $82,000)
2. $96,000 ($60,000 + $36,000)
3. Net loss of $4,000 ($80,000 − $84,000); revenues minus expenses

The Financial Statements

Objective

④ **Evaluate** business operations

The financial statements present a company in financial terms. Each financial statement relates to a specific date or a particular time period. What would managers and investors want to know about Sun-Rype Products Ltd. at the end of a period? Exhibit 1-8 summarizes four questions decision makers may ask. The answers come from one of the financial statements.

To learn how to use financial statements, let's work through Sun-Rype's statements for the year ended December 31, 2007. The following diagram shows how the data flow from one financial statement to the next. The order is important.

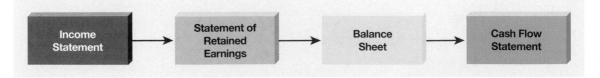

We begin with the income statement in Exhibit 1-9. Note that Sun-Rype calls its income statement a statement of operations and that Sun-Rype, as a number of companies do, includes the **statement of retained earnings** with the statement of operations. While some companies follow this procedure, others provide two separate statements. You will note that net earnings and comprehensive income of $4.64 million (line 12) are added to the opening balance of retained earnings of $19.31 million (line 13); retained earnings also appears on the balance sheet (Exhibit 1-11, line 20

EXHIBIT 1-8   Information Reported on the Financial Statements

Question	Financial Statement	Answer
1. How well did the company perform during the year?	Income statement (also called the statement of operations)	Revenues − Expenses Net income (or Net loss)
2. Why did the company's retained earnings change during the year?	Statement of retained earnings	Beginning retained earnings + Net income (or − Net loss) − Dividends Ending retained earnings
3. What is the company's financial position at the end of the year?	Balance sheet (also called the statement of financial position)	Assets = Liabilities + Owners' Equity
4. How much cash did the company generate and spend during the year?	Cash flow statement	Operating cash flows ± Investing cash flows ± Financing cash flows Increase (or decrease) in cash

on page 21). As you can see, there is a natural progression from net earnings through retained earnings to the balance sheet, and finally to the cash flow statement (Exhibit 1-12, line 1 on page 24).

The Income Statement Measures Operating Performance

The **income statement**, **statement of operations**, or **statement of earnings** reports the company's revenues, expenses, and net income or net loss for a period. At the top of Exhibit 1-9 is the company's name, Sun-Rype Products Ltd.

EXHIBIT 1-9   Statement of Operations and Retained Earnings (Adapted)

Sun-Rype Products Ltd.
Statements of Operations and Retained Earnings (Adapted)
For the Years ended December 31
(in millions of dollars)

	2007	2006
1. **Net sales**	$135.14	$130.62
2. Cost of sales	93.30	85.31
3. Gross profit	41.84	45.31
Expenses		
4. Selling, general, and administrative	28.54	30.48
5. Amortization	4.18	3.86
6. Interest	0.15	0.04
7. Loss on disposal of property, plant, and equipment	0.21	0.13
8. Foreign exchange loss	1.98	0.11
9.	35.06	34.62
10. Earnings before income taxes	6.78	10.69
11. Income taxes	2.14	3.42
12. **Net earnings and comprehensive income**	4.64	7.27
13. Retained earnings, beginning of year	19.31	29.58
14. Dividends paid	(1.62)	(17.54)
15. **Retained earnings, end of year**	$ 22.33	$ 19.31

Some companies such as KFC include a parent company and subsidiaries. The statements of such companies would report the consolidated results of the parent and subsidiaries. The Forzani Group is a retailer and as such reports its income, as do other retailers such as The Bay and Zellers, based on a 52-week rather than a 12-month period.

Most companies use the calendar year as their accounting year. Examples are EnCana Corporation, Magna International Inc., and Great-West Lifeco Inc. Other companies have year-ends during the year; for example, almost all of Canada's major banks have October 31 year-ends. Companies usually adopt an accounting year that ends on the low point of their operations.

Sun-Rype's income statement in Exhibit 1-9 reports operating results for two years, 2007 and 2006, to show trends for sales, expenses, and net income. To avoid cluttering the statement with zeros, we show Sun-Rype's figures in millions of dollars. During 2007, Sun-Rype increased sales from $130.62 million to $135.14 million (see line 1). Net earnings decreased from $7.27 million to $4.64 million (line 12). Sun-Rype was able to sell more juice and fruit products in 2007.

The income statement reports two main categories:

- Revenues and gains
- Expenses and losses

Revenues and expenses measure net income as follows:

Net Income = Total Revenues and Gains − Total Expenses and Losses

In accounting, the word *net* means the result after a subtraction. *Net* income is the profit left over after subtracting expenses and losses from revenues and gains. Net income is the single most important item in the financial statements.

Revenues. Companies do not always use the term *revenue* in their statement titles. For example, net sales revenue is often abbreviated as *net sales. Net* sales means sales revenue after subtracting all the goods customers have returned to the company. The Bay, Canadian Tire, and Jean Coutu get some goods back from customers. Swiss Chalet and other restaurateurs don't have much in the way of sales returns. In Sun-Rype's case, revenue comes from retail sales through the manufacturing and marketing of fruit-based foods and beverages targeted to health-conscious consumers.

Expenses. *Cost of sales* (also called *cost of goods sold,* line 2) represents the cost to Sun-Rype Products Ltd. of the fruit and vegetable products it manufactures and sells to customers. Cost of goods sold is the cost to the company of the manufactured or purchased inventory that the company has sold; selling expenses are the cost of selling the inventory such as shipping costs, advertising costs, and commissions; general and administrative expenses include such costs as office payroll, office supplies, and couriers and postage. Sun-Rype shows cost of goods sold and selling, general and administrative expenses separately, while some companies, such as Canadian Tire, combine them and show them as one figure.

Selling, general, and administrative (S, G, & A) expense (line 4) includes all operating costs not directly related to selling products. Examples include, in addition to those in the previous paragraph, the salaries paid to company executives and home-office expenses.

Amortization expense (also called *depreciation expense*) is an allocation of an asset's cost to expense over the expected life of the asset. Amortization expense may

EXHIBIT 1-10	Statement of Retained Earnings (Adapted)

Sun-Rype Products Ltd.
Statement of Retained Earnings (Adapted)
For the Years Ended December 31 (in millions of dollars)

	2007	2006
Retained earnings:		
1. Balance, beginning of year	$19.31	$29.58
2. Net income	4.64	7.27
3. Less: Cash dividends paid	(1.62)	(17.54)
4. Balance, end of year	$22.33	$19.31

relate to manufacturing operations (for example, amortization of production equipment) or administration (for example, amortization of computers, desks, and other office equipment), but it is shown as a separate category on the income statement (line 5).

Similarly, *interest expense* is not included in selling expense or general and administrative expense, but is shown as a separate category on the income statement (line 6).

Often, companies have other categories of revenue and expenses on their income statements. These revenues and expenses arise from activities outside a company's central, ongoing operations. For example, a company might dispose of capital assets, as Sun-Rype did (line 7) in 2007 and 2006. The company might suffer a loss (a loss has the same effect as an expense). Conversely, the company might have a gain (a gain has the same effect as a revenue item).

Income tax expense (line 11). Corporations pay income tax just as individuals do. During 2007, Sun-Rype's income tax expense was $2.14 million.

Now let's move on to the statement of retained earnings and Exhibit 1-10.

MyAccountingLab

Accounting Cycle Tutorial
Income Statement Accounts and
Transactions Tutorial

The Statement of Retained Earnings Shows What a Company Did with Its Net Income

As you are aware from your examination of Exhibit 1-9, Sun-Rype Products Ltd. includes the statement of retained earnings on the statement of operations. Exhibit 1-10 was created so that you see what Sun-Rype's statement of retained earnings might look like.

Retained earnings represent exactly what the term implies: that portion of net income the company has retained. Net income from the income statement also appears on the statement of retained earnings (line 2 in Exhibit 1-10). Net income increases retained earnings, and dividends decrease retained earnings. Why the decrease? Because the company did not retain the net income it gave to shareholders.

Sun-Rype's statement of retained earnings needs explanation. Start with 2007. At the beginning of 2007, Sun-Rype had retained earnings of $19.31 million (line 1). During 2007, Sun-Rype earned net income of $4.64 million (line 2) and gave the shareholders dividends of $1.62 million (line 3). Sun-Rype ended 2007 with retained earnings of $22.33 million (line 4).

Which item on the statement of retained earnings comes directly from the income statement? It's net income. Line 2 of the retained earnings statement comes directly from line 12 of the income statement. Trace this amount from one statement to the other.

Give yourself a pat on the back. You're already learning how to analyze financial statements!

After a company earns net income, the board of directors decides whether to pay a dividend to the shareholders. In 2007 and 2006, Sun-Rype declared and paid dividends to the shareholders (line 3). The dividends decrease retained earnings (the parentheses indicate a subtraction).

Trace 2007 retained earnings to the balance sheet in Exhibit 1-11 (line 20). Ending retained earnings from 2007 carries over and becomes the beginning retained earnings of 2008.

The Balance Sheet Measures Financial Position

A company's **balance sheet**, also called the **statement of financial position**, reports three main categories: assets, liabilities, and shareholders' or owners' equity. The balance sheet is dated at the *moment in time* when the accounting period ends.

Sun-Rype's comparative balance sheet appears in Exhibit 1-11.

Assets.   Assets are subdivided into two categories: current and long-term. **Current assets** includes cash and cash equivalents as well as those assets the company expects to convert to cash, sell, or consume during the next 12 months or within the business's normal operating cycle if longer than a year. Current assets for Sun-Rype consist of cash, accounts receivable, income taxes receivable, inventories, prepaid expenses, and future income taxes (lines 1 to 6). Sun-Rype's current assets total $29.02 million at December 31, 2007 (line 7).

Sun-Rype has $2.69 million in *cash* and cash equivalents at December 31, 2007 (line 1). Cash is a liquid asset that is the medium of exchange.

Accounts receivable, $7.39 million (line 2), are the amounts due to Sun-Rype primarily for products purchased from the company on account (credit) and are amounts the company expects to collect from customers.

Income taxes receivable of $0.82 million (line 3) represent an overpayment of corporate income taxes in 2007. Inventories (line 4) are the company's second-largest current asset, totalling $17.30 million. *Inventory* is a common abbreviation for *merchandise inventory*; the two names are used interchangeably.

Prepaid expenses $0.38 million (line 5) represent prepayments for advertisements and for rent, insurance, and supplies that have not yet been used up. Prepaid expenses are assets because Sun-Rype will benefit from these expenditures in the future. *Future income taxes* of $0.44 million (line 6) on the asset side represent taxes recoverable in future years and arise because of timing differences between income for accounting purposes and income for tax purposes.

Capital assets are those assets that will be consumed over a period greater than one year. The most significant capital assets are usually property, plant, and equipment, also known as long-term assets and fixed assets.

Property, plant, and equipment of $27.87 million (line 8) includes Sun-Rype's land, buildings, computers, and production equipment. Sun-Rype reports property, plant, and equipment at its net book value (historical cost minus accumulated amortization). The actual Sun-Rype financial statements have a footnote for property, plant, and equipment that shows the costs and accumulated amortization of all the property, plant, and equipment owned by Sun-Rype Products Ltd. The note shows that Sun-Rype deducts the accumulated amortization from the total costs of the property, plant, and equipment to calculate the net book value of $27.87 million shown on the balance sheet. That amount ($27.87 million) is the portion of the

EXHIBIT 1-11   Balance Sheet (Adapted)

Sun-Rype Products Ltd.
Balance Sheets (Adapted)
December 31 (in millions of dollars)

	2007	2006
Assets		
Current		
1. Cash and cash equivalents	$ 2.69	$ 1.53
2. Accounts receivable	7.39	12.68
3. Income taxes receivable	0.82	—
4. Inventories	17.30	18.71
5. Prepaid expenses	0.38	0.38
6. Future income taxes	0.44	0.20
7.	29.02	33.50
8. **Property, plant, and equipment**	27.87	25.95
9.	$56.89	$59.45
Liabilities and Shareholders' Equity		
Current		
10. Promissory note payable	$0.50	$0.60
11. Accounts payable and accrued liabilities	12.69	18.25
12. Unrealized foreign exchange loss	0.46	—
13. Income taxes payable	—	0.24
14. Current portion, long-term obligations	0.32	0.21
15.	13.97	19.30
16. **Long-term obligations**	0.74	0.92
17. **Future income taxes**	1.15	1.22
18.	15.86	21.44
Shareholders' equity		
19. Share capital and contributed surplus	18.70	18.70
20. Retained earnings	22.33	19.31
21.	41.03	38.01
22.	$56.89	$59.45

property, plant, and equipment that has not yet been amortized (used up). *Cost* means the acquisition price to Sun-Rype. It does not mean that Sun-Rype could sell its property, plant, and equipment at the cost prices. After all, the company may have acquired the assets several years ago.

Liabilities. Liabilities are also divided into two categories: current and long-term. **Current liabilities** (lines 10 to 14) are debts payable within one year or within the entity's normal operating cycle if longer than a year. Current liabilities for Sun-Rype Products Ltd. at December 31, 2007, consist of a promissory note payable, accounts payable and accrued liabilities, unrealized foreign exchange loss, and the current portion (due in 2008) of the long-term obligations. Sun-Rype Products Ltd.'s current liabilities total $13.97 million (line 15). A *promissory note* is a formal, written promise to pay representing an obligation of the company. Sun-Rype shows a promissory note of $0.50 million (line 10).

 Accounts payable and accrued liabilities of $12.69 million (line 11) represents amounts owed for goods and services that Sun-Rype has purchased but not yet paid for.

 Sun-Rype had an *unrealized foreign exchange loss* of $0.46 million (line 12) incurred in connection with foreign exchange contracts the company has entered into.

The *current portion of long-term obligations* of $0.32 million (line 14) represents the current portion of the long-term liability reported on line 16.

Long-term liabilities are those liabilities which are due beyond one year after the balance sheet date. The long-term liabilities include long-term obligations and future income taxes.

Sun-Rype's *long-term obligations* of $0.74 million (line 16) are related to post-retirement benefits.

Future income taxes of $1.15 million (line 17) on the liability side represent taxes payable in future years. They arise because of timing differences between income for accounting purposes and income for tax purposes. At December 31, 2007, total liabilities are $15.86 million (line 18). This is just 28% of total assets (line 9).

STOP & THINK

Examine Sun-Rype's balance sheet in Exhibit 1-11. Look at total assets on line 9. What is your opinion of the change in total assets and total liabilities during 2007? Is it good news, bad news, or no news? Why? To what other item should you relate the change in total assets? Identify that item, its change during 2007, and state why it too is important.

Answer:
It is important to look at the complete picture and not to focus just on a part. Total assets declined from $59.45 million to $56.89, a decrease of $2.56 million, but total liabilities also declined, from $21.44 million to $15.86, a decrease of $5.58 million. Shareholders' equity increased from $38.01 million to $41.03, an increase of $3.02 million. Sun-Rype is in a stronger financial position in 2007 than it was in 2006.

Owners' Equity.   The accounting equation states that

$$\text{Assets} - \text{Liabilities} = \text{Owners' Equity}$$

The assets (resources) and the liabilities (debts) of Sun-Rype are fairly easy to understand. Owners' equity is harder to understand. Owners' equity is simple to calculate, but what does it *mean*?

MyAccountingLab

**Accounting Cycle Tutorial
Balance Sheet Accounts and
Transactions Tutorial**

Sun-Rype Products Ltd. calls its owners' equity *shareholders' equity*, and this title is descriptive. Remember that a company's owners' equity represents the shareholders' ownership of business assets. Owners' equity for Sun-Rype consists of common shares, represented by almost 11 million shares issued to shareholders for approximately $18.70 million through December 31, 2007 (line 19).

Retained earnings is $24.33 million (line 19). Trace the $22.33 million ending balance of retained earnings from the statement of retained earnings in Exhibit 1-10 (line 4) to the balance sheet in Exhibit 1-11 (line 20). Retained earnings links the statement of retained earnings to the balance sheet.

At December 31, 2007, Sun-Rype has total shareholders' equity of $41.03 million (line 21). We can now prove that Sun-Rype's total assets equal the company's total liabilities and equity (amounts in millions of dollars):

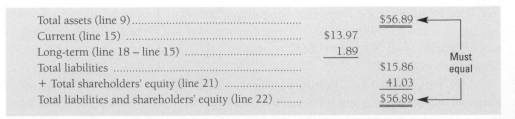

Total assets (line 9)		$56.89
Current (line 15)	$13.97	
Long-term (line 18 – line 15)	1.89	
Total liabilities		$15.86
+ Total shareholders' equity (line 21)		41.03
Total liabilities and shareholders' equity (line 22)		$56.89

The cash flow statement is the last required financial statement.

The Cash Flow Statement Measures Cash Receipts and Payments

Companies engage in three basic types of activities:

1. **Operating activities**
2. **Investing activities**
3. **Financing activities**

The **cash flow statement** reports cash flows under these three categories. Think about the cash flows (cash receipts and cash payments) in each category:

- **Companies operate by buying, and then selling, goods and services to customers.** Operating activities result in net income or net loss, and they either increase or decrease cash. The income statement tells whether the company is profitable. The cash flow statement reports whether operations provided cash or used cash. Cash flow from operating activities is the most important piece of information on the cash flow statement. It should always be positive; continuing negative cash flow from operations can send an organization into bankruptcy.

- **Companies invest in property, plant and equipment for use in operations.** Sun-Rype pays cash to buy buildings and equipment. When these assets wear out, the company sells them for cash. Both purchases and sales of capital assets are investing cash flows. Investing cash flows are next most important after operations because what a company invests in determines where its cash comes from.

- **Companies need money for financing.** Financing includes both issuing and repurchasing shares of stock and borrowing and repaying funds. Sun-Rype has issued shares to its shareholders for cash, providing a financing cash inflow. Sun-Rype paid a dividend to shareholders in 2007. This payment is a financing cash outflow.

Overview. Companies organize the cash flow statement into operating, investing, and financing activities. Each category either increases or decreases cash. In Exhibit 1-12, Sun-Rype's operating activities provided cash of $10.27 million in 2007 (line 3). This increase in cash signals strong cash flow from operations. Financing activities used $1.85 million (line 6). Investing activities used cash of $7.26 million in 2007 (line 9). On a cash flow statement, cash receipts appear as positive amounts. Cash payments are negative amounts and enclosed by parentheses.

Overall, Sun-Rype's cash increased by $1.16 million during 2007 (line 10); Sun-Rype ended the year with cash of $2.69 million (line 12). Trace the ending cash balance of $2.69 million to the balance sheet in Exhibit 1-11. The cash balance links the cash flow statement to the balance sheet.

Let's now examine the three major sections of the cash flow statement more closely.

Cash Flows from Operating Activities. The vast majority of companies report cash flows from operating activities starting with net income. They then make some adjustments to reconcile from net income to net cash provided by operating activities. Sun-Rype follows this practice in Exhibit 1-12 (lines 1 to 3).

Cash Flows from Investing Activities. During the year ended December 31, 2007, Sun-Rype Products Ltd. spent $7.36 million to acquire capital assets and received $0.10 million for the sale of capital assets. Negative cash flow for investing activities is generally healthy because it indicates that a company is buying new assets and growing.

EXHIBIT 1-12	Statement of Cash Flows

Sun-Rype Products Ltd.
Statements of Cash Flows
For the Years Ended December 31 (in millions of dollars)

	2007	2006
Cash provided by (used in):		
Operating activities		
1. Net earnings	$ 4.64	$ 7.27
2. Adjustments to reconcile net income to cash provided by operating activities..	5.63	(1.53)
3.	10.27	5.74
Financing activities		
4. Dividends paid	(1.62)	(17.54)
5. Reduction of long-term obligations	(0.23)	—
6.	(1.85)	(17.54)
Investing activities		
7. Proceeds on disposal of property, plant and equipment	0.10	0.01
8. Payments for property, plant and equipment	(7.36)	(6.64)
9.	(7.26)	(6.63)
10. Increase (decrease) in cash position	1.16	(18.43)
11. Cash and cash equivalents, beginning of year	1.53	19.96
12. **Cash and cash equivalents, end of year**........................	$ 2.69	$ 1.53

Cash Flows from Financing Activities. During the year ended December 31, 2007, Sun-Rype paid dividends of $1.62 million and paid off long-term obligations in the amount of $0.23 million. Financing activities generated a negative cash flow of $1.85 million.

Net Increase (Decrease) in Cash. The overall result of the cash flow statement is the net increase (or decrease) in cash during the year. As we have seen, Sun-Rype's cash increased by $1.16 million during 2007 (line 10). Lines 11 and 12 of the cash flow statement show both the beginning cash balance and the ending cash balance for the year. Note that Sun-Rype Products Ltd. uses the account Cash and cash equivalents. The company began the year with cash and cash equivalents of $1.53 million (line 11) and ended with cash and cash equivalents of $2.69 million (line 12). Trace both amounts to the balance sheet in Exhibit 1-11 (line 1).

The purpose of the cash flow statement is to show why *cash changed during the year.*

Relationships Among the Financial Statements

Exhibit 1-13 summarizes the relationships among the financial statements of Huron Ltd. Study the exhibit carefully because these relationships apply to all organizations. Specifically, note the following:

1. The income statement for the year ended December 31, 2009,

    a. reports all revenues and all expenses during the period. Revenues and expenses are reported *only* on the income statement.

    b. reports net income if total revenues exceed total expenses. If expenses exceed revenues, there is a net loss.

EXHIBIT 1-13	Relationships Among the Financial Statements (The statements are summarized, with all amounts assumed for illustration)

Huron Ltd.
Income Statement
For the Year Ended December 31, 2009

Revenues	$ 700,000
Expenses	670,000
Net income	$ 30,000

Huron Ltd.
Statement of Retained Earnings
For the Year Ended December 31, 2009

①

Beginning retained earnings	$ 120,000
Net income	30,000
Cash dividends	(10,000)
Ending retained earnings	$140,000

Huron Ltd.
Balance Sheet
December 31, 2009

Assets

②

Cash	$ 25,000
All other assets	275,000
Total assets	$300,000

Liabilities

Total liabilities	$120,000

Shareholders' Equity

Common shares	40,000
Retained earnings	140,000
Total liabilities and shareholders' equity	$300,000

③

Huron Ltd.
Cash Flow Statement
For the Year Ended December 31, 2009

Net cash provided by operating activities	$ 90,000
Net cash used for investing activities	(110,000)
Net cash provided by financing activities	40,000
Net increase in cash	20,000
Beginning cash balance	5,000
Ending cash balance	$ 25,000

2. The statement of retained earnings for the year ended December 31, 2009,

   a. opens with the beginning retained earnings balance.

   b. adds net income (or subtracts net loss). Net income comes directly from the income statement (arrow ① in Exhibit 1-13).

   c. subtracts dividends.

   d. ends with the retained earnings balance at the end of the period.

3. The balance sheet at December 31, 2009, at the end of the accounting year

   a. reports all assets, liabilities, and shareholders' equity at the end of the period. Only the balance sheet reports assets and liabilities.

   b. reports that assets equal the sum of liabilities plus shareholders' equity. This balancing feature gives the balance sheet its name; it follows the accounting equation.

   c. reports ending retained earnings, which comes from the statement of retained earnings (arrow ② in Exhibit 1-13).

4. The cash flow statement for the year ended December 31, 2009,

   a. reports cash flows from operating activities, investing activities, and financing activities. Each category results in net cash provided (an increase) or net cash used (a decrease).

   b. reports that cash increased or decreased during the period and ends with the cash balance on December 31, 2009. Ending cash is reported on the balance sheet (arrow ③ in Exhibit 1-13).

DECISION GUIDELINES

IN EVALUATING A COMPANY, WHAT DO DECISION MAKERS LOOK FOR?

The Decision Guidelines illustrate how people use financial statements. Decision Guidelines appear throughout the book to show how accounting information aids decision making.

Suppose you are considering an investment in Sun-Rype shares. How do you proceed? Where do you get the information you need? What do you look for?

Question/Decision	What to look for
Can the company sell its products?	Sales revenue on the income statement. Are sales increasing or decreasing?
What are the main income measures to watch for trends?	**1.** Gross margin (sales − cost of goods sold) **2.** Operating income (gross margin − operating expenses) **3.** Net income (bottom line of the income statement) All three income measures should be increasing over time.
What percentage of sales revenue ends up as profit?	Divide net income by sales revenue. Examine the trend of the net income percentage from year to year.
Can the company collect its receivables?	From the balance sheet, compare the percentage increase in accounts receivable to the percentage increase in sales. If receivables are growing much faster than sales, collections may be too slow and a cash shortage may result.
Can the company pay its **a.** Current liabilities? **b.** Current and long-term liabilities?	From the balance sheet, compare **a.** Current assets to current liabilities. Current assets should be somewhat greater than current liabilities. **b.** Total assets to total liabilities. Total assets must be quite a bit greater than total liabilities.
Where is the company's cash coming from? How is cash being used?	On the cash flow statement, operating activities should provide the bulk of the company's cash during most years. Otherwise the business will fail. Examine investing cash flows to see if the company is purchasing capital assets—property, plant, and equipment (this signals growth). Examine financing cash flows for heavy borrowing (a bad sign) or issuance of shares (a better sign).

END-OF-CHAPTER SUMMARY PROBLEM *MyAccountingLab*

J. J. Booth and Marie Savard incorporated Tara Inc., a consulting engineering company, and began operations on April 1, 2009. During April, the business provided engineering services for clients. It is now April 30, and J. J. and Marie wonder how well Tara Inc. performed during its first month. They also want to know the business's financial position at the end of April 30 and cash flows during the month.

The following data are listed in alphabetical order.

Accounts payable	$ 1,800	Land	$18,000
Accounts receivable	2,000	Office supplies	3,700
Adjustments to reconcile net income to net cash provided by operating activities	(3,900)	Payments of cash: Acquisition of land	40,000
		Dividends	2,100
Cash balance at beginning of April	0	Rent expense	1,100
Cash balance at end of April	33,300	Retained earnings at beginning of April	0
Cash receipts:			
Issuance (sale) of shares	50,000	Retained earnings at end of April	?
Sale of land	22,000	Salary expense	1,200
Common shares (contributed capital)	50,000	Service revenue	10,000
		Utilities expense	400

Required

1. Prepare the income statement, the statement of retained earnings, and the cash flow statement for the month ended April 30, 2009, and the balance sheet at April 30, 2009. Draw arrows linking the pertinent items in the statements.
2. Answer the investors' underlying questions.
   a. How well did Tara Inc. perform during its first month of operations?
   b. Where does Tara Inc. stand financially at the end of the first month?
3. If you were a banker, would you be willing to lend money to Tara Inc.?

Name: Tara Inc.
Industry: Consulting engineering corporation
Fiscal Period: Month of April 2009

Review the list of accounts provided and determine whether each account is an asset, liability, shareholders' equity, revenue, or expense. Then group the accounts by financial statement.

Answers

Requirement 1

Financial Statements of Tara Inc.

Tara Inc.
Income Statement
For the Month Ended April 30, 2009

Revenue:		
Service revenue		$10,000
Expenses:		
Salary expense	$1,200	
Rent expense	1,100	
Utilities expense	400	
Total expenses		2,700
Net income		$ 7,300 ──①

The title must include the name of the company, "Income Statement," and the specific period of time covered. It is critical that the time period be defined.

Gather all the revenue and expense accounts from the account listing. List the revenue accounts first. List the expense accounts next.

The title must include the name of the company, "Statement of Retained Earnings," and the specific period of time covered. It is critical that the time period be defined.

The net income amount (or net loss amount) is transferred from the income statement. Retained earnings at the end of the period is the result of a calculation, and is an accumulation of the corporation's performance since it began.

Tara Inc.
Statement of Retained Earnings
For the Month Ended April 30, 2009

Retained earnings, April 1, 2009	$ 0
Add: Net income for the month	7,300
	7,300
Less: Dividends	(2,100)
Retained earnings, April 30, 2009	$5,200

The title must include the name of the company, "Balance Sheet," and the date of the balance sheet. It shows the financial position at the end of the day.

Gather all the asset, liability, and equity accounts from the account listing. List assets first, then liabilities, then equity accounts. The retained earnings amount is transferred from the statement of retained earnings.

It is imperative that total assets = total liabilities + shareholders' equity

Tara Inc.
Balance Sheet
April 30, 2009

Assets		Liabilities	
Cash	$33,300	Accounts payable	$ 1,800
Accounts receivable	2,000	**Shareholders' Equity**	
Office supplies	3,700	Common shares	50,000
Land	18,000	Retained earnings	5,200
		Total shareholders' equity	55,200
		Total liabilities and	
Total assets	$57,000	shareholders' equity	$57,000

The title must include the name of the company, "Cash Flow Statement," and the specific period of time covered. It is critical that the time period be defined.

Net income comes from the income statement. The adjustments amount was provided. In later chapters, you will learn how to calculate this amount.

Include all transactions that involve investing the company's cash, which involve any changes in the property, plant, and equipment.

Include all cash transactions relating to shares and long-term debt obligations.

Tara Inc.
Cash Flow Statement
For the Month Ended April 30, 2009

Cash flows from operating activities:		
Net income		$ 7,300
Adjustments to reconcile net income to net cash		
provided by operating activities		(3,900)
Net cash provided by operating activities		3,400
Cash flows from investing activities:		
Acquisition of land	$(40,000)	
Sale of land	22,000	
Net cash used for investing activities		(18,000)
Cash flows from financing activities:		
Issuance (sale) of shares	$ 50,000	
Payment of dividends	(2,100)	
Net cash provided by financing activities		47,900
Net increase in cash		$33,300
Cash balance, April 1, 2009		0
Cash balance, April 30, 2009		$33,300

Requirements 2 and 3

Consider the net income from the income statement.

Consider net worth, which is total assets − total liabilities.

2. **a.** The company performed rather well in April. Net income was $7,300—very good in relation to service revenue of $10,000. Tara was able to pay cash dividends of $2,100.

   b. The business ended April with cash of $33,300. Total assets of $57,000 far exceed total liabilities of $1,800. Shareholders' equity of $55,200 provides a good cushion for borrowing. The business's financial position at April 30, 2009, is strong.

   c. The company has plenty of cash, and assets far exceed liabilities. Operating activities generated positive cash flow in the first month of operations. Lenders like to see these features before making a loan. Most bankers would be willing to lend to Tara Inc. at this time.

REVIEW THE FINANCIAL STATEMENTS

QUICK CHECK   (Answers are given on page 49.)

1. All the following statements are true except one. Which statement is false?
   a. Bookkeeping is only a part of accounting.
   b. A proprietorship is a business with several owners.
   c. Professional accountants are held to a high standard of ethical conduct.
   d. The organization that formulates generally accepted accounting principles is the Canadian Institute of Chartered Accountants (CICA).

2. The valuation of assets on the balance sheet is generally based on
   a. Historical cost
   b. What it would cost to replace the asset
   c. Current fair market value as established by independent appraisers
   d. Selling price

3. The accounting equation can be expressed as
   a. Assets + Liabilities = Shareholders' Equity
   b. Shareholders' Equity − Assets = Liabilities
   c. Assets = Liabilities − Shareholders' Equity
   d. Assets − Liabilities = Shareholders' Equity

4. The nature of an asset is best described as
   a. Something with physical form that's valued at cost in the accounting records.
   b. An economic resource representing cash or the right to receive cash in the near future.
   c. An economic resource that's expected to benefit future operations.
   d. Something owned by a business that has a ready market value.

5. Which financial statement covers a period of time?
   a. Balance sheet   c. Cash flow statement
   b. Income statement   d. Both b and c

6. How would net income be most likely to affect the accounting equation?
   a. Increase assets and increase shareholders' equity
   b. Increase liabilities and decrease shareholders' equity
   c. Increase assets and increase liabilities
   d. Decrease assets and decrease liabilities

7. During the year, ChemDry Ltd. has $100,000 in revenues, $40,000 in expenses, and $3,000 in dividend payments. Shareholders' equity changed by
   a. +$27,000   c. +$12,000
   b. +$57,000   d. −$8,000

8. ChemDry Ltd. in Question 7 had net income (or net loss) of
   a. Net income of $100,000   c. Net income of $60,000
   b. Net income of $57,000   d. Net loss of $40,000

9. Leah Corporation holds cash of $5,000 and owes $25,000 on accounts payable. Leah has accounts receivable of $30,000, inventory of $20,000, and land cost of $50,000. How much are Leah's total assets and shareholders' equity?

	Total assets	Shareholders' equity
a.	$100,000	$25,000
b.	$105,000	$80,000
c.	$105,000	$25,000
d.	$25,000	$105,000

10. Which item(s) is (are) reported on the balance sheet?
    a. Retained earnings   c. Inventory
    b. Accounts payable   d. All of the above

11. During the year, Mason Inc.'s shareholders' equity increased from $30,000 to $40,000. Mason earned net income of $15,000. How much in dividends did Mason declare in the year?
    - **a.** $6,000
    - **b.** $0
    - **c.** $8,000
    - **d.** $5,000

12. Stuebs Corporation had total assets of $300,000 and total shareholders' equity of $100,000 at the beginning of the year. During the year assets increased by $50,000 and liabilities increased by $40,000. Shareholders' equity at the end of the year is
    - **a.** $90,000
    - **b.** $110,000
    - **c.** $140,000
    - **d.** $150,000

ACCOUNTING VOCABULARY

account payable A liability for goods or services purchased on credit and backed by the general reputation and credit standing of the debtor. (p. 14)

accounting The information system that measures business activities, processes that information into reports and financial statements, and communicates the results to decision makers. (p. 3)

accounting equation The most basic tool of accounting: Assets = Liabilities + Owners' Equity. (p. 14)

accounts receivable An asset, amounts due from customers to whom a business has sold goods or services. (p. 14)

asset An economic resource that is expected to produce a benefit in the future. (p. 14)

balance sheet List of an entity's assets, liabilities, and owners' equity as of a specific date. Also called the *statement of financial position*. (p. 20)

board of directors Group elected by the shareholders to set policy for a corporation and to appoint its officers. (p. 8)

capital Another name for the *owners' equity* of a business. (p. 14)

capital assets Another name for *property, plant and equipment*. (p. 14)

cash Money and any medium of exchange that a bank accepts at face value. (p. 14)

cash flow statement Reports cash receipts and cash payments classified according to the entity's major activities: operating, investing, and financing. (p. 23)

common shares The most basic form of share capital. Common shareholders own a corporation. (p. 15)

contributed capital The amount of shareholders' equity that shareholders have invested in the corporation. (p. 15)

corporation A business owned by shareholders. A corporation is a legal entity, an "artificial person" in the eyes of the law. (p. 7)

cost principle Principle that states that assets and services should be recorded at their actual historical cost. (p. 12)

current asset An asset that is expected to be converted to cash, sold, or consumed during the next 12 months, or within the business's normal operating cycle if longer than a year. (p. 20)

current liability A debt due to be paid within 1 year or within the entity's operating cycle if the cycle is longer than a year. (p. 21)

dividends Distributions (usually cash) by a corporation to its shareholders. (p. 15)

entity An organization or a section of an organization that, for accounting purposes, stands apart from other organizations and individuals as a separate economic unit. (p. 10)

expenses Decrease in retained earnings that results from operations; the cost of doing business; opposite of revenues. (p. 15)

fair value The amount that a business could sell an asset for, or the amount that a business could pay to settle a liability. (p. 12)

financial accounting The branch of accounting that provides information to people outside the firm. (p. 4)

financial statements Business documents that report financial information about a business entity to decision makers. (p. 2)

financing activities Activities that obtain from investors and creditors the cash needed to launch and sustain the business; a section of the cash flow statement. (p. 23)

fixed assets Another name for *property, plant, and equipment*. (p. 14)

generally accepted accounting principles (GAAP) Accounting guidelines, formulated by the Canadian Institute of Chartered Accountants (CICA) Accounting Standards Board, that govern how accounting is practised. (p. 8)

going-concern concept Holds that the entity will remain in operation for the foreseeable future. (p. 12)

income statement A financial statement listing an entity's revenues, expenses, and net income or net loss for a specific period. Also called the *statement of operations* or the *statement of earnings*. (p. 17)

inventory The merchandise that a company sells; also includes raw materials for use in a manufacturing process. (p. 14)

investing activities Activities that increase or decrease the capital assets available to the business; a section of the cash flow statement. (p. 23)

liability An economic obligation (a debt) payable to an individual or an organization outside the entity. (p. 14)

long-term debt A liability that falls due beyond one year from the date of the financial statements. (p. 14)

management accounting The branch of accounting that generates information for the internal decision makers of a business, such as top executives. (p. 4)

net assets Another name for *owners' equity*. (p. 14)

net earnings Another name for *net income*. (p. 15)

net income Excess of total revenues over total expenses. Also called *net earnings* or *net profit*. (p. 15)

net loss Excess of total expenses over total revenues. (p. 15)

net profit Another name for *net income*. (p. 15)

note payable A liability evidenced by a written promise to make a future payment. (p. 14)

objectivity principle Another name for the *reliability principle*. (p. 12)

operating activities Activities that create revenue or expense in the entity's major line of business; a section of the cash flow statement. Operating activities affect the income statement. (p. 23)

owners' equity The claim of the owners of a business to the assets of the business. Also called *capital, shareholders' equity,* or *net assets.*   (p. 14)

partnership An association of two or more persons who co-own a business.   (p. 7)

plant assets Another name for *property, plant, and equipment.*   (p. 14)

property, plant, and equipment Long-lived assets, such as land, buildings, and equipment, used in the operation of the business. Also called *plant assets, fixed assets,* or *tangible capital assets.*   (p. 14)

proprietorship A business with a single owner.   (p. 6)

reliability principle The accounting principle that ensures that accounting records and statements are based on the most objective data available. Also called the *objectivity principle.*   (p. 11)

retained earnings The amount of shareholders' equity that the corporation of the business has earned through profitable operation and has not given back to shareholders.   (p. 15)

revenues Increase in retained earnings from delivering goods or services to customers or clients.   (p. 15)

shareholder A person who owns shares of stock in a corporation.   (p. 7)

shareholders' equity The shareholders' ownership interest in the assets of a corporation. Also called *owners' equity.*   (p. 14)

stable-monetary-unit concept The reason for ignoring the effect of inflation in the accounting records, based on the assumption that the dollar's purchasing power is relatively stable.   (p. 13)

statement of earnings Another name for the *income statement.*   (p. 17)

statement of financial position Another name for the *balance sheet.*   (p. 20)

statement of operations Another name for the *income statement.*   (p. 17)

statement of retained earnings Summary of the changes in the retained earnings of a corporation during a specific period.   (p. 16)

stock Shares into which the owners' equity of a corporation is divided.   (p. 7)

ASSESS YOUR PROGRESS

Make the grade with MyAccountingLab: The exercises and problems marked in red can be found on MyAccountingLab at www.myaccountinglab.com. You can practise them as often as you want, and they feature step by step guided solutions to help you find the right answer.

SHORT EXERCISES

S1-1 Use the accounting equation to show how to determine the amount of the missing term in each of the following situations.

Applying the accounting equation **(Obj. 3)**

	Total Assets	=	Total Liabilities	+	Shareholders' Equity
a.	$?		$150,000		$150,000
b.	290,000		90,000		?
c.	220,000		?		120,000

S1-2 Accountants follow ethical guidelines in the conduct of their work. What are these standards of professional conduct designed to produce? Why is this goal important?

Making ethical judgments **(Obj. 1)**

S1-3 John Grant is chairman of the board of The Grant Group Ltd. Suppose Grant has just founded this company, and assume that he treats his home and other personal assets as part of The Grant Group Ltd. Answer these questions about the evaluation of The Grant Group Ltd.

Applying accounting concepts **(Obj. 2)**

1. Which accounting concept governs this situation?
2. How can the proper application of this accounting concept give John Grant a realistic view of The Grant Group Ltd.? Explain in detail.

S1-4 Review the accounting equation on page 14.

Using the accounting equation **(Obj. 3)**

1. Use the accounting equation to show how to determine the amount of a company's owners' equity. How would your answer change if you were analyzing your own household or a single IHOP restaurant?
2. If you know assets and owners' equity, how can you measure liabilities? Give the equation.

Using accounting vocabulary
(Obj. 1)

S1-5 Accounting definitions are precise, and you must understand the vocabulary to properly use accounting. Sharpen your understanding of key terms by answering the following questions:

1. How do the *assets* and *shareholders' equity* of Sun-Rype Products Ltd. differ from each other? Which one (assets or shareholders' equity) must be at least as large as the other? Which one can be smaller than the other?

2. How are Sun-Rype Products Ltd.'s *liabilities* and *shareholders' equity* similar? How are they different?

Classifying assets, liabilities, and owner's equity
(Obj. 2)

S1-6 Consider **Wal-Mart**, the world's largest retailer. Classify the following items as an asset (A), a liability (L), or an owners' equity (E) item for Wal-Mart:

_____ **a.** Accounts payable   _____ **g.** Accounts receivable

_____ **b.** Common shares   _____ **h.** Long-term debt

_____ **c.** Cash   _____ **i.** Merchandise inventories

_____ **d.** Retained earnings   _____ **j.** Notes payable

_____ **e.** Land   _____ **k.** Accrued expenses payable

_____ **f.** Prepaid expenses   _____ **l.** Equipment

Using the income statements
(Obj. 4)

S1-7

1. Identify the two basic categories of items on an income statement.

2. What do we call the bottom line of the income statement?

Preparing an income statement
(Obj. 4)

S1-8 Split Second Wireless Inc. began 2009 with total assets of $110 million and ended 2009 with assets of $160 million. During 2009 Split Second earned revenues of $90 million and had expenses of $20 million. Split Second paid dividends of $10 million in 2009. Prepare the company's income statement for the year ended December 31, 2008, complete with the appropriate heading.

Preparing a statement of retained earnings
(Obj. 4)

S1-9 Mondala Ltd. began 2009 with retained earnings of $200 million. Revenues during the year were $400 million and expenses totalled $300 million. Mondala declared dividends of $40 million. What was the company's ending balance of retained earnings? To answer this question, prepare Mondala's statement of retained earnings for the year ended December 31, 2009, complete with its appropriate heading.

Preparing a balance sheet
(Obj. 4)

S1-10 At December 31, 2009, Skate Sharp Limited has cash of $13,000, receivables of $2,000, and inventory of $40,000. The company's equipment totals $75,000, and other assets amount to $10,000. Skate Sharp owes accounts payable of $10,000 and short-term notes payable of $5,000, and also has long-term debt of $70,000.

Contributed capital is $15,000.

Prepare Skate Sharp Limited's balance sheet at December 31, 2009, complete with its appropriate heading.

Preparing a cash flow statement
(Obj. 4)

S1-11 Brazos Medical, Inc., ended 2008 with cash of $24,000. During 2009, Brazos earned net income of $120,000 and had adjustments to reconcile net income to net cash provided by operations totaling $20,000 (this is a negative amount).

Brazos paid $300,000 for equipment during 2009 and had to borrow half of this amount on a long-term note. During the year, the company paid dividends of $15,000 and sold old equipment, receiving cash of $60,000.

Prepare Brazos' cash flow statement with its appropriate heading for the year ended December 31, 2009. Follow the format in the summary problem on page 28.

Identifying items with the appropriate financial statements
(Obj. 5)

S1-12 Suppose you are analyzing the financial statements of a Canadian company. Identify each item with its appropriate financial statement, using the following abbreviations: income statement (IS), statement of retained earnings (SRE), balance sheet (BS), and cash flow statement (CFS).

Three items appear on two financial statements, and one item shows up on three statements.

a. Dividends _____

b. Salary expense _____

c. Inventory _____

d. Sales revenue _____

e. Retained earnings _____

f. Net cash provided by operating activities _____

g. Net income _____

h. Cash _____

i. Net cash provided by financing activities _____

j. Accounts payable _____

k. Common shares _____

l. Interest revenue _____

m. Long-term debt _____

n. Net increase or decrease in cash _____

EXERCISES

E1-13 Quality Environmental Inc. needs funds, and Mary Wu, the president, has asked you to consider investing in the business. Answer the following questions about the different ways that Wu might organize the business. Explain each answer.

Organizing a business
(Obj. 1)

a. What form of organization will enable the owners of Quality Environmental to limit their risk of loss to the amount they have invested in the business?

b. What form of business organization will give Wu the most freedom to manage the business as she wishes?

c. What form of organization will give creditors the maximum protection in the event that Quality Environmental fails and cannot pay its liabilities?

If you were Wu and could organize the business as you wish, what form of organization would you choose for Quality Environmental? Explain your reasoning.

E1-14 Ed Eisler wants to open a café in Digby, Nova Scotia. In need of cash, he asks the Bank of Montreal for a loan. The bank requires financial statements to show likely results of operations for the year and the expected financial position at year-end. With little knowledge of accounting, Eisler doesn't understand the request. Explain to him the information provided by the income statement and the balance sheet. Indicate why a lender would require this information.

Evaluating business operations
(Obj. 4)

E1-15 Identify the accounting concept or principle that best applies to each of the following situations.

Applying accounting concepts and principles
(Obj. 2)

a. Wendy's, the restaurant chain, sold a store location to Burger King. How can Wendy's determine the sale price of the store—by a professional appraisal, Wendy's cost, or the amount actually received from the sale?

b. Inflation has been around 6% for some time. Trammel Crow Realtors is considering measuring its land values in inflation-adjusted amounts.

c. Toyota wants to determine which division of the company—Toyota or Lexus—is more profitable.

d. You get an especially good buy on a laptop, paying only $399 for a computer that normally costs $799. What is your accounting value for this computer?

E1-16 Compute the missing amount in the accounting equation for each company (amounts in millions):

Accounting equations
(Obj. 3)

	Assets	Liabilities	Shareholders' Equity
Telus................................	$?	$10,061	$ 6,926
Scotiabank	411,510	?	18,804
Shoppers Drugmart..........	5,644	2,434	?

Which company appears to have the strongest financial position? Explain your reasoning.

Accounting equation; evaluating business
(Obj. 3, 4)

E1-17 Assume **Maple Leaf Foods Inc.** has current assets of $633.6 million; capital assets of $1,126.7 million; and other assets totalling $1,237.5 million. Current liabilities are $591.2 million and long-term liabilities total $1,245.2 million.

❙ Required

1. Use these data to write Maple Leaf Foods' accounting equation.

2. How much in resources does Maple Leaf Foods have to work with?

3. How much does Maple Leaf Foods owe creditors?

4. How much of the company's assets do the Maple Leaf Foods shareholders actually own?

Apply accounting equation
(Obj. 3)

E1-18 We Store For You Ltd.'s comparative balance sheets at December 31, 2009, and December 31, 2008, report (in millions):

	2009	2008
Total assets	$40	$30
Total liabilities	10	8

❙ Required

Below are three situations about We Store For You's issuance of shares and payment of dividends during the year ended December 31, 2009. For each situation, use the accounting equation and statement of retained earnings to compute the amount of We Store For You's net income or loss during the year ended December 31, 2009.

1. We Store For You issued shares for $2 million and paid no dividends.

2. We Store For You issued no shares and paid dividends of $3 million.

3. We Store For You issued shares for $11 million and paid dividends of $2 million.

Applying the accounting equation to business operations
(Obj. 3, 4)

E1-19 Answer these questions about two companies.

1. Mortimer Limited began the year with total liabilities of $400,000 and total shareholders' equity of $300,000. During the year, total assets increased by 20%. How much are total assets at the end of the year?

2. Aztec Associates began a year with total assets of $500,000 and total liabilities of $200,000. Net income for the year was $100,000 and no dividends were paid. How much is shareholders' equity at the end of the year?

Identifying financial statement information
(Obj. 5)

E1-20 Assume MySpace Inc. is expanding into the United States. The company must decide where to locate, and how to finance the expansion. Identify the financial statement where decision makers can find the following information about MySpace Inc. In some cases, more than one statement will report the needed data.

a. Common shares

b. Income tax payable

c. Dividends

d. Income tax expense

e. Ending balance of retained earnings

f. Total assets

g. Long-term debt

h. Revenue

i. Cash spent to acquire equipment

j. Selling, general, and administrative expenses

k. Adjustments to reconcile net income to net cash provided by operations

l. Ending cash balance

m. Current liabilities

n. Net income

o. Cost of goods sold

E1-21 Amounts of the assets and liabilities of Torrance Associates Inc., as of December 31, 2009, are given as follows. Also included are revenue and expense figures for the year ended on that date (amounts in millions):

Business organization, balance sheet
(Obj. 2, 5)

Property and equipment, net	$ 4	Total revenue	$ 35
Investment	72	Receivables	253
Long-term liabilities	73	Current liabilities	290
Other expenses	14	Common shares	12
Cash	28	Interest expense	3
Retained earnings, beginning	19	Salary and other employee expense	9
Retained earnings, ending	?	Other assets	43

❚ *Required*

Prepare the balance sheet of Torrance Associates Inc. at December 31, 2009. Use the accounting equation to compute ending retained earnings.

E1-22 This exercise should be worked only in connection with Exercise 1-21. Refer to the data of Torrance Associates Inc. in Exercise 1-21.

Business organization, income statement
(Obj. 2, 5)

❚ *Required*

1. Prepare the income statement of Torrance Associates Inc. for the year ended December 31, 2009.
2. What amount of dividends did Torrance declare during the year ended December 31, 2009? Hint: Prepare a statement of retained earnings.

E1-23 Groovy Limited began 2009 with $95,000 in cash. During 2009, Groovy earned net income of $300,000 and adjustments to reconcile net income to net cash provided by operations totalled $60,000, a positive amount. Investing activities used cash of $400,000, and financing activities provided cash of $70,000. Groovy ended 2009 with total assets of $250,000 and total liabilities of $110,000.

Business organization, cash flow statement
(Obj. 2, 4, 5)

❚ *Required*

Prepare Groovy Limited's cash flow statement for the year ended December 31, 2009. Identify the data items that do not appear on the cash flow statement and indicate which financial statement reports these items.

E1-24 Assume a FedEx Kinko's at the University of Saskatchewan ended the month of July 2009 with these data:

Preparing an income statement and a statement of retained earnings
(Obj. 5)

Payments of cash:		Cash receipts:	
Acquisition of equipment	$36,000	Issuance (sale) of shares to	
Dividends	2,000	owners	$35,000
Retained earnings at July 1, 2009	0	Rent expense	700
Retained earnings of July 31, 2009	?	Common shares	35,000
Utilities expense	200	Equipment	36,000
Adjustments to reconcile net income		Office supplies expense	1,200
to cash provided by operations	3,200	Accounts payable	3,200
Salary expense	4,000	Service revenue	14,000
Cash balance July 1, 2009	0		
Cash balance July 31, 2009	8,100		

❚ *Required*

Prepare the income statement and the statement of retained earnings of this FedEx Kinko's for the month ended July 31, 2009.

Preparing a balance sheet
(Obj. 5)

E1-25 Refer to the data in the preceding exercise. Prepare the balance sheet of the FedEx Kinko's at July 31, 2009.

Preparing a cash flow statement
(Obj. 5)

E1-26 Refer to the data in Exercise 1-24. Prepare the cash flow statement of the FedEx Kinko's at the University of Saskatchewan for the month ended July 31, 2009. Draw arrows linking the pertinent items in the statements you prepared for Exercises 1-24 through 1-26.

Advising a business
(Obj. 4, 5)

E1-27 This exercise should be used in conjunction with Exercises 1-24 through 1-26. The owner of the FedEx Kinko's now seeks your advice as to whether the University of Saskatchewan store should cease operations or continue operating. Write a report giving the owner your opinion of operating results, dividends, financial position, and cash flows during the company's first month of operations. Cite specifics from the financial statements to support your opinion. Conclude your report with advice on whether to stay in business or cease operations.

Applying accounting concepts to explain business activity
(Obj. 2, 5)

E1-28 Apply your understanding of the relationships among the financial statements to answer these questions.
a. How can a business earn large profits but have a small balance of retained earnings?
b. Give two reasons why a business can have a steady stream of net income over a five-year period and still experience a cash shortage.
c. If you could pick a single source of cash for your business, what would it be? Why?
d. How can a business lose money several years in a row and still have plenty of cash?

QUIZ

Test your understanding of the financial statements by answering the following questions. Select the best choice from among the possible answers given.

Q1-29 The *primary* objective of financial reporting is to provide information
a. Useful for making investment and credit decisions
b. About the profitability of the enterprise
c. On the cash flows of the company
d. To the federal government

Q1-30 For a company of a certain size, which type of business organization provides the least amount of protection for bankers and other creditors of the company?
a. Proprietorship
b. Partnership
c. Both a and b
d. Corporation

Q1-31 Assets are usually reported at their
a. Appraised value
b. Current market value
c. Historical cost
d. None of the above (fill in the blank)

Q1-32 During January, assets increased by $20,000 and liabilities increased by $4,000. Shareholders' equity must have
a. Increased by $16,000
b. Increased by $24,000
c. Decreased by $16,000
d. Decreased by $24,000

Q1-33 The amount a company expects to collect from customers appears on the
a. Income statement in the expenses section
b. Balance sheet in the current assets section
c. Balance sheet in the shareholders' equity section
d. Cash flow statement

Q1-34 All of the following are current assets except
a. Cash
b. Accounts receivable
c. Inventory
d. Sales revenue

Q1-35 Revenues are
a. Increases in share capital resulting from the owners investing in the business
b. Increases in retained earnings resulting from selling products or performing services
c. Decreases in liabilities resulting from paying off loans
d. All of the above

Q1-36 The financial statement that reports revenues and expenses is called the
a. Statement of retained earnings
b. Income statement
c. Cash flow statement
d. Balance sheet

Q1-37 Another name for the balance sheet is the
a. Statement of operations
b. Statement of earnings
c. Statement of profit and loss
d. Statement of financial position

Q1-38 Baldwin Corporation began the year with cash of $35,000 and a computer that cost $20,000. During the year Baldwin earned sales revenue of $140,000 and had the following expenses: salaries, $59,000; rent, $8,000; and utilities, $3,000. At year end Baldwin's cash balance was down to $16,000. How much net income (or net loss) did Baldwin experience for the year?
a. ($19,000)
b. $70,000
c. $107,000
d. $140,000

Q1-39 Quartz Instruments had retained earnings of $145,000 at December 31, 2008. Net income for 2009 totalled $90,000, and dividends for 2009 were $30,000. How much retained earnings should Quartz report at December 31, 2009?
a. $205,000
b. $235,000
c. $140,000
d. $175,000

Q1-40 Net income appears on which financial statement(s)?
a. Income statement
b. Statement of retained earnings
c. Both a and b
d. Balance sheet

Q1-41 Cash paid to purchase a building appears on the cash flow statement among the
a. Operating activities
b. Financing activities
c. Investing activities
d. Shareholders' equity

Q1-42 The shareholders' equity of Chernasky Company at the beginning and end of 2009 totalled $15,000 and $18,000, respectively. Assets at the beginning of 2009 were $25,000. If the liabilities of Chernasky Company increased by $8,000 in 2009, how much were total assets at the end of 2009? Use the accounting equation.
a. $36,000
b. $16,000
c. $2,000
d. Some other amount (fill in the blank)

Q1-43 Drexler Company had the following on the dates indicated:

	12/31/09	12/31/08
Total assets	$750,000	$520,000
Total liabilities	300,000	200,000

Drexler had no share transactions in 2009 and, thus, the change in shareholders' equity for 2009 was due to net income and dividends. If dividends were $50,000, how much was Drexler's net income for 2009? Use the accounting equation and the statements of retained earnings.
a. $100,000
b. $130,000
c. $180,000
d. Some other amount (fill in the blank)

PROBLEMS

(GROUP A)

Applying accounting vocabulary, concepts, and principles to the income statement
(Obj. 1, 2, 4, 5)

P1-44A Assume that the Special Contract Division of **FedEx Kinko's** experienced the following transactions during the year ended December 31, 2009.

a. Suppose the division provided copy services to Telus for the discounted price of $250,000. Under normal conditions, Kinko's would have provided these services for $280,000. Other revenues totalled $50,000.

b. Salaries cost the division $20,000 to provide these services. The division had to pay employees overtime. Ordinarily the salary cost for these services would have been $18,000.

c. Other expenses totalled $240,000. Income tax expense was 30% of income before tax.

d. Kinko's has two operating divisions. Each division is accounted for separately to indicate how well each is performing. At year end, Kinko's combines the statements of divisions to show results for Kinko's as a whole.

e. Inflation affects the amounts that Kinko's must pay for copy machines. To show the effects of inflation, net income would drop by $3,000.

f. If Kinko's were to go out of business, the sale of its assets would bring in $150,000 in cash.

I *Required*

1. Prepare the Special Contracts Division income statement for the year ended December 31, 2009.

2. As CEO, identify the accounting concept or principle that provides guidance in accounting for the items described in a through f. State how you have applied the concept or principle in preparing the division income statement.

Using the accounting equation
(Obj. 3)

P1-45A Compute the missing amounts (shown by a ?) for each company (in millions).

	Link Ltd.	Chain Inc.	Fence Corp.
Beginning			
Assets	$ 78	$ 30	?
Liabilities	47	19	$ 2
Common shares	6	1	2
Retained earnings	?	10	3
Ending			
Assets	?	$ 48	$ 9
Liabilities	$ 48	30	?
Common shares	6	1	2
Retained earnings	27	?	4
Owners' equity			
Dividends	$ 3	$2	$0
Income statement			
Revenues	$216	?	$20
Expenses	211	$144	19
Net income	?	9	1

At the end of the year, which company has the

- highest net income?
- highest percentage of net income to revenues?

Hint: Prepare a statement of retained earnings to help with your calculations.

P1-46A Dan Shoe, the manager of STRIDES Inc., prepared the company's balance sheet while the accountant was ill. The balance sheet contains numerous errors. In particular, Shoe knew that the balance sheet should balance, so he plugged in the shareholders' equity amount needed to achieve this balance. The shareholders' equity amount is *not* correct. All other amounts are accurate.

Balance sheet
(Obj. 2, 5)

Strides Inc.
Balance Sheet
For the Month Ended July 31, 2009

Assets		Liabilities	
Cash	$ 25,000	Accounts receivable	$ 20,000
Store fixtures	10,000	Sales revenue	80,000
Accounts payable	16,000	Interest expense	800
Rent expense	4,000	Note payable	9,000
Salaries expense	15,000	Total	109,800
Land	44,000		
Advertising expense	3,000	**Shareholders' Equity**	
		Shareholders' equity	7,200
Total assets	$117,000	Total liabilities and shareholders' equity	$117,000

Required

1. Prepare the correct balance sheet and date it properly. Compute total assets, total liabilities, and shareholders' equity.
2. Is STRIDES Inc. actually in better or worse financial position than the erroneous balance sheet reports? Give the reason for your answer.
3. Identify the accounts listed on the incorrect balance sheet that are not reported on the balance sheet. State why you excluded them from the correct balance sheet you prepared for Requirement 1. On which financial statement should these accounts appear?

P1-47A Alexa Markowitz is a realtor. She buys and sells properties on her own, and she also earns commission as an agent for buyers and sellers. She organized her business as a corporation on March 16, 2009. The business received $60,000 cash from Markowitz and issued common shares. Consider the following facts as of March 31, 2009:

Balance sheet, entity concept
(Obj. 2, 5)

a. Markowitz has $5,000 in her personal bank account and $14,000 in the business bank account.
b. Office supplies on hand at the real estate office total $1,000.
c. Markowitz's business spent $25,000 for a ReMax franchise, which entitles her to represent herself as an agent. ReMax is a national affiliation of independent real estate agents. This franchise is a business asset.
d. The business owes $60,000 on a note payable for some undeveloped land acquired for a total price of $110,000.
e. Markowitz owes $100,000 on a personal mortgage on her personal residence, which she acquired in 2002 for a total price of $350,000.
f. Markowitz owes $1,800 on a personal charge account with Holt Renfrew.
g. Markowitz acquired business furniture for $10,000 on March 25. Of this amount, the business owes $6,000 on accounts payable at March 31.

Required

1. Prepare the balance sheet of the real estate business of Alexa Markowitz Realtor Inc. at March 31, 2009.
2. Does it appear that the realty business can pay its debts? How can you tell?
3. Explain why some of the items given in the preceding facts were not reported on the balance sheet of the business.

Income statement, statement of retained earnings, balance sheet (Obj. 5)

P1-48A The assets and liabilities of Web Services Inc. as of December 31, 2009, and revenues and expenses for the year ended on that date are listed here.

Land..........................	$ 8,000	Equipment..............................	$ 11,000
Note payable	32,000	Interest expense	4,000
Property tax expense	2,000	Interest payable.......................	2,000
Rent expense............................	15,000	Accounts payable	15,000
Accounts receivable.................	25,000	Salary expense	40,000
Service revenue	150,000	Building.................................	126,000
Supplies	2,000	Cash..	8,000
Utilities expense......................	3,000	Common shares......................	15,000

Beginning retained earnings was $60,000, and dividends totalled $30,000 for the year.

❙ Required

1. Prepare the income statement of Web Services Inc. for the year ended December 31, 2009.
2. Prepare the company's statement of retained earnings for the year.
3. Prepare the company's balance sheet at December 31, 2009.
4. As CEO of Web Services Inc., after answering these questions, will you be pleased by Web Services' performance in 2009?

   a. Was Web Services profitable during 2009? By how much?

   b. Did retained earnings increase or decrease? By how much?

   c. Which is greater, total liabilities or total equity? Who owns more of Web Services's assets, creditors or Web Services's shareholders?

Preparing a cash flow statement (Obj. 5)

P1-49A The following data are adapted from the financial statements of **The Jean Coutu Group** (PJC) Inc. for the fiscal year ended March 1, 2008 (in millions):

Purchases of capital assets and		Accounts receivable.......................	$168
other assets.................................	$ 144	Redemption of common shares	177
Issuance of long-term debt	164	Payment of dividends....................	31
Net loss	(251)	Common shares	715
Adjustments to reconcile		Issuance of common shares...........	1
net income (loss) to cash		Sales of capital assets and	
provided by operations..............	397	other assets................................	1
Revenues	1,676	Retained earnings..........................	752
Cash, beginning of year.................	41	Repayment of long-term debt	1
end of year	0		
Cost of goods sold.........................	1,370		

❙ Required

1. Prepare a cash flow statement for the fiscal year ended March 1, 2008. Follow the format of the summary problem on page 28. Not all items given are reported in the cash flow statement.
2. What was the largest source of cash? Is this a sign of financial strength or weakness?

Analyzing a company's financial statements (Obj. 4, 5)

P1-50A Summarized versions of the Gonzales Corporation's financial statements are given (on the next page) for two years.

| | (In Thousands) | |
	2009	2008
Statement of Operations		
Revenues	$ k	$16,000
Cost of goods sold	11,500	a
Other expenses	1,300	1,200
Earnings before income taxes	4,000	3,700
Income taxes (35% tax rate)	l	1,300
Net earnings	$ m	$ b
Statement of Retained Earnings		
Beginning balance	$ n	$ 3,500
Net earnings	o	c
Dividends	(300)	(200)
Ending balance	$ p	$ d
Balance Sheet		
Assets:		
Cash	$ q	$ e
Capital assets	3,000	1,800
Other assets	r	11,200
Total assets	$ s	$15,000
Liabilities:		
Current liabilities	$ t	$ 5,600
Notes payable and long-term debt	4,500	3,200
Other liabilities	80	200
Total liabilities	$ 9,100	$ f
Shareholders' Equity:		
Common shares	$ 300	$ 300
Retained earnings	u	g
Total shareholders' equity	v	6,000
Total liabilities and shareholders' equity	$ w	$ h
Cash Flow Statement		
Net cash provided by operating activities	$ x	$ 1,900
Net cash used for investing activities	(1,000)	(900)
Net cash used for financing activities	(700)	(1.010)
Increase (decrease) in cash	400	i
Cash at beginning of year	y	2,010
Cash at end of year	$ z	$ j

❙ Required

1. Determine the missing amounts denoted by the letters.
2. As Gonzales Corporation's CEO, use financial statements to answer these questions about the company. Explain each of your answers, and identify the financial statement where you found the information.

   a. Did operations improve or deteriorate during 2009?

   b. What is the company doing with most of its income—retaining it for use in the business or using it for dividends?

   c. How much in total resources does the company have to work with as it moves into the year 2010?

   d. At the end of 2008, how much did the company owe outsiders? At the end of 2009, how much did the company owe? Is this trend good or bad in comparison to the trend in assets?

e. What is the company's major source of cash? Is cash increasing or decreasing? What is your opinion of the company's ability to generate cash?

(GROUP B)

Applying accounting vocabulary, concepts, and principles to the income statement
(Obj. 1, 2, 4, 5)

P1-51B Snap Fasteners Inc. experienced the following transactions during the year ended December 31, 2009:

a. Snap sold products for $56.2 million. Company management believes that the value of these products is approximately $60.5 million.
b. It cost Snap $40.0 million to manufacture the products it sold. If Snap had purchased the products instead of manufacturing them, Snap's cost would have been $43.0 million.
c. All other expenses, excluding income taxes, totalled $14.9 million for the year. Income tax expense was 35% of income before tax.
d. Snap has several operating divisions. Each division is accounted for separately to show how well each division is performing. However, Snap's financial statements combine the statements of all the divisions to report on the company as a whole.
e. Inflation affects Snap's cost to manufacture goods. If Snap's financial statements were to show the effects of inflation, assume the company's reported net income would drop by $0.250 million.
f. If Snap were to go out of business, the sale of its assets may bring in over $5 million in cash.

❚ *Required*

1. Prepare Snap's income statement for the year ended December 31, 2009.
2. For items a through f, identify the accounting concept or principle that explains how you accounted for the item described. State how you have applied the concept or principle in preparing Snap's income statement.

Using the accounting equation
(Obj. 3)

P1-52B Compute the missing amounts (?) for each company (in millions).

	Gas Limited	Groceries Inc.	Bottlers Corp.
Beginning			
Assets	$11,200	$ 3,256	$ 909
Liabilities	4,075	1,756	564
Ending			
Assets	$12,400	$?	$1,025
Liabilities	4,400	1,699	565
Owners' Equity			
Issuance/(Repurchase) of shares	$ (36)	$ (0)	$?
Dividends	341	30	0
Income Statement			
Revenues	$11,288	$11,099	$1,663
Expenses	?	10,879	1,568

Which company has the

- highest net income?
- highest percentage of net income to revenues?

Hint: Prepare a statement of owners' equity, which begins with opening shareholders' equity and adds and subtracts changes to conclude with closing shareholders' equity.

P1-53B Ned Robinson, the manager of Lunenberg Times Inc., prepared the balance sheet of the company while the accountant was ill. The balance sheet contains numerous errors. In particular, the manager knew that the balance sheet should balance, so he plugged in the shareholders' equity amount needed to achieve this balance. The shareholders' equity amount, however, is *not* correct. All other amounts are accurate.

Balance sheet
(Obj. 2, 5)

Lunenberg Times Inc.
Balance Sheet
For the Month Ended October 31, 2009

Assets		Liabilities	
Cash	$ 25,000	Accounts receivable	$ 10,000
Office furniture	15,000	Sales revenue	70,000
Note payable	16,000	Salary expense	20,000
Rent expense	4,000	Accounts payable	8,000
Inventory	30,000		
Land	34,000	**Shareholders' Equity**	
Advertising expense	2,500	Shareholders' equity	18,500
Total assets	$126,500	Total liabilities.........................	$126,500

I Required

1. Prepare the correct balance sheet and date it properly. Compute total assets, total liabilities, and shareholders' equity.
2. Is Lunenberg Times Inc. actually in better or worse financial position than the erroneous balance sheet reports? Give the reason for your answer.
3. Identify the accounts listed in the incorrect balance sheet that are *not* reported on the corrected balance sheet. State why you excluded them from the correct balance sheet you prepared for Requirement 1. Which financial statement should these accounts appear on?

P1-54B Luis Fantano is a realtor. He buys and sells properties on his own and also earns commission as an agent for buyers and sellers. Fantano organized his business as a corporation on July 10, 2009. The business received $75,000 from Fantano and issued common shares. Consider these facts as of July 31, 2009:

Balance sheet, entity concept
(Obj. 2, 5)

a. Fantano owes $5,000 on a personal charge account with Visa.
b. Fantano's business owes $80,000 on a note payable for some undeveloped land acquired for a total price of $135,000.
c. Fantano has $5,000 in his personal bank account and $10,000 in the business bank account.
d. Office supplies on hand at the real estate office total $1,000.
e. Fantano's business spent $35,000 for a Century 21 real estate franchise, which entitles him to represent himself as a Century 21 agent. Century 21 is a national affiliation of independent real estate agents. This franchise is a business asset.
f. Fantano owes $125,000 on a personal mortgage on his personal residence, which he acquired in 2001 for a total price of $300,000.
g. Fantano acquired business furniture for $18,000 on July 15. Of this amount, his business owes $10,000 on open account at July 31.

I Required

1. Prepare the balance sheet of the realty business of Luis Fantano Realtor Inc. at July 31, 2009.
2. Does it appear that Fantano's realty business can pay its debts? How can you tell?
3. Identify the personal items given in the preceding facts that would not be reported on the balance sheet of the business.

Income statement, statement of retained earnings, balance sheet
(Obj. 5)

P1-55B The assets and liabilities of Auto Mechanics Ltd. as of December 31, 2009, and revenues and expenses for the year ended on that date follow.

Interest expense	$ 4,000	Accounts receivable	$ 25,000
Land	95,000	Advertising expense	10,000
Note payable	95,000	Building	140,000
Accounts payable	21,000	Salary expense	85,000
Rent expense	6,000	Salary payable	12,000
Cash	10,000	Service revenue	210,000
Common shares	75,000	Supplies	3,000
Furniture	20,000	Property tax expense	5,000

Beginning retained earnings were $40,000, and dividends totalled $50,000 for the year.

❙ Required

1. Prepare the income statement of Auto Mechanics Ltd. for the year ended December 31, 2009.
2. Prepare the Auto Mechanics Ltd. statement of retained earnings for the year.
3. Prepare Auto Mechanics' balance sheet at December 31, 2009.
4. Using the information prepared in Requirements 1 through 3:
   a. Was Auto Mechanics Ltd. profitable during 2009? By how much?
   b. Did retained earnings increase or decrease? By how much?
   c. Which is greater, total liabilities or total equity? Who owns more of Auto Mechanics Ltd.'s assets, the creditors or the shareholders?

Preparing a cash flow statement
(Obj. 5)

P1-56B The data below are adapted from the financial statements of Long Boat Ltd. at the end of a recent year (in thousands).

Adjustments to reconcile net income to cash provided by operations	$ 65	Sales of capital assets	$ 2
Revenues	3,870	Payment of long-term debt	26
Bank overdraft, beginning of year	(11)	Cost of goods sold	3,182
Cash, end of year	23	Common shares	212
Purchases of capital assets	123	Accounts receivable	271
Long-term debt	234	Issuance of common shares	4
Net income	180	Change in bank loan	(44)
Retained earnings	1,000	Payment of dividends	24

❙ Required

1. Prepare Long Boat's cash flow statement for the year. Follow the solution to the summary problem starting on page 27. Not all the items given appear on the cash flow statement.
2. Which activities provided the bulk of Long Boat's cash? Is this a sign of financial strength or weakness?

Analyzing a company's financial statements
(Obj. 4, 5)

P6-57B Condensed versions of Your Phone Ltd.'s financial statements, with certain amounts omitted, are given for two years.

	(Thousands)	
	2009	2008
Statement of Income		
Revenues	$94,500	$ a
Cost of goods sold	k	65,400
Other expenses	15,660	13,550
Income before income taxes	5,645	9,300
Income taxes (35%)	l	3,450
Net income	$ m	$ b
Statement of Retained Earnings		
Beginning balance	$ n	$10,000
Net income	o	c
Dividends	(480)	(450)
Ending balance	$ p	$ d
Balance Sheet		
Assets:		
Cash	$ q	$ 400
Capital assets	23,790	e
Other assets	r	17,900
Total assets	$ s	$38,500
Liabilities:		
Current liabilities	$11,100	$10,000
Long-term debt and other liabilities	t	12,500
Total liabilities	24,500	f
Shareholders' Equity:		
Common shares	$ 400	$ 600
Retained earnings	u	g
Total shareholders' equity	v	16,000
Total liabilities and shareholders' equity ...	$ w	$ h
Cash Flow Statement		
Net cash provided by operating activities	$ x	$ 3,600
Net cash used for investing activities	(2,700)	(4,150)
Net cash provided by financing activities	250	900
Increase (decrease) in cash	50	i
Cash at beginning of year	y	50
Cash at end of year	$ z	$ j

❙ Required

1. Determine the missing amounts denoted by the letters.
2. Use Your Phone's financial statements to answer these questions about the company. Explain each of your answers.

   a. Did operations improve or deteriorate during 2009?

   b. What is the company doing with most of its income—retaining it for use in the business or using it for dividends?

   c. How much in total resources does the company have to work with as it moves into 2010? How much in total resources did the company have at the end of 2008?

   d. At the end of 2008, how much did the company owe outsiders? At the end of 2009, how much did the company owe?

   e. What is the company's major source of cash? What is your opinion of the company's ability to generate cash? How is the company using most of its cash? Is the company growing or shrinking?

APPLY YOUR KNOWLEDGE

DECISION CASES

Evaluating business operations; using financial statements
(Obj. 4, 5)

Case 1. Two businesses, Web Services and PC Providers, have sought business loans from you. To decide whether to make the loans, you have requested their balance sheets.

Web Services
Balance Sheet
October 31, 2009

Assets		Liabilities	
Cash	$ 11,000	Accounts payable	$ 13,000
Accounts receivable	4,000	Notes payable	377,000
Furniture	36,000	Total liabilities	390,000
Software	79,000	**Shareholders' Equity**	
Computers	300,000	Shareholders' equity	40,000
		Total liabilities and	
Total assets	$430,000	shareholders' equity	$430,000

PC Providers Inc.
Balance Sheet
October 31, 2009

Assets		Liabilities	
Cash	$ 9,000	Accounts payable	$ 12,000
Accounts receivable	24,000	Note payable	28,000
Merchandise inventory	85,000	Total liabilities	40,000
Furniture and fixtures	9,000		
Building	82,000	**Shareholders' Equity**	
Land	14,000	Shareholders' equity	183,000
		Total liabilities and	
Total assets	$223,000	shareholders' equity	$223,000

▌*Required*

1. Using only these balance sheets, to which entity would you be more comfortable lending money? Explain fully, citing specific items and amounts from the respective balance sheets.

2. Is there other financial information you would consider before making your decision? Be specific.

Analyzing a company's financial statements
(Obj. 4, 5)

Case 2. After you have been out of college for a year, you have $5,000 to invest. A friend has started My Dream Inc., and she asks you to invest in her company. You obtain My Dream Inc.'s financial statements, which are summarized at the end of the first year as follows:

My Dream Inc.
Income Statement
For the Year Ended December 31, 2009

Revenues	$80,000
Expenses	60,000
Net income	$20,000

My Dream Inc. Balance Sheet December 31, 2009			
Cash	$13,000	Liabilities	$35,000
Other assets	67,000	Equity	45,000
Total assets............................	$80,000	Total liabilities and equity	$80,000

Visits with your friend turn up the following facts:

a. The company owes an additional $10,000 for TV ads that was incurred in December but not recorded in the books.

b. Software costs of $20,000 were recorded as assets. These costs should have been expensed. My Dream paid cash for these expenses and recorded the cash payment correctly.

c. Revenues and receivables of $10,000 were overlooked and omitted.

▌Required

1. Prepare corrected financial statements.

2. Use your corrected statements to evaluate My Dream's results of operations and financial position.

3. Will you invest in My Dream? Give your reason.

ETHICAL ISSUE

During 2002, Enron Corporation admitted excluding large liabilities from its balance sheet. WorldCom confessed to recording expenses as assets. In 2002, Livent Inc.'s senior executives were charged with reducing expenses and inflating profits. All of these companies needed to improve their appearance as reported in their financial statements.

▌Required

1. What is the fundamental ethical issue in these situations?

2. Use the accounting equation to show how Enron abused good accounting. Use a separate accounting equation to demonstrate WorldCom's error. Do the same for Livent.

3. What can happen when companies report financial data that are untrue?

FOCUS ON FINANCIALS

Mullen Group Income Fund

This and similar cases in succeeding chapters are based on the financial statements of Mullen Group Income Fund (www.mullen-group.com). As you work with Mullen Group Income Fund throughout this course, you will develop the ability to use actual financial statements.

Evaluating business operations
(Obj. 4)

▌Required

Refer to the Mullen Group Income Fund financial statements in Appendix B at the end of the book.

1. Suppose you own units in Mullen. If you could pick one item on the company's income statement to increase year after year, what would it be? Why is this item so important? Did this item increase or decrease during 2007? Is this good news or bad news for the company?

2. What was Mullen's largest expense each year? In your own words, explain the meaning of this item. Give specific examples of items that make up this expense. Why is this expense less than sales revenue?

3. Use the balance sheet of Mullen Group Income Fund in Appendix B to answer these questions. At the end of 2007, how much in total resources did Mullen have to work with? How much did the company owe? How much of its assets did the company's shareholders actually own? Use these amounts to write Mullen's accounting equation at December 31, 2007.

4. How much cash did Mullen have at the beginning of the most recent year? How much cash did it have at the end of the year? Where does Mullen get most of its cash? How does the company spend its cash?

FOCUS ON ANALYSIS

Evaluating by using financial statements
(Obj. 4, 5)

Sun-Rype Products Ltd.

This and similar cases in succeeding chapters are based on the financial statements of Sun-Rype Products Ltd. (www.sunrype.com). As you work with Sun-Rype Products Ltd. throughout this course, you will develop the ability to analyze financial statements of actual companies.

❚ *Required*

Refer to the Sun-Rype Products Ltd. financial statements in Appendix A at the end of the book.

1. Write Sun-Rype's accounting equation at December 31, 2007 (express all items in millions of dollars). Does Sun-Rype's financial condition look strong or weak? How can you tell?

2. What was the result of Sun-Rype Products' operations during 2007? Identify both the name and the dollar value of the result of operations for 2007. Does an increase (decrease) signal good news or bad news for the company and its shareholders?

3. Examine shareholders' equity on the balance sheet and the statement of retained earnings. What were the changes in shareholders' equity during 2007? What caused these changes?

4. Which statement reports cash as part of Sun-Rype Products' financial position? Which statement tells why cash increased (or decreased) during the year? What two individual items caused Sun-Rype Products' cash to change the most in 2007?

5. Which asset changed the most in 2007 compared to 2006? What account balance on the income statement likely led to the change?

GROUP PROJECT

Project 1. As instructed by your professor, obtain an annual report of a Canadian company.

❚ *Required*

1. Take the role of a loan committee of the Royal Bank of Canada. Assume the company has requested a loan from your bank. Analyze the company's financial statements and any other information you need to reach a decision regarding the largest amount of money you would be willing to lend. Go as deeply into the analysis and the related decision as you can. Specify the following:
   a. Any restrictions you would impose on the borrower.
   b. The length of the loan period (that is, over what period will you allow the company to pay you back).

Note: The long-term debt note to the financial statements gives details of the company's liabilities.

2. Write your group decision in a report addressed to the bank's board of directors. Limit your report to two double-spaced word-processed pages.

3. If your professor directs you to, present your decision and analysis to the class. Limit your presentation to 10 to 15 minutes.

Project 2. You are the owner of a company that is about to "go public" (that is, issue its shares to outside investors). You wish to make your company look as attractive as possible to raise $1 million in cash to expand the business. At the same time, you want to give potential investors a reliable and relevant picture of your company.

❙ *Required*

1. Design a presentation to portray your company in a way that will enable outsiders to reach an informed decision as to whether to invest in your company. The presentation should include the following:
   a. Name and location of your company
   b. Nature of the company's business (be specific and detailed to provide a clear picture of the nature, history, and future goals of the business)
   c. How you plan to spend the money you raise
   d. The company's comparative income statement, statement of retained earnings, balance sheet, and cash flow statement for two years: the current year and the preceding year. Make the data as realistic as possible with the intent of receiving $1 million.

2. Prepare a word-processed presentation that does not exceed five pages.

3. If directed by your professor, distribute copies of your presentation to the class with the intent of interesting your classmates in investing in your company. Make a 10- to 15-minute investment pitch to the class. Measure your success by the amount of investment commitment you receive.

QUICK CHECK ANSWERS

1. *b*
2. *a*
3. *d*
4. *c*
5. *d*
6. *a*
7. *b* ($100,000 − $40,000 − $3,000 = $57,000)
8. *c* ($100,000 − $40,000 = $60,000)
9. *b* [Total assets = $105,000 ($5,000 + $30,000 + $20,000 + $50,000). Shareholders' equity: $80,000 ($105,000 − $25,000)]
10. *d*
11. *d* [$30,000 + Net income ($15,000) − Dividends = $40,000; Dividends = $5,000]
12. *b*

	Assets	=	Liabilities	+	Equity
Beginning	$300,000	=	$200,000	+	$100,000
Increase	50,000	=	40,000	+	10,000*
Ending	350,000	=	240,000	+	110,000*

*Must solve for these amounts.

2

Transaction Analysis

SPOTLIGHT

How do busy men and women in business, government, and education around the world manage their communications? They likely use one of the many versions of the BlackBerry® smartphone from Research In Motion (RIM), which generate lots of income for the company.

How does RIM determine the amount of its revenues, expenses, and net income? Like all other companies, RIM has a comprehensive accounting system. RIM's income statement (statement of operations) is given at the start of this chapter. The income statement shows that during fiscal year 2008, RIM made over $6 billion of sales and earned net income of $1.3 billion. Where did those figures come from? In this chapter, we'll show you.

Research In Motion ▼ Consolidated Statement of Operations (Adapted) For the Year Ended March 31, 2008	
	US$ in millions
Revenue	
Devices and other	$4,914
Service and software	1,095
	6,009
Cost of sales	
Devices and other	2,758
Service and software	171
	2,929
Gross margin	3,080
Expenses	
Research and development	360
Selling, marketing, and administration	881
Amortization	108
	1,349
Income from operations	1,731
Investment income	79
Income before income taxes	1,810
Provision for (recovery of) income taxes	
Current	588
Deferred	(71)
	517
Net income	$1,293

Chapter 1 introduced the basic financial statements. Chapter 2 will show you how companies actually record the transactions that eventually become part of the financial statements.

Transactions

Business activity is all about transactions. A **transaction** is any event that has a financial impact on the business and can be measured reliably. For example, Apple Computer, Inc. pays programmers to create iTunes® software. Apple sells computers and borrows money and repays the loan—three separate transactions.

But not all events qualify as transactions. MTV may feature iTunes, motivating you to consider buying an Apple iPod®. The feature may create lots of new business for Apple. But no transaction occurs until someone actually buys an Apple product. A transaction must occur before Apple records anything.

Transactions provide objective information about the financial impacts on a company. Every transaction has two sides:

- You give something, and
- You receive something.

In accounting we always record both sides of a transaction. And we must be able to measure the financial effect of the event on the business before recording it as a transaction. You must be able to assign a dollar amount to the transaction to record it on the books.

The Account

As we saw in Chapter 1, the accounting equation expresses the basic relationships of accounting:

$$\text{Assets} = \text{Liabilities} + \text{Shareholders' (Owners') Equity}$$

For each asset, each liability, and each element of shareholders' equity, we use a record called the account. An **account** is the record of all the changes in a particular asset, liability, or shareholders' equity during a period. The account is the basic summary device of accounting. Before launching into transaction analysis, let's review the accounts that a company such as RIM uses.

Assets

Assets are economic resources that provide a future benefit for a business. Most firms use the following asset accounts:

Cash. Cash means money and any medium of exchange including bank account balances, paper currency, coins, GICs, and cheques.

Accounts Receivable. RIM, like most other companies, sells its goods or services and receives a promise for future collection of cash. The Accounts Receivable account holds these amounts.

Notes Receivable. RIM may receive a note receivable from a customer, who signed the note promising to pay RIM. A note receivable is similar to an account receivable, but a note receivable is more binding because the customer signed the note. Notes receivable usually specify an interest rate.

Inventory. RIM's most important asset is its inventory: the products the company sells to customers. Other titles for this account include Merchandise and Merchandise Inventory.

Prepaid Expenses. RIM pays certain expenses in advance. A **prepaid expense** is an asset because the payment provides a future benefit for the business. Prepaid Rent, Prepaid Insurance, and Office Supplies are prepaid expenses.

Land. The Land account shows the cost of the land RIM uses in its operations.

Buildings. The cost of RIM's buildings—office buildings, manufacturing factory, and the like—appears in the Buildings account.

Equipment, Furniture, and Fixtures. Businesses have separate asset accounts for each type of equipment, for example, Office Equipment, Manufacturing Equipment, and Store Equipment. The Furniture and Fixtures account shows the cost of these assets, which are similar to equipment.

Liabilities

Recall that a liability is a debt. A receivable is always an asset; a payable is always a liability. The most common types of liabilities include the following:

Accounts Payable. The Accounts Payable account is the direct opposite of Accounts Receivable. RIM's promise to pay a debt arising from a credit purchase of inventory appears in the Accounts Payable account.

Notes Payable. The Notes Payable account is the opposite of the Notes Receivable account. Notes Payable includes the amounts that RIM must pay because RIM signed promissory notes that require future payments. Notes payable, like notes receivable, also carry interest.

Accrued Liabilities. An **accrued liability** is a liability for an expense you have not yet paid. Interest Payable and Salary Payable are accrued liability accounts for most companies. Income Taxes Payable is another accrued liability.

Shareholders' (Owners') Equity

The owners' claims to the assets of a corporation are called shareholders' equity or simply owners' equity. A corporation uses Contributed Capital, Retained Earnings, and Dividends accounts to record changes in the company's shareholders' equity. In a proprietorship, there is a single Capital account. For a partnership, owners' equity is held in separate accounts for each owner's capital balance.

Contributed Capital. The Contributed Capital section shows the owners' investment in the corporation. Common Shares or Share Capital are typical contributed capital account titles. A corporation receives cash and issues common shares to the investor. A company's common shares are its most basic element of equity. All for-profit corporations have common shares with the exception of income trusts, which have trust units.

Retained Earnings. The Retained Earnings account shows the cumulative net income earned by the corporation over its lifetime, minus its cumulative net losses and dividends.

Dividends. After profitable operations, the board of directors of RIM may (or may not) declare and pay a cash dividend. Dividends are optional: they are decided by the board of directors. The corporation may keep a separate account titled Dividends, which indicates a decrease in Retained Earnings.

Revenues. The increase in shareholders' equity that results from delivering goods or services to customers is called revenue. The company uses as many revenue accounts as needed. RIM has two revenue accounts: "Devices and Other" and "Service and Software." A lawyer provides legal services for clients and uses a Service Revenue account. Scotiabank loans money to an outsider and uses an Interest Revenue account. If the business rents a building to a tenant, it needs a Rent Revenue account.

Expenses. An expense is the cost of operating a business. Expenses decrease shareholders' equity, the opposite of revenues. A business needs a separate account for each type of expense, such as Cost of Sales, Salary Expense, Rent Expense, Advertising Expense, and Utilities Expense. Businesses strive to minimize expenses and thereby maximize net income.

STOP & THINK

Accounting for Business Transactions

Objective

① **Analyze** transactions

To illustrate accounting for business transactions, let's return to J.J. Booth and Marie Savard. You met them in Chapter 1 when they opened a consulting engineering company on April 1, 2009, and incorporated it as Tara Inc.

We consider 11 events and analyze each in terms of its effect on the accounting equation of Tara Inc. We begin by using the accounting equation. In the second half of the chapter, we record transactions using the journal and ledger of accounting.

Transaction 1. Booth, Savard, and several fellow engineers invest $50,000 to begin Tara Inc., and the business issues common shares to the shareholders.

The effect of this transaction on the accounting equation of the business entity Tara Inc. is a receipt of $50,000 cash and issuance of common shares:

	ASSETS Cash	=	LIABILITIES	+	SHAREHOLDERS' EQUITY Common Shares	TYPE OF SHAREHOLDERS' EQUITY TRANSACTION
(1)	+ 50,000				+ 50,000	Issued shares

Every transaction's net amount on the left side of the equation must equal the net amount on the right side. The first transaction increases both the cash and the issued common shares of the business. To the right of the transaction we write "Issued shares" to record the reason for the $50,000 increase in shareholders' equity.

Every transaction affects the financial statements, and we can prepare the statements after one, two, or any number of transactions. For example, Tara Inc. could report the company's balance sheet after its first transaction, shown below.

This balance sheet shows that Tara Inc. holds cash of $50,000 and owes no liabilities. The company's equity (ownership) is denoted as Common Shares on the

Tara Inc. Balance Sheet April 1, 2009			
Assets		**Liabilities**	
Cash..	$50,000	None	
		Shareholders' Equity	
		Common shares.....................	$50,000
		Total shareholders' equity....	50,000
		Total liabilities and	
Total assets..............................	$50,000	shareholders' equity	$50,000

balance sheet. A bank would look favourably on the Tara Inc. balance sheet because the business has $50,000 cash and no debt—a strong financial position.

As a practical matter, most entities report their financial statements at the end of the accounting period—not after each transaction. But an accounting system can produce statements whenever managers and owners need to know where the business stands.

Transaction 2. Tara Inc. purchases land for an office location and pays cash of $40,000. The effect of this transaction on the accounting equation is:

	ASSETS				LIABILITIES +	SHAREHOLDERS' EQUITY	TYPE OF SHAREHOLDERS' EQUITY TRANSACTION
	Cash	+	Land			Common Shares	
Bal.	50,000					50,000	Issued shares
(2)	−40,000	+	40,000	=			
Bal.	10,000		40,000			50,000	
		50,000				50,000	

The purchase increases one asset (Land) and decreases another asset (Cash) by the same amount. After the transaction is completed, Tara Inc. has cash of $10,000, land of $40,000, and no liabilities. Shareholders' equity is unchanged at $50,000. Note that total assets must always equal total liabilities plus equity.

Transaction 3. The business buys stationery and other office supplies on account, agreeing to pay $3,700 within 30 days. This transaction increases both the assets and the liabilities of the business. Its effect on the accounting equation is as follows:

	ASSETS				LIABILITIES	+	SHAREHOLDERS' EQUITY
	Cash	+ Office Supplies +	Land		Accounts Payable	+	Common Shares
Bal.	10,000		40,000				50,000
(3)		+3,700		=	+3,700		
Bal.	10,000	3,700	40,000		3,700		50,000
		53,700				53,700	

The new asset is Office Supplies, and the liability is Accounts Payable. Tara signs no formal promissory note, so the liability is an account payable, not a note payable.

Transaction 4. Tara Inc. earns service revenue by providing engineering services. Assume the business earns $7,000 and collects this amount in cash. The effect on the accounting equation is an increase in the asset Cash and an increase in Retained Earnings, as follows:

	ASSETS					LIABILITIES +		SHAREHOLDERS' EQUITY			TYPE OF SHAREHOLDERS' EQUITY TRANSACTION
	Cash	+	Office Supplies	+ Land		Accounts Payable	+	Common Shares	+	Retained Earnings	
Bal.	10,000		3,700	40,000		3,700		50,000			
(4)	+7,000				=					7,000	Service revenue
Bal.	17,000		3,700	40,000		3,700		50,000		7,000	
			60,700					60,700			

Transaction 5. Tara Inc. performs service on account, which means that Tara lets customers pay later. Tara earns revenue but doesn't collect the cash immediately. In Transaction 5, Tara provides engineering service for King Contracting Ltd., and King promises to pay Tara within one month. This promise is an account receivable—an asset—of Tara Inc.

It's performing the service that earns the revenue—not collecting the cash. Therefore, Tara records revenue when it performs the service—regardless of whether Tara receives the cash now or later. The King Contracting Ltd. transaction record follows:

		ASSETS				LIABILITIES +	SHAREHOLDERS' EQUITY			TYPE OF SHAREHOLDERS' EQUITY TRANSACTION
	Cash +	Accounts Receivable +	Office Supplies +	Land		Accounts Payable +	Common Shares +	Retained Earnings		
Bal.	17,000		3,700	40,000		3,700	50,000	7,000		
(5)		+3,000			=			+3,000		Service revenue
Bal.	17,000	3,000	3,700	40,000		3,700	50,000	10,000		
		63,700					63,700			

Transaction 6. During the month, Tara Inc. pays $2,700 for the following expenses: office rent, $1,100; employee salary, $1,200; and utilities, $400. The effect on the accounting equation is:

		ASSETS				LIABILITIES +	SHAREHOLDERS' EQUITY			TYPE OF SHAREHOLDERS' EQUITY TRANSACTION
	Cash +	Accounts Receivable +	Office Supplies +	Land		Accounts Payable +	Common Shares +	Retained Earnings		
Bal.	17,000	3,000	3,700	40,000		3,700	50,000	10,000		
(6)	−1,100							−1,100		Rent expense
	−1,200				=			−1,200		Salary expense
	− 400							− 400		Utilities expense
Bal.	14,300	3,000	3,700	40,000		3,700	50,000	7,300		
		61,000					61,000			

The expenses decrease Tara's Cash and Retained Earnings. List each expense separately to keep track of its amount.

Transaction 7. Tara pays $1,900 on account, which means to make a payment on an account payable. In this transaction, Tara pays part of the balance owing to the store from which it purchased Office Supplies in Transaction 3. The transaction decreases Cash and also decreases Accounts Payable as follows:

		ASSETS				LIABILITIES +	SHAREHOLDERS' EQUITY		
	Cash +	Accounts Receivable +	Office Supplies +	Land		Accounts Payable +	Common Shares +	Retained Earnings
Bal.	14,300	3,000	3,700	40,000		3,700	50,000	7,300
(7)	1,900				=	−1,900		
Bal.	12,400	3,000	3,700	40,000		1,800	50,000	7,300
		59,100					59,100		

Transaction 8. J.J. Booth paid $30,000 to remodel his home. This event is a personal transaction of J.J. Booth. It is not recorded by Tara Inc. We focus solely on the business entity, which this event does not affect. The transaction illustrates the entity concept from Chapter 1.

Transaction 9. In Transaction 5, Tara Inc. performed service for King Contracting on account. The business now collects $1,000 from King Contracting. We say that Tara Inc. collects the cash on account, which means Tara will record an increase in Cash and a decrease in Accounts Receivable. This is not service revenue now because Tara already recorded the revenue in Transaction 5. The effect of collecting cash on account is:

	ASSETS					LIABILITIES	+	SHAREHOLDERS' EQUITY		
	Cash +	Accounts Receivable +	Office Supplies +	Land		Accounts Payable	+	Common Shares	+	Retained Earnings
Bal.	12,400	3,000	3,700	40,000	=	1,800		50,000		7,300
(9)	+1,000	−1,000								
Bal.	13,400	2,000	3,700	40,000		1,800		50,000		7,300
		59,100						59,100		

Transaction 10. Tara Inc. sells part of the land purchased in Transaction 2 for $22,000, which is the same amount it paid for that part of the land it sold. Tara Inc. receives $22,000 cash, and the effect on the accounting equation is:

	ASSETS					LIABILITIES	+	SHAREHOLDERS' EQUITY		
	Cash +	Accounts Receivable +	Office Supplies +	Land		Accounts Payable	+	Common Shares	+	Retained Earnings
Bal.	13,400	2,000	3,700	40,000	=	1,800		50,000		7,300
(10)	+22,000			−22,000						
Bal.	35,400	2,000	3,700	18,000		1,800		50,000		7,300
		59,100						59,100		

Note that the company did not sell all its land; Tara still owns $18,000 worth of land.

Transaction 11. Tara Inc. declares a dividend and pays the shareholders $2,100 cash. The effect on the accounting equation is:

	ASSETS					LIABILITIES +		SHAREHOLDERS' EQUITY			TYPE OF SHAREHOLDERS' EQUITY TRANSACTION
	Cash +	Accounts Receivable +	Office Supplies +	Land		Accounts Payable	+	Common Shares	+	Retained Earnings	
Bal.	35,400	2,000	3,700	18,000	=	1,800		50,000		7,300	
(11)	−2,100									−2,100	Dividends
Bal.	33,300	2,000	3,700	18,000		1,800		50,000		5,200	
		57,000						57,000			

The dividend decreases both the asset Cash and the Retained Earnings of the business. *But dividends are not an expense.*

Transactions and Financial Statements

Exhibit 2-1 summarizes the 11 preceding transactions. Panel A gives the details of the transactions, and Panel B shows the transaction analysis for the transactions that affect the business. As you study the exhibit, note that every transaction on Panel B maintains the following equality:

$$\text{Assets} = \text{Liabilities} + \text{Shareholders' Equity}$$

- *Income statement* data appear as revenues and expenses under Retained Earnings. The revenues increase Retained Earnings; the expenses decrease Retained Earnings.
- The *balance sheet* data are composed of the ending balances of the assets, liabilities, and shareholders' equity shown at the bottom of the exhibit. The account-

EXHIBIT 2-1   **Analysis of Tara Inc. Transactions**

Panel A—Transactions Details

(1) Received $50,000 cash and issued shares to the owners
(2) Paid $40,000 cash for land
(3) Bought $3,700 of office supplies on account
(4) Received $7,000 cash from customers for service revenue earned
(5) Performed services for customers on account, $3,000
(6) Paid cash expenses: rent, $1,100; employee salary, $1,200; utilities, $400

(7) Paid $1,900 on the account payable created in Transaction 3
(8) Shareholder pays personal funds to remodel home, *not a transaction of the business*
(9) Received $1,000 on account
(10) Sold land for cash at its cost of $22,000
(11) Declared and paid a dividend of $2,100 to the shareholders

Panel B—Analysis of Transactions

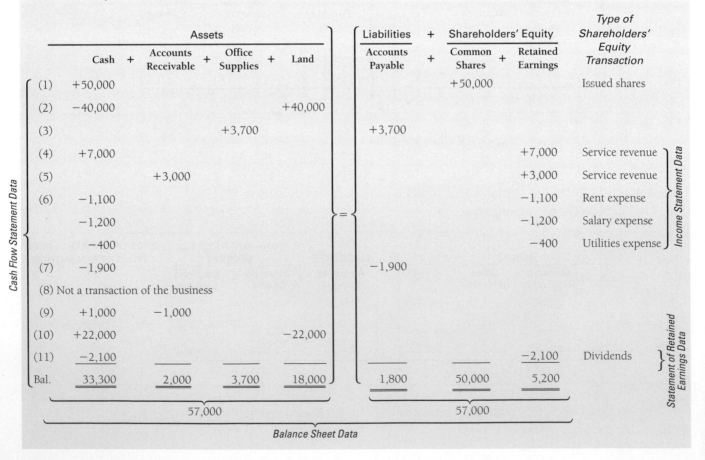

		Assets					Liabilities	+	Shareholders' Equity		Type of Shareholders' Equity Transaction
	Cash +	Accounts Receivable +	Office Supplies +	Land			Accounts Payable	+	Common Shares +	Retained Earnings	
(1)	+50,000								+50,000		Issued shares
(2)	−40,000			+40,000							
(3)			+3,700				+3,700				
(4)	+7,000									+7,000	Service revenue
(5)		+3,000								+3,000	Service revenue
(6)	−1,100									−1,100	Rent expense
	−1,200				=					−1,200	Salary expense
	−400									−400	Utilities expense
(7)	−1,900						−1,900				
(8) Not a transaction of the business											
(9)	+1,000	−1,000									
(10)	+22,000			−22,000							
(11)	−2,100									−2,100	Dividends
Bal.	33,300	2,000	3,700	18,000			1,800		50,000	5,200	

Cash Flow Statement Data (bracket at left)

Income Statement Data (bracket at right, transactions 4–6)

Statement of Retained Earnings Data (bracket at right, transaction 11)

57,000   57,000

Balance Sheet Data

ing equation shows that total assets ($57,000) equal total liabilities plus share-holders' equity ($57,000).

- The *statement of retained earnings* repeats net income (or net loss) from the income statement. Dividends are subtracted. Ending retained earnings is the final result.

- Data for the *cash flow statement* are aligned under the Cash account. Cash receipts increase cash, and cash payments decrease cash.

Exhibit 2-2 shows the Tara Inc. financial statements at the end of April, the company's first month of operations. Follow the flow of data to observe the following:

1. The income statement reports revenues, expenses, and either a net income or a net loss for the period. During April, Tara Inc. earned a net income of $7,300. Compare the Tara Inc. income statement with that of Research In Motion

EXHIBIT 2-2 Financial Statements of Tara Inc.

Tara Inc.
Income Statement
For the Month Ended April 30, 2009

Revenue		
Service revenue ($7,000 + $3,000)		$10,000
Expenses		
Salary	$1,200	
Rent	1,100	
Utilities	400	
Total expenses		2,700
Net income		$ 7,300

①

Tara Inc.
Statement of Retained Earnings
For the Month Ended April 30, 2009

Retained earnings, April 1, 2009	$ 0
Add: Net income for the month	7,300
	7,300
Less: Dividends	(2,100)
Retained earnings, April 30, 2009	$5,200

②

Tara Inc.
Balance Sheet
April 30, 2009

Assets		Liabilities	
Cash	$33,300	Accounts payable	$ 1,800
Accounts receivable	2,000		
Office supplies	3,700	**Shareholders' Equity**	
Land	18,000	Common shares	50,000
		Retained earnings	5,200
		Total shareholders' equity	55,200
		Total liabilities and	
Total assets	$57,000	shareholders' equity	$57,000

Limited at the beginning of the chapter. The income statement includes only two types of accounts: revenues and expenses.

2. The statement of retained earnings starts with the beginning balance of retained earnings (zero for a new business). Add net income for the period (arrow ①), subtract dividends, and obtain the ending balance of retained earnings ($5,200).

3. The balance sheet lists the assets, liabilities, and shareholders' equity of the business at the end of the period. Included in shareholders' equity is retained earnings, which comes from the statement of retained earnings (arrow ②).

MyAccountingLab

MID-CHAPTER SUMMARY PROBLEM

Margaret Jarvis opens a research service near a college campus. She names the corporation Jarvis Research Inc. During the first month of operations, July 2009, the business engages in the following transactions:

a. Jarvis Research Inc. issues its common shares to Margaret Jarvis, who invests $25,000 to open the business.
b. The company purchases, on account, office supplies costing $350.
c. Jarvis Research Inc. pays cash of $20,000 to acquire a lot next to the campus. The company intends to use the land as a building site for a business office.
d. Jarvis Research Inc. performs services for clients and receives cash of $1,900.
e. Jarvis Research Inc. pays $100 on the account payable it created in transaction b.
f. Margaret Jarvis pays $2,000 of personal funds for a vacation.
g. Jarvis Research Inc. pays cash expenses for office rent ($400) and utilities ($100).
h. The business sells a small parcel of the land it purchased for its cost of $5,000.
i. The business declares and pays a cash dividend of $1,200.

Required

1. Analyze the preceding transactions in terms of their effects on the accounting equation of Jarvis Research Inc. Use Exhibit 2-1, Panel B as a guide.
2. Prepare the income statement, statement of retained earnings, and balance sheet of the business after recording the transactions. Draw arrows linking the statements.

Name: Jarvis Research Inc.
Industry: Research service
Fiscal Period: Month of July 2009
Key Facts: New business

Solutions

Requirements 1 and 2

As you analyze each transaction in Panel A, determine which asset, liability, and shareholders' equity accounts will be affected. Add those accounts to the headings in Panel B. For example, for transaction a, the accounts Cash and Common Shares are affected, so add Cash under the Assets heading and add Common Shares under the Shareholders' Equity heading in Panel B.

PANEL A—Details of Transactions

a. Received $25,000 cash and issued common shares
b. Purchased $350 of office supplies on account
c. Paid $20,000 to acquire land as a building site
d. Earned service revenue and received cash of $1,900
e. Paid $100 on account
f. Shareholder paid for a personal vacation; not a transaction of the business
g. Paid cash expenses for rent ($400) and utilities ($100)
h. Sold land for $5,000, its cost
i. Declared and paid cash dividends of $1,200

PANEL B—*Analysis of Transactions*

	Assets				=	Liabilities +	Shareholders' Equity		Type of Shareholders' Equity Transaction
	Cash	+	Office Supplies	+ Land		Accounts Payable	+ Common Shares	+ Retained Earnings	
a.	+25,000						+25,000		Issued shares
b.			+350			+350			
c.	−20,000			+20,000					
d.	+ 1,900							+1,900	Service revenue
e.	− 100					−100			
f.	Not a transaction of the business								
g.	− 400							− 400	Rent expense
	− 100							− 100	Utilities expense
h.	+ 5,000			− 5,000					
i.	− 1,200							−1,200	Dividends
Bal.	10,100		350	15,000		250	25,000	200	

25,450 = 25,450

> Add all the asset balances and add all the liabilities and shareholders' equity balances. Make sure that Total assets = Total liabilities + Shareholders' equity.

Jarvis Research Inc.
Income Statement
For the Month Ended July 31, 2009

Revenue		
Service revenue..		$1,900
Expenses		
Rent..	$400	
Utilities..	100	
Total..		500
Net income..		$1,400

> The title must include the name of the company, "Income Statement," and the specific period of time covered. It is critical that the time period be defined.

> Use the revenue and expense amounts data from the Retained Earnings column and names from the Type of Shareholders' Equity Transaction column.

Jarvis Research Inc.
Statement of Retained Earnings
For the Month Ended July 31, 2009

Retained earnings, July 1, 2009..	$ 0
Add: Net income for the month	1,400
	1,400
Less: Dividends..	(1,200)
Retained earnings, July 31, 2009..	$ 200

> ① The title must include the name of the company, "Statement of Retained Earnings," and the specific period of time covered. It is critical that the time period be defined.

> Beginning retained earnings is $0 because this is the first year of operations. The net income amount is transferred from the income statement. The dividends amount is from the Retained Earnings column of Panel B.

Jarvis Research Inc.
Balance Sheet
July 31, 2009

Assets		Liabilities	
Cash..........................	$10,100	Accounts payable	$ 250
Office supplies	350		
Land	15,000	**Shareholders' Equity**	
		Common shares......................	25,000
		Retained earnings....................	200
		Total shareholders' equity........	25,200
		Total liabilities and	
Total assets..............................	$25,450	shareholders' equity	$25,450

> ② The title must include the name of the company, "Balance Sheet," and the date of the balance sheet. It shows the financial position at the end of business on a specific date.

> Gather the asset, liability, and common shares accounts from the heading of Panel B. Insert the final balances for each account from the Bal. row in Panel B. The retained earnings amount is transferred from the statement of retained earnings. It is imperative that Total assets = Total liabilities + Shareholders' equity.

The analysis in the first half of this chapter can be used, but it is cumbersome. Research In Motion Limited has hundreds of accounts and millions of transactions. The spreadsheet to account for RIM's transactions would be huge! In the second half of this chapter we discuss double-entry accounting as it is actually used in business.

Double-entry Accounting

The *double-entry system* of accounting uses debits and credits to record the dual effects of each business transaction.

All business transactions include two parts:

- You give something, and
- You receive something

Each transaction affects at least two accounts. For example, Tara Inc.'s receipt of $50,000 cash and issuance of shares increased both the Cash and the Common Shares. It would be incomplete to record only the increase in Cash or only the increase in Common Shares.

The T-Account

An account can be represented by the letter T. We call this a T-account. The vertical line in the letter divides the account into its two sides: left and right. The account title rests on the horizontal line at the top of the T. For example, the Cash account of a business can appear as follows:

Cash	
(Left side)	(Right side)
Debit	*Credit*

The left side of the account is called the **debit** side, and the right side is called the **credit** side. Often, students are confused by the words debit and credit. To become comfortable using them, remember that

Debit = Left side   Credit = Right side

Every business transaction involves both a debit and a credit. The debit side of an account shows what you received. The credit side shows what you gave.

Increases and Decreases in the Accounts: The Rules of Debit and Credit

The type of account determines how we record increases or decreases. The rules of debit and credit follow in Exhibit 2-3.

- Increases in *assets* are recorded on the left (debit) side of the account. Decreases in *assets* are recorded on the right (credit) side.
- Conversely, increases in *liabilities* and *shareholders' equity* are recorded by credits. Decreases in *liabilities* and *shareholders' equity* are recorded by debits.

To illustrate the ideas diagrammed in Exhibit 2-3, let's review the first transaction. Tara Inc. received $50,000 and issued (gave) shares. Which accounts are affected? How will the accounts appear after the transaction? The Cash account and the Common Shares account will hold these amounts (see Exhibit 2-4):

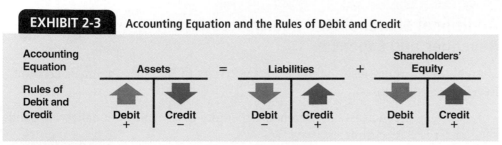

EXHIBIT 2-3   Accounting Equation and the Rules of Debit and Credit

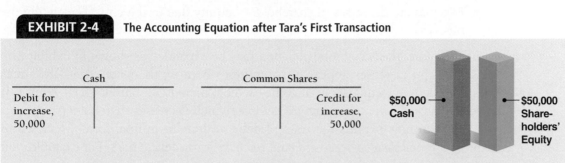

EXHIBIT 2-4   The Accounting Equation after Tara's First Transaction

The amount remaining in an account is called its balance. This first transaction gives Cash a $50,000 debit balance and Common Shares a $50,000 credit balance.

Tara Inc.'s second transaction is a $40,000 cash purchase of land. This transaction decreases Cash with a credit and increases Land with a debit, as shown in the following T-accounts.

	Cash				Common Shares	
Bal.	50,000	Credit for decrease, 40,000			Bal.	50,000
Bal.	10,000					

	Land	
Debit for increase, 40,000		
Bal.	40,000	

After this transaction, Cash has a $10,000 debit balance. Land has a debit balance of $40,000, and Common Shares has a $50,000 credit balance, as shown in Exhibit 2-5.

MyAccountingLab

Accounting Cycle Tutorial
Balance Sheet Accounts and
Transactions Tutorial

MyAccountingLab

Accounting Cycle Tutorial
Balance Sheet Accounts and
Transactions Application—Exercise 2

EXHIBIT 2-5   The Accounting Equation After Tara Inc.'s First Two Transactions

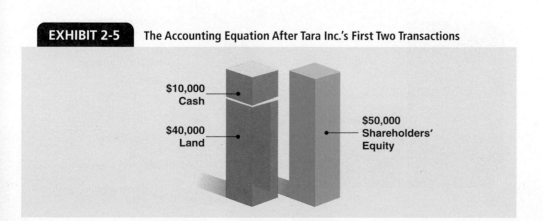

Additional Shareholders' Equity Accounts: Revenues and Expenses

Shareholders' equity also includes the two types of income statement accounts, Revenues and Expenses:

- *Revenues* are increases in shareholders' equity that result from delivering goods or services to customers.
- *Expenses* are decreases in shareholders' equity due to the cost of operating the business.

Therefore, the accounting equation may be expanded as shown in Exhibit 2-6. Revenues and expenses appear in parentheses because their net effect—revenues minus expenses—equals net income, which increases shareholders' equity. If expenses exceed revenues, there is a net loss, which decreases shareholders' equity.

We can now express the rules of debit and credit in final form, as shown in Exhibit 2-7. *You should not proceed until you have learned these rules.* For example, you must remember the following:

- A debit increases an asset account.
- A credit decreases an asset.

Liabilities and shareholders' equity are the opposite.

- A credit increases a liability account.
- A debit decreases a liability.

Dividends and Expenses accounts are exceptions to the rule. Dividends and Expenses are equity accounts that are increased by a debit. Dividends and Expenses accounts are negative (or contra) equity accounts.

Revenues and Expenses are often treated as separate account categories because they appear on the income statement. Exhibit 2-7 shows Revenues and Expenses below the other equity accounts.

MyAccountingLab

**Accounting Cycle Tutorial
Income Statement Accounts and
Transactions Tutorial**

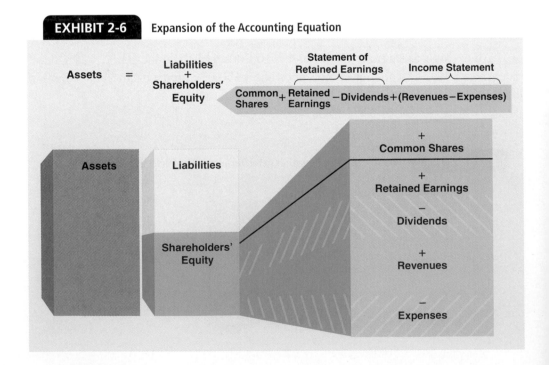

EXHIBIT 2-6 **Expansion of the Accounting Equation**

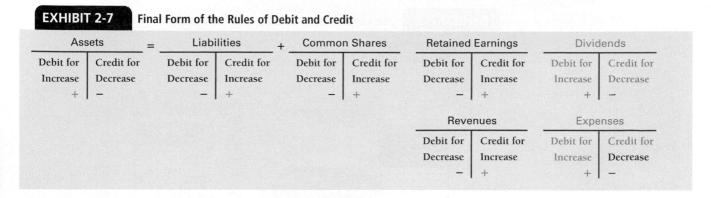

EXHIBIT 2-7 Final Form of the Rules of Debit and Credit

Assets =		Liabilities +		Common Shares		Retained Earnings		Dividends	
Debit for	Credit for	Debit for	Credit for	Debit for	Credit for	Debit for	Credit for	Debit for	Credit for
Increase	Decrease	Decrease	Increase	Decrease	Increase	Decrease	Increase	Increase	Decrease
+	−	−	+	−	+	−	+	+	−

Revenues		Expenses	
Debit for	Credit for	Debit for	Credit for
Decrease	Increase	Increase	Decrease
−	+	+	−

Recording Transactions

Accountants use a chronological record of transactions called a **journal**. The journalizing process follows three steps:

1. Specify each account affected by the transaction, and classify each account by type (asset, liability, shareholders' equity, revenue, or expense).

2. Determine whether each account is increased or decreased by the transaction. Use the rules of debit and credit to increase or decrease each account.

3. Record the transaction in the journal, including a brief explanation for the entry. The debit side is entered on the left margin, and the credit side is indented to the right.

Objective

③ **Record** transactions in the journal

Step 3 is also called "making the journal entry" or "journalizing the transaction." Let's apply the steps to journalize the first transaction of Tara Inc.

step 1 The business receives cash and issues shares. Cash and Common Shares are affected. Cash is an asset and Common Shares is equity.

step 2 Both Cash and Common Shares increase. Debit Cash to record an increase in this asset. Credit Common Shares to record an increase in this equity account.

step 3 Journalize the transaction:

Date	Accounts and Explanation	Debit	Credit
Apr. 1, 2009	Cash..	50,000	
	Common Shares		50,000
	Issued common shares.		

When analyzing a transaction, first pinpoint its effects (if any) on Cash. Did Cash increase or decrease? Typically, it is easiest to identify a transaction's cash effects. Then identify the effects on other accounts.

Copying Information (Posting) from Journal to Ledger

The journal is a chronological record of all company transactions listed by date. But the journal does not indicate, for example, how much cash or accounts receivable the business has.

The **ledger** is a grouping of all the T-accounts with their balances. For example, the balance of the Cash account indicates how much cash the business has. The balance of Accounts Receivable shows the amount due from customers. The balance

EXHIBIT 2-8 The Ledger (Asset, Liability, and Shareholders' Equity Accounts)

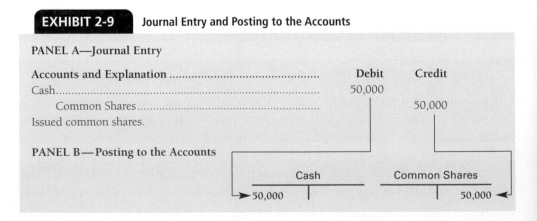

of Accounts Payable tells how much the business owes suppliers on open account, and so on.

In the phrase "keeping the books," books refers to the accounts in the ledger. In most accounting systems, the ledger is computerized. Exhibit 2-8 shows how the asset, liability, and shareholders' equity accounts are grouped in the ledger.

Entering a transaction in the journal does not get the data into the ledger accounts. Data must be copied to the ledger—a process called **posting**. Debits in the journal are posted as debits in the accounts, and likewise for credits. Exhibit 2-9 shows how Tara Inc.'s share issuance transaction is posted to the accounts.

The Flow of Accounting Data

Exhibit 2-10 summarizes the flow of accounting data from the business transaction to the ledger.

Let's continue the example of Tara Inc. and account for the same 11 transactions we illustrated earlier. Here we use the journal and the accounts.

Each journal entry posted to the accounts is keyed by date or by transaction number. This linking allows you to locate any information you may need.

EXHIBIT 2-9 Journal Entry and Posting to the Accounts

PANEL A—Journal Entry

Accounts and Explanation	Debit	Credit
Cash	50,000	
Common Shares		50,000
Issued common shares.		

PANEL B—Posting to the Accounts

Cash		Common Shares	
50,000			50,000

EXHIBIT 2-10 Flow of Accounting Data

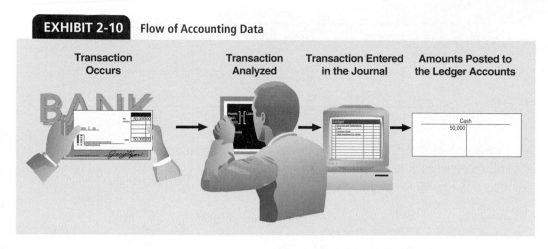

Transaction Occurs	Transaction Analyzed	Transaction Entered in the Journal	Amounts Posted to the Ledger Accounts

Transaction 1 Analysis. Tara Inc. received $50,000 cash from shareholders and in turn issued common shares to them. The journal entry, accounting equation, and ledger accounts follow:

Journal entry

Cash 50,000
  Common Shares 50,000
Issued common shares.

Accounting equation

ASSETS	=	LIABILITIES	+	SHAREHOLDERS' EQUITY
+50,000	=	0	+	50,000

The ledger accounts

Cash	Common Shares
(1) 50,000	(1) 50,000

Transaction 2 Analysis. The business paid $40,000 cash for land. The purchase decreased cash; therefore, credit Cash. The purchase increased the asset land; to record this increase, debit Land.

Journal entry

Land 40,000
  Cash 40,000
Paid cash for land.

Accounting equation

ASSETS	=	LIABILITIES	+	SHAREHOLDERS' EQUITY
+40,000	=	0	+	0
−40,000				

The ledger accounts

Cash		Land
(1) 50,000	(2) 40,000	(2) 40,000

Transaction 3 Analysis. The business purchased office supplies for $3,700 on account payable. The purchase increased Office Supplies, an asset, and Accounts Payable, a liability.

Journal entry

Office Supplies 3,700
  Accounts Payable 3,700
Purchased office supplies on account.

Accounting equation	**ASSETS**	=	**LIABILITIES**	+	**SHAREHOLDERS' EQUITY**
	+3,700	=	+3,700	+	0

	Office Supplies		Accounts Payable
The ledger accounts	(3) 3,700		(3) 3,700

Transaction 4 Analysis.

The business performed engineering services for clients and received cash of $7,000. The transaction increased cash and service revenue. To record the revenue, credit Service Revenue.

Journal entry	Cash	7,000	
	Service Revenue		7,000
	Performed services for cash.		

Accounting equation	**ASSETS**	=	**LIABILITIES**	+	**SHAREHOLDERS' EQUITY**	+	**REVENUES**
	+7,000	=	0	+	0	+	7,000

	Cash		Service Revenue
The ledger accounts	(1) 50,000 | (2) 40,000		(4) 7,000
	(4) 7,000		

Transaction 5 Analysis.

Tara performed services for King Contracting on account. King Contracting did not pay immediately so Tara billed King Contracting for $3,000. The transaction increased accounts receivable; therefore, debit Accounts Receivable. Service revenue also increased, so credit Service Revenue.

Journal entry	Accounts Receivable	3,000	
	Service Revenue		3,000
	Performed services on account.		

Accounting equation	**ASSETS**	=	**LIABILITIES**	+	**SHAREHOLDERS' EQUITY**	+	**REVENUES**
	+3,000	=	0	+		+	3,000

	Accounts Receivable		Service Revenue
The ledger accounts	(5) 3,000		(4) 7,000
			(5) 3,000

Transaction 6 Analysis.

Tara paid $2,700 for the following expenses: office rent, $1,100; employee salary, $1,200; and utilities, $400. Credit Cash for the sum of the expense amounts. The expenses increased, so debit each account separately.

Journal entry	Rent Expense	1,100	
	Salary Expense	1,200	
	Utilities Expense	400	
	Cash		2,700
	Paid expenses.		

Accounting equation	**ASSETS**	=	**LIABILITIES**	+	**SHAREHOLDERS' EQUITY**	−	**EXPENSES**
	−2,700	=	0	+		−	2,700

	Cash		Rent Expense	
The ledger accounts	(1) 50,000	(2) 40,000	(6) 1,100	
	(4) 7,000	(6) 2,700		

	Salary Expense	Utilities Expense	
	(6) 1,200	(6) 400	

Transaction 7 Analysis. The business paid $1,900 on the account payable created in Transaction 3. Credit Cash for the payment. The payment decreased a liability, so debit Accounts Payable.

Journal entry	Accounts Payable	1,900	
	Cash		1,900
	Paid cash on account.		

Accounting equation	**ASSETS**	**=**	**LIABILITIES**	**+**	**SHAREHOLDERS' EQUITY**
	−1,900	=	−1,900	+	0

	Cash		Accounts Payable	
The ledger accounts	(1) 50,000	(2) 40,000	(7) 1,900	(3) 3,700
	(4) 7,000	(6) 2,700		
		(7) 1,900		

Transaction 8 Analysis. J.J. Booth, a shareholder of Tara Inc., remodelled his personal residence. This is not a transaction of the engineering consultancy, so Tara makes no journal entry.

Transaction 9 Analysis. The business collected $1,000 cash on account from the client in Transaction 5. Cash increased so debit Cash. The asset accounts receivable decreased; therefore, credit Accounts Receivable.

Journal entry	Cash	1,000	
	Accounts Receivable		1,000
	Collected cash on account.		

Accounting equation	**ASSETS**	**=**	**LIABILITIES**	**+**	**SHAREHOLDERS' EQUITY**
	+1,000	=	0	+	0
	−1,000				

	Cash		Accounts Receivable	
The ledger accounts	(1) 50,000	(2) 40,000	(5) 3,000	(9) 1,000
	(4) 7,000	(6) 2,700		
	(9) 1,000	(7) 1,900		

Transaction 10 Analysis. Tara sold a portion of its land for its cost of $22,000, receiving cash. The asset cash increased; debit Cash. The asset land decreased; credit Land.

Journal entry	Cash	22,000	
	Land		22,000
	Sold land.		

Accounting equation	**ASSETS**	**=**	**LIABILITIES**	**+**	**SHAREHOLDERS' EQUITY**
	+22,000	=	0	+	0
	−22,000				

	Cash		Land	
The ledger accounts	(1) 50,000	(2) 40,000	(2) 40,000	(10) 22,000
	(4) 7,000	(6) 2,700		
	(9) 1,000	(7) 1,900		
	(10) 22,000			

Transaction 11 Analysis. Tara Inc. paid its shareholders cash dividends of $2,100. Credit Cash for the payment. The transaction also decreased shareholders' equity and requires a debit to an equity account; therefore, debit Dividends.

Journal entry	Dividends	2,100	
	Cash		2,100
	Declared and paid dividends.		

Accounting equation	**ASSETS**	**=**	**LIABILITIES**	**+**	**SHAREHOLDERS' EQUITY**	**−**	**DIVIDENDS**
	−2,100	=	0	+		−	2,100

	Cash		Dividends	
The ledger accounts	(1) 50,000	(2) 40,000	(11) 2,100	
	(4) 7,000	(6) 2,700		
	(9) 1,000	(7) 1,900		
	(10) 22,000	(11) 2,100		

Accounts After Posting to the Ledger

Exhibit 2-11 shows the accounts after all transactions have been posted. Group the accounts under assets, liabilities, and shareholders' equity.

Each account has a balance, denoted as Bal., which is the difference between the account's total debits and its total credits. For example, the Accounts Payable balance is the difference between the credit ($3,700) and the debit ($1,900). Thus, the Accounts Payable balance is a credit of $1,800. The cash account has a debit balance of $33,300.

A horizontal line separates the transaction amounts from the account balance. If, as shown by the Cash account, the sum of an account's debits is greater than the sum of its credits, that account has a debit balance. If the sum of its credits is greater, that account has a credit balance, as for Accounts Payable.

The Trial Balance

Objective

4 **Use** a trial balance

A **trial balance** lists all accounts with their balances—assets first, followed by liabilities and then shareholders' equity. The trial balance summarizes all the account balances for the financial statements and shows whether total debits equal total credits. A trial balance may be taken at any time, but the most common time is at the end of the period. Exhibit 2-12 is the trial balance of Tara Inc. after its first 11 transactions have been journalized and posted at the end of April.

EXHIBIT 2-11   Tara Inc.'s Ledger Accounts After Posting

| Assets | | | | = | Liabilities | | | + | Shareholders' Equity | | | |

Cash

(1)	50,000	(2)	40,000
(4)	7,000	(6)	2,700
(9)	1,000	(7)	1,900
(10)	22,000	(11)	2,100
Bal.	33,300		

Accounts Receivable

(5)	3,000	(9)	1,000
Bal.	2,000		

Office Supplies

(3)	3,700		
Bal.	3,700		

Land

(2)	40,000	(10)	22,000
Bal.	18,000		

Accounts Payable

(7)	1,900	(3)	3,700
		Bal.	1,800

Common Shares

		(1)	50,000
		Bal.	50,000

REVENUE

Service Revenue

		(4)	7,000
		(5)	3,000
		Bal.	10,000

Dividends

(11)	2,100		
Bal.	2,100		

EXPENSES

Rent Expense

(6)	1,100		
Bal.	1,100		

Salary Expense

(6)	1,200		
Bal.	1,200		

Utilities Expense

(6)	400		
Bal.	400		

Analyzing Accounts

You can often tell what a company did by analyzing its accounts. This is a powerful tool for a manager who knows accounting. For example, if you know the beginning and ending balance of Cash, and if you know total cash receipts, you can compute your total cash payments during the period.

In our chapter example, suppose Tara Inc. began May with cash of $1,000. During May, Tara received cash of $8,000 and ended the month with a cash balance

EXHIBIT 2-12   Trial Balance

Tara Inc.
Trial Balance
April 30, 2009

Account Title	Balance Debit	Balance Credit
Cash	$33,300	
Accounts receivable	2,000	
Office supplies	3,700	
Land	18,000	
Accounts payable		$ 1,800
Common shares		50,000
Dividends	2,100	
Service revenue		10,000
Rent expense	1,100	
Salary expense	1,200	
Utilities expense	400	
Total	$61,800	$61,800

of $3,000. You can compute total cash payments by analyzing Tara's Cash account as follows:

Cash			
Beginning balance	1,000		
Cash receipts	8,000	Cash payments	x = 6,000
Ending balance	3,000		

Or, if you know Cash's beginning and ending balances and total payments, you can compute cash receipts during the period—for any company!

You can compute either sales on account or cash collections on account by analyzing the Accounts Receivable account as follows (using assumed amounts):

Accounts Receivable			
Beginning balance	6,000		
Sales on account	10,000	Collections on account	11,000
Ending balance	5,000		

Also, you can determine how much you paid on account by analyzing Accounts Payable as follows (using assumed amounts):

Accounts Payable			
		Beginning balance	9,000
Payments on account	4,000	Purchases on account	6,000
		Ending balance	11,000

Please master this powerful technique. It works for any company and for your own personal finances! You will find this tool very helpful when you become a manager.

Correcting Accounting Errors

Accounting errors can occur even in computerized systems. Input data may be wrong, or they may be entered twice or not at all. In a manual system, a debit may be entered as a credit, and vice versa. You can detect the reason or reasons behind many out-of-balance conditions by computing the difference between total debits and total credits. Then perform one or more of the following actions:

1. Search the records for a missing account. Trace each account back and forth from the journal to the ledger. A $200 transaction may have been recorded incorrectly in the journal or posted incorrectly to the ledger. Search the journal for a $200 transaction.

2. Divide the out-of-balance amount by 2. A debit treated as a credit, or vice versa, doubles the amount of error. Suppose Tara Inc. added $300 to Cash instead of subtracting $300. The out-of-balance amount is $600, and dividing by 2 identifies $300 as the amount of the transaction. Search the journal for the $300 transaction, and trace it to the account affected.

3. Divide the out-of-balance amount by 9. If the result is an integer (no decimals), the error may be a
   - *slide* (writing $400 as $40).The accounts would be out of balance by $360 ($400 − $40 = $360). Dividing $360 by 9 yields $40. Scan the trial balance in Exhibit 2-12 for an amount similar to $40. Utilities Expense (balance of $400) is the misstated account.

- *transposition* (writing $2,100 as $1,200). The accounts would be out of balance by $900 ($2,100 − $1,200 = $900). Dividing $900 by 9 yields $100. Trace all amounts on the trial balance back to the T-accounts. Dividends (balance of $2,100) is the misstated account.

Chart of Accounts

As you know, the ledger contains the business accounts grouped under these headings:

1. Balance sheet accounts: Assets, Liabilities, and Shareholders' Equity
2. Income statement accounts: Revenues and Expenses

Organizations use a **chart of accounts** to list all accounts and account numbers. Account numbers usually have two or more digits. Assets are often numbered beginning with 1, liabilities with 2, shareholders' equity with 3, revenues with 4, and expenses with 5. The second, third, and higher digits in an account number indicate the position of the individual account within the category. For example, Cash may be account number 101, which is the first asset account. Accounts Payable may be number 201, the first liability account. All accounts are numbered by this system.

Organizations with many accounts use lengthy account numbers. For example, the chart of accounts of Research In Motion may use five-digit account numbers. The chart of accounts for Tara Inc. appears in Exhibit 2-13. The gap between the account numbers 111 and 141 leaves room to add another category of receivables, for example, Notes Receivable, which may be numbered 121.

Appendix C in this book gives two expanded charts of accounts that you may find helpful as you work through this course. The first chart lists the typical accounts that a service corporation, such as Tara Inc., would have after a period of growth. The second chart is for a merchandising corporation, one that sells a product instead of a service.

The Normal Balance of an Account

An account's *normal balance* falls on the side of the account—debit or credit—where increases are recorded. The normal balance of assets is on the debit side, so assets are called *debit-balance accounts.* Conversely, liabilities and shareholders' equity usually have a credit balance, so their normal balances are on the credit side. They are called

---

EXHIBIT 2-13   Chart of Accounts—Tara Inc.

Balance Sheet Accounts

Assets	Liabilities	Shareholders' Equity
101 Cash	201 Accounts Payable	301 Common Shares
111 Accounts Receivable	231 Notes Payable	311 Dividends
141 Office Supplies		312 Retained Earnings
151 Office Furniture		
191 Land		

Income Statement Accounts
(Part of Shareholders' Equity)

Revenues	Expenses
401 Service Revenue	501 Rent Expense
	502 Salary Expense
	503 Utilities Expense

EXHIBIT 2-14   Normal Balances of the Accounts

Assets..	Debit
Liabilities	Credit
Shareholders' equity—overall...	Credit
Common shares	Credit
Retained earnings	Credit
Dividends..	Debit
Revenues	Credit
Expenses	Debit

EXHIBIT 2-15   Account in Three-Column Format

Account: Cash   **Account No. 101**

Date	Item	Debit	Credit	Balance
2009				
Apr. 1		50,000		50,000 Dr.
3			40,000	10,000 Dr.

credit-balance accounts. Exhibit 2-14 illustrates the normal balances of all the assets, liabilities, and shareholders' equities, including revenues and expenses.

As explained earlier, shareholders' equity usually contains several accounts. But there are exceptions. Dividends and Expenses carry debit balances because they represent decreases in shareholders' equity. Overall, these accounts show a normal credit balance.

Account Formats

So far we have illustrated accounts in a two-column T-account format, with the debit column on the left and the credit column on the right. Another format has three *amount* columns, as illustrated for the Cash account in Exhibit 2-15. The first pair of amount columns are for the debit and credit amounts. The third amount column is for the account balance. A debit balance is denoted by "Dr.," the abbreviation of debit. A credit balance is denoted by "Cr.," the abbreviation for credit. This three-column format keeps a running balance in the third column.

Quick Decision Making with T-Accounts

Business people must often make decisions without the benefit of a complete accounting system. For example, assume the managers of lululemon athletica inc. may consider borrowing $100,000 to buy equipment. To see how the two transactions [(a) borrowing cash and (b) buying equipment] affect lululemon, the manager can go directly to T-accounts, as follows:

T-accounts:	Cash	Note Payable
	(a) 100,000 |	| (a) 100,000

T-accounts:	Cash	Equipment	Note Payable
	(a) 100,000 | (b) 100,000	(b) 100,000 |	| (a) 100,000

This informal analysis shows immediately that lululemon will add $100,000 of equipment and a $100,000 note payable to its financial position. Assuming that lululemon began with zero balances, the equipment and note payable transactions would result in the following balance sheet (date assumed for illustration only):

lululemon athletica inc.
Balance Sheet
As at September 12, 2009

Assets		Liabilities	
Cash	$ 0	Note payable	$100,000
Equipment	100,000	Total liabilities	100,000
		Shareholders' Equity	0
		Total liabilities and	
Total assets	$100,000	shareholders' equity	$100,000

Companies do not actually keep records in this shortcut fashion. But a decision maker who needs information immediately does not have time to journalize, post to the accounts, take a trial balance, and prepare financial statements. A manager who knows accounting can analyze the transaction and make a decision quickly.

Now apply what you have learned. Study the Decision Guidelines, which summarize the chapter.

DECISION GUIDELINES

Any entrepreneur must determine whether a venture is profitable. To do this, he or she needs to know its results of operations and financial position. If Jim Balsillie, co-CEO of Research In Motion, for example, wanted to know whether RIM was making money, the Decision Guidelines that follow would help him.

HOW TO MEASURE RESULTS OF OPERATIONS AND FINANCIAL POSITION

Decision	Guidelines
Has a transaction occurred?	If the event affects the entity's financial position *and* can be reliably recorded—Yes. If either condition is absent—No.
Where to record the transaction?	In the *journal*, the chronological record of transactions
How to record an increase or decrease in the following accounts?	Rules of *debit* and *credit*:

	Increase	*Decrease*
Asset.....................................	Debit	Credit
Liability	Credit	Debit
Shareholders' equity	Credit	Debit
Revenue	Credit	Debit
Expense	Debit	Credit

Decision	Guidelines
Where to store all the information for each account?	In the *ledger*, the book of accounts
Where to list all the accounts and their balances?	In the *trial* balance
Where to report the:	
Results of operations?	In the *income statement* (Revenues − Expenses = Net income or net loss)
Financial position?	In the *balance sheet* (Assets = Liabilities + Shareholders' Equity)

MyAccountingLab | **END-OF-CHAPTER SUMMARY PROBLEM**

The trial balance of Bos Personnel Services Inc. on March 1, 2009, lists the entity's assets, liabilities, and shareholders' equity on that date.

	Balance	
Account Title	*Debit*	*Credit*
Cash...	$26,000	
Accounts receivable..	4,500	
Accounts payable		$ 2,000
Common shares		10,000
Retained earnings..		18,500
Total...	$30,500	$30,500

During March, the business completed the following transactions:

a. Borrowed $70,000 from the bank, with C. Bos signing a note payable in the name of the business.
b. Paid cash of $60,000 to a real estate company to acquire land.
c. Performed service for a customer and received cash of $5,000.
d. Purchased supplies on credit, $300.
e. Performed customer service and earned revenue on account, $4,000.
f. Paid $1,200 on account.
g. Paid the following cash expenses: salary, $3,000; rent, $1,500; and interest, $400.
h. Received $3,100 on account.
i. Received a $200 utility bill that will be paid next week.
j. Declared and paid a dividend of $1,000.

> **Name:** Bos Personnel Services Inc.
> **Industry:** Human Resources
> **Fiscal Period:** Month of March 2009
> **Key Fact:** An existing, ongoing business

Required

1. Open the following accounts, with the balances indicated, in the ledger of Bos Personnel Services Inc. Use the T-account format.
  • Assets—Cash, $26,000; Accounts Receivable, $4,500; Supplies, no balance; Land, no balance
  • Liabilities—Accounts Payable, $2,000; Note Payable, no balance
  • Shareholders' Equity—Common Shares, $10,000; Retained Earnings, $18,500; Dividends, no balance
  • Revenues—Service Revenue, no balance
  • Expenses—(none have balances) Salary Expense, Rent Expense, Interest Expense, Utilities Expense

> Prepare a T-account for each account name. Place the opening balance in the T-account, remembering that the normal balance in an asset account is a debit, in a liability or equity account is a credit, in a revenue account is a credit, and in an expense account is a debit.
>
> For each transaction, ensure that Assets = Liabilities + Shareholders' equity.

2. Journalize the transactions listed above. Key journal entries by transaction letter.
3. Post to the ledger and show the balance in each account after all the transactions have been posted.
4. Prepare the trial balance of Bos Personnel Services Inc. at March 31, 2009.
5. To determine the net income or net loss of the entity during the month of March, prepare the income statement for the month ended March 31, 2009. List expenses in order from the largest to the smallest.
6. Suppose the organizers of Bos Personnel Services Inc. ask you to purchase $4,000 of the company's shares. Cite specifics from the income statement and the trial balance to support your decision.

> Refer to the rules of debit and credit shown in Exhibit 2-7 on page 65.

Answers

Requirement 1

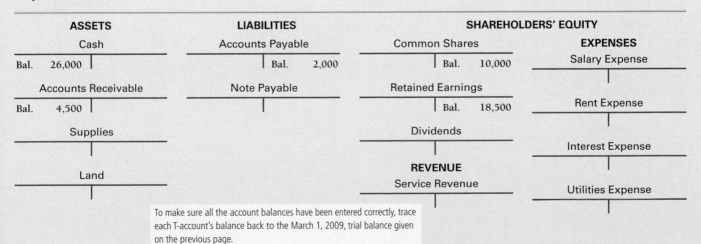

ASSETS	LIABILITIES	SHAREHOLDERS' EQUITY	
Cash	**Accounts Payable**	**Common Shares**	**EXPENSES**
Bal. 26,000	Bal. 2,000	Bal. 10,000	Salary Expense
Accounts Receivable	**Note Payable**	**Retained Earnings**	
Bal. 4,500		Bal. 18,500	Rent Expense
Supplies		**Dividends**	
			Interest Expense
Land		**REVENUE**	
		Service Revenue	Utilities Expense

To make sure all the account balances have been entered correctly, trace each T-account's balance back to the March 1, 2009, trial balance given on the previous page.

Requirement 2

Accounts and Explanation	Debit	Credit		Accounts and Explanation	Debit	Credit
a. Cash	70,000			g. Salary Expense	3,000	
Note Payable		70,000		Rent Expense	1,500	
Borrowed cash on note payable.				Interest Expense	400	
b. Land	60,000			Cash		4,900
Cash		60,000		Paid cash expenses.		
Purchased land for cash.				h. Cash	3,100	
c. Cash	5,000			Accounts Receivable		3,100
Service Revenue		5,000		Received on account.		
Performed service and received cash.				i. Utilities Expense	200	
d. Supplies	300			Accounts Payable		200
Accounts Payable		300		Received utility bill.		
Purchased supplies on account.				j. Dividends	1,000	
e. Accounts Receivable	4,000			Cash		1,000
Service Revenue		4,000		Declared and paid dividends.		
Performed service on account.						
f. Accounts Payable	1,200					
Cash		1,200				
Paid on account.						

Selected transactions are explained more fully:

d. Increase Supplies (asset) and increase Accounts Payable (liability), since supplies were purchased on credit. Cash will be paid for the supplies in the future.

e. Increase Accounts Receivable (asset) and increase Service Revenue (income) since the service was performed on account. Cash will be received for the service in the future.

g. This transaction could also have been recorded with three journal entries, with a debit to the expense and a credit to Cash for each of the expenses.

i. Increase Utilities Expense (expenses) and increase Accounts Payable (liability), since cash will be paid for the utility bill in the future.

Requirement 3

ASSETS				LIABILITIES				SHAREHOLDERS' EQUITY				

ASSETS

Cash

Bal.	26,000	(b)	60,000
(a)	70,000	(f)	1,200
(c)	5,000	(g)	4,900
(h)	3,100	(j)	1,000
Bal.	37,000		

Accounts Receivable

Bal.	4,500	(h)	3,100
(e)	4,000		
Bal.	5,400		

Supplies

(d)	300		
Bal.	300		

Land

(b)	60,000		
Bal.	60,000		

LIABILITIES

Accounts Payable

(f)	1,200	Bal.	2,000
		(d)	300
		(i)	200
		Bal.	1,300

Note Payable

		(a)	70,000
		Bal.	70,000

SHAREHOLDERS' EQUITY

Common Shares

		Bal.	10,000

Retained Earnings

		Bal.	18,500

Dividends

(j)	1,000		
Bal.	1,000		

REVENUE

Service Revenue

		(c)	5,000
		(e)	4,000
		Bal.	9,000

EXPENSES

Salary Expense

(g)	3,000		
Bal.	3,000		

Rent Expense

(g)	1,500		
Bal.	1,500		

Interest Expense

(g)	400		
Bal.	400		

Utilities Expense

(i)	200		
Bal.	200		

Make sure each transaction is posted to the proper T-account, and make sure no transactions were missed. Make sure that Assets = Liabilities + Shareholders' Equity for each transaction before going to the next transaction.

Requirement 4

Bos Personnel Servics Inc.
Trial Balance
March 31, 2009

Account Title	Balance Debit	Credit
Cash	$ 37,000	
Accounts receivable	5,400	
Supplies	300	
Land	60,000	
Accounts payable		$ 1,300
Note payable		70,000
Common shares		10,000
Retained earnings		18,500
Dividends	1,000	
Service revenue		9,000
Salary expense	3,000	
Rent expense	1,500	
Interest expense	400	
Utilities expense	200	
Total	$108,800	$108,800

The title must include the name of the company, "Trial Balance," and the date of the trial balance. It shows the account balances on one specific date.

List all the accounts that have a balance in their T-accounts. Write the "Bal." amount for each account from Requirement 3 into the debit or credit column of the trial balance. Make sure that the total of the Debit column equals the total of the Credit column. Double underline the totals to show that the columns have been added and the totals are final.

Requirement 5

Bos Personnel Services Inc.
Income Statement
For the Month Ended March 31, 2009

Revenue		
Service revenue		$9,000
Expenses		
Salary expense	$3,000	
Rent expense	1,500	
Interest expense	400	
Utilities expense	200	
Total expenses		5,100
Net income		$3,900

The title must include the name of the company, "Income Statement," and the specific period of time covered. It is critical that the time period be defined. Prepare the income statement by listing the revenue and expense account names from the trial balance. Then transfer the amounts from the trial balance to the income statement.

Requirement 6

A $4,000 investment in Bos appears to be warranted because
  a. the company earned net income of $3,900, so the business appears profitable.
  b. total assets of $102,700 ($37,000 + $5,400 + $300 + $60,000) far exceed total liabilities of $71,300 ($1,300 + $70,000), which suggests that Bos can pay its debts and remain in business.
  c. Bos is paying a dividend, so an investment in the shares may yield a quick return in the form of dividends.

Items to consider when answering a question like this are
a. net income
b. the excess of assets over liabilities
c. whether dividends were distributed during the year.

REVIEW TRANSACTION ANALYSIS

QUICK CHECK (Answers are given on page 102.)

1. A debit entry to an account
   a. Increases liabilities
   b. Increases shareholders' equity
   c. Increases assets
   d. Both a and c

2. Which of the following account types normally have a credit balance?
   a. Liabilities
   b. Revenues
   c. Expenses
   d. Both a and b

3. An attorney performs services of $800 for a client and receives $200 cash with the rest on account. The journal entry for this transaction would be which of the following?
   a. Debit Cash, debit Accounts Receivable, credit Service Revenue
   b. Debit Cash, credit Accounts Receivable, credit Service Revenue
   c. Debit Cash, credit Service Revenue
   d. Debit Cash, debit Service Revenue, credit Accounts Receivable

4. Accounts Payable had a normal beginning balance of $1,000. During the period, there were debit postings of $400 and credit postings of $600. What was the ending balance?
   a. $800 debit
   b. $800 credit
   c. $1,200 debit
   d. $1,200 credit

5. The list of all accounts with their balances is the
   a. Trial balance
   b. Chart of accounts
   c. Journal
   d. Balance sheet

6. The basic summary device used in accounting is the
   a. Ledger
   b. Account
   c. Journal
   d. Trial balance

7. The beginning Cash balance was $5,000. At the end of the period, the balance was $6,000. If total cash paid out during the period was $24,000, the amount of cash receipts was
   a. $23,000
   b. $13,000
   c. $25,000
   d. $35,000

8. In a double-entry accounting system
   a. A debit entry is recorded on the left side of a T-account
   b. Half of all the accounts have a normal credit balance
   c. Liabilities, owners' equity, and revenue accounts all have normal debit balances
   d. Both a and c are correct

9. Which accounts appear on which financial statement?

	Balance sheet	*Income statement*
a.	Cash, revenues, land	Expenses, payables
b.	Receivables, land, payables	Revenues, supplies
c.	Expenses, payables, cash	Revenues, receivables, land
d.	Cash, receivables, payables	Revenues, expenses

10. A doctor purchases medical supplies of $670 and pays $200 cash with the rest on account. The journal entry for this transaction would be

a. Supplies	c. Supplies
Accounts Payable	Accounts Receivable
Cash	Cash
b. Supplies	d. Supplies
Cash	Accounts Payable
Accounts Payable	Cash

11. Which is the correct sequence of accounting procedures?
    a. Journal, ledger, trial balance, financial statements
    b. Ledger, trial balance, journal, financial statements
    c. Financial statements, trial balance, ledger, journal
    d. Ledger, journal, trial balance, financial statements

12. The error of posting $100 as $10 can be detected by
    a. Dividing the out-of-balance amount by 2
    b. Totalling each account's balance in the ledger
    c. Dividing the out-of-balance amount by 9
    d. Examining the chart of accounts

ACCOUNTING VOCABULARY

account The record of the changes that have occurred in a particular asset, liability, or shareholders' equity during a period. The basic summary device of accounting.   (p. 52)

accrued liability A liability for an expense that has not yet been paid by the company.   (p. 53)

chart of accounts List of a company's accounts and their account numbers.   (p. 73)

credit The right side of an account.   (p. 62)

debit The left side of an account.   (p. 62)

double-entry system An accounting system that uses debits and credits to record the dual effects of each business transaction.   (p. 62)

journal The chronological accounting record of an entity's transactions.   (p. 65)

ledger The book of accounts and their balances.   (p. 65)

posting Copying amounts from the journal to the ledger.   (p. 66)

prepaid expense A category of miscellaneous assets that typically expire or get used up in the near future. Examples include Prepaid Rent, Prepaid Insurance, and Supplies.   (p. 52)

transaction Any event that has a financial impact on the business and can be measured reliably.   (p. 51)

trial balance A list of all the ledger accounts with their balances.   (p. 70)

ASSESS YOUR PROGRESS

Make the grade with MyAccountingLab: The exercises and problems marked in red can be found on MyAccountingLab at www.myaccountinglab.com. You can practise them as often as you want, and they feature step by step guided solutions to help you find the right answer.

SHORT EXERCISES

S2-1 Sue Deliveau opened a software consulting firm that immediately paid $10,000 for a computer. Was Deliveau's payment an expense of the business? Explain your answer.

Explaining an asset versus an expense
(Obj. 1)

S2-2 Hourglass Software began with cash of $10,000. Hourglass then bought supplies for $2,000 on account. Separately, Hourglass paid $5,000 for a computer. Answer these questions.
a. How much in total assets does Hourglass have?
b. How much in liabilities does Hourglass owe?

Analyzing the effects of transactions
(Obj. 1)

S2-3 Marsha Solomon, a physiotherapist, opened a practice. The business completed the following transactions:

Analyzing transactions
(Obj. 1)

May	1	Solomon invested $25,000 cash to start her practice. The business issued shares to Solomon.
	1	Purchased medical supplies on account totalling $9,000.
	2	Paid monthly office rent of $4,000.
	3	Recorded $8,000 revenue for service rendered to patients, received cash of $2,000, and sent bills to patients for the remainder.

After these transactions, how much cash does the business have to work with? Use T-accounts to show your answer.

Analyzing transactions
(Obj. 1)

S2-4 Refer to Short Exercise 2-3. Which of the transactions of Marsha Solomon, P.T., increased the total assets of the business? For each transaction, identify the asset or liability that was increased or decreased.

Recording transactions
(Obj. 2, 3)

S2-5 After operating for several months, artist Paul Marciano completed the following transactions during the latter part of June:

June	15	Borrowed $25,000 from the bank, signing a note payable.
	22	Painted a portrait for a client on account totalling $9,000.
	28	Received $5,000 cash on account from clients.
	29	Received a utility bill of $600, which will be paid during July.
	30	Paid monthly salary of $2,500 to gallery assistant.

Journalize the transactions of Paul Marciano, artist. Include an explanation with each journal entry.

Journalizing transactions; posting
(Obj. 2, 3)

S2-6 Architect Sonia Biaggi purchased supplies on account for $5,000. Later Biaggi paid $3,000 on account.

1. Journalize the two transactions on the books of Sonia Biaggi, architect. Include an explanation for each transaction.
2. Open a T-account for Accounts Payable and post to Accounts Payable. Compute the balance and denote it as Bal.
3. How much does Biaggi's business owe after both transactions? In which account does this amount appear?

Journalizing transactions; posting
(Obj. 2, 3)

S2-7 Family Services Centre (The Centre) performed service for a client who could not pay immediately. The Centre expected to collect the $500 the following month. A month later, The Centre received $100 cash from the client.

1. Record the two transactions on the books of Family Services Centre. Include an explanation for each transaction.
2. Open these T accounts: Cash, Accounts Receivable, and Service Revenue. Post to all three accounts. Compute each account balance and denote as Bal.
3. Answer these questions based on your analysis:
   a. How much did The Centre earn? Which account shows this amount?
   b. How much in total assets did The Centre acquire as a result of the two transactions?
   Show the amount of each asset.

Preparing and using a trial balance
(Obj. 4)

S2-8 Assume that lululemon athletica inc. reported the following summarized data at December 31, 2009. Accounts appear in no particular order; dollar amounts are in millions.

Revenues	$275
Other liabilities	38
Other assets	101
Cash and other current assets	53
Accounts payable	5
Expenses	244
Shareholders' equity	80

Prepare the trial balance of lululemon at December 31, 2009. List the accounts in their proper order, as on page 71. How much was lululemon's net income or net loss?

S2-9 Blackberry's trial balance follows:

Blackberry Inc.
Trial Balance
June 30, 2009

	Debit	Credit
Cash	$ 6,000	
Accounts receivable	13,000	
Supplies	4,000	
Equipment	22,000	
Land	50,000	
Accounts payable		$ 19,000
Note payable		20,000
Common shares		10,000
Retained earnings		8,000
Service revenue		70,000
Salary expense	21,000	
Rent expense	10,000	
Interest expense	1,000	
Total	$127,000	$127,000

Compute these amounts for Blackberry:

1. Total assets
2. Total liabilities
3. Total shareholders' equity
4. Net income or loss during June

S2-10 Refer to Blackberry's trial balance in Short Exercise S2-9. The purpose of this exercise is to help you learn how to correct three common accounting errors:

Error 1. Slide. Suppose the trial balance lists Land as $5,000 instead of $50,000. Recompute column totals, take the difference, and divide by 9. The result is an integer (no decimals), which suggests that the error is either a transposition or a slide.

Error 2. Transposition: Assume the trial balance lists Accounts receivable as $31,000 instead of $13,000. Recompute column totals, take the difference, and divide by 9. The result is an integer (no decimals), which suggests that the error is either a transposition or a slide.

Error 3. Mislabelling an item: Assume that Blackberry accidentally listed Accounts Receivable as a credit balance instead of a debit. Recompute the trial balance totals for debits and credits. Then take the difference between total debits and total credits, and divide the difference by 2. You get back to the original amount of Accounts Receivable.

S2-11 Accounting has its own vocabulary and basic relationships. Match the accounting terms at left with the corresponding definition or meaning at right.

____ 1. Debit
____ 2. Expense
____ 3. Net income
____ 4. Ledger
____ 5. Posting
____ 6. Normal balance
____ 7. Payable
____ 8. Journal
____ 9. Receivable
____ 10. Owners' equity

A. The cost of operating a business; a decrease in shareholders' equity
B. Always a liability
C. Revenues – Expenses
D. Grouping of accounts
E. Assets – Liabilities
F. Record of transactions
G. Always an asset
H. Left side of an account
I. Side of an account where increases are recorded
J. Copying data from the journal to the ledger

Analyzing transactions without a journal
(Obj. 5)

S2-12 Canadian Prairies Investments began by issuing common shares for cash of $100,000. The company immediately purchased computer equipment on account for $60,000.

1. Set up the following T-accounts for the company: Cash, Computer Equipment, Accounts Payable, Common Shares.

2. Record the transactions directly in the T-accounts without using a journal.

3. Show that total debits equal total credits.

EXERCISES

Reporting on business activities
(Obj. 1)

E2-13 Assume The Gap has opened a store in Ottawa. Starting with cash and shareholders' equity (common shares) of $100,000, Susan Harper, the store manager, signed a note payable to purchase land for $40,000 and a building for $130,000. She also paid $50,000 for store fixtures and $40,000 for inventory to use in the business. All these were paid for in cash.

Suppose the head office of Gap requires a weekly report from store managers. Write Harper's memo to the head office to report on her borrowing and purchases. Include the store's balance sheet as the final part of your memo. Prepare a T-account to compute the balance for cash.

Transactions and the accounting equation
(Obj. 1)

E2-14 During April, Spokes Ltd. completed a series of transactions. For each of the following items, give an example of a business transaction that has the described effect on the accounting equation of Spokes Ltd.

a. Increase one asset, and decrease another asset.

b. Decrease an asset, and decrease shareholders' equity.

c. Decrease an asset, and decrease a liability.

d. Increase an asset, and increase shareholders' equity.

e. Increase an asset, and increase a liability.

Transaction analysis
(Obj. 1)

E2-15 The following selected events were experienced by either Problem Solvers Inc., a corporation, or Pierce Laflame, the major shareholder. State whether each event (1) increased, (2) decreased, or (3) had no effect on the total assets of the business. Identify any specific asset affected.

a. Received $9,000 cash from customers on account

b. Laflame used personal funds to purchase a swimming pool for his home.

c. Sold land and received cash of $60,000 (the land was carried on the company's books at $60,000)

d. Borrowed $50,000 from the bank

e. Made cash purchase of land for a building site, $85,000

f. Received $20,000 cash and issued shares to a shareholder

g. Paid $60,000 cash on accounts payable

h. Purchased equipment and signed a $100,000 promissory note in payment

i. Purchased supplies on account for $15,000

j. The business paid Laflame a cash dividend of $4,000.

Transaction analysis; accounting equation
(Obj. 1)

E2-16 Joseph Ohara opens a dental practice. During the first month of operation (March), the practice, titled Joseph Ohara Dental Clinic Ltd., experienced the following events:

March	6	Ohara invested $50,000 in the business, which in turn issued its common shares to him.
	9	The business paid cash for land costing $30,000. Ohara plans to build a professional services building on the land.
	12	The business purchased dental supplies for $3,000 on account.
	15	Joseph Ohara Dental Clinic Ltd. officially opened for business.
	15–31	During the rest of the month, Ohara treated patients and earned service revenue of $10,000, receiving cash for half the revenue earned.
	15–31	The practice paid cash expenses: employee salaries, $1,400; office rent, $1,000; utilities, $300.
	31	The practice used supplies with a cost of $250.
	31	The practice borrowed $10,000, signing a note payable to the bank.
	31	The practice paid $2,000 on account.

Required

1. Analyze the effects of these events on the accounting equation of the practice of Joseph Ohara Dental Clinic Ltd. Use a format similar to that of Exhibit 2-1, Panel B, with headings for Cash, Accounts Receivable, Dental Supplies, Land, Accounts Payable, Note Payable, Common Shares, and Retained Earnings.

2. After completing the analysis, answer these questions about the business.
   a. How much are total assets?
   b. How much does the business expect to collect from patients?
   c. How much does the business owe in total?
   d. How much of the business's assets does Ohara really own?
   e. How much net income or net loss did the business experience during its first month of operations?

E2-17 Refer to Exercise 2-16. Record the transactions in the journal of Joseph Ohara Dental Clinic Ltd. List the transactions by date, and give an explanation for each transaction.

Journalizing transactions
(Obj. 2, 3)

E2-18 Perfect Printers Inc. completed the following transactions during October 2009, its first month of operations:

Journalizing transactions
(Obj. 1)

Oct.	1	Received $25,000, and issued common shares
	2	Purchased $800 of office supplies on account
	4	Paid $20,000 cash for land to use as a building site
	6	Performed service for customers, and received cash of $5,000
	9	Paid $100 on accounts payable
	17	Performed service for Waterloo School Board on account totalling $1,500
	23	Collected $1,000 from Waterloo School Board on account
	31	Paid the following expenses: salary, $1,000; rent, $500

Required

1. Record the transactions in the journal of Perfect Printers Inc. Key transactions by date and include an explanation for each entry, as illustrated in the chapter.

E2-19 Refer to Exercise 2-18.

Required

1. After journalizing the transactions of Exercise 2-18, post the entries to the ledger, using T-accounts. Key transactions by date. Date the ending balance of each account October 31.
2. Prepare the trial balance of Perfect Printers Inc., at October 31, 2009.
3. How much are total assets, total liabilities, and total shareholders' equity on October 31?

Posting to the ledger and preparing and using a trial balance
(Obj. 3, 4)

E2-20 The first seven transactions of Splash Water Park Ltd. have been posted to the company's accounts as follows:

Journalizing transactions
(Obj. 2, 3)

	Cash				Supplies				Equipment			Land	
(1)	20,000	(3)	8,000	(4)	1,000	(5)	100	(6)	8,000		(3)	31,000	
(2)	7,000	(6)	8,000										
(5)	100	(7)	400										

	Accounts Payable				Note Payable				Common Shares	
(7)	400	(4)	1,000			(2)	7,000		(1)	20,000
						(3)	23,000			

❚ Required

Prepare the journal entries that served as the sources for the seven transactions. Include an explanation for each entry. As Splash Water Park moves into the next period, how much cash does the business have? How much does Splash Water Park owe?

Preparing and using a trial balance
(Obj. 4)

E2-21 The accounts of Victoria Garden Care Ltd. follow with their normal balances at September 30, 2009. The accounts are listed in no particular order.

Account	Balance	Account	Balance
Dividends	6,000	Common shares	$8,500
Utilities expense	1,400	Accounts payable	4,300
Accounts receivable	17,500	Service revenue	24,000
Delivery expense	300	Equipment	29,000
Retained earnings	21,400	Note payable	13,000
Salary expense	8,000	Cash	9,000

❚ Required

1. Prepare the company's trial balance at September 30, 2009, listing accounts in proper sequence, as illustrated in the chapter. For example, Accounts receivable comes before Equipment. List the expense with the largest balance first, the expense with the next largest balance second, and so on.

2. Prepare the financial statement for the month ended September 30, 2009, that will tell the company's top managers the results of operations for the month.

Correcting errors in a trial balance
(Obj. 4)

E2-22 The trial balance of Sam's Deli Inc. at October 31, 2009, does not balance:

Cash	$ 4,200	
Accounts receivable	13,000	
Inventory	17,000	
Supplies	600	
Land	55,000	
Accounts payable		$12,000
Common shares		47,900
Sales revenue		32,100
Salary expense	1,700	
Rent expense	800	
Utilities expense	700	
Total	$93,000	$92,000

The accounting records hold the following errors:

a. Recorded a $1,000 cash revenue transaction by debiting Accounts Receivable. The credit entry was correct
b. Posted a $1,000 credit to Accounts Payable as $100
c. Did not record utilities expense or the related account payable in the amount of $200
d. Understated Common Shares by $1,100
e. Omitted insurance expense of $1,000 from the trial balance.

Required

Prepare the correct trial balance at October 31, 2009, complete with a heading. Journal entries are not required.

Recording transactions without a journal
(Obj. 5)

E2-23 Set up the following T-accounts: Cash, Accounts Receivable, Office Supplies, Office Furniture, Accounts Payable, Common Shares, Dividends, Service Revenue, Salary Expense, and Rent Expense.

Record the following transactions directly in the T-accounts without using a journal. Use the letters to identify the transactions. Calculate the account balances and denote as Bal.

a. In the month of May 2009, Sonia Rothesay opened an accounting firm by investing $10,000 cash and office furniture valued at $5,000. Organized as a professional corporation, the business issued common shares to Rothesay.

b. Paid monthly rent of $1,600

c. Purchased office supplies on account, $600

d. Paid employees' salaries of $2,000

e. Paid $200 of the account payable created in transaction c

f. Performed accounting service on account, $12,100

g. Declared and paid dividends of $2,000

E2-24 Refer to Exercise 2-23.

Preparing and using a trial balance
(Obj. 4)

1. After recording the transactions in Exercise 2-23, prepare the trial balance of Sonia Rothesay, Accountant, at May 31, 2009.

2. How well did the business perform during its first month? Give the basis for your answer.

SERIAL EXERCISE

Exercise 2-25 begins an accounting cycle that is completed in Chapter 3.

E2-25 Web Marketing Services Inc. completed these transactions during the first part of January 2009:

Recording transactions and preparing a trial balance
(Obj. 2, 3, 4)

Jan.	2	Received $5,000 cash from investors, and issued common shares
	2	Paid monthly office rent, $500
	3	Paid cash for a Dell computer, $3,000, with the computer expected to remain in service for 5 years
	4	Purchased office furniture on account, $6,000, with the furniture projected to last for 5 years
	5	Purchased supplies on account, $900
	9	Performed marketing service for a client, and received cash for the full amount of $800
	12	Paid utility expenses, $200
	18	Performed marketing service for a client on account, $1,700

❚ *Required*

1. Set up T-accounts for Cash, Accounts Receivable, Supplies, Equipment, Furniture, Accounts Payable, Common Shares, Dividends, Service Revenue, Rent Expense, Utilities Expense, and Salary Expense.

2. Journalize the transactions. Explanations are not required.

3. Post to the T-accounts. Key all items by date and denote an account balance on January 18 as Bal.

4. Prepare a trial balance at January 18. In the Serial Exercise of Chapter 3, we add transactions for the remainder of January and will require a trial balance at January 31, 2009.

CHALLENGE EXERCISES

E2-26 The manager of Canadiana Gallery Ltd. needs to compute the following information:

a. Total cash paid during March. Analyze Cash.

b. Cash collections from customers during March. Analyze Accounts Receivable

c. Cash paid on a note payable during March. Analyze Notes Payable

Computing financial statement amounts
(Obj. 5)

Here are additional data you need to analyze.

| | Balance | | |
Account	Feb. 28	Mar. 31	Additional Information for the Month of March
1. Cash	10,000	$5,000	Cash receipts, $80,000
2. Accounts Receivable	26,000	24,000	Sales on account, $50,000
3. Note Payable........................	13,000	21,000	New borrowing, $25,000

Prepare a T-account to compute each amount a through c.

Analyzing transactions; using a trial balance
(Obj. 1, 4)

E2-27 The trial balance of You Build Inc. at December 31, 2009, does not balance.

Cash	$ 3,900	Common shares.........................	$20,000
Accounts receivable	7,200	Retained earnings......................	7,300
Land	34,000	Service revenue..........................	9,100
Accounts payable.......................	5,800	Salary expense	3,400
Note payable.............................	5,000	Advertising expense...................	900

▌ *Required*

1. How much out of balance is the trial balance? Determine the out-of-balance amount. The error lies in the Accounts Receivable account. Add the out-of-balance amount to, or subtract it from, Accounts Receivable to determine the correct balance of Accounts Receivable.

2. You Build Inc. also failed to record the following transactions during December:
    a. Purchased additional land for $60,000 by signing a note payable
    b. Earned service revenue on account, $10,000
    c. Paid salary expense of $1,400
    d. Purchased a TV advertisement for $1,000 on account. This account will be paid during January.

    Add these amounts to, or subtract them from, the appropriate accounts to properly include the effects of these transactions. Then prepare the corrected trial balance of You Build Inc.

3. After correcting the accounts, advise the top management of You Build Inc. on the company's
    a) Total assets
    b) Total liabilities
    c) Net income or loss

Analyzing transactions
(Obj. 1)

E2-28 This question concerns the items and the amounts that two entities, City of Regina and Public Health Organization, Inc. (PHO), should report in their financial statements.

During August, PHO provided City of Regina with medical checks for new school pupils and sent a bill for $30,000. On September 7, Regina sent a cheque to PHO for $25,000. Regina began August with a cash balance of $50,000; PHO began with cash of $0.

▌ *Required*

For this situation, show everything that both Regina and PHO will report on their August and September income statements and on their balance sheets at August 31 and September 30. Use the following format for your answer:

Regina:		
Income statement	August	September
Balance sheet	August 31	September 30
PHO:		
Income statement	August	September
Balance sheet	August 31	September 30

After showing what each company should report, briefly explain how the City of Regina and Public Health Organization Inc. data relate to each other. Be specific.

QUIZ

Test your understanding of transaction analysis by answering the following questions. Select the best choice from among the possible answers.

Q2-29 An investment of cash into the business will
a. Decrease total assets
b. Decrease total liabilities
c. Increase shareholders' equity
d. Have no effect on total assets

Q2-30 Purchasing a computer on account will
a. Increase total assets
b. Increase total liabilities
c. Have no effect on shareholders' equity
d. All of the above

Q2-31 Performing a service on account will
a. Increase total assets
b. Increase shareholders' equity
c. Both a and b
d. Increase total liabilities

Q2-32 Receiving cash from a customer on account will
a. Have no effect on total assets
b. Increase total assets
c. Decrease liabilities
d. Increase shareholders' equity

Q2-33 Purchasing computer equipment for cash will
a. Increase both total assets and total liabilities
b. Decrease both total assets and shareholders' equity
c. Decrease both total liabilities and shareholders' equity
d. Have no effect on total assets, total liabilities, or shareholders' equity

Q2-34 Purchasing a building for $100,000 by paying cash of $20,000 and signing a note payable for $80,000 will
a. Increase both total assets and total liabilities by $100,000
b. Increase both total assets and total liabilities by $80,000
c. Decrease total assets, and increase total liabilities by $20,000
d. Decrease both total assets and total liabilities by $20,000

Q2-35 What is the effect on total assets and shareholders' equity of paying the electric bill as soon as it is received each month?

	Total assets	Shareholders' equity
a.	Decrease	No effect
b.	No effect	No effect
c.	Decrease	Decrease
d.	No effect	Decrease

Q2-36 Which of the following transactions will increase an asset and increase a liability?
a. Buying equipment on account
b. Purchasing office equipment for cash
c. Issuing shares
d. Making a payment on account

Q2-37 Which of the following transactions will increase an asset and increase shareholders' equity?
a. Collecting cash from a customer on an account receivable
b. Performing a service on account for a customer
c. Borrowing money from a bank
d. Purchasing supplies on account

Q2-38 Where do we first record a transaction?
a. Ledger
b. Trial balance
c. Account
d. Journal

Q2-39 Which of the following is not an asset account?
a. Common Shares
b. Salary Expense
c. Service Revenue
d. None of the above accounts is an asset.

Q2-40 Which of the following statements is false?
a. Revenues are increased by credits.
b. Assets are increased by debits.
c. Dividends are increased by credits.
d. Liabilities are decreased by debits.

Q2-41 The journal entry to record the receipt of land and a building and issuance of common shares
a. Debits Land and Building, and credits Common Shares
b. Debits Land, and credits Common Shares
c. Debits Common Shares, and credits Land and Building
d. Credits Land, Building, and debits Common Shares

Q2-42 The journal entry to record the purchase of supplies on account
a. Credits Supplies, and debits Cash
b. Debits Supplies, and credits Accounts Payable
c. Debits Supplies Expense, and credits Supplies
d. Credits Supplies, and debits Accounts Payable

Q2-43 If the credit to record the purchase of supplies on account is not posted,
a. Liabilities will be understated.
b. Expenses will be overstated.
c. Assets will be understated.
d. Shareholders' equity will be understated.

Q2-44 The journal entry to record a payment on account will
a. Debit Accounts Payable, and credit Retained Earnings
b. Debit Cash, and credit Expenses
c. Debit Expenses, and credit Cash
d. Debit Accounts Payable, and credit Cash

Q2-45 If the credit to record the payment of an account payable is not posted,
a. Liabilities will be understated.
b. Expenses will be understated.
c. Cash will be overstated.
d. Cash will be understated.

Q2-46 Which statement is false?
a. A trial balance lists all the accounts with their current balances.
b. A trial balance is the same as a balance sheet.
c. A trial balance can verify the equality of debits and credits.
d. A trial balance can be taken at any time.

Q2-47 A business's purchase of a $100,000 building with an $85,000 mortgage payable and issuance of $15,000 of common shares will
a. Increase shareholders' equity by $15,000
b. Increase assets by $15,000
c. Increase assets by $85,000
d. Increase shareholders' equity by $100,000

Q2-48 A new company completed these transactions. What will total assets equal?
1. Shareholders invested $50,000 cash and inventory worth $25,000
2. Sales on account, $12,000
   a. $75,000
   b. $87,000
   c. $63,000
   d. $62,000

PROBLEMS

(GROUP A)

P2-49A The trial balance of Amusement Specialties Inc., follows:

Analyzing a trial balance
(Obj. 4)

Amusement Specialties Inc. Trial Balance December 31, 2009		
Cash	$ 14,000	
Accounts receivable	11,000	
Prepaid expenses	4,000	
Equipment	171,000	
Building	100,000	
Accounts payable		$ 30,000
Note payable		120,000
Common shares		102,000
Retained earnings		40,000
Dividends	22,000	
Service revenue		86,000
Rent expense	14,000	
Advertising expense	3,000	
Wage expense	32,000	
Supplies expense	7,000	
Total	$378,000	$378,000

Sue Sibalius, your best friend, is considering investing in Amusement Specialties Inc. She seeks your advice in interpreting this information. Specifically, she asks how to use this trial balance to compute the company's total assets, total liabilities, and net income or net loss for the year.

I Required

Write a short note to answer Sue's questions. In your note, state the amounts of Amusement Specialties' total assets, total liabilities, and net income or net loss for the year. Also show how you computed each amount.

P2-50A The following amounts summarize the financial position of Blythe Spirit Consulting, Inc. on May 31, 2009:

Analyzing transactions with the accounting equation and preparing the financial statements
(Obj. 1)

	ASSETS			=	LIABILITIES	+	SHAREHOLDERS' EQUITY	
CASH +	ACCOUNTS RECEIVABLE	+ SUPPLIES	+ LAND =		ACCOUNTS PAYABLE	+	COMMON SHARES	+	RETAINED EARNINGS
Bal. 1,300	1,000		12,000		8,000		4,000	2,300

During June 2009, the business completed these transactions:

a. Received cash of $5,000, and issued common shares

b. Performed services for a client, and received cash of $7,600

c. Paid $4,000 on accounts payable

d. Purchased supplies on account, $1,500

e. Collected cash from a customer on account, $1,000

f. Consulted on the design of a business report, and billed the client for services rendered, $2,500

g. Recorded the following business expenses for the month: paid office rent, $900; paid advertising, $300

h. Declared and paid a cash dividend of $2,000

❙ *Required*

1. Analyze the effects of the preceding transactions on the accounting equation of Blythe Spirit Consulting, Inc. Adapt the format of Exhibit 2-1, Panel B.

2. Prepare the income statement of Blythe Spirit Consulting, Inc. for the month ended June 30, 2009. List expenses in decreasing order by amount.

3. Prepare the entity's statement of retained earnings for the month ended June 30, 2009.

4. Prepare the balance sheet of Blythe Spirit Consulting, Inc. at June 30, 2009.

Recording transactions, posting
(Obj. 2, 3)

P2-51A Use this problem in conjunction with Problem 2-50A.

❙ *Required*

1. Journalize the transactions of Blythe Spirit Consulting, Inc. Explanations are not required.

2. Set up the following T-accounts: Cash, Accounts Receivable, Supplies, Land, Accounts Payable, Common Shares, Retained Earnings, Dividends, Service Revenue, Rent Expense, and Advertising Expense. Insert in each account its balance as given (example: Cash $1,300). Post the transactions to the accounts.

3. Compute the balance in each account. For each asset account, each liability account, and for Common Shares, compare its balance to the ending balance you obtained in Problem 2-50A. Are the amounts the same or different? (In Chapter 3, we complete the accounting process. There you will learn how the Retained Earnings, Dividends, Revenue, and Expense accounts work together in the processing of accounting information.)

Analyzing transactions with the
accounting equation
(Obj. 1, 2)

P2-52A Mountain View Estates Ltd. experienced the following events during the organizing phase and its first month of operations. Some of the events were personal and did not affect the business. Others were business transactions.

Sept.	4	Gayland Jet, the major shareholder of the company, received $50,000 cash from an inheritance.
	5	Jet deposited $50,000 cash in a new business bank account titled Mountain View Estates Ltd. The business issued common shares to Jet.
	6	The business paid $300 cash for letterhead stationery for the new office.
	7	The business purchased office furniture. The company paid cash of $20,000 and agreed to pay the account payable for the remainder, $5,000, within three months.
	10	Jet sold Telus shares, which he had owned for several years, receiving $30,000 cash from his stockbroker.
	11	Jet deposited the $30,000 cash from sale of the Telus shares in his personal bank account.
	12	A representative of a large company telephoned Jet and told him of the company's intention to put a down payment of $10,000 on a lot.
	18	Jet finished a real estate deal on behalf of a client and submitted his bill for services, $10,000. Jet expects to collect from this client within two weeks.
	21	The business paid half its account payable for the furniture purchased on September 7.
	25	The business paid office rent of $4,000.
	30	The business declared and paid a cash dividend of $2,000.

❙ *Required*

1. Classify each of the preceding events as one of the following:

   a. A business-related event but not a transaction to be recorded by Mountain View Estates Ltd.

   b. A personal transaction for a shareholder, not to be recorded by Mountain View Estates Ltd.

   c. A business transaction to be recorded by the business of Mountain View Estates Ltd.

2. Analyze the effects of the preceding events on the accounting equation of Mountain View Estates Ltd. Use a format similar to that in Exhibit 2-1, Panel B.

3. At the end of the first month of operations, Jet has a number of questions about the financial standing of the business. Explain the following to him:

   a. How the business can have more cash than retained earnings.

   b. How much in total resources the business has, how much it owes, and what Jet's ownership interest is in the assets of the business.

4. Record the transactions of the business in its journal. Include an explanation for each entry.

P2-53A During October, All Pets Veterinary Clinic Ltd. completed the following transactions:

Analyzing and recording transactions
(Obj. 2, 3)

Oct.	1	Dr. Squires deposited $8,000 cash in the business bank account. The business issued common shares to her.
	5	Paid monthly rent, $1,000
	9	Paid $5,000 cash, and signed a $25,000 note payable to purchase land for an office site
	10	Purchased supplies on account, $1,200
	19	Paid $600 on account
	22	Borrowed $10,000 from the bank for business use. Dr. Squires signed a note payable to the bank in the name of the business.
	31	Revenues earned during the month included $7,000 cash and $5,000 on account
	31	Paid employees' salaries ($2,000), advertising expense ($1,500), and utilities ($1,100)
	31	Declared and paid a cash dividend of $3,000

The clinic uses the following accounts: Cash, Accounts Receivable, Supplies, Land, Accounts Payable, Notes Payable, Common Shares, Dividends, Service Revenue, Salary Expense, Rent Expense, Utilities Expense, and Advertising Expense.

❚ Required

1. Journalize each transaction of All Pets Veterinary Clinic Ltd. Explanations are not required.

2. Prepare T-accounts for Cash, Accounts Payable, and Notes Payable. Post to these three accounts.

3. After these transactions, how much cash does the business have? How much in total does it owe?

P2-54A During the first month of operations, New Pane Windows Inc. completed the following transactions:

Journalizing transactions, posting, and preparing and using a trial balance
(Obj. 2, 3, 4)

May	2	New Pane received $30,000 cash and issued common shares to shareholders.
	3	Purchased supplies, $1,000, and equipment, $2,600, on account
	4	Performed services, and received cash, $1,500
	7	Paid cash to acquire land for an office site, $22,000
	11	Repaired a window, and billed the customer $500
	16	Paid for the equipment purchased May 3 on account
	17	Paid the telephone bill, $95
	18	Received partial payment from client on account, $250
	22	Paid the water and electricity bills, $400
	29	Received $2,000 cash for installing a new window
	31	Paid employee salary, $1,300
	31	Declared and paid dividends of $1,500

▌*Required*

Set up the following T-accounts: Cash, Accounts Receivable, Supplies, Equipment, Land, Accounts Payable, Common Shares, Dividends, Service Revenue, Salary Expense, and Utilities Expense.

1. Record each transaction in the journal, using the account titles given. Key each transaction by date. Explanations are not required.

2. Post the transactions to the T-accounts, using transaction dates as posting references. Label the ending balance of each account Bal., as shown in the chapter.

3. Prepare the trial balance of New Pane Windows, at May 31 of the current year.

4. The manager asks you how much in total resources the business has to work with, how much it owes, and whether May was profitable (and by how much).

Recording transactions directly in T-accounts; preparing and using a trial balance
(Obj. 3, 4)

P2-55A During the first month of operations (January 2009) Music Services Ltd. completed the following selected transactions:

a. The business has cash of $10,000 and a building valued at $50,000. The corporation issued common shares to the shareholders.

b. Borrowed $50,000 from the bank, and signed a note payable

c. Paid $60,000 for music equipment

d. Purchased supplies on account, $1,000

e. Paid employees' salaries, $1,500

f. Received $800 for service performed for customers

g. Performed service to customers on account, $4,500

h. Paid $100 of the account payable created in transaction d

i. Received a $600 utility bill that will be paid in the near future

j. Received cash on account, $3,100

k. Paid the following cash expenses: rent, $1,000; advertising, $800

▌*Required*

1. Set up the following T-accounts: Cash, Accounts Receivable, Office Supplies, Music Equipment, Building, Accounts Payable, Note Payable, Common Shares, Service Revenue, Salary Expense, Rent Expense, Advertising Expense, and Utilities Expense.

2. Record the foregoing transactions directly in the T-accounts without using a journal. Use the letters to identify the transactions.

3. Prepare the trial balance of Music Services Ltd. at January 31, 2009.

4. The bank manager is afraid that the total liabilities of the business exceed the total assets. He also fears that the business suffered a net loss during January. Compute the amounts needed to answer his questions.

(GROUP B)

Analyzing a trial balance
(Obj. 4)

P2-56B The owners of Opera Tours Inc. are selling the business. They offer the trial balance that appears at the top of the next page to prospective buyers.

Your best friend is considering buying Opera Tours. She seeks your advice in interpreting this information. Specifically, she asks whether this trial balance provides the data to prepare a balance sheet and an income statement.

▌*Required*

Write a memo to answer your friend's questions. Indicate which accounts go on the balance sheet and which accounts go on the income statement. State the amount of net income that Opera Tours earned in 2009 and explain your computation.

Opera Tours Inc.
Trial Balance
December 31, 2009

Cash	$ 12,000	
Accounts receivable	45,000	
Prepaid expenses	4,000	
Equipment	231,000	
Accounts payable		$105,000
Note payable		92,000
Common shares		30,000
Retained earnings		32,000
Service revenue		139,000
Salary expense	69,000	
Tour expenses	26,000	
Rent expense	7,000	
Advertising expense	4,000	
Total	$398,000	$398,000

P2-57B Doug Hanna operates and is the major shareholder of an interior design studio called DH Designers Inc. The following amounts summarize the financial position of the business on April 30, 2009:

Analyzing transactions with the accounting equation and preparing the financial statements
(Obj. 1)

	ASSETS			=	LIABILITIES	+	SHAREHOLDERS' EQUITY	
CASH +	ACCOUNTS RECEIVABLE	+ SUPPLIES	+ LAND	=	ACCOUNTS PAYABLE	+	COMMON SHARES	+ RETAINED EARNINGS
Bal. 1,700	2,200		24,100		5,400		10,000	12,600

During May 2009, the business completed these transactions:

a. Hanna received $30,000 as a gift and deposited the cash in the business bank account. The business issued common shares to Hanna.

b. Paid $1,000 on accounts payable

c. Performed services for a client and received cash of $5,100

d. Collected cash from a customer on account, $700

e. Purchased supplies on account, $800

f. Consulted on the interior design of a major office building and billed the client for services rendered, $15,000

g. Received cash of $1,700 and issued common shares to a shareholder

h. Recorded the following expenses for the month: paid office rent, $2,100; paid advertising, $1,600

i. Declared and paid a cash dividend of $2,000

❙ Required

In order to guide Doug Hanna,

1. Analyze the effects of the preceding transactions on the accounting equation of DH Designers, Inc. Adapt the format of Exhibit 2-1, Panel B.

2. Prepare the income statement of DH Designers, Inc. for the month ended May 31, 2009. List expenses in decreasing order by amount.

3. Prepare the statement of retained earnings of DH Designers, Inc. for the month ended May 31, 2009.

4. Prepare the balance sheet of DH Designers, Inc. at May 31, 2009.

P2-58B Use this problem in conjunction with Problem 2-57B.

❙ *Required*

1. Journalize the transactions of DH Designers, Inc. Explanations are not required.

2. Set up the following T-accounts: Cash, Accounts Receivable, Supplies, Land, Accounts Payable, Common Shares, Retained Earnings, Dividends, Service Revenue, Rent Expense, and Advertising Expense. Insert in each account its balance as given (example: Cash $1,700). Post to the accounts.

3. Compute the balance in each account. For each asset account, each liability account, and for Common Shares, compare its balance to the ending balance you obtained in Problem 2-57B. Are the amounts the same or different? (In Chapter 3, we complete the accounting process. There you will learn how the Retained Earnings, Dividends, Revenue, and Expense accounts work together in the processing of accounting information.)

P2-59B Lane Kohler opened a consulting practice that he operates as a corporation. The name of the new entity is Lane Kohler, Consultant, Inc. Kohler experienced the following events during the organizing phase of his new business and its first month of operations. Some of the events were personal transactions of the shareholder and did not affect the consulting practice. Others were transactions that should be accounted for by the business.

March	1	Kohler sold 1,000 shares of RIM stock and received $100,000 cash from his stockbroker.
	2	Kohler deposited in his personal bank account the $100,000 cash from sale of the RIM shares.
	3	Kohler received $150,000 cash through an inheritance from his grandfather.
	5	Kohler deposited $50,000 cash in a new business bank account titled Lane Kohler, Consultant, Inc. The business issued common shares to Kohler.
	6	A representative of a large company telephoned Kohler and told him of the company's intention to give $15,000 of consulting business to Kohler.
	7	The business paid $450 cash for letterhead stationery for the consulting office.
	9	The business purchased office furniture. Kohler paid cash of $5,000 and agreed to pay the account payable for the remainder, $10,500, within three months.
	23	Kohler finished an analysis for a client and submitted his bill for services, $4,000. He expected to collect from this client within one month.
	29	The business paid $5,000 of its account payable on the furniture purchased on March 9.
	30	The business paid office rent of $2,100.
	31	The business declared and paid a cash dividend of $1,000.

❙ *Required*

1. Classify each of the preceding events as one of the following:

   a. A personal transaction of a shareholder not to be recorded by the business of Lane Kohler, Consultant, Inc.

   b. A business transaction to be recorded by the business of Lane Kohler, Consultant, Inc.

   c. A business-related event but not a transaction to be recorded by the business of Lane Kohler, Consultant, Inc.

2. Analyze the effects of the preceding events on the accounting equation of the business of Lane Kohler, Consultant, Inc. Use a format similar to Exhibit 2-1, Panel B.

3. At the end of the first month of operations, Kohler has a number of questions about the financial standing of the business. Answer the following questions for him:

   a. How can the business have more cash than retained earnings?

   b. How much in total resources does the business have? How much does it owe? What is Kohler's ownership interest in the assets of the business?

4. Record the transactions of the business in its journal. Include an explanation for each entry.

P2-60B Wimberley Glass, Inc. has shops in the shopping malls of a major metropolitan area. The business completed the following transactions:

Analyzing and recording transactions
(Obj. 2, 3)

June	1	Received cash of $25,000, and issued common shares to a shareholder
	2	Paid $10,000 cash, and signed a $30,000 note payable to purchase land for a new glassworks site
	7	Received $20,000 cash from sales, and deposited that amount in the bank
	10	Purchased supplies on account, $1,000
	15	Paid employees' salaries, $2,800, and rent on a shop, $1,800
	15	Paid advertising expense, $1,100
	16	Paid $1,000 on account
	17	Declared and paid a cash dividend of $2,000

Wimberley Glass, Inc. uses the following accounts: Cash, Supplies, Land, Accounts Payable, Note Payable, Common Shares, Dividends, Sales Revenue, Salary Expense, Rent Expense, and Advertising Expense.

I Required

1. Journalize each transaction. Explanations are not required.
2. Prepare T-accounts for Cash, Accounts Payable, and Notes Payable. Post to these three accounts.
3. After these transactions, how much cash does the business have? How much does it owe in total?

P2-61B During the first month of operations, Barron Environmental Services Inc. completed the following transactions.

Journalizing transactions, posting, and preparing and using a trial balance
(Obj. 2, 3, 4)

Oct.	3	Received $20,000 cash, and issued common shares
	4	Performed services for a client, and received $5,000 cash
	6	Purchased supplies, $300, and furniture, $2,500, on account
	7	Paid $15,000 cash to acquire land for an office site
	7	Worked for a client, and billed the client $1,500
	16	Received partial payment from a client on account, $500
	24	Paid the telephone bill, $110
	24	Paid the water and electricity bills, $400
	28	Received $2,500 cash for helping a client meet environmental standards
	31	Paid secretary's salary, $1,200
	31	Paid $2,500 of the account payable created on October 3.
	31	Declared and paid dividends of $2,400

I Required

Set up the following T-accounts: Cash, Accounts Receivable, Supplies, Furniture, Land, Accounts Payable, Common Shares, Dividends, Service Revenue, Salary Expense, and Utilities Expense.

1. Record each transaction in the journal, using the account titles given. Key each transaction by date. Explanations are not required.
2. Post the transactions to the T-accounts, using transaction dates as posting references. Label the ending balance of each account Bal., as shown in the chapter.
3. Prepare the trial balance of Barron Environmental Services Inc. at October 31 of the current year.
4. Report to the shareholder how much in total resources the business has to work with, how much it owes, and whether October was profitable (and by how much).

Recording transactions directly in T-accounts; preparing and using a trial balance
(Obj. 3, 4)

P2-62B During the first month of operations (June 2009), Schulich Graphics Service Inc. completed the following selected transactions:

a. Began the business with an investment of $20,000 cash and a building valued at $60,000. The corporation issued common shares to the shareholders.

b. Borrowed $90,000 from the bank, and signed a note payable

c. Paid $35,000 for computer equipment

d. Purchased office supplies on account for $1,300

e. Performed computer graphic service on account for a client, $2,500

f. Received $1,200 cash on account

g. Paid $800 of the account payable created in transaction d

h. Received a $500 bill for advertising expense that will be paid in the near future

i. Performed service for clients, and received $1,100 in cash

j. Paid employees' salaries totalling $2,200

k. Paid the following cash expenses: rent, $700; utilities, $400

I Required

1. Set up the following T-accounts: Cash, Accounts Receivable, Office Supplies, Computer Equipment, Building, Accounts Payable, Note Payable, Common Shares, Service Revenue, Salary Expense, Advertising Expense, Rent Expense, and Utilities Expense.

2. Record each transaction directly in the T-accounts without using a journal. Use the letters to identify the transactions.

3. Prepare the trial balance of Schulich Graphics Service Inc. at June 30, 2009.

APPLY YOUR KNOWLEDGE

DECISION CASES

Recording transactions directly in T-accounts, preparing a trial balance, and measuring net income or loss
(Obj. 4, 5)

Case 1. A friend named Tom Tipple has asked what effect certain transactions will have on his company. Time is short, so you cannot apply the detailed procedures of journalizing and posting. Instead, you must analyze the transactions without the use of a journal. Tipple will continue the business only if he can expect to earn monthly net income of $10,000. The following transactions occurred this month:

a. Tipple deposited $10,000 cash in a business bank account, and the corporation issued common shares to him.

b. Paid $300 cash for supplies

c. Purchased office furniture on account, $4,400

d. Earned revenue on account, $7,000

e. Borrowed $5,000 cash from the bank, and signed a note payable due within one year

f. Paid the following cash expenses for one month: employee's salary, $1,700; office rent, $600.

g. Collected cash from customers on account, $1,200

h. Paid on account, $1,000

i. Earned revenue, and received $2,500 cash

j. Purchased advertising in the local newspaper for cash, $800

I Required

1. Set up the following T-accounts: Cash, Accounts Receivable, Supplies, Furniture, Accounts Payable, Notes Payable, Common Shares, Service Revenue, Salary Expense, Advertising Expense, and Rent Expense.

2. Record the transactions directly in the accounts without using a journal. Key each transaction by letter.

3. Prepare a trial balance at the current date. List expenses with the largest amount first, the next largest amount second, and so on. The business name will be Tipple Networks, Inc.

4. Compute the amount of net income or net loss for this first month of operations. Why would you recommend that Tipple continue or not continue in business?

Case 2. Barbara Boland opened a flower shop. Business has been good, and Boland is considering expanding with a second shop. A cousin has produced the following financial statements at December 31, 2009, the end of the first three months of operations:

Correcting financial statements; deciding whether to expand a business
(Obj. 2)

Barbara Boland Blossoms Inc.	
Income Statement	
Quarter Ended December 31, 2009	
Sales revenue	$36,000
Common shares	10,000
Total revenue	46,000
Accounts payable	8,000
Advertising expense	5,000
Rent expense	6,000
Total expenses	19,000
Net income	$27,000

Barbara Boland Blossoms Inc.	
Balance Sheet	
December 31, 2009	
Assets	
Cash	$ 6,000
Cost of goods sold (expense)	22,000
Flower inventory	5,000
Store fixtures	10,000
Total assets	$43,000
Liabilities	
None	
Owners' Equity	$43,000

In these financial statements all amounts are correct, except for Owners' Equity. Boland's cousin heard that total assets should equal total liabilities plus owners' equity, so he plugged in the amount of owners' equity at $43,000 to make the balance sheet come out even.

I *Required*

Barbara Boland has asked whether she should expand the business. Her banker says Boland may be wise to expand if (a) net income for the first quarter reaches $5,000 and (b) total assets are at least $25,000. It appears that the business has reached these milestones, but Boland doubts her cousin's understanding of accounting. Boland needs your help in making this decision. Prepare a corrected income statement and balance sheet. (Remember that Retained Earnings, which was omitted from the balance sheet, should equal net income for the period; there were no dividends.) After preparing the statements, give Boland your recommendation as to whether she should expand the flower shop.

ETHICAL ISSUES

Issue 1. Scruffy Murphy is the president and principal shareholder of Scruffy's Bar and Grill. To expand, the business is applying for a $250,000 bank loan. The bank requires the company to have shareholders' equity of at least as much as the loan. To get the loan, Murphy is considering two options for beefing up the shareholders' equity of the business:

Option 1. Issue $100,000 common shares for cash. A friend has been wanting to invest in the company. This may be the right time to extend the offer.

Option 2. Transfer $100,000 of Murphy's personal land to the business, and issue common shares to Murphy. Then, after obtaining the loan, Murphy can transfer the land back to himself and zero out the common shares.

Journalize the transactions required by each option. Which plan is ethical? Which is unethical and why?

Issue 2. Community Charities has a standing agreement with Royal Bank of Canada (RBC). The agreement allows Community Charities to overdraw its cash balance at the bank when donations are running low. In the past, Community Charities managed funds wisely and rarely used this privilege. Recently, however, Beatrice Grand has been named president of Community Charities. To expand operations, she is acquiring office equipment and spending a lot for fundraising. During Grand's presidency, Community Charities has maintained a negative bank balance of about $3,000.

❙ Required

What is the ethical issue in this situation? Do you approve or disapprove of Grand's management of Community Charities' and RBC's funds? Why?

FOCUS ON FINANCIALS

Analyzing a leading company's financial statements
(Obj. 2, 6)

Sun-Rype Products Ltd.

Refer to the Sun-Rype Products Ltd. financial statements in Appendix A at the end of the book. Assume that Sun-Rype completed the following selected transactions during 2007.

a. Made sales on account, $135.1 million

b. Incurred cost of goods sold (an expense) of $93.3 million. Credit the Inventories account.

c. Paid operating and other expenses of $32.7 million

d. Paid income tax expense, $2.1 million

e. Collected accounts receivable, $140.4 million

f. Paid cash for inventory, $91.9 million

g. Paid cash for other assets, $10.1 million

h. Incurred other expenses (credit Cash), $2.4 million

❙ Required

1. Set up T-accounts for Cash (debit balance of $1.5 million); Accounts Receivable (debit balance of $12.7 million); Inventories (debit balance of $18.7 million); Other Assets ($0 balance); Net Sales ($0 balance); Cost of Goods Sold ($0 balance); Operating and Other Expenses ($0 balance); Income Tax Expense ($0 balance).

2. Journalize Sun-Rype's transactions a through h. Explanations are not required.

3. Post to the T-accounts, and compute the balance for each account. Key postings by transaction letters a through h.

4. For each of the following accounts, compare your computed balance to Sun-Rype's actual balance as shown on Sun-Rype's income statement or balance sheet dated June 29, 2004. All your amounts should agree to the actual figures, rounded to the nearest million dollars. There may be a slight rounding error.
   a. Cash
   b. Accounts Receivable
   c. Inventories
   d. Net Sales
   e. Cost of Goods Sold
   f. Income Tax Expense (listed as Income Taxes on the income statement)

5. Use the relevant accounts from requirement 4 to prepare a summary income statement for Sun-Rype for the year ended December 31, 2007. Compare the net income you computed to Sun-Rype's actual net income. The two net income amounts should be equal.

FOCUS ON ANALYSIS

Mullen Group Income Fund

Refer to the Mullen Group Income Fund financial statements in Appendix B at the end of the book. Suppose you are an investor considering buying Mullen's units. The following questions are important:

Recording transactions and computing net income
(Obj. 3, 4)

1. Explain which of Mullen's sales or collections from customers was the largest amount during the year ended December 31, 2007. Analyze net receivables to answer this question.

2. A major concern of lenders, such as banks, is the amount of long-term debt a company owes. How much long-term debt does Mullen owe at the end of 2007? What must have happened to Mullen's long-term debt during 2007?

3. Investors are vitally interested in a company's revenues and profits, and its trends of revenues and profits over time. Consider Mullen's revenues and net income during the period from 2006 to 2007. Compute the percentage increases in revenue and also in net income or loss during 2007. Which item grew faster during this period, revenue or net income? (For convenience, show dollar amounts in thousands.) Which would you prefer to grow faster, revenue or net income? Give the reason for your answer.

GROUP PROJECTS

Project 1. You are promoting a concert in your area. Your purpose is to earn a profit, so you need to establish the formal structure of a business entity. Assume you organize as a corporation.

I *Required*

1. Make a detailed list of 10 factors you must consider as you establish the business.

2. Describe 10 of the items your business must arrange to promote and stage the concert.

3. Identify the transactions that your business can undertake to organize, promote, and stage the concert. Journalize the transactions, and post to the relevant T-accounts. Set up the accounts you need for your business ledger.

4. Prepare the income statement, statement of retained earnings, and balance sheet immediately after the concert, that is, before you have had time to pay all the business bills and collect all receivables.

5. Assume that you will continue to promote concerts if the venture is successful. If it is unsuccessful, you will terminate the business within three months after the concert. Discuss how to evaluate the success of your venture and how to decide whether to continue in business.

Project 2. Contact a local business, and arrange with the owner to learn what accounts the business uses.

I *Required*

1. Obtain a copy of the business's chart of accounts.

2. Prepare the company's financial statements for the most recent month, quarter, or year.

You may use either made-up account balances or balances supplied by the owner.

If the business has a large number of accounts within a category, combine related accounts and report a single amount on the financial statements. For example, the company may have several cash accounts. Combine all cash amounts and report a single Cash amount on the balance sheet.

You will probably encounter numerous accounts that you have not yet learned. Deal with these as best you can. The charts of accounts given in Appendix C at the end of the book can be helpful.

QUICK CHECK ANSWERS

1. *c*	4. *d*	7. *c*	10. *d*
2. *d*	5. *a*	8. *a*	11. *a*
3. *a*	6. *b*	9. *d*	12. *c*

Accrual Accounting and Income

Learning Objectives

1. **Relate** accrual accounting and cash flows

2. **Apply** the revenue and matching principles

3. **Adjust** the accounts

4. **Prepare** the financial statements

5. **Close** the books

6. **Use** two new ratios to evaluate a business

SPOTLIGHT

Tim Hortons Inc. is a Canadian icon. It was founded in Hamilton, Ontario, in 1964 and now includes 2,823 restaurants in Canada and 398 in the United States.

As you can see from Tim Hortons' income statement, the company sold more than $1.8 billion of coffee, doughnuts, and related products during the 2007 fiscal year. How does Tim Hortons know whether these revenues translated into profit? The income statement reports net income of $270 million. That's a lot of coffee and doughnuts!

Tim Hortons Inc.

▼   **Consolidated Statement of Operations (Adapted)**
For the Year Ended December 30, 2007

	Millions
Revenues	$1,896
Expenses:	
Cost of sales	1,099
Operating expenses	201
General and administrative expenses	119
Other expenses	51
Interest expense	17
Income taxes	139
Total expenses	$1,626
Net income	$ 270

This chapter completes our coverage of the accounting cycle. It gives the basics of what you need before tackling individual topics such as cash, receivables, and inventory.

Accrual Accounting Versus Cash-Basis Accounting

Managers want to earn a profit. Investors search for companies whose share prices will increase. Banks seek borrowers who'll pay their debts. Accounting provides the information these people use for decision making. Accounting can be based on either of the following:

- Accrual basis
- Cash basis

Accrual accounting records the impact of a business transaction as it occurs. When the business performs a service, makes a sale, or incurs an expense, the accountant records the transaction even if it receives or pays no cash.

Cash-basis accounting records only cash transactions—cash receipts and cash payments. Cash receipts are treated as revenues, and cash payments are handled as expenses.

Generally accepted accounting principles (GAAP) require accrual accounting. The business records revenues as the revenues are earned and expenses as the expenses are incurred—not necessarily when cash changes hands. Consider a sale on account. Which transaction increases your wealth—making an $800 sale on account, or collecting the $800 cash? Making the sale increases your wealth by $300 because you gave up inventory that cost you $500 and you got a receivable worth $800. Collecting cash later merely swaps your $800 receivable for $800 cash—no gain on this transaction. Making the sale—not collecting the cash—increases your wealth.

The basic defect of cash-basis accounting is that the cash basis ignores important information. That makes the financial statements incomplete. As a result, people using cash basis financial statements make bad decisions.

Suppose your business makes a sale *on account*. The cash basis does not record the sale because you received no cash. You may be thinking, "Let's wait until we collect cash and then record the sale. After all, we pay the bills with cash, so ignore transactions that don't affect cash."

What's wrong with this argument? There are two defects—one on the balance sheet and the other on the income statement.

Balance-Sheet Defect. If we fail to record a sale on account, the balance sheet reports no account receivable. Why is this so bad? The receivable is a real asset, and it should appear on the balance sheet. Without this information, your assets are understated as shown on the balance sheet.

Income-Statement Defect. A sale on account provides revenue that increases the company's wealth. Ignoring the sale understates your revenue and net income on the income statement.

The take-away lessons from this discussion are:

- Watch out for companies that use the cash basis of accounting. Their financial statements omit important information.
- All but the smallest businesses use the accrual basis of accounting.

Accrual Accounting and Cash Flows

Accrual accounting is more complex—and more complete—than cash-basis accounting. Accrual accounting records *cash* transactions, including:

- Collecting from customers
- Receiving cash from interest earned
- Paying salaries, rent, and other expenses
- Borrowing money
- Paying off loans
- Issuing shares

    Accrual accounting also records *noncash* transactions such as:

- Purchases of inventory on account
- Sales on account
- Accrual of expenses incurred but not yet paid
- Amortization expense
- Usage of prepaid rent, insurance, and supplies
- Earning of revenue when cash was collected in advance

    Accrual accounting is based on a framework of concepts and principles. We turn now to the time-period concept, the revenue principle, and the matching principle.

The Time-Period Concept

The only way for a business to know for certain how well it performed is to close its doors, sell the assets, pay the liabilities, and return any leftover cash to the owners. This process, called *liquidation*, means going out of business. On-going businesses cannot measure income this way. Instead, they need regular progress reports. Accountants, therefore, prepare financial statements for specific periods. The **time-period concept** ensures that accounting information is reported at regular intervals.

The basic accounting period is one year, and virtually all businesses prepare annual financial statements. Around 60% of large companies, including TransCanada Corporation, use the calendar year from January 1 through December 31.

Objective

① **Relate** accrual accounting and cash flows

A *fiscal year* ends on a date other than December 31. Most retailers, including the Hudson's Bay Company, use a fiscal year that ends on January 31 because the low point in their business activity falls after Christmas. Sobeys Inc.'s fiscal year is 52 weeks, ending on the first Saturday in May.

Companies prepare financial statements for interim periods of less than a year, such as a month, a quarter (three months), or a semi-annual period (six months). Most of the discussions in this text are based on an annual accounting period.

The Revenue Principle

The **revenue principle** governs two things:

1. *When* to record revenue (make a journal entry)
2. The *amount* of revenue to record

When should you record revenue?* After it has been earned—and not before. In most cases, revenue is earned when the business has delivered a good or service to a customer. It has done everything required to earn the revenue by transferring the good or service to the customer.

Exhibit 3-1 shows two situations that provide guidance on when to record earned revenue. Situation 1 illustrates when not to record revenue: No transaction has occurred, so Tim Hortons records nothing. Situation 2 illustrates when revenue should be recorded—after a business transaction has occurred.

The *amount* of revenue to record is the cash value of the good or service transferred to the customer. Suppose that in order to obtain golfer Lorie Kane's travel business, Marlin Travel arranges a trip for the price of $500. Ordinarily, Marlin would charge $600 for this service. How much revenue should it record? The answer is $500—the cash value of the transaction.

The Matching Principle

The **matching principle** is a basis for recording expenses. Expenses are the costs of assets used up, and liabilities created, in the earning of revenue. Expenses have no future benefit to the company. The matching principle includes two steps:

1. Identify all the expenses incurred during the accounting period.
2. Measure the expenses, and match expenses against the revenues earned.

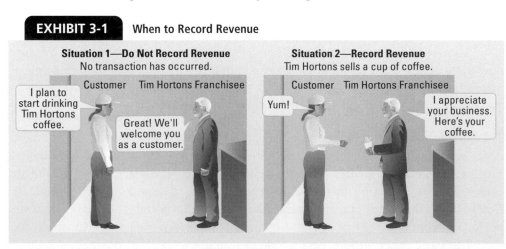

EXHIBIT 3-1   **When to Record Revenue**

Situation 1—Do Not Record Revenue
No transaction has occurred.

Customer   Tim Hortons Franchisee

I plan to start drinking Tim Hortons coffee.

Great! We'll welcome you as a customer.

Situation 2—Record Revenue
Tim Hortons sells a cup of coffee.

Customer   Tim Hortons Franchisee

Yum!

I appreciate your business. Here's your coffee.

IFRS

---

*Later in the text you will learn that converged accounting standards require certain assets and liabilities to be valued at their fair values. This valuation results in unrealized gains and losses.

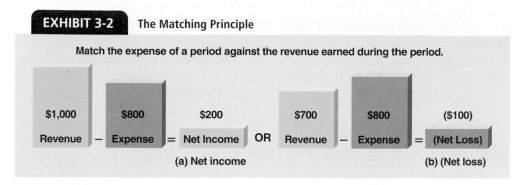

EXHIBIT 3-2   The Matching Principle

Match the expense of a period against the revenue earned during the period.

| $1,000 Revenue | − | $800 Expense | = | $200 Net Income | OR | $700 Revenue | − | $800 Expense | = | ($100) (Net Loss) |

(a) Net income   (b) (Net loss)

To *match* expenses against revenues means to subtract expenses from revenues to compute net income or net loss. Exhibit 3-2 illustrates the matching principle.

Some expenses are paid in cash. Other expenses arise from using up an asset such as supplies. Still other expenses occur when a company creates a liability. For example, Tim Hortons' salary expense occurs when employees work for the company. Tim Hortons may pay the salary expense immediately, or it may record a liability for the expense. In either case, Tim Hortons has salary expense. The critical event for recording an expense is the occurrence of the expense, not the payment of cash.

Unrealized losses are not matched because they are unrealized.

IFRS

MyAccountingLab

Accounting Cycle Tutorial
Income Statement Accounts and
Transactions

STOP & THINK

1. A client pays Windsor Group Ltd. $900 on March 15 for consulting service to be performed April 1 to June 30. Has Windsor Group Ltd. earned revenue on March 15? When will Windsor Group Ltd. earn the revenue?
2. Windsor Group Ltd. pays $4,500 on July 31 for office rent for the next three months. Has the company incurred an expense on July 31?

Answers:

1. No. Windsor Group Ltd. has received the cash but will not perform the service until later. Windsor Group Ltd. earns the revenue when it performs the service.
2. No. Windsor Group Ltd. has paid cash for rent in advance. This prepaid rent is an asset because Windsor Group Ltd. has the use of an office in the future.

Ethical Issues in Accrual Accounting

Accrual accounting provides some ethical challenges that cash accounting avoids. For example, suppose that in 2008, Shop Online Inc. (SOL) prepays a $3 million advertising campaign to be conducted by Ogilvy & Mather (Canada) Ltd., a leading advertising agency. The advertisements are scheduled to run during December, January, and February. SOL is buying an asset, a prepaid expense. Suppose SOL pays for the advertisements on December 1 and the ads start running immediately. SOL should record one-third of the expense ($1 million) during the year ended December 31, 2008, and two-thirds ($2 million) during 2009.

Suppose 2008 is a great year for SOL—net income is better than expected. SOL's top managers believe that 2009 will not be as profitable. In this case, the company has a strong incentive to expense the full $3 million during 2008 in order to report all the expense in the 2008 income statement. This unethical action would keep $2 million of advertising expense off the 2009 income statement and make 2009's net income look better.

Another ethical challenge in accrual accounting arises because it is easy to overlook an expense at the end of the period. Suppose it is now December 31, 2008, and the year has not turned out very well for Highfield Computer Products Ltd. If top managers are unethical, the company can "manufacture" net income by failing to record some expenses. Suppose the company owes $40,000 in interest expense that it will pay in January 2009. At December 31, 2008, company accountants can "overlook" the $40,000 interest expense and increase the 2008 net income substantially.

USER ALERT

Earnings Management and Cookie Jar Reserves

In a competitive market, it is important for a company to meet or beat Bay Street earnings forecasts. Companies that report higher-than-expected profits are rewarded with higher share prices and companies that fail to meet their earnings forecasts are punished. Therefore, managers try not to surprise the market with bad news. How can a company keep earnings trending upward and stay within GAAP? The best way is to deliver superior products or services to customers. If that fails, some companies try to "manage their earnings," a practice generally frowned on by the Ontario Securities Commission (OSC) and the other provincial securities commissions because users of financial statements are presented with a deceptive picture of the company's operations.

During the 1990s and early 2000s, the world economy grew at a record pace. Profits rose, and share prices soared. Some companies abused the adjusting process by creating "cookie jar reserves." An example of a cookie jar reserve is a liability created when a company records an expense that is not directly linked to a specific accounting period—the expense may fall in one period or another. Companies may record such a *discretionary* expense when profits are high because they can afford to take the hit to income. When profits are low, the company reduces the liability (the reserve) rather than recording an expense in the lean year. The result is a "smoothing" of net income over the course of several years, with net income still trending upward. Analysts recommend the company's shares, and everyone is happy. Now let's return to accounting as it is supposed to be practised.

Updating the Accounts: The Adjusting Process

At the end of a period, the business prepares its financial statements. This process begins with the trial balance introduced in Chapter 2. We refer to this trial balance as *unadjusted* because the accounts are not yet ready for the financial statements. In most cases, the simple label "Trial Balance" means "unadjusted."

Which Accounts Need to Be Updated (Adjusted)?

Objective

③ **Adjust** the accounts

The shareholders need to know how well Tara Inc. is performing. The financial statements report this information, and all accounts must be up-to-date. That means some accounts must be adjusted. Exhibit 3-3 gives the trial balance of Tara Inc. at April 30, 2009.

This trial balance is unadjusted. That means it's not completely up-to-date. It's not quite ready for preparing the financial statements for presentation to external users.

Cash, Accounts Payable, Common Shares, and Dividends are up-to-date and need no adjustment at the end of the period. Why? Because the day-to-day transactions provide all the data for these accounts.

Accounts Receivable, Supplies, Prepaid Rent, Furniture and the other accounts are another story. These accounts are not yet up-to-date on April 30. Why? Because certain transactions have not yet been recorded. Consider Supplies. During April, Tara Inc. used stationery and other supplies to serve clients. But Tara Inc. did not make a journal entry every time someone printed a proposal for a client. That would waste time and money. Instead, Tara Inc. waits until the end of the period and then accounts for the supplies used up during the month.

EXHIBIT 3-3	Unadjusted Trial Balance

Tara Inc.
Unadjusted Trial Balance
April 30, 2009

Cash	$24,800	
Accounts receivable	2,250	
Supplies	700	
Prepaid rent	3,000	
Furniture	16,500	
Accounts payable		$13,100
Unearned service revenue		450
Common shares		20,000
Retained earnings		11,250
Dividends	3,200	
Service revenue		7,000
Salary expense	950	
Utilities expense	400	
Total	$51,800	$51,800

The cost of supplies used up is an expense. An adjusting entry at the end of June updates both Supplies (an asset) and Supplies Expense. We must adjust all other accounts whose balances are not yet up-to-date.

Categories of Adjusting Entries*

Accounting adjustments fall into three basic categories: deferrals, amortization, and accruals.

Deferrals. A **deferral** is an adjustment for which the business paid or received cash in advance. TELUS Corporation purchases supplies for use in its operations. During the period, some supplies (assets) are used up and thus become expenses. At the end of the period, an adjustment is needed to decrease the Supplies account for the supplies used up. This is Supplies Expense. Prepaid Rent, Prepaid Insurance, and all other prepaid expenses require deferral adjustments.

There are also deferral adjustments for liabilities. Companies such as TELUS collect cash in advance of earning the revenue. TELUS collects cash up front and then provides wireless phone service. When TELUS receives cash up front, the company has a liability to provide a service for the client. This liability is called Unearned Service Revenue. Then, over the course of the contract period, TELUS earns Service Revenue by providing the phone service. This earning process requires an adjustment at the end of the period. The adjustment decreases the liability account and increases the revenue account for the revenue earned. Publishers such as Rogers Publishing Limited, publisher of *Maclean's* magazine, and your local newspaper sell subscriptions and collect cash in advance. They too must make adjusting entries for revenues earned later.

Amortization. **Amortization** is the allocation of the cost of a capital (long-lived) asset to expense over the asset's useful life. Amortization is the most common long-term deferral. Sobeys buys long-term capital assets, such as buildings, equipment, and

IFRS

---

*Later in the text you will learn of another category of adjusting entry; that is the entry to adjust assets and liabilities to their fair values.

furniture. As Sobeys uses the assets, it records amortization for wear-and-tear and obsolescence. The accounting adjustment records Amortization Expense, which decreases the book value of the asset over its life. The process is identical to a deferral-type adjustment; the only difference is the type of asset involved.

Accruals. An **accrual** is the opposite of a deferral. For an accrued *expense*, TELUS records an expense before paying cash. For an accrued *revenue*, TELUS records the revenue before collecting cash.

Salary Expense can create an accrual adjustment. As employees work for TELUS, the company's salary expense accrues with the passage of time. Suppose that at December 31, 2008, TELUS owes employees some salaries to be paid after the year end. It will pay them on January 2, 2009. At December 31, 2008, TELUS recorded Salary Expense and Salary Payable for the amount owed. Other examples of expense accruals include interest expense and income tax expense.

An accrued revenue is a revenue that the business has earned and will collect next year. At year end, TELUS must accrue the revenue. The adjustment debits a receivable and credits a revenue. For example, accrual of interest revenue debits Interest Receivable and credits Interest Revenue.

Let's see how the adjusting process actually works for Tara Inc. at April 30, 2009. We begin with prepaid expenses.

Prepaid Expenses

A prepaid expense is an expense paid in advance. Therefore, prepaid expenses are assets, because they provide a future benefit for the owner. Let's do the adjustment for prepaid rent and supplies.

Prepaid Rent. Rent is usually paid in advance. This prepayment creates an asset for the renter, who can then use the rented item in the future. Suppose Tara Inc. prepays three months' office rent ($3,000) on April 1. The entry for the prepayment of three months' rent debits Prepaid Rent as follows:

Apr. 1	Prepaid Rent ($1000 × 3)............................	3,000	
	Cash		3,000
	Paid three months' rent in advance.		

The accounting equation shows that one asset increases and another decreases. Total assets are unchanged.

ASSETS	=	LIABILITIES	+	SHAREHOLDERS' EQUITY
3,000	=	0	+	0
−3,000				

After posting, the Prepaid Rent account appears as follows:

Prepaid Rent	
Apr. 1 3,000	

Throughout April, the Prepaid Rent account maintains this beginning balance, as shown in Exhibit 3-3 (page 109). The adjustment transfers $1,000 from Prepaid Rent to Rent Expense as follows:[*]

---

[*]See Exhibit 3-8, page 119, for a summary of adjustments a through g.

Apr. 30   Rent Expense ($1000 × 1/3)..........................   1,000   *Adjusting entry a*
           Prepaid Rent...   1,000
         To record rent expense.

Both assets and shareholders' equity decrease.

ASSETS	=	LIABILITIES	+	SHAREHOLDERS' EQUITY	–	EXPENSES
–1,000	=	0			–	1,000

After posting, Prepaid Rent and Rent Expense appear as follows:

Prepaid Rent					Rent Expense		
Apr. 1	3,000	Apr. 30	1,000	→	Apr. 30	1,000	
Bal.	2,000				Bal.	1,000	

This expense illustrates the matching principle. We record an expense in order to measure net income.

Supplies. Supplies are another type of prepaid expense. On April 2, Tara Inc. paid cash of $700 for office supplies:

Apr. 2   Supplies..   700
           Cash   700
         Paid cash for supplies.

ASSETS	=	LIABILITIES	+	SHAREHOLDERS' EQUITY
700	=	0	+	0
–700				

The cost of the supplies Tara Inc. used is supplies expense. To measure supplies expense for April, the business counts the supplies on hand at the end of the month. The count shows that supplies costing $400 remain. Subtracting the $400 of supplies on hand at the end of April from the supplies available ($700) measures supplies expense for the month ($300) as follows:

ASSET AVAILABLE DURING THE PERIOD	–	ASSET ON HAND AT THE END OF THE PERIOD	=	ASSET USED (EXPENSE) DURING THE PERIOD
$700	–	$400	=	$300

The April 30 adjusting entry debits the expense and credits the asset, as follows:

Apr. 30   Supplies Expense ($700 – $400).   300   *Adjusting entry b*
           Supplies..   300
         To record supplies expense.

ASSETS	=	LIABILITIES	+	SHAREHOLDERS' EQUITY	–	EXPENSES
–300	=	0			–	300

After posting, the Supplies and Supplies Expense accounts appear as follows:

Supplies					Supplies Expense		
Apr. 2	700	Apr. 30	300	→	Apr. 30	300	
Bal.	400				Bal.	300	

The Supplies account then enters the month of May with a $400 balance, and the adjustment process is repeated each month.

STOP & THINK

At the beginning of the month, supplies were $5,000. During the month, $7,000 of supplies were purchased. At month's end, $3,000 of supplies were still on hand. What are the adjusting entry and the ending balance in the Supplies account?

Answer:

Supplies Expense ($5,000 + $7,000 − $3,000)	9,000	
Supplies		9,000

Ending balance of supplies = $3,000 (the supplies still on hand)

Amortization of Property, Plant, and Equipment

Property, Plant, and Equipment (also referred to as tangible capital assets) are long-lived tangible assets, such as land, buildings, furniture, machinery, and equipment. All capital assets but land decline in usefulness as they age, and this decline is an expense. Accountants spread the cost of each capital asset, except land, over its useful life. Amortization is the process of allocating cost to expense for a long-term capital asset.

To illustrate amortization, consider Tara Inc. Suppose that on April 3 the business purchased furniture including several computers, a printer, a fax machine, and a copier, on account for $16,500:

Apr. 3	Furniture	16,500	
	Accounts Payable		16,500
	Purchased office furniture on account.		

ASSETS	=	LIABILITIES	+	SHAREHOLDERS' EQUITY
16,500	=	16,500	+	0

After posting, the Furniture account appears as follows:

Furniture	
Apr. 3 16,500	

Tara Inc. records an asset when it purchases furniture. Then, as the asset is used, a portion of the asset's cost is transferred to Amortization Expense each period the asset is used. Accounting matches the expense against revenue—this is the matching principle. Computerized systems program the amortization for automatic entry each period.

Tara Inc.'s furniture is expected to remain useful for five years and then be worthless. One way to compute the amount of amortization for each year is to divide the cost of the asset ($16,500 in our example) by its expected useful life (five years). This procedure—called the straight-line amortization method—gives annual amortization of $3,300. The amortization amount is an *estimate*. (Chapter 7 covers property, plant, and equipment and amortization in more detail.)

Annual amortization = $16,500/5 years = $3,300 per year

Amortization for April is $275.

Monthly amortization = $3,300/12 months = $275 per month

The Accumulated Amortization Account. Amortization expense for April is recorded as follows:

Apr. 30	Amortization Expense—Furniture....................	275	*Adjusting entry c*
	Accumulated Amortization—Furniture		275
	To record amortization.		

Note that assets decrease by the amount of the expense:

ASSETS	=	LIABILITIES	+	SHAREHOLDERS' EQUITY	–	EXPENSES
−275	=	0			–	275

The Accumulated Amortization account (not Furniture) is credited to preserve the original cost of the furniture in the Furniture account. Managers can then refer to the Furniture account if they need to know how much the asset cost.

The **Accumulated Amortization** account shows the sum of all amortization expense from the date of acquiring the asset. Therefore, the balance in the Accumulated Amortization account increases over the asset's life.

Accumulated Amortization is a contra asset account—an asset account with a normal credit balance. A **contra account** has two distinguishing characteristics:

1. It always has a companion account.

2. Its normal balance is opposite that of the companion account.

In this case, Accumulated Amortization is the contra account to Furniture, so Accumulated Amortization appears directly after Furniture in the financial statements. A business carries an accumulated amortization account for each amortizable asset, for example, Accumulated Amortization—Building and Accumulated Amortization—Machinery.

After posting, the accounts of Tara Inc. related to furniture are as follows:

	Furniture			Accumulated Amortization—Furniture			Amortization Expense—Furniture	
Apr. 3	16,500				Apr. 30	275	Apr. 30	275	
Bal.	16,500				Bal.	275	Bal.	275	

Book Value. The net amount of a capital asset (cost minus accumulated amortization) is called that asset's **book value** or *carrying amount*. Exhibit 3-4 shows how Tara Inc. would report the book value of its furniture at April 30, 2009. At April 30, 2009, the book value of furniture is $16,225.

While some companies report the cost, accumulated amortization, and the difference, net book value, on the balance sheet, many others report that information

EXHIBIT 3-4 Capital Assets on the Balance Sheet of Tara Inc. (April 30, 2009)

Tara Inc.
Property, Plant and Equipment
April 30, 2009

Furniture	$16,500
Less Accumulated Amortization...	(275)
Book value of capital assets...	$16,225

STOP & THINK

What will the book value of Tara Inc.'s furniture be at the end of May 2009?

Answer:

$16,500 − $275 − $275 = $15,950.

in the notes to the financial statements and simply the net book value on the balance sheet.

Exhibit 3-5 shows how TELUS Corporation shows capital assets in its December 31, 2007, annual report. The second column from the left shows the cost of property, plant, and equipment. Assets under construction is construction in process; when completed it will be included with the buildings. Leasehold improvements are renovations to leased property.

The middle column shows the sum of the accumulated amortization for each type of asset, and the column on the right shows the net book value of each type of asset.

Accrued Expenses

Businesses incur expenses before they pay cash. Consider an employee's salary. Big Rock Brewery Income Trust's salary expense and salary payable grow as the employee works, so the liability is said to accrue. Another example is interest expense on a note payable. Interest accrues as the clock ticks. The term **accrued expense** refers to a liability that arises from an expense that has not yet been paid.

Companies don't record accrued expenses daily or weekly. Instead, they wait until the end of the period and use an adjusting entry to update each expense (and related liability) for the financial statements. Let's look at salary expense.

Most companies pay their employees at set times. Suppose Tara Inc. pays its employee a monthly salary of $1,900, half on the 15th and half on the last day of the month. The calendar on the opposite page is for illustrative purposes and is not that for April 2009. It has the paydays circled.

EXHIBIT 3-5	TELUS Corporation Reporting of Property, Plant, and Equipment and Other (Adapted, in Millions), as at December 31, 2007

	Cost	Accumulated Amortization	Net Book Value
Property, plant, equipment, and other			
Telecommunications assets	$19,082.2	$13,730.2	$5,352.0
Assets on customers' premises	765.8	614.4	151.4
Buildings and leasehold improvements	1,992.7	1,112.8	879.9
Office equipment and furniture	1,146.8	894.2	252.6
Assets under capital lease	18.4	12.7	5.7
Other	344.9	267.3	77.6
Land	48.2	–	48.2
Assets under construction	375.5	–	375.5
Materials and supplies	34.4	–	34.4
	$23,808.9	$16,631.6	$7,177.3

			April			
Sun.	Mon.	Tue.	Wed.	Thur.	Fri.	Sat.
					1	2
3	4	5	6	7	8	9
10	11	12	13	14	⑮	16
17	18	19	20	21	22	23
24	25	26	27	28	29	㉚

Assume that if a payday falls on the weekend, Tara Inc. pays the employee on the following Monday. During the April illustrated, Tara paid its employees' first half-month salary of $950 and made the following entry:

Apr. 15   Salary Expense..   950
            Cash   950
        To pay salary.

ASSETS	=	LIABILITIES	+	SHAREHOLDERS' EQUITY	−	EXPENSES
−950	=	0			−	950

After posting, the Salary Expense account is

Salary Expense	
Apr. 15 950	

Because April 30, the second payday of the month illustrated, falls on a Saturday, the second half-month amount of $950 will be paid on Monday, May 2. At April 30, therefore, Tara Inc. adjusts for additional *salary expense* and *salary payable* of $950 as follows:

Apr. 30   Salary Expense..   950   *Adjusting entry d*
            Salary Payable...   950
        To accrue salary expense.

The accounting equation shows that an accrued expense increases liabilities and decreases shareholders' equity:

ASSETS	=	LIABILITIES	+	SHAREHOLDERS' EQUITY	−	EXPENSES
0	=	950			−	950

After posting, the Salary Payable and Salary Expense accounts appear as follows:

Salary Payable			Salary Expense	
	Apr. 30 950		Apr. 15 950	
	Bal. 950		Apr. 30 950	
			Bal. 1,900	

The accounts at April 30 for this illustration now contain the full month's salary information. Salary Expense has a full month's salary, and Salary Payable shows the amount owed at April 30. All accrued expenses are recorded this way—debit the expense account and credit the liability account.

Computerized systems contain a payroll module. The adjustment for accrued salaries is automatically journalized and posted at the end of each accounting period.

Accrued Revenues

Businesses often earn revenue before they receive the cash—collection occurs later. A revenue that has been earned but not yet received in cash is called an **accrued revenue**.

Assume that Parkin, Ghandi, and Lee Inc., project engineers for a new hospital in Lethbridge, Alberta, hire Tara Inc. on April 15, 2009, to do some consulting on the hospital project. Parkin, Ghandi, and Lee Inc. arrange to pay Tara Inc. $500 monthly, with the first payment on May 15. During April, Tara Inc. will earn half a month's fee, $250, for work done from April 15 through April 30. On April 30, Tara Inc. makes the following adjusting entry:

Apr. 30	Accounts Receivable	250	*Adjusting entry e*
	Service Revenue..		250
	To accrue service revenue ($500 × 1/2).		

Revenue increases both total assets and shareholders' equity:

ASSETS	=	LIABILITIES	+	SHAREHOLDERS' EQUITY	+	REVENUES
250	=	0			+	250

Recall that Accounts Receivable has an unadjusted balance of $2,250, and Service Revenue's unadjusted balance is $7,000 (Exhibit 3-3, p. 109). This April 30 adjusting entry has the following effects:

Accounts Receivable			Service Revenue		
	2,250				7,000
Apr. 30	250			Apr. 30	250
Bal.	2,500			Bal.	7,250

All accrued revenues are accounted for similarly—debit a receivable and credit a revenue.

STOP & THINK

Suppose Tara Inc. holds a note receivable from a client. At the end of April, $125 of interest revenue has been earned. Prepare the adjusting entry at April 30.

Answer:

Interest Receivable..	125	
Interest Revenue..		125
To accrue interest revenue.		

Unearned Revenues

Some businesses collect cash from customers before earning the revenue. This creates a liability called **unearned revenue**, which is an obligation arising from receiving cash before providing a service. Only when the job is completed can the business earn the revenue. Suppose Circle Four Farms Ltd. engaged Tara Inc. to provide ongoing consulting services for the next year, agreeing to pay the consultancy $450 monthly, beginning immediately. If Tara Inc. collects the first amount on April 20, Tara Inc. records this transaction as follows:

Apr. 20	Cash	450	
	Unearned Service Revenue...........................		450
	Received cash for revenue in advance.		

ASSETS	=	LIABILITIES	+	SHAREHOLDERS' EQUITY
450	=	450	+	0

After posting, the liability account appears as follows:

Unearned Service Revenue

	Apr. 20	450

Unearned Service Revenue is a liability because Tara Inc. is obligated to perform services for the client. The April 30 unadjusted trial balance (Exhibit 3-3, p. 109) lists Unearned Service Revenue with a $450 credit balance. During the last 10 days of the month—April 21 through April 30—the consultancy will *earn* one-third (10 days divided by April's total of 30 days) of the $450, or $150. Therefore, the accountant makes the following adjustment on April 30:

Apr. 30	Unearned Service Revenue	150	*Adjusting entry f*
	Service Revenue...		150
	To record unearned service revenue that has been earned ($450 × 1/3).		

ASSETS	=	LIABILITIES	+	SHAREHOLDERS' EQUITY	+	REVENUES
0	=	−150			+	150

This adjusting entry shifts $150 of the total amount received ($450) from liability to revenue. After posting, Unearned Service Revenue is reduced to $300, and Service Revenue is increased by $150, as follows:

Unearned Service Revenue				
Apr. 30	150	Apr. 20	450
		Bal.	300

Service Revenue			
			7,000
		Apr. 30	250
		Apr. 30	150
		Bal.	7,400

All revenues collected in advance are accounted for in this way. An unearned revenue is a liability, not a revenue.

One company's prepaid expense is the other company's unearned revenue. For example, Circle Four Farms Ltd.'s prepaid expense is Tara Inc.'s liability for unearned revenue.

Exhibit 3-6 diagrams the distinctive timing of prepaid and accrual adjustments. Study prepaid expenses all the way across. Then study unearned revenues, and so on.

Summary of the Adjusting Process

Two purposes of the adjusting process are to

- Measure income
- Update the balance sheet

Therefore, every adjusting entry affects at least one

- Revenue or expense—to measure income
- Asset or liability—to update the balance sheet

**Accounting Cycle Tutorial
Adjustments Tutorial**

Exhibit 3-7 summarizes the standard adjustments.

EXHIBIT 3-6 Prepaid and Accrual Adjustments

PREPAIDS—Cash First

	First			*Later*	
Prepaid expenses	*Pay cash and record an asset:*		→	*Record an expense and decrease the asset:*	
	Prepaid Expense	XXX		Expense	XXX
	Cash	XXX		Prepaid Expense	XXX
Unearned revenues	*Receive cash and record unearned revenue:*		→	*Record a revenue and decrease unearned revenue:*	
	Cash	XXX		Unearned Revenue	XXX
	Unearned Revenue	XXX		Revenue	XXX

ACCRUALS—The Cash Transaction Occurs Later

	First			*Later*	
Accrued expenses	*Accrue expense and a payable:*		→	*Pay cash and decrease the payable:*	
	Expense	XXX		Payable	XXX
	Payable	XXX		Cash	XXX
Accrued revenues	*Accrue revenue and a receivable:*		→	*Receive cash and decrease the receivable:*	
	Receivable	XXX		Cash	XXX
	Revenue	XXX		Receivable	XXX

The authors thank Darrel Davis and Alfonso Oddo for suggesting this exhibit.

Accounting Cycle Tutorial
Adjustments Application—Exercise 1

Exhibit 3-8 on page 119 summarizes the adjustments of Tara Inc. at April 30, 2009—the adjusting entries we've examined over the past few pages.

- Panel A repeats the data for each adjustment.
- Panel B gives the adjusting entries.
- Panel C shows the accounts after posting the adjusting entries. The adjustments are keyed by letter.

Exhibit 3-8 includes an additional adjusting entry that we have not yet discussed—the accrual of income tax expense. Like individual taxpayers, corporations are subject to income tax. They typically accrue income tax expense and the related income tax payable as the final adjusting entry of the period. Tara Inc. accrues income tax expense with adjusting entry g, as follows:

Apr. 30	Income Tax Expense	540	*Adjusting entry g*
	Income Tax Payable		540
	To accrue income tax expense.		

The Adjusted Trial Balance

This chapter began with the unadjusted trial balance (see Exhibit 3-3, p. 109). After the adjustments are journalized and posted, the accounts appear as shown in Exhibit 3-8,

EXHIBIT 3-7 Summary of Adjusting Entries

	Type of Account	
Category of Adjusting Entry	*Debit*	*Credit*
Prepaid expense	Expense	Asset
Amortization	Expense	Contra asset
Accrued expense	Expense	Liability
Accrued revenue	Asset	Revenue
Unearned revenue	Liability	Revenue

Adapted from material provided by Beverly Terry.

EXHIBIT 3-8   The Adjusting Process of Tara Inc.

PANEL A—Information for Adjustments at April 30, 2009

(a) Prepaid rent expired, $1,000

(b) Supplies on hand, $400. (See Exhibit 3-3.)

(c) Amortization on furniture, $275.

(d) Accrued salary expense, $950. This entry assumes the pay period ended April 30 and the employee was paid May 2.

(e) Accrued service revenue, $250

(f) Amount of unearned service revenue that has been earned, $150.

(g) Accrued income tax expense, $540. (Described on page 118.)

PANEL B—Adjusting Entries

(a) Rent Expense 1,000
    Prepaid Rent   1,000
    To record rent expense.

(b) Supplies Expense 300
    Supplies   300
    To record supplies used.

(c) Amortization Expense—Furniture 275
    Accumulated Amortization—Furniture   275
    To record amortization.

(d) Salary Expense 950
    Salary Payable   950
    To accrue salary expense.

(e) Accounts Receivable... 250
    Service Revenue   250
    To accrue service revenue.

(f) Unearned Service Revenue.. 150
    Service Revenue   150
    To record unearned revenue that has been earned.

(g) Income Tax Expense 540
    Income Tax Payable..   540
    To accrue income tax expense.

PANEL C—Ledger Accounts

Assets	Liabilities	Shareholders' Equity	

Assets

Cash

Bal.	24,800	

Accounts Receivable

	2,250	
(e)	250	
Bal.	2,500	

Supplies

| | 700 | (b) | 300 |
| Bal. | 400 | | |

Prepaid Rent

| | 3,000 | (a) | 1,000 |
| Bal. | 2,000 | | |

Furniture

Bal.	16,500	

Accumulated Amortization—Furniture

| | (c) | 275 |
| | Bal. | 275 |

Liabilities

Accounts Payable

	Bal.	13,100

Salary Payable

| | (d) | 950 |
| | Bal. | 950 |

Unearned Service Revenue

| (f) | 150 | | 450 |
| | | Bal. | 300 |

Income Tax Payable

| | (g) | 540 |
| | Bal. | 540 |

Shareholders' Equity

Common Shares

	Bal.	20,000

Retained Earnings

	Bal.	11,250

Dividends

Bal.	3,200	

Revenue

Service Revenue

		7,000
	(e)	250
	(f)	150
	Bal.	7,400

Expenses

Rent Expense

| (a) | 1,000 | |
| Bal. | 1,000 | |

Salary Expense

	950	
(d)	950	
Bal.	1,900	

Supplies Expense

| (b) | 300 | |
| Bal. | 300 | |

Amortization Expense—Furniture

| (c) | 275 | |
| Bal. | 275 | |

Utilities Expense

Bal.	400	

Income Tax Expense

| (g) | 540 | |
| Bal. | 540 | |

EXHIBIT 3-9   Work Sheet for the Preparation of Adjusted Trial Balance

Tara Inc.
Preparation of Adjusted Trial Balance
April 30, 2009

Account Title	Unadjusted Trial Balance Debit	Credit	Adjustments Debit	Credit	Adjusted Trial Balance Debit	Credit	
Cash	24,800				24,800		
Accounts receivable	2,250		(e) 250		2,500		
Supplies	700			(b) 300	400		
Prepaid rent	3,000			(a) 1,000	2,000		
Furniture	16,500				16,500		
Accumulated amortization—furniture				(c) 275		275	Balance Sheet
Accounts payable		13,100				13,100	(Exhibit 3-12)
Salary payable				(d) 950		950	
Unearned service revenue		450	(f) 150			300	
Income tax payable				(g) 540		540	
Common shares		20,000				20,000	
Retained earnings		11,250				11,250	Statement of
Dividends	3,200				3,200		Retained Earnings
Service revenue		7,000		(e) 250		7,400	(Exhibit 3-11)
				(f) 150			
Rent expense			(a) 1,000		1,000		
Salary expense	950		(d) 950		1,900		Income Statement
Supplies expense			(b) 300		300		(Exhibit 3-10)
Amortization expense—furniture			(c) 275		275		
Utilities expense	400				400		
Income tax expense			(g) 540		540		
	51,800	51,800	3,465	3,465	53,815	53,815	

Panel C. A useful step in preparing the financial statements is to list the accounts, along with their adjusted balances, on an **adjusted trial balance**. This document lists all the accounts and their final balances in a single place. Exhibit 3-9 shows the preparation of the adjusted trial balance of Tara Inc.

Note how clearly the adjusted trial balance presents the data. The Account Title and the Unadjusted Trial Balance data come from the trial balance. The two Adjustments columns summarize the adjusting entries. The Adjusted Trial Balance columns give the final account balances. Each amount on the *adjusted* trial balance of Exhibit 3-9 is the unadjusted balance plus or minus the adjustments. For example, Accounts Receivable starts with a balance of $2,250. Add the $250 debit adjustment to get Accounts Receivable's ending balance of $2,500. Spreadsheets are designed for this type of analysis.

Accounting Cycle Tutorial
Adjustments Application—Exercise 3

Preparing the Financial Statements

The April 2009 financial statements of Tara Inc. can be prepared from the adjusted trial balance. At the far right, Exhibit 3-9 shows how the accounts are distributed to the financial statements.

- The income statement (Exhibit 3-10) lists the revenue and expense accounts.
- The statement of retained earnings (Exhibit 3-11) shows the changes in retained earnings.
- The balance sheet (Exhibit 3-12) reports assets, liabilities, and shareholders' equity.
- The arrows in Exhibits 3-10, 3-11, and 3-12 show the flow of data from one statement to the next.

Why is the income statement prepared first and the balance sheet last?

1. The income statement reports net income or net loss, the result of revenues minus expenses. Revenues and expenses affect shareholders' equity, so net income is transferred to retained earnings. Arrow ¨ tracks net income.

2. Retained Earnings is the final balancing element of the balance sheet. To solidify your understanding, trace the $11,035 retained earnings figure from Exhibit 3-11 to Exhibit 3-12. Arrow ② tracks retained earnings.

You will note that the cash flow statement is not included in the list of statements that are prepared from the adjusted trial balance. The reason it is not included, as you will discover in Chapter 12, is that the cash flow statement is not prepared, as the other three are, from the adjusted trial balance but rather from the comparative balance sheets, the income statement, and other sources.

Objective

④ **Prepare** the financial statements

MyAccountingLab

Accounting Cycle Tutorial
Financial Statements Application—
Exercise 2

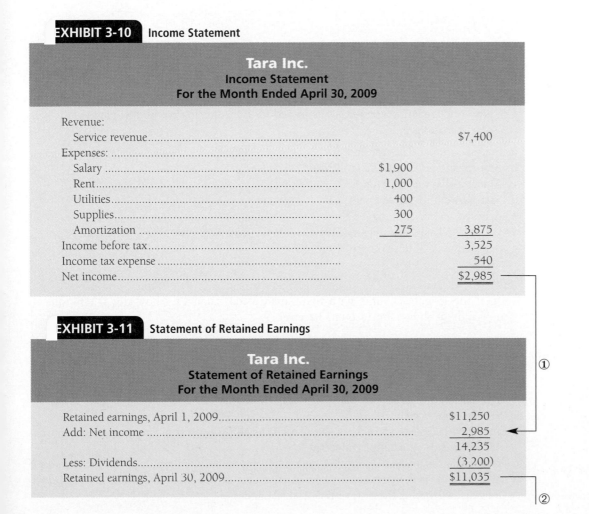

EXHIBIT 3-10   Income Statement

Tara Inc.
Income Statement
For the Month Ended April 30, 2009

Revenue:		
Service revenue		$7,400
Expenses:		
Salary	$1,900	
Rent	1,000	
Utilities	400	
Supplies	300	
Amortization	275	3,875
Income before tax		3,525
Income tax expense		540
Net income		$2,985

EXHIBIT 3-11   Statement of Retained Earnings

Tara Inc.
Statement of Retained Earnings
For the Month Ended April 30, 2009

Retained earnings, April 1, 2009	$11,250
Add: Net income	2,985
	14,235
Less: Dividends	(3,200)
Retained earnings, April 30, 2009	$11,035

①

②

EXHIBIT 3-12 Balance Sheet

Tara Inc.
Balance Sheet
April 30, 2009

Assets			Liabilities	
Cash		$24,800	Accounts payable	$13,100
Accounts receivable		2,500	Salary payable	950
Supplies		400	Unearned service revenue	300
Prepaid rent		2,000	Income tax payable	540
Furniture	$16,500		Total liabilities	14,890
Less Accumulated				
amortization	(275)	16,225	**Shareholders' Equity**	
			Common shares	20,000
			Retained earnings	11,035
			Total shareholders' equity	31,035
			Total liabilities and	
Total assets		$45,925	shareholders' equity	$45,925

②

MyAccountingLab

MID-CHAPTER SUMMARY PROBLEM

The trial balance of Treasure Inc. shown below pertains to December 31, 2009, which is the end of its year-long accounting period. Data needed for the adjusting entries include the following (all amounts in thousands):

 a. Supplies on hand at year-end, $2.
 b. Amortization on furniture and fixtures, $20.
 c. Amortization on building, $10.
 d. Salary owed but not yet paid, $5.
 e. Accrued service revenue, $12.
 f. Of the $45 balance of unearned service revenue, $32 was earned during the year.
 g. Accrued income tax expense, $35.

Required

1. Open the ledger accounts with their unadjusted balances. Show dollar amounts in thousands, as shown for Accounts Receivable:

Accounts Receivable
370 |

2. Journalize the Treasure Inc. adjusting entries at December 31, 2009. Key entries by letter, as in Exhibit 3-8, page 119. Make entries in thousands.
3. Post the adjusting entries.
4. Enter the trial balance on a work sheet, enter the adjusting entries, and prepare an adjusted trial balance, as shown in Exhibit 3-9.
5. Prepare the income statement, the statement of retained earnings, and the balance sheet. (At this stage, it is not necessary to classify assets or liabilities as current or long term.) Draw arrows linking these three financial statements.

Name: Treasure Inc.
Industry: Service corporation
Fiscal Period: Year ended December 31, 2009
Key Fact: Existing, ongoing business

Treasure Inc.
Trial Balance
December 31, 2009

	(in thousands)	
Cash	$ 198	
Accounts receivable	370	
Supplies	6	
Furniture and fixtures	100	
Accumulated amortization—furniture and fixtures		$ 40
Building	250	
Accumulated amortization—building		130
Accounts payable		380
Salary payable		
Unearned service revenue		45
Income tax payable		
Common shares		100
Retained earnings		193
Dividends	65	
Service revenue		286
Salary expense	172	
Supplies expense		
Amortization expense—furniture and fixtures		
Amortization expense—building		
Income tax expense		
Miscellaneous expense	13	
Total	$1,174	$1,174

For Requirement 1, create a T-account for each account name listed in the December 31, 2009 trial balance. Insert the opening balances into the T-accounts from the trial balance, ensuring debit and credit balances on the trial balance are debit and credit balances in the T-accounts. To make sure all the account balances have been entered correctly, trace each T-account's balance back to the December 31, 2009, trial balance.

For Requirement 3, make sure each transaction is posted to the proper T-account, and make sure no transactions were missed.

Answers

Requirements 1 and 3 (*Amounts in Thousands*)

Assets

Cash

Bal.	198	

Accounts Receivable

	370		
(e)	12		
Bal.	382		

Supplies

	6	(a)	4
Bal.	2		

Furniture and Fixtures

Bal.	100	

Accumulated Amortization—Furniture and Fixtures

			40
		(b)	20
		Bal.	60

Building

Bal.	250	

Accumulated Amortization—Building

			130
		(c)	10
		Bal.	140

Liabilities

Accounts Payable

		Bal.	380

Salary Payable

		(d)	5
		Bal.	5

Unearned Service Revenue

(f)	32		45
		Bal.	13

Income Tax Payable

		(g)	35
		Bal.	35

Shareholders' Equity

Common Shares

		Bal.	100

Retained Earnings

		Bal.	193

Dividends

Bal.	65	

Revenue

Service Revenue

			286
		(e)	12
		(f)	32
		Bal.	330

Expenses

Salary Expense

	172		
(d)	5		
Bal.	177		

Supplies Expense

(a)	4		
Bal.	4		

Amortization Expense—Furniture and Fixtures

(b)	20		
Bal.	20		

Amortization Expense—Building

(c)	10		
Bal.	10		

Income Tax Expense

(g)	35		
Bal.	35		

Miscellaneous Expense

Bal.	13	

Requirement 2

Refer to the rules of debit and credit shown in Chapter 2, Exhibit 2-7 on page 65.

Make sure that Assets = Liabilities + Shareholders' Equity for each transaction before going to the next transaction.

2009

Amounts in thousands

(a)	Dec. 31	Supplies Expense		4	
		Supplies			4
		To record supplies used ($6 − $2).			
(b)	Dec. 31	Amortization Expense—Furniture and Fixtures		20	
		Accumulated Amortization—Furniture and Fixtures			20
		To record amortization expense on furniture and fixtures.			
(c)	Dec. 31	Amortization Expense—Building		10	
		Accumulated Amortization—Building			10
		To record amortization expense on building.			
(d)	Dec. 31	Salary Expense		5	
		Salary Payable			5
		To accrue salary expense.			
(e)	Dec. 31	Accounts Receivable		12	
		Service Revenue			12
		To accrue service revenue.			
(f)	Dec. 31	Unearned Service Revenue		32	
		Service Revenue			32
		To record unearned service revenue that has been earned.			
(g)	Dec. 31	Income Tax Expense		35	
		Income Tax Payable			35
		To accrue income tax expense.			

Requirement 4

Treasure Inc.
Preparation of Adjusted Trial Balance
December 31, 2009

(Amounts in Thousands)

	Unadjusted Trial Balance		Adjustments				Adjusted Trial Balance	
	Debit	Credit	Debit		Credit		Debit	Credit
Cash	198						198	
Accounts receivable	370		(e)	12			382	
Supplies	6				(a)	4	2	
Furniture and fixtures	100						100	
Accumulated amortization— furniture and fixtures		40			(b)	20		60
Building	250						250	
Accumulated amortization—building		130			(c)	10		140
Accounts payable		380						380
Salary payable					(d)	5		5
Unearned service revenue		45	(f)	32				13
Income tax payable					(g)	35		35
Common shares		100						100
Retained earnings		193						193
Dividends	65						65	
Service revenue		286			(e)	12		330
					(f)	32		
Salary expense	172		(d)	5			177	
Supplies expense			(a)	4			4	
Amortization expense— furniture and fixtures			(b)	20			20	
Amortization expense—building			(c)	10			10	
Income tax expense			(g)	35			35	
Miscellaneous expense	13						13	
	1,174	1,174		118		118	1,256	1,256

Create a worksheet with columns for the original trial balance, adjustments, and the adjusted trial balance. List all the account names that have a balance in their T-accounts. Write the account balances from the December 31, 2009, trial balance in the first two columns. Write the adjustment amounts in the next two columns. Write the "Bal." amounts from the T-accounts in the Adjusted Trial Balance columns. Ensure total debits equal total credits for each pair of columns. Double-check the adjusted trial balance amounts by adding the adjustments to the original trial balance amounts. Double underline the totals to show that the columns have been added and the totals are final.

Requirement 5

Treasure Inc.
Income Statement
For the Year Ended December 31, 2005

> The title must include the name of the company, "Income Statement," and the specific period of time covered. It is critical that the time period is defined.

	(Amounts in Thousands)	
Revenue:		
Service revenue		$330
Expenses:		
Salary	$177	
Amortization—furniture and fixtures	20	
Amortization—building	10	
Supplies	4	
Miscellaneous	13	224
Income before tax		106
Income tax expense		35
Net income		$ 71

> Gather all the revenue and expense account names and amounts from the Debit and Credit Adjusted Trial Balance columns of the worksheet.
>
> Notice that Income Tax Expense is always reported separately from the other expenses, and it appears as the last item before net income (or net loss).

Treasure Inc.
Statement of Retained Earnings
For the Year Ended December 31, 2005

> The title must include the name of the company, "Statement of Retained Earnings," and the specific period of time covered. It is critical that the time period is defined.

	(Amounts in Thousands)
Retained earnings, January 1, 2005	$193
Add: Net income	71
	264
Less: Dividends	(65)
Retained earnings, December 31, 2005	$199

> Beginning retained earnings and dividends are from the Adjusted Trial Balance columns of the worksheet.
>
> The net income amount is transferred from the income statement.

Treasure Inc.
Balance Sheet
December 31, 2009

> The title must include the name of the company, "Balance Sheet," and the date of the balance sheet. It shows the financial position on one specific date.

(Amounts in Thousands)

Assets			Liabilities	
Cash		$198	Accounts payable	$380
Accounts receivable		382	Salary payable	5
Supplies		2	Unearned service revenue	13
Furniture and fixtures	$100		Income tax payable	35
Less accumulated amortization	(60)	40	Total liabilities	433
			Shareholders' Equity	
Building	$250		Common shares	100
Less accumulated amortization	(140)	110	Retained earnings	199
			Total shareholders' equity	299
			Total liabilities and	
Total assets		$732	shareholders' equity	$732

> Gather all the asset, liability, and the common shares accounts and amounts from the Adjusted Trial Balance columns of the worksheet. The retained earnings amount is transferred from the statement of retained earnings.
>
> It is imperative that Total assets = Total liabilities and Shareholders' equity.

DECISION   **Which Accounts Need to Be Closed?**

It is now April 30, the end of the month. Ranjini Sivakumar, Tara's manager, will continue operating the business into May, June, and beyond. But wait—the revenue and the expense accounts still hold amounts for April. At the end of each accounting period, it is necessary to close the books.

Closing the books means preparing the accounts for the next period's transactions. The **closing entries** set the balances of the revenue and expense accounts back to zero at the end of the period. The idea is the same as setting the scoreboard back to zero after a hockey game.

Closing is easily handled by computers. Recall that the income statement reports only one period's income. For example, net income for Tim Hortons or Tara Inc. for 2009 relates exclusively to 2009. At each year-end, Tim Hortons' accountants close the company's revenues and expenses for that year.

Temporary Accounts. Because revenues and expenses relate to a limited period, they are called **temporary accounts**. The Dividends account is also temporary. The closing process applies only to temporary accounts (revenues, expenses, and dividends).

Permanent Accounts. Let's contrast the temporary accounts with the **permanent accounts**: assets, liabilities, and shareholders' equity. The permanent accounts are not closed at the end of the period because they carry over to the next period. Consider Cash, Accounts Receivable, Buildings, Accounts Payable, Common Shares, and Retained Earnings. Their final balances at the end of one period become the beginning balances of the next period.

Closing entries transfer the revenue, expense, and dividends balances to Retained Earnings. Following are the steps to close the books of a corporation such as Tim Hortons or Tara Inc.:

① Debit each revenue account for the amount of its credit balance. Credit Retained Earnings for the sum of the revenues. Now the sum of the revenues is in Retained Earnings.

② Credit each expense account for the amount of its debit balance. Debit Retained Earnings for the sum of the expenses. The sum of the expenses is also in Retained Earnings.

③ Credit the Dividends account for the amount of its debit balance. Debit Retained Earnings. This entry places the dividends amount on the debit side of Retained Earnings. Remember that dividends are not expenses. Dividends never affect net income.

MyAccountingLab

Accounting Cycle Tutorial
Adjustments and Closing Entries Tutorial

After closing the books, the Retained Earnings account of Tara Inc. appears as follows (data from p. 119):

		Retained Earnings	
		Beginning balance	11,250
Expenses	4,415	Revenues	7,400
Dividends	3,200		
		Ending balance	11,035

MyAccountingLab

Accounting Cycle Tutorial
Adjustments and Closing Entries
Application—Exercise 2

Assume that Tara Inc. closes the books at the end of April. Exhibit 3-13 presents the complete closing process for the business. Panel A gives the closing journal entries, and Panel B shows the accounts after closing.

EXHIBIT 3-13 Journalizing and Posting and Closing Entries

PANEL A—Journalizing the Closing Entries

Closing Entries

①	Apr. 30	Service Revenue...	7,400	
		Retained Earnings..		7,400
②	30	Retained Earnings...	4,415	
		Rent Expense...		1,000
		Salary Expense..		1,900
		Supplies Expense...		300
		Amortization Expense—Furniture.......................		275
		Utilities Expense..		400
		Income Tax Expense.......................................		540
③	30	Retained Earnings...	3,200	
		Dividends...		3,200

PANEL B—Posting to the Accounts

Rent Expense			Service Revenue	
Adj. 1,000				7,000
Bal. 1,000	Clo. 1,000		Adj. 250	
			Adj. 150	
Salary Expense			Clo. 7,400	Bal. 7,400
950				
Adj. 950		①		
Bal. 1,900	Clo. 1,900	②		
Supplies Expense		**Retained Earnings**		
Adj. 300		Clo. 4,415	11,250	
Bal. 300	Clo. 300	Clo. 3,200	Clo. 7,400	
			Bal. 11,035	
Amortization Expense		**Dividends**		
Adj. 275		Bal. 3,200	Clo. 3,200	
Bal. 275	Clo. 275	③		
Utilities Expense				
400				
Bal. 400	Clo. 400			
Income Tax Expense				
Adj. 540				
Bal. 540	Clo. 540			

Adj. = Amount posted from an adjusting entry
Clo. = Amount posted from a closing entry
Bal. = Balance
As arrow ② in Panel B shows, it is not necessary to make a separate closing entry for each expense. In one closing entry, we record one debit to Retained Earnings and a separate credit to each expense account.

Classifying Assets and Liabilities Based on Their Liquidity

On the balance sheet, assets and liabilities are classified as current or long term to indicate their relative liquidity. **Liquidity** measures how quickly an item can be converted to cash. Cash is the most liquid asset. Accounts receivable are relatively liquid because the business expects to collect the cash quickly. Inventory is less liquid than accounts receivable because the company must first sell the goods. Furniture and buildings are even less liquid because these assets are held for use and not for sale. A balance sheet lists assets and liabilities in the order of their relative liquidity.

Current Assets. As we saw in Chapter 1, current assets are the most liquid assets. They will be converted to cash, sold, or consumed during the next 12 months or within the business's normal operating cycle if longer than a year. The **operating cycle** is the time span during which (1) cash is paid for goods and services, and (2) these goods and services are sold to bring in cash.

For most businesses, the operating cycle is a few months. Cash, Accounts Receivable, Merchandise Inventory, and Prepaid Expenses are current assets.

Long-Term Assets. **Long-term assets** are all assets not classified as current assets. One category of long-term assets is Property, Plant, and Equipment, sometimes called capital assets or fixed assets. Land, Buildings, Furniture and Fixtures, and Equipment are capital assets. Other types of long-term assets are Long-Term Investments, Intangible Assets, and Other Assets (a catch-all category for assets that are not classified more precisely but are also long-term).

Current Liabilities. As we saw in Chapter 1, current liabilities are debts that must be paid within one year or within the entity's operating cycle if longer than a year. Accounts Payable, Notes Payable due within one year, Salary Payable, Unearned Revenue, Interest Payable, and Income Tax Payable are current liabilities.

Bankers and other lenders are interested in the due dates of an entity's liabilities. The sooner a liability must be paid, the more pressure it creates for the company. Therefore, the balance sheet lists liabilities in the order in which they must be paid. Balance sheets usually report two liability classifications, current liabilities and long-term liabilities.

Long-Term Liabilities. All liabilities that are not current are classified as **long-term liabilities**. Many notes payable are long-term. Some notes payable are paid in installments, with the first installment due within one year, the second installment due the second year, and so on. The first installment would be a current liability, and the remainder would be long-term.

Let's see how Sobeys Inc. reports these asset and liability categories on its balance sheet.

Reporting Assets and Liabilities: Sobeys Inc.

Exhibit 3-14 shows the actual classified balance sheet of Sobeys Inc. A **classified balance sheet** separates current assets from long-term assets and current liabilities from long-term liabilities. You should be familiar with most of Sobeys' accounts. Study the Sobeys statements all the way through—line by line.

Sobeys' financial statements need two explanations:

1. *Consolidated* in the statement title means that Sobeys owns a number of different companies and all of those companies' financial statements are combined, or consolidated, into a single set of statements.

2. The dates of the statements may look strange. Sobeys, like many other companies, ends its accounting year on the Saturday nearest its basic year-end date, which is May 1 each year. In 2006, that date fell on May 6. In 2007, the year-end date fell on May 5.

EXHIBIT 3-14 Financial Statements of Sobeys Inc.

Sobeys Inc.
Consolidated Balance Sheets (Adapted)
(in millions of dollars)

	May 5, 2007	May 6, 2006
Assets		
Current		
Cash and cash equivalents..	$284.6	$ 332.1
Receivables...	244.2	208.2
Inventories..	683.1	626.8
Prepaid expenses...	47.5	45.9
Mortgages, loans, and other receivables......................	14.5	15.9
Income taxes receivable...	30.2	5.8
	1,304.1	1,234.7
Long-term		
Mortgages, loans, and other receivables......................	64.7	68.4
Other assets	244.0	180.0
Property and equipment	1,754.6	1,612.2
Assets held for realization...	8.5	8.5
Intangibles (less accumulated amortization of $10.7;		
May 6/06 $7.2)	33.2	21.5
Goodwill...	655.5	613.3
Total assets	$4,064.6	$3,738.6
Liabilities		
Current		
Accounts payable and accrued liabilities	$1,187.6	$1,158.8
Future tax liabilities	40.4	46.1
Long-term debt due within one year	30.0	25.0
	1,258.0	1,229.9
Long-term		
Long-term debt...	582.7	465.0
Long-term lease obligation	36.9	20.8
Employee future benefits obligation	100.6	96.0
Future tax liabilities	63.3	44.1
Deferred revenue..	6.5	3.3
Minority interest	42.9	45.2
Total liabilities	2,090.9	1,904.3
Shareholders' equity		
Capital stock...	908.8	904.8
Contributed surplus...	1.6	0.9
Retained earnings..	1,063.3	928.6
Total shareholders' equity..	1,973.7	1,834.3
Total liabilities and shareholders' equity......................	$4,064.6	$3,738.6

Formats for the Financial Statements

Companies can format their financial statements in different ways. Both the balance sheet and the income statement can be formatted in two basic ways.

Balance Sheet Formats

The **report format** lists the assets at the top, followed by the liabilities and shareholders' equity below. The balance sheet of Sobeys Inc. in Exhibit 3-14 illustrates the report format. The report format is the most popular.

The **account format** lists the assets on the left and the liabilities and share-holders' equity on the right in the same way that a T-account appears, with assets (debits) on the left, and liabilities and equity (credits) on the right. Exhibit 3-12 (p. 122) shows an account-format balance sheet. Either format is acceptable.

Income Statement Formats

A **single-step income statement** lists all the revenues together under a heading such as Revenues, or Revenues and Gains. The expenses are listed together in a single category titled Expenses, or Expenses and Losses. There is only one step, the subtraction of Expenses and Losses from the sum of Revenues and Gains, in arriving at net income. Tom Hortons Inc.'s income statement in the opening vignette is in single-step format.

A **multi-step income statement** contains a number of subtotals to highlight important relationships among revenues and expenses. For example, Tim Hortons' multi-step income statement in Exhibit 3-15 highlights gross margin (also called *gross profit*), earnings before other expenses and interest expense, and earnings before income taxes.

Many corporations using the multi-step income statement consider it important to report operating income separately from non-operating income. Typically they show non-operating income just before earnings before income taxes on the income statement.

Most actual company income statements do not conform to either a pure single-step format or a pure multi-step format. Today, business operations are too complex for all companies to conform to rigid reporting formats.

Using Accounting Ratios

As we've seen, accounting provides information for decision making. A bank considering lending money must predict whether the borrower can repay the loan. If the borrower already has a lot of debt, the probability of repayment may be low. If the borrower owes little, the loan may be approved. To analyze a company's financial position, decision makers use ratios computed from various items in the financial statements. Let's see exactly how this process works.

EXHIBIT 3-15	Multi-Step Income Statement (Adapted, in millions)

Tim Hortons Inc.
Consolidated Statement of Operations (Adapted)
For the Fiscal Year Ended December 30, 2007

Net revenue	$1,896
Cost of sales	1,099
Gross margin	797
Operating expenses	201
General and administrative expenses	119
Earnings before other expenses and interest expense	477
Other expenses	51
Interest expense, net	17
Earnings before income taxes	409
Income taxes	139
Net earnings for the year	$ 270

Current Ratio

One of the most widely used financial ratios is the **current ratio**, which divides total current assets by total current liabilities, taken from the balance sheet.

$$\text{Current ratio} = \frac{\text{Total current assets}}{\text{Total current liabilities}}$$

For Sobeys Inc. (amounts in millions for 2007, from p. 129):

$$\frac{\$1,304.1}{\$1,258.0} = 1.037$$

The current ratio measures the company's ability to pay current liabilities with current assets. A company prefers to have a high current ratio, which means that the business has plenty of current assets to pay current liabilities. An increasing current ratio from period to period indicates improvement in financial position.

As a rule of thumb, a strong current ratio is 1.50, which indicates that the company has $1.50 in current assets for every $1.00 in current liabilities. A company with a current ratio of 1.50 would probably have little trouble paying its current liabilities. Most successful businesses operate with current ratios between 1.00 and 1.50. A current ratio of 0.80 is considered low.

The Decision Guidelines feature on page 134 provides some tips for using the current ratio.

Debt Ratio

A second aid to decision making is the **debt ratio**, which is the ratio of total liabilities to total assets:

$$\text{Debt ratio} = \frac{\text{Total liabilities}}{\text{Total assets}}$$

For Sobeys (amounts in millions for 2007, from p. 129),

$$\frac{\$2,090.9}{\$4,064.6} = 0.514$$

The debt ratio indicates the proportion of a company's assets that is financed with debt. This ratio measures a business's ability to pay both current and long-term debts (total liabilities).

A lower ratio is safer than a higher debt ratio. Why? Because a company with a small amount of liabilities has low required payments. This company is less likely to get into financial difficulty. By contrast, a business with a high debt ratio may have trouble paying its liabilities, especially when sales are low and cash is scarce. Sobeys Inc.'s debt ratio of 0.51 is reasonable.

When a company fails to pay its debts, the creditors can take the company away from its owners. Most bankruptcies result from high debt ratios.

How Do Transactions Affect the Ratios?

Companies such as Sobeys are keenly aware of how transactions affect their ratios. Lending agreements often require that a company's current ratio not fall below a certain level. Another frequent loan requirement is that the company's debt ratio may not rise above a threshold, such as 0.7. When a company fails to meet one of these conditions, it is said to *violate its lending agreements*. The penalty can be severe: The lender can require immediate payment of the loan. Some companies are in danger of violating a covenant.

Let's use Sobeys to examine the effects of some transactions on the company's current ratio and debt ratio. As shown in the preceding section, Sobeys's ratios are as follows (dollar amounts in millions):

$$\text{Current ratio} = \frac{\$1,304.1}{\$1,258.0} = 1.037 \qquad \text{Debt ratio} = \frac{\$2,090.9}{\$4,064.6} = 0.514$$

The managers of any company would be concerned about how inventory purchases, payments on account, expense accruals, and amortization would affect its ratios. Let's see how Sobeys would be affected by some typical transactions. For each transaction, the journal entry helps identify the effects on the company.

a. Issued shares and received cash of $50 million.

Journal entry: Cash 50
　　　　　　Common shares 50

Cash, a current asset, affects both the current ratio and the debt ratio as follows:

$$\text{Current ratio} = \frac{\$1,304.1 + \$50}{\$1,258.0} = 1.076 \quad \text{Debt ratio} = \frac{\$2,090.9}{\$4,064.6 + \$50} = 0.508$$

The issuance of shares improves both ratios.

b. Purchased a building for $20 million cash.

Journal entry: Building 20
　　　　　　　Cash 20

Cash, a current asset, decreases, but total assets stay the same. Liabilities are unchanged.

$$\text{Current ratio} = \frac{\$1,304.1 - \$20}{\$1,258.0} \qquad \text{Debt ratio} = \frac{\$2,090.9}{\$4,064.6 + \$20 - \$20}$$

$$= 1.021 \qquad\qquad\qquad = 0.514; \text{ no change}$$

A cash purchase of a building hurts the current ratio but doesn't affect the debt ratio.

c. Made a $40 million sale on account to a chain of nursing homes.

Journal entry: Accounts Receivable 40
　　　　　　　Sales Revenue 40

The increase in Accounts Receivable increases current assets and total assets. The effects on both ratios are as follows:

$$\text{Current ratio} = \frac{\$1,304.1 + \$40}{\$1,258.0} = 1.068 \quad \text{Debt ratio} = \frac{\$2,090.9}{\$4,064.6 + \$40} = 0.509$$

A sale on account improves both ratios.

d. Collected the account receivable, $40 million.

Journal entry: Cash 40
　　　　　　　Accounts Receivable 40

This transaction has no effect on total current assets, total assets, or total liabilities. Both ratios are unaffected.

e. Accrued salary expense at year-end, $25 million.

Journal entry: Salary Expense... 25

Salary Payable... 25

Salary Payable, a current liability, increases. Recalculating the ratios, we get

$$\text{Current ratio} = \frac{\$1,304.1}{\$1,258.0 + \$25} = 1.016 \quad \text{Debt ratio} = \frac{\$2,090.9 + \$25}{\$4,064.6} = 0.521$$

Most expenses hurt both ratios.

f. Recorded amortization, $50 million.

Journal entry: Amortization Expense..................................... 50

Accumulated Amortization 50

No current accounts are part of an amortization transaction, so only the debt ratio is affected.

$$\text{Current ratio} = \frac{\$1,304.1}{\$1,258.0} = 1.037 \qquad \text{Debt ratio} = \frac{\$2,090.9}{\$4,064.6 - \$50} = 0.521$$

No current accounts are affected but amortization decreases total assets and therefore the debt ratio increases.

g. Earned interest revenue and collected cash, $60 million.

Journal entry: Cash 60

Interest Revenue 60

Cash, a current asset, affects both the current ratio and the debt ratio as follows:

$$\text{Current ratio} = \frac{\$1,304.1 + \$60}{\$1,258.0} = 1.084 \quad \text{Debt ratio} = \frac{\$2,090.9}{\$4,064.6 + \$60} = 0.507$$

A revenue increase improves both ratios.

Now, let's wrap up the chapter by seeing how to use the current ratio and the debt ratio for decision making. The Decision Guidelines feature offers some clues.

Decision Guidelines

USING THE CURRENT RATIO AND THE DEBT RATIO

In general, a *high* current ratio is preferable to a low current ratio. *Increases* in the current ratio indicate an improving financial position. By contrast, a *low* debt ratio is preferable to a high debt ratio. Improvement is indicated by a *decrease* in the debt ratio.

No single ratio gives the whole picture about a company. Therefore, lenders and investors use many ratios to evaluate a company. Now, let's apply what we have learned. Suppose you are a loan officer at Scotiabank, and Tim Hortons Inc. has asked you to lend the company $5 million to develop a new line of breakfast sandwiches. How will you make this loan decision? The Decision Guidelines show how bankers and investors use the two key ratios.

USING THE CURRENT RATIO

Decision	Guidelines
How can you measure a company's ability to pay current liabilities with current assets?	Current ratio $= \dfrac{\text{Total current assets}}{\text{Total current liabilities}}$
Who uses the current ratio for decision making?	*Lenders* and other *creditors*, who must predict whether a borrower can pay its current liabilities. *Shareholders*, who know that a company that cannot pay its debts is not a good investment because it may go bankrupt. *Managers*, who must have enough cash to pay the company's current liabilities.
What is a good value of the current ratio?	Depends on the industry: • A company with strong cash flow can operate successfully with a low current ratio of, say, 1.10 to 1.20. • A company with weaker cash flow needs a higher current ratio of, say, 1.30 to 1.50. • Traditionally, a current ratio of 2.00 was considered ideal. Recently, acceptable values have decreased as companies have been able to operate more efficiently; today, a current ratio of 1.50 is considered strong. Cash rich companies like Research In Motion can operate with lower current ratios.

USING THE DEBT RATIO

Decision	Guidelines
How can you measure a company's ability to pay total liabilities?	Debt ratio $= \dfrac{\text{Total liabilities}}{\text{Total assets}}$
Who uses the debt ratio for decision making?	*Lenders* and other *creditors*, who must predict whether a borrower can pay its debts. *Shareholders*, who know that a company that cannot pay its debts is not a good investment because it may go bankrupt. *Managers,* who must have enough assets to pay the company's debts.
What is a good value of the debt ratio?	Depends on the industry: • A profitable company with strong cash flow can operate successfully with a high debt ratio of, say, 0.70 to 0.80. • A company with weak cash flow needs a lower debt ratio of, say, 0.50 to 0.60. • Traditionally, a debt ratio of 0.50 was considered ideal. Recently, values have increased as companies have been able to operate more efficiently. Today, a normal value of the debt ratio is around 0.60 to 0.65.

END-OF-CHAPTER SUMMARY PROBLEM   *MyAccountingLab*

Refer to the mid-chapter summary problem that begins on page 122.

Required

1. Make Treasure Inc.'s closing entries at December 31, 2009. Explain what the closing entries accomplish and why they are necessary.
2. Post the closing entries to Retained Earnings and compare Retained Earnings' ending balance with the amount reported on the balance sheet on page 125. The two amounts should be the same.
3. Prepare Treasure Inc.'s classified balance sheet to identify the company's current assets and current liabilities. (Treasure has no long-term liabilities.) Then compute the company's current ratio and debt ratio at December 31, 2009.
4. The top management of Treasure Inc. has asked you for a $500,000 loan to expand the business. They propose to pay off the loan over a ten-year period. Recompute Treasure Inc.'s debt ratio assuming you make the loan. Use the company financial statements plus the ratio values to decide whether to grant the loan at an interest rate of 8%, 10%, or 12%. Treasure Inc.'s cash flow is strong. Give the reasoning underlying your decision.

Name: Treasure Inc.
Industry: Service corporation
Fiscal Period: Year ended December 31, 2009
Key Fact: Existing, ongoing business

Answers

Requirement 1

2009			(In thousands)	
Dec. 31	Service Revenue		330	
	Retained Earnings			330
31	Retained Earnings		259	
	Salary Expense			177
	Amortization Expense—Furniture and Fixtures			20
	Amortization Expense—Building			10
	Supplies Expense			4
	Income Tax Expense			35
	Miscellaneous Expense			13
31	Retained Earnings		65	
	Dividends			65

To close revenue accounts, debit each revenue account for the amounts reported on the income statement, and credit Retained Earnings for the total of the debits.

To close expense accounts, credit each expense account for the amounts reported on the income statement, and debit Retained Earnings for the total of the credits.

To close the dividend accounts, credit each dividend account for the amounts reported on the statement of retained earnings, and debit Retained Earnings for the total of the credits.

Explanation of Closing Entries

The closing entries set the balance of each revenue, expense, and Dividends account back to zero for the start of the next accounting period. We must close these accounts because their balances relate only to one accounting period.

Requirement 2

The balance in the Retained Earnings T-account should equal the Retained Earnings balance reported on the balance sheet.

Retained Earnings

Clo.	259		193
Clo.	65	Clo.	330
		Bal.	199

The balance in the Retained Earnings account agrees with the amount reported on the balance sheet, as it should.

Requirement 3

The title must include the name of the company, "Balance Sheet," and the date of the balance sheet. It shows the financial position on one specific date.

The classified balance sheet uses the same accounts and balances as those on the page 125 balance sheet. However, segregate current assets (assets expected to be converted to cash within one year) from capital assets, and segregate current liabilities (liabilities expected to be paid or settled within one year) from other liabilities.

Treasure Inc.
Balance Sheet
December 31, 2009

(Amounts in Thousands)

Assets			Liabilities		
Current assets			Current liabilities		
Cash..................................		$198	Accounts payable		$380
Accounts receivable.............		382	Salary payable		5
Supplies		2	Unearned service revenue.....		13
Total current assets..............		582	Income tax payable..............		35
Capital assets			Total current liabilities..........		433
Furniture and fixtures.............	$100				
Less Accumulated				**Shareholders' Equity**	
amortization..................	(60)	40	Common shares		100
Building	$250		Retained earnings...................		199
Less Accumulated			Total shareholders' equity.........		299
amortization..................	(140)	110	Total liabilities and		
Total assets............................		$732	shareholders' equity.............		$732

Current ratio = Current assets ÷ Current liabilities

Debt ratio = Current liabilities ÷ Total assets

$$\text{Current ratio} = \frac{\$582}{\$433} = 1.34 \qquad \text{Debt ratio} = \frac{\$433}{\$732} = 0.59$$

You must add $500,000 to the current liabilities and total assets to account for the additional $500,000 loan. Factors to consider:
- The debt ratio increase. Creditors prefer a low debt ratio because it means creditors' claims are only a small percentage of total assets.
- Effect on future cash flows. More debt leads to greater debt repayments and greater interest payments in the future.

Requirement 4

$$\text{Debt ratio assuming the loan is made} = \frac{\$433 + \$500}{\$732 + \$500} = \frac{\$933}{\$1,232} = 0.76$$

Decision: Make the loan at 10%.

Reasoning: Prior to the loan, the company's financial position and cash flow are strong. The current ratio is in a middle range, and the debt ratio is not too high. Net income (from the income statement) is high in relation to total revenue. Therefore, the company should be able to repay the loan.

The loan will increase the company's debt ratio from 59% to 76%, which is more risky than the company's financial position at present. On this basis, a midrange interest rate appears reasonable—at least as the starting point for the negotiation between Treasure Inc. and the bank.

REVIEW ACCRUAL ACCOUNTING AND INCOME

QUICK CHECK (Answers are given on page 166.)

1. On September 1, LostForest Apartments Ltd. received $3,600 from a tenant for three months' rent. The receipt was credited to Unearned Rent Revenue. What adjusting entry is needed on September 30?

   a. Unearned Rent Revenue 2,400
        Rent Revenue   2,400
   b. Rent Revenue 1,200
        Unearned Rent Revenue   1,200
   c. Unearned Rent Revenue 1,200
        Rent Revenue   1,200
   d. Cash.. 1,200
        Rent Revenue   1,200

2. The following normal balances appear on the *adjusted* trial balance of Ojibway Industries:

Equipment...	$90,000
Accumulated amortization, equipment	15,000
Amortization expense, equipment..	5,000

  The book value of the equipment is

   a. $85,000   **c.** $75,000
   b. $70,000   **d.** $60,000

3. Jones Company Ltd. purchased supplies for $1,000 during 2009. At year-end Jones had $300 of supplies left. The adjusting entry should

   a. Debit Supplies $700
   b. Debit Supplies Expense $700
   c. Credit Supplies $300
   d. Debit Supplies $300

4. The accountant for Moreau Ltd. failed to make the adjusting entry to record amortization for the current year. The effect of this error is

   a. Assets are overstated; shareholders' equity and net income are understated.
   b. Assets and expenses are understated, and net income is understated.
   c. Net income is overstated, and liabilities are understated.
   d. Assets, net income, and shareholders' equity are all overstated.

5. Interest due on a note payable at December 31 equals $125. What adjusting entry is required to accrue this expense?

   a. Interest Payable 125 Interest Expense 125
   b. Interest Expense 125 Cash 125
   c. Interest Receivable 125 Interest Revenue 125
   d. Interest Expense 125 Interest Payable 125

6. If a real estate company fails to accrue commission revenue,

   a. Liabilities are overstated, and owners' equity is understated.
   b. Assets are understated, and net income is understated.
   c. Net income is understated, and shareholders' equity is overstated.
   d. Revenues are understated, and net income is overstated.

7. All the following statements are true except one. Which statement is false?

   a. Adjusting entries are required for a business that uses the cash basis.
   b. Accrual accounting produces better information than cash-basis accounting.
   c. The matching principle directs accountants to identify and measure all expenses incurred and deduct them from revenues earned during the same period.
   d. A fiscal year ends on some date other than December 31.

8. The account Unearned Revenue is a(n)
   a. Revenue
   b. Expense
   c. Asset
   d. Liability

9. Adjusting entries
   a. Do not debit or credit Cash
   b. Are needed to measure the period's net income or net loss
   c. Update the accounts
   d. All of the above

10. An adjusting entry that debits an expense and credits a related liability is which type?
    a. Accrued expense
    b. Cash expense
    c. Prepaid expense
    d. Amortization expense

Use the following data for Questions 11 and 12.

Here are key figures from the balance sheet of Davis Ltd. at the end of 2009 (in thousands)

	December 31, 2009
Total assets (of which 40% are current)	$4,000
Current liabilities	800
Bonds payable (long-term)	1,200
Common shares	1,500
Retained earnings	500
Total liabilities and shareholders' equity	$4,000

11. Davis' current ratio at the end of 2009 is
    a. 6.25
    b. 2.0
    c. 3.75
    d. 2.24

12. Davis' debt ratio at the end of 2009 is
    a. 42% (rounded)
    b. 17% (rounded)
    c. 60%
    d. 50%

13. On a trial balance, which of the following would indicate that an error has been made?
    a. Service Revenue has a debit balance.
    b. Salary Expense has a debit balance.
    c. Accumulated Amortization has a credit balance.
    d. All of the above indicate errors.

14. The entry to close Management Fees Revenue would be
    a. Management Fees Revenue does not need to be closed out.
    b. Dr. Retained Earnings   Cr. Management Fees Revenue
    c. Dr. Management Fees Revenue   Cr. Retained Earnings
    d. Dr. Management Fees Revenue   Cr. Service Revenue

15. Which of the following accounts is not closed out?
    a. Accumulated Amortization
    b. Amortization Expense
    c. Dividends
    d. Interest Revenue

16. Suppose Starbucks Corporation borrows $50 million on a 10-year note payable. How does this transaction affect Starbucks' ratios?
    a. Improves both ratios
    b. Improves the current ratio and hurts the debt ratio
    c. Hurts both ratios
    d. Hurts the current ratio and improves the debt ratio

ACCOUNTING VOCABULARY

account format A balance-sheet format that lists assets on the left and liabilities and shareholders' equity on the right. (p. 130)

accrual An expense or a revenue that occurs before the business pays or receives cash. An accrual is the opposite of a deferral. (p. 110)

accrual accounting Accounting that records the impact of a business event as it occurs, regardless of whether the transaction affected cash. (p. 104)

accrued expense An expense incurred but not yet paid in cash. (p. 114)

accrued revenue A revenue that has been earned but not yet received in cash. (p. 116)

accumulated amortization The cumulative sum of all amortization expense from the date of acquiring a plant asset. (p. 113)

adjusted trial balance A list of all the ledger accounts with their adjusted balances. (p. 120)

amortization Allocation of the cost of a plant asset over its useful life. (p. 109)

book value (of a plant asset) The asset's cost minus accumulated amortization. (p. 113)

cash-basis accounting Accounting that records only transactions in which cash is received or paid. (p. 104)

classified balance sheet A balance sheet that shows current assets separate from long-term assets, and current liabilities separate from long-term liabilities. (p. 128)

closing entries Entries that transfer the revenue, expense, and dividend balances from these respective accounts to the Retained Earnings account. (p. 126)

closing the books The process of preparing the accounts to begin recording the next period's transactions. Closing the accounts consists of journalizing and posting the closing entries to set the balances of the revenue, expense, and dividend accounts to zero. Also called *closing the accounts*. (p. 126)

contra account An account that always has a companion account and whose normal balance is opposite that of the companion account. (p. 113)

current ratio Current assets divided by current liabilities. Measures a company's ability to pay current liabilities with current assets. (p. 131)

debt ratio Ratio of total liabilities to total assets. States the proportion of a company's assets that is financed with debt. (p. 131)

deferral An adjustment for which the business paid or received cash in advance. Examples include prepaid rent, prepaid insurance, and supplies. (p. 109)

liquidity Measure of how quickly an item can be converted to cash. (p. 127)

long-term assets An asset that is not a current asset. (p. 128)

long-term liabilities A liability that is not a current liability. (p. 128)

matching principle The basis for recording expenses. Directs accountants to identify all expenses incurred during the period, to measure the expenses, and to match them against the revenues earned during that same period. (p. 106)

multi-step income statement An income statement that contains subtotals to highlight important relationships between revenues and expenses. (p. 130)

operating cycle Time span during which cash is paid for goods and services, and these goods and services are sold to bring in cash. (p. 128)

permanent accounts Assets, liabilities, and shareholders' equity. (p. 126)

report format Lists assets at the top, followed by liabilities and shareholders' equity below. (p. 129)

revenue principle Governs when to record revenue and the amount to record. (p. 106)

single-step income statement Lists all revenues together and all expenses together; there is only one step in arriving at net income. (p. 130)

temporary accounts Revenue and expenses related to a limited period. (p. 126)

time-period concept Ensures that accounting information is reported at regular intervals. (p. 105)

unearned revenue An obligation arising from receiving cash before providing a service. (p. 116)

ASSESS YOUR PROGRESS

Make the grade with MyAccountingLab: The exercises and problems marked in red can be found on MyAccountingLab at www.myaccountinglab.com. You can practise them as often as you want, and they feature step by step guided solutions to help you find the right answer.

SHORT EXERCISES

S3-1 Marquis Inc. made sales of $700 million during 2009. Of this amount, Marquis Inc. collected cash for all but $30 million. The company's cost of goods sold was $300 million, and all other expenses for the year totalled $350 million. Also during 2009, Marquis Inc. paid $400 million for its inventory and $280 million for everything else. Beginning cash was $100

Linking accrual accounting and cash flows
(Obj. 1)

million. Marquis Inc.'s top management is interviewing you for a job and you are asked two questions:

a. How much was Marquis Inc.'s net income for 2009?
b. How much was Marquis Inc.'s cash balance at the end of 2009?
    You will get the job only if you answer the two questions correctly.

Linking accrual accounting and cash flows
(Obj. 1)

S3-2 Great Sporting Goods Inc. began 2009 owing notes payable of $4.0 million. During 2009, the company borrowed $2.6 million on notes payable and paid off $2.5 million of notes payable from prior years of notes payable. Interest expense for the year was $1.0 million including $0.2 million of interest payable accrued at December 31, 2009. Show what Great Sporting Goods Inc. should report for these facts on the following financial statements:

- Income Statement
    Interest expense
- Balance Sheet
    Notes payable
    Interest payable

Applying the revenue and the matching principles
(Obj. 2)

S3-3 Ford Canada sells large fleets of vehicles to auto rental companies, such as **Budget** and **Avis**. Suppose Budget is negotiating with Ford to purchase 1,000 Explorers. Write a short paragraph to explain to Ford when the company should, and should not, record this sales revenue and the related cost of goods sold. Mention the accounting principles that provide the basis for your explanation.

Adjusting prepaid expenses
(Obj. 3)

S3-4 Answer the following questions about prepaid expenses:

a. On November 1, World Travel Ltd. prepaid $6,000 for 3 months' rent. Give the adjusting entry to record rent expense at December 31. Include the date of the entry and an explanation. Then post all amounts to the two accounts involved, and show their balances at December 31. World Travel adjusts the accounts only at December 31.
b. On December 1, World Travel paid $800 for supplies. At December 1, World Travel has $500 of supplies on hand. Make the required journal entry at December 31. Post all accounts to the accounts and show their balances at December 31.

Recording amortization; cash flows
(Obj. 1, 3)

S3-5 Suppose that on January 1 **Roots Ltd.** paid cash of $30,000 for computers that are expected to remain useful for 3 years. At the end of 3 years, the computers' values are expected to be zero.

1. Make journal entries to record (a) purchase of the computers on January 1 and (b) the annual amortization on December 31. Include dates and explanations, and use the following accounts: Computer Equipment; Accumulated Amortization—Computer Equipment; and Amortization Expense—Computer Equipment.
2. Post to the accounts and show their balances at December 31.
3. What is the computers' book value at December 31?
4. Which account(s) will Roots report on the income statement for the year? Which accounts will appear on the balance sheet of December 31? Show the amount to report for each item on both financial statements.

Applying the matching principle and the time-period concept
(Obj. 2)

S3-6 During 2008, Many Miles Trucking paid salary expense of $40 million. At December 31, Many Miles accrued salary expense of $2 million. Many Miles paid $1.9 million to its employees on January 3, 2009, the company's next payday after the end of the 2008 year. For this sequence of transactions, show what Many Miles would include on its 2008 income statement and its balance sheet at the end of 2008.

Accruing and paying interest expense
(Obj. 3)

S3-7 Schwartz & Associates Inc. borrowed $100,000 on October 1 by signing a note payable to **Scotiabank**. The interest expense for each month is $500. The loan agreement requires Schwartz & Associates Inc. to pay interest on December 31.

1. Make Schwartz & Associates Inc.'s adjusting entry to accrue interest expense and interest payable at October 31, at November 30, and at December 31. Date each entry and include its explanation.

2. Post all three entries to the Interest Payable account. You need not take the balance of the account at the end of each month.

3. Record the payment of three months' interest at December 31.

S3-8 Return to the situation in Short Exercise 3-7. Here you are accounting for the same transactions on the books of Scotiabank, which lent the money to Schwartz & Associates Inc. Perform all three steps in Short Exercise 3-7 for Scotiabank using the bank's own accounts.

Accruing and receiving cash from interest revenue **(Obj. 3)**

S3-9 Write a paragraph to explain why unearned revenues are liabilities instead of revenues. In your explanation, use the following actual example: *Maclean's* magazine collects cash from subscribers in advance and later delivers magazines to subscribers over a 1-year period. Explain what happens to the unearned subscription revenue over the course of a year as *Maclean's* delivers magazines to subscribers. Into what account does the unearned subscription revenue go as *Maclean's* delivers magazines?

Explaining unearned revenues **(Obj. 3)**

Give the journal entries that *Maclean's* would make to:

a. Collect $10,000 of subscription revenue in advance.

b. Record earning $40,000 of subscription revenue.

Include an explanation for each entry, as illustrated in the chapter.

S3-10 Birdie Golf Ltd. prepaid 3 months' rent ($6,000) on January 1. At March 31, Birdie prepared a trial balance and made the necessary adjusting entry at the end of the quarter. Birdie adjusts its accounts every quarter of the fiscal year, which ends December 31.

Reporting prepaid expenses **(Obj. 4)**

What amount appears for Prepaid Rent on

a. Birdie's unadjusted trial balance March 31?

b. Birdie's adjusted trial balance March 31?

What amount appears for Rent Expense on

a. Birdie's unadjusted trial balance at March 31?

b. Birdie's adjusted trial balance at March 31?

S3-11 Josie Inc. collects cash from customers two ways:

Updating the accounts **(Obj. 3)**

1. Accrued Revenue. Some customers pay Josie after Josie has performed service for the customer. During 2009, Josie made sales of $50,000 on account and later received cash of $40,000 on account from these customers.

2. Unearned Revenue. A few customers pay Josie in advance, and Josie later performs service for the customer. During 2009, Josie collected $7,000 cash in advance and later earned $6,000 of this amount.

Journalize the following for Josie:

a. Earning service revenue of $50,000 on account and then collecting $40,000 on account

b. Receiving $7,000 in advance and then earning $6,000 as service revenue

Explanations are not required.

S3-12 Entertainment Centre Ltd. reported the following data at March 31, 2009, with amounts adapted and in thousands:

Preparing the financial statements **(Obj. 4)**

Retained earnings, March 31, 2008... $	1,300	Cost of goods sold....................	$126,000
Accounts receivable..........................	27,700	Cash...	900
Net revenues......................................	174,500	Property and equipment, net....	7,200
Total current liabilities.....................	53,600	Common shares	26,000
All other expenses............................	45,000	Inventories	33,000
Other current assets	4,800	Long-term liabilities	13,500
Other assets	24,300	Dividends..................................	0

You are the CFO responsible for reporting Entertainment Centre (ECL) Ltd. results. Use these data to prepare: ECL's income statement for the year ended March 31, 2009; the statement of retained earnings for the year ended March 31, 2009; and the classified balance sheet at March 31, 2009. Use the report format for the balance sheet. Draw arrows linking the three statements to explain the information flows between the statements.

S3-13 Use the Entertainment Centre Ltd. data in Short Exercise 3-12 to make the company's closing entries at March 31, 2009. Then set up a T-account for Retained Earnings and post to that account. Compare Retained Earnings' ending balance to the amount reported on ECL's statement of retained earnings and balance sheet. What do you find? Why is this important?

Computing the current ratio and the debt ratio
(Obj. 6)

S3-14 Use the Entertainment Centre Ltd. data in Short Exercise 3-12 to compute ECL's

a. Current ratio
b. Debt ratio
   Round to two decimal places. Report to the CEO whether these values look strong, weak, or middle-of-the-road.

Using the current ratio and the debt ratio
(Obj. 6)

S3-15 Use the Entertainment Centre Ltd. data in Short Exercise 3-12 to compute ECL's (a) current ratio and (b) debt ratio after each of the following transactions which were not included in the year-end data (all amounts are in thousands):

1. ECL earned revenue of $10,000 on account
2. ECL paid off accounts payable of $10,000 (Challenge)
   Round to two decimal places. Explain to the CEO any differences in the ratios compared to those computed in Short Exercise 3-14 and why the entries should be made.

EXERCISES

Linking accrual accounting and cash flows
(Obj. 1)

E3-16 During 2009, Organic Foods Inc. made sales of $4,000 (assume all on account) and collected cash of $4,100 from customers. Operating expenses totalled $800, all paid in cash. At December 31, 2009, Organic Foods' customers owed the company $400. Organic Foods owed creditors $700 on account. All amounts are in millions.

1. For these facts, show what Organic Foods Inc. would report on the following 2009 financial statements:
   - Income statement
   - Balance sheet
2. Suppose Organic Foods had used cash-basis accounting. What would Organic Foods Ltd. have reported for these facts?

Linking accrual accounting and cash flows
(Obj. 1)

E3-17 During 2009, Valley Sales Inc. earned revenues of $500,000 on account. Valley Sales collected $410,000 from customers during the year. Expenses totalled $420,000, and the related cash payments were $400,000. Show what Valley Sales would report on its 2009 income statement under the

a. Cash basis
b. Accrual basis
   Compute net income under both bases of accounting. Which basis measures net income more appropriately? Explain your answer.

Accrual basis of accounting, applying accounting principles
(Obj. 1, 2)

E3-18 During 2009, Dish Networks Inc. earned revenues of $700 million. Expenses totalled $540 million. Dish collected all but $20 million of the revenues and paid $530 million on its expenses. Dish's top managers are evaluating the year, and they ask you the following questions:

a. Under accrual accounting, what amount of revenue should the company report for 2009? Is the $700-million revenue earned or is it the amount of cash actually collected? How does the revenue principle help to answer these questions?
b. Under accrual accounting, what amount of total expense should Dish report for the year—$540 million or $530 million? Which accounting principle helps to answer this question?
c. Which financial statement reports revenues and expenses? Which statement reports cash receipts and cash payments?

Applying accounting concepts and principles
(Obj. 2)

E3-19 Write a short paragraph to explain in your own words the concept of amortization as used in accounting.

E3-20 Identify the accounting concept or principle that gives the most direction on how to account for each of the following situations:

Applying accounting concepts and principles
(Obj. 2)

a. Salary expense of $20,000 is accrued at the end of the period to measure income properly.
b. October has been a particularly slow month, and the business will have a net loss for the third quarter of the year. Management is considering not following its customary practice of reporting quarterly earnings to the public.
c. A dentist performs a surgical operation and bills the patient's insurance company. It may take three months to collect from the insurance company. Should the dentist record revenue now or wait until cash is collected?
d. A construction company is building a highway system, and construction will take three years. How do you think it should record the revenue it earns over the year or over three years?
e. A utility bill is received on December 30 and will be paid next year. When should the company record utility expense?

E3-21 An accountant made the following adjustments at December 31, the end of the accounting period:

Journalizing adjusting entries and analyzing their effects on net income; accrual versus cash basis
(Obj. 1, 3)

a. Prepaid insurance, beginning, $700. Payments for insurance during the period, $2,100. Prepaid insurance, ending, $800
b. Interest revenue accrued, $900
c. Unearned service revenue, beginning, $800. Unearned service revenue, ending, $300
d. Amortization, $6,200
e. Employees' salaries owed for 3 days of a 5-day work week; weekly payroll, $9,000
f. Income before income tax expense, $20,000. Income tax rate is 25%.

❙ Required

1. Journalize the adjusting entries.
2. Suppose the adjustments were not made. Compute the overall overstatement or understatement of net income as a result of the omission of these adjustments.

E3-22 Green Leaf Fertilizer Ltd. experienced four situations for its supplies. Compute the amounts indicated by question marks for each situation. For situations 1 and 2, journalize the needed transaction. Consider each situation separately.

Allocating supplies cost to the asset and the expenses
(Obj. 2, 3)

	Situation			
	1	2	3	4
Beginning supplies	$ 500	$1,000	$ 300	$ 900
Payments for supplies during the year	?	3,100	?	1,100
Total amount to account for	$1,300	?	?	2,000
Ending supplies	400	500	700	?
Supplies expense	$ 900	$?	$ 700	$1,400

E3-23 Clark Motors Ltd. faced the following situations. Journalize the adjusting entry needed at year-end (December 31, 2008) for each situation. Consider each fact separately.

Journalizing adjusting entries
(Obj. 3)

a. The business has interest expense of $9,000 early in January 2009.
b. Interest revenue of $3,000 has been earned but not yet received.
c. When the business collected $12,000 in advance three months ago, the accountant debited Cash and credited Unearned Revenue. The client was paying for two cars, one delivered in December, the other to be delivered in February 2009.
d. Salary expense is $1,000 per day—Monday through Friday—and the business pays employees each Friday. This year, December 31 falls on a Tuesday.
e. The unadjusted balance of the Supplies account is $3,100. The total cost of supplies on hand is $800.
f. Equipment was purchased at the beginning of this year at a cost of $60,000. The equipment's useful life is five years. Record the amortization for this year and then determine the equipment's book value.

Making adjustments in T-accounts
(Obj. 3)

E3-24 The accounting records of Lalonde Ltée include the following unadjusted balances at May 31: Accounts Receivable, $1,300; Supplies, $900; Salary Payable, $0; Unearned Service Revenue, $800; Service Revenue, $14,400; Salary Expense, $4,200; Supplies Expense, $0. As Lalonde's accountant you have developed the following data for the May 31 adjusting entries:

a. Supplies on hand, $300
b. Salary owed to employees, $2,000
c. Service revenue accrued, $600
d. Unearned service revenue that has been earned, $700

Open the foregoing T-accounts with their beginning balances. Then record the adjustments directly in the accounts, keying each adjustment amount by letter. Show each account's adjusted balance. Journal entries are not required.

Preparing the financial statements
(Obj. 4)

E3-25 The adjusted trial balance of Honeybee Hams Inc. follows.

Honeybee Hams Inc.		
Adjusted Trial Balance		
December 31, 2009		

	Adjusted Trial Balance	
(thousands)	Debit	Credit
Cash	$ 3,300	
Accounts receivable	1,800	
Inventories	1,100	
Prepaid expenses	1,900	
Capital assets	6,600	
Accumulated amortization		$ 2,400
Other assets	9,900	
Accounts payable		7,700
Income tax payable		600
Other liabilities		2,200
Common shares		4,900
Retained earnings (December 31, 2008)		4,500
Dividends	1,700	
Sales revenue		41,000
Cost of goods sold	25,000	
Selling, administrative, and general expense	10,000	
Income tax expense	2,000	
	$63,300	$63,300

❙ *Required*

Prepare Honeybee Hams' income statement and statement of retained earnings for the year ended December 31, 2009, and its balance sheet on that date. Draw arrows linking the three statements.

Measuring financial statement amounts
(Obj. 3)

E3-26 The adjusted trial balances of Tower Development Inc. for March 31, 2008 and March 31, 2009 include these amounts (in millions):

	2009	2008
Receivables	$300	$200
Prepaid insurance	180	110
Accrued liabilities (for other operating expenses)	700	600

Tower Development completed these transactions during the year ended March 31, 2009.

Collections from customers	$20,800
Payment of prepaid insurance	400
Cash payments for other operating expenses	4,100

Compute the amount of sales revenue, insurance expense, and other operating expense to report on the income statement for the year ended March 31, 2009.

E3-27 This question deals with the items and the amounts that two entities, Mountain Services Inc. (Mountain) and City of Squamish (Squamish), should report in their financial statements.

Reporting on the financial statements
(Obj. 4)

1. On March 31, 2008, Mountain collected $12,000 in advance from Squamish, a client. Under the contract, Mountain is obligated to provide consulting services for Squamish evenly during the year ended March 31, 2009. Assume you are Mountain.

    Mountain's income statement for the year ended December 31, 2008, will report _____ of $_____.

    Mountain's balance sheet at December 31, 2008, will report _____ of $_____.

2. Assume that you are Squamish. Squamish's income statement for the year ended December 31, 2008, will report _____ of $_____.

    Squamish's balance sheet at December 31, 2008, will report _____ of $_____.

E3-28 This exercise builds from a simple situation to a slightly more complex situation. **Rogers**, the Canadian wireless phone service provider, collects cash in advance from customers. All amounts are in millions.

Linking deferrals and cash flows
(Obj. 1, 3)

Assume Rogers collected $400 in advance during 2009 and at year-end still owed customers phone service worth $90.

❙ Required

1. Show what Rogers will report for 2009 on its
   - Income statement
   - Balance sheet
2. Use the same facts for Rogers as in Requirement 1. Further, assume Rogers reported unearned service revenue of $80 at the end of 2008.

    Show what Rogers will report for 2009 on the same financial statements. Explain why your answer differs from your answer to Requirement 1.

E3-29 Prepare the required closing entries for the following selected accounts from the records of SouthWest Transport Inc. at December 31, 2009 (amounts in thousands):

Closing the accounts
(Obj. 5)

Cost of services sold	$11,600	Service Revenue	$23,600
Accumulated amortization	17,800	Amortization expense	4,100
Selling, general, and		Other revenue	600
administrative expense	6,900	Income tax expense	400
Retained earnings,		Dividends	400
December 31, 2008	1,900	Income tax payable	300

How much net income did SouthWest Transport Inc. earn during the year ended December 31, 2009? Prepare a T-account for Retained Earnings to show the December 31, 2009, balance of Retained Earnings.

*Identifying and recording
adjusting and closing entries*
(Obj. 3, 5)

E3-30 The unadjusted trial balance and income statement amounts from the December 31, 2009, adjusted trial balance of Yosaf Portraits Ltd. are given below.

	Yosaf Portraits Ltd. Trial Balance December 31, 2009			
Account Title	Unadjusted Trial Balance		From the Adjusted Trial Balance	
Cash	10,200			
Prepaid rent	1,100			
Equipment	32,100			
Accumulated amortization		3,800		
Accounts payable		4,600		
Salary payable				
Unearned service revenue		8,400		
Income tax payable				
Note payable, long term		10,000		
Common shares		8,700		
Retained earnings		1,300		
Dividends	1,000			
Service revenue		12,800		19,500
Salary expense	4,000		4,900	
Rent expense	1,200		1,400	
Amortization expense			300	
Income tax expense			1,600	
	49,600	49,600	8,200	19,500
Net income			11,300	
			19,500	19,500

❚ *Required*

Journalize the adjusting and closing entries of Yosaf Portraits Ltd. at December 31, 2009. There was only one adjustment to Service Revenue.

*Preparing a classified balance
sheet and using the ratios*
(Obj. 4, 6)

E3-31 Refer to Exercise 3-30.

❚ *Required*

1. After solving Exercise 3-30, use the data in that exercise to prepare Yosaf Portraits Ltd.'s classified balance sheet at December 31, 2009. Use the report format. First you must compute the adjusted balance for several balance sheet accounts.
2. Compute Yosaf Portraits Ltd.'s current ratio and debt ratio at December 31, 2009. A year ago, the current ratio was 1.55 and the debt ratio was 0.45. Indicate whether the company's ability to pay its debts—both current and total—improved or deteriorated during the current year.

*Measuring the effect of
transactions on the ratios*
(Obj. 6)

E3-32 Le Gasse Inc. reported these ratios at December 31, 2008 (dollar amounts in millions)

$$\text{Current ratio} = \frac{\$20}{\$10} = 2.00 \qquad\qquad \text{Debt ratio} = \frac{\$20}{\$50} = 0.40$$

Le Gasse completed these transactions during the 2009 year:

a. Purchased equipment on account, $4 million
b. Paid long-term debt, $5 million
c. Collected cash from customers in advance, $2 million
d. Accrued interest expense, $1 million
e. Made cash sales, $6 million

Determine whether each transaction would improve or hurt Le Gasse's current ratio and debt ratio. Round all ratios to two decimal places.

SERIAL EXERCISE

Exercise 3-33 continues the Web Marketing Services Inc. situation begun in Exercise 2-25 of Chapter 2 (p. 87).

E3-33

Refer to Exercise 2-25 of Chapter 2. Start from the trial balance and the posted T-accounts prepared at January 18, 2009. Later in January, the business completed these transactions:

Adjusting the accounts, preparing the financial statements, closing the accounts, and evaluating the business
(Obj. 3, 4, 5, 6)

2009		
Jan.	21	Received $900 in advance for marketing work to be performed evenly over the next 30 days
	21	Hired a secretary to be paid on the 15th day of each month
	26	Paid $900 on account
	28	Collected $600 on account
	31	Declared and paid dividends of $1,000

❙ *Required*

1. Open these T-accounts: Accumulated Amortization—Equipment, Accumulated Amortization—Furniture, Salary Payable, Unearned Service Revenue, Retained Earnings, Amortization Expense—Equipment, Amortization Expense—Furniture, and Supplies Expense. Also, use the T-accounts opened for Exercise 2-25.

2. Journalize the transactions of January 21 through 31.

3. Post the January 21 to January 31 transactions to the T-accounts, keying all items by date. Denote account balances as Bal.

4. Prepare a trial balance at January 31. Also set up columns for the adjustments and for the adjusted trial balance, as illustrated in Exhibit 3-9, page 120.

5. At January 31, 2009, the following information is gathered for the adjusting entries:
   a. Accrued service revenue, $1,000
   b. Earned $300 of the service revenue collected in advance on January 21
   c. Supplies on hand, $300
   d. Amortization expense—equipment, $100; furniture, $200
   e. Accrued expense for secretary's salary, $1,000.

   Make these adjustments directly in the adjustments columns and complete the adjusted trial balance at January 31, 2009.

6. Journalize and post the adjusting entries. Denote each adjusting amount as Adj. and an account balance as Bal.

7. Prepare the income statement and statement of retained earnings of Web Marketing Services Inc. for the month ended January 31, 2009, and the classified balance sheet at that date. Draw arrows to link the financial statements.

8. Journalize and post the closing entries at January 31, 2009. Denote each closing amount as Clo. and an account balance as Bal.

9. Using the information you have prepared, compute the current ratio and the debt ratio of Web Marketing Services Inc. (to two decimals) and evaluate these ratio values as indicative of a strong or weak financial position.

CHALLENGE EXERCISES

Computing financial statement amounts
(Obj. 3, 4)

E3-34 Valley Bleu Ltée reported the following current accounts at December 31, 2008 (amounts in thousands):

a. Cash	$1,700
b. Receivables	5,600
c. Inventory	1,800
d. Prepaid expenses	800
e. Accounts payable	2,400
f. Unearned revenue	1,200
g. Accrued expenses payable	1,700

During 2009, Valley Bleu completes these transactions:

- Used inventory of $3,800
- Sold services on account, $6,500
- Amortization expense, $400
- Paid for accrued expenses, $500
- Collected from customers on account, $7,500
- Accrued expenses, $1,300
- Purchased inventory of $3,500 on account
- Paid on account, $5,000
- Used up prepaid expenses, $600

Compute Valley Bleu's current ratio at December 31, 2008, and again at December 31, 2009. Did the current ratio improve or deteriorate during 2009? Comment on the company's current ratio.

Computing financial statement amounts
(Obj. 3, 4)

E3-35 The accounts of Maritime Specialists Ltd. prior to the year-end adjustments are given below.

Cash	$ 4,000	Common shares	$ 10,000
Accounts receivable	7,000	Retained earnings	43,000
Supplies	4,000	Dividends	16,000
Prepaid insurance	3,000	Service revenue	155,000
Building	107,000	Salary expense	32,000
Accumulated amortization—building	14,000	Amortization expense—building	
Land	51,000	Supplies expense	
Accounts payable	6,000	Insurance expense	
Salary payable		Advertising expense	7,000
Unearned service revenue	5,000	Utilities expense	2,000

Adjusting data at the end of the year include:

a. Unearned service revenue that has been earned, $1,000
b. Accrued service revenue, $2,000
c. Supplies used in operations, $3,000
d. Accrued salary expense, $3,000
e. Prepaid insurance expired, $1,000
f. Amortization expense, building, $2,000

Jon Whale, the principal shareholder, has received an offer to sell Maritime Specialists. He needs to know the following information within one hour:

a. Net income for the year covered by these data
b. Total assets

c. Total liabilities

d. Total shareholders' equity

e. Proof that Total assets = Total liabilities + Total shareholders' equity, after all items are updated

❙ Required

Without opening any accounts, making any journal entries, or using a worksheet, provide Whale with the requested information. The business is not subject to income tax. Show all computations.

QUIZ

Test your understanding of accrual accounting by answering the following questions. Select the best choice from among the possible answers given.

Questions 36 through 38 are based on the following facts:

Freddie Handel began a music business in July 2009. Handel prepares monthly financial statements and uses the accrual basis of accounting. The following transactions are Handel Company's only activities during July through October:

July	14	Bought music on account for $10, with payment to the supplier due in 90 days
Aug.	3	Performed a job on account for Joey Bach for $25, collectible from Bach in 30 days. Used up all the music purchased on July 14
Sept.	16	Collected the $25 receivable from Bach
Oct.	22	Paid the $10 owed to the supplier from the July 14 transaction

Q3-36 In which month should Handel record the cost of the music as an expense?

a. July

b. August

c. September

d. October

Q3-37 In which month should Handel report the $25 revenue on its income statement?

a. July

b. August

c. September

d. October

Q3-38 If Handel Company uses the *cash* basis of accounting instead of the accrual basis, in what month will Handel report revenue and in what month will it report expense?

	Revenue	**Expense**
a.	September	October
b.	September	July
c.	August	October
d.	September	August

Q3-39 In which month should revenue be recorded?

a. In the month that goods are ordered by the customer

b. In the month that goods are shipped to the customer

c. In the month that the invoice is mailed to the customer

d. In the month that cash is collected from the customer

Q3-40 On January 1 of the current year, Aladdin Company paid $600 rent to cover six months (January through June). Aladdin recorded this transactions as follows:

Prepaid Rent	600	
Cash		600

Aladdin adjusts the accounts at the end of each month. Based on these facts, the adjusting entry at the end of January should include

a. A credit to Prepaid Rent for $500   c. A debit to Prepaid Rent for $100
b. A debit to Prepaid Rent for $500   d. A credit to Prepaid Rent for $100

Q3-41 Assume the same facts as in the previous problem. Aladdin's adjusting entry at the end of February should include a debit to Rent Expense in the amount of

a. $0   c. $200
b. $500   d. $100

Q3-42 What effect does the adjusting entry in question 3-41 have on Aladdin's net income for February?

a. Increase by $100   c. Decrease by $100
b. Increase by $200   d. Decrease by $200

Q3-43 An adjusting entry recorded March salary expense that will be paid in April. Which statement best describes the effect of this adjusting entry on the company's accounting equation at the end of March?

a. Assets are not affected, liabilities are decreased, and shareholders' equity is decreased.
b. Assets are decreased, liabilities are increased, and shareholders' equity is decreased.
c. Assets are not affected, liabilities are increased, and shareholders' equity is decreased.
d. Assets are decreased, liabilities are not affected, and shareholders' equity is decreased.

Q3-44 On April 1, 2008, Metro Insurance Company sold a 1-year insurance policy covering the year ended April 1, 2009. Metro collected the full $1,200 on April 1, 2008. Metro made the following journal entry to record the receipt of cash in advance:

Cash	1,200	
Unearned Revenue		1,200

Nine months have passed, and Metro has made no adjusting entries. Based on these facts, the adjusting entry needed by Metro at December 31, 2008, is

a.	Unearned Revenue	300	
	Insurance Revenue		300
b.	Insurance Revenue	300	
	Unearned Revenue		300
c.	Unearned Revenue	900	
	Insurance Revenue		900
d.	Insurance Revenue	900	
	Unearned Revenue		900

Q3-45 The Unearned Revenue account of Dean Incorporated began 2009 with a normal balance of $5,000 and ended 2009 with a normal balance of $12,000. During 2009, the Unearned Revenue account was credited for $19,000 that Dean will earn later. Based on these facts, how much revenue did Dean earn in 2009?

a. $5,000   c. $24,000
b. $19,000   d. $12,000

Q3-46 What is the effect on the financial statements of *recording* amortization on equipment?

a. Assets are decreased, but net income and shareholders' equity are not affected.
b. Net income, assets, and shareholders' equity are all decreased.
c. Net income and assets are decreased, but shareholders' equity is not affected.
d. Net income is not affected, but assets and shareholders' equity are decreased.

Q3-47 For 2009, Monterrey Company had revenues in excess of expenses. Which statement describes Monterrey's closing entries at the end of 2009?
a. Revenues will be debited, expenses will be credited, and retained earnings will be debited.
b. Revenues will be credited, expenses will be debited, and retained earnings will be debited.
c. Revenues will be debited, expenses will be credited, and retained earnings will be credited.
d. Revenues will be credited, expenses will be debited, and retained earnings will be credited.

Q3-48 Which of the following accounts would *not* be included in the closing entries?
a. Accumulated Amortization   c. Amortization Expense
b. Service Revenue   d. Retained Earnings

Q3-49 A major purpose of preparing closing entries is to
a. Zero out the liability accounts.
b. Close out the Supplies account.
c. Adjust the asset accounts to their correct current balances.
d. Update the Retained Earnings account.

Q3-50 Selected data for Austin Company follow:

Current assets	$50,000	Current liabilities	$40,000
Capital assets	70,000	Long-term liabilities	35,000
Total revenues	30,000	Total expenses	20,000

Based on these facts, what are Austin's current ratio and debt ratio?

Current ratio	**Debt ratio**
a. 2 to 1	0.5 to 1
b. 0.83 to 1	0.5 to 1
c. 1.25 to 1	0.625 to 1
d. 2 to 1	0.633 to 1

PROBLEMS

(GROUP A)

P3-51A Lewitas Ltd. earned revenues of $35 million during 2009 and ended the year with income of $8 million. During 2009, Lewitas Ltd. collected $33 million from customers and paid cash for all of its expenses plus an additional $1 million for accounts payable. Answer these questions about Lewitas' operating results, financial position, and cash flows during 2009:

Linking accrual accounting and cash flows
(Obj. 1)

❚ *Required*

1. How much were the company's total expenses? Show your work.
2. Identify all the items that Lewitas will report on its 2009 income statement. Show each amount.
3. Lewitas began 2009 with receivables of $4 million. All sales were on account. What was the company's receivables balance at the end of 2009? Identify the appropriate financial statement, and show how Lewitas will report ending receivables in the 2009 annual report.
4. Lewitas began 2009 owing accounts payable totalling $9 million. How much in accounts payable did the company owe at the end of the year? Identify the appropriate financial statement, and show how Lewitas will report these accounts payable in its 2009 annual report.

Cash basis versus accrual basis
(Obj. 1)

P3-52A Prairies Consultants Inc. had the following selected transactions in August 2009:

Aug.	1	Prepaid insurance for August through December, $1,000
	4	Purchased software for cash, $800
	5	Performed service and received cash, $900
	8	Paid advertising expense, $300
	11	Performed service on account, $3,000
	19	Purchased computer on account, $1,600
	24	Collected for the August 11 service
	26	Paid account payable from August 19
	29	Paid salary expense, $900
	31	Adjusted for August insurance expense (see Aug. 1)
	31	Earned revenue of $800 that was collected in advance in July

❚ Required

1. Show how each transaction would be handled using the cash basis and the accrual basis. Under each column, give the amount of revenue or expense for August. Journal entries are not required. Use the following format for your answer, and show your computations:

Prairies Consultants Inc. **Amount of Revenue (Expense) for August 2009**		
Date	**Cash Basis**	**Accrual Basis**

2. Compute August income (loss) before tax under each accounting method.

3. Indicate which measure of net income or net loss is preferable. Use the transactions on August 11 and 24 to explain.

Applying accounting principles
(Obj. 1, 2)

P3-53A Write a memo to explain to a new employee the difference between the cash basis of accounting and the accrual basis. Mention the roles of the revenue principle and the matching principle in accrual accounting.

Making accounting adjustments
(Obj. 3)

P3-54A Journalize the adjusting entry needed on December 31, 2009, end of the current accounting period, for each of the following independent cases affecting Callaway Corp. Include an explanation for each entry.

a. Details of Prepaid Insurance are shown in the account:

Prepaid Insurance			
Jan. 1	Bal.	400	
Mar. 31		3,600	

Callaway prepays insurance on March 31 each year. At December 31, $900 is still prepaid.

b. Callaway pays employees each Friday. The amount of the weekly payroll is $6,000 for a five-day work week. The current accounting period ends on Wednesday.

c. Callaway has a note receivable. During the current year, the company has earned accrued interest revenue of $500 that it will receive next year.

d. The beginning balance of supplies was $2,600. During the year, Callaway purchased supplies costing $6,100, and at December 31 the cost of supplies on hand is $2,100.

e. Callaway is providing financial services for Manatawabi Investments Inc., and the owner of Manatawabi paid Callaway $12,000 for its annual service fee. Callaway recorded this amount as Unearned Service Revenue. Callaway estimates that it has earned one-third of the total fee during the current year.

f. Amortization for the current year includes Office Furniture, $1,000, and Equipment, $2,700. Make a compound entry.

P3-55A The unadjusted trial balance of The Rock Industries Ltd. at January 31, 2009, appears below.

Preparing an adjusted trial balance and the financial statements; using the current ratio to evaluate the business (Obj. 3, 4, 6)

The Rock Industries Ltd. Trial Balance January 31, 2009		
Cash	$ 8,000	
Accounts receivable	10,000	
Prepaid rent	3,000	
Supplies	2,000	
Furniture	36,000	
Accumulated amortization		$ 3,000
Accounts payable		10,000
Salary payable		
Common shares		26,000
Retained earnings (December 31, 2008)		13,000
Dividends	4,000	
Service revenue		14,000
Salary expense	2,000	
Rent expense		
Utilities expense	1,000	
Amortization expense		
Supplies expense		
Total	$66,000	$66,000

Adjustment data:

a. Accrued service revenue at January 31, $2,000
b. Prepaid rent expired during the month. The unadjusted prepaid balance of $3,000 relates to the period January through March.
c. Supplies used during January, $2,000
d. Amortization on furniture for the month. The estimated useful life of the furniture is three years.
e. Accrued salary expense at January 31 for Monday, Tuesday, and Wednesday. The five-day weekly payroll of $5,000 will be paid on Friday, February 2.

❚ Required

1. Using Exhibit 3-9, page 120, as an example, prepare the adjusted trial balance of The Rock Industries Ltd. at January 31, 2009. Key each adjusting entry by letter.
2. Prepare the income statement, the statement of retained earnings, and the classified balance sheet. Draw arrows linking the three financial statements.
3. Using the information prepared in Req. 1 and 2:
   a. Compare the business's net income for January using the information prepared in questions 1 and 2 to the amount of dividends paid to the owners. Suppose this trend continues each month for the remainder of 2009. What will be the effect on the business's financial position, as shown by its accounting equation?
   b. Will the trend make it easier or more difficult to borrow money if the business gets in a bind and needs cash? Why?
   c. Does either the current ratio or the cash position suggest the need for immediate borrowing? Explain.

*Analyzing and recording
adjustments*
(Obj. 3)

P3-56A Sundance Apartments Inc.'s unadjusted and adjusted trial balance at April 30, 2009, follow:

Sundance Apartments Inc.
Adjusted Trial Balance
April 30, 2009

Account Title	Trial Balance Debit	Trial Balance Credit	Adjusted Trial Balance Debit	Adjusted Trial Balance Credit
Cash	$ 8,300		$ 8,300	
Accounts receivable	6,300		6,800	
Interest receivable			300	
Note receivable	4,100		4,100	
Supplies	900		200	
Prepaid insurance	2,400		700	
Building	66,400		66,400	
Accumulated amortization		$16,000		$ 18,200
Accounts payable		6,900		6,900
Wages payable				400
Unearned rental revenue		600		100
Common shares		18,000		18,000
Retained earnings		42,700		42,700
Dividends	3,600		3,600	
Rental revenue		9,900		10,900
Interest revenue				300
Wages expense	1,600		2,000	
Insurance expense			1,700	
Amortization expense			2,200	
Property tax expense	300		300	
Supplies expense			700	
Utilities expense	200		200	
	$94,100	$94,100	$97,500	$97,500

❚ *Required*

1. Make the adjusting entries that account for the differences between the two trial balances.
2. Compute Sundance Apartments Inc.'s total assets, total liabilities, total equity, and net income. Prove your answer with the accounting equation.

*Preparing the financial statements
and using the debt ratio*
(Obj. 4, 6)

P3-57A The adjusted trial balance of Marshall Ltd. at December 31, 2009, is given on page 155.

❚ *Required*

1. Prepare Marshall Ltd.'s 2009 income statement, statement of retained earnings, and balance sheet. List expenses (except for income tax) in decreasing order on the income statement, and show total liabilities on the balance sheet. Draw arrows linking the three financial statements.
2. Marshall Ltd.'s lenders require that the company maintain a debt ratio no higher than 0.50. Compute Marshall Ltd.'s debt ratio at December 31, 2009, to determine whether the company is in compliance with this debt restriction. If not, suggest a way that Marshall Ltd. could have avoided this difficult situation.

Marshall Ltd.
Adjusted Trial Balance
December 31, 2009

Cash	$ 1,400	
Accounts receivable	8,900	
Supplies	2,300	
Prepaid rent	1,600	
Equipment	37,100	
Accumulated amortization		$ 4,300
Accounts payable		3,700
Interest payable		800
Unearned service revenue		600
Income tax payable		2,100
Note payable		18,600
Common shares		5,000
Retained earnings		1,000
Dividends	24,000	
Service revenue		107,900
Amortization expense	1,600	
Salary expense	39,900	
Rent expense	10,300	
Interest expense	3,100	
Insurance expense	3,800	
Supplies expense	2,900	
Income tax expense	7,100	
Total	$144,000	$144,000

P3-58A The accounts of Marciano Services Ltd. at March 31, 2009, are listed in alphabetical order.

Closing the books and evaluating retained earnings
(Obj. 5)

Accounts payable	$14,700	Insurance expense	600
Accounts receivable	16,500	Note payable, long-term	6,200
Accumulated amortization—		Other assets	14,100
equipment	7,100	Prepaid expenses	5,300
Advertising expense	10,900	Retained earnings, March 31, 2008	20,200
Amortization expense	1,900	Salary expense	17,800
Cash	7,500	Salary payable	2,400
Common shares	9,100	Service revenue	94,100
Current portion of note payable	800	Supplies	3,800
Dividends	31,200	Supplies expense	4,600
Equipment	43,200	Unearned service revenue	2,800

❙ Required

1. All adjustments have been journalized and posted, but the closing entries have not been made. Journalize Marciano Ltd.'s closing entries at March 31, 2009.
2. Set up a T-account for Retained Earnings and post to that account. Compute Marciano's net income for the year ended March 31, 2009. What is the ending balance of Retained Earnings?
3. Did retained earnings increase or decrease during the year? What caused the increase or the decrease?

P3-59A Refer to Problem 3-58A.
1. Use the Marciano Ltd. data in Problem 3-58A to prepare the company's classified balance sheet at March 31, 2009. Show captions for total assets, total liabilities, and total liabilities and shareholders' equity.

Preparing a classified balance sheet and using the ratios to evaluate the business
(Obj. 4, 6)

2. Evaluate Marciano's debt position as strong or weak, giving your reason. Assess whether Marciano's ability to pay both current and total debts improved or deteriorated during 2009. In order to complete your evaluation, compute Marciano's current and debt ratios at March 31, 2009, rounding to two decimal places. At March 31, 2008, the current ratio was 1.30 and the debt ratio was 0.30.

Analyzing financial ratios
(Obj. 6)

P3-60A This problem demonstrates the effects of transactions on the current ratio and the debt ratio of Ojibway Inc. Ojibway's condensed and adapted balance sheet at December 31, 2008, is:

	(In millions)
Total current assets	$15.5
Properties, plant, equipment, and other assets	15.8
	$31.3
Total current liabilities	$ 9.2
Total long-term liabilities	5.3
Total shareholders' equity	16.8
	$31.3

Assume that during the first quarter of the following year, 2009, Ojibway completed the following transactions:

a. Paid half of the current liabilities
b. Borrowed $3 million on long-term debt
c. Earned revenue, $2.5 million on account
d. Paid selling expense of $1 million
e. Accrued general expense of $0.8 million. Credit General Expense Payable, a current liability.
f. Purchased equipment for $4.2 million, paying cash of $1.4 million and signing a long-term note payable for $2.8 million
g. Recorded amortization expense of $0.6 million

❚ Required

1. Compute Ojibway's current ratio and debt ratio at December 31, 2008, to two decimal places.
2. Compute Ojibway's current ratio and debt ratio after each transaction during 2009, that is, 7 times. Consider each transaction separately. Round to two decimal places.
3. Based on your analysis, you should be able to readily identify the effects of certain transactions on the current ratio and the debt ratio. Test your understanding by completing these statements with either "increase" or "decrease":

   a. Revenues usually _____ the current ratio.
   b. Revenues usually _____ the debt ratio.
   c. Expenses usually _____ the current ratio. (*Note:* Amortization is an exception to this rule.)
   d. Expenses usually _____ the debt ratio.
   e. If a company's current ratio is greater than 1.0, as it is for Ojibway, paying off a current liability will always _____ the current ratio.
   f. Borrowing money on long-term debt will always _____ the current ratio and _____ the debt ratio.

(GROUP B)

Linking accrual accounting and cash flows
(Obj. 1)

P3-61B During 2009, Schubert Inc. earned revenues of $19 million from the sale of its products. Schubert ended the year with net income of $4 million. Schubert collected cash of $20 million from customers.

Answer these questions about Schubert's operating results, financial position, and cash flows during 2009:

1. How much were Schubert's total expenses? Show your work.
2. Identify all the items that Schubert will report on its income statement for 2009. Show each amount.
3. Schubert began 2009 with receivables of $6 million. All sales are on account. What was Schubert's receivables balance at the end of 2009? Identify the appropriate financial statement and show how Schubert will report its ending receivables balance in the company's 2009 annual report.
4. Schubert began 2009 owing accounts payable of $9 million. Schubert incurs all expenses on account. During 2009, Schubert paid $18 million on account. How much in accounts payable did Schubert owe at the end of 2009? Identify the appropriate financial statement and show how Schubert will report this accounts payable in its 2009 annual report.

P3-62B Fred's Catering Ltd. had the following selected transactions during May 2009:

Cash basis versus accrual basis
(Obj. 1)

May	1	Received $800 in advance for a banquet to be served later
	5	Paid electricity expenses, $700
	9	Received cash for the day's sales, $2,000
	14	Purchased two food warmers, $1,800
	23	Served a banquet, receiving a note receivable, $700
	31	Accrued salary expense, $900
	31	Prepaid $3,000 building rent for June and July

❚ *Required*

1. Show how each transaction would be handled using the cash basis and the accrual basis. Under each column, give the amount of revenue or expense for May. Journal entries are not required. Use the following format for your answer, and show your computations:

Fred's Catering Ltd.		

Amount of Revenue (Expense) for May 2009		
Date	Cash Basis	Accrual Basis

2. Compute income (loss) before tax for May under the two accounting methods.
3. Which method better measures income and assets? Use the last transaction to explain.

P3-63B As the controller of Stuart Enterprises Inc. you have hired a new employee, whom you must train. She objects to making an adjusting entry for accrued utilities at the end of the period. She reasons, "We will pay the utilities soon. Why not wait until payment to record the expense? In the end, the result will be the same." Write a reply to explain to the employee why the adjusting entry is needed for accrued utility expense.

Applying accounting principles
(Obj. 1, 2)

P3-64B Journalize the adjusting entry needed on December 31, 2009, the end of the current accounting period, for each of the following independent cases affecting Lee Computer Systems Inc. (LCSI). Include explanations for each entry.

Making accounting adjustments
(Obj. 3)

a. Each Friday, LCSI pays employees for the current week's work. The amount of the payroll is $5,000 for a 5-day work week. The current accounting period ends on Tuesday.
b. LCSI has received notes receivable from some clients for services. During the current year, LCSI has earned accrued interest revenue of $1,100, which will be received next year.
c. The beginning balance of Supplies was $1,800. During the year, LCSI purchased supplies costing $12,500, and at December 31 the inventory of supplies on hand is $2,900.
d. LCSI is developing software for a client and the client paid LCSI $20,000 at the start of the project. LCSI recorded this amount as Unearned Service Revenue. The software

development will take several months to complete. LCSI executives estimate that the company has earned three-quarters of the total fee during the current year.

e. Amortization for the current year includes Computer Equipment, $6,300, and Building, $3,700. Make a compound entry.

f. Details of Prepaid Insurance are shown in the Prepaid Insurance account. LCSI pays the annual insurance premium (the payment for insurance coverage is called a premium) on September 30 each year. At December 31, 9 months of insurance is still prepaid.

Prepaid Insurance			
Jan. 1	Bal.	1,800	
Sept. 30		3,600	

Preparing an adjusted trial balance and the financial statements; using the current ratio to evaluate the business
(Obj. 3, 4, 6)

P3-65B Consider the unadjusted trial balance of Creative Advertising Ltd. at October 31, 2009, and the related month-end adjustment data.

Creative Advertising Ltd.
Trial Balance
October 31, 2009

Cash	$16,300	
Accounts receivable	7,000	
Prepaid rent	4,000	
Supplies	600	
Computers	36,000	
Accumulated amortization		$ 3,000
Accounts payable		8,800
Salary payable		
Common shares		15,000
Retained earnings (September 30, 2008)		21,000
Dividends	4,600	
Advertising revenue		25,400
Salary expense	4,400	
Rent expense		
Utilities expense	300	
Amortization expense		
Supplies expense		
Total	$73,200	$73,200

Adjustment data:

a. Accrued advertising revenue at October 31, $2,900

b. Prepaid rent expired during the month. The unadjusted prepaid balance of $4,000 relates to the period October 2009 through January 2010.

c. Supplies used during October, $200

d. Amortization on computers for the month. The computer's expected useful life is three years.

e. Accrued salary expense at October 31 for Monday through Thursday; the five-day weekly payroll is $2,000.

❙ Required

1. Using Exhibit 3-9, page 120, as an example, prepare the adjusted trial balance of Creative Advertising Ltd. at October 31, 2009. Key each adjusting entry by letter.

2. Prepare the income statement, the statement of retained earnings, and the classified balance sheet. Draw arrows linking the three financial statements.

3. a. Compare the business's net income for October to the amount of dividends paid to the owners. Suppose this trend continues into November. What will be the effect on the business's financial position, as shown by its accounting equation?

b. Will the trend make it easier or more difficult for Creative Advertising Ltd. to borrow money if the business gets in a bind and needs cash? Why?

c. Does either the current ratio or the cash position suggest the need for immediate borrowing? Explain.

P3-66B Your Talent Agency Ltd.'s unadjusted and adjusted trial balances at December 31, 2009, are shown below.

Analyzing and recording adjustments
(Obj. 3)

Your Talent Agency Ltd.
Adjusted Trial Balance
December 31, 2009

Account Title	Trial Balance Debit	Trial Balance Credit	Adjusted Trial Balance Debit	Adjusted Trial Balance Credit
Cash	$ 4,100		$ 4,100	
Accounts receivable	11,200		12,400	
Supplies	1,000		700	
Prepaid insurance	2,600		900	
Office furniture	21,600		21, 600	
Accumulated amortization		$ 8,200		$ 9,300
Accounts payable		6,300		6,300
Salary payable				900
Interest payable				400
Note payable		6,000		6,000
Unearned commission revenue		1,500		1,100
Common shares		5,000		5,000
Retained earnings		3,500		3,500
Dividends	18,300		18,300	
Commission revenue		72,800		74,400
Amortization expense			1,100	
Supplies expense			300	
Utilities expense	4,900		4,900	
Salary expense	26,600		27,500	
Rent expense	12,200		12,200	
Interest expense	800		1,200	
Insurance expense			1,700	
	$103,300	$103,300	$106,900	$106,900

❙ *Required*

1. Make the adjusting entries that account for the difference between the two trial balances.

2. Compute Your Talent Agency Ltd.'s total assets, total liabilities, total equity, and net income.

3. Prove your answer with the accounting equation.

P3-67B The adjusted trial balance of Reid and Campbell Ltd. at December 31, 2009, appears on page 160.

Preparing the financial statements and using the debt ratio
(Obj. 4, 6)

❙ *Required*

1. Prepare Reid and Campbell Ltd.'s 2009 income statement, statement of retained earnings, and balance sheet. List expenses in decreasing order on the income statement and show total liabilities on the balance sheet. Draw arrows linking the three financial statements.

2. Compute Reid and Campbell Ltd.'s debt ratio at December 31, 2009, rounding to two decimal places. Evaluate the company's debt ratio as strong or weak.

Reid and Campbell Ltd.
Adjusted Trial Balance
December 31, 2009

Cash	$ 11,600	
Accounts receivable	41,400	
Prepaid rent	1,300	
Store furnishings	67,600	
Accumulated amortization		$ 12,900
Accounts payable		3,600
Deposits		4,500
Interest payable		2,100
Salary payable		900
Income tax payable		8,800
Note payable		26,200
Common shares		12,000
Retained earnings, Dec. 31, 2008		20,300
Dividends	48,000	
Sales		165,900
Amortization expense	11,300	
Salary expense	44,000	
Rent expense	12,000	
Interest expense	1,200	
Income tax expense	18,800	
Total	$257,200	$257,200

Preparing a classified balance sheet and using the ratios to evaluate the business
(Obj. 4, 6)

P3-68B The accounts of For You eTravel Inc. at December 31, 2009, are listed in alphabetical order.

Accounts payable	$ 5,100	Note payable, long-term	$10,600
Accounts receivable	6,600	Other assets	3,600
Accumulated amortization—furniture	11,600	Retained earnings,	
Advertising expense	2,200	December 31, 2008	5,300
Amortization expense	1,300	Salary expense	24,600
Cash	7,300	Salary payable	3,900
Common shares	15,000	Service revenue	93,500
Dividends	47,400	Supplies	7,700
Furniture	41,400	Supplies expense	5,700
Interest expense	800	Unearned service revenue	3,600

❙ Required

1. All adjustments have been journalized and posted, but the closing entries have not been made. Journalize For You eTravel Inc.'s closing entries at December 31, 2009.

2. Set up a T-account for Retained Earnings and post to that account. Compute For You's net income for the year ended December 31, 2009. What is the ending balance of Retained Earnings?

3. Did Retained Earnings increase or decrease during the year? What caused the increase or the decrease?

Closing the books and evaluating retained earnings
(Obj. 5)

P3-69B Refer to Problem 3-68B.

1. Use the For You eTravel Ltd. data in Problem 3-68B to prepare the company's classified balance sheet at December 31, 2009. Show captions for total assets, total liabilities, and total liabilities and shareholders' equity.

2. Evaluate For You's debt position as strong or weak, giving your reason. Assess whether For You's ability to pay both current and total debts improved or deteriorated during 2009. In order to complete your evaluation, compute For You's current and debt ratios at December 31, 2009, rounding to two decimal places. At December 31, 2008, the current ratio was 1.50 and the debt ratio was 0.45.

Analyzing financial ratios
(Obj. 6)

P3-70B This problem demonstrates the effects of transactions on the current ratio and the debt ratio of a company. A condensed balance sheet at March 31, 2008, is given in millions of dollars.

	(In millions)
Total current assets	$3.0
Properties (net) and other assets	3.8
	$6.8
Total current liabilities	$2.2
Total long-term liabilities	2.4
Total shareholders' equity	2.2
	$6.8

Assume that during the following year, ending March 31, 2009, the company completed the following transactions:

a. Paid half the current liabilities
b. Borrowed $3 million on long-term debt
c. Earned revenue of $2.5 million on account
d. Paid expenses of $1 million
e. Accrued salary expense of $0.8 million. Credit Salary Payable, which is a current liability.
f. Purchased equipment, paying cash of $1.8 million and signing a long-term note payable for $3.4 million
g. Recorded amortization expense of $0.6 million

❙ *Required*

Take all calculations to three decimal places.

1. Compute the company's current ratio and debt ratio at March 31, 2008.
2. Compute the company's current ratio and debt ratio after each transaction during 2009. Consider each transaction separately.
3. Based on your analysis, you should be able to readily identify the effects of certain transactions on the current ratio and the debt ratio. Test your understanding by completing these statements with either "increase" or "decrease":

   a. Revenues usually _____ the current ratio.
   b. Revenues usually _____ the debt ratio.
   c. Expenses usually _____ the current ratio. (*Note:* Amortization is an exception to this rule.)
   d. Expenses usually _____ the debt ratio.
   e. If a company's current ratio is greater than 1.0, paying off a current liability will always _____ the current ratio.
   f. Borrowing money on long-term debt will always _____ the current ratio and _____ the debt ratio.

APPLY YOUR KNOWLEDGE

DECISION CASES

Adjusting and correcting the accounts; computing and evaluating the current ratio
(Obj. 3, 6)

Case 1. Below is a list of accounts of Patel Consulting Ltd. at January 31, 2009. The unadjusted trial balance of Patel Consulting Ltd. at January 31, 2009, does not balance. In addition, the trial balance needs to be updated before the financial statements at January 31, 2009 can be prepared. The manager needs to know the current ratio of Patel Consulting Ltd.

Patel Consulting Ltd.		
List of Accounts		
January 31, 2009		
Cash	$ 6,000	
Accounts receivable	2,200	
Supplies	800	
Prepaid rent	12,000	
Land	41,000	
Accounts payable		10,000
Salary payable		0
Unearned service revenue		1,500
Note payable, due in three years		25,400
Common shares		15,000
Retained earnings		7,300
Service revenue		9,100
Salary expense	3,400	
Rent expense	0	
Advertising expense	900	
Supplies expense	0	
	?	?

❚ Required

1. How much *out of balance* is the trial balance? The error is in the Land account.
2. Patel Consulting Ltd. needs to make the following adjustments at January 31:
   a. Supplies of $600 were used during January.
   b. The balance of Prepaid Rent was paid on January 1 and covers the rest of 2009. No adjustment was made January 31.
   c. At January 31, Patel Consulting owes employees $400.
   d. Unearned service revenue of $800 was earned during January.

   Prepare a corrected, adjusted trial balance. Give Land its correct balance.
3. After the error is corrected and after these adjustments are made, compute the current ratio of Patel Consulting Ltd. If your business had this current ratio, could you sleep at night?

Preparing financial statements; continue or close the business?
(Obj. 3, 4)

Case 2. On October 1, Sue Skate opened a restaurant named Silver Skates Ltd. After the first month of operations, Sue is at a crossroads. The October financial statements paint a glowing picture of the business, and Sue has asked you whether she should expand Silver Skates.

To expand the business, Sue Skate wants to be earning net income of $10,000 per month and have total assets of $35,000. Based on the financial information available to her, Skate believes she is meeting both goals.

To start the business, she invested $20,000, not the $10,000 amount reported as "Common shares" on the balance sheet. The bookkeeper plugged the $10,000 "Common shares" amount into the balance sheet to make it come out even. The bookkeeper made other mistakes too. Skate shows you the following financial statements that the bookkeeper prepared.

Silver Skates Ltd.
Income Statement
For the Month Ended October 31, 2009

Revenues:		
Investments by owner	$20,000	
Unearned banquet sales revenue	3,000	
		$23,000
Expenses:		
Wages expense	$ 5,000	
Rent expense	4,000	
Dividends	3,000	
Amortization expense—fixtures	1,000	
		13,000
Net income (Net loss)		$10,000

Silver Skates Ltd.
Balance Sheet
October 31, 2009

Assets:		Liabilities:	
Cash	$ 6,000	Accounts payable	$ 5,000
Prepaid insurance	1,000	Sales revenue	32,000
Insurance expense	1,000	Accumulated amortization—	
Food inventory	3,000	fixture	1,000
Cost of goods sold (expense)	14,000		38,000
Fixtures (tables, chairs, etc.)	19,000	Owners' equity:	
Dishes and silverware	4,000	Common shares	10,000
	$48,000		$48,000

❙ *Required*

Prepare corrected financial statements for Silver Skates Ltd.: income statement, statement of retained earnings, and balance sheet. Then, based on your corrected statements, recommend to Sue Skates whether she should expand her business.

Case 3. Walter Liu has owned and operated LW Media Inc. since its beginning 10 years ago. Recently, Liu mentioned that he would consider selling the company for the right price.

Valuing a business on the basis of its net income **(Obj. 3, 4)**

Assume that you are interested in buying this business. You obtain its most recent monthly trial balance, which follows on the next page. Revenues and expenses vary little from month to month, and June is a typical month. Your investigation reveals that the trial balance does not include the effects of monthly revenues of $5,000 and expenses totalling $1,100. If you were to buy LW Media Inc., you would hire a manager so you could devote your time to other duties. Assume that your manager would require a monthly salary of $6,000.

❙ *Required*

1. Assume that the most you would pay for the business is 20 times the monthly net income *you could expect to earn* from it. Compute this possible price.
2. Walter Liu states that the least he will take for the business is 1.5 times shareholders' equity on June 30, 2009. Compute this amount.
3. Under these conditions, how much should you offer Liu? Give your reason.

LW Media Inc.		
Trial Balance		
June 30, 2009		
Cash	$ 10,000	
Accounts receivable	4,900	
Prepaid expenses	3,200	
Equipment	115,000	
Accumulated amortization		$ 76,500
Land	158,000	
Accounts payable		13,800
Salary payable		
Unearned revenue		56,700
Common shares		50,000
Retained earnings		88,000
Dividends	9,000	
Revenue		20,000
Rent expense		
Salary expense	4,000	
Utilities expense	900	
Amortization expense		
Supplies expense		
Total	$305,000	$305,000

ETHICAL ISSUES

Issue 1. ARAS Inc. is in its third year of operations and the company has grown. To expand the business, ARAS borrowed $1 million from **Royal Bank of Canada**. As a condition for making this loan, the bank required that ARAS maintain a current ratio of at least 1.50 and a debt ratio of no more than 0.50.

Business recently has been worse than expected. Expenses have brought the current ratio down to 1.47 and the debt ratio up to 0.51 at December 15. Shane Rollins, the general manager, is considering the implication of reporting this current ratio to the bank. Rollins is considering recording this year some revenue on account that ARAS will earn next year. The contract for this job has been signed, and ARAS will perform the service during January.

❙ *Required*

1. Journalize the revenue transaction, omitting amounts, and indicate how recording this revenue in December would affect the current ratio and the debt ratio.
2. State whether it is ethical to record the revenue transaction in December. Identify the accounting principle relevant to this situation.
3. Propose to ARAS a course of action that is ethical.

Issue 2. The net income of Accent Photography Company Ltd. decreased sharply during 2008. Mark Smith, owner of the company, anticipates the need for a bank loan in 2009. Late in 2008, he instructed the accountant to record a $20,000 sale of portraits to the Smith family, even though the photos will not be shot until January 2009. Smith also told the accountant *not* to make the following December 31, 2008, adjusting entries:

Salaries owed to employees	$5,000
Prepaid insurance that has expired	1,000

❙ *Required*

1. Compute the overall effect of these transactions on the company's reported income for 2009. Is income overstated or understated?
2. Why did Smith take these actions? Are they ethical? Give your reason, identifying the parties helped and the parties harmed by Smith's action.
3. As a personal friend, what advice would you give the accountant?

FOCUS ON FINANCIALS

Sun-Rype Products Ltd.

Like all other business, Sun-Rype adjusts accounts prior to year-end to measure assets, liabilities, revenues, and expenses for the financial statements. Examine Sun-Rype's balance sheet in Appendix A, and pay particular attention to (a) Prepaid Expenses and (b) Accounts Payable and Accrued Liabilities.

Tracing account balance to the financial statements
(Obj. 3, 6)

❙ *Required*

1. Why aren't Prepaid Expenses "true" expenses? What word could be added to Accrued Liabilities to make the nature of this account clear?
2. Open T-accounts for the Prepaid Expenses account and the Accounts Payable and Accrued Liabilities account. Insert Sun-Rype's balances (in thousands) at December 31, 2006.
3. Journalize the following for the year ended December 31, 2007. Key entries by letter, and show accounts in thousands. Explanations are not required.
   a. Paid the beginning balance of Accounts Payable and Accrued Liabilities
   b. Paid Prepaid Expenses of $2,300
   c. Recorded Accounts Payable and Accrued Liabilities for the ending balance in the amount of $12,688. Assume this is a cost of sale expense.
   d. Recorded Selling and Administrative Expenses so the ending balance of Prepaid Expenses is equal to its opening balance.
4. Post these entries and show that the balances in Prepaid Expenses and in Accounts Payable and Accrued Liabilities agree with the corresponding amounts reported in the December 31, 2007, balance sheet.
5. Compute the current ratios and debt ratios for Sun-Rype at December 31, 2007, and at December 31, 2006. Did the ratio values improve, deteriorate, or hold steady during the year ended December 31, 2007? Do the ratio values indicate financial strength or weakness?

FOCUS ON ANALYSIS

Mullen Group Income Fund

During the year 2007, Mullen Group (Appendix B) had numerous accruals and deferrals. As a new member of Mullen Group accounting and financial staff, it is your job to explain the effects of accruals and deferrals on Mullen Group net income for 2007. The accrual and deferral data follow, along with questions that Mullen unitholders have raised (all amounts in thousands):

Explaining accruals and deferrals
(Obj. 3)

1. Beginning total receivables for 2007 were $209,545 (all amounts in thousands). Ending receivables for 2007 are $185,475. Which of these amounts did Mullen earn in 2006? Which amount did Mullen earn in 2007? Which amount is included in Mullen's revenue for 2007?
2. Accumulated amortization on Property, plant, and equipment stood at $143,298 at December 31, 2006, and at $194,841 at December 31, 2007. Accumulated amortization was reduced by $6,141 for assets sold during the year. Calculate the amortization expense for the year, and compare to the amortization expense reported on the income statement.

3. Certain income-statement accounts are directly linked to specific balance-sheet accounts other than cash. Examine Mullen's income statement in Appendix B. For each revenue and expense account that you can do so, excluding retained earnings, identify the related balance sheet account(s) (other than cash).

GROUP PROJECT

Matt Davis formed a lawn service company as a summer job. To start the business on May 1, he deposited $1,000 in a new bank account in the name of the corporation. The $1,000 consisted of an $800 loan from his father and $200 of his own money. The corporation issued 200 common shares to Davis.

Davis rented lawn equipment, purchased supplies, and hired high-school students to mow and trim his customers' lawns. At the end of each month, Davis mailed bills to his customers. On August 31, Davis was ready to dissolve the business and return to Simon Fraser University for the fall semester. Because he had been so busy, he had kept few records other than his chequebook and a list of amounts owed by customers.

At August 31, Davis's chequebook shows a balance of $1,390, and his customers still owe him $560. During the summer, he collected $5,150 from customers. His chequebook lists payments for supplies totalling $400, and he still has gasoline, weedeater cord, and other supplies that cost a total of $50. He paid his employees wages of $1,900, and he still owes them $200 for the final week of the summer.

Davis rented some equipment from Ludwig Tool Company. On May 1, he signed a six-month lease on mowers and paid $600 for the full lease period. Ludwig will refund the unused portion of the prepayment if the equipment is in good shape. To get the refund, Davis has kept the mowers in excellent condition. In fact, he had to pay $300 to repair a mower that ran over a hidden tree stump.

To transport equipment to jobs, Davis used a trailer that he bought for $300. He figures that the summer's work used up one-third of the trailer's service potential. The business chequebook lists an expenditure of $460 for dividends paid to Davis during the summer. Also, Davis paid his father back during the summer.

I *Required*

1. Prepare the income statement of Davis Lawn Service Inc. for the four months, May through August. The business is not subject to income tax.
2. Prepare the classified balance sheet of Davis Lawn Service Inc. at August 31.

QUICK CHECK ANSWERS

1. *c*	5. *d*	9. *d*	13. *a*
2. *c*	6. *b*	10. *a*	14. *c*
3. *b*	7. *a*	11. *b*	15. *a*
4. *d*	8. *d*	12. *d*	17. *b*

Internal Control and Cash

4

Learning Objectives

1. **Set up** an internal control system

2. **Prepare** and use a bank reconciliation

3. **Apply** internal controls to cash receipts and cash payments

4. **Use** a budget to manage your cash

5. **Make** ethical business judgments

SPOTLIGHT

"I've never been so shocked in my life!" exclaimed Lee Grant, manager of the GreBru Products Inc. office in Vancouver, British Columbia. "This goes to show how important internal controls are."

Grant just returned from the trial of Marty Popplewell, who was convicted of embezzlement. Popplewell had been the cashier of the GreBru Products Inc. office in Vancouver. As cashier, Popplewell received client cash that came in by mail. Unknown to Grant, Popplewell had been "robbing Peter to pay Paul"—that is, transferring client collections to Popplewell's own account and then applying the next client cash receipt to cover the missing amount. With access to client accounts, Popplewell could juggle the books to keep anyone from discovering his scheme. This embezzlement had been going on for three years, and the trial proved that Popplewell had stolen $62,000 from the company.

What tipped off Grant to the embezzlement? Popplewell was involved in an auto accident and couldn't work for two weeks. The employee covering for Popplewell saw too many irregularities in client accounts. The ensuing investigation pointed to Popplewell, and Grant then turned the case over to the police.

Shortly after the trial, Grant revamped the internal controls at GreBru Products. Now Grant rotates employees from job to job. That way there's always someone checking up on someone else. And now the cashier has no access to client accounting records.

Popplewell's scheme is well known to accountants. It is called lapping—similar to laying shingles on a roof. Lapping takes lots of ingenuity and purpose. The thief has to keep the scheme going or it unravels quickly. That's what happened when Popplewell wasn't on the job to juggle the books.

GreBru Products Inc. Balance Sheet (Partial, Adapted)	
Assets	**December 31, 2009**
Cash and cash equivalents	$ 6,260
Accounts receivable	2,000
Inventories	36,200
Prepaid expenses	1,400
Investments	10,000
Property, plant, and equipment (net of accumulated amortization of $2,400)	13,170
Other assets	3,930
Total assets	$81,250

This chapter covers the basics of internal control. It also shows how to account for cash. These two topics—internal control and cash—go together because cash is the asset that is stolen most often.

The excerpt from the GreBru Products balance sheet reports the company's assets. Focus on the top line, Cash and cash equivalents. At December 31, 2009, GreBru reported cash of $8,260. If Popplewell's scheme hadn't been detected, the reported cash balance would have been overstated. One purpose of internal control is to produce accurate and reliable accounting records.

Internal Control

Managers must control the operations of their business. Those charged with governance set goals, managers lead the way, and employees carry out plans. If managers don't control operations, the entity may suffer losses unnecessarily, as GreBru Products Inc. did.

Internal control is the organizational plan and all the related measures that an entity adopts that are designed to accomplish five objectives:

1. **Safeguard assets and records**. A company must safeguard its assets and records; otherwise it's throwing away resources. If you fail to safeguard your cash, it will slip away.

2. **Encourage employees to follow company policy**. Everyone in an organization—managers and employees—needs to work toward the same goal. It's also important for managers to develop policies so that the company treats customers and employees fairly.

3. **Promote operational efficiency**. You cannot afford to waste resources. You work hard to make a sale, and you don't want to waste any of the benefits. If the company can buy something for $30, why pay $35? Eliminate waste, and increase your profits.

4. **Ensure accurate, reliable accounting records**. Good records are essential. Without reliable records, you cannot tell which part of the business is profitable and which part needs improvement. You could be losing money on every product you sell—unless you keep good records for the cost of your products.

5. **Comply with legal requirements**, such as legislation relating to the environment. Companies, like people, are subject to the law. When companies disobey the law, they must pay fines or, in extreme cases, their top executives go to prison.

How critical are internal controls? They're so important that the Ontario Legislature passed a law[*] to require public companies—those that sell their shares to the public—to maintain a system of internal controls. Exhibit 4-1 gives Loblaw Companies management's Statement of Responsibility for Financial Reporting.

The Sarbanes-Oxley Act (SOX)

The Enron and WorldCom accounting scandals rocked the United States. Enron overstated profits and went out of business almost overnight. WorldCom (now MCI) reported expenses as assets and overstated both profits and assets. The company only recently emerged from bankruptcy.

As the scandals unfolded, many people asked, "How can these things happen? Where were the auditors?" To address public concern, U.S. Congress passed the *Sarbanes-Oxley Act of 2002*, abbreviated as SOX. SOX revamped corporate governance in the United States and also had sweeping effects on the accounting profession. It will take several years to determine how SOX affects financial reporting. Securities regulators in Canada and around the world considered the SOX requirements in light of their own countries' capital markets.

A **public company** offers its securities, such as shares or debt, for sale to the general public. A **private company** does not offer its securities, such as shares or debt, for sale to the general public.

Canadian-listed public companies are regulated by one of the 13 (10 provinces and 3 territories) security commissions in Canada. The 13 security commissions have formed an umbrella organization called the Canadian Securities Administrators (CSA), which issues Staff Notices and National Instruments on behalf of the 13 security commissions.

The CSA began work on developing a Canadian strategy incorporating some or all of the rules in SOX for Canadian public companies. On July 11, 2008, the CSA issued Staff Notice 52-322, which stated that National Instrument 52-109 would be issued subject to commission approvals "as soon as practicable" and that NI 52-109 would have an effective date (that is, would apply to filing companies with year-ends

| EXHIBIT 4-1 | Loblaw Companies Limited Management's Statement of Responsibility for Financial Reporting |

Management's Statement of Responsibility for Financial Reporting

To provide reasonable assurance that assets are safeguarded and that relevant and reliable financial information is produced, management is required to design a system of internal controls and certify as to the design effectiveness of internal controls over financial reporting. Internal auditors, who are employees of the company, review and evaluate internal controls on management's behalf.

---

[*]Bill 198 (Chapter 22, Statutes of Ontario, 2002) *An Act to implement Budget Measures and other initiatives of the Government.*

on or after the effective date) of December 15, 2008. Some of the requirements of interest of NI 52-109 are:

- "The CEO and CFO [certifying officers] must certify that they have evaluated the effectiveness of the issuer's [internal control over financial reporting] (ICFR) and disclosed in the annual [management discussion and analysis] (MD&A) their conclusions about the effectiveness of ICFR at the financial year end."

- "MD&A disclosure is required for each material weakness related to ICFR. Issuers are not required to remediate a material weakness; however, they must disclose plans, if any, to remediate one."

- "The . . . rules require the CEO and CFO to certify each quarter, among other things, that they have designed [disclosure controls and procedures] DC&P and ICFR and disclosed changes in ICFR that have materially affected or are reasonably likely to materially affect the issuer's ICFR."

- In addition, the rules require "certifying officers to disclose any ICFR design weaknesses in MD&A."

Exhibit 4-2 shows the shield that internal controls provide for an organization. Protected by the shield, people do business securely. How does a business achieve good internal control? The next section identifies the components of internal control.

The Components of Internal Control

Objective

❶ **Set up** an internal control system

Internal control can be broken down into five components:

- Control environment
- Risk assessment
- Control procedures
- Monitoring of controls
- Information system

Control Environment. The control environment is the "tone at the top" of the business. It starts with the owner and the top managers. They must behave honourably to set a good example for company employees. The owner must demonstrate the importance of internal controls if he or she expects employees to take the controls seriously. Former executives of Enron, WorldCom, and Tyco failed to establish a strong control environment, and their companies suffered as a result.

Risk Assessment. A company must identify its risks. For example, CN Rail faces the risk of a derailment. Air Canada faces the risk of high fuel costs. And all companies

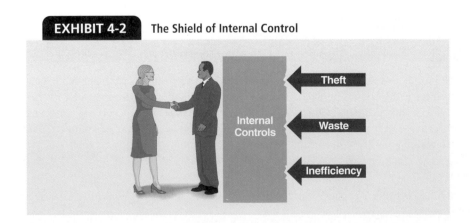

EXHIBIT 4-2 The Shield of Internal Control

face the risk of bankruptcy. Companies facing difficulties are tempted to falsify the financial statements to make themselves look better than they really are.

Control Procedures. These are the procedures designed to ensure that the business's goals are achieved. Examples include assigning responsibilities, separating duties, and using security devices to protect assets from theft. The next section discusses internal control procedures.

Monitoring of Controls. Companies hire auditors to monitor their controls. Internal auditors monitor company controls to safeguard the company's assets, and external auditors monitor the controls to ensure that the accounting records are accurate.

Information System. As we have seen, the information system is critical. The owner of a business needs accurate information to make the best decisions, to keep track of assets, and to accurately measure profits and losses.

Internal Control Procedures

Exhibit 4-3 shows the components of internal control.

    Whether business is GreBru Products, Research In Motion, or a Petro-Canada gas station, you need the following internal control procedures.

Competent, Reliable, and Ethical Personnel. Employees should be *competent, reliable*, and *ethical*. Paying good salaries will attract high-quality employees. You must also train them to do the job, supervise their work, and reward them fairly. This will build a competent staff.

Assignment of Responsibilities. In a business with good internal controls, no important duty is overlooked. Each employee has certain responsibilities. Large corporations have a vice-president of finance and accounting, sometimes called the chief financial officer or CFO. Two other officers, the treasurer and the controller, report to that vice-president. The **treasurer** manages cash, and the **controller** is in charge of accounting.

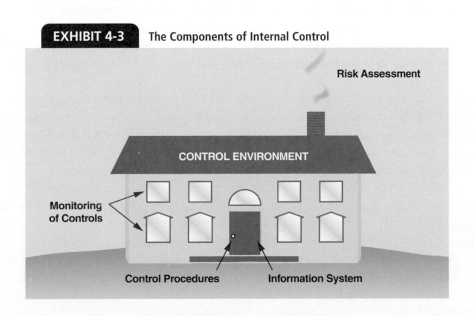

EXHIBIT 4-3   **The Components of Internal Control**

The controller may be responsible for approving invoices (bills) for payment, while the treasurer may actually sign the cheques. With clearly assigned responsibilities, all important jobs get done.

Proper Authorization.   An organization needs rules that outline approval procedures. Any deviation from company policy requires *proper authorization*. For example, managers of retail stores must approve customer cheques for amounts above the store's usual limit. Managers must approve customers' credit limits being exceeded and discounts in excess of advertised discounts and stated prices.

Separation of Duties.   Smart management divides responsibilities for transactions between two or more people. *Separation of duties* limits the chances for fraud and promotes the accuracy of accounting records. Separation of duties, often mentioned as the cornerstone of internal control, can be divided into two parts:

1. **Separate operations from accounting**. Accounting should be completely separate from the operating departments, such as manufacturing and sales. For example, computer programmers should not operate a company's computers, because they can program the computer to write cheques or ship goods to themselves.

2. **Separate the custody of assets from accounting**. Accountants should not be allowed to handle cash and cashiers should have no access to the accounting records. If one employee has both cash-handling and accounting duties, that person can steal cash and conceal the theft by making a bogus entry on the books. We saw this breakdown of internal control in the chapter-opening story.

Audits.   An important component of internal control is the assurance provided by external and internal auditors. Both groups, as part of their activities, test and assess the company's internal controls. To validate their accounting records, most companies have an audit. An **audit** is an examination of the company's financial statements and accounting system. To evaluate the system, auditors examine the internal controls.

Audits can be internal or external. *Internal auditors* are employees of the business. They ensure that employees are following company policies and operations are running efficiently. Internal auditors also determine whether the company is following legal requirements.

External auditors are independent public accounting firms who are hired by a company's board of directors on behalf of the shareholders to determine whether or not the company's financial statements agree with generally accepted accounting principles (GAAP).

The accounting firm audits the financial statements by first gaining an understanding of the company and its accounting system and evaluating the company's internal controls. The firm then provides an opinion on whether the company's financial statements "present fairly" the company's financial position, results of operations, and cash flows according to some specified criteria, usually GAAP. Management may be intentionally or unintentionally biased in their reporting and research has shown that the independent audit reduces management bias. Users of financial statements value the audit for that reason.

USER ALERT

Are the Outside Auditors Really Independent?

Incorporation legislation and securities regulations in Canada require companies issuing securities to the public to have annual audits of their financial statements by independent accountants. The purpose is to ensure that the information in the company's financial statements is relevant and reliable. Auditors should be independent of their clients so that they can issue an unbiased opinion on the financial statements they audit. In September 2003, the Canadian Institute of Chartered Accountants' Public Interest and Integrity Committee issued a *Rule of Professional Conduct* that establishes standards of independence for auditors and other assurance providers. The new standard mirrors the current independence standards related to the audit of public companies issued by both the International Federation of Accountants (IFAC) and the U.S. Securities and Exchange Commission (SEC).

The specific prohibitions under the new rule include:

- Auditors having a financial interest in the client
- Auditors having a close business relationship with the client

In addition, the audit committee is required to approve services to be provided to the audit client by the accounting firm. Consider the two cases described below and you will see a difference.

Case 1. John Smith is the auditor of Allied Building Products. Smith's investment portfolio is made up primarily of majority shareholdings in Batten Construction Co. Ltd. and Craggy Range Properties Inc., a property developer. Both are significant customers of Allied Building Products Inc.

Case 2. Marilyn Chu is the auditor of Darwin Corp., a plumbing supply company. Marilyn's investments are primarily in bonds issued by the federal and provincial governments and in mutual funds.

In which company's financial information, Allied or Darwin, would you have more confidence?

Under the CICA's Public Interest and Integrity Committee's Rule of Professional Conduct, Smith could not be the auditor of Allied because of his financial interests in Batten and Craggy Range. On the other hand, Marilyn's investments bear no relationship to her audit client.

The take-away lesson is:

- Ensure that the auditor is independent of the client. Otherwise, the auditor is not likely to provide an unbiased opinion on the client's financial statements.

Documents and Records. *Documents* provide the details of business transactions. Documents include invoices and fax orders. Documents should be prenumbered to prevent theft and inefficiency. A gap in the numbered sequence draws attention.

In a bowling alley a key document is the score sheet. The manager can compare the number of games scored with the amount of cash received. Multiply the number of games by the charge per game and compare the revenue with cash receipts. You can see whether the business is collecting all the revenue.

Bowling Scorecard			101
Ron			SCORE
X \ — X X \ X \ — X			113
Sue			
X X X X X X X X X			300
Games	Charge per Game		Total Revenue
2	×	$3 =	$6

Electronic Devices. Businesses use electronic devices to safeguard assets. Retailers such as Hudson's Bay Co. and Sears Canada Inc. control inventories by attaching *electronic sensors* to merchandise. If a customer tries to leave the store with a sensor still attached, an alarm sounds. According to Checkpoint Systems, these electronic sensors reduce theft by as much as 50%.

Bar codes speed checkout at a store, and *surveillance cameras* help identify shoplifters.

Other Controls

Businesses keep important documents in *fireproof vaults. Burglar alarms* protect buildings, and *security cameras* protect other property. *Loss-prevention specialists* train employees to spot suspicious activity.

Employees who handle cash are in a tempting position. Many businesses purchase *fidelity bonds* on cashiers. The bond is an insurance policy that reimburses the company for any losses due to employee theft. Before issuing a fidelity bond, the insurance company investigates the employee's background.

Mandatory vacations and *job rotation* improve internal control. Companies move employees from job to job. This improves morale by giving employees a broad view of the business. Also, knowing someone else will do your job next month keeps you honest. Initially, GreBru Products didn't rotate employees to different jobs, and it cost the company $622,000.

Internal Controls for E-Commerce

E-commerce creates its own risks. Hackers may gain access to confidential information such as account numbers and passwords.

Pitfalls

E-commerce pitfalls include:

- Stolen credit-card numbers
- Computer viruses and Trojan Horses
- Phishing expeditions

Stolen Credit-Card Numbers. Suppose you buy CDs from eMusic.com. To make the purchase, your credit-card number must travel through cyberspace. Wireless networks (Wi-Fi) are creating new security hazards.

Amateur hacker Carlos Salgado, Jr., used his home computer to steal 100,000 credit-card numbers with a combined limit exceeding $1 billion. Salgado was caught when he tried to sell the numbers to an undercover police woman.

Computer Viruses and Trojan Horses. A *computer virus* is a malicious program that (a) enters program code without consent and (b) performs destructive actions in the victim's computer files or programs. A *Trojan Horse* is a malicious computer program that hides inside a legitimate program and works like a virus. Viruses can destroy or alter data, make bogus calculations, and infect files. Most firms have had a problem with viruses.

Phishing Expeditions. Thieves phish by creating bogus Web sites, such as AOL4Free.com and freecds.com. The neat-sounding Web sites attract lots of visitors, and the thieves obtain account numbers and passwords from unsuspecting people. The thieves then use the data for illicit purposes.

Security Measures

To address the risks posed by e-commerce, companies have devised a number of security measures, including:

- Encryption
- Firewalls

Encryption. The server holding confidential information may not be secure. One technique for protecting customer data is encryption. *Encryption* rearranges messages by a mathematical process. The encrypted message can't be read by those who don't know the code. An accounting example uses check-sum digits for account numbers. Each account number has its last digit equal to the sum of the previous digits. For example, consider Customer Number 2237, where $2 + 2 + 3 = 7$. Any account number that fails this test triggers an error message.

Firewalls. *Firewalls* limit access into a local network. Members can access the network but nonmembers can't. Usually several firewalls are built into the system.

Think of a fortress with multiple walls protecting the king's chamber in the centre. At the point of entry, passwords, PINs (personal identification numbers), and signatures are used. More sophisticated firewalls are used deeper in the network. Start with Firewall 1, and work toward the centre.

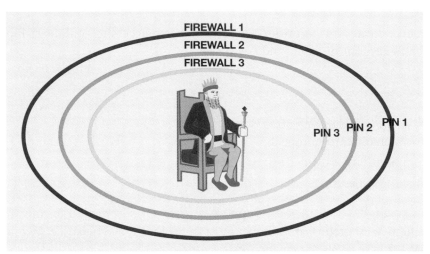

USER ALERT

Two Faces of Internal Control

Internal controls are designed to safeguard assets, encourage adherence to company policies, promote operational efficiency, ensure accurate and reliable accounting records and comply with legal requirements. Two examples illustrate how things can go wrong.

1. *Weak separation of duties* An employee of the *St. Catharines Standard* stole $2.2 million from her employer. Lucy Magda apparently diverted cheques received in the mail and used them to conceal thefts of cash from the daily bank deposits. The theft was concealed by removing and destroying invoices for which the cheques were payment. Giving the advertising manager access to incoming receipts and the related invoices gave the manager the opportunity to steal and doctor the records to cover the theft.

   The most obvious way to limit this risk is to deny the cashier access to accounting records. But in many companies, especially small businesses, it isn't feasible to separate all duties. To manage its risk, the *St. Catharines Standard* could have done several things:

   - Require employees to take vacations. That way other employees must review the work of the one on vacation. Discrepancies will probably come to light.
   - Routinely check on the advertising manager's work. For example, another employee can reconcile customer accounts. Discrepancies can then be detected.
   - Mail questionnaires to customers, and ask them to confirm their account balances to a responsible official of the company. Investigate all discrepancies.

2. *No proper authorization* Auditors at the Department of National Defence and the Department of Public Works uncovered a fraud that may have operated over 10 years and resulted in the government paying up to $160 million for military computer hardware and support services it never received. Defence Minister David Pratt stated that there was a "very deliberate and well-crafted strategy to hide irregularities from audit teams at both Defence and Public Works."

   Good internal control systems include a system of authorizations for credit limits and approvals for purchases and payments, usually with a limit imposed. The *Financial Administration Act* had such limits; public servants could authorize payments up to $250,000. It seems that the perpetrators of the fraud made a series of fraudulent purchases for amounts under $250,000. In addition, the perpetrators argued that national security required that secrecy surround the transactions. Thus the transactions escaped detection. The three perpetrators of the fraud pleaded guilty in 2007 and were sentenced to jail terms.

   Sources: www.ctv.ca, March 11, 2004; www.canada.com, September 17, 2007.

Limitations of Internal Control—Costs and Benefits

Unfortunately, most internal control measures can be overcome. Systems designed to thwart one person's fraud can be beaten by two or more employees working together—*colluding*—to defraud the firm. Consider the Galaxy Theatre. Ralph, who sells tickets, and Lana, who takes the tickets, can design a scheme in which Ralph sells tickets and pockets the cash from 10 customers. Lana admits 10 customers without tickets. Ralph and Lana split the cash. To prevent this situation, Colleen, the manager, must take additional steps, such as matching the number of people in the theatre against the number of ticket stubs retained. But that takes time away from her other duties.

The stricter the internal control system, the more it costs. A too-complex system of internal control can strangle the business with red tape. How tight should the controls be? Internal controls must be judged in light of their costs and benefits. An example of a good cost/benefit relationship: A security guard at a Wal-Mart store costs about $28,000 a year. On average, each guard prevents about $50,000 of theft. The net savings to Wal-Mart is $22,000.

The Bank Account as a Control Device

Cash is the most liquid asset because it is the medium of exchange. Cash is easy to conceal and relatively easy to steal. As a result, most businesses have specific controls for cash.

Keeping cash in a bank account helps control cash. This is important because banks have established practices for safeguarding customers' money. The documents used to control bank accounts include:

- Signature cards
- Deposit slips
- Cheques
- Bank statements
- Bank reconciliations

Signature Cards

Banks require each person authorized to sign on an account to provide a *signature card*. This protects against forgery.

Deposit Slips

Banks supply standard forms such as *deposit slips*. The customer fills in the amount of each deposit. As proof of the transaction, the customer keeps a deposit receipt.

Cheques

To pay cash, the depositor can write a **cheque**, which tells the bank to pay the designated party a specified amount. There are three parties to a cheque:

- The maker, who signs the cheque
- The payee, to whom the cheque is paid
- The bank on which the cheque is drawn

Exhibit 4-4 shows a cheque drawn by Nixon Partners Inc., the maker. The cheque has two parts, the cheque itself and the *remittance advice* below. This optional attachment tells the payee the reason for the payment.

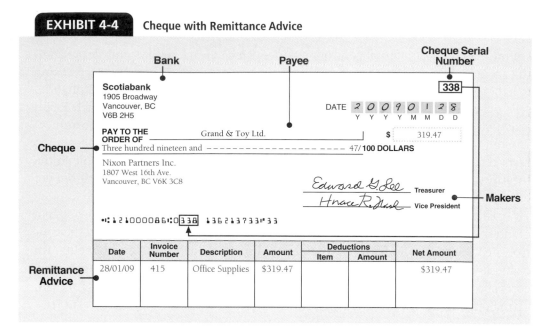

EXHIBIT 4-4 Cheque with Remittance Advice

Electronic Funds Transfer

Electronic funds transfer (EFT) is a system that moves cash by electronic communications. It is cheaper for a company to pay employees by EFT (direct deposit) than by issuing payroll cheques. Many people pay their regular bills, such as mortgage, rent, and utilities, by EFT.

Bank Statements

Banks send monthly statements to customers. A **bank statement** reports what the bank did with the customer's cash. The statement shows the account's beginning and ending balances, cash receipts, and payments. Included with the statement are copies of the maker's *cancelled cheques* (or the actual paid cheques). Exhibit 4-5 is the January 2009 bank statement of Nixon Partners Inc.

Bank Reconciliations

There are two records of a business's cash:

1. The Cash account in the company's general ledger. Exhibit 4-6 shows that Nixon Partners Inc.'s ending cash balance is $3,294.21.

2. The bank statement, which shows the cash receipts and payments transacted through the bank. In Exhibit 4-5, the bank shows an ending balance of $5,931.51 for Nixon Partners.

The books and the bank statement usually show different cash balances. Differences arise because of a time lag in recording transactions. Here are two examples:

- When you write a cheque, you immediately deduct it in your chequebook. But the bank does not subtract the cheque from your account until the bank pays the cheque a few days later. And you immediately add the cash receipt for all your deposits. But it may take a day or two for the bank to add deposits to your balance.

- Your EFT payments and cash receipts are recorded by the bank before you learn of them.

EXHIBIT 4-5   Bank Statement

ACCOUNT STATEMENT

Scotiabank
1905 Broadway Vancouver, BC V6B 2H5

Nixon Partners Inc.
1807 West 16th Avenue
Vancouver, BC V6K 3C8

BUSINESS CHEQUING ACCOUNT 136–213733

CHEQUING ACCOUNT SUMMARY AS OF 31/01/09

BEGINNING BALANCE	TOTAL DEPOSITS	TOTAL WITHDRAWALS	SERVICE CHARGES	ENDING BALANCE
6,556.12	4,352.64	4,963.00	14.25	5,931.51

BUSINESS CHEQUING ACCOUNT TRANSACTIONS

DEPOSITS	DATE	AMOUNT
Deposit	Jan04	1,000.00
Deposit	Jan04	112.00
Deposit	Jan06	194.60
EFT—Collection of rent	Jan10	904.03
Bank Collection	Jan16	2,114.00
Interest	Jan20	28.01

CHARGES	DATE	AMOUNT
Service Charge	Jan31	14.25
Cheques:		

CHEQUES			BALANCES			
Number	Date	Amount	Date	Balance	Date	Balance
332	Jan06	3,000.00	Dec31	6,556.12	Jan16	7,378.75
656	Jan06	100.00	Jan04	7,616.12	Jan20	7,405.76
333	Jan10	150.00	Jan06	4,710.72	Jan25	5,945.76
334	Jan12	100.00	Jan10	5,464.75	Jan31	5,931.51
335	Jan12	100.00	Jan12	5,264.75		
336	Jan25	1,100.00				

OTHER CHARGES	DATE	AMOUNT
NSF	Jan04	52.00
EFT—Insurance	Jan20	361.00

MONTHLY SUMMARY

Withdrawals: 8	Minimum Balance: 4,710.72	Average Balance: 6,215.00

EXHIBIT 4-6   Cash Records of Nixon Partners Inc.

ACCOUNT   Cash

Date		Item	Debit	Credit	Balance
2009					
Jan.	1	Balance			6,556.12
	2	Cash receipt	1,112.00		7,668.12
	5	Cash receipt	194.60		7,862.72
	31	Cash payments		6,160.14	1,702.58
	31	Cash receipt	1,591.63		3,294.21

Cash Payments

Cheque No.	Amount	Cheque No.	Amount
332	$3,000.00	338	$ 319.47
333	510.00	339	83.00
334	100.00	340	203.14
335	100.00	341	458.53
336	1,100.00		
337	286.00	Total	$6,160.14

To ensure accurate cash records, you need to update your cash record—either online or after you receive your bank statement. The result of this updating process allows you to prepare a **bank reconciliation**. The bank reconciliation explains all differences between your cash records and your bank balance.

The person who prepares the bank reconciliation should have no other cash duties and be independent of cash activities. Otherwise, he or she can steal cash and manipulate the reconciliation to conceal the theft.

Preparing the Bank Reconciliation

Here are the items that appear on a bank reconciliation. They all cause differences between the bank balance and the book balance. We call your cash record (also known as a "chequebook") the "Books."

Bank Side of the Reconciliation.

1. Items to show on the *Bank* side of the bank reconciliation:
    a. **Deposits in transit** (outstanding deposits). You have recorded these deposits, but the bank has not. Add deposits in transit on the bank reconciliation.
    b. **Outstanding cheques**. You have recorded these cheques, but the bank has not yet paid them. Subtract outstanding cheques.
    c. **Bank errors**. Correct all bank errors on the Bank side of the reconciliation. For example, the bank may erroneously subtract from your account a cheque written by someone else.

Book Side of the Reconciliation.

2. Items to show on the *Book* side of the bank reconciliation:
    a. **Bank collections**. Bank collections are cash receipts that the bank has recorded for your account. But you haven't recorded the cash receipt yet. Many businesses have their customers pay directly to their bank. This is called a *lockbox system* and reduces theft. An example is a bank collecting an account receivable for you. Add bank collections on the bank reconciliation.
    b. **Electronic funds transfers**. The bank may receive or pay cash on your behalf. An EFT may be a cash receipt or a cash payment. Add EFT receipts and subtract EFT payments.
    c. **Service charge**. This cash payment is the bank's fee for processing your transactions. Subtract service charges.
    d. **Interest revenue on your chequing account**. You earn interest if you keep enough cash in your account. The bank statement tells you of this cash receipt. Add interest revenue.
    e. **Nonsufficient funds (NSF) cheques** are your earlier cash receipts that have turned out to be worthless. NSF cheques (sometimes called bad cheques) are treated as cash payments on your bank reconciliation. Subtract NSF cheques.
    f. **The cost of printed cheques**. This cash payment is handled like a service charge. Subtract this cost.
    g. **Book errors**. Correct all book errors on the Book side of the reconciliation. For example, you may have recorded a $150 cheque that you wrote as $510.

In a business, the bank reconciliation can be a part of internal control if it is done on a regular basis and if someone independent of the person preparing the bank reconciliation, for example, someone from another department, reviews the reconciliation.

Bank Reconciliation Illustrated. The bank statement in Exhibit 4-5 indicates that the January 31 bank balance of Nixon Partners Inc. is $5,931.51. However, Exhibit 4-6 shows that the company's Cash account on the books has a balance of $3,294.21. This situation calls for a bank reconciliation.

Exhibit 4-7, panel A, lists the reconciling items for easy reference, and panel B shows the completed reconciliation.

After the reconciliation in Exhibit 4-7, the adjusted bank balance equals the adjusted book balance. This equality checks the accuracy of both the bank and the books.

Journalizing Transactions from the Bank Reconciliation. The bank reconciliation is an accountant's tool separate from the journals and ledgers. It does *not* account for transactions in the journal. To get the transactions into the accounts, we must make journal entries and post to the ledger. All items on the *Book* side of the bank reconciliation require journal entries.

The bank reconciliation in Exhibit 4-7 requires Nixon Partners to make journal entries to bring the Cash account up-to-date. Numbers in parentheses correspond to the reconciling items listed in Exhibit 4-7, Panel A.

> **Objective**
>
> 2 **Prepare** and use a bank reconciliation

(4) Jan.	31	Cash....................................	904.03		(8) Jan.	31	Miscellaneous Expense*.........	14.25	
		Rent Revenue		904.03			Cash		14.25
		Receipt of rent revenue					Bank service charge.		
(5) Jan.	31	Cash....................................	2,114.00		(9) Jan.	31	Accounts Receivable—L. Ross	52.00	
		Notes Receivable		1,900.00			Cash		52.00
		Interest Revenue..........................		214.00			NSF customer cheque returned by bank.		
		Note receivable collected by bank.							
(6) Jan.	31	Cash....................................	28.01		(10) Jan.	31	Insurance Expense.................	361.00	
		Interest Revenue..........................		28.01			Cash		361.00
		Interest earned on bank balance.......					Payment of monthly insurance.		
(7) Jan.	31	Cash....................................	360.00						
		Accounts Payable—Brown Company Ltd.	360.00						
		Correction of cheque no. 333.							

*Note: Miscellaneous Expense is debited for the bank service charge because the service charge pertains to no particular expense category.

The entry for the NSF cheque (entry 9) needs explanation. Upon learning that a customer's $52.00 cheque to us was not good, we must credit Cash to update the Cash account. Unfortunately, we still have a receivable from the customer, so we must debit Accounts Receivable to reinstate our receivable.

Online Banking

Online banking allows you to pay bills and view your account electronically. You don't have to wait until the end of the month to get a bank statement. With online banking you can reconcile transactions at any time and keep your account current whenever you wish. Exhibit 4-8 on page 183 shows a page from the account history of Toni Anderson's bank account.

| EXHIBIT 4-7 | Bank Reconciliation |

PANEL A—Reconciling Items

Bank side:

1. Deposit in transit, $1,591.63
2. Bank error: The bank deducted $100.00 for a cheque written by another company. Add $100.00 to the bank balance.
3. Outstanding cheques—total of $1,350.14

Cheque No.	Amount
337	$286.00
338	319.47
339	83.00
340	203.14
341	458.53

Book side:

4. EFT receipt of your rent revenue earned on an investment, $904.03.
5. Bank collection of your note receivable including interest of $214.00, $2,114.00.
6. Interest revenue earned on your bank balance, $28.01.
7. Book error: You recorded cheque no. 333 for $510.00 The amount you actually paid on account was $150.00. Add $360.00 to your book balance.
8. Bank service charge, $14.25.
9. NSF cheque from a customer, $52.00. Subtract $52.00 from your book balance.
10. EFT payment of insurance expense, $361.00.

PANEL B—Bank Reconciliation

Nixon Partners Inc.
Bank Reconciliation
January 31, 2009

Bank			Books		
Balance, January 31		$5,931.51	Balance, January 31		$3,294.21
Add:			Add:		
1. Deposit in transit		1,591.60	4. EFT receipt of rent revenue		904.03
2. Correction of bank error		100.00	5. Bank collection of note		
		7,623.14	receivable		2,114.00
			6. Interest revenue earned on		
			bank balance		28.01
			7. Correction of book error—		
Less:			overstated our cheque no. 333		360.00
3. Outstanding cheques					6,700.25
No. 337	$286.00				
No. 338	319.47		Less:		
No. 339	83.00		8. Service charge	$ 14.25	
No. 340	203.14		9. NSF cheque	52.00	
No. 341	458.53	(1,350.14)	10. EFT payment of insurance expense	361.00	(427.25)
Adjusted bank balance		$6,273.00	Adjusted bank balance		$6,273.00

These amounts should agree.

Summary of the Various Reconciling Items:

Bank Balance—Always
- *Add* deposits in transit.
- *Subtract* outstanding cheques.
- *Add* or *subtract* corrections of bank errors.

Book Balance—Always
- *Add* bank collections, interest revenue, and EFT receipts.
- *Subtract* service charges, NSF cheques, and EFT payments.
- *Add* or *subtract* corrections of book errors.

The account history—like a bank statement—lists deposits, cheques, EFT payments, ATM withdrawals, and interest earned on your bank balance.

But the account history doesn't show your beginning balance, so you can't work from your beginning balance to your ending balance.

STOP & THINK

Your bank statement balance is $4,500 and shows a service charge of $15, interest earned of $5, and an NSF cheque for $300. Deposits in transit total $1,200; outstanding cheques are $575. You recorded as $152 a cheque of $125 in payment of an account payable.

1. What is your adjusted bank balance?
2. What was your book balance of cash before the reconciliation?

Answers:

1. $5,125 ($4,500 + $1,200 − $575).
2. $5,408 ($5,125 + $15 − $5 + $300 − $27).

The adjusted book and bank balances are the same. The answer can be determined by working backward from the adjusted balance.

Using the Bank Reconciliation to Control Cash

The bank reconciliation is a powerful control device. Julie Brox is a CMA in Regina, Saskatchewan. She owns several apartment complexes that are managed by her uncle, Herman Klassen. Her uncle signs up tenants, collects the monthly rents, arranges custodial and maintenance work, hires and fires employees, writes the cheques, and performs the bank reconciliation. In short, he does it all. This concentration of duties in one person is evidence of weak internal control. Brox's uncle could be stealing from her or making mistakes, and as a CMA she is aware of this possibility.

Brox trusts her uncle because he is a member of the family. Nevertheless, she exercises some controls over his management of her apartments. Brox periodically

EXHIBIT 4-8	Online Banking—Account History (Like a Bank Statement)

**Account History for Toni Anderson Chequing # 5401-632-9
as of Close of Business 07/27/2009**
Account Details

Date ↓	Description	Withdrawals	Deposits	Balance
	Current Balance			$4,136.08
07/27/09	DEPOSIT		1,170.35	
07/26/09	28 DAYS INTEREST		2.26	
07/25/09	Cheque #6131 View Image	443.83		
07/24/09	Cheque #6130 View Image	401.52		
07/23/09	EFT PYMT ROGERS	61.15		
07/22/09	EFT PYMT	3,172.85		
07/20/09	Cheque #6127 View Image	550.00		
07/19/09	Cheque #6122 View Image	50.00		
07/16/09	Cheque #6116 View Image	2,056.75		
07/15/09	Cheque #6123 View Image	830.00		
07/13/09	Cheque #6124 View Image	150.00		
07/11/09	ATM 4900 SANGER AVE	200.00		
07/09/09	Cheque #6119 View Image	30.00		
07/05/09	Cheque #6125 View Image	2,500.00		
07/04/09	ATM 4900 SANGER AVE	100.00		
07/01/09	DEPOSIT		9,026.37	

E-Mail

drops by her properties to see whether the custodial/maintenance staff is keeping the property in good condition. To control cash, Brox regularly examines the bank reconciliation that her uncle has performed. Brox would know immediately if her uncle is writing cheques to himself. By examining each cheque, Brox establishes control over cash payments.

Brox has a simple method for controlling cash receipts. She knows the occupancy level of her apartments. She also knows the monthly rent she charges. She multiplies the number of apartments—say 20—by the monthly rent (which averages $500 per unit) to arrive at an expected monthly rent revenue of $10,000. By tracing the $10,000 revenue to the bank statement, Brox can tell if all her rent money went into her bank account. To keep her uncle on his toes, Brox lets him know that she periodically audits his work.

Control activities such as these are critical. If there are only a few employees, separation of duties may not be feasible. The owner must control operations, or the assets may slip away. These controls are called *executive controls*.

MyAccountingLab   # MID-CHAPTER SUMMARY PROBLEM

The Cash account of Chima Inc. at February 28, 2009, is as follows:

		Cash			
Feb. 1	Balance	3,995	Feb. 5		400
6		800	12		3,100
15		1,800	19		1,100
22		1,100	26		500
28		2,400	27		900
Feb. 28	Balance	4,095			

Aneil Chima deposits all cash receipts in the bank and makes all cash payments by cheque. Chima Inc. receives this bank statement on February 28, 2009 (as always, negative amounts are in parentheses):

Name: Chima Inc.
Accounting Period: Month of February 2009
Key Fact: Existing, ongoing business

Bank Statement for February 2009		
Beginning balance		$ 3,995
Deposits:		
Feb. 7	$ 800	
15	1,800	
23	1,100	3,700
Cheques (total per day):		
Feb. 8	$ 400	
16	3,100	
23	1,100	(4,600)
Other items:		
Service charge		(10)
NSF cheque from M. E. Crown		(700)
Bank collection of note receivable		1,000*
EFT—monthly rent expense		(330)
Interest on account balance		15
Ending balance		$ 3,070

*Includes interest of $119

Required

1. Prepare the bank reconciliation of Chima Inc. at February 28, 2009.
2. Record the journal entries based on the bank reconciliation.

Answers

Requirement 1

Chima Inc.		
Bank Reconciliation		
February 28, 2009		

> Before creating the bank reconciliation, compare the Cash account and the bank statement. Cross out all items that appear in both places. The items that remain are the reconciling items.

Bank:
Balance, February 28, 2009 .... $3,070
Add: Deposit of February 28 in transit 2,400
5,470

Less: Outstanding cheques issued on
Feb. 26 ($500) and Feb. 27 ($900) .... (1,400)
Adjusted bank balance, February 28, 2009 .... $4,070

> Begin with the ending balance on the bank statement.
> • Add deposits (debits) from the Cash account not on the bank statement.
> • Deduct cheques (credits) from the Cash account not on the bank statement.

Books:
Balance, February 28, 2009 .... $4,095
Add: Bank collection of note receivable, including interest of $119..... 1,000
Interest earned on bank balance 15
5,110

Less: Service charge... $ 10
NSF cheque 700
EFT—Rent expense 330   (1,040)
Adjusted book balance, February 28, 2009 .... $4,070

> Begin with the ending balance in the Cash general ledger account.
> • Add money received by the bank on behalf of the company (increases to the bank statement balance).
> • Deduct bank charges, NSF cheques, or pre-authorized payments (decreases to the bank statement balance).

Requirement 2

Feb. 28	Cash	1,000	
	Note Receivable ($1,000 − $119)....		881
	Interest Revenue		119
	Note receivable collected by bank.		
28	Cash	15	
	Interest Revenue		15
	Interest earned on bank balance.		
28	Miscellaneous Expense	10	
	Cash		10
	Bank service charge.		

Feb. 28	Accounts Receivable—M. E. Crown.....	700	
	Cash...		700
	NSF cheque returned by bank.		
28	Rent Expense	330	
	Cash...		330
	Monthly rent expense.		

> Prepare journal entries for all reconciling items from the "Books" section of the bank reconciliation.

Internal Control over Cash Receipts

Cash requires some specific internal controls because cash is relatively easy to steal and it's easy to convert to other forms of wealth. Moreover, all transactions ultimately affect cash. Let's see how to control cash receipts.

All cash receipts should be deposited for safekeeping in the bank—quickly. Companies receive cash over the counter and through the mail. Each source of cash requires its own security measures.

Cash Receipts over the Counter

Exhibit 4-9 illustrates a cash receipt over the counter in a department store. The point-of-sale terminal (cash register) provides control over the cash receipts. Consider a Zellers store. For each transaction, Zellers issues a receipt to ensure that each sale is recorded. The cash drawer opens when the clerk enters a transaction, and the machine records it. At the end of the day, a manager proves the cash by comparing the cash in the drawer against the machine's record of sales. This step helps prevent theft by the clerk.

At the end of the day—or several times a day if business is brisk—the cashier deposits the cash in the bank. The machine tape then goes to the accounting department for the journal entry to record sales revenue. These measures, coupled with oversight by a manager, discourage theft.

Cash Receipts by Mail

Many companies receive cash by mail. Exhibit 4-10 shows how companies control cash received by mail. All incoming mail is opened by a mailroom employee. The person opening the mail should also make a list of the receipts as an independent control from the treasurer/accounting department. The mailroom then sends all customer cheques to the treasurer, who has the cashier deposit the money in the bank. The remittance advices go to the accounting department for journal entries to Cash and to the appropriate customers' accounts receivable. As a final step, the controller compares the following records for the day:

- Bank deposit amount from the treasurer
- Debit to Cash from the accounting department

The debit to Cash should equal the amount deposited in the bank. All cash receipts are safe in the bank, and the company books are up-to-date.

EXHIBIT 4-9   Cash Receipts over the Counter

Cash receipts over the counter

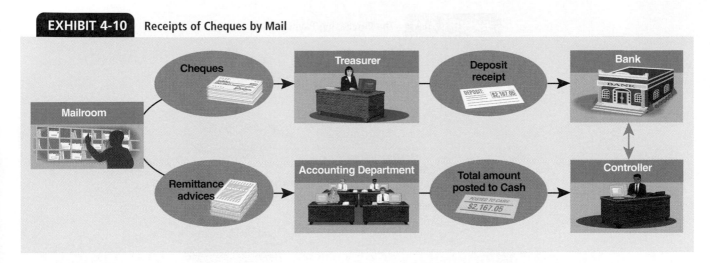

EXHIBIT 4-10 Receipts of Cheques by Mail

Many companies use a lockbox system. Customers send their cheques directly to the company's bank account. Internal control is tight because company personnel never touch incoming cash. The lockbox system puts your cash to work immediately.

Internal Control over Cash Payments

Companies make most payments by cheque. Let's see how to control cash payments by cheque.

Controls over Payment by Cheque

As we have seen, you need a good separation of duties between (a) operations and (b) writing cheques for cash payments. Payment by cheque is an important internal control, as follows:

- The cheque provides a record of the payment.
- The cheque must be signed by an authorized official.
- Before signing the cheque, the official should study the evidence supporting the payment.

Controls over Purchase and Payment. To illustrate the internal control over cash payments by cheque, suppose GreBru Products buys some of its inventory from Stanfield's Limited. The purchasing and payment process follows these steps, as shown in Exhibit 4-11. Start with the box for GreBru Products on the left side.

1 GreBru faxes a *purchase order* to Stanfield's. GreBru says, "Please send us 100 T-shirts."

2 Stanfield's ships the goods and faxes an *invoice* back to GreBru. Stanfield's sent the goods.

3 GreBru receives the *inventory* and prepares a *receiving report* to list the goods received. GreBru got its T-shirts.

4 After approving all documents, GreBru says, "Okay, we'll pay you" and sends a cheque to Stanfield's.

For good internal control, the purchasing agent should neither receive the goods nor approve the payment. If these duties aren't separated, a purchasing agent

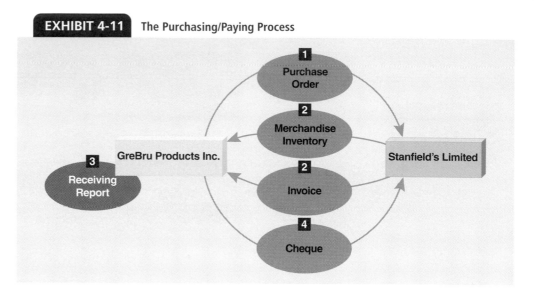

EXHIBIT 4-11   The Purchasing/Paying Process

can buy goods and have them shipped to his or her home. Or a purchasing agent can spend too much on purchases, approve the payment, and split the excess with the supplier. To avoid these problems, companies split the following duties among different employees:

- Purchasing goods
- Receiving goods
- Approving and paying for goods

Exhibit 4-12 shows GreBru's payment packet of documents.

Before approving the payment, the controller or the treasurer should examine the packet to ensure that all the documents agree. Only then does the company know:

1. It received the goods ordered.
2. It pays only for the goods received.

After payment, the cheque signer can punch a hole through the disbursement packet or stamp the documents "Paid," or otherwise prevent their being presented again for payment. The hole or "Paid" stamp denotes that the invoice has been paid.

Petty Cash. It would be wasteful to write separate cheques for an executive's taxi fare, CDs needed right away, or delivery of a package across town. Therefore, companies keep a **petty cash** fund on hand to pay such minor amounts.

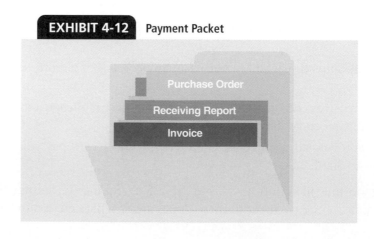

EXHIBIT 4-12   Payment Packet

The petty cash fund is opened with a particular amount of cash. A cheque for that amount is issued to Petty Cash. Assume that on February 28, CHC Helicopter Corp. establishes a petty cash fund of $500 in a sales department. The custodian of the petty cash fund cashes the cheque and places $500 in the fund, which may be a cash box or other device.

For each petty cash payment, the custodian prepares a petty cash slip to list the item purchased. The sum of the cash in the petty cash fund plus the total of the slip amounts should equal the opening balance at all times—in this case, $500. The Petty Cash account keeps its prescribed $500 balance at all times. Maintaining the Petty Cash account at this balance, supported by the fund (cash plus slips), is how an **imprest system** works. The control feature of an imprest system is that it clearly identifies the amount for which the custodian is responsible.

Using a Budget to Manage Cash

Managers control their organizations with a budget. A **budget** is a financial plan that helps coordinate business activities. Cash is the item that is budgeted most often.

How, for example, does TELUS Corp. decide when to invest millions in new wireless technology? How will TELUS Corp. decide how much to spend? Will borrowing be needed, or can TELUS Corp. finance the purchase with internally generated cash? Similarly, by what process do you decide how much to spend on your education? On an automobile? On a house? All these decisions depend to some degree on the information that a cash budget provides.

A cash budget helps a company or an individual manage cash by planning receipts and payments during a future period. The company must determine how much cash it will need and then decide whether or not its operations will bring in the needed cash. Managers proceed as follows:

1. Start with the entity's cash balance at the beginning of the period, the amount left over from the preceding period.

2. Add the budgeted cash receipts and subtract the budgeted cash payments.

3. The beginning balance plus the expected receipts minus the expected payments equals the expected cash balance at the end of the period.

4. Compare the expected ending cash balance to the budgeted cash balance at the end of the period. Managers know the minimum amount of cash they need (the budgeted balance). If the budget shows excess cash, managers can invest the excess. But if the expected cash balance falls below the budgeted balance, the company will need additional financing. The budget is a valuable tool for helping the company plan for the future.

The budget period can span any length of time—a day, a week, a month, or a year. Exhibit 4-13 shows a hypothetical cash budget for The Country Store Ltd. for the year ended January 31, 2009. Study it carefully, because at some point you will use a cash budget.

The Country Store Ltd.'s cash budget in Exhibit 4-13 begins with $12.0 million of cash (line 1). Then add budgeted cash receipts and subtract budgeted payments. In this case The Country Store expects to have $4.6 million of cash available at the year end (Line 11). The Country Store managers need to maintain a cash balance of at least $13.5 million (Line 12). Line 13 shows that The Country Store must arrange the financing of $8.9 million in order to achieve its goals for 2009.

Objective

4 **Use** a budget to manage your cash

EXHIBIT 4-13	Cash Budget

The Country Store Ltd.
Consolidated Cash Budget (Hypothetical)
For the Year Ended January 31, 2009

			(In Millions)
(1)	Cash balance, February 1, 2008		$ 12.0
	Estimated cash receipts:		
(2)	Collections from customers	$360.0	
(3)	Interest and dividends on investments	6.2	
(4)	Sale of store fixtures	4.9	371.1
			383.1
	Estimated cash payments:		
(5)	Purchases of inventory	245.0	
(6)	Operating expenses	82.5	
(7)	Expansion of existing stores	14.6	
(8)	Opening of new stores	12.4	
(9)	Payment of long-term debt	16.0	
(10)	Payment of dividends	8.0	(378.5)
(11)	Cash available (needed) before new financing		(4.6)
(12)	Budgeted cash balance, January 31, 2009		13.5
(13)	Cash available for additional investments (New financing needed)		$ (8.9)

The cash budget helps managers arrange any new financing needed in an orderly manner. With enough cash, The Country Store Ltd. can expand its stores and search out new products that keep customers coming back.

Reporting Cash on the Balance Sheet

Most companies have numerous bank accounts, but they usually combine all cash amounts into a single total called "Cash and cash equivalents." Cash equivalents include liquid assets such as time deposits and guaranteed investment certificates, which are interest-bearing accounts that can be withdrawn with no penalty. Slightly less liquid than cash, they are sufficiently similar to be reported along with cash. The balance sheet of Sobeys Inc. reported the following at May 3, 2008:

Sobeys Inc.
Consolidated Balance Sheet (Excerpt, Adapted)
May 3, 2008

	(In Millions)
Assets	
Current assets:	
Cash and cash equivalents	$158.8

Compensating Balance Agreements

The Cash account on the balance sheet is the amount of liquid assets available for day-to-day use. None of the cash balance is restricted in any way.

Any restricted amount of cash should *not* be reported as Cash on the balance sheet. For example, banks often lend money under a compensating balance agreement.

The borrower agrees to maintain a minimum balance in a chequing account at all times, so the minimum balance becomes a long-term asset and not cash in the normal sense.

Suppose Methanex Corporation borrowed $5 million at 7% from the CIBC and agreed to keep 10% ($500,000) on deposit at all times. The net result of the compensating balance agreement is that Methanex actually borrowed only $4.5 million. And by paying 7% interest on the full $5 million, Methanex's actual interest rate is higher than 7%.*

Ethics and Accounting

Roger Smith, former chairman of General Motors, said, "Ethical practice is, quite simply, good business." First and foremost, practising good ethics is the right thing to do. Second, unethical behaviour always comes back to haunt you.

Corporate and Professional Codes of Ethics

Most companies have a code of ethics designed to encourage ethical and responsible behaviour by employees. But codes of conduct are not enough: Owners and managers must set a high ethical tone, as we saw in the section on Control Environment (see page 170). Managers must make it clear that their company will not tolerate unethical or illegal conduct.

As professionals, accountants are expected to maintain higher standards than society in general. Their ability to do business depends entirely on their reputations. Most professional accountants are members of the Canadian Institute of Chartered Accountants, the Certified General Accountants Association of Canada, or the Society of Management Accountants of Canada. They are bound by the rules of professional conduct of their respective organizations. Unacceptable actions can result in penalties that include expulsion from the professional organization.

Ethical Issues in Accounting

In many situations, the ethical choice is easy. For example, stealing cash is both unethical and illegal. In other cases, the choices are more difficult. But in every instance, ethical judgments boil down to a personal decision: What should I do in a given situation? Let's consider three ethical issues in accounting.

Situation 1. Brian Bivona is preparing the income tax return of a client who has earned more income than expected. On January 2, the client pays for advertising and asks Bivona to backdate the expense to the preceding year. Backdating the deduction would lower the client's immediate tax payments. After all, there is a difference of only 2 days between January 2 and December 31. This client is important to Bivona. What should Bivona do?

> Bivona should refuse the request because the transaction took place in January of the new year.

What control device could prove that Bivona behaved unethically if he backdated the transaction in the accounting records? A Canada Revenue Agency (CRA) audit

---

*The actual effective interest rate = (Actual interest rate paid each period/Amount actually borrowed).

could prove that the expense occurred in January rather than in December. Falsifying documents filed with the CRA is both unethical and illegal.

Situation 2. Marlene Reed Software Company owes $40,000 to Scotiabank. The loan agreement requires Reed's company to maintain a current ratio (current assets divided by current liabilities) of 1.50 or higher. At present, the company's current ratio is 1.40. At this level, Reed is in violation of her loan agreement. She can increase the current ratio to 1.53 by paying off some current liabilities right before year end. Is it ethical to do so?

Yes, because the action is a real business transaction.

Reed should be aware that paying off the liabilities is only a delaying tactic. It will hold off the bank for now, but the business must improve to keep from violating the agreement in the future.

The situation at Enron Corporation illustrates a conflict of interest. A conflict of interest occurs when someone plays two roles that directly compete. A conflict of interest, therefore, poses an ethical dilemma that is best avoided. For example, a judge will not decide a lawsuit when a relative of the judge is involved in the case. Judges *recuse* themselves from the case because of the natural temptation to favour a relative.

As CFO of Enron Corporation, Andrew Fastow managed Enron's finances. In this position he was honour-bound to act in the best interest of the Enron shareholders. Fastow also acted as a principal of partnerships outside Enron that bought assets and assumed debt from Enron. Therefore, he was also honour-bound to act in the best interest of the investors who owned those partnerships. But Fastow negotiated transactions between Enron and the partnerships. Exhibit 4-14 illustrates the conflict of interest.

A conflict of interest arose because Enron did business with the outside partnerships. Fastow negotiated both sides of the deal, and the values of the items bought and sold may have been rigged to come out too low or too high. Investors considering buying Enron shares received financial statements based on faulty values. Flawed net asset amounts likely led investors to pay unreasonable amounts for Enron shares.

How could the conflict of interest have been avoided? Enron's board of directors should not have let CFO Andrew Fastow transact business with partnerships that he controlled. Without this conflict of interest, the values assigned to the transactions would have been more objective. This is only one of the problems that affected Enron Corporation, but it illustrates an important ethical issue.

EXHIBIT 4-14 **Conflict of Interest**

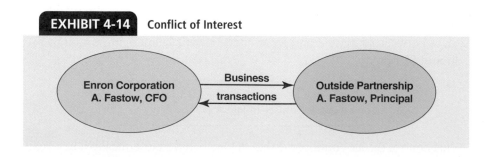

Decision Guidelines

ETHICAL JUDGMENTS

Suppose you are former Enron vice president Sherron Watkins, a CPA (the equivalent of a CA in the U.S.) who understood what was going on in the company. Watkins was faced with a tough decision that had an ethical dimension. For her, as for others in similar situations, weighing tough ethical judgments requires a decision framework. Consider these five steps as general guidelines. Let's apply them to Sherron Watkins.

Question	Decision Guidelines
1. What is the ethical issue?	**1.** *Identify the ethical issues.* The root word of ethical is *ethics,* which Webster's dictionary defines as "the discipline dealing with what is good and bad and with moral duty and obligation." Watkins' ethical dilemma is to decide what she should do with the information she has uncovered.
2. What are the options?	**2.** *Specify the alternatives.* For Sherron Watkins, four alternatives are (a) express her concern about the outside partnerships to her boss, CFO Andrew Fastow; (b) express her concern to Kenneth Lay, CEO of Enron; (c) do nothing; or (d) resign.
3. Who is involved in the situation?	**3.** *Identify the people involved.* Individuals who could be affected include all Enron employees (including Watkins), shareholders, creditors, and the SEC.
4. What are the possible consequences?	**4.** *Assess the possible outcomes.* **a.** If Watkins approaches Fastow, he might penalize her, or he might reward her for careful work. This would preserve her integrity and may lead Fastow to correct the situation and preserve Enron's public trust, but Fastow may fire Watkins for insubordination. **b.** If Watkins takes her concerns to the CEO, who is Fastow's boss—going over Fastow's head—her integrity would be preserved. Her relationship with Fastow would surely be strained and it might be difficult for them to work together in the future. Watkins might be rewarded for careful work, but if Fastow's boss has colluded with Fastow in setting up the partnerships, Watkins could be penalized. If the situation is corrected and outsiders are notified, Enron could be reprimanded by the SEC if the company's financial-statement data prove inaccurate. **c.** If Watkins does nothing, or resigns, she would avoid a confrontation with Fastow or Lay. But, the public may suffer if investors and creditors rely on faulty data and Watkins' conscience would likely trouble her.
5. What should Watkins do?	**5.** *Make the decision.* Identifying the best choice is difficult. Watkins must balance the likely effects on the various people against the dictates of her own conscience. This framework identifies the relevant factors. As it turned out, Watkins took her concerns to CEO Kenneth Lay, and he launched an investigation into the situation. Unfortunately, however, enough damage had already been done and Enron filed for Chapter 11 bankruptcy protection from its creditors. Enron fired Andrew Fastow who has since pleaded guilty to a number of charges and is now in jail.

MyAccountingLab

END-OF-CHAPTER SUMMARY PROBLEM

Assume the following situation and transactions for TransAlta Corporation. At December 31, 2007, TransAlta had total assets of $7,179 million, which included cash of $51 million. At December 31, 2007, TransAlta had long-term obligations of $2,136 million, of which it expected to pay $197 million during 2008. At the end of 2007, Brian Burden, CFO of TransAlta, is preparing the budget for the next year.

During 2008, Burden expects TransAlta to collect $2,800 million from customers. TransAlta expects to pay $1,200 million for fuel and purchased power, and $1,000 million for operations and other cash expenses. To remain competitive, TransAlta plans to spend $850 million to upgrade facilities and purchase new property, plant, and equipment. Sale of property, plant and equipment will provide cash of $90 million. TransAlta will pay dividends of $204 million and distributions to a subsidiary's non-controlling limited partner of $87 million.

Because of the increased level of activity planned for 2008, Burden budgets the need for a minimum cash balance of $160 million at December 31, 2008.

Required

1. How much must TransAlta borrow during 2008 to keep its cash balance from falling below $160 million? Prepare the 2008 cash budget to answer this important question.
2. Consider the company's need to borrow $557 million. TransAlta can avoid the need to borrow money in 2008 by delaying one particular cash payment until 2009 or later. Identify the item, and state why it would nevertheless be unwise to delay its payment.

Name: TransAlta Corporation
Industry: Energy corporation
Fiscal Period: Year ended December 31, 2008

Answers

Requirement 1

A cash budget helps a company estimate its cash inflows and cash outflows for a future period. The period of time covered must be specified in the heading of the cash budget.

Use only the cash amounts from the data that are given.

Cash receipts from:
- Ordinary sales
- Extraordinary sales

Cash payments for:
- Purchases from suppliers
- Cash dividends
- Debt repayments

TransAlta Corporation
Cash Budget (Hypothetical)
For the Year Ended December 31, 2008

		(In Millions)
Cash balance, December 31, 2007		$ 51
Estimated cash receipts:		
Collections from customers		2,800
Sale of assets		50
		$2,901
Estimated cash payments:		
Purchases of fuel and purchased power	$1,200	
Payment of operating expenses	1,000	
Upgrading of facilities and purchase of property, plant and equipment	600	
Payment of dividends and distributions	291	
Payment of long-term debt	197	(3,288)
Cash available (needed) before new financing		(387)
Budgeted cash balance, December 31, 2008		160
Cash available for additional investments, or (New financing needed)		$ (547)

Requirement 2

Consider delaying cash payments to upgrade facilities since the upgrades are not necessary to generate the current level of income.

TransAlta can eliminate the need for borrowing the $547 million by delaying part of the $850 million payment to *upgrade the company's facilities and purchase property, plant, and equipment*. The delay would be unwise because TransAlta needs the upgrading and new property, plant, and equipment to remain competitive.

REVIEW INTERNAL CONTROL AND CASH

QUICK CHECK (Answers are given on page 214.)

1. Internal control has its own terminology. On the left are some key internal control concepts. On the right are some key terms. Match each internal control concept with its term by writing the appropriate letter in the space provided. Not all letters are used.

_____ This procedure limits access to sensitive data.

_____ This type of insurance policy covers losses due to employee theft.

_____ Trusting your employees can lead you to overlook this procedure.

_____ One of the most basic purposes of internal control.

_____ Internal control cannot always safeguard against this problem.

_____ Often mentioned as the cornerstone of a good system of internal control.

_____ Pay employees enough to require them to do a good job.

a. Competent personnel
b. Encryption
c. Separation of duties
d. Safeguarding assets
e. Fidelity bond
f. Collusion
g. Firewalls
h. Supervision
i. External audits

2. Each of the following is an example of a control procedure, *except*

a. A sound marketing plan
b. Sound personnel procedures
c. Limited access to assets
d. Separation of duties

3. Which of the following is an example of poor internal control?

a. The accounting department compares goods received with the related purchase order.
b. Employees must take vacations.
c. Employees are rotated through various jobs.
d. The mailroom clerk immediately records daily cash receipts in the journal.

4. A not-for-profit organization has internal controls because

a. It wants to be businesslike.
b. It has a fiduciary responsibility to safeguard assets.
c. It makes operations easier for employees.
d. None of the above

5. Each of the items in the following list must be accounted for in a bank reconciliation. Match each item with the appropriate treatment from the list on the right.

_____ Outstanding cheque

_____ NSF cheque

_____ Bank service charge

_____ Cost of printed cheques

_____ Bank error that decreased bank balance

_____ Deposit in transit

_____ Bank collection

_____ Customer cheque returned because of unauthorized signature

_____ Book error that increased balance of Cash account

a. Bank side of reconciliation—add item

b. Bank side of reconciliation—subtract item

c. Book side of reconciliation—add item

d. Book side of reconciliation—subtract item

6. Internal controls have limitations because
   a. A company may not understand internal controls
   b. The benefits of the system must be greater than the cost
   c. Employees can ignore internal controls
   d. Errors are just a fact of life

7. A bank reconciliation
   a. Records cash
   b. Ensures all cash transactions have been accounted for
   c. Manages the company cashflow
   d. Reports all bills paid

8. A deposit made on the last day of the current month but that did not appear on the bank statement
   a. Would be added to the book balance
   b. Does not belong on the bank reconciliation
   c. Would be added to the bank balance
   d. Would be deducted from the bank balance

9. Which of the following reconciling items does not require a journal entry?
   a. NSF cheque
   b. Deposit in transit
   c. Bank collection of a note receivable
   d. Bank service charge

10. A cheque was written for $542 to purchase supplies. The cheque was recorded in the journal as $425. The entry to correct the error would
    a. Increase Supplies, $117
    b. Decrease Cash, $117
    c. Decrease Supplies, $117
    d. Both a and b

11. A cash budget helps control cash by
    a. Developing a plan for increasing sales
    b. Ensuring accurate cash records
    c. Helping to determine whether additional cash is available for investments or new financing is needed
    d. All of the above

ACCOUNTING VOCABULARY

audit A periodic examination of a company's financial statements and the accounting systems, controls, and records that produce them.   (p. 172)

bank collections Collection of money by the bank on behalf of a depositor.   (p. 180)

bank reconciliation A document explaining the reasons for the difference between a depositor's records and the bank's records about the depositor's cash. (p. 180)

bank statement Document showing the beginning and ending balances of a particular bank account listing the month's transactions that affected the account.   (p. 178)

budget A quantitative expression of a plan that helps managers coordinate the entity's activities.   (p. 189)

cheque Document instructing a bank to pay the designated person or business the specified amount of money.   (p. 177)

controller The chief accounting officer of a business who accounts for cash.   (p. 171)

deposits in transit A deposit recorded by the company but not yet by its bank.   (p. 180)

electronic funds transfer (EFT) System that transfers cash by electronic communication rather than by paper documents. (p. 178)

imprest system A way to account for petty cash by maintaining a constant balance in the petty cash account, supported by the fund (cash plus payment slips) totalling the same amount. (p. 189)

internal control Organizational plan and related measures adopted by an entity to safeguard assets, encourage adherence to company policies, promote operational efficiency, ensure accurate and reliable accounting records, and comply with legal requirements.   (p. 168)

nonsufficient funds (NSF) cheque A cheque for which the payer's bank account has insufficient money to pay the cheque. NSF cheques are cash receipts that turn out to be worthless. (p. 180)

outstanding cheques A cheque issued by the company and recorded on its books but not yet paid by its bank. (p. 180)

petty cash Fund containing a small amount of cash that is used to pay minor amounts. (p. 188)

private company Company that does not offer its securities for sale to the general public. (p. 169)

public company Company that offers its securities for sale to the general public. (p. 169)

treasurer In a large company, the person in charge of managing cash. (p. 171)

ASSESS YOUR PROGRESS

Make the grade with MyAccountingLab: The exercises and problems marked in red can be found on MyAccountingLab at www.myaccountinglab.com. You can practise them as often as you want, and they feature step by step guided solutions to help you find the right answer.

SHORT EXERCISES

S4-1 What are some of the major requirements of NI 52–109?

Certification of internal controls
(Obj. 1)

S4-2 List the components of internal control. In your own words briefly describe each component.

Components of internal control
(Obj. 1)

S4-3 Explain in your own words why separation of duties is such an important procedure for safeguarding assets. Describe what can happen if the same person has custody of an asset and also accounts for it.

Characteristics of an effective system of internal control
(Obj. 1)

S4-4 Identify three electronic control devices used in business and show all the internal control objectives that each electronic device relates to.

Electronic devices and internal control
(Obj. 1)

S4-5 The Cash account of SWITZER Ltd. reported a balance of $2,500 at August 31, 2009. Included were outstanding cheques totalling $900 and an August 31 deposit of $500 that did not appear on the bank statement. The bank statement, which came from HSBC Bank, listed an August 31, 2009, balance of $3,405. Included in the bank balance was an August 30 collection of $550 on account from a customer who pays the bank directly. The bank statement also shows a $20 service charge, $10 of interest revenue that SWITZER earned on its bank balance, and an NSF cheque for $35.

Preparing a bank reconciliation
(Obj. 2)

Prepare a bank reconciliation to determine how much cash SWITZER actually has at August 31, 2009.

S4-6 After preparing the SWITZER Ltd. bank reconciliation in Short Exercise 4-5, make the company's journal entries for transactions that arise from the bank reconciliation. Include an explanation with each entry.

Recording transactions from a bank reconciliation
(Obj. 2)

S4-7 Jordan Quinn manages the local Homeless Shelter. He fears that a trusted employee has been stealing from the shelter. This employee receives cash from supporters and also prepares the monthly bank reconciliation. To check on the employee, Quinn prepares his own bank reconciliation as on page 198.

Using a bank reconciliation as a control device
(Obj. 2)

Homeless Shelter			
Bank Reconciliation			
August 31, 2009			

Bank		Books	
Balance, August 31	$3,300	Balance, August 31	$2,820
Add		Add	
Deposits in transit.....................	400	Bank collections	800
		Interest revenue.........................	10
Less		Less	
Outstanding cheques.................	(1,100)	Service charge.............................	(30)
Adjusted bank balance	$2,600	Adjusted book balance	$3,600

Does it appear that the employee has stolen from the shelter? If so, how much? Explain your answer. Which side of the bank reconciliation shows the shelter's true cash balance?

Control over cash receipts
(Obj. 3)

S4-8 Gina Rolande sells memberships to the symphony in Winnipeg. The symphony's procedure requires Rolande to write a patron receipt for all memberships sold. The receipt forms are prenumbered. Rolande is having personal financial problems, and she stole $500 received from a member. To hide her theft, Rolande destroys the symphony copy of the receipt she gave the member. What will alert manager Tom Jelnick that something is wrong?

Internal control over cash payments
(Obj. 3)

S4-9 Answer the following questions about internal control over cash payments:

1. Payment by cheque carries three basic controls over cash. What are they?
2. Suppose a receptionist opens the mail, records payments received, and makes the bank deposit. How could a dishonest receptionist cheat the company? How do companies avoid this internal control weakness?

Using a cash budget
(Obj. 4)

S4-10 In your own words, briefly explain how a cash budget works and what it accomplishes with its last few lines of data.

Preparing a cash budget
(Obj. 4)

S4-11 Dairy Farmers of Ontario (DFO) is the marketing group for Ontario's dairy farms. Suppose the organization begins 2009 with cash of $28 million. DFO estimates cash receipts during the year will total $15 million. Planned payments for the year will total $14 million. To meet member commitment, DFO must maintain a cash balance of at least $25 million. Prepare the organization's cash budget for 2009.

Making an ethical judgment
(Obj. 5)

S4-12 Jane Hill, an accountant for Stainton Hardware Inc., discovers that her supervisor, Drew Armour, made several errors last year. Overall, the errors overstated Stainton Hardware's net income by 20%. It is not clear whether the errors were deliberate or accidental. What should Jane Hill do?

EXERCISES

E-commerce pitfalls
(Obj. 1)

E4-13 How do computer viruses, Trojan Horses, and phishing expeditions work? How can these e-commerce pitfalls hurt you? Be specific.

Explaining the role of internal control
(Obj. 1)

E4-14 Answer the following questions on internal control:
a. Separation of duties is an important internal control procedure. Why is this so?
b. Cash may be a small item on the financial statements. Nevertheless, internal control over cash is very important. Why is this true?
c. Crane Company requires that all documents supporting a cheque be cancelled by punching a hole through the packet. Why is this practice required? What might happen if it were not?

E4-15 Identify the internal control weakness in the following situations. State how the person can hurt the company.

Identifying internal control weaknesses
(Obj. 1)

a. Jerry Miller works as a security guard at U Park parking in Calgary. Miller has a master key to the cash box where commuters pay for parking. Each night Miller prepares the cash report that shows (a) the number of cars that parked on the lot and (b) the day's cash receipts. Sandra Covington, the U Park treasurer, checks Miller's figures by multiplying the number of cars by the parking fee per car. Covington then deposits the cash in the bank.

b. Sharon Fisher is the purchasing agent for Manatee Golf Equipment. Fisher prepares purchase orders based on requests from division managers of the company. Fisher faxes the purchase orders to suppliers who then ship the goods to Manatee. Fisher receives each incoming shipment and checks it for agreement with the purchase order and the related invoice. She then routes the goods to the respective division managers and sends the receiving report and the invoice to the accounting department for payment.

c. The external auditor for Mattson Financial Services takes a global view of the audit. To form his professional opinion of Mattson's financial statements, the auditor runs no tests of Mattson's financial statements or of the underlying transactions. Instead, the auditor computes a few ratios and compares the current-year ratio values to the ratio values a year ago. If the ratio values appear reasonable, the auditor concludes that Mattson's financial statements are okay.

E4-16 The following situations describe two cash payment situations and two cash receipt situations. In each pair, one set of internal controls is better than the other. Evaluate the internal controls in each situation as strong or weak, and give the reason for your answer.

Identifying internal control strengths and weaknesses
(Obj. 1)

Cash payments:

a. Jim McCord Construction's policy calls for construction supervisors to request the equipment needed for their jobs. The home office then purchases the equipment and has it shipped to the construction site.

b. Granite & Marble Inc.'s policy calls for project supervisors to purchase the equipment needed for jobs. The supervisors then submit the paid receipts to the home office for reimbursement. This policy enables supervisors to get the equipment quickly and keep construction jobs moving.

Cash receipts:

a. At McClaren Chevrolet, cash received by mail goes straight to the accountant, who debits Cash and credits Accounts Receivable to record the collections from customers. The McClaren accountant then deposits the cash in the bank.

b. Cash received by mail at Fleur de Lys Orthopedic Clinic goes to the mailroom, where a mail clerk opens envelopes and totals the cash receipts for the day. The mail clerk forwards customer cheques to the cashier for deposit in the bank and forwards the remittance slips to the accounting department for posting credits to customer accounts.

E4-17 In June 2008, it was reported in the *Globe and Mail* that Janet Donio, the former chief information officer of the Council of Ontario Universities (COU), was accused of embezzling $600,000 from the organization. Donio is alleged to have arranged the payment of funds for invoices for services never produced and which instead were allegedly siphoned off by Donio. In addition, her chief academic credentials—a Canadian university degree and a PhD from the United States were found to be bogus. The fraud was not discovered until after her departure from COU when an audit was launched due to irregularities noticed by her successor at COU.

Correcting an internal control weakness
(Obj. 1)

How could Donio have embezzled the funds from COU? Give your opinion on how COU might have prevented the fraud and the actions taken when irregularities were discovered.

Classifying bank reconciliation items
(Obj. 2)

E4-18 The following items appear on a bank reconciliation:

_____ 1. Outstanding cheques

_____ 2. Bank error: The bank credited our account for a deposit made by another bank customer.

_____ 3. Service charge

_____ 4. Deposits in transit

_____ 5. NSF cheque

_____ 6. Bank collection of a note receivable on our behalf

_____ 7. Book error: We debited Cash for $100. The correct debit was $1,000

Classify each item as (a) an addition to the bank balance, (b) a subtraction from the bank balance, (c) an addition to the book balance, or (d) a subtraction from the book balance.

Preparing a bank reconciliation
(Obj. 2)

E4-19 LeAnn Bryant's chequebook lists the following:

Date		Cheque No.	Item	Cheque	Deposit	Balance
Nov.	1					$ 705
	4	622	Direct Energy	$19		686
	9		Dividends		$116	802
	13	623	Canadian Tire	43		759
	14	624	Petro-Canada	58		701
	18	625	Cash	50		651
	26	626	St. Mark's Church	25		626
	28	627	Bent Tree Apartments	275		351
	30		Paycheque		846	1,197

The November bank statement shows

Balance...			$705
Add Deposits..			116
Deduct cheques	No.	Amount	
	622	$19	
	623	43	
	624	85*	
	625	50	(197)
Other charges:			
NSF cheque...		$ 8	
Service charge..		12	(20)
Balance			$604

*This is the correct amount for cheque number 624.

Required

Prepare Bryant's bank reconciliation at November 30, 2009.

Preparing a bank reconciliation
(Obj. 2)

E4-20 Tim Wong operates a FedEx Kinko's store. He has just received the monthly bank statement at May 31, 2009, from Royal Bank of Canada, and the statement shows an ending balance of $595. Listed on the statement are an EFT customer collection of $300, a service charge of $12, two NSF cheques totalling $120, and a $9 charge for printed cheques. In reviewing his cash records, Wong identifies outstanding cheques totalling $603 and a May 31 deposit in transit of $1,788. During May, he recorded a $290 cheque for the salary of a part-time employee as $29. Wong's Cash account shows a May 31 cash balance of $1,882. How much cash does Wong actually have at May 31?

E4-21 Use the data from Exercise 4-20 to make the journal entries that Wong should record on May 31 to update his Cash account. Include an explanation for each entry.

Journalizing transactions from bank reconciliations
(Obj. 2)

E4-22 A chain of shoe stores uses point-of-sale terminals as cash registers. The register shows the amount of each sale, the cash received from the customer, and any change returned to the customer. The machine also produces a customer receipt but keeps no record of transactions. At the end of the day, the clerk counts the cash in the register and gives it to the cashier for deposit in the company bank account. Write a memo to convince the store manager that there is an internal control weakness over cash receipts. Identify the weakness that gives an employee the best opportunity to steal cash and state how to prevent such a theft.

Identifying internal control weaknesses
(Obj. 1)

E4-23 Tee Golf Company manufactures a popular line of golf clubs. Tee Golf employs 140 workers and keeps their employment records on time sheets that show how many hours the employee works each week. On Friday, the shop foreman collects the time sheets, checks them for accuracy, and delivers them to the payroll department for preparation of paycheques. The treasurer signs the paycheques and returns the cheques to the payroll department for distribution to the employees.

Identify the main internal control weakness in this situation, state how the weakness can hurt Tee Golf, and propose a way to correct the weakness.

Evaluating internal control over cash payments
(Obj. 3)

E4-24 Wireless Communications Inc. is preparing its cash budget for 2009. Wireless ended 2008 with cash of $81 million, and managers need to keep a cash balance of at least $75 million for operations.

Collections from customers are expected to total $11,284 million during 2009, and payments for the cost of services and products should reach $6,166 million. Operating expense payments are budgeted at $2,543 million.

During 2009, Wireless expects to invest $1,825 million in new equipment and sell older assets for $115 million. Debt payments scheduled for 2009 will total $597 million. The company forecasts net income of $890 million for 2009 and plans to pay dividends of $338 million.

Prepare Wireless Communications' cash budget for 2009. Will the budgeted level of cash receipts leave Wireless with the desired ending cash balance of $75 million, or will the company need additional financing? If it does, how much will it need?

Preparing a cash budget
(Obj. 4)

E4-25 Sunbelt Bank recently appointed the accounting firm of Baker, Jackson, and Trent as the bank's auditor. Sunbelt quickly became one of Baker, Jackson, and Trent's largest clients. Subject to banking regulations, Sunbelt must provide for any expected losses on notes receivable that Sunbelt may not collect in full.

During the course of the audit, Baker, Jackson, and Trent determined that three large notes receivable of Sunbelt seem questionable. Baker, Jackson, and Trent discussed these loans with Stephanie Carson, controller of Sunbelt. Carson assured the auditors that these notes were good and that the makers of the notes will be able to pay their notes after the economy improves.

Baker, Jackson, and Trent stated that Sunbelt must record a loss for a portion of these notes receivable to account for the likelihood that Sunbelt may never collect their full amount. Carson objected and threatened to dismiss Baker, Jackson, and Trent if the auditor demands that the bank record the loss. Baker, Jackson, and Trent want to keep Sunbelt as a client. In fact, Baker, Jackson, and Trent were counting on the revenue from the Sunbelt audit to finance an expansion of the firm.

Apply the decision guidelines for ethical judgments outlined on page 193 to decide how the accounting firm of Baker, Jackson, and Trent should proceed.

Resolving an ethical challenge
(Obj. 5)

E4-26 Assume **Second Cup** borrowed $1 million from Bank of Montreal and agreed to (a) pay an interest rate of 7% and (b) maintain a compensating balance amount equal to 5% of the loan. Determine Second Cup's actual effective interest rate on this loan.

Compensating balance agreement
(Obj. 4)

CHALLENGE EXERCISES

Internal controls over cash payments, ethical considerations
(Obj. 3, 5)

E4-27 Morris Cody, the owner of Parkwood Apartments, has delegated management of the apartment building to Mario daSilva, a friend. Cody drops by to meet tenants and check up on rent receipts, but daSilva manages building maintenance and handles cash payments. Rentals have been very good lately, and cash receipts have kept pace with the apparent level of rent. However, for a year or so, the amount of cash on hand has been too low. When asked about this, daSilva explains that building maintenance has been required and suppliers are charging more for goods than in the past. During the past year, daSilva has taken two expensive vacations, and Cody wonders how daSilva can afford these trips on his $60,000 annual salary.

List at least three ways daSilva could be defrauding Cody of cash. In each instance also identify how Cody can determine whether daSilva's actions are ethical. Limit your answers to the building's cash payments. The business pays all suppliers by cheque (no EFTs).

Preparing and using a cash budget
(Obj. 4)

E4-28 Dan Davis, the chief financial officer, is responsible for The Furniture Mart's cash budget for 2009. The budget will help Davis determine the amount of long-term borrowing needed to end the year with a cash balance of $150 thousand. Davis's assistants have assembled budget data for 2009, which the computer printed in alphabetical order. Not all the data items reproduced below are used in preparing the cash budget.

(Assumed Data)	(In thousands)
Actual cash balance December 31, 2008	$ 140
Budgeted total assets	22,977
Budgeted total current assets	7,776
Budgeted total current liabilities	4,860
Budgeted total liabilities	11,488
Budgeted total shareholders' equity	7,797
Collections from customers	18,527
Dividend payments	237
Issuance of shares	627
Net income	1,153
Payment of long-term and short-term debt	950
Payment of operating expenses	2,349
Purchases of inventory items	14,045
Purchase of property and equipment	1,518

❙ Required

1. Prepare the cash budget of The Furniture Mart, Inc., for 2009.

2. Compute The Furniture Mart's budgeted current ratio and debt ratio at December 31, 2009. Based on these ratio values, and on the cash budget, would you lend $100,000 to The Furniture Mart? Give the reason for your decision.

QUIZ

Test your understanding of internal control and cash by answering the following questions. Select the best choice from among the possible answers given.

Q4-29 All the following are objectives of internal control except
a. To comply with legal requirements
b. To safeguard assets
c. To maximize net income
d. To ensure accurate and reliable accounting records

Q4-30 All the following are internal control procedures except
a. Electronic devices
b. Sarbanes-Oxley reforms
c. Assignment of responsibilities
d. Internal and external audits

Q4-31 Requiring that an employee with no access to cash do the accounting is an example of which characteristic of internal control?
a. Separation of duties
b. Competent and reliable personnel
c. Mandatory vacations
d. Monitoring of controls

Q4-32 All the following are controls for cash received over the counter except
a. The customer should be able to see the amounts entered into the cash register.
b. A printed receipt must be given to the customer.
c. The cash drawer should open only when the sales clerk enters an amount on the keys.
d. The sales clerk must have access to the cash register tape.

Q4-33 In a bank reconciliation, an outstanding cheque is
a. Added to the book balance
b. Deducted from the book balance
c. Added to the bank balance
d. Deducted from the bank balance

Q4-34 In a bank reconciliation, a bank collection of a note receivable is
a. Added to the book balance
b. Deducted from the book balance
c. Added to the bank balance
d. Deducted from the bank balance

Q4-35 In a bank reconciliation, an EFT cash payment is
a. Added to the book balance
b. Deducted from the book balance
c. Added to the bank balance
d. Deducted from the bank balance

Q4-36 If a bookkeeper mistakenly recorded a $58 deposit as $85, the error would be shown on the bank reconciliation as a
a. $27 addition to the book balance
b. $85 deduction from the book balance
c. $27 deduction from the book balance
d. $85 addition to the book balance

Q4-37 If a bank reconciliation included a deposit in transit of $670, the entry to record this reconciling item would include which of the following?
a. Credit to prepaid insurance for $670
b. Credit to cash for $670
c. Debit to cash for $670
d. No journal entry is required.

Q4-38 In a bank reconciliation, interest revenue earned on your bank balance is
a. Added to the book balance
b. Deducted from the book balance
c. Added to the bank balance
d. Deducted from the bank balance

Q4-39 Before paying an invoice for goods received on account, the controller or treasurer should ensure that
a. The company is paying for the goods it ordered.
b. The company is paying for the goods it actually received.
c. The company has not already paid this invoice.
d. All of the above

Q4-40 La Petite France Bakery is budgeting cash for 2009. The cash balance at December 31, 2008, was $10,000. La Petite budgets 2009 cash receipts at $85,000. Estimated cash payments include $40,000 for inventory, $30,000 for operating expenses, and $20,000 to expand the store. La Petite needs a minimum cash balance of $10,000 at all times. La Petite expects to earn net income of $40,000 during 2009. What is the final result of the company's cash budget for 2009?
a. $10,000 is available for additional investments.
b. $5,000 is available for additional investments.
c. La Petite must arrange new financing for $5,000.
d. La Petite must pay off $10,000 of debt.

PROBLEMS

(GROUP A)

Identifying internal control weaknesses
(Obj. 1)

P4-41A Avant Garde Imports is an importer of silver, brass, and furniture items from Mexico. Kay Jones is the general manager of Avant Garde Imports. Jones employs two other people in the business. Marco Gonzalez serves as the buyer for Avant Garde. He travels throughout Mexico to find interesting new products. When Gonzalez finds a new product, he arranges for Avant Garde to purchase and pay for the item. He helps the Mexican artisans prepare their invoices and then faxes the invoices to Jones in the company office.

Jones operates out of an office in Montreal, Quebec. The office is managed by Rita Bowden, who handles the mail, keeps the accounting records, makes bank deposits, and prepares the monthly bank reconciliation. Virtually all of Avant Garde's cash receipts arrive by mail—from sales made to Pier 1 Imports and Wal-Mart.

Bowden also prepares cheques for payment based on invoices that come in from the suppliers who have been contacted by Gonzalez. To maintain control over cash payments, Jones examines the paperwork and signs all cheques.

❚ Required

Identify all the major internal control weaknesses in Avant Garde's system and how the resulting action could hurt Avant Garde. Also state how to correct each weakness.

P4-42A Each of the following situations reveals an internal control weakness.

Identifying internal control weakness
(Obj. 1, 3)

a. Accounting firms use paraprofessional employees to perform routine tasks. For example, an accounting paraprofessional might prepare routine tax returns for clients. In the firm of Dunham & Lee, Rodney Lee, one of the partners, turns over a significant portion of his high-level accounting work to his paraprofessional staff.

b. In evaluating the internal control over cash payments of Butler Manufacturing, an auditor learns that the purchasing agent is responsible for purchasing diamonds for use in the company's manufacturing process, approving the invoices for payment, and signing the cheques. No supervisor reviews the purchasing agent's work.

c. Charlotte James owns an architecture firm. James's staff consists of 12 professional architects, and James manages the office. Often, James's work requires her to travel to meet with clients. During the past 6 months, James has observed that when she returns from a business trip, the architecture jobs in the office have not progressed satisfactorily. James learns that when she is away, two of her senior architects take over office management and neglect their normal duties. One employee could manage the office.

d. B.J. Tanner has been an employee of the Crystal City for many years. Because the city is small, Tanner performs all accounting duties, plus opening the mail, preparing the bank deposit, and preparing the bank reconciliation.

e. Part of an internal auditor's job is to evaluate how efficiently the company is running. For example, is the company purchasing inventory from the least expensive supplier? After a particularly bad year, Long Photographic Products eliminates its internal audit department to reduce expenses.

❚ Required

1. Identify the missing internal control characteristic in each situation.
2. Identify each firm's possible problem.
3. Propose a solution to the problem.

P4-43A The cash data of Alta Vista Toyota for June 2009 follow:

*Preparing the bank reconciliation
and using it as a control device*
(Obj. 2)

Cash

Date	Item	Jrnl. Ref.	Debit	Credit	Balance
June 1	Balance				5,011
30		CR6	10,578		15,589
30		CP11		10,924	4,665

Cash Receipts (CR)		Cash Payments (CP)	
Date	Cash Debit	Cheque No.	Cash Credit
June 2	$ 4,174	3113	$ 891
8	407	3114	147
10	559	3115	1,930
16	2,187	3116	664
22	1,854	3117	1,472
29	1,060	3118	1,000
30	337	3119	632
Total	$10,578	3120	1,675
		3121	100
		3122	2,413
		Total	$10,924

Alta Vista received the following bank statement on June 30, 2009:

Bank Statement for June 2009

Beginning balance		$5,011
Deposits and other additions		
June 1	$ 326 EFT	
4	4,174	
9	407	
12	559	
17	2,187	
22	1,701 BC	
23	1,854	11,208
Cheques and other deductions		
June 7	$ 891	
13	1,390	
14	903 US	
15	147	
18	664	
21	219 EFT	
26	1,472	
30	1,000	
30	20 SC	(6,706)
Ending balance		$ 9,513

Explanation: EFT—electronic funds transfer, BC—bank collection, US—unauthorized signature, SC—service charge

Additional data for the bank reconciliation include the following:

a. The EFT deposit was a receipt of a monthly car lease. The EFT debit was a monthly
insurance payment.
b. The bank collection was of a note receivable.
c. The unauthorized signature cheque was received from a customer.
d. The correct amount of cheque number 3115, a payment on account, is $1,390. (Alta Vista's
accountant mistakenly recorded the cheque for $1,930.)

Preparing a bank reconciliation and the related journal entries
(Obj. 4)

I *Required*

1. Prepare the Alta Vista Toyota bank reconciliation at June 30, 2009.
2. Describe how a bank account and the bank reconciliation help the general manager control Alta Vista's cash.

P4-44A The May 31, 2009, bank statement of Family Services Association (FSA) has just arrived from Scotiabank. To prepare the FSA bank reconciliation, you gather the following data:

a. FSA's Cash account shows a balance of $2,256.14 on May 31.
b. The May 31 bank balance is $4,023.05
c. The bank statement shows that FSA earned $38.19 of interest on its bank balance during May. This amount was added to FSA's bank balance.
d. FSA pays utilities ($250) and insurance ($100) by EFT.
e. The following FSA cheques did not clear the bank by May 31:

Cheque No.	Amount
237	$ 46.10
288	141.00
291	578.05
293	11.87
294	609.51
295	8.88
296	101.63

f. The bank statement includes a donation of $850, electronically deposited to the bank for FSA.
g. The bank statement lists a $10.50 bank service charge.
h. On May 31, the FSA treasurer deposited $16.15, which will appear on the June bank statement.
i. The bank statement includes a $300 deposit that FSA did not make. The bank added $300 to FSA's account for another company's deposit.
j. The bank statement includes two charges for returned cheques from donors. One is a $395 cheque received from a donor with the imprint "Unauthorized Signature." The other is a nonsufficient funds cheque in the amount of $146.67 received from a client.

I *Required*

1. Prepare the bank reconciliation for FSA.
2. Journalize the May 31 transactions needed to update FSA's Cash account. Include an explanation for each entry.

Identifying internal control weakness
(Obj. 3)

P4-45A Sun Skin Care makes all sales on credit. Cash receipts arrive by mail, usually within 30 days of the sale. Nancy Brown opens envelopes and separates the cheques from the accompanying remittance advices. Brown forwards the cheques to another employee, who makes the daily bank deposit but has no access to the accounting records. Brown sends the remittance advices, which show the amount of cash received, to the accounting department for entry in the accounts receivable. Brown's only other duty is to grant allowances to customers. (An *allowance* decreases the amount that the customer must pay.) When Brown receives a customer cheque for less than the full amount of the invoice, she records the allowance in the accounting records and forwards the document to the accounting department.

I *Required*

You are a new employee of Sun Skin Care. Write a memo to the company president identifying the internal control weakness in this situation. State how to correct the weakness.

P4-46A Kenneth Austin, chief financial officer of Morin Equipment Ltd., is responsible for the company's budgeting process. Austin's staff is preparing the Morin cash budget for 2009. A key input to the budgeting process is last year's cash flow statement, which follows (amounts in thousands):

Preparing a cash budget and using cash flow information
(Obj. 4)

Morin Equipment Ltd. Cash Flow Statement 2008	
	(In thousands)
Cash Flows from Operating Activities	
Collections from customers	$ 60,000
Interest received	100
Purchases of inventory	(44,000)
Operating expenses	(13,900)
Net cash provided by operations	2,200
Cash Flows from Investing Activities	
Purchases of equipment	(4,300)
Purchases of investments	(200)
Sales of investments	400
Net cash used for investing activities	(4,100)
Cash Flows from Financing Activities	
Payment of long-term debt	(300)
Issuance of shares	1,200
Payment of cash dividends	(500)
Net cash provided by financing activities	400
Cash	
Increase (decrease) in cash	(1,500)
Cash, beginning of year	2,700
Cash, end of year	$ 1,200

❙ Required

1. Prepare the Morin Equipment Ltd. cash budget for 2009. Date the budget simply "2009" and denote the beginning and ending cash balances as "beginning" and "ending." Assume the company expects 2009 to be the same as 2008, but with the following changes:

   a. In 2009, the company expects a 15% increase in collections from customers and a 20% increase in purchases of inventory.

   b. There will be no sales of investments in 2009.

   c. Morin plans to issue no shares in 2009.

   d. Morin plans to end the year with a cash balance of $2,000 thousand.

2. Does the company's cash budget for 2009 suggest that Morin is growing, holding steady, or decreasing in size?

P4-47A Larry Raborn is a branch manager of HSBC. Active in community affairs, Raborn serves on the board of directors of **The Salvation Army**. The Salvation Army is expanding rapidly and is considering relocating. At a recent meeting, The Salvation Army decided to buy 200 hectares of land on the edge of town. The owner of the property is Freda Rader, a major depositor in his branch. Rader is completing a bitter divorce, and Raborn knows that Rader is eager to sell her property. In view of Rader's difficult situation, Raborn believes Rader would accept a low offer for the land. Realtors have appraised the property at $2.2 million.

Making an ethical judgment
(Obj. 5)

❙ Required

Apply the ethical judgment framework outlined in the chapter to help Raborn decide what role he should play in The Salvation Army's attempt to buy the land from Rader.

Setting up an effective internal control system
(Obj. 1)

(GROUP B)

P4-48B Trey Osborne, administrator of Valley View Clinic, seeks your advice. Valley View Clinic employs two people in the office, Jim Bates and Rhonda Clark. Osborne asks you how to assign the various office functions to the three people (including Osborne) to achieve good internal control. Here are the duties to be performed by the two office workers and Osborne:

a. Record cash payments
b. Record cash receipts
c. Receive incoming cash from patients
d. Reconcile the bank account
e. Deposit cash receipts
f. Sign cheques for payment

❙ Required

1. Propose a plan that divides duties a through f to Bates, Clark, and Osborne. Your goal is to divide the duties so as to achieve good internal control for the clinic.
2. Identify several combinations of duties that should not be performed by the same person.

P4-49B Each of the following situations has an internal control weakness:

Identifying internal control weaknesses
(Obj. 1, 3)

a. Retail stores such as **Sobeys** and **Home Depot** receive a significant portion of their sales revenue in cash. At the end of each day, sales clerks compare the cash in their own register with the record of sales kept within the register. They then forward the cash to a Brinks security officer for deposit in the bank.
b. The office supply company from which Martin Audiology Service purchases cash receipt forms recently notified Martin that the last-shipped sales receipts were not prenumbered. Derek Martin, the owner, replied that he did not use the receipt numbers, so the omission is unimportant to him.
c. Azbell Electronics specializes in programs with musical applications. The company's most popular product prepares musical programs for large gatherings. In the company's early days, the owner and eight employees wrote the programs, lined up production of the programs, sold the products, and performed the general management of the company. As Azbell has grown, the number of employees has increased dramatically. Recently, the development of a new musical series stopped while the programmers redesigned Azbell's sound system. Azbell could have hired outsiders to do this task.
d. Paul Allen, who has no known sources of outside income, has been a trusted employee of Chapparall Cosmetics for 20 years. Allen performs all cash-handling and accounting duties, including opening the mail, preparing the bank deposit, accounting for cash and accounts receivable, and preparing the bank reconciliation. Allen has just purchased a new Lexus. Linda Altman, owner of the company, wonders how Allen can afford the new car on his salary.
e. Monica Wade employs three professional interior designers in her design studio. The studio is located in an area with a lot of new construction, and her business is booming. Ordinarily, Wade does all the purchasing of materials needed to complete jobs. During the summer, Wade takes a long vacation, and in her absence she allows each designer to purchase materials. On her return, Wade reviews operations and observes that expenses are higher and net income is lower than in the past.

❙ Required

1. Identify the missing internal control characteristics in each situation.
2. Identify each firm's possible problem.
3. Propose a solution to the problem.

P4-50B The cash data of Navajo Products for September 2009 follow:

Preparing the bank reconciliation and using it as a control device **(Obj. 2)**

Cash

Date	Item	Jrnl. Ref.	Debit	Credit	Balance
Sept. 1	Balance				7,078
30		CR 10	9,106		16,184
30		CP 16		11,353	4,831

Cash Receipts (CR)		Cash Payments (CP)	
Date	Cash Debit	Cheque No.	Cash Credit
Sept. 1	$ 2,716	1413	$ 1,465
9	544	1414	1,004
11	1,655	1415	450
14	896	1416	8
17	367	1417	775
25	890	1418	88
30	2,038	1419	4,126
Total	$9,106	1420	970
		1421	200
		1422	2,267
		Total	$11,353

On September 30, 2009, Navajo received this bank statement:

Bank Statement for September 2009

Beginning balance		$7,078
Deposits and other additions:		
Sept. 1	$ 625 EFT	
5	2,716	
10	544	
1	1,655	
15	896	
18	367	
25	890	
30	1,400 BC	9,093
Cheques and other deductions		
Sept. 8	$ 441 NSF	
9	1,465	
13	1,004	
14	450	
15	8	
19	340 EFT	
22	775	
29	88	
30	4,216	
30	25 SC	(8,812)
Ending balance		$ 7,359

Explanation: BC—bank collection, EFT—electronic funds transfer, NSF—nonsufficient funds cheque, SC—service charge

Additional data for the bank reconciliation:

a. The EFT deposit was for monthly rent revenue. The EFT deduction was for monthly insurance expense.

b. The bank collection was of a note receivable.

c. The NSF cheque was received from a customer.

d. The correct amount of cheque number 1419, a payment on account, is $4,216. (The Navajo accountant mistakenly recorded the cheque for $4,126.)

❙ Required

1. Prepare the bank reconciliation of Navajo Products at September 30, 2009.
2. Describe how a bank account and the bank reconciliation help managers control a firm's cash.

Preparing a blank reconciliation and the related journal entries
(Obj. 2)

P4-51B The January 31, 2009, bank statement of Bed & Bath Accessories has just arrived from Royal Bank of Canada (RBC). To prepare the Bed & Bath bank reconciliation, you gather the following data:

a. The January 31 bank balance is $8,400.82.
b. Bed & Bath's Cash account shows a balance of $7,391.55 on January 31, 2009.
c. The following Bed & Bath cheques are outstanding at January 31:

Cheque No.	Amount
616	$403.00
802	74.02
806	36.60
809	161.38
810	229.05
811	48.91

d. The bank statement includes two special deposits: $899.14, which is the amount of dividend revenue the bank collected from IBM on behalf of Bed & Bath, and $16.86, the interest revenue Bed & Bath earned on its bank balance during January.
e. The bank statement lists a $6.25 bank service charge.
f. On January 31 the Bed & Bath treasurer deposited $381.14, which will appear on the February bank statement.
g. The bank statement includes a $410.00 deduction for a cheque drawn by Bonjovi Music Company.
h. The bank statement includes two charges for returned cheques from customers. One is a nonsufficient funds cheque in the amount of $67.50 received from a customer. The other is a $195.03 cheque received from another customer. It was returned by the customer's bank with the imprint "Unauthorized Signature."
i. A few customers pay monthly bills by EFT. The January bank statement lists an EFT deposit for sales revenue of $200.23.

❙ Required

1. Prepare the bank reconciliation for Bed & Bath Accessories at January 31, 2009.
2. Journalize the transactions needed to update the Cash account. Include an explanation for each entry.

Identifying an internal control weakness
(Obj. 3)

P4-52B Nordhaus Energy Co. makes all sales on credit. Cash receipts arrive by mail, usually within 30 days of the sale. Dan Webster opens envelopes and separates the cheques from the accompanying remittance advices. Webster forwards the cheques to another employee, who makes the daily bank deposit but has no access to the accounting records. Webster sends the remittance advices, which show the amount of cash received, to the accounting department for entry in the accounts receivable. Webster's only other duty is to grant allowances to customers. (An *allowance* decreases the amount that the customer must pay.) When Webster receives a customer cheque for less than the full amount of the invoice, he records the allowance in the accounting records and forwards the document to the accounting department.

❙ Required

You are a new employee of Nordhaus Energy Co. Write a memo to the company president identifying the internal control weakness in this situation. Explain how to correct the weakness.

P4-53B Melissa Becker is chief financial officer of Valero Machines. She is responsible for the company's budgeting process. Becker's staff is preparing the Valero cash budget for 2009. The starting point is the cash flow statement of the current year, 2009, which follows:

Preparing a cash budget and using cash flow information
(Obj. 1, 3)

Valero Machines Cash Flow Statement 2009	
	(in thousands)
Cash Flows from Operating Activities	
Collections from customers	$ 35,600
Interest received	100
Purchases of inventory	(11,000)
Operating expenses	(16,600)
Net cash provided by operating activities	8,100
Cash Flows from Investing Activities	
Purchases of property and equipment	(5,000)
Purchases of investments	(7,500)
Sales of investments	8,100
Net cash used by investing activities	(4,400)
Cash Flows from Financing Activities	
Payment of dividends	(2,700)
Payment of short-term debt	(1,000)
Long-term borrowings by issuing notes payable	1,200
Issuance of common shares	300
Net cash used by financing activities	(2,200)
Increase (decrease) in Cash	1,500
Cash, beginning of year	2,600
Cash, end of year	$ 4,100

❙ Required

1. Prepare the Valero Machines cash budget for 2009. Date the budget simply "2009" and denote the beginning and ending cash balances as "beginning" and "ending." Assume the company expects 2009 to be the same as 2008, but with the following changes:

   a. In 2009, the company expects a 10% increase in collections from customers, a 5% increase in purchases of inventory, and a doubling of additions to property and equipment.

   b. Operating expenses will drop by $2,000.

   c. There will be no sales of investments in 2009.

   d. Becker plans to end the year with a cash balance of $3,000.

2. Does the company's cash budget for 2009 suggest that Valero is growing, holding steady, or decreasing in size? (Challenge)

P4-54B A community bank has a loan receivable from IMS Chocolates. IMS is 6 months late in making payments to the bank, and Jan French, a bank vice-president, is assisting IMS to restructure its debt.

Making an ethical judgment
(Obj. 5)

French learns that IMS is depending on landing a contract with Snicker Foods, another bank client. French also serves as Snicker Foods' loan officer at the bank. In this capacity, French is aware that Snicker is considering bankruptcy. No one else outside Snicker Foods knows this. French has been a great help to IMS, and IMS's owner is counting on French's expertise in loan workouts to advise the company through this difficult process. To help the bank collect on this large loan, French has a strong motivation to alert IMS of Snicker's financial difficulties.

❙ Required

Apply the ethical judgment framework outlined in the chapter to help French plan her next action.

APPLY YOUR KNOWLEDGE

DECISION CASES

Using the bank reconciliation to detect a theft
(Obj. 2)

Case 1. Green Construction Inc. has poor internal control. Recently Jean Ouimet, the owner, has suspected the cashier of stealing. Here are some details of the business's cash position at June 30, 2009.

a. The Cash account shows a balance of $10,402. This amount includes a June 30 deposit of $3,794 that does not appear on the June 30 bank statement.

b. The June 30 bank statement shows a balance of $8,224. The bank statement lists a $200 bank collection, an $8 service charge, and a $36 NSF cheque. The accountant has not recorded any of these items.

c. At June 30, the following cheques are outstanding:

Cheque No.	Amount
154	$116
256	150
278	853
291	990
292	206
293	145

d. The bookkeeper records all incoming cash and makes bank deposits. He also reconciles the monthly bank statement. Here is his June 30, 2009, reconciliation:

Balance per books, June 30, 2009		$10,402
Add: Outstanding cheques		1,460
Bank collection		200
Subtotal		12,062
Less: Deposits in transit	$3,794	
Service charge	8	
NSF cheque	36	(3,838)
Balance per bank, June 30, 2009		$ 8,224

▎*Required*

Ouimet has requested that you determine whether the cashier has stolen cash from the business and, if so, how much. He also asks you to explain how the cashier has attempted to conceal the theft. To make this determination, you perform your own bank reconciliation. There are no bank or book errors. Ouimet also asks you to evaluate the internal controls and to recommend any changes needed to improve them.

Correcting an internal control weakness
(Obj. 1, 3)

Case 2. Gilead Construction Inc., which is headquartered in Calgary, Alberta, built a small apartment building in Red Deer. The construction foreman, whose name was Jon Machenko, moved to Red Deer in May to hire the 20 workers needed to complete the project. Machenko hired the construction workers, had them fill out the necessary tax forms, and sent the employment documents to the home office, which opened a payroll file for each employee.

Work on the building began on June 1. Each Friday evening, Jon Machenko filled out a time card that listed the hours worked for each employee during the 5-day work week ended at 5 p.m. on Friday. Machenko faxed the time sheets to the home office, which prepared the payroll cheques on Monday morning. Machenko drove to the home office after lunch on Monday, picked up the payroll cheques, and returned to the construction site. At 5 p.m. on Monday, Machenko distributed the payroll cheques to the workers.

a. Describe in detail the internal control weakness in this situation. Specify what negative result could occur because of the internal control weakness.

b. Describe what you would do to correct the internal control weakness.

ETHICAL ISSUE

Eric Thorman owns shoe stores in Halifax and Lunenburg. Each store has a manager who is responsible for sales and store expenses, and runs advertisements in the local newspaper. The managers transfer cash to Thorman monthly and prepare their own bank reconciliations. The manager in Lunenburg has been stealing large sums of money. To cover the theft, he understates the amount of the outstanding cheques on the monthly bank reconciliation. As a result, each monthly bank reconciliation appears to balance. However, the balance sheet reports more cash than Thorman actually has in the bank. While negotiating the sale of the shoe stores, Thorman shows the balance sheet to prospective investors.

❙ *Required*

1. Identify two parties other than Thorman who can be harmed by this theft. In what ways can they be harmed?
2. Discuss the role accounting plays in this situation.

FOCUS ON FINANCIALS

Sun-Rype Products

Refer to the Sun-Rype Products Ltd. financial statements in Appendix A at the end of this book. Suppose Sun-Rype's year-end bank statement, dated December 31, 2007, has just arrived at company headquarters. Further assume the bank statement shows Sun-Rype's cash balance at $3,187 and that Sun-Rype's Cash and Cash Equivalents account has a balance of $2,442 on the books.

Cash and internal control
(Obj. 1, 2)

1. You must determine how much to report for cash and cash equivalents on the December 31, 2007, balance sheet. Suppose you uncover these reconciling items (all amounts are assumed and in thousands):

   a. Interest earned on bank balance, $50

   b. Outstanding cheques, $800

   c. Bank collections of various items, $200

   d. Deposits in transit, $300

   e. Book error—Sun-Rype overstated cash by $5

Prepare a bank reconciliation to show how Sun-Rype arrived at the correct amount of cash and cash equivalents to report on its December 31, 2007, balance sheet. Prove that your answer is the actual amount Sun-Rype reported. Journal entries are not required.

2. In their Management's Discussion and Analysis, study Sun-Rype's Management's Reporting on Accounting Policy: Disclosure Controls and Procedures and indicate how that report links to specific items of internal control discussed in this chapter.

FOCUS ON ANALYSIS

Mullen Group Income Fund

Refer to the Mullen Group Income Fund financial statements in Appendix B at the end of this book.

Analyzing internal control and cash flows
(Obj. 1, 5)

1. Focus on Cash and cash equivalents. Why did cash change during 2007? The cash flow statement holds the answer to this question. Analyze the seven largest *individual* items on the cash flow statement (exclude net (loss) income). For each of the seven individual items, state how Mullen's action affected cash. Show amounts in thousands.

2. Mullen Group's Management's Report to the Unitholders describes the company's internal controls. Show how the report corresponds to two of the five elements in the definition of internal control.

GROUP PROJECT

You are promoting a rock concert in your area. Assume you organize as a corporation, with each member of your group purchasing $10,000 of the corporation's shares. Therefore, each of you is risking some hard-earned money on this venture. Assume it is April 1 and that the concert will be performed on June 30. Your promotional activities begin immediately, and ticket sales start on May 1. You expect to sell all the firm's assets, pay all the liabilities, and distribute all remaining cash to the group members by July 31.

I *Required*

Write an internal control manual that will help safeguard the assets of the business. The manual should address the following aspects of internal control:

1. Assign responsibilities among the group members.
2. Authorize individuals, including group members and any outsiders that you need to hire, to perform specific jobs.
3. Separate duties among the group and any employees.
4. Describe all documents needed to account for and safeguard the business's assets.

QUICK CHECK ANSWERS

1. *g, e, h, d, f, c, a Unused: b, i*
2. *a*
3. *d*
4. *b*
5. *b, d, d, d, a, a, c, d, d*
6. *b*
7. *b*
8. *c*
9. *b*
10. *d*
11. *c*

Short-Term Investments and Receivables

5

Learning Objectives

1 **Account** for short-term investments

2 **Apply** internal controls to receivables

3 **Use** the allowance method for uncollectible receivables

4 **Account** for notes receivable

5 **Use** two new ratios to evaluate a business

SPOTLIGHT

"Mullen is recognized as the largest provider of specialized transportation and related services to the oil and natural gas industry in western Canada and is one of the leading suppliers of trucking and logistics services in Canada."[*] While capital assets make up the majority of Mullen's total assets, accounts receivable are a significant asset and the largest current asset. It turns out that receivables are the largest assets for many companies, including Research In Motion and Petro-Canada. Receivables are the largest current asset for Petro-Canada, but not their largest asset. Their PPE is 10 times their A/R.

Another category of current assets is short-term investments. Investments held for trading may be categorized as short-term, if management intends to convert them into cash within one year, or long-term, if management intends to hold them for one year or longer. Short-term investments held for trading are listed on the balance sheet immediately after cash and before receivables because they are very liquid.

Mullen Group had no short-term investments held for trading at December 31, 2007, but it did hold $7.6 million worth of investments for trading, which are included with the capital assets on the partial balance sheet that follows.

[*]Mullen Group Income Fund Interim Report for the Three- and Six-Month Period ended June 30, 2008.

		Mullen Group Income Fund		
▼		Consolidated Balance Sheets (Excerpt, Adapted)		
		December 31, 2007 and 2006		

	($ thousands)	
	2007	**2006**
Assets		
Current assets:		
Cash and cash equivalents..	$ 79,155	$ 49,398
Accounts receivable	185,475	209,545
Income taxes recoverable...	1,488	6,834
Prepaid expenses...	27,715	27,675
Total Current Assets..	293,833	293,452
Investments..	9,884	1,825
Property, plant, and equipment.......................................	586,823	558,522
Goodwill	794,448	1,041,827
Intangible assets..	82,674	116,284
Other assets..	2,828	9,335
Total Assets	$1,770,490	$2,021,245

Objective

1 **Account** for short-term investments

This chapter shows how to account for short-term investments and receivables. We cover short-term investments along with receivables to emphasize their relative liquidity. Short-term investments are the next-most-liquid current assets after cash. (Recall that liquid means close to cash.) We begin our discussion with short-term investments.

Short-Term Investments

Short-term investments, also called **marketable securities** or *temporary investments*, are investments that a company plans to hold for one year or less. These investments allow the company to invest excess cash for a short period of time and earn a return until the cash is needed.

IFRS ALERT

This chapter deals with investments and accounts receivable, which are a subset of financial instruments. The accounting discussed in the chapter is based on several *CICA Handbook* Sections, including Section 3855 "Financial Instruments—Recognition and Measurement." The focus of Section 3855, which is relevant for this chapter, is the valuation of financial instruments using fair value as the basis of valuation.

Section 3855 is a good example of the convergence of Canadian generally accepted accounting principles (GAAP) with IFRS. It is based in a large part *but not completely* on International Accounting Standard (IAS) 32 "Financial Instruments: Presentation and Disclosure" and IAS 39 "Financial Instruments: Recognition and Measurement," which were issued in revised form in December 2003 and March 2004 by the International Accounting Standards Board (IASB).

In a companion note to Section 3855 titled "Financial Instruments—Recognition and Measurement—Background Information and Basis for Conclusions," the Accounting Standards Board (AcSB) notes, "Work in this subject area continues globally. In developing Section 3855, the AcSB has taken into account matters identified by the IASB in its roundtables and exposure processes related to improving IAS 39. The AcSB continues to monitor FASB and IASB activities and will consider them to the extent they have a direct impact on the conclusions in Section 3855."

In other words, the convergence to IFRS is an ongoing process. And convergence differs from adoption, as was pointed out in the IFRS Alert in Chapter 1.

Because short-term investments are the next most liquid asset after cash we report short-term investments immediately after cash and before receivables on the balance sheet. A short-term investment falls into one of three categories:

Three Categories of Short-Term Investments		
Financial Asset Held for Trading Investment	Available-for-Sale Investment	Held-to-Maturity Investment
Covered in this section of the chapter	Covered in Chapter 10	Same as accounting for a note receivable, which is explained starting on page 230.

IFRS

An investor, such as Loblaw Companies Limited, expects to sell a financial asset held for **trading investment** within a very short time—a few months at most. Therefore, all such investments are current assets. The other two categories of investments are either short-term or long-term, depending on how long management intends to hold them. Let's begin with financial assets held for trading investments.

Trading Investments

The purpose of owning a financial asset held for trading investment (trading investment) is to hold it for a short time and then sell it for more than its cost. Trading investments can be shares or bonds in another company. Suppose Loblaw purchases shares in TransCanada Corporation, intending to sell the shares in a few months. If the market value of the TransCanada shares increases, Loblaw will have a gain; if TransCanada's share price decreases, Loblaw will have a loss. Along the way, Loblaw will receive dividend revenue from TransCanada.

Suppose Loblaw buys the TransCanada shares on December 18, 2008, paying $100,000 cash. Loblaw records the purchase of the investment at cost:

2008
Dec. 18   Short-Term Investments 100,000
       Cash   100,000
       Purchased investment.

Short-Term Investments
100,000

Assume on December 27 Loblaw receives a cash dividend of $800 from TransCanada. Loblaw records the receipt of the dividend as follows:

2008
Dec. 27   Cash 800
       Dividend Revenue   800
       Received cash dividend.

ASSETS	=	LIABILITIES	+	SHAREHOLDERS' EQUITY	+	REVENUES
+800	=	0	+	0	+	800

Unrealized Gains and Losses

Loblaw's fiscal year ends on January 3, 2009, and Loblaw prepares financial statements. Assume the TransCanada shares have risen in value, and on January 3, 2009, Loblaw's investment has a current market value (fair value) of $102,000. Market value is the

IFRS

IFRS

amount the owner can receive when selling the investment. Loblaw has an *unrealized gain* on the investment.

- *Gain* because the market value ($102,000) is greater than Loblaw's investment cost. A gain has the same effect on owners' equity as a revenue.
- *Unrealized gain* because Loblaw has not yet sold the investment.

Trading investments are reported on the balance sheet at their current market value because that is the amount the investor can receive by selling the investment.

On January 3, 2009, Loblaw makes year-end adjustments to bring the TransCanada investment to its current market value with the following entries:

2009			
Jan. 3	Short-Term Investments	2,000	
	Unrealized Gain on Investments		2,000
	Adjusted investment to market value.		

Short-Term Investments		Unrealized Gain on Investments	
100,000			2,000
2,000			
102,000			

After the adjustment, Loblaw's investment account appears as shown above. The short-term investments account is ready to be reported on the balance sheet at current market value of $102,000.

If Loblaw's investment in TransCanada shares had decreased in value, say to $95,000, then Loblaw would have reported an unrealized loss. A *loss* has the same effect on owners' equity as an expense. In this case, Loblaw would make a different entry at January 3, 2009, for an *unrealized loss* of $5,000.

2009			
Jan. 3	Unrealized Loss on Investments	5,000	
	Short-Term Investments		5,000
	Adjusted investment to market value.		

Short-Term Investments		Unrealized Loss on Investments	
100,000	5,000	5,000	
95,000			

Reporting on the Balance Sheet and the Income Statement

The Balance Sheet. Short-term investments are current assets. They appear on the balance sheet immediately after cash because short-term investments are almost as liquid as cash. (*Liquid* means close to cash.) Report short-term investments at their *current market value*.

IFRS

Income Statement. Investments earn interest revenue and dividend revenue. Investments also create gains and losses. For short-term investments, these items are reported on the income statement as Other revenue, gains, and losses as shown in Exhibit 5-1.

EXHIBIT 5-1	Reporting Short-Term Investments and the Related Revenues, Gains, and Losses (Amounts from the Preceding Example)

Balance sheet			Income statement		
Current assets:			Revenues	$	XXX
Cash.......................................	$	XXX	Other revenue, gains, and (losses)		
Short-term investments, at			Interest revenue.........................		XXX
market value		102,000	Dividend revenue......................		800
Accounts receivable		XXX	Unrealized gain on investments ...		2,000
			Net income....................................	$	XXX

Realized Gains and Losses

A *realized* gain or loss usually occurs only when the investor sells an investment. The gain or loss is different from the unrealized gain that we reported for Loblaw above. The result may be a:

- Realized gain → Sale price *greater than* investment carrying amount
- Realized loss → Sale price *less than* investment carrying amount

Suppose Loblaw sells its TransCanada shares on February 19, 2009. The sale price is $98,000, and Loblaw makes the following journal entry:

```
2009
Feb. 19   Cash .................................................................    98,000
          Loss on Sale of Investments ................................     4,000
              Short-Term Investments ...................................              102,000
          Sold short-term investments at a loss.
```

Loss on Sale of Investments		Short-Term Investments	
4,000		102,000	102,000
		Bal. 0	

Accountants rarely use the word "Realized" in the account title. A gain (or a loss) is understood to be a realized gain (or loss) arising from a sale transaction. Unrealized gains and losses are clearly labelled as *unrealized*. Loblaw would report Gain (or Loss) on Sale of Investments among the "Other" items in the income statement.

Lending Agreements and the Current Ratio

Lending agreements often require the borrower to maintain a current ratio at some specified level, say 1.50 or greater. What happens when the borrower's current ratio falls below 1.50? The consequences can be severe:

- The lender can call the loan for immediate payment.
- If the borrower cannot pay, then the lender may take over the company.

Suppose it's December 10 and it looks like Duck Lake Wood Products Inc.'s (DLWP) current ratio will end the year at a value of 1.48. That would put DLWP in default on the lending agreement and create a bad situation. With three weeks remaining in the year, how can DLWP improve its current ratio?

Recall that the current ratio is computed as:

$$\text{Current ratio} = \frac{\text{Total current assets}}{\text{Total current liabilities}}$$

There are several strategies for increasing the current ratio, such as:

1. **Launch a major sales effort.** The increase in cash and receivables will more than offset the decrease in Inventory, total current assets will increase, and the current ratio will improve.

2. **Pay off some current liabilities before year-end.** Both current assets in the numerator and current liabilities in the denominator will decrease by the same amount. The proportionate impact on current liabilities in the denominator will be greater than the impact on current assets in the numerator, and the current ratio will increase. This strategy increases the current ratio when the current ratio is already above 1.0, as for DLWP.

USER ALERT

A third strategy is questionable, and we wish to alert you to one of the accounting games that companies sometimes play. Suppose DLWP has some long-term investments (investments that DLWP plans to hold for longer than a year—that is, capital assets). Before year-end DLWP can reclassify these long-term investments as current assets. The investments increase DLWP's current assets, which increases the current ratio. This strategy would be okay if DLWP does in fact plan to sell the investments within the next year. But the strategy would be dishonest if DLWP plans to keep the investments for longer than a year.

The above examples and User Alert illustrate that accounting is not cut-and-dried or all black-and-white. It takes good judgment—and honesty—to be a successful accountant.

MyAccountingLab

MID-CHAPTER SUMMARY PROBLEM

TELUS Corporation is a leading Canadian communications company. One of the current assets on Telus Corporation's balance sheet is Short-Term Investments. Their cost is $41.8 million. Their market value is $42.4 million.

What will TELUS report on the balance sheet at December 31, 2007? What will TELUS Corporation report on its 2007 income statement? Show the Short-Term Investments T-account.

Name: TELUS Corporation
Industry: Communications corporation
Accounting Period: Year ended December 31, 2007

Short-term investments are included in current assets.

An unrealized gain is the excess of the market value over the cost.

IFRS

Answer

Short-Term Investments, reported on the balance sheet as follows (amounts in millions):

	(In millions)
Current assets	
Short-term investments at market value	$42.4

TELUS Corporation's income statement will report:

	(In millions)
Other Revenue, Gains, and (Losses):	
Unrealized gain on investment ($42.4 − $41.8 million)	$ 0.6

Suppose TELUS sells the investments on February 7, 2008, for $41.4 million. Journalize the sale and then show the Short-Term Investments account as it would appear after the sale.

Answer

2008			
Feb. 7	Cash	41,400,000	
	Loss on Sale of Short-Term Investments	1,000,000	
	Short-Term Investments...............................		42,400,000
	Sold short-term investments at a loss.		

Short-Term Investments	
41,800,000	
600,000	42,400,000
Bal. 0	

Accounts and Notes Receivable

Receivables are the third-most liquid asset—after cash and short-term investments. Most of the remainder of the chapter shows how to account for receivables.

Types of Receivables

Receivables are monetary claims against others. They are acquired mainly by selling goods and services (accounts receivable) and by lending money (notes receivable). Journal entries to record receivables can be shown as follows:

Performing a Service on Account		Lending Money on a Note Receivable	
Accounts Receivable...................... XXX		Note Receivable......................... XXX	
Service Revenue	XXX	Cash.....................................	XXX
Performed a service on account.		Loaned money to another company.	

The two major types of receivables are accounts receivable and notes receivable. A business's *accounts receivable* are the amounts collectible from customers from the sale of goods and services. Accounts receivable, which are *current assets*, are sometimes called *trade receivables* or merely *receivables*.

The Accounts Receivable account in the general ledger serves as a *control account* that summarizes the total amount receivable from all customers. Companies also keep a *subsidiary ledger* of accounts receivable with a separate account for each customer, illustrated as follows:

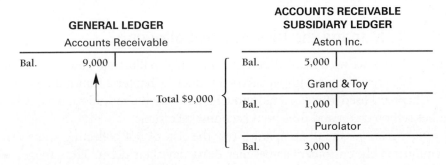

Notes receivable are more formal contracts than accounts receivable. The borrower signs a written promise to pay the creditor a definite sum at the *maturity* date. That is why notes receivable are also called promissory notes. The note may require the borrower to pledge *security* for the loan. This means that the borrower gives the lender permission to claim certain assets, called *collateral*, if the borrower fails to pay the amount due. We cover the details of notes receivable on page 230.

Other Receivables is a miscellaneous category that includes loans to employees and subsidiary companies. Some companies report other receivables under the heading Other Assets on the balance sheet.

Internal Controls over Cash Collections on Account

Objective

2 **Apply** internal controls to receivables

Businesses that sell on credit receive most of their cash payment on account by mail. Internal control over collections on account is important. Chapter 4 discussed control procedures for cash receipts, but another element of internal control deserves emphasis here—the separation of cash-handling and cash-accounting duties. Consider the following case:

> Butler Supply Co. Ltd. is a small, family-owned business that takes pride in the loyalty of its workers. Most employees have been with the Butlers for at least five years. The company makes 90% of its sales on account.
>
> The office staff consists of a bookkeeper and a supervisor. The bookkeeper maintains the general ledger and a subsidiary record of individual accounts receivable. He also makes the daily bank deposit. The supervisor prepares monthly financial statements and any special reports the Butlers require. She also takes sales orders from customers and serves as office manager.

Can you identify the internal control weakness here? The problem is that the bookkeeper makes the deposit. With this cash-handling duty, the bookkeeper could steal an incoming customer cheque and write off the customer's account as uncollectible. The customer doesn't complain because the bookkeeper has written the account off the books and Butler, therefore, stops pursuing collection.

How can this weakness be corrected? The supervisor—not the bookkeeper—could open incoming mail and make the daily bank deposit. The bookkeeper should *not* be allowed to handle cash. Only the remittance advices would be forwarded to the bookkeeper to credit customer accounts receivable. Removing cash handling from the bookkeeper and keeping the accounts away from the supervisor separates duties and strengthens internal control.

Using a bank lockbox achieves the same separation of duties. Customers send their payments directly to Butler Supply Co. Ltd.'s bank, which records and deposits the cash into Butler's bank account. The bank then forwards the remittance advice to Butler's bookkeeper, who credits the customer account. No Butler employee ever touches incoming cash.

How Do We Manage the Risk of Not Collecting?

In Chapters 1 to 4, we used many different companies to illustrate how to account for a business. Chapter 1 began with Sun-Rype Products. Chapter 2 featured Research In Motion. Chapter 3 used Tim Hortons, and Chapter 4 used GreBru Products. All these companies sell on credit and thus hold accounts receivable.

By selling on credit, all companies run the risk of not collecting some receivables. Unfortunately, customers sometimes don't pay their debts. The prospect that we may fail to collect from a customer provides the biggest challenge in accounting for receivables. The Decision Guidelines address this challenge.

Accounting for Uncollectible Receivables

A company gets an account receivable only when it sells its product or service on credit (on account). You'll recall that the entry to record the earning of revenue on account is (amount assumed):

Accounts Receivable	1,000	
Sales Revenue (or Service Revenue)		1,000
Earned revenue on account.		

Ideally, the company would collect cash for all its receivables. But unfortunately the entry to record cash collections on account is for only $950.

Cash	950	
Accounts Receivable		950
Collections on account.		

You can see that companies rarely collect all of their accounts receivables. So companies must account for their uncollectible accounts—$50 in this example.

Selling on credit creates both a benefit and a cost:

- *Benefit*: Customers who cannot pay cash immediately can buy on credit, so company profits rise as sales increase.

- *Cost*: The company will be unable to collect from some credit customers. Accountants label this cost **uncollectible-account expense, doubtful-account expense**, or **bad-debt expense**.

The *CICA Handbook* in Section 3020, paragraph .01, "Accounts and Notes Receivable," states, "Since it is to be assumed that adequate allowance for doubtful accounts has been made if no statement has been made to the contrary, it is not considered necessary to refer to such an allowance." Accordingly, most companies do not disclose an allowance for doubtful accounts; they show the net value of accounts receivable in their financial statements.

The IFRS Alert on page 216 mentioned *CICA Handbook* Section 3855, which deals with financial instruments. A basic principle of Section 3855 in paragraph .02 (b) states that "fair value is the most relevant measure for financial instruments..." However *CICA Handbook* Section 3862, paragraph .29, states, "Disclosure of fair value [are] not required...when the carrying amount [net realizable value] is a reasonable approximation of fair value...such as short-term trade receivables..." GAAP requires that accounts receivable be valued in the financial statements at cost minus an appropriate allowance for doubtful accounts (that is, net realizable value).

IFRS

Bad debt expense is not shown as a separate line item on the income statement; it is usually included in Selling Expense or Administrative Expense.

A company that chose to present the allowance for doubtful accounts could present the information in the notes to the financial statements or disclose the information on the balance sheet as follows:

Accounts receivable (net of allowance for doubtful accounts of $120,000)	$2,005,234

Uncollectible-account expense is an operating expense along with salary expense, rent expense, and utilities expense. To measure uncollectible-account expense, accountants use the allowance method or, in certain limited cases, the direct write-off method (which we discuss starting on page 228).

Allowance Method

Objective

③ **Use** the allowance method for uncollectible receivables

The best way to measure bad debts is by the **allowance method**. This method records collection losses on the basis of estimates. Management does not wait to see which customers will not pay. Managers estimate bad-debt expense on the basis of the company's collection experience. The business records the estimated amount as Uncollectible-Account Expense and sets up an **Allowance for Uncollectible Accounts**. Other titles for this account are **Allowance for Doubtful Accounts** and **Allowance for Bad Debts**. This is a contra account to Accounts Receivable. The allowance shows the amount of the receivables that the business expects *not* to collect.

In Chapter 3 we used the Accumulated Amortization account to show how much of a property, plant, and equipment asset has been expensed—the portion of the asset that is no longer a benefit to the company. Allowance for Uncollectible Receivables serves a similar purpose for Accounts Receivable. The allowance shows how much of the receivable has been expensed. You'll find the following table helpful (amounts are assumed).

Property, Plant, and Equipment	$100,000	Accounts Receivable	$10,000
Less: Accumulated		Less: Allowance for	
Amortization	(40,000)	Uncollectible Accounts	(900)
Property, Plant, and Equipment, net	$ 60,000	Accounts Receivable, net	$ 9,100

Focus on Accounts Receivable. Customers owe this company $10,000, but the company expects to collect only $9,100. This amount is known as the net realizable value. Another way to report these receivables is:

Accounts receivable, net of allowance for uncollectible accounts of $900 .... $9,100

You can work backward to determine the full amount of the receivable, $10,000 (net realizable value of $9,100 plus the allowance of $900).

The income statement reports uncollectible-account expense among the operating expenses as follows (using assumed figures):

Income statement (partial):
Expenses:
Uncollectible-account expense.. $2,000

STOP & THINK

You are considering an investment in Open Text Corporation and are looking at Open Text's June 30, 2008, financial statements, which are stated in thousands of U.S. dollars. In particular, you are focusing on Open Text's accounts receivable. The balance sheet includes the following:

	June 30	
	2008	2007
Accounts receivable trade, net of allowance for doubtful accounts of $3,974 as of June 30, 2008, and $2,089 as of June 30, 2007....	$134,396	$128,781

At June 30, 2008, how much did customers owe Open Text Corporation? How much did Open Text expect *not* to collect? How much of the receivables did Open Text expect to collect? What was the net realizable value of Open Text Corporation's receivables?

Answer:

	Thousands
Customers owed Open Text Corporation	$138,370
Open Text expected not to collect	3,974
Open Text expected to collect—net realizable value	$134,396

The best way to estimate uncollectibles uses the company's history of collections from customers. There are two basic ways to estimate uncollectibles:

- Percentage-of-sales method
- Aging-of-receivables method

Percentage-of-Sales. The **percentage-of-sales method** computes uncollectible-account expense as a percentage of revenue. This method takes an *income-statement approach* because it focuses on the amount of expense to be reported on the income statement. Assume it is June 30, 2008, and Open Text Corporation's accounts have these balances *before the year-end adjustments* (the following discussion expresses all amounts in thousands):

Accounts Receivable		Allowance for Uncollectible Accounts	
138,370			346

Customers owe Open Text Corporation $138,370, and the Allowance amount is $346. Suppose the economy slows down, and Open Text's top managers know that the company will fail to collect more than $346. Suppose Open Text's credit department estimates that uncollectible-account expense is 1/2 of 1% (0.005) of total revenues, which were $725,532 for 2008. The entry to record bad-debt expense for the year also updates the allowance as follows:

2008
June 30   Uncollectible-Account Expense ($725,532 × 0.005)   3,628
               Allowance for Uncollectible Accounts   3,628
           Recorded expense for the year

The expense decreases assets, as shown by the accounting equation:

ASSETS	=	LIABILITIES	+	SHAREHOLDERS' EQUITY	–	EXPENSES
−3,628	=	0			–	3,628

Now the accounts are ready for reporting in the financial statements.

Accounts Receivable		Allowance for Uncollectible Accounts	
138,370			346
			3,628
			3,974

Net accounts receivable, $134,396

Compare these amounts to the Stop & Think answer on page 224. They are the same.

Customers still owe Open Text Corporation $138,370, but now the Allowance for Uncollectible Accounts balance is realistic. Open Text's balance sheet actually reported accounts receivable at their net realizable value amount of $134,396 ($138,370 − $3,974). Open Text's income statement included uncollectible-account expense among the operating expenses for the period.

Aging of Accounts Receivable. The other popular method for estimating uncollectibles is called **aging of accounts receivable**. This method is a *balance-sheet approach* because it focuses on Accounts Receivable. In the aging method, individual receivables from specific customers are analyzed based on how long they have been outstanding.

Computerized accounting packages are programmed to age the company's accounts receivable. Exhibit 5-2 shows an assumed aging of receivables for Open Text at June 30, 2008. Open Text's receivables total $138,370 (in thousands of U.S. dollars). Of this amount, the aging schedule shows that the company will *not* collect $6,156, but the allowance for uncollectible accounts is not yet up-to-date. Suppose Open Text's accounts are as follows *before the year-end adjustment* (in thousands):

Accounts Receivable	Allowance for Uncollectible Accounts
138,370	346

The aging method will bring the balance of the allowance account ($346) to the needed amount ($6,156) as determined by the aging schedule in Exhibit 5-2. The lower left corner gives the needed balance in the allowance account. To update the allowance, Open Text Corporation would make this entry:

2008
June 30 Uncollectible-Account Expense ($6,156 − $346)   5,810
              Allowance for Uncollectible Accounts   5,810
         Recorded expense for the year

The expense decreases assets, as shown by the accounting equation.

ASSETS	=	LIABILITIES	+	SHAREHOLDERS' EQUITY	−	EXPENSES
−5,810	=	0			−	5,810

Now the balance sheet can report the amount that Open Text Corporation actually expects to collect from customers: $132,214 ($138,370 − $6,156). This is the net realizable value of Open Text's trade receivables. Open Text's accounts are now ready for the balance sheet, as follows:

Accounts Receivable	Allowance for Uncollectible Accounts	
138,370		346
	Adj.	5,810
	End. Bal.	6,156

Net accounts receivable, $132,214

EXHIBIT 5-2   **Aging the Accounts Receivable of Open Text Corporation**

		Dollar Amounts (in Thousands)			
		Number of Days Past Due			
Customer	*Total*	*1–30*	*31–60*	*61–90*	*over 90*
City of Regina	$ 500	$ 500			
IBM Canada	1,000	1,000			
Keady Pipe Corp.	2,100		$ 1,000	$ 1,100	
TorBar Inc.	200			200	
Others	134,570	66,070	57,000	9,000	$2,500
	$138,370	$67,570	$58,000	$10,300	$2,500
Estimated % Uncollectible		2%	5%	10%	35%
Total Estimated Uncollectible Accounts	$ 6,156	$ 1,351	$ 2,900	$ 1,030	$ 875

Writing Off Uncollectible Accounts. Suppose that early in July 2008, Open Text's credit department determines that Open Text cannot collect from customers Keady Pipe Corporation and TorBar Inc. (see Exhibit 5-2). Open Text Corporation then writes off the receivables from these two delinquent customers with the following entry (in thousands of U.S. dollars):

2008
July 12   Allowance for Uncollectible Accounts   2,300
                 Accounts Receivable—Keady Pipe Corporation............   2,100
                 Accounts Receivable—TorBar Inc.   200
             Wrote off uncollectible receivables.

After the write-off, Open Text's accounts show these amounts:

Accounts Receivable—Keady Pipe Corp.		Accounts Receivable—TorBar Inc.		Allowance for Uncollectible Accounts	
2,100	2,100	200	200	2,300	6,156
					3,856

Accounts Receivable Other	
136,070	

Total Accounts Receivable = $136,070   Allowance = $3,856

Accounts Receivable, Net = $132,214

The accounting equation shows that the write-off of uncollectibles has no effect on total assets. The net realizable value of accounts receivable is still $132,214. There is no effect on net income either, because no income statement account is affected.

ASSETS	=	LIABILITIES	+	SHAREHOLDERS' EQUITY
+2,300				
−2,300	=	0	+	0

STOP & THINK

Combining the Percentage-of-Sales and the Aging-of-Accounts-Receivable Methods. Most companies use the percentage-of-sales and aging-of-accounts-receivable methods together, as follows:

- For *interim statements* (monthly or quarterly), companies use the percentage-of-sales method because it is easier to apply. The percentage-of-sales method focuses on the uncollectible-account *expense*, but that is not enough.

- At the end of the year, companies use the aging-of-accounts-receivable method to ensure that Accounts Receivable is reported at *net realizable value* on the balance sheet. The aging-of-accounts-receivable method focuses on the amount of the receivables that is uncollectible.

- Using the two methods together provides good measures of both the expense and the asset. Exhibit 5-3 compares the two methods.

Direct Write-Off Method

There is another, less preferable, way to account for uncollectible receivables. Under the **direct write-off method**, the company waits until it decides that a specific customer's receivable is uncollectible. Then the accountant records Uncollectible-Account Expense and writes off the customer's Account Receivable as follows (using assumed data):

2009
Jan. 30   Uncollectible-Account Expense.......................................   2,000
                  Accounts Receivable—Jones Inc.   2,000
                  Wrote off an uncollectible account by direct write-off method.

This method is defective for two reasons:

1. The direct write-off method does not set up an allowance for uncollectible accounts. As a result, receivables are always reported at their full amount, which is more than the business expects to collect. *Assets on the balance sheet are overstated.*

2. The direct write-off method causes a poor matching of uncollectible-account expense against revenue. In this example, the company made the sale to Jones Inc. in 2008 and should have recorded the expense during 2008. By recording the expense in 2009, the company overstates net income *in 2008*. Then, by recording the expense when it writes off the receivable in 2009, the company understates net income *in 2009*.

According to the matching principle, expenses should be matched against the revenue of the same period. Thus, the direct write-off method is acceptable only when uncollectibles are so low that there is no significant difference between uncollectible account expense by the allowance method and the direct write-off method.

Computing Cash Collections from Customers

A company earns revenue and then collects the cash from customers. For Open Text and most other companies there is a time lag between earning the revenue and collecting the cash. Collections from customers are the single most important source of cash for any business. You can compute a company's collections from customers by

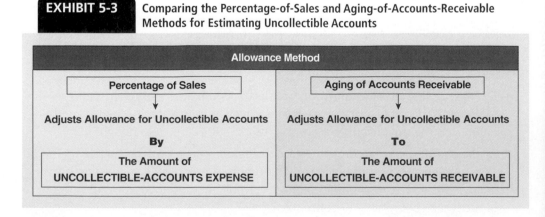

EXHIBIT 5-3   Comparing the Percentage-of-Sales and Aging-of-Accounts-Receivable Methods for Estimating Uncollectible Accounts

analyzing its Accounts Receivable account. Receivables typically hold only five different items, as follows (amounts assumed):

Accounts Receivable			
Beg. balance (left from last period)	200	Write-offs of uncollectible accounts	100**
		Collections from customers	$X = 1,500$†
Sales (or service) revenue	1,800*		
End. balance (carries over to next period)	400		

*The journal entry that places revenue into the receivable account is

Accounts Receivable	1,800	
Sales (or Service) Revenue		1,800

**The journal entry for write-offs is

Allowance for Uncollectible Accounts	100	
Accounts Receivable		100

†The journal entry that places collections into the receivable account is

Cash	1,500	
Accounts Receivable		1,500

Suppose you know all these amounts except collections from customers. You can compute collections by solving for X in the T-account.*

Often write-offs are not known and must be omitted. Then the computation of collections becomes an approximation.

USER ALERT

Shifting Sales into the Current Period Makes a Company Look Good Now, But You Pay for It Later

Suppose it is December 26. Late in the year a company's business dried up: Its profits are running below what everyone predicted. The company needs a loan and its banker requires financial statements to support the loan request. Unless the company acts quickly, it won't get the loan.

Fortunately, next year looks better. The company has standing orders for sales of $50,000. As soon as the company gets the merchandise, it can ship it to customers and record the sales. An old accounting trick can solve the problem. Book the $50,000 of sales in December. After all, the company will be shipping the goods on January 2 of next year. What difference does two days make?

It makes all the difference in the world. Shifting the sales into the current year will make the company look better immediately. Reported profits will rise, the current ratio will improve, and the company can then get the loan needed. But what are the consequences? If caught, the company will be prosecuted for fraud and its reputation will be ruined. Remember that the company shifted next year's sales into the current year. Next year's sales will be lower than the true amount, and profits will suffer. If next year turns out to be like this year, the company will be facing the same shortage again. Also, something may come up to keep the company from shipping the goods on January 2.

Very few companies pull these tricks, because they are dishonest, unethical, and illegal. Honesty is always the best policy.

The take-away lesson from this User Alert is this:

- Study a company's financial-statement notes to learn when it books revenue. If booked too early, the company's revenues aren't there yet and shouldn't be recognized.

Notes Receivable

As stated earlier, notes receivable are more formal than accounts receivable. Notes receivable due within 1 year or less are current assets. Notes due beyond 1 year are *long-term receivables* and are reported as capital assets. Some notes receivable are

---

*An equation may help you solve for X. The equation is $200 + 1,800 - X - 100 = 400$. $X = 1,500$.

collected in installments. The portion due within 1 year is a current asset and the remainder is long term. RONA Inc. may hold a $20,000 note receivable from a customer, but only the $6,000 the customer must pay within 1 year is a current asset of RONA.

Before launching into the accounting for notes receivable, let's define some key terms:

Creditor.	The party to whom money is owed. The creditor is also called the **lender**.
Debtor.	The party that borrowed and owes money on the note. The debtor is also called the **maker** of the note or the **borrower**.
Interest.	Interest is the cost of borrowing money. The interest is stated in an annual percentage rate.
Maturity date.	The date on which the debtor must pay the note.
Maturity value.	The sum of principal and interest on the note.
Principal.	The amount of money borrowed by the debtor.
Term.	The length of time from when the note was signed by the debtor to when the debtor must pay the note.

There are two parties to a note:

- The *creditor* has a note receivable.
- The *debtor* has a note payable.

The debtor signs the note and thereby creates a contract with the creditor. Exhibit 5-4 shows a typical promissory note.

The **principal** amount of the note ($1,000) is the amount borrowed by the debtor and lent by the creditor. This six-month note runs from July 1, 2009, to December 31, 2009, when Lauren Holland (the maker) promises to pay Canadian Western Bank (the creditor) the principal of $1,000 plus 9% interest per year. **Interest** is revenue to the creditor (Canadian Western Bank, in this case).

EXHIBIT 5-4 A Promissory Note

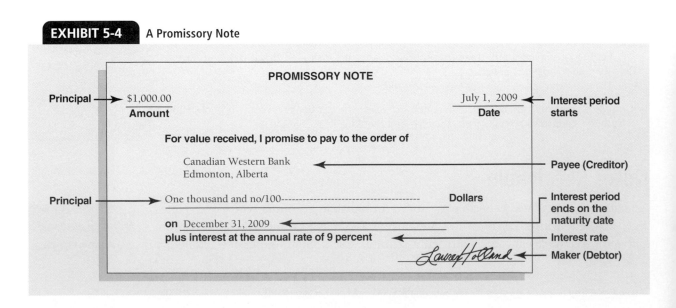

Accounting for Notes Receivable

Consider the promissory note shown in Exhibit 5-4. After Lauren Holland (the maker) signs the note, Canadian Western Bank gives her $1,000 cash. The bank's entries follow, assuming an October 31, 2009, year-end for Canadian Western Bank:

2009
July 1   Note Receivable—L. Holland 1,000
             Cash...   1,000
         Made a loan.

Note Receivable—L. Holland	
1,000	

The bank gave one asset, cash, in return for another asset, a note receivable, so the total assets did not change.

ASSETS	=	LIABILITIES	+	SHAREHOLDERS' EQUITY
+1,000 −1,000	=	0	+	0

Canadian Western Bank earns interest revenue during July, August, September, and October. At October 31, 2009, the bank accrues interest revenue for four months as follows:

2009
Oct. 31   Interest Receivable ($1,000 × 0.09 × 4/12) 30
              Interest Revenue...   30
          Accrued interest revenue.

The bank's assets and its revenue increase.
The bank reports these amounts in its financial statements at October 31, 2009:

Balance sheet
Current assets:
    Note receivable... $1,000
    Interest receivable...   30
Income statement
    Interest revenue... $30

The bank collects the note on December 31, 2009, and records:

2009
Dec. 31   Cash.. 1,045
              Note Receivable—L. Holland   1,000
              Interest Receivable...   30
              Interest Revenue ($1,000 × 0.09 × 2/12)..................   15
          Collected note at maturity.

This entry zeroes out Note Receivable and Interest Receivable and also records the interest revenue earned in the year ended October 31, 2010.

Note Receivable—L. Holland	
1,000	1,000

In its 2010 financial statements the only item that Canadian Western Bank will report is the interest revenue of $15 that was earned in 2010. There's no note receivable or interest receivable on the balance sheet because those items were zeroed out when the bank collected the note at maturity.

Three aspects of these entries deserve mention:

1. Interest rates are always for an annual period unless stated otherwise. In this example, the annual interest rate is 9%. At October 31, 2009, Canadian Western Bank accrues interest revenue for the four months the bank has held the note. The interest computation is:

$$\text{Principal} \times \text{Interest rate} \times \text{Time} = \text{Amount of Interest}$$
$$\$1{,}000 \times 0.09 \times 4/12 = \$30$$

2. The time element (4/12) is the fraction of the year that the note has been in force during the year ended October 31, 2009.

3. Interest is often completed for a number of days. For example, suppose you loaned out $10,000 on April 10. The note receivable runs for 90 days and specifies interest at 8%.

    a. Interest starts accruing on April 11 and runs for 90 days, ending on the due date, July 9, as follows:

Month	Number of Days That Interest Accrues
April	20
May	31
June	30
July	9
Total	90

    b. The interest computation is: $\$10{,}000 \times 0.08 \times 90/365 = \$197$

Some companies sell goods and services on notes receivable (versus selling on accounts receivable). This often occurs when the payment term extends beyond the customary accounts receivable period of 30 to 60 days.

Suppose that on March 20, 2009, West Fraser Timber Co. Ltd. sells lumber for $15,000 to Darmal Const. Inc. West Fraser receives Darmal's 90-day promissory note at 10% annual interest. The entries to record the sale and collection from Darmal follow the pattern illustrated previously for Canadian Western Bank and Lauren Holland, with one exception. At the outset, West Fraser would credit Sales Revenue (instead of Cash) because West Fraser is making a sale (and not lending money to Darmal).

IFRS

GAAP requires that notes receivable of the kind discussed in this chapter be valued in the same way as accounts receivable in that an appropriate allowance should be set up for notes thought to be uncollectible. It was quoted earlier in this chapter that "Disclosures of fair value [are] not required...when the carrying amount [net realizable value] is a reasonable approximation of fair value...such as short-term trade receivables...." The statement would be applicable in the case of short-term notes receivable arising from the sale of goods or services.

Notes with a maturity of more than 365 days would be classified as "held-to-maturity investments" since it is likely that they will be held to maturity by the lender. Accordingly the notes should be valued at amortized cost (that is, discounted to reflect the time value of money).

A company may also accept a note receivable from a trade customer whose account receivable is past due. The customer signs a note payable, and the company then credits the account receivable and debits a note receivable. We would say the company "received a note receivable from a customer on account."

For example, assume that on February 1, 2009, Power Ltd. purchased $5,000 of building supplies from Piercy's Building Supplies with 60-day credit terms. Piercy's records the sale as follows:

Date	Account/Explanation	Debit	Credit
2009			
Feb. 1	Accounts Receivable	5,000	
	Sales		5,000
	To record sale to Power Ltd.		

If on April 1, 2009, Power Ltd. agrees to sign a 30-day note receivable to replace the account receivable due on that date, then Piercy's would record the following journal entry:

Date	Account/Explanation	Debit	Credit
2009			
Apr. 1	Notes Receivable	5,000	
	Accounts Receivable—Power Ltd.		5,000
	To record conversion of account receivable to note receivable.		

Now let's examine some strategies to speed up cash flow.

How to Speed Up Cash Flow

All companies want speedy cash receipts. Rapid cash flow finances new products, new technology, research, and development. Thus, companies find ways to collect cash immediately. Two common strategies generate cash more quickly than waiting to collect from customers.

Credit Card Sales. The merchant sells merchandise and lets the customer pay with a credit card, such as VISA, MasterCard, or a company credit card such as HBC (Hudson's Bay Company). This strategy may dramatically increase sales, but the added revenue comes at a cost. Let's see how credit cards work from the seller's perspective. The merchant actually records the cash amount equal to the sale amount and the bank deducts the fee monthly on that month's sales. The examples that follow are illustrative of the principle, not practice.

Suppose you purchase a BlackBerry® Curve™ from TELUS in Fredericton, New Brunswick, for $500 and you pay with a MasterCard. TELUS would record the sale as follows:

Cash	485	
Financing Expense	15	
Sales Revenue		500
Recorded credit card sale.		

ASSETS	=	LIABILITIES	+	SHAREHOLDERS' EQUITY	+	REVENUES	−	EXPENSES
+485	=	0	+		+	500	−	15

TELUS enters the transaction in the credit-card machine. The machine, linked to a MasterCard server, automatically credits TELUS's account for a discounted portion, say $485, of the $500 sales amount. MasterCard gets 3%, or $15 ($500 × 0.03 = $15). To the merchant, the financing expense is an operating expense similar to interest expense.

Debit Card Sales. The merchant sells merchandise, and the customer pays by swiping a bank card such as a Scotiabank ScotiaCard™ or a TD Canada Trust Green Card using the Interac System. In this case, the bank card is being used as a debit card. To a merchant or service provider, a debit card is just like cash; when the card is swiped and the personal identification number (PIN) is entered, the merchant receives payment immediately as the Interac System takes money directly from the card-holder's bank account and transfers the money to the merchant's bank account less a processing fee. As with credit cards, the merchant is charged a fee. To record a sale of groceries for $65.48, Safeway would record this entry:

Cash	64.48	
Interac fee (assumed rate)	1.00	
Sales revenue		65.48
Record sale paid using Interac.		

ASSETS = LIABILITIES + SHAREHOLDERS' EQUITY + REVENUE − EXPENSES				
+64.48 =	0	+	+ 65.48	− 1.00

One advantage for the merchant is that the payment is just like cash without the task of depositing the money. One advantage to the customer is that there is no need to carry cash. A second advantage to the card-holder is the cash-back feature; the card-holder can ask for cash back, and the merchant will record an entry that includes the purchase plus the requested cash. Using the above date and assuming the card-holder requested $30.00 cash back, the entry would be:

Cash	94.48	
Interac fee (assumed rate)	1.00	
Sales revenue		65.48
Cash (to card-holder)		30.00
Record sale paid using Interac and cash back of $30.00.		

Selling (Factoring) Receivables. Suppose Open Text makes normal sales on account, debiting Accounts Receivable and crediting Sales Revenue. Open Text can then sell its accounts receivable to another business, called a *factor*. The factor earns revenue by paying a discounted price for the receivables and then hopefully collecting the full amount from the customers. The benefit to the company is the immediate receipt of cash.

To illustrate, suppose Open Text wishes to speed up cash flow and therefore sells $100,000 of accounts receivable, receiving cash of $95,000. Open Text would record the sale of the receivables as follows:

Cash	95,000	
Financing Expense	5,000	
Accounts Receivable		100,000
Sold accounts receivable.		

Again, Financing Expense is an operating expense, with the same effect as a loss. Some companies may debit a Loss account. Discounting a note receivable is similar to selling an account receivable; however, the credit is to Notes Receivable (instead of Accounts Receivable).

Using Two Key Ratios to Make Decisions

Investors and creditors use ratios to evaluate the financial health of a company. We introduced the current ratio in Chapter 3. Other ratios, including the acid-test or quick ratio and the number of days' sales (or revenues) in receivables, help investors measure liquidity. These measures help to build a picture of the strength of a business.

Acid-Test (or Quick) Ratio

A balance sheet lists assets in the order of relative liquidity:

- Cash and cash equivalents
- Short-term investments
- Accounts (or trade) receivables

The acid-test ratio is similar to the current ratio introduced in Chapter 3 (page 131), but it excludes inventory and prepaid expenses.

Open Text Corporation's balance sheet in the chapter-opening story shows the ordering of the first and third of these accounts; it has no short-term investments.

Managers, shareholders, and creditors care about the liquidity of assets. In Chapter 3, for example, we saw the current ratio, which measures the ability to pay current liabilities with current assets. A more stringent measure of ability to pay current liabilities is the **acid-test** (or **quick**) **ratio**.

For Open Text Corporation, 2008* (Thousands of US Dollars)

$$\text{Acid-test ratio} = \frac{\text{Cash} + \frac{\text{Temporary}}{\text{investments}} + \frac{\text{Net current}}{\text{receivables}}}{\text{Total current liabilities}} = \frac{\$254,916 + \$0 + \$134,396}{\$297,863} = 1.31$$

*Taken from Open Text Corporation's 2008 balance sheet, which includes cash and cash equivalents together.

The higher the acid-test ratio, the easier it is to pay current liabilities. Open Text Corporation's acid-test ratio of 1.31 means that Open Text has $1.31 of quick assets to pay each $1.00 of current liabilities. This ratio value indicates that Open Text Corporation can meet its short-term liquidity needs. Open Text's acid-test ratio was 1.44 in 2004. In general, an acid-test ratio of 1.0 is considered safe so Open Text is in a strong position.

Inventory is excluded from the acid-test ratio because inventory is not a liquid asset. A company with lots of inventory may have an acceptable current ratio but find it hard to pay its bills.

What is an acceptable acid-test ratio? The answer depends on the industry. Auto dealers can operate smoothly with an acid-test ratio of 0.20, roughly one-sixth of Open Text Corporation's ratio value. How can auto dealers survive with so low an acid-test ratio? GM, Toyota, and the other auto manufacturers help finance their dealers' inventory. Most dealers, therefore, have a financial safety net. Nike, the sports manufacturer, has a quick ratio of around 1.0. In general, an acid-test ratio of 1.0 is considered safe.

Days' Sales in Receivables

After a business makes a credit sale, the *next* step is collecting the receivable. **Days' sales in receivables**, also called the *collection period*, tells how long it takes to collect the average level of receivables. Shorter is better because cash is coming in quickly. The longer the collection period, the less cash is available to pay bills and expand.

Days' sales in receivables can be computed in two logical steps, as follows. First, compute one day's sales (or one day's total revenues). Then divide one day's sales into average receivables for the period. We show days' sales in receivables for Open Text Corporation.

For Open Text Corporation (Thousands of US Dollars)

1. $\text{One day's sale} = \dfrac{\text{Net sales}}{365 \text{ days}}$ $\qquad \dfrac{\$725,532^*}{365} = \$1,987.76 \text{ per day}$

2. $\begin{aligned} \text{Day's sales in} \\ \text{average accounts} \\ \text{receivable} \end{aligned} = \dfrac{\begin{array}{c}\text{Average net} \\ \text{accounts receivable}\end{array}}{\text{One day's sales}} = \dfrac{\left(\begin{array}{cc}\text{Beginning net} & \text{Ending net} \\ \text{receivables} + \text{receivables}\end{array}\right) \div 2}{\text{One day's sales}}$

$\qquad\qquad\qquad\qquad\qquad = \dfrac{(\$134,396 + \$128,781 \div 2)}{\$1,987.76} = 66 \text{ days}$

*Taken from Open Text Corporation's 2008 income statement.

Net sales come from the income statement and the receivables amounts are taken from the balance sheet. Average receivables is the simple average of the beginning and ending balances.

The length of the collection period depends on the credit terms of the company's sales. For example, sales on "net 30" terms should be collected within approximately 30 days. Open Text's days' sales in average receivables was 75 days in the 2004 financial statements.

Companies watch their collection periods closely. Whenever the collections get slow, the business must find other sources of financing, such as borrowing cash or factoring receivables. During recessions, customers pay more slowly, and a longer collection period may be unavoidable.*

Reporting on the Cash Flow Statement

Receivables and temporary investments appear on the balance sheet as assets. We saw these in Open Text Corporation's balance sheet at the beginning of the chapter. We've also seen how to report the related revenues, gains, and losses on the income statement. Because receivables and investment transactions affect cash, their effects must also be reported on the cash flow statement.

Receivables bring in cash when the business collects from customers. These transactions are reported as *operating activities* on the cash flow statement because they result from sales. Investment transactions are reported as *investing activities* on the cash flow statement. Chapter 12 shows how companies report their cash flows to the public on the cash flow statement. In that chapter, we will see exactly how to report cash flows related to receivables and investment transactions.

---

*Another ratio, **accounts receivable turnover**, captures the same information as days' sales in receivables. Receivable turnover is computed as follows: Net sales ÷ Average net accounts receivable. During 2008, Open Text Corporation had a receivable turnover rate of 5.5 times [$726 ÷ ([$134 + $129] ÷ 2)]. The authors prefer days' sales in receivables because it is easier to interpret. Days' sales in receivables can be compared directly to the company's credit sale terms.

DECISION GUIDELINES

MANAGING AND ACCOUNTING FOR RECEIVABLES

Here are the management and accounting issues that a business faces when the company extends credit to customers. For each issue, the Decision Guidelines propose a plan of action. Let's look at a business situation: Suppose you and a friend open a health club near your college. Assume you will let customers use the club and charge bills to their accounts. What challenges will you encounter by extending credit to customers?

The main issues in *managing* receivables, along with a plan of action, are:

Issues	Plan of Action
1. What are the benefits and the costs of extending credit to customers?	1. Benefit—Increase in sales. Cost—Risk of not collecting.
2. Extend credit only to creditworthy customers.	2. Run a credit check on prospective customers.
3. Separate cash-handling and accounting duties to keep employees from stealing the cash collected from customers.	3. Design the internal control system to separate duties.
4. Pursue collection from customers to maximize cash flow.	4. Keep a close eye on customer paying habits. Send second, and third, statements to slow-paying customers, if necessary. Do not extend credit to overdue accounts.

The main issues in *accounting* for receivables, and the related plans of action, are (amounts are assumed):

Issues	Plan of Action
1. Measure and report receivables on the balance sheet at their *net realizable value*, the amount we expect to collect. This is the appropriate amount to report for current receivables.	1. Report receivables at their net realizable value: **Balance sheet** Receivables .... $1,000 Less: Allowance for uncollectible accounts ..... (80) Receivables, net .... $ 920
2. Measure and report the expense associated with failure to collect receivables. This expense is called *uncollectible-account expense* and is reported on the income statement.	2. Measure the expense of not collecting from customers: **Income statement** Sales (or service) revenue .... $8,000 Expenses: Uncollectible-account expense 190

MyAccountingLab **END-OF-CHAPTER SUMMARY PROBLEM**

CHC Helicopter Corporation is Vancouver-based and is the world's largest provider of helicopter services to the global offshore oil and gas industry. The company balance sheet at April 30, 2007, adapted, reported:

	(In millions)
Trade accounts receivable	$240.6
Allowance for doubtful accounts	(8.4)

Required

1. How much of the April 30, 2007, balance of accounts receivable did CHC Helicopter Corporation expect to collect? Stated differently, what was the expected realizable value of these receivables?
2. Journalize, without explanations, 2008 entries for CHC Helicopter, assuming

   a. estimated Doubtful-Account Expense of $1.3 million, based on the percentage-of-sales method, all during the year.

   b. write-offs of uncollectible accounts receivable totalling $8.0 million.

   c. April 30, 2008, aging of receivables, which indicates that $3.1 million of the total receivables of $303.4 million is uncollectible at year-end.
3. Show how CHC Helicopter's receivables and related allowance will appear on the April 30, 2008, balance sheet.
4. Show what CHC Helicopter's income statement will report for the foregoing transactions.

Name: CHC Helicopter Corporation
Industry: Helicopter services
Accounting Period: Years ended April 30, 2007, and April 30, 2008

Answers

Requirement 1

The expected realizable value of receivables is the full value less the allowance for doubtful accounts.

	(In millions)
Expected realizable value of receivables ($240.6 − $8.4)	$232.2

Requirement 2

The estimate increases both the expense and the allowance for doubtful accounts.

Write-offs reduce the allowance for doubtful accounts and accounts receivable. They do *not* affect the doubtful-account expense.

a. Doubtful-Account Expense	1.3	
Allowance for Doubtful Accounts..		1.3
b. Allowance for Doubtful Accounts..	8.0	
Accounts Receivable		8.0

Allowance for Doubtful Accounts			
2008 Write-offs	8.0	April 30, 2007	8.4
		2008 Expense	1.3
		2008 Balance	1.7

First, determine the balance in Allowance for Doubtful Accounts by filling in its T-account using the opening balance (given), adding the expense amount from 2 a, and deducting the write-offs from 2 b.

The final balance in the Allowance for Doubtful Accounts must be $3.1 (estimated in 2 c). The balance in the T-account is already $1.7 (calculated above). Therefore, Doubtful-Account Expense and Allowance for Doubtful Accounts must be increased by the difference of $1.4.

c. Doubtful-Account Expense ($3.1 − $1.7)................................	1.4	
Allowance for Doubtful Accounts..		1.4

Allowance for Doubtful Accounts		
		1.7
		1.4
		3.1

Requirement 3

	(In millions)
Accounts receivable..	$303.4
Allowance for doubtful accounts..	(3.1)
Accounts receivable, net..	$300.3

> Accounts receivable are always shown at net realizable value, the amount actually expected to be collected.

Requirement 4

	(In millions)
Expenses: Doubtful-account expense for 2008 ($1.3 + $1.4).......................	$2.7

> Add all the Doubtful-Account Expense amounts from Requirement 2 a, b, and c. The $2.7 includes estimates based on percentage of sales and aging of the receivables.

REVIEW SHORT-TERM INVESTMENTS AND RECEIVABLES

QUICK CHECK (Answers are given on page 259.)

1. Harvey Penick Golf Academy held trading investments valued at $55,000 at December 31, 2008. These investments cost Penick $50,000. What is the appropriate amount for Penick to report for these investments on the December 31, 2008, balance sheet?
   - **a.** $50,000
   - **b.** $55,000
   - **c.** $5,000 gain
   - **d.** Cannot be determined from the data given

2. Return to Harvey Penick Golf Academy in question 1. What should appear on the Penick income statement for the year ended December 31, 2008, for the trading investments?
   - **a.** $50,000
   - **b.** $55,000
   - **c.** $5,000 unrealized gain
   - **d.** Cannot be determined from the data given

Use the following information to answer questions 3 through 7.

Neal Company had the following information relating to credit sales in 2009:

Accounts receivable December 31, 2009...	$ 9,500
Allowance for uncollectible accounts December 31, 2009	
(before adjustment)...	900
Credit sales during 2009...	46,000
Cash sales during 2009...	15,000
Collections from customers on account during 2009..........................	49,500

3. Uncollectible accounts are determined by the percentage-of-sales method to be 2% of credit sales. How much is uncollectible-account expense for 2009?
   - **a.** $920
   - **b.** $2,000
   - **c.** $750
   - **d.** $20

4. Using the percentage-of-sales method, what is the adjusted balance in the Allowance account at year end 2009?
   - **a.** $900
   - **b.** $920
   - **c.** $1,500
   - **d.** $1,820

5. If uncollectible accounts are determined by the aging-of-receivables method to be $1,350, the uncollectible account expense for 2009 would be
   - **a.** $450
   - **b.** $900
   - **c.** $920
   - **d.** $1,350

6. Using the aging-of-receivables method, the balance of the Allowance account after the adjusting entry would be
   a. $450
   b. $900
   c. $920
   d. $1,350

7. Assuming the aging-of-receivables method is used, the net realizable value of accounts receivable on the December 31, 2009, balance sheet would be
   a. $8,580
   b. $8,150
   c. $8,600
   d. $9,500

8. Accounts Receivable has a debit balance of $3,200, and the Allowance for Uncollectible Accounts has a credit balance of $300. A $100 account receivable is written off. What is the amount of net receivables (net realizable value) after the write-off?
   a. $2,800
   b. $2,900
   c. $3,000
   d. $3,100

9. Ridgewood Corporation began 2009 with Accounts Receivable of $800,000. Sales for the year totalled $2,500,000. Ridgewood ended the year with accounts receivable of $900,000. Ridgewood's bad-debt losses are minimal. How much cash did Ridgewood collect from customers in 2009?
   a. $3,400,000
   b. $2,940,000
   c. $2,500,000
   d. $2,400,000

10. Saturn Company received a 4-month, 5%, $4,800 note receivable on December 1. The adjusting entry on December 31 will
    a. Debit Interest Receivable $20
    b. Credit Interest Revenue $20
    c. Both a and b
    d. Credit Interest Revenue $240

11. What is the maturity value of a $25,000, 5%, 6-month note?
    a. $20,000
    b. $25,000
    c. $25,625
    d. $26,250

12. If the adjusting entry to accrue interest on a note receivable is omitted, then
    a. Liabilities are understated, net income is overstated, and shareholders' equity is overstated.
    b. Assets are overstated, net income is understated, and shareholders' equity is understated.
    c. Assets, net income, and shareholders' equity are overstated.
    d. Assets, net income, and shareholders' equity are understated.

13. Net sales total $730,000. Beginning and ending accounts receivable are $62,000 and $58,000, respectively. Calculate days' sales in receivables.
    a. 32 days
    b. 23 days
    c. 43 days
    d. 30 days

14. From the following list of accounts, calculate the quick ratio.

Cash	$3,000	Accounts payable	$ 8,000
Accounts receivable	6,000	Salary payable	3,000
Inventory................................	8,000	Notes payable (due in 2 years)	10,000
Prepaid insurance	2,000	Short-term investments................	2,000

   a. 2.1
   b. 1.3
   c. 0.82
   d. 1.4

ACCOUNTING VOCABULARY

accounts receivable turnover Net sales divided by average net accounts receivable. (p. 236)

acid-test ratio Ratio of the sum of cash plus short-term investments plus net current receivables to total current liabilities.

Tells whether the entity can pay all its current liabilities if they come due immediately. Also called the *quick ratio*. (p. 235)

aging of accounts receivable A way to estimate bad debts by analyzing individual accounts receivable according to the length of time they have been receivable from the customer. Also called the *balance-sheet approach* because it focuses on accounts receivable. (p. 225)

Allowance for Doubtful Accounts Another name for *Allowance for Uncollectible Accounts*. (p. 224)

Allowance for Uncollectible Accounts A contra account, related to accounts receivable, that holds the estimated amount of collection losses. Another name for *Allowance for Doubtful Accounts*. (p. 224)

allowance method A method of recording collection losses based on estimates of how much money the business will not collect from its customers. (p. 224)

bad-debt expense Another name for *uncollectible-account expense*. (p. 223)

creditor The party to whom money is owed. (p. 230)

days' sales in receivables Ratio of average net accounts receivable to one day's sales. Indicates how many days' sales remain in Accounts Receivable awaiting collection. Also called the *collection period*. (p. 235)

debtor The party who owes money. (p. 230)

direct write-off method A method of accounting for bad debts in which the company waits until a customer's account receivable proves uncollectible and then debits Uncollectible-Account Expense and credits the customer's Account Receivable. (p. 228)

doubtful-account expense Another name for *uncollectible-account expense*. (p. 223)

interest The borrower's cost of renting money from a lender. Interest is revenue for the lender and expense for the borrower. (p. 230)

marketable securities Another name for *short-term investments*. (p. 216)

maturity date The date on which a debt instrument must be paid. (p. 230)

maturity value The sum of principal and interest on a note. (p. 230)

percentage-of-sales method Computes uncollectible-account expense as a percentage of net sales. Also called the *income statement approach* because it focuses on the amount of expense to be reported on the income statement. (p. 225)

principal The amount borrowed by a debtor and lent by a creditor. (p. 230)

quick ratio Another name for *acid-test ratio*. (p. 235)

receivables Monetary claims against a business or an individual, acquired mainly by selling goods or services and by lending money. (p. 221)

short-term investments Investments that a company plans to hold for one year or less. Also called *marketable securities*. (p. 216)

term The length of time from inception to maturity. (p. 230)

trading investments Share or bond investments that are to be sold in the near future with the intent of generating profits on the sale. (p. 217)

uncollectible-account expense Cost to the seller of extending credit. Arises from the failure to collect from credit customers. Also called *doubtful-account expense* or *bad-debt expense*. (p. 223)

ASSESS YOUR PROGRESS

Make the grade with MyAccountingLab: The exercises and problems marked in red can be found on MyAccountingLab at www.myaccountinglab.com. You can practise them as often as you want, and they feature step by step guided solutions to help you find the right answer.

SHORT EXERCISES

S5-1 Answer these questions about investments.

1. Why is a financial asset held for trading investment always a current asset? Explain.

2. What is the amount to report on the balance sheet for a financial asset held for trading investment?

Reporting short-term investments
(Obj. 1)

S5-2 Bannister Corp. holds short-term trading investments. On November 16, Bannister paid $80,000 for a short-term trading investment in RIM shares. At December 31, the market value of the RIM shares is $84,000. For this situation, show everything that Bannister would report on its December 31 balance sheet and on its income statement for the year ended December 31.

Accounting for a financial asset held for trading investment
(Obj. 1)

S5-3 Beckham Investments paid $104,000 for a short-term investment in RIM shares.

1. Suppose the RIM shares decreased in value to $98,000 at December 31. Make the Beckham journal entry to adjust the Short-Term Investment account to market value.

2. Show how Beckham would report the short-term investment on its balance sheet and the unrealized gain or loss on its income statement.

Accounting for a financial asset held for trading investment
(Obj. 1)

Internal control over the collection of receivables
(Obj. 2)

Applying the allowance method (percentage-of-sales) to account for uncollectibles
(Obj. 3)

S5-4 Don Roose keeps the Accounts Receivable records of Zachary & Polk, a partnership. What duty will a good internal control system withhold from Roose? Why?

Short Exercises 5-5 through 5-7 should be used together.

S5-5 During its first year of operations, Environmental Products Inc. had sales of $875,000, all on account. Industry experience suggests that Environmental Products' uncollectibles will amount to 2% of credit sales. At December 31, 2008, Environmental Products' accounts receivable total $80,000. The company uses the allowance method to account for uncollectibles.

1. Make Environmental Products' journal entry for uncollectible-account expense using the percentage-of-sales method.
2. Show how Environmental Products could report accounts receivable on its balance sheet at December 31, 2009, by disclosing the allowance for doubtful accounts. Follow the reporting format illustrated after the second paragraph on page 224.

Applying the allowance method (percentage-of-sales) to account for uncollectibles
(Obj. 3)

S5-6 This exercise continues the situation of Short Exercise 5-5, in which Environmental Products ended the year 2008 with accounts receivable of $80,000 and an allowance for uncollectible accounts of $17,500. During 2009, Environmental Products completed the following transactions:

1. Credit sales, $1,000,000
2. Collections on account, $880,000
3. Write-offs of uncollectibles, $16,000
4. Uncollectible-account expense, 1.5% of credit sales

Journalize the 2009 transactions for Environmental Products. Explanations are not required.

Applying the allowance method (percentage-of-sales) to account for uncollectibles
(Obj. 3)

S5-7 Use the solution to Short Exercise 5-6 to answer these questions about Environmental Products Inc. for 2009.

1. Start with Accounts Receivable's beginning balance ($80,000) and then post to the Accounts Receivable T-account. How much do Environmental Products' customers owe the company at December 31, 2009?
2. Start with the Allowance account's beginning credit balance ($17,500) and then post to the Allowance for Uncollectible Accounts T-account. How much of the receivables at December 31, 2009, does the company expect *not* to collect?
3. At December 31, 2009, what is the net realizable value of the company's accounts receivable?

Applying the allowance method (aging-of-accounts-receivable) to account for uncollectibles
(Obj. 3)

S5-8 Gulig and Durham, a law firm, started 2009 with accounts receivable of $60,000 and an allowance for uncollectible accounts of $5,000. The 2009 service revenue on account was $400,000, and cash collections on account totalled $410,000. During 2009, Gulig & Durham wrote off uncollectible accounts receivable of $7,000. At December 31, 2009, the aging of accounts receivable indicated that Gulig & Durham will *not* collect $10,000 of its accounts receivable.

Journalize Gulig & Durham's (a) service revenue, (b) cash collections on account, (c) write-offs of uncollectible receivables, and (d) uncollectible-account expense for the year. Explanations are not required. Prepare a T-account for Allowance for Uncollectible Accounts to show your computation of uncollectible-account expense for the year.

Applying the allowance method (aging-of-accounts-receivable) to account for uncollectibles
(Obj. 3)

S5-9 Perform the following accounting for the receivables of Benoit, Brown & Hill, an accounting firm, at December 31, 2009.

1. Start with the beginning balances for these T-accounts:
   - Accounts Receivable, $80,000
   - Allowance for Uncollectible Accounts, $9,000

   Post the following 2009 transactions to the T-accounts:
   a. Service revenue of $850,000, all on account
   b. Collections on account, $790,000

c. Write-offs of uncollectible accounts, $7,000
d. Uncollectible-account expense (allowance method), $8,000

2. What are the ending balances of Accounts Receivable and Allowance for Uncollectible Accounts?

3. Show two ways Benoit, Brown & Hill could report accounts receivable on its balance sheet at December 31, 2009.

S5-10 Metro Credit Union in Charlottetown, Prince Edward Island, loaned $90,000 to David Mann on a 6-month, 8% note. Record the following for Metro Credit Union:
a. Lending the money on March 6.
b. Collecting the principal and interest at maturity. Specify the date. Explanations are not required.

Accounting for a note receivable
(Obj. 4)

S5-11

1. Compute the amount of interest during 2007, 2008, and 2009 for the following note receivable: On June 30, 2007, Scotiabank loaned $100,000 to Heather Hutchison on a 2-year, 8% note.

2. Which party has a (an)
   a. Note receivable?   c. Interest revenue?
   b. Note payable?   d. Interest expense?

3. How much in total would Scotiabank collect if Hutchison paid off the note early—say, on October 30, 2007?

Internal control over the collection of receivables
(Obj. 2)

S5-12 On May 31, 2008, Nancy Thomas borrowed $6,000 from Assiniboine Credit Union. Thomas signed a note payable, promising to pay the credit union principal plus interest on May 31, 2009. The interest rate on the note is 8%. The accounting year of Assiniboine Credit Union ends on December 31, 2008. Journalize Assiniboine Credit Union's (a) lending money on the note receivable at May 31, 2008, (b) accrual of interest at December 31, 2008, and (c) collection of principal and interest at May 31, 2009, the maturity date of the note.

Accruing interest receivable and collecting a note receivable
(Obj. 4)

S5-13 Using your answers to Short Exercise 5-12, show how the Assiniboine Credit Union will report the following:
a. Whatever needs to be reported on the classified balance sheet at December 31, 2008. Ignore Cash.
b. Whatever needs to be reported on the income statement for the year ended December 31, 2008.
c. Whatever needs to be reported on the classified balance sheet at December 31, 2009. Ignore Cash.
d. Whatever needs to be reported on the income statement for the year ended December 31, 2009.

Reporting receivables amounts
(Obj. 4)

S5-14 Botany Clothiers reported the following amounts in its 2009 financial statements. The 2008 figures are given for comparison.

Evaluating the acid-test ratio and days' sales in receivables
(Obj. 5)

	2009		2008	
Current assets:				
Cash..		$ 9,000		$ 7,000
Short-term investments.................................		12,000		10,000
Accounts receivable......................................	$60,000		$54,000	
Less allowance for uncollectibles................	(5,000)	55,000	(5,000)	49,000
Inventory		170,000		172,000
Prepaid insurance...		1,000		1,000
Total current assets		$247,000		$239,000
Total current liabilities		$ 80,000		$ 70,000
Net sales		$803,000		$750,000

❙ Required

1. Compute Botany's acid-test ratio at the end of 2009. Round to two decimal places. How does the acid-test ratio compare with the industry average of 0.95?
2. Compare Botany's days' sales in receivables measure for 2009 with the company's credit terms of net 30 days.

Reporting receivables and other accounts in the financial statements
(Obj. 5)

S5-15 Victoria Medical Service reported the following selected items (amounts in thousands):

Unearned revenues (current)........	$ 207		Service revenue	$8,613
Allowance for			Other assets.................................	767
doubtful accounts	109		Property, plant, and equipment	3,316
Other expenses	2,569		Operating expense	1,620
Accounts receivable.....................	817		Cash..	239
Accounts payable	385		Notes payable (long-term)...........	719

1. Classify each item as (a) income statement or balance sheet and as (b) debit balance or credit balance.
2. How much net income (or net loss) did Victoria earn for the year?
3. Compute Victoria's current ratio. Round to two decimal places.

EXERCISES

Accounting for a financial asset held for trading investment
(Obj. 1)

E5-16 Research Capital, the investment banking company, has extra cash to invest. Suppose Research Capital buys 1,000 shares of Potash Corporation of Saskatchewan at $185 per share. Assume Research Capital expects to hold the Potash shares for 1 month and then sell them. The purchase occurs on December 15, 2009. At December 31, the market price of a share of Potash is $195 per share.

❙ Required

1. What type of investment is this to Research Capital? Give the reason for your answer.
2. Record Research Capital's purchase of the Potash shares on December 15 and the adjustment to market value on December 31.
3. Show how Research Capital would report this investment on its balance sheet at December 31 and any gain or loss on its income statement for the year ended December 31, 2009.

Reporting a financial asset held for trading investment
(Obj. 1)

E5-17 On November 16, **Edward Jones Co.** paid $50,000 for a trading investment in shares of Royal Bank of Canada (RBC). On November 27, Edward Jones received a $500 cash dividend from RBC. It is now December 31, and the market value of the RBC shares is $49,500. For this investment, show what Edward Jones should report in its income statement and balance sheet.

Accounting for a financial asset held for trading investment
(Obj. 1)

E5-18 TELUS reports short-term investments on its balance sheet. Suppose a division of TELUS completed the following short-term investment transactions during 2008 and 2009:

2008		
Nov.	6	Purchased 1,000 shares of Canadian Pacific Railway Limited (CPR) for $60,000. TELUS plans to sell the shares at a profit in the near future.
	27	Received a cash dividend of $0.25 per share on the CPR shares.
Dec.	31	Adjusted the investment in CPR shares. Current market value is $65,000. TELUS plans to sell the shares in early 2009.
2009		
Jan.	11	Sold the CPR shares for $66,000.

Required

1. Prepare T-accounts for Cash, Short-Term Investment, Dividend Revenue, Unrealized Loss or Gain on Investment, and Gain on Sale of Investment. Show the effects of TELUS's investment transactions. Start with a cash balance of $75,000. All the other accounts start at zero.

E5-19 As a recent college graduate, you land your first job in the customer collections department of Backroads Publishing. Shawn Dugan, the manager, asks you to propose a system to ensure that cash received from customers by mail is handled properly. Draft a short memorandum to explain the essential element in your proposed plan. State why this element is important. Refer to Chapter 4 if necessary.

Controlling cash receipts from customers
(Obj. 2)

E5-20 At December 31, 2009, Credit Valley Nissan has an accounts receivable balance of $101,000. Allowance for Doubtful Accounts has a credit balance of $2,000 before the year-end adjustment. Service revenue for 2009 was $800,000. Credit Valley estimates that doubtful-account expense for the year is 1% of sales. Make the December 31 entry to record doubtful-account expense. Show how the accounts receivable and the allowance for doubtful accounts are reported on the balance sheet. Use the reporting format "Accounts receivable, net of allowance for doubtful accounts $ - - -" in 2009. Insert the value you've calculated for the allowance.

Reporting uncollectible accounts debts by the allowance method
(Obj. 3)

E5-21 On June 30, 2009, Perfect Party Planners (PPP) had a $40,000 balance in Accounts Receivable and a $3,000 credit balance in Allowance for Uncollectible Accounts. During July, PPP made credit sales of $75,000. July collections on account were $60,000, and write-offs of uncollectible receivables totalled $2,200. Uncollectible-account expense is estimated as 2% of revenue.

Using the allowance method for uncollectible accounts
(Obj. 3)

Required

1. Journalize sales, collections, write-offs of uncollectibles, and uncollectible-account expense by the allowance method during July. Explanations are not required.

2. Show the ending balances in Accounts Receivable, Allowance for Uncollectible Accounts, and *Net* Accounts Receivable at July 31. How much does PPP expect to collect?

3. Show how PPP will report Accounts Receivable on its July 31 balance sheet. Use the format "Accounts Receivable, net of allowance for uncollectible accounts of $ - - -" at July 31, 2009. Insert the value you've calculated for the allowance.

E5-22 Refer to Exercise 5-21.

Using the direct write-off method for uncollectible accounts
(Obj. 3)

Required

1. Record uncollectible-account expense for July by the direct write-off method.
2. What amount of accounts receivable would Perfect Party Planners (PPP) report on its July 31 balance sheet under the direct write-off method? Does PPP expect to collect the full amount?

E5-23 At December 31, 2009, before any year-end adjustments, the Accounts Receivable balance of Sunset Hills Clinic is $235,000. Allowance for Doubtful Accounts has a $6,500 credit balance. Sunset Hills prepares the following aging schedule for accounts receivable:

Using the aging method to estimate uncollectible accounts
(Obj. 3)

Total Balance	Age of Accounts			
	1–30 Days	31–60 Days	61–90 Days	Over 90 Days
$235,000	$110,000	$60,000	$50,000	$15,000
Estimated uncollectible	0.5%	1.0%	6.0%	40%

Required

1. Based on the aging of accounts receivable, is the unadjusted balance of the allowance account adequate? Is it either too high or too low?
2. Make the entry required by the aging schedule. Prepare a T-account for the allowance.

3. Show how Sunset Hills Clinic will report Accounts Receivable on its December 31 balance sheet. Include the two accounts that come before receivables on the balance sheet, using assumed amounts.

Measuring and accounting for uncollectibles
(Obj. 3)

E5-24 University Travel experienced the following revenue and accounts receivable write-offs.

Month	Service Revenue	January	February	March	Total

Month	Service Revenue	Accounts Receivable Write-Offs in Month			
		January	February	March	Total
January	$ 6,800	$53	$ 86		$139
February	7,000		105	$ 33	138
March	7,500			115	115
	$21,300	$53	$191	$148	$392

University Travel estimates that 2% of revenues will become uncollectible.
Journalize service revenue (all on account), bad-debt expense, and write-offs during March. Include explanations. Is an estimate of 2% of revenues being uncollectible reasonable?

Recording notes receivable and accruing interest revenue
(Obj. 4)

E5-25 Record the following note receivable transactions in the journal of Town & Country Realty. How much interest revenue did Town & Country earn this year? Use a 365-day year for interest computations, and round interest amounts to the nearest dollar.

Oct.	1	Loaned $50,000 cash to Springfield Co. on a 1-year, 9% note.
Nov.	3	Performed service for Joplin Corporation, receiving a 90-day, 12% note for $10,000.
Dec.	16	Received a $2,000, 6-month, 12% note on account from Afton, Inc.
	31	Accrued interest revenue for the year.

Reporting the effects of note receivable transactions on the balance sheet and income statement
(Obj. 4)

E5-26 Mattson Loan Company completed these transactions:

2008		
Apr.	1	Loaned $20,000 to Charlene Baker on a 1-year, 5% note.
Dec.	31	Accrued interest revenue on the Baker note.
2009		
Apr.	1	Collected the maturity value of the note from Baker (principal plus interest).

Show what Mattson would report for these transactions on its 2008 and 2009 balance sheets and income statements. Mattson's accounting year ends on December 31.

Practical questions about receivables
(Obj. 3, 4)

E5-27 Answer these questions about receivables and uncollectibles. For the true-false questions, explain any answers that are false.

1. True or false? Credit sales increase receivables. Collections and write-offs decrease receivables.
2. Which receivables figure, the *total* amount that customers *owe* the company, or the *net* amount the company expects to collect, is more interesting to investors as they consider buying the company's shares? Give your reason.
3. Show how to determine net accounts receivable.
4. True or false? The direct write-off method of accounting for uncollectibles understates assets.
5. Caisse Desjardins lent $100,000 to Chicoutimi Ltée on a 6-month, 6% note. Which party has interest receivable? Which party has interest payable? Which party has interest expense, and which has interest revenue? How much interest will these organizations record 1 month after Chicoutimi Ltée signs the note?
6. When Caisse Desjardins accrues interest on the Chicoutimi Ltée note, show the directional effects on the bank's assets, liabilities, and equity (increase, decrease, or no effect).

E5-28 Research In Motion Limited (RIM) reported the following items at year-ends 2008 and 2007.

Using the acid-test ratio and days' sales in receivables to evaluate a company
(Obj. 5)

Research In Motion Limited
Consolidated Balance Sheets (Summarized)
(amounts in millions)

	March 1 2008	March 3 2007		March 1 2008	March 3 2007
Current assets:			Current liabilities:		
Cash	$1,184.4	$677.1	Accounts payable	$271.1	$130.3
Short-term investments	420.7	310.1	Other current liabilities	1,203.3	416.3
Accounts receivable, net	1,174.7	572.6	Long-term liabilities	103.2	58.8
Inventories	396.3	255.9			
Other current assets	301.3	103.6	Shareholders' equity	3,933.6	2,483.5
Capital assets	2,033.8	1,169.6			
Total assets	$5,511.2	$3,088.9	Total liabilities and equity	$5,511.2	$3,088.9

Income Statement (partial): 2008
Revenue $6,009.4

Compute RIM's (a) acid-test ratio and (b) days' sales in average receivables for 2008. Evaluate each ratio value as strong or weak. Assume RIM sells on terms of net 30 days.

E5-29 Loblaw Companies Limited reported these figures in millions of dollars:

Analyzing a company's financial statements
(Obj. 5)

	2007	2006
Net sales	$29,384	$28,640
Receivables at end of year	885	728

❙ Required

1. Compute Loblaw's average collection period during 2007.
2. Is Loblaw's collection period long or short? Potash Corporation of Saskatchewan takes 36 days to collect its average level of receivables. FedEx, the overnight shipper, takes 40 days. What causes Loblaw's collection period to be so different?

CHALLENGE EXERCISES

E5-30 Ripley Shirt Company sells on credit and manages its own receivables. Average experience for the past three years has been as follows:

Determining whether to sell on credit cards
(Obj. 2)

	Cash	Credit	Total
Sales	$300,000	$300,000	$600,000
Cost of goods sold	165,000	165,000	330,000
Uncollectible-account expense	—	10,000	10,000
Other expenses	84,000	84,000	168,000

John Ripley, the owner, is considering whether to accept credit cards (VISA, MasterCard). Ripley expects total sales to increase by 10% but cash sales to remain unchanged. If Ripley switches to credit cards, the business can save $8,000 on other expenses, but VISA and MasterCard charge 2% on credit card sales. Ripley figures that the increase in sales will be due to the increased volume of credit card sales.

❙ Required

Should Ripley Shirt Company start selling on credit cards? Show the computations of net income under the present plan and under the credit card plan.

*Reconstructing receivables and
bad-debt amounts*
(Obj. 3)

E5-31 Nixtel Inc. reported net receivables of $2,583 million and $2,785 million at December 31, 2007, and 2006, after subtracting allowances of $62 million and $88 million at these respective dates. Nixtel earned total revenue of $10,948 million (all on account) and recorded doubtful-account expense of $2 million for the year ended December 31, 2007.

❚ Required

Use this information to measure the following amounts for the year ended December 31, 2007.
a. Write-offs of uncollectible receivables
b. Collections from customers

QUIZ

Test your understanding of receivables by answering the following questions. Select the best choice from among the possible answers given.

Q5-32 HSBC Bank Canada owns lots of investments. Assume that HSBC paid $600,000 for trading investments on December 3, 2009. Two weeks later HSBC received a $45,000 cash dividend. At December 31, 2009, these trading investments were quoted at a market price of $603,000. HSBC's December income statement should report
a. Dividend revenue of $45,000
b. Unrealized gain of $3,000
c. Both a and b
d. None of the above

Q5-33 Refer to the HSBC data in Question 5-32. At December 31, the HSBC balance sheet should report
a. Dividend revenue of $45,000
b. Unrealized gain of $3,000
c. Short-term investment of $603,000
d. Short-term investment of $600,000

Q5-34 Under the allowance method for uncollectible receivables, the entry to record uncollectible-account expense has what effect on the financial statements?
a. Increases expenses and increases owners' equity.
b. Decreases assets and has no effect on net income.
c. Decreases owners' equity and increases liabilities.
d. Decreases net income and decreases assets.

Q5-35 Snead Company uses the aging method to adjust the allowance for uncollectible accounts at the end of the period. At December 31, 2009, the balance of accounts receivable is $210,000 and the allowance for uncollectible accounts has a credit balance of $3,000 (before adjustment). An analysis of accounts receivable produced the following age groups:

Current	$150,000
60 days past due	50,000
Over 60 days past due	10,000
	$210,000

Based on past experience, Snead estimates that the percentage of accounts that will prove to be uncollectible within the three groups is 2%, 8%, and 20%, respectively. Based on these facts, the adjusting entry for uncollectible accounts should be made in the amount of
a. $3,000
b. $6,000
c. $9,000
d. $13,000

Q5-36 Refer to Question 5-35. The net receivables on the balance sheet is _____.

Q5-37 Harper Company uses the percentage-of-sales method to estimate uncollectibles. Net credit sales for the current year amount to $100,000 and management estimates 2% will be uncollectible. Allowance for doubtful accounts prior to adjustment has a credit balance of $2,000. The amount of expense to report on the income statement will be

a. $30,000   c. $28,000
b. $32,000   d. $2,000

Q5-38 Refer to Question 5-37. The balance of Allowance for Doubtful Accounts, after adjustment, will be

a. $2,000   d. $12,000
b. $4,000   e. Cannot be determined from the
c. $6,000   information given

Q5-39 Draw a T-account to illustrate the information in Questions 5-37 and 5-38. Early the following year, Harper wrote off $3,000 of old receivables as uncollectible. The balance in the Allowance account is now _____.

The next four questions use the following data:

On August 1, 2009, Maritimes Ltd. sold equipment and accepted a 6-month, 9%, $10,000 note receivable. Maritimes' year-end is December 31.

Q5-40 How much interest revenue should Maritimes Ltd. accrue on December 31, 2009?

a. $225   c. $375
b. $450   d. Some other amount _____

Q5-41 If Maritimes Ltd. fails to make an adjusting entry for the accrued interest, which of the following will happen?

a. Net income will be understated, and liabilities will be overstated.
b. Net income will be understated, and assets will be understated.
c. Net income will be overstated, and liabilities will be understated.
d. Net income will be overstated, and assets will be overstated.

Q5-42 How much interest does Maritimes Ltd. expect to collect on the maturity date (February 1, 2010)?

a. $450   c. $75
b. $280   d. Some other amount _____

Q5-43 Which of the following accounts will Maritimes Ltd. credit in the journal entry at maturity on February 1, 2010, assuming collection in full?

a. Interest Receivable   c. Interest Payable
b. Note Payable   d. Cash

Q5-44 Write the journal entry for Question 5-43.

Q5-45 Which of the following is included in the calculation of the acid-test ratio?

a. Cash and accounts receivable   c. Inventory and short-term investment
b. Prepaid expenses and cash   d. Inventory and prepaid expenses

Q5-46 A company with net sales of $1,217,000, beginning net receivables of $90,000, and ending net receivables of $110,000, has a days' sales in accounts receivable of

a. 50 days   c. 30 days
b. 55 days   d. 33 days

Q5-47 The company in Question 5-46 sells on credit terms of "net 30 days." Its days' sales in receivables is

a. Too high   c. About right
b. Too low   d. Cannot be evaluated from the data given

PROBLEMS

(GROUP A)

*Accounting for a trading
investment*
(Obj. 1)

P5-48A During the fourth quarter of 2008, Cablevision Inc. generated excess cash, which the company invested in securities, as follows:

Nov.	12	Purchased 1,000 common shares as a trading investment, paying $9 per share.
Dec.	14	Received cash dividend of $0.26 per share on the trading investment.
	31	Adjusted the trading investment to its market value of $7.50 per share.

▌Required

1. Prepare T-accounts for Cash, beginning balance of $20,000; Short-Term Investment; Dividend Revenue; and Unrealized Gain on Investment or Unrealized Loss on Investment.
2. Journalize the foregoing transactions, and post to the T-accounts.
3. Show how to report the short-term investment on the Cablevision balance sheet at December 31.
4. Show how to report whatever should appear on Cablevision's income statement.
5. Cablevision sold the trading investment for $8,000 on January 10, 2009. Journalize the sale.

*Controlling cash receipts from
customers*
(Obj. 2)

P5-49A Computer Giant Inc. makes all sales on account. Susan Phillips, accountant for the company, receives and opens incoming mail. Company procedure requires Phillips to separate customer cheques from the remittance slips, which list the amounts that Phillips posts as credits to customer accounts receivable. Phillips deposits the cheques in the bank. At the end of each day she computes the day's total amount posted to customer accounts and matches this total to the bank deposit slip. This procedure ensures that all receipts are deposited in the bank.

▌Required

As a consultant hired by Computer Giant Inc., write a memo to management evaluating the company's internal controls over cash receipts from customers. If the system is effective, identify its strong features. If the system has flaws, propose a way to strengthen the controls.

*Accounting for revenue,
collections, and uncollectibles;
percentage-of-sales method*
(Obj. 3)

P5-50A This problem takes you through the accounting for sales, receivables, and uncollectibles for **FedEx Corporation**, the overnight shipper. By selling on credit, FedEx cannot expect to collect 100% of its accounts receivable. At May 31, 2008, and 2007, respectively, FedEx reported the following on its balance sheet (adapted and in millions of U.S. dollars):

	May 31	
	2008	2007
Accounts receivable..	$4,517	$4,078
Less: Allowance for uncollectibles	(316)	(136)
Accounts receivable, net..	$4,201	$3,942

During the year ended May 31, 2008, FedEx earned service revenue and collected cash from customers. Assume uncollectible-account expense for the year was 1% of service revenue and that FedEx wrote off uncollectible receivables.

▌Required

1. Prepare T-accounts for Accounts Receivable and Allowance for Uncollectibles, and insert the May 31, 2007, balances as given.

2. Journalize the following assumed transactions of FedEx for the year ended May 31, 2008. Explanations are not required.

    a. Service revenue on account, $37,953 million

    b. Collections on account, $37,314 million

    c. Uncollectible-account expense, 1% of service revenue

    d. Write-offs of uncollectible accounts receivable, $200 million

3. Post your entries to the Accounts Receivable and the Allowance for Uncollectibles T-accounts.

4. Compute the ending balances for the two T-accounts, and compare your balances to the actual May 31, 2008 amounts. They should be the same.

5. Show what FedEx would report on its income statement for the year ended May 31, 2008.

P5-51A The December 31, 2009, records of First Data Communications include these accounts:

Accounts Receivable..	$230,000
Allowance for Doubtful Accounts	(8,500)

During the year, First Data estimates doubtful-account expense at 1% of credit sales. At year-end, the company ages its receivables and adjusts the balance in Allowance for Doubtful Accounts to correspond to the aging schedule. During the last quarter of 2009, the company completed the following selected transactions:

Using the aging approach for uncollectibles
(Obj. 3)

2009		
Nov. 30		Wrote off as uncollectible the $1,100 account receivable from Rainbow Carpets and the $600 account receivable from Show-N-Tell Antiques.
Dec. 31		Adjusted the Allowance for Doubtful Accounts, and recorded Doubtful-Account Expense at year end, based on the aging of receivables, which follows.

	Age of Accounts			
Total Balance	1–30 Days	31–60 Days	61–90 Days	Over 90 Days
$230,000	$150,000	$40,000	$14,000	$26,000
Estimated uncollectible	0.2%	0.5%	5.0%	30.0%

❙ *Required*

1. Record the transactions in the journal. Explanations are not required.

2. Prepare a T-account for Allowance for Doubtful Accounts, and post to that account.

3. Show two ways First Data could report its accounts receivable on a comparative balance sheet for 2008 and 2009. At December 31, 2008, the company's Accounts Receivable balance was $212,000 and the Allowance for Doubtful Accounts stood at $4,200.

P5-52A Assume **Deloitte & Touche**, the accounting firm, advises Pappadeaux Seafood that Pappadeaux's financial statements must be changed to conform to GAAP. At December 31, 2008, Pappadeaux's accounts include the following:

Short-term investments, uncollectibles, and the ratios
(Obj. 1, 3, 5)

Cash	$ 51,000
Short-term trading investments, at cost..	19,000
Accounts receivable	37,000
Inventory...	61,000
Prepaid expenses...	14,000
Total current assets	$182,000
Accounts payable	$ 62,000
Other current liabilities...	41,000
Total current liabilities	$103,000

Deloitte & Touche advised Pappadeaux that

- Cash includes $20,000 that is deposited in a compensating balance account that is tied up until 2010.
- The market value of the short-term trading investments is $17,000. Pappadeaux purchased the investments a couple of weeks ago.
- Pappadeaux has been using the direct write-off method to account for uncollectible receivables. During 2008, Pappadeaux wrote off bad receivables of $7,000. Deloitte & Touche determines that uncollectible-account expense for the year should be 2.5% of sales revenue, which totalled $600,000 in 2008. The aging of Pappadeaux's receivables at year-end indicated uncollectibles of $8,000 at the year-end.
- Pappadeaux reported net income of $92,000 in 2008.

❙ *Required*

1. Restate Pappadeaux's current accounts to conform to GAAP.

2. Compute Pappadeaux's current ratio and acid-test ratio both before and after your corrections.

3. Determine Pappadeaux's correct net income for 2008.

Notes receivable and accrued interest revenue
(Obj. 4)

P5-53A Assume that **General Mills Canada**, famous for Cheerios®, Chex® snacks, and Yoplait yogurt, completed the following selected transactions.

2008		
Nov.	30	Sold goods to Sobeys Inc., receiving a $50,000, 3-month, 5% note.
Dec.	31	Made an adjusting entry to accrue interest on the Sobeys note.
2009		
Feb.	28	Collected the Sobeys note.
Mar.	1	Received a 90-day, 5%, $6,000 note from Louis' Joli Goût on account.
	1	Sold the Louis note to Caisse Populaire, receiving cash of $5,900.
Dec.	16	Loaned $25,000 cash to Betty Crocker Brands, receiving a 90-day, 8% note.
	31	Accrued the interest on the Betty Crocker Brands note.

❙ *Required*

1. Record the transactions in General Mills' journal. Round interest amounts to the nearest dollar. Explanations are not required.

2. Show what General Mills will report on its comparative classified balance sheet at December 31, 2008, and December 31, 2009.

Using ratio data to evaluate a company's financial position
(Obj. 5)

P5-54A The comparative financial statements of Sunset Pools Inc., for 2009, 2008, and 2007 included the following selected data.

	(In millions)		
	2009	2008	2007
Balance sheet:			
Current assets:			
Cash	$ 86	$ 60	$ 70
Short-term investments	130	174	112
Receivables, net of allowance for doubtful accounts			
of $27, $21, and $15, respectively	243	245	278
Inventories	330	375	362
Prepaid expenses	10	25	26
Total current assets	$ 799	$ 879	$ 848
Total current liabilities	$ 403	$ 498	$ 413
Income statement:			
Net sales	$2,898	$2,727	$2,206

I *Required*

1. Compute these ratios for 2009 and 2008:

   a. Current ratio

   b. Acid-test ratio

   c. Days' sales in receivables

2. Write a memo explaining to top management which ratio values improved from 2008 to 2009 and which ratio values deteriorated. State whether the overall trend is favourable or unfavourable, and give the reason for your evaluation.

(GROUP B)

P5-55B During the fourth quarter of 2009, the operations of Baris Carpet Centre generated excess cash, which the company invested in securities, as follows:

Accounting for a trading investment
(Obj. 1)

Dec.	10	Purchased 2,500 common shares as a trading investment, paying $15 per share.
	17	Received cash dividend of $0.50 per share on the trading investment.
	31	Adjusted the trading investment to its market value of $40,000.

I *Required*

1. Prepare T-accounts for Cash, balance of $85,000; Short-Term Investment; Dividend Revenue; and Unrealized Gain on Investment or Unrealized Loss on Investment.

2. Journalize the foregoing transactions, and post to the T-accounts.

3. Show how to report the short-term investment on Baris's balance sheet at December 31.

4. Show how to report whatever should appear on Baris's income statement.

5. On January 6, 2010, Baris sold the trading investment for $36,000. Journalize the sale.

P5-56B Mountainview Software Sales makes all sales on credit, so virtually all cash receipts arrive in the mail. Shatel Patel, the company president, has just returned from a trade association meeting with new ideas for the business. Among other things, Patel plans to institute stronger internal controls over cash receipts from customers.

Controlling cash receipts from customers
(Obj. 2)

I *Required*

Take the role of Shatel Patel, the company president. Write a memo to employees outlining procedures to ensure that all cash receipts are deposited in the bank and that the total amounts of each day's cash receipts are posted to customer accounts receivable.

P5-57B Brubacher Service Company sells for cash and on account. By selling on credit, Brubacher cannot expect to collect 100% of its accounts receivable. At December 31, 2009, and 2008, respectively, Brubacher reported the following on its balance sheet (in thousands of dollars):

Accounting for revenue, collections, and uncollectibles; percentage-of-sales method
(Obj. 3)

	December 31,	
	2009	2008
Accounts receivable...	$500	$400
Less: Allowance for uncollectibles	(95)	(60)
Accounts receivable, net..	$405	$340

During the year ended December 31, 2009, Brubacher earned service revenue and collected cash from customers. Uncollectible-account expense for the year was 5% of service revenue and Brubacher wrote off uncollectible accounts receivable.

I *Required*

1. Prepare T-accounts for Accounts Receivable and Allowance for Uncollectibles, and insert the December 31, 2008, balances as given.

2. Journalize the following transactions of Brubacher for the year ended December 31, 2009. Explanations are not required.

a. Service revenue on account, $6,700 thousand

b. Collections from customers on account, $6,300 thousand

c. Uncollectible-account expense, 5% of service revenue

d. Write-offs of uncollectible accounts receivable, $300 thousand

3. Post to the Accounts Receivable and Allowance for Uncollectibles T-accounts.

4. Compute the ending balances for the two T-accounts, and compare to the Brubacher Service amounts at December 31, 2009. They should be the same.

5. Show what Brubacher should report on its income statement for the year ended December 31, 2009.

Using the aging approach for uncollectibles
(Obj. 3)

P5-58B The December 31, 2009, records of Synetics Computers include these accounts:

Accounts Receivable..	$114,000
Allowance for Doubtful Accounts	(4,100)

At year-end, Synetics ages its receivables and adjusts the balance in Allowance for Doubtful Accounts to correspond to the aging schedule. During the last quarter of 2009, Synetics completed the following selected transactions:

2009		
Oct. 31		Wrote off the following accounts receivable as uncollectible: Cisco Foods, $300; Tindall Storage, $400; and Tiffany Energy, $1,100.
Dec. 31		Adjusted the Allowance for Doubtful Accounts and recorded doubtful-account expense at year-end, based on the aging of receivables, which follows.

	Age of Accounts			
Total Balance	**1–30 Days**	**31–60 Days**	**61–90 Days**	**Over 90 Days**
$114,000	$80,000	$20,000	$4,000	$10,000
Estimated uncollectible	0.5%	1.0%	5.0%	40.0%

❙ *Required*

1. Record the transactions in the journal. Explanations are not required.

2. Prepare a T-account for Allowance for Doubtful Accounts, and post to that account.

3. Show two ways Synetics Computers could report its accounts receivable in a comparative balance sheet for 2008 and 2009. At December 31, 2008, the company's Accounts Receivable balance was $111,000 and the Allowance for Doubtful Accounts stood at $3,700.

Short-term investments, uncollectibles, and the ratios
(Obj. 1, 3, 5)

P5-59B The top managers of Whelan Gift Stores seek the counsel of **Ernst & Young**, the accounting firm, and learn that Whelan must make some changes to bring its financial statements into conformity with GAAP. At December 31, 2009, Whelan Gift Stores accounts include the following:

Cash	$ 23,000
Short-term trading investments, at cost.............................	24,000
Accounts receivable	54,000
Inventory...	45,000
Prepaid expenses...	17,000
Total current assets	$163,000
Accounts payable	46,000
Other current liabilities..	69,000
Total current liabilities	$115,000

As the accountant from Ernst & Young, you draw the following conclusions:

- Cash includes $6,000 that is deposited in a compensating balance account that will be tied up until 2011.
- The market value of the short-term trading investments is $32,000. Whelan Gift Stores purchased the investments in early December.
- Whelan Gift Stores has been using the direct write-off method to account for uncollectibles. During 2009, the company wrote off bad receivables of $4,000. Ernst & Young determines that uncollectible-account expense should be 2% of sales, which for 2009 totalled $450,000. An aging of receivables at year-end indicated uncollectibles of $5,000.
- Whelan Gift Stores reported net income of $81,000 for 2009.

❚ Required

1. Restate all current accounts to conform to GAAP. (Challenge)
2. Compute Whelan Gift Stores' current ratio and acid-test ratio both before and after your corrections.
3. Determine Whelan Gift Stores' correct net income for 2009. (Challenge)

P5-60B Lilley & Taylor, partners in an accounting practice, completed the following selected transactions:

Notes receivable and accrued interest revenue
(Obj. 4)

2008		
Oct.	31	Performed service for Berger Manufacturing Inc., receiving a $30,000, 3-month, 5% note.
Dec.	31	Made an adjusting entry to accrue interest on the Berger note.
2009		
Jan.	31	Collected the Berger note.
Feb.	18	Received a 90-day, 8%, $10,000 note from Emerson Ltd., on account.
	19	Sold the Emerson note to a financial institution, receiving cash of $9,700.
Nov.	11	Loaned $20,000 cash to Diaz Insurance Agency, receiving a 90-day, 9% note.
Dec.	31	Accrued the interest on the Diaz note.

❚ Required

1. Record the transactions in Lilley & Taylor's journal. Round all amounts to the nearest dollar. Explanations are not required.
2. Show what Lilley & Taylor will report on its comparative classified balance sheet at December 31, 2009, and December 31, 2008.

P5-61B The comparative financial statements of New World Piano Company for 2009, 2008, and 2007 included the following selected data:

Using ratio data to evaluate a company's financial position
(Obj. 5)

	(In millions)		
	2009	2008	2007
Balance sheet:			
Current assets:			
Cash	$ 67	$ 66	$ 62
Short-term investments	73	81	70
Receivables, net of allowance for doubtful accounts of $7, $6, and $4, respectively	226	174	195
Inventories	398	375	349
Prepaid expenses	22	19	16
Total current assets	$ 786	$ 715	$ 692
Total current liabilities	$ 420	$ 405	$ 388
Income statement:			
Net sales	$2,071	$2,005	$1,965

❙ Required

1. As a financial advisor to an investor in New World Piano Company, compute these ratios for 2009 and 2008.

   a. Current ratio

   b. Acid-test ratio

   c. Days' sales in receivables

2. Write a memo explaining to your client which ratio values showed improvement from 2009 to 2008 and which ratio values deteriorated. State whether the overall trend is favourable or unfavourable for the company, give the reason for your evaluation, and advise your client regarding its investment.

APPLY YOUR KNOWLEDGE

DECISION CASES

Revenues, collections, and bad debts on receivables
(Obj. 3)

Case 1. A fire during 2009 destroyed most of the accounting records of Morris Financial Services Inc. The only accounting data for 2009 that Morris can come up with are the following balances at December 31, 2009. The general manager also knows that bad-debt expense should be 5% of service revenue.

Accounts receivable	$180,000
Less: Allowance for bad debts	(22,000)
Total expenses, excluding bad-debt expense	670,000
Collections from customers	840,000
Write-offs of bad receivables	30,000
Accounts receivable, December 31, 2008	110,000

As the insurance claims officer, prepare a summary income statement for Morris Financial Services Inc., for the year ended December 31, 2009. The insurance claim will be affected by whether the company was profitable in 2009. Use a T-account for Accounts Receivable to compute service revenue.

Estimating the collectibility of accounts receivable
(Obj. 3)

Case 2. Suppose you work in the loan department of CIBC. Dean Young, owner of Dean Young Sports Equipment, has come to you seeking a loan for $500,000 to expand operations. Young proposes to use accounts receivable as collateral for the loan and has provided you with the following information from the company's most recent financial statements:

	(In thousands)		
	2009	2008	2007
Sales	$1,475	$1,001	$902
Cost of goods sold	876	647	605
Gross profit	599	354	297
Other expenses	518	287	253
Net profit or (loss) before taxes	$ 81	$ 67	$ 44
Accounts receivable	$ 128	$ 107	$ 94
Allowance for doubtful accounts	13	11	9

❙ Required

Analyze the trends of sales, days' sales in receivables, and cash collections from customers for 2009 and 2008. Would you make the loan to Young? Support your decision with facts and figures.

ETHICAL ISSUE

Sunnyvale Loan Company is in the consumer loan business. Sunnyvale borrows from banks and loans out the money at higher interest rates. Sunnyvale's bank requires Sunnyvale to submit quarterly financial statements to keep its line of credit. Sunnyvale's main asset is Notes Receivable. Therefore, Uncollectible-Account Expense and Allowance for Uncollectible Accounts are important accounts for the company. Kimberly Burnham, the company's owner, prefers for net income to increase in a smooth pattern, rather than increase in some periods and decrease in other periods. To report smoothly increasing net income, Burnham underestimates Uncollectible-Account Expense in some periods. In other periods, Burnham overestimates the expense. She reasons that the income overstatements roughly offset the income understatements over time.

I *Required*

Is Sunnyvale Loan's practice of smoothing income ethical? Why or why not?

FOCUS ON FINANCIALS

Sun-Rype Products

Refer to Sun-Rype Products' financial statements in Appendix A at the end of this book.

Short-term investments and accounts receivable
(Obj. 1, 3, 4)

1. In the Notes to the Financial Statements, we find the following:
   2. Change of Accounting Policies
   (b) Financial instruments recognition, measurement, disclosure and presentation, the company disclosed "*...the Company has designated its cash and cash equivalents as held-for-trading, which are measured at their fair value...*"
   1. Significant Accounting Policies
   (c) Cash and cash equivalents the company disclosed "*cash and cash equivalents include cash and short-term deposits in high quality, low risk money market instruments, which are cashable on demand 90 days or less from the date of issue.*"

   Assume that Cash and cash equivalents included short-term money market instruments at December 31, 2007, of $100 (and at December 31, 2006, of $300). Further assume that there were no market value write-downs in 2007 and that the cash flow statement reports that Sun-Rype sold money market instruments for $201. How much gain or loss would Sun-Rype have on the sale of the money market instruments?

2. How much were Sun-Rype's receivables at December 31, 2007 and 2006? What can you assume from this information?

3. Assume that Sun-Rype wrote off 1% of 2007 sales as uncollectible. How much did Sun-Rype collect from customers during 2007?

FOCUS ON ANALYSIS

Mullen Group Income Fund

This case is based on the Mullen Group Income Fund financial statements in Appendix B at the end of this book.

Analyzing accounts receivable
(Obj. 3)

In "Management's Discussion and Analysis," included in the Mullen Group Income Fund ("the Fund") Annual Report (this document is not included in Appendix B, but can be accessed through the Mullen Group website), management states:

"Bad Debt Expense: The Fund routinely reviews accounts receivables and sets up a reserve for bad debts on a customer-by-customer basis. This is an estimate as some of the reserved accounts may subsequently be collected whereas some accounts currently deemed collectible may become uncollectible. The Fund considers its reserve at the end of December 31, 2007 to be reasonable."

1. Does the Mullen Group disclose the Allowance for Doubtful Accounts in its financial statements? How can you determine what the Mullen Group expects to collect from its reported Accounts Receivable?

2. What decision ratios can you calculate with the information reported in the Mullen Group financial statements? Calculate for 2007.

3. Would you conclude that the Mullen Group's doubtful-account expense will include large write-offs in 2008? What basis do you have for this conclusion?

GROUP PROJECT

Jillian Michaels and Dee Childress worked for several years as sales representatives for Xerox Corporation. During this time, they became close friends as they acquired expertise with the company's full range of copier equipment. Now they see an opportunity to put their expertise to work and fulfill lifelong desires to establish their own business. Northern Lights College has a campus in their community, Fort St. John, British Columbia, and there is no copy centre within 8 kilometres of the campus. Business in the area is booming, office buildings and apartments are springing up, and the population of the Fort St. John section of the city is growing.

Michaels and Childress want to open a copy centre, similar to FedEx Kinko's, near the campus. A small shopping centre across the street from the college has a vacancy that would fit their needs. Michaels and Childress each have $35,000 to invest in the business, but they forecast the need for $200,000 to renovate the store and purchase some of the equipment they will need. Xerox Corporation will lease two large copiers to them at a total monthly rental of $6,000. With enough cash to see them through the first six months of operation, they are confident they can make the business succeed. The two women work very well together, and both have excellent credit ratings. Michaels and Childress must borrow $130,000 to start the business, advertise its opening, and keep it running for its first six months.

❚ *Required*

Assume two roles: (1) Michaels and Childress, the partners who will own Fort St. John Copy Centre; and (2) loan officers at North Peace Savings and Credit Union (NPSCU).

1. As a group, visit a copy centre to familiarize yourselves with its operations. If possible, interview the manager or another employee. Then write a loan request that Michaels and Childress will submit to NPSCU with the intent of borrowing $130,000 to be paid back over three years. The loan will be a personal loan to the partnership of Michaels and Childress, not to Fort St. John Copy Centre. The request should specify all the details of Michaels' and Childress's plan that will motivate the bank to grant the loan. Include a budget for each of the first six months of operation of the proposed copy centre.

2. As a group, interview a loan officer in a bank. Write NPSCU's reply to the loan request. Specify all the details that the bank should require as conditions for making the loan.

3. If necessary, modify the loan request or the bank's reply in order to reach agreement between the two parties.

QUICK CHECK ANSWERS

1. *b*

2. *c*

3. *a ($46,000 × 0.02)*

4. *d ($900 + $920)*

5. *a ($1,350 − $900)*

6. *d*

7. *b ($9,500 − $1,350)*

8. *b ($3,200 − $100) − ($300 − $100)*

9. *d ($800,000 + $2,500,000 − $900,000)*

10. *c ($4,800 × 0.05 × 1/12)*

11. *c $25,000 + ($25,000 × 0.05 × 6/12)*

12. *d*

13. *d [($62,000 + $58,000)/2) ÷ ($730,000/365)]*

14. *c [($3,000 + $6,000) ÷ ($8,000 + $3,000)]*

Inventory and Cost of Goods Sold

6

SPOTLIGHT

You have just graduated from college, taken a job, and you are moving into an apartment. The place is unfurnished so you will need a bed, dresser, sofa, table, and chairs to go with your TV and sound system from college. Where will you find these things? Leon's Furniture is a good source.

Leon's Furniture is known for its contemporary-styled, well-priced furnishings—just about right for a new graduate. The company operates 35 company stores and has 28 franchised locations.

Leon's Furniture Limited's balance sheet is summarized here. You can see that merchandise inventory (labelled simply as Inventory) is one of Leon's Furniture's biggest assets. That's not surprising since Leon's, like other retailers, attracts customers with goods they can purchase and take home immediately.

Leon's Furniture Limited
Consolidated Balance Sheets (Adapted)
As at December 31

	(millions)	
	2007	2006
Assets		
Current		
Cash and cash equivalents	$ 25.7	$ 28.2
Short-term investments	116.6	92.1
Accounts receivable (net)	33.7	25.7
Inventory	75.6	74.7
Total current assets	251.6	220.7
Property, plant, and equipment (net)	211.6	207.0
Other long-term assets	12.0	11.9
	$475.2	$439.6
Liabilities and Shareholders' Equity		
Current		
Accounts payable and accrued liabilities	$ 92.0	$ 94.7
Other current liabilities	34.8	33.0
Total current liabilities	126.8	127.7
Future tax liabilities	7.1	5.6
Other liabilities	19.3	18.8
Total liabilities	153.2	152.1
Shareholders' equity		
Common shares	14.0	11.5
Retained earnings	307.1	276.0
Other equity	0.9	—
Total shareholders' equity	322.0	287.5
	$475.2	$439.6

We also present Leon's Furniture Limited's income statement. The year 2007 was a good year; sales and net income were up.

Leon's Furniture Limited
Consolidated Statements of Income (Adapted)
For the Years Ended December 31

	(millions)	
	2007	2006
Sales	$637.5	$591.3
Cost of sales	363.3	341.4
Gross margin	274.2	249.9
Selling, general, and administrative expenses	146.2	136.1
Amortization	14.0	13.3
Other operating expenses	28.1	24.5
Interest income	(4.7)	(3.5)
	183.6	170.4
Income before gain on sale of assets and income taxes	90.6	79.5
Gain on sales of assets	0.4	2.0
	91.0	81.5
Provision for income taxes	32.5	27.9
Net income for the year	$ 58.5	$ 53.6

EXHIBIT 6-1 Contrasting a Service Company with a Merchandiser

Service Company
Royal LePage Real Estate
Income Statement
For the Year Ended December 31, 2008

Service revenue...	$XXX
Expenses	
Operating and administrative...................	X
Amortization...	X
Income tax..	X
Net income	$ X

Merchandising Company
The Forzani Group Ltd.
Income Statement
For the Year Ended February 3, 2008

Amounts in millions

Sales revenue...	$1,331
Cost of goods sold.......................................	853
Gross margin	478
Operating *expenses*	
Operating and administrative...................	X
Amortization...	X
Income tax..	X
Net income	$ 4

Royal LePage Real Estate
Balance Sheet
As at December 31, 2008

Assets

Current assets	
Cash..	$X
Temporary investments............................	X
Accounts receivable, net..........................	X
Prepaid expenses.....................................	X

The Forzani Group Ltd.
Balance Sheet
As at February 3, 2008

Assets

Amounts in thousands

Current assets	
Cash..	$ X
Temporary investments............................	X
Accounts receivable, net..........................	X
Inventory	319
Prepaid expenses.....................................	X

You can see that the **cost of sales** (another name for *cost of goods sold*) is by far Leon's Furniture's largest expense. The account titled Cost of Sales perfectly describes that expense. In short,

- Leon's buys inventory, an asset carried on the books at cost.
- The goods that Leon's sells are no longer Leon's Furniture's assets. The cost of inventory that's sold gets shifted into the expense account, Cost of Sales.

Merchandise inventory is the heart of a merchandising business, and cost of goods sold is the most important expense for a company that sells goods rather than services. This chapter covers the accounting for inventory and cost of goods sold. It also shows you how to analyze financial statements. Here we focus on inventory, cost of goods sold, and gross margin.

IFRS ALERT

CICA Handbook Section 3031 "Inventories" includes an explanatory note that indicates that the Section is based on International Accounting Standard (IAS) 2 "Inventories." The note indicates that, at least at present, Section 3031 converges with IAS 2, the relevant IFRS.

Two significant changes adapted from IAS 2 are worth noting:

1. The use of the Last-In, First-Out (LIFO) method of cost determination is no longer acceptable in Canada.
2. When the value of inventory has been written down from book value (normally cost) to net realizable value and the net realizable value subsequently increases to a value equal to or greater than the pre-write-down book value, the write-down should be reversed. The reversal must not exceed the write-down.

This chapter will apply these two changes to the discussion of inventory.

We begin by showing how the financial statements of a merchandiser such as Leon's Furniture Limited or The Forzani Group Ltd. differ from those of service entities such as Purolator or Royal LePage Real Estate. The financial statements in Exhibit 6-1 highlight how service entities differ from merchandisers.

Accounting for Inventory

The basic concept of accounting for merchandise inventory can be illustrated with an example. Suppose Leon's Furniture has in stock 3 chairs that cost $300 each. Leon's Furniture marks the chairs up by $200 and sells 2 of the chairs for $500 each.

- Leon's Furniture's balance sheet reports the 1 chair that the company still holds in inventory.
- The income statement reports the cost of the 2 chairs sold, as shown in Exhibit 6-3.

Here is the basic concept of how we identify inventory, the asset, from cost of goods sold, the expense.

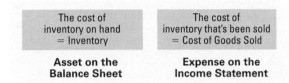

Inventory's cost shifts from asset to expense when the seller delivers the goods to the buyer.

Merchandisers have two accounts that service entities don't need: Inventory on the balance sheet and Cost of Goods Sold on the income statement.

Other Categories of Inventory

While the focus of this chapter is on merchandise inventory, other categories of inventory should also be mentioned:

- Manufacturing companies have inventories of raw materials, work in process, and finished goods. For example, Algoma Steel Inc.'s March 31, 2008, consolidated balance sheet (amounts in millions) shows Inventories of $345.5, which consists of Raw Materials and Supplies ($151.3), Work in Process ($81.8), and Finished Products ($112.4). The consolidated statement of income (loss) shows Cost of Sales, which includes cost of goods sold.
- Service companies have inventories of office supplies and other such items on hand at their year end, which may be described as Inventory or Prepaid Expenses.

Accounting Principles and Inventories

It is important at this point that you consider several accounting principles that have special relevance to inventories:

- Consistency
- Disclosure
- Conservatism

Consistency Principle

The **consistency principle** states that businesses should use the same accounting methods and procedures from period to period. Consistency enables investors to compare a company's financial statements from one period to the next.

Suppose you are analyzing Interfax Corporation's net income pattern over a two-year period. Now, suppose Interfax switched from one inventory method to another during that time and its net income increased dramatically, but only because of the change in inventory method. If you did not know of the change, you might believe that Interfax's income increased due to improved operations, which is not the case.

The consistency principle does not mean that a company is not permitted to change its accounting methods. GAAP require that a change in accounting method, such as a change in the method of valuing inventory, be disclosed. CICA Handbook Section 1506 (which corresponds to IFRS IAS 8 "Accounting Policies, Changes in Accounting Estimates and Errors") indicates that such a change is acceptable if it "results in the financial statements providing reliable and more relevant information." The change should normally be applied retrospectively, which means that prior years' financial statements should be restated to reflect the change. In addition, the effect of the change on the current financial statements should be disclosed.

Such an accounting change might be disclosed in the notes to the financial statements according to the disclosure principle.

IFRS

Disclosure Principle

The **disclosure principle** holds that a company's financial statements should report enough information for outsiders to make informed decisions about the company.

The company should report *relevant*, *reliable*, and *comparable* information about itself. That means disclosing inventory accounting methods. Without knowledge of the accounting method being used a banker could make an unwise lending decision. Suppose the banker is comparing two companies—one uses one inventory method and the other uses another method that leads to higher income. The latter reports higher net income, but only because of the inventory method being used. Without knowing the reason for the higher income, the banker could loan money to the wrong business.

Conservatism Principle

Conservatism in accounting means that companies should ensure that assets, revenues, and gains are not overstated and that liabilities, expenses, and losses are not understated. That is, they should be stated at their fair value. However, conservatism does not mean that any accounts should be deliberately understated or overstated. The goal is to present information that is neutral so that it can be relied on by users.

IFRS

Conservatism directs accountants to decrease the accounting book values of assets that appear to be unrealistically high. Assume that Surrey Mfg. Inc. paid $35,000 for inventory that has become outdated and whose current value is only $12,000. Conservatism dictates that Surrey Mfg. Inc. immediately write down the value of the inventory to $12,000 and record a $23,000 loss, which would go to the income statement. Many accountants regard conservatism as a counter balance to management's optimistic tendencies. The goal is to present reliable data.

Lower-of-Cost-or-Market Rule. The **lower-of-cost-or-market rule** (abbreviated as **LCM**) is based on accounting conservatism. LCM requires that inventory be reported in the financial statements at whichever is lower—the inventory's historical cost or its market value. Applied to inventories, *market value* means *net realizable value* (that is, the estimated price at which the company could sell the inventory in the normal course of business minus the estimated cost of completing the inventory and the selling costs). If the net realizable value of inventory falls below its historical cost, the business must write down the value of its goods to market value. The business reports ending inventory at its LCM value on the balance sheet. All this can be done automatically by a computerized accounting system. How is the write-down accomplished?

Suppose Klassen Furniture Inc. paid $3,000 for inventory on September 26. By December 31, the inventory can be replaced for $2,000. Klassen's December 31 balance sheet must report this inventory at the LCM value of $2,000. Exhibit 6-2 presents the effects of LCM on the balance sheet and the income statement. Before any LCM effect, cost of goods sold is $9,000. An LCM write-down decreases Inventory and increases Cost of Goods Sold, as follows (see also Exhibit 6-2):

Cost of Goods Sold	1,000	
Inventory		1,000
Write inventory down to net realizable value.		

IFRS

The IFRS alert at the beginning of the chapter indicated that one of the changes resulting from the merge of the *CICA Handbook* with IFRS was that inventory that has been written down to net realizable value should be reassessed each period. If the net realizable value has increased, the previous write-down should be reversed up to the new net realizable value. Of course, the inventory cannot be written up to a value that exceeds its original cost.

Assume that Klassen's inventory described above was still on hand at the end of the next period and that the net realizable value had increased to $2,400. The journal entry to reverse a previous write-down would be as follows:

Inventory	400	
Cost of Goods Sold		400
Write inventory up to new net realizable value.		

EXHIBIT 6-2   Lower-of-Cost-or-Market (LCM) Effects on Inventory and Cost of Goods Sold

Balance Sheet

Current assets:	$ XXX
Cash	XXX
Short-term investments	XXX
Accounts receivable	XXX
Inventories, at market (which is lower than $3,000 cost)	2,000
Prepaid expenses	XXX
Total current assets	$ X,XXX

Income Statement

Sales revenue	$21,000
Cost of goods sold ($9,000 + $1,000)	10,000
Gross margin	$11,000

Companies disclose how they apply LCM in a note to their financial statements as shown in the following excerpt from Sobeys Inc.'s 2008 audited annual report.

> **Summary of Significant Accounting Policies**
>
> **Inventories**
>
> Warehouse inventories are valued at the lower of cost and net realizable value with cost being determined on a first-in, first-out or a moving average cost basis. Retail inventories are valued at the lower of cost and net realizable value . . .

LCM is not optional. It is required by GAAP.

Sales Price versus Cost of Inventory

Note the difference between the sale price of inventory and the cost of inventory. In our Leon's Furniture example,

- Sales revenue is based on the sale price of the inventory sold ($500 per chair).
- Cost of goods sold is based on the cost of the inventory sold ($300 per chair).
- Inventory on the balance sheet is based on the cost of the inventory still on hand ($300 per chair).

Exhibit 6-3 shows the items.

Gross margin, also called **gross margin**, is the excess of sales revenue over cost of goods sold. It is called *gross margin* because operating expenses have not yet been subtracted. Exhibit 6-4 shows actual inventory and cost of goods sold data (cost of sales) from the financial statements of Leon's Furniture Limited.

Leon's inventory of $75.6 million represents

$$\frac{\text{Inventory}}{\text{(balance sheet)}} = \frac{\text{Number of units of}}{\text{inventory } \textit{on hand}} \times \frac{\text{Cost per unit}}{\text{of inventory}}$$

Leon's cost of goods sold ($363.3 million) represents

$$\frac{\text{Cost of goods sold}}{\text{(income statement)}} = \frac{\text{Number of units of}}{\text{inventory sold}} \times \frac{\text{Cost per unit}}{\text{of inventory}}$$

Let's see what "units of inventory" and "cost per unit" mean.

Number of Units of Inventory. The number of inventory units on hand is determined from accounting records, backed up by a physical count of the goods at year-end. Companies do not include in their inventory any goods that they hold on *consignment* because those goods belong to another company. But they do include their own inventory that is out on consignment and held by another company.

EXHIBIT 6-3   Inventory and Costs of Goods Sold When Inventory Cost Is Constant

Balance Sheet (partial)		Income Statement (partial)	
Current assets		Sales revenue	
Cash	$XXX	(2 chairs @ sales price of $500	$1,000
Short-term investments	XXX	Cost of goods sold	
Accounts receivable	XXX	(2 chairs @ cost of $300)	600
Inventory (1 chair @ cost of $300)	300	Gross margin	$ 400
Prepaid expenses	XXX		

Cost per Unit of Inventory. The cost per unit of inventory poses a challenge because companies purchase goods at different prices throughout the year. Which unit costs go into the ending inventory for the balance sheet? Which unit costs go to cost of goods sold?

The next section shows how the different accounting methods determine ending inventory on the balance sheet and cost of goods sold for the income statement. First, however, you need to understand how inventory accounting systems work.

Accounting for Inventory in the Perpetual System

There are two main types of inventory accounting systems: the periodic system and the perpetual system. The **periodic inventory system** is mainly used by businesses that sell inexpensive goods. A dollar store or a convenience store, for example, may not keep a running record of every one of the hundreds of items they sell. Instead, these stores count their inventory periodically—at least once a year—to determine the quantities on hand. Businesses such as some restaurants and hometown nurseries also use the periodic inventory system because the accounting cost is low. For details on the periodic inventory system, refer to Appendix 6A beginning on page 310.

A **perpetual inventory system** uses computer software to keep a running record of inventory on hand. This system achieves control over goods such as parts at a Buick dealer, lumber at Rona, furniture at Leon's Furniture, and all the various groceries and other items that a Loblaw store sells. Today, most businesses use the perpetual inventory system.

Even with a perpetual system, the business still counts the inventory on hand annually. The physical count serves as a check on the accuracy of the perpetual records and confirms the accuracy of the inventory records for preparing the financial statements. The chart at the top of the next page compares the perpetual and periodic systems.

EXHIBIT 6-4	Leon's Furniture Limited Inventory and Cost of Goods Sold (Cost of Sales)

Leon's Furniture Limited
Consolidated Balance Sheets (Partial, Adapted)
As at December 31

	(Millions)	
Assets	2007	2006
Cash and cash equivalents	$ 25.7	$28.2
Short-term investments	116.6	92.1
Accounts receivable (net)	33.7	25.7
Inventory	75.6	74.7

Leon's Furniture Limited
Consolidated Statements of Income (Partial, Adapted)
For the Years Ended December 31

	(Millions)	
	2007	2006
Sales	$637.5	$591.3
Cost of sales	363.3	341.4
Gross margin	$274.2	$249.9

Perpetual Inventory System	*Periodic Inventory System*
• Used for all types of goods	• Used for inexpensive goods
• Keeps a running record of all goods bought, sold, and on hand	• Does not keep a running record of all goods bought, sold, and on hand
• Inventory counted at least once a year	• Inventory counted at least once a year

EXHIBIT 6-5 Bar Code for Electronic Scanner

0 72512 06581 5

How the Perpetual System Works. Let's use an everyday situation to show how a perpetual inventory system works. Suppose you are buying a pair of Nike cross-trainer shoes from Forzani. The clerk scans the bar code on the product label of your purchase. Exhibit 6-5 illustrates a typical bar code. The bar code on the product or product label holds lots of information. The optical scanner reads the bar code, and the computer records the sale and updates the inventory records.

Recording Transactions in the Perpetual System. All accounting systems record each purchase of inventory as a debit to Inventory and a credit to either Cash or Accounts Payable.

When Leon's Furniture makes a sale, two entries are needed in the perpetual system:

- The company records the sale—debits Cash or Accounts Receivable and credits Sales Revenue for the sale price of the goods.
- Leon's Furniture also debits Cost of Goods Sold and credits Inventory for the cost of the inventory sold.

Exhibit 6-6 shows the accounting for inventory in a perpetual system. Panel A gives the journal entries and the T-accounts, and Panel B presents the income statement and the balance sheet. All amounts are assumed. (Exhibit 6A-1 illustrates the accounting for these transactions in a periodic inventory system while Exhibit 6A-2 compares the journal entries required for the two types of inventory systems.)

In Exhibit 6-6, Panel A, the first entry to Inventory summarizes a lot of detail. The cost of the inventory, $560,000*, is the net amount of the purchases, determined as follows (using assumed amounts):

Purchase price of the inventory from the seller	$600,000
+ **Freight-in** (Transportation cost to move the goods from the seller to the buyer)	4,000
− **Purchase returns** for unsuitable goods returned to the seller................................	(25,000)
− **Purchase allowances** granted by the seller	(5,000)
− **Purchase discounts** for early payment...	(14,000)
= Net purchases of inventory	$560,000

Freight-in is the transportation cost paid by the buyer to move goods from the seller to the buyer. Freight-in is accounted for as part of the cost of inventory. A **purchase return** is a decrease in the cost of inventory because the buyer returned the goods to the seller. A **purchase allowance** also decreases the cost of inventory because the buyer got an allowance (a deduction) from the amount owed—often because of a merchandise defect. Throughout this book, we often refer to net purchases simply as purchases.

---

*The price shown does *not* include Canada's goods and services tax (GST). Sales taxes, goods and services taxes, and harmonized sales taxes are explained in the User Alert on page 271.

EXHIBIT 6-6	Recording and Reporting Inventory—Perpetual System (Amounts Assumed)

Perpetual System

PANEL A—Recording Transactions and the T-accounts

1.	Inventory	560,000	
	Accounts Payable		560,000
	Purchase of inventory on account.		
2.	Accounts Receivable..	900,000	
	Sales Revenue..		900,000
	Sold inventory on account.		
	Cost of Goods Sold	540,000	
	Inventory		540,000
	Recorded cost of goods sold.		

The T-accounts show the following:

Inventory			
Beginning balance	100,000*	Cost of goods sold	540,000
Purchases	560,000		
Ending balance	120,000		

Cost of Goods Sold	
Cost of goods sold 540,000	

*Beginning inventory was $100,000.

PANEL B—Reporting in the Financial Statements

Income Statement (Partial)

Sales revenue	$900,000
Cost of goods sold	540,000
Gross margin	$360,000

Ending Balance Sheet (Partial)

Current assets:		
Cash	$	XXX
Temporary investments..............		XXX
Accounts receivable		XXX
Inventory....................................		120,000
Prepaid expenses		XXX

A **purchase discount** is a decrease in the cost of inventory that is earned by paying quickly. A common arrangement states payment terms of 2/10 n/30. This means the buyer can take a 2% discount for payment within 10 days, or pay the full amount within 30 days. Another common credit term is "net 30," which directs the customer to pay the full amount within 30 days. In summary,

> **NET PURCHASES = PURCHASES**
> **– PURCHASE RETURNS AND ALLOWANCES**
> **– PURCHASE DISCOUNTS**
> **+ FREIGHT-IN**

Net sales are computed exactly the same way as net purchases, but with no freight-in.

> **NET SALES = SALES REVENUE**
> **– SALES RETURNS AND ALLOWANCES**
> **– SALES DISCOUNTS**

Freight-out paid by the *seller* is not part of the cost of inventory. Instead, freight-out is a delivery expense. It is the seller's expense of delivering merchandise to customers. (Appendix 6A shows the accounting for these same transactions in a periodic accounting system.) Now study Exhibit 6-6 and the dated illustration on the following page.

The first entry in Exhibit 6-6 is a summary entry. Since the various transactions that make up the $560,000 may occur on different dates, it is instructive to now view each entry separately with assumed dates as follows:

General Journal

Date	Account Titles and Explanation	Ref.	Debit	Credit
2009				
Jan. 4	Inventory		600,000	
	Accounts Payable			600,000
	To record purchase of merchandise.			
6	Inventory		4,000	
	Cash			4,000
	To record freight costs.			
11	Accounts Payable		25,000	
	Inventory			25,000
	To record purchase returns.			
13	Accounts Payable		5,000	
	Inventory			5,000
	To record purchase allowances.			
16	Accounts Payable		14,000	
	Inventory			14,000
	To record purchase discounts.			

 **USER ALERT**

Goods and Services Taxes (GST), Sales Taxes, and Harmonized Sales Taxes

Canada has three types of sales taxes:

- Federal goods and services tax (GST) applies to most goods and services (exempt goods and services include residential accommodation, health, medical, and dental services, and certain child-care services).
- Provincial or regional sales tax (PST) applies to goods and services purchased by a consumer, such as an individual or a business, for its own use. Note: Quebec has a specific sales tax (QST); Alberta, Yukon, Northwest Territories, and Nunavut do not charge sales tax.
- Harmonized sales tax (HST) is a blended PST and GST. New Brunswick, Newfoundland and Labrador, and Nova Scotia use HST.

The GST may be charged at several points along the supply chain, and each link, except the final link (the consumer), is allowed to offset tax paid against tax collected (termed an input tax credit or ITC). The following example from Manitoba is illustrative (PST is excluded from the illustration).

Argosy Products sells steel rods to Harmony Tools for $1,000. Harmony Tools uses the steel rods in the manufacture of lawn rakes which it sells to Kitchen Hardware for $3,000. Kitchen Hardware sells the lawn rakes to the end users (the consumers) for $6,000.

Transactions	Argosy Steel	Harmony Tools	Kitchen Hardware	GST	GST Remitted
1. Sale of steel rods	$1,000			Collect $ 50	$ 50
2. Purchase of steel rods		$1,000		ITC ($50)	
Sale of lawn rakes		$3,000		Collect $150	$100
3. Purchase of lawn rakes			$3,000	ITC ($150)	
Sale of lawn rakes			$6,000	Collect $300	$150
Total Consumer Sales			$6,000		$300

The PST is charged on the sale to the final consumer and remitted to the provincial treasurer. Using the information in the example above, Kitchen Hardware would charge the Manitoba sales tax rate of 7% on the $6000 sale and remit the tax collected of $420.00 to Manitoba Finance, Taxation Division.

The HST is administered by the federal government and applies to all goods and services with some exceptions. For example, in Nova Scotia the HST combines the GST of 5% and Nova Scotia's provincial tax of 8% for a total 13% HST.

Inventory Costing

Inventory is the first asset for which a manager can decide which accounting method to use. The accounting method selected affects the profits to be reported and the amount of income taxes to be paid and the values of the ratios derived from the balance sheet.

What Goes into Inventory Cost?

The cost of inventory in Leon's Furniture Limited's balance sheet represents all the costs that Leon's Furniture incurred to bring the inventory to the point of sale. The following cost principle applies to all assets:

> *The cost of any asset, such as inventory, is the sum of all costs incurred to bring the asset to its intended use, less any discounts.*

Inventory's cost includes its basic purchase price, plus freight-in, insurance while in transit, and any costs paid to get the inventory ready to sell, less returns, allowances, and discounts.

Once a chair is sitting in a Leon's Furniture's showroom, other costs incurred, such as advertising and sales commissions, are not included as the cost of inventory. Advertising, sales commissions, and delivery costs are expenses.

What items to include in inventory is determined not by the nature of the assets but by the nature of the business. For example, a delivery truck would be inventory for a truck dealership but would be a capital asset for Purolator Courier Ltd.

This chapter focuses on inventory held by a merchandising firm, but you should be aware that a manufacturing firm has three types of inventory: (1) raw materials, which are items obtained for use in the manufacturing process that eventually become part of the final product; (2) work in process, which includes partially completed products that require further processing but contain direct material costs, direct labour costs, and manufacturing overhead costs; and (3) finished goods, which are manufactured products that are ready for sale. When the finished goods are sold, their cost is charged to cost of goods sold.

Determining the ownership of inventory at the time of shipment depends on who has legal title. If inventory is shipped FOB (free on board) shipping point, it should be included on the books of the buyer, who has legal title, as soon as it leaves the shipper's dock. If the goods are shipped FOB destination, the inventory in transit still belongs on the books of the seller until it is delivered to the buyer.

Sometimes inventory is delivered by a company, say, Able Company, to another company, say, Baker Company, with the understanding that payment for the goods is only to be made once Baker Company sells the merchandise. Such goods are said to be held on consignment and, for financial reporting purposes, belong on the books of Able Company.

The Various Inventory Costing Methods

Objective

❷ **Understand** the various inventory methods

Determining the cost of inventory is easy when the unit cost remains constant, as in Exhibit 6-3. But unit cost usually changes. For example, prices often rise. Salomon snowboards that cost Intrawest $150 in October may cost $160 in November and $180 in December. Intrawest sells 50 snowboards in November. How many of the Salomon snowboards sold cost $150, how many cost $160, and how many cost $180?

To compute cost of goods sold and the cost of ending inventory still on hand, we must assign a unit cost to the items. Three generally accepted inventory methods are the following:

1. Specific unit cost
2. Weighted-average cost
3. First-in, first-out (FIFO) cost

A company can use any of these methods. As we shall see, these methods can have very different effects on reported profits, income taxes, and cash flow. Therefore, companies select their inventory method with great care.

Specific Unit Cost. Some businesses deal in unique inventory items, such as antique furniture, jewels, and real estate. These businesses cost their inventories at the specific cost of the particular unit. For instance, a Chevrolet dealer may have two vehicles in the showroom—a "stripped-down" model that cost $22,000 and a "loaded" model that cost $29,000. If the dealer sells the loaded model, cost of goods sold is $29,000. The stripped-down auto will be the only unit left in inventory, so ending inventory is $22,000.

The **specific-unit-cost method** is also called the *specific identification method*. This method is too expensive to use for inventory items that have common characteristics, such as metres of lumber, litres of paint, or automobile tires.

The other acceptable inventory accounting methods—weighted-average and FIFO—do not use the specific cost of a particular unit. Instead, they assume different flows of inventory costs.

Illustration of Weighted-Average and FIFO Costing. To illustrate weighted-average and FIFO costing, we use a common set of data, given in Exhibit 6-7.

In Exhibit 6-7, Leon's began the period with 10 lamps that cost $10 each; the beginning inventory was therefore $100. During the period, Leon's bought 50 more lamps, sold 40 lamps, and ended the period with 20 lamps, summarized in the T-account in Exhibit 6-7 and as follows:

	Number of Units	Total Cost
Goods available for sale	= 10 + 25 + 25 = 60 units	$100 + $350 + $450 = $900
Cost of goods sold	= 40 units	?
Ending inventory	= 20 units	?

The big accounting questions are

1. What is the cost of goods sold for the income statement?
2. What is the cost of the ending inventory for the balance sheet?

EXHIBIT 6-7	**Inventory Data Used to Illustrate Inventory Costing Methods**

		Inventory		
Begin. bal.	(10 units @ $10)	100		
Purchases:			Cost of goods sold	
No. 1	(25 units @ $14)	350	(40 units @ $?)	?
No. 2	(25 units @ $18)	450		
Ending bal.	(20 units @ $?)	?		

The answers to these questions depend on which inventory method Leon's uses. Leon's actually uses FIFO, but we will look at weighted-average costing first.

Weighted-Average Cost.

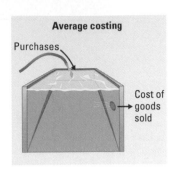

Average costing

The **weighted-average-cost method**, sometimes called the average-cost method, is based on the average cost of inventory for the period. The weighted-average cost per unit is determined as follows (data from Exhibit 6-7):

$$\text{Weighted-average cost per unit} = \frac{\text{Cost of goods available}^*}{\text{Number of units available}} = \frac{\$900}{60} = \$15$$

*Goods available = Beginning inventory + Purchases

$$
\begin{aligned}
\text{Cost of goods sold} &= \text{Number of units sold} \times \text{Weighted-average cost per unit} \\
&= \quad\quad 40 \text{ units} \quad\quad \times \quad\quad\quad \$15 \quad\quad\quad\quad = \$600
\end{aligned}
$$

$$
\begin{aligned}
\text{Ending inventory} &= \text{Number of units on hand} \times \text{Weighted-average cost per unit} \\
&= \quad\quad 20 \text{ units} \quad\quad \times \quad\quad\quad \$15 \quad\quad\quad\quad = \$300
\end{aligned}
$$

The following T-account shows the effects of weighted-average costing:

Inventory (at weighted-average cost)		
Begin. bal. (10 units @ $10) 100		
Purchases:		
No. 1 (25 units @ $14) 350		
No. 2 (25 units @ $18) 450	Cost of goods sold (40 units @ average cost of $15 per unit) 600	
Ending bal. (20 units @ average cost of $15 per unit) 300		

FIFO Cost.

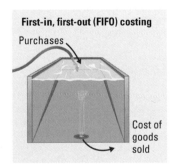

First-in, first-out (FIFO) costing

Under the **first-in, first-out (FIFO) cost method**, the first costs into inventory are the first costs assigned to cost of goods sold—hence, the name *first-in, first-out*. The diagram in the margin shows the effect of FIFO costing. The following T-account shows how to compute FIFO cost of goods sold and ending inventory for Leon's lamps (data from Exhibit 6-7):

Inventory (at FIFO cost)		
Begin. bal. (10 units @ $10) 100		
Purchases:	Cost of goods sold (40 units):	
No. 1 (25 units @ $14) 350	(10 units @ $10) 100	
No. 2 (25 units @ $18) 450	(25 units @ $14) 350 } 540	
	(5 units @ $18) 90	
Ending bal. (20 units @ $18) 360		

IFRS

Under FIFO, the cost of ending inventory is always based on the latest costs incurred—in this case $18 per unit.

LIFO Cost.

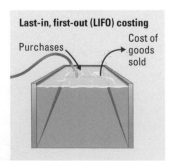

Last-in, first-out (LIFO) costing

We present **last-in, first-out (LIFO) cost method** for completeness; recall from the IFRS Alert at the beginning of this chapter that LIFO is no longer acceptable in Canada. It presently is used in the United States where it offers tax advantages. It was permitted in Canada for financial reporting purposes prior to the convergence of Canadian GAAP with IAS 2. Prior to the convergence, LIFO was little used in Canada as it was not permitted under Canadian income tax rules. LIFO costing is the opposite of FIFO. Under the LIFO cost method, the last costs into inventory go immediately to cost of goods sold, as shown in the diagram. Compare LIFO and FIFO, and you will see a vast difference.

The following T-account shows how to compute the LIFO inventory amounts for Leon's lamps (data from Exhibit 6-7).

Inventory (at LIFO cost)			
Begin bal. (10 units @ $10)	100		
Purchases:		Cost of goods sold (40 units):	
No. 1 (25 units @ $14)	350	(25 units @ $18)	450
No. 2 (25 units @ $18)	450	(15 units @ $14)	210 } 660
Ending bal. (10 units @ $10) 100			
(10 units @ $14) 140 } 240			

Under LIFO, the cost of ending inventory is always based on the oldest costs—from beginning inventory plus the early purchases of the period—$10 and $14 per unit.

The Effects of FIFO and Weighted-Average Cost on Cost of Goods Sold, Gross Margin, and Ending Inventory

In our Leon's example, the cost of inventory rose from $10 to $14 to $18. When inventory unit costs change this way, the various inventory methods produce different cost-of-goods-sold figures. Exhibit 6-8 summarizes the income effects (Sales − Cost of goods sold = gross margin) of the two inventory methods (remember that prices are rising). Study the exhibit carefully, focusing on cost of goods sold and gross margin.

Exhibit 6-9 demonstrates the effect of increasing and decreasing costs of inventory on cost of goods sold and ending inventory. Study this exhibit carefully; it will help you really understand FIFO and weighted-average.

Let's use the gross margin data from Exhibit 6-8 to illustrate the potential tax effects of the two methods in a period of rising prices:

	FIFO	Weighted-Average
Gross margin	$460	$400
Operating expenses (assumed)	260	260
Income before income tax	200	140
Income tax expense (35%)	70	49

Income tax expense is lower under weighted-average ($49) and higher under FIFO ($70).

In Canada, approximately the same number of companies uses FIFO as use weighted-average. Exhibit 6-9 demonstrates that in a period of rising prices, FIFO will generally lead to higher profits and higher taxes than weighted-average while the opposite is true in a period of falling prices. The difference between the two methods on profit and income taxes may be small, and each of the two methods is appropriate for certain types of inventory. In addition, some companies use a mixture of specific unit cost, FIFO, and weighted-average. The authors have therefore concluded that a company does not place much emphasis on potential tax savings when it decides

EXHIBIT 6-8 Effects of the FIFO and Weighted-Average Inventory Methods

	FIFO	Weighted-Average
Sales revenue (assumed)	$1,000	$1,000
Cost of goods sold	540 (lowest)	600 (highest)
Gross margin	$ 460 (highest)	$ 400 (lowest)

| EXHIBIT 6-9 | Cost of Goods Sold and Ending Inventory—FIFO and Weighted-Average; Increasing Costs and Decreasing Costs |

When inventory costs are decreasing,

	Cost of Goods Sold (COGS)	**Ending Inventory (EI)**
FIFO	FIFO COGS is highest because it's based on the oldest costs, which are high. Gross margin is, therefore, the lowest.	FIFO EI is lowest because it's based on the most recent costs, which are low.
Weighted-Average	Weighted-average is lowest because it's based on, which is lower than the oldest costs. Gross margin is, therefore, the highest.	Weighted-average is highest because the average costs for the period are high than the most recent ones.

When inventory costs are increasing,

	Cost of Goods Sold (COGS)	**Ending Inventory (EI)**
FIFO	FIFO COGS is lowest because it's based on oldest costs, which are low. Gross margin is, therefore, the highest.	FIFO EI is highest because it's based on the most recent costs, which are high.
Weighted-Average	Weighted-average is highest because it's based on an average of the costs for the period, which is higher than the oldest costs. Gross margin is, therefore, the lowest.	Weighted-average is lowest because the average costs for the period are lower than themost recent ones.

which of the three methods is appropriate for its organization (especially given that a company may use a different inventory costing method for tax purposes than the one used for financial reporting).

Comparison of the Inventory Methods

Let's compare the weighted-average and FIFO inventory methods.

1. How well does each method measure income by matching inventory expense—cost of goods sold—against revenue? Weighted-average results in the most realistic net income figure. Weighted-average is an average that combines all costs (old costs and recent costs). In contrast, FIFO matches old inventory costs against revenue—a poor matching of expense with revenue. FIFO income is therefore less realistic than income under weighted-average.

2. Which method reports the most up-to-date inventory cost on the balance sheet? FIFO reports the most current inventory cost on the balance sheet. Weighted-average can value inventory at very old costs because weighted-average leaves the oldest prices in ending inventory.

3. What effects do the methods have on income taxes? Weighted-average is an average that combines all costs (old costs and recent costs).

The following table summarizes the effects of these inventory methods on the balance sheet, income statement, and cash flows when prices are rising.

Weighted-Average	FIFO
Balance Sheet Effects	
Reports inventory at weighted-average costs so that current assets are not as current as under FIFO	Reports recent cost as the current asset value, thus approximating current replacement cost
Income Statement Effects	
Cost of goods sold (CGS) is less out of date than under FIFO	Results in poor matching since older-cost goods are assigned to CGS to be deducted from current revenue; tends to overstate net income
Cash Flow Effects	
Less cash paid for taxes than under FIFO so could be used by firms seeking to minimize taxes	More cash paid for taxes but still may be popular for firms seeking to maximize reported income

International Perspective. You saw in the IFRS Alert that only specific unit cost, FIFO, and weighted-average are permitted in countries that have adopted or converged with IFRSs.

IFRS

MID-CHAPTER SUMMARY PROBLEM

MyAccountingLab

Suppose a division of DIY Building Products Inc. has these inventory records for January 2009:

Date	Item	Quantity	Unit Cost
Jan. 1	Beginning inventory	100 units	$ 8
6	Purchase	60 units	9
21	Purchase	150 units	9
27	Purchase	90 units	10

Operating expense for January was $1,900, and sales of 310 units generated sales revenue of $6,770.

> **Name:** DIY Building Products Inc.
> **Industry:** Building products
> **Fiscal Period:** Month of January 2009
> **Key Fact:** Perpetual inventory system

Required

1. Prepare the January income statement, showing amounts for FIFO and weighted-average cost. Label the bottom line "Operating income." (Round figures to whole-dollar amounts.) Show your computations, and compute cost of goods sold.
2. Explain which inventory method would result in:
   a. reporting the highest operating income.
   b. reporting inventory on the balance sheet at the most current cost.
   c. attaining the best measure of net income for the income statement.

Answers

Requirement 1

Sales revenue is given.

Beginning inventory is given.

See the Computations section.

See Computations section.

Cost of goods available for sale − Ending

Sales revenue – Cost of goods sold

Operating expenses are given.

Gross margin – Operating expenses

DIY Building Products Inc.
Income Statement for Division
For the Month Ended January 31, 2009

	FIFO		Weighted-Average	
Sales revenue		$6,770		$6,770
Cost of goods sold:				
Beginning inventory	$ 800		$ 800	
Purchases	2,790		2,790	
Cost of goods available for sale	3,590		3,590	
Ending inventory	(900)		(808)	
Cost of goods sold		2,690		2,782
Gross margin		4,080		3,988
Operating expenses		1,900		1,900
Operating income		$2,180		$2,088

Computations

Beginning inventory: 100 × $8 = $800

Purchases: (60 × $9) + (150 × $9) + (90 × $10) = $2,790

Ending inventory—FIFO: 90* × $10 = $900

Weighted-average: 90 × $8.975** = $808 (rounded from $807.75)

*Number of units in ending inventory = 100 + 60 + 150 + 90 − 310 = 90
**$3,590/400 units† = $8.975 per unit
†Number of units available = 100 + 60 + 150 + 90 = 400

Use the quantities and unit costs given in the question to calculate beginning inventory and purchases. Recall that FIFO ending inventory calculations use the most current purchase prices. Weighted-average ending inventory calculations use the average purchase prices (including the price of the beginning inventory).

Since beginning inventory, purchases, and operating expense are the same for all three inventory methods, use the ending inventory and operating income amounts you calculated in Requirement 1 to help you answer these questions.

Requirement 2

a. Use FIFO to report the highest operating income. Income under FIFO is highest when inventory unit costs are increasing, as in this situation.

b. Use FIFO to report inventory on the balance sheet at the most current cost. The oldest inventory costs are expensed as cost of goods sold, leaving the most recent (most current) costs of the period in ending inventory.

c. Use weighted-average to attain the best measure of net income. Weighted-average produces the best matching of current expense with current revenue. Weighted-average inventory costs, which are expensed as part of goods sold, are closer to the most recent (most current) inventory costs than FIFO costs are.

Inventory and the Financial Statements

Detailed Income Statement

Exhibit 6-10 provides an example of a detailed income statement, complete with all the discounts and expenses in their proper places. Study it carefully.

Analyzing Financial Statements

Owners, managers, and investors use ratios to evaluate a business. Two ratios relate directly to inventory: the gross margin percentage and the rate of inventory turnover.

Gross Margin Percentage. Gross margin—sales minus cost of goods sold—is a key indicator of a company's ability to sell inventory at a profit. Merchandisers strive to increase **gross margin percentage**. Gross margin percentage is markup stated as a percentage of sales. Gross margin percentage is computed as follows for Leon's Furniture. Data (in millions) for 2007 are taken from Exhibit 6-4, page 268.

$$\text{Gross margin percentage} = \frac{\text{Gross margin}}{\text{Net sales revenue}} = \frac{\$274.2}{\$637.5} = 0.430 = 43.0\%$$

Managers and investors watch the gross margin percentage carefully. A 43.0% gross margin means that each dollar of sales generates 43.0 cents of gross margin. On average, cost of goods sold consumes 57.0 cents of each sales dollar for Leon's. For most firms, the gross margin percentage changes little from year to year, so a small downturn may signal trouble.

Leon's gross margin percentage of 43.0% compares very favourably with those of other retailers. Exhibit 6-11 shows the gross margin percentages for Leon's, Pier 1, and Home Depot.

Objective

3 **Use** gross margin percentage and inventory turnover to evaluate operations

EXHIBIT 6-10   Detailed Income Statement

Valley Software Company
Income Statement
For the Year Ended December 31, 2009

Sales revenue	$100,000	
Less: Sales discounts	(2,000)	
Sales returns and allowances	(3,000)	
Net sales		$95,000*
Cost of goods sold		45,000
Gross margin		50,000
Operating expenses:		
Selling:		
Sales commission expense	$ 5,000	
Freight-out (delivery expense)	1,000	
Other expenses (detailed)	6,000	12,000
Administrative:		
Salary expense	$ 2,000	
Amortization expense	2,000	
Other expenses (detailed)	4,000	8,000
Income before income tax		30,000
Income tax expense (40%)		12,000
Net income		$18,000

*Most companies report only the net sales figure.

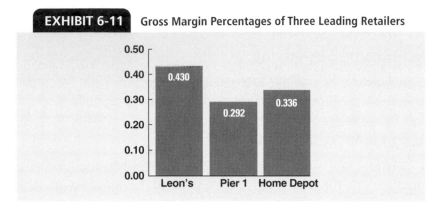

EXHIBIT 6-11 **Gross Margin Percentages of Three Leading Retailers**

Inventory Turnover. Leon's strives to sell its inventory as quickly as possible because furniture and fixtures generate no profit until they are sold. The faster the sales, the higher the company's income, and vice versa for slow-moving goods. Ideally, a business could operate with zero inventory, but most businesses, especially retailers, must keep some goods on hand. **Inventory turnover**, the ratio of cost of goods sold to average inventory, indicates how rapidly inventory is sold. The 2007 computation for Leon's follows (data in millions from Exhibit 6-4, page 268):

$$\frac{\text{Inventory}}{\text{turnover}} = \frac{\text{Cost of goods sold}}{\text{Average inventory}} = \frac{\text{Cost of goods sold}}{\left(\begin{array}{c}\text{Beginning} \\ \text{inventory}\end{array} + \begin{array}{c}\text{Ending} \\ \text{inventory}\end{array}\right) \div 2}$$

$$= \frac{\$363.3}{(\$74.7 + \$75.6)/2} = \begin{array}{l}\text{4.83 times per year} \\ \text{(every 76 days)}\end{array}$$

The inventory turnover statistic shows how many times the company sold (or turned over) its average level of inventory during the year. Inventory turnover varies from industry to industry.

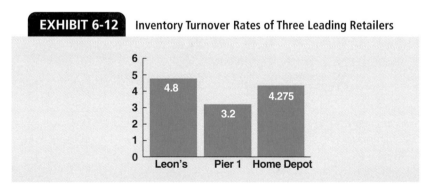

EXHIBIT 6-12 **Inventory Turnover Rates of Three Leading Retailers**

STOP & THINK

You have received a gift of cash from your grandparents and are considering investing in the stock market. You have carefully researched the market and have decided you will invest in one of three companies: Leon's Furniture, Pier 1, or Home Depot. Assume your analysis has resulted in Exhibits 6-11 and 6-12. What do the ratio values in the two exhibits say about the merchandising (pricing) strategies of Leon's, Pier 1, and Home Depot?

Answers:
It's obvious that Leon's sells higher-end merchandise. Leon's gross margin percentage is much higher than those of Pier 1 and Home Depot. At the same time, Leon's has a higher turnover ratio. Home Depot's gross margin percentage is lower than Leon's. Generally, the lower the price, the faster the turnover and vice versa.

Leon's and other specialty retailers turn their inventory over slowly. Retailers must keep lots of inventory on hand because visual appeal is critical in retailing. Department stores such as The Bay and discounters such as Wal-Mart and Zellers also keep a lot of inventory on hand. Exhibit 6-12 shows the inventory turnover rates for three leading retailers.

Additional Inventory Issues

Using the Cost-of-Goods-Sold Model

Exhibit 6-13 presents the **cost-of-goods-sold model**. Some accountants view this model as related to the periodic inventory system. But it's used by all companies, including those with perpetual inventory systems. The model is extremely powerful because it captures all the inventory information for an entire accounting period. Study this model carefully (all amounts are assumed).

Leon's Furniture uses a perpetual inventory accounting system. Let's see how Leon's can use the cost-of-goods-sold model to manage the business effectively.

1. What's the single most important question for Leon's to address?
   - What merchandise should Leon's offer to its customers? This is a *marketing* question that requires market research. If Leon's continually stocks the wrong merchandise, sales will suffer and profits will drop.

2. What's the second most important question for Leon's?
   - How much inventory should Leon's buy? **This is an accounting question faced by all merchandisers**. If Leon's buys too much merchandise, it will have to lower prices, the gross margin percentage will suffer, and it may lose money. If Leon's buys too little inventory, customers will go elsewhere. Buying the right quantity of inventory is critical for success. This question can be answered with the cost-of-goods-sold model. Let's see how it works.

We must rearrange the cost-of-goods-sold formula. Then we can help a Leon's store manager know how much inventory to buy, as follows (using amounts from Exhibit 6-13):

1	Cost of goods sold (based on the budget for the next period)	$6,000
2	+ Ending inventory (based on the budget for the next period)	1,500
3	= Goods available for sale as budgeted	7,500
4	− Beginning inventory (actual amount left over from the prior period)	1,200
5	= Purchases (how much inventory the manager needs to buy)	$6,300

In this case, the manager should buy $6,300 of merchandise to work his plan for the upcoming period.

EXHIBIT 6-13   **The Cost-of-Goods-Sold Model**

Cost-of-goods sold:

Beginning inventory	$1,200
+ Purchases	6,300
= Goods available for sale	7,500
− Ending inventory	(1,500)
= Cost of goods sold	$6,000

Estimating Inventory by the Gross Margin Method

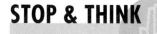
Often a business must *estimate* the value of its goods. For example, if a fire destroys inventory, an insurance company will require an estimate of the loss. In this case, the business must estimate the cost of ending inventory because it was destroyed.

The **gross margin method** is widely used to estimate ending inventory. This method uses the familiar cost-of-goods-sold model (amounts are assumed):

Beginning inventory	$ 4,000
+ Purchases	16,000
= Goods available for sale	20,000
− Ending inventory	(5,000)
= Cost of goods sold	$15,000

We rearrange *ending inventory* and *cost of goods sold* as follows:

Beginning inventory	$ 4,000
+ Purchases	16,000
= Goods available for sale	20,000
− Cost of goods sold	(15,000)
= Ending inventory	$ 5,000

Suppose a fire destroys some of Leon's inventory. To collect insurance, Leon's must estimate the cost of the ending inventory. Beginning inventory, net purchases, and net sales can be taken directly from the accounting records. Using Leon's *actual gross margin rate* of 43.0% (that is, gross margin divided by net sales), you can estimate the cost of goods sold. Then subtract cost of goods sold from goods available to estimate ending inventory. Exhibit 6-14 shows the calculations for the gross margin method with new amounts assumed for this illustration.

You can use the gross margin method to test the overall reasonableness of an ending inventory amount. This method also helps to detect large errors.

To ensure reliability, the gross margin rate should be based on historical trends adjusted for any current changes in pricing or product mix strategies that may have altered the historical range of the gross margin rate.

STOP & THINK

Assume your business had a bad fire and you wish to calculate your inventory loss. Beginning inventory is $70,000, net purchases total $365,000, and net sales are $500,000. With a normal gross margin rate of 30% of sales, how much is ending inventory?

Answer:
$70,000 + $365,000 − (0.70 × $500,000) = $85,000

EXHIBIT 6-14   The Gross Margin Method of Estimating Inventory (Amounts Assumed)

Beginning inventory		$18,000
Purchases		72,000
Goods available for sale		90,000
Cost of goods sold:		
Net sales revenue	$100,000	
Less estimated gross margin of 43.0%	(43,000)	
Estimated cost of goods sold		57,000
Estimated cost of *ending inventory*		$33,000

Effects of Inventory Errors

Inventory errors sometimes occur. In Exhibit 6-15 start with period 1, in which ending inventory is *overstated* by $5,000 and cost of goods sold is therefore *understated* by $5,000. Then compare period 1 with period 3, which is correct. *Period 1 should look exactly like period 3.*

Inventory errors counter balance in two consecutive periods. Why? Recall that period 1's ending inventory becomes period 2's beginning inventory amount. Thus, the error in period 1 carries over into period 2. Trace the ending inventory of $15,000 from period 1 to period 2. Then compare periods 2 and 3. *All periods should look exactly like period 3.* The amounts **in bold type** in Exhibit 6-15 are incorrect.

Beginning inventory and ending inventory have opposite effects on cost of goods sold (beginning inventory is added; ending inventory is subtracted); therefore, after two periods, an inventory accounting error "washes out" (counter balances) as illustrated in Exhibit 6-15. Notice that total gross margin for periods 1 and 2 combined is correct ($100,000) even though each period's gross margin is wrong by $5,000. The correct gross margin is $50,000 for each period as shown in period 3.

Note that there is a direct relationship between ending inventory (EI) and gross margin (GM) but an inverse relationship between beginning inventory (BI) and gross margin, that is, an understatement of ending inventory results in an understatement of gross margin but an understatement of beginning inventory results in an overstatement of gross margin. (COGS = cost of goods sold)

EI ↓ results in COGS ↑ results in GM ↓ (Direct relationship between EI and GM)

BI ↓ results in COGS ↓ results in GM ↑ (Inverse relationship between BI and GM)

⚠ USER ALERT

Inventory Errors

Inventory errors cannot be ignored simply because they counter balance. Suppose you are analyzing trends in the operations of the company presented above. Exhibit 6-15 shows a drop in gross margin from period 1 to period 2, followed by an increase in period 3. Did the company really get worse and then better again? No, that picture of operations is inaccurate because of the accounting error. The correct gross margin is $50,000 for each period. We must have accurate information for all periods. Exhibit 6-16 summarizes the effects of inventory accounting errors.

EXHIBIT 6-15	**Inventory Errors: An Example**					
		Period 1		Period 2		Period 3
		Ending Inventory Overstated by $5,000		*Beginning Inventory Overstated by $5,000*		*Correct*
Sales revenue			$100,000		$100,000		$100,000
Cost of goods sold:						
Beginning inventory	$10,000		**$ 15,000**		$10,000	
Purchases	50,000		50,000		50,000	
Cost of goods available for sale	60,000		**65,000**		60,000	
Ending inventory	**(15,000)**		(10,000)		(10,000)	
Cost of goods sold		**45,000**		**55,000**		50,000
Gross margin		**$ 55,000**		**$ 45,000**		$ 50,000
			$ 100,000			

Source: The authors thank Professor Carl High for this example.

EXHIBIT 6-16 Effects of Inventory Errors

	Period 1		Period 2	
Inventory Error	**Cost of Goods Sold**	**Gross Margin and Net Income**	**Cost of Goods Sold**	**Gross Margin and Net Income**
Period 1 Ending inventory overstated	Understated	Overstated	Overstated	Understated
Period 1 Ending inventory understated	Overstated	Understated	Understated	Overstated

USER ALERT

Ethical Considerations: Cooking the Books

No area of accounting has a deeper ethical dimension than inventory. Managers of companies whose profits do not meet shareholder expectations are sometimes tempted to "cook the books" to increase reported income. The increase in reported income may lead investors and creditors into thinking the business is more successful than it really is.

What do managers hope to gain from fraudulent accounting? In some cases, they are trying to keep their jobs. In other cases, their bonuses are tied to reported income: the higher the company's net income, the higher the managers' bonuses. There are two main schemes for cooking the books.

- The easiest is simply to overstate ending inventory. The upward-pointing arrows in the accounting equation indicate an overstatement: reporting more assets and equity than are actually present.

ASSETS	**=**	**LIABILITIES**	**+**	**SHAREHOLDERS' EQUITY**
↑	=	0	+	↑

- The second way of using inventory to cook the books involves sales revenue. Sales schemes are more complex than overstating ending inventory. Consider two examples of real companies. Datapoint Corporation and MiniScribe, both computer-related companies, were charged with creating fictitious sales to boost reported profits. Datapoint is alleged to have hired drivers to transport its inventory around town so that the goods could not be physically counted. Datapoint tried to show that the goods had been sold. The scheme fell apart when the trucks returned the goods to Datapoint's warehouse, and Datapoint had unrealistic amounts of sales returns. What would you think of a company with $10 million in sales and $3 million of sales returns? No company produces that many defective computers.

    MiniScribe is alleged to have shipped boxes of bricks labelled as computer parts to customers immediately before year-end. The bogus transactions increased the company's sales by $4 million—but only temporarily. The scheme boomeranged when MiniScribe had to record the returns. In virtually every area, accounting imposes a discipline that ultimately brings frauds to light.

    Watch out for excessive sales returns. Some of the sales revenue may have been fictitious.

The Decision Guidelines feature summarizes the situations that call for (a) a particular inventory accounting system and (b) the motivation for using each costing method.

Decision Guidelines

INVENTORY MANAGEMENT

PetSmart Tropical Fish Inc. stocks two basic categories of merchandise:

- Tropical fish that are unique
- Fish tanks and related equipment and prepackaged fish foods and supplies

Jacob Stiles, the owner of PetSmart Tropical Fish Inc., is considering how accounting will affect the business. Let's examine several decisions that Stiles must make to achieve his goals for his company.

Decision	Guidelines	System or Method
Which inventory system to use?	• Expensive merchandise • Cannot control inventory by visual inspection	Perpetual system for the fish tanks and related equipment and prepackaged fish food and supplies
	• Can control inventory by visual inspection	Periodic system for the tropical fish
Which costing method to use?	• Most current cost of ending inventory • Maximizes reported income when costs are rising	FIFO
	• More current measure of cost of goods sold and net income based on average costs for period	Weighted-average
	• Unique inventory items	Specific unit cost for the fish tanks and the tropical fish because they are unique

END-OF-CHAPTER SUMMARY PROBLEM   *MyAccountingLab*

Rainy River Hardware Company Ltd. began 2009 with 60,000 units of inventory that cost $36,000. During 2009, Rainy River purchased merchandise on account for $352,500 as follows:

Purchase 1	100,000 units costing	$ 65,000
Purchase 2	270,000 units costing	175,500
Purchase 3	160,000 units costing	112,000

Cash payments on account for merchandise totalled $326,000 during the year.

Rainy River's sales during 2009 consisted of 520,000 units of inventory for $660,000, all on account. The company uses the FIFO inventory method.

Cash collections from customers were $630,000. Operating expenses totalled $240,500, of which Rainy River paid $211,000 in cash. Rainy River credited Accrued Liabilities for the remainder. At December 31, Rainy River accrued income tax expense at the rate of 35% of income before tax.

Required

1. Make summary journal entries to record Rainy River Hardware Company Ltd.'s transactions for the year, assuming the company uses a perpetual inventory system. Ignore GST and PST for this problem.

2. Determine the FIFO cost of Rainy River's ending inventory at December 31, 2009, in the following two ways:
   a. Use a T-account.
   b. Multiply the number of units on hand by the unit cost.
3. Show how Rainy River would compute cost of goods sold for 2009.
4. Prepare Rainy River Hardware Company Ltd.'s income statement for the year ended December 31, 2009. Show totals for the gross margin and income before tax.
5. Determine Rainy River's gross margin percentage, rate of inventory turnover, and net income as a percentage of sales for the year. In the hardware industry, a gross margin percentage of 40%, an inventory turnover of six times per year, and a net income percentage of 7% are considered excellent. How well does Rainy River compare to these industry averages?

Name: Rainy River Hardware Company Ltd.
Industry: Retail corporation
Fiscal Period: Year ended December 31, 2009
Key Fact: Perpetual inventory system

Since the company uses the perpetual inventory system, record inventory purchases and sales as they occur.

All merchandise is purchased on account.

Partial payment for the merchandise purchased.

All sales are made on account.

Use FIFO (oldest costs) to calculate cost of the 520,000 units sold:
Opening inventory: $36,000 (60,000 units)
Purchase 1: $65,000 (100,000 units)
Purchase 2: $175,500 (270,000 units)
Purchase 3: 90,000 units (520,000 − 60,000 − 100,000 − 270,000)
$112,000/160,000 units = $0.70/unit
$0.70/unit × 90,000 units = $63,000

Operating expenses were paid partly with cash ($211,000) and partly on account ($29,500).

Income tax expense is 35% of net income before taxes (Sales revenue − Cost of goods sold − Operating expenses).

FIFO ending inventory:
a. Beginning inventory + Purchases − Cost of goods sold
b. Number of units in ending inventory × Unit cost of ending inventory, where unit cost of ending inventory is from Purchase 3, the most recent purchase.

Beginning inventory must be the same amount as the inventory on the previous year's balance sheet.

Ending inventory must be the same amount as the inventory on this year's balance sheet.

Answers

Requirement 1

Inventory ($65,000 + $175,500 + $112,000)	352,500	
Accounts Payable		352,500
Accounts Payable	326,000	
Cash		326,000
Accounts Receivable	660,000	
Sales Revenue		660,000
Cost of Goods Sold (See Requirement 3)	339,500	
Inventory		339,500
Cash	630,000	
Accounts Receivable		630,000
Operating Expenses	240,500	
Cash		211,000
Accrued Liabilities		29,500
Income Tax Expense (See Requirement 4)	28,000	
Income Tax Payable		28,000

Requirement 2

a.

Inventory	
36,000	339,500
352,500	
49,000	

b. Number of units in ending inventory

(60,000 + 100,000 + 270,000 + 160,000 − 520,000)	70,000
Unit cost of ending inventory at FIFO ($112,000 ÷ 160,000)	× $ 0.70
FIFO cost of ending inventory	$49,000

Requirement 3

Cost of goods sold (520,000 units):	
60,000 units costing	$ 36,000
100,000 units costing	65,000
270,000 units costing	175,500
90,000 units costing $0.70 each	63,000
Cost of goods sold	$339,500

Requirement 4

Rainy River Hardware Company Ltd. **Income Statement** **For the Year Ended December 31, 2009**	

Sales revenue	$660,000	
Cost of goods sold..	339,500	
Gross margin...	320,500	Sales revenue – Cost of goods sold
Operating expenses...	240,500	
Income before tax	80,000	Gross margin – Operating expenses
Income tax expense...	28,000	GAAP require that income tax expense be presented separately from all other expenses.
Net Income...	$ 52,000	

Requirement 5

Gross margin percentage:	$320,500 ÷ $660,000 = 48.6%	Gross margin ÷ Sales revenue
Inventory turnover:	$\dfrac{\$339{,}500}{(\$36{,}000 + \$49{,}000)/2} = 8$ times	Cost of goods sold ÷ Average inventory, where Average inventory = (Beginning inventory + Ending inventory) ÷ 2
Net income as a percentage of sales:	$52,000 ÷ $660,000 = 7.9%	Net income ÷ Sales revenue

Rainy River's statistics are better than the industry averages.

REVIEW INVENTORY AND COST OF GOODS SOLD

QUICK CHECK   (Answers are given on page 309.)

1. Which statement is true?
   a. The Sales account is used to record only sales on account.
   b. The invoice is the purchaser's request for collection from the customer.
   c. Gross margin is the excess of sales revenue over cost of goods sold.
   d. A service company purchases products from suppliers and then sells them.

2. Sales discounts should appear in the financial statements:
   a. As an addition to inventory
   b. As an addition to sales
   c. As an operating expense
   d. Among the current liabilities
   e. As a deduction from sales

3. How is inventory classified in the financial statements?
   a. As an asset
   b. As a liability
   c. As an expense
   d. As a revenue
   e. As a contra account to Cost of Goods Sold

Questions 4 through 6 use the following data of King Ltd.

	Units	Unit Cost	Total Cost	Units Sold
Beginning inventory	25	$5	$125	
Purchase on May 23	30	6	180	
Purchase on Nov. 5	10	7	70	
Sales	50	?	?	

4. King uses a FIFO inventory system. Cost of goods sold for the period is

    a. $275   c. $255

    b. $347   d. $375

5. King's FIFO cost of ending inventory would be

    a. $161   c. $208

    b. $100   d. $225

6. King's weighted-average cost of ending inventory is

    a. $87   c. $100

    b. $104   d. $330

7. When applying lower-of-cost-or-market to inventory, "market" generally means

    a. Sales value   c. Net realizable value

    b. Original cost   d. Original cost, less physical deterioration

8. During a period of rising prices, the inventory method that will yield the highest net income and asset value is

    a. Specific identification

    b. Weighted-average cost

    c. FIFO

9. Which statement is true?

    a. The inventory method that best matches current expense with current revenue is FIFO.

    b. Application of the lower-of-cost-or-market rule often results in a lower inventory value.

    c. An error overstating ending inventory in 2009 will understate 2010 net income.

    d. When prices are rising, the inventory method that results in the lowest ending inventory value is FIFO.

10. The ending inventory of LaVal Co. is $60,000. If beginning inventory was $70,000 and goods available for sale totalled $124,000, the cost of goods sold is

    a. $112,000   d. $50,000

    b. $198,000   e. None of the above ($fill in the blank)

    c. $60,000

11. Martin Company had cost of goods sold of $130,000. The beginning and ending inventories were $10,000 and $20,000, respectively. Purchases for the period must have been

    a. $82,000   d. $140,000

    b. $94,000   e. $138,000

    c. $132,000

Use the following information for questions 12 through 14.

12. Tee Company had a $20,000 beginning inventory and a $24,000 ending inventory. Net sales were $180,000; purchases, $80,000; purchase returns and allowances, $4,000; and freight-in, $5,000. Cost of goods sold for the period is

    a. $69,000   c. $77,000

    b. $49,000   e. None of the above

    d. $85,000

13. What is Tee's gross margin percentage (rounded to the nearest percentage)?

    a. 57%   **c.** 47%

    b. 88%   **d.** None of the above

14. What is Tee's rate of inventory turnover?

    a. 3.4 times   **c.** 6.4 times

    b. 3.5 times   **d.** 6.2 times

15. Beginning inventory is $60,000, purchases are $180,000, and sales total $300,000. The normal gross margin is 30%. Using the gross margin method, how much is ending inventory?

    a. $120,000   **d.** $30,000

    b. $106,400   **e.** None of the above ($ _____)

    c. $244,000

16. An overstatement of ending inventory in one period results in

    a. No effect on net income of the next period

    b. An understatement of net income of the next period

    c. An overstatement of net income of the next period

    d. An understatement of the beginning inventory of the next period

ACCOUNTING VOCABULARY

conservatism The accounting concept by which the least favourable figures are presented in the financial statements. (p. 265)

consistency principle A business must use the same accounting methods and procedures from period to period. (p. 265)

cost of goods sold Cost of the inventory the business has sold to customers. Also called *cost of sales*. (p. 263)

cost-of-goods-sold model Formula that brings together all the inventory data for the entire accounting period: Beginning inventory + Purchases = Goods available for sale. Then, Goods available for sale − Ending inventory = Cost of goods sold. (p. 281)

disclosure principle A business's financial statements must report enough information for outsiders to make knowledgeable decisions about the business. The company should report relevant, reliable, and comparable information about its economic affairs. (p. 265)

first-in, first-out (FIFO) cost (method) Inventory costing method by which the first costs into inventory are the first costs out to cost of goods sold. Ending inventory is based on the costs of the most recent purchases. (p. 274)

gross margin Sales revenue minus cost of goods sold. Also called *gross profit*. (p. 267)

gross margin method A way to estimate inventory based on a rearrangement of the cost-of-goods-sold model: Beginning inventory + Net purchases = Goods available for sale − Cost of goods sold = Ending inventory. (p. 282)

gross margin percentage Gross margin divided by net sales revenue. (p. 279)

inventory turnover Ratio of cost of goods sold to average inventory. Indicates how rapidly inventory is sold. (p. 280)

last-in, first-out (LIFO) cost (method) Inventory costing method by which the last costs into inventory are the first costs out to cost of goods sold. This method leaves the oldest costs—those of beginning inventory and the earliest purchases of the period—in ending inventory. (p. 274)

lower-of-cost-or-market (LCM) rule Requires that an asset be reported in the financial statements at whichever is lower—its historical cost or its market value (current net realizable value for inventory). (p. 266)

periodic inventory system An inventory system in which the business does not keep a continuous record of the inventory on hand. Instead, at the end of the period, the business makes a physical count of the inventory on hand and applies the appropriate unit costs to determine the cost of the ending inventory. (p. 268)

perpetual inventory system An inventory system in which the business keeps a continuous record for each inventory item to show the inventory on hand at all times. (p. 268)

purchase allowance A decrease in the cost of purchases because the seller has granted the buyer a subtraction (an allowance) from the amount owed. (p. 269)

purchase discount A decrease in the cost of purchases earned by making an early payment to the vendor. (p. 270)

purchase return A decrease in the cost of purchases because the buyer returned the goods to the seller. (p. 269)

specific-unit-cost method Inventory costing method based on the specific cost of particular units of inventory. Also called the *specific identification method*. (p. 273)

weighted-average-cost method Inventory costing method based on the average cost of inventory for the period. Weighted-average cost is determined by dividing the cost of goods available by the number of units available. Also called the *average cost method*. (p. 274)

ASSESS YOUR PROGRESS

Make the grade with MyAccountingLab: The exercises and problems marked in red can be found on MyAccountingLab at www.myaccountinglab.com. You can practise them as often as you want, and they feature step by step guided solutions to help you find the right answer.

SHORT EXERCISES

Accounting for inventory transactions
(Obj. 1)

S6-1 Journalize the following assumed transactions for **Shoppers Drug Mart Corporation**. Show amounts in millions.

- Cash purchases of inventory, $3,900 million
- Sales on account (including credit cards), $19,400 million
- Cost of goods sold (perpetual inventory system), $4,200 million
- Collections on account, $18,900 million

Accounting for inventory transactions
(Obj. 1)

S6-2 Riley Kilgo Inc., purchased inventory costing $100,000 and sold 80% of the goods for $240,000. All purchases and sales were on account. Kilgo later collected 20% of the accounts receivable.

1. Journalize these transactions for Kilgo, which uses the perpetual inventory system.
2. For these transactions, show what Kilgo will report for inventory, revenues, and expenses on its financial statements. Report gross margin on the appropriate statement.

Applying the weighted-average cost, FIFO, and LIFO methods
(Obj. 2)

S6-3 Allstate Sporting Goods started April with an inventory of 10 sets of golf clubs that cost a total of $1,500. During April Allstate purchased 20 sets of clubs for $3,200. At the end of the month, Allstate had 6 sets of golf clubs on hand. The store manager must select an inventory costing method, and he asks you to tell him both cost of goods sold and ending inventory under these two accounting methods:

a. Weighted-average cost
b. FIFO

Applying the weighted-average cost and FIFO method
(Obj. 2)

S6-4 University Copy Centre Ltd. uses laser printers. The Copy Centre started the year with 100 containers of ink (weighted-average cost of $9.20 each, FIFO cost of $9 each). During the year, the Copy Centre purchased 700 containers of ink at $10 and sold 600 units for $20 each. The Copy Centre paid operating expenses throughout the year, a total of $3,000. The Copy Centre is not subject to income tax. Prepare University Copy Centre Ltd.'s income statement for the year ended December 31, 2009, under the weighted-average and FIFO inventory costing methods. Include a complete statement heading.

Income tax effects of the inventory costing methods
(Obj. 2)

S6-5 This exercise should be used in conjunction with Short Exercise S6-4. Now assume that University Copy Centre in Short Exercise S6-4 is a corporation subject to an 18% income tax. Compute the Copy Centre's income tax expense under the weighted-average cost and FIFO inventory costing methods. Which method would you select to (a) maximize income before tax and (b) minimize income tax expense? Format your answer as shown on page 273.

Accounting principles related to inventory
(Obj. 1)

S6-6 You are opening a new bookstore catering to the students at Queen's University. Once you have established this operation, you plan to approach investors to support an expansion to locations in other Canadian university communities. Explain to your accountant what principles you expect him to follow in accounting for inventory and the reasons for your expectations.

S6-7 It is December 31, 2009, end of year, and the controller of Garcia Corporation is applying the lower-of-cost-or-market (LCM) rule to inventories. Before any year-end adjustments Garcia has these data:

Applying the lower-of-cost-or-market rule to inventory
(Obj. 2)

Cost of goods sold..	$410,000
Historical cost of ending inventory,	
as determined by a physical count	60,000

Garcia determines that the net realizable value of ending inventory is $49,000. Show what Garcia should report for ending inventory and for cost of goods sold. Identify the financial statement where each item appears.

S6-8 Gildan Activewear Inc. made sales of $964.4 million during 2007. Cost of goods sold for the year totalled $655.3 million. At the end of 2006, Gildan's inventory stood at $200.7 million, and Gildan ended 2007 with inventory of $240 million. Compute Gildan's gross margin percentage and rate of inventory turnover for 2007.

Using ratio data to evaluate operations
(Obj. 3)

S6-9 Provincial Technology Inc. began the year with inventory of $300,000 and purchased $1,600,000 of goods during the year. Sales for the year are $3,000,000, and Provincial's gross margin percentage is 40% of sales. Compute Provincial's estimated cost of ending inventory by using the gross margin method.

Estimating ending inventory by the gross margin method
(Obj. 4)

S6-10 CWD Inc., reported these figures for its fiscal year (amounts in millions):

Assessing the effect of an inventory error—1 year only
(Obj. 5)

Net sales	$1,700
Cost of goods sold..	1,180
Ending inventory	360

Suppose CWD later learns that ending inventory was overstated by $10 million. What are CWD's correct amounts for (a) net sales, (b) ending inventory, (c) cost of goods sold, and (d) gross margin?

S6-11 Suppose **Staples Inc.'s** $1.9 million cost of inventory at February 3, 2007 (fiscal year-end), was understated by $0.5 million.

Assessing the effect of an inventory error on 2 years
(Obj. 5)

1. Would 2007's reported gross margin of $5.2 million be overstated, understated, or correct? What would be the correct amount of gross margin for 2007?
2. Would 2008's gross margin of $5.6 million be overstated, understated, or correct? What would be the correct amount of gross margin for 2008?

S6-12 Determine whether each of the following actions in buying, selling, and accounting for inventories is ethical or unethical. Give your reason for each answer.

1. In applying the lower-of-cost-or-market rule to inventories, Terre Haute Industries recorded an excessively low market value for ending inventory. This allowed the company to pay less income tax for the year.

Ethical implications of inventory actions
(Obj. 2, 4)

2. Laminated Photo Film purchased lots of inventory shortly before year end to increase the weighted-average cost of goods sold and decrease reported income for the year.
3. Madison Inc. delayed the purchase of inventory until after December 31, 2009, to keep 2009's cost of goods sold from growing too large. The delay in purchasing inventory helped net income of 2009 to reach the level of profit demanded by the company's investors.
4. Dover Sales Company deliberately overstated ending inventory in order to report higher profits (net income).
5. Roberto Corporation deliberately overstated purchases to produce a high figure for cost of goods sold (low amount of net income). The real reason was to decrease the company's income tax payments to the government.

EXERCISES

Accounting for inventory transactions
(Obj. 1, 2)

E6-13 Accounting records for Red Deer Tire Ltd. yield the following data for the year ended December 31, 2008 (amounts in thousands):

Inventory, December 31, 2008...	$ 550
Purchases of inventory (on account)	1,200
Sales of inventory—80% on account; 20% for cash (cost $900)........	2,000
Inventory at FIFO cost, December 31, 2009	850

❚ Required

1. Journalize Red Deer Tire's inventory transactions for the year under the perpetual system. Show all amounts in thousands. Use Exhibit 6-6 as a model, page 270.

2. Report ending inventory, sales, cost of goods sold, and gross margin on the appropriate financial statement (amounts in thousands).

Analyzing inventory transactions
(Obj. 1, 2)

E6-14 Langley Inc. inventory records for a particular development program show the following at October 31, 2009:

Oct.	1	Beginning inventory..............................	5 units @	$150	=	$ 750
	15	Purchase...	11 units @	160	=	1,760
	26	Purchase...	5 units @	170	=	850

At October 31, 10 of these programs are on hand.

❚ Required

1. Journalize for Langley:
   a. Total October purchases in one summary entry. All purchases were on credit.
   b. Total October sales and cost of goods sold in two summary entries. The selling price was $500 per unit, and all sales were on credit. Langley uses the FIFO inventory method.
2. Under FIFO, how much gross margin would Langley earn on these transactions? What is the FIFO cost of Langley's ending inventory?

Determining ending inventory and cost of goods sold by three methods
(Obj. 2)

E6-15 Use the data for Langley Inc. in Exercise E6-14 to answer the following.

❚ Required

1. Compute cost of goods sold and ending inventory, using each of the following methods:
   a. Specific unit cost, with two $150 units, three $160 units, and five $170 units still on hand at the end
   b. Weighted-average cost
   c. First-in, first-out cost
2. Which method produces the highest cost of goods sold? Which method produces the lowest cost of goods sold? What causes the difference in cost of goods sold?

Computing the tax advantage of weighted-average cost over FIFO
(Obj. 2)

E6-16 Use the data in Exercise E6-14 to illustrate Langley's income tax advantage from using weighted-average cost over FIFO cost. Sales revenue is $6,000, operating expenses are $1,100, and the income tax rate is 25%. How much in taxes would Langley save by using the weighted-average-cost method versus FIFO?

E6-17 MusicBiz.net Ltd. specializes in sound equipment. Because each inventory item is expensive, MusicBiz uses a perpetual inventory system. Company records indicate the following data for a line of speakers:

Determining ending inventory and cost of goods sold—FIFO versus weighted-average cost **(Obj. 2)**

Date		Item	Quantity	Unit Cost	Sale Price
June	1	Balance	6	$ 95	
	10	Purchase	11	100	
	21	Sale	3		$155
	30	Sale	5		160

❚ Required

1. Determine the amounts that MusicBiz should report for cost of goods sold and ending inventory in the following two ways:

   a. FIFO

   b. weighted-average cost

2. MusicBiz uses the FIFO method. Prepare MusicBiz's income statement for the month ended June 30, 2009, reporting gross margin. Operating expenses totalled $319, and the income tax rate was 25%.

E6-18 Suppose a Johnson store in Ottawa, Ontario, ended November 2009 with 800,000 units of merchandise that cost an average of $8 each. Suppose the store then sold 600,000 units for $5.0 million during December. Further, assume the store made 2 large purchases during December as follows:

Measuring gross margin—FIFO versus weighted-average cost, falling prices **(Obj. 2)**

December	6	100,000 units	@ $7	=	$ 700,000
	26	400,000 units	@ 6	=	2,400,000

1. At December 31, the store manager needs to know the store's gross margin under both FIFO and weighted-average cost. Supply this information.

2. What caused the FIFO and weighted-average cost gross margin figures to differ?.

E6-19 Deitrick Guitar Company is nearing the end of its worst year ever. With three weeks until year end, it appears that net income for the year will have decreased by 20% from last year. Jim Deitrick, the president and principal shareholder, is distressed with the year's results.

Managing income taxes under the weighted-average-cost method **(Obj. 2)**

Deitrick asks you, the financial vice president, to come up with a way to increase the business's net income. Inventory quantities are a little higher than normal because sales have been slow during the last few months. Deitrick uses the weighted-average-cost inventory method, and inventory costs have risen dramatically during the latter part of the year.

❚ Required

Write a memorandum to Jim Deitrick to explain how the company can increase its net income for the year. Explain your reasoning in detail. Deitrick is a man of integrity, so your plan must be completely ethical.

E6-20 This exercise tests your understanding of accounting for inventory. Provide a word or phrase that best fits the description. Assume that the cost of inventory is rising.

Identifying effects of the inventory methods and evaluating operations **(Obj. 2, 3)**

___ 1. Generally associated with saving income taxes.

___ 2. Results in a cost of ending inventory that is close to the current cost of replacing the inventory.

___ 3. Used to account for automobiles, jewellery, and art objects.

___ 4. Maximizes reported income.

___ 5. Inventory system that keeps a running record of all goods bought, sold, and on hand.

___ **6.** Principle that enables investors to compare a company's financial statements from one period to the next.

___ **7.** Writes inventory down when net realizable value cost drops below historical cost.

___ **8.** Key indicator of a company's ability to sell inventory at a profit.

___ **9.** A decrease in the buyer's cost of inventory earned by paying quickly.

Applying the lower-of-cost-or-market rule to inventories
(Obj. 2)

E6-21 Tavistock Inc. uses a perpetual inventory system. Tavistock has these account balances at December 31, 2009, prior to making the year-end adjustments:

Inventory		Cost of Goods Sold		Sales Revenue	
Beg. bal. 12,400					
End bal. 14,000		Bal. 78,000			Bal. 125,000

A year ago, the net realizable value of Tavistock's ending inventory was $13,000, which exceeded cost of $12,400. Tavistock has determined that the net realizable value of the December 31, 2009, ending inventory is $12,000.

❚ Required

Prepare Tavistock Inc.'s 2009 income statement through gross margin to show how the company would apply the lower-of-cost-or-market rule to its inventories.

Determining amounts for the income statement; using the cost-of-goods-sold model
(Obj. 2)

E6-22 Supply the missing income statement amounts for each of the following companies (amounts in millions, at January 31, 2009):

Company	Net Sales	Beginning Inventory	Purchases	Ending Inventory	Cost of Goods Sold	Gross Profit
Myers Confectionary	$543	$29	$470	$24	(a)	(b)
Canada Computers	74	7	(c)	8	(d)	19
Best Taste Beverages	(e)	(f)	16	2	16	19
Value for $	31	2	24	(g)	23	(h)

Prepare the income statement for Myers Confectionary Ltd., in millions of dollars, for the year ended January 31, 2009. Use the cost-of-goods-sold model to compute cost of goods sold. Myers' operating and other expenses for the year were $204. Ignore income tax.

Note: Exercise E6-23 builds on Exercise E6-22 with a profitability analysis of these actual companies.

Measuring profitability
(Obj. 3)

E6-23 Refer to the data in Exercise E6-22. Compute all ratio values to answer the following questions:

• Which company has the highest gross margin percentage? Which company has the lowest?
• Which company has the highest rate of inventory turnover? Which company has the lowest?

Based on your figures, which company appears to be the most profitable?

Measuring gross margin and reporting cash flows
(Obj. 4)

E6-24 Suppose a company you are considering as an investor made sales of $54.8 billion in the year ended December 31, 2009. Collections from customers totalled $55 billion. The company began the year with $6.6 billion in inventories and ended with $7.9 billion. During the year, purchases of inventory added up to $39.8 billion. Of the purchases, the company paid $37.9 billion to suppliers.

As an investor searching for a good investment, you would identify several critical pieces of information about the company's operations during the year.

Compute the company's gross margin, gross margin percentage, and rate of inventory turnover during 2009. Use the cost-of-goods-sold model as needed. Would the information help you make your investment decision?

E6-25 Your company, Home Products Ltd., prepares budgets to help manage the company. Home Products is budgeting for the fiscal year ended December 31, 2009. During preceding fiscal year 2008, sales totalled $1,777 million and cost of goods sold was $1,175 million. At December 31, 2008, inventory stood at $366 million.

Budgeting inventory purchase
(Obj. 2)

During the upcoming 2009 year, suppose you expect cost of goods sold to increase by 8%. The company budgets next year's ending inventory at $369 million.

I *Required*

One of the most important decisions you make is how much inventory to buy. How much inventory will you purchase during the upcoming year to reach your budgeted figures?

E6-26 Vacation Properties began March with concession inventory of $36,000. The business made net purchases of concessions for $79,500 and had net sales of $150,000 before a break-in when its concession inventory was stolen. For the past several years, Vacation Properties' gross margin percentage has been 45%. Estimate the cost of the concession inventory stolen. Would a manager use the gross margin method to estimate ending inventory under normal circumstances?

Estimating inventory by the gross margin method
(Obj. 4)

E6-27 Dijon Mustard Ltée. reported the following comparative income statement for the years ended September 30, 2008, and 2009:

Correcting an inventory error
(Obj. 5)

Dijon Mustard Ltée
Income Statement
For the Years Ended September 30

	2009		2008	
Sales revenue		$194,000		$158,000
Cost of goods sold				
Beginning inventory	$ 23,000		$ 16,000	
Purchases	97,000		86,000	
Goods available for sale	120,000		102,000	
Ending inventory	(21,000)		(23,000)	
Cost of goods sold		99,000		79,000
Gross margin		95,000		79,000
Operating expenses		20,000		20,000
Net income		$ 75,000		$ 59,000

Dijon's shareholders are thrilled by the company's boost in sales and net income during 2009. Then they discover that the 2008 ending inventory was understated by $10,000. How well did Dijon really perform in 2009, as compared with 2008?

CHALLENGE EXERCISES

E6-28 For each of the following situations, identify the inventory method that you would use or, given the use of a particular method, state the strategy that you would follow to accomplish your goal:

Inventory policy decisions
(Obj. 2)

a. Inventory costs are increasing. Your company uses weighted-average cost and is having an unexpectedly good year. It is near year end, and you need to keep net income from increasing too much in order to save on income tax.

b. Suppliers of your inventory are threatening a labour strike, and it may be difficult for your company to obtain inventory. This situation could increase your income taxes.

c. Inventory costs are decreasing, and your company's board of directors wants to minimize income taxes.

d. Inventory costs are increasing, and the company prefers to report high income.

e. Inventory costs have been stable for several years, and you expect costs to remain stable for the indefinite future. (Give the reason for your choice of method.)

Understanding inventory methods
(Obj. 2)

E6-29 Suppose **Holt Renfrew**, the specialty retailer, had these records for ladies' evening gowns during 2009.

Beginning inventory (30 @ $1,000)	$ 30,000
Purchase in February (25 @ $1,100)	27,500
Purchase in June (60 @ $1,200)	72,000
Purchase in December (25 @ $1,300)	32,500
Goods available	$162,000

Assume sales of evening gowns totalled 130 units during 2009 and that Holt's uses the weighted-average-cost method to account for inventory. The income tax rate is 30%.

| Required

1. Compute Holt's cost of goods sold for evening gowns in 2009.

2. Compute what cost of goods sold would have been if Holt's had purchased enough inventory in December—at $1,300 per evening gown—to keep year-end inventory at the same level it was at the beginning of the year, 30 units.

Evaluating a company's profitability
(Obj. 3)

E6-30 Cheri's Beauty Products Ltd. reported the figures below at December 31, 2009, 2008, and 2007. The business has declared bankruptcy. You have been asked to review the business and explain why it failed.

Cheri's Beauty Products Ltd.
Statement of Income
For the Years Ended December 31, 2009, 2008, and 2007

Thousands	2009	2008	2007
Sales	$41.0	$39.5	$37.1
Cost of sales	32.7	30.9	28.9
Selling expenses	8.0	7.2	6.8
Other expenses	0.4	1.0	0.8
Net income (net loss)	$ (0.1)	$ 0.4	$ 0.6
Additional data:			
Ending inventory	9.2	8.6	7.7

| Required

Evaluate the trend of Cheri's Beauty Products results of operations during 2007 through 2009. Consider the trends of sales, gross margin, and net income. Track the gross margin percentage (to three decimal places) and the rate of inventory turnover (to one decimal place) in each year—2007, 2008, and 2009. Also discuss the role that selling expenses must have played in Cheri's Beauty Products' difficulties.

QUIZ

Test your understanding of accounting for inventory by answering the following questions. Select the best choice from among the possible answers given.

Q6-31 Riverside Software began January with $3,500 of merchandise inventory. During January, Riverside made the following entries for its inventory transactions:

Inventory..	6,000	
Accounts Payable		6,000
Accounts Receivable	7,200	
Sales Revenue		7,200
Cost of Goods Sold..	5,500	
Inventory..		5,500

What was the value of Riverside's inventory at the end of January?
a. $0   c. $4,500
b. $4,000   d. $5,000

Q6-32 Use the data in question Q6-31. What is Riverside's gross margin for January?
a. $0   c. $5,000
b. $1,700   d. $7,200

Q6-33 When does the cost of inventory become an expense?
a. When cash is collected from the customer.
b. When inventory is purchased from the supplier.
c. When payment is made to the supplier.
d. When inventory is delivered to a customer.

Questions Q6-34 and Q6-35 use the following facts. Leading Edge Frame Shop wants to know the effect of different inventory costing methods on its financial statements. Inventory and purchases data for April follow.

			Units	Unit Cost	Total Cost
April	1	Beginning inventory	2,000	$10.00	$20,000
	4	Purchase	1,000	10.60	10,600
	9	Sale	(1,500)		

Q6-34 If Leading Edge uses the FIFO method, the cost of the ending inventory will be
a. $10,600   c. $15,300
b. $15,000   d. $15,600

Q6-35 If Leading Edge uses the weighted-average-cost method, cost of goods sold will be
a. $10,600   c. $15,300
b. $15,000   d. $15,600

Q6-36 In a period of rising prices,
a. Gross margin under FIFO will be higher than under weighted-average cost.
b. Weighted-average-cost inventory will be greater than FIFO inventory.
c. Cost of goods sold under weighted-average cost will be less than under FIFO.
d. Net income under weighted-average cost will be higher than under FIFO.

Q6-37 The income statement for Heritage Health Foods shows gross margin of $144,000, operating expenses of $130,000, and cost of goods sold of $216,000. What is the amount of net sales revenue?
a. $274,000   c. $360,000
b. $246,000   d. $490,000

Q6-38 The word "market" as used in "the lower of cost or market" generally means
a. Original cost
b. Net realizable value
c. Retail market price
d. Liquidation price

Q6-39 The sum of ending inventory and cost of goods sold is
a. Goods available for sale
b. Net purchases
c. Gross margin
d. Beginning inventory

Q6-40 The following data come from the inventory records of Dodge Company:

Net sales revenue	$620,000
Beginning inventory..	60,000
Ending inventory	40,000
Net purchases	400,000

Based on these facts, the gross margin for Dodge Company is
a. $150,000
b. $220,000
c. $190,000
d. Some other amount (*enter here*)

Q6-41 Elizabeth Baker Cosmetics ended May with inventory of $20,000. Elizabeth Baker expects to end June with inventory of $15,000 after cost of goods sold of $90,000. How much inventory must Elizabeth Baker purchase during June to accomplish these results?
a. $85,000
b. $95,000
c. $105,000
d. Cannot be determined from the data given

Q6-42 Two financial ratios that clearly distinguish a discount chain such as Wal-Mart from a high-end retailer such as Tiffany & Co. are the gross margin percentage and the rate of inventory turnover. Which set of relationships is most likely for Tiffany's?

	Gross margin percentage	**Inventory turnover**
a.	High	High
b.	Low	Low
c.	Low	High
d.	High	Low

Q6-43 Sales are $500,000, and cost of goods sold is $300,000. Beginning and ending inventories are $25,000 and $35,000, respectively. How many times did the company turn its inventory over during this period?
a. 16.7 times
b. 6.7 times
c. 8 times
d. 10 times

Q6-44 Tulsa Inc. reported the following data:

Freight in	$ 20,000	Sales returns	$ 10,000
Purchases	205,000	Purchase returns........................	6,000
Beginning inventory	50,000	Sales revenue.............................	490,000
Purchase discounts........................	4,000	Ending inventory.......................	40,000

Tulsa's gross margin percentage is
a. 47.9%
b. 52.1%
c. 53.1%
d. 54.0%

Q6-45 Sherman Tank Company had the following for the first quarter of 2009:

Beginning inventory, $50,000   Net purchases, $75,000
Net sales revenue, $90,000   Gross margin rate, 30%

By the gross margin method, the ending inventory should be
a. $62,000
b. $63,000
c. $64,000
d. $65,000

Q6-46 An error understated Rice Corporation's December 31, 2009, ending inventory by $40,000. What effect will this error have on total assets and net income for 2009?

	Assets	Net income
a.	No effect	No effect
b.	No effect	Overstate
c.	Understate	Understate
d.	Understate	No effect

Q6-47 What is the effect of Rice Corporation's 2009 inventory error on net income for 2010?
a. No effect
b. Understate
c. Overstate

PROBLEMS

(GROUP A)

P6-48A Best Buy purchases merchandise inventory by the crate; each crate of inventory is a unit. The fiscal year of Best Buy ends each February 28.

Accounting for inventory in a perpetual system **(Obj. 1, 2)**

Assume you are dealing with a single Best Buy store in Toronto, Ontario, and that the store experienced the following: The store began fiscal year 2009 with an inventory of 20,000 units that cost a total of $1,000,000. During the year, the store purchased merchandise on account as follows:

April (30,000 units @ cost of $60)..	$1,800,000
August (50,000 units @ cost of $64)..	3,200,000
November (60,000 units @ cost of $70)	4,200,000
Total purchases	$9,200,000

Cash payments on account totalled $8,800,000.

During fiscal year 2009, the store sold 150,000 units of merchandise for $14,400,000. Cash accounted for $5,000,000 of this, and the balance was on account. Best Buy uses the weighted-average-cost method for inventories.

Operating expenses for the year were $4,000,000. The store paid 80% in cash and accrued the rest as accrued liabilities. The store accrued income tax at the rate of 33%.

❙ Required

1. Make summary journal entries to record the store's transactions for the year ended February 28, 2009. Best Buy uses a perpetual inventory system.
2. Prepare a T-account to show the activity in the Inventory account.
3. Prepare the store's income statement for the year ended February 28, 2009. Show totals for gross margin, income before tax, and net income.

P6-49A Assume a The Runner's Store outlet store began August 2009 with 40 pairs of running shoes that cost the store $40 each. The sale price of these shoes was $70. During August, the store completed these inventory transactions:

Measuring cost of goods sold and ending inventory—perpetual system **(Obj. 2)**

			Units	Unit Cost	Unit Sale Price
Aug.	3	Sale	16	$40	$70
	8	Purchase......................	80	41	
	11	Sale	24	40	70
	19	Sale	9	41	72
	24	Sale	30	41	72
	30	Purchase......................	18	42	

❙ *Required*

1. The preceding data are taken from the store's perpetual inventory records. Which cost method does the store use? Explain how you arrived at your answer.
2. Determine the store's cost of goods sold for August. Also compute gross margin for August.
3. What is the cost of the store's August 31 inventory of running shoes?

Computing inventory by two methods—perpetual system
(Obj. 2)

P6-50A Army-Navy Surplus Ltd. began March 2009 with 70 tents that cost $20 each. During the month, Army-Navy Surplus made the following purchases at cost:

March	4	100 tents	@ $22	=	$2,200
	19	160 tents	@ 24	=	3,840
	25	40 tents	@ 25	=	1,000

Army-Navy Surplus sold 320 tents, and at March 31 the ending inventory consists of 50 tents. The sale price of each tent was $45.

❙ *Required*

1. Determine the cost of goods sold and ending inventory amounts for March under (a) weighted-average cost and (b) FIFO cost. Round weighted-average cost per unit to four decimal places, and round all other amounts to the nearest dollar.
2. Explain why cost of goods sold is highest under weighted-average cost. Be specific.
3. Prepare Army-Navy Surplus's income statement for March 2009. Report gross margin. Operating expenses totalled $4,000. Army-Navy Surplus uses weighted-average costing for inventory. The income tax rate is 21%.

Applying the different inventory costing methods—perpetual system
(Obj. 2)

P6-51A The records of Armstrong Aviation Supply Inc. include the following accounts for inventory of aviation fuel at December 31, 2009:

Inventory				
Jan.	1	Balance	700 units @ $7.00	4,900
Mar.	6	Purchase	300 units @ 7.05	2,115
June	22	Purchase	8,400 units @ 7.50	63,000
Oct.	4	Purchase	500 units @ 8.50	4,250

Sales Revenue		
Dec. 31 9,000 units		127,800

❙ *Required*

1. Prepare a partial income statement through gross margin under the weighted-average-cost and FIFO methods. Round weighted-average cost per unit to four decimal places and all other amounts to the nearest dollar.
2. Which inventory method would you use to minimize income tax? Explain why this method causes income tax to be the lowest.

Applying the lower-of-cost-or-market rule to inventories—perpetual system
(Obj. 2)

P6-52A AMC Trade Mart has recently had lacklustre sales. The rate of inventory turnover has dropped, and the merchandise is gathering dust. At the same time, competition has forced AMC's suppliers to lower the prices that AMC will pay when it replaces its inventory. It is now December 31, 2009, and the current net realizable value of AMC's ending inventory is $80,000 below what AMC actually paid for the goods, which was $190,000. Before any adjustments at the end of the period, the Cost of Goods Sold account has a balance of $780,000.

What accounting action should AMC take in this situation? Give any journal entry required. At what amount should AMC report Inventory on the balance sheet? At what amount should the company report cost of goods sold on the income statement? Discuss the accounting principle or concept that is most relevant to this situation.

Are there circumstances that would allow AMC to increase the value of its inventory? Are there limits to which the value of the inventory may be increased?

P6-53A Chocolate Treats Ltd. and Coffee Bars Inc. are both specialty food chains. The two companies reported these figures, in thousands:

Using gross margin percentage and inventory turnover to evaluate two companies (Obj. 3)

Chocolate Treats Ltd.
Statement of Operations

Thousands	Fiscal Year	
	2009	2008
Revenues:		
Net sales	$543	$708
Costs and Expenses:		
Cost of goods sold	475	598
General and administrative expenses	68	55

Chocolate Treats Ltd.
Balance Sheet

Thousands	January 31,	
	2009	2008
Assets		
Current assets:		
Cash and cash equivalent	$17	$28
Receivables	27	30
Inventories	24	29

Coffee Bars Inc.
Statement of Earnings

Thousands	Fiscal Year	
	2009	2008
Net sales	$7,787	$6,369
Cost of goods sold	3,179	2,605
Selling, general, and administrative expenses	2,948	2,363

Coffee Bars Inc.
Balance Sheet

Thousands	Year End	
	2009	2008
Assets		
Current assets:		
Cash and temporary investments	$313	$174
Receivables, net	224	191
Inventories	636	546

❙ Required

1. Compute the gross margin percentage and the rate of inventory turnover for Chocolate Treats and for Coffee Bars for 2009.

2. Based on these statistics, which company looks more profitable? Why? What other expense category should we consider in evaluating these two companies?

Estimating inventory by the gross margin method; preparing the income statement
(Obj. 4)

P6-54A Suppose an **Indigo** bookstore lost inventory in a fire. To file an insurance claim, Indigo must estimate its inventory by the gross margin method. For the past 2 years, Indigo's gross margin has averaged 40% of net sales. Indigo's inventory records reveal the following data:

Inventory, July 1, 2009	$360,000
Transactions during July	
Purchases..	628,000
Purchase discounts..	4,500
Purchase returns	9,000
Sales revenue	1,000,000
Sales returns...	170,000

▌Required

1. Estimate the cost of the lost inventory, using the gross margin method.
2. Prepare the July 2009 income statement through gross margin. Show the detailed computation of cost of goods sold in a separate schedule.

Determining the amount of inventory to purchase
(Obj. 1)

P6-55A Here are condensed versions of Pontiac Convenience Store's most recent income statement and balance sheet. Because the business is organized as a proprietorship, it pays no corporate income tax.

Pontiac Convenience Store
Income Statement
For the Year Ended December 31, 2008

Sales	$900,000
Cost of sales	700,000
Gross margin	200,000
Operating expenses	80,000
Net income..	$120,000

Pontiac Convenience Store
Balance Sheet
December 31, 2008

Assets		Liabilities and Capital	
Cash..................................	$ 70,000	Accounts payable	$ 35,000
Inventories	35,000	Note payable......................	280,000
Land and		Total liabilities...................	315,000
buildings, net	360,000	Owner, capital	150,000
Total assets	$465,000	Total liabilities and capital..	$465,000

The owner is budgeting for 2010. She expects sales and cost of goods sold to increase by 8%. To meet customer demand for the increase in sales, ending inventory will need to be $50,000 at December 31, 2010. The owner hopes to earn a net income of $160,000 next year.

▌Required

1. One of the most important decisions a manager makes is the amount of inventory to purchase. Compute the amount of inventory to purchase in 2009.
2. Prepare the store's budgeted income statement for 2009 to reach the target net income of $160,000.

Correcting inventory errors over a 3-year period
(Obj. 5)

P6-56A Columbia Video Sales Ltd. reported the following data (millions). The shareholders are very happy with Columbia's steady increase in net income.

Auditors discovered that the ending inventory for 2007 was understated by $1 million and that the ending inventory for 2008 was also understated by $1 million. The ending inventory for 2009 was correct.

Columbia Video Sales Ltd.
Income Statements for the Years Ended

(Amounts in millions)	2009		2008		2007	
Net sales revenue............................		$36		$33		$30
Cost of goods sold:						
Beginning inventory...................	$ 6		$ 5		$4	
Purchases....................................	26		24		22	
Goods available for sale..............	32		29		26	
Less: Ending inventory...............	(7)		(6)		(5)	
Cost of goods sold		25		23		21
Gross margin		11		10		9
Total operating expenses................		8		8		8
Net income....................................		$ 3		$ 2		$ 1

▌ Required

1. Show corrected income statements for each of the 3 years.
2. How much did these assumed corrections add to or take away from Columbia's total net income over the 3-year period? How did the corrections affect the trend of net income?
3. Will Columbia's shareholders still be happy with the company's trend of net income? Give the reason for your answer.

(GROUP B)

P6-57B Italian Leather Goods Inc. began 2009 with an inventory of 50,000 units that cost $1,500,000. During the year the store purchased merchandise on account as follows:

Accounting for inventory in a perpetual system
(Obj. 1, 2)

March (40,000 units @ cost of $32)...	$1,280,000
August (40,000 units @ cost of $34)..	$1,360,000
October (180,000 units @ cost of $35)...	$6,300,000
Total purchases	$8,940,000

Cash payments on account totalled $8,610,000.

During 2009, the company sold 260,000 units of merchandise for $12,900,000. Cash accounted for $4,700,000 of this, and the balance was on account. Italian Leather Goods uses the weighted-average-cost method for inventories.

Operating expenses for the year were $2,080,000. Italian Leather Goods paid 60% in cash and accrued the rest as accrued liabilities. The company accrued income tax at the rate of 32%.

▌ Required

1. Make summary journal entries to record the Italian Leather Goods transactions for the year ended December 31, 2009. The company uses a perpetual inventory system.
2. Prepare a T-account to show the activity in the Inventory account.
3. Prepare the Italian Leather Goods Inc. income statement for the year ended December 31, 2009. Show totals for gross margin, income before tax, and net income.

Measuring cost of goods sold and ending inventory—perpetual system
(Obj. 2)

P6-58B Whitewater Sports Ltd. began July 2009 with 50 backpacks that cost $19 each. The sale price of each backpack was $36. During July, Whitewater completed these inventory transactions:

			Units	Unit Cost	Unit Sale Price
July	2	Purchase......................	12	$20	
	8	Sale	37	19	$36
	13	Sale	13	19	36
		Sale	4	20	37
	17	Purchase......................	24	20	
	22	Sale	15	20	37

❚ Required

1. The preceding data are taken from Whitewater's perpetual inventory records. Which cost method does Whitewater use? How can you tell?
2. Determine Whitewater's cost of goods sold for July. Also compute gross margin for July.
3. What is the cost of Whitewater's July 31 inventory of backpacks?

Computing inventory by two methods—perpetual system
(Obj. 2)

P6-59B Spice Inc. began October 2009 with 100 shirts that cost $76 each. During October, the store made the following purchases at cost:

Oct.	3	200 @	$81	=	$16,200
	12	90 @	82	=	7,380
	24	240 @	85	=	20,400

Spice sold 500 shirts and ended October with 130 shirts. The sale price of each shirt was $130.

❚ Required

1. Determine the cost of goods sold and ending inventory amounts by the weighted-average-cost and FIFO cost methods. Round weighted-average cost per unit to three decimal places, and round all other amounts to the nearest dollar.
2. Explain why cost of goods sold is highest under weighted-average cost. Be specific.
3. Prepare Spice's income statement for October 2009. Report gross margin. Operating expenses totalled $10,000. Spice uses the weighted-average-cost method for inventory. The income tax rate is 23%.

P6-60B The records of Sonic Sound Systems Inc. include the following for cases of CDs at December 31, 2009:

Applying the different inventory costing methods—perpetual system
(Obj. 2)

Inventory						
Jan.	1	Balance	300 cases	@ $300	121,500	
			100 cases	@ 315		
May	19	Purchase	600 cases	@ 335	201,000	
Aug.	12	Purchase	400 cases	@ 350	140,000	
Oct.	4	Purchase	700 cases	@ 370	259,000	

Sales Revenue			
Dec.	31	1,800 cases	910,000

❚ Required

1. Prepare a partial income statement through gross margin under the weighted-average-cost and FIFO cost methods. Round weighted-average cost per unit to four decimal places and all other amounts to the nearest dollar.
2. Which inventory method would you use to report the highest net income? Explain why this method produces the highest reported income.

P6-61B Westside Copiers Ltd. has recently been plagued with lacklustre sales. The rate of inventory turnover has dropped, and some of the company's merchandise is gathering dust. At the same time, competition has forced some of Westside's suppliers to lower the prices that Westside will pay when it replaces its inventory. It is now December 31, 2009. The current net realizable value of Westside's ending inventory is $6,800,000, which is far less than the amount Westside paid for the goods, $8,900,000. Before any adjustments at the end of the period, Westside's Cost of Goods Sold account has a balance of $36,400,000.

Applying the lower-of-cost-or-market rule to inventories— perpetual system
(Obj. 2)

What accounting action should Westside Copiers take in this situation? Give any journal entry required. At what amount should Westside report Inventory on the balance sheet? At what amount should Westside report Cost of Goods Sold on the income statement? Discuss the accounting principle or concept that is most relevant to this situation.

Are there circumstances that would allow Westside Copiers to increase the value of its inventory? Are there limits to which the value of inventory may be increased?

P6-62B Hewlett Packard and Apple Computer are competitors. The companies reported these amounts, in billions. In January 2009, you wish to make an investment in one of these companies. Results for 2008 are not yet available.

Using gross margin percentage and inventory turnover to evaluate two leading companies
(Obj. 3)

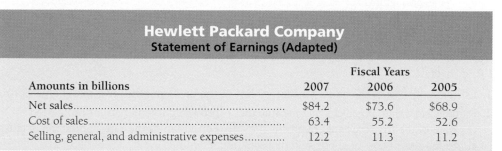

Hewlett Packard Company Statement of Earnings (Adapted)			
		Fiscal Years	
Amounts in billions	2007	2006	2005
Net sales..	$84.2	$73.6	$68.9
Cost of sales..	63.4	55.2	52.6
Selling, general, and administrative expenses..............	12.2	11.3	11.2

Hewlett Packard Company Balance Sheet (Adapted)			
		Year End	
Amounts in billions	2007	2006	2005
Assets			
Cash and cash equivalents	$11.3	$16.4	$13.9
Accounts receivable	13.4	10.9	9.9
Inventories..	8.0	7.8	6.9

Apple Computer Inc. Statement of Operations (Adapted)			
		Fiscal Years	
Amounts in billions	2007	2006	2005
Net sales..	$24.0	$19.3	$13.9
Cost of sales..	15.9	13.7	9.9
Selling, general, and administrative expenses..............	3.0	2.4	1.9

Apple Computer Inc. Balance Sheet (Adapted)			
		Year End	
Amounts in billions	2007	2006	2005
Assets			
Cash and cash equivalents	$9.4	$6.4	$3.5
Accounts receivable	6.0	1.3	0.9
Inventories..	0.4	0.3	0.2

I *Required*

1. Compute both companies' gross margin percentage and their rates of inventory turnover during 2007 and 2006.
2. Can you tell from these statistics which company should be more profitable in percentage terms? Why? What other important category of expenses do the gross margin percentage and the inventory turnover ratio fail to consider?

Estimating inventory by the gross margin method; preparing the income statement
(Obj. 4)

P6-63B Assume McMillan Tire Ltd. lost some inventory in a fire. To file an insurance claim, McMillan must estimate its ending inventory by the gross margin method. Assume for the past 2 years, McMillan's gross margin has averaged 40% of net sales. Suppose the company's inventory records reveal the following data at June 15, 2009, the date of the fire.

Inventory, January 1	$1,200,000
Transactions during the year:	
Purchases	6,500,000
Purchase discounts	100,000
Purchase returns	10,000
Sales revenue	8,600,000
Sales returns	20,000

I *Required*

1. Estimate the cost of the ending inventory lost in the fire using the gross margin method.
2. Prepare McMillan Tire Ltd.'s income statement through gross margin for the period up to the date of the fire. Date the statement "For the Period Up to the Fire." Show the detailed computations of cost of goods sold in a separate schedule.

Determining the amount of inventory to purchase
(Obj. 1)

P6-64B Margison Shoe Stores Ltd.'s income statement and balance sheet reported the following. The business is organized as a partnership, so it pays no corporate income tax. The owners are budgeting for 2009. They expect sales and cost of goods sold to increase by 10%. To meet customer demand, ending inventory will need to be $80,000 at December 31, 2009. The owners can lower operating expenses by $6,000 by doing some of the work themselves. They hope to earn a net income of $160,000 next year.

Margison Shoe Stores Ltd.
Income Statement
For the Year Ended December 31, 2008

Sales	$960,000
Cost of goods sold	720,000
Gross margin	240,000
Operating expenses	110,000
Net income	$130,000

Margison Shoe Stores Ltd.
Balance Sheet
December 31, 2008

Assets		Liabilities and Capital	
Cash	$ 40,000	Accounts payable	$ 30,000
Inventories	70,000	Note payable	190,000
Land and		Total liabilities	220,000
buildings, net	270,000	Owner, capital	160,000
Total assets	$380,000	Total liabilities and capital	$380,000

I *Required*

1. One of the most important decisions a business owner makes is the amount of inventory to purchase. Compute the amount of inventory to purchase in 2009.
2. Prepare the store's budgeted income statement for 2009 to reach the target net income of $160,000.

P6-65B The accounting records of Oriental Rugs show these data (in thousands).

As the auditor, you discovered that the ending inventory for 2007 was overstated by $100,000 and that the ending inventory for 2008 was understated by $50,000. The ending inventory at December 31, 2009, was correct.

Correcting inventory errors over a 3-year period
(Obj. 5)

Oriental Rugs			
Income Statements for the Years Ended			
(Amounts in thousands)	2009	2008	2007
Net sales revenue.........................	$1,400	$1,200	$1,100
Cost of goods sold:			
Beginning inventory.................	$ 400	$ 300	$200
Purchases.................................	800	700	600
Goods available for sale...........	1,200	1,000	800
Less ending inventory.............	(500)	(400)	(300)
Cost of goods sold...................	700	600	500
Gross margin	700	600	600
Total operating expenses.............	500	430	450
Net income.................................	$ 200	$ 170	$ 150

▌ Required

1. Show correct income statements for each of the 3 years.
2. How much did these corrections add to, or take away from, Oriental Rugs' total net income over the 3-year period? How did the corrections affect the trend of net income?

APPLY YOUR KNOWLEDGE

DECISION CASES

Case 1. Duracraft Corporation is nearing the end of its first year of operations. Duracraft made inventory purchases of $926,000 during the year, as follows:

Assessing the impact of a year-end purchase of inventory
(Obj. 1, 2)

January	1,500 units	@	$120.00	=	$ 180,000
July	3,000		142.00		426,000
November	2,000		160.00		320,000
Totals	6,500				$926,000

Sales for the year are 6,000 units for $1,800,000 of revenue. Expenses other than cost of goods sold and income taxes total $425,000. The president of the company is undecided about whether to adopt the FIFO method or the weighted-average-cost method for inventories. The income tax rate is 30%.

▌ Required

1. To aid company decision making, prepare income statements under FIFO and under weighted-average cost.
2. Compare the net income under FIFO with net income under weighted-average cost. Which method produces the higher net income? What causes this difference? Be specific.

Assessing the impact of the inventory costing method on the financial statements
(Obj. 2)

Case 2. The inventory costing method a company chooses can affect the financial statements and, thus, the decisions of the people who use those statements.

❙ *Required*

1. Company A uses the weighted-average-cost inventory method and discloses that in notes to the financial statements. Company B uses the FIFO method to account for its inventory. Company B does not disclose which inventory method it uses. Company B reports a higher net income than Company A. In which company would you prefer to invest? Give your reason. Assume rising inventory costs.

2. Conservatism is an accepted accounting concept. Would you want management to be conservative in accounting for inventory if you were a shareholder or a creditor of a company? Give your reason.

3. Super Sports Company follows conservative accounting and writes the value of its inventory of tents down to net realizable value, which has declined below cost. The following year, an unexpected camping craze results in a demand for tents that far exceeds supply, and the net realizable value increases above the previous cost. What effect will conservatism have on the income of Super Sports over the two years?

ETHICAL ISSUE

During 2009, Vanguard Inc. changed to the weighted-average-cost method of accounting for inventory. Suppose that during 2010, Vanguard changes back to the FIFO method and the following year Vanguard switches back to weighted-average cost again.

❙ *Required*

1. What would you think of a company's ethics if it changed accounting methods every year?

2. What accounting principle would changing methods every year violate?

3. Who can be harmed when a company changes its accounting methods too often? How?

FOCUS ON FINANCIALS

Sun-Rype Products Ltd.

Analyzing inventories
(Obj. 2, 3)

The notes are part of the financial statements. They give details that would clutter the statements. This case will help you learn to use a company's inventory notes. Refer to Sun-Rype Products Ltd.'s statements and related notes in Appendix A at the end of the book and answer the following questions:

1. How much was Sun-Rype's inventory at December 31, 2007? What about at December 31, 2006?

2. How does Sun-Rype value its inventories? Which cost method does the company use?

3. How much were Sun-Rype's purchases of inventory during the year ended December 31, 2007?

4. Did Sun-Rype's gross margin percentage on company sales improve or deteriorate in 2007 compared to 2006?

5. Would you rate Sun-Rype's rate of inventory turnover as fast or slow in comparison to most other companies? Explain your answer.

GROUP PROJECT

Obtain the annual reports of 10 companies, 2 from each of 5 different industries. Most companies' financial statements can be downloaded from their Web sites.

Comparing companies' inventory turnover ratios
(Obj. 3)

1. Compute each company's gross margin percentage and rate of inventory turnover for the most recent 2 years. If annual reports are unavailable or do not provide enough data for multiple-year computations, you can gather financial statement data from SEDAR.

2. For the industries of the companies you are analyzing, obtain the industry averages for gross margin percentage and inventory turnover.

3. How well does each of your companies compare to the other company in its industry? How well do your companies compare to the average for their industry? What insight about your companies can you glean from these ratios?

4. Write a memo to summarize your findings, stating whether your group would invest in each of the companies it has analyzed.

QUICK CHECK ANSWERS

1. *c*
2. *e*
3. *a*
4. *a* [(25 × $5) + (25 × $6) = $275]
5. *b* (10 × $7 + 5 × $6 = $100)
6. *a* (15 × [($125 + $180 + $70) ÷ 65] = $86.54)
7. *c*
8. *c*
9. *b*
10. *c* ($124,000 − $64,000 = $60,000)
11. *d* ($10,000 + X − $20,000 = $130,000; X = $140,000)
12. *c* ($20,000 + $80,000 − $4,000 + $5,000 − $24,000 = $77,000)
13. *a* [($180,000 − $77,000)/$180,000 = 0.572]
14. *b* [$77,000 ÷ ($20,000 + $24,000)/2 = 3.5]
15. *d* [$60,000 + $180,000 − ($300,000 × [1 − 0.30]) = $30,000]
16. *b*

Appendix 6A

Accounting for Inventory in the Periodic System

In the periodic inventory system, the business keeps no running record of the merchandise. Instead, at the end of the period, the business counts inventory on hand and applies the unit costs to determine the cost of ending inventory. This inventory figure appears on the balance sheet and is used to compute cost of goods sold.

Recording Transactions in the Periodic System

In the periodic system, throughout the period the Inventory account carries the beginning balance left over from the preceding period. The business records purchases of inventory in the Purchases account (an expense). Then, at the end of the period, the Inventory account must be updated for the financial statements. A journal entry removes the begin-

---

EXHIBIT 6A-1 Recording and Reporting Inventories—Periodic System (Amounts assumed)

PANEL A—Recording Transactions and the T-accounts (All amounts are assumed)

1. Purchases... 560,000
      Accounts Payable   560,000
   Purchased inventory on account.

2. Accounts Receivable 900,000
      Sales Revenue   900,000
   Sold inventory on account.

3. End-of-period entries to update Inventory and record Cost of Goods Sold (COGS):
   a. Cost of Goods Sold 100,000
         Inventory (beginning balance)   100,000
      Transferred beginning inventory to COGS.
   b. Inventory (ending balance)......................... 120,000
         Cost of Goods Sold   120,000
      Set up ending inventory based on physical count.
   c. Cost of Goods Sold 560,000
         Purchases...   560,000
      Transferred purchases to COGS.

The T-accounts show the following:

Inventory			Cost of Goods Sold	
100,000*	100,000		100,000	120,000
120,000			560,000	
120,000			540,000	

*Beginning Inventory was $100,000.

PANEL B—Reporting in the Financial Statements

Income Statement (Partial)			Ending Balance Sheet (Partial)	
Sales revenue.......................		$900,000	Current Assets:	
Cost of goods sold:			Cash	$ XXX
Beginning inventory	$100,000		Temporary investments......	XXX
Purchases	560,000		Accounts receivable	XXX
Goods available for sale ...	660,000		Inventory..........................	120,000
Ending inventory	(120,000)		Prepaid expenses	XXX
Cost of goods sold..............		540,000		
Gross margin...................		$360,000		

ning balance by crediting Inventory and debiting Cost of Goods Sold. A second journal entry sets up the ending inventory balance, based on the physical count. The final entry in this sequence transfers the amount of Purchases to Cost of Goods Sold. These end-of-period entries can be made during the closing process.

Exhibit 6A-1 illustrates the accounting in the periodic system. After the process is complete, Inventory has its correct ending balance of $120,000, and Cost of Goods Sold shows $540,000.

Exhibit 6A-2 illustrates the inventory-related journal entries for a perpetual inventory system and a periodic inventory system.

EXHIBIT 6A-2   Inventory-Related Journal Entries under a Perpetual Inventory System Versus a Periodic Inventory System

	Perpetual Inventory System				Periodic Inventory System		
Date	Accounts	Debit	Credit	Date	Accounts	Debit	Credit
Jan. 2	Inventory	600,000		Jan. 2	Purchases	600,000	
	Accounts payable		600,000		Accounts payable		600,000
	Purchased 1,000 units on account.				Purchased 1000 units on account.		
3	Inventory	4,000		3	Freight-in	4,000	
	Accounts payable		4,000		Accounts Payable		4,000
	Record freight fee on purchases.				Record freight fee on purchases.		
9	Accounts payable	25,000		9	Accounts payable	25,000	
	Inventory		25,000		Purchase returns and allowance.		25,000
	Returned goods to supplier for credit.				Returned goods to supplier for credit.		
11	Accounts payable	5,000		11	Accounts payable	5,000	
	Inventory		5,000		Purchase allowance		5,000
	Record purchase allowance.				Record purchase allowance.		
16	Accounts payable	14,000		16	Accounts payable	14,000	
	Inventory		14,000		Purchase discount		14,000
	Record purchase discount.				Record purchase discount.		
16	Accounts payable	560,000		16	Accounts payable	560,000	
	Cash		560,000		Cash		560,000
	Record payment.				Record payment.		
31	Accounts receivable	900,000		31	Accounts receivable	900,000	
	Sales revenue		900,000		Sales revenue		900,000
	Record sales on account.				Record sales on account.		
31	Cost of goods sold	540,000		31	No entry.		
	Inventory		540,000				
	Update inventory and COGS.						
31	No adjustments required.			31	Cost of goods sold	540,000	
					Inventory,* ending balance	120,000	
					Purchase allowance	5,000	
					Purchase returns and allow.	25,000	
					Purchase discount	14,000	
					Purchases		600,000
					Freight-in		4,000
					Inventory, beginning		100,000
					Close out temporary accounts to COGS and record ending inventory.		

*Determined by physical count.

Appendix Assignments

Short Exercises

S6A-1 Capital Technologies Inc. began 2009 with inventory of $20,000. During the year, Capital purchased inventory costing $100,000 and sold goods for $140,000, with all transactions on account. Capital ended the year with inventory of $30,000. Journalize all the necessary transactions under the periodic inventory system.

S6A-2 Use the data in Short Exercise S6A-1 to do the following for Capital Technologies Inc.:

1. Post to the Inventory and Cost of Goods Sold accounts.

2. Compute cost of goods sold by the cost-of-goods-sold model.

3. Prepare the December 2010 income statement of Capital Technologies Inc. through gross margin.

Exercises

E6A-3 Suppose a technology company's inventory records for a particular computer chip indicate the following at October 31:

Oct. 1	Beginning inventory	5 units	@ $160	=	$ 800
8	Purchase	4 units	@ 160	=	640
15	Purchase	11 units	@ 170	=	1,870
26	Purchase	5 units	@ 180	=	900

The physical count of inventory at October 31 indicates that 8 units of inventory are on hand.

❙ Required

Compute ending inventory and cost of goods sold, using each of the following methods. Round all amounts to the nearest dollar.

1. Specific unit cost, assuming four $160 units and four $170 units are on hand

2. Weighted-average cost

3. First-in, first-out cost

E6A-4 Use the data in Exercise E6A-3 to journalize the following for the periodic system:

1. Total October purchases in one summary entry. All purchases were on credit.

2. Total October sales in a summary entry. Assume that the selling price was $300 per unit and that all sales were on credit.

3. October 31 entries for inventory. The company uses weighted-average cost. Post to the Cost of Goods Sold T-account to show how this amount is determined. Label each item in the account.

4. Show the computation of cost of goods sold by the cost-of-goods-sold model.

Problems

P6A-5 Assume a Roots outlet store began August 2009 with 40 units of inventory that cost $30 each. The sale price of these units was $60. During August, the store completed these inventory transactions:

Computing cost of goods sold and gross margin on sales— periodic system

			Units	Unit Cost	Unit Sale Price
Aug.	3	Sale	16	$30	$60
	8	Purchase	70	31	62
	11	Sale	24	30	60
	19	Sale	8	31	62
	24	Sale	30	31	62
	30	Purchase	28	32	73
	31	Sale	15	31	62

❙ Required

1. Determine the store's cost of goods sold for August under the periodic inventory system. Assume the FIFO method.

2. Compute gross margin for August.

P6A-6 Accounting records for Cookies for You Ltd. yield the following data for the year ended December 31, 2009 (amounts in thousands):

Recording transactions in the periodic system; reporting inventory items in the financial statements

Inventory, December 31, 2008	$ 410
Purchases of inventory (on account)	3,200
Sales of inventory—80% on account; 20% for cash	4,830
Inventory at the lower of FIFO cost or market, December 31, 2009	600

❙ Required

1. Journalize Cookies for You's inventory transactions for the year under the periodic system. Show all amounts in thousands. Use Exhibit 6A-1 as a model.

2. Report ending inventory, sales, cost of goods sold, and gross margin on the appropriate financial statement (amounts in thousands). Show the computation of cost of goods sold.

7

Property, Plant, and Equipment, Natural Resources, and Intangible Assets

Learning Objectives

1 **Determine** the cost of property, plant, and equipment

2 **Account** for amortization

3 **Select** the best amortization method

4 **Analyze** the effect of property, plant, and equipment disposal

5 **Account** for natural resources and amortization

6 **Account** for intangible assets and amortization

7 **Report** long-lived assets such as property, plant, and equipment transactions on the cash flow statement

S P O T L I G H T

EnCana Corporation is a leading North American energy company whose primary focus is natural gas production, but it is also involved in oil exploration and production. EnCana's property, plant, and equipment includes long-lived assets such as refinery property, plant, and equipment, the capitalized costs directly associated with the acquisition of, exploration for, and development of natural gas and crude oil reserves, office furniture and computers, corporate aircraft, and land.

This chapter covers long-lived assets, such as property, plant, and equipment, to complete our coverage of assets, except for investment, which we will examine in Chapter 10. Let's begin by examining the various types of capital assets.

EnCana Corporation
▼ Consolidated Balance Sheet
(Assets only, Adapted)

	December 31	
Amounts in $U.S. millions	**2007**	**2006**
Assets		
Current Assets		
1. Cash and cash equivalents	$ 553	$ 402
2. Accounts receivable and accrued revenues	2,381	1,721
3. Current portion of partnership contribution receivable	297	–
4. Risk management	385	1,403
5. Inventories	828	176
6.	4,444	3,702
7. Property, Plant, and Equipment, net	35,865	28,213
8. Investments and Other Assets	607	533
9. Partnership Contribution Receivable	3,147	–
10. Risk Management	18	133
11. Goodwill	2,893	2,525
12.	$46,974	$35,106

 **IFRS ALERT**

The Accounting Standards Board (AcSB) is converging the several Canadian Institute of Chartered Accountants of Canada *CICA Handbook* sections dealing with property, plant, and equipment (previously called capital assets), intangibles, and natural resources with the related International Financial Reporting Standards (IFRS) or International Accounting Standards (IAS).

The accounting for property, plant, and equipment, intangibles, and natural resources is described in the following IASs and *CICA Handbook* sections:

Property, plant, and equipment	IAS 16	Section 3061
Intangibles	IAS 38	Section 3064
		(Goodwill and Intangible Assets)
Natural resources	IFRS 6[*]	Section 3061
Leases	IAS 17	Section 3065

[*]Exploration for and Evaluation of Mineral Resources

Issues related to convergence and the impact of those issues will be introduced and discussed as appropriate throughout the chapter.

IAS 16 uses the term "depreciation" for property, plant and equipment while the *CICA Handbook* Section 3061 uses "amortization." Because convergence has not been completed, amortization is the appropriate term for Canadian reporting.

Types of Assets

Businesses have several types of assets that are classified as long-lived:

- Certain of those such as property, plant, and equipment and goodwill are long-lived assets that are used in the business (see lines 7 and 11). This chapter is concerned with these assets.

IFRS

We will discuss the expense that applies to these assets:

- For example, buildings, airplanes, equipment, and natural resources are tangible capital assets that decline in value while in use and are amortized.
- Intangible assets excluding goodwill are amortized over their useful or legal lives unless their useful life is determined to be indefinite
- Goodwill must be assessed every year and written down if its value is deemed impaired.
- Businesses also have other assets, such as financial assets, which have a maturity of more than one year beyond the balance sheet date (see lines 8, 9, and 10). These assets are discussed in Chapter 10.

The tangible capital assets and intangible assets introduced above are used in the business and are not held for sale.

- Property, plant, and equipment (also called tangible capital assets or fixed assets) are long-lived assets that are tangible. The expense associated with these assets is called *amortization*. Of these assets, land is unique. Land is not expensed over time because its usefulness does not decrease. Many companies report tangible long-lived assets as property, plant, and equipment on the balance sheet. EnCana uses that term for its production equipment, buildings, and other tangible capital assets (line 7).
- **Intangible assets** are useful because of the special rights they carry. They have no physical form. Patents, copyrights, and trademarks are intangible assets, as is goodwill. Accounting for intangibles, except goodwill, is similar to accounting for tangible capital assets. EnCana has a single intangible asset on its balance sheet, goodwill (line 11).

Accounting for long-lived tangible assets and intangibles has its own terminology. Different names apply to the individual assets and their corresponding expense accounts, as shown in Exhibit 7-1.

Unless stated otherwise, we describe accounting in accordance with generally accepted accounting principles (GAAP) for financial-statement reporting to outsiders, as distinguished from reporting to Canada Revenue Agency (CRA) for income tax purposes. Before examining the various types of capital assets, let's see how to value them.

IFRS

EXHIBIT 7-1	Long-Lived Asset Terminology

Asset Account *(Balance Sheet)*	*Related Expense Account* *(Income Statement)*
Tangible Capital Assets	
Land	None
Buildings, machinery and equipment, furniture and fixtures, and land improvements	Amortization (also called depreciation)
Natural resources, mining properties, oil and gas properties	Amortization (also called depletion)
Intangible Assets	Amortization (except goodwill)

Measuring the Cost of Property, Plant, and Equipment

Here is a basic working rule for determining the cost of an asset:

The cost of any asset is the sum of all the costs incurred to bring the asset to its intended use. The cost of a capital asset includes purchase price, plus any taxes, commissions, and other amounts paid to make the asset ready for use. Because the specific costs differ for the various categories of capital assets, we discuss the major groups individually.

Land

The cost of land includes its purchase price (cash plus any note payable given), real estate commission, survey fees, legal fees, and any back property taxes that the purchaser pays. Land cost also includes expenditures for grading and clearing the land and demolishing or removing unwanted buildings.

The cost of land does *not* include the cost of fencing, paving, sprinkler systems, and lighting. These are separate capital assets—called *land improvements*—and they are subject to amortization.

Suppose Big Rock Brewery Income Trust signs a $300,000 note payable to purchase 20 ha of land for a new production facility. Big Rock Brewery also pays $10,000 for real estate commission, $8,000 of back property tax, $5,000 for removal of an old building, a $1,000 survey fee, and $260,000 to pave the parking lot—all in cash. What is Big Rock Brewery's cost of this land?

Purchase price of land		$300,000
Add related costs:		
Real estate commission	$10,000	
Back property tax	8,000	
Removal of building	5,000	
Survey fee	1,000	
Total related costs		24,000
Total cost of land		$324,000

Note that the cost to pave the parking lot, $260,000, is *not* included in the land's cost, because the pavement is a land improvement. Big Rock Brewery would record the purchase of this land as follows:

Land	324,000	
Note Payable		300,000
Cash		24,000
To record the purchase of land.		

ASSETS	=	LIABILITIES	+	SHAREHOLDERS' EQUITY
+324,000 −24,000	=	+300,000	+	0

The purchase increases both assets and liabilities. There is no effect on equity.

Buildings, Machinery, and Equipment

The cost of constructing a building includes architectural fees, building permits, contractors' charges, and payments for material, labour, and overhead. The company may also include as cost the interest on money borrowed to construct a building or buy machinery and equipment for the building until the point in time when the building, machinery, and equipment are ready for their intended use.

When an existing building (new or old) is purchased, its cost includes the purchase price, brokerage commission, sales and other taxes paid, and all expenditures to repair and renovate the building for its intended purpose.

The cost of machinery and equipment includes its purchase price (less any discounts), plus transportation, insurance while in transit, sales and other taxes, purchase commission, installation costs, and any expenditures to test the asset before it is placed in service. The equipment cost will also include the cost of any special platforms used to support the equipment. After the asset is up and running, insurance, taxes, and maintenance costs are recorded as expenses, not as part of the asset's cost.

Land Improvements and Leasehold Improvements

For the Big Rock Brewery production facility building, the cost to pave a parking lot ($260,000) would be recorded in a separate account titled Land Improvements. This account includes costs for other items such as driveways, signs, fences, and sprinkler systems. Although these assets are located on the land, they are subject to decay, and their cost should therefore be amortized.

An airline such as WestJet leases some of its airplanes and other assets. The company customizes these assets to meet its special needs. For example, WestJet paints its logo on airplanes. These improvements are assets of WestJet Airlines Ltd., even though the company does not own the airplane. The cost of improvements to leased assets may appear under Capital Assets or Other Long-Term Assets. The cost of leasehold improvements should be amortized over the term of the lease or the life of the asset, whichever is shorter.

Lump-Sum (or Basket) Purchases of Assets

Businesses often purchase several assets as a group, or in a "basket," for a single lump-sum amount. For example, Great-West Lifeco Inc. may pay one price for land and a building. The company must identify the cost of each asset. The total cost is divided among the assets according to their relative sales (or market) values. This technique is called the *relative-sales-value method*.

Suppose Great-West purchases land and a building in St. John's, Newfoundland, for a sales office. The building sits on 2 ha of land, and the combined purchase price of land and building is $2,800,000. An appraisal indicates that the land's market value is $300,000 and that the building's market value is $2,700,000.

Great-West first calculates the ratio of each asset's market value to the total market value. Total appraised value is $2,700,000 + $300,000 = $3,000,000. Thus, the land, valued at $300,000, is 10% of the total market value. The building's appraised value is 90% of the total. These percentages are then used to determine the cost of each asset, as follows:

Asset	Market (Sales) Value		Total Market Value		Percentage of Total Market Value		Total Cost		Cost of Each Asset
Land	$ 300,000	÷	$3,000,000	=	10%	×	$2,800,000	=	$ 280,000
Building	2,700,000	÷	3,000,000	=	90	×	2,800,000	=	2,520,000
Total	$3,000,000				100%				$2,800,000

If Great-West pays cash, the entry to record the purchase of the land and building is

Land..	280,000	
Building..	2,520,000	
Cash		2,800,000

ASSETS	=	LIABILITIES	+	SHAREHOLDERS' EQUITY
+280,000				
+2,520,000	=	0	+	0
−2,800,000				

Total assets don't change—merely the makeup of Great-West's assets.

STOP & THINK

How would WestJet Airlines Ltd. divide a $120,000 lump-sum purchase price for land, building, and equipment with estimated market values of $40,000, $95,000, and $15,000, respectively?

Answer:

	Estimated Market Value	Percentage of Total Market Value	×	Total Cost	=	Cost of Each Asset
Land	$ 40,000	26.7%*	×	$120,000	=	$ 32,040
Building............	95,000	63.3	×	120,000	=	75,960
Equipment........	15,000	10.0	×	120,000	=	12,000
	$150,000	00.0%				$120,000

*$40,000/$150,000 = 0.267, and so on

DECISION ## Capital Expenditure Versus an Immediate Expense

When a company spends money on a capital asset, it must decide whether to record an asset or an expense. Examples of these expenditures range from WestJet Airlines' purchase of a flight simulator from CAE Electronics to replacing a tire on a plane.

Expenditures that increase the asset's capacity or extend its useful life are called **capital expenditures** or **betterments**. For example, the cost of a major overhaul that extends the useful life of a Big Rock Brewery truck is a capital expenditure. Capital expenditures are said to be *capitalized,* which means the cost is added to an asset account and not expensed immediately. A major decision in accounting for property, plant, and equipment is whether to capitalize or expense a certain cost.

Costs that do not extend the asset's capacity or its useful life, but merely maintain the asset or restore it to working order, are considered *repairs* and are recorded as expenses. For example, Repair Expense is reported on the income statement and matched against revenue. The costs of repainting a Big Rock Brewery truck, repairing a dented fender, and replacing tires are also expensed immediately. Exhibit 7-2 illustrates the distinction between capital expenditures and immediate expenses for van expenditures.

The distinction between a capital expenditure and an expense requires judgment: Does the cost extend the asset's usefulness or its useful life? If so, record an asset. If the cost merely repairs or maintains the asset or returns it to its prior condition, then record an expense.

Most companies expense all small costs, say, below $1,000. For higher costs, they follow the rule we gave above: they capitalize costs that extend the asset's usefulness

EXHIBIT 7-2	Capital Expenditure or Immediate Expense for Costs Associated with a Van
Record an Asset for Capital Expenditures/Betterments	*Record Repair and Maintenance Expense (Not an Asset) for an Expense*
Extraordinary repairs:	*Ordinary repairs:*
Major engine overhaul	Repair of transmission or other mechanism
Modification of body for new use of van	Oil change, lubrication, and so on
Addition to storage capacity of van	Replacement tires, windshield, or a paint job

or its useful life, and they expense all other costs. A conservative policy is one that avoids overstating assets and profits. A company that overstates its assets may get into trouble and have to defend itself in court. Whenever investors lose money because a company overstated its profits or its assets, the investors might file a lawsuit. The courts tend to be sympathetic to investor losses caused by shoddy accounting. The User Alert below is an example.

Accounting misstatements sometimes occur for asset costs. For example, a company may

- expense a cost that should have been capitalized. This error overstates expenses and understates net income in the year of the error.

- capitalize a cost that should have been expensed. This error understates expenses and overstates net income in the year of the error.

USER ALERT ⚠️

Is That Cost Really an Asset?

There is a world of difference between a capital expenditure and an expense. Just ask MCI. MCI WorldCom (now just MCI) got in hot water by missing the mark in its accounting for capital expenditures.

A few years ago—before cellular phones became so popular—long-distance (LD) phone service was extremely profitable for Sprint and MCI. These companies invested huge amounts on LD phone networks. MCI was one of the hottest stocks on Wall Street.

Almost overnight cellular companies Cingular and Verizon began to siphon profits away from MCI. Profits grew thin and then turned to losses. MCI needed to protect its pacesetter image. But how?

MCI's chief financial officer, Scott Sullivan, made some highly unusual journal entries, as follows:

Line-Cost Assets..	$Billions	
Line-Cost Expenses..............................		$Billions
To reclassify expenses as assets.		

These line costs were payments MCI made to other companies (such as AT&T and Sprint) to transmit LD calls for MCI customers. It's a common practice for these companies to rent competitors' phone lines. But it's most unusual to record an expense and then later reclassify the expense as an asset.

The fundamental question is this: Is MCI's rental payment to transmit customer calls an expense or an asset?

Scott Sullivan rationalized that the rental payments were assets because they provided future business for MCI. Independent CPAs from KPMG disagreed. KPMG stated flat out that the rental payments were expenses because the LD calls lasted only minutes and provided no future benefit for MCI. KPMG was right. MCI was wrong. MCI's improper accounting created a scandal.

The take-away lesson from this User Alert:

- Treat expenses as expenses and assets as assets!

Measuring Property, Plant, and Equipment Amortization

As we've seen in previous chapters, property, plant, and equipment are reported on the balance sheet at book value, which is

$$\text{Book value of property, plant and equipment} = \text{Cost} - \text{Accumulated amortization}$$

Property, plant, and equipment wears out, grows obsolete, and loses value over time. To account for this process, we allocate an asset's cost to expense over its life—a process called amortization. The amortization process for a for-profit company matches the asset's expense against revenue to measure income, as the matching principle directs. Exhibit 7-3 illustrates the amortization process for the purchase of a Boeing 737 jet by WestJet Airlines.

Recall that amortization expense (not accumulated amortization) is reported on the income statement.

Only land has an unlimited life and is not amortized for accounting purposes. For most capital assets, amortization is caused by

- **Physical wear and tear.** For example, physical deterioration takes its toll on the usefulness of WestJet airplanes, vehicles, and buildings.

- **Obsolescence.** Computers and other electronic equipment may be *obsolete* before they deteriorate. An asset is obsolete when another asset can do the job more efficiently. An asset's useful life may be shorter than its physical life. WestJet and other companies amortize their computers over a short period of time—perhaps four years—even though the computers will remain in working condition much longer.

Suppose WestJet buys a computer for use in scheduling flight crews. WestJet believes it will get four years of service from the computer, which will then be worthless. Under straight-line amortization, WestJet expenses one-quarter of the asset's cost in each of its four years of use.

You've just seen what amortization accounting is. Let's see what it is *not*.

1. **Amortization is not a process of valuation.** Businesses do not record amortization based on changes in the market value of their property, plant, and equipment. Instead, businesses allocate the asset's cost to the periods of its useful life based on a specific amortization method.

EXHIBIT 7-3   **Amortization and the Matching of Expense with Revenue**

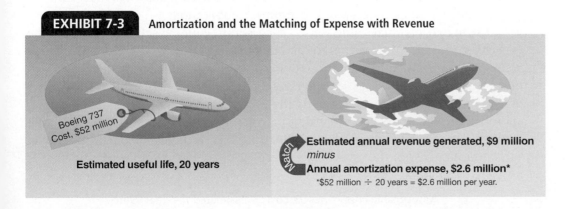

Boeing 737
Cost, $52 million

Estimated useful life, 20 years

Match

Estimated annual revenue generated, $9 million
minus
Annual amortization expense, $2.6 million*

*$52 million ÷ 20 years = $2.6 million per year.

2. **Amortization does not mean setting aside cash to replace assets as they wear out.** Any cash fund is entirely separate from amortization.

Amortization and Not-for-Profit and Government Organizations

Although not-for-profit and government organizations do not have revenues in the same sense as profit-oriented organizations do, they do have receipts and expenses. They also have capital assets, so they amortize those assets in order to assess their costs of operating.

The Canadian Red Cross included the following in its March 31, 2007, annual report:

> Capital Assets
>
> Purchased capital assets are recorded at cost ... Amortization is provided on a straight-line basis over the estimated useful lives as follows:
>
> | | |
> |---|---|
> | Buildings | 20 to 40 years |
> | Furniture, office, and healthcare equipment | 3 to 5 years |
> | Vehicles | 2 to 5 years |
> | Computer hardware and software | 2 to 3 years |

The public sector accounting standards put forth by the CICA's Public Sector Accounting Standards Committee require public sector organizations such as the federal, provincial, and territorial governments and local governments to amortize their capital assets.

How to Measure Amortization

To measure amortization for a capital asset, we must know its

1. Cost
2. Estimated useful life
3. Estimated residual value

We have already discussed cost, which is a known amount. The other two factors must be estimated.

Estimated useful life is the length of service expected from using the asset. Useful life may be expressed in years, units of output, kilometres, or some other measure. For example, the useful life of a building is stated in years. The useful life of a WestJet airplane or van may be expressed as the total number of kilometres the aircraft or vehicle is expected to travel. Companies base such estimates on past experience and information from industry and government publications.

Estimated residual value—also called **scrap value** or **salvage value**—is the expected cash value of an asset at the end of its useful life. For example, WestJet may believe that a baggage-handling machine will be useful for seven years. After that time, WestJet may expect to sell the machine as scrap metal. The amount WestJet believes it can get for the machine is the estimated residual value. In computing amortization, the asset's estimated residual value is *not* amortized because WestJet expects to receive this amount from selling the asset. If there's no expected residual value, the full cost of the asset is amortized. A capital asset's **amortizable cost** is measured as follows:

$$\text{Amortizable cost} = \text{Asset's cost} - \text{Estimated residual value}$$

Amortization Methods

There are three main amortization methods that will be discussed in this text:

Objective

2 **Account** for amortization

- Straight-line
- Units-of-production
- Declining-balance—an accelerated amortization method

These methods allocate different amounts of amortization to each period. However, they all result in the same total amount of amortization, which is the asset's amortizable cost. Exhibit 7-4 presents assumed data, which we will use to illustrate amortization computations for a Big Rock Brewery van.

Straight-Line Method. In the **straight-line (SL) method**, an equal amount of amortization is assigned to each year (or period) of asset use. Amortizable cost is divided by useful life in years to determine the annual amortization expense. Applied to the Big Rock Brewery van data from Exhibit 7-4, straight-line amortization is

$$\text{Straight-line amortization per year} = \frac{\text{Cost} - \text{Residual value}}{\text{Useful life, in years}}$$

$$= \frac{\$41,000 - \$1,000}{5}$$

$$= \$8,000$$

The entry to record amortization is

| Amortization Expense | 8,000 | |
| Accumulated Amortization | | 8,000 |

ASSETS	=	LIABILITIES	+	SHAREHOLDERS' EQUITY	−	EXPENSES
−8,000	=	0			−	8,000

Observe that amortization decreases the asset (through Accumulated Amortization) and also decreases equity (through Amortization Expense). Let's assume that Big Rock Brewery purchased this van on January 1, 2009; Big Rock Brewery's fiscal year ends on December 31. Exhibit 7-5 gives a *straight-line amortization schedule* for the van. The final column of the exhibit shows the *asset's book value*, which is its cost less accumulated amortization.

As an asset is used in operations, accumulated amortization increases, and the book value of the asset decreases. An asset's final book value is its *residual value* ($1,000 in Exhibit 7-5). At the end of its useful life, the asset is said to be *fully amortized*.

EXHIBIT 7-4	Data for Amortization Computations—A Big Rock Brewery Van

Data Item	Amount
Cost of van, January 1, 2009	$41,000
Less estimated residual value	(1,000)
Amortizable cost	$40,000
Estimated useful life:	
Years	5 years
Units of production	100,000 units [kilometres]

STOP & THINK

Imagine a company purchased a machine for $13,000 that had a useful life of five years and residual value of $3,000. If the asset book value was $7,000, how many more years of use would the machine have?

Answer:
The yearly amortization would be $2,000 [($13,000 − $3,000)/5]. Therefore the years of use left would be 2 [($7,000 − $3,000)/$2,000)].

EXHIBIT 7-5 Straight-Line Amortization Schedule for a Big Rock Brewery Van

| Date | Asset Cost | Amortization for the Year | | | | Accumulated Amortization | Asset Book Value |
		Amortization Rate		Amortizable Cost	Amortization Expense		
01-01-2009	$41,000						$41,000
31-12-2009		0.20*	×	$40,000	= $8,000	$ 8,000	33,000
31-12-2010		0.20	×	40,000	= 8,000	16,000	25,000
31-12-2011		0.20	×	40,000	= 8,000	24,000	17,000
31-12-2012		0.20	×	40,000	= 8,000	32,000	9,000
31-12-2013		0.20	×	40,000	= 8,000	40,000	1,000

* $\dfrac{1}{5 \text{ years}}$ = 0.20 per year

Units-of-Production Method.

In the **units-of-production (UOP) method**, a fixed amount of amortization is assigned to each *unit of output*, or service, produced by the asset. Amortizable cost is divided by useful life—in units of production—to determine this amount. This per-unit amortization expense is then multiplied by the number of units produced each period to compute amortization. The units-of-production amortization for the Big Rock Brewery van data in Exhibit 7-4 is

$$\text{Units-of-production amortization per unit of output} = \frac{\text{Cost} - \text{Residual value}}{\text{Useful life, in units of production}}$$

$$= \frac{\$41,000 - \$1,000}{100,000 \text{ km}} = \$0.40/\text{km}$$

Assume that the van is expected to be driven 20,000 km during the first year, 30,000 during the second, 25,000 during the third, 15,000 during the fourth, and 10,000 during the fifth. Exhibit 7-6 shows the UOP amortization schedule.

The amount of UOP amortization varies with the number of units the asset produces. In our example, the total number of units produced is 100,000. UOP amortization does not depend directly on time, as do the other methods.

EXHIBIT 7-6 Units-of-Production Amortization Schedule for a Big Rock Brewery Van

| Date | Asset Cost | Amortization for the Year | | | | Accumulated Amortization | Asset Book Value |
		Amortization Per Unit		Number of Units	Amortization Expense		
01-01-2009	$41,000						$41,000
31-12-2009		$0.40*	×	20,000	= $ 8,000	$ 8,000	33,000
31-12-2010		0.40	×	30,000	= 12,000	20,000	21,000
31-12-2011		0.40	×	25,000	= 10,000	30,000	11,000
31-12-2012		0.40	×	15,000	= 6,000	36,000	5,000
31-12-2013		0.40	×	10,000	= 4,000	40,000	1,000

*($41,000 − $1,000)/100,000 km = $0.40/km.

Declining-Balance Method. An **accelerated amortization method** writes off a larger amount of the asset's cost near the start of its useful life than the straight-line method does. Double-declining-balance is the main accelerated amortization method. The **double-declining-balance (DDB) method** computes annual amortization by multiplying the asset's declining book value by a constant percentage, which is two times the straight-line amortization rate. Double-declining-balance amounts are computed as follows:

- *First*, compute the straight-line amortization rate per year. A five-year asset has a straight-line amortization rate of 1/5, or 20% each year. A ten-year asset has a straight-line rate of 1/10, or 10%, and so on.

- *Second*, multiply the straight-line rate by 2 to compute the DDB rate. For a five-year asset, the DDB rate is 40% (20% × 2). A ten-year asset has a DDB rate of 20% (10% × 2).

- *Third*, multiply the DDB rate by the period's beginning asset book value (cost less accumulated amortization). Under the DDB method, ignore the residual value of the asset in computing amortization, except during the last year. The DDB rate for the Big Rock Brewery van in Exhibit 7-4 (page 323) is

$$\text{DDB amortization rate per year} = \frac{1}{\text{Useful life, in years}} \times 2$$

$$= \frac{1}{5 \text{ years}} \times 2$$

$$= 20\% \times 2$$

$$= 40\%$$

- *Fourth,* determine the final year's amortization amount—that is, the amount needed to reduce the asset book value to its residual value. In Exhibit 7-7, the fifth and final year's DDB amortization is $4,314: the book value of $5,314 less the $1,000 residual value. *The residual value should not be amortized* but should remain on the books until the asset is disposed of.

The DDB method differs from the other methods in two ways:

1. Residual value is ignored initially; in the first year, amortization is computed on the asset's full cost.

2. Amortization expense in the final year is whatever amount is needed to reduce the asset's book value to its residual value.

EXHIBIT 7-7 **Double-Declining-Balance Amortization Schedule for a Big Rock Brewery Van**

| Date | Asset Cost | Amortization for the Year | | | Accumulated Amortization | Asset Book Value |
		DDB Rate	Asset Book Value	Amortization Expense		
01-01-2009	$41,000					$41,000
31-12-2009		0.40	× $41,000 =	$16,400	$16,400	24,600
31-12-2010		0.40	× 24,600 =	9,840	26,240	14,760
31-12-2011		0.40	× 14,760 =	5,904	32,144	8,856
31-12-2012		0.40	× 8,856 =	3,542	35,686	5,314
31-12-2013				4,314*	40,000	1,000

*Last-year amortization is the amount needed to reduce asset book value to the residual value ($5,314 − $1,000 = $4,314).

STOP & THINK

What would you as a user of the company described in the Stop & Think on page 323 expect DDB amortization to be for each year?

Answers: Yr. 1: $5,200 ($13,000 × 40%)
Yr. 2: $3,120 ($7,800 × 40%)
Yr. 3: $1,680 ($13,000 − $5,200 − $3,120 − $3,000)*
Yr. 4: $0
Yr. 5: $0

*The asset is not amortized below residual value.

Comparing Amortization Methods

Let's compare the three methods in terms of the yearly amount of amortization. The yearly amount of amortization varies by method, but the total $40,000 amortizable cost is the same under all methods.

| | Amount of Amortization Per Year | | |
| | | | *Accelerated Method* |
Year	*Straight-Line*	*Units-of-Production*	*Double-Declining-Balance*
1	$ 8,000	$ 8,000	$16,400
2	8,000	12,000	9,840
3	8,000	10,000	5,904
4	8,000	6,000	3,542
5	8,000	4,000	4,314
Total	$40,000	$40,000	$40,000

GAAP direct a business to match an asset's amortization against the revenue the asset produces. For a capital asset that generates revenue evenly over time, the straight-line method best meets the matching principle. The units-of-production method best fits those assets that wear out because of physical use rather than obsolescence. The accelerated method (DDB) applies best to assets that generate greater amounts of revenue earlier in their useful lives and less in later years.

Exhibit 7-8 graphs annual amortization amounts for the straight-line, units-of-production, and DDB methods. The graph of straight-line amortization is flat through time because annual amortization is the same in all periods. Units-of-production amortization follows no particular pattern because annual amortization depends on the use of the asset. Accelerated amortization is greatest in the first year and less in the later years.

Recent surveys of companies in Canada and the United States indicate that straight-line amortization is used by more than 80%. Around 10% use some form of

EXHIBIT 7-8   Amortization Patterns Through Time

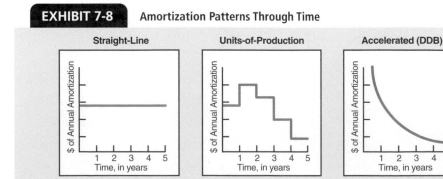

accelerated amortization and the rest use units of production and other methods. Many companies use more than one method.

For reporting in the financial statements, straight-line amortization is most popular. As we shall see, however, many organizations use capital cost allowance (CCA), a form of accelerated amortization allowed for income-tax purposes by the *Income Tax Act*.

MID-CHAPTER SUMMARY PROBLEM

MyAccountingLab

Suppose you are a manager at Big Rock Brewery Income Trust. The company purchased equipment on January 1, 2009, for $44,000. The expected useful life of the equipment is 10 years or 100,000 units of production, and its residual value is $4,000. Under three amortization methods, the annual amortization expense and the balance of accumulated amortization at the end of 2009 and 2010 are as follows:

	Method A		Method B		Method C	
Year	Annual Amortization Expense	Accumulated Amortization	Annual Amortization Expense	Accumulated Amortization	Annual Amortization Expense	Accumulated Amortization
2009	$4,000	$4,000	$8,800	$ 8,800	$1,200	$1,200
2010	4,000	8,000	7,040	15,840	5,600	6,800

Required

1. Your assistant has provided you with the above information. Identify the amortization method used in each instance, and show the equation and computation for each. (Round off to the nearest dollar.)
2. Assume continued use of the same method through year 2011. Determine the annual amortization expense, accumulated amortization, and book value of the equipment for 2009 through 2011 under each method, assuming 12,000 units of production in 2011.

Name: Big Rock Brewery Income Trust
Industry: Brewer of craft beers
Accounting Period: The years 2009, 2010, 2011

Answers

Requirement 1

Method A: Straight-Line

$$\text{Amortizable cost} = \$40,000 \ (\$44,000 - \$4,000)$$
$$\text{Each year: } \$40,000/10 \text{ years} = \$4,000$$

The straight-line method assigns the same amortization expense to each year.

Method B: Double-Declining-Balance

$$\text{Rate} = \frac{1}{10 \text{ years}} \times 2 = 10\% \times 2 = 20\%$$

$$2009: 0.20 \times \$44,000 = \$8,800$$
$$2010: 0.20 \times (\$44,000 - \$8,800) = \$7,040$$

The double-declining balance method assigns an expense amount that gets smaller every year. Do not include the salvage value when using this method.

Method C: Units-of-Production

$$\text{Amortization per unit} = \frac{\$44,000 - \$4,000}{100,000 \text{ units}} = \$0.40/\text{unit}$$

$$2009: \$1,200 \div \$0.40 = 3,000 \text{ units}$$
$$2010: \$5,600 \div \$0.40 = 14,000 \text{ units}$$

With the units-of-production method, there is a direct correlation to the number of units produced.

Subtract the salvage value from the original cost. Calculate the amortization per unit. Then divide the annual amortization expense by the unit cost to determine the number of units produced each year.

Requirement 2

> Use the same $4,000 annual amortization expense used for the prior years.

	Method A: Straight-Line		
Year	Annual Amortization Expense	Accumulated Amortization	Book Value
Start			$44,000
2009	$4,000	$ 4,000	40,000
2010	4,000	8,000	36,000
2011	4,000	12,000	32,000

> The amortization expense is calculated as 20% of the prior year's book value.

	Method B: Double-Declining-Balance		
Year	Annual Amortization Expense	Accumulated Amortization	Book Value
Start			$44,000
2009	$8,800	$ 8,800	35,200
2010	7,040	15,840	28,160
2011	5,632	21,472	22,528

> Use the same $0.40 per unit amount used for the prior years. Multiply by the number of units produced during 2011.

	Method C: Units-of-Production		
Year	Annual Amortization Expense	Accumulated Amortization	Book Value
Start			$44,000
2009	$1,200	$ 1,200	42,800
2010	5,600	6,800	37,200
2011	4,800	11,600	32,400

Computations for 2011	
Straight-line	$40,000/10 years = $4,000
Double-declining-balance	0.20 × $28,160 = $5,632
Units-of-production	$0.40 × 12,000 units = $4,800

Other Issues in Accounting for Capital Assets

> **Objective**
>
> ❸ **Select** the best amortization method

Long-lived assets such as property, plant, and equipment are complex because:

- They have long lives.
- Amortization affects income taxes.
- Companies may have gains or losses when they sell such assets.

Amortization for Tax Purposes

Many businesses use the straight-line method for reporting property, plant, and equipment on the balance sheet and amortization expense on the income statement. The *Income Tax Act* permits taxpayers to use accelerated amortization (up to specified CCA maximums) for tax purposes. In other words, a taxpayer may use one method of amortization for accounting purposes and another method for tax purposes.

| DECISION | Is It Ethical to Keep Two Sets of Amortization Records? |

Is it ethical for WestJet Airlines Ltd., The Jean Coutu Group (PJC) Inc., and Jazz Golf Equipment Inc. of Winnipeg to keep two sets of amortization records—one for their financial statements and the other for reporting to CRA? Yes, that's perfectly okay because the two sets of amortization records serve two very different purposes.

The amortization records illustrated in this chapter are designed for the income statement and the balance sheet. The purpose here is to measure accounting income and asset values for reporting to shareholders and creditors. Accounting theory is the driving force behind these amortization amounts to provide relevant information for investment and credit decisions.

Amortization amounts for income tax purposes march to the beat of a different drummer. Parliament designs tax amortization to raise tax revenue for the government. Political considerations enter the world of taxes, so tax amortization is very different from basic accounting amortization. Companies must comply with CCA regulations and so have two sets of records for amortization.

The result of using one method for accounting and another method for tax purposes is that income tax expense and net income calculated for accounting purposes will usually be different from those calculated for tax purposes. In the early years of an asset's life, amortization for tax purposes will be greater than amortization for accounting purposes (and actual income tax expense will be less). In the later years, amortization for accounting purposes will be greater than amortization for tax purposes (and actual income tax will be more).

While the relationship is generally considered to be a topic for an advanced accounting course, the authors felt it important to introduce it in this text. There is more extensive coverage of the topic in the Appendix to this chapter.

Amortization for Partial Years

Companies purchase capital assets whenever they need them. They do not wait until the beginning of a year or a month. Therefore, companies must compute *amortization for partial years*. Suppose the County Line Bar-B-Q restaurant in Edmonton purchases a building on April 1 for $500,000. The building's estimated life is 20 years, and its estimated residual value is $80,000. The restaurant's fiscal year ends on December 31. Let's consider how the company computes amortization for April through December:

- First compute amortization for a full year.
- Then multiply the full year's amortization by the fraction of the year that you held the asset.

Assuming the straight-line method, the year's amortization for County Line's building is $15,750, as follows:

$$\text{Full-year amortization} = \frac{\$500,000 - \$80,000}{20} = \$21,000$$

Partial year amortization: $21,000 \times 9/12 = $15,750

What if County Line bought the asset on April 18? Many businesses record no monthly amortization on assets purchased after the 15th of the month, and they record a full month's amortization on an asset bought on or before the 15th.

Most companies use computerized systems to account for capital assets. Each asset has a unique identification number that links to the asset's cost, estimated life, residual value, and amortization method. The system will automatically calculate the amortization expense for each period. Accumulated Amortization is automatically updated.

Changing the Useful Life of an Amortizable Asset

Managers must decide on an asset's useful life to compute its amortization. After an asset is put into use, managers may refine their estimate on the basis of experience and new information. Such a change in accounting estimate is very rare in Canada; a senior partner of one of the Big Four chartered accountancy firms initiated a search of two large databases containing statements of public companies and could find only one such reported change in the past three years.

An example from the United States is illustrative. The Walt Disney Company made such a change, called a *change in accounting estimate*. Disney recalculated amortization on the basis of revised useful lives of several of its theme park assets. The following note in Walt Disney's financial statements reports this change in accounting estimate:

Note 5

. . . [T]he Company extended the estimated useful lives of certain theme park ride and attraction assets based upon historical data and engineering studies. The effect of this change was to decrease [amortization] by approximately $8 million (an increase in net income of approximately $4.2 million . . .).

Assume that a Disney hot-dog stand cost $40,000 and that the company originally believed the asset had an eight-year useful life with no residual value. Using the straight-line method, the company would record $5,000 amortization each year ($40,000/8 years = $5,000). Suppose Disney used the asset for two years. Accumulated amortization reached $10,000, leaving a remaining amortizable book value (cost *less* accumulated amortization *less* residual value) of $30,000 ($40,000 − $10,000). From its experience, management believes the asset will remain useful for an additional ten years. The company would spread the remaining amortizable book value over the asset's remaining life as follows:

Asset's remaining amortizable book value	÷	(New) Estimated useful life remaining	=	(New) Annual amortization
$30,000	÷	10 years	=	$3,000

The yearly amortization entry based on the new estimated useful life is

Amortization Expense—Hot Dog Stand.................	3,000	
Accumulated Amortization—Hot Dog Stand		3,000

ASSETS	=	LIABILITIES	+	SHAREHOLDERS' EQUITY	−	EXPENSES
−3,000	=	0		−		3,000

1. Suppose a company was having a bad year—net income was well below expectations and lower than last year's income. For amortization purposes, the company extended the estimated useful lives of its amortizable assets. How would this accounting change affect the company's (a) amortization expense, (b) net income, and (c) owners' equity?
2. Suppose that the company's accounting change turned a loss year into a profitable year. Without the accounting change, the company would have reported a net loss for the year. The accounting change enabled the company to report net income. Under Canadian and U.S. GAAP, the company's annual report must disclose the accounting change and its effect on net income. Would investors evaluate the company as better or worse for having made this accounting change?

Answers:
1. An accounting change that lengthens the estimated useful lives of amortizable assets
   (a)   decreases amortization expense and
   (b,c)   increases net income and owners' equity.
2. Investor reactions are not always predictable. There is research to indicate that companies cannot fool investors. In this case, investment advisers would *probably* subtract from the company's reported net income the amount added by the accounting change. Investors could then use the remaining net *loss* figure to evaluate the company's lack of progress during the year. Investors would probably view the company as worse for having made this accounting change. It is probably for this reason that such changes in accounting estimates are so rare in Canada.

Fully Amortized Assets

A *fully amortized asset* is an asset that has reached the end of its estimated useful life. Suppose Big Rock Brewery has fully amortized equipment with zero residual value (cost was $40,000). Big Rock Brewery accounts will appear as follows:

Equipment		Accumulated Amortization	
40,000			40,000

The equipment's book value is zero, but that doesn't mean the equipment is worthless. Big Rock Brewery may continue using the equipment for a few more years, but will not take any more amortization.

When Big Rock Brewery disposes of the equipment, it will remove both the asset's cost ($40,000) and its accumulated amortization ($40,000) from the books. The next section shows how to account for capital asset disposals.

Accounting for Disposal of Property, Plant, and Equipment

Eventually, property, plant, and equipment ceases to serve a company's needs. The asset may wear out, become obsolete, or for some other reason cease to be useful. Before accounting for the disposal of the asset, the business should bring amortization up to date to

- Record the expense up to the date of sale
- Measure the asset's final book value

To account for disposal, remove the asset and its related accumulated amortization from the books. Suppose the final year's amortization expense has just been recorded to fully amortize a machine that cost $50,000 and is estimated to have zero residual value. The machine's accumulated amortization thus totals $50,000. Assuming that this asset is disposed of, not sold, the entry to record its disposal is:

Accumulated Amortization—Machinery................	50,000	
Machinery		50,000

To dispose of a fully amortized machine.

Objective

4 **Analyze** the effect of property, plant, and equipment disposal

ASSETS	=	LIABILITIES	+	SHAREHOLDERS' EQUITY
+50,000 −50,000	=	0	+	0

There is no gain or loss on this disposal, so there is no effect on equity.

If assets are "junked" before being fully amortized, the company incurs a loss on the disposal. Suppose M&M Meat Shops disposes of store fixtures that cost $4,000. Accumulated amortization is $3,000, and book value is, therefore, $1,000. Junking these store fixtures results in a loss as follows:

Accumulated Amortization—Store Fixtures...........	3,000	
Loss on Disposal of Store Fixtures	1,000	
Store Fixtures		4,000
To dispose of store fixtures.		

ASSETS	=	LIABILITIES	+	SHAREHOLDERS' EQUITY	−	LOSSES
+3,000 −4,000	=	0			−	1,000

M&M Meat Shops got rid of an asset with a $1,000 book value and received nothing. The result is a $1,000 loss, which decreases both total assets and equity.

The Loss on Disposal of Store Fixtures is reported as Other Income (Expense) on the income statement. Losses decrease net income exactly as expenses do. Gains increase net income in the same manner as revenues.

Selling Property, Plant, and Equipment. Suppose M&M Meat Shops sells fixtures on September 30, 2009, that cost $10,000 when purchased on January 1, 2006, and have been amortized on a straight-line basis. M&M Meat Shops originally estimated a ten-year useful life and no residual value. Prior to recording the sale, the M&M Meat Shops accountants must update the asset's amortization. Suppose the business uses the calendar year as its accounting period. Partial-year amortization must be recorded for the asset's expense from January 1, 2009, to the sale date. The straight-line amortization entry at September 30, 2009, is

Sept. 30	Amortization Expense ($10,000/10 years × 9/12)	750	
	Accumulated Amortization—Fixtures		750
	To update amortization.		

The Fixtures account and the Accumulated Amortization—Fixtures account appear as follows. Observe that the fixtures' book value is $6,250 ($10,000 − $3,750).

Fixtures		Accumulated Amortization—Fixtures	
Jan. 1, 2006 10,000		Dec. 31, 2006 1,000	
		Dec. 31, 2007 1,000	
		Dec. 31, 2008 1,000	
		Sep. 30, 2009 750	
		Balance 3,750	

Suppose M&M Meat Shops sells the fixtures for $7,000 cash. The gain on the sale is $750, determined as follows:

Cash received from sale of the asset		$7,000
Book value of asset sold:		
Cost	$10,000	
Less accumulated amortization	(3,750)	6,250
Gain on sale of the asset...		$ 750

The entry to record the sale of the fixtures for $7,000 cash is

Sept. 30	Cash..	7,000	
	Accumulated Amortization—Fixtures	3,750	
	Gain on Sale of Fixtures		750
	Fixtures...		10,000
	To sell fixtures.		

ASSETS	=	LIABILITIES	–	SHAREHOLDERS' EQUITY	+	GAINS
+7,000						
+3,750	=	0			+	750
−10,000						

Gains are recorded as credits, in the same manner as revenues; losses are recorded as debits, in the same manner as expenses. Gains and losses on asset disposals appear on the income statement as other income (expense).

STOP & THINK

Suppose you are reviewing WestJet Airlines's comparative income statement for 2009 and 2008 and notice these items:

	(In millions)	
	2009	2008
Net revenues...	$1,600	$1,300
Income from operations...	150	165
Other income (expense)		
Gain on sale of maintenance building	20	
Income before income taxes..	$ 170	$ 165

Which would you decide was a better year for WestJet, 2009 or 2008?

Answer:
From a revenue standpoint, 2009 was better because revenues were higher. But from an *income* standpoint, 2008 was better.

In 2008, the company's core business generated $165 million of income from operations. In 2009, operations produced only $150 million of operating income. Twenty million dollars of the company's income in 2009 came from selling a maintenance building (gain of $20 million). A business cannot hope to continue on this path very long. This example shows why investors and creditors care about the sources of a company's profits, and not just the final amount of net income.

Exchanging Property, Plant, and Equipment. Managers often trade in old property, plant, and equipment for new ones. For example, Mazzio's Pizzeria trades in a five-year-old delivery van for a newer model. In such a transaction, GAAP requires that the most reliable of the fair value of the asset given up and the fair value of the asset received be used to record the transaction. In this case, the fair value of the new van is likely to be the most reliable.

Assume the old van cost $20,000 and has a net book value of $3,400 and that the new van has a listed price of $27,400 (GST and PST included). Further assume that the dealer wants Mazzio's to pay cash in the amount of $24,000. The pizzeria records the exchange transaction as follows:

Delivery Auto (new)	27,400	
Accumulated Amortization (old) ($20,000 – $3,400)...	16,600	
Delivery Auto (old)...		20,000
Cash		24,000
Traded in old delivery van for new van.		

ASSETS	=	LIABILITIES	+	SHAREHOLDERS' EQUITY
+27,400				
+16,600	=	0	+	0
−20,000				
−24,000				

There was no gain or loss on this exchange, so there was no effect on equity.

The subject of more complex exchanges of property, plant, and equipment and other long-lived assets is beyond the scope of this text.

Using T-Accounts to Analyze Property, Plant, and Equipment Transactions

You can perform quite a bit of analysis if you know how transactions affect the property, plant, and equipment accounts. Here are the accounts with descriptions of the activity in each account.

Building (or Equipment)	
Beginning balance	
Cost of assets purchased	Cost of assets disposed of
Ending balance	

Accumulated Amortization	
Accum. amort. of assets disposed of	Beginning balance
	Amortization expense for the current period
	Ending balance

Amortization Expense	
Amortization expense for the current period	

Gain on Sale of Building (or Equipment)	
	Gain on sale

Loss on Sale of Building (or Equipment)	
Loss on sale	

Example: Suppose you started the year with buildings that cost $100,000. During the year you bought another building for $150,000 and ended the year with buildings that cost $180,000. What was the cost of the building you sold?

Building			
Beginning balance	100,000		
Cost of assets purchased	150,000	Cost of assets sold	? = $70,000
Ending balance	180,000		

You can perform similar analyses to answer other interesting questions about what the business did during the period.

Accounting for Natural Resources

Natural resources are capital assets of a special type, such as iron ore, petroleum (oil), and timber. As property, plant, and equipment are expensed through amortization, so too are natural resource assets expensed through amortization. Another term that is often used for amortization of natural resource assets is *depletion*. Amortization expense is that portion of the cost of a natural resource that is used up in a particular period. The credit is to accumulated amortization, which is a contra account. Amortization expense is computed in the same way as units-of-production amortization.

Legislation and accounting standards require many companies that make use of natural resources to return the land on or under which the natural resources are found to the state the land was in before the company began the extraction or removal of the natural resource. The process of returning the land has several names, but the most common one is *remediation*, the act or process of remedying, of repairing, of restoring the site to its original state. Companies are required to capitalize an amount equal to the estimated remediation costs and charge that cost against the revenue derived from the natural resources in a systematic way similar to amortization.

Suppose an oil lease costs EnCana Corporation $200,000 and contains an estimated 10,000 barrels of oil. The amortization rate would be $20 per barrel ($200,000/10,000 barrels). If 3,000 barrels are extracted, amortization expense is $60,000 (3,000 barrels × $20 per barrel). The amortization entry is

Amortization Expense (3,000 barrels × $20)	60,000	
Accumulated Amortization—Oil		60,000

ASSETS	=	LIABILITIES	+	SHAREHOLDERS' EQUITY	−	EXPENSES
−60,000	=	0			−	60,000

Both assets and equity decrease. Why equity? Because the amortization expense decreases net income and thus decreases retained earnings.

If 4,500 barrels are removed the next year, that period's amortization is $90,000 (4,500 barrels × $20 per barrel). Accumulated Amortization for Natural Resources is a contra account similar to Accumulated Amortization for Property, Plant, and Equipment.

EnCana Corporation, like many other oil and gas companies, uses the full cost accounting method under which " . . . all costs including . . . [remediation] costs, directly associated with the acquisition of, exploration for, and the development of natural gas and crude oil reserves, are capitalized on a country-by-country cost centre basis."[1] Natural resource costs are included with other capital assets under the heading Property, Plant, and Equipment.

Natural resource assets could be reported on EnCana's balance sheet as follows (amounts and titles assumed):

Property, plant, and equipment		
Equipment	$960,000	
Less: Accumulated amortization	(410,000)	$550,000
Oil	$340,000	
Less: Accumulated amortization	(140,000)	200,000
Total property, plant, and equipment		$750,000

---

[1] EnCana Corporation, December 31, 2007, annual report, page 73.

Accounting for Intangible Assets

As we saw earlier, *intangible assets* are long-lived assets with no physical form. Intangibles are valuable because they carry special rights from patents, copyrights, trademarks, franchises, leaseholds, and goodwill. Like buildings and equipment, an intangible asset is recorded at its acquisition cost. Intangibles are often the most valuable assets of high-tech companies and other companies that depend on research and development. The residual value of most intangibles is zero.

Intangible assets fall into two categories:

- Intangibles with *finite lives* that can be measured. We record amortization for these intangibles. Amortization is usually computed on a straight-line basis. Amortization can be credited directly to the asset account, as we shall see.

- Intangibles with *indefinite lives*. Record no amortization for these intangibles. Instead, check them annually for any loss in value (impairment), and record a loss when it occurs. Goodwill is the most prominent example of an intangible asset with an indefinite life.

In the following discussions, we illustrate the accounting for both categories of intangibles.

Accounting for Specific Intangibles

Each type of intangible asset is unique, and the accounting can vary from one intangible to another.

Patents. **Patents** are federal government grants giving the holder the exclusive right for 20 years to produce and sell an invention. The invention may be a product or a process—for example, Research In Motion's BlackBerry and IMAX's projection process. Like any other asset, a patent may be purchased. Suppose Bombardier pays $170,000 to acquire a patent on January 1, and the business believes the expected useful life of the patent is five years. Amortization expense is $34,000 per year ($170,000/5 years). Bombardier records the acquisition and amortization for this patent as follows:

Jan. 1	Patents	170,000	
	Cash		170,000
	To acquire a patent.		
Dec. 31	Amortization Expense—Patents ($170,000/5).................	34,000	
	Patents		34,000
	To amortize the cost of a patent.		

ASSETS	=	LIABILITIES	+	SHAREHOLDERS' EQUITY	−	EXPENSES
−34,000	=	0			−	34,000

Amortization for an intangible decreases both assets and equity exactly as it does for equipment.

Copyrights. **Copyrights** are exclusive rights to reproduce and sell a book, musical composition, film, or other work of art. Copyrights also protect computer software programs, such as Corel's WordPerfect. Issued by the federal government, copyrights extend 50 years beyond the author's (composer's, artist's, or programmer's) death. The cost of obtaining a copyright from the government is low, but a company may pay a large sum to purchase an existing copyright from the owner. For example, a publisher may pay the author of a popular novel $1 million or more for the book copyright. Because the useful life of the copyright of a novel may be usually no longer than two or three years, each period's amortization amount is a high proportion of the copyright cost.

Trademarks and Trade Names. **Trademarks** and **trade names** (or **brand names**) are distinctive identifications of products or services. You are probably familiar with the CBC's sectioned circle logo and CTV's red, blue, and green logo. You would also recognize MuchMusic's and TSN's logos. Tim Hortons and Roots are names we all recognize. Advertising slogans, such as Molson's "I am Canadian," are protected.

The cost of a trademark or trade name may be amortized over its useful life. But if the trademark is expected to generate cash flow for the indefinite future, the business should not amortize the trademark's cost.

Franchises and Licences. **Franchises** and **licences** are privileges granted by a private business or a government to sell a product or service in accordance with specified conditions. The Edmonton Oilers hockey organization is a franchise granted to its owner by the National Hockey League. Swiss Chalet restaurants and Canadian Tire are popular franchises. The useful lives of many franchises and licences are indefinite and, therefore, are not amortized.

Goodwill. In accounting, **goodwill** has a very specific meaning. It is defined as the excess of the cost of purchasing another company over the sum of the market values of its net assets (assets minus liabilities). A purchaser is willing to pay for goodwill when it buys another company with abnormal earning power.

Canadian Tire expanded into another line of business when it acquired Mark's Work Wearhouse Ltd. on February 1, 2002. The purchase price was $110.8 million. The fair value of the assets was $189.8 million, and the fair value of the liabilities was $97.9 million, so Canadian Tire paid $18.9 million for goodwill, computed as follows:

Purchase price paid for Mark's Work Wearhouse Ltd. (MWW)	$110.8 million
Sum of the fair values of MWW's assets	$189.8 million
Less: Fair value of MWW's liabilities	97.9 million
Value of MWW's net assets..	91.9 million
Excess is called *goodwill*	$ 18.9 million

Canadian Tire would consolidate Mark's Work Wearhouse's financial statements, but if Canadian Tire were to combine Mark's records with its own, the entry, including goodwill, would be

Assets (Cash, Receivables, Inventories, Property,		
Plant and Equipment, Other Assets all at fair value)	189,800,000	
Goodwill	18,900,000	
Liabilities...		97,900,000
Cash...		110,800,000

ASSETS	=	LIABILITIES	+	SHAREHOLDERS' EQUITY
+189,800,000				
+18,900,000	=	+97,900,000	+	0
−110,800,000				

Note that Canadian Tire has acquired both Mark's Work Wearhouse's assets and its liabilities.

Goodwill has special features, as follows:

1. Goodwill is recorded *only* when it is purchased in the acquisition of another company. A purchase transaction provides objective evidence of the value of goodwill. Companies never record goodwill that they have created for their own business.

2. According to GAAP, goodwill is not amortized because it has an indefinite life. As you will see below, if the value of goodwill is impaired it must be written down.

Accounting for the Impairment of an Intangible Asset

IFRS

Some intangibles—such as goodwill, licences, and some trademarks—have indefinite lives and, therefore, are not subject to amortization. But all intangibles are subject to a write-down when their fair value is less than book value. The annual report of Brampton Brick Limited for the year ended December 31, 2007, reports that "The Company performed its annual test for impairment of goodwill as at December 31, 2007 . . . [and] determined that there had been an impairment in the carrying value of goodwill . . . " As a result of the impairment test, the company wrote down its investment in Landscape Products' business by $13.5 million in fiscal 2007.

Brampton Brick recorded the write-down as follows:

2007
Dec. 31   Goodwill Impairment...   13.5
                Goodwill 13.5

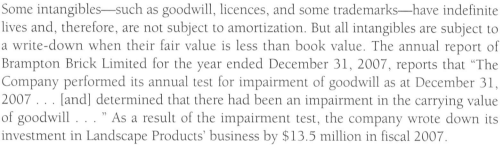

ASSETS	=	LIABILITIES	+	SHAREHOLDERS' EQUITY	−	EXPENSES
−13.5	=	0			−	13.5

Brampton Brick's financial statements reported the following (in millions of dollars):

	2007	2006
Balance sheet		
Intangible assets: Goodwill	$6.7	$20.2
Income statement		
Goodwill Impairment	(13.5)	(−)

Accounting for Research and Development Costs

Accounting for research and development (R&D) costs is one of the most difficult issues the accounting profession has faced. R&D is the lifeblood of companies such as Research In Motion, Open Text, Nortel, and Bombardier because it is vital to the development of new products and processes. The cost of R&D activities is one of these companies' most valuable (intangible) assets.

Canada requires *development costs* meeting certain criteria to be capitalized and then expensed over the life of the product, while other countries require such costs to be expensed in the year incurred. Canada and most other countries require *research costs* to be expensed as incurred.

Some critics argue that R&D costs represent future benefits and should be capitalized, others agree with the present accounting standards, and still others think all R&D costs should be expensed.

Reporting Property, Plant, and Equipment Transactions on the Cash Flow Statement

Three main types of capital asset transactions appear on the cash flow statement:

- Acquisitions
- Sales
- Amortization

Objective

7 **Report** long-lived assets such as property, plant, and equipment transactions on the cash flow statement

Acquisitions and sales of property, plant, and equipment are *investing* activities. A company invests in property, plant, and equipment by paying cash or incurring a liability. The cash payments for buildings and equipment are investing activities that appear on the cash flow statement. The sale of property, plant, and equipment results in a cash receipt, as illustrated in Exhibit 7-9, which excerpts data from the cash flow statement of WestJet Airlines Ltd. The acquisitions, sales, and amortization of capital assets are denoted in colour (lines 5, 6, and 2).

EXHIBIT 7-9	Reporting Capital Asset Transactions on WestJet's Cash Flow Statement

WestJet Airlines Ltd.
Consolidated Cash Flow Statement (partial, adapted)
For the Year Ended December 31, 2007

	Amounts in millions
Operating Activities:	
1. Net earnings	$192.8
Adjustments to reconcile net income	
to cash provided by operating activities:	
2. Amortization	127.2
3. Other items (summarized)	221.1
4. Cash provided by operating activities	541.1
Investing Activities:	
5. Purchases of aircraft and other capital assets	(216.1)
6. Proceeds from capital asset disposals	15.8
7. Cash used in investing activities	(200.3)
Financing Activities:	
8. Cash used in financing activities	(59.3)
9. Cash flow from operating, investing and financing activities	281.5
10. Effect of exchange rate on cash	(5.5)
11. Net change in cash	276.0
12. Cash at beginning of year	377.5
13. Cash at end of year	$653.5

Let's examine the investing activities first. During the fiscal year ended December 31, 2007, WestJet paid $216.1 million for capital assets (line 5). WestJet received $15.8 million from the disposal of capital assets during the year. WestJet describes the cash received as "aircraft disposals" and "other property and equipment disposals." The $15.8 million is the amount of *cash* received from the disposal of the capital assets. A gain or loss on the sale of capital assets is not reported as an investing activity on the cash flow statement. The gain or loss is reported on the income statement.

WestJet's cash flow statement reports Amortization in the operating activities section (line 2). Observe that "Amortization" is listed as a positive item under Adjustments to Reconcile Net Income to Cash Provided by Operating Activities. You may be wondering why amortization appears on the cash flow statement. After all, amortization does not affect cash.

In this format, the operating activities section of the cash flow statement starts with net earnings (line 1) and reconciles to cash provided by operating activities (line 4). Amortization decreases net income in the same way that all other expenses do. But it does not affect cash. Amortization is therefore added back to net income to measure cash flow from operations. The add-back of amortization to net income offsets the earlier subtraction of the expense. The sum of net income plus amortization, therefore, helps to reconcile net income (on the accrual basis) to cash flow from operations (a cash-basis amount). We revisit this topic in the full context of the cash flow statement in Chapter 12.

Incidentally, WestJet's cash flows are strong. Operations generated $541.1 million of cash, and WestJet spent $216.1 million on new aircraft, property, and equipment. The company is not standing still; it is continuing to expand.

STOP & THINK

Test your ability to understand the cash flow statement.

1. How much cash did WestJet spend on purchases of aircraft and other capital assets during the year?
2. Suppose the book value of the capital assets that WestJet sold for $15.8 million was $58.6 million (a cost of $100.0 million minus accumulated amortization of $41.4 million). Write a sentence to explain why the sale transaction resulted in a loss for WestJet.
3. Where would WestJet report any gain or loss on the sale of the capital assets—on which financial statement, under which heading?

Answers:

1. WestJet spent $216.1 million.
2. The company sold for $15.8 million assets that had a book value of $58.6 million. The result of the sale was a loss of $42.8 million ($15.8 million received and $42.8 million given up).
3. Report the loss on the *income statement* under the heading *Non-operating income (expense)*.

DECISION GUIDELINES

PROPERTY, PLANT, AND EQUIPMENT AND RELATED EXPENSES

EnCana Corporation, like all other companies, must make some decisions about how to account for its property, plant, and equipment assets. Let's review some of these decisions.

Decision	Guidelines
Capitalize or expense a cost?	General rule: Capitalize all costs that provide *future* benefit for the business, such as a new luggage conveyor. Expense all costs that provide *no future* benefit (that maintain or restore to working order), such as a repair to a van.
Capitalize or expense:	
• Cost associated with a new asset?	Capitalize all costs that bring the asset to its intended use, including asset purchase price, transportation charges, and taxes paid to acquire the asset.
• Cost associated with an existing asset?	Capitalize only those costs that add to the asset's usefulness or to its useful life. Expense all other costs as maintenance or repairs.
• Interest cost incurred to finance the asset's construction or acquisition?	Capitalize the interest costs incurred to construct or to purchase and prepare a capital asset for use up to the point the asset is put into its intended service.
Which amortization method to use	
• For financial reporting?	Use the method that best matches amortization expense against the revenues produced by the asset. Most companies use the straight-line method.
• For income tax?	Use the method that results in the maximum deductions from taxable income, that is, the maximum amount of capital cost allowance permitted by the Canada Revenue Agency. A company can, and usually does, use different amortization methods for financial reporting and for income tax purposes. In Canada, this practice is considered both legal and ethical.
• How to account for natural resources?	Capitalize the asset's acquisition cost and all later costs that add to the natural resource's future benefit. Then record amortization expense, as computed by the units-of-production method.
• How to account for intangibles?	Capitalize acquisition cost and all later costs that add to the asset's future benefit. For intangibles with finite lives, record amortization expense. For intangibles with indefinite lives, do not record amortization. However, if an intangible asset's value is impaired, then record a loss in the amount of the decrease in the asset's fair value.

MyAccountingLab | **END-OF-CHAPTER SUMMARY PROBLEM**

Problem 1

The figures that follow appear in the *Answers to the Mid-Chapter Summary Problem*, Requirement 2, on page 328, for Big Rock Brewery Income Trust.

	Method A: Straight-Line			Method B: Double-Declining-Balance		
Year	Annual Amortization Expense	Accumulated Amortization	Book Value	Annual Amortization Expense	Accumulated Amortization	Book Value
Start			$44,000			$44,000
2007	$4,000	$4,000	40,000	$8,800	$8,800	35,200
2008	4,000	8,000	36,000	7,040	15,840	28,160
2009	4,000	12,000	32,000	5,632	21,472	22,528

Name: Big Rock Brewery Income Trust
Industry: Brewer of craft beers
Accounting Period: The years 2009, 2010, 2011

Required

Suppose the income tax authorities permitted a choice between these two amortization methods. Which method would Big Rock Brewery select for income tax purposes? Why?

Problem 2

Suppose Big Rock Brewery purchased the equipment described in the table on January 1, 2007. Management has amortized the equipment by using the double-declining-balance method. On July 1, 2009, Big Rock Brewery sold the equipment for $27,000 cash.

Required

Record amortization for 2009 and the sale of the equipment on July 1, 2009.

Answers

If a choice were permitted, the greater amortization expense leads to a lower net income and, therefore, a lower income tax expense. However, Canada's *Income Tax Act* does not allow amortization as a deduction for income tax purposes. Canada Revenue Agency does allow capital cost allowance to be deducted.

Problem 1

For tax purposes, most companies select an accelerated method because it results in the most amortization in the earliest years of the equipment's life. Accelerated amortization minimizes taxable income and income tax payments in the early years of the asset's life, thereby maximizing the business's cash at the earliest possible time. Big Rock Brewery would use the maximum rate allowed by the Canada Revenue Agency.

Problem 2

To record amortization to date of sale, and then the sale of the equipment:

Amortization expense must first be recorded for the portion of the year that the asset was used before it was sold.

The gain on the sale is the excess of the cash received over the net book value of the asset.

2009			
July 1	Amortization Expense—Equipment ($5,632 × 1/2 year)...........	2,816	
	Accumulated Amortization—Equipment.................................		2,816
	To update amortization.		
July 1	Cash..	27,000	
	Accumulated Amortization—Equipment ($15,840 + $2,816)...	18,656	
	Equipment		44,000
	Gain on Sale of Equipment..		1,656
	To record sale of equipment.		

REVIEW PROPERTY, PLANT, AND EQUIPMENT, NATURAL RESOURCES, AND INTANGIBLE ASSETS

QUICK CHECK (Answers are given on page 363.)

1. Argyle Corp. purchased a tract of land, a small office building, and some equipment for $1,500,000. The appraised value of the land was $850,000, the building $675,000, and the equipment $475,000. What is the cost of the land?

   a. $850,000
   b. $637,500
   c. $482,776
   d. None of the above

2. Which of the following statements about amortization is false?

   a. Recording amortization creates a fund to replace the asset at the end of its useful life.
   b. The cost of a capital asset minus accumulated amortization equals the asset's book value.
   c. Amortization is a process of allocating the cost of a capital asset over its useful life.
   d. Amortization is based on the matching principle because it matches the cost of the asset with the revenue generated over the asset's useful life.

Use the following data for Questions 3 through 6.

On August 1, 2008, Major Link Inc. purchased a new piece of equipment that cost $25,000. The estimated useful life is 5 years, and estimated residual value is $2,500.

3. Assume Major Link purchased the equipment on August 1, 2008. If Major Link uses the straight-line method for amortization, what is the amortization for the year ended December 31, 2008?

   a. $1,875
   b. $1,500
   c. $2,083
   d. $4,500

4. Assume Major Link purchased the equipment on January 1, 2008. If Major Link uses the straight-line method for amortization, what is the asset's book value at the end of 2009?

   a. $13,500
   b. $15,000
   c. $18,625
   d. $16,000

5. Assume Major Link purchased the equipment on January 1, 2008. If Major Link uses the double-declining-balance method of amortization, what is the amortization for the year ended December 31, 2009?

   a. $5,400
   b. $6,000
   c. $8,333
   d. $15,000

6. Return to Major Link's original purchase date of August 1, 2008. Assume that Major Link uses the straight-line method of amortization and sells the equipment for $11,500 on August 1, 2012. Based on the result of the sale of the equipment what benefit or cost will Major Link realize?

   a. $4,500
   b. $13,500
   c. $(9,000)
   d. $0

7. A company bought a new machine for $17,000 on January 1. The machine is expected to last 4 years and to have a residual value of $2,000. If the company uses the double-declining-balance method, how much will have been expensed at the end of year 2?

   a. $10,880
   b. $11,250
   c. $12,750
   d. $15,000

8. Which of the following is *not* a capital expenditure?

   a. The addition of a building wing
   b. A complete overhaul of an air-conditioning system
   c. A tune-up of a company vehicle
   d. Replacement of an old motor with a new one in a piece of equipment
   e. The cost of installing a piece of equipment

9. Which of the following assets is *not* subject to a decreasing book value through amortization?
   - **a.** Goodwill
   - **b.** Intangibles
   - **c.** Land improvements
   - **d.** Natural resources

10. Why would a business select an accelerated method of amortization for tax purposes?
   - **a.** CCA amortization follows a specific pattern of amortization.
   - **b.** Accelerated amortization generates a greater amount of amortization over the life of the asset than does straight-line amortization.
   - **c.** Accelerated amortization is easier to calculate because salvage value is ignored.
   - **d.** Accelerated amortization generates higher amortization expense immediately, and therefore lower tax payments in the early years of the asset's life.

11. A company purchases an oil well for $200,000. It estimates that the well contains 50,000 barrels, has a 10-year life, and has no salvage value. If the company extracts and sells 6,000 barrels during the first year, how much amortization expense should be recorded?
   - **a.** $16,000
   - **b.** $24,000
   - **c.** $20,000
   - **d.** $100,000

12. Which item among the following is *not* an intangible asset?
   - **a.** A trademark
   - **b.** A copyright
   - **c.** A patent
   - **d.** Goodwill
   - **e.** All of the above are intangible assets

ACCOUNTING VOCABULARY

accelerated amortization method An amortization method that writes off a relatively larger amount of the asset's cost nearer the start of its useful life than the straight-line method does. (p. 324)

amortizable cost The cost of a tangible asset minus its estimated residual value. (p. 322)

brand name A distinctive identification of a product or service. Also called a *trademark* or *trade name*. (p. 337)

capital cost allowance (CCA) Amortization allowed for income tax purposes by the Canada Revenue Agency; the rates allowed are called *capital cost allowance rates*. (p. 364)

capital expenditure Expenditure that increases an asset's capacity or efficiency or extends its useful life. Capital expenditures are debited to an asset account. Also called *betterments*. (p. 319)

copyright Exclusive right to reproduce and sell a book, musical composition, film, other work of art, or computer program. Issued by the federal government, copyrights extend 50 years beyond the author's life. (p. 336)

double-declining-balance (DDB) method An accelerated amortization method that computes annual amortization by multiplying the asset's decreasing book value by a constant percentage, which is two times the straight-line rate. (p. 325)

estimated residual value Expected cash value of an asset at the end of its useful life. Also called *scrap value* or *salvage value*. (p. 322)

estimated useful life Length of service that a business expects to get from an asset. May be expressed in years, units of output, kilometres, or other measures. (p. 322)

franchises and licenses Privileges granted by a private business or a government to sell a product or service in accordance with specified conditions. (p. 337)

goodwill Excess of the cost of an acquired company over the sum of the market values of its net assets (assets minus liabilities). (p. 337)

intangible asset An asset with no physical form, a special right to current and expected future benefits. (p. 316)

patent A federal government grant giving the holder the exclusive right for 20 years to produce and sell an invention. (p. 336)

straight-line (SL) method Amortization method in which an equal amount of amortization expense is assigned to each year of asset use. (p. 323)

trademark/trade name A distinctive identification of a product or service. Also called a *brand name*. (p. 337)

units-of-production (UOP) method Amortization method by which a fixed amount of amortization is assigned to each unit of output produced by the plant asset. (p. 324)

ASSESS YOUR PROGRESS

Make the grade with MyAccountingLab: The exercises and problems marked in red can be found on MyAccountingLab at www.myaccountinglab.com. You can practise them as often as you want, and they feature step by step guided solutions to help you find the right answer.

SHORT EXERCISES

S7-1 Examine the balance sheet of **EnCana Corporation** at the beginning of this chapter on page 315. Answer these questions about the company:

1. What is EnCana's largest category of assets?

2. If accumulated amortization is $23,956 million at December 31, 2007, what was the cost of property, plant, and equipment? Why is book value less than cost?

Cost and book value of a company's capital assets
(Obj. 1)

S7-2 Page 317 of this chapter lists the costs included for the acquisition of land. First is the purchase price of the land, which is obviously included in the cost of the land. The reasons for including the related costs are not so obvious. For example, property tax is ordinarily an expense, not part of the cost of an asset. State why the related costs listed on page 317 are included as part of the cost of the land. After the land is ready for use, will these related costs be capitalized or expensed?

Measuring the cost of a capital asset
(Obj. 1)

S7-3 Suppose you have purchased land, a building, and some equipment. At the time of the acquisition, the land has a current market value of $75,000, the building's market value is $60,000, and the equipment's market value is $15,000. Journalize the lump-sum purchase of the three assets for a total cost of $140,000. Assume you sign a note payable for this amount.

Lump-sum purchase of assets
(Obj. 1)

S7-4 Assume **WestJet** repaired one of its Boeing 737 aircraft at a cost of $0.8 million, which WestJet paid in cash. Further, assume the WestJet accountant erroneously capitalized this cost as part of the cost of the plane.

Show the effects of the accounting error on WestJet's income statement and balance sheet. To answer this question, determine whether revenues, total expenses, net income, total assets, and shareholders' equity would be overstated or understated by the accounting error.

Capitalizing versus expensing capital asset costs
(Obj. 1)

S7-5 Assume that at the beginning of 2009, **Porter Airlines** purchased a Bombardier Q400 aircraft at a cost of $25,000,000. Porter expects the plane to remain useful for 5 years (5,000,000 km) and to have a residual value of $5,000,000. Porter expects the plane to be flown 750,000 km the first year and 1,250,000 km each year during years 2 through 4, and 500,000 km the last year.

1. Compute Porter's first-year amortization on the plane using the following methods:
   a. Straight-line
   b. Units-of-production
   c. Double-declining-balance

2. Show the airplane's book value at the end of the first year under each amortization method.

Computing amortization by three methods—first year only
(Obj. 2)

S7-6 Use the assumed Porter Airlines data in Short Exercise 7-5 to compute Porter's fifth-year amortization on the plane using the following methods:
a. Straight-line
b. Units-of-production
c. Double-declining-balance

Computing amortization by three methods—final year only
(Obj. 2)

Selecting the method that permits the greatest deduction for income tax purposes
(Obj. 3)

S7-7 This exercise uses the assumed Porter Airlines data from Short Exercise 7-5. Assume Porter is trying to decide whether to use the maximum CCA allowed for income tax purposes.

1. Which amortization method offers the tax advantage for the first year? Describe the nature of the tax advantage.

2. How much income tax will Porter save for the first year of the airplane's use as compared with using the straight-line method? Canada Revenue Agency permits a maximum capital cost allowance rate of 25%. Porter's income tax rate is 35%. Ignore any earnings from investing the extra cash. Also ignore the 50% rule applicable to the year of acquisition.

Partial-year amortization
(Obj. 2)

S7-8 Assume that on September 30, 2008, **Swiss**, the national airline of Switzerland, purchased an Airbus aircraft at a cost of €40,000,000 (€ is the symbol for the euro). Swiss expects the plane to remain useful for 7 years (5,000,000 km) and to have a residual value of €5,000,000. Swiss expects the plane to be flown 500,000 km during the remainder of the first year ended December 31, 2008. Compute Swiss's amortization on the plane for the year ended December 31, 2008, using the following methods:

a. Straight-line
b. Units-of-production
c. Double-declining-balance

Which method would produce the highest net income for 2009? Which method produces the lowest net income?

Computing and recording amortization after a change in useful life of the asset
(Obj. 2)

S7-9 Canada's Wonderland paid $60,000 for a concession stand. Amortization was recorded by the straight-line method over 10 years with zero residual value. Suppose that after using the concession stand for 4 years, Canada's Wonderland determines that the asset will remain useful for only 3 more years. How will this affect amortization on the concession stand for year 5 by the straight-line method?

Recording a gain or loss on disposal under two amortization methods
(Obj. 4)

S7-10 On January 1, 2006, **Big Rock Brewery** purchased a van for $45,000. Big Rock expects the van to have a useful life of 5 years and a residual value of $5,000. The amortization method used was straight-line. On December 31, 2009, the van was sold for $15,000 cash.

1. What was the book value of the van on the date of sale?

2. Record the sale of the van on December 31, 2009.

Accounting for the amortization of a company's natural resources
(Obj. 5)

S7-11 Petro-Canada, the giant oil company, holds reserves of oil and gas assets. At the end of 2007, suppose the book value of Petro-Canada's oil sands totalled approximately $3,348 million, representing 276 million barrels of oil in the ground.

1. Which amortization method do Petro-Canada and other oil companies use to compute their annual amortization expense for the oil removed from the ground? Explain why this method is appropriate.

2. Suppose Petro-Canada removed 40 million barrels of oil during 2008. Record Petro-Canada's amortization expense for the year.

3. At December 31, 2007, Petro-Canada's Accumulated Amortization account stood at $1,011 million. If Petro-Canada did not add any new oil and gas reserves during 2008, what would be the book value of the company's oil reserves at December 31, 2008? Cite a specific figure from your answer to illustrate why exploration activities are so important for companies such as Petro-Canada.

Analyzing a company's goodwill
(Obj. 6)

S7-12 Consider the purchase of a supplier by **Canadian Tire**.

1. Suppose the fair value of the net assets at the date of purchase (February 1, 2007) had been $180.3 million. What would the goodwill cost have been if Canadian Tire had paid $200 million?

2. Explain how Canadian Tire will have been accounting for this goodwill up to February 1, 2009.

S7-13 This exercise summarizes the accounting for patents, which like copyrights, trademarks, and franchises, provide the owner with a special right or privilege. It also covers research costs.

Suppose Jaguar Automobiles Ltd. paid $500,000 to research a new global positioning system. Jaguar also paid $1,200,000 to acquire a patent on a new motor. After readying the motor for production, Jaguar's sales revenue for the first year totalled $6,500,000. Cost of goods sold was $3,200,000, and selling expenses were $300,000. All these transactions occurred during fiscal 2009. Jaguar expects the patent to have a useful life of three years.

Prepare Jaguar's income statement for the fiscal year ended December 31, 2009, complete with a heading.

Accounting for patents and research cost
(Obj. 6)

S7-14 You are reviewing the financial statements of Rising Yeast Co. During 2009, Rising Yeast purchased two other companies for $17 million. Also during fiscal 2009, Rising Yeast made capital expenditures of $2 million to expand its market share. During the year, the company sold operations, receiving cash of $25 million, and experienced a gain of $6 million on the disposal. Overall, Rising Yeast reported net income of $1 million during 2009. What would you expect the section for cash flows from investing activities on its cash flow statement for 2009 to report? What total amount for net cash provided by (used in) investing activities do you anticipate?

Reporting investing activities on the cash flow statement
(Obj. 7)

EXERCISES

E7-15 Moody Inc. purchased land, paying $150,000 cash as a down payment and signing a $100,000 note payable for the balance. Moody also had to pay delinquent property tax of $5,000, title insurance costing $3,000, and $25,000 to level the land and to remove an unwanted building. The company paid $70,000 to remove earth for the foundation and then constructed an office building at a cost of $3,750,000. It also paid $100,000 for a fence around the property, $10,500 for the company sign near the property entrance, and $18,000 for lighting of the grounds. Determine the cost of the company's land, land improvements, and building.

Determining the cost of capital assets
(Obj. 1)

E7-16 Assume Trois Cuisines Manufacturing bought three machines in a $100,000 lump-sum purchase. An independent appraiser valued the machines as follows:

Allocating costs to assets acquired in a lump-sum purchase; disposing of a capital asset
(Obj. 1, 4)

Machine No.	Appraised Value
1	$27,000
2	45,000
3	36,000

Trois Cuisines paid one-third in cash and signed a note payable for the remainder. What is each machine's individual cost? Immediately after making this purchase, Trois Cuisines sold machine 2 for its appraised value. What is the result of the sale? Round to three decimal places.

E7-17 Assume **Hershey Chocolate Ltd.** purchased a piece of manufacturing machinery. Classify each of the following expenditures as a capital expenditure or an immediate expense related to machinery: (a) sales tax paid on the purchase price, (b) transportation and insurance while machinery is in transit from seller to buyer, (c) purchase price, (d) installation, (e) training of personnel for initial operation of the machinery, (f) special reinforcement to the machinery platform, (g) income tax paid on income earned from the sale of products manufactured by the machinery, (h) major overhaul to extend useful life by 3 years, (i) ordinary repairs to keep the machinery in good working order, (j) lubrication of the machinery before it is placed in service, and (k) periodic lubrication after the machinery is placed in service. What criteria differentiated a capital expenditure from an immediate expense?

Distinguishing capital expenditures from expenses
(Obj. 1)

Measuring, amortizing, and reporting capital assets
(Obj. 1, 2)

E7-18 During 2009, Roberts Inc. paid $200,000 for land and built a restaurant in Collingwood, Ontario. Prior to construction, the City of Collingwood charged Roberts Inc. $2,250 for a building permit, which it paid. Roberts Inc. also paid $20,000 for architect's fees. The construction cost of $700,000 was financed by a long-term note payable issued on January 1, 2009, with interest cost of $29,000 paid at December 31, 2009. The building was completed September 30, 2009. Roberts Inc. will amortize the building by the straight-line method over 25 years, with an estimated residual value of $60,000.

1. Journalize transactions for
   a. Purchase of the land
   b. All the costs chargeable to the building, in a single entry
   c. Amortization on the building

   Explanations are not required.
2. Report this transaction in the capital assets on the company's balance sheet at December 31, 2009.
3. What will Roberts Inc.'s income statement for the year ended December 31, 2009, report for the building?

Determining amortization amounts by three methods
(Obj. 2, 3)

E7-19 Assume you have a flower shop and you bought a delivery van for $30,000. You expect the van to remain in service for 3 years (150,000 km). At the end of its useful life, you estimate that the van's residual value will be $3,000. You estimate the van will travel 40,000 km the first year, 60,000 km the second year, and 50,000 km the third year. Prepare an estimate of the *amortization expense* per year for the van under the three amortization methods. Show your computations.

Which method do you think tracks the useful life cost on the van most closely? Would you use the maximum CCA for income tax purposes? The Canada Revenue Agency's maximum capital cost allowance rate is 30%. Explain in detail which method you choose.

Reporting capital assets, amortization, and investing cash flow
(Obj. 1, 2, 7)

E7-20 In January 2009, suppose a **Starbucks** franchise in Regina purchased a building, paying $50,000 cash and signing a $100,000 note payable. The franchise paid another $50,000 to remodel the facility. Equipment and store fixtures cost $50,000; dishes and supplies—a current asset—were obtained for $10,000.

The franchise is amortizing the building over 25 years by the straight-line method, with estimated residual value of $50,000. The equipment and store fixtures will be replaced at the end of 5 years; these assets are being amortized by the double-declining-balance method, with zero residual value. At the end of the first year, the franchise has dishes and supplies worth $2,000.

Show what the franchise will report for supplies, capital assets, and cash flows at the end of the first year on its

• Income statement
• Balance sheet
• Cash flow statement (investing only)

   Show all computations.
   Note: The purchase of dishes and supplies is an operating cash flow because supplies are a current asset.

Comparing amortization methods for income tax purposes
(Obj. 3)

E7-21 On June 30, 2009, Baie Comeau Products Ltd. paid $210,000 for equipment that is expected to have a 7-year life. In this industry, the residual value of equipment is approximately 10% of the asset's cost. Baie Comeau Products Ltd.'s revenues for the year are $100,000, and expenses total $60,000 before amortization.

Determine the extra amount of cash that Baie Comeau Products can invest by using CCA versus straight-line and claiming less than maximum CCA for the year ended December 31, 2009. The *Income Tax Act* CCA rate is 20%. The income tax rate is 30%. Apply the half-year rule.

E7-22 Assume **The Salvation Army** purchased a building for $900,000 and amortized it on a straight-line basis over 30 years. The estimated residual value was $100,000. After using the building for 10 years, the Salvation Army realized that the building will remain useful for only 10 more years. Starting with the 11th year, the Salvation Army began amortizing the building over the newly revised total life of 20 years and decreased the estimated residual value to $75,000. What is the effect on amortization expense on the building for years 11 and 12?

Changing a capital asset's useful life
(Obj. 2)

E7-23 Assume that on January 2, 2008, a **Pizza Hut** franchise purchased fixtures for $15,000 cash, expecting the fixtures to remain in service 5 years. The shop has amortized the fixtures on a double-declining-balance basis, with $1,000 estimated residual value. On June 30, 2009, Pizza Hut sold the fixtures for $5,000 cash. Record both the amortization expense on the fixtures for 2009 and then the sale of the fixtures. Apart from your journal entry, also show how to compute the gain or loss on the Pizza Hut's disposal of these fixtures.

Analyzing the effect of a sale of a capital asset; DDB amortization
(Obj. 4)

E7-24 Bison Transport is a large trucking company that operates from Ontario to British Columbia in Canada and in the United States. Bison uses the units-of-production (UOP) method to amortize its trucks because its managers believe UOP amortization best measures wear and tear.

Measuring a capital asset's cost, using UOP amortization, and trading in a used asset
(Obj. 1, 2, 4)

Bison Transport trades in its trucks often to keep driver morale high and maximize fuel efficiency. Assume that in 2007, the company acquired a tractor-trailer rig costing $280,000 and expected it to remain in service for 5 years or 1,000,000 km. Estimated residual value would be $40,000. During 2007, the truck was driven 130,000 km; during 2008, 180,000 km; and during 2009, 180,000 km. After 90,000 km in 2010, the company traded in the tractor-trailer rig for a new rig, receiving a trade-in credit equal to the book value of the tractor-trailer rig purchased in 2007. If Bison Transport paid cash of $150,000, determine the cost of the new truck. Journal entries are not required.

E7-25 Suppose you are part of a group who paid $506,000 for the right to extract ore from a 250,000-tonne mineral deposit. In addition to the purchase price, the group also paid a $1,000 filing fee, a $3,000 licence fee, and $60,000 for a geological survey of the property. Because the group purchased the rights to the minerals only, it expects the asset to have zero residual value when fully depleted. Assume the group incorporated and during the first year of production your group removed 50,000 tonnes of ore. Make journal entries to record the (a) purchase of the mineral rights, (b) payment of fees and other costs, and (c) amortization for first-year production. What will this mineral asset's book value be on the balance sheet at the end of the year? Explain the method of amortization you chose.

Recording natural resource assets and amortization
(Obj. 5)

E7-26 Holze Music Company purchased for $600,000 a patent for a new sound system. Although it gives legal protection for 20 years, the patent is expected to provide the company with a competitive advantage for only 6 years. Make journal entries to record (a) the purchase of the patent and (b) amortization for year 1.

Recording intangibles, amortization, and a change in the asset's useful life
(Obj. 6)

After using the patent for 2 years, Holze Music Company's research director learns at a professional meeting that BOSE is designing a more powerful system. On the basis of this new information, Holze Music Company determines that the patent's total useful life is only 4 years. Record amortization for year 3.

E7-27 Research In Motion (RIM), the manufacturer of BlackBerry smartphones, recently reported in the Cash Flow Statement and Notes to the Financial Statements in its annual report that it had made acquisitions of U.S.$6.2 million. Assume the balance sheet reported an increase in goodwill for the year in the amount of U.S.$4.5 million.

Business acquisitions and cash flows
(Obj. 6, 7)

❚ *Required*

1. What is the definition of goodwill?
2. Explain the meaning of (a) the $6.2 million that RIM reported on the cash flow statement and (b) the $4.5 million increase in goodwill on the balance sheet.
3. RIM's income statement and cash flow statement do not show any charges for amortization of goodwill during the year. Explain the reason for the lack of charges.

Measuring and recording goodwill
(Obj. 6)

E7-28 Assume that Google paid $18 million to purchase MySpace.com. Assume further that MySpace had the following summarized data at the time of the Google acquisition (amounts in millions U.S.$).

Assets		Liabilities and Equity	
Current assets	$10	Total liabilities	$24
Long-term assets	20	Shareholders' equity	6
	$30		$30

MySpace's long-term assets had a current value of only $15 million.

▌*Required*

1. Compute the cost of the goodwill purchased by Google.
2. Record the purchase of MySpace.
3. Explain how Google will account for goodwill in the future.

Interpreting a cash flow statement
(Obj. 7)

E7-29 The following items are excerpted from an annual report of **RONA Inc.**, one of the leading retailers and distributors of hardware, home improvement, and gardening products in Canada:

RONA Inc.
Consolidated Cash Flow Statement (Partial, Adapted)
For the Year Ended December 30, 2007

	Amounts in millions
Cash flow from operating activities:	
Net income	$185.1
Noncash items:	
Amortization	90.9
Cash flow from investing activities:	
Fixed assets	($233.6)
Other investments	(0.6)
Disposal of assets	17.0

▌*Required*

1. Why is amortization listed on the cash flow statement?
2. Explain in detail each investing activity.

Reporting cash flows for property and equipment
(Obj. 7)

E7-30 Assume Flowers to Go Ltd., a chain of flower shops, completed the following transactions. For each transaction, show what the company would report for investing activities on its cash flow statement. Show negative amounts in parentheses.

a. Sold a building for $600,000. The building had cost $1,000,000, and at the time of the sale its accumulated amortization totalled $400,000.
b. Lost a store building in a fire. The warehouse cost $300,000 and had accumulated amortization of $180,000. The insurance proceeds received were $120,000.
c. Renovated a store at a cost of $400,000, paying cash.
d. Purchased store fixtures for $60,000. The fixtures are expected to remain in service for 5 years and then be sold for $10,000. Flowers to Go uses the straight-line amortization method.

CHALLENGE EXERCISES

Units-of-production amortization
(Obj. 2)

E7-31 Good Life Clubs purchased exercise equipment at a cost of $100,000 each. In addition, Good Life paid $2,000 for a special platform on which to stabilize the equipment for use.

Freight costs of $2,500 to ship the equipment were paid by the equipment supplier. Good Life will amortize the equipment by the units-of-production method, based on an expected useful life of 50,000 hours of exercise. The estimated residual value of the equipment is $10,000. How many hours of usage can Good Life expect from the equipment if budgeted amortization expense is $10,304 for the year?

E7-32 Collicutt Energy Services Ltd. of Calgary, Alberta, reported the following for land, buildings, and equipment (in millions):

Determining the sale price of property and equipment **(Obj. 4)**

	December 31	
	2007	2006
Capital assets (land, buildings, and equipment)..........................	$544.1	$575.1
Accumulated amortization...	(195.1)	(209.4)

During 2007, Collicutt Energy paid $74.2 million for new property and equipment. Amortization for the year totalled $38.1 million. During 2007, Collicutt sold property and equipment for $20.2 million. How much was Collicutt's gain or loss on the sale of the property and equipment?

E7-33 Rindy Inc. has a popular line of beaded jewellery. Rindy Inc. reported net earnings of $21,000 for 2008. Amortization expense for furniture, fixtures, equipment, and automotive totalled $1,000. Rindy amortizes furniture, fixtures, equipment, and automotive on a straight-line basis over 5 years and assumes no residual value. The company's income tax rate is 25%.

Determining net income after a change in amortization method **(Obj. 2)**

Assume that Rindy's furniture, fixtures, equipment, and automotive are 3 years old and that Rindy switches over to double-declining-balance (DDB) amortization at the start of fiscal 2009. Further, assume that fiscal 2009 is expected to be the same as fiscal 2008 except for the change in amortization method. How much net income can Rindy expect to earn during fiscal 2009?

E7-34 Air New Zealand (ANZ) is a Star Alliance member airline. Assume that early in 2009, ANZ purchased equipment at a cost of $200,000 (NZ). Management expects the equipment to remain in service 4 years and estimated residual value to be negligible. ANZ uses the straight-line amortization method. Through an accounting error, ANZ expensed the entire cost of the equipment at the time of purchase.

Capitalizing versus expensing; measuring the effect of an error **(Obj. 1)**

❚ *Required*

Prepare a schedule to show the overstatement or understatement in the following items at the end of each year over the 5-year life of the equipment. Ignore income taxes.

1. Total current assets   2. Equipment, net   3. Net income   4. Owners' equity

QUIZ

Test your understanding of accounting for property, plant, and equipment, natural resources, and intangibles by answering the following questions. Select the best choice from among the possible answers given.

Q7-35 A capital expenditure
a. Is expensed immediately
b. Records additional capital
c. Adds to an asset
d. Is a credit like capital (owners' equity)

Q7-36 Which of the following items should be accounted for as a capital expenditure?
a. Taxes paid in conjunction with the purchase of office equipment
b. The monthly rental cost of an office building
c. Costs incurred to repair leaks in the building roof
d. Maintenance fees paid with funds provided by the company's capital

Q7-37 Suppose you buy land for $3,000,000 and spend $1,000,000 to develop the property. You then divide the land into lots as follows:

Category	Sale price per lot
10 Hilltop lots..	$500,000
10 Valley lots...	300,000

How much did each hilltop lot cost you?

a. $171,429   c. $250,000
b. $228,571   d. $400,000

Q7-38 Which statement about amortization is false?
a. Amortization is a process of allocating the cost of an asset to expense over its useful life.
b. Amortization should not be recorded in years that the market value of the asset has increased.
c. A major objective of amortization accounting is to match the cost of using an asset with the revenues it helps to generate.
d. Obsolescence as well as physical wear and tear should be considered when determining the period over which an asset should be amortized.

Q7-39 A business would choose to use CCA for tax purposes for which of the following reasons?
a. It is easier to calculate.
b. The useful life of the asset is allocated appropriately.
c. Taxable income is lowest in the early years of the asset's life.
d. The Canada Revenue Agency requires this method.

Q7-40 The Blossom Shoppe's business activity fluctuates over its fiscal year, with December being its busiest month. Which method of amortization would be most appropriate for its delivery van?
a. Straight-line   c. Units of production
b. Declining-balance   d. Some other method

Q7-41 Kramer Company failed to record amortization of equipment. How does this omission affect Kramer's financial statements?
a. Net income is overstated, and assets are understated.
b. Net income is understated, and assets are understated.
c. Net income is understated, and assets are overstated.
d. Net income is overstated, and assets are overstated.

Q7-42 Jack's Stereo Inc. uses the double-declining-balance method for amortization on its computers. Which item is not needed to compute amortization for the first year?
a. Original cost   c. Expected useful life in years
b. Estimated residual value   d. All the above are needed

Q7-43 Which of the following costs is reported on a company's income statement?
a. Accumulated amortization   c. Accounts payable
b. Land   d. Amortization expense

Q7-44 Which of the following items is reported on the balance sheet? (Challenge)
a. Net sales revenue   c. Gain on disposal of equipment
b. Accumulated amortization   d. Cost of goods sold

Q7-45 Which of the following transactions does not appear on a cash flow statement?
a. Purchase of plant, property, and equipment
b. Accumulated amortization
c. Cash receipts from sale of property, plant, and equipment
d. Amortization expense

Q7-46 An intangible asset is different from other assets for which of the following reasons?
a. They have special rights to current and expected future benefits.
b. They do not become obsolete.
c. They have no physical form.
d. They are not amortized.

Q7-47 Your self-storage company has purchased a moving company for $400,000. The fair value of the moving company's net assets is $325,000. How do you record the $75,000 difference?
a. As an expense on the income statement
b. As a property, plant, and equipment cost
c. As a long-term asset named goodwill
d. None of the above

Q7-48 A company has purchased the rights to mineral assets of approximately 500,000 tonnes of ore valued at $850,000 and has paid remediation costs of $150,000. The company expects to maintain mining operations over 5 years. The correct amortization for this asset would be which of the following?
a. Straight-line over 5 years
b. Units-of-production method based on a capital asset of $850,000
c. Declining-balance method based on a capital asset of $1,000,000
d. Units-of-production method based on a capital asset of $1,000,000

Q7-49 Suppose **The Globe and Mail** paid $1 million for a rural newspaper in Ontario 3 years ago. The newspaper's assets were valued at $1,000,000 and its liabilities at $150,000. The company recorded $150,000 as goodwill at the time of the purchase. What *amortization* expense will be recorded for the current year?
a. $30,000 based on straight-line amortization over 5 years
b. No amortization, as review of the goodwill indicates there has been reduction in its value
c. No amortization, as the goodwill was fully expensed in the year of purchase
d. None of the above

PROBLEMS

(GROUP A)

P7-50A Assume Milne's Moving & Storage Ltd. (MMS) of Regina, Saskatchewan, incurred the following costs in acquiring land, making land improvements, and constructing and furnishing its own storage warehouse:

Identifying the elements of a capital asset's cost
(Obj. 1, 2)

a.	Purchase price of 4 acres of land, including an old building that will be used for an office (land market value is $320,000, building market value is $80,000)......	$350,000
b.	Landscaping (additional dirt and earth moving)...	8,100
c.	Fence around the land	31,600
d.	Lawyer fee for title search on the land...	1,000
e.	Delinquent real estate taxes on the land to be paid by MMS...................................	7,500
f.	Company signs at front of the company property..	3,400
g.	Building permit for the warehouse...	1,500
h.	Architect fee for the design of the warehouse	24,500
i.	Masonry, carpentry, roofing, and other labour to construct the warehouse...............	920,000
j.	Renovation of the office building	50,200
k.	Interest cost on construction loan for warehouse	9,700
l.	Landscaping (trees and shrubs)..	8,200
m.	Parking lot, concrete walks, and lights on the property...	57,600
n.	Concrete, wood, and other materials used in the construction of the warehouse.....	234,300
o.	Supervisory salary of construction supervisor (85% to warehouse, 5% to land improvements, 10% to office building)	60,000
p.	Office furniture..	115,700
q.	Transportation and installation of furniture...	2,300

Assume MMS amortizes buildings over 40 years, land improvements over 20 years, and furniture over 8 years, all on a straight-line basis with zero residual value.

❙ Required

1. Set up columns for Land, Land Improvements, Warehouse, Office Building, and Furniture. Show how to account for each of MSM's costs by listing the cost under the correct account. Determine the total cost of each asset.

2. Assuming that all construction was complete and the assets were placed in service on September 1, 2009, record amortization for the year ended December 31, 2009. Round to the nearest dollar.

3. Identify the management issues included in this problem and what effect they have on business operations.

Recording capital asset transactions; reporting on the balance sheet
(Obj. 2)

P7-51A Lifestyle Lighting Ltd. reported the following on its balance sheet at December 31, 2008:

Capital assets, at cost:	
Land	$ 150,000
Buildings	400,000
Less Accumulated amortization	(87,500)
Equipment	600,000
Less Accumulated amortization	(260,000)

In early July 2009, Lifestyle Lighting expanded operations and purchased additional equipment at a cost of $100,000. The company amortizes buildings by the straight-line method over 20 years with residual value of $50,000. Due to obsolescence, the equipment has a useful life of only 10 years and is being amortized by the double-declining-balance method with zero residual value.

❙ Required

1. Journalize Lifestyle Lighting Ltd.'s capital asset purchase and amortization transactions for 2009.

2. Report capital assets on the December 31, 2009, balance sheet.

Recording capital asset transactions, exchanges, and changes in useful life
(Obj. 1, 2, 4)

P7-52A Assume that Inter-Provincial Transport Ltd.'s balance sheet includes the following assets under Property, Plant, and Equipment: Land, Buildings, and Motor-Carrier Equipment. Inter-Provincial has a separate accumulated amortization account for each of these assets except land. Further, assume that Inter-Provincial completed the following transactions:

2009		
Jan.	2	Traded in motor-carrier equipment with accumulated amortization of $67,000 (cost of $130,000) for similar new equipment with a cash price of $176,000. Inter-Provincial received a trade-in allowance of $70,000 on the old equipment and paid $106,000 in cash.
July	3	Sold a building that had cost $650,000 and had accumulated amortization of $145,000 through December 31 of the preceding year. Amortization is computed on a straight-line basis. The building had a 40-year useful life and a residual value of $250,000. Inter-Provincial received $100,000 cash and a $400,000 note receivable.
Oct.	29	Purchased land and a building for a single price of $420,000. An independent appraisal valued the land at $150,000 and the building at $300,000.
Dec.	31	Recorded amortization as follows:
		Motor-carrier equipment has an expected useful life of 6 years and an estimated residual value of 5% of cost. Amortization is computed on the double-declining-balance method.
		Amortization on buildings is computed by the straight-line method. The new building carries a 40-year useful life and a residual value equal to 10% of its cost.

Required

Record the transactions in Inter-Provincial Transport Ltd.'s journal.

P7-53A The board of directors of Special Services, a not-for-profit organization, is reviewing its 2009 annual report. A new board member—a nurse with little business experience—questions the accountant about the amortization amounts. The nurse wonders why amortization expense has decreased from $200,000 in 2007 to $184,000 in 2008 to $172,000 in 2009. She states that she could understand the decreasing annual amounts if the company had been disposing of buildings each year, but that has not occurred. Further, she notes that growth in the city is increasing the values of company buildings. Why is the company recording amortization when the property values are increasing?

Explaining the concept of amortization
(Obj. 2)

Required

Write a paragraph or two to explain the concept of amortization to the nurse and to answer her questions.

P7-54A On January 3, 2009, B.W. Soffer Inc. paid $224,000 for a computer system. In addition to the basic purchase price, the company paid a setup fee of $6,200, $6,700 sales tax, and $3,100 for special installation. Management estimates that the computer will remain in service for 5 years and have a residual value of $20,000. The computer will process 50,000 documents the first year, decreasing annually by 5,000 during each of the next 4 years (that is, 45,000 documents in 2008, 40,000 documents in 2009, and so on). In trying to decide which amortization method to use, the company president has requested an amortization schedule for each of three amortization methods (straight-line, units-of-production, and double-declining-balance).

Computing amortization by three methods and the cash-flow advantage of accelerated amortization for tax purposes
(Obj. 2, 3)

Required

1. Prepare an amortization schedule for each of the three amortization methods listed, showing asset cost, amortization expense, accumulated amortization, and asset book value.

2. B.W. Soffer Inc. reports to shareholders and creditors in the financial statements using the amortization method that maximizes reported income in the early years of asset use. For income tax purposes, however, the company uses the amortization method that minimizes income. Consider the first year B.W. Soffer Inc. uses the computer system. Identify the amortization method that meets the company's objectives. Discuss the advantages of each amortization method.

3. Assume that cash provided by operations before income tax is $150,000 for the computer system's first year. The income tax rate is 25%. For the method chosen by B.W. Soffer Inc. and for tax identified in Requirement 2, compare the net income and cash provided by operations (cash flow). Show which method gives the net-income advantage and which method gives the cash-flow advantage. (For purposes of this problem, assume the CCA rate of 30% and ignore the 50% CCA rule for year of purchase.)

P7-55A The **Canadian Red Cross** is the leading humanitarian organization through which people voluntarily demonstrate their caring. The excerpts that follow are adapted from The Canadian Red Cross financial statements for 2007.

Analyzing capital asset transactions from a company's financial statements
(Obj. 2, 4, 7)

Amounts in thousands	March 31	
Balance Sheet	2007	2006
Assets		
Total current assets	$277,631	$261,015
Capital assets	68,406	61,225
Less accumulated amortization	(26,909)	(22,725)
Long-term investments	108,302	147,165

Consolidated Cash Flow Statement	For the Year Ended March 31	
	2007	2006
Operating excess of revenues over expense	$13,068	$15,321
Noncash items affecting net income:		
Amortization	4,184	3,748
Cash flows from investing activities:		
Additions to capital assets	(7,781)	(8,623)
Reduction of (additions to) long-term investments	38,863	(96,316)

❚ Required

1. How much was the Canadian Red Cross's cost of capital assets at March 31, 2007? How much was the book value of capital assets? Show computations.

2. The financial statements give four pieces of evidence that the Canadian Red Cross purchased capital assets and sold long-term investments during 2007. What is the evidence?

3. Prepare T-accounts for Capital Assets, Accumulated Amortization, and Long-term Investments. Then show all the activity in these accounts during 2007. Label each increase or decrease and give its dollar amount.

4. Why is amortization added to net income on the cash flow statement?

Accounting for intangibles, natural resources, and the related expenses
(Obj. 5, 6)

P7-56A Part 1. Sobeys Inc.'s balance sheet reports the asset Cost in Excess of Net Assets of Purchased Businesses. Assume that Sobeys acquired another company, which carried these figures:

Book value of net assets	$3.8 million
Market value of assets	4.1 million

❚ Required

1. What is the term used in Canadian financial reporting for the asset Cost in Excess of Net Assets of Purchased Businesses?

2. Record Sobeys's purchase of the other company for $5.3 million cash.

3. Assume that Sobeys determined that the asset Cost in Excess of Net Assets of Purchased Businesses increased in value by $800,000. How would this transaction be recorded? Then, suppose Cost in Excess of Net Assets of Purchased Businesses decreased in value by $800,000. How would this transaction be recorded? Discuss the basis for your decision in each case.

Part 2. Luscar Ltd. produces more than 50% of Canada's total coal. Suppose Luscar paid $2.6 million cash for a lease giving the firm the right to work a mine that contained an estimated 200,000 tonnes of coal. Assume Luscar treats the lease as a separate operation called Coal Lease. Assume that the company paid $60,000 to remove unwanted buildings from the land and $70,000 to prepare the surface for mining. Further assume that Luscar signed a $30,000 note payable to a landscaping company to return the land surface to its original condition after the lease ends. During the first year, Luscar removed 40,000 tonnes of coal, which it sold on account for $300/tonne. Operating expenses for the first year totalled $258,000, all paid in cash. In addition, the company accrued income tax at the tax rate of 38%.

❚ Required

1. As the CFO, how would you expect that Luscar's transactions for the year relating to the Coal Lease would be recorded?

2. Prepare the company's income statement for the Coal Lease operations for the first year. Evaluate the profitability of the coal operations.

3. Explain what items were capitalized and why. Discuss your choice of amortization method.

P7-57A At the end of 2008, Geothermal Heating Ltd. had total assets of $17.4 million and total liabilities of $9.2 million. Included among the assets were property, plant, and equipment with a cost of $4.8 million and accumulated amortization of $3.4 million.

Reporting capital asset transactions on the cash flow statement
(Obj. 7)

Assume that Geothermal Heating completed the following selected transactions during 2009. The company earned total revenues of $26.5 million and incurred total expenses of $21.3 million, which included amortization of $1.7 million. During the year, Geothermal Heating paid $1.4 million for new equipment and sold old capital assets for $0.3 million. The cost of the assets sold was $0.8 million, and their accumulated amortization was $0.4 million.

I *Required*

1. Explain how to determine whether Geothermal Heating had a gain or loss on the sale of old capital assets during the year. What was the amount of the gain or loss, if any?
2. How will Geothermal Heating report property, plant, and equipment on the balance sheet at December 31, 2009, after all the year's activity? What will be the book value of capital assets?
3. How will Geothermal Heating report operating activities and investing activities on its cash flow statement for 2009? The company's cash flow statement starts with net income.

(GROUP B)

P7-58B McMillan Tire Inc. operates in several provinces. The head office incurred the following costs in acquiring land and a building, making land improvements, and constructing and furnishing a garage showroom.

Identifying the elements of a capital asset's cost
(Obj. 1, 2)

a. Purchase price of land, including a building that will be enlarged to be a warehouse (land market value is $150,000; building market value is $50,000) ..	$180,000
b. Fence around the land	26,000
c. Company signs near front and rear approaches to the company property	25,000
d. Title insurance on the land acquisition...................	1,200
e. Renovation of the warehouse	21,300
f. Landscaping (additional dirt and earth moving)................	3,550
g. Architect fee for the design of the garage/showroom	45,000
h. Building permit for the building	200
i. Delinquent real estate taxes on the land to be paid by McMillan	3,700
j. Concrete, wood, and other materials used in the construction of the garage/showroom................	322,000
k. Supervisory salary of construction supervisor (90% to garage/showroom; 6% to land improvements, and 4% to building renovation)	55,000
l. Landscaping (trees and shrubs)................	5,350
m. Masonry, carpentry, roofing, and other labour to construct the garage/showroom ...	234,000
n. Lights for the parking lot, walkways, and company signs................	8,900
o. Parking lots and concrete walks on the property................	17,450
p. Interest cost on construction loan for garage/showroom	3,300
q. Installation of equipment................	8,000
r. Equipment for the garage/showroom	80,000

McMillan Tire amortizes buildings over 40 years, land improvements over 10 years, and equipment over 8 years, all on a straight-line basis with zero residual value.

I *Required*

1. Determine the total cost of each asset. Set up columns for Land, Land Improvements, Garage/Showroom, Warehouse, and Equipment. Decide how to account for each of McMillan's costs by listing the cost under the correct account.
2. All construction was complete and the assets were placed in service on March 29. Record amortization for the year ended December 31. Round figures to the nearest dollar.
3. Identify the issues of this problem, and discuss how your decisions would affect the results of McMillan Tire Inc.

Recording capital asset transactions; reporting on the balance sheet
(Obj. 2)

P7-59B Moreau Lock & Key Ltd. has a hefty investment in security equipment, as reported in the company's balance sheet at December 31, 2008:

Property, plant, and equipment, at cost:	
Land	$ 200,000
Buildings...	310,000
Less Accumulated amortization...	(40,000)
Security equipment	620,000
Less Accumulated amortization...	(370,000)

In early October 2009, Moreau Lock & Key purchased additional security equipment at a cost of $80,000. The company amortizes buildings by the straight-line method over 20 years with residual value of $70,000. Due to obsolescence, security equipment has a useful life of only 8 years and is being amortized by the double-declining-balance method with zero residual value.

❙ Required

1. How will Moreau Lock & Key's capital asset purchase be recorded? What will the 2009 amortization expense be?
2. Report capital assets on the company's December 31, 2009, balance sheet.

Recording capital asset transactions, exchanges and changes in useful life
(Obj. 1, 2, 4)

P7-60B Schmaltz Cable Company's balance sheet reports the following assets under Property, Plant, and Equipment: Land, Buildings, Office Furniture, Communication Equipment, and Televideo Equipment. The company has a separate accumulated amortization account for each of these assets except land. Assume that Schmaltz Cable completed the following transactions:

2009		
Jan.	4	Traded in communication equipment with accumulated amortization of $85,000 (cost of $96,000) for similar new equipment with a quoted price of $118,000. The seller gave a trade-in allowance of $18,000 on the old equipment, and Schmaltz Cable paid $100,000 in cash.
June	30	Sold a building that had cost $495,000 and had accumulated amortization of $255,000 through December 31 of the preceding year. Amortization is computed on a straight-line basis. The building has a 40-year useful life and a residual value of $95,000. The company received $50,000 cash and a $250,000 note receivable.
Nov.	4	Purchased used communication and televideo equipment from Rogers Cable Company. Total cost was $80,000 paid in cash. An independent appraisal valued the communication equipment at $75,000 and the televideo equipment at $25,000.
Dec.	31	Amortization is recorded as follows:
		Equipment is amortized by the double-declining-balance method over a 5-year life with zero residual value. Amortization is recorded separately on the equipment purchased on January 4 and on November 4.

❙ Required

If Schmaltz Cable has recorded these transactions correctly, what should your review of their records show?

Explaining the concept of amortization
(Obj. 2)

P7-61B The board of directors of the **Canadian Red Cross** is having its regular quarterly meeting. Accounting policies are on the agenda, and amortization is being discussed. A new board member, a social worker, has some strong opinions about two aspects of amortization policy. The new board member argues that amortization must be coupled with a fund to replace company assets. Otherwise, there is no substance to amortization, he argues. He also challenges the three-year estimated life over which the Canadian Red Cross is amortizing association computers. He notes that the computers will last much longer and should be amortized over at least 10 years.

❚ Required

Write a paragraph or two to explain the concept of amortization to the new board member and to answer his arguments.

P7-62B On January 2, 2009, Yuki Sporting Goods Ltd. purchased equipment at a cost of $63,000. Before placing the equipment in service, the company spent $2,200 for delivery, $4,000 to customize the equipment, and $800 for installation. Management estimates that the equipment will remain in service for 6 years and have a residual value of $16,000. The equipment can be expected to brand 18,000 pieces in each of the first 4 years and 14,000 pieces in each of the next 2 years. In trying to decide which amortization method to use, George Yuki requests an amortization schedule for each method (straight-line, units-of-production, and double-declining-balance).

Computing amortization by three methods and the cash-flow advantage of accelerated amortization for tax purposes
(Obj. 2, 3)

❚ Required

1. Prepare an amortization schedule for each of the amortization methods listed, showing asset cost, amortization expense, accumulated amortization, and asset book value.

2. Yuki Sporting Goods reports to its banker in the financial statements using the amortization method that maximizes reported income in the early years of asset use. For income tax purposes, however, the company uses maximum CCA, the method that minimizes income. Consider the first year that Yuki Sporting Goods uses the equipment. Identify the amortization method that meets the company objectives. Explain your choice. (The *Income Tax Act* permits maximum capital cost allowance for computers of 30%. Ignore CRA's 50% rule in year of purchase.)

3. Cash provided by operations before income tax is $100,000 for the equipment's first year. The corporate income tax rate is 25%. For the two methods identified in Requirement 2, compare the net income and cash provided by operations (cash flow). Identify the method which gives the net-income advantage and identify the method which gives the cash-flow advantage.

P7-63B Royal Bank of Canada (RBC), Canada's largest bank, provides financial services globally. The excerpts that follow are adapted from RBC's financial statements for fiscal year 2007.

Analyzing capital asset transactions from a company's financial statements
(Obj. 2, 4, 6, 7)

Amounts in millions	October 31,	
Balance Sheet	**2007**	**2006**
Assets		
Total current assets	$237,936	$208,530
Premises and equipment	5,941	5,246
Less Accumulated amortization	(3,810)	(3,428)
Goodwill	4,752	4,304
	For the Year Ended October 31	
Cash Flow Statement (in millions)	**2007**	**2006**
Cash provided from operating activities:		
Net income from continuing operations	$5,492	$4,757
Noncash items affecting net income:		
Amortization	434	405
Cash used in investing activities:		
Acquisition of premises and equipment	(706)	(511)
Cash used in acquisitions (including $41 of premises and equipment)	(373)	(256)

❚ Required

1. How much was RBC's cost of capital assets at October 31, 2007? How much was the book value of capital assets? Show computations.

2. The financial statements give four pieces of evidence that RBC purchased capital assets and made acquisitions during 2007. What are they?

3. Prepare T-accounts for Premises and Equipment and Accumulated Amortization. Then show all the activity in these accounts during 2007. Did RBC dispose of any assets and if so what was the book value?

4. Why has goodwill not been amortized?

Accounting for intangibles, natural resources, and the related expenses
(Obj. 5, 6)

P7-64B Part 1. The **Coca-Cola Company's** (CCC) balance sheet reports the asset Goodwill. Assume that CCC purchased an asset to be included in Goodwill as part of the acquisition of another company, which carried these figures (thousands of dollars):

Book value of long-term assets	$34,550
Market value of assets	49,000
Liabilities	4,500

❚ Required

1. Explain the terms *book value of assets*, *market value of assets*, and *goodwill*. On what would you base the purchase price of the acquisition?

2. Make the journal entry to record CCC's purchase of the other company for $50,000 cash.

Part 2. Mainstay Pipeline Corp., which operates a pipeline that provides natural gas to several east coast cities, is an oil and gas production company. The company's balance sheet includes the asset Oil Properties.

Mainstay paid $5 million cash for petroleum reserves that contained an estimated 500,000 barrels of oil. The company paid $350,000 for additional geological tests of the property and $110,000 to prepare the surface for drilling. Prior to production, the company signed a $40,000 note payable to have a building constructed on the property. Because the building provides onsite headquarters for the drilling effort and will be abandoned when the oil is depleted, its cost is debited to the Oil Properties account and included in depletion charges. During the first year of production, Mainstay removed 80,000 barrels of oil, which it sold on credit for $38 per barrel. Operating expenses related to this project totalled $660,000 for the first year, all paid in cash. In addition, Mainstay accrued income tax at the rate of 38%.

❚ Required

1. Record all of Mainstay Pipeline Corp.'s transactions for the year.

2. Prepare the company's income statement for the New Oil entity for the first year. Evaluate the profitability of the project.

Reporting capital asset transactions on the cash flow statement
(Obj. 7)

P7-65B At the end of 2007, **Rogers Communications Inc.**, the telecommunications company, had total assets of $15.3 billion and total liabilities of $10.7 billion. Included among the assets were property, plant, and equipment with a cost of $16.4 billion and accumulated amortization of $9.1 billion.

Suppose that Rogers completed the following selected transactions during 2008. The company earned total revenues of $11.6 billion and incurred total expenses of $9.89 billion, which included amortization of $1.84 billion. During the year, Rogers paid $1.8 billion for new capital assets and sold old capital assets for $0.2 billion. The cost of the assets sold was $0.29 billion and their accumulated amortization was $0.29 billion.

❚ Required

1. Explain how to determine whether Rogers had a gain or a loss on the sale of the old capital assets. What was the amount of the gain or loss, if any?

2. Show how Rogers would report capital assets on the balance sheet at December 31, 2008.

3. Show how Rogers would report operating activities and investing activities on its cash flow statement for 2008. The company's cash flow statement starts with net income.

APPLY YOUR KNOWLEDGE

DECISION CASES

Case 1. Suppose you are considering investing in two businesses, La Petite France Bakery and Burgers Ahoy Inc. The two companies are virtually identical, and both began operations at the beginning of the current year.

Measuring profitability based on different amortization methods **(Obj. 2, 3)**

In early January, both companies purchased equipment costing $175,000 that had a 10-year estimated useful life and a $10,000 residual value. La Petite France uses the amortization method that maximizes reported income for both reporting and tax purposes. In contrast, Burgers Ahoy uses the double-declining-balance method for amortization purposes. Assume that both companies' trial balances at December 31 included the following:

Sales revenue	$350,000
Cost of goods sold	94,000
Operating expenses before amortization	50,000

The income tax rate is 25%. The maximum capital cost allowance rate is 20%.

❙ *Required*

1. Prepare both companies' income statements.

2. Write an investment newsletter to address the following questions for your clients. Which company appears to be more profitable? Which company has more cash to invest in promising projects? If prices continue rising over the long term, in which company would you prefer to invest? Why?

Case 2. The following questions are unrelated except that they all apply to capital assets and intangible assets:

Capital assets and intangible assets **(Obj. 1, 6)**

1. The manager of Fashion Forward Ltd. regularly buys capital assets and debits the cost to Repairs and Maintenance Expense. Why would she do that, since she knows this action violates GAAP?

2. The manager of Greytown Express Inc. regularly debits the cost of repairs and maintenance of capital assets to Plant and Equipment. Why would he do that, since he knows he is violating GAAP?

3. It has been suggested that because many intangible assets have no value except to the company that owns them, they should be valued at $1.00 or zero on the balance sheet. Many accountants disagree with this view. Which view do you support? Why?

ETHICAL ISSUE

Vitner's Ltd. purchased land and a building for the lump sum of $6.0 million. To get the maximum tax deduction, Mary Drink allocated 80% of the purchase price to the building and only 20% to the land. A more realistic allocation would have been 60% to the building and 40% to the land.

❙ *Required*

1. Explain the tax advantage of allocating too much to the building and too little to the land.

2. Was Vitner's allocation ethical? If so, state why. If not, why not? Identify who was harmed.

FOCUS ON FINANCIALS

Sun-Rype Products Ltd.

Explaining capital asset activity
(Obj. 2, 4, 7)

Refer to the Sun-Rype financial statements in Appendix A at the end of this book, and answer the following questions.

1. Which amortization method does Sun-Rype use for reporting to shareholders and creditors in the financial statements? Would the company use the same method for income tax reporting? Give your reasons.

2. During 2007, Sun-Rype sold capital assets. What were the proceeds? What was the cost of the property, plant and equipment disposed of?

3. How much did Sun-Rype pay for property and equipment during 2007? What about in 2006? Evaluate the trend in these capital expenditures as to whether it conveys good news for Sun-Rype.

4. During 2007, Sun-Rype added new property, plant, and equipment. Therefore, it is possible that the company's property and equipment at the end of 2007 were proportionately newer than the assets the company held at the end of 2006. Were property and equipment proportionately newer or older at the end of 2007 (versus 2006)?

FOCUS ON ANALYSIS

Mullen Group Income Fund

Analyzing capital assets
(Obj. 2, 3, 6, 7)

Refer to Mullen's financial statements in Appendix B at the end of the book, and answer the following questions:

1. Which amortization method for property, plant, and equipment does Mullen use for reporting to shareholders and creditors in the financial statements? What method did Mullen probably use for income tax purposes?

2. How much was Mullen's depreciation and amortization expense during fiscal year 2007? How much was Mullen's accumulated depreciation and amortization at the end of year 2007? Explain why accumulated depreciation and amortization exceeds depreciation and amortization expense for the year 2007.

3. Explain why Mullen adds depreciation and amortization expenses back to net income in the computation of net cash from operating activities.

4. How much did Mullen spend on capital assets during 2007? Do these expenditures convey good news or bad news for Mullen? Explain.

5. Does Mullen have any goodwill? How did it arise? How does Mullen account for it? In 2007, was amortization on goodwill charged? Mullen describes one intangible asset. What is it? How does Mullen account for intangible assets? Explain the $25 million charge regarding intangible assets in 2007.

GROUP PROJECT

To do this project, choose and visit a local business or use your educational institution. If neither of these situations is appropriate, choose a type of business and develop the property, plant, and equipment, goodwill, and intangible assets as outlined below.

❙ *Required*

1. List all the property, plant, and equipment assets for the business or organization you have chosen.

2. If possible, interview the manager. Gain as much information as you can about the company's property, plant, and equipment assets. For example, try to determine the assets'

costs, the amortization method the company is using, and the estimated useful life of each asset category. If an interview is impossible, then develop your own estimates of the assets' costs, useful lives, and book values, assuming appropriate amortization methods.

3. Determine whether the business has any intangible assets. If it does, list them and find as much information as possible about their nature, cost, and estimated lives.

4. Write a detailed report of your findings, and be prepared to present your results to the class. Include your evaluation of the capital assets of this business based on cost allocation, method of amortization, and value to the business.

QUICK CHECK ANSWERS

1. *b* [($850,000/[$850,000 | $675,000 + $475,000]) × $1,500,000 = $637,500]
2. *a*
3. *a* [($25,000 − $2,500)/5 × 5/12 = $1,875]
4. *d* [($25,000 − $2,500)/5 × 2 = $9,000; $25,000 − $9,000 = $16,000]
5. *b* [$25,000 × 2/5 = $10,000; ($25,000 − $10,000) × 2/5 = $6,000]
6. *a* [($25,000 − $2,500)/5 × 4 = $18,000; $25,000 − $18,000 = $7,000; $11,500 − $7,000 = gain of $4,500, therefore, a benefit will be realized]
7. *c* [$17,000 × 2/4 = $8,500; ($17,000 − $8,500) × 2/4 = $4,250; $8,500 + $4,250 = $12,750]
8. *c*
9. *a*
10. *d*
11. *b* [$200,000 × (6,000/50,000) = $24,000]
12. *e*

Appendix 7A

Amortization for Accounting Purposes and Capital Cost Allowance for Income Tax Purposes

This topic was introduced on page 328. The following discussion provides a more thorough investigation of the topic.

The majority of businesses use the straight-line method for reporting property, plant, and equipment values and amortization expense to their owners and creditors on their financial statements. But businesses must keep a separate set of records for calculating the CCA they claim on their tax returns. This is because whatever amortization method a business uses, amortization expense on the income statement is different from CCA deducted for income tax purposes. The *Income Tax Act* allows corporations, as well as individuals earning business or professional income, to deduct from income **capital cost allowance (CCA)**, the term CRA uses to describe amortization for tax purposes. CRA specifies the maximum capital cost allowance rate a taxpayer may use. Different classes of assets have different *capital cost allowance rates*. The capital cost allowance rates published by CRA are maximums. A taxpayer may claim from zero to the maximum capital cost allowance allowed in a year. Most taxpayers claim the maximum CCA since this provides the largest deduction from income as quickly as possible, thus decreasing the immediate tax payments. CCA rates tend to be similar to rates used for accelerated amortization. Claiming the maximum CCA leaves more cash available for investment or other business uses.

To understand the relationships between cash flow, amortization, and income tax, we use a van purchased by Bakal Corp. costing $40,000 with a 5-year life and zero residual value:

- First-year amortization is $8,000 under the straight-line amortization method.
- CRA allows a maximum rate of 30% for vans, so Bakal would be allowed to claim a maximum of 30% or $12,000 in 2009.[2]

Assume that Bakal Corp. facility has $400,000 in revenue and $300,000 in cash operating expenses during the van's first year and an income tax rate of 30%. The cash flow analysis appears in Exhibit 7A-1.

Exhibit 7A-1 highlights an important fact: The higher the amortization expense used for tax purposes, the lower the income before tax and thus the lower the tax payment. Therefore, accelerated amortization helps conserve cash for use in the business. Exhibit 7A-1 shows that Bakal Corp. will have $1,200 (line 10) more cash at the end of the first year if it uses the maximum CCA rate instead of straight-line amortization.

---

[2]Present CRA rules permit a taxpayer to deduct only 50% of the normal CCA in the year of acquisition of a capital asset. The authors have generally ignored that rule for purposes of this chapter to simplify the discussion. Where required to do so in the text, use the rule.

EXHIBIT 7A-1	The Cash Flow Advantage of Accelerated Amortization over Straight-Line Amortization for Income Tax Purposes

	SL	CCA
1. Cash revenues	$400,000	$400,000
2. Cash operating expenses	300,000	300,000
3. Cash provided by operations before income tax	100,000	100,000
4. Amortization/Capital cost allowance expense (a noncash expense)	8,000	12,000
5. Income before income tax	$ 92,000	$ 88,000
6. Income tax expense (30%)	$ 27,600	$ 26,400
Cash-flow analysis:		
7. Cash provided by operations before tax	$100,000	$100,000
8. Income tax expense	27,600	26,400
9. Cash provided by operations	$ 72,400	$ 73,600
10. Extra cash available for investment if maximum CCA is used ($73,600 − $72,400)		$ 1,200

STOP & THINK

Which amortization method produces a higher net income? How much better? Show how you arrive at your answer.

Answer

Straight-line amortization makes Bakal look better. Net income under

- Straight-line amortization is $64,400 ($92,000 − $27,600).
- Accelerated amortization (maximum CCA) is $61,600 ($88,000 − $26,400).

Under straight-line amortization, Bakal reports $2,800 ($64,400 − $61,600) more net income. Therefore, most managers prefer to use straight-line amortization for their financial statements.

8

Liabilities

SPOTLIGHT

Air Canada was founded in 1937 as Trans-Canada Airlines. Today it is the seventh largest airline in the world based on its fleet of airplanes.

Air Canada, like the other major airlines, has some interesting liabilities. Although it has transferred its frequent flier program to Aeroplan, originally a subsidiary but now a separate entity, it still has a liability of $55 million for Aeroplan miles dating from the date Aeroplan was set up in 2001. The liability is called "Aeroplan miles obligation" and appears under current liabilities on Air Canada's balance sheet.

Air Canada collects ticket revenue in advance and provides flights for customers later. This creates unearned revenue that Air Canada reports as "Advance ticket sales" on its balance sheet under Current Liabilities. The company also has accounts payable and accrued liabilities under Current Liabilities, and long-term debt and capital leases, and pension and other benefit liabilities under Long-term Liabilities.

Air Canada

▼ **Consolidated Balance Sheet (Adapted)**
December 31, 2007 (in millions)

Assets		Liabilities and Shareholders' Equity	
Current Assets		**Current Liabilities**	
Cash and cash equivalents.........	$ 1,239	Accounts payable and	
Other current assets...................	1,239	accrued charges	$ 1,243
Total current assets....................	2,478	Unearned ticket revenue	1,245
		Aeroplan miles obligation	55
		Current maturities of capital leases	148
		Current maturities of long-term debt	265
		Total current liabilities	2,956
Property and equipment...............	7,919	**Long-Term Liabilities**	
Other assets	1,440	Capital leases....................................	824
		Long-term debt	3,182
		Other long-term liabilities................	2,248
			9,210
		Shareholders' Equity	
		Non-controlling interest...................	184
		Shareholders' equity	2,443
		Total liabilities and	
Total assets	$11,837	shareholders' equity	$11,837

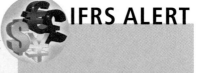 **IFRS ALERT**

The IFRS Alert in Chapter 5 (page 216) introduced you to the Canadian Institute of Chartered Accountants *CICA Handbook* Section 3855 "Financial Instruments—Recognition and Measurement," which is based in large part on International Accounting Standard (IAS) 32 "Financial Instruments: Presentation," International Financial Reporting Standards (IFRS) 7 "Financial Instruments: Disclosures," and IAS 39 "Financial Instruments: Recognition and Measurement."

The focus of Section 3855 that is relevant for the first half of this chapter (as was true for Chapter 5) is the valuation of financial instruments using fair value as the basis of valuation. *CICA Handbook*, Section 3862, paragraph .29 states "[Disclosure] of fair value [is] not required . . . when the carrying amount is a reasonable approximation of fair value . . . such as short-term trade . . . payables."

Bonds payable with a due date more than one year in the future, which are discussed in the second half of this chapter, are different than short-term payables. The IFRS Alert on page 377 discusses the accounting for long-term financial instruments.

This chapter shows how to account for liabilities—both current and long-term. We begin with current liabilities.

Current Liabilities

Current liabilities are obligations due within one year or within the company's normal operating cycle if longer than a year. Obligations due beyond that period of time are classified as *long-term liabilities*.

Current liabilities are of two kinds:

- Known amounts
- Estimated amounts

We look first at current liabilities of a known amount.

Objective

① **Account** for current liabilities and contingent liabilities

Current Liabilities of Known Amount

Current liabilities of known amount include accounts payable, short-term notes payable, GST payable, sales tax payable, accrued expenses payable, payroll liabilities, unearned revenues, and the current portion of long-term debt.

Accounts Payable. Amounts owed for products or services purchased on account are *accounts payable*. For example, Air Canada purchases soft drinks on account. We have seen many other examples of accounts payable in previous chapters.

One of a merchandiser's most common transactions is the credit purchase of inventory. The Hudson's Bay Company and Sobeys buy their inventory on account.

Short-Term Notes Payable. **Short-term notes payable**, a common form of financing, are notes payable due within one year. Robertson Construction Inc. may issue short-term notes payable to borrow cash or to purchase assets. For its notes payable, Robertson must accrue interest expense and interest payable at the end of the period. The following sequence of entries covers the purchase of inventory, accrual of interest expense, and payment of a short-term note payable:

2008
Oct. 1   Inventory 8,000
               Note Payable, Short-Term   8,000
               Purchase of inventory by issuing a 6-month 10% note payable.

This transaction increases both an asset and a liability.

ASSETS	=	LIABILITIES	+	SHAREHOLDERS' EQUITY
+8,000	=	+8,000	+	0

Assume Robertson Construction's year-end is December 31. At year-end, Robertson must accrue interest expense at 10% per year for October through December.

2008
Dec. 31   Interest Expense ($8,000 × 0.10 × 3/12)...................... 200
                Interest Payable   200
                Adjusting entry to accrue interest expense at year-end.

Liabilities increase and equity decreases because of the expense.

ASSETS	=	LIABILITIES	+	SHAREHOLDERS' EQUITY	–	EXPENSES
0	=	+200	+		–	200

The balance sheet at year-end will report the note payable of $8,000 and the related interest payable of $200 as current liabilities. The income statement will report interest expense of $200.

The following entry records the note's payment at March 31, 2009:

2009
Mar. 31   Note Payable, Short-Term... 8,000
                Interest Payable 200
                Interest Expense ($8,000 × 0.10 × 3/12)...................... 200
                    Cash [$8,000 + ($8,000 × 0.10 × 6/12)].................... 8,400
                Payment of a note payable and interest at maturity.

ASSETS	=	LIABILITIES	+	SHAREHOLDERS' EQUITY	−	EXPENSES
−8,400	=	−8,000			−	200
		− 200				

The debits zero out the two payables and also record interest expense for 2009.

Goods and Services Tax Payable.

You were introduced to the Goods and Services Tax (GST) in the User Alert on page 271 of Chapter 6. Recall that the final consumer of a GST-taxable product or service bears the tax; entities farther up the supply chain from the final consumer pay GST on their purchases but get an input tax credit (ITC) equal to the GST they have paid.

GST payable is a current liability as it is payable quarterly or monthly depending on the payer's volume of business.

In the User Alert, Kitchen Hardware purchases lawn rakes for $3,000 plus 5% GST for a total of $3,150. Subsequently, Kitchen sells the rakes for $6,000 plus GST of $300 (provincial sales tax is ignored for this example but is covered below). The entries to record the purchase of the rakes, the sale of the rakes, and the remittance of the GST payable by Kitchen are:

Inventory	3,000	
GST ITC	150	
Accounts Payable		3,150
To record purchase of inventory.		
Accounts Receivable	6,300	
Cost of Goods Sold	3,000	
Sales		6,000
Inventory		3,000
GST Payable		300
To record sale of inventory.		
GST Payable	300	
GST ITC		150
Cash		150
To record payment of GST collected less GST paid.		

Sales Tax Payable.

You were introduced to the provincial sales taxes in the User Alert on page 271 of Chapter 6. Recall that:

- Provincial sales tax (PST) applies to goods and services purchased by a consumer, such as an individual or a business, for its own use.

- Alberta, the Yukon, the Northwest Territories, and Nunavut do not charge the equivalent of a provincial sales tax.

- PST is charged on the sale to the final consumer and remitted to the provincial treasurer. Using the information in the example above, Kitchen Hardware would charge the Manitoba sales tax rate of 7% on the $6,000 sale and remit the tax collected of $420 to Manitoba Finance, Taxation Division.

PST payable is a current liability as it is payable quarterly or monthly depending on the payer's volume of business.

In the User Alert, Kitchen Hardware, a hardware store chain located in Manitoba where the PST is 7%, sells lawn rakes for $6,000 plus 5% GST for a total of $6,300. The PST on the sale would be $420 so the total price to the consumer would be $6,720. The entries to record the sale of the rakes (including GST and PST payable) and the remittance of the PST payable by Kitchen are:

Accounts Receivable..	6,720	
Cost of Goods Sold	3,000	
Sales..		6,000
Inventory		3,000
GST Payable...		300
PST Payable		420
To record sale of inventory.		
PST Payable	420	
Cash..		420
To record payment of PST collected.		

Accrued Liabilities (Accrued Expenses).

An accrued liability usually results from an expense the business has incurred but not yet paid. Therefore, an accrued expense creates a liability, which explains why it is also called an *accrued expense*.

For example, Air Canada's salaries and wages payable occur as employees work for the company. Interest expense accrues with the passage of time. There are several categories of accrued expenses:

- Salaries and Wages Payable
- Interest Payable
- Income Taxes Payable

Salaries and Wages Payable (also called Accrued Salaries and Wages Payable) is the liability for salaries, wages, and related payroll expenses not yet paid at the end of the period. This category also includes payroll deductions withheld from employee paycheques. *Interest Payable* is the company's interest payable on notes payable. *Income Taxes Payable* is the amount of income tax the company still owes at year-end.

Payroll Liabilities.

Payroll, also called *employee compensation*, is a major expense. For service organizations—such as law firms, real estate brokers, and accounting firms—compensation is *the* major expense, just as cost of goods sold is the major expense for a merchandising company.

Employee compensation takes different forms. A *salary* is employee pay stated at a yearly or monthly rate. A *wage* is employee pay stated at an hourly rate. Sales employees earn a *commission*, which is a percentage of the sales the employee has made. A *bonus* is an amount over and above regular compensation. Accounting for all forms of compensation follows the same pattern, as illustrated in Exhibit 8-1 (using assumed figures).

Every expense accrual has the same effect: Liabilities increase and equity decreases because of the expense. The accounting equation shows these effects.

Salary expense represents *gross pay* (that is, pay before subtractions for taxes and other deductions). Salary expense creates several payroll entries, expenses, and liabilities:

- *Salary Payable to Employees* is their net (take-home) pay.
- *Employee Withheld Income Tax Payable* is the employees' income tax that has been withheld from paycheques.

EXHIBIT 8-1	Accounting for Payroll Expenses and Liabilities

Salary Expense...	10,000	
Employee Withheld Income Tax Payable......................................		1,350
Canada Pension Plan Payable		320
Employment Insurance Payable		270
Employee Union Dues Payable..		272
Salary Payable to Employees [take-home pay]		7,788
To record salary expense and employee withholdings.		
Canada Pension Plan and Employment Insurance Expense	698	
Canada Pension Plan Payable		320
Employment Insurance Payable		378
To record employer's share of Canada Pension Plan and		
Employment Insurance.		
Provincial Employer's Health and Post-Secondary Education Tax	200	
Employee Dental Benefits Expense...	182	
Employee Benefits Expense Payable		382
To record employee benefits payable by employer.		

ASSETS	=	LIABILITIES	+	SHAREHOLDERS' EQUITY	−	EXPENSES
		+1,350				
		+ 320				
0	=	+ 270				−10,000
		+ 272				
		+7,788				
0	=	+ 320				−698
		+ 378				
0	=	+ 382				−200
						−182

- *Canada Pension Plan Payable* and *Employment Insurance Payable* are the employees' contributions to those two government programs.
- *Employee Union Dues Payable* are collected for the union by the employer.
- *Canada Pension Plan and Employment Insurance Expense* is the cost of the employer's contribution to those two government programs. The two credits to liabilities totalling $698 represent the liability for the employer's contribution.
- *Provincial Employer's Health and Post-Secondary Education Tax* is an employment expense levied on employers by some provinces.
- *Employment Dental Benefits Expense* is typical of employee benefits many employers provide. The payable represents the liability for those two expenses.

Unearned Revenues. *Unearned revenues* are also called *deferred revenues* and *revenues collected in advance*. For all unearned revenue the business has received cash from customers before earning the revenue. The company has a liability to provide goods or services to the customer. Let's consider an example.

Air Canada sells tickets and collects cash in advance. Air Canada therefore reports Unearned Ticket Revenue for airline tickets sold in advance. At December 31, 2007, Air Canada owed customers $1,245 million of air travel (see page 367). Let's see how Air Canada accounts for unearned ticket revenue.

Assume that Air Canada collects $800 for a round-trip Tango Plus ticket from Vancouver to Winnipeg (taxes and fees are not considered in this example). Air Canada's entries would be as follows:

```
2008
Sept. 1    Cash.........................................................   800
                Unearned Ticket Revenue...........................        800
           To receive cash for plane fare (return) from
              Vancouver to Winnipeg (Tango Plus).
```

Unearned Ticket Revenue	
	800

Air Canada's assets and liabilities increase equally. There is no revenue yet.

ASSETS	=	LIABILITIES	+	SHAREHOLDERS' EQUITY
+800	=	+800	+	0

Suppose the passenger flies from Vancouver to Winnipeg on September 26, 2008. Air Canada records revenue as follows:

```
2008
Sept. 26    Unearned Ticket Revenue................................   400
                Ticket Revenue ($800/2)..............................        400
            To record revenue earned that was collected in advance.
```

The liability decreases and the revenue goes up:

Unearned Ticket Revenue			Ticket Revenue	
400	800			400

At December 31, 2008, Air Canada reports:

- $400 of unearned ticket revenue (a liability) on the balance sheet
- $400 of ticket revenue on the income statement

The customer returns to Vancouver on January 28, 2009, and Air Canada records the revenue earned with this journal entry:

```
2009
Jant. 28    Unearned Ticket Revenue................................   400
                Ticket Revenue ($800/2)..............................        400
            Earned revenue that was collected in advance.
```

Now the liability balance is zero because Air Canada has earned all the revenue it collected in advance.

Current Portion of Long-Term Debt. Some long-term debt must be paid in installments. The **current installment of long-term debt** (also called *current portion of long-term debt*) is the amount of the principal that is payable within one year. At the end of each year, a company reclassifies (from long-term debt to a current liability) the amount of its long-term debt that must be paid during the upcoming year.

Air Canada (page 367) reports Current Portion of Long-Term Debt among Current Liabilities on its balance sheet. Air Canada also reports Long-Term Debt, which excludes the current maturities. *Long-term debt* refers to long-term notes payable and bonds payable, which we cover in the second half of this chapter.

You are thinking of purchasing Air Canada shares and are concerned about Air Canada's debt. You examine Air Canada's balance sheet to answer the following questions about the company's current and long-term debt:

1. At December 31, 2007, how much in total did Air Canada owe on current and long-term debt?
2. How much of the long-term debt did Air Canada expect to pay during the year ended December 31, 2008? How much was the company scheduled to pay during later years?

Answers:

1. $3,447 million ($265 + $3,182)
2. Pay next year—$265 million; pay later—$3,182 million

Current Liabilities That Must Be Estimated

A business may know that a liability exists and not know the exact amount. The business must report the liability on the balance sheet. Estimated liabilities vary among companies. Let's look first at Estimated Warranty Payable, a liability account that most manufacturers have.

Estimated Warranty Payable. Many companies guarantee their products under *warranty* agreements. The warranty period may extend for 90 days to a year for consumer products. Automobile companies accrue liabilities for vehicle warranties, which usually extend for several years.

Whatever the warranty's life, the matching principle demands that the company record the *warranty expense* in the same period that the business records sales revenue. After all, the warranty motivates customers to buy products, so the company must record warranty expense. At the time of the sale, however, the company does not know which products will be defective. The exact amount of warranty expense cannot be known with certainty, so the business must estimate warranty expense and the related warranty liability.

Assume that Black & Decker Manufacturing Company Ltd., which manufactures power tools, made sales of $200,000,000 subject to product warranties. If, in past years, between 2% and 4% of products proved defective, Black & Decker could estimate that 3% of the products it sells this year will require repair or replacement. In that case, Black & Decker would estimate warranty expense of $6,000,000 ($200,000,000 × 0.03) for the period and make the following entry:

Warranty Expense..	6,000,000	
Estimated Warranty Payable		6,000,000
To accrue warranty expense.		

Estimated Warranty Payable	
	6,000,000

Assume that defective merchandise totals $4,800,000. Black & Decker will replace the defective products and record the following:

Estimated Warranty Payable..	4,800,000	
Inventory		4,800,000
To replace defective products sold under warranty.		

Estimated Warranty Payable	
4,800,000	6,000,000
	Bal. 1,200,000

At the end of the year, Black & Decker will report Estimated Warranty Payable of $1,200,000 as a current liability. The income statement reports Warranty Expense of $6,000,000 for the year. Then, next year Black & Decker will repeat this process. The Estimated Warranty Payable account probably won't ever zero out.

If Black & Decker paid cash to satisfy the warranty, then the credit would be to Cash rather than to Inventory.

Vacation pay is another expense that must be estimated. And income taxes must be estimated because the final amount isn't determined until early the next year.

Contingent Liabilities. A *contingent liability* is not an actual liability. Instead, it is a potential liability that depends on a *future* event arising out of past events. The Accounting Standards Board (AcSB) of the CICA provides these guidelines to account for contingent losses (or expenses) and their related liabilities:

1. Record an actual liability if it is *likely* that the loss (or expense) will occur and the *amount can be reasonably estimated*. Warranty expense is an example.

2. Report the contingency in a financial statement note if it is likely that a loss (or expense) will occur but the amount cannot be reasonably estimated or it cannot be determined that the loss (or expense) is likely. Lawsuits in progress are a prime example.

   Canadian Tire Corporation reported on its contingencies at December 29, 2007, in the following note:

   > *Note 14. GUARANTEES, COMMITMENTS AND CONTINGENCIES* (in part): **Other commitments and contingencies** As at December 29, 2007, [Canadian Tire] had the following other commitments and contingencies. In accordance with Canadian generally accepted accounting principles, the Company has not recognized a liability relating to these commitments and contingencies except for a provision for legal proceedings: . . .
   >
   > The Company and certain of its subsidiaries are party to a number of legal proceedings. The Company believes that each such proceeding constitutes routine litigation incidental to the business conducted by the Company and that the ultimate disposition of the proceedings will not have a material adverse effect on its consolidated earnings, cash flow or financial position.

3. There is no need to report a contingent loss that is unlikely to occur. Instead, wait until an actual transaction clears up the situation. For example, suppose Barrick Gold Corporation has a mine in a country whose government threatens expropriation of foreign assets. Barrick will report nothing about the contingency if the probability of a loss is considered remote.

A contingent liability may arise from lawsuits that claim wrongdoing by the company. The plaintiff may seek damages through the courts. If the court or Canada Revenue Agency (CRA) rules in favour of a company, there is no liability. But if the ruling favours the plaintiff, then the company will have an actual liability. It would be unethical to omit these disclosures from the financial statements because investors need this information to properly evaluate a company.

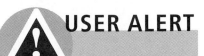

Are All a Company's Liabilities Reported on the Balance Sheet?

The big danger with liabilities is that a company may fail to report a large debt on its balance sheet. What is the consequence of missing a large liability? The company will definitely understate its liabilities and its debt ratio. The company will probably overstate its net income. In short, its financial statements will make the company look better than it really is. Any such error, if significant, hurts a company's credibility.

Contingent liabilities are very easy to overlook because they aren't actual debts. How would you feel if you owned shares in a company that failed to report a contingency that put the company out of business? If you had known of the contingency, you could have sold the shares and avoided the loss. In this case, you would hire a lawyer to file suit against the company for negligent financial reporting.

Summary of Current Liabilities

Let's summarize what we've covered thus far. A company can report its current liabilities on the balance sheet as follows:

Hudson Ltd.
Balance Sheet
December 31, 2009

Assets		Liabilities	
Current assets:		**Current liabilities**	
Cash		Accounts payable	
Short-term investments		Salary payable*	
Etc.		Interest payable*	
		GST payable*	
		Sales tax payable*	
		Income tax payable*	
Property, plant, and equipment:		Unearned revenue	
Land		Estimated warranty payable*	
Etc.		Notes payable, short-term	
		Current portion of long-term debt	
		Total current liabilities	
Other assets:		Long-term liabilities	
		Shareholders' Equity	
		Common shares	
		Retained earnings	
Total assets	$XXX	Total liabilities and shareholders' equity	$XXX

*These items are often combined and reported in a single total as "Accrued Liabilities" or "Accrued Expenses Payable."

On its income statement this company would report:

- *Expenses* related to some of the current liabilities. Examples include salary expense, interest expense, income tax expense, and warranty expense.
- *Revenue* related to the unearned revenue. Examples include service revenue and sales revenue that were collected in advance.

MyAccountingLab

MID-CHAPTER SUMMARY PROBLEM

Assume that Korvar Plastics Inc., a manufacturer of plastic pipe for the construction industry, faced the following liability situations at June 30, 2009, the end of the company's fiscal year:

a. Long-term debt totals $10 million and is payable in annual installments of $1 million each. The interest rate on the debt is 7%, and interest is paid each December 31.

b. The company pays royalties on its purchased trademarks. Royalties for the trademarks are equal to a percentage of Korvar's sales. Assume that sales in 2009 were $40 million and were subject to a royalty rate of 3%. At June 30, 2009, Korvar owes two-thirds of the year's royalty, to be paid in July.

c. Salary expense for the last payroll period of the year was $90,000. Of this amount, employees' withheld income tax totalled $12,000, and other withholdings and employee benefits were $6,000. These payroll amounts will be paid early in July.

d. GST less ITC credits payable was $124,000.

e. On fiscal year 2009 sales of $40 million, management estimates warranty expense of 2%. One year ago, at June 30, 2008, Estimated Warranty Liability stood at $100,000. Warranty payments were $300,000 during the year ended June 30, 2009.

Name: Korvar Plastics Inc.
Industry: Manufacturing
Accounting Period: June 30, 2009

Show how Korvar Plastics Inc. would report these liabilities on its balance sheet at June 30, 2009.

Answer

Current liabilities include the amount due to be paid within one year:
• Principal repayment
• Interest payment

a. Current liabilities:

Current installment of long-term debt......................................	$1,000,000
Interest payable ($10,000,000 × 0.07 × 6/12).......................	350,000
Long-term debt ($10,000,000 − $1,000,000).............................	9,000,000

Royalties are due to be paid within one year; thus, are a current liability.

b. Current liabilities:

Royalties payable ($40,000,000 × 0.03 × 2/3)	$ 800,000

Salaries payable to employees are net of all withholdings.

c. Current liabilities:

Salary payable ($90,000 − $12,000 − $6,000).......................	$72,000
Employee withheld income tax payable	12,000
Other employee withholdings and benefits payable	6,000

GST payable is net of applicable ITC credits.

d. Current liabilities:

GST payable..	$ 124,000

Estimated warranty liability must be reduced by any warranty payments made during the year.

e. Current liabilities:

Estimated warranty payable	$ 600,000
[$100,000 + ($40,000,000 × 0.02) − $300,000]	

Long-Term Liabilities: Bonds

Large companies, such as Bombardier, Canadian Tire, and TransCanada, cannot borrow billions of dollars from a single lender. So how do large corporations borrow huge amounts? They issue (sell) bonds to the public. **Bonds payable** are groups of notes issued to multiple lenders, called *bondholders*. Bombardier can borrow large amounts by issuing bonds to thousands of individual investors, who each lend a modest amount to Bombardier. Bombardier receives what it needs, and each investor limits his or her risk by diversifying investments—not putting all the investor's "eggs in one basket." Here we treat bonds and long-term notes that are payables together because their accounting is the same.

Bonds: An Introduction

Each bond that is issued is, in effect, a long-term note payable. Bonds payable are debts of the issuing company.

Purchasers of bonds receive a bond certificate, which carries the issuing company's name. The certificate also states the *principal*, which is typically stated in units of $1,000; principal is also called the bond's **face value** or **maturity value**. The bond obligates the issuing company to pay the debt at a specific future time called the *maturity date*.

Interest is the rental fee on money borrowed. The bond certificate states the interest rate that the issuer will pay the holder and the dates that the interest payments are due (generally twice a year). Exhibit 8-2 shows an actual bond certificate issued by the Bank of Montreal.

Issuing bonds usually requires the services of a securities firm, for example, RBC Dominion Securities, to act as the underwriter of the bond issue. The **underwriter** purchases the bonds from the issuing company and resells them to its clients, or it may sell the bonds to its clients and earn a commission on the sale.

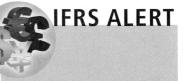 **IFRS ALERT**

The IFRS Alert in Chapter 5 (page 216) introduced you to *CICA Handbook* Section 3855 "Financial Instruments—Recognition and Measurement," which is based in a large part on IAS 32 "Financial Instruments: Presentation," IFRS 7 "Financial Instruments: Disclosures," and IAS 39 "Financial Instruments: Recognition and Measurement."

The IFRS Alert on page 367 discussed valuation of short-term financial instruments. The focus of this half of Chapter 8 is long-term financial instruments, with an emphasis on bonds payable. The discussion of valuation and disclosure of financial instruments other than bonds payable is quite complex and beyond the scope of this text.

Paragraph 3855.71 indicates that liabilities that are to be held until they come due, such as bonds payable, should be valued at their amortized cost calculated using the effective interest method.

Paragraph 3861.69 indicates that the financial statements should disclose the fair value of each class of financial liability "*in a way that permits it to be compared with the corresponding carrying amount in the balance sheet.*" The excerpt from the Air Canada financial statements on page 395 is illustrative.

Types of Bonds. All the bonds in a particular issue may mature at a specified time (**term bonds**) or in installments over a period of time (**serial bonds**). Serial bonds are like installment notes payable. Some of TransCanada Corporation's long-term debts are serial in nature because they come due in installments.

Secured, or *mortgage*, *bonds* give the bondholder the right to take specified assets of the issuer if the company *defaults*, that is, fails to pay interest or principal. *Unsecured*

EXHIBIT 8-2 Bond Certificate (a blank specimen)

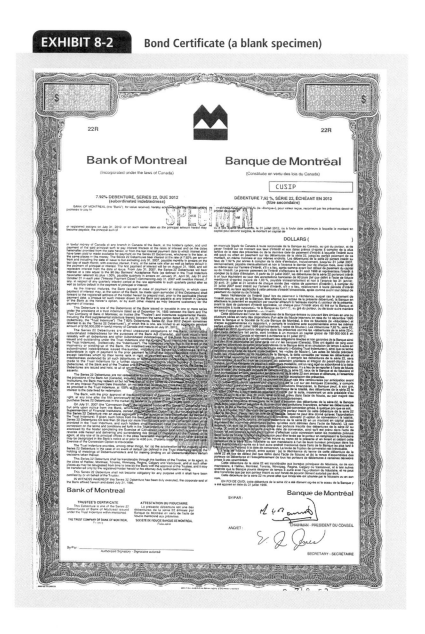

bonds, called **debentures**, are backed only by the good faith of the borrower. Debentures carry a higher rate of interest than secured bonds because debentures are riskier investments.

Bond Prices. Investors may buy and sell bonds through bond markets. The bond market in Canada is called the over-the-counter market. It is a network of investment dealers who trade bonds issued by the Government of Canada and Crown corporations, the provinces, municipalities and regions, and corporations. In addition, there is an electronic fixed-income trading system called CanDeal. It is owned by the 11 leading investment dealers in Canada. Bond prices are quoted at a percentage of their maturity value. For example,

- A $1,000 bond quoted at 100 is bought or sold for $1,000, which is 100% of its face value.

- The same bond quoted at 101.5 has a market price of $1,015 (101.5% of face value = $1,000 × 1.015).

- A $1,000 bond quoted at 88.375 is priced at $883.75 ($1,000 × 0.88375).

EXHIBIT 8-3	Bond Price Information for Province of Manitoba			
Issuer Coupon	*Maturity Date*	*Bid Price*	*Bid Yield*	*Yield Change*
Manitoba 5.50	18-Nov-15	105.61	4.79	–0.050

Exhibit 8-3 contains actual price information for Province of Manitoba bonds taken from the ScotiaMcLeod website on October 22, 2008. On this particular day, Province of Manitoba $1,000 face value bonds with a coupon rate of 5.50% maturing in the year 2018 (maturity date, November 15, 2018) were traded. The bond's asking price was $1,056.10 ($1,000 × 1.0561). Bond prices may change daily due to changes in market demand and supply.

Bond Premium and Bond Discount. A bond issued at a price above its face value is said to be issued at a **premium**, and a bond issued at a price below face value is issued at a **discount**.

Premium on Bonds Payable has a *credit* balance and Discount on Bonds Payable carries a *debit* balance. Bond Discount is therefore a contra liability account.

As a bond nears maturity, its market price moves toward par value; therefore, the price of a bond issued at a

- Premium decreases toward maturity value
- Discount increases toward maturity value

On the maturity date, a bond's market value exactly equals its face value because the company that issued the bond pays that amount to retire the bond.

The Time Value of Money. A dollar received today is worth more than a dollar to be received in the future because you may invest today's dollar immediately and earn income from it. But if you must wait to receive the dollar, you forgo the interest revenue. Money earns income over time, a fact called the *time value of money*. Let's examine how the time value of money affects the pricing of bonds.

Assume that a bond with a face value of $1,000 reaches maturity three years from today and carries no interest. Would you pay $1,000 to purchase the bond? No, because the payment of $1,000 today to receive the same amount in the future provides you with no income on the investment. You would not be taking advantage of the time value of money. Just how much would you pay today to receive $1,000 at the end of three years? The answer is some amount *less* than $1,000. Let's suppose that you feel $750 is a good price. By investing $750 now to receive $1,000 later, you earn $250 interest revenue over the three years. The issuing company sees the transaction this way: It will pay you $250 interest for the use of your $750 for three years.

The amount that a person would invest *at the present time* to receive a greater amount at a future date is called the **present value** of a future amount. In our example, $750 is the present value of the $1,000, which is the future amount.

Our $750 bond price is a reasonable estimate. The exact present value of any future amount depends on

1. The amount of the future payment ($1,000 in our example)
2. The length of time from the investment date to the date when the future amount is to be collected (3 years)
3. The interest rate during the period (say 10%)

In this case the present value is very close to $750. Present value is always less than the future amount. We discuss how present value is computed in Appendix D at the end of the book.

Bond Interest Rates Determine Bond Prices. Bonds are always sold at their *market price*, which is the amount investors are willing to pay. A **bond market price** is the bond's present value, which equals the present value of the principal payment plus the present value of the cash interest payments. Interest is usually paid semi-annually (twice a year), but also annually or quarterly.

Two interest rates work to set the price of a bond:

- The **stated interest rate** is the interest rate printed on the bond certificate. The stated interest rate determines the amount of cash the borrower pays—and the investor receives—each year. For example, the Province of Quebec's 6.25% bonds have a contract interest rate of 6.25%. Thus, Quebec pays $6,250 of interest annually on each $100,000 bond. Each semi-annual interest payment is $3,125 ($100,000 × 0.0625 × 6/12).

- The **market interest rate**, or *effective interest rate*, is the rate that investors demand for loaning their money. The market rate varies by the minute.

Exhibit 8-4 shows how the contract (stated) interest rate and the market interest rate interact to determine the issuance price of a bond payable for three separate cases.

Manitoba may issue 6.25% bonds when the market rate has risen to 7%. Will the Manitoba bonds attract investors in this market? No, because investors can earn 7% on other bonds of similar risk. Therefore, investors will purchase Manitoba bonds only at a price less than their par value. The difference between the lower price and face value is a *discount* (Exhibit 8-4). Conversely, if the market interest rate is 5%, Manitoba's 6.25% bonds will be so attractive that investors will pay more than face value for them. The difference between the higher price and face value is a *premium*. It is useful to remember that there is an inverse relationship between the market rate and bond prices—a higher market rate results in a lower bond price and a lower market rate results in a higher bond price.

EXHIBIT 8-4 How the Contract Interest Rate and the Market Interest Rate Interact to Determine the Price of a Bond

Issuance Price of Bonds Payable

Case A:

Contract (stated) interest rate on a bond payable	equals	Market interest rate	implies	Price of face, or maturity, value
Example: 6%	=	6%	→	*Face: $1,000 bond issued for $1,000*

Case B:

Contract (stated) interest rate on a bond payable	less than	Market interest rate	implies	Discount price (price *below* face value)
Example: 6%	<	7%	→	*Discount: $1,000 bond issued for a price below $1,000*

Case C:

Contract (stated) interest rate on a bond payable	greater than	Market interest rate	implies	Premium price (price *above* face value)
Example: 6%	>	5%	→	*Premium: $1,000 bond issued for a price above $1,000*

Issuing Bonds Payable at Face Value

Suppose Great-West Lifeco Inc. has $50,000 in 6% bonds that mature in five years. Assume that Great-West issues these bonds at face value on January 1, 2009. The issuance entry is

Objective

② **Account** for bonds-payable transactions

2009
Jan. 1   Cash...   50,000
            Bonds Payable   50,000
            To issue 6%, five-year bonds at face value.

Bonds Payable	
	50,000

ASSETS	=	LIABILITIES	+	SHAREHOLDERS' EQUITY
+50,000	=	+50,000	+	0

Great-West, the borrower, makes a one-time entry to record the receipt of cash and the issuance of bonds. Afterward, investors buy and sell the bonds through the bond markets. These buy-and-sell transactions between outside investors do *not* involve Great-West at all.

Interest payments occur each January 1 and July 1. Great-West's entry to record the first semi-annual interest payment is as follows:

2009
July 1   Interest Expense..   1,500
            Cash..   1,500
            To pay semi-annual interest. ($50,000 × 0.06 × 6/12)

ASSETS	=	LIABILITIES	+	SHAREHOLDERS' EQUITY	–	EXPENSES
–1,500	=	0	+		–	–1,500

At year-end, Great-West must accrue interest expense and interest payable for six months (July through December), as follows:

2009
Dec. 31   Interest Expense ($50,000 × 0.06 × 6/12)....................   1,500
            Interest Payable   1,500
            To accrue interest.

ASSETS	=	LIABILITIES	+	SHAREHOLDERS' EQUITY	–	EXPENSES
0	=	+1,500	+		–	–1,500

At maturity, Great-West will pay off the bonds as follows:

2014
Jan. 1   Bonds Payable...   50,000
            Cash..   50,000
            To pay bonds payable at maturity.

Bonds Payable	
50,000	50,000
	Bal. 0

ASSETS	=	LIABILITIES	+	SHAREHOLDERS' EQUITY
−50,000	=	−50,000		

Issuing Bonds Payable at a Discount

Market conditions may force a company to issue bonds at a discount. Suppose TELUS issues $100,000 of its 9% five-year bonds when the market interest rate is 10%. The market price of the bonds drops, and TELUS receives $96,149[1] at issuance. The transaction is recorded as follows:

2009				
Jan. 1	Cash..	96,149	
	Discount on Bonds Payable	3,851	
	Bonds Payable		100,000
	To issue 9%, five-year bonds at a discount.		

ASSETS	=	LIABILITIES	+	SHAREHOLDERS' EQUITY
+96,149	=	−3,851	+	0
		+100,000		

Now the bond accounts have a net balance of $96,149 as follows:

Bonds Payable		Discount on Bonds Payable	= Net carrying amount of bonds payable
	100,000	+ 3,851	= $96,149

TELUS's balance sheet immediately after issuance of the bonds would report the following:

Total current liabilities		$ XXX
Long-term liabilities		
Bonds payable, 9%, due 2014	$100,000	
Less: Discount on bonds payable	(3,851)	96,149

Discount on Bonds Payable is a contra account to Bonds Payable, a decrease in the company's liabilities. Subtracting the discount from Bonds Payable yields the *carrying amount* of the bonds. Thus, TELUS's liability is $96,149, which is the amount the company borrowed.

DECISION **What Is the Interest Expense on These Bonds Payable?**

Objective

③ **Measure** interest expense

TELUS pays interest on its bonds semi-annually, which is common practice. Each semi-annual interest *payment* remains the same over the life of the bonds:

$$\text{Semi-annual interest payment} = \$100,000 \times 0.09 \times 6/12$$
$$= \$4,500$$

This payment amount is fixed by the bond contract. But TELUS's interest *expense* increases from period to period as the bonds march toward maturity. Remember, these bonds were issued at a discount.

---

[1] Appendix D at the end of this book shows how to determine the price of this bond.

Panel A of Exhibit 8-5 repeats the TELUS bond data we've been using. Panel B provides an amortization table that

- Determines the periodic interest expense (column B)
- Shows the bond carrying amount (column E)

Study the exhibit carefully because the amounts we will be using come directly from the amortization table. This exhibit shows the *effective-interest method of amortization*, which is the correct way to measure interest expense.

Interest Expense on Bonds Issued at a Discount

In Exhibit 8-5, TELUS Communications Inc. borrowed $96,149 cash but must pay $100,000 when the bonds mature. What happens to the $3,851 balance of the discount account over the life of the bond issue?

The $3,851 is additional interest expense to TELUS over and above the stated interest that TELUS pays each six months. Exhibit 8-6 graphs the interest expense and the interest payment on the TELUS bonds over their lifetime. Observe that the semi-annual interest payment is fixed—by contract—at $4,500 (column A in Exhibit 8-5), but the amount of interest expense (column B) increases each period as the bond carrying amount moves upward toward maturity.

EXHIBIT 8-5 **Debt Amortization for a Bond Discount**

PANEL A—Bond Data

Issue date—January 1, 2009	Market interest rate at time of issue—10% annually, 5% semi-annually
Maturity (face) value—$100,000	Issue price—$96,149
Contract interest rate—9%	Maturity date—January 1, 2014
Interest paid—4 1/2% semi-annually, $4,500 = $100,000 × 0.09 × 6/12	

PANEL B—Amortization Table

	A	B	C	D	E
Semi-Annual Interest Date	Interest Payment (4 1/2% of Maturity Value)	Interest Expense (5% of Preceding Bond Carrying Amount)	Discount Amortization (B − A)	Discount Account Balance (Preceding D − C)	Bond Carrying Amount ($100,000 − D)
Jan. 1, 2009				$3,851	$ 96,149
July 1	$4,500	$4,807	$307	3,544	96,456
Jan. 1, 2010	4,500	4,823	323	3,221	96,779
July 1	4,500	4,839	339	2,882	97,118
Jan. 1, 2011	4,500	4,856	356	2,526	97,474
July 1	4,500	4,874	374	2,152	97,848
Jan. 1, 2012	4,500	4,892	392	1,760	98,240
July 1	4,500	4,912	412	1,348	98,652
Jan. 1, 2013	4,500	4,933	433	915	99,085
July 1	4,500	4,954	454	461	99,539
Jan. 1, 2014	4,500	4,961*	461	0	100,000

*Adjusted for the effect of rounding

Notes
- Column A The semi-annual interest payments are constant—fixed by the bond contract.
- Column B The interest expense each period = The preceding bond carrying amount × The market interest rate. Interest expense increases as the bond carrying amount (E) increases.
- Column C The excess of interest expense (B) over interest payment (A) is the discount amortization (C) for the period.
- Column D The discount balance (D) decreases when amortized.
- Column E The bond carrying amount (E) increases from $96,149 at issuance to $100,000 at maturity.

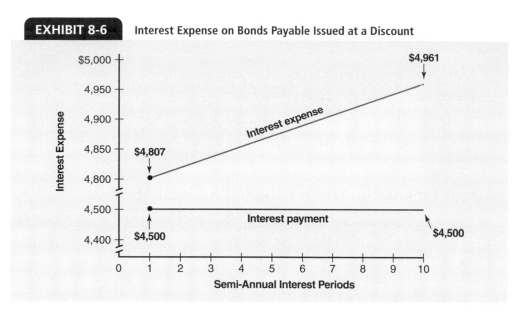

EXHIBIT 8-6 Interest Expense on Bonds Payable Issued at a Discount

The discount is allocated to interest expense through amortization each period over the term of the bonds. Exhibit 8-7 illustrates the amortization of the bonds' carrying value from $96,149 at the start to $100,000 at maturity. These amounts come from Exhibit 8-5, column E.

Now let's see how to account for the TELUS bonds issued at a discount. In our example, TELUS issued its bonds on January 1, 2009, On July 1, TELUS made the first $4,500 semi-annual interest payment. But TELUS's interest expense is greater than $4,500. TELUS's journal entry to record interest expense and the interest payment for the first six months follows (with all amounts taken from Exhibit 8-5):

2009
July 1   Interest Expense 4,807
          Discount on Bonds Payable   307
          Cash   4,500
    To pay semi-annual interest and amortize bond discount.

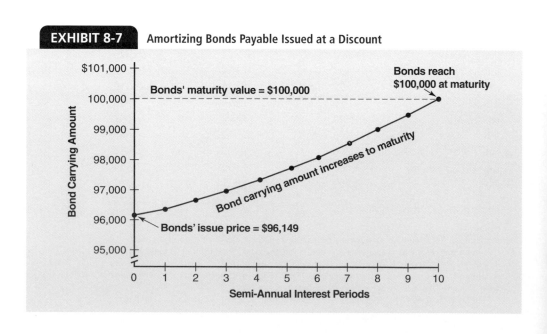

EXHIBIT 8-7 Amortizing Bonds Payable Issued at a Discount

The credit to Discount on Bonds Payable accomplishes two purposes:

- It adjusts the bonds' carrying amount as the bonds approach maturity value.
- It allocates (amortizes) the discount to interest expense.

ASSETS	=	LIABILITIES	+	SHAREHOLDERS' EQUITY	−	EXPENSES
−4,500	=	+307			−	4,807

At December 31, 2009, TELUS accrues interest and amortizes the bond discount for July through December with this entry (amounts from Exhibit 8-5):

2009
Dec. 31   Interest Expense..   4,823
       Discount on Bonds Payable   323
       Interest Payable   4,500
       To accrue semi-annual interest and amortize bond discount.

ASSETS	=	LIABILITIES	+	SHAREHOLDERS' EQUITY	−	EXPENSES
0	=	+323			−	4,823
		+4,500				

At December 31, 2009, TELUS's bond accounts appear as follows:

Bonds Payable		Discount on Bonds Payable	
	100,000	3,851	307
			323
		Bal. 3,221	

Bond carrying amount, $96,779 = $100,000 − $3,221 from Exhibit 8-5

STOP & THINK

You are analyzing the financial statements of a small company, and you note there is a difference between interest expense and the stated interest rate for the bonds. You wonder why interest expense is greater than the stated interest rate.

Answer:
Amortization of the bond discount is the difference between interest expense and the cash payment of interest. Interest expense exceeds the interest payment because the company isssued the bonds at a discount and must pay the face amount at maturity.

STOP & THINK

What would you expect TELUS Communications Inc.'s 2009 income statement and year-end balance sheet to report for these bonds?

Answer:

Income Statement for 2009	
Interest expense ($4,807 + $4,823)	$ 9,630

Balance Sheet at December 31, 2009		
Current liabilities:		
Interest payable...		$ 4,500
Long-term liabilities:		
Bonds payable...	$100,000	
Less: Discount on bonds payable	(3,221)	96,779

At the bonds' maturity on January 1, 2014, the discount will have been amortized to zero, and the bonds' carrying amount will be $100,000. TELUS will retire the bonds by making a $100,000 payment to the bondholders.

Partial-Period Interest Amounts

Companies don't always issue bonds at the beginning or the end of their accounting year. They issue bonds when market conditions are most favourable, and that may be on May 16, August 1, or any other date. To illustrate partial-period interest, assume Google Inc. issues $100,000 of 8% bonds payable at 96 on August 31, 2008. The market rate of interest was 9%, and these bonds pay semi-annual interest on February 28 and August 31 each year. The first few lines of Google's amortization table are:

Semi-annual Interest Date	4% Interest Payment	$4\frac{1}{2}$% Interest Expense	Discount Amortization	Discount Account Balance	Bond Carrrying Amount
Aug. 31, 2008				$4,000	$96,000
Feb. 28, 2009	$4,000	$4,320	$320	3,680	96,320
Aug. 31, 2009	4,000	4,334	334	3,346	96,654

Google's accounting year ends on December 31, so at year-end Google must accrue interest and amortize bond discount for 4 months (September through December). At December 31, 2008, Google will make this entry:

```
2008
Dec. 31   Interest Expense ($4,320 × 4/6)...................................  2,880
              Discount on Bonds Payable ($320 × 4/6) ...................         213
              Interest Payable ($4,000 × 4/6) ................................       2,667
          To accrue interest and amortize discount at year end.
```

The year-end entry at December 31, 2008, uses 4/6 of the upcoming semi-annual amounts at February 28, 2009. This example clearly illustrates the benefit of an amortization schedule.

Issuing Bonds at a Premium

Let's modify the TELUS bond example to illustrate issuance of the bonds at a premium. Assume that TELUS Communications Inc. issues $100,000 of five-year, 9% bonds that pay interest semi-annually. If the bonds are issued when the market interest rate is 8%, their issue price is $104,100.[2] The premium on these bonds is $4,100, and Exhibit 8-8 shows how to amortize the bonds by the effective-interest method. In practice, bond premiums are rare because few companies issue their bonds to pay cash interest above the market interest rate. We cover bond premiums for completeness.

TELUS's entries to record issuance of the bonds on January 1, 2009, and to make the first interest payment and amortize the bonds on July 1, are as follows:

```
2009
Jan. 1    Cash...............................................................................  104,100
              Bonds Payable .............................................................       100,000
              Premium on Bonds Payable .........................................         4,100
          To issue 9%, five-year bonds at a premium.
```

---

[2]Again, Appendix D at the end of the book shows how to determine the price of this bond.

At the beginning, TELUS's liability is $104,100—not $100,000. The accounting equation makes this clear.

ASSETS	=	LIABILITIES	+	SHAREHOLDERS' EQUITY
104,100	=	100,000	+	0
		+4,100		

2009
July 1

Interest Expense	4,164	
Premium on Bonds Payable	336	
Cash		4,500
To pay semi-annual interest and amortize bond premium.		

ASSETS	=	LIABILITIES	+	SHAREHOLDERS' EQUITY	−	EXPENSES
−4,500	=	−336			−	4,164

Immediately after issuing the bonds at a premium on January 1, 2009, TELUS would report the bonds payable on the balance sheet as follows:

Total current liabilities		$	XXX
Long-term liabilities:			
Bonds payable	$100,000		
Premium on bonds payable	4,100		104,100

The premium is *added* to the balance of bonds payable to determine the carrying amount.

In Exhibit 8-8, TELUS borrowed $104,100 cash but must pay only $100,000 at maturity. The $4,100 premium on the bonds is a reduction in TELUS's interest expense over the term of the bonds. Exhibit 8-9 graphs TELUS's interest payments (column A from Exhibit 8-8) and interest expense (column B).

Through amortization the premium decreases interest expense each period over the term of the bonds. Exhibit 8-10 diagrams the amortization of the bond carrying amount from the issue price of $104,100 to the maturity value of $100,000. All amounts are taken from Exhibit 8-8.

The Straight-Line Amortization Method: A Quick and Dirty Way to Measure Interest Expense

There is a less precise way to amortize bond discount or premium. The *straight-line amortization method* divides a bond discount or premium into equal periodic amounts over the bond's term. The amount of interest expense is thus the same for each interest period. This method is not acceptable for financial reporting.

Let's apply the straight-line method to the TELUS bonds issued at a discount and illustrated in Exhibit 8-5 (page 383). Suppose TELUS's executive vice-president and chief financial officer is considering issuing the 9% bonds at $96,149. To estimate semi-annual interest expense on the bonds, the executive can use the straight-line amortization method for the bond discount.

IFRS

Semi-annual cash interest payment ($100,000 × 0.09 × 6/12)	$4,500
+ Semi-annual amortization of discount ($3,851 ÷ 10)	385
= Estimated semi-annual interest expense	$4,885

EXHIBIT 8-8   Debt Amortization for a Bond Premium

PANEL A—Bond Data

Issue date—January 1, 2009   Market interest rate at time of issue—8% annually, 4% semi-annually
Maturity (face) value—$100,000   Issue price—$104,100
Contract interest rate—9%   Maturity date—January 1, 2014
Interest paid—4 1/2% semi-annually, $4,500 = $100,000 × 0.09 × 6/12

PANEL B—Amortization Table

	A	B	C	D	E
Semi-Annual Interest Date	Interest Payment (4 1/2% of Maturity Value)	Interest Expense (4% of Preceding Bond Carrying Amount)	Premium Amortization (A − B)	Premium Account Balance (Preceding D − C)	Bond Carrying Amount ($100,000 + D)
Jan. 1, 2009				$4,100	$104,100
July 1	$4,500	$4,164	$336	3,764	103,764
Jan. 1, 2010	4,500	4,151	349	3,415	103,415
July 1	4,500	4,137	363	3,052	103,052
Jan. 1, 2011	4,500	4,122	378	2,674	102,674
July 1	4,500	4,107	393	2,281	102,281
Jan. 1, 2012	4,500	4,091	409	1,872	101,872
July 1	4,500	4,075	425	1,447	101,447
Jan. 1, 2013	4,500	4,058	442	1,005	101,005
July 1	4,500	4,040	460	545	100,545
Jan. 1, 2014	4,500	3,955*	545	0	100,000

*Adjusted for the effect of rounding

Notes
- Column A   The semi-annual interest payments are constant—fixed by the bond contract.
- Column B   The interest expense each period = The preceding bond carrying amount × The market interest rate.
             Interest expense decreases as the bond carrying amount (E) decreases.
- Column C   The excess of each interest payment (A) over interest expense (B) is the premium amortization for the period (C).
- Column D   The premium balance (D) decreases when amortized.
- Column E   The bond carrying amount (E) decreases from $104,100 at issuance to $100,000 at maturity.

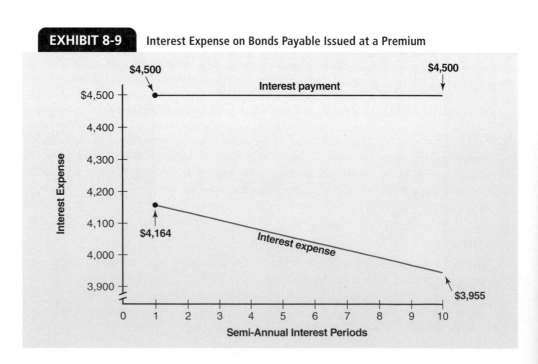

EXHIBIT 8-9   Interest Expense on Bonds Payable Issued at a Premium

EXHIBIT 8-10	Amortizing Bonds Payable Issued at a Premium

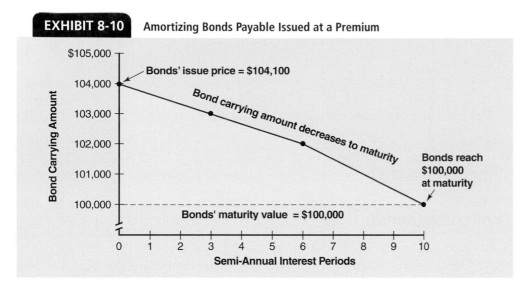

TELUS's entry to record interest and amortization of the bond discount under the straight-line amortization method would be:

2009

July 1	Interest Expense	4,164	
	Premium on Bonds Payable	336	
	Cash		4,500
	To pay semi-annual interest and amortize bond premium.		

GAAP permit the straight-line method to be used when the amounts differ insignificantly from amounts obtained from applying the effective interest method.

DECISION Should We Retire Bonds Payable Before Their Maturity?

Normally, companies wait until maturity to pay off, or *retire*, their bonds payable. But companies sometimes retire bonds early. The main reason for retiring bonds early is to relieve the pressure of making interest payments. Also the company may be able to borrow at a lower interest rate.

Some bonds are **callable**, which means that the bonds' issuers may *call*, or pay off, those bonds at a prearranged price (this is the *call price*) whenever the issuers so choose. The call price is usually a few percentage points above the face value, perhaps 102 or 103. Callable bonds give the issuer the benefit of being able to pay off the bonds whenever it is most favourable to do so. The alternative to calling the bonds is to purchase them in the open market at their current market price.

Assume Air Products and Chemicals Inc., a producer of industrial gases and chemicals, has $70 million of debenture bonds outstanding with an unamortized discount of $350,000. Lower interest rates in the market may convince management to pay off these bonds now. Assume that the bonds are callable at 103. If the market price of the bonds is 99.25, will Air Products and Chemicals Inc. call the bonds or purchase them in the open market? Market price is the better choice because the market price is lower than the call price. Retiring the bonds on February 1, 2007, at 99.25 results in a gain of $175,000, computed as follows:

Face value of bonds being retired	$70,000,000
Less: Unamortized discount	(350,000)
Carrying amount of the bonds	69,650,000
Market price ($70,000,000 × 0.9925)	69,475,000
Gain on retirement of bonds payable	$ 175,000

Journal entry to retire the bonds:

2007			
Feb. 1	Bonds Payable	70,000,000	
	Discount on Bonds Payable		350,000
	Cash		69,475,000
	Gain on retirement of bonds...................................		175,000
	To record the retirement of bonds.		

Gains and losses on early retirement of debt are reported as Other Income (Loss) on the income statement.

Convertible Bonds

Some corporate bonds may be converted into the issuing company's common shares. These bonds are called **convertible bonds** (or **convertible notes**). For investors, they combine (a) the safety of assured receipt of interest and principal on the bonds with (b) the opportunity for gains on the shares. The conversion feature is so attractive that investors usually accept a lower interest rate than they would for nonconvertible bonds. The lower cash interest payments benefit the issuer.

The holder of a convertible bond has the right to convert the bond into a specified number of common shares usually within a specified time period. The holder of the bond is likely to convert the bond into shares if the market price of the issuing company's shares gets high enough.

The subject of convertible bonds is mentioned for completeness; the accounting for convertible bonds and their presentation in the financial statements under the new *CICA Handbook* standards is complex and is beyond the scope of this text.

Objective

④ **Understand** the advantages and disadvantages of borrowing

DECISION Financing Operations with Bonds or Shares?

Managers must decide how to get the money they need to pay for assets. There are three main ways to finance operations:

- By retained earnings
- By issuing shares
- By issuing bonds (or notes)

Each strategy has its advantages and disadvantages.

1. **Financing by retained earnings** means that the company already has enough cash to purchase the needed assets. There's no need to issue more shares or borrow money. This strategy is low-risk to the company.

2. **Issuing shares** creates no liabilities or interest expense and is less risky to the issuing corporation. But issuing shares is more costly, as we shall see.

3. **Issuing bonds or notes payable** does not dilute control of the corporation. It often results in higher earnings per share because the earnings on borrowed money usually exceed interest expense. But creating more debt increases the risk of the company.

Earnings per share (EPS) is the amount of a company's net income for each of its outstanding shares. EPS is perhaps the single most important statistic used to evaluate companies because it is a standard measure of operating performance for comparing companies of different sizes and from different industries.

Suppose Athens Corporation needs $500,000 for expansion. Assume Athens has net income of $300,000 and 100,000 common shares outstanding. Management is considering two financing plans. Plan 1 is to issue $500,000 of 6% bonds, and plan 2 is to issue 50,000 common shares for $500,000. Management believes the new cash can be invested in operations to earn income of $200,000 before interest and taxes.

Exhibit 8-11 shows the earnings-per-share advantage of borrowing. As you can see, Athens Corporation's EPS amount is higher if the company borrows by issuing bonds (compare lines 9 and 10). Athens earns more on the investment ($102,000) than the interest it pays on the bonds ($30,000). This is called **trading on the equity** or using **leverage**. It is widely used to increase earnings per share of common shares.

In this case, borrowing results in higher earnings per share than issuing shares. Borrowing has its disadvantages, however. Interest expense may be high enough to eliminate net income and lead to losses. Also, borrowing creates liabilities that must be paid during bad years as well as good years. In contrast, a company that issues shares can omit its dividends during a bad year. The Decision Guidelines provide some guidance in deciding how to finance operations.

DECISION The Times-Interest-Earned Ratio

We have just seen how the wise use of borrowing can increase EPS. But too much debt can lead to bankruptcy if the business cannot pay liabilities as they come due. Managers and lenders use ratios to determine how much credit risk they are taking.

The debt ratio measures the effect of debt on the company's *financial position* but says nothing about the ability to pay interest expense. Analysts use a second ratio—the **times-interest-earned ratio**—to relate income to interest expense. To compute this ratio, we divide *income from operations* (also called *operating income*) by interest expense. This ratio measures the number of times that operating income can *cover* interest expense. The ratio is also called the **interest-coverage ratio**. A high times-interest-earned ratio indicates ease in paying interest expense; a low value suggests difficulty. Let's see how Sobeys Inc. and Loblaw Companies Limited, two leading grocery chains, compare on the times-interest-earned ratio (in millions of dollars).

EXHIBIT 8-11	Earnings-Per-Share Advantage of Borrowing			
		Plan 1		Plan 2
		Borrow $500,000 at 6%		Issue 50,000 Common Shares for $500,000
1. Net income before expansion...			$300,000	$300,000
2. Expected project income before interest and income tax.........................	$200,000		$200,000	
3. Less interest expense ($500,000 × 0.06)...	(30,000)		0	
4. Expected project income before income tax...	170,000		200,000	
5. Less income tax expense (40%)...	(68,000)		(80,000)	
6. Expected project net income..		102,000		120,000
7. Total company net income...		$402,000		$420,000
8. Earnings per share after expansion:				
9. Plan 1 Borrow ($402,000/100,000 shares)...		$ 4.02		
10. Plan 2 ($420,000/150,000 shares)..				$ 2.80

			Sobeys Inc.	Loblaw Companies Ltd.
Times-interest-earned ratio	=	$\dfrac{\text{Operating income}}{\text{Interest expense}}$ =	$\dfrac{364}{57}$	$\dfrac{736}{285}$
			= 6.4 times	= 2.6 times

Sobeys' income from operations covers its interest expense 6.4 times. Loblaw's interest-coverage ratio is 2.6 times. Sobeys is less risky on this ratio than Loblaw.

STOP & THINK

As part of your review of the financial statements of Sobeys and Loblaw as a possible investment, which company would you expect to have the higher debt ratio?

Summarized balance sheet (Amounts in millions)

	Sobeys Inc. May 3, 2008	Loblaw Companies Ltd. December 29, 2007
Total assets.....................................	$4,641	$13,674
Total liabilities	$2,691	$ 8,129
Shareholders' equity........................	1,950	5,545
Total liabilities and equity...............	$4,641	$13,674

Answer:

Loblaw has a slightly higher debt ratio than Sobeys (in millions of dollars):

		Sobeys	Loblaw
Debt ratio =	$\dfrac{\text{Total liabilities}}{\text{Total assets}}$ =	$\dfrac{\$2,691}{\$4,641}$	$\dfrac{\$8,129}{\$13,674}$
		= 0.58	= 0.59

Further research would reveal that Sobeys' long-term (and interest bearing) debt is 36% of Sobeys' total liabilities while Loblaw's long-term (and interest bearing) debt is 47% of Loblaw's total liabilities. This exercise demonstrates that a user must look deeply into the numbers on the financial statements to truly understand differences between companies.

Long-Term Liabilities: Leases and Pensions

A **lease** is a rental agreement in which the tenant (**lessee**) agrees to make rent payments to the property owner (**lessor**) in exchange for the use of the asset. Leasing allows the lessee to acquire the use of a needed asset without having to make the large initial cash down payment that purchase agreements require. Accountants distinguish between two types of leases: operating leases and capital leases.

Types of Leases

Operating leases are often short-term or cancellable. They give the lessee the right to use the asset but provide the lessee with no continuing rights to the asset. The lessor retains the usual risks and rewards of owning the leased asset. To account for an operating lease, the lessee debits Rent Expense (or Lease Expense) and credits Cash for the amount of the lease payment. Operating leases require the lessee to make rent payments. Therefore, an operating lease creates a liability even though the liability does not appear on the lessee's balance sheet.

Capital Leases.   Most businesses use capital leasing to finance the acquisition of some assets. A **capital lease** is a long-term noncancellable debt. How do we distinguish a capital lease from an operating lease? The *CICA Handbook's* Section 3065 on leases provides the guidelines. To be classified as a capital lease, a particular lease agreement must meet any *one* of the following criteria:

1. The lessee is likely to obtain ownership of the leased asset at the end of the lease either because the lease transfers title of the leased asset to the lessee at the end of the lease term or the lease contains a *bargain purchase option.*

2. The lease term is 75% or more of the estimated useful life of the leased asset. The lessee uses up most of the leased asset's service potential.

3. The present value of the lease payments is 90% or more of the market value of the leased asset. In effect, the lease payments are the same as installment payments for the leased asset.

Accounting for a capital lease is much like accounting for the purchase of an asset by the lessee. The lessee enters the asset into its own accounts and records a lease liability at the beginning of the lease term. Thus, the lessee capitalizes the asset in its own financial statements even though it may never take legal title to the property.

Many companies lease some of their property, plant, and equipment. Air Canada reports both operating leases and capital leases in its December 31, 2007, financial statements. Operating leases are reported in note 16 "Commitments" while capital leases are reported in note 8 "Long-term Debt and Capital Leases."

As was indicated above, operating leases are not recorded on the lessee's books. GAAP requires the lessee (in this case Air Canada) to disclose total operating lease payments due and the annual payments for the next five years. Air Canada does so in its financial statements in note 16 as follows:

Operating lease commitments	Aircraft	Other Property	Total
Year ended December 31, 2008	$ 280	$ 59	$ 339
Year ended December 31, 2009	271	42	313
Year ended December 31, 2010	255	36	291
Year ended December 31, 2011	197	33	230
Year ended December 31, 2012	180	32	212
Thereafter	602	121	723
	$1,785	$323	$2,108

The accounting for capital leases is to set up the present value of the lease payments as an asset and a liability. The gross amount of the capital leases and the associated accumulated amortization should be disclosed in the financial statements. Air Canada, in note 4, discloses the gross amount of the capital leases to be $1,899 million at December 31, 2007; accumulated amortization is disclosed as $438 million. GAAP requires the lessee to disclose total capital lease payments due, the annual payments for the next five years, and the amount of interest included in the payments. Air Canada does so in their financial statements in note 8 as follows:

Capital lease payments	
2008	$ 223
2009	147
2010	142
2011	136
2012	177
Thereafter	569
Total minimum lease payments	$1,394
Less amount representing interest	(422)
Total obligation under capital leases	$ 972

DECISION **Do Lessees Prefer Operating Leases or Capital Leases?**

Suppose you were the chief financial officer of Kepel Corporation. Kepel, whose assets total $504,000 and liabilities total $122,000, is leasing assets valued at close to $10 million. Kepel is the lessee (the renter) in the transaction. The lease can be structured either as an operating lease or as a capital lease. Which type of lease would you prefer for Kepel? Why? Computing Kepel's debt ratio two ways (new lease as an operating lease; new lease as a capital lease) will make your decision clear:

(Amounts in millions of dollars)	New Lease Is an Operating Lease	New Lease Is a Capital Lease
$\text{Debt ratio} = \dfrac{\text{Total liabilities}}{\text{Total assets}} =$	$\dfrac{\$122}{\$504}$	$\dfrac{\$122 + \$10}{\$504 + \$10} = \dfrac{\$132}{\$514}$
	$= 0.24$	$= 0.26$

You can see that a capital lease increases the debt ratio as both the asset and the liability are reported on the balance sheet. By contrast, operating leases don't affect the debt ratio. For this reason, companies generally prefer operating leases.

Pensions and Post-Retirement Liabilities

Many companies have retirement plans for their employees. A **pension** is an employee benefit that will be received during retirement. Companies also provide post-retirement benefits, such as medical insurance for retired former employees. Because employees earn these benefits by their service, the company records pension and retirement-benefit expense while employees work for the company.

Pensions are one of the most complex areas of accounting. As employees earn their pensions and the company pays into the pension plan, the plan's assets grow. The obligation for future pension payments to employees also accumulates. At the end of each period, the company compares

- the fair market value of the assets in the pension plan—cash and investments with

- the plan's *accumulated benefit obligation*, which is the present value of promised future pension payments to retirees.

If the plan assets exceed the accumulated benefit obligation, the plan is said to be *overfunded*. In this case, the asset and obligation amounts are to be reported only in the notes to the financial statements. However, if the accumulated benefit obligation (the pension liability) exceeds plan assets, the plan is *underfunded*, and the company must report the excess liability amount as a long-term pension liability on the balance sheet.

At May 3, 2008, Sobeys Inc. indicates that certain of its benefit plans were underfunded. Sobeys' balance sheet, therefore, included an employee future benefits obligation of $105.5 million. This amount is included with other long-term liabilities.

Reporting Liabilities

Reporting on the Balance Sheet

This chapter began with the liabilities reported on the balance sheets of Air Canada. Exhibit 8-12 repeats the liabilities section of Air Canada's balance sheet.

Objective

⑤ **Report** liabilities on the balance sheet

Exhibit 8-12 includes Note 8 from Air Canada's financial statements, which gives additional details about the company's liabilities. Note 8 shows the interest rates and the maturity dates of Air Canada's long-term debt and capital leases. Investors need these data to evaluate the company. The note also reports:

- Current installments of long-term debt and capital leases ($413 million) as a current liability
- Long-term debt and capital leases, excluding current installments, of $4,006 million

Trace these amounts from Note 8 to the company's balance sheet. Working back and forth between the financial statements and the related notes is an important part of financial analysis. You now have the tools to understand the liabilities reported on an actual balance sheet.

EXHIBIT 8-12   Reporting Liabilities of Air Canada

Air Canada
Consolidated Balance Sheet (Partial, Adapted)
December 31, 2007

	(Amounts in millions)
Current Liabilities	
Accounts payable and accrued charges	$1,243
Unearned ticket revenue	1,245
Aeroplan miles obligation	55
Current maturities of long-term debt and capital leases	413
Total current liabilities	2,956
Long-term debt and capital leases	4,006
Other long-term liabilities	2,248
	$9,210

Source: Air Canada's 2007 Annual Report

8. LONG-TERM DEBT AND CAPITAL LEASES (Partial, Adapted)

	Final Maturity	Stated Interest Rate	2007
Embraer aircraft financing	2017–2021	6.61–8.49	$1,138
Boeing aircraft financing	2019	5.13–5.69	647
Predelivery financing	2008–2013	6.16	521
Conditional sales agreements	2019	7.74–7.97	149
Lufthansa cooperation agreement	2009	6.50	25
GE loan	2015	10.58	38
Canadian Regional Jet	2012	6.43	33
Direct Corporation debt			2,551
Aircraft and engine leasing entities–debt			771
Fuel facility corporations–debt			125
Debt consolidated under AcG-15			896
Capital lease obligations			972
Total debt and capital leases			4,419
Current portion			(413)
Long-term debt and capital leases			$4,006

Reporting the Fair Market Value of Long-Term Debt

IFRS

As was pointed out in the IFRS Alert on page 377, *CICA Handbook* Section 3861 requires companies to report the fair market value of their financial assets and liabilities. At December 31, 2007, WestJet's Note 12 included this excerpt:

> At December 31, 2007, the carrying value of long-term debt was $1,430 million (2006 $1,445 million) with the fair value being approximately $1,474 million (2006 $1,495 million). The fair value of long-term debt is determined by discounting the future contractual cash flows under current financing arrangements at discount rates which represent borrowing rates presently available to the Corporation for loans with similar terms and maturity.

Overall, the fair market value of WestJet's long-term debt is about $44 million higher than the carrying amount on its books.

Reporting Financing Activities on the Cash Flow Statement

WestJet's balance sheet shows that the company finances most of its operations with debt. In fact, the company's debt ratio is 68.2% (total liabilities of $2,034 million divided by total assets of $2,984 million). Let's examine WestJet's financing activities as reported on its cash flow statement. Exhibit 8-13 is an excerpt from the company's cash flow statement.

During the year ended December 31, 2007, WestJet financed its investing activities from cash from operations and improved its cash position.

EXHIBIT 8-13 Cash Flow Statement (Adapted) for WestJet Airlines Ltd.

WestJet Airlines Ltd.
Consolidated Cash Flow Statement (Partial, Adapted)
For the Year Ended December 31, 2007

	(Amounts in millions)
Cash Flow from Operating Activities:	
Net cash provided by operating activities	$541
Cash Flow from Investing Activities:	
Net cash used in investing activities	(200)
Cash Flow from Financing Activities:	
Repurchase of common shares (net)	(21)
Increase in long-term debt	141
Payments of long-term debt	(157)
Other	(22)
	(59)
Cash Flow from Operating, Investing and Financing Activities	282

DECISION GUIDELINES

FINANCING WITH DEBT OR WITH SHARES?

The Forzani Group Ltd., the leading chain of sporting goods stores in Canada, was started by John Forzani in 1974 in Calgary. Suppose John Forzani is thinking of expanding into the United States. Take the role of John Forzani, and assume you must make some key decisions about how to finance the expansion.

Decision	Guidelines
How will you finance Forzani's expansion?	Your financing plan depends on Forzani's ability to generate cash flow, your willingness to give up some control of the business, the amount of financing risk you are willing to take, and Forzani's credit rating.
Do Forzani's operations generate enough cash to meet all its financing needs?	If yes, the business needs little outside financing. There is no need to borrow. If no, the business will need to issue additional shares or borrow the money.
Are you willing to give up some of your control of the business?	If yes, then issue shares to other shareholders, who can vote their shares to elect the company's directors. If no, then borrow from bondholders, who have no vote in the management of the company.
How much financing risk are you willing to take?	If much, then borrow as much as you can, and you may increase Forzani's earnings per share. But this will increase the business's debt ratio and the risk of being unable to pay its debts. If little, then borrow sparingly. This will hold the debt ratio down and reduce the risk of default on borrowing agreements. But Forzani's earnings per share may be lower than if you were to borrow.
How good is the business's credit rating?	The better the credit rating, the easier it is to borrow on favourable terms. A good credit rating also makes it easier to issue shares. Neither shareholders nor creditors will entrust their money to a company with a bad credit rating.

MyAccountingLab END-OF-CHAPTER SUMMARY PROBLEM

TransCanada Corporation has a number of debt issues outstanding in various amounts with various interest rates and maturities. Assume TransCanada has outstanding an issue of 8% bonds that mature in 2019. Suppose the bonds are dated October 1, 2009, and pay interest each April 1 and October 1.

Required

1. Complete the following effective-interest amortization table through October 1, 2011:
   Bond Data
   Maturity value—$100,000
   Contract interest rate—8%
   Interest paid—4% semi-annually, $4,000 ($100,000 × 0.08 × 6/12)
   Market interest rate at the time of issue—9% annually, 4 1/2% semi-annually
   Issue price—93.80

Amortization Table

Semi-Annual Interest Date	A Interest Payment (4% of Maturity Amount)	B Interest Expense (4 1/2% of Preceding Bond Carrying Amount)	C Discount Amortization (B − A)	D Discount Account Balance (Preceding D − C)	E Bond Carrying Amount ($100,000 − D)
01-10-09					
01-04-10					
01-10-10					
01-04-11					
01-10-11					

2. Using the amortization table, record the following transactions:
   a. Issuance of the bonds on October 1, 2009.
   b. Accrual of interest and amortization of the bonds on December 31, 2009.
   c. Payment of interest and amortization of the bonds on April 1, 2010.
   d. Retirement of two-thirds of the bonds payable on October 2, 2011. Purchase price of the bonds was based on their call price of 102.

Name: TransCanada Corporation
Industry: Pipeline provider
Accounting Period: The years 2009, 2010, 2011

Answers

Requirement 1

The semi-annual interest payment is constant ($4,000). The interest expense is calculated as 4.5% of the previous period's carrying value. The discount account balance reflects that the issue price of $90.75 is less than $100.00.

Semi-Annual Interest Date	A Interest Payment (4% of Maturity Amount)	B Interest Expense (4 1/2% of Preceding Bond Carrying Amount)	C Discount Amortization (B − A)	D Discount Account Balance (Preceding D − C)	E Bond Carrying Amount ($100,000 − D)
01-10-09				$6,200	$93,800
01-04-10	$4,000	$4,221	$221	5,979	94,021
01-10-10	4,000	4,231	231	5,748	94,252
01-04-11	4,000	4,241	241	5,507	94,493
01-10-11	4,000	4,252	252	5,255	94,745

Requirement 2

a. 2009

Oct. 1	Cash	93,800	
	Discount on Bonds Payable..............................	6,200	
	Bonds Payable...		100,000
	To issue 8%, ten-year bonds at a discount.		

> The bonds were issued for less than $100,000, reflecting a discount. Use the amounts from columns D and E for 01-10-09 from the amortization table.

b. Dec. 31 Interest Expense ($4,221 × 3/6) 2,111

Discount on Bonds Payable ($121 × 3/6).....................		111
Interest Payable ($4,000 × 3/6)...................................		2,000
To accrue interest and amortize the bonds.		

> The accrued interest is calculated, and the bond discount is amortized. Use 3/6 of the amounts from columns A, B, and C for 01-04-10 from the amortization table.

c. 2010

Apr. 1	Interest Expense	2,110	
	Interest Payable	2,000	
	Discount on Bonds Payable ($121 × 3/6).....................		110*
	Cash		4,000
	To pay semi-annual interest, part of which was accrued, and amortize the bonds.		

> The semi-annual interest payment is made ($4,000 from Column A). Only the January-to-March 2010 interest expense is recorded, since the October-to-December interest expense was already recorded in Requirement 2 b. The same is true for the discount on bonds payable. Reverse Interest Payable from Requirement 2 b, since cash is paid now.

d. Oct. 2 Bonds Payable ($100,000 × 2/3)...................................... 66,667

Loss on Retirement of Bonds	4,836	
Discount on Bonds Payable ($5,255 × 2/3).................		3,503
Cash ($100,000 × 2/3 × 1.02)		68,000
To retire bonds payable before maturity.		

> The cash paid on retirement was $102 for every $100 of bonds. Use 2/3 of the amount from column D for 01-10-11 to calculate Discount on Bonds Payable. The loss on retirement reflects the excess of the book value over the cash received and is the "plug" figure in the journal entry.

*The total amortization was $221 of which $111 was recognized at December 31, 2009.

REVIEW LIABILITIES

QUICK CHECK   (Answers are given on page 421.)

1. Which of the following is *not* an estimated liability?
   - **a.** Allowance for bad debts
   - **b.** Product warranties
   - **c.** Income taxes
   - **d.** Vacation pay

2. Recording estimated warranty expense in the current year *best* follows which accounting principle?
   - **a.** Consistency
   - **b.** Materiality
   - **c.** Full disclosure
   - **d.** Historical cost
   - **e.** Matching

3. Lotta Sound grants a 90-day warranty on all stereos. Historically, approximately 2 1/2% of all sales prove to be defective. Sales in June are $200,000. In July, $2,900 of defective units are returned for replacement. What entry must Lotta Sound make at the end of June to record the warranty expense?
   - **a.** Debit Warranty Expense, and credit Estimated Warranty Payable, $2,900.
   - **b.** Debit Warranty Expense, and credit Cash, $4,865.
   - **c.** Debit Warranty Expense, and credit Estimated Warranty Payable, $5,000.
   - **d.** No entry is needed at June 30

4. Outback Camera Co. was organized to sell a single product that carries a 60-day warranty against defects. Engineering estimates indicate that 5% of the units sold will prove defective and require an average repair cost of $40 per unit. During Outback's first month of operations, total sales were 400 units; by the end of the month, 6 defective units had

been repaired. The liability for product warranties at month-end should be which of the following?

a. $270

b. $530

c. $560

d. $810

e. None of these

5. A contingent liability should be recorded in the accounts

a. If the related future event will probably occur

b. If the amount is due in cash within 1 year

c. If the amount can be reasonably estimated

d. Both a and b

e Both a and c

6. An unsecured bond is a

a. Registered bond

b. Mortgage bond

c. Term bond

d. Serial bond

e. Debenture bond

7. The Discount on Bonds Payable account

a. Is a contra account to Bonds Payable

b. Is a miscellaneous revenue account

c. Is an expense account

d. Is expensed at the bond's maturity

e. Has a normal credit balance

8. The discount on a bond payable becomes

a. Additional interest expense the year the bonds are sold

b. Additional interest expense over the life of the bonds

c. A reduction in interest expense the year the bonds mature

d. A reduction in interest expense over the life of the bonds

e. A liability in the year the bonds are sold

9. A bond that matures in installments is called a

a. Secured bond

b. Zero coupon

c. Serial bond

d. Term bond

e. Callable bond

10. The carrying value of Bonds Payable equals

a. Bonds Payable − Premium on Bonds Payable

b. Bonds Payable − Discount on Bonds Payable

c. Bonds Payable + Discount on Bonds Payable

d. Bonds Payable + Accrued Interest

11. A corporation issues bonds that pay interest each March 1 and September 1. The corporation's December 31 adjusting entry may include a

a. Debit to Cash

b. Credit to Cash

c. Credit to Interest Expense

d. Debit to Interest Payable

e. Credit to Discount on Bonds Payable

Use this information to answer Questions 12 through 16.

McLennan Corporation issued $200,000 of 9 1/2% 5-year bonds. The bonds are dated and sold on January 1, 2009. Interest payment dates are January 1 and July 1. The bonds are issued for $196,140 to yield the market interest rate of 10%. Use the effective-interest method for Questions 12 through 15.

12. What is the amount of interest expense that McLennan Corporation will record on July 1, 2009, the first semi-annual interest payment date?

a. $9,807

b. $9,926

c. $10,000

d. $19,000

13. What is the amount of discount amortization that McLennan Corporation will record on July 1, 2009, the first semi-annual interest payment date?
    - a. $0
    - b. $74
    - c. $193
    - d. $307

14. What is the total cash payment for interest for each 12-month period?
    - a. $10,000
    - b. $19,000
    - c. $19,614
    - d. $20,000

15. What is the carrying amount of the bonds on the December 31, 2009, balance sheet?
    - a. $196,140
    - b. $196,526
    - c. $196,769
    - d. $196,912

16. Using straight-line amortization, the carrying amount of McLennan Corporation's bonds at December 31, 2009 is which of the following?
    - a. $196,140
    - b. $196,526
    - c. $196,769
    - d. $196,912

ACCOUNTING VOCABULARY

bond market price The price investors are willing to pay for the bond. It is equal to the present value of the principal payment plus the present value of the interest payments. (p. 380)

bonds payable Groups of notes payable issued to multiple lenders called *bondholders*. (p. 377)

callable bonds Bonds that may be paid at a specified price whenever the issuer wants. (p. 389)

capital lease Lease agreement that meets any one of four criteria: (1) The lease transfers title of the leased asset to the lessee at the end of the lease term. (2) The lease contains a bargain purchase option. (3) The lease term is 75% or more of the estimated useful life of the leased asset. (4) The present value of the lease payments is 90% or more of the market value of the leased asset. (p. 392)

convertible bonds (or **notes**) Bonds or notes that may be converted into the issuing company's common stock at the investor's option. (p. 390)

current installment of long-term debt The amount of the principal that is payable within one year. Also called *current portion of long-term debt*. (p. 372)

debentures Unsecured bonds—bonds backed only by the good faith of the borrower. (p. 378)

discount (on a bond) Excess of a bond's face (par) value over its issue price. (p. 379)

earnings per share (EPS) Amount of a company's net income per outstanding common share. (p. 390)

face value of bond The principal amount payable by the issuer. Also called *maturity value*. (p. 378)

interest-coverage ratio Another name for the *times-interest-earned ratio*. (p. 391)

lease Rental agreement in which the tenant (lessee) agrees to make rent payments to the property owner (lessor) in exchange for the use of the asset. (p. 392)

lessee Tenant in a lease agreement. (p. 392)

lessor Property owner in a lease agreement. (p. 392)

leverage Earning more income on borrowed money than the related interest expense, thereby increasing the earnings for the owners of the business. Also called *trading on the equity*. (p. 391)

market interest rate Interest rate that investors demand for loaning their money. Also called *effective interest rate*. (p. 380)

operating lease Usually a short-term or cancellable rental agreement. (p. 392)

payroll Employee compensation, a major expense of many businesses. (p. 370)

pension Employee benefit that will be received during retirement. (p. 394)

premium (on a bond) Excess of a bond's issue price over its face value. (p. 379)

present value Amount a person would invest now to receive a greater amount at a future date. (p. 379)

serial bonds Bonds that mature in installments over a period of time. (p. 377)

short-term note payable Note payable due within one year. (p. 368)

stated interest rate Interest rate printed on the bond certificate that determines the amount of cash interest the borrower pays and the investor receives each year. Also called the *coupon rate* or *contract interest rate*. (p. 380)

term bonds Bonds that all mature at the same time for a particular issue. (p. 377)

times-interest-earned ratio Ratio of income from operations to interest expense. Measures the number of times that operating income can cover interest expense. Also called the *interest-coverage ratio*. (p. 391)

trading on the equity Earning more income on borrowed money than the related interest expense, thereby increasing the earnings for the owners of the business. Also called *leverage*. (p. 391)

underwriter Organization that purchases the bonds from an issuing company and resells them to its clients or sells the bonds for a commission, agreeing to buy all unsold bonds. (p. 377)

ASSESS YOUR PROGRESS

MyAccountingLab

Make the grade with MyAccountingLab: The exercises and problems marked in red can be found on MyAccountingLab at www.myaccountinglab.com. You can practise them as often as you want, and they feature step by step guided solutions to help you find the right answer.

SHORT EXERCISES

Accounting for a note payable
(Obj. 1)

S8-1 Jasper Sports Limited purchased inventory costing $10,000 by signing a 10% short-term note payable. The purchase occurred on March 31, 2008. Jasper pays annual interest each year on March 31. Journalize Jasper's (a) purchase of inventory, (b) accrual of interest expense on December 31, 2008, and (c) payment of the note plus interest on March 31, 2009.

Reporting a short-term note payable and the related interest in the financial statements
(Obj. 1)

S8-2 This short exercise works with Short Exercise 8-1.

1. Refer to the data in Short Exercise 8-1. Show what the company would report on its balance sheet at December 31, 2008, and on its income statement for the year ended on that date.

2. What one item will the financial statements for the year ended December 31, 2009, report? Identify the financial statement, the item, and its amount.

Accounting for warranty expense and estimated warranty payable
(Obj. 1)

S8-3 General Motors of Canada Limited guarantees automobiles against defects for 5 years or 160,000 km, whichever comes first. Suppose GM Canada can expect warranty costs during the 5-year period to add up to 3% of sales.

Assume that Forbes Motors in Waterloo, Ontario, made sales of $2,000,000 on their Pontiac line during 2009. Forbes received cash for 10% of the sales and took notes receivable for the remainder. Payments to satisfy customer warranty claims totalled $50,000 during 2009.

1. Record the sales, warranty expense, and warranty payments for Forbes. Ignore any reimbursement that Forbes may receive from GM Canada.

2. Post to the Estimated Warranty Payable T-account. The beginning balance was $40,000. At the end of 2009, how much in estimated warranty payable does Forbes owe its customers?

Applying GAAP; reporting warranties in the financial statements
(Obj. 1)

S8-4 Refer to the data given in Short Exercise 8-3. What amount of warranty expense will Forbes report during 2009? Which accounting principle addresses this situation? Does the warranty expense for the year equal the year's cash payments for warranties? Explain the relevant accounting principle as it applies to measuring warranty expense.

Interpreting a company's contingent liabilities
(Obj. 1)

S8-5 MDS Inc., the global life sciences company, included the following note in its October 31, 2007, financial statements:

NOTES TO CONSOLIDATED FINANCIAL STATEMENTS
23. (In Part): Commitments, Contingencies, and Guarantees

c) Liability insurance

The Company is self-insured for up to the first $5 million of costs incurred relating to a single liability claim in a year and to $10 million in aggregate claims arising during an annual policy period. The Company provides for unsettled reported losses and losses incurred but not reported based on an independent review of all claims made against the Company. Accruals for estimated losses related to self-insurance were not material at October 31, 2007.

1. Why are these contingent (versus real) liabilities?

2. How can a contingent liability become a real liability for MDS Inc.? What are the limits of self-insured liability claims? Explain how these limits work.

3. What is the meaning of the last sentence in the note?

S8-6 Compute the price of the following bonds:
a. $1,000,000 quoted at 89.75
b. $500,000 quoted at 110.375
c. $100,000 quoted at 97.50
d. $400,000 quoted at 102.625

Pricing bonds
(Obj. 2)

S8-7 Determine whether the following bonds will be issued at face value, a premium, or a discount:
a. The market interest rate is 9%. Star Inc. issues bonds with a stated rate of 8 1/2%.
b. Charger Corporation issued 7 1/2% bonds when the market rate was 7 1/2%.
c. Explorer Corporation issued 8% bonds when the market interest rate was 6 7/8%.
d. Tundra Company issued bonds that pay cash interest at the stated interest rate of 7%. At the date of issuance, the market interest rate was 8 1/4%.

Determining bond prices at face value, a discount, or a premium
(Obj. 2)

S8-8 Suppose **Scotiabank** issued a 6-year $10,000 bond with stated interest rate of 6.25% when the market interest rate was 6 1/4%. Assume that the accounting year of Scotiabank ends on October 31. Journalize the following transactions, including an explanation for each entry.
a. Issuance of the bond, payable on May 1, 2009
b. Accrual of interest expense on October 31, 2009 (rounded to the nearest dollar)
c. Payment of cash interest on November 1, 2009
d. Payment of the bonds at maturity (give the date)

Journalizing basic bond payable transactions; bonds issued at face value
(Obj. 2)

S8-9 Standard Autoparts Inc. issued $100,000 of 7%, 10-year bonds at a price of 87 on January 31, 2009. The market interest rate at the date of issuance was 9%, and the standard bonds pay interest semi-annually.

1. Prepare an effective-interest amortization table for the bonds through the first three interest payments. Use Exhibit 8-5, page 383, as a guide, and round amounts to the nearest dollar.
2. Record Standard's issuance of the bonds on January 31, 2009, and payment of the first semi-annual interest amount and amortization of the bonds on July 31, 2009. Explanations are not required.

Issuing bonds and amortizing bonds by the effective-interest method
(Obj. 2)

S8-10 Use the amortization table that you prepared for Standard Autoparts in Short Exercise 8-9 to answer these questions about the company's long-term debt:

1. How much cash did Standard Autoparts borrow on January 31, 2009? How much cash will Standard Autoparts pay back at maturity on January 31, 2019?
2. How much cash interest will Standard Autoparts pay each 6 months?
3. How much interest expense will Standard Autoparts report on July 31, 2009, and on January 31, 2010? Why does the amount of interest expense increase each period? Explain in detail.

Analyzing data on long-term debt
(Obj. 3)

S8-11 Max Industries Ltd. borrowed money by issuing a $10,000 6.5%, 10-year bond. Assume the issue price was 94 on July 1, 2009.

1. How much cash did Max Industries receive when it issued the bond?
2. How much must Max Industries pay back at maturity? When is the maturity date?
3. How much cash interest will Max Industries pay each 6 months? Carry the interest amount to the nearest cent.
4. How much interest expense will Max Industries report each 6 months? Assume the straight-line amortization method, and carry the interest amount to the nearest cent.

Determining bonds payable amounts: amortizing bonds by the straight-line method
(Obj. 3)

S8-12 Return to the Max Industries bond in Short Exercise 8-11. Assume that Max Industries issued the bond on July 1, 2009, at a price of 90. Also assume that Max Industries' accounting year ends on December 31. Journalize the following transactions for Max Industries, including an explanation for each entry:
a. Issuance of the bonds on July 1, 2009
b. Accrual of interest expense and amortization of bonds on December 31, 2009. (Use the straight-line amortization method, and round amounts to the nearest dollar.)
c. Payment of the first semi-annual interest amount on January 1, 2010.

Issuing bonds, accruing interest, and amortizing bonds by the straight-line method
(Obj. 3)

Earnings-per-share effects of financing with bonds versus shares
(Obj. 4)

S8-13 Assume that YouTube needs $1.5 million to expand the company. YouTube is considering the issuance of either

- $1,500,000 of 5% bonds to borrow the money, or
- 100,000 common shares at $15 per share

Before any new financing, YouTube expects to earn net income of $500,000, and the company already has 200,000 common shares outstanding. YouTube believes the expansion will increase income before interest and income tax by $250,000. YouTube's income tax rate is 30%.

Prepare an analysis similar to Exhibit 8-11, page 391, to determine which plan is likely to result in the higher earnings per share. Based solely on the earnings-per-share comparison, which financing plan would you recommend for YouTube?

Computing the times-interest-earned ratio
(Obj. 4)

S8-14 Zigzag International Ltd. reported the following data in 2009 (in millions):

Net operating revenues	$29.2
Operating expenses	26.3
Operating income	2.9
Nonoperating items	
Interest expense	(1.6)
Other	(0.2)
Net income	$ 1.1

Compute Zigzag's times-interest-earned ratio, and write a sentence to explain what the ratio value means. Would you be willing to lend Zigzag $1 million? State your reason.

Reporting liabilities, including capital lease obligations
(Obj. 5)

S8-15 Trinidad Industries Inc. has the following selected accounts at December 31, 2008.

GST Payable (net of ITC)	$ 17,000
Bonds payable	300,000
Equipment	120,000
Current portion of bonds payable	40,000
Notes payable, long-term	100,000
Interest payable (due March 1, 2009)	10,000
Accounts payable	44,000
Discount on bonds payable (all long-term)	10,000
Accounts receivable	34,000

Prepare the liabilities section of Trinidad's balance sheet at December 31, 2008, to show how Trinidad would report these items. Report total current liabilities and total liabilities.

EXERCISES

Accounting for warranty expense and the related liability
(Obj. 1)

E8-16 The accounting records of Audio-Video Inc. included the following balances before the year-end adjustments:

Estimated Warranty Payable	Sales Revenue	Warranty Expense
Beg. bal. 8,000	150,000	

In the past, Audio-Video's warranty expense has been 6% of sales. During the current period, the business paid $9,400 to satisfy the warranty claims of customers.

❙ *Required*

1. Record Audio-Video's warranty expense for the period and the company's cash payments to satisfy warranty claims. Explanations are not required.
2. Show everything Audio-Video will report on its income statement and balance sheet for this situation.
3. Which data item from Requirement 2 will affect Audio-Video's current ratio? Will Audio-Video's current ratio increase or decrease as a result of this item?

E8-17 *Ontario Traveller Magazine* completed the following transactions during 2009:

Recording and reporting current liabilities
(Obj. 1)

Aug.	31	Sold 1-year subscriptions, collecting cash of $1,500, plus PST of 8% and GST of 5%
Dec.	31	Remitted (paid) the sales tax to the Province of Ontario, GST to Canada Revenue Agency (CRA)
	31	Made the necessary adjustment at year end.

Journalize these transactions (explanations are not required). Then report any liability on the company's balance sheet at December 31.

E8-18 Penske Talent Search has an annual payroll of $150,000. At December 31, Penske owes salaries of $7,600 on which employee withholdings payable are $1,200 and employee benefits payable by the company are $1,000. The company has calculated its share of Canada Pension Plan, Employment Insurance, and other employee benefits to be 6% of payroll expense. The company will pay these amounts early next year. Show what Penske will report for the foregoing on its income statement and year-end balance sheet.

Reporting payroll expense and liabilities
(Obj. 1)

E8-19 Joy's Bar and Grill completed the following note-payable transactions.

Recording note-payable transactions
(Obj. 1)

2008		
Aug.	1	Purchased kitchen equipment costing $60,000 by issuing a 1-year, 5% note
Dec.	31	Accrued interest on the note payable
2009		
Aug.	1	Paid the note payable at maturity

Answer these questions for Joy's Bar and Grill:

1. How much interest expense must be accrued at December 31, 2008?
2. Determine the amount of Joy's final payment on July 1, 2009.
3. How much interest expense will Joy's report for 2008 and for 2009?

E8-20 At December 31, 2008, Young Real Estate reported a current liability for income tax payable of $200,000. During 2009, Young earned income of $900,000 before income tax. The company's income tax rate during 2009 was 20%. Also during 2009, Young paid income taxes of $250,000. How much income tax payable did Young Real Estate report on its balance sheet at December 31, 2009? How much income tax expense did Young report on its 2009 income statement?

Accounting for income tax
(Obj. 1)

E8-21 Mills Geothermal Ltd. installs environmental heating/cooling systems. The company's 2009 revenues totalled $360 million, and at December 31, 2009, the company had $65 million in current assets. The December 31, 2009, balance sheet reported the liabilities and shareholders' equity as follows.

Analyzing liabilities
(Obj. 1, 5)

	At year end (In millions)	
	2009	2008
Liabilities and Shareholders' Equity		
Current Liabilities		
Accounts payable	$ 29	$ 26
Accrued expenses	16	20
Employee compensation and benefits	9	11
Current portion of long-term debt	5	—
Total Current Liabilities	59	57
Long-Term Debt	115	115
Post-retirement Benefits Payable	31	27
Other Liabilities	21	17
Shareholders' Equity	$ 73	70
Total Liabilities and Shareholders' Equity	$299	$286

❚ Required

1. Describe each of Mills Geothermal Ltd.'s liabilities, and state how the liability arose.
2. What were the company's total assets at December 31, 2009? Was the company's debt ratio at the end of 2009 high, low, or in a middle range?

Reporting a contingent liability
(Obj. 1)

E8-22 PharmaNet Development Group Inc. is the parent company of Anapharm Inc., the Canadian industry leader in early phase drug development. PharmaNet's revenues for 2007 totalled $470.3 million. At December 31, 2007, PharmaNet was a defendant in a number of lawsuits related to accounting issues.

> **NOTE G (in part): Litigation and Inquiries** of the financial statements December 31, 2007, reported:
>
> The [company] named as defendant[s] in the Federal Derivative Actions and the Florida Circuit Court Derivative Actions intend[s] to vigorously defend against the lawsuits. As the outcome of these matters is difficult to predict, significant changes in the Company's estimated exposures could occur.

❚ Required

1. Suppose PharmaNet's lawyers believe a significant legal judgment against the company is reasonably possible. How should PharmaNet report this situation in its financial statements?
2. Suppose PharmaNet's lawyers believe it is probable that a $2-million judgment will be rendered against the company. How should this situation be reported in Pharmanet's financial statement? Journalize any entry required by GAAP. Explanations are not required.

Reporting current and long-term liabilities
(Obj. 1, 5)

E8-23 Assume that Premium Golf Equipment completed these selected transactions during December 2008.

a. Sales of $3,000,000 are subject to estimated warranty cost of 3%. The estimated warranty payable at the beginning of the year was $30,000, and warranty payments for the year totalled $60,000.
b. On December 1, 2008, Premium signed a $150,000 note that requires annual payments of $30,000 plus 5% interest on the unpaid balance each December 1.
c. Golf Town, a chain of golf stores, ordered $125,000 of golf equipment. With its order, Golf Town sent a cheque for $125,000, and Premium shipped $100,000 of the goods. Premium will ship the remainder of the goods on January 3, 2009.
d. The December payroll of $100,000 is subject to employee withheld income tax, Canada Pension Plan and Employment Insurance, and company share of Canada Pension Plan and Employment Insurance totalling $25,000 and benefits of $9,000. On December 31, Premium pays employees their take-home pay and accrues all tax amounts.

❚ Required

Classify each liability as current or long-term and report the liability and its amount that would appear on the Premium Golf Equipment balance sheet at December 31, 2008. Show a total for current liabilities.

Issuing bonds, paying and accruing interest, and amortizing the bonds by the straight-line method
(Obj. 2)

E8-24 On January 31, 2009, Triumph Sports Cars issued 10-year, 6% bonds with a face value of $100,000. The bonds were issued at 97 and pay interest on January 31 and July 31. Triumph amortizes bonds by the straight-line method. Record (a) issuance of the bonds on January 31, (b) the semi-annual interest payment and discount amortization on July 31, and (c) the interest accrual and discount amortization on December 31.

Measuring cash amounts for a bond; amortizing the bonds by the straight-line method
(Obj. 2, 3)

E8-25 Moreau Manufacturing Inc. has $200,000 of 8% debenture bonds outstanding. The bonds were issued at 102 in 2009 and mature in 2029.

❚ Required

1. How much cash did Moreau receive when it issued these bonds?
2. How much cash *in total* will Moreau pay the bondholders through the maturity date of the bonds?

3. Take the difference between your answers to Requirements 1 and 2. This difference represents Moreau's total interest expense over the life of the bonds. (Challenge)

4. Compute Moreau's annual interest expense by the straight-line amortization method. Multiply this amount by 20. Your 20-year total should be the same as your answer to Requirement 3. (Challenge)

E8-26 Family General Stores Inc. is authorized to issue $500,000 of 7%, 10-year bonds. On December 31, 2008, when the market interest rate is 8%, the company issues $400,000 of the bonds and receives cash of $372,660. Family General amortizes bonds by the effective-interest method. The semi-annual interest dates are January 31 and July 31.

Issuing bonds (discount); recording interest payments and the related bond amortization
(Obj. 2, 3)

❙ *Required*

1. Prepare a bond amortization table for the first four semi-annual interest periods.

2. Record issuance of the bonds on December 31, 2008, and the semi-annual interest payments on January 31, 2009, and on July 31, 2009.

E8-27 On June 30, 2008, the market interest rate is 7%. Dellaca Enterprises issues $500,000 of 8% 20-year bonds at 110.625. The bonds pay interest on June 30 and December 31. Dellaca amortizes bonds by the effective-interest method.

Issuing bonds (premium); recording interest accrual and payment and the related bond amortization
(Obj. 2, 3)

❙ *Required*

1. Prepare a bond amortization table for the first four semi-annual interest periods.

2. Record issuance of the bonds on June 30, 2008, the payment of interest at December 31, 2009, and the semi-annual interest payment on June 30, 2009.

E8-28 Carlson Candies issued $300,000 of 8 3/8%, 5-year bonds on January 1, 2007, when the market interest rate was 9 1/2%. The company pays interest annually at year end. The issue price of the bonds was $287,041.

Debt payment and bond amortization schedule
(Obj. 3)

❙ *Required*

Create a spreadsheet model to prepare a schedule to amortize the bonds. Use the effective-interest method of amortization. Round to the nearest dollar, and format your answer as shown here.

	A	B	C	D	E	F
1						
2						Bond
3		Interest	Interest	Discount	Discount	Carrying
4	Date	Payment	Expense	Amortization	Balance	Amount
5	1-1-2007					287,041
6	12-31-2007	$ ☐	$ ☐	$ ☐	$ ☐	$ ☐
7	12-31-2008					
8	12-31-2009					
9	12-31-2010					
10	12-31-2011					
		300,000*0.08375	+F5*0.095	+C6–B6	300,000–F5	+F5+D6

E8-29 Montrose Corporation issued $300,000 of 8 1/2% notes on December 31, 2006, at a price of 98.5. The notes' term to maturity is 10 years. After 3 years, Montrose retired the bonds when the market price per bond is 99.0.

Recording retirement of notes payable
(Obj. 2)

❙ *Required*

1. Without making journal entries, compute the carrying amount of the notes payable at December 31, 2009, immediately before the retirement. Montrose uses the straight-line method to amortize bonds.

2. All amortization has been recorded properly. Journalize the retirement transaction at December 31, 2009.

Using ratios to compare companies
(Obj. 4)

E8-30 Companies that operate in different industries may have very different financial ratio values. These differences may grow even wider when we compare companies located in different countries.

Compare three leading companies on their current ratio, debt ratio, and times-interest-earned ratio. Compute three ratios for **Sobeys** (the Canadian grocery chain), **Sony** (the Japanese electronics manufacturer), and **Daimler** (the German auto company).

Income data	(Amounts in millions or billions)		
	Sobeys	Sony	Daimler
Total revenues	$12,853	¥7,475	€151,589
Operating income	332	191	2,072
Interest expense	35	29	913
Net Income	197	124	3,227

Asset and liability data	(Amounts in millions or billions)		
	Sobeys	Sony	Daimler
Total current assets	$1,235	¥3,770	€93,131
Long-term assets	2,504	6,838	96,891
Total current liabilities	1,230	3,200	59,977
Long-term liabilities	674	4,204	95,890
Shareholders' equity	1,835	3,204	34,155

Note: ¥ is the symbol for a Japanese yen; € for a euro.

Based on your computed ratio values, which company looks the least risky? (Challenge)

Analyzing alternative plans for raising money
(Obj. 4)

E8-31 Altman & Associates is considering two plans for raising $700,000 to expand operations. Plan A is to borrow at 5%, and plan B is to issue 100,000 common shares. Before any new financing, Altman has net income of $500,000 and 100,000 common shares outstanding. Assume you own most of Altman's existing shares. Management believes the company can use the new funds to earn additional income of $300,000 before interest and taxes. Altman's income tax rate is 30%.

❙ Required

1. Analyze Altman's situation to determine which plan will result in higher earnings per share. Use Exhibit 8-11, page 391, as a model.

2. Which plan results in higher earnings per share? Which plan allows you to retain control of the company? Which plan creates more financial risk for the company? Which plan do you prefer? Why? Present your conclusion in a memo to Altman's board of directors.

CHALLENGE EXERCISES

Reporting current liabilities
(Obj. 1, 5)

E8-32 Assume the top management of **Best Buy Inc**. examines company accounting records at February 7, 3 weeks before the end of the fiscal year (amounts in billions):

Total current assets..	$ 8.0
Noncurrent assets...	3.9
	$ 11.9
Total current liabilities..	6.0
Noncurrent liabilities...	0.6
Shareholders' equity	5.3
	$11.9

Suppose Best Buy's top management wants to achieve a current ratio of 1.4. How much in current liabilities should Best Buy pay off within the next three weeks to achieve its goal?

E8-33 United Products completed one of the most famous debt refinancings in history. A debt refinancing occurs when a company issues new bonds to retire old bonds. The company debits the old bonds payable and credits the new bonds.

Refinancing old bonds with new bonds
(Obj. 2, 3, 5)

United had $125 million of 5 1/2% bonds payable outstanding, with 20 years to maturity. United retired these old bonds by issuing $75 million of new 9% bonds to the holders of the old bonds and paying the bondholders $13 million in cash. United issued both groups of bonds at par so there was no bond premium or discount. At the time of the debt refinancing, United had total assets of $600 million and total liabilities of $450 million. Net income for the most recent year was $6.5 million on sales of $1 billion.

❙ *Required*

1. Journalize the debt refinancing transaction.
2. Compute annual interest expense for both the old and the new bond issues.
3. Why did United Products refinance the old 5 1/2% bonds with the new 9% bonds? Consider interest expense, net income, and the debt ratio.

E8-34 This (adapted) advertisement appeared in *The Wall Street Journal*. (*Note:* A *subordinated debenture* is an unsecured bond. The rights of the bondholders are less than the rights of other bondholders.)

Analyzing bond transactions
(Obj. 2, 3)

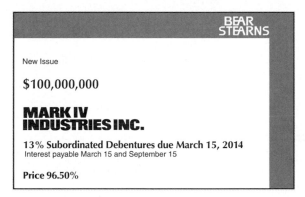

New Issue

$100,000,000

MARK IV INDUSTRIES INC.

13% Subordinated Debentures due March 15, 2014
Interest payable March 15 and September 15

Price 96.50%

❙ *Required*

Answer these questions.

1. Journalize Mark IV Industries Inc.'s issuance of these bonds on March 15, 2009. No explanation is required, but describe the transaction in detail, indicating who received cash, who paid cash, and how much.
2. Why is the stated interest rate on these bonds so high?
3. Compute the semi-annual cash interest payment on the bonds.
4. Compute the semi-annual interest expense under the straight-line amortization method.
5. Compute both the first-year (from March 15, 2009, to March 15, 2010) and the second-year interest expense (March 15, 2010, to March 15, 2011) under the effective-interest amortization method. The market rate of interest at the date of issuance was 14%. Why is interest expense greater in the second year?

QUIZ

Test your understanding of accounting for liabilities by answering the following questions. Select the best choice from among the possible answers given.

Q8-35 For the purpose of classifying liabilities as current or noncurrent, the term *operating cycle* refers to which of the following?
a. A period of 1 year
b. The time period between date of sale and the date the related revenue is collected

c. The time period between purchase of merchandise and the conversion of this merchandise back to cash

d. The average time period between business recessions

Q8-36 Failure to accrue interest expense results in which of the following?
a. An overstatement of net income and an overstatement of liabilities
b. An understatement of net income and an overstatement of liabilities
c. An understatement of net income and an understatement of liabilities
d. An overstatement of net income and an understatement of liabilities

Q8-37 Sportscar Warehouse operates in a province with a 6% sales tax. For convenience, Sportscar Warehouse credits Sales Revenue for the total amount (selling price plus sales tax) collected from each customer. If Sportscar Warehouse fails to make an adjustment for sales taxes, which of the following will be true?
a. Net income will be overstated, and liabilities will be overstated.
b. Net income will be overstated, and liabilities will be understated.
c. Net income will be understated, and liabilities will be overstated.
d. Net income will be understated, and liabilities will be understated.

Q8-38 What kind of account is *Unearned Revenue*?
a. Asset account   c. Revenue account
b. Liability account   d. Expense account

Q8-39 An end-of-period adjusting entry that debits Unearned Revenue will most likely credit which of the following?
a. A revenue   c. An expense
b. An asset   d. A liability

Q8-40 Adrian Inc. manufactures and sells computer monitors with a 3-year warranty. Warranty costs are expected to average 8% of sales during the warranty period. The following table shows the sales and actual warranty payments during the first 2 years of operations:

Year	Sales	Warranty Payments
2008	$500,000	$ 4,000
2009	700,000	32,000

Based on these facts, what amount of warranty liability should Adrian Inc. report on its balance sheet at December 31, 2009?
a. $32,000   c. $60,000
b. $36,000   d. $96,000

Q8-41 Today's Fashions has a debt that has been properly reported as a long-term liability up to the present year (2009). Some of this debt comes due in 2009. If Today's Fashions continues to report the current position as a long-term liability, the effect will be to do which of the following?
a. Overstate the current ratio   c. Understate total liabilities
b. Overstate net income   d. Understate the debt ratio

Q8-42 A bond with a face amount of $10,000 has a current price quote of 102.875. What is the bond's price?
a. $1,028,750   c. $10,028.75
b. $10,200.88   d. $10,287.50

Q8-43 Bond carrying value equals Bonds Payable
a. Minus Premium on Bonds Payable   d. Minus Discount on Bonds Payable
b. Plus Discount on Bonds Payable   e. Both a and b
c. Plus Premium on Bonds Payable   f. Both c and d

Q8-44 What type of account is *Discount on Bonds Payable*, and what is its normal balance?

Type of account	Normal balance
a. Contra liability	Debit
b. Reversing account	Debit
c. Adjusting amount	Credit
d. Contra liability	Credit

Questions 8-45 through 8-48 use the following data:

Q8-45 Sweetwater Company sells $100,000 of 10%, 15-year bonds for 97 on April 1, 2008. The market rate of interest on that day is 10 1/2%. Interest is paid each year on April 1. The entry to record the sale of the bonds on April 1 would be which of the following?

a.	Cash	97,000	
	Bonds Payable		97,000
b.	Cash	100,000	
	Bonds Payable		100,000
c.	Cash	97,000	
	Discount on Bonds Payable	3,000	
	Bonds Payable		100,000
d.	Cash	100,000	
	Discount on Bonds Payable		3,000
	Bonds Payable		97,000

Q8-46 Sweetwater Company uses the straight-line amortization method. The sale price of the bonds was $97,000. The amount of interest expense on April 1 of each year will be which of the following?

a. $4,080
b. $4,000
c. $4,200
d. $10,200
e. None of these. The interest expense is _____.

Q8-47 Write the adjusting entry required at December 31, 2008.

Q8-48 Write the journal entry required at April 1, 2009.

Q8-49 McPherson Corporation issued $100,000 of 10%, 5-year bonds on January 1, 2009, for $92,280. The market interest rate when the bonds were issued was 12%. Interest is paid semi-annually on January 1 and July 1. The first interest payment is July 1, 2009. Using the effective-interest amortization method, how much interest expense will McPherson record on July 1, 2009?

a. $6,000
b. $5,228
c. $6,772
d. $5,000
e. Some other amount _____

Q8-50 Using the facts in the preceding question, McPherson's journal entry to record the interest expense on July 1, 2009, will include a

a. Debit to Bonds Payable
b. Credit to Interest Expense
c. Debit to Premium on Bonds Payable
d. Credit to Discount on Bonds Payable

Q8-51 Amortizing the discount on bonds payable does which of the following?
a. Increases the recorded amount of interest expense
b. Is necessary only if the bonds were issued at more than face value
c. Reduces the semi-annual cash payment for interest
d. Reduces the carrying value of the bond liability

Q8-52 The journal entry on the maturity date to record the payment of $1,000,000 of bonds payable that were issued at a $70,000 discount includes
a. A debit to Discount on Bonds Payable for $70,000
b. A credit to Cash for $1,070,000
c. A debit to Bonds Payable for $1,000,000
d. All of the above

Q8-53 The payment of the face amount of a bond on its maturity date is regarded as which of the following?
a. An operating activity
b. An investing activity
c. A financing activity

PROBLEMS

(GROUP A)

Measuring current liabilities
(Obj. 1)

P8-54A Sea Spray Marina experienced these events during 2009.

a. December revenue totalled $110,000 and, in addition, Sea Spray collected sales tax of 7%. The sales tax amount will be remitted to the province of British Columbia and the GST to the Canada Revenue Agency early in January.
b. On October 31, Sea Spray signed a 6-month, 7% note to purchase a boat costing $90,000. The note requires payment of principal and interest at maturity.
c. On August 31, Sea Spray received cash of $1,800 in advance for service revenue. This revenue will be earned evenly over 6 months.
d. Revenues of $900,000 were covered by Sea Spray's service warranty. At January 1, estimated warranty payable was $11,300. During the year, Sea Spray recorded warranty expense of $31,000 and paid warranty claims of $34,700.
e. Sea Spray owes $100,000 on a long-term note payable. At December 31, 6% interest for the year plus $20,000 of this principal are payable within 1 year.

❚ Required

For each item, indicate the account and the related amount to be reported as a *current* liability on the Sea Spray Marina balance sheet at December 31, 2009.

Recording liability-related transactions
(Obj. 1)

P8-55A The following transactions of Smooth Sounds Music Company occurred during 2008 and 2009:

2008		
Mar.	3	Purchased a Steinway piano (inventory) for $40,000, signing a 6-month, 5% note.
Apr.	30	Borrowed $50,000 on a 9% note payable that calls for annual installment payments of $25,000 principal plus interest. Record the short-term note payable in a separate account from the long-term note payable.
Sept.	3	Paid the 6-month, 5% note at maturity
Dec.	31	Accrued warranty expense, which is estimated at 2% of sales of $190,000
	31	Accrued interest on the outstanding note payable
2009		
Apr.	30	Paid the first installment plus interest for 1 year on the outstanding note payable

❚ Required

Record the transactions in Smooth Sounds' journal. Explanations are not required.

P8-56A The board of directors of Circuits Plus authorizes the issue of $1 million of 7%, 10-year bonds payable. The semi-annual interest dates are May 31 and November 30. The bonds are issued on May 31, 2008, at face value.

Recording bond transactions (at face value) and reporting bonds payable on the balance sheet **(Obj. 2)**

❚ Required

1. Journalize the following transactions:
    a. Issuance of half of the bonds on May 31, 2008
    h. Payment of interest on November 30, 2008
    c. Accrual of interest on December 31, 2008
    d. Payment of interest on May 31, 2009

2. Report interest payable and bonds payable as they would appear on the Circuits Plus balance sheet at December 31, 2008.

P8-57A On February 28, 2008, **ETrade Inc.** issues 8 $\frac{1}{2}$%, 20-year bonds with a face value of $200,000. The bonds pay interest on February 28 and August 31. ETrade amortizes bonds by the straight-line method.

Issuing bonds at a discount, amortizing by the straight-line method, and reporting bonds payable on the balance sheet **(Obj. 2, 5)**

❚ Required

1. If the market interest rate is 7 $\frac{5}{8}$% when ETrade issues its bonds, will the bonds be priced at face value, a premium, or a discount? Explain.

2. If the market interest rate is 9% when ETrade issues its bonds, will the bonds be priced at face value, a premium, or a discount? Explain.

3. Assume that the issue price of the bonds is 97. Journalize the following bond transactions.
    a. Issuance of the bonds on February 28, 2008
    b. Payment of interest and amortization of the bonds on August 31, 2008
    c. Accrual of interest and amortization of the bonds on December 31, 2008
    d. Payment of interest and amortization of the bonds on February 28, 2009

4. Report interest payable and bonds payable as they would appear on the ETrade balance sheet at December 31, 2008.

P8-58A

1. Journalize the following transactions of Trekker Boot Company:

Accounting for bonds payable at a discount and amortizing by the straight-line method **(Obj. 2)**

2008		
Jan. 1	Issued $600,000 of 8%, 10-year bonds at 97	
July 1	Paid semi-annual interest and amortized bonds by the straight-line method on the 8% bonds payable	
Dec. 31	Accrued semi-annual interest expense and amortized bonds by the straight-line method on the 8% bonds payable	
2009		
Jan. 1	Paid semi-annual interest.	
2018		
Jan 1	Paid the 8% bonds at maturity	

2. At December 31, 2008, after all year-end adjustments, determine the carrying amount of Trekker's bonds payable, net.

3. For the 6 months ended July 1, 2008, determine for Trekker:
    a. Interest expense
    b. Cash interest paid
    What causes interest expense on the bonds to exceed cash interest paid?

Analyzing a company's long-term debt and reporting long-term debt on the balance sheet (effective-interest method)
(Obj. 2, 3, 5)

P8-59A Notes to the Maritime Industries Ltd. financial statements reported the following data on December 31, 2009 (the end of the fiscal year):

Note 6, Indebtedness		
Bonds payable, 5%, due in 2014	$600,000	
Less Discount	(25,274)	$574,726
Notes payable, 8.3%, payable in $50,000 annual installments starting in Year 2013		250,000

Maritime Industries amortizes bonds by the effective-interest method.

❙ Required

1. Answer the following questions about Maritime's long-term liabilities:
   a. What is the maturity value of the 5% bonds?
   b. What are Maritime's annual cash interest payments on the 5% bonds?
   c. What is the carrying amount of the 5% bonds at December 31, 2009?
2. Prepare an amortization table through December 31, 2012, for the 5% bonds. The market interest rate for these bonds was 6%. Maritime pays interest annually on December 31. How much is Maritime's interest expense on the 5% bonds for the year ended December 31, 2012?
3. Show how Maritime Industries would report the bonds payable and notes payable at December 31, 2012.

Issuing bonds at a discount, amortizing by the effective-interest method, retiring bonds early, and reporting the bonds payable on the balance sheet
(Obj. 2, 3, 5)

P8-60A On December 31, 2008, Digital Connections issued 8%, 10-year bonds payable with a maturity value of $500,000. The semi-annual interest dates are June 30 and December 31. The market interest rate is 9%, and the issue price of the bonds is 94. Digital Connections amortizes bonds by the effective-interest method.

❙ Required

1. Prepare an effective-interest-method amortization table for the first four semi-annual interest periods.
2. Journalize the following transactions:
   a. Issuance of the bonds on December 31, 2008. Credit Bonds Payable.
   b. Payment of interest and amortization of the bonds on June 30, 2009
   c. Payment of interest and amortization of the bonds on December 31, 2009
   d. Retirement by the bondholders on July 1, 2010, of bonds with face value of $200,000 when the market price is 96.5.
3. Show how Digital Connections would report the remaining bonds payable on its balance sheet at December 31, 2010.

Financing operations with debt or with shares
(Obj. 4)

P8-61A Outback Sporting Goods is embarking on a massive expansion. Assume plans call for opening 20 new stores during the next 2 years. Each store is scheduled to be 50% larger than the company's existing locations, offering more items of inventory, and with more elaborate displays. Management estimates that company operations will provide $1 million of the cash needed for expansion. Outback must raise the remaining $6 million from outsiders. The board of directors is considering obtaining the $6 million either through borrowing or by issuing common shares.

❙ Required

Write a memo to Outback's management discussing the advantages and disadvantages of borrowing and of issuing common shares to raise the needed cash. Which method of raising the funds would you recommend?

P8-62A The accounting records of Pacer Foods Inc. include the following items at December 31, 2009.

Reporting liabilities on the balance sheet; times-interest-earned ratio
(Obj. 5)

Mortgage note payable, current	$ 50,000	Accumulated amortization, equipment	$219,000
Accumulated pension benefit obligation	463,000	Discount on bonds payable (all long-term)	7,000
Bonds payable, long-term	490,000	Operating income	291,000
Mortgage note payable, long-term	150,000	Equipment	487,000
Bonds payable current portion	70,000	Pension plan assets (market value)	382,000
Interest expense	67,000	Interest payable	9,000

❚ Required

1. Show how each relevant item would be reported on the Pacer Foods Inc. classified balance sheet, including headings and totals for current liabilities and long-term liabilities.
2. Answer the following questions about Pacer's financial position at December 31, 2009.
   a. What is the carrying amount of the bonds payable (combine the current and long-term amounts)?
   b. Why is the interest-payable amount so much less than the amount of interest expense?
3. How many times did Pacer cover its interest expense during 2009?

(GROUP B)

P8-63B Goldwater Corporation experienced these five events during 2009:

Measuring current liabilities
(Obj. 1)

a. December sales totalled $50,000, and Goldwater collected sales tax of 8%. The sales tax will be sent to the Province of Ontario and the GST to the Canada Revenue Agency early in January.
b. On November 30, Goldwater received rent of $6,000 in advance for a lease on unused store space. This rent will be earned evenly over 3 months.
c. On September 30, Goldwater signed a 6-month, 9% note to purchase store fixtures costing $12,000. The note requires payment of principal and interest at maturity.
d. Sales of $400,000 were covered by Goldwater's product warranty. At January 1, estimated warranty payable was $12,400. During the year, Goldwater recorded warranty expense of $22,300 and paid warranty claims of $24,600.
e. Goldwater owes $100,000 on a long-term note. At December 31, 5% interest since July 31 and $20,000 of this principal are payable within 1 year.

❚ Required

For each item, indicate the account and the related amount to be reported as a *current* liability on the Goldwater Corporation balance sheet at December 31, 2009.

P8-64B Assume that the following transactions of Sleuth Book Store occurred during 2008 and 2009.

Recording liability-related transactions
(Obj. 1)

❚ Required

Record the transactions in the company's journal. Explanations are not required.

2008		
Jan.	9	Purchased store fixtures at a cost of $50,000, signing an 8% 6-month note for that amount
June	30	Borrowed $200,000 on a 9% note that calls for annual installment payment of $50,000 principal plus interest. Record the short-term note payable in a separate account from the long-term note payable.
July	9	Paid the 6-month, 8% note at maturity
Dec.	31	Accrued warranty expense, which is estimated at 3% of sales of $600,000
	31	Accrued interest on the outstanding note payable
2009		
June	30	Paid the first installment and interest for 1 year on the outstanding note payable

P8-65B Assume the board of directors of **The Saddledome Foundation** authorizes the issue of $1 million of 8%, 20-year bonds. The semi-annual interest dates are March 31 and September 30. The bonds are issued on March 31, 2008, at face value.

I *Required*

1. Journalize the following transactions:

   a. Issuance of the bonds on March 31, 2008

   b. Payment of interest on September 30, 2008

   c. Accrual of interest on December 31, 2008

   d. Payment of interest on March 31, 2009

2. Report interest payable and bonds payable as they would appear on the Saddledome Foundation balance sheet at December 31, 2008.

P8-66B On February 28, 2008, Panorama Ltd. issues 7%, 10-year notes with a face value of $300,000. The notes pay interest on February 28 and August 31, and Panorama amortizes bonds by the straight-line method.

I *Required*

1. If the market interest rate is 6% when Panorama issues its notes, will the notes be priced at face value, a premium, or a discount? Explain.

2. If the market interest rate is 8% when Panorama issues its notes, will the notes be priced at face value, a premium, or a discount? Explain.

3. Assume that the issue price of the notes is 96. Journalize the following note payable transactions:

   a. Issuance of the notes on February 28, 2008

   b. Payment of interest and amortization of the bonds on August 31, 2008

   c. Accrual of interest and amortization of the bonds on December 31, 2008

   d. Payment of interest and amortization of the bonds on February 28, 2009

4. Report interest payable and notes payable as they would appear on Panorama's balance sheet at December 31, 2008.

P8-67B

1. Journalize the following transactions of Farm Equipment Limited:

2007	
Jan. 1	Issued $100,000 of 8%, 5-year bonds at 94
July 1	Paid semi-annual interest and amortized the bonds by the straight-line method on our 8% bonds payable
Dec. 31	Accrued semi-annual interest expense and amortized the bonds by the straight-line method on our 8% bonds payable
2008	
Jan. 1	Paid semi-annual interest
2012	
Jan. 1	Paid the 8% bonds at maturity

2. At December 31, 2007, after all year-end adjustments, determine the carrying amount of Farm Equipment Limited's bonds payable, net

3. For the 6 months ended July 1, 2007, determine the following for Farm Equipment Limited:

   a. Interest expense

   b. Cash interest paid

   What causes interest expense on the bonds to exceed cash interest paid?

P8-68B The notes to the Community Charities financial statements reported the following data on December 31, 2009 (end of the fiscal year):

Analyzing a company's long-term debt and reporting the long-term debt on the balance sheet (effective-interest method)
(Obj. 2, 3, 5)

Note D—Long-Term Debt		
7% bonds payable, due in 2015	$ 500,000	
Less: Discount	(26,032)	$473,968
6^{1}/$_{2}$% notes payable; principal due in annual amounts of $50,000 in 2013 through 2018		300,000

Community Charities amortizes bonds by the effective-interest method and pays all interest amounts at December 31.

I *Required*

1. Answer the following questions about Community Charities' long-term liabilities:
   a. What is the maturity value of the 7% bonds?
   b. What is Community Charities' annual cash interest payment on the 7% bonds?
   c. What is the carrying amount of the 7% bonds at December 31, 2009?
2. Prepare an amortization table through December 31, 2012, for the 7% bonds. The market interest rate on the bonds was 8%. Round all amounts to the nearest dollar. How much is Community Charities' interest expense on the 7% bonds for the year ended December 31, 2012?
3. Show how Community Charities would report the 7% bonds payable and the 6 1/2% notes payable at December 31, 2012.

P8-69B On December 31, 2007, Caribbean Cruise Lines (CCL) issues 9%, 10-year convertible bonds with a maturity value of $300,000. The semi-annual interest dates are June 30 and December 31. The market interest rate is 8%, and the issue price of the bonds is 106. CCL amortizes bonds by the effective-interest method.

Issuing bonds at a premium by the effective-interest method, retiring bonds early, and reporting the bonds payable on the balance sheet
(Obj. 2, 3, 5)

I *Required*

1. Prepare an effective-interest-method amortization table for the first four semi-annual interest periods.
2. Journalize the following transactions.
   a. Issuance of the bonds on December 31, 2007. Credit Bonds Payable.
   b. Payment of interest and amortization of the bonds on June 30, 2008
   c. Payment of interest and amortization of the bonds on December 31, 2008
   d. Retirement by the bondholders on July 1, 2009, of bonds with face value of $150,000 when market price of bonds is 102
3. Show how Caribbean Cruise Lines would report the remaining bonds payable on its balance sheet at December 31, 2009.

P8-70B Two businesses in very different circumstances are pondering how to raise $2 million. HighTech.com has fallen on hard times. Net income has been low for the last 3 years, even falling by 10% from last year's level of profits, and cash flow also took a nose dive. Top management has experienced some turnover and has stabilized only recently. To become competitive again, High Tech needs $2 million to invest in new technology.

Financing operations with debt or shares
(Obj. 4)

Decorator Services is in the midst of its most successful period since it began operations in 2005. Net income has increased by 25%. The outlook for the future is bright with new markets opening up and competitors unable to compete with Decorator. As a result, Decorator is planning a large-scale expansion.

I *Required*

Propose a plan for each company to raise the needed cash. Which company should borrow? Which company should issue shares? Consider the advantages and disadvantages of raising money by borrowing and by issuing shares, and discuss them in your answer.

Reporting liabilities on the balance sheet, times-interest-earned ratio
(Obj. 5)

P8-71B The accounting records of Toronto Financial Services include the following items at December 31, 2009.

Premium on bonds payable (all long-term)...	$ 13,000
Interest payable	3,900
Pension plan assets (market value)	402,000
Operating income...	104,000
Accumulated pension benefit obligation	436,000
Interest expense..	39,000
Bonds payable, current portion...	50,000
Accumulated amortization, building..	70,000
Mortgage note payable, long-term	215,000
Bonds payable long-term..	250,000
Building...	160,000

❙ Required

1. Show how each relevant item would be reported on Toronto Financial Services' classified balance sheet. Include headings and totals for current liabilities and long-term liabilities.

2. Answer the following questions about the financial position of Toronto Financial Services at December 31, 2009.

   a. What is the carrying amount of the bonds payable (combine the current and long-term amounts)?

   b. Why is the interest payable amount so much less than the amount of interest expense? (Challenge)

3. How many times did Toronto cover its interest expense during 2009?

APPLY YOUR KNOWLEDGE

DECISION CASES

Exploring an actual bankruptcy
(Obj. 2)

Case 1. In 2002, **Enron Corporation** filed for Chapter 11 bankruptcy protection, shocking the business community: How could a company this large and this successful go bankrupt? This case explores the causes and the effects of Enron's bankruptcy.

At December 31, 2000, and for the 4 years ended on that date, Enron reported the following (amounts in millions):

Balance Sheet (summarized)

Total assets	$65,503
Total liabilities..	54,033
Total shareholders' equity...	11,470

Income Statements (excerpts)

	2000	1999	1998	1997
Net income	$979[*]	$893	$703	$105

[*]Operating Income = $1,953
Interest expense = $838

Unknown to investors and lenders, Enron also controlled hundreds of partnerships that owed vast amounts of money. These special-purpose entities (SPEs) did not appear on the Enron financial statements. Assume that the SPEs' assets totalled $7,000 million and their liabilities stood at $6,900 million; assume a 10% interest rate on these liabilities.

During the 4-year period up to 2000, Enron's share price shot up from $17.50 to $90.56. Enron used its escalating share price to finance the purchase of the SPEs by guaranteeing lenders that Enron would give them Enron shares if the SPEs could not pay their loans.

In 2001, the SEC launched an investigation into Enron's accounting practices. It was alleged that Enron should have been including the SPEs in its financial statements all along. Enron then restated net income for years up to 2000, wiping out nearly $600 million of total net income (and total assets) for this 4-year period. Enron's share price tumbled, and the guarantees to the SPEs' lenders added millions to Enron's liabilities (assume the full amount of the SPEs' debt). To make matters worse, the assets of the SPEs lost much of their value; assume that their market value is only $500 million.

❙ Required

1. Compute the debt ratio that Enron reported at the end of 2000. Recompute this ratio after including the SPEs in Enron's financial statements. Also compute Enron's times-interest-earned ratio both ways for 2000. Assume that the changes to Enron's financial position occurred during 2000.
2. Why does it appear that Enron failed to include the SPEs in its financial statements? How do you view Enron after including the SPEs in the company's financial statements? (Challenge)

Case 2. Business is going well for **Park 'N Fly**, the company that operates remote parking lots near major airports. The board of directors of this family-owned company believes that Park 'N Fly could earn an additional $2 million income before interest and taxes by expanding into new markets. However, the $5 million that the business needs for growth cannot be raised within the family. The directors, who strongly wish to retain family control of the company, must consider issuing securities to outsiders. The directors are considering three financing plans.

Analyzing alternative ways of raising $5 million
(Obj. 4)

Plan A is to borrow at 6%. Plan B is to issue 100,000 common shares. Plan C is to issue 100,000 nonvoting, $3.75 preferred shares ($3.75 is the annual dividend paid on each preferred share).* Park 'N Fly currently has net income of $3.5 million and 1 million common shares outstanding. The company's income tax rate is 25%.

❙ Required

1. Prepare an analysis to determine which plan will result in the highest earnings per common share.
2. Recommend one plan to the board of directors. Give your reasons.

ETHICAL ISSUE

Issue 1. Microsoft Corporation is the defendant in numerous lawsuits claiming unfair trade practices. Microsoft has strong incentives not to disclose these contingent liabilities; however, GAAP requires that companies report their contingent liabilities.

❙ Required

1. Why would a company prefer not to disclose its contingent liabilities?
2. Describe how a bank could be harmed if a company seeking a loan did not disclose its contingent liabilities.
3. What is the ethical tightrope that companies must walk when they report their contingent liabilities?

Issue 2. The top managers of Medtech.com borrowed heavily to develop a prescription-medicine distribution system. Medtech's outlook was bright, and investors poured millions into the company. Sadly, Medtech never lived up to its potential, and the company is in bankruptcy. It can't pay about half of its liabilities.

❙ Required

Is it unethical for managers to saddle a company with a high level of debt? Or is it just risky? Who could be hurt by a company's taking on too much debt? Discuss.

---

*For a discussion of preferred shares, see Chapter 9.

FOCUS ON FINANCIALS

Sun-Rype Products Ltd.

Analyzing current and contingent liabilities
(Obj. 1, 2, 5)

Refer to Sun-Rype Products Ltd.'s financial statements in Appendix A at the end of this book.

1. Sun-Rype's balance sheet reports a promissory note payable under current liabilities. What are the terms of this note that require it to be reported as a current liability?

2. Sun-Rype's Notes to the Financial Statements include the note, "Commitments, guarantees and contingencies." What information does this provide the user of these financial statements?

3. Did Sun-Rype borrow more or pay off more short-term and long-term debt in 2007? How can you tell?

4. How would you rate Sun-Rype's overall debt position: risky, safe, or average? Compute the ratio at December 31, 2007, that answers this question.

FOCUS ON ANALYSIS

Mullen Group Income Fund

Analyzing current liabilities and long-term debt
(Obj. 1, 2, 3, 5)

The Mullen Group Income Fund financial statements in Appendix B at the end of this book report a number of liabilities. Show amounts in thousands.

1. How would you rate Mullen Group's overall debt position at year-end 2007: risky, safe, or average? Compute the ratio that enables you to answer this question.

2. The statement of cash flow reports that Mullen Group completed two long-term debt transactions during 2007. Journalize those transactions.

3. Use the data in Mullen Group's 2007 income statement and balance sheet to estimate Mullen's average interest rate during 2007 on all company borrowings. Use the beginning balance of long-term debt for 2007.

GROUP PROJECTS

Project 1. Consider three different businesses:

1. A bank

2. A magazine publisher

3. A department store

For each business, list all its liabilities—both current and long-term. Then compare the three lists to identify the liabilities that the three businesses have in common. Also identify the liabilities that are unique to each type of business.

Project 2. Alcenon Corporation leases the majority of the assets that it uses in operations. Alcenon prefers operating leases (versus capital leases) in order to keep the lease liability off its balance sheet and maintain a low debt ratio.

Alcenon is negotiating a 10-year lease on an asset with an expected useful life of 15 years. The lease requires Alcenon to make 10 annual lease payments of $20,000 each, with the first payment due at the beginning of the lease term. The leased asset has a market value of $135,180. The lease agreement specifies no transfer of title to the lessee and includes no bargain purchase option.

Write a report for Alcenon's management to explain what conditions must be present for Alcenon to be able to account for this lease as an operating lease.

QUICK CHECK ANSWERS

1. *a*

2. *e*

3. *c* ($200,000 × 0.025 = $5,000)

4. *c* [400 × 0.05 × $40 = *warranty expense of $800; repaired $40 × 6 = $240; year-end liability* = $560 ($800 − $240)]

5. *e*

6. *e*

7. *a*

8. *b*

9. *c*

10. *b*

11. *e*

12. *a* ($196,140 × 0.10 × 6/12 = $9,807)

13. *d* [*Int. exp.* = $9,807 *Int. payment* = $9,500 ($200,000 × 0.095 × 6/12) $9,807 − $9,500 = $307]

14. *b* ($200,000 × 0.095 = $19,000)

15. *c* (*See Amortization Schedule*)

Date	Interest Payment	Interest Expense	Discount Amortiz.	Bond Carry Amt.
1/1/09				$196,140
7/1/09	$9,500	$9,807	$307	196,447
1/1/10	9,500	9,822	322	196,769

16. *d* {$196,140 + [($200,000 − $196,140) × 1/5] = $196,912}

9

Shareholders' Equity

SPOTLIGHT

Sun-Rype: "Simply nutritious. That's Sun-Rype. There's nothing complex. Just simple goodness."* That's the Sun-Rype slogan. When you want pure fruit products for your meals and snacks you will choose Sun-Rype because you know all its products are pure fruit.

"Sun-Rype grew out of the fresh fruit business in the lush Okanagan Valley. In 1946, the BC Fruit Growers Association, who had already been in the apple business for over 50 years, created BC Fruit Processing Ltd. to produce and sell a pure 100% apple juice, made with apples straight from the orchard. They named their new juice "Sun-Rype," and that is how it all started."*

In this chapter, we'll show you how to account for Sun-Rype's issuance of shares to investors. We'll also cover the other elements of shareholders' equity, such as retained earnings and dividends. By the time you finish this chapter, you may be ready for a bottle of Sun-Rype Peach-Pear juice. Or you may want to go online to buy some Sun-Rype shares.

*Source: www.sunrype.ca

Sun-Rype Products Ltd.
▼ **Balance Sheet (Adapted)**
December 31, 2007

	(In thousands, except number of shares)
Assets	
Current assets	$29,017
Property, plant, and equipment, net	27,867
Total assets	$56,884
Liabilities and Shareholders' Equity	
Current liabilities	$13,969
Long-term obligations	744
Future income taxes	1,148
1. Shareholders' equity:	
2. Common shares, no stated value, 100,000,000 shares authorized;	
10,827,600 shares issued and fully paid	17,756
3. Contributed surplus	942
4. Retained earnings	22,325
5. Total shareholders' equity	41,023
Total liabilities and shareholders' equity	$56,884

Chapters 4 to 8 discussed accounting for assets and liabilities. By this time, you should be familiar with all the assets and liabilities listed on Sun-Rype's balance sheet. Let's focus now on Sun-Rype's shareholders' equity. In this chapter we discuss some of the decisions a company faces when:

- Paying dividends
- Issuing shares
- Buying back its shares

Let's begin with the organization of a corporation.

DECISION What Is the Best Way to Organize a Business?

Anyone starting a business must decide how to organize the company. Corporations differ from proprietorships and partnerships in several ways.

Separate Legal Entity. A corporation is a business entity formed under federal or provincial law. The federal or provincial government grants *articles of incorporation*, which consist of documents giving the governing body's permission to form a corporation. A corporation is a distinct entity, an artificial person that exists apart from its owners, the shareholders. The corporation has many of the rights that a person has. For example, a corporation may buy, own, and sell property. Assets and liabilities in the business belong to the corporation and not to its owners. The corporation may enter into contracts, sue, and be sued.

    Nearly all well-known companies, such as Shoppers Drug Mart Corporation, TransCanada Corporation, Bombardier Inc., and Sobeys Inc., are corporations. Their full names include *Limited*, *Corporation*, or *Incorporated* (abbreviated *Ltd.*, *Corp.*, and *Inc.*) to indicate that they are corporations. However, some companies do not use those terms; Air Canada is an example.

Objective

❶ **Explain** the features of a corporation

Continuous Life and Transferability of Ownership. Corporations have *continuous lives* regardless of changes in their ownership. The shareholders of a corporation may transfer shares as they wish. They may sell or trade the shares to another person, give them away, bequeath them in a will, or dispose of them in any other way. The transfer of the shares from one person to another does not affect the continuity of the corporation. In contrast, proprietorships and partnerships terminate when ownership changes.

Limited Liability. Shareholders have **limited liability** for the corporation's debts. They have no personal obligation for corporate liabilities. The most that a shareholder can lose on an investment in a corporation's shares is the cost of the investment. Limited liability is one of the most attractive features of the corporate form of organization. It enables corporations to raise more capital from a wider group of investors than proprietorships and partnerships can. By contrast, proprietors and partners are personally liable for all the debts of their businesses (unless the business is organized as a limited liability partnership (LLP)).

Separation of Ownership and Management. Shareholders own the corporation, but a *board of directors*—elected by the shareholders—appoints officers to manage the business. Thus, shareholders may invest $1,000 or $1 million in the corporation without having to manage it.

Management's goal is to maximize the firm's value for the shareholders. But the separation between owners and managers may create problems. Corporate officers may run the business for their own benefit and not for the shareholders'. For example, the chief financial officer (CFO) of Enron Corporation set up outside partnerships and paid himself millions of dollars to manage the partnerships—unknown to Enron shareholders. He subsequently went to prison.

Corporate Taxation. Corporations are separate taxable entities. They pay a variety of taxes not borne by proprietorships or partnerships, such as federal and provincial income taxes.

Corporate earnings are subject to **double taxation** of their income.

- First, corporations pay income taxes on their corporate income.
- Then, shareholders pay personal income tax on the cash dividends that they receive from corporations. Canada's tax laws attempt to minimize double taxation so the tax rate on dividends is lower than the tax rate on regular income. Proprietorships and partnerships pay no business income tax. Instead, the tax falls solely on the owners, who are taxed on their share of the proprietorship or partnership income.

Government Regulation. Because shareholders have only limited liability for corporation debts, outsiders doing business with the corporation can look no further than the corporation if it fails to pay. To protect a corporation's creditors and the shareholders, both federal and provincial governments monitor corporations. This regulation consists mainly of ensuring that corporations disclose the information that investors and creditors need to make informed decisions. Accounting provides much of this information.

Exhibit 9-1 summarizes the advantages and disadvantages of the corporate form of business organization.

EXHIBIT 9-1 Advantages and Disadvantages of a Corporation

Advantages	Disadvantages
1. Can raise more capital than a proprietorship or partnership can	1. Separation of ownership and management
2. Continuous life	2. Corporate taxation
3. Ease of transferring ownership	3. Government regulation
4. Limited liability of shareholders	

Organizing a Corporation

The creation of a corporation begins when its organizers, called the *incorporators*, submit articles of incorporation to the federal or provincial government for approval. The articles of incorporation include the authorization for the corporation to issue a certain number of shares of stock, which are shares of ownership in the corporation. The incorporators

- Pay fees
- Sign the charter
- File the required documents with the incorporating jurisdiction
- Agree to a set of **bylaws**, which act as the constitution for governing the corporation

    Then the corporation comes into existence.

    Ultimate control of the corporation rests with the shareholders. The shareholders elect a *board of directors*, which sets the company policy and appoints officers. The board elects a **chairperson**, who usually is the most powerful person in the organization. The board also designates the **president**, who is the chief executive officer (CEO) in charge of day-to-day operations. Most corporations also have a chief operating officer (COO), in which case the COO is responsible for administering day-to-day operations and reports to the CEO, and vice-presidents in charge of sales, manufacturing, accounting and finance (the chief financial officer, or CFO), and other key areas. Exhibit 9-2 shows the authority structure in a corporation.

Shareholders' Rights

Ownership of shares entitles shareholders to five basic rights, unless specific rights are withheld by agreement with the shareholders:

1. *The right to sell the shares*. This right might be restricted in certain circumstances but such discussion is beyond the scope of this text.

2. *Vote*. The right to participate in management by voting on matters that come before the shareholders. This is the shareholder's sole voice in the management of the corporation. A shareholder is normally entitled to one vote for each common share owned. There are various classes of common shares that give the holder multiple votes or no vote.

3. *Dividends*. The right to receive a proportionate part of any distributed payment, or dividend. Each share in a particular class receives an equal dividend.

4. *Liquidation*. The right to receive a proportionate share of any assets remaining after the corporation pays all liabilities in liquidation. Liquidation means to go out of business, sell the assets, pay its liabilities, and distribute any remaining cash to the owners.

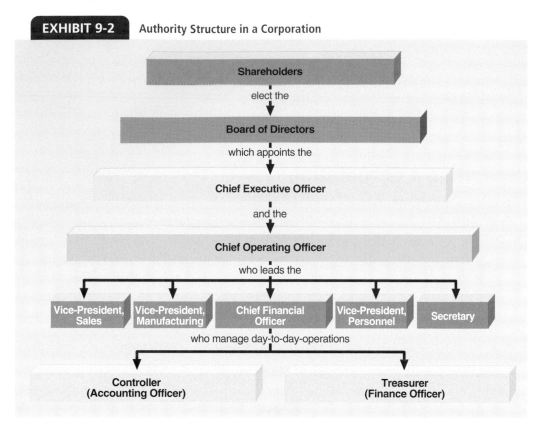

EXHIBIT 9-2 Authority Structure in a Corporation

5. *Preemption.* The right to maintain one's proportionate ownership in the corporation. Suppose you own 5% of a corporation's shares. If the corporation issues 100,000 new shares, it must offer you the opportunity to buy 5% (5,000) of the new shares. This right is called the *preemptive right.* This right might be specifically withheld.

Shareholders' Equity

As we saw in Chapter 1, *shareholders' equity* represents the shareholders' ownership interest in the assets of a corporation. Shareholders' equity is divided into two main parts:

1. *Contributed capital*, also called *capital stock.* This is the amount of shareholders' equity the shareholders have contributed to the corporation. The contributed surplus on Sun-Rype's balance sheet is contributed capital.

2. *Retained earnings.* This is the amount of shareholders' equity the corporation has earned through profitable operations and has not used for dividends.

Companies report shareholders' equity by source. They report contributed capital separately from retained earnings because most incorporating acts prohibit the declaration of cash dividends from contributed capital. Thus, cash dividends are declared from retained earnings.

The owners' equity of a corporation is divided into shares of *stock.* A corporation issues *share certificates* to its owners in exchange for their investment in the business—usually cash. The basic unit of contributed capital is called a *share.* A corporation may issue a share certificate for any number of shares it wishes—one share, 100 shares, or any other number—but the total number of *authorized* shares is limited by charter. Exhibit 9-3 shows an actual common share certificate for Danier Leather Inc.

EXHIBIT 9-3   Share Certificate

The terms *authorized*, *issued*, and *outstanding* are frequently used to describe a corporation's shares. *Authorized* refers to the maximum number of shares a corporation is allowed to distribute to shareholders. Companies incorporated under the *Canada Business Corporations Act* are permitted to issue an unlimited number of shares. *Issued* refers to the number of shares sold or transferred to shareholders. **Outstanding shares** are those actually in the hands of shareholders. Sometimes a company repurchases shares it has previously issued so that the number of shares outstanding will be less than the number of shares issued. For example, if a corporation issued 100,000 shares and later repurchased 20,000 shares, then the number of shares outstanding would be 80,000. The total number of shares outstanding at any time represents 100% ownership of the corporation.

Classes of Shares

Corporations issue different types of shares to appeal to a variety of investors. The shares of a corporation may be either

- Common
- Preferred

Common and Preferred. Every corporation issues *common shares*, the basic form of capital stock. Unless designated otherwise, the word *share* is understood to mean "common share." Common shareholders have the five basic rights of share ownership, unless a right is specifically withheld. For example, some companies issue Class A common shares, which usually carry the right to vote, and Class B common shares, which may be nonvoting. In describing a corporation, we would say the common shareholders are the owners of the business. They stand to benefit the most if the corporation succeeds because they take the most risk by investing in common shares.

Preferred shares give their owners certain advantages over common shareholders. Preferred shareholders receive dividends before the common shareholders and receive assets before the common shareholders if the corporation liquidates. Owners of preferred shares also have the five basic shareholder rights, unless a right is specifically denied. Companies may issue different classes of preferred shares (Class A and Class B or Series A and Series B, for example). Each class is recorded in a separate account. The most preferred shareholders can expect to earn is their fixed dividend.

Preferred shares are a hybrid between common shares and long-term debt. Like debt, preferred shares pay a fixed dividend amount to the investor. But like common shares, the dividend is not required to be paid unless the board of directors has declared the dividend. Also, companies have no obligation to pay back true preferred shares. Preferred shares that must be redeemed (paid back) by the corporation are a liability masquerading as a stock.

Preferred shares are not all that common. Surveys reveal that less than one-third of companies issue preferred shares. All corporations have common shares.

Exhibit 9-4 summarizes the similarities and differences among common shares, preferred shares, and long-term debt.

No-Stated-Value Shares. No-stated-value shares are shares of stock that do not have a value assigned to them by the articles of incorporation. The board of directors assigns a value to the shares when they are issued; this value is known as the **stated value**. For example, Dajol Inc. has authorization to issue 100,000 common shares, having no stated value assigned to them by the articles of incorporation. Dajol Inc. needs $50,000 at incorporation, and might issue 10,000 shares for $5.00 per share, 2,000 shares at $25.00 per share, or 1,000 shares at $50.00 per share, and so on. The point is that Dajol Inc. can assign whatever value to the shares the board of directors wishes. Normally, the stated value would be credited to Common Shares when the shares are issued.

The recorded value of a corporation's contributed capital or stated capital is the sum of the shares issued times the stated values of those shares at the time of issue. For example, if YDR Ltd. issued 1,000 common shares at a stated value of $8.00 per share, 2,000 shares at $12.00 per share, and 500 shares at $15.00 per share, its contributed capital or stated capital would be $39,500 [(1,000 × $8) + (2,000 × $12) + (500 × $15)].

The *Canada Business Corporations Act* and most provincial incorporating acts now require common and preferred shares to be issued without nominal or stated value. The full amount of the proceeds from the sale of shares by a company must be allocated to the capital account for those shares. For example, if Canadian Tire Corporation Ltd. were to issue 100 common shares for $2,500 (that is, the shares sold for $25.00 per share), $2,500 would be credited to Common Shares.

Issuing Shares

Large corporations such as Hudson's Bay Company and EnCana Corp. need huge amounts of money to operate. Corporations may sell shares directly to the shareholders or use the service of an *underwriter*, such as the brokerage firms ScotiaMcLeod and BMO Nesbitt Burns. Companies often advertise the issuance of their shares to

EXHIBIT 9-4	Comparison of Common Shares, Preferred Shares, and Long-Term Debt		
	Common Shares	*Preferred Shares*	*Long-Term Debt*
1. Corporate obligation to repay principal	No	No	Yes
2. Dividends/interest	Dividends not tax-deductible	Dividends not tax-deductible	Tax-deductible interest expense
3. Corporate obligation to pay dividends/interest	Only after declaration	Only after declaration	At fixed dates

attract investors. The *Globe and Mail Report on Business* and the *National Post* are the most popular media for such advertisements, which are also called *tombstones*.

Exhibit 9-5 on page 430 is a reproduction of Mega Bloks Inc.'s tombstone, which appeared in *The Globe and Mail*. The lead underwriter of Mega Bloks Inc.'s public offering was Merrill Lynch Canada Inc. Several other Canadian firms were involved in the issue. In this 2003 public offering, Mega Bloks Inc. sought to raise $133,799,660 of capital.

Common Shares

Issuing Common Shares at a Stated Value. Suppose in the year ended December 31, 2008, George Weston Ltd. issues 100,000 common shares for cash, and the directors determine that the shares will be issued with a stated value (selling price) of $50 per share. The share issuance entry is

```
2008
Jan. 8   Cash .................................................................. 5,000,000
             Common Shares.............................................          5,000,000
         To issue common shares at $50.00 per share (100,000 × $50.00)
```

We assume George Weston Ltd. received $5,000,000. The amount invested in the corporation, $5,000,000 in this case, is called *contributed capital*. The credit to Common Shares records an increase in the contributed capital of the corporation.

George Weston, in its annual report dated December 31, 2007, indicated there were 129,074,526 common shares outstanding with a stated value of $133 million. After this assumed transaction, George Weston would report $129,174,526 outstanding shares and the balance in its share capital account would be increased by $5 million.

All the transactions recorded in this section include a receipt of cash by the corporation as it issues *new* shares. These transactions are different from those reported in the financial press. In those transactions, one shareholder sells shares to another investor, and the corporation makes no journal entry. Note that issuances of shares are capital contributions and don't affect earnings.

STOP & THINK

You are thinking of investing in Shoppers Drug Mart Corporation, and have obtained a copy of its December 29, 2007, annual report. Your examination of the report reveals that Shoppers had contributed capital of $1,516 million at December 29, 2007, and $1,498 million at December 30, 2006.

1. Where would you look in the annual report to determine why the two numbers differ?
2. Assume that no shares were repurchased during the year. How would you determine the number of common shares issued during the year and the average price paid for those shares?

Answers:

1. The Notes to the financial statements
2. The Notes to the Shoppers Drug Mart financial statements disclose the number of shares issued and their stated value. If that information is not specifically provided you can calculate the change in common shares issued and outstanding and the stated value of the shares at each year-end.

Common Shares Issued for Assets Other Than Cash. When a corporation issues shares in exchange for assets other than cash, it records the assets received at their current market value and credits the capital accounts accordingly. The assets' prior book value does not matter because the shareholder will demand shares equal

Announcement of Public Offering of Mega Bloks Inc. Common Shares

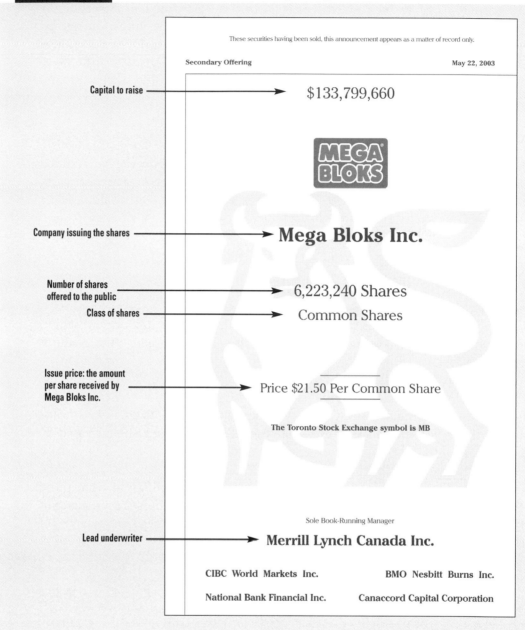

These securities having been sold, this announcement appears as a matter of record only.

Secondary Offering   May 22, 2003

Capital to raise → $133,799,660

Company issuing the shares → **Mega Bloks Inc.**

Number of shares offered to the public → 6,223,240 Shares

Class of shares → Common Shares

Issue price: the amount per share received by Mega Bloks Inc. → Price $21.50 Per Common Share

The Toronto Stock Exchange symbol is MB

Sole Book-Running Manager

Lead underwriter → **Merrill Lynch Canada Inc.**

CIBC World Markets Inc.   BMO Nesbitt Burns Inc.

National Bank Financial Inc.   Canaccord Capital Corporation

to the market value of the asset given. Kahn Corporation issued 15,000 common shares for equipment worth $4,000 and a building worth $120,000. Kahn Corporation's entry is

Nov. 12   Equipment 4,000
           Building 120,000
               Common Shares..   124,000
           To issue common shares in exchange for equipment and a building.

ASSETS	=	LIABILITIES	+	SHAREHOLDERS' EQUITY
+4,000 +120,000	=	0	+	+124,000

A Share Issuance for Other Than Cash Can Pose an Accounting Problem—1

Generally accepted accounting principles say to record shares at the fair market value of whatever the corporation receives in exchange for the shares. When the corporation receives cash, the cash received provides clear evidence of the value of the shares because cash is worth its face amount.

Many entrepreneurs start up companies with an asset other than cash. They invest the asset and receive the new corporation's shares. A computer whiz may contribute some computer hardware and software. The software may be market-tested or it may be new. It may be worth millions or it may be worthless. An artist may contribute paintings or sculpture to start an art gallery. A real-estate agent may invest in a building to start a realty company.

The corporation must record the asset received and the shares given with a journal entry such as the following:

Software...	XXX	
Common Shares...		XXX
Issued shares in exchange for software.		

In effect, the new corporation is buying the software and paying for it by issuing common shares. Therefore, the business must assign a value to the software and to the common shares. The market value of the software determines the value assigned to the shares. What is the software really worth? Let's consider two possibilities:

Situation 1. The software has been on the market for several months and is selling well. The creator of the software has standing orders for 2,000 copies, and an industry expert values the software at $500,000. To start up the new corporation, the company makes this entry:

Software...	500,000	
Common Shares...		500,000
Issued shares in exchange for software.		

Situation 2. The software is new and untested. The entrepreneur believes it is worth millions but decides to be conservative and values it at $500,000. For its first transaction, the company makes this entry:

Software...	500,000	
Common Shares...		500,000
Issued shares in exchange for software.		

Suppose both entrepreneurs need $200,000 to market the software. They invite you to invest in their new business. Both companies' balance sheets will look like the balance sheet below:

Balance Sheet December 31, 2009			
Assets		**Liabilities**	
Computer software	$500,000		$ 0
		Shareholders' Equity	
		Common shares......................	500,000
Total assets............................	$500,000	Total liabilities and equity......	$500,000

Both companies are debt-free and both appear to have a valuable asset. In which company will you invest? Here are two take-away lessons.

- Some accounting values are more solid than others.

- Not all financial statements mean exactly what they say, unless they are audited by independent public accountants who will require the preparers to follow GAAP.

Preferred Shares

Accounting for preferred shares follows the pattern we illustrated for common shares. The company records a Preferred Shares account at its stated value. When reporting shareholders' equity on the balance sheet, a corporation generally lists preferred shares, common shares, and retained earnings in that order. The example below is from Lambeth Plastics Ltd.

	(Amounts in thousands)	
	2008	**2007**
Preferred shares, series I	$ 228	$ 228
Common shares	310	310
Share capital	538	538
Retained earnings	1,020	975
Total shareholders' equity	$1,558	$1,513

On April 18, 2009, Lambeth Plastics Ltd. announced the completion of the sale of 4,000 Series II Preferred Shares for proceeds of $200 thousand. The journal entry to record this issuance would be:

```
2009
Apr. 18    Cash............................................................... 200,000
                Preferred shares, Series II ................................      200,000
           To record issuance of 4,000 Series II preferred shares.
```

After this issuance, share capital in the shareholders' equity section would appear as follows (amounts in thousands):

Preferred shares, Series I	$228
Preferred shares, Series II	200
Common shares	310
Share capital	738

Companies issue convertible preferred shares. The preferred shares are usually convertible into the company's common shares and always at the discretion of the preferred shareholders. Whenever the common share market price gets high enough—or the preferred's market price gets low enough—holders of convertible preferred will convert their shares into common. Here are some representative journal entries for convertible preferred shares, using assumed amounts:

```
2009       Cash............................................................... 50,000
                Convertible Preferred Shares ......................      50,000
           Issued convertible preferred shares.

2009       Convertible Preferred Shares ........................... 50,000
                Common Shares...................................      50,000
           Investors converted preferred into common.
```

As you can see, we merely remove Preferred Shares from the books and give the new Common Shares the prior book value of the preferred.

A Share Issuance for Other Than Cash Can Pose an Accounting Problem—2

As was pointed out earlier, issuance of shares for *cash* poses no serious ethical challenge. The company simply receives cash and records the shares at the amount received, as illustrated in the preceding sections of this chapter. There is no difficulty in valuing shares issued for cash because the value of the cash—and the shares—is obvious.

Issuing shares for assets other than cash can pose an ethical challenge. The company issuing the shares often wishes to record a large amount for the noncash asset received (such as land or a building) and for the shares that it is issuing. Why? Because large asset and shareholders' equity amounts on the balance sheet make the business look more prosperous and more creditworthy.

A company is supposed to record an asset received at its current market value. But one person's perception of a particular asset's market value can differ from another person's opinion. One person may appraise land at a market value of $400,000. Another may honestly believe the land is worth only $300,000. A company receiving land in exchange for its shares must decide whether to record the land received and the shares issued at $300,000, at $400,000, or at some amount in between.

The ethical course of action is to record the asset at its current fair market value, as determined by a good-faith estimate of market value from independent appraisers. It is rare for a corporation to be found guilty of *understating* the asset values on its balance sheet, but companies have been embarrassed by *overstating* these values. Investors who rely on the financial statements may be able to prove in court that an overstatement of asset values caused them to pay too much for the company's shares. Creditors who rely on financial statements may also be able to prove in court that an overstatement of asset values caused them to loan the corporation more than if the asset values were correctly stated. In both cases, the court may render a judgment against the company. For this reason, companies often value assets conservatively.

MID-CHAPTER SUMMARY PROBLEMS

1. Test your understanding of the first half of this chapter by deciding whether each of the following statements is true or false.

 a. The policy-making body in a corporation is called the board of directors.

 b. The owner of 100 preferred shares has greater voting rights than the owner of 100 common shares.

 c. Issuance of 1,000 common shares at $12 per share increases contributed capital by $12,000.

 d. A corporation issues its preferred shares in exchange for land and a building with a combined market value of $200,000. This transaction increases the corporation's owners' equity by $200,000 regardless of the assets' prior book values.

 e. Preferred shares are a riskier investment than common shares.

2. Adolfo Inc. has two classes of common shares. Class A shares are entitled to one vote, whereas Class B shares are entitled to 100 votes. The two classes rank equally for dividends. The following is extracted from a recent annual report:

Shareholders' Equity

Capital stock	
Class A common shares, no stated value (authorized and issued 1,260 shares)...	$ 1,260
Class B common shares (authorized and issued 46,200)	11,000
	12,260
Retained earnings...	872,403
	$884,663

Required

a. Record the issuance of the Class A common shares. Use the Adolfo Inc. account titles.
b. Record the issuance of the Class B common shares. Use the Adolfo Inc. account titles.
c. How much of Adolfo Inc.'s shareholders' equity was contributed by the shareholders? How much was provided by profitable operations? Does this division of equity suggest that the company has been successful? Why or why not?
d. Write a sentence to describe what Adolfo Inc.'s shareholders' equity means.

Name: Adolfo Inc.
Industry: Auto parts manufacturing corporation
Fiscal Period: A recent fiscal year

Answers

1. **a.** True **b.** False **c.** True **d.** True **e.** False

2. **a.** Cash.. 1,260

      Class A Common Shares................................. 1,260
      To record issuance of Class A common shares.

   b. Cash.. 11,000

      Class B Common Shares................................. 11,000
      To record issuance of Class B common shares.

   c. Contributed by the shareholders: $12,260 ($1,260 + $11,000).
      Provided by profitable operations: $872,403.
      This division suggests that the company has been successful because almost all of its shareholders' equity has come from profitable operations.

   d. Adolfo Inc.'s shareholders' equity of $884,663 means that the company's shareholders own $884,663 of the business's assets.

b. Preferred shareholders typically do not have voting rights. e. Preferred shares are less risky because they usually have a fixed dividend rate.

a. and b. Share issuances increase assets (cash) and shareholders' equity.

Compare the fraction of shareholders' equity contributed by shareholders to the fraction contributed by retained earnings. A greater retained earnings fraction is positive.

Shareholders' equity is the net worth of the company (Assets – Liabilities).

Repurchase of Shares by a Corporation

Corporations may repurchase their own shares for several reasons:

1. The company needs the **repurchased shares** to fulfill future share issuance commitments, such as those related to share option plans and conversions of bonds and preferred shares into common shares.

2. The purchase may help support the share's current market price by decreasing the supply of shares available to the public; that is, repurchase is anti-dilutive.

3. Management wants to avoid a takeover by an outside party.

Firms incorporated under certain provincial jurisdictions are permitted to reacquire shares that they previously issued and hold these shares for future issuance. Such shares are accounted for as a contra account to shareholders' equity beneath Retained Earnings. Corporations that are incorporated under the *Canada Business Corporations Act* are required to immediately cancel any reacquired shares so these do not exist for federally incorporated companies.

For example, Research In Motion repurchased, as part of a share repurchase plan, 18.96 million common shares in the year ended March 4, 2006, and 9.54 million in the year ended March 3, 2007. No common shares were repurchased in the year ended March 1, 2008. All of the repurchased common shares have been cancelled.

DECISION **Should a Company Buy Back Its Own Shares?**

Let's illustrate the accounting for repurchased shares by using the data of Ava Smallco Ltd. Before repurchasing any of its shares, the company reported the following shareholders' equity at December 31, 2008:

(Before Repurchase of Shares)	
Common shares (100,000 shares authorized; 10,000 shares issued).........	$ 70,000
Retained earnings	193,632
Total equity..	$263,632

During 2009, Ava Smallco Ltd. paid $12,000 to repurchase 1,000 of its common shares for cancellation. Ava Smallco Ltd. recorded the share repurchase as follows:

2009			
May 12	Common Shares...	7,000	
	Retained Earnings	5,000	
	Cash		12,000
	Repurchased common shares for cancellation.		

When a company repurchases its shares for more than the shares were issued for originally, it is deemed to be distributing profits (from Retained Earnings) to those shareholders who are selling their shares back to the company.

Ava Smallco Ltd.'s shareholders' equity would be shown as follows after the repurchase:

(After Repurchase of Shares)	
Common shares (100,000 shares authorized; 9,000 shares issued)...........	$ 63,000
Retained earnings	188,632
Total equity..	$251,632

Compare Ava Smallco Ltd.'s total equity before the repurchase of shares ($263,632) and after ($251,632). You will see that Ava Smallco Ltd.'s total equity decreased by $12,000, the amount of cash the company paid to buy back its own shares. The repurchase of shares has the opposite effect of issuing shares:

- Issuing shares grows a company's assets and equity.
- Repurchasing shares *shrinks* assets and equity.

When the company repurchases its shares for less than the issue price, the difference is considered contributed surplus arising from the share repurchases, and Contributed Surplus—Share Repurchase is credited for the difference between the issue price and repurchase price.

Assume Ava Smallco Ltd. paid $4,000 to repurchase 1,000 of its common shares for cancellation some time after the repurchase described above took place. Ava Smallco would record the share repurchase as follows:

2009			
Nov. 15	Common Shares...	7,000	
	Contributed Surplus—Share Repurchase....................		3,000
	Cash		4,000
	Repurchased common shares for cancellation.		

Ava Smallco Ltd.'s shareholders' equity would be shown as follows after this second repurchase:

(After Second Repurchase of Shares)	
Common shares (100,000 shares authorized; 8,000 shares issued)...........	$ 56,000
Contributed surplus	3,000
Retained earnings	188,632
Total equity	$247,632

Compare Ava Smallco Ltd.'s total equity after the first repurchase ($251,632) and after the second repurchase ($247,632). You will see that Ava Smallco Ltd.'s total equity decreased by $4,000, the amount of cash the company paid to buy back its own shares.

In most cases the company cancels the shares when they are repurchased. Shares that are reissued are accounted for in exactly the same way as shares that are issued for the first time.

STOP & THINK

You are examining the financial statements of SurCo Inc. and note that SurCo had net income of $5,000 for the year ended December 31, 2009, and paid dividends of the same amount during the year. The balance sheet provides the following additional information:

	December 31, 2009	December 31, 2008
Common shares (Issued and outstanding:		
2009 1,800 shares; 2008 2,000 shares)	$18,000	$20,000
Retained earnings......................................	36,800	40,800
Total shareholders' equity	$54,800	$60,800

Explain what caused the change in total shareholders' equity between December 31, 2008, and December 31, 2009.

Answer:

SurCo Inc. repurchased 200 common shares issued at $10.00 per share for $30.00 per share.

Retained Earnings, Dividends, and Splits

The Retained Earnings account carries the balance of the business's net income less its net losses and less any declared dividends accumulated over the corporation's lifetime. *Retained* means "held onto." Successful companies grow by reinvesting back into the business the assets they generate through profitable operations. George Weston Limited is an example; about 96 percent of its equity comes from retained earnings.

The Retained Earnings account is not a reservoir of cash waiting for paying dividends to the shareholders. In fact, the corporation may have a large balance in Retained Earnings but not have the cash to pay a dividend. Cash and Retained Earnings are two entirely separate accounts with no particular relationship. A $500,000 balance in Retained Earnings says nothing about the company's Cash balance.

A *credit* balance in Retained Earnings is normal, indicating that the corporation's lifetime earnings exceed its lifetime losses and dividends. A *debit* balance in Retained Earnings arises when a corporation's lifetime losses and dividends exceed its lifetime earnings. Called a **deficit**, this amount is subtracted from the sum of the other equity accounts to determine total shareholders' equity. Retained earnings deficits are not uncommon.

DECISION ## Should the Company Declare and Pay Cash Dividends?

A *dividend* is a corporation's return to its shareholders of the benefits of earnings. Dividends usually take one of three forms:

- Cash
- Shares
- Noncash assets

In this section we focus on cash dividends and stock dividends because noncash dividends are rare. For a noncash asset dividend, debit Retained Earnings and credit the asset (for example, Long-Term Investment) for the current market value of the asset given.

Cash Dividends

Most dividends are cash dividends. Finance courses discuss how a company decides on its dividend policy. Accounting tells a company if it can pay a dividend. To do so, a company must have both

- Enough Retained Earnings to *declare* the dividend, and
- Enough Cash to *pay* the dividend

A corporation declares a dividend before paying it. Only the board of directors has the authority to declare a dividend. The corporation has no obligation to pay a dividend until the board declares one, but once declared, the dividend becomes a legal liability of the corporation. There are three relevant dates for dividends (using assumed amounts):

Objective

4 **Account** for dividends

1. **Declaration date, June 19.** On the declaration date, the board of directors announces the dividend. Declaration of the dividend creates a liability for the corporation. Declaration is recorded by debiting Retained Earnings and crediting Dividends Payable. Assume a $50,000 dividend.

June 19	Retained Earnings*	50,000	
	Dividends Payable		50,000
	Declared a cash dividend.		

Liabilities increases, and equity goes down.

ASSETS	=	LIABILITIES	+	SHAREHOLDERS' EQUITY
0	=	+50,000		−50,000

2. **Date of record, July 1.** As part of the declaration, the corporation announces the record date, which follows the declaration date by a few weeks. The shareholders on the record date will receive the dividend. There is no journal entry for the date of record.

---

*In the early part of this book, we debited a Dividends account to clearly identify the purpose of the payment. From here on, we follow the more common practice of debiting the Retained Earnings account for dividend declarations.

3. **Payment date, July 10**. Payment of the dividend usually follows the record date by a week or two. Payment is recorded by debiting Dividends Payable and crediting Cash.

July 10	Dividends Payable	50,000	
	Cash		50,000
	Paid cash dividend.		

Both assets and liabilities decrease. The corporation shrinks.

ASSETS	=	LIABILITIES	+	SHAREHOLDERS' EQUITY
−50,000	=	−50,000		

Analyzing the Shareholder's Equity Accounts

By knowing accounting you can look at a company's comparative year-to-year financial statements and tell a lot about what the company did during the current year. For example, Sun-Rype Products Ltd. reported the following for Retained Earnings (in thousands):

	December 31	
	2007	**2006**
Retained earnings	$22,325	$19,310

What do these figures tell you about Sun-Rype's results of operations during 2007? Was it a net income or a net loss? How can you tell? Sun-Rype had a net income. This is for certain, because

- Retained Earnings increased in 2007.
- Net income is the only item that increases Retained Earnings.

Was Sun-Rype's net income the full $3,015 ($22,325 − $19,310 = $3,015)? Not necessarily. Sun-Rype may have declared a dividend, and dividends decrease Retained Earnings.

If you know accounting—if you know Sun-Rype's net income ($4,636 from Sun-Rype's income statement)—you can compute Sun-Rype's dividend declarations during 2007 as follows (in thousands):

Retained Earnings			
		Begin. bal.	19,310
Dividends	?	Net income	4,636
		Ending bal.	22,325

Dividends (x) were $1,621 ($19,310 + $4,636 − x = $22,325; x = $1,621). It really helps to know accounting!

Dividends on Preferred Shares

When a company has issued both preferred and common shares, the preferred shareholders receive their dividends first. The common shareholders receive dividends only if the total declared dividend is large enough to pay the preferred shareholders first.

Pinecraft Industries Inc. has 100,000 shares of $1.50 cumulative preferred shares outstanding in addition to its common shares. This $1.50 designation means that preferred dividends are paid at the annual amount of $1.50 per share. Assume that in 2009, Pinecraft declares an annual dividend of $1,000,000. The allocation to preferred and common shareholders is as follows:

Preferred dividend (100,000 shares × $1.50 per share)	$ 150,000
Common dividend (remainder: $1,000,000 − $150,000)	850,000
Total dividend	$1,000,000

If Pinecraft declares only a $200,000 dividend, preferred shareholders receive $150,000, and the common shareholders receive the remainder, $50,000 ($200,000 − $150,000).

Expressing the Dividend on Preferred Shares. Dividends on preferred shares are stated as a dollar amount since preferred shares do not have a nominal or stated value. For example, preferred shares may be "$3 preferred," which means that shareholders receive an annual dividend of $3 per share.

Dividends on Cumulative and Noncumulative Preferred Shares. The allocation of dividends may be complex if the preferred shares are *cumulative*. Corporations sometimes fail to pay a dividend to preferred shareholders. This is called *passing the dividend*, and the passed dividends are said to be *in arrears*. The owners of **cumulative preferred shares** must receive all dividends in arrears plus the current year's dividend before the corporation can pay dividends to the common shareholders. *The law considers preferred shares noncumulative unless they are specifically labelled as cumulative.*

The preferred shares of Pinecraft Industries Inc. are cumulative. Suppose the company passed the 2008 preferred dividend of $150,000. Before paying dividends to its common shareholders in 2009, the company must first pay preferred dividends of $150,000 for both 2008 and 2009, a total of $300,000.

Assume that Pinecraft Industries Inc. passes its 2008 preferred dividend. In 2009, the company declares a $500,000 dividend. The entry to record the declaration is

2009			
Sept. 6	Retained Earnings	500,000	
	Dividends Payable, Preferred ($150,000 × 2)		300,000
	Dividends Payable, Common ($500,000 − $300,000)		200,000
	To declare a cash dividend.		

If the preferred shares are *noncumulative*, the corporation is not obligated to pay dividends in arrears. A liability for dividends arises only when the board of directors declares the dividend.

Some preferred shares have a *participation feature*. The following events will occur when a company pays out extra dividends on participating preferred shares:

- Preferred shareholders receive their usual dividend
- Common shareholders receive the dividend declared for the common shares
- The excess above these amounts is shared by common and preferred in proportion to the total value of both classes of shares or according to some other agreed formula

The details of determining dividends for participating preferred shares will be left to an intermediate accounting course.

Limited Voting Rights

Preferred shares are generally non-voting. However, limited voting is sometimes granted to preferred shareholders under the following conditions:

- When the company wants to liquidate a large portion of corporate assets
- When the company wants to merge with another company
- When the company wants to issue new bonds or preferred shares

Call Provisions

Preferred shares may be *callable*. This allows the issuing company to repurchase the shares from shareholders at a predetermined price and retire them. The call price includes the payment of any dividends in arrears and generally includes a premium to compensate the preferred shareholders for the inconvenience of having their shares called. A call price of 102 means that the call price is 102% of the book value of the preferred shares called. If on April 1, 2009, a company called $100,000 of preferred shares at 102 that have $3,000 of dividends in arrears, the following entry would be made to record the call.

2009			
Apr. 1	Preferred shares...	100,000	
	Loss on call of preferred shares	2,000	
	Dividends or Retained Earnings	3,000	
	Cash (102% × $100,000 + $3,000)................................		105,000
	To call $100,000 of preferred shares at 102, with		
	$3,000 dividends in arrears.		

Stock Dividends

A **stock dividend** is a proportional distribution by a corporation of its own shares to its shareholders. Stock dividends increase the shares account and decrease Retained Earnings. Total equity is unchanged, and no asset or liability is affected.

The corporation distributes stock dividends to shareholders in proportion to the number of shares they already own. If you own 300 common shares of TransCanada Corporation and TransCanada distributes a 10% common shares dividend, you will receive 30 (300 × 0.10) additional shares. You would then own 330 common shares. All other TransCanada shareholders would also receive additional shares equal to 10% of their prior holdings.

In distributing a stock dividend, the corporation gives up no assets. Why, then, do companies issue stock dividends? A corporation may choose to distribute stock dividends for the following reasons:

1. **To continue dividends but conserve cash.** A company may want to keep cash for operations and yet wish to continue dividends in some form. So the corporation may distribute a stock dividend. Shareholders pay tax on stock dividends the same way they pay tax on cash dividends.

2. **To reduce the per-share market price of its shares.** Distribution of a stock dividend may cause the market price of a share of the company's stock to fall because of the increased supply of the shares. The objective is to make the shares less expensive and thus more attractive to more investors.

Suppose TransCanada declared a 2% stock dividend in 2009. At the time, assume TransCanada had 540 million common shares outstanding. TransCanada is incorporated under the *Canada Business Corporations Act*, which suggests that the market value of the shares at the time of declaration be used to value the dividend. At the time of the stock dividend, assume TransCanada's shares are trading for $35 per share. TransCanada would record this stock dividend as follows, where SE stands for "Shareholders' equity":

2008

Nov. 19   Retained Earnings (540,000,000 common shares
       outstanding × 0.02 stock dividend × $35 market
       value per common share) (−SE) 378,000,000
         Common Shares (+SE) 378,000,000
       Distributed a 2% stock dividend.

The accounting equation clearly shows that a stock dividend has no effect on total assets, liabilities, or equity. The increases in equity offset the decreases, and the net effect is zero.

ASSETS	=	LIABILITIES	+	SHAREHOLDERS' EQUITY
0	=	0		−378,000,000 +378,000,000

STOP & THINK

A corporation issued 1,000 common shares as a stock dividend when the share market price was $25. Assume that the 1,000 shares issued are (1) 10% of the outstanding shares and (2) 100% of the outstanding shares. Does either stock dividend change total shareholders' equity?

Answer:
No, neither a large stock dividend nor a small stock dividend affects total shareholders' equity because all the accounts affected by a stock dividend are part of shareholders' equity.

Stock Splits

A **stock split** is an increase in the number of authorized, issued, and outstanding shares of stock, coupled with a proportionate reduction in the share's book value. For example, if a company splits its stock 2 for 1, the number of outstanding shares is doubled and each share's book value is halved. A stock split, like a stock dividend, decreases the market price of the shares—with the intention of making the shares more attractive in the market. Leading companies in Canada—Bank of Nova Scotia, Canadian National Railway Company, Molson Coors Brewing Company, Suncor Energy Inc., and others—have split their stock.

The recent share price of Potash Corporation of Saskatchewan Inc. on the Toronto Stock Exchange was $90.00. Assume Potash Corporation wants to decrease the price to approximately $45.00. Potash Corporation may decide to split its common shares.

A 2-for-1 stock split means that the company would have twice as many shares outstanding after the split as it had before and that each share's book value would be cut in half. Before the split, Potash Corporation had approximately 316 million common shares issued and outstanding. Compare Potash Corporation's shareholders' equity before and after a 2-for-1 stock split:

Potash Corporation's Shareholders' Equity (Adapted)

Before 2-for-1 Stock Split:	(In millions U.S. dollars)	After 2-for-1 Stock Split:	(In millions U.S. dollars)
Common shares, unlimited number of shares authorized, 316 million shares issued	$1,461.3	Common shares, unlimited number of shares authorized, 632 million shares issued	$1,461.3
Retained earnings	2,279.6	Retained earnings	2,279.6
Other	2,277.8	Other	2,277.8
Total shareholders' equity	$6,018.7	Total shareholders' equity	$6,018.7

All account balances are the same after the stock split as before. Only the number of shares issued is affected. Total equity does not change.

Summary of the Effects on Assets, Liabilities, and Shareholders' Equity

We've seen how to account for the basic shareholders' equity transactions:

- Issuance of shares—common and preferred (pp. 428–432)
- Repurchase of shares (pp. 434–436)
- Cash dividends (pp. 437–440)
- Stock dividends and stock splits (pp. 440–442)

How do these transactions affect assets, liabilities, and equity? Exhibit 9-6 provides a helpful summary.

Retained Earnings Restrictions

As emphasized in previous chapters, Retained Earnings represent a corporation's lifetime earnings minus lifetime dividends to date (both cash dividends and stock dividends). In some cases restrictions to protect creditors are imposed that make a portion of the current Retained Earnings balance unavailable for dividends.

Restrictions are disclosed in the notes accompanying financial statements and result from one or more of the following causes:

Legal — Regulatory agencies limit dividend payments to the balance of retained earnings.

Contractual — Debt covenants related to bank loans may restrict dividends to a specified percentage of retained earnings.

Voluntary — Corporate directors may limit dividends so that cash can be used in the business to take advantage of investment opportunities.

EXHIBIT 9-6 Effects on Assets, Liabilities, and Equity

Transaction	Effect on Total		
	Assets =	Liabilities +	Shareholders' Equity
Issuance of shares—common and preferred	Increase	No effect	Increase
Repurchase of shares	Decrease	No effect	Decrease
Declaration of cash dividend	No effect	Increase	Decrease
Payment of cash dividend	Decrease	Decrease	No effect
Stock dividend	No effect	No effect	No effect
Stock split	No effect	No effect	No effect

Measuring the Value of Shares

The business community measures *share values* in various ways, depending on the purpose of the measurement. These values include market value, redemption value, liquidation value, and book value.

Objective

⑤ **Use** share values in decision making

Market, Redemption, Liquidation, and Book Value

A share's **market value**, or *market price*, is the price for which a person can buy or sell one share of stock. Market value varies with the corporation's net income, financial position, and future prospects and the general economic conditions. *In almost all cases, shareholders are more concerned about the market value of a share than any other value.*

Sun-Rype's recent share price was $10.00. Therefore, if Sun-Rype were issuing 1,000 of its common shares, Sun-Rype would receive cash of $10,000 (1,000 × $10.00 per share). This would be the market value of the shares Sun-Rype issued.

IFRS ALERT

The subject of convertible preferred shares, like the subject of convertible bonds (mentioned in Chapter 8), is generally complex when the convertible preferred shares are defined by the converged standards in the *CICA Handbook* as liabilities or as combined equities and liabilities. Convertible preferred shares of that definition are an advanced topic beyond the scope of this text.

The convertible preferred shares discussed in this section are defined by the converged standards in the *CICA Handbook* as equities and, as such, are subject to the accounting described in the text.

Preferred shares that require the company to redeem the shares at the holder's option at a set price are called *redeemable preferred shares*. The company is *obligated* to redeem the preferred shares. The price the corporation agrees to pay for the shares, which is set when the shares are issued, is called the *redemption value*. *Liquidation value* is the amount that a company must pay a preferred shareholder in the event the company liquidates (sells out) and closes its doors if the necessary cash is available.

The **book value** per common share is the amount of owners' equity on the company's books for each common share. If the company has only common shares outstanding, its book value is computed by dividing total equity by the number of common shares *outstanding*. For example, a company with shareholders' equity of $180,000 and 5,000 common shares outstanding has a book value of $36 per share ($180,000 ÷ 5,000 shares).

If the company has both preferred shares and common shares outstanding, the preferred shareholders have the first claim to owners' equity. Preferred shares often have a specified liquidation or redemption value. The value of the preferred equity is its redemption value plus any cumulative preferred dividends in arrears (assuming the preferred dividends are cumulative). Book value per common share is then computed as follows:

$$\text{Book value per common share} = \frac{\text{Total shareholders' equity} - \text{Preferred equity}}{\text{Number of common shares outstanding}}$$

Crusader Corp.'s balance sheet reports the following amounts:

Shareholders' Equity	
Preferred shares, $6.00, 400 shares issued, redemption value $130 per share	$ 40,000
Common shares, 5,000 shares issued	131,000
Retained earnings	70,000
Total shareholders' equity	$241,000

USER ALERT

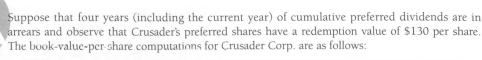

Suppose that four years (including the current year) of cumulative preferred dividends are in arrears and observe that Crusader's preferred shares have a redemption value of $130 per share. The book-value-per-share computations for Crusader Corp. are as follows:

Preferred equity	
Redemption value (400 shares × $130)	$ 52,000
Cumulative dividends (400 × $6.00 × 4 years)	9,600
Preferred equity	$61,600*

Common equity	
Total shareholders' equity	$241,000
Less preferred equity	(61,600)
Common equity	$179,400
Book value per share [$179,400 ÷ 5,000 shares outstanding]	$ 35.88

*If the preferred shares had no redemption value, then preferred equity would be $40,000 plus preferred dividends in arrears of $9,600 ($49,600).

DECISION Using Book Value Per Share

Some investors search for stocks whose market value is below book value. They believe this indicates a good buy. Financial analysts often shy away from companies with a share price at or below book value. To them, such a company is in trouble. As you can see not all users of financial statements agree on a share's value. Let's compare two companies, Canadian Tire Corporation Limited and Leon's Furniture Ltd.:

Company	Recent Share Price	Common Share-holders' Equity	Number of Common Shares Outstanding	Book Value
Canadian Tire Corporation Limited	$44.94	$3,093,900,000	81,502,273	$37.96
Leon's Furniture Ltd.	$8.80	$307,985,000	70,713,532	$4.36

*Book value = $\dfrac{\text{Common shareholders' equity}}{\text{Number of common shares outstanding}}$

Neither company's shares are selling below their book value. But Canadian Tire's book value per share is somewhat closer to its market value than Leon's. Does this mean Canadian Tire's shares are the better investment? Not necessarily. In fact, wise investors base their decisions on more than a single ratio. In Chapter 13 you'll see the full range of financial ratios, plus a few more analytical techniques.

Relating Profitability to a Company's Shares

Objective

⑥ **Compute** return on assets and return on equity

Investors search for companies whose shares are likely to increase in value. They're constantly comparing companies. But a comparison of Canadian Tire with a new start-up is not meaningful. Canadian Tire's profits run into the millions, which far exceed a new company's net income. Does this automatically make Canadian Tire a better investment? Not necessarily. To compare companies of different sizes, investors use some standard profitability measures, including:

- Return on assets
- Return on equity

Return on Assets. The **rate of return on total assets**, or simply **return on assets (ROA)**, measures a company's success in using its assets to earn income for the two groups who finance the business:

- Creditors to whom the corporation owes money (creditors want interest)
- Shareholders who own the corporation's shares (shareholders want net income)

The sum of interest expense and net income is the return to the two groups who finance a corporation. This sum is the numerator of the return-on-assets ratio. The denominator is average total assets. Return on assets is computed as follows, using data from Canadian Tire Corporation Limited's financial statements for a recent year-end (dollar amounts in millions):

$$\begin{array}{l}\text{Rate of return} \\ \text{on total assets}\end{array} = \frac{\text{Net income} + \text{Interest expense}}{\text{Average total assets}}$$

$$= \frac{\$417.6 + \$78.4}{(\$6,742.7 + \$5,804.6)/2} = \frac{\$496.0}{\$6,273.7} = 0.079$$

Net income and interest expense are taken from the income statement. Average total assets is computed from the beginning and ending balance sheets.

What is a good rate of return on total assets? Ten percent is considered strong for most companies. However, rates of return vary widely by industry. For example, high-technology companies earn much higher returns than do utility companies, retailers, and manufacturers of consumer goods such as toothpaste and paper towels. Canadian Tire's return on assets is close to strong.

Return on Equity. **Rate of return on common shareholders' equity**, often called **return on equity (ROE)**, shows the relationship between net income and average common shareholders' equity. Return on equity is computed only on common shares because the return to preferred shareholders is their specified dividend (for example, $1.50).

The numerator of return on equity is net income minus preferred dividends. The denominator is *average common shareholders' equity*—average total shareholders' equity minus preferred equity. A recent rate of return on common shareholders' equity for Canadian Tire is computed as follows (dollar amounts in millions):

$$\begin{array}{l}\text{Rate of return} \\ \text{on common} \\ \text{shareholders' equity}\end{array} = \frac{\text{Net income} - \text{Preferred dividends}}{\text{Average common shareholders' equity}}$$

$$= \frac{\$417.6 - \$0}{(\$3,093.9 + \$2,785.2)/2} = \frac{\$417.6}{\$2,939.6} = 0.142$$

Because Canadian Tire has no preferred shares, preferred dividends are zero. With no preferred shares outstanding, average *common* shareholders' equity is the same as average *total* equity—the average of the beginning and ending amounts.

Canadian Tire's return on equity (14.2%) is higher than its return on assets (7.9%). This difference results from the interest-expense component of return on assets. Companies such as Canadian Tire borrow at one rate (say, 6%) and invest the funds to earn a higher rate (say, 12%). Borrowing at a lower rate than the company's return on investments is called *using leverage*. Leverage increases net income as long as operating income exceeds the interest expense from borrowing.

ROE is always higher than ROA for a successful company. Shareholders take a lot more investment risk than bondholders, so the shareholders demand that

ROE *exceed* ROA. If ROA were higher, that would mean that the return on debt—interest—is higher than the return on equity—net income. If that were true, there wouldn't be any shareholders. Everyone would be investing in bonds!

Investors and creditors use ROE in much the same way they use ROA—to compare companies. The higher the rate of return, the more successful the company. In most industries, 15% is considered good. Therefore, Canadian Tire's 14.2% return on common shareholders' equity is good.

The Decision Guidelines feature (page 448) offers suggestions for what to consider when investing in shares.

Reporting Shareholders' Equity Transactions

Cash Flow Statement

Many of the transactions discussed in this chapter are reported on the cash flow statement. Equity transactions are *financing activities* because the company is dealing with its owners. Financing transactions that affect both cash and equity fall into three main categories:

* Issuances of shares
* Repurchases of shares
* Dividends

Issuances of Shares. *Issuances of shares* includes basic transactions in which a company issues its shares for cash. During 2007, Canadian Tire issued 457,606 Class A common shares for a stated value of $35.1 million. The sale was reported as a financing activity.

Repurchases of Shares. As we discussed earlier, a company can repurchase its shares. During 2007, Canadian Tire repurchased 457,000 class A common shares for cancellation at $34.9 million and reported the payment as a financing activity.

Dividends. Most companies pay cash dividends to their shareholders. Dividend payments are a type of financing transaction because the company is paying its shareholders for the use of their money. Stock dividends are not reported on the cash flow statement because the company pays no cash. Canadian Tire paid dividends in the amount of $58.8 million during 2007. See Exhibit 9-7.

Variations in Reporting Shareholders' Equity

Businesses often use terminology and formats in reporting shareholders' equity that differ from our examples. We use a more detailed format in this book to help you learn all the components of shareholders' equity.

EXHIBIT 9-7	**Canadian Tire Corporation Limited Financing Activities (Adapted)**

	($ millions)
Financing activities:	
Share capital – issued in excess of retired	0.2
Dividends – to shareholders	(58.8)

One of the most important skills you will take from this course is the ability to understand the financial statements of real companies. Exhibit 9–8 presents a side-by-side comparison of our general teaching format and the format you are more likely to encounter in real-world balance sheets, such as those of Canadian Tire Corporation.

In general:

- Preferred shares come first and the individual classes are listed separately. The dividend rate, features such as whether the dividend is cumulative and whether the shares are redeemable, and the number of shares authorized and issued are reported.

- Common shares come next and individual classes are listed separately. The number of shares authorized and issued is reported.

- Contributed surplus is listed next.

- Preferred shares, common shares, and contributed surplus are included in Contributed Capital.

- Accumulated other comprehensive income.

- Retained Earnings comes last.

IFRS

EXHIBIT 9-8   **Formats for Reporting Shareholders' Equity**

General Teaching Format		*Real-World Format*	
Shareholders' equity		**Shareholders' equity**	
Capital stock:			
Preferred shares, $0.80, cumulative,		Contributed capital	
30,000 shares authorized and issued	$ 300,000	Share capital (Note 9)	$2,500,000
Common shares, 100,000 shares		Contributed surplus	11,000
authorized, 60,000 shares issued	2,200,000	Accumulated other comprehensive income	15,000
		Retained earnings	1,542,000
Contributed surplus from retirement of		Total shareholders' equity	$4,068,000
preferred shares	8,000		
Contributed surplus from repurchase of		**Notes to the Financial Statements**	
common shares..	3,000	1.	
		.	
Total capital stock	2,511,000	.	
Accumulated other comprehensive income.......	15,000	.	
Retained earnings	1,542,000	**9. Share capital**	
Total shareholders' equity	$4,068,000		
			2010
		Preferred shares, $0.80 cumulative	
		30,000 shares authorized and issued	$ 300,000
		Common shares, 100,000 shares authorized,	
		60,000 issued	$2,200,000
		Total share capital	$2,500,000

DECISION GUIDELINES

INVESTING IN SHARES

Suppose you've saved $5,000 to invest. You visit a nearby ScotiaMcLeod office, where the broker probes you for your risk tolerance capacity. Are you investing mainly for dividends, or for growth in the share price? You must make some key decisions.

Investor Decision	Guidelines
Which category of shares to buy for:	
• A safe investment?	Preferred shares are safer than common, but for even more safety, invest in blue chip stocks, high-grade corporate bonds, or government securities.
• Steady dividends?	Cumulative preferred shares. However, the company is not obligated to declare preferred dividends, and the dividends are unlikely to increase.
• Increasing dividends?	Common shares, as long as the company's net income is increasing and the company has adequate cash flow to pay a dividend after meeting all obligations and other cash demands.
• Increasing share price?	Common shares, but again only if the company's net income and cash flow are increasing.
• How to identify a good stock to buy?	There are many ways to pick share investments. One strategy that works reasonably well is to invest in companies that consistently earn higher rates of return on assets and on equity than competing firms in the same industry. Also, select industries that are expected to grow.

 **END-OF-CHAPTER SUMMARY PROBLEMS**

1. The balance sheet of Quetico Inc. reported the following at December 31, 2009:

Shareholders' Equity

Preferred shares, $0.40, 10,000 shares authorized and issued (redemption value, $110,000)	$100,000
Common shares, 100,000 shares authorized*	400,000
Retained earnings	476,500
Total shareholders' equity	$976,500

*The common shares were issued at a stated value of $8.00 per share.

Required

a. Are the preferred shares cumulative or noncumulative? How can you tell?
b. What is the total amount of the annual preferred dividend?
c. How many common shares are outstanding?
d. Compute the book value per share of the common shares. No preferred dividends are in arrears, and Quetico Inc. has not yet declared the 2009 dividend.

2. Use the following accounts and related balances to prepare the classified balance sheet of Ghandi Ltd. at September 30, 2009. Use the account format of the balance sheet.

Common shares,		Property, plant, and	
50,000 shares authorized,		equipment, net....................	$226,000
20,000 shares issued...........	$100,000	Accounts receivable, net..........	23,000
Dividends payable...................	4,000	Preferred shares, $3.75,	
Cash	9,000	10,000 shares authorized,	
Accounts payable	28,000	2,000 shares issued	24,000
Long-term note payable	80,000	Accrued liabilities	3,000
Inventory	85,000	Retained earnings...................	104,000

Answers

1. a. The preferred shares are not cumulative because they are not specifically labelled cumulative.

b. Total annual preferred dividend: $4,000 (10,000 × $0.40).

c. Common shares outstanding: 50,000 shares ($400,000 ÷ $8 stated value).

d. Book value per common share:

Common:	
Total shareholders' equity...	$ 976,500
Less shareholders' equity allocated to preferred................................	(110,000)*
Shareholders' equity allocated to common	$ 866,500
Book value per share ($866,500 ÷ 50,000 shares).............................	$ 17.33
*Redemption value..	$110,000

> All features must be specified in the financial statements.

> Details given on the balance sheet.

> Each common share was sold for the $8 stated value.

> Book value per common share must exclude any amounts pertaining to preferred shares.

2.

> The classified balance sheet must specify current assets and current liabilities. Make sure that Total assets = Total liabilities + Shareholders' equity.

Ghandi Ltd.
Balance Sheet
September 30, 2009

Assets		Liabilities	
Current		Current	
Cash	$ 9,000	Accounts payable	$ 28,000
Accounts receivable, net	23,000	Dividends payable....................	4,000
Inventory...	85,000	Accrued liabilities....................	3,000
Total current assets	117,000	Total current liabilities..........	35,000
Property, plant, and equipment, net..........	226,000	Long-term note payable	80,000
		Total liabilities...........................	$115,000
		Shareholders' Equity	
		Preferred shares, $3.75,	
		10,000 shares authorized,	
		2,000 shares issued	$ 24,000
		Common shares,	
		50,000 shares authorized,	
		20,000 shares issued	100,000
		Retained earnings........................	104,000
		Total shareholders' equity.........	228,000
		Total liabilities and	
Total assets	$343,000	shareholders' equity	$343,000

REVIEW SHAREHOLDERS' EQUITY

QUICK CHECK   (Answers are given on page 473.)

1. Copeland Company is authorized to issue 40,000 $10 common shares. On January 15, 2009, Copeland issued 10,000 shares at $15 per share. Copeland's journal entry to record these facts should include a
   a. Credit to Common Shares for $100,000
   b. Credit to Common Shares for $150,000
   c. Debit to Common Shares for $150,000
   d. Both a and b

Questions 2 through 5 use the following account balances of Casio Co. at March 31, 2009:

Number of common shares authorized	1,000,000	Number of common shares issued.....	180,000
Dividends Payable	$ 22,000	Cash..	$ 74,000
Preferred Shares............................	100,000	Common Shares..............................	180,000
		Retained Earnings	200,000

2. Casio has issued _____ common shares.
   a. 74,000   c. 225,000
   b. 180,000   d. Some other amount

3. Casio's total contributed capital at March 31, 2009, is
   a. $495,000   c. $1,175,000
   b. $180,000   d. Some other amount

4. Casio's total shareholders' equity as of March 31, 2009, is
   a. $1,406,000   c. $480,000
   b. $1,249,000   d. $1,480,000

5. What would Casio's total shareholders' equity be if there were $5,000 of common shares repurchased? _____

6. Woodstock Corporation repurchased common shares in 2009 at a price of $30 per share that had an average cost of $40 per share. What amount should Woodstock report on its income statement for 2009?
   a. $40   c. $10
   b. $30   d. $0

7. The shareholders' equity section of a corporation's balance sheet reports

	Common Shares	*Discount on Bonds Payable*
a.	Yes	No
b.	No	Yes
c.	Yes	Yes
d.	No	No

8. The repurchase of a company's own shares
   a. Increases one asset, and decreases another asset
   b. Decreases total assets, and decreases total shareholders' equity
   c. Has no effect on total assets, total liabilities, or total shareholders' equity
   d. Decreases total assets, and increases total shareholders' equity

9. When does a cash dividend become a legal liability?
   a. On date of payment
   b. On date of record
   c. On date of declaration
   d. It never becomes a liability because it is paid.

10. When do dividends increase shareholders' equity?

    a. Never   **c.** On date of record

    b. On date of declaration   **d.** On date of payment

11. Willow Run Mall Inc. has 5,000 $2 cumulative preferred shares and 100,000 common shares outstanding. At the beginning of the current year, preferred dividends were 3 years in arrears. Willow Run's board of directors wants to pay a $1.25 cash dividend on each share of outstanding common shares. To accomplish this, what total amount of dividends must Willow Run declare?

    a. $170,000   **c.** $165,000

    b. $185,000   **d.** Some other amount $_____

12. Which of the following is true of stock dividends?

    a. They have no effect on total shareholders' equity.

    b. They are distributions of cash to shareholders.

    c. They reduce the total assets of the company.

    d. They increase the corporation's total liabilities.

13. What is the effect of a stock split and a stock dividend on total assets?

	Stock Split	*Stock Dividend*
a.	Decrease	No effect
b.	Decrease	Decrease
c.	No effect	Decrease
d.	No effect	No effect

14. A 2-for-1 stock split has the same effect on the number of shares being issued as a

    a. 20% stock dividend   **c.** 100% stock dividend

    b. 50% stock dividend   **d.** 200% stock dividend

15. The numerator for computing the rate of return on total assets is

    a. Net income

    b. Net income minus interest expense

    c. Net income plus interest expense

    d. Net income minus preferred dividends

16. The numerator for computing the rate of return on common equity is

    a. Net income minus preferred dividends

    b. Net income minus interest expense

    c. Net income plus preferred dividends

    d. Net income

ACCOUNTING VOCABULARY

book value (of a share) Amount of owners' equity on the company's books for each share of its stock.   (p. 443)

bylaws Constitution for governing a corporation.   (p. 425)

chairperson Elected by a corporation's board of directors, usually the most powerful person in the corporation.   (p. 425)

cumulative preferred shares Preferred shares whose owners must receive all dividends in arrears plus the current year's dividend before the corporation can pay dividends to the common shareholders.   (p. 439)

deficit Debit balance in the Retained Earnings account.   (p. 436)

double taxation Corporations pay income taxes on corporate income. Then, the shareholders pay personal income tax on the cash dividends that they receive from corporations. Canada's tax laws attempt to minimize double taxation.   (p. 424)

limited liability No personal obligation of a shareholder for corporation debts. A shareholder can lose no more on an invest-

ment in a corporation's shares than the cost of the investment.   (p. 424)

market value (of a share) Price for which a person could buy or sell a share of stock.   (p. 443)

no-stated-value shares Shares of stock that do not have a value assigned to them by articles of the corporation.   (p. 428)

outstanding shares Shares in the hands of shareholders.   (p. 427)

preferred shares Shares that give their owners certain advantages, such as the priority to receive dividends before the common shareholders and the priority to receive assets before the common shareholders if the corporation liquidates.   (p. 427)

president Chief executive officer in charge of managing the day-to-day operations of a corporation.   (p. 425)

rate of return on common shareholders' equity Net income minus preferred dividends, divided by average common shareholders' equity. A measure of profitability. Also called *return on equity*.   (p. 445)

rate of return on total assets Net income plus interest expense divided by average total assets. This ratio measures a company's success in using its assets to earn income for those who finance the business. Also called *return on assets*. (p. 445)

repurchased shares A corporation's own shares that it has issued and later reacquired. (p. 434)

return on assets Another name for *rate of return on total assets*. (p. 445)

return on equity Another name for *rate of return on common shareholders' equity*. (p. 445)

stated value An arbitrary amount assigned by a company to a share of its stock at the time of issue. (p. 428)

stock dividend A proportional distribution by a corporation of its own shares to its shareholders. (p. 440)

stock split An increase in the number of authorized, issued, and outstanding shares of stock coupled with a proportionate reduction in the share's book value. (p. 441)

ASSESS YOUR PROGRESS

MyAccountingLab Make the grade with MyAccountingLab: The exercises and problems marked in red can be found on MyAccountingLab at www.myaccountinglab.com. You can practise them as often as you want, and they feature step by step guided solutions to help you find the right answer.

SHORT EXERCISES

Advantages and disadvantages of a corporation
(Obj. 1)

S9-1 What are two main advantages that a corporation has over a proprietorship and a partnership? What are two main disadvantages of a corporation?

Authority structure in a corporation
(Obj.1)

S9-2 Consider the authority structure in a corporation, as diagrammed in Exhibit 9-2, page 426.

1. What group holds the ultimate power in a corporation?
2. Who is the most powerful person in the corporation?
3. Who's in charge of day-to-day operations? What's the abbreviation of this person's title?
4. Who's in charge of accounting and finance? What's the abbreviation of this person's title?

Characteristics of preferred and common shares
(Obj. 1)

S9-3 Answer the following questions about the characteristics of a corporation's shares:

1. Who are the real owners of a corporation?
2. What privileges do preferred shareholders have over common shareholders?
3. Which class of shareholders reaps greater benefits from a highly profitable corporation? Explain.

Effect of a share issuance on net income
(Obj. 2)

S9-4 Study **George Weston Ltd.'s** January 8, 2008, share issuance entry given on page 429, and answer these questions about the nature of the transaction.

1. If George Weston had sold the shares for $80, would the $30 ($80 − $50) be profit for George Weston?
2. Suppose the shares had been issued at different times and different prices. Will shares issued at higher prices have more rights than those issued at lower prices? Give the reason for your answer.

Issuing shares and analyzing retained earnings
(Obj. 2)

S9-5 On December 31, 2009, shareholders' equity accounts of Green Products Inc. (GPI) had the balances shown below. GPI paid dividends of $4,096 on December 1, 2009.

	2009	2008
Common shares	$82,968	$64,968
Retained earnings	80,435	78,881
Total shareholders' equity	$163,403	$145,849

1. GPI sold 10,000 common shares on June 30, 2009. What was the average selling price of these shares if this was the only common-shares transaction during 2009?

2. Journalize GPI's sale of the common shares on June 30, 2009.

3. Based only on the above information, did GPI earn a profit or loss during 2009? Calculate the profit or loss.

S9-6 This Short Exercise demonstrates the similarity and the difference between two ways to acquire capital assets.

Issuing shares to finance the purchase of assets
(Obj. 2)

Case A—Issue shares and buy the assets in separate transactions:	Case B—Issue shares to acquire the assets in a single transaction:
Longview Corporation issued 10,000 common shares for cash of $200,000. In a separate transaction, Longview used the cash to purchase a warehouse building for $160,000 and equipment for $40,000. Journalize the 2 transactions.	Tyler Corporation issued 10,000 common shares to acquire a warehouse valued at $160,000 and equipment worth $40,000. Journalize this transaction.

Compare the balances in all the accounts after making both sets of entries. Are the account balances the same or different?

S9-7 The financial statements of Eppley Employment Services Inc. reported the following accounts (adapted, with dollar amounts in thousands):

Preparing the shareholders' equity section of a balance sheet
(Obj. 2)

Common shares:		Total revenues	$1,390
600 shares issued	$600	Accounts payable	420
Long-term debt	25	Retained earnings	646
		Other current liabilities	2,566
		Total expenses	805

Prepare the shareholders' equity section of Eppley's balance sheet. Net income has already been closed to Retained Earnings.

S9-8 Use the Eppley Employment Services data in Short Exercise 9-7 to compute Eppley's

Using shareholders' equity data
(Obj. 2)

a. Net income
b. Total liabilities
c. Total assets (use the accounting equation)

S9-9 General Marketing Corporation reported the following shareholders' equity at December 31, 2009 (adapted and in millions):

Accounting for the repurchase and sale of shares
(Obj. 3)

Common shares	$ 257
Retained earnings	2,159
Total shareholders' equity	$2,416

During the next year, General Marketing repurchased common shares at a cost of $38 million and issued shares for $5 million. The repurchased shares had a stated value of $40 million.

Record the repurchase and issuance of common shares. Overall, how much did shareholders' equity increase or decrease as a result of the two share transactions?

S9-10 Gleneagles Corporation earned net income of $70,000 during the year ended December 31, 2008. On December 15, Gleneagles declared the annual cash dividend on its $0.50 preferred shares (10,000 shares issued for $100,000) and a $0.60 per share cash dividend on its common shares (25,000 shares issued for $50,000). Gleneagles then paid the dividends on January 4, 2009.

Accounting for cash dividends
(Obj. 4)

Journalize for Gleneagles Corporation:

a. Declaring the cash dividends on December 15, 2008

b. Paying the cash dividends on January 4, 2009

Did Retained Earnings increase or decrease during 2008? If so, by how much?

Dividing cash dividends between preferred and common shares
(Obj. 4)

S9-11 Refer to the allocation of dividends for Pinecraft Industries Inc. on page 439. Answer these questions about Pinecraft's cash dividends.

1. How much in dividends must Pinecraft declare each year before the common shareholders receive any cash dividends for the year?

2. Suppose Pinecraft declares cash dividends of $300,000 for 2010. How much of the dividends go to preferred? How much go to common?

3. Are Pinecraft's preferred shares cumulative or noncumulative? How can you tell?

4. Pinecraft passed the preferred dividend in 2007 and 2008. Then in 2009, Pinecraft declares cash dividends of $800,000. How much of the dividends go to preferred? How much go to common?

Recording a small stock dividend
(Obj. 4)

S9-12 Fidelity Software Ltd. has 80,000 common shares issued. Suppose Fidelity distributes a 10% stock dividend when the market value of its shares is $10.50 per share.

1. Journalize Fidelity's distribution of the shares dividend on May 11. An explanation is not required.

2. What was the overall effect of the stock dividend on Fidelity's total assets? What about on its total liabilities and its total shareholders' equity?

Computing book value per share
(Obj. 5)

S9-13 Refer to the Real-World Format of shareholders' equity in Exhibit 9-8, page 447. That company has passed its preferred dividends for three years including the current year. Compute the book value of one of the company's common shares.

S9-14 Give the formula for computing (a) rate of return on total assets (ROA) and (b) rate of return on common shareholders' equity (ROE). Then answer these questions about the rate-of-return computations.

Computing and explaining return on assets and return on equity
(Obj. 6)

1. Why is interest expense added to net income in the computation of ROA?

2. Why are preferred dividends subtracted from net income to compute ROE? Why are they not subtracted from net income in computing ROA?

Computing return on assets and return on equity
(Obj. 6)

S9-15 Federated Machinery Ltd.'s 2009 financial statements reported the following items, with 2008 figures given for comparison (adapted and in millions). Compute Federated's return on assets and return on common equity for 2009. Evaluate the rates of return as strong or weak.

	2009	2008
Balance sheet		
Total assets	$10,608	$9,499
Total liabilities	$7,404	$6,629
Total shareholders' equity (all common)	3,204	2,870
Total liabilities and equity	$10,608	$9,499
Income statement		
Revenues and other income	$ 7,629	
Operating expense	7,284	
Interest expense	29	
Other expense	192	
Net income	$ 124	

Measuring cash flows from financing activities
(Obj. 7)

S9-16 During 2009, Robertson Inc. earned net income of $5.6 billion and paid off $2.7 billion of long-term notes payable. Robertson Inc. raised $1.2 billion by issuing common shares, paid $3.0 billion to repurchase shares, and paid cash dividends of $1.9 billion. Report Robertson's *cash flows from financing activities* on the cash flow statement for 2009.

EXERCISES

E9-17 Lance Brown and Monica Kobelsky are opening a **Second Cup** franchise. Brown and Kobelsky need outside capital, so they plan to organize the business as a corporation. They come to you for advice. Write a memorandum informing them of the steps in forming a corporation in the province of Alberta. Identify specific documents used in this process, and name the different parties involved in the ownership and management of a corporation.

Organizing a corporation
(Obj. 1)

E9-18 Burgers & Fries, Inc. is authorized to issue an unlimited number of common shares and 10,000 preferred shares. During its first year, the business completed the following share issuance transactions:

Issuing shares and reporting shareholders' equity
(Obj. 2)

July	19	Issued 10,000 common shares for cash of $6.50 per share
Oct.	3	Issued 500 $1.50 preferred shares for $50,000 cash
	11	Received inventory valued at $11,000 and equipment with market value of $8,500 for 3,300 common shares

❚ Required

1. Journalize the transactions. Explanations are not required.
2. Prepare the shareholders' equity section of Burgers & Fries' balance sheet. The ending balance of Retained Earnings is a deficit of $42,000.

E9-19 Citadel Sporting Goods is authorized to issue 5,000 preferred shares and 10,000 common shares. During a 2-month period, Citadel completed these share-issuance transactions:

Preparing the shareholders' equity section of a balance sheet
(Obj. 2)

Sept.	23	Issued 1,000 common shares for cash of $16 per share
Oct.	2	Issued 300 $4.50 preferred shares for $20,000 cash
	12	Received inventory valued at $15,000 and equipment with market value of $43,000 for 4,000 common shares

❚ Required

Prepare the shareholders' equity section of the Citadel Sporting Goods balance sheet for the transactions given in this exercise. Retained Earnings has a balance of $49,000. Journal entries are not required.

E9-20 Trans World Publishing Inc. was recently organized. The company issued common shares to a lawyer who provided legal services of $15,000 to help organize the corporation. Trans World also issued common shares to an inventor in exchange for his patent with a market value of $80,000. In addition, Trans World received cash both for the issuance of 5,000 of its preferred shares at $110 per share and for the issuance of 20,000 common shares at $20 per share. During the first year of operations, Trans World earned net income of $55,000 and declared a cash dividend of $20,000. Without making journal entries, determine the total contributed capital created by these transactions.

Measuring the contributed capital of a corporation
(Obj. 2)

E9-21 Sagebrush Software Ltd. had the following selected account balances at December 31, 2009 (in thousands). Prepare the shareholders' equity section of Sagebrush Software's balance sheet (in thousands).

Shareholders' equity section of a balance sheet
(Obj. 2, 3)

Inventory	$ 653	Class A common shares,	
Property, plant, and equipment, net	857	unlimited number authorized,	
Contributed surplus – share repurchase	901	3,600 shares issued	$ 90
Class B common shares,		Deficit	2,400
unlimited number authorized,		Accounts receivable, net	600
5,000 shares issued	1,380	Notes payable	1,122

Explain what is meant by "deficit."

Recording share transactions and measuring their effects on shareholders' equity
(Obj. 2, 3)

E9-22 Journalize the following transactions of Concilio Video Productions Inc.:

April	19	Issued 2,000 common shares at $10 per share
July	22	Repurchased 900 shares at $11 per share
Nov.	11	Issued 800 common shares at $12 per share

What was the overall effect of these transactions on Concilio's shareholders' equity?

Recording share issuance and dividend transactions
(Obj. 2, 3, 4)

E9-23 At December 31, 2009, Blumenthall Corporation reported the shareholders' equity accounts shown here (as adapted, with dollar amounts in millions).

Common shares	
1,800 million shares issued	$ 2,700
Retained earnings	1,200
Total shareholders' equity	$3,900

Blumenthall's 2009 transactions included the following:

a. Net income, $350 million

b. Issuance of 6 million common shares for $12.50 per share

c. Repurchase of 1 million common shares for $15 million

d. Declaration and payment of cash dividends of $25 million

  Journalize Blumenthall's transactions. Explanations are not required.

Reporting shareholders' equity after a sequence of transactions
(Obj. 2, 3, 4)

E9-24 Use the Blumenthall Corporation data in Exercise 9-23 to prepare the shareholders' equity section of the company's balance sheet at December 31, 2009.

Inferring transactions from a company's shareholders' equity
(Obj. 2, 3, 4, 5)

E9-25 Optical Products Company reported the following shareholders' equity on its balance sheet:

	December 31,	
Shareholders' Equity (Dollars and shares in millions)	**2009**	**2008**
Preferred shares; authorized 20 shares;		
Convertible Preferred shares; issued and outstanding:		
2009 and 2008—0 and 2 shares, respectively	$ 0	$ 12
Common shares; authorized unlimited shares; issued:		
2009 and 2008—564 and 364 shares, respectively	3,270	1,900
Retained earnings	6,280	5,006
Total shareholders' equity	$ 9,550	$ 6,918
Total liabilities and shareholders' equity	$48,918	$45,549

❙ Required

1. What caused Optical Products' preferred shares to decrease during 2009? Cite all the possible causes.

2. What caused Optical Products' common shares to increase during 2009? Identify all the possible causes.

3. How many shares of Optical Products were outstanding at December 31, 2009?

4. Optical Products' net income during 2009 was $1,410 million. How much were Optical Products' dividends during the year?

5. During 2009, the cost of repurchasing 10 million common shares was $60 million. What average price did Optical Products pay for the shares the company repurchased during the year? Determine the amount received from new common shares issued during 2009.

E9-26 Great Lakes Manufacturing Inc. reported the following:

Computing dividends on preferred and common shares
(Obj. 4)

Shareholders' Equity	
Preferred shares, cumulative, $0.10, 80,000 shares issued................	$ 80,000
Common shares, 8,130,000 shares issued...	813,000

Great Lakes Manufacturing has paid all preferred dividends through 2006.

▌Required

Compute the total amounts of dividends to both preferred and common shareholders for 2009 and 2010 if total dividends are $50,000 in 2009 and $100,000 in 2010.

E9-27 The shareholders' equity for Best in Show Cinemas Ltd. (BSC) (adapted) at December 31, 2008 appears as follows:

Recording a stock dividend and reporting shareholders' equity
(Obj. 4)

Shareholders' Equity	
Common shares, 2,000,000 shares authorized,	
500,000 shares issued	$1,012,000
Retained earnings..	7,122,000
Total shareholders' equity	$8,134,000

On April 15, 2009, the market price of BSC common shares was $17 per share. Assume BSC distributed a 10% stock dividend on this date.

▌Required

1. Journalize the distribution of the stock dividend.
2. Prepare the shareholders' equity section of the balance sheet after the stock dividend.
3. Why is total shareholders' equity unchanged by the stock dividend?
4. Suppose BSC had a cash balance of $540,000 on April 16, 2009. What is the maximum amount of cash dividends BSC can declare?

E9-28 Identify the effects—both the direction and the dollar amount—of these assumed transactions on the total shareholders' equity of a large corporation. Each transaction is independent.

Measuring the effects of share issuance, dividends, and share transactions
(Obj. 2, 3, 4)

a. Declaration of cash dividends of $80 million
b. Payment of the cash dividend declared
c. 10% stock dividend. Before the dividend, 69 million common shares were outstanding; the market value was $7.625 at the time of the dividend.
d. A 50% stock dividend. Before the dividend, 69 million common shares were outstanding; the market value was $13.75 at the time of the dividend.
e. Repurchase of 2,000 common shares at $4.25 per share
f. Sale of 600 common shares for $5.00 per share
g. A 3-for-1 stock split. Prior to the split, 69 million common shares were outstanding

E9-29 Solartech Inc. had the following shareholders' equity at January 31 (dollars in millions):

Reporting shareholders' equity after a stock split
(Obj. 4)

Common shares, 500 million shares authorized,	
440 million shares issued	$ 318
Contributed surplus...	44
Retained earnings..	2,393
Total shareholders' equity	$2,755

Assume that on March 7, Solartech split its common shares 2 for 1. Prepare the shareholders' equity section of the balance sheet immediately after the split.

Measuring the book value per share of common shares
(Obj. 5)

E9-30 The balance sheet of Oriental Rug Company reported the following:

Redeemable preferred shares, $0.06, redemption value $10,000; outstanding 6,000 shares	$ 6,000
Common shareholders' equity:	
8,000 shares issued and outstanding..	87,200
Total shareholders' equity	$93,200

Required

1. Compute the book value per share for the common shares, assuming all preferred dividends are fully paid up (none in arrears).
2. Compute the book value per share of the common shares, assuming that 3 years' preferred dividends, including the current year, are in arrears.
3. Oriental Rug's common shares recently traded at a market price of $7.75 per share. Does this mean that Oriental Rug's shares are a good buy at $7.75?

Evaluating profitability
(Obj. 6)

E9-31 Lexington Inns Limited reported these figures for 2008 and 2009 (in millions):

	2009	2008
Balance sheet		
Total assets	$15,695	$13,757
Common shares..	43	388
Retained earnings..	8,605	7,216
Income statement		
Operating income	$ 4,021	$ 3,818
Interest expense	219	272
Net income	1,486	1,543

Compute Lexington's return on assets and return on common shareholders' equity for 2009. Do these rates of return suggest strength or weakness? Give your reason.

Evaluating profitability
(Obj. 6)

E9-32 B.C. Pacific Company included the following items in its financial statements for 2009, the current year (amounts in millions):

Payment of long-term debt..............	$17,055		Dividends paid	$ 225
Proceeds from issuance of			Interest expense:	
common shares...........................	8,425		Current year	1,437
Total liabilities:			Preceding year	597
Current year-end..........................	32,320		Net income:	
Preceding year-end.......................	38,023		Current year	1,882
Total shareholders' equity:			Preceding year	2,001
Current year-end..........................	23,478		Operating income:	
Preceding year-end.......................	14,048		Current year	4,884
Borrowings......................................	6,582		Preceding year	4,012

Compute B.C. Pacific's return on assets and return on common equity during 2009 (the current year). B.C. Pacific has no preferred shares outstanding. Do the company's rates of return look strong or weak? Give your reason.

Reporting cash flows from financing activities
(Obj. 7)

E9-33 Use the B.C. Pacific Company data in Exercise 9-32 to show how the company reported cash flows from financing activities during 2009 (the current year). List items in descending order from largest to smallest dollar amount.

CHALLENGE EXERCISES

E9-34 A-1 Networking Solutions Inc. began operations on January 1, 2009, and immediately issued its shares, receiving cash. A-1's balance sheet at December 31, 2009, reported the following shareholders' equity:

Reconstructing transactions from the financial statements
(Obj. 2, 3, 4)

Common shares..	$249,500
Contributed surplus...	800
Retained earnings..	38,000
Total shareholders' equity	$288,300

During 2009, A-1

a. Issued 50,000 common shares for $5 per share
b. Repurchased 800 of its own common shares, paying $4 per share
c. Issued common shares for $7 each
d. Earned net income of $56,000 and declared and paid cash dividends. Revenues were $171,000 and expenses totalled $115,000.

I *Required*

Journalize all A-1's shareholders' equity transactions during the year. A-1's entry in d to close net income to Retained Earnings was:

Revenues	171,000	
Expenses		115,000
Retained Earnings		56,000

E9-35 Use the data in Challenge Exercise 9-34 to report all A-1 Networking Solutions' financing activities on the company's cash flow statement for 2009 (journal entries and/or T-accounts may aid your approach to a solution).

Reporting financing activities on the cash flow statement
(Obj. 7)

E9-36 Startech Limited reported the following shareholders' equity data (all dollars in millions):

Explaining the changes in shareholders' equity
(Obj. 2, 3, 4)

	December 31,	
	2009	**2008**
Preferred shares...	$ 604	$ 740
Common shares	2,390	2,130
Retained earnings	20,661	19,108

Startech earned net income of $2,960 during 2009. Common shares were issued for $20.00 each. For each account except Retained Earnings, one transaction explains the change from the December 31, 2008, balance to the December 31, 2009, balance. Two transactions affected Retained Earnings. Give a full explanation, including the dollar amount, for the change in each account.

E9-37 Fun City Inc. ended 2008 with 8 million common shares issued and outstanding. The average issue price was $1.50. Beginning retained earnings totalled $40 million.

Accounting for changes in shareholders' equity
(Obj. 2, 3, 4)

- In March 2009, Fun City issued 2 million common shares at a price of $2 per share.
- In May, the company distributed a 10% stock dividend at a time when Fun City's common shares had a market value of $3 per share.
- Then in October, Fun City's stock price dropped to $1 per share and the company repurchased 2 million shares.
- For the year, Fun City earned net income of $26 million and declared cash dividends of $17 million.

Complete the following tabulation to show what Fun City should report for shareholders' equity at December 31, 2009. Journal entries are not required.

(Amounts in millions)	Common Shares	+	Retained Earnings	−	Contributed Surplus Share Repurchase	=	Total Equity
Balance, Dec. 31, 2008	$12		$40		$0		$52
Issuance of shares 2008							
Stock dividend...........................							
Repurchase of common shares....							
Net income							
Cash dividends							
Balance, Dec. 31, 2009	$		$		$		$

QUIZ

Test your understanding of shareholders' equity by answering the following questions. Select the best choice from among the possible answers given.

Q9-38 Which of the following is a characteristic of a corporation?
a. Mutual agency
b. No income tax
c. Limited liability of shareholders
d. Both a and b

Q9-39 Team Spirit Inc. issues 240,000 common shares for $5 per share. The journal entry is

a.	Cash	240,000	
	Common Shares		240,000
b.	Cash	1,200,000	
	Common Shares		240,000
	Gain on the Sale of Shares		960,000
c.	Cash	1,200,000	
	Common Shares		1,200,000
d.	Cash	1,200,000	
	Common Shares		480,000
	Contributed Surplus on Common Shares		720,000

Q9-40 Which of the following is true about stated value?
a. It represents what a share is worth.
b. It represents the original selling price for a share.
c. It is established for a share after it is issued.
d. It is an arbitrary amount assigned by a company to a share at the time of issue.
e. It may exist for common shares but not for preferred shares.

Q9-41 The contributed capital portion of shareholders' equity does not include
a. Preferred Shares
b. Contributed Surplus
c. Retained Earnings
d. Common Shares

Q9-42 Preferred shares are *least* likely to have which of the following characteristics?
a. Preference as to assets on liquidation of the corporation
b. Extra liability for the preferred shareholders
c. The right of the holder to convert to common shares
d. Preference as to dividends

Q9-43 Which of the following classifications represents the largest quantity of common shares?
a. Issued shares
b. Outstanding shares
c. Unissued shares
d. Authorized shares

Use the following information for Questions 9-44 through 9-46:

These account balances at December 31 relate to Sportaid Inc.

Accounts Payable	$ 51,700	Preferred shares, $0.10,	
Accounts Receivable	81,350	89,000 shares issued	89,000
Common Shares	593,000	Retained Earnings	71,800
Bonds Payable	3,400	Notes Receivable	12,500

Q9-44 What is total share capital for Sportaid Inc.?
a. $682,000
b. $701,345
c. $694,445
d. $753,800
e. None of the above

Q9-45 What is total shareholders' equity for Sportaid Inc.?
a. $766,300
b. $758,800
c. $753,800
d. $764,735
e. None of the above

Q9-46 Sportaid's net income for the period is $119,600 and beginning common shareholders' equity is $681,400. What is Sportaid's return on common shareholders' equity?
a. 15.7%
b. 16.4%
c. 17.5%
d. 18.6%

Q9-47 A company paid $20 per share to repurchase 500 common shares. The shares were originally issued at $15 per share. The journal entry to record the repurchase of common shares is

a.	Common Shares	10,000	
	Cash		10,000
b.	Common Shares	7,500	
	Retained Earnings	2,500	
	Cash		10,000
c.	Common Shares	5,000	
	Retained Earnings	5,000	
	Cash		10,000
d.	Retained Earnings	10,000	
	Cash		10,000

Q9-48 When common shares are repurchased for less than their stated value, the entry should include a credit to which of the following?
a. Gain on Sale of Shares
b. Loss on Sale of Shares
c. Contributed Surplus
d. Retained Earnings

Q9-49 A company repurchased 200 common shares at $55 per share. The stated value of each share is $50. The entry to record the repurchase includes which of the following?
a. Credit to Cash for $1,000
b. Credit to Common Shares for $11,000
c. Credit to Retained Earnings for $1,000
d. Debit to Retained Earnings for $1,000
e. Credit to Contributed Surplus for $11,000

Q9-50 Shareholders are eligible for a dividend if they own the shares on the date of
a. Declaration
b. Record
c. Payment
d. Issuance

Q9-51 Mario's Foods has outstanding 500 $7.00 preferred shares and 1,200 common shares. Mario's declares dividends of $14,300. The correct entry is

a.	Retained Earnings	14,300	
	Dividends Payable, Preferred		3,500
	Dividends Payable, Common		10,800
b.	Dividends Expense	14,300	
	Cash		14,300
c.	Retained Earnings	14,300	
	Dividends Payable, Preferred		7,150
	Dividends Payable, Common		7,150
d.	Dividends Payable, Preferred	3,500	
	Dividends Payable, Common	10,800	
	Cash		14,300

Q9-52 A corporation has 20,000 $8.00 preferred shares outstanding with a stated value of $2,000,000. Also, there are 20,000 common shares outstanding. If a $350,000 dividend is paid, how much goes to the preferred shareholders?
a. $0
b. $350,000
c. $160,000
d. $120,000
e. $320,000

Q9-53 Assume the same facts as in Question 9-52. What is the amount of dividends per share on common shares?
a. $9.50
b. $8.00
c. $17.50
d. $1.50
e. None of the above

Q9-54 Which of the following is *not* true about a 10% stock dividend?
a. Shareholders do not receive additional shares.
b. No assets are affected.
c. Retained Earnings decreases.
d. The market value of the share is needed to record the stock dividend.
e. Total shareholders' equity remains the same.

Q9-55 A company declares a 5% stock dividend. The debit to Retained Earnings is an amount equal to
a. The stated value of original shares
b. The excess of the market price over the original issue price of the shares to be issued
c. The book value of the shares to be issued
d. The market value of the shares to be issued

Q9-56 Which of the following statements is *not* true about a 3-for-1 stock split?
a. Stated value is reduced to one-third of what it was before the split.
b. Total shareholders' equity increases.
c. The market price of each share will decrease.
d. A shareholder with 10 shares before the split owns 30 shares after the split.
e. Retained Earnings remains the same.

Q9-57 Franco Company's net income and interest expense are $44,000 and $4,000, respectively, and average total assets are $384,000. How much is Franco's return on assets?

a. 10.4%

b. 11.5%

c. 12.5%

d. 13.1%

PROBLEMS

(GROUP A)

P9-58A The board of directors of Freestroke Swim Centres Inc. is meeting to address the concerns of shareholders. Shareholders have submitted the following questions for discussion at the board meeting. Answer each question.

Explaining the features of a corporation's shares
(Obj. 1, 3, 4)

1. Why did Freestroke organize as a corporation if a corporation must pay an additional layer of income tax?

2. How are preferred shares similar to common shares? How are preferred shares similar to debt?

3. Freestroke repurchased common shares for $50,000 and a year later reissued them for $65,000. Explain to the shareholders whether the $15,000 excess is profit to be reported on the company's income statement. Explain your answer.

4. Would Freestroke investors prefer to receive cash dividends or stock dividends? Explain your reasoning.

P9-59A The articles of incorporation from the province of Ontario authorize Challenger Canoes Inc. to issue 10,000 shares of $6 preferred shares and 100,000 common shares. In its first month, Challenger completed the following transactions:

Recording corporate transactions and preparing the shareholders' equity section of the balance sheet
(Obj. 2)

2009		
Oct.	6	Issued 300 common shares to the lawyer for assistance with chartering the corporation. The lawyer's fee was $1,500. Debit Organization Expense.
	9	Issued 9,000 common shares to Jerry Spence and 12,000 shares to Sheila Markle in return for cash equal to the shares, market value of $5 per share. Spence and Markle are executives of the company.
	10	Issued 400 preferred shares to acquire a patent with a market value of $40,000
	26	Issued 2,000 common shares for cash of $12,000

❙ Required

1. Record the transactions in the journal.
2. Prepare the shareholders' equity section of the Challenger balance sheet at October 31, 2009. The ending balance of Retained Earnings is $49,000.

P9-60A Samuells' Sportswear's articles of incorporation authorize the company to issue 5,000 $5 preferred shares and 500,000 common shares. Samuells' issued 1,000 preferred shares at $100 per share. It issued 100,000 common shares for $427,000. The company's Retained Earnings balance at the beginning of 2009 was $61,000. Net income for 2009 was $80,000, and the company declared a $5 cash dividend on preferred shares for 2009.

Preparing the shareholders' equity section of the balance sheet
(Obj. 2, 4)

❙ Required

Prepare the shareholders' equity section of Samuells' Sportswear Inc.'s balance sheet at December 31, 2009. Show the computation of all amounts. Journal entries are not required.

P9-61A Calpak Winter Sports Ltd. is positioned ideally in the winter business. Located in Whistler B.C., Calpak is the only company with a distribution network for its imported goods. The company is doing a brisk business around the Winter Olympics being held in Whistler in 2010. Calpak's recent success has made the company a prime target for a takeover. Against the wishes of Calpak's board of directors, an investment group from Vancouver is

Fighting off a takeover of the corporation
(Obj. 3)

attempting to buy 51% of Calpak's outstanding shares. Board members are convinced that the Vancouver investors would sell off the most desirable pieces of the business and leave little of value. At the most recent board meeting, several suggestions were advanced to fight off the hostile takeover bid.

❙ Required

Suppose you are a significant shareholder of Calpak Winter Sports. Write a short memo to the board to propose an action that would make it difficult for the investor group to take over Calpak. Include in your memo a discussion of the effect your proposed action would have on the company's assets, liabilities, and total shareholders' equity.

Measuring the effects of share issuance, repurchase of shares, and dividend transactions on shareholders' equity
(Obj. 2, 3, 4)

P9-62A Wholegrain Health Foods Inc. is authorized to issue 5,000,000 common shares. In its initial public offering during 2005, Wholegrain issued 500,000 common shares for $7.00 per share. Over the next year, Wholegrain's share price increased and the company issued 400,000 more shares at an average price of $8.50.

During 2007, the price of Wholegrain's common shares dropped to $7, and the company repurchased 60,000 of its common shares. After the market price of the common shares rose in 2008, Wholegrain sold 40,000 common shares for $8 per share.

During the 5 years 2005 through 2009, Wholegrain earned net income of $920,000 and declared and paid cash dividends of $140,000. A 10% stock dividend was distributed to the shareholders in 2008 on the 880,000 shares outstanding. The market price was $8.00 per share when the stock dividend was distributed. At December 31, 2009, the company has total assets of $14,500,000 and total liabilities of $6,920,000.

❙ Required

Show the computation of Wholegrain's total shareholders' equity at December 31, 2009. Present a detailed computation of each element of shareholders' equity.

Analyzing the shareholders' equity and dividends of a corporation
(Obj. 2, 4)

P9-63A Steeltrap Security Inc. included the following shareholders' equity on its balance sheet at December 31, 2009:

Shareholders' Equity	($ Millions)
Preferred Shares:	
Authorized 20,000 shares in each class:	
$5.00 Cumulative Preferred Shares, 2,500 shares issued......................	$ 125,000
$2.50 Cumulative Preferred Shares, 4,000 shares issued......................	100,000
Common Shares:	
Authorized 80,000 shares, issued 48,000 shares..................................	384,000
Retained earnings	529,000
	$1,138,000

❙ Required

1. Identify the different issues of shares Steeltrap Security has outstanding.
2. What was the value at which the $2.50 Cumulative Preferred Shares were issued?
3. Suppose Steeltrap decided not to pay its preferred dividends for one year. Would the company have to pay these dividends in arrears before paying dividends to the common shareholders? Why?
4. What amount of preferred dividends must Steeltrap declare and pay each year to avoid having preferred dividends in arrears?
5. Assume preferred dividends are in arrears for 2008. Journalize the declaration of a $50,000 cash dividend for 2009. No explanation is needed.

P9-64A Exquisite Jewellery Limited reported the following summarized balance sheet at December 31, 2008:

Accounting for share issuance, dividends, and share repurchase
(Obj. 2, 3, 4)

Assets	
Current assets	$33,400
Property and equipment, net.......................................	51,800
Total assets..	$85,200
Liabilities and Equity	
Liabilities	$37,800
Shareholders' equity:	
$0.50 cumulative preferred shares, 400 shares issued	2,000
Common shares, 6,000 shares issued................................	23,400
Retained carnings..	22,000
Total liabilities and equity..	$85,200

During 2009, Exquisite completed these transactions that affected shareholders' equity:

Feb.	13	Issued 5,000 common shares for $4 per share
June	7	Declared the regular cash dividend on the preferred shares
July	24	Paid the cash dividend
Aug.	9	Distributed a 10% stock dividend on the common shares. Market price of the common shares was $5 per share
Oct.	26	Repurchased 500 common shares paying $6 per share
Nov.	20	Sold 200 common shares for $8 per share.

❙ Required

1. Journalize Exquisite's transactions. Explanations are not required.
2. Report Exquisite Jewellery Limited's shareholders' equity at December 31, 2009. Net income for 2009 was $27,000.

P9-65A Niles Corporation completed the following selected transactions during the current year:

Measuring the effects of dividend and share transactions on a company
(Obj. 3, 4)

Mar.	3	Distributed a 10% stock dividend on the 90,000 common shares outstanding. The market value of the common shares was $25 per share.
May	16	Declared a cash dividend on the $5 preferred shares (5,000 shares outstanding)
	30	Paid the cash dividends
Oct.	26	Repurchased 1,500 common shares at $24 per share
Dec.	8	Issued 1,500 common shares for $27 per share
	19	Issued 10,000 common shares for $28 per share

❙ Required

Analyze each transaction in terms of its effect (in dollars) on the accounting equation of Niles Corporation.

Preparing a corporation's balance sheet; measuring profitability
(Obj. 3, 6)

P9-66A The following accounts and related balances of Kingston Appliances Inc. are arranged in no particular order.

Dividends payable	$ 3,000	Accounts payable	$ 31,000
Total assets, December 31, 2008	461,000	Retained earnings	?
Net income	36,200	Common shares,	
Common shareholders' equity		100,000 shares authorized,	
December 31, 2008	283,000	42,000 shares issued	171,000
Interest expense	3,800	Inventory	93,000
Prepaid expenses	13,000	Property, plant, and equipment, net	181,000
Patent, net	31,000	Goodwill	6,000
Accrued liabilities	17,000	Preferred shares, $4,	
Long-term note payable	79,000	25,000 shares authorized	
Accounts receivable, net	71,000	370 shares issued	37,000
Cash	44,000		

❙ *Required*

1. Prepare Kingston's classified balance sheet in the account format at December 31, 2009.
2. Compute the rate of return on total assets and the rate of return on common shareholders' equity for the year ended December 31, 2009.
3. Do these rates of return suggest strength, weakness, or a midrange? Give your reason.

Analyzing the cash flow statement
(Obj. 7)

P9-67A The cash flow statement of Picture Perfect Photography reported the following for the year ended December 31, 2009:

Cash flows from financing activities	
Dividends [declared and] paid	$(8,300)
Proceeds from issuance of common shares	14,100
Payments of short-term notes payable	(6,900)
Payments of long-term notes payable	(1,300)
Proceeds from issuance of long-term notes payable	2,100
Repurchases of common shares	(6,300)

❙ *Required*

Make the journal entry that Picture Perfect used to record each of these transactions.

(GROUP B)

Explaining the features of a corporation's shares
(Obj. 1, 2, 5)

P9-68B Reinhart Industries Limited is conducting a special meeting of its board of directors to address some concerns raised by the shareholders. Shareholders have submitted the following questions. Answer each question.

1. Why are common shares and retained earnings shown separately in the shareholders' equity section of the balance sheet?
2. Lou Harris, a Reinhart shareholder, proposes to give some land she owns to the company in exchange for company shares. How should Reinhart Industries Limited determine the number of shares to issue for the land?
3. Preferred shares generally are preferred with respect to dividends and in the event of a liquidation. Why would investors buy our *common* shares when *preferred* shares are available?
4. What does the redemption value of our preferred shares require us to do?
5. One of our shareholders owns 100 shares of Reinhart, and someone has offered to buy her shares for their book value. Our shareholder asks us the formula for computing the book value of her shares.

P9-69B The partners who own Bassett Furniture Co. wished to avoid the unlimited personal liability of the partnership form of business, so they incorporated as BFC Inc. The articles of incorporation from the province of Manitoba authorize the corporation to issue 10,000 $6 preferred shares and 250,000 common shares. In its first month, BFC completed the following transactions:

Recording corporate transactions and preparing the shareholders' equity section of the balance sheet **(Obj. 2)**

2009		
Jan.	3	Issued 1,000 common shares to the promoter for assistance with issuance of the common shares. The promotional fee was $10,000. Debit Organization Expense.
	6	Issued 5,000 common shares to Jo Bassett, and 3,800 shares to Mel Bassett in return for cash equal to the market value of $11 per share. (The Bassetts were partners in Bassett Furniture Co.)
	12	Issued 1,000 preferred shares to acquire a patent with a market value of $110,000
	22	Issued 1,500 common shares for $12 cash per share

Required

1. Record the transactions in the journal.
2. Prepare the shareholders' equity section of the BFC Inc. balance sheet at January 31. The ending balance of Retained Earnings is $89,000.

P9-70B Northwest Territories Inc. has the following shareholders' equity information:

Northwest's incorporation authorizes the company to issue 10,000 $5 preferred shares and 400,000 common shares. The company issued 1,000 preferred shares at $100 per share. It issued 100,000 common shares for a total of $370,000. The company's Retained Earnings balance at the beginning of 2009 was $40,000, and net income for the year was $90,000. During 2009, Northwest declared the specified dividend on preferred shares and a $0.50 per-share dividend on common shares. Preferred dividends for 2008 were in arrears.

Preparing the shareholders' equity section of the balance sheet **(Obj. 2, 4)**

Required

Prepare the shareholders' equity section of Northwest Territories Inc.'s balance sheet at December 31, 2009. Show the computation of all amounts. Journal entries are not required.

P9-71B Gary Swan Imports Inc. is located in Stratford, Ontario. Swan is the only company with reliable sources for its imported gifts. The company does a brisk business with specialty stores such as Bowring. Swan's recent success has made the company a prime target for a takeover. An investment group from Toronto is attempting to buy 51% of Swan's outstanding shares against the wishes of Swan's board of directors. Board members are convinced that the Toronto investors would sell the most desirable pieces of the business and leave little of value.

Repurchasing common shares to fight off a takeover of the corporation **(Obj. 3)**

At the most recent board meeting, several suggestions were made to fight off the hostile takeover bid. The suggestion with the most promise is to repurchase a huge quantity of common shares. Swan has the cash to carry out this plan.

Required

1. Suppose you are a significant shareholder of Gary Swan Imports Inc. Write a memorandum to explain to the board how the repurchase of common shares would make it difficult for the Toronto group to take over Swan. Include in your memo a discussion of the effect that repurchasing common shares would have on shares outstanding and on the size of the corporation.
2. Suppose Swan management is successful in fighting off the takeover bid and later issues new shares at prices greater than the repurchase price. Explain what effect these sales will have on assets, shareholders' equity, and net income.

Measuring the effects of share issuance, share repurchase, and dividend transactions on shareholders' equity
(Obj. 2, 3, 4)

P9-72B Western Agriculture Industries Ltd. is authorized by the province of Saskatchewan to issue 500,000 common shares.

In its initial public offering during 2005, Western Agricultural issued 200,000 of its common shares for $12 per share. Over the next year, Western Agricultural's common share price increased, and the company issued 100,000 more shares at an average price of $14.50.

During 2007, the price of Western Agricultural common shares dropped to $8, and Western Agricultural repurchased 30,000 of its common shares. After the market price of the common share increased in 2009, Western Agricultural sold 20,000 common shares for $11 per share.

During the 5 years 2005 to 2009, Western Agricultural earned net income of $395,000 and declared and paid cash dividends of $119,000. Stock dividends of $135,000 were distributed to the shareholders in 2008, when the share market price was $10. At December 31, 2009, total assets of the company are $7,030,000, and liabilities add up to $2,924,000.

❚ Required

Show the computation of Western Agricultural Industries Ltd.'s total shareholders' equity at December 31, 2009. Present a detailed computation of each element of shareholders' equity.

Analyzing the shareholders' equity and dividends of a corporation
(Obj. 2, 4)

P9-73B Teak Outdoor Furniture Limited included the following shareholders' equity on its year-end balance sheet at February 28, 2009:

Shareholders' Equity	
Preferred shares, $1.10 cumulative; authorized 100,000 shares in each class	
Class A—issued 75,000 shares..	$ 1,500,000
Class B—issued 92,000 shares	1,840,000
Common shares; authorized 1,000,000 shares, issued 280,000 shares	6,940,000
Retained earnings	8,330,000
	$18,610,000

❚ Required

1. Identify the different issues of shares Teak Outdoor Furniture Limited has outstanding.

2. Give the summary entries to record issuance of all the Teak shares. Assume that all the shares were issued for cash. Explanations are not required.

3. Suppose Teak did not pay its preferred dividends for 3 years. Would the company have to pay those dividends in arrears before paying dividends to the common shareholders? Give your reason.

4. What amount of preferred dividends must Teak declare and pay each year to avoid having preferred dividends in arrears?

5. Assume that preferred dividends are in arrears for 2008. Record the declaration of an $800,000 dividend on February 28, 2009. An explanation is not required.

Accounting for share issuance and dividends
(Obj. 2, 3, 4)

P9-74B Winnipeg Enterprises Inc. reported the following summarized balance sheet at December 31, 2008:

Assets	
Current assets	$18,200
Property and equipment, net	34,700
Total assets	$52,900
Liabilities and Equity	
Liabilities	$ 6,200
Shareholders' equity:	
$5 cumulative preferred shares, 180 shares issued	1,800
Common shares, 2,400 shares issued..	25,900
Retained earnings..	19,000
Total liabilities and equity..	$52,900

During 2009, Winnipeg Enterprise completed these transactions that affected shareholders' equity:

Feb.	22	Issued 1,000 common shares for $16 per share
May	4	Declared the regular cash dividend on the preferred shares
	24	Paid the cash dividend
July	9	Distributed a 10% stock dividend on the common shares. Market price of the common shares was $18 per share.
Nov.	19	Repurchased 800 common shares paying $14 per share
Dec.	8	Issued 600 common shares for $15 per share

Required

1. Journalize Winnipeg Enterprise's transactions. Explanations are not required.
2. Report Winnipeg Enterprise's shareholders' equity at December 31, 2009. Net income for 2009 was $62,000.

P9-75B Cones Inc. of Baie-Comeau completed the following transactions during 2009, the company's tenth year of operations:

Measuring the effects of dividend and share transactions on a company
(Obj. 3, 4)

Feb.	2	Issued 10,000 common shares for cash of $250,000
Mar.	18	Repurchased 2,000 of the company's own common shares at $22 per share
Apr.	22	Sold 700 common shares for $26 per share
Aug.	6	Declared a cash dividend on the 10,000 $0.60 preferred shares
Sept.	1	Paid the cash dividends
Nov.	18	Distributed a 10% stock dividend on the 30,000 common shares outstanding. The market value of the common shares was $25 per share.

Required

Analyze each transaction in terms of its effect (in dollars) on the accounting equation of Cones Inc.

P9-76B The following accounts and related balances of Bluebird Designers Inc., as of December 31, 2009, are arranged in no particular order.

Preparing a corporation's balance sheet; measuring profitability
(Obj. 3, 6)

Cash....................................	$ 41,000	Interest expense	$ 16,100
Accounts receivable, net...................	24,000	Property, plant, and equipment, net ..	357,000
Accrued liabilities.............................	26,000	Common shares,	
Long-term note payable	98,000	500,000 shares authorized,	
Inventory	99,000	115,000 shares issued	112,000
Dividends payable............................	9,000	Prepaid expenses..............................	10,000
Retained earnings............................	?	Common shareholders' equity,	
Accounts payable	131,000	December 31, 2008......................	222,000
Trademark net	9,000	Net income..	31,000
Preferred shares, $0.50, 10,000 shares		Total assets, December 31, 2008	494,000
authorized and issued	27,000		
Goodwill...	14,000		

Required

1. Prepare the company's classified balance sheet in the account format at December 31, 2009.
2. Compute the rate of return on total assets and the rate of return on common shareholders' equity for the year ended December 31, 2009.
3. Do these rates of return suggest strength or weakness? Give your reason.

Analyzing the cash flow statement
(Obj. 7)

P9-77B The cash flow statement of a large corporation reported the following (adapted) for the year ended December 31, 2008:

Cash flows from financing activities—*amounts in millions:*	
Cash dividends paid	$(1,854)
Issuance of common shares	1,194
Proceeds from issuance of long-term notes payable	51
Repurchase of common shares	(3,010)
Payments of long-term notes payable	(157)

❚ *Required*

Make the journal entry that the corporation would use to record each of these transactions.

APPLY YOUR KNOWLEDGE

DECISION CASES

Evaluating alternative ways of raising capital
(Obj. 2)

Case 1. Nate Smith and Darla Jones have written a computer program to advertise on text mail. They need additional capital to market the product, and they plan to incorporate their business. Smith and Jones are considering alternative capital structures for the corporation. Their primary goal is to raise as much capital as possible without giving up control of the business. Smith and Jones plan to receive 50,000 common shares of the corporation in return for the net assets of their old business. After the old company's books are closed and the assets adjusted to current market value, Smith's and Jones's capital balances will each be $25,000.

The company's incorporation plans include an authorization to issue 10,000 preferred shares and 500,000 common shares. Smith and Jones are uncertain about the most desirable features for the preferred shares. Prior to incorporating, Smith and Jones are discussing their plans with two investment groups. The corporation can obtain capital from outside investors under either of the following plans:

- **Plan 1.** Group 1 will invest $80,000 to acquire 800 $6, nonvoting, preferred shares.
- **Plan 2.** Group 2 will invest $55,000 to acquire 500 $5 preferred shares and $35,000 to acquire 35,000 common shares. Each preferred share receives 50 votes on matters that come before the shareholders.

❚ *Required*

Assume that the company is incorporated.
1. Journalize the issuance of common shares to Smith and Jones. Debit each person's capital account for its balance.
2. Journalize the issuance of shares to the outsiders under both plans.
3. Assume that net income for the first year is $120,000 and total dividends are $30,000. Prepare the shareholders' equity section of the corporation's balance sheet under both plans.
4. Recommend one of the plans to Smith and Jones. Give your reasons.

Analyzing cash dividends and stock dividends
(Obj. 4)

Case 2. Suppose the balance sheet of the financial statements you are analyzing had the following shareholders' equity amounts on December 31, 2009 (adapted, in millions):

Common Shares; 1,135 shares issued	$ 278
Retained earnings	9,457
Total shareholders' equity	$ 9,735

During 2009, the corporation paid a cash dividend of $0.715 per share. Assume that, after paying the cash dividends, the corporation distributed a 10% stock dividend. Assume further that the following year the corporation declared and paid a cash dividend of $0.65 per share. Suppose you own 10,000 of this corporation's common shares acquired 3 years ago, prior to the 10% stock dividend. The market price of the shares was $61.02 per share before the stock dividend.

I *Required*

1. How does the stock dividend affect your proportionate ownership in the corporation? Explain.

2. What amount of cash dividends did you receive last year? What amount of cash dividends will you receive after the above dividend action?

3. Assume that immediately after the stock dividend was distributed, the market value of the corporation's shares decreased from $61.02 per share to $55.473 per share. Does this decrease represent a loss to you? Explain.

4. Suppose the corporation announces at the time of the stock dividend that the company will continue to pay the annual $0.715 *cash* dividend per share, even after distributing the *stock* dividend. Would you expect the market price of the common shares to decrease to $55.473 per share as in Requirement 3? Explain.

Case 3. At December 31, 2009, Make It Limited reported the following data (condensed in millions):

Evaluating financial position and profitability
(Obj. 2, 3, 4, 5)

Total assets	$65,503
Total liabilities	54,033
Shareholders' equity	11,470
Net income, as reported, for 2008	979

During 2009, Make It restated company financial statements for 2005 to 2008, after reporting that some data had been omitted from those prior-year statements. Assume that the startling events of 2009 included the following:

- Several related companies should have been, but were not, included in the Make It statements for 2008. These companies had total assets of $5,700 million, liabilities totalling $5,600 million, and net losses of $130 million.

- In January 2009, Make It's shareholders got the company to give them $2,000 million of 12% long-term notes payable in return for their giving up their common shares. Interest is accrued at year-end.

Take the role of a financial analyst. It is your job to analyze Make It Limited and rate the company's long-term debt.

I *Required*

1. Measure Make It's expected net income for 2009 two ways:
   a. Assume 2009 net income should be the same as the amount of net income that was actually reported for 2008.
   b. Recompute expected net income for 2009 taking into account the new developments of 2009.
   c. Evaluate the likely trend of net income for the future. Discuss *why* this trend is developing. Ignore income tax.

2. Write Make It's accounting equation two ways:
   a. As actually reported at December 31, 2008
   b. As adjusted for the events of 2009

3. Measure Make It's debt ratio as reported at December 31, 2008, and again after making the adjustments for the events of 2009.

4. Based on your analysis, make a recommendation to the Debt-Rating Committee of Moody's Investor Services. Would you recommend upgrading, downgrading, or leaving Make It's debt rating undisturbed (currently, it is "high-grade")?

ETHICAL ISSUE

Ethical Issue 1. *Note:* This case is based on a real situation.

George Campbell paid $50,000 for a franchise that entitled him to market Success Associates software programs in the countries of the European Union. Campbell intended to sell individual franchises for the major language groups of Western Europe: German, French, English, Spanish, and Italian. Naturally, investors considering buying a franchise from Campbell asked to see the financial statements of his business.

Believing the value of the franchise to be greater than $50,000, Campbell sought to capitalize his own franchise at $500,000. The law firm of McDonald & LaDue helped Campbell form a corporation chartered to issue 500,000 common shares. Attorneys suggested the following chain of transactions:

a. A third party borrows $500,000 and purchases the franchise from Campbell.

b. Campbell pays the corporation $500,000 to acquire all its shares.

c. The corporation buys the franchise from the third party, who repays the loan.

In the final analysis, the third party is debt-free and out of the picture. Campbell owns all the corporation's shares, and the corporation owns the franchise. The corporation balance sheet lists a franchise acquired at a cost of $500,000. This balance sheet is Campbell's most valuable marketing tool.

❚ *Required*

1. What is unethical about this situation?

2. Who can be harmed in this situation? How can they be harmed? What role does accounting play here?

Ethical Issue 2. St. Genevieve Petroleum Company is an independent oil producer. In February, company geologists discovered a pool of oil that tripled the company's proven reserves. Prior to disclosing the new oil to the public, St. Genevieve's managers quietly purchased most of its shares. After the discovery was announced, the company's share price increased from $6 to $27.

❚ *Required*

1. Did St. Genevieve managers behave ethically? Explain your answer.

2. Identify the accounting principle relevant to this situation.

3. Who was helped and who was harmed by management's action?

FOCUS ON FINANCIALS

Sun-Rype Products Ltd.

Analyzing common shares, retained earnings, and return on assets
(Obj. 2, 3, 6)

Sun-Rype's financial statements appear in Appendix A at the end of this book.

1. How many common shares were issued during 2007? Why would Sun-Rype have a contributed surplus?

2. In 2004, Sun-Rype repurchased and cancelled 26,800 common shares for $281,000. The average stated cost for the shares was $1.68. Show how this would be journalized. Sun-Rype had a contributed surplus balance against which the excess purchase price was applied. Show how this would be journalized.

3. Prepare a T-account to show the beginning and ending balances plus all the activity in the Retained Earnings account for the year ended December 31, 2007.

4. Compute Sun-Rype's return on equity and return on assets for 2007. Interpret the relationship between these two ratios.

FOCUS ON ANALYSIS

Mullen Group Income Fund

Mullen Group Income Fund is an unincorporated, open-ended investment trust governed by the laws of the province of Alberta pursuant to a declaration of trust dated as of June 3, 2005. The beneficiaries of the Fund are the holders of the trust units issued by the Fund. The following questions relate to the Unitholders' Equity in Mullen Group Income Fund's financial statements for the year ended December 31, 2007.

Analyzing changes in unitholders' equity
(Obj. 2,3,4)

1. Examine Mullen Group's cash flow statement in Appendix B at the end of the book. What transactions occurred related to the Trust Units during 2007?

2. Explain the deficit at December 31, 2007. Begin with the Opening Retained Earnings of $214,550.

3. As a unitholder, what would your reaction be to the information in the Statements of Income and Deficit at December 31, 2007?

GROUP PROJECT

Competitive pressures are the norm in business and corporate downsizing has occurred on a massive scale. Many companies or industries have pared down plant and equipment, laid off employees, or restructured operations.

❚ *Required*

1. Identify all the stakeholders of a corporation. A *stakeholder* is a person or a group who has an interest (that is, a stake) in the success of the organization.

2. Identify several measures by which a company may be considered deficient and in need of downsizing. How can downsizing help to solve this problem?

3. Debate the downsizing issue. One group of students takes the perspective of the company and its shareholders, and another group of students takes the perspective of the other stakeholders of the company (the community in which the company operates and society at large).

QUICK CHECK ANSWERS

1. *b (10,000 shares × 15 = $150,000)*
2. *b*
3. *d ($180,000 + $100,000 = $280,000)*
4. *c ($180,000 + $200,000 + $100,000 = $480,000)*
5. *($480,000 − $5,000 = $475,000)*
6. *d [No gain or loss (for the income statement) on repurchased share transactions.]*
7. *a*
8. *b*
9. *c*
10. *a*
11. *c [annual preferred dividend = $10,000 (5,000 × $2)] [($10,000 × 4) +*
    (100,000 × $1.25) = $165,000]
12. *a*
13. *d*
14. *c*
15. *c*
16. *a*

Appendix 9A

Owners' Equity of Partnerships

In Chapter 1 you were introduced to the three main forms of business ownership: proprietorship, partnership, and corporation. Exhibit 1-2 on page 7 provides a concise summary of the essential features of these entities. In this appendix we expand on the basic principles of partnership accounting.

A partnership is an association of two or more persons who co-own a business. The legal life of a partnership terminates with the admission of a new partner, the withdrawal or death of a partner, voluntary dissolution by the partners, or involuntary dissolution. The essential characteristics of a partnership include the following features:

- Limited life—Life of a partnership is limited by the length of time that all partners continue to own a share of the business. When a partner withdraws from the partnership, the partnership must be dissolved.

- Unlimited personal liability—When a partnership cannot pay its debts with business assets, the partners must use their own personal assets to pay off this debt. Some professionals, such as accountants and lawyers, have organized their partnerships as limited liability partnerships (LLP) where liability is limited to partnership assets.

- Mutual agency—Every partner can bind the business to a contract within the scope of the partnership's regular business operations.

- Co-ownership of property—All assets that a partner invests in the partnership become the joint property of all the partners.

- No partnership income taxes—A partnership does not pay income taxes on the net income of the business. Instead, net income is divided among the partners and each partner is personally liable for the income taxes on his or her share of the business's net income, even if income is not withdrawn from the partnership.

A partnership may be formed by a simple oral agreement among two or more people to operate a business for profit. A partnership agreement should preferably be in writing to avoid misunderstandings and should specify information such as:

- The types of products and services to be provided
- Each partner's initial investment
- Additional investment conditions
- Each partner's rights and responsibilities
- Rules for withdrawing assets, such as cash, from the partnership
- Procedures for dissolving the partnership
- Profit and loss sharing formulas

Initial Investment by Partners

Assets contributed to a partnership are debited for their market values. Market values are also applied to any liabilities assumed by the partnership, and separate capital accounts and drawing accounts are maintained for each partner. Assume that on January 2, 2009, Jones and Wong establish a partnership whereby Jones contributes $80,000 cash and Wong contributes a building that has a fair market value of $200,000 and an outstanding mortgage of $60,000. The journal entry to establish the partnership is as follows:

2009

Jan. 2	Cash		80,000	
	Building		200,000	
	Mortgage Payable			60,000
	Jones, Capital			80,000
	Wong, Capital			140,000

Profit and loss sharing formulas may be based on contributions from the partners such as their relative investments, time and effort each plans to devote to the business, and the talents and expertise each partner brings to the business. Profits and losses must be divided equally among the partners if the partnership agreement does not specify a profit and loss formula. Usually, however, the partnership agreement will contain provisions that share profits and losses based on salary, percentage return on invested capital, and stated ratio for dividing up any balance remaining.

Assume Jones and Wong agree to share profits and losses in a 2:3 ratio. If net income during the first year of operations is $300,000, the following entry would be made to allocate net income to the partners:

2009

Dec. 31	Income summary		300,000	
	Jones, Capital (2/5 × $300,000)			120,000
	Wong, Capital (3/5 × $300,000)			180,000
	To close income summary and allocate net income to the partners.			

If Jones and Wong withdrew cash of $30,000 and $40,000, respectively, these withdrawals would be recorded as follows:

2009

Dec. 31	Jones, Drawings		30,000	
	Wong, Drawings		40,000	
	Cash			70,000

At the end of the period the statement of partners' equity would appear as follows:

Partners' Capital Statement For the Year Ended December 31, 2009			
	Jones	Wong	Total
Capital, January 2, 2009	$ 80,000	$140,000	$220,000
Add: Net income	120,000	180,000	300,000
	200,000	320,000	520,000
Less: Drawings	30,000	40,000	70,000
Capital, December 31, 2009	$170,000	$280,000	$450,000

Let's take a more complex example. Assume the partnership agreement specifies that Jones and Wong will receive a salary of $40,000 and $60,000, respectively, and each partner will receive an interest allowance equal to 10% of the balance of their beginning capital balance. Any remaining balance will be allocated equally.

Division of Net Income				
	Jones	Wong	Total	Amount to Be Distributed
Partnership net income				$300,000
Salary allowance	$ 40,000	$ 60,000	$100,000	200,000
Interest allowance	8,000	14,000	22,000	178,000
Remainder	89,000	89,000	178,000	0
Total division	$137,000	$163,000	$300,000	

The following period-end entry transfers net income to the partners' capital accounts:

2009

Dec. 31   Income Summary   300,000

           Jones, Capital..   137,000

           Wong, Capital   163,000

         To close Income Summary and allocate net income to the partners.

Although Jones and Wong were allocated net incomes of $137,000 and $163,000 respectively, this does not indicate that the partners actually withdrew those amounts from the partnership. However, for income tax purposes Jones and Wong must record these amounts as income on their income tax returns whether they withdrew assets from the partnership or not.

Assume instead that the partnership had a net loss of $200,000. The net loss would be allocated as follows:

Division of Net Income

	Jones	Wong	Total	Amount to Be Distributed
Partnership net income				$(200,000)
Salary allowance	$ 40,000	$ 60,000	$ 100,000	(300,000)
Interest allowance	8,000	14,000	22,000	(322,000)
Remainder	(161,000)	(161,000)	(322,000)	0
Total division	$(113,000	$ (87,000)	$(200,000)	

Since there was a net loss, income summary must have had a debit balance and the closing entry results in reductions to Jones's and Wong's capital accounts as follows:

2009

Dec. 31   Jones, Capital...   113,000

         Wong, Capital   87,000

           Income Summary...   200,000

Problem

On January 2, 2009, B. Able, D. Nile, and R. Wright formed the ANW Partnership by making capital contributions of $91,875, $65,625, and $105,000, respectively. They anticipate annual net incomes of $300,000 and are considering the following alternative plans of sharing net incomes and losses: (a) equally; (b) in the ratio of their initial investments; (c) a ratio of 2:3:4; or (d) salary allowances of $45,000 to Able, $35,000 to Nile, and $50,000 to Wright; interest allowances of 10% on initial investments, with any remaining balance shared equally.

❙ *Required*

1. For alternatives (a), (b), and (c), prepare a schedule showing the distribution of a $300,000 net income among the partners. Round your answers to the nearest whole dollar.

2. For alternative (d), prepare a schedule showing the distribution of a $40,000 net income.

3. Prepare a statement of changes in partners' equity showing the allocation of income to the partners, assuming they agree to use alternative (d) and the net income earned is $120,000. During the year, Able, Nile, and Wright withdraw $18,000, $20,000, and $35,000, respectively.

4. Prepare the December 31 journal entries to record the withdrawals by the partners, allocate profit or losses to the partners, and close the withdrawals accounts and the income summary using the information in Requirement 3.

Appendix 9A Solution

(1)(a)   *Division of Net Income*

	B. Able	D. Nile	R. Wright	Total	Amount Yet to Be Distributed
Partnership net income					$300,000
Equally	$100,000	$100,000	$100,000	$300,000	0

(1)(b)   *Division of Net Income*

	B. Able	D. Nile	R. Wright	Total	
Capital ratios*	0.35	0.25	0.40	1.00	

	B. Able	D. Nile	R. Wright	Total	Amount Yet to Be Distributed
Partnership net income					$300,000
Capital balance ratios*	$105,000	$75,000	$120,000	$300,000	0

*$91,875/($91,875 + $65,625 + $105,000) = 0.35

(1)(c)   *Division of Net Income*

	B. Able	D. Nile	R. Wright	Total	Amount Yet to Be Distributed
Partnership net income					$300,000
2:3:4 ratio	$66,667	$100,000	$133,333	$300,000	0

2.   *Division of Net Income*

	B. Able	D. Nile	R. Wright	Total	Amount Yet to Be Distributed
Partnership net income					$ 40,000
Salary allowance	$45,000	$35,000	$50,000	$130,000	(90,000)
Interest allowance	9,188	6,562	10,500	26,250	(116,250)
Remainder	(38,750)	(38,750)	(38,750)	(116,250)	0
Total division	$15,438	$ 2,812	$21,750	$ 40,000	

3.   *Division of Net Income*

	B. Able	D. Nile	R. Wright	Total	Amount Yet to Be Distributed
Partnership net income					$120,000
Salary allowance	$45,000	$35,000	$50,000	$130,000	(10,000)
Interest allowance	9,188	6,562	10,500	26,250	(36,250)
Remainder	(12,083)	(12,083)	(12,084)	(36,250)	0
Total division	$42,105	$29,479	$48,416	$120,000	

	Able	Nile	Wright	Total
ANW Partnership				
Partners' Capital Statement				
For the Year Ended December 31, 2009				
Capital, January 2	$ 91,875	$65,625	$105,000	$262,500
Add: Net income	42,105	29,479	48,416	120,000
	133,980	94,104	153,416	382,500
Less: Drawings	18,000	20,000	35,000	73,000
Capital, December 31	$115,980	$75,104	$118,416	$309,500

4. 2009

Date	Account	Debit	Credit
Dec. 31	B. Able, Drawings	18,000	
	D. Nile, Drawings	20,000	
	R. Wright, Drawings	35,000	
	Cash		73,000
	To record withdrawals of cash from the partnership.		

2009

Date	Account	Debit	Credit
Dec. 31	Income Summary	120,000	
	B. Able, Capital		42,105
	D. Nile, Capital		29,479
	R. Wright, Capital		48,416
	To close Income Summary and allocate net income to the partners.		

2009

Date	Account	Debit	Credit
Dec. 31	B. Able, Capital	18,000	
	D. Nile, Capital	20,000	
	R. Wright, Capital	35,000	
	B. Able, Drawings		18,000
	D. Nile, Drawings		20,000
	R. Wright, Drawings		35,000
	To close the Drawings accounts to the partners' Capital accounts.		

Long-Term Investments and International Operations

10

SPOTLIGHT

ATCO holds several different types of investments. After graduation, you may start investing through a Registered Retirement Savings Plan (RRSP) or you may make some investments on your own. The reasons people invest are for current income (interest and dividends) and appreciation of the investment's value (by purchasing shares or real estate, for example).

Businesses, such as ATCO Ltd., Canadian Tire Corporation, and Great-West Life Assurance Company, invest for the same reasons. In this chapter, you will learn how to account for investments of all types. We use ATCO as our example company because ATCO has so many interesting investments.

ATCO Ltd.
Consolidated Balance Sheet (Partial, adapted)
December 31, 2007

	(millions of dollars)
1. **Assets**	
2. **Current assets**	
3. Cash and short-term investments	$ 838.3
4. Accounts receivable	443.3
5. Inventories..	119.9
6. Other current assets...	45.1
7. Total current assets	1,446.6
8. Property, plant, and equipment	6,142.5
9. Goodwill	71.2
10. Other long-term assets..	339.6
	$7,999.9

Source: www.atco.com

ATCO Ltd. has been serving the people of Alberta and Canada since 1947. ATCO has grown from humble beginnings to become a multinational with operations across Canada and in the United States, South America, Europe, and Australia. Its operations include power generation; utilities including water, electricity, gas, and pipelines; workforce housing; industrial noise abatement; logistics technologies; facility management; and energy services. ATCO also either has controlling interest in or operates as joint ventures eight other enterprises. For example, Canadian Utilities Limited is a major subsidiary of ATCO. Canadian Utilities has a major subsidiary, CU Inc. Canadian Utilities and CU either have controlling interest in or operate as joint ventures more than 20 domestic and global enterprises. These investments are reflected in the various asset accounts such as inventory; property, plant, and equipment; and goodwill. The credit side of the ATCO balance sheet shows "Non-controlling interests $1,836.7 (millions)," which reflects the non-controlling or minority interests in the subsidiaries. In addition, ATCO has short-term investments.

Throughout this course, you have become increasingly familiar with the financial statements of companies such as Sun-Rype Products Ltd., TransCanada Corporation and Sobeys Inc. You have seen most of the items that appear in a set of financial statements. One of your learning goals should be to develop the ability to interpret whatever you encounter in real-company statements. This chapter will help you advance toward that goal.

The first part of the chapter shows how to account for long-term investments, including a brief overview of consolidated financial statements. The second half of the chapter covers accounting for international operations.

Share Investments: A Review

Investments come in all sizes and shapes—from a few shares to the acquisition of an entire company. In earlier chapters, we discussed shares and bonds from the perspective of the company that issued the securities. In this chapter, we examine *long-term* investments.

To consider investments, we need to define two key terms. The entity that owns shares in a corporation is the *investor*. The corporation that issued the shares is the *investee.* If you own ATCO common shares, you are an investor and ATCO is the investee.

Share Prices

Investors buy more shares in transactions among themselves than directly from large companies, such as ATCO Ltd. Each share is issued only once, but it may be traded among investors many times thereafter. You may log onto the Internet or consult a newspaper to learn ATCO's current share price.

Exhibit 10-1 presents information on ATCO common shares from *The Globe and Mail Report on Business* for January 17, 2009. It reports transactions on January 16, 2009. During the previous 52 weeks, ATCO shares reached a high price of $54.50 and a low price of $32.51 per share. The annual cash dividend is $0.94 per share. At the end of the previous day, the price of the shares closed at $37.34, down $0.10 from the closing price of the shares on January 15, 2009.

Reporting Investments on the Balance Sheet

An investment is an asset to the investor. The investment may be short term or long term. *Short-term investments* are described as financial assets held for trading by the new Section 3855 of the *CICA Handbook* (see Chapter 5 and especially the IFRS Alert on p. 216). They are current assets and are sometimes called *temporary investments* or *marketable securities*. To be listed as short term on the balance sheet,

- The investment must be *liquid* (readily convertible to cash).
- The investor must intend either to convert the investment to cash within one year or to use it to pay a current liability. We saw how to account for short-term investments in Chapter 5.

Investments that are not short term are classified as **long-term investments**, a category of noncurrent assets. Long-term investments include shares and bonds that the investor expects to hold for longer than one year. Exhibit 10-2 shows the positions of short-term and long-term investments on the balance sheet.

Assets are listed in the order of liquidity. Long-term investments are less liquid than current assets but more liquid than property, plant, and equipment. Many companies report short-term investments immediately after cash; ATCO, like many other companies, reports a total for cash plus short-term investments.

Accounting for Long-Term Investments in Shares

The *CICA Handbook* describes three categories of long-term share investments. The categories depend on the percentage of ownership by the investor. They are:

1. *Investments in subsidiaries*, which are described in Section 1590. A subsidiary is a company controlled by another company (the parent), which is entitled to the rewards and bears the risks of the subsidiary. Generally a parent will own more

EXHIBIT 10-1 Share Price Information for ATCO Ltd.

| 52-Week | | Stock | | | Net |
Hi	Lo	Symbol	Div	Close	Change
$54.50	$32.51	ACO	$0.94	$37.34	−$0.10

EXHIBIT 10-2	Reporting Investments on the Balance Sheet

Current Assets:

Cash	$X
Short-term investments	X
Accounts receivable	X
Inventories	X
Prepaid expenses	X
Total current assets	$X
Long-term investments [or simply Investments]	X
Property, plant, and equipment (net)	X
Intangible assets (net)	X
Other assets	X

than 50% of the voting shares of the subsidiary. The financial statements of the investee are consolidated with those of the investor.

2. *Investments subject to significant influence*, which are described in Section 3051. An investee is generally described as being subject to significant influence when the investor owns between 20% and 50% of the voting shares of the investee. Significant influence allows the investor to direct the affairs of the investee. The investor accounts for the investment using the *equity method* by which the investor's proportionate share of the investee's profits and losses are treated as income or loss by the investor. The investor's share of dividends paid by the investee are treated as a return of investment and are credited to the investment account.

3. *Other investments*, which are described in Section 3051. These are investments where the investor owns less than 20% of the voting shares of the investee and thus is presumed to exercise no influence over the affairs of the investee. The investor accounts for the investment using the *cost method* by which the investor's share of dividends paid by the investee is treated as income by the investor.

We begin our discussion with "other investments."

IFRS ALERT

It was mentioned in the IFRS Alert in Chapter 5 that the convergence of generally accepted accounting principles (GAAP) with IFRSs by the CICA's Accounting Standards Board (AcSB) is occurring on an ongoing basis. In this chapter, you will learn some new terms that were incorporated into the *CICA Handbook* as part of the convergence process.

Available-for-sale investments are share investments other than financial assets held for trading (introduced in Chapter 5). They may be current assets if the business plans to sell them within the next year. All other available-for-sale investments are classified as long-term.

Held-to-maturity investments are financial assets with fixed or determinable payments and fixed maturity. The business plans to hold them to their maturity date (in other words, they are neither held for trading investments or available-for-sale investments).

The accounting for both types of investments is explained on the following pages.

Accounting for Available-for-Sale Investments

Objective

1 **Account** for available-for-sale investments

An investor may make an **available-for-sale investment** where the purpose is similar to that of short-term investing; the investor will hold the investment to earn dividend revenue and/or capital appreciation but has no long-term interest in the investee. The investor usually holds less than 20% of the voting shares and would normally play no important role in the investee's operations. Such an investor would account for the investment using the *cost method*.

Available-for-sale investments are accounted for at market value because the company expects to sell the investment at its market price. *Cost* is used only as the initial amount for recording the investments. These investments are reported on the balance sheet at *current market value*.

Suppose ATCO Ltd. purchases 1,000 Agrium Inc. common shares at the market price of $50.00. ATCO intends to hold this investment for longer than a year and therefore classifies it as an available-for-sale investment. ATCO's entry to record the investment is:

2008
July 10   Long-Term Investment (1,000 × $50.00)   50,000
         Cash   50,000
         Purchased investment.

ASSETS	=	LIABILITIES	+	SHAREHOLDERS' EQUITY
+50,000	=	0	+	0
−50,000				

Assume that ATCO receives a $0.14 per share cash dividend on the Agrium Inc. shares. ATCO's entry to record receipt of the dividend is:

2008
Oct. 5   Cash (1,000 × $0.14)   140
        Dividend Revenue   140
        Received cash dividend.

ASSETS	=	LIABILITIES	+	SHAREHOLDERS' EQUITY	+	REVENUES
140	=	0	+		+	140

Receipt of a *stock* dividend is different from receipt of a cash dividend. For a stock dividend, the investor records no dividend revenue. Instead, the investor makes a memorandum entry in the accounting records to denote the new number of shares held as an investment. Because the number of shares held has increased, the investor's cost per share decreases. For example, suppose ATCO receives a 5% stock dividend from Agrium Inc. ATCO would receive 50 shares (5% of 1,000 shares previously held) and make this memorandum entry in its accounting records:

> MEMORANDUM—Receipt of stock dividend: Received 50 common shares of Agrium Inc. in 5% stock dividend. New cost per share is $47.62 (cost of $50,000 ÷ 1,050 shares).

In all of ATCO's future transactions that affect the Agrium Inc. investment, ATCO will use the new cost per share of $47.62.

What Value of an Investment Is Most Relevant?

Market value is the amount that you can buy or sell an investment for. Because of the relevance of market values for decision making, available-for-sale investments in shares are reported on the balance sheet at their market value. On the balance sheet date we therefore adjust available-for-sale investments from their last carrying amount to current market value. Assume that the market value of the Agrium common shares is $53,000 on December 31, 2008. In this case, ATCO makes the following entry to bring the investment to market value.

2008			
Dec. 31	Long-Term Investment		
	($53,000 − $50,000)	3,000	
	Other Comprehensive Income		3,000
	Adjusted investment to market value.		

The increase in the investment's market value creates additional equity for the investor.

ASSETS	=	LIABILITIES	+	SHAREHOLDERS' EQUITY
+3,000	=	0		+3,000

The Long-Term Investment account and the Other Comprehensive Income account would appear as follows:

Long-Term Investment	Other Comprehensive Income
50,000	
3,000	3,000

If the investment's market value declines, the Long-Term Investment is credited. The corresponding debit is to Other Comprehensive Income. *Unrealized* gains and losses result from changes in market value, not from sales of investments.

Unrealized gains and unrealized losses on available-for-sale investments that occur in a fiscal year are reported in two places in the financial statements:

- *Other Comprehensive Income,* which can be reported on the *income statement* in a separate section below net income or on the *statement of comprehensive income.* For example, the Consolidated Statement of Comprehensive Income section of Leon's Furniture Limited's 2007 annual report states:

  Other comprehensive income, net of tax
    Unrealized (losses) on available-for-sale financial assets arising
      during the year (net of tax of $67) .... $(290)

- *Accumulated Other Comprehensive Income,* which is a separate section of shareholders' equity below retained earnings on the *balance sheet.* The Shareholders' Equity section of the Leon's Furniture Limited's 2007 balance sheet reports:

  Accumulated other comprehensive income $917

At December 31, 2008, ATCO would close the Other Comprehensive Income account to the shareholder equity account Accumulated Other Comprehensive Income as follows:

2008
Dec. 31   Other Comprehensive Income   3,000
           Accumulated Other Comprehensive Income   3,000
      To close out the unrealized gain on the available-for-sale
        investment to Accumulated Other Comprehensive Income.

After the preceding entries are posted, the Other Comprehensive Income and the Accumulated Other Comprehensive Income would appear as follows:

Other Comprehensive Income		Accumulated Other Comprehensive Income	
	3,000		
3,000			3,000
			Bal. 3,000

Selling an Available-for-Sale Investment

The sale of an available-for-sale investment can result in a *realized* gain or loss. Realized gains and losses measure the difference between the amount received from the sale of the investment and the cost of the investment.

Suppose ATCO sells its investment in Agrium Inc. shares for $57,000 during 2009. ATCO would record the sale as follows:

```
2009
May 19   Cash...............................................................   57,000
            Accumulated Other Comprehensive Income ...................   3,000
               Long-Term Investment ...............................................        53,000
               Gain on Sale of Investment.........................................         7,000
            To record sale of investment.
```

ASSETS	=	LIABILITIES	+	SHAREHOLDERS' EQUITY	+	GAINS
57,000 −53,000	=	0	−	3,000	+	7,000

ATCO would report the Gain on Sale of Investments as an "Other" item on the income statement.

STOP & THINK

Suppose Ardnas Holdings Ltd. holds the following portfolio securities as long-term investments at March 31, 2009:

Shares	Cost	Current Market Value
Canadian Tire Corp..........................	$70,000	$47,500
Quebecor...	26,000	16,000
	$96,000	$63,500

Show how Ardnas Holdings will report long-term investments on its March 31, 2009 balance sheet if the decline in value is thought to not be temporary.

Answer:

Assets
Long-term investments.. $63,500

Equity-Method Investments

We use the **equity method** to account for investments in which the investor owns 20% to 50% of the investee's shares.

> ### DECISION Why Buy a Large Stake in Another Company?
>
> An investor who holds less than 20% of the investee's voting shares usually plays no important role in the investee's operations. But an investor with a larger share holding—between 20% and 50% of the investee's voting shares—may significantly influence how the investee operates the business. Such an investor can probably affect the investee's decisions on dividend policy, product lines, and other important matters.
>
> ATCO holds equity-method investments in the Barking Power Station in London, England, and in the Joffre Plant in Central Alberta. Because ATCO has a voice in shaping the policy and operations of these two power-generating facilities, some measure of their profits and losses should be included in ATCO's income.

IFRS ALERT

International Accounting Standard (IAS) 28 "Investments in Associates" deals with equity-method investments. IAS 28's corresponding section in the *CICA Handbook* is Section 3051 "Investments."

Section 3051 had not been converged with IAS 28 when this textbook edition was written. There are a number of differences between the two. IAS 28 has more stringent rules for determining if an investor has "significant influence" over an investee's affairs. Another difference is that IAS 28 has the requirement that an investor must adjust the book value of an available-for-sale investment to reflect fair value. Another IAS 28 requirement deals with the excess of the purchase price paid over the fair value of net assets acquired. These issues are beyond the scope of this text and are not covered in this chapter.

Accounting for Equity-Method Investments

Objective

❷ **Use** the equity method for investments

Investments accounted for by the equity method are recorded initially at cost. Suppose NPC Corporation paid $409 million for 32% of the common shares of Bruce Power in Ontario. NPC's entry to record the purchase of this investment follows (in millions):

```
2008
Jan. 2   Long-Term Investment ...................................................    409
            Cash ...................................................................            409
         To purchase equity investment.
```

ASSETS	=	LIABILITIES	+	SHAREHOLDERS' EQUITY
+409	=	0	+	0
−409				

The Investor's Percentage of Investee Income. Under the equity method, NPC, as the investor, applies its percentage of ownership (32% in our example) in recording its share of the investee's net income. Suppose Bruce reports net income of $100 million for 2008, NPC records 32% of this amount as follows (in millions):

```
Dec. 31  Long-Term Investment ($100 × 0.32) ...........................    32
            Equity-Method Investment Revenue ...........................            32
         To record investment revenue.
```

ASSETS	=	LIABILITIES	+	SHAREHOLDERS' EQUITY	+	REVENUES
32	=	0	+		+	32

Because of the close relationship between NPC and Bruce, the investor increases the Investment account and records Investment Revenue when the investee reports income. As Bruce's equity increases, so does the Investment account on NPC's books.

Receiving Dividends Under the Equity Method. NPC Corporation records its proportionate part of cash dividends received from Bruce. Assume Bruce declares and pays a cash dividend of $10 million. NPC receives 32% of this dividend and records this entry (in millions):

Dec. 31	Cash ($10 × 0.32)..	3[*]	
	Long-Term Investment		3[*]
	To receive cash dividend on equity investment.		

[*]$3.2 million rounded to $3 million

ASSETS	=	LIABILITIES	+	SHAREHOLDERS' EQUITY
3	=	0	+	0
−3				

The Investment account is *decreased* for the receipt of a dividend on an equity method investment. Why? Because the dividend decreases the investee's owners' equity and thus the investor's investment.

After the preceding entries are posted, NPC's Long-Term Investment account would include its equity in the net assets of Bruce as follows (in millions):

Long-Term Investment

2008	Jan. 2	Purchase	409	Dec. 31	Dividends	3
	Dec. 31	Net income	32			
	Dec. 31	Balance	438			

NPC reports long-term investments on the balance sheet and the equity-method investment revenue on the income statement as follows:

	Millions
Balance sheet (partial):	
Assets	
Total current assets...	$XXX
Long-term investments...	438
Property, plant, and equipment, net	XXX
Income statement (partial):	
Income from operations	$XXX
Other revenue:	
Equity-method investment revenue	32
Net income	$XXX

Gain or loss on the sale of an equity-method investment is measured as the difference between the sale proceeds and the carrying amount of the investment. For example, NPC Corporation's financial statements show that the investment in Bruce Power at December 31, 2008, was $438 million. Suppose NPC sold 10% of its interest in Bruce Power on January 10, 2009, for $62 million. The entry to record the sale would be:

2009
Jan. 10   Cash..   62
        Loss on Sale of Investment   2
        Long-Term Investment ($640 million × 0.10)   64
Sold 10% of investment.

ASSETS	=	LIABILITIES	+	SHAREHOLDERS' EQUITY	–	LOSSES
62	=	0	+		–	2
−64						

CICA Handbook Section 3150 requires the investor, when there has been a loss in value in an equity investment that is other than a temporary decline, to write the investment down to reflect the loss. This is different than adjusting the value to fair value, which is done whether the decline is temporary or other than temporary (see IFRS Alert on p. 486).

IFRS

Summary of the Equity Method. The following T-account illustrates the accounting for equity-method investments.

Equity-Method Investment

Original cost	Share of losses
Share of income	Share of dividends
Balance	

Consolidated Subsidiaries

Companies buy a significant stake in another company to *influence* the other company's operations. In this section, we cover the situation in which a corporation buys enough of another company to actually *control* that company. ATCO's 100% ownership of Canadian Utilities Limited is an example.

Objective

③ **Understand** consolidated financial statements

DECISION   Why Buy Another Company?

Most large corporations own controlling interests in other companies. A **controlling** (or **majority**) **interest** is the ownership of more than 50% of the investee's voting shares. Such an investment enables the investor to elect a majority of the members of the investee's board of directors and thus control the investee. The investor is called the **parent company**, and the investee company is called the **subsidiary company**. For example, ATCO Structures is a subsidiary of ATCO Ltd., the parent. Therefore, the shareholders of ATCO Ltd. control ATCO Structures, as shown in Exhibit 10-3. Exhibit 10-4 shows how ATCO operates worldwide.

EXHIBIT 10-3   Ownership Structure of ATCO Ltd. and ATCO Structures

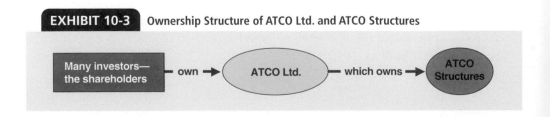

EXHIBIT 10-4   How ATCO Ltd. Operates Worldwide

ATCO Ltd. controls:
- some corporations directly
- some corporations through Canadian Utilities Limited

ATCO groups its subsidiaries as follows:
- Power Generation
- Utilities
- Global Enterprises
  - ATCO Industrials Group

There are more than 40 companies in the ATCO Group.

EXHIBIT 10-5   Accounting Methods for Share Investment by Percentage of Ownership

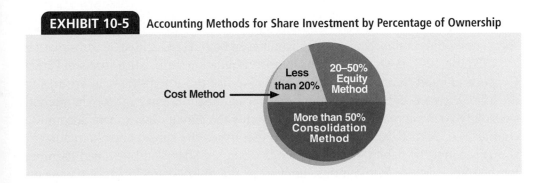

Consolidation Accounting

Consolidation accounting is a method of combining the financial statements of all the companies controlled by the same shareholders. This method reports a single set of financial statements for the consolidated entity, which carries the name of the parent company. Exhibit 10-5 summarizes the accounting methods used for share investments.

Consolidated statements combine the balance sheets, income statements, and other financial statements of the parent company with those of its subsidiaries. The result is as if the parent and its subsidiaries were one company. Users can gain a better perspective on total operations than they could by examining the reports of the parent and each individual subsidiary.

In consolidated financial statements the assets, liabilities, revenues, and expenses of each subsidiary are added to the parent's accounts. For example, the balance in the Cash account of Canadian Utilities Limited is added to the balance in the ATCO Ltd. Cash account, and the sum of the two amounts is presented as a single amount in the ATCO consolidated balance sheet at the beginning of the chapter. Each account balance of a subsidiary loses its identity in the consolidated statements, which bear the name of the parent company, ATCO Ltd.

Exhibit 10-6 diagrams a corporate structure whose parent corporation owns controlling interests in five subsidiary companies and an equity-method investment in another investee company.

The Consolidated Balance Sheet and the Related Worksheet

ATCO Ltd. has purchased 52.5% of the outstanding common shares of Canadian Utilities Limited. Both ATCO and Canadian Utilities Limited keep separate sets of books. ATCO, the parent company, uses a worksheet to prepare the consolidated

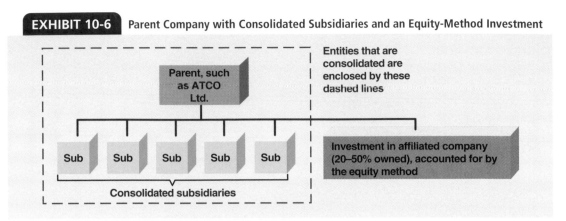

EXHIBIT 10-6 Parent Company with Consolidated Subsidiaries and an Equity-Method Investment

statements of ATCO and its consolidated subsidiaries. ATCO's consolidated balance sheet shows the combined assets and liabilities of both ATCO and all its subsidiaries.

Exhibit 10-7 shows the worksheet for consolidating the balance sheets of Parent Corporation and Subsidiary Corporation. We use these hypothetical entities to illustrate the consolidation process. Consider elimination entry (a) for the parent-subsidiary ownership accounts. Entry (a) credits the parent's Investment account to eliminate its debit balance. Entry (a) also eliminates the subsidiary's shareholders' equity accounts by debiting the subsidiary's Common Shares and Retained Earnings for their full balances. Without this elimination, the consolidated financial statements would include both the parent company's investment in the subsidiary and the subsidiary company's equity. But these accounts represent the same thing—Subsidiary's equity—and so they must be eliminated from the consolidated totals. If they weren't, the same resources would be counted twice. However, the subsidiary's net assets are consolidated and are thus included.

The resulting Parent and Subsidiary consolidated balance sheet (far right column) reports no Investment in Subsidiary account, and the consolidated totals for

EXHIBIT 10-7 Worksheet for Consolidated Balance Sheet

	Parent Corporation	Subsidiary Corporation	Eliminations		Parent and Subsidiary Consolidated Amounts
			Debit	Credit	
Assets					
Cash..	$ 12,000	$ 18,000			$ 30,000
Note receivable from Subsidiary........	80,000	—		(b) 80,000	—
Inventory	104,000	91,000			195,000
Investment in Subsidiary...................	150,000	—		(a) 150,000	—
Other assets......................................	218,000	138,000			356,000
Total...	$564,000	$247,000			$581,000
Liabilities and Shareholders' Equity					
Accounts payable	$ 43,000	$ 17,000			$ 60,000
Notes payable...................................	190,000	80,000	(b) 80,000		190,000
Common shares	176,000	100,000	(a) 100,000		176,000
Retained earnings.............................	155,000	50,000	(a) 50,000		155,000
Total...	$564,000	$247,000	$230,000	$230,000	$581,000

Common Shares and Retained Earnings are those of Parent Corporation only. Study the final column of the consolidation worksheet.

In this example, Parent Corporation has an $80,000 note receivable from Subsidiary, and Subsidiary has a note payable to Parent. The parent's receivable and the subsidiary's payable represent the same resources—all entirely within the consolidated entity. Both, therefore, must be eliminated. Entry (b) accomplishes this.

- The $80,000 credit in the Eliminations column of the worksheet zeros out Parent's Note Receivable from Subsidiary.

- The $80,000 debit in the Eliminations column zeros out the Subsidiary's Notes Payable to Parent.

- The resulting consolidated amount for notes payable is the amount owed to creditors outside the consolidated entity, which is appropriate.

After the worksheet is complete, the consolidated amount for each account represents the total asset, liability, and equity amounts controlled by Parent Corporation.

STOP & THINK

Examine Exhibit 10-7. Why does the consolidated shareholders' equity ($176,000 + $155,000) exclude the equity of Subsidiary Corporation?

Answer:
The shareholders' equity of the consolidated entity is that of the parent only. Also, the subsidiary's equity and the parent company's investment balance represent the same resources. Including both would amount to double counting.

Goodwill and Minority Interest

Goodwill and Minority Interest are two accounts that only a consolidated entity can have. *Goodwill*, which we studied in Chapter 7 (see p. 337), arises when a parent company pays more to acquire a subsidiary company than the market value of the subsidiary's net assets. As we saw in Chapter 7, goodwill is the intangible asset that represents the parent company's excess payment to acquire the subsidiary. ATCO reports goodwill of $71.2 million on its December 31, 2007, balance sheet.

Minority interest arises when a parent company purchases less than 100% of the shares of a subsidiary company. For example, ATCO owns less than 100% of some of the companies it controls. The remainder of the subsidiaries' shares is minority interest to ATCO. Minority Interest is included below the liabilities and above shareholders' equity on the balance sheet of the parent company. ATCO reports minority interest on its balance sheet using the heading "Non-controlling interests" in the amount of $1,836.7 (millions).

IFRS ALERT

The *CICA Handbook* and IFRSs disagree on where minority interests should appear on the balance sheet. *CICA Handbook* Sections 3861 and 3863 state that minority interest should be presented before shareholders' equity. IAS 27 states that minority interest should be included in shareholders' equity. In the absence of convergence, the dictates of the *CICA Handbook* should be followed.

Income of a Consolidated Entity

The income of a consolidated entity is the net income of the parent plus the parent's proportion of the subsidiaries' net income. Suppose Parent Company owns all the shares of Subsidiary S-1 and 60% of the shares of Subsidiary S-2. During the year just ended, Parent earned net income of $330,000, S-1 earned $150,000, and S-2 had a net loss of $100,000. Parent Company would report net income of $420,000, computed as follows:

	Net Income (Net Loss) of Each Company		Parent's Ownership of Each Company		Parent's Consolidated Net Income (Net Loss)
Parent Company	$ 330,000	×	100%	=	$330,000
Subsidiary S-1	150,000	×	100	=	150,000
Subsidiary S-2	(100,000)	×	60	=	(60,000)
Consolidated net income.....					$420,000

Intercompany sales and expenses must also be eliminated but that is a subject for an advanced accounting text.

Long-Term Investments in Bonds

The major investors in bonds are financial institutions, pension plans, mutual funds, and insurance companies, such as Manulife Financial Corporation. The relationship between the issuing corporation and the investor (bondholder) may be diagrammed as follows:

An investment in bonds is classified either as short term (a current asset) or as long term. Short-term investments in bonds are rare. Here, we focus on long-term investments called **held-to-maturity investments** (see IFRS Alert, p. 482).

Both *CICA Handbook* Section 3855 "Financial Instruments—Recognition and Measurement" and IAS 39 "Financial Instruments: Recognition and Measurement" impose stringent conditions on the decision to classify long-term investment as *held-to-maturity*. The instruments must have fixed or determinable payments and a fixed maturity. In addition, the investor must have positive intention and the ability to hold the investment to maturity. There is a penalty to reclassifying held-to-maturity investments, although both standards do provide a short list of conditions when reclassification is acceptable.

Bond investments are recorded at cost. Years later, at maturity, the investor will receive the bond's face value. Often bond investments are purchased at a premium or a discount. When there is a premium or discount, held-to-maturity investments are amortized to account for interest revenue and the bonds' carrying amount. Held-to-maturity investments are reported by the *amortized cost method*, which determines the carrying amount.

Suppose an investor purchases $100,000 of 5% Government of Canada bonds at a price of $95,735 on June 1, 2009. The bonds pay interest on June 1 and December 1. The investor intends to hold the bonds until their maturity on June 2, 2014. The bonds will be outstanding for 5 years (10 interest periods). The bonds meet the criteria to be classified as held-to-maturity investments. The investor paid a discounted price for the bonds of $95,735 (an effective interest rate of 6%). The investor must amortize the bonds' carrying amount from cost of $95,735 up to $100,000 over their term to maturity.

Both *CICA Handbook* Section 3150 and IAS 39 require held-to-maturity investments to be valued at amortized cost and also require the amortization to be calculated using the effective interest method (see Chapter 8, p. 383, and Appendix D). The following are the entries for this long-term investment:

2009
June 1	Long-Term Investment in Bonds ($100,000 × 95.735)........................	95,735	
	Cash		95,735
	To purchase bond investment.		
Dec. 2	Cash ($100,000 × 0.05 × 1/2)...	2,500	
	Interest Revenue		2,500
	To receive semi-annual interest.		
Dec. 2	Long-Term Investment in Bonds (($95,735 × 0.06 × 1/2) − $2,500) ...	373[*]	
	Interest Revenue		373[*]
	To amortize bond investment.		

[*]Rounded

At December 31, the year-end adjustments are

2009
Dec. 31	Interest Receivable ($100,000 × 0.05 × 1/12)....................................	417[*]	
	Interest Revenue.		417[*]
	To accrue interest revenue.		
Dec. 31	Long-Term Investment in Bonds (($96,108 × 0.06 × 1/12) − $417) ...	64[*]	
	Interest Revenue		64[*]
	To amortize bond investment.		

[*]Rounded

This amortization entry has two effects:

1. It increases the Long-Term Investment account on its march toward maturity value.

2. It increases the interest by the amount of the increase in the carrying amount of the investment.

The financial statements at December 31, 2009, report the following for this investment in bonds:

Balance sheet at December 31, 2009:	
Current assets:	
Interest receivable	$ 417
Long-term investments in bonds ($95,735 + $373 + $64).............................	96,172
Property, plant, and equipment..	X,XXX
Income statement for the year ended December 31, 2009:	
Other revenues:	
Interest revenue ($2,500 + $373 + $417 + $64)	$ 3,354

MyAccountingLab   # MID-CHAPTER SUMMARY PROBLEM

1. Identify the appropriate accounting method for each of the following long-term investment situations:
   a. Investment in 25% of investee's shares
   b. 10% investment in shares
   c. Investment in more than 50% of investee's shares

2. At what amount should the following long-term investment portfolio be reported on the June 30, 2009, balance sheet? All the investments are less than 5% of the investee's shares.

Shares	Investment Cost	Current Market Value
Bank of Montreal	$75,000	$52,000
Canadian Tire Corp.	24,000	31,000
Jean Coutu Group	32,000	36,000

   Journalize any adjusting entry required by these data.

3. Investor Corporation paid $67,900 to acquire a 40% equity-method investment in the common shares of Investee Corporation. At the end of the first year, Investee's net income was $80,000, and Investee declared and paid cash dividends of $55,000. What is Investor's ending balance in its Equity-Method Investment account? Use a T-account to answer.

4. Parent Corporation paid $85,000 for all the common shares of Subsidiary Corporation, and Parent owes Subsidiary $20,000 on a note payable. Complete the consolidation work sheet below.

	Parent Corporation	Subsidiary Corporation	Eliminations Debit	Eliminations Credit	Consolidated Amounts
Assets					
Cash	$ 7,000	$ 4,000			
Note receivable from Parent	—	20,000			
Investment in Subsidiary	85,000	—			
Other assets	108,000	99,000			
Total	$200,000	$123,000			
Liabilities and Shareholders' Equity					
Accounts payable	$ 15,000	$ 8,000			
Notes payable	20,000	30,000			
Common shares	120,000	60,000			
Retained earnings	45,000	25,000			
Total	$200,000	$123,000			

Answers

For investments:
Less than 20%→Available-for-sale;
20% to 50%→Equity;
Greater than 50%→Consolidation

1. a. Equity
   b. Available-for-sale
   c. Consolidation

2. Report the investments at market value ($119,000) as follows:

Shares	Investment Cost	Current Market Value
Bank of Montreal	$ 75,000	$ 52,000
Canadian Tire	24,000	31,000
Jean Coutu Group	32,000	36,000
Totals	$131,000	$119,000

> Determine the market value for each investment in the portfolio. Then create the journal entry for any change from investment cost to current market value.

IFRS

Adjusting entry.

Other Comprehensive Income ($131,000 − $119,000)	12,000	
Long-term Investments		12,000

To adjust investments to current market value.

3. Equity-Method Investment

Equity-Method Investment			
Cost	67,900	Dividends	22,000**
Income	32,000*		
Balance	77,900		

*$80,000 × 0.40 = $32,000
**$55,000 × 0.40 = $22,000

> The equity-method investment T-account includes:
> 100% of the cost of the investment
> + 40% of the investee's net income
> − 40% of the investee's cash dividends

4. Consolidation work sheet:

> Eliminate all parent-and-subsidiary intercompany transactions to avoid double-counting items when consolidating.

	Parent Corporation	Subsidiary Corporation	Eliminations Debit	Eliminations Credit	Consolidated Amounts
Assets					
Cash...	$ 7,000	$ 4,000			$ 11,000
Note receivable from Parent	—	20,000		(a) 20,000	—
Investment in Subsidiary.........	85,000	—		(b) 85,000	—
Other assets	108,000	99,000			207,000
Total.......................................	$200,000	$123,000			$218,000
Liabilities and Shareholders' Equity					
Accounts payable	$ 15,000	$ 8,000			$ 23,000
Notes payable	20,000	30,000	(a) 20,000		30,000
Common shares	120,000	60,000	(b) 60,000		120,000
Retained earnings....................	45,000	25,000	(b) 25,000		45,000
Total..	$200,000	$123,000	$105,000	$105,000	$218,000

Accounting for International Operations

IFRS

Many Canadian companies do large parts of their business abroad. Bank of Nova Scotia, Magna International Inc., and Research In Motion Limited, among many others, are very active in other countries. Exhibit 10-8 shows the percentages of international sales for these companies.

As you have learned from the IFRS Alerts presented throughout this text, accounting for business activities across national boundaries is called *international accounting*. Electronic communication makes international accounting important because investors around the world need the same data to make decisions.

International trade is growing, as is the investment by Canadian companies in companies in other countries. It is the authors' belief that it is important you be provided with some exposure to the accounting for international trade and international operations. The IFRS Alert on this page points out that convergence of Canadian standards related to foreign currency translation with the related IAS has not yet occurred.

The complexities of foreign currency translation are normally covered in an advanced accounting course. Accordingly, the following discussion is based on existing Canadian GAAP and is intended to provide you with a basic understanding of foreign currency translation in the context of international trade and the context of international investment by Canadian companies.

IFRS ALERT

CICA Handbook Section 1651 "Foreign Currency Translation" had not been converged with IAS 21 "The Effect of Changes in Foreign Exchange Rates" when this textbook edition was written. While some of the differences are small, others are very complex. Accordingly, this text will use the existing *CICA Handbook* as the authoritative source for the material in the balance of this chapter.

Foreign Currencies and Exchange Rates

Most countries use their own national currencies. An exception is a group of European nations, the European Union (EU)—France, Germany, Italy, Belgium, and others use a common currency, the *euro*, whose symbol is €. If Bombardier Inc., a Canadian company, sells aircraft to Air France, will Bombardier receive Canadian dollars or euros? If the transaction takes place in dollars, Air France must buy dollars to pay Bombardier in Canadian currency. If the transaction is in euros, Bombardier will collect euros and sell the euros for dollars.

The price of one nation's currency may be stated in terms of another country's monetary unit. This measure of one currency against another is called the **foreign-currency exchange rate**. In Exhibit 10-9, the dollar value of a euro is $1.58. This means that one euro can be bought for about $1.58. Other currencies are also listed in Exhibit 10-9.

EXHIBIT 10-8	Extent of International Business
Company	**Percentage of International Revenue**
Bank of Nova Scotia...	43%
Magna International Inc...	71
Research In Motion Limited...................................	93

EXHIBIT 10-9 Foreign-Currency Exchange Rates

Country	Monetary Unit	Canadian Dollar Value	Country	Monetary Unit	Canadian Dollar Value
China	Yuan (CNY)	$0.184	Japan	Yen (¥)	0.013
France	Euro (€)	1.58	Mexico	Peso (P)	0.086
Germany	Euro (€)	1.58	United Kingdom	Pound (£)	1.793
Italy	Euro (€)	1.58	United States	Dollar ($)	1.26

Source: The Sander School of Business, University of British Columbia, February 18, 2009.

We can convert the cost of an item in one currency to its cost in a second currency. We call this conversion a *translation*. Suppose an item costs 200 euros. To compute its cost in dollars, we multiply the amount in euros by the conversion rate: 200 euros × $1.58 = $316.00.

Two main factors determine the supply of and demand for a particular currency:

1. The ratio of a country's imports to its exports.
2. The rate of return available in the country's capital markets.

The Import/Export Ratio. Japanese exports often surpass Japan's imports. Customers of Japanese companies must buy yen (the Japanese unit of currency) in the international currency market to pay for their purchases. This strong demand drives up the price—the foreign exchange rate—of the yen. Canada also exports more than it imports. In contrast, the United States imports more goods than it exports. But when Canada's exports of commodities (oils, minerals, lumber, potash) declined in late 2008 and early 2009, Canada's trade surplus declined and the Canadian dollar dropped in value relative to the U.S. dollar.

The Rate of Return. The rate of return available in a country's capital markets affects the amount of investment funds flowing into the country. When rates of return are high in a politically stable country such as Canada, international investors buy shares, bonds, and real estate in that country. This activity increases the demand for the nation's currency and drives up its exchange rate.

Currencies are often described as *strong* or *weak*. The exchange rate of a **strong currency** is rising relative to other nations' currencies. The exchange rate of a **weak currency** is falling relative to other currencies.

The Bank of Canada's Web site listed the exchange rate for the British pound as $1.85 on January 16, 2009. On January 23, 2009, that rate was $1.69. We would say that the dollar has risen against—is stronger than—the British pound. Because the pound has become less expensive, the dollar now buys more pounds. A stronger dollar would make travel to England more attractive to Canadians.

Managing Cash in International Transactions. International transactions are common. Linamar Corporation, the original equipment automobile components supplier based in Guelph, Ontario, is an example. Linamar has factories in Canada, the United States, Mexico, China, Korea, and Europe. Sales are made to companies outside the Linamar family of companies and between Linamar companies in these geographic areas. For example, a transmission might be manufactured in Canada for General Motors in the United States using parts manufactured by Linamar in Europe. The European parts would be priced in euros while the transmission could be priced in Canadian dollars and sold to GM for U.S. dollars.

Do We Collect Cash in Dollars or in a Foreign Currency? Do We Pay in Dollars or in a Foreign Currency?

Linamar owns Skyjack Inc., which manufactures the Skyjack, a self-propelled scissor-type elevating work platform used mainly in construction. Consider the sale of an SJ8243 Skyjack to All-England Construction Ltd. for $65,000 Canadian. The sale can be conducted in dollars or in pounds. If All-England Construction agrees to pay in dollars, Skyjack avoids the complication of dealing in a foreign currency, and the transaction is the same as selling to Devlan Construction Ltd. across town. Suppose that All-England Construction demands to pay in pounds and that Skyjack agrees to receive pounds instead of dollars.

Because Skyjack will need to convert the pounds to dollars, the transaction poses a challenge. What if the pound loses value—weakens, taking fewer dollars to obtain each pound—before Skyjack collects from All-England Construction? In this case, Skyjack will not earn as much as expected on the sale. The following example shows how to account for international transactions that result in the receipt of a foreign currency. It also shows how to measure the effects of such transactions on a company's cash position and profits.

Skyjack sells goods to All-England Construction Ltd. for a price of £10,000 on January 8, 2009. On that date, a pound was worth $1.81, as quoted on the Bank of Canada exchange rate tables. On March 8, 2009, suppose the pound has weakened against the dollar so that a pound is worth $1.70. Skyjack receives £10,000 from All-England Construction on March 8 but the dollar value of Skyjack's receipt is $17,000 (£10,000 × $1.70), which is $1,100 less than expected. Skyjack ends up earning less than hoped for on the transaction. The following journal entries show how Skyjack would account for these transactions:

2009
Jan. 8   Accounts Receivable—All-England Construction
                 (£10,000 × $1.81)... 18,100
             Sales Revenue... 18,100
         Sale on account.

ASSETS	=	LIABILITIES	+	SHAREHOLDERS' EQUITY	+	REVENUES
18,100	=	0	+		+	18,100

Mar. 8   Cash (£10,000 × $1.70)... 17,000
         Foreign-Currency Transaction Loss 1,100
             Accounts Receivable—All-England Construction 18,100
         Collection on account.

ASSETS	=	LIABILITIES	+	SHAREHOLDERS' EQUITY	−	LOSSES
17,000 −18,100	=	0	+		−	1,100

If Skyjack had required All-England Construction to pay at the time of the sale, Skyjack would have received pounds worth $18,100. But by waiting the normal 60-day collection period to receive cash, Skyjack exposed itself to *foreign-currency exchange risk*, the risk of loss in an international transaction. In this case, Skyjack experienced a $1,100 foreign-currency transaction loss and received $1,100 less cash than expected, as shown in the collection entry.

If the pound had increased in value, Skyjack would have experienced a foreign-currency transaction gain. When a company holds a receivable denominated in a foreign currency, it wants the foreign currency to remain strong so that it can be converted into more dollars. Unfortunately, that did not occur for Skyjack.

Purchasing from a foreign company may also expose a company to foreign-currency exchange risk. To illustrate, assume Linamar buys a milling machine from Gesellschaft Ltd., a Swiss company. After lengthy negotiations, the two companies decide on a price of 20,000 Swiss francs. On January 2, 2009, when Linamar receives the machine, the Swiss franc is quoted in international currency markets at $1.13 Canadian. When Linamar pays two months later, on March 2, 2009, the Swiss franc has weakened against the dollar—decreased in value to $1.07. Linamar would record the purchase and payment as follows:

2009
Jan. 2   Property, plant, and equipment
        (20,000 Swiss francs × $1.13)   22,600
        Accounts Payable—Gesellschaft Ltd.   22,600
   Purchase on account.

ASSETS	=	LIABILITIES	+	SHAREHOLDERS' EQUITY
22,600	=	22,600	+	0

Mar. 2   Accounts Payable—Gesellschaft Ltd.   22,600
        Cash (20,000 Swiss francs × $1.07).   21,400
        Foreign-Currency Transaction Gain   1,200
   Payment on account.

ASSETS	=	LIABILITIES	+	SHAREHOLDERS' EQUITY	+	GAINS
–21,400	=	–22,600	+		+	1,200

The Swiss franc could have strengthened against the dollar, in which case Linamar would have had a foreign-currency transaction loss. A company with a payable denominated in a foreign currency hopes that the dollar gets stronger: The payment then costs fewer dollars.

Reporting Gains and Losses on the Income Statement

The Foreign-Currency Transaction Gain account is the record of the gains on transactions settled in a currency other than the dollar. Likewise, the Foreign-Currency Transaction Loss account shows the amount of the losses on transactions conducted in foreign currencies. The company reports the *net amount* of these two accounts on the income statement as Other Revenues and Gains, or Other Expenses and Losses, as the case may be. For example, Linamar, on its consolidated statements, would combine the $1,100 foreign-currency loss and the $1,200 gain and report the net gain of $100 on the income statement as part of Selling, General, and Administrative Expenses.

These gains and losses are not included in Cost of Sales because they arise from buying and selling foreign currencies, not from the main line of the company's business (in the case of Linamar, selling automobile components and Skyjacks). Companies seek to minimize their foreign-currency losses by a strategy called *hedging*.

> **DECISION** **Should We Hedge Our Foreign-Currency Transaction Risk?**
>
> One way for Canadian companies to avoid foreign-currency transaction losses is to insist that international transactions be settled in dollars. This requirement puts the burden of currency translation on the foreign party. But this approach may alienate customers and decrease sales. Another way for a company to protect itself is by **hedging**. Hedging means to protect oneself from losing money in one transaction by engaging in a counterbalancing transaction.
>
> A Canadian company selling goods to be collected in Mexican pesos expects to receive a fixed number of pesos in the future. If the peso is losing value, the Canadian company would expect the pesos to be worth fewer dollars than the amount of the receivable—an expected loss situation.
>
> The Canadian company may have accumulated payables stated in a foreign currency in the normal course of its business, such as the amount payable by Linamar to the Swiss company. Losses on the receipt of pesos may be offset by gains on the payment of Swiss francs to Gesellschaft Ltd. Most companies do not have equal amounts of receivables and payables in foreign currency. To obtain a more precise hedge, some companies buy *futures contracts*, which are contracts for foreign currencies to be received in the future. Futures contracts can effectively create a payable to offset a receivable exactly, and vice versa. Many companies that do business internationally use hedging techniques. Accounting for hedges is covered in advanced accounting courses.

Consolidation of Foreign Subsidiaries

A Canadian company, such as Linamar, with a foreign subsidiary must consolidate the subsidiary's financial statements into its own statements for reporting to the public. The consolidation of a foreign subsidiary poses two special challenges:

1. Many countries outside Canada specify accounting treatments that differ from Canadian accounting principles. For reporting to the Canadian public, accountants must first bring the subsidiary's statements into conformity with Canadian GAAP.

2. The second accounting challenge arises when the subsidiary statements are expressed in a foreign currency. First, we must translate the subsidiary statements into dollars. Then the two companies' statements can be consolidated, as illustrated in Exhibit 10-7 on page 490.

The process of translating a foreign subsidiary's financial statements into dollars usually creates a *foreign-currency translation adjustment*. This item appears in the financial statements of most multinational companies and is reported as part of other income on the income statement or as part of shareholders' equity on the consolidated balance sheet. Linamar Corporation's December 31, 2007, annual report shows a cumulative translation adjustment as a debit to Shareholders' Equity in the amount of $82.017 million.

A translation adjustment arises due to changes in the foreign exchange rate over time. In general,

- *Assets* and *liabilities* are translated into dollars at the current exchange rate on the date of the statements.
- *Shareholders' equity* is translated into dollars at older, historical exchange rates.

This difference in exchange rates creates an out-of-balance condition on the balance sheet. The translation adjustment amount brings the balance sheet back into balance. Let's use an example to see how the translation adjustment works.

Vivos Imports Corporation owns Italian Imports Inc., whose financial statements are expressed in euros. Vivos Imports must consolidate the Italian subsidiary's financial statements into its own statements. When Vivos Imports acquired Italian Imports in 2007, 1 euro was worth $1.43. When Italian Imports acquired its retained earnings during 2007 through 2009, the average exchange rate was $1.65. On the balance sheet date in 2009, a euro is worth $1.60. Exhibit 10-10 shows how to translate Italian Imports' balance sheet into dollars and shows how the translation adjustment arises.

The **foreign-currency translation adjustment** is the balancing amount that brings the dollar amount of the total liabilities and shareholders' equity of a foreign subsidiary into agreement with the dollar amount of its total assets (in Exhibit 10-10, total assets equal $1,280,000). Only after the translation adjustment of $7,000 do total liabilities and shareholders' equity equal total assets stated in dollars.

What caused the positive translation adjustment? The euro strengthened after the acquisition of the Italian company.

- When Vivos Imports acquired the foreign subsidiary in 2007, a euro was worth $1.43.

- When the Italian company earned its income during 2007 through 2009, the average exchange rate was $1.65.

- On the balance sheet date in 2009, a euro is worth $1.60.

- Thus, the Italian company's equity (assets minus liabilities) is translated into $480,000 ($1,280,000 − $800,000).

- To bring shareholders' equity to $480,000 requires a $7,000 positive adjustment.

In a sense, a positive translation adjustment is like a gain. It is reported as a credit item in the shareholders' equity section of the balance sheet, as shown in Exhibit 10-10. The interpretation of a positive translation adjustment is this:

Measured in today's dollars, the book value of Vivos Imports Corporation's investment in Italian Imports Inc. is more than the amount Vivos Imports invested to acquire the company.

The Italian Imports Inc. dollar figures in Exhibit 10-10 are the amounts that Vivos Imports Corporation would include in its consolidated balance sheet. The consolidation procedures would follow those illustrated beginning on page 489.

EXHIBIT 10-10   Translation of a Foreign-Currency Balance Sheet into Dollars

Italian Imports Inc. Amounts	Euros	Exchange Rate	Dollars
Assets	€800,000	$1.60	$1,280,000
Liabilities	€500,000	1.60	$ 800,000
Shareholders' equity			
Common shares	100,000	1.43	143,000
Retained earnings	200,000	1.65	330,000
Foreign-currency translation adjustment	—		7,000
	€800,000		$1,280,000

EXHIBIT 10-11	Some International Accounting Differences		
Country	Inventories	Research and Development Costs	Goodwill
Canada	LIFO is unacceptable	Expense research costs. Some development costs may be capitalized	Record an impairment
United States	Specific unit cost, FIFO, LIFO, weighted-average	Expensed as incurred	Similar to Canada
Germany	Similar to U.S.	Similar to U.S.	Amortized over 5 years
Japan	Similar to U.S.	May be capitalized and amortized over 5 years	Amortized over 5 years

International Accounting Standards

In this text, we focus on the accounting principles that are generally accepted in Canada. Most accounting methods are consistent throughout the world. Double-entry accounting, the accrual system, and the basic financial statements are used worldwide. Differences, however, do exist among countries, as shown in Exhibit 10-11.

In discussing amortization (Chapter 7), we emphasized that in Canada, the methods used for reporting to tax authorities differ from the methods used for reporting to shareholders. However, tax reporting and shareholder reporting are identical in many countries. For example, France has a "Plan Compatible," which specifies that a National Uniform Chart of Accounts be used for both tax returns and reporting to shareholders. German financial reporting is also determined primarily by tax laws.

IFRS

Throughout this text, beginning with Chapter 1, you have seen references to the International Accounting Standards Board (IASB), International Accounting Standards (IAS), and International Financial Reporting Standards (IFRS). Many chapters have included one or more IFRS Alerts that drew to your attention information about the converging of Canadian accounting standards with the standards issued by the IASB. You may wish to refer to the IFRS Alert in Chapter 1 on page 10.

It is the authors' belief that, as the date approaches when Canadian publicly accountable enterprises will have to report using IFRS, all accounting students should have some familiarity with the new standards, as it is probable that Canadian accounting standards for all organizations will be converged to a lesser or greater degree with IFRS.

Using the Cash Flow Statement

Investing activities include many types of transactions. In Chapter 7, we covered investing transactions in which companies purchase and sell long-term assets, such as property, plant, and equipment. In this chapter, we examined another type of investing activity actually called *investment*. The purchase and sale of investments in shares and bonds of other companies are also investing activities reported on the cash flow statement.

Investing activities are usually reported on the cash flow statement as the second category, after operating activities and before financing activities. Exhibit 10-12 provides excerpts from ATCO Ltd.'s cash flow statement. During 2007, ATCO spent $232.5 million on new property, plant, and equipment. Overall, ATCO invested $218.8 million. This is one reason ATCO stays ahead of competitors: it invests in the future.

EXHIBIT 10-12   ATCO Ltd. Consolidated Cash Flow Statement

ATCO Ltd.
Cash Flow Statement (Partial, adapted)
For the Year Ended December 31, 2007

	(In millions)
Cash flows—Investing activities	
Purchase of property, plant, and equipment	$(235.2)
Proceeds (costs) on disposal of other property, plant, and equipment	(11.2)
Contributions by utility customers for extensions to plant	25.8
Non-current deferred electricity costs	(4.5)
Changes in noncash working capital	6.1
Other	0.2
Cash used for investing activities	$(218.8)

DECISION GUIDELINES

ACCOUNTING METHODS FOR LONG-TERM INVESTMENTS

These guidelines show which accounting method to use for each type of long-term investment.

Power Corporation of Canada has all types of investments—shares, bonds, 25% interests, controlling interests. How should Power Corporation account for its various investments?

IFRS

Type of Long-Term Investment	Accounting Method
Power Corporation owns less than 20% of investee shares (Portfolio investment classified as noncurrent asset)	Available-for-sale*
Power Corporation owns between 20% and 50% of investee/affiliate shares	Equity*
Power Corporation owns more than 50% of investee shares	Consolidation
Power Corporation owns long-term investment in bonds (held-to-maturity investment)	Amortized cost*

*Net realizable value if impaired

END-OF-CHAPTER SUMMARY PROBLEM   *MyAccountingLab*

Translate the balance sheet of the Brazilian subsidiary of The Jean Shop Corporation, a Canadian company, into dollars. When The Jean Shop acquired this subsidiary, the exchange rate of the Brazilian currency, the real, was $0.45. The average exchange rate applicable to retained earnings is $0.52. The real's current exchange rate is $0.53.

Before performing the translation, predict whether the translation adjustment will be positive or negative. Does this situation generate a foreign-currency translation gain or loss? Give your reasons.

	Reals
Assets	900,000
Liabilities	600,000
Shareholders' equity:	
Common shares	30,000
Retained earnings	270,000
	900,000

Answers

The current exchange rate is higher than the rate in effect at the time of the investment purchase. This results in an increase in the value of the investment and, accordingly, a gain.

Translation of foreign-currency balance sheet:

This situation will generate a *positive* translation adjustment, which is like a gain. The gain occurs because the real's current exchange rate, which is used to translate net assets (assets minus liabilities), exceeds the historical exchange rates used for shareholders' equity.

The calculation follows.

The foreign-currency translation adjustment is the "plug" figure that makes total assets equal total liabilities plus shareholders' equity after translation. A positive figure is like a foreign-currency translation gain. A negative figure is like a foreign-currency translation loss.

	Reals	Exchange Rate	Dollars
Assets	900,000	$0.53	$477,000
Liabilities...	600,000	0.53	$318,000
Shareholders' equity:			
Common shares..	30,000	0.45	13,500
Retained earnings	270,000	0.52	140,400
Foreign-currency translation adjustment ...	—		5,100
	900,000		$477,000

REVIEW LONG-TERM INVESTMENTS AND INTERNATIONAL OPERATIONS

QUICK CHECK (Answers are given on page 522.)

1. A company's investment in less than 1% of GE's shares, which it expects to hold for 2 years and then sell, is which type of investment?
   - **a.** Held-for-trading
   - **b.** Equity
   - **c.** Available-for-sale
   - **d.** Consolidation

2. DuBois Corporation purchased an available-for-sale investment in 1,000 shares of Scotiabank (BNS) for $31 per share. On the next balance sheet date, BNS is quoted at $35 per share. DuBois' *balance sheet* should report
   - **a.** Unrealized loss of $4,000
   - **b.** Unrealized gain of $31,000
   - **c.** Investments of $31,000
   - **d.** Investments of $35,000

3. Use the DuBois Corporation data in question 2. DuBois' *income statement* should report
   - **a.** Unrealized gain of $4,000
   - **b.** Unrealized loss of $4,000
   - **c.** Investments of $31,000
   - **d.** Nothing because DuBois hasn't sold the investment

4. Use the DuBois Corporation data in question 2. DuBois sold the Scotiabank shares for $40,000 two years later. DuBois' *income statement* should report
   - **a.** Unrealized gain of $4,000
   - **b.** Gain on sale of $9,000
   - **c.** Gain on sale of $5,000
   - **d.** Investments of $40,000

5. Alexander Moving & Storage Inc. paid $100,000 for 20% of the common shares of Sellers Ltd. Sellers earned net income of $50,000 and paid dividends of $25,000. The carrying value of Alexander's investment in Sellers is
   - **a.** $100,000
   - **b.** $105,000
   - **c.** $125,000
   - **d.** $150,000

6. Tarrant Inc. owns 80% of Rockwall Corporation, and Rockwall owns 80% of Kaufman Company. During 2009, these companies' net incomes are as follows before any consolidations:

   - Tarrant, $100,000
   - Rockwall, $68,000
   - Kaufman, $40,000

   How much net income should Tarrant report for 2009?

   a. $100,000   c. $180,000
   b. $164,000   d. $204,000

7. TRULINE Inc. holds an investment in Manulife bonds that pay interest each June 30. TRULINE's *balance sheet* at December 31 should report

   a. Interest receivable   c. Interest revenue
   b. Interest payable   d. Interest expense

8. You are going on a vacation to France, and you buy euros for $1.60. On your return you cash in your unused euros for $1.50. During your vacation

   a. The dollar lost value   c. The euro gained value
   b. The euro rose against the dollar   d. The dollar rose against the euro

9. Grey County, Ontario, purchased earth-moving equipment from a U.S. company. The cost was $1,000,000 in U.S. dollars, and the U.S. dollar was quoted at $1.25. A month later, Grey County paid its debt, and the Canadian dollar was quoted at $1.27. What was Grey County's cost of the equipment?

   a. $20,000   c. $950,000
   b. $1,250,000   d. $1,020,000

10. ATCO owns numerous foreign subsidiary companies. When ATCO consolidates its Australian subsidiary, ATCO should translate the subsidiary's assets into Canadian dollars at the

    a. Historical exchange rate when ATCO purchased the Australian company
    b. Average exchange rate during the period ATCO owned the Australian subsidiary
    c. Current exchange rate
    d. None of the above. There's no need to translate the subsidiary's assets into Canadian dollars.

ACCOUNTING VOCABULARY

available-for-sale investments All investments held to earn dividend revenue and/or capital appreciation. (p. 482)

consolidated statements Financial statements of the parent company plus those of majority-owned subsidiaries as if the combination were a single legal entity. (p. 489)

controlling (majority) interest Ownership of more than 50% of an investee company's voting shares. (p. 488)

equity method The method used to account for investments in which the investor has 20–50% of the investee's voting shares and can significantly influence the decisions of the investee. (p. 485)

foreign-currency exchange rate The measure of one country's currency against another country's currency. (p. 496)

foreign-currency translation adjustment The balancing figure that brings the dollar amount of the total liabilities and shareholders' equity of the foreign subsidiary into agreement with the dollar amount of its total assets. (p. 501)

hedging To protect oneself from losing money in one transaction by engaging in a counterbalancing transaction. (p. 500)

held-to-maturity investments Bonds and notes that an investor intends to hold until maturity. (p. 492)

long-term investments Any investment that does not meet the criteria of a short-term investment; any investment that the investor expects to hold for longer than a year. (p. 481)

majority interest Ownership of more than 50% of an investee company's voting shares. (p. 488)

minority interest A subsidiary company's equity that is held by shareholders other than the parent company. (p. 491)

parent company An investor company that owns more than 50% of the voting shares of a subsidiary company. (p. 488)

strong currency A currency whose exchange rate is rising relative to other nations' currencies. (p. 497)

subsidiary company An investee company in which a parent company owns more than 50% of the voting shares. (p. 488)

weak currency A currency whose exchange rate is falling relative to other nations' currencies. (p. 497)

ASSESS YOUR PROGRESS

 Make the grade with MyAccountingLab: The exercises and problems marked in red can be found on MyAccountingLab at www.myaccountinglab.com. You can practise them as often as you want, and they feature step by step guided solutions to help you find the right answer.

SHORT EXERCISES

Accounting for an available-for-sale investment; unrealized gain or loss
(Obj. 1)

S10-1 Assume Knowlton Holdings Ltd. completed these long-term available-for-sale investment transactions during 2008:

2008		
Feb.	10	Purchased 300 shares of BCE, paying $25 per share. Knowlton intends to hold the investment for the indefinite future.
Dec.	1	Received a cash dividend of $0.36 per share on the BCE shares.
Dec.	31	Adjusted the BCE investment to its current market value of $7,000.

1. Journalize Knowlton investment transactions. Explanations are not required.
2. Show how to report the investment and any unrealized gain or loss on Knowlton's balance sheet at December 31, 2008. Ignore income tax.

Accounting for the sale of an available-for-sale investment
(Obj. 1)

S10-2 Use the data given in Short Exercise 10-1. On May 19, 2009, Knowlton sold its investment in BCE shares for $26 per share.

1. Journalize the sale. No explanation is required.
2. How does the gain or loss that you recorded here differ from the gain or loss that was recorded at December 31, 2008?

Accounting for a 40% investment in another company
(Obj. 2)

S10-3 Suppose on February 1, 2008, **General Motors** paid $41 million for a 40% investment in ABC Ltd., an auto parts manufacturer. Assume ABC earned net income of $6 million and paid cash dividends of $2 million during 2008.

1. What method should General Motors use to account for the investment in ABC? Give your reason.
2. Journalize these three transactions on the books of General Motors. Show all amounts in millions of dollars, and include an explanation for each entry.
3. Post to the Long-Term Investment T-account. What is its balance after all the transactions are posted?

Accounting for the sale of an equity-method investment
(Obj. 2)

S10-4 Use the data given in Short Exercise 10-3. Assume that in November 2009, **General Motors** sold half its investment in ABC to Toyota. The sale price was $14 million. Compute General Motors' gain or loss on the sale.

Understanding consolidated financial statements
(Obj. 3)

S10-5 Answer these questions about consolidation accounting:

1. Define *parent company*. Define *subsidiary company*.
2. How do consolidated financial statements differ from the financial statements of a single company?
3. Which company's name appears on the consolidated financial statements? How much of the subsidiary's shares must the parent own before reporting consolidated statements?

Understanding goodwill and minority interest
(Obj. 3)

S10-6 Two accounts that arise from consolidation accounting are goodwill and minority interest.

1. What is *goodwill*, and how does it arise? Which company reports goodwill, the parent or the subsidiary? Where is goodwill reported?
2. What is minority interest, and which company reports it, the parent or the subsidiary? Where is minority interest reported?

S10-7 Suppose **Prudential Bache (PB)** buys $1,000,000 of **CitiCorp** bonds at a price of 101. The CitiCorp bonds pay cash interest at the annual rate of 7% and mature at the end of 5 years.

Working with a bond investment
(Obj. 4)

1. How much did PB pay to purchase the bond investment? How much will PB collect when the bond investment matures?
2. How much cash interest will PB receive each year from CitiCorp?
3. Will PB's annual interest revenue on the bond investment be more or less than the amount of cash interest received each year? Give your reason.
4. Compute PB's first-year interest revenue on this bond investment. Use the effective interest of 6.75% to amortize the investment.

S10-8 Return to Short Exercise 10-7, the **Prudential Bache (PB)** investment in **CitiCorp** bonds. Journalize on PB's books:

Recording bond investment transactions
(Obj. 4)

a. Purchase of the bond investment on January 2, 2006. PB expects to hold the investment to maturity.
b. Receipt of annual cash interest on December 31, 2006.
c. Amortization of the bonds on December 31, 2006.
d. Collection of the investment's face value at the maturity date on January 2, 2011. (Assume the receipt of 2010 interest and the amortization of bonds for 2010 have already been recorded, so ignore these entries.)

S10-9 Suppose **Coca-Cola Canada (CCC)** sells soft-drink syrup to a Russian company on September 14. CCC agrees to accept 2,000,000 Russian rubles. On the date of sale, the ruble is quoted at $0.0346. CCC collects half the receivable on October 19, when the ruble is worth $0.0339. Then, on November 10, when the foreign-exchange rate of the ruble is $0.035, CCC collects the final amount.

Accounting for transactions stated in a foreign currency
(Obj. 5)

Journalize these three transactions for CCC.

S10-10 Shipp Belting Ltd. sells goods for 1,000,000 Mexican pesos. The foreign-exchange rate for a peso is $0.085 on the date of sale, July 31, 2009. Shipp Belting then collects cash on August 28, when the exchange rate for a peso is $0.089. Record Shipp's cash collection.

Accounting for transactions stated in a foreign currency
(Obj. 5)

Shipp Belting buys inventory for 20,000 Swiss francs. A Swiss franc costs $1.0826 on the purchase date, August 25, 2009. Record Shipp Belting's payment of cash on September 29, 2009, when the exchange rate for a Swiss franc is $1.0831.

In these two scenarios, which currencies strengthened and which weakened?

S10-11 Exhibit 10-11, page 502, outlines some differences between accounting in Canada and accounting in other countries. Canadian companies conduct a lot of business with American companies. But there are important differences between American and Canadian accounting. In your own words, describe the differences and similarities for inventories, goodwill, and research and development among Canada, the United States, Japan, and Germany.

International accounting differences
(Obj. 5)

S10-12 Companies divide their cash flows into three categories for reporting on the cash flow statement.

Reporting cash flows
(Obj. 6)

1. List the three categories of cash flows in the order they appear on the cash flow statement. Which category of cash flows is most closely related to this chapter?
2. Identify two types of transactions that companies report as cash flows from investing activities.

EXERCISES

E10-13 Journalize the following long-term available-for-sale investment transactions of Solomon Brothers Department Stores:

Journalizing transactions for an available-for-sale investment
(Obj. 1)

a. Purchased 400 shares of **Royal Bank of Canada** at $40 per share, with the intent of holding the shares for the indefinite future.
b. Received cash dividend of $0.50 per share on the Royal Bank of Canada investment.
c. At year-end, adjusted the investment account to current market value of $35 per share.
d. Sold the shares for the market price of $30 per share.

Accounting for long-term investments
(Obj. 1)

E10-14 Dow-Smith Ltd. bought 3,000 common shares of **Shoppers Drug Mart** at $50, 600 common shares of **Bank of Montreal (BMO)** at $42.50, and 1,400 common shares of **EnCana** at $93.36, all as available-for-sale investments. At December 31, **TSX Online** reports Shoppers shares at $48.05, BMO's shares at $31.25, and EnCana's shares at $56.96.

❙ *Required*

1. Determine the cost and the market value of the long-term investment portfolio at December 31.

2. Record Dow-Smith's adjusting entry at December 31.

3. What would Dow-Smith report on its income statement and balance sheet for the information given? Make the necessary disclosures. Ignore income tax.

Accounting for transactions under the equity method
(Obj. 2)

E10-15 Research In Motion (RIM) owns equity-method investments in several companies. Suppose RIM paid $1,000,000 to acquire a 25% investment in Thai Software Company. Thai Software reported net income of $640,000 for the first year and declared and paid cash dividends of $420,000.

1. Record the following in RIM's journal: (a) purchase of the investment, (b) RIM's proportion of Thai Software's net income, and (c) receipt of the cash dividends.

2. What is the ending balance in RIM's investment account?

Measuring gain or loss on the sale of an equity-method investment
(Obj. 2)

E10-16 Without making journal entries, record the transactions of Exercise 10-15 directly in the RIM account, Long-Term Investment in Thai Software. Assume that after all the noted transactions took place, RIM sold its entire investment in Thai Software for cash of $2,700,000. How much is RIM's gain or loss on the sale of the investment?

Applying the appropriate accounting method for a 30% investment
(Obj. 2)

E10-17 Oaktree Financial Inc. paid $500,000 for a 25% investment in the common shares of eTrav Inc. For the first year, eTrav reported net income of $200,000 and at year-end declared and paid cash dividends of $100,000. On the balance sheet date, the market value of Oaktree's investment in eTrav shares was $384,000.

❙ *Required*

1. Which method is appropriate for Oaktree Financial to use in accounting for its investment in eTrav? Why?

2. Show everything that Oaktree would report for the investment and any investment revenue in its year-end financial statements.

Preparing a consolidated balance sheet
(Obj. 3)

E10-18 Merryhill Inc. owns Green Meadows Ltd. The two companies' individual balance sheets follow:

	Merryhill	Green Meadows
Assets		
Cash	$ 49,000	$ 14,000
Accounts receivable, net	82,000	53,000
Note receivable from Merryhill	—	42,000
Inventory	55,000	77,000
Investment in Green Meadows	100,000	—
Property, plant, and equipment, net	286,000	99,000
Other assets	22,000	8,000
Total	$594,000	$293,000
Liabilities and Shareholders' Equity		
Accounts payable	$ 44,000	$ 26,000
Notes payable	147,000	36,000
Other liabilities	82,000	131,000
Common shares	210,000	80,000
Retained earnings	111,000	20,000
Total	$594,000	$293,000

I Required

1. Prepare the consolidated balance sheet of Merryhill Inc. It is sufficient to complete the consolidation worksheet.
2. What is the amount of shareholders' equity for the consolidated entity?

E10-19 Assume that on September 30, 2004, **Manulife Financial** paid 91 for 7% bonds of **Hydro-Québec** as a long-term held-to-maturity investment. The effective interest rate was 8%. The maturity value of the bonds will be $20,000 on September 30, 2009. The bonds pay interest on March 31 and September 30.

Recording bond investment transactions
(Obj. 4)

I Required

1. What method should Manulife use to account for its investment in the Hydro-Québec bonds?
2. Using the effective interest method of amortizing the bonds, journalize all of Manulife's transactions on the bonds for 2004.
3. Show how Manulife would report everything related to the bond investment on its balance sheet at December 31, 2004.

E10-20 Assume that **Future Shop** completed the following foreign-currency transaction:

Managing and accounting for foreign-currency transactions
(Obj. 5)

Mar.	17	Purchased DVD players as inventory on account from Sony. The price was 300,000 yen, and the exchange rate of the yen was $0.01341.
Apr.	16	Paid Sony when the exchange rate was $0.0129
	19	Sold merchandise on account to Bon Temps, a French company, at a price of 60,000 euros. The exchange rate was $1.6051.
	30	Collected from Bon Temps when the exchange rate was $1.5903

1. Journalize these transactions for Future Shop. Focus on the gains and losses caused by changes in foreign-currency rates.
2. On March 18, immediately after the purchase, and on April 20, immediately after the sale, which currencies did Future Shop want to strengthen? Which currencies did in fact strengthen? Explain your reasoning in detail.

E10-21 Translate into dollars the balance sheet of Assiniboine Leather Goods Inc.'s Spanish subsidiary. When Assiniboine Leather Goods acquired the foreign subsidiary, a euro was worth $1.60. The current exchange rate is $1.70. During the period when retained earnings were earned, the average exchange rate was $1.58 per euro.

Translating a foreign-currency balance sheet into dollars
(Obj. 5)

	Euros
Assets	500,000
Liabilities	300,000
Shareholders' equity:	
Common shares	50,000
Retained earnings	150,000
	500,000

During the period covered by this situation, which currency was stronger, the dollar or the euro?

E10-22 During fiscal year 2009, Donuts 'R' Us Inc. reported net loss of $135.8 million. Donuts received $1.0 million from the sale of other businesses. Donuts made capital expenditures of $10.4 million and sold property, plant, and equipment for $7.3 million. The company purchased long-term investments at a cost of $12.2 million and sold other long-term investments for $2.5 million.

Preparing and using the cash flow statement
(Obj. 6)

I *Required*

Prepare the investing activities section of the Donuts 'R' Us cash flow statement. Based solely on Donuts' investing activities, does it appear that the company is growing or shrinking? How can you tell?

Using the cash flow statement
(Obj. 6)

E10-23 At the end of the year, Blue Chip Properties Ltd.'s cash flow statement reported the following for investment activities:

Blue Chip Properties Ltd.	
Consolidated Cash Flow Statement (Partial)	
Cash Flows from Investing Activities	
Notes receivable collected...	$ 3,110,000
Purchases of short-term investments...	(3,457,000)
Proceeds from sales of equipment...	1,409,000*
Proceeds from sales of investments (cost of $450,000).......................	461,000
Expenditures for property, plant, and equipment...............................	(1,761,000)
Net cash used by investing activities..	$ (238,000)

*Cost $5,100,000; Accumulated amortization, $3,691,000

I *Required*

For each item listed, make the journal entry that placed the item on Blue Chip's cash flow statement.

CHALLENGE EXERCISES

Accounting for various types of investments
(Obj. 1, 2, 3, 5)

E10-24 This exercise summarizes the accounting for investments. Suppose **YouTube.ca** owns the following investment at December 31, 2009:

a. 100% of the common shares of YouTube United Kingdom, which holds assets of £800,000 and owes a total of £600,000. At December 31, 2009, the current exchange rate of the pound (£) is £1 = $1.80. The translation rate of the pound applicable to shareholders' equity is £1 = $1.70. During 2009, YouTube United Kingdom earned net income of £100,000 and the average exchange rate for the year was £1 = $1.85. YouTube United Kingdom paid cash dividends of £40,000 during 2009.

b. Investments that YouTube is holding for trade. These investments cost $900,000 and declined in value by $400,000 during 2009, but they paid cash dividends of $16,000 to YouTube. One year ago, at December 31, 2008, the market value of these investments was $1,100,000.

c. 25% of the common shares of YouTube Financing Associates. During 2009, YouTube Financing earned net income of $300,000 and declared and paid cash dividends of $80,000. The carrying amount of this investment was $700,000 at December 31, 2008.

I *Required*

1. Which method is used to account for each investment?
2. By how much did each of these investments increase or decrease YouTube's net income during 2009?
3. For investment b and c, show how YouTube would report these investments on its balance sheet at December 31, 2009.

E10-25 Big-Box Retail Corporation reported shareholders' equity on its balance sheet at December 31, 2009, as follows:

Explaining and analyzing accumulated other comprehensive income **(Obj. 1, 6)**

Big Box Retail Corporation
Balance Sheet (Partial)
December 31, 2009

	Millions
Shareholders' Equity:	
Common shares, $0.10	
800 million shares authorized, 300 million shares issued............................	$1,113
Retained earnings...	6,250
Accumulated other comprehensive income (loss).......................................	(?)

❙ Required

1. Identify the two components that typically make up Accumulated other comprehensive income.
2. For each component of Accumulated other comprehensive income, describe the event that can cause a *positive* balance. Also describe the events that can cause a negative balance for each component.
3. At December 31, 2008, Big-Box's Accumulated other comprehensive loss was $53 million. Then, during 2009, Big-Box had a positive foreign-currency translation adjustment of $29 million and an unrealized loss of $16 million on available-for-sale investments. What was Big-Box's balance of Accumulated other comprehensive income (loss) at December 31, 2009?

QUIZ

Test your understanding of long-term investments and international operations by answering the following questions. Select the best choice from among the possible answers given.

Questions 10-26 through 10-28 use the following data:

Assume that Maritimes Holdings Inc. owns the following long-term available-for-sale investment:

December 31, 2009

Company	Number of Shares	Cost per Share	Current Market Value per Share	Dividend per Share
Airbus Corp.	1,000	$60	$71	$2
Whole Grains Inc.	200	9	11	1.50
MySpace Ltd.	500	20	24	1

Q10-26 Maritime's balance sheet at December 31, 2009, should report

a. Investments of $85,200
b. Investments of $81,200
c. Dividend revenue of $2,800
d. Unrealized loss of $13,400

Q10-27 Maritime's 2009 income statement should report

a. Investments of $71,800
b. Gain on sale of investment of $13,400
c. Unrealized gain of $13,400
d. Dividend revenue of $2,800

Q10-28 Suppose Maritime sells the Airbus shares for $68 per share, February 2, 2010. Journalize the sale.

Q10-29 Dividends received on an equity-method investment

a. Increase the investment account
b. Decrease the investment account
c. Increase dividend revenue
d. Increase owners' equity

Q10-30 The starting point in accounting for all investments is
a. Market value on the balance sheet date   c. Cost
b. Equity value   d. Cost minus dividends

Q10-31 Consolidation accounting
a. Combines the accounts of the parent company and those of the subsidiary companies
b. Eliminates all liabilities
c. Reports the receivables and payables of the parent company only
d. All of the above

Q10-32 On January 1, 2008, Vallée Bleue Ltée purchased $100,000 face value of the 7% bonds of Mail Frontier Inc. at 105. Interest is paid on January 1. The bonds mature on January 1, 2009. For the year ended December 31, 2008, Vallée Bleu received cash interest of
a. $5,000   c. $6,400
b. $6,000   d. $7,000

Q10-33 Return to Vallée Bleue's bond investment in question 10-32. Assume an effective interest rate of 6%. For the year ended December 31, 2008, Vallée Bleu earned interest revenue of
a. $5,000   c. $7,000
b. $6,300   d. $7,700

Q10-34 Yukon Systems purchased inventory on account from **Panasonic**. The price was ¥100,000, and a yen was quoted at $0.0129. Yukon paid the debt in yen a month later, when the price of a yen was $0.0134. Yukon
a. Debited Inventory for $1,290
b. Debited Inventory for $1,340
c. Recorded a Foreign-Currency Transaction Loss of $50
d. None of the above

Q10-35 One way to avoid a foreign-currency transaction loss is to
a. Pay in the foreign currency
b. Collect in your own currency
c. Offset foreign currency inventory and plant assets
d. Pay debts as late as possible

Q10-36 Foreign-currency transaction gains and losses are reported on the
a. Balance sheet   c. Cash flow statement
b. Consolidation worksheet   d. Income statement

Q10-37 Consolidation of a foreign subsidiary usually results in a
a. Gain on consolidation   c. Foreign-currency translation adjustment
b. Loss on consolidation   d. Foreign-currency transaction gain or loss

PROBLEMS

(GROUP A)

Reporting investments on the balance sheet and the related revenue on the income statement
(Obj. 1, 2)

P10-38A Winnipeg Exchanges Ltd. completed the following long-term investment transactions during 2009.

2009		
May	12	Purchased 20,000 shares, which make up 35% of the common shares of Fellingham Corporation at a total cost of $370,000
July	9	Received annual cash dividend of $1.26 per share on the Fellingham investment
Sept.	16	Purchased 800 common shares of Tomassini Inc. as an available-for-sale investment, paying $41.50 per share
Oct.	30	Received cash dividend of $0.30 per share on the Tomassini investment
Dec.	31	Received annual report from Fellingham Corporation. Net income for the year was $510,000.

At year-end the current market value of the Tomassini shares is $30,600. The market value of the Fellingham shares is $652,000.

I Required

1. For which investment is current market value used in the accounting? Why is market value used for one investment and not the other?

2. Show what Winnipeg Exchange Ltd. would report on its year-end balance sheet and income statement for these investment transactions. It is helpful to use a T-account for the Long-Term Investment in Fellingham shares account. Ignore income tax.

P10-39A The beginning balance sheet of New Technology Corporation included the following:

Accounting for available-for-sale and equity-method investments
(Obj. 1, 2)

Long-Term Investment in MSC Software (equity-method investment)................... $619,000

New Technology completed the following investment transactions during the year 2009:

Mar.	16	Purchased 2,000 shares of ATI Inc. as a long-term available-for-sale investment, paying $12.25 per share
May	21	Received cash dividend of $0.75 per share on the ATI investment
Aug.	17	Received cash dividend of $81,000 from MSC Software
Dec.	31	Received annual report from MSC Software. Net income for the year was $550,000. Of this amount, New Technology's proportion is 22%.

At year-end, the market values of New Technology's investments are ATI, $25,700, and MSC, $700,000.

I Required

1. Record the transactions in the journal of New Technology Corporation.

2. Post entries to the T-account for Long-Term Investment in MSC and determine its balance at December 31, 2009.

3. Show how to report the Long-Term Available-for-Sale Investment and the Long-Term Investment in MSC accounts on New Technology's balance sheet at December 31, 2009.

P10-40A This problem demonstrates the dramatic effect that consolidation accounting can have on a company's ratios. ABC Company owns 100% of ABC Credit Corporation, its financing subsidiary. ABC's main operations consist of manufacturing automotive products. ABC Credit Corporation mainly helps people finance the purchase of automobiles from ABC and its dealers. The two companies' individual balance sheets are adapted and summarized as follows (amounts in billions):

Analyzing consolidated financial statements
(Obj. 3)

	ABC (Parent)	ABC Credit (Subsidiary)
Total assets...	$94.8	$179.0
Total liabilities..	$68.4	$164.7
Total shareholders' equity....................................	26.4	14.3
Total liabilities and equity...................................	$94.8	$179.0

Assume that ABC Credit's liabilities include $1.8 billion owed to ABC, the parent company.

I Required

1. Compute the debt ratio of ABC Company considered alone.

2. Determine the consolidated total assets, total liabilities, and shareholders' equity of ABC Company after consolidating the financial statements of ABC Credit into the totals of ABC, the parent company.

3. Recompute the debt ratio of the consolidated entity. Why do companies prefer not to consolidate their financing subsidiaries into their own financial statements?

Consolidating a wholly-owned subsidiary
(Obj. 3)

P10-41A Direct Express Inc. paid $266,000 to acquire all the common shares of We-Pack Corporation, and We-Pack owes Direct $81,000 on a note payable. Immediately after the purchase on September 30, 2009, the two companies' balance sheets looked as follows.

	Direct	We-Pack
Assets		
Cash	$ 24,000	$ 20,000
Accounts receivable, net	91,000	42,000
Note receivable from We-Pack	81,000	—
Inventory	19,000	214,000
Investment in We-Pack	266,000	—
Property, plant, and equipment, net	278,000	219,000
Total	$759,000	$495,000
Liabilities and Shareholders' Equity		
Account payable	$ 57,000	$ 49,000
Notes payable	175,000	149,000
Other liabilities	129,000	31,000
Common shares	150,000	118,000
Retained earnings	248,000	148,000
Total	$759,000	$495,000

I Required

Prepare the consolidated balance sheet of Direct Express. (It is sufficient to complete a consolidation worksheet.)

Accounting for a bond investment purchased at a premium
(Obj. 4)

P10-42A Insurance companies and pension plans hold large quantities of bond investments. Prairie Insurance Corp. purchased $600,000 of 5% bonds of Eaton Inc. for 104.5 on March 1, 2008, when the effective interest rate was 4%. These bonds pay interest on March 1 and September 1 each year. They mature on March 1, 2013. At February 28, 2009, the market price of the bonds is 103.5.

I Required

1. Journalize Prairie's purchase of the bonds as a long-term investment on March 1, 2008 (to be held to maturity), receipt of cash interest and amortization of the bond investment on September 1, 2008, and accrual of interest revenue and amortization at February 28, 2009. Use the effective-interest method for amortizing the bond investment.

2. Show all financial statement effects of this long-term bond investment on Prairie Insurance Corp.'s balance sheet and income statement at February 28, 2009.

Recording foreign-currency transactions and reporting the transaction gain or loss
(Obj. 5)

P10-43A Suppose **Bridgestone Corporation** completed the following international transactions:

May	1	Sold inventory on account to Mezzo, an Italian company, for €82,000. The exchange rate of the euro is $1.60, and Mezzo demands to pay in euros.
	10	Purchased supplies on account from an American company at a price of $50,000 in U.S. dollars. The exchange rate of the U.S. dollar is $1.20, and payment will be in U.S. dollars.
	17	Sold inventory on account to an English firm for £100,000. Payment will be in British pounds. The exchange rate is £1 = $1.80.
	22	Collected from Mezzo. The exchange rate is €1 = $1.65.
June	18	Paid the American company. The exchange rate of the U.S. dollar is $1.22.
	24	Collected from the English firm: The exchange rate is £1 = $1.75.

I Required

1. Record these transactions in Bridgestone's journal, and show how to report the transaction gain or loss on the income statement.

2. How will what you learned in this problem help you structure international transactions?

P10-44A Assume that **Research In Motion (RIM)** has a subsidiary company based in Japan.

Measuring and explaining the foreign-currency translation adjustment
(Obj. 5)

I *Required*

1. Translate into dollars the foreign-currency balance sheet of the Japanese subsidiary of RIM.

	Yen
Assets	300,000,000
Liabilities	80,000,000
Shareholders' equity:	
Common shares	20,000,000
Retained earnings	200,000,000
	300,000,000

When RIM acquired this subsidiary, the Japanese yen was worth $0.0134. The current exchange rate is $0.0137. During the period when the subsidiary earned its income, the average exchange rate was $0.0135 per yen.

Before you perform the foreign-currency translation calculations, indicate whether RIM has experienced a positive or a negative translation adjustment. State whether the adjustment is a gain or a loss, and show where it is reported in the financial statements.

2. To which company does the foreign-currency translation adjustment "belong"? In which company's financial statements will the translation adjustment be reported?

P10-45A Excerpts from Smart Pro Inc.'s cash flow statement appear as follows:

Using a cash flow statement
(Obj. 6)

Smart Pro Inc.		
Consolidated Cash Flow Statement (Partial, adapted)		
For the Years Ended December 31		
(In millions)	2009	2008
Cash and cash equivalents, beginning of year	$ 2,976	$ 3,695
Net cash provided by operating activities	8,654	12,827
Cash flows provided by (used for) investing activities:		
Additions to property, plant, and equipment	(7,309)	(6,674)
Acquisitions of other companies	(883)	(2,317)
Purchases of available-for-sale investments	(7,141)	(17,188)
Sales of available-for-sale investments	15,138	16,144
Net cash (used for) investing activities	(195)	(10,035)
Cash flows provided by (used for) financing activities:		
Borrowing	329	215
Retirement of long-term debt	(10)	(46)
Proceeds from issuance of shares	762	797
Repurchase of common shares	(4,008)	(4,007)
Payment of dividends to shareholders	(538)	(470)
Net cash (used for) financing activities	(3,465)	(3,511)
Net increase (decrease) in cash and cash equivalents	4,994	(719)
Cash and cash equivalents, end of year	$ 7,970	$ 2,976

I *Required*

As the chief executive officer of Smart Pro Inc. your duty is to write the management letter to your shareholders to explain Smart Pro's investing activities during 2009. Compare the company's level of investment with the preceding year, and indicate the major way the company financed its investments during 2009. Net income for 2009 was $1,291 million.

(GROUP B)

P10-46B Homestead Financial Corporation owns numerous investments in the shares of other companies. Homestead Financial completed the following long-term investment transactions:

2009		
May	1	Purchased 8,000 shares, which make up 25% of the common shares of Mars Company at total cost of $450,000
Sept.	15	Received a cash dividend of $1.40 per share on the Mars investment
Oct.	12	Purchased 1,000 common shares of Mercury Corporation as an available-for-sale investment paying $22.50 per share
Dec.	14	Received a cash dividend of $0.75 per share on the Mercury investment
	31	Received annual report from Mars Company. Net income for the year was $350,000.

At year-end the current market value of the Mercury shares is $19,200. The market value of the Mars shares is $740,000.

❙ Required

1. For which investment is current market value used in the accounting? Why is market value used for one investment and not the other?
2. Show what Homestead Financial will report on its year-end balance sheet and income statement for these investments. (It is helpful to use a T-account for the Long-Term Investment in Mars shares account.) Ignore income tax.

P10-47B The beginning balance sheet of Dealmaker Securities Limited included the following:

Long-Term Investments in Affiliates (equity-method investments)........................ $409,000

Dealmaker completed the following investment transactions during the year:

Feb.	16	Purchased 10,000 shares of BCM Software common shares as a long-term available-for-sale investment, paying $9.25 per share
May	14	Received cash dividend of $0.82 per share on the BCM investment
Oct.	15	Received cash dividend of $29,000 from an affiliated company
Dec.	31	Received annual reports from affiliated companies. Their total net income for the year was $620,000. Of this amount, Dealmaker's proportion is 25%.

The market values of Dealmaker's investments are BCM, $89,000, and affiliated companies, $947,000.

❙ Required

1. Record the transactions in the journal of Dealmaker Securities.
2. Post entries to the Long-Term Investments in Affiliates T-account, and determine its balance at December 31.
3. Show how to report Long-Term Available-for-Sale Investments and Long-Term Investments in Affiliates on Dealmaker's balance sheet at December 31.

P10-48B This problem demonstrates the dramatic effect that consolidation accounting can have on a company's ratios. Organic Food Growers Inc. owns 100% of Perfect Packaging Ltd. Organic Food Growers uses Perfect Packaging products to ensure freshness in its delivered products. The two companies' individual balance sheets are summarized as follows (amounts in millions):

	Organic Food Growers (Parent)	Perfect Packaging (Subsidiary)
Total assets	$145.8	$105.9
Total liabilities	$122.4	96.7
Total shareholders' equity	23.4	9.2
Total liabilities and equity	$145.8	$105.9

Assume that Perfect Packaging's liabilities include $5.1 million owed to Organic Food Growers, the parent company.

Required

1. Compute the debt ratio of Organic Food Growers considered alone.
2. Determine the consolidated total assets, total liabilities, and shareholders' equity of Organic Food Growers after consolidating the financial statements of Perfect Packaging into the totals of Organic Food Growers, the parent company.
3. Recompute the debt ratio of the consolidated entity.

P10-49B Flemingwood Corporation paid $179,000 to acquire all the common shares of Bos Ltd., and Bos owes Flemingwood $55,000 on a note payable. Immediately after the purchase on June 30, 2009, the two companies' balance sheets were as follows:

Consolidating a wholly-owned subsidiary
(Obj. 3)

	Flemingwood	Bos
Assets		
Cash	$ 48,000	$ 32,000
Accounts receivable, net	264,000	43,000
Note receivable from Bos	55,000	—
Inventory	193,000	153,000
Investment in Bos	179,000	—
Property, plant, and equipment, net	105,000	138,000
Total	$844,000	$366,000
Liabilities and Shareholders' Equity		
Accounts payable	$ 76,000	$ 37,000
Notes payable	118,000	123,000
Other liabilities	174,000	27,000
Common shares	82,000	90,000
Retained earnings	394,000	89,000
Total	$844,000	$366,000

Required

Prepare Flemingwood's consolidated balance sheet. (It is sufficient to complete a consolidation worksheet.)

P10-50B Financial institutions hold large quantities of bond investments. Suppose **Sun Life Financial** purchases $500,000 of 6% bonds of General Components Corporation for 88 on January 1, 2009, when the effective interest rate was 8%. These bonds pay interest on January 1 and July 1 each year. They mature on January 1, 2017. At December 31, 2009, the market price of the bonds is 90.

Accounting for a bond investment purchased at a discount
(Obj. 4)

Required

1. Journalize Sun Life's purchase of the bonds as a long-term investment on January 1, 2009 (to be held to maturity), receipt of cash interest and amortization of the bond investment on July 1, 2009, and accrual of interest revenue and amortization at December 31, 2009. Use the effective-interest method for amortizing the bond investment.
2. Show all financial statement effects of this long-term bond investment on Sun Life's balance sheet and income statement at December 31, 2009.

P10-51B Sun Power Drinks Inc. (SPD) completed the following international transactions:

Apr.	4	Sold soft-drink syrup on account to a Mexican company for $81,000. The exchange rate of the Mexican peso is $0.085, and the customer agrees to pay in Canadian dollars.
	13	Purchased inventory on account from an American company at a price of 100,000 U.S. dollars. The exchange rate of the U.S. dollar is $1.20 and payment will be in U.S. dollars.
	20	Sold goods on account to an English firm for £70,000. Payment will be in British pounds, and the exchange rate of the pound is $1.80.
	27	Collected from the Mexican company.
May	21	Paid the American company. The exchange rate of the U.S. dollar is $1.22.
June	17	Collected from the English firm. The exchange rate of the British pound is $1.85.

❙ Required

1. Record these transactions in Sun's journal and show how to report the transaction gain or loss on the income statement.
2. How will what you learned in this problem help you structure international transactions?

P10-52B Arte Fabrics Ltd. owns a subsidiary based in France.

❙ Required

1. Translate the foreign-currency balance sheet of the French subsidiary of Arte Fabrics Ltd. into dollars. When Arte Fabrics acquired this subsidiary, the euro was worth $1.60. The current exchange rate is $1.80 per euro. During the period when the subsidiary earned its income, the average exchange rate was $1.70 per euro.

	Euros
Assets	3,000,000
Liabilities	1,000,000
Shareholders' equity:	
Common shares	300,000
Retained earnings	1,700,000
	3,000,000

Before you perform the foreign-currency translation calculation, indicate whether Arte Fabrics has experienced a positive or a negative foreign-currency translation adjustment. State whether the adjustment is a gain or a loss, and show where it is reported in the financial statements.

2. To which company does the translation adjustment "belong"? In which company's financial statements will the translation adjustment be reported?

P10-53B WestJet Airlines Ltd.'s cash flow statement, as adapted, appears as follows:

Using a cash flow statement
(Obj. 6)

WestJet Airlines Ltd.
Consolidated Cash Flow Statement
For the Years Ended December 31 (Stated in thousands of Canadian dollars)

	2007	2006
Cash flows from (used in):		
Operating activities:		
Net earnings	$ 192,833	$ 114,676
Items not involving cash:		
Depreciation and amortization	127,223	111,442
Amortization of other liabilities	(897)	(868)
Amortization of hedge settlements	1,400	1,427
Net realized loss on cash flow hedge	18	—
Loss on disposal of property and equipment and		
aircraft parts	32,773	394
Stock-based compensation expense	20,058	21,205
Future income tax expense	41,775	46,635
Unrealized foreign exchange loss (gain)	13,813	(346)
Decrease in non-cash working capital	112,069	43,707
	541,065	338,272
Financing activities:		
Increase in long-term debt	141,178	418,581
Repayment of long-term debt	(156,516)	(132,559)
Decrease in obligations under capital lease	(356)	(480)
Share issuance costs	—	(10)
Shares repurchased	(21,250)	—
Issuance of common shares	1,551	—
Increase in other assets	(20,897)	(27,830)
Increase in non-cash working capital	(3,000)	(1,071)
	(59,290)	256,631
Investing activities:		
Aircraft additions	(191,437)	(438,906)
Aircraft disposals	1,975	3,822
Other property and equipment additions	(24,639)	(43,590)
Other property and equipment disposals	13,819	1,611
	(200,282)	(477,063)
Cash flow from operating, financing, and investing activities	281,493	117,840
Effect of exchange rate on cash	(5,452)	37
Net change in cash	276,041	117,877
Cash, beginning of year	377,517	259,640
Cash, end of year	$ 653,558	$ 377,517

Cash is defined as cash and cash equivalents.

❙ *Required*

As a member of an investment club, you have been asked to review WestJet's major investing activities during 2007. Compare the company's level of investment with the previous year, and indicate how the company financed its investments during 2007.

APPLY YOUR KNOWLEDGE

DECISION CASES

Making an investment decision
(Obj. 1, 5)

Case 1. Infografix Corporation's consolidated sales for 2009 were $26.6 million and expenses totalled $24.8 million. Infografix operates worldwide and conducts 37% of its business outside Canada. During 2009, Infografix reported the following items in its financial statements (amounts in millions):

Foreign-currency translation adjustments...	$(202)
Unrealized holding on available-for-sale investments..	(328)

As you consider an investment in Infografix shares, some concerns arise. Answer the following questions:

1. What do the parentheses around the two dollar amounts signify?

2. Are these items reported as assets, liabilities, shareholders' equity, revenues, or expenses? Are they normal-balance accounts, or are they contra accounts?

3. Are these items reason for rejoicing or sorrow at Infografix? Are Infografix's emotions about these items deep or only moderate? Why?

4. Did Infografix include these items in net income? Did it include these items in retained earnings? In the final analysis, how much net income did Infografix report for 2009?

5. Should these items scare you away from investing in Infografix shares? Why or why not?

Making an investment sale decision
(Obj. 1, 2, 4)

Case 2. Cathy Talbert is the general manager of Barham Ltd., which provides data-management services for physicians in the Regina, Saskatchewan, area. Barham is having a rough year. Net income trails projections for the year by almost $75,000. This shortfall is especially important. Barham plans to issue shares early next year and needs to show investors that the company can meet its earnings targets.

Barham holds several investments purchased a few years ago. Even though investing in shares is outside Barham's core business of data-management services, Talbert thinks these investments may hold the key to helping the company meet its net income goal for the year. She is considering what to do with the following investments:

1. Barham owns 50% of the common shares of Prairie Office Systems, which provides the business forms that Barham uses. Prairie Office Systems has lost money for the past 2 years but still has a retained earnings balance of $550,000. Talbert thinks she can get Prairie's treasurer to declare a $160,000 cash dividend, half of which would go to Barham.

2. Barham owns a bond investment with a 4% coupon rate and an annual interest payment. The bond was purchased 8 years ago for $293,000. The purchase price represents a discount from the bonds' maturity value of $400,000 based on an effective rate of 8%. These bonds mature 2 years from now, and their current market value is $380,000. Ms. Talbert has checked with a Scotiabank investment representative and Talbert is considering selling the bonds. A charge of 1% commission would be made on the sale transaction.

3. Barham owns 5,000 **Royal Bank of Canada (RBC)** shares valued at $53 per share. One year ago, RBC was worth only $28 per share. Barham purchased the RBC shares for $37 per share. Talbert wonders whether Barham should sell the RBC shares.

❚ *Required*

Evaluate all three actions as a way for Barham Ltd. to generate the needed amount of income. Recommend the best way for Barham to achieve its net income goal.

ETHICAL ISSUE

Media One owns 15% of the voting shares of Online Inc. The remainder of the Online shares are held by numerous investors with small holdings. Austin Cohen, president of Media One and a member of Online's board of directors, heavily influences Online's policies.

Under the market value method of accounting for investments, Media One's net income increases as it receives dividend revenue from Online. Media One pays President Cohen a bonus computed as a percentage of Media One's net income. Therefore, Cohen can control his personal bonus to a certain extent by influencing Online's dividends.

A recession occurs in 2009, and Media One's income is low. Cohen uses his power to have Online pay a large cash dividend. The action requires Online to borrow in order to pay the dividend.

❘ *Required*

1. In getting Online to pay the large cash dividend, is Cohen acting within his authority as a member of the Online board of directors? Are Cohen's actions ethical? Whom can his actions harm?

2. Discuss how using the equity method of accounting for investment would decrease Cohen's potential for manipulating his bonus.

FOCUS ON FINANCIALS

Sun-Rype Products Ltd.

Sun-Rype's financial statements are given in Appendix A at the end of this book.

1. Does Sun-Rype have any subsidiaries? How can you tell?

2. Is Sun-Rype expanding or contracting its operations? How can you tell?

3. Does Sun-Rype engage in foreign-currency transactions? If so, what is the nature of the transactions?

Analyzing investments, consolidated statements, and international operations
(Obj. 3, 5, 6)

FOCUS ON ANALYSIS

Mullen Group Income Fund

Mullen Group's financial statements are given in Appendix B at the end of this book.

1. Does Mullen Group have any subsidiaries? How can you tell?

2. If Mullen Group has subsidiaries, what is Mullen Group's percentage of ownership? How can you tell?

3. Is Mullen Group expanding or contracting its operations? How can you tell?

4. Describe the type of long-term investments that Mullen Transportation holds.

5. Did Mullen Group's goodwill suffer any impairment during the year? How can you tell?

Analyzing goodwill, consolidated subsidiaries, and investments
(Obj. 1, 2, 3, 6)

GROUP PROJECT

Pick a stock from *The Globe and Mail* or other database or publication. Assume that your group purchases 1,000 shares as a long-term investment and that your 1,000 shares are less than 20% of the company's outstanding shares. Research the shares to determine whether the company pays cash dividends and, if so, how much and at what intervals.

❘ *Required*

1. Track the shares for a period assigned by your professor. Over the specified period, keep a daily record of the share price to see how well your investment has performed. Keep a

record of any dividends you would have received. End the period of your analysis with a month end, such as September 30 or December 31.

2. Journalize all transactions that you have experienced, including the share purchase, dividends received (both cash dividends and stock dividends), and any year-end adjustment required by the accounting method that is appropriate for your situation. Assume you will prepare financial statements on the ending date of your study.

3. Show what you will report on your company's balance sheet, income statement, and cash flow statement as a result of your investment transactions.

QUICK CHECK ANSWERS

1. *c*
2. *d (1,000 shares × $35 = $35,000)*
3. *a ($35,000 − $31,000 = $4,000)*
4. *b [$40,000 − (1,000 shares × $31) = $9,000]*
5. *b [$100,000 + 0.20 ($50,000 − $25,000) = $105,000]*
6. *c ($100,000 + 0.80 [$68,000 + 0.80($40,000)] = $180,000)*
7. *a*
8. *d*
9. *b ($1,000,000 in U.S. dollars × $1.25 = $1,250,000)*
10. *c*

The Income Statement and the Statement of Shareholders' Equity

11

Learning Objectives

1. **Analyze** a corporate income statement

2. **Account** for a corporation's income tax

3. **Analyze** a statement of shareholders' equity

4. **Understand** managers' and auditors' responsibilities for the financial statements

SPOTLIGHT

Bombardier has had another successful year, with profits up 18% for the year ended January 31, 2008. Its planes, trains, subway cars, and services are sold all over the world. You may have seen Bombardier's TV commercials in which people from all over the world in many languages recognize a train or plane as a Bombardier product.

Bombardier's income statement shows that sales and revenues were up in 2008. The company believes in innovation. It spent US$139 million on research and development. Earnings per share increased by 21%.

Bombardier Inc.
Consolidated Statements of Income
(In millions of US dollars, except per share amounts)

For the fiscal years ended January 31	2008	2007	2006
Revenues			
1. Manufacturing	$12,508	$10,512	$10,708
2. Services	3,016	2,738	2,537
3. Other	1,982	1,632	1,481
4.	17,506	14,882	14,726
5. Cost of sales	14,919	12,667	12,719
6. Selling, general and administrative	1,096	929	842
7. Research and development	139	173	175
8. Other expense (income)	(62)	18	–
9. Amortization	512	518	545
10. Special items	162	24	88
11.	16,766	14,329	14,369
12. Income from continuing operations before the following:...	740	553	357
13. Financing income	(225)	(157)	(156)
14. Financing expense	526	375	363
15. Income from continuing operations before income taxes....	439	335	150
16. Income taxes	122	92	15
17. Income from continuing operations	317	243	135
18. Income from discontinued operations, net of tax	–	25	114
19. **Net income**	$ 317	$ 268	$ 249
Earnings per share:			
Basic			
20. From continuing operations	$0.17	$0.12	$0.06
21. Net income	$0.17	$0.14	$0.13
Diluted			
22. From continuing operations	$0.16	$0.12	$0.06
23. Net income	$0.16	$0.14	$0.13

This chapter rounds out your coverage of the corporate income statement. After studying this material, you will have seen all the types of items that appear on an income statement. You'll also learn about earnings per share (lines 20 to 23), the most often-mentioned statistic in business. Finally, you'll learn about the statement of shareholders' equity, which is like an expanded version of the statement of retained earnings. Your new learning will help you analyze financial statements and use the information in decision making.

Net income. Income from continuing operations. Which number measures a company's progress? This chapter will help you make that decision. We begin with a basic question: how to evaluate the quality of earnings. The term *quality of earnings* refers to the characteristics of an earnings number that make it most useful for decision making.

Evaluating the Quality of Earnings

A corporation's net income (including earnings per share) receives more attention than any other item in the financial statements. To shareholders, a larger net income suggests a greater likelihood of dividends. To creditors, a larger net income indicates a better ability to pay debts.

Objective

1 **Analyze** a corporate income statement

Suppose you are considering investing in the shares of two companies that sell over the Internet. In reading their annual reports, you learn that the companies earned the same net income last year and that each company has increased its net income by 15% annually over the last five years.

The two companies are similar but they generate profits in different ways:

- Company A's income has resulted from continuing operations.

- Company B's sales have struggled. Its net income growth resulted from selling off land acquired years earlier.

In which company would you invest?

Company A holds the promise of better earnings in the future because it earns profits from *continuing operations*. We may expect Company A to match its past earnings in the future. Company B shows no growth in income from operations. Its net income results from *one-time transactions*—the selling off of assets. Sooner or later, Company B will run out of assets to sell. Investors would say that Company A's earnings are of *higher quality* because they are more likely to repeat in the future.

To explore the makeup and quality of earnings let's examine its various sources. Exhibit 11-1 provides a comprehensive example that we will use throughout the

EXHIBIT 11-1 Westmount Concepts Inc. Income Statement

Westmount Concepts Inc.
Income Statement
For the Year Ended December 31, 2009

1	Sales revenue			$500,000
2	Cost of goods sold			240,000
3	Gross margin			260,000
4	Operating expenses (detailed)			181,000
5	Operating income			79,000
	Other gains (losses):			
6	Loss on restructuring operations			(8,000)
7	Gain on sale of computers			9,000
8	Income from continuing operations before income tax			80,000
9	Income tax expense			25,600
10	Income before discontinued operations and extraordinary items			54,400
	Discontinued operations:			
11	Operating income	$30,000		
12	Less income tax	(9,600)	$20,400	
13	Gain on disposal of discontinued assets	10,000		
14	Less income tax	(3,200)	6,800	27,200
15	Income before extraordinary items			81,600
16	Extraordinary tornado loss		20,000	
17	Less income tax saving		(6,400)	(13,600)
18	Net income			$ 68,000
	Earnings per share (12,500 shares outstanding)			
19	Income before discontinued operations and extraordinary items			$4.35
20	Income from discontinued operations			2.18
21	Income before extraordinary items			6.53
22	Extraordinary loss			(1.09)
23	Net income			$5.44

Continuing operations (rows 1–10)
Special items (rows 11–18)
Earnings per share (rows 19–23)

chapter. It is the income statement of Westmount Concepts Inc., which produces specialized software for business applications.

Continuing Operations

In Exhibit 11-1, the topmost section of the income statement reports income from continuing operations (lines 1 to 10). This part of the business is expected to continue from period to period. **We may use this information to predict that Westmount Concepts Inc. will earn income of approximately $54,400 next year.**

The continuing operations of Westmount include three new items:

- During 2009, the *company restructured operations* at a loss of $8,000 (line 6). Restructuring costs include severance pay to laid-off workers and moving expenses for employees transferred to other locations. The restructuring loss is part of continuing operations because Westmount Concepts Inc. is remaining in the same line of business. But the restructuring loss is an "Other" item on the income statement because restructuring the business falls outside Westmount's core activity, which is selling software products.
- Westmount had a *gain on sale of computers* that it no longer needed (line 7), also outside the company's core business activity. This explains why the gain isn't part of operating income (lines 1 to 5).
- *Income tax expense* (line 9) is subtracted in arriving at income from continuing operations. Corporate income tax is a significant expense. The current range for tax rates for corporations in Canada that are similar to Westmount Concepts Inc. is 31% to 35%. Thus, we use an income tax rate of 32% in this illustration. The $25,600 income tax expense in Exhibit 11-1 equals the pre-tax income from continuing operations multiplied by the tax rate ($80,000 × 0.32 = $25,600).

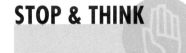

STOP & THINK

How much was Westmount Concepts Inc.'s total income tax expense during 2009? Consider lines 9, 12, 14, and 17 of the income statement in Exhibit 11-1.

Answer:

$32,000 = ($25,600 + $9,600 + $3,200 − $6,400)

DECISION   Which Income Number Predicts Future Profits?

How is income from continuing operations used in investment analysis? Suppose Laney Gibbs, an analyst with BMO Nesbitt Burns in Halifax, is estimating the value of Westmount Concepts Inc.'s common shares. Gibbs believes that Westmount can earn annual income each year equal to its income from continuing operations, $54,000 (rounded).

To estimate the value of Westmount Concepts Inc.'s common shares, financial analysts determine the present value (present value means the value today) of Westmount Concepts Inc.'s stream of future income. Gibbs must use some interest rate to compute the present value. Assume that an appropriate interest rate (i) for the valuation of Westmount is 12%. This rate is determined subjectively, based on the risk that Westmount might not be able to earn annual income from continuing operations of $54,000 (rounded) for the indefinite future. The rate is also called the **investment capitalization rate** because it is used to estimate the value of an investment. The higher the risk, the higher the rate, and vice versa. The computation of the estimated value of Westmount's common shares is

$$\text{Estimated value of Westmount Concepts Inc. common shares} = \frac{\text{Estimated future annual income}}{\text{Investment capitalization rate}} = \frac{\$54,000}{0.12} = \$450,000^*$$

*This valuation model has many forms, which are covered in finance classes. Here, we introduce the basic form.

Gibbs thus estimates that Westmount Concepts Inc. is worth $450,000. She would then compare this estimate to the current market value of Westmount Concepts Inc.'s shares, which is $513,000. Westmount's balance sheet reports that Westmount Concepts Inc. has 12,500 common shares outstanding. In addition, suppose *The Globe and Mail* reports that Westmount Concepts Inc. common shares are selling for $41.04 per share. The current market value of Westmount Concepts Inc. is thus

$$\text{Current market value of the company} = \text{Number of common shares outstanding} \times \text{Current market price per share}$$

$$\$513,000 = 12,500 \times \$41.04$$

The investment decision rule may take this form:

			DECISION:
If estimated value of the company (such as Westmount)	Exceeds → Equals → Is less than →	Current market → value of the company	Buy the shares because you think the share price will go up.
		→	Hold the shares because you think the share price will hold steady
		→	Sell the shares because you think the share price will fall

In this case,

			DECISION:
Estimated value of Westmount $450,000	Is less than	Current market value of the company $513,000	Sell the shares
$36.00 per share*	Is less than	$41.04 per share	

*$450,000 / 12,500 shares = $36.00 per share

Gibbs believes the share price should fall to bring the current market value of $513,000 to somewhere in a range near $450,000. Based largely on Westmount's income from continuing operations, Gibbs thinks that Westmount Concepts Inc. would be more fairly valued at $450,000. Based on this analysis, BMO Nesbitt Burns would recommend that investors sell their shareholdings of Westmount Concepts Inc.

Investors often make their decisions based on the value of a single share. They can estimate the value of one share by using earnings per share (EPS) of common shares, as follows:

$$\text{Estimated value of one common share} = \frac{\text{Estimated annual earnings per share}}{\text{Investment capitalization rate}}$$

The analysis based on one share follows the pattern illustrated for the company as a whole.

Discontinued Operations

Most large corporations engage in several lines of business. For example, Bombardier Inc. has two business segments: BA, which designs and builds "innovative aviation products" and provides aviation-related services; and BT, which designs and builds rail-related products (such as rail passenger cars, locomotives, and subway cars and related vehicles) and transportation-related products, and provides related services. In Chapter 10, you read about ATCO Ltd., which is involved with utilities, power generation, logistics and energy services, and technologies and industrials on a worldwide basis. We call each identifiable division of a company a **segment of the business**.

A company may sell a segment of its business. The sale of a business segment is viewed as a one-time transaction. Bombardier did not have any discontinued operations in 2008 but in the January 31, 2007, annual report the company reported that "During fiscal year 2007, the Corporation continued with its strategy of reducing the former Bombardier Capital Segment ("BC") . . . " and sold other assets. The sale of BC began in the year ended January 31, 2006.

Let's return to the Westmount Concepts Inc. example in Exhibit 11-1 (page 525). Westmount faces an income tax rate of 32%, so the discontinued operations are taxed at the 32% rate. Discontinued operations are reported along with their income tax effect by Westmount Concepts Inc. as shown below (lines 11 to 14, page 525). Canadian GAAP require the separate disclosure of the gain or loss from discontinued operations and the gain or loss on the disposal of net assets from the discontinued operations.

Discontinued operations:		
Operating income	$30,000	
Less income tax	(9,600)	$20,400
Gain on disposal of discontinued assets	10,000	
Less income tax	(3,200)	6,800
		$27,200

Financial analysts typically do *not* include discontinued operations in predictions of future corporate income because the discontinued segments will not continue to generate income for the company.

Discontinued operations relate to an identifiable segment of the business. Gains and losses on the sales of property, plant, and equipment are *not* reported as discontinued operations. These items are not unusual, and they recur from time to time, so they appear in the "Other" section of the income statement (Exhibit 11-1, line 7).

Extraordinary Gains and Losses (Extraordinary Items)

Extraordinary gains and losses, also called *extraordinary items*, are *unusual* for the company and *infrequent*. Losses from natural disasters (such as earthquakes, floods, and tornadoes), where such occurrences are rare, and the taking of company assets by a foreign government (expropriation) are extraordinary. Bombardier has no extraordinary items on its income statement in 2008, 2007, or 2006.

Some managers may prefer to report good news as ordinary and bad news as extraordinary. To avoid such abuse Canadian accounting standards severely restrict the recognition of extraordinary items to the extent that they are rarely seen on Canadian income statements. Section 3480 of the *CICA Handbook* identifies three characteristics that must be satisfied before gains or losses can be classified as extraordinary:

1. They are not expected to occur frequently over several years.
2. They do not typify the normal business activities of the entity.
3. They do not depend primarily on decisions or determinations by management or owners.

Extraordinary items are reported along with their income tax effect. During 2009, Westmount Concepts Inc. lost $20,000 of inventory when a tornado blew off a portion of the factory's roof. The costs of repairing the building were covered by insurance. This loss, which reduced income, also reduced Westmount's income tax. The tax effect decreases the net amount of the loss in the same way that income tax reduces the amount of net income. Another way to report an extraordinary loss along with its tax effect is as follows:

> Extraordinary tornado loss, net of tax saving of $6,400.......................... (13,600)

Trace this item to the income statement in Exhibit 11-1 (lines 16 and 17). An extraordinary gain is reported in the same way, net of its income tax.

Gains and losses due to expropriation of assets by a Canadian government body (for example, for a highway), restructuring, and the sale of capital assets are *not* extraordinary items. They are considered normal business occurrences. However, because they are outside the business's central operations, they are reported on the income statement as Other Gains and Losses. Examples include losses due to labour strikes, the gain on sale of machinery, and the restructuring loss in the Other Gains (Losses) section of Exhibit 11-1 (lines 6 and 7).

CICA Handbook Section 3480 actually singles out particular gains and losses that are NOT to be classified as extraordinary because they fall into the category of normal business risk:

- Losses and provisions for losses with respect to bad debts and inventories
- Gains and losses from fluctuations in foreign exchange rates
- Adjustments with respect to contract prices
- Gains and losses from write-down or sale of property, plant, and equipment or other investments
- Income tax reductions on utilization of prior period losses or reversal of previously recorded tax benefits
- Changes in income tax rates or laws

It should be pointed out that extraordinary items are very rare.

Accounting for a Change in Accounting Policy

With respect to the latter circumstance, companies sometimes change from one accounting policy or method to another, such as from double-declining-balance (DDB) to straight-line amortization, or from first-in, first-out (FIFO) to weighted-average cost for inventory. An accounting change makes it difficult to compare one period's financial statements with those of preceding periods. Without detailed information, investors and creditors can be misled into thinking that the current year is better or worse than the preceding year when, in fact, the only difference is a change

IFRS ALERT

In 2006, Section 1506 of the *CICA Handbook* was converged with International Financial Reporting Standard (IFRS) International Accounting Standard (IAS) 8 "Accounting Policies, Changes in Accounting Estimates and Errors."

Both Section 1506 and IAS 8 indicate that the entity should change an accounting policy only if the change results in more relevant and reliable information than the policy it replaces. This position would rule out a change in accounting policy simply to increase net income.

In addition, both standards require the change in accounting policy to be applied retrospectively unless such implication is impracticable. Section 1506 defines retrospective application as "applying a new policy to transactions . . . as if that policy had always been applied."

Changes is accounting policies are permitted only in two circumstances:

- When required by GAAP; an involuntary change
- When the change is voluntary in order to provide more relevant and reliable information

IFRS

in accounting method. It is for this reason, as is noted in the IFRS Alert, that both *CICA Handbook* Section 1506 and IAS 8 suggest that a voluntary change should be made only " . . . if the change . . . results in the financial statements providing reliable and more relevant information . . . on the entity's financial position, financial performance, or cash flows."

To help users understand the effects of a change in accounting policy, Section 1506 requires Canadian companies to account for changes in accounting policy retroactively except when the necessary information is not available. This means the company must go back and restate previous income statements and the opening balance of retained earnings.

Suppose Balmy Beach Boats Ltd. has a single capital asset that cost $20,000 in 2006 and that Balmy Beach has been amortizing the machine at the rate of 10% per year on a straight-line basis. Relevant information for Balmy Beach follows:

	2006	2007	2008
Amortization expense	$ 2,000	$ 2,000	$ 2,000
Net income[*]	$18,000	$22,000	$24,000
Retained earnings—Beginning balance	$ 0	$18,000	$40,000
Net income	18,000	22,000	24,000
Retained earnings—Ending balance	$18,000	$40,000	$64,000

[*]Income taxes will be ignored for this illustration.

In 2009, Balmy Beach decides to convert to double-declining-balance (DDB) amortization using a rate of 20%. Net income after deducting amortization expense of $2,048 was $25,952 for 2009. On page 531, Balmy Beach provides comparatives for the previous two years together with the current year's balances. Amortization using the DDB method would be:

	2006	2007	2008	2009
DDB amortization	$4,000	$3,200	$2,560	$2,048
Amortization expense previously claimed	2,000	2,000	2,000	
Cumulative difference	2,000	3,200	3,760	

The (partial) comparative statement of retained earnings would be as follows:

	2007	2008	2009
Opening balance	$18,000	$36,800	$60,240
Restatement of amortization expense	2,000*		
Revised opening balance	16,000	36,800	60,240
Net income	22,000	24,000	25,952
Less additional amortization	1,200	560	
Restated net income	20,800	23,440	25,952
Restated closing balance	$36,800	$60,240	$86,192

*Restatement of 2006 closing balance is $16,000: $18,000 original − $2,000
(which is $4,000 DDB − $2,000 straight-line).

USER ALERT

Watch Out for Voluntary Accounting Changes That Increase Reported Income

Investment analysts follow companies to see if they meet their forecast earnings targets. And managers sometimes take drastic action to increase reported earnings. Assume it's late in November and our earnings may fall *below* the target for the year. A reasonable thing to do is to try to increase sales and net income. Managers can also cut expenses. These actions are ethical and honest. Profits earned by these actions are real. Managers can take another action that is honest and legal, but its ethics are questionable. Suppose the company has been using the double-declining-balance method for amortization. Changing to straight-line amortization can increase reported income.

Accounting changes are a quick-and-dirty way to create reported profits when the company can't earn enough from continuing operations. This is why GAAP permits companies to change an accounting method only if the change results in more relevant and reliable information and requires companies to report changes in accounting methods, along with their effects on earnings—to let investors know where the income came from. In addition, the companies must restate all prior-year financial statements to show how they would have appeared if the new accounting method had been in effect all along. This helps investors compare all periods' profits and losses on the same accounting basis.

Earnings per Share

CICA Handbook Section 3500 "Earnings per Share" and IAS 33 "Earnings per Share" were very similar in their approach and so convergence did not result in significant changes in the Canadian standard.

The final segment of a corporation's income statement presents the company's earnings per share. **Earnings per share (EPS)** is the amount of a company's net income per share of its *outstanding common shares*. EPS is a key measure of a business's success because it shows how much income the company earned for each common share. Share prices are quoted at an amount per share, and investors buy a certain number of shares. EPS is used to help determine the value of a share. EPS is computed as follows:

IFRS

$$\text{Earnings per share} = \frac{\text{Net income} - \text{Preferred dividends}}{\text{Average number of common shares outstanding}}$$

The corporation lists its various sources of income separately: continuing operations, discontinued operations, and so on. It also lists the EPS figure separately for each element of net income. Consider the EPS calculations for Westmount Concepts Inc. The final section (lines 19 to 23) of Exhibit 11-1 shows how companies report EPS. Westmount has 12,500 common shares outstanding.

Earnings per share of common shares (12,500 shares outstanding):

19	Income before discontinued operations and extraordinary items ($54,400/12,500)	$4.35
20	Income from discontinued operations ($27,200/12,500)	2.18
21	Income before extraordinary item ($81,600/12,500)	6.53
22	Extraordinary loss ($13,600/12,500)	(1.09)
23	Net income ($68,000/12,500)	$5.44

Effect of Preferred Dividends on Earnings per Share. Recall that EPS is earnings per *common* share. But holders of preferred shares have first claim on dividends. Therefore, preferred dividends must be subtracted from net income in the computation of EPS. Preferred dividends are not subtracted from discontinued operations, extraordinary items, or the cumulative effect of accounting changes. When the number of common shares outstanding changes during the year, such as when a company issues shares or repurchases shares during the year, earnings per share is calculated based on the weighted average number of common shares outstanding during the year.

Suppose Westmount Concepts Inc. had 10,000 preferred shares outstanding, each with a $1.00 dividend. The annual preferred dividend would be $10,000 (10,000 × $1.00). The $10,000 would be subtracted from each of the different income subtotals, resulting in the following EPS computations:

Earnings per share of common shares (12,500 shares outstanding):

Income before discontinued operations and extraordinary items ($54,400 − $10,000)/12,500	$3.55
Income from discontinued operations ($27,200/12,500)	2.18
Income before extraordinary item ($81,600 − $10,000)/12,500	5.73
Extraordinary loss ($13,600/12,500)	(1.09)
Net income ($68,000 − $10,000)/12,500	$4.64

USER ALERT

Earnings per Share May Not Be What They Seem

Although EPS is widely used as a measure of profitability, it has some serious limitations. Two firms could have the same earnings and EPS, but they would not be equally profitable if one firm invested more assets or capital to generate those earnings. Another problem arises when firms boost their EPS by manipulating the denominator. A firm could actually have a decline in earnings but could increase EPS by simply repurchasing shares.

Earnings per Share Dilution. Some corporations make their bonds or preferred shares more attractive to investors by offering conversion privileges, which permit the holder to convert the bond or preferred shares into some specified number of common shares. Bombardier, which was mentioned in the opening vignette, is one such company. If the bonds or preferred shares are converted to common shares, the EPS is diluted, or reduced, because more common shares are divided into net income. Corporations with complex capital structures present two sets of EPS figures:

- EPS based on actual outstanding common shares (*basic* EPS)
- EPS based on outstanding common shares plus the additional common shares that would arise from conversion of convertible bonds or preferred shares into common shares (*diluted* EPS)

Reporting Comprehensive Income

All companies report net loss on their income statements. In January 2005, the CICA issued a new *Handbook* Section 1530 "Comprehensive Income." **Comprehensive income** is the company's change in total shareholders' equity from all sources other than investments from and distributions to owners. Comprehensive income includes net income plus:

- Unrealized gains (losses) on portfolio investments
- Foreign-currency translation adjustments

These items do not enter into the determination of net income or of earnings per share until realized. They can be reported as Other comprehensive income, as shown in Exhibit 11-2. All amounts are assumed for this illustration.

IFRS

| DECISION | What Should You Analyze to Gain an Overall Picture of a Company? |

Two key figures used in financial analysis are

- Net income (or income from continuing operations)
- Cash flow from operations

For any one period, Westmount Concepts Inc.'s net income and net cash flow from operating activities may chart different paths. Accounting income arises from the accrual process as follows:

Total revenues and gains − Total expenses and losses = Net income (or Net loss)

As we have seen, revenues and gains are recorded when they occur, regardless of when the company receives or pays cash.

Net cash flow, on the other hand, is based solely on cash receipts and cash payments. During any particular period, a company may have lots of revenues and expenses and a hefty net income. But the company may have weak cash flow because it has not yet collected from customers. The reverse may also be true: The company may have abundant cash but little income.

EXHIBIT 11-2   Westmount Concepts Inc. Statement of Comprehensive Income

IFRS

Westmount Concepts Inc.
Statement of Comprehensive Income (Partial)
For the Year Ended December 31, 2009

Net income		$68,000
Other comprehensive income:		
Unrealized gain on investment	$ 2,000	
Less income tax (32%)	(640)	$ 1,360
Foreign-currency translation adjustment (loss)	(9,000)	
Less income tax saving (32%)	2,880	(6,120)
Other comprehensive income (loss)		(4,760)
Comprehensive income		$63,240

The income statement and the cash flow statement often present different pictures of the company. Which one provides better information? Neither: Both statements are needed, along with the balance sheet and statement of shareholders' equity, for an overall view of the business. Chapter 12 will cover the cash flow statement in detail.

Objective

2 **Account** for a corporation's income tax

Accounting for Corporate Income Taxes

Corporations pay income tax as individuals do, but corporate and personal tax rates differ. The 2008 federal tax rate ranges from 11% for private corporations to 19% for all others. The provinces also levy corporate income taxes at varying rates. The combined rate in 2008 for other than private corporations varied from 31% to 35%. We will use 32% in the following discussion.

To account for income tax, the corporation measures the following for each period:

- *Income tax expense*, an expense on the income statement. Income tax helps measure net income.
- *Income tax payable*, a liability on the balance sheet. Income tax payable is the current year's unpaid income tax.

Accounting for income tax by a corporation follows the principles of accrual accounting. Suppose that in 2008 Red Lake Outfitters Ltd. reported income before tax (also called **pretax accounting income**) of $9 million. Assume Red Lake's combined income tax rate is 32%. To begin this discussion, let's assume income tax expense and income tax payable are the same. Then Red Lake Outfitters Ltd. would record income tax for the year as follows:

2008			
Dec. 31	Income Tax Expense..	2,880,000	
	Income Tax Payable		2,880,000
	Recorded income tax for the year ($9,000,000 × 0.32).		

ASSETS	=	LIABILITIES	+	SHAREHOLDERS' EQUITY	−	EXPENSES
0	=	2,880,000	+		−	2,880,000

Red Lake Outfitters Ltd.'s 2008 financial statements would report these figures (partial, in thousands):

Income statement		Balance sheet	
Income before income tax...........	$9,000	Current liabilities:	
Income tax expense	(2,880)	Income tax payable................	$2,880
Net income	$6,120		

In general, income tax expense and income tax payable can be computed as follows:[*]

$$\text{Income tax expense} = \text{Income before income tax (from the income statement)} \times \text{Income tax rate} \qquad \text{Income tax payable} = \text{Taxable income (from the income tax return filed with tax authorities)} \times \text{Income tax rate}$$

[*]The authors thank Jean Marie Hudson for suggesting this presentation.

The income statement and the income tax return are entirely separate documents:

- The income statement reports the results of operations.
- The income tax return is filed with Canada Revenue Agency (CRA) or the province in the case of Alberta, Ontario, and Quebec, to report the company's estimate of how much tax to pay the government in the current period.

For most companies, income tax expense and income tax payable differ. Certain revenues and expenses affect income differently for accounting purposes and tax purposes. One of the most important differences between accounting income and **taxable income** occurs when a corporation uses straight-line amortization for the financial statements and capital cost allowance rates for the tax return. For any one year, tax amortization usually differs from accounting amortization on the income statement.

Continuing with the Red Lake Outfitters Ltd. illustration, suppose for 2009 that Red Lake has:

- Pretax accounting income of $10 million on the income statement
- Taxable income of $9.2 million on the company's income tax return

Taxable income is $0.8 million less than accounting income because Red Lake Outfitters Ltd., like many other companies, uses straight-line amortization for accounting purposes and capital cost allowance for income tax purposes. Red Lake Outfitters Ltd. will record income tax for 2009 as follows (dollar amounts in millions and an income tax rate of 32%):

```
2009
Dec. 31    Income Tax Expense ($10 × 0.32)...................................    3.20
               Income Tax Payable ($9.2 × 0.32) ..............................           2.94
               Future Income Tax Liability..........................................           0.26
           Recorded income tax for the year.
```

ASSETS	=	LIABILITIES	+	SHAREHOLDERS' EQUITY	−	EXPENSES
0	=	$2.94 + $0.26			−	$3.20

Income tax expense is reported on the income statement, and income tax payable and future income tax liability on the balance sheet, as follows for Red Lake Outfitters Ltd. at the end of 2009 (dollar amounts in millions):

Income statement		Balance sheet	
Income before income tax............	$10.00	Current liabilities:	
Income tax expense	(3.20)	Income tax payable................	$2.94
Net income	$ 6.80	Long-term liabilities:	
		Future income tax liability.....	0.26*

*Assumes the beginning balance of Future Income Tax Liability was zero.

Early in 2010, Red Lake Outfitters Ltd. would pay its income tax payable of $2.94 million because this is a current liability. Future income tax liability, however, is usually long-term, and the company may pay this liability over a longer period.

For a given year, Income Tax Payable can exceed Income Tax Expense. When that occurs, the company records a Future Income Tax Asset.

EXHIBIT 11-3	Reporting a Prior-Period Adjustment on the Statement of Retained Earnings

Darlind Corp.
Statement of Retained Earnings
For the Year Ended December 31, 2009

Retained earnings balance, December 31, 2008, as originally reported.................	$390,000
Prior-period adjustment—debit to correct error in recording income tax expense of 2008	(10,000)
Retained earnings balance, December 31, 2008, as adjusted................................	380,000
Net income for 2009	114,000
	494,000
Dividends for 2009...	(41,000)
Retained earnings balance, December 31, 2009..	$453,000

Analyzing Retained Earnings

Prior-Period Adjustments

What happens when a company records revenues or expenses incorrectly? If the error occurs in one period and is corrected in a later period, the balance of Retained Earnings will be wrong until the error is corrected. Corrections to Retained Earnings for errors of earlier periods are called **prior-period adjustments**. The prior-period adjustment appears on the statement of retained earnings.

Assume that Darlind Corp. recorded 2008 income tax expense as $30,000. The correct amount was $40,000. This error understated 2008 expenses and current liabilities by $10,000 and overstated net income by $10,000. A re-assessment by CRA in 2009 for the additional $10,000 alerted Darlind Corp. to the mistake.

This accounting error requires a prior-period adjustment. Prior-period adjustments are not reported on the income statement because they relate to an earlier accounting period. This prior-period adjustment would appear on the statement of retained earnings, as shown in Exhibit 11-3, with all amounts assumed.

IFRS ALERT

As was reported in the IFRS Alert on p. 530, in 2006, Section 1506 of the *CICA Handbook* was converged with IFRS IAS 8 "Accounting Policies, Changes in Accounting Estimates and Errors." The correction of errors in prior-period financial statements is one area where there has not been convergence between Section 1506 and IAS 8. Section 1506 requires the error from the prior period to be corrected retrospectively whether or not such application is practicable. IAS 8 also requires the error from the prior period to be corrected retrospectively unless such implementation is impracticable.

Analyzing the Statement of Shareholders' Equity

Most companies report a statement of shareholders' equity, which includes retained earnings. The statement of shareholders' equity is formatted like a statement of retained earnings but with a column for each element of shareholders' equity. The **statement of shareholders' equity** thus reports reasons for the changes in equity during the period.

Exhibit 11-4 is the 2009 statement of shareholders' equity for Westmount Concepts Inc. Study its format. There is a column for each element of equity, with common shares on the left and the far right column reporting the total. The top row (line 1) reports the beginning balances taken from last period's balance sheet. The

EXHIBIT 11-4   Statement of Shareholders' Equity

Westmount Concepts Inc.
Statement of Shareholders' Equity
For the Year Ended December 31, 2009

	Common Shares	Contributed Surplus— Share Repurchases	Retained Earnings	Accumulated Other Comprehensive Income		Total Share- holders' Equity
				Unrealized Gain (Loss) on Investments	Foreign- Currency Translation Adjustment	
1 Balance, December 31, 2008	$180,000		$136,000	$6,000	$(10,000)	$312,000
2 Net income			68,000			68,000
3 Cash dividends			(21,000)			(21,000)
4 Stock dividends—6%	10,800		(10,800)			0
5 Issuance of shares	92,000					92,000
6 Repurchase of common shares	(20,800)	$2,080				(18,720)
7 Unrealized gain on investments				1,360		1,360
8 Foreign-currency translation adjustment					(6,120)	(6,120)
9 Balance, December 31, 2009	$262,000	$2,080	$172,200	$7,360	$(16,120)	$427,520

rows report the various transactions, starting with Cash dividends (line 3). The statement ends with the December 31, 2009, balances (line 9), which appear on the ending balance sheet given in Exhibit 11-5.

Let's examine Westmount Concepts Inc.'s shareholders' equity during 2009 using Exhibit 11-4.

IFRS

Net Income (Line 2). During 2009, Westmount Concepts Inc. earned net income of $68,000, which increased Retained Earnings. Trace net income from the income statement (Exhibit 11-1, page 525) to the statement of shareholders' equity (Exhibit 11-4). Then trace the ending amount of Retained Earnings to the balance sheet in Exhibit 11-5. Moving back and forth among the financial statements is an important part of financial analysis.

EXHIBIT 11-5   Shareholders' Equity Section of the Balance Sheet

Westmount Concepts Inc.
Balance Sheet (Partial)
December 31, 2009

IFRS

Total assets	$920,310
Total liabilities	$492,790
Shareholders' Equity	
Common shares, shares issued—10,800	262,000
Contributed surplus—share repurchases	2,080
Retained earnings	172,200
Accumulated other comprensive income	
Unrealized gain on investments	7,360
Foreign-currency translation adjustment..................................	(16,120)
Total shareholders' equity	427,520
Total liabilities and shareholders' equity....................................	$920,310

Declaration of Cash Dividends (Line 3). The statement of shareholders' equity reports the amount of cash dividends the company declared during the year. Westmount Concepts Inc.'s cash dividends were $21,000, roughly one-third of net income. Exhibit 11-4 reports the decrease in retained earnings from the declaration of the cash dividends.

Distribution of Stock Dividends (Line 4). During the early part of 2009, Westmount Concepts Inc. distributed a stock dividend to its shareholders. Prior to the stock dividend, Westmount Concepts Inc.'s Common Shares account had a balance of $180,000. The company issued a stock dividend of 6%, which added 540 shares to the 9,000 shares outstanding at the beginning of the year, which resulted in 9,540 shares being outstanding. The shares were valued at $20.00 per share, the market price at the date the dividend was declared.

But there was more to this stock dividend. Westmount decreased (debited) Retained Earnings for the market value of the new shares issued in the stock dividend. This market value, $10,800, is reported under Retained Earnings in Exhibit 11-4. The market value of the dividend ($10,800) was credited to Common Shares.

Issuance of Shares (Line 5). During the latter part of 2009, Westmount Concepts Inc. issued 2,300 common shares for $92,000, which went into the Common Shares account. The issuance of shares increased contributed capital and total equity by $92,000.

Repurchase of Shares (Line 6). The statement of shareholders' equity reports the repurchase of shares. Recall from Chapter 9 that when shares are repurchased, Common Shares is debited for the issue price of the shares repurchased. During 2009, Westmount Concepts Inc. paid $18,720 to repurchase 1,040 company shares (line 6). This transaction decreased shareholders' equity by $18,720. The Common Shares account was debited in the amount of $20,800, the amount of the credit to Common Shares when the repurchased shares were first issued. The difference of $2,080 ($20,800 − $18,720) is credited to Contributed Surplus—Share Repurchase. Practically, the company gained on the repurchase since it paid less to reacquire the shares than it sold them for originally. But a company cannot profit from transactions in its own shares, so the "gain" is put directly into Shareholders' Equity.

IFRS

Accumulated Other Comprehensive Income (Lines 7 and 8). Two categories of other comprehensive income are unrealized gains and losses on portfolio investments and the foreign-currency translation adjustment.

At December 31, 2008, Westmount held portfolio investments with an unrealized gain of $6,000. This explains the beginning balance. Then, during 2009, the market value of the investments increased by another $1,360 (line 7). At December 31, 2009, Westmount's portfolio of investments had an unrealized gain of $7,360 (line 9). An unrealized loss on investments would appear as a negative amount.

At December 31, 2008, Westmount had a negative foreign-currency translation adjustment of $10,000 (line 1). During 2009, the foreign-currency translation adjustment was $(4,760) (line 8) and at December 31, 2009, Westmount's cumulative foreign-currency adjustment stood at an unrealized loss of $14,760.

Responsibility for the Financial Statements
Management's Responsibility

Management issues a management report in the annual report in which it acknowledges its responsibility for the company's financial statements. Management also acknowledges its responsibility for internal controls. Exhibit 11-6 is an excerpt from the statement of management's responsibility included in the 2007 annual report of Big Rock Brewery Income Trust, the regional brewer of fine beers based in Calgary.

Management declares its responsibility for the financial statements and states that they conform to GAAP. As we've seen throughout this book, GAAP are the standard for preparing the financial statements and are designed to produce relevant, reliable, and useful information for making investment and credit decisions.

Objective

4 **Understand** managers' and auditors' responsibilities for the financial statements

Auditor's Report

The various federal and provincial incorporating acts and, in the case of listed companies, the provincial securities commissions and the stock exchanges require companies that issue their shares or trust units publicly to file audited financial statements with the various bodies. To comply with this requirement, companies engage outside auditors who are usually chartered accountants, or, depending on the province, certified general accountants, to examine their statements. In some provinces, certified management accountants and others may perform the audit. The independent auditors decide whether the company's financial statements comply with GAAP and then issue an auditor's report. Auditors' reports usually fall into one of two categories:

1. **Unqualified (clean)**. The statements are reliable.
2. Reservation of opinion:
   i. **Qualified.** The statements are reliable except for one item for which the opinion is said to be qualified.
   ii. **Adverse.** There is a significant deviation from GAAP, and the statements do not present fairly.

EXHIBIT 11-6   Excerpt from Management Report—Big Rock Brewery Income Trust Ltd

Management Report
Big Rock Brewery Income Trust Ltd.

The accompanying consolidated financial statements in the annual report are the responsibility of management. The consolidated financial statements of the Trust have been prepared in accordance with Canadian generally accepted accounting principles ("GAAP"). In the opinion of management, the financial statements have been prepared within acceptable limits of materiality and, when necessary, management has made informed judgments and estimates in accounting for transactions which were not complete at the balance sheet date. Where alternative accounting methods exist, management has chosen those it deems most appropriate in the circumstances as indicated in the notes to the consolidated financial statements.

Management maintains appropriate systems of internal control. Policies and procedures are designed to give reasonable assurance that transactions are appropriately authorized, assets are protected, and financial records are properly maintained to provide reasonable assurance that financial information is relevant and reliable.

iii. **Denial of opinion.** The auditor was unable to reach a professional opinion because of scope limitations (inability to obtain sufficient appropriate evidential matter).

Exhibit 11-7 is the auditor's report on the financial statements of Big Rock Brewery Income Trust.

The auditor's report is addressed to the unitholders of the Trust. The auditing firm signs its name, in this case the Calgary office of Ernst & Young LLP (LLP is the abbreviation for limited liability partnership).

The auditor's report typically contains three paragraphs:

- The first (introductory) paragraph identifies the audited financial statements. It also delineates the responsibilities of management and the auditor insofar as the financial statements are concerned.

- The second (scope) paragraph describes how the audit was performed, mentioning that generally accepted auditing standards are the benchmark for evaluating the audit's quality.

- The third (opinion) paragraph states Ernst & Young's opinion that Big Rock's financial statements conform to Canadian GAAP and that people can rely on them for decision making.

Big Rock's auditor's report contains an unqualified opinion, which indicates that the financial statements are reliable.

EXHIBIT 11-7 Auditor's Report on the Financial Statements of Big Rock Brewery Income Trust

Auditors' Report

To the Unitholders of
Big Rock Brewery Income Trust

We have audited the consolidated balance sheets of **Big Rock Brewery Income Trust** as at December 31, 2007 and 2006 and the consolidated statements of operations and undistributed income and cash flows for the years then ended. These financial statements are the responsibility of the Trust's management. Our responsibility is to express an opinion on these financial statements based on our audits.

We conducted our audits in accordance with Canadian generally accepted auditing standards. Those standards require that we plan and perform an audit to obtain reasonable assurance whether the financial statements are free of material misstatement. An audit includes examining, on a test basis, evidence supporting the amounts and disclosures in the financial statements. An audit also includes assessing the accounting principles used and significant estimates made by management, as well as evaluating the overall financial statement presentation.

In our opinion, these consolidated financial statements present fairly, in all material respects, the financial position of the Trust as at December 31, 2007 and 2006 and the results of its operations and its cash flows for the years then ended in accordance with Canadian generally accepted accounting principles.

Calgary, Canada
March 28, 2008

/s/ Ernst & Young LLP
Chartered Accountants

The independent audit adds credibility to the financial statements. It is no accident that financial reporting and auditing are very advanced in Canada and the United States and that these two countries' capital markets are highly regarded.

DECISION GUIDELINES

In this set of Decision Guidelines, we'll revisit the decision setting in which investors use accounting information to make investment decisions. You have completed your studies, taken a job, and been fortunate to save $10,000. Now you are ready to start investing. These guidelines provide a framework for using accounting information for investment analysis.

USING THE INCOME STATEMENT AND THE RELATED NOTES IN INVESTMENT ANALYSIS

Decision	Factors to Consider		Decision Variable or Model
Which measure of profitability should be used for investment analysis?	Are you interested in accounting income? →	Income, including all revenues, expenses, gains, and losses?	Net income (bottom line)
		Income that can be → expected to repeat from year to year?	Income from continuing operations
	Are you interested in cash flows?	⟶	Cash flows from operating activities (Chapter 12)

Note: A conservative strategy may use both income and cash flows and compare the two sets of results.

What is the estimated value of the shares?	If you believe the company can earn the income (or cash flow) indefinitely ⟶	$$\text{Estimated value} = \frac{\text{Annual income}}{\text{Investment capitalization rate}}$$
	If you believe the company can earn the income (or cash flow) for a finite number of years ⟶	$$\text{Estimated value} = \text{Annual income} \times \begin{array}{c}\text{Present value}\\ \text{of annuity}\\ \text{(See Appendix D)}\end{array}$$
How does risk affect the value of the shares?	If the investment is high-risk ⟶	Increase the investment capitalization rate
	If the investment is low-risk ⟶	Decrease the investment capitalization rate

MyAccountingLab ▌ ## END-OF-CHAPTER SUMMARY PROBLEM

The following information was taken from the ledger of Canmore Outdoor Products Ltd. as at December 31, 2009:

Prior-period adjustment—			Income tax expense (saving):	
credit to Retained Earnings.......	$ 5,000		Discontinued operations	6,400
Gain on sale of capital assets	21,000		Extraordinary gain	9,600
Cost of goods sold........................	380,000		Preferred shares, $8.00,	
Income tax expense (saving):			500 shares issued	50,000
Continuing operations..............	25,600		Dividends	16,000
Selling expenses	78,000		Operating income from	
Common shares, ...			discontinued operations..........	20,000
40,000 shares issued	165,000		Loss due to lawsuit	11,000
Sales revenue...............................	620,000		General expenses	62,000
Interest expense	30,000		Retained earnings, beginning,	
Extraordinary gain	30,000		as originally reported	103,000

Required

Prepare a single-step income statement (with all revenues grouped together) and a statement of retained earnings for Canmore Outdoor Products Ltd. for the year ended December 31, 2009. Include the earnings-per-share presentation and show computations. Assume no changes in the share accounts during the year.

Name: Canmore Outdoor Products Ltd.
Industry: Outdoor products corporation
Fiscal Period: Year ended December 31, 2009

Answers

Sort the ledger items into those that appear on the statement of retained earnings and those that appear on the income statement. Selected items are highlighted.

Revenue includes gain on sale of capital assets.

Expenses include all normal operating costs related to the revenue reported. Income tax expense is included here.

This is reported net of income tax.

This is reported net of income tax.

Canmore Outdoor Products Ltd.
Income Statement
For the Year Ended December 31, 2009

Revenue and gains:		
Sales revenue..		$620,000
Gain on sale of capital assets		21,000
Total revenues and gains...		641,000
Expenses and losses:		
Cost of goods sold...	$380,000	
Selling expenses	78,000	
General expenses...	62,000	
Interest expense	30,000	
Loss due to lawsuit..	11,000	
Income tax expense...	25,600	
Total expenses and losses..		586,600
Income before discontinued operations and extraordinary items...		54,400
Operating income from discontinued operations, $20,000,		
less income tax, $6,400..		13,600
Income before extraordinary item		68,000
Extraordinary gain, $30,000, less income tax, $9,600..................		20,400
Net income		$ 88,400

Earnings per share:*
    Income from continuing operations [($54,400 − $4,000)/40,000 shares] $1.26
    Income from discontinued operations ($13,600/40,000 shares).........................   0.34
    Income before extraordinary item [($68,000 − $4,000)/40,000 shares] 1.60
    Extraordinary gain ($20,400/40,000 shares) 0.51
Net income [($88,400 − $4,000)/40,000 shares] $2.11

The earnings per share is calculated by using net income from various parts of the income statement less preferred dividends. Use the common shares and preferred shares information from the data given to calculate preferred dividends and the number of common shares outstanding.

*Computations:

$$EPS = \frac{Income - Preferred\ dividends}{Common\ shares\ outstanding}$$

    Preferred dividends: 500 × $8.00 = $4,000
    Common shares outstanding: 40,000 shares

Canmore Outdoor Products Ltd.
Statement of Retained Earnings
For the Year Ended December 31, 2009

Retained earnings balance, beginning, as originally reported	$103,000
Prior-period adjustment	5,000
Retained earnings balance, beginning, as adjusted..	108,000
Net income for current year	88,400
	196,400
Dividends for current year...	(16,000)
Retained earnings balance, ending...	$180,400

Prior period adjustments must be disclosed in a separate line in the statement of retained earnings.

Given in the list of data.

REVIEW THE INCOME STATEMENT AND THE STATEMENT OF SHAREHOLDERS' EQUITY

QUICK CHECK   (Answers are given on page 560.)

1. The quality of earnings suggests that
    a. Net income is the best measure of the results of operations.
    b. Income from continuing operations is better than income from one-time transactions.
    c. Continuing operations and one-time transactions are of equal importance.
    d. Shareholders want the corporation to earn enough income to be able to pay its debts.

2. Which statement is true?
    a. Discontinued operations are a separate category on the income statement.
    b. Extraordinary items are part of discontinued operations.
    c. Cumulative effect of accounting changes is combined with continuing operations on the income statement.
    d. All of the above are true.

3. Marshall Transportation Ltd. earned $5.94 per common share. Suppose you capitalize Marshall's income at 6%. How much are you willing to pay for a share of Marshall Transportation?
    a. $32.17
    b. $5.17
    c. $165.00
    d. Some other amount

4. Return to Bombardier's income statement on page 524. Bombardier has no preferred shares outstanding. How many common shares did Bombardier have outstanding during fiscal year 2008? Focus on the bottom line, net income.

   a. 99 million
   b. 320 million
   c. 1.9 million
   d. 31 million

5. Why is it important for companies to report their accounting changes to the public?

   a. Accounting changes affect dividends, and investors want dividends.
   b. Some accounting changes are more extraordinary than others.
   c. Most accounting changes increase net income, and investors need to know why the increase in net income occurred.
   d. Without the reporting of accounting changes, investors could believe all the company's income came from continuing operations.

6. Other comprehensive income

   a. Affects earnings per share
   b. Includes extraordinary gains and losses
   c. Includes unrealized gains and losses on investments
   d. Has no effect on income tax

7. OnStar GPS Systems earned income before tax of $50,000. Taxable income was $40,000, and the income tax rate was 25%. OnStar recorded income tax with this journal entry:

a.	Income Tax Expense	12,500	
	Income Tax Payable		10,000
	Future Income Tax Liability		2,500
b.	Income Tax Expense	12,500	
	Income Tax Payable		12,500
c.	Income Tax Payable	10,000	
	Income Tax Expense		10,000
d.	Income Tax Payable	12,500	
	Income Tax Expense		10,000
	Future Income Tax Liability		2,500

8. Future Income Tax Liability is usually

	Type of Account	Reported on the
a.	Short-term	Income statement
b.	Short-term	Statement of shareholders' equity
c.	Long-term	Income statement
d.	Long-term	Balance statement

9. The main purpose of the statement of shareholders' equity is to report

   a. Financial position
   b. Reasons for changes in the equity accounts
   c. Results of operations
   d. Comprehensive income

10. An auditor report by independent accountants

    a. Ensures that the financial statements are error-free
    b. Gives investors assurance that the company's shares are a safe investment
    c. Gives investors assurance that the company's financial statements conform to GAAP
    d. Is ultimately the responsibility of the management of the client company

ACCOUNTING VOCABULARY

adverse opinion An audit opinion stating that the financial statements are unreliable. (p. 539)

clean opinion An *unqualified opinion*. The statements are reliable. (p. 539)

comprehensive income A company's change in total shareholders' equity from all sources other than from the owners of the business.   (p. 533)

denial of opinion An audit opinion stating that the auditor was unable to reach a professional opinion regarding the quality of the financial statements.   (p. 540)

earnings per share (EPS) Amount of a company's net income per outstanding common share.   (p. 531)

extraordinary gains and losses Also called *extraordinary items*, these gains and losses are both unusual and infrequent for the company, and they are not determined by management.   (p. 528)

extraordinary items An *extraordinary gain* or *loss*.   (p. 528)

investment capitalization rate An earnings rate used to estimate the value of an investment in the share capital of a company.   (p. 526)

pretax accounting income Income before tax on the income statement.   (p. 534)

prior-period adjustment A correction to the beginning balance of Retained Earnings for an error of an earlier period.   (p. 536)

qualified opinion An audit opinion stating that the financial statements are reliable, except for one or more items for which the opinion is said to be qualified.   (p. 539)

segment of a business An identifiable division of a company.   (p. 528)

statement of shareholders' equity Reports the changes in all categories of shareholders' equity during the period.   (p. 536)

taxable income The basis for computing the amount of tax to pay the government.   (p. 535)

unqualified (clean) opinion An audit opinion stating that the financial statements are reliable.   (p. 539)

ASSESS YOUR PROGRESS

Make the grade with MyAccountingLab: The exercises and problems marked in red can be found on MyAccountingLab at www.myaccountinglab.com. You can practise them as often as you want, and they feature step by step guided solutions to help you find the right answer.

SHORT EXERCISES

S11-1 List the major parts of a complex corporate income statement for Omnibus Corporation Inc. for the year ended March 31, 2009. Include all the major parts of the income statement, starting with net sales revenue and ending with net income (net loss). You may ignore dollar amounts and earnings per share.

Preparing a complex income statement
(Obj. 1)

S11-2 Study the 2006 (not 2007) income statement of **Sun-Rype Products Ltd.** (see Appendix A), and answer these questions about the company:

1. How much gross margin did Sun-Rype earn on the sale of its products? How much was income before taxes? How much was net income?

2. At the end of 2006, what dollar amount of net income would most sophisticated investors use to predict Sun-Rype's net income for 2007 and beyond? Name this item, give its amount, and state your reason.

Explaining the items on a complex income statement
(Obj. 1)

S11-3 Financial Resources Inc. reported the following items, listed in no particular order, at December 31, 2009 (in thousands):

Preparing a complex income statement
(Obj. 1)

Other gains (losses)	$ (2,000)	Extraordinary gain	$ 4,000
Net sales revenue	168,000	Cost of goods sold	66,000
Loss on discontinued operations	20,000	Operating expenses	56,000
		Accounts receivable	21,000

Income tax of 25% applies to all items.

Prepare Financial Resources' income statement for the year ended December 31, 2009. Omit earnings per share.

S11-4 Return to the Financial Resources data in Short Exercise 11-3. Financial Resources had 10,000 common shares outstanding during 2009. Financial Resources declared and paid preferred dividends of $5,000 during 2009.

Report Financial Resources' earnings per share on the income statement.

Reporting earnings per share
(Obj. 1)

Reporting comprehensive income
(Obj. 1)

S11-5 Use the Financial Resources data in Short Exercise 11-3. In addition, Financial Resources had unrealized gains of $1,000 on investments and a $2,000 foreign-currency translation adjustment (a gain) during 2009. Both amounts are net of tax. Start with Financial Resources' net income from S11-3 and show how the company could report other comprehensive income on its 2009 income statement.

Should Financial Resources report earnings per share for other comprehensive income? State why or why not.

Valuing a company's shares
(Obj. 1)

S11-6 For fiscal year 2007, **Shoppers Drug Mart Corporation** reported net sales of $8,479 million, net income of $494 million, and no significant discontinued operations, extraordinary items, or accounting changes.

Earnings per share was $2.28. At a capitalization rate of 6%, how much should one share of Shoppers Drug Mart be worth? Compare your estimated share price to Shoppers Drug Mart's actual share price as quoted in *The Globe and Mail*, in your newspaper, or on the Internet. Based on your estimated market value, should you buy, hold, or sell Shoppers Drug Mart shares?

S11-7 Marstaller Motor Limited has preferred shares outstanding and issued additional common shares during the year.

Interpreting earnings-per-share data
(Obj. 1)

1. Give the basic equation to compute earnings per common share for net income.
2. List the income items for which Marstaller must report earnings-per-share data.
3. What makes earnings per share so useful as a business statistic?

Accounting for a corporation's income tax
(Obj. 2)

S11-8 PEI Marine Inc. had income before income tax of $110,000 and taxable income of $90,000 for 2009, the company's first year of operations. The income tax rate is 25%.

1. Make the entry to record PEI Marine's income taxes for 2009.
2. Show what PEI Marine will report on its 2009 income statement starting with income before income tax. Also show what PEI Marine will report for current and long-term liabilities on its December 31, 2009, balance sheet.

Reporting a prior-period adjustment
(Obj. 3)

S11-9 Quick Pies Ltd. was set to report the following statement of retained earnings for the year ended December 31, 2009.

Quick Pies Ltd. Statement of Retained Earnings For the Year Ended December 31, 2009	
Retained earnings, December 31, 2008	$140,000
Net income for 2009	91,000
Dividends for 2009	(14,000)
Retained earnings, December 31, 2009	$217,000

Before issuing its 2009 financial statements, Quick Pies learned that net income of 2008 was overstated by $16,000. Prepare Quick Pies' 2009 statement of retained earnings to show the correction of the error—that is, the prior-period adjustment.

Using the statement of shareholders' equity
(Obj. 4)

S11-10 Use the statement of shareholders' equity in Exhibit 11-4 (p. 537) to answer the following questions about Westmount Concepts Inc.:

1. How much cash did the issuance of common shares bring in during 2009?
2. What was the effect of the stock dividends on Westmount's retained earnings? What was the effect on total share capital, on total shareholders' equity, and on total assets?
3. What was the cost of the common shares that Westmount repurchased during 2009?

EXERCISES

E11-11 Mountain Cycles Inc. reported a number of special items on its income statement. The following data, listed in no particular order, came from Mountain's financial statements (amounts in thousands):

Preparing and using a complex income statement
(Obj. 1)

Income tax expense (saving):		Net sales	$18,300
Continuing operations....................	$515	Foreign-currency translation	
Discontinued operations................	60	adjustment.............................	320
Extraordinary loss...........................	(4)	Extraordinary loss.....................	19
Unrealized gain on portfolio		Income from discontinued	
investments	15	operations.............................	330
Short-term investments	25	Dividends declared and paid	860
		Total operating expenses............	16,250

❙ Required

Show how the Mountain Cycles Inc. income statement for the year ended September 30, 2009, should appear. Omit earnings per share.

E11-12 The Golden Books Corporation accounting records include the following for 2009 (in thousands):

Preparing and using a complex income statement
(Obj. 1)

Other revenues	$ 1,400
Income tax expense—extraordinary gain	600
Income tax expense—income from continuing operations.................................	2,150
Extraordinary gain	1,500
Sales revenue	114,000
Total operating expenses...	106,800

❙ Required

1. Prepare Golden Books' single-step income statement for the year ended December 31, 2009, including earnings per share. Golden Books had 1,600 thousand common shares and no preferred shares outstanding during the year.

2. Assume investors capitalize Golden Books' earnings at 7%. Estimate the price of one common share of the company.

E11-13 High Seas Cruise Lines Inc. reported the following income statement for the year ended December 31, 2008.

Using an income statement
(Obj. 1)

	Millions
Operating revenues..	$ 70,752
Operating expenses...	60,258
Operating income	10,494
Other revenue (expense), net	985
Income from continuing operations	11,479
Discontinued operations, net of tax...	935
Cumulative effect of accounting change, net of tax..................................	(503)
Net income	$11,911

❙ Required

1. Were High Seas' discontinued operations and cumulative effect of the accounting change more like an expense or a revenue? How can you tell?

2. Should the discontinued operations and the cumulative effect of High Seas' accounting change be included in or excluded from net income? State your reason.

3. Suppose you are working as a financial analyst and your job is to predict High Seas' net income for 2009 and beyond. Which item from the income statement will you use for your prediction? Identify its amount. Why will you use this item?

Using income data for investment analysis
(Obj. 1)

E11-14 During 2007, **Canadian National Railway Company (CN)** had sales of $1.9 billion, operating profit of $0.7 billion, and net income of $0.8 billion. Earnings per share (EPS) were $1.70. On May 16, 2008, a common share of CN was priced at $56.84 on the Toronto Stock Exchange.

What investment capitalization rate did investors appear to be using to determine the value of one common share of CN? The formula for the value of one common share uses EPS in the calculation.

Computing earnings per share
(Obj. 1

E11-15 Tennyson Loan Corporation's balance sheet reports the following:

Preferred shares, $6, 10,000 shares issued	$500,000
Common shares, 1,200,000 shares issued..	600,000

During 2009 Tennyson earned net income of $5,800,000. Compute Tennyson's EPS for 2009.

Computing and using earnings per share
(Obj. 1)

E11-16 Midtown Holding Limited operates numerous businesses, including motel, auto rental, and real estate companies. Year 2009 was interesting for Midtown, which reported the following on its income statement (in millions):

Net revenues	$3,930
Total expenses and other	3,354
Income from continuing operations	576
Discontinued operations, net of tax..	84
Income before extraordinary item, net of tax..	660
Extraordinary gain, net of tax...	8
Net income	$ 668

During 2009, Midtown had the following (in millions, except for stated value per share):

Common shares 900 shares issued..	$9

❙ Required

Show how Midtown should report earnings per share for 2009.

Accounting for income tax by a corporation
(Obj. 2)

E11-17 For 2009, its first year of operations, Smartpages Advertising Ltd. earned pretax accounting income (on the income statement) of $600,000. Taxable income (on the tax return filed with the Canada Revenue Agency) is $550,000. The income tax rate is 25%. Record Smartpages' income tax for the year. Show what Smartpages will report on its 2009 income statement and balance sheet for this situation. Start the income statement with income before tax.

Accounting for income tax by a corporation
(Obj. 2)

E11-18 During 2009, the Castle Heights Corp. income statement reported income of $300,000 before tax. The company's income tax return filed with the Canada Revenue Agency showed taxable income of $250,000. During 2009, Castle Heights was subject to an income tax rate of 25%.

❙ Required

1. Journalize Castle Heights' income taxes for 2009.
2. How much income tax did Castle Heights have to pay currently for 2009?

3. At the beginning of 2009, Castle Heights' balance of Future Income Tax Liability was $40,000. How much Future Income Tax Liability did Castle Heights report on its balance sheet at December 31, 2009?

E11-19 Roy Beaty Products Inc. reported a prior-period adjustment in 2009. An accounting error caused net income of 2008 to be understated by $10 million. Retained earnings at December 31, 2008, as previously reported, stood at $324 million. Net income for 2009 was $88 million, and 2009 dividends were $48 million.

Reporting a prior-period adjustment on the statement of retained earnings
(Obj. 3)

❙ *Required*

Prepare the company's statement of retained earnings for the year ended December 31, 2009. How does the prior-period adjustment affect Roy Beaty's net income for 2009?

E11-20 At December 31, 2008, Lake Air Mall Inc. reported shareholders' equity as follows:

Preparing a statement of shareholders' equity
(Obj. 3)

Common shares, 500,000 shares authorized, 300,000 shares issued...................	$ 870,000
Retained earnings...	680,000
	$1,550,000

During 2009, Lake Air Mall completed these transactions (listed in chronological order):

a. Declared and issued a 5% stock dividend on the outstanding shares. At the time, Lake Air Mall shares were quoted at a market price of $10 per share
b. Issued 20,000 common shares at the price of $12 per share
c. Net income for the year, $320,000
d. Declared cash dividends of $100,000

❙ *Required*

Prepare Lake Air Mall's statement of shareholders' equity for 2009, using the format of Exhibit 11-4 (p. 537) as a model.

E11-21 Spring Water Limited reported the following items on its statement of shareholders' equity for the year ended December 31, 2009 (in thousands):

Using a company's statement of shareholders' equity
(Obj. 3)

	Common Shares	Retained Earnings	Accumulated Other Comprehensive Income	Total Shareholders' Equity
Balance, Dec. 31, 2008..............	$3,000	$5,000	$14	$8,014
Net earnings...............................		1,500		
Unrealized gain on investments.			2	
Issuance of 15 shares.................	150			
Cash dividends..........................		(220)		
Balance, Dec. 31, 2009..............				

❙ *Required*

1. Determine the December 31, 2009, balances in Spring Water's shareholders' equity accounts and total shareholders' equity on this date.
2. Spring Water's total liabilities on December 31, 2009, are $7,500 thousand. What is Spring Water's debt ratio on this date?
3. Was there a profit or a loss for the year ended December 31, 2009? How can you tell?
4. At what price per share did Spring Water issue common shares during 2009?

Identifying responsibility and standards for the financial statements
(Obj. 4)

E11-22 The 2007 annual report of **WestJet Airlines Ltd**. included the following:

MANAGEMENT'S REPORT TO THE SHAREHOLDERS

The consolidated financial statements have been prepared by management in accordance with Canadian generally accepted accounting principles. When a choice between accounting methods exists, management has chosen those it deems conservative and appropriate in the circumstances. Financial statements will by necessity include certain amounts based on estimates and judgments. Management has determined such amounts on a reasonable basis to ensure that the consolidated financial statements are presented fairly in all material respects. Financial information contained in the annual report is consistent, where appropriate, with the information and data contained in the consolidated financial statements. All information in the annual report is the responsibility of management.

Management has established systems of internal control, including disclosure controls and procedures which are designed to provide reasonable assurance that financial and non-financial information that is disclosed is timely, complete, relevant and accurate. These systems of internal control also serve to safeguard the Corporation's assets. The systems of internal control are monitored by management, and further supported by an internal audit department whose functions include reviewing internal controls and their application.

The Board of Directors is responsible for the overall stewardship and governance of the Corporation, including ensuring management fulfills its responsibility for financial reporting and internal control, and reviewing and approving the consolidated financial statements. The Board carries out this responsibility principally through its Audit Committee.

The Audit Committee of the Board of Directors, comprised of independent Directors, meets regularly with management, the internal auditors and the external auditors to satisfy itself that each is properly discharging its responsibilities, and to review the consolidated financial statements and management's discussion and analysis. The Audit Committee reports its findings to the Board of Directors prior to the approval of such statements for issuance to the shareholders. The Audit Committee also recommends, for review by the Board of Directors and approval of shareholders, the reappointment of the external auditors. The internal and external auditors have full and free access to the Audit Committee.

The consolidated financial statements have been audited by KPMG LLP, the independent external auditors, in accordance with generally accepted auditing standards on behalf of the shareholders. The auditors' report outlines the scope of their examination and sets forth their opinion.

/s/Sean Durfy
SEAN DURFY
President and
Chief Executive Officer

/s/Vito Culmone
VITO CULMONE
Executive Vice-President, Finance
and Chief Financial Officer

Calgary, Canada
February 11, 2008

AUDITORS' REPORT TO THE SHAREHOLDERS

We have audited the consolidated balance sheets of WestJet Airlines Ltd. as at December 31, 2007 and 2006 and the consolidated statements of earnings, comprehensive income, shareholders' equity and cash flows for the years then ended. These financial statements are the responsibility of the Corporation's management. Our responsibility is to express an opinion on these financial statements based on our audits.

We conducted our audits in accordance with Canadian generally accepted auditing standards. Those standards require that we plan and perform an audit to obtain reasonable assurance whether the financial statements are free of material misstatement. An audit includes examining, on a test basis, evidence supporting the amounts and disclosures in the financial statements. An audit also includes assessing the accounting principles used and significant estimates made by management, as well as evaluating the overall financial statement presentation.

In our opinion, these consolidated financial statements present fairly, in all material respects, the financial position of the Corporation as at December 31, 2007 and 2006 and the results of its operations and its cash flows for the years then ended in accordance with Canadian generally accepted accounting principles.

/s/KPMG LLP

Chartered Accountants

Calgary, Canada
February 11, 2008

1. Who is responsible for WestJet's financial statements?
2. By what accounting standard are the financial statements prepared?
3. Identify one concrete action that WestJet's management takes to fulfill its responsibility for the reliability of the company's financial information.
4. Which entity gave an outside, independent opinion on the WestJet financial statements? Where was this entity located, and when did it release its opinion to the public?
5. Exactly what did the audit cover? Give names and dates.
6. By what standard did the auditor conduct the audit?
7. What was the auditor's opinion of WestJet's financial statements?

QUIZ

Test your understanding of the corporate income statement and the statement of shareholders' equity by answering the following questions. Select the best choice from among the possible answers given.

Q11-23 What is the best source of income for a corporation?
a. Prior-period adjustments
b. Continuing operations
c. Extraordinary items
d. Discontinued operations

Q11-24 Jergens Lotion Limited reports several earnings numbers on its current-year income statement (parentheses indicate a loss):

Gross margin	$140,000	Income from continuing operations	$35,000
Net income	41,000	Extraordinary gains	14,000
Income before income tax	60,000	Discontinued operations	(8,000)

How much net income would most investment analysts predict for Jergens to earn next year?
a. $14,000
b. $35,000
c. $49,000
d. $41,000

Q11-25 Return to the preceding question. Suppose you are evaluating Jergens Lotion Limited shares as an investment. You require a 10% rate of return on investments, so you capitalize Jergen's earnings at 10%. How much are you willing to pay for all of Jergens' common shares?
a. $1,400,000
b. $600,000
c. $410,000
d. $350,000

Q11-26 Hi-Valu Inc. had the following extraordinary items:

Extraordinary flood loss	$ 90,000
Extraordinary gain on lawsuit	110,000

Net income before income tax and before extraordinary items totals $260,000, and the income tax rate is 25%. Hi-Valu's net income is

a. $210,000
b. $280,000
c. $380,000
d. $460,000

Q11-27 Hi-Valu Inc. in question 11-26 has 10,000 $5 preferred shares and 100,000 common shares outstanding. Earnings per share for net income is
a. $1.02
b. $1.60
c. $1.68
d. $2.02

Q11-28 Earnings per share is *not* reported for
a. Continuing operations
b. Discontinued operations
c. Comprehensive income
d. Extraordinary items

Q11-29 Copystar Corporation has income before income tax of $150,000 and taxable income of $100,000. The income tax rate is 25%. Copystar's income statement will report net income of

a. $40,000

b. $60,000

c. $112,500

d. $120,000

Q11-30 Copystar Corporation in the preceding question must immediately pay income tax of

a. $60,000

b. $8,000

c. $32,000

d. $25,000

Q11-31 Use the Copystar Corporation data in question 11-29. At the end of its first year of operations, Copystar's future income tax liability is

a. $12,500

b. $28,000

c. $32,000

d. $40,000

Q11-32 Which of the following items is most closely related to prior-period adjustments?

a. Earnings per share

b. Retained earnings

c. Accounting changes

d. Preferred share dividends

Q11-33 Examine the statement of shareholders' equity of Westmount Concepts Inc. in Exhibit 11-4 (p. 537). What was the market value of each share that Westmount gave its shareholders in the stock dividend?

a. $8

b. $8,000

c. $34,000

d. $20

Q11-34 Which statement is true?

a. Management audits the financial statements.

b. Independent auditors prepare the financial statements.

c. GAAP governs the form and content of the financial statements.

d. The Public Company Oversight Board evaluates internal controls.

PROBLEMS

(GROUP A)

Preparing a complex income statement
(Obj. 1)

P11-35A The following information was taken from the records of Beauty Cosmetics Ltd. at December 31, 2009.

Prior-period adjustment—			Dividends on common shares ..	$ 37,000
debit to Retained Earnings	$ 4,000		Interest expense	23,000
Income tax expense (saving):			Gain on lawsuit settlement	8,000
Continuing operations	25,000		Dividend revenue	11,000
Income from discontinued operations..	2,000		General expenses	71,000
Extraordinary loss	(8,900)		Sales revenue	567,000
Cumulative effect of change			Retained earnings, beginning,	
in inventory method	2,500		as originally reported	63,000
Loss on sale of plant assets	10,000		Selling expenses	87,000
Income from discontinued operations..	7,000		Common shares	
Preferred shares $1.50			20,000 shares authorized	
4,000 shares issued	100,000		and issued	350,000
Cumulative effect of change in			Extraordinary loss	27,000
inventory method (credit)	7,600		Cost of goods sold	319,000

▌Required

1. Prepare Beauty Cosmetics' single-step income statement, which lists all revenues together and all expenses together, for the fiscal year ended December 31, 2009. Include earnings-per-share data.

2. Evaluate income for the year ended December 31, 2009. Beauty Cosmetics' top managers hoped to earn income from continuing operations equal to 10% of sales.

P11-36A Use the data in Problem 11-35A to prepare the Beauty Cosmetics statement of retained earnings for the year ended December 31, 2009.

Preparing a statement of retained earnings
(Obj. 3)

P11-37A Beauty Cosmetics in Problem 11-35A holds significant promise for carving a niche in its industry. A group of Canadian investors is considering purchasing the company's outstanding common shares. Beauty Cosmetics' common shares are currently selling for $32 per share.

Using income data to make an investment decision
(Obj. 1)

A *Financial Markets Magazine* story predicted the company's income is bound to grow. It appears that Beauty Cosmetics can earn at least its current level of income for the indefinite future. Based on this information, the investors think that an appropriate investment capitalization rate for estimating the value of Beauty Cosmetics' common shares is 8%. How much will this belief lead the investors to offer for Beauty Cosmetics? Will Beauty Cosmetics' existing shareholders be likely to accept this offer? Explain your answers.

P11-38A Turnaround Specialists Ltd. (TSL) specializes in taking underperforming companies to a higher level of performance. TSL's capital structure at December 31, 2008, included 10,000 $2.50 preferred shares and 120,000 common shares. During 2009, TSL issued common shares and ended the year with 127,000 common shares outstanding. Average common shares outstanding during 2009 were 123,500. Income from continuing operations during 2009 was $219,000. The company discontinued a segment of the business at a loss of $69,000, and an extraordinary item generated a gain of $49,500. All amounts are after income tax.

Computing earnings per share and estimating the price of a common share
(Obj. 1)

❙ Required

1. Compute TSL's earnings per share. Start with income from continuing operations.
2. Analysts believe TSL can earn its current level of income for the indefinite future. Estimate the market price of a common share of TSL at investment capitalization rates of 6%, 8%, and 10%. Which estimate presumes an investment in TSL is the most risky? How can you tell?

P11-39A Richard Wright, accountant for Sweetie Pie Foods Inc., was injured in an auto accident. Another employee prepared the following income statement for the fiscal year ended June 30, 2009:

Preparing a corrected income statement, including comprehensive income
(Obj. 1)

Sweetie Pie Foods Inc.
Income Statement
For the Year Ended June 30, 2009

Revenue and gains:		
Sales		$733,000
Contributed surplus on common shares		100,000
Total revenues and gains		833,000
Expenses and losses:		
Cost of goods sold	$383,000	
Selling expenses	103,000	
General expenses	74,000	
Sales returns	22,000	
Unrealized loss on investments	4,000	
Dividends paid	15,000	
Sales discounts	10,000	
Income tax expense	46,500	
Total expenses and losses		657,500
Income from operations		175,500
Other gains and losses:		
Extraordinary gain	30,000	
Loss on discontinued operations	(15,000)	
Total other gains (losses)		15,000
Net income		$190,500
Earnings per share		$4.76

The individual *amounts* listed on the income statement are correct. However, some *accounts* are reported incorrectly, and some accounts do not belong on the income statement at all. Also, income tax (33%) has not been applied to all appropriate figures. Sweetie Pie Foods issued 44,000 common shares back in 2003 and repurchased 4,000 common shares all during the fiscal year 2009.

I Required

Prepare a corrected statement of income (single-step, which lists all revenues together and all expenses together), including comprehensive income, for fiscal year 2009. Include earnings per share.

Accounting for a corporation's income tax
(Obj. 2)

P11-40A The accounting (not the income tax) records of Haynes Publications Inc. provide the comparative income statement for 2008 and 2009, respectively:

	2008	2009
Total revenue	$600,000	$720,000
Expenses:		
Cost of goods sold	$290,000	$310,000
Operating expenses	180,000	190,000
Total expenses before tax	470,000	500,000
Pretax accounting income	$130,000	$220,000

Taxable income for 2008 includes these modifications from pretax accounting income:

a. Additional taxable income of $10,000 for rent revenue earned in 2009, but collected in advance in 2008. Revenue collected in advance is included in the taxable income of the year when the cash is received. In calculating taxable income on the tax return, this revenue belongs in 2008.

b. There is additional capital cost allowance of $20,000 for amortization expense. Canada Revenue Agency (CRA) capital cost allowance (CCA) rate is higher than the straight-line method used by Haynes Publications Inc.

The income tax rate is 33%.

I Required

1. Compute Haynes' taxable income for 2008.
2. Journalize the corporation's income taxes for 2008.
3. Prepare the corporation's income statement for 2008.

Using a statement of shareholders' equity
(Obj. 3)

P11-41A Asian Food Specialties Inc. reported the following statement of shareholders' equity for the year ended June 30, 2009. The company was founded in 2005 and issued 455 million common shares. There have been no further share transactions until 2009.

Asian Food Specialties Inc.
Statement of Shareholders' Equity
For the Year Ended June 30, 2009

(In millions)	Common Shares	Retained Earnings	Total
Balance, June 30, 2008			
455 shares outstanding	$2,275	$1,702	$3,977
Net income		540	540
Cash dividends		(117)	(117)
Issuance of shares (5 shares)	50		50
Stock dividend (36 shares)	186	(186)	–
Issuance of shares (2 shares)	20		20
Balance, June 30, 2009	$2,531	$1,939	$4,470

❙ Required

Answer these questions about Asian Food Specialties' shareholders' equity transactions.

1. The income tax rate is 33%. How much income before income tax did Asian Food Specialties report on the income statement?

2. What is the stated value of a common share at June 30, 2008?

3. At what price per share did Asian Food Specialties issue its common shares during the year?

4. Asian Food Specialties' statement of shareholders' equity lists the share transactions in the order in which they occurred. What was the percentage of the stock dividend? Round to the nearest percentage.

(GROUP B)

P11-42B The following information was taken from the records of Kendall Industries Ltd. at April 30, 2009. Kendall manufactures electronic controls for model airplanes.

Preparing a complex income statement
(Obj. 1)

Dividends	$ 15,000		Prior-period adjustment—	
Interest revenue	4,000		credit to Retained Earnings	$ 6,000
Extraordinary gain	30,000		Interest expense	11,000
Income from discontinued operations	5,000		Cost of goods sold	424,000
Loss on insurance settlement	12,000		Cumulative effect of change	
General expenses	113,000		in inventory method (debit)	(18,000)
Preferred shares—$2,			Loss on sale of plant assets	8,000
10,000 shares authorized,			Income tax expense (saving):	
5,000 shares issued	200,000		Continuing operations	33,250
Retained earnings, beginning,			Discontinued operations	1,250
as originally reported	88,000		Extraordinary gain	7,500
Selling expenses	136,000		Cumulative effect of change	
Common shares, 24,000 shares			in inventory method	(4,500)
authorized and issued	240,000			
Sales revenue	833,000			

❙ Required

1. Prepare Kendall's single-step income statement, which lists all revenues together and all expenses together for the fiscal year ended April 30, 2009. Include earnings-per-share data.

2. Evaluate income for the year ended April 30, 2009. Kendall's top managers hoped to earn income from continuing operations equal to 10% of sales.

P11-43B Use the data in Problem 11-42B to prepare Kendall Industries Ltd.'s statement of retained earnings for the year ended April 30, 2009.

Preparing a statement of retained earnings
(Obj. 3)

P11-44B Kendall Industries Ltd. in Problem 11-42B holds significant promise for carving a niche in the electronic controls industry, and a group of Swiss investors is considering purchasing Kendall's outstanding common shares. Kendall's common shares are currently selling for $50 per share.

Using income data to make an investment decision
(Obj. 1)

A *Canadian Business* magazine story predicts that Kendall's income is bound to grow. It appears that the company can earn at least its current level of income for the indefinite future.

Based on this information, the investors think an appropriate investment capitalization rate for estimating the value of Kendall common shares is 9%. How much will this belief lead the investors to offer for Kendall Industries Ltd.? Will the existing shareholders of Kendall be likely to accept this offer? Explain your answers.

Computing earnings per share and estimating the price of a share
(Obj. 1)

P11-45B The capital structure of Morgan Products Inc. at December 31, 2008, included 20,000 $1.25 preferred shares and 44,000 common shares. During 2009, Morgan issued common shares and ended the year with 58,000 shares. The average number of common shares outstanding for the year was 51,000. Income from continuing operations during 2009 was $81,100. The company discontinued a segment of the business at a gain of $6,630, and an extraordinary item generated a loss of $16,000. All amounts are after income tax.

❙ *Required*

1. Compute Morgan's earnings per share. Start with income from continuing operations.
2. Analysts believe Morgan can earn its current level of income for the indefinite future. Estimate the market price of a common share at investment capitalization rates of 7%, 9%, and 11%. Which estimate presumes an investment in Morgan shares is the most risky? How can you tell?

Preparing a corrected income statement, including comprehensive income
(Obj. 1)

P11-46B Rhonda Sparks, accountant for Canon Pet Supplies Ltd., was injured in a skiing accident. Another employee prepared the accompanying income statement for the year ended December 31, 2009.

   The individual *amounts* listed on the income statement are correct. However, some *accounts* are reported incorrectly, and some accounts do not belong on the income statement at all. Also, income tax (30%) has not been applied to all appropriate figures. Canon issued 52,000 common shares in 2008 and repurchased 2,000 shares during 2009.

Canon Pet Supplies Ltd.
Income Statement
2009

Revenue and gains:		
Sales		$362,000
Unrealized gain on investments		10,000
Contributed surplus		80,000
Total revenues and gains		452,000
Expenses and losses:		
Cost of goods sold	$103,000	
Selling expenses	56,000	
General expenses	61,000	
Sales returns	11,000	
Dividends paid	7,000	
Sales discounts	6,000	
Income tax expense	37,500	
Total expenses and losses		281,500
Income from operations		170,500
Other gains and losses:		
Extraordinary loss	(20,000)	
Loss on discontinued operations	(3,000)	
Total other losses		(23,000)
Net income		$147,500
Earnings per share		$2.95

❙ *Required*

Prepare a corrected statement of income (single-step, which lists all revenues together and all expenses together), including comprehensive income for 2009. Include earnings per share.

P11-47B The accounting (not the income tax) records of Ottawa Rafting Inc. provide the following comparative income statement for 2008 and 2009, respectively.

Accounting for a corporation's income tax
(Obj. 2)

	2008	2009
Total revenue	$900,000	$990,000
Expenses:		
Cost of goods sold	$430,000	$460,000
Operating expenses	270,000	280,000
Total expenses before tax	700,000	740,000
Pretax accounting income	$200,000	$250,000

Taxable income for 2008 includes these modifications from pretax accounting income:

a. Additional taxable income of $15,000 for revenue earned in 2009, but collected in advance in 2008. Revenue collected in advance is included in the taxable income of the year when the cash is received. In calculating taxable income on the tax return, this revenue belongs in 2008.

b. There is additional capital cost allowance of $30,000 for amortization expense. Canada Revenue Agency capital cost allowance rate is higher than the straight-line method used by Ottawa Rafting Inc.

The income tax rate is 25%.

❙ Required

1. Compute Ottawa Rafting's taxable income for 2008.
2. Journalize the corporation's income taxes for 2008.
3. Prepare the corporation's income statement for 2008.

P11-48B Datacom Services Inc. reported the following statement of shareholders' equity for the year ended October 31, 2009.

Using a statement of shareholders' equity
(Obj. 3)

Datacom Services Inc.
Statement of Shareholders' Equity
For the Year Ended October 31, 2009

(In millions)	Common Shares	Retained Earnings	Total
Balance, Oct. 31, 2008	$2,025	$904	$2,929
Net income		360	360
Cash dividends		(194)	(194)
Issuance of shares (13 shares)	49		49
Stock dividend (55 shares)	166	(166)	–
Balance, Oct. 31, 2009	$2,240	$904	$3,144

❙ Required

Answer these questions about Datacom Services' shareholders' equity transactions:

1. The income tax rate is 33%. How much income before income tax did Datacom report on the income statement?
2. What is the stated value of a common share at October 31, 2008?
3. At what price per share did Datacom Services issue its common shares during the year?
4. Datacom Services' statement lists the share transactions in the order they occurred. What was the percentage of the stock dividend?

APPLY YOUR KNOWLEDGE

DECISION CASES

Evaluating the components of income
(Obj. 1)

Case 1. Prudhoe Bay Oil Ltd. is having its initial public offering (IPO) of company shares. To create public interest in its shares, Prudhoe Bay's chief financial officer has blitzed the media with press releases. One, in particular, caught your eye. On September 19, Prudhoe Bay announced unaudited earnings per share (EPS) of $1.19, up 89% from last year's EPS of $0.63. An 89% increase in EPS is outstanding!

Before deciding to buy Prudhoe Bay stock, you investigated further and found that the company omitted several items from the determination of unaudited EPS:

- Unrealized loss on investments, $0.06 per share
- Gain on sale of building, $0.05 per share
- Cumulative effect of change in method of recognizing revenue, increase in retained earnings, $1.10 per share
- Restructuring expenses, $0.29 per share
- Loss on settlement of lawsuit begun 5 years ago, $0.12 per share
- Lost income due to employee labour strike, $0.24 per share
- Income from discontinued operations, $0.09 per share

Wondering how to treat these "special items," you called your stockbroker at Merrill Lynch. She thinks that these items are nonrecurring and outside Prudhoe Bay's core operations. Furthermore, she suggests that you ignore the items and consider Prudhoe Bay's earnings of $1.19 per share to be a good estimate of long-term profitability.

❙ Required

What EPS number will you use to predict Prudhoe Bay's future profits? Show your work, and explain your reasoning for each item.

Using the financial statements in investment analysis
(Obj. 1)

Case 2. Mike Magid Toyota is an automobile dealership. Magid's annual report includes Note 1—Summary of Significant Accounting Policies as follows:

> **Income Recognition**
>
> Sales are recognized when cash payment is received or, in the case of credit sales, which represent the majority of . . . sales, when a down payment is received and the customer enters into an Installment sales contract. These installment sales contracts . . . are normally collectible over 36 to 60 months . . . .
>
> Revenue from auto insurance policies sold to customers is recognized as income over the life of the contracts.

Bay Area Nissan, a competitor of Mike Magid Toyota, includes the following note in its Summary of Significant Accounting Policies:

> **Accounting Policies for Revenues**
>
> Sales are recognized when cash payment is received or, in the case of credit sales, which represent the majority of . . . sales, when the customer enters into an installment sales contract. Customer down payments are rare. Most of these installment sales contracts are normally collectible over 36 to 60 months . . . . Revenue from auto insurance policies sold to customers are recognized when the customer signs an insurance contract. Expenses are recognized over the life of the insurance contracts.

Suppose you have decided to invest in an auto dealership and you've narrowed your choices to Magid and Bay Area. Which company's earnings are of higher quality? Why? Will their accounting policies affect your investment decision? If so, how? Mention specific accounts in the financial statements that will differ between the two companies.

ETHICAL ISSUE

The income statement of Transparency Accounting Services Ltd. reported the following results of operations:

Earnings before income taxes, extraordinary gain, and cumulative effect of accounting change	$178,064
Income tax expense	58,761
Earnings before extraordinary gain and cumulative effect of accounting change	119,303
Extraordinary gain, net of income tax	149,755
Cumulative effect of change in accounting, net of income tax	(32,961)
Net earnings	$236,097

Suppose Transparency's management had reported the company's results of operations in this manner:

Earnings before income taxes	$352,384
Income tax expense	116,287
Net earnings	$236,097

❙ *Required*

1. Does it really matter how a company reports its operating results? Why? Who could be helped by management's action? Who could be hurt?

2. Suppose Transparency's management decides to report its operating results in the second manner. Evaluate the ethics of this decision.

FOCUS ON FINANCIALS

Sun-Rype Products Ltd.

Refer to the Sun-Rype Products Ltd. financial statements in Appendix A at the end of this book.

Analyzing income and investments **(Obj. 1)**

1. Sun-Rype's income statement does not mention income from continuing operations. Why not?

2. Take the role of an investor, and suppose you are determining the price to pay for a share of Sun-Rype Products. Assume you are considering three investment capitalization rates that depend on the risk of an investment in Sun-Rype Products: 5%, 6%, and 7%. Compute your estimated value of a share of Sun-Rype Products using each of the three capitalization rates. Which estimated value would you base your investment strategy on if you rate Sun-Rype Products risky? Which estimated value would you use if you consider Sun-Rype Products a safe investment? Use basic earnings per share for 2007.

3. Go to Sun-Rype's Web site and compare your computed estimates to Sun-Rype Products' actual share price. Which of your prices is most realistic?

FOCUS ON ANALYSIS

Mullen Group Income Fund

This case is based on the Mullen Group financial statements in Appendix B at the end of this book.

Evaluating the quality of earnings, valuing investments, and analyzing units outstanding **(Obj. 1, 3)**

1. Mullen's income statement reports only one special item. What is it, and what is its amount for 2007?

2. What is your evaluation of the quality of Mullen Group's earnings? State how you formed your opinion.

3. At the end of 2006, how much would you have been willing to pay for one unit of Mullen Group if you had rated the investment as high risk? What about if you rated it as low risk? Use even-numbered investment capitalization rates in the range of 6% to 12% for your analysis, and use basic earnings per unit for continuing operations.

4. Go to Mullen Group's Web site and get the price of a unit of Mullen Group Income Fund at February 2007. Which value that you estimated in requirement 2 was closest to Mullen's actual unit price?

GROUP PROJECT

Select a company and research its business. Search the business press for articles about this company. Obtain its annual report by requesting it directly from the company or from the company's Web site.

❙ *Required*

1. Based on your group's analysis, come to class prepared to instruct the class on six interesting facts about the company that can be found in its financial statements and the related notes. Your group can mention only the obvious, such as net sales or total revenue, net income, total assets, total liabilities, total shareholders' equity, and dividends, in conjunction with other terms. Once you use an obvious item, you may not use that item again.

2. The group should write a paper discussing the facts that it has uncovered. Limit the paper to two double-spaced word-processed pages.

QUICK CHECK ANSWERS

1. *b*
2. *a*
3. *d ($5.94/0.06 = $99)*
4. *c ($317/$0.17 = 1,865 thousand = 1.9 million)*
5. *d*
6. *c*
7. *a*
8. *d*
9. *b*
10. *c*

The Cash Flow Statement

Learning Objectives

1. **Identify** the purposes of the cash flow statement

2. **Distinguish** among operating, investing, and financing cash flows

3. **Prepare** a cash flow statement by the indirect method

4. **Prepare** a cash flow statement by the direct method

SPOTLIGHT

Potash Corporation of Saskatchewan Inc. (PotashCorp) is the world's largest producer of potash, a principal ingredient in fertilizer, which is needed all over the world to grow food for an ever-increasing population.

Other potash suppliers are reaching or have reached maximum production while PotashCorp can expand its production to meet an ever-increasing demand. The future looks very bright for PotashCorp.

Potash Corporation of Saskatchewan Inc.
▼ Consolidated Cash Flow Statement (Adapted)
For the Year Ended December 31, 2007

(Amounts in millions of U.S. dollars)		2007
Operating Activities		
Net income		$1,103.6
Adjustments to reconcile net income to cash provided by operating activities		
Depreciation and amortization	291.3	
Stock-based compensation	38.6	
Loss (gain) on disposal of property, plant, and equipment and long-term investments....	7.9	
Provision for auction rate securities	26.5	
Foreign exchange on future income tax	52.4	
Provision for future income tax	119.6	
Undistributed earnings of equity investees	(35.6)	
Unrealized gain on derivative instruments	(21.1)	
Other long-term liabilities	(57.9)	
Subtotal of adjustments		421.7
Changes in non-cash operating working capital		
Accounts receivable	(154.6)	
Inventories	60.3	
Prepaid expenses and other current assets	7.0	
Accounts payable and accrued charges	250.9	
Subtotal of changes in non-cash operating working capital		163.6
Cash provided by operating activities		1,688.9
Investing Activities		
Additions to property, plant, and equipment		(607.2)
Purchase of long-term investments		(30.7)
Purchase of investments in auction rate securities		(132.5)
Proceeds from disposal of property, plant, and equipment and long-term investments		4.5
Other assets and intangible assets		7.8
Cash used in investing activities		(758.1)
Cash before financing activities		930.8
Financing Activities		
Proceeds from long-term debt obligations		1.5
Repayment and issue costs of long-term debt obligations		(403.6)
(Repayment of) proceeds from short-term debt obligations		(67.9)
Dividends		(93.6)
Issuance of common shares		26.6
Cash used in financing activities		(537.0)
Increase in Cash and Cash Equivalents		393.8
Cash and Cash Equivalents, Beginning of Year		325.7
Cash and Cash Equivalents, End of Year		$ 719.5
Cash and cash equivalents comprised of:		
Cash		$ 23.1
Short-term investments		696.4
		$ 719.5

Source: PotashCorp 2007 Annual Report.

In preceding chapters, we covered cash flows as they related to various topics: receivables, property, plant, and equipment, and so on. In this chapter, we show you how to prepare and use the cash flow statement. We begin with the statement format used by the vast majority of companies, called the *indirect approach*. We end with the alternate format of the cash flow statement, the *direct approach*. After working through this chapter, you can analyze the cash flows of actual companies.

This chapter has three distinct sections:

- Basic Concepts, beginning on this page
- Preparing the Cash Flow Statement: Indirect Method, page 566
- Preparing the Cash Flow Statement: Direct Method, page 578

The introduction applies to all cash-flow topics. Professors who wish to cover only the indirect method can assign the first two parts of the chapter. Those interested only in the direct method can proceed from the introduction, which ends on page 566, to the direct method, on page 578.

Basic Concepts: The Cash Flow Statement

The balance sheet reports financial position, and balance sheets from two periods show whether cash increased or decreased. But that doesn't tell why the cash balance changed. The income statement reports revenues, expenses, and net income and provides some clues about cash, but the income statement does not tell why cash increased or decreased. We need a third statement.

The cash flow statement reports **cash flows**—cash receipts and cash payments—in other words, where cash came from (receipts) and how it was spent (payments). The statement covers a span of time and therefore is dated "For the Year Ended December 31, 2008" or "For the Month Ended June 30, 2009." Exhibit 12-1 illustrates the relative timing of the four basic statements.

The cash flow statement helps investors and creditors perform the following functions:

1. **Predict future cash flows.** Past cash receipts and payments are reasonably good predictors of future cash flows.

2. **Evaluate management decisions.** Businesses that make wise investment decisions prosper, and those that make unwise decisions suffer losses. The cash flow statement reports how managers got cash and how they used cash to run the business.

Objective

① Identify the purposes of the cash flow statement

EXHIBIT 12-1   **Timing of the Financial Statements**

| December 31, 2008 (a point in time) | For the Year Ended December 31, 2009 (a period of time) | December 31, 2009 (a point in time) |

3. **Determine ability to pay dividends and interest.** Shareholders want dividends on their investments. Creditors collect interest and principal on their loans. The cash flow statement reports on the ability to make these payments.

4. **Show the relationship of net income to cash flows.** Usually, cash and net income move together. High levels of income tend to lead to increases in cash, and vice versa. However, a company's cash flow can suffer even when net income is high.

On a cash flow statement, *cash* means more than just cash in the bank. It includes **cash equivalents**, which are highly liquid short-term investments that can be converted into cash immediately. Examples include money-market accounts and investments in Canadian government securities. Throughout this chapter, the term *cash* refers to cash and cash equivalents.

Let's now turn to the different categories of cash flows.

USER ALERT ⚠

How's Your Cash Flow? Telltale Signs of Financial Difficulty

Companies want to earn net income because profit measures success. Without net income, a business sinks. There will be no dividends, and the share price will likely suffer. High net income helps attract investors, but you can't pay bills with net income. That requires cash.

A company needs both net income and strong cash flow. Income and cash flow usually move together because net income generates cash. Sometimes, however, net income and cash flow follow different patterns. To illustrate, consider Fastech Company Ltd.:

Fastech Company Ltd. Income Statement For the Year Ended December 31, 2009		**Fastech Company Ltd.** Balance Sheet December 31, 2009			
Sales revenue	$100,000	Cash	$ 3,000	Total current liabilities	$ 50,000
Cost of goods sold	30,000	Receivables	37,000	Long-term liabilities	20,000
Operating expenses	10,000	Inventory	40,000		
		Capital assets, net	60,000	Shareholders' equity	70,000
Net income	$ 60,000	Total assets	$140,000	Total liabilities and equity	$140,000

What can we glean from Fastech's income statement and balance sheet?

- Fastech is profitable. Net income is 60% of revenue. Fastech's profitability looks outstanding.
- The current ratio is 1.6, and the debt ratio is only 50%. These measures suggest little trouble in paying bills.
- But Fastech is on the verge of bankruptcy. Can you spot the problem? Can you see what is causing the problem? Three trouble spots leap out to a financial analyst.

1. The cash balance is very low. Three thousand dollars isn't enough cash to pay the bills of a company with sales of $100,000.
2. Fastech isn't selling inventory fast enough. Fastech turned over its inventory only 0.75 times during the year. As we saw in Chapter 6, many companies have inventory turnover rates of 3 to 8 times a year. A turnover ratio of 0.75 times means it takes a very long time to sell inventory, and that delays cash collections.
3. Fastech's days' sales in receivables ratio is 135 days. Very few companies can wait that long to collect from customers. With standard credit terms of net 30 days, Fastech should collect cash within around 45 days. Fastech cannot survive with a collection period of 135 days.

This User Alert's lesson is the following:

- You need both net income and strong cash flow to succeed in business.

Operating, Investing, and Financing Activities

A business engages in three types of business activities:

- Operating activities
- Investing activities
- Financing activities

PotashCorp's cash flow statement reports cash flows under these three headings, as shown for PotashCorp on page 562.

Operating activities create revenues, expenses, gains, and losses—*net income,* which is a product of accrual-basis accounting. The cash flow statement reports on operating activities. Operating activities are the most important of the three categories because they reflect the core of the organization. *A successful business must generate most of its cash from operating activities.*

Investing activities increase and decrease *long-term assets,* such as computers and software, land, buildings, equipment, and investments in other companies. Purchases and sales of these assets are investing activities. Investing activities are important, but they are less critical than operating activities.

Financing activities obtain cash from investors and creditors. Issuing and repurchasing shares, borrowing money, and paying cash dividends to shareholders are financing activities. Paying off a loan is another example. Financing cash flows relate to *long-term liabilities* and *owners' equity*. They are the least important of the three categories of cash flows, and that's why they come last. Exhibit 12-2 shows how operating, investing, and financing activities relate to the various parts of the balance sheet.

Examine PotashCorp's cash flow statement on page 562. Focus on the final line of each section: Operating, Investing, and Financing. During 2007, PotashCorp's operating activities provided almost $1,700 million (U.S.) of cash. PotashCorp invested almost $760 million (U.S.) and reduced debt and paid dividends of almost $540 million (U.S.) through financing activities. These figures show that:

- *Operations* are PotashCorp's largest source of cash.
- The company is *investing* in the future.
- The company is rewarding its investors and managing its debt.

Two Formats for Operating Activities

There are two ways to format operating activities on the cash flow statement:

- **Indirect method**, which reconciles net income to net cash provided by operating activities.
- **Direct method**, which reports all cash receipts and cash payments from operating activities.

EXHIBIT 12-2   Operating, Investing, and Financing Cash Flows and the Balance Sheet

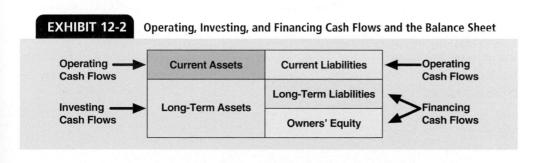

The two methods use different computations, but they produce the same figure for cash from *operating activities*. The two methods do not affect *investing* or *financing* activities. The following table summarizes the differences between the two approaches:

Indirect Method		*Direct Method*	
Net income	$600	Collections from customers.........	$2,000
Adjustments:		*Deductions:*	
Amortization added back, etc.......	300	Payments to suppliers, etc.......	(1,100)
Net income provided by		Net income provided by	
operating activities	$900	operating activities	$ 900

Let's begin with the indirect method because the vast majority of companies use it.

Preparing the Cash Flow Statement: Indirect Method

Objective

③ **Prepare** a cash flow statement by the indirect method

To illustrate the cash flow statement we use Bradshaw Corporation, a dealer in playground equipment. Proceed as shown in the following steps to prepare the cash flow statement by the indirect method.

STEP 1 Lay out the template as shown in Part 1 of Exhibit 12-3. The exhibit is comprehensive. The diagram in Part 2 gives a visual picture of the statement.

STEP 2 Use the comparative balance sheet to determine the increase or decrease in cash during the period. The change in cash is the "check figure" for the cash flow statement. Exhibit 12-4 gives Bradshaw Corporation's comparative balance sheet with cash highlighted. Bradshaw's cash decreased by $20,000 during 2009. *Why* did cash decrease? The cash flow statement provides the answer.

STEP 3 From the income statement, take net income, amortization expense, and any gains or losses on the sale of long-term assets. Print these items on the cash flow statement. Exhibit 12-5 (p. 569) gives Bradshaw Corporation's income statement, with relevant items highlighted.

STEP 4 Use the income statement and the balance sheet data to prepare the cash flow statement. The cash flow statement is complete only after you have explained the year-to-year changes in all the balance sheet accounts.

Go to "Cash Flows from Operating Activities," below.

Cash Flows from Operating Activities

Operating activities are related to the transactions that make up net income.[1]

The operating section of the cash flow statement begins with net income, taken from the income statement (Exhibit 12-5), and is followed by "Adjustments to reconcile net income to net cash provided by operating activities" (Exhibit 12-6). Let's discuss these adjustments.

---

[1]The authors thank Alfonso Oddo for suggesting this summary.

EXHIBIT 12-3   Part 1—Template of the Cash Flow Statement: Indirect Method

Bradshaw Corporation
Cash Flow Statement
For the Year Ended December 31, 2009

Cash flows from operating activities:

Net income
  Adjustments to reconcile net income to net cash provided by operating activities:
  + Amortization expense
  + Loss on sale of long-term assets
  − Gain on sale of long-term assets
  − Increases in current assets other than cash
  + Decreases in current assets other than cash
  + Increases in current liabilities
  − Decreases in current liabilities
  Net cash provided by operating activities

Cash flows from investing activities:

Sales of long-term assets (investments, land, building, equipment, and so on)
  − Purchases of long-term assets
  + Collections of long-term receivables
  − Long-term loans to others
  Net cash provided by (used for) investing activities

Cash flows from financing activities:

Issuance of shares
  − Repurchase of shares
  + Borrowing (issuance of notes or bonds payable)
  − Payment of notes or bonds payable
  − Payment of dividends
  Net cash provided by (used for) financing activities

Net increase (decrease) in cash during the year
  + Cash at December 31, 2008
  = Cash at December 31, 2009

Ⓐ **Amortization Expense.** This expense is added back to net income when we go from net income to cash flow. Let's see why. Amortization is recorded as follows:

Amortization Expense	18,000	
Accumulated Amortization		18,000

Amortization expense has no effect on cash. However, amortization expense, like all other expenses, decreases net income. Therefore, to convert net income to cash flow, we add amortization back to net income. The add-back cancels the earlier deduction.

Example: Suppose you had only two transactions during the period, a $1,000 cash sale and amortization expense of $300. Net income is $700 ($1,000 − $300). Cash flow from operations is $1,000. To go from net income ($700) to cash flow ($1,000), we must add back the amortization ($300).

Ⓑ **Gains and Losses on the Sale of Long-Term Assets.** Sales of long-term assets are *investing* activities, and there is often a gain or loss on the sale. On the cash flow statement, a gain or loss on the sale is an adjustment to net income. Exhibit 12-6 includes an adjustment for a gain. During 2009, Bradshaw sold equipment for $62,000. The book value was $54,000 (see calculation of book value on page 571), so there was a gain of $8,000.

EXHIBIT 12-3   Part 2—Positive and Negative Items on the Cash Flow Statement: Indirect Method

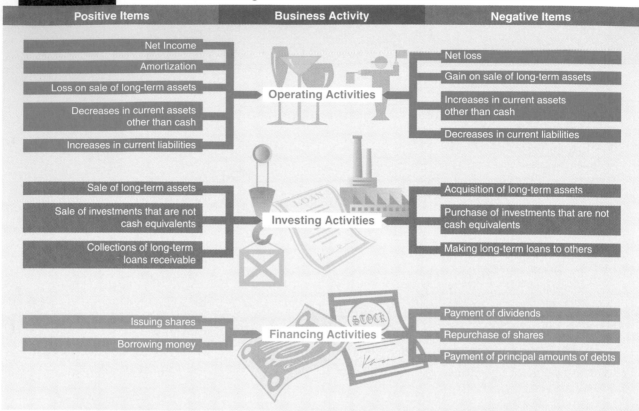

EXHIBIT 12-4   Comparative Balance Sheet for Bradshaw Corporation

Bradshaw Corporation
Comparative Balance Sheet
December 31, 2009 and 2008

(Amounts in thousands)	2009	2008	Increase (Decr Tease)	
Assets				
Current:				
Cash	$ 22	$ 42	$ (20)	⎫
Accounts receivable	93	80	13	⎬
Interest receivable	3	1	2	⎬ Changes in current assets—Operating
Inventory	135	138	(3)	⎬
Prepaid expenses	8	7	1	⎭
Long-term note receivable from another company	11	—	11	⎫
Property, plant, and equipment				⎬
assets, net of amortization	353	219	134	⎬ Changes in noncurrent assets—Investing
Total	$625	$487	$138	⎭
Liabilities				
Current:				
Accounts payable	$ 91	$ 57	$ 34	⎫
Salary and wages payable	4	6	(2)	⎬ Changes in current liabilities—Operating
Accrued liabilities	1	3	(2)	⎭
Long-term debt	160	77	83	⎫ Changes in long-term liabilities and
Shareholders' Equity				⎬ contributed capital accounts—Financing
Common shares	259	258	1	⎭
Retained earnings	110	86	24	⎫ Changes due to net income—Operating
Total	$625	$487	$138	⎭ Change due to dividends—Financing

EXHIBIT 12-5   Income Statement for Bradshaw Corporation

Bradshaw Corporation
Income Statement
For the Year Ended December 31, 2009

	(Amounts in thousands)	
Revenues and gains:		
Sales revenue	$284	
Interest revenue	12	
Dividend revenue	9	
Gain on sale of property, plant, and equipment	8	
Total revenues and gains		$313
Expenses:		
Cost of goods sold	150	
Salary and wages expense	56	
Amortization expense	18	
Other operating expense	17	
Interest expense	16	
Income tax expense	15	
Total expenses		272
Net income		$41

EXHIBIT 12-6   Cash Flow Statement—Operating Activities by the Indirect Method

Bradshaw Corporation
Cash Flow Statement
For the Year Ended December 31, 2009

		(Amounts in thousands)	
Cash flows from operating activities:			
	Net income		$41
	Adjustments to reconcile net income to net cash provided by operating activities:		
Ⓐ	Amortization	$ 18	
Ⓑ	Gain on sale of property, plant, and equipment	(8)	
	Increase in accounts receivable	(13)	
	Increase in interest receivable	(2)	
	Decrease in inventory	3	
Ⓒ	Increase in prepaid expenses	(1)	
	Increase in accounts payable	34	
	Decrease in salary and wages payable	(2)	
	Decrease in accrued liabilities	(2)	27
	Net cash provided by operating activities		$68

The $62,000 cash received from the sale is an investing activity; the $62,000 includes the $8,000 gain. Net income also includes the gain, so we must subtract the gain from net cash provided from operations, as shown in Bradshaw Corporation's cash flow statement (Exhibit 12-6). (We explain investing activities in the next section.)

A loss on the sale of property, plant, and equipment also creates an adjustment in the operating section. Losses are *added back* to net income to compute cash flow from operations.

© **Changes in the Current Asset and Current Liability Accounts.** Most current assets and current liabilities result from operating activities. For example, accounts receivable result from sales, inventory relates to cost of goods sold, and so on. Changes in the current accounts are reported as adjustments to net income on the cash flow statement. The reasoning follows:

1. **An *increase* in another current asset decreases cash.** It takes cash to acquire assets. Suppose you make a sale on account. Accounts receivable are increased, but cash isn't affected yet. Exhibit 12-4 (page 568) reports that Bradshaw Corporation's Accounts Receivable increased by $13,000 during 2009. To compute cash flow from operations, we must subtract the $13,000 increase in Accounts Receivable, as shown in Exhibit 12-6. The reason is this: We have *not* collected this $13,000 in cash. The same logic applies to the other current assets. If they increase, cash decreases.

2. **A *decrease* in another current asset increases cash.** Suppose Bradshaw's Accounts Receivable balance decreased by $4,000. Cash receipts caused Accounts Receivable to decrease, so we add decreases in Accounts Receivable and the other current assets to net income.

3. **A *decrease* in a current liability decreases cash.** Payment of a current liability decreases both cash and the liability, so we subtract decreases in current liabilities from net income. In Exhibit 12-6, the $2,000 decrease in Accrued Liabilities is *subtracted* from net income to compute net cash provided by operations.

4. **An *increase* in a current liability increases cash.** Bradshaw's Accounts Payable increased. That can occur only if cash is not spent to pay this liability. Cash payments are therefore less than expenses and Bradshaw has more cash on hand. Thus, increases in current liabilities increase cash.

Evaluating Cash Flows from Operating Activities. Let's step back and evaluate Bradshaw's operating cash flows during 2009. Bradshaw Corporation's operations provided net cash flows of $68,000 (Exhibit 12-6). This amount exceeds net income, and it should because of the add-back of amortization. Now let's examine Bradshaw's investing and financing activities, as reported in Exhibit 12-7.

Cash Flows from Investing Activities

> Investing activities affect long-term asset accounts, such as Long-Term Assets, Investments, and Notes Receivable.

Most of the data come from the balance sheet.

Computing Acquisitions and Sales of Property, Plant, and Equipment Assets. Companies keep separate accounts for each item of property, plant, and equipment. But for computing cash flows, it is helpful to combine these accounts into a single summary account. Also, we subtract accumulated amortization from the assets' cost and use the net figure. It is easier to work with a single property, plant, and equipment asset account.

To illustrate, observe that Bradshaw Corporation's

- Balance sheet reports beginning property, plant, and equipment, net of amortization, of $219,000. The ending balance is $353,000 (Exhibit 12-4).

- Income statement shows amortization expense of $18,000 and an $8,000 gain on sale of property, plant, and equipment (Exhibit 12-5).

EXHIBIT 12-7	Cash Flow Statement—Indirect Method

Bradshaw Corporation
Cash Flow Statement
For the Year Ended December 31, 2009

		(Amounts in thousands)	
Cash flows from operating activities:			
Net income..		$ 41	
Adjustments to reconcile net income to net cash			
provided by operating activities:			
Ⓐ Amortization	$ 18		
Ⓑ Gain on sale of property, plant, and equipment	(8)		
Increase in accounts receivable	(13)		
Increase in interest receivable	(2)		
Decrease in inventory	3		
Ⓒ Increase in prepaid expenses	(1)		
Increase in accounts payable...	34		
Decrease in salary and wages payable	(2)		
Decrease in accrued liabilities...	(2)	27	
Net cash provided by operating activities.......................		68	
Cash flows from investing activities:			
Acquisition of property, plant, and equipment.......................	(206)		
Loan to another company...	(11)		
Proceeds from sale of property, plant, and equipment............	62		
Net cash used for investing activities		(155)	
Cash flows from financing activities:			
Proceeds from issuance of common shares	1		
Proceeds from issuance of long-term debt	94		
Payment of long-term debt..	(11)		
Payment of dividends..	(17)		
Net cash provided by financing activities...........................		67	
Net decrease in cash...		(20)	
Cash balance, December 31, 2008		42	
Cash balance, December 31, 2009		$ 22	

Bradshaw's purchases of property, plant, and equipment total $206,000 (take this amount as given; see Exhibit 12-7). How much, then, are the proceeds from the sale of property, plant, and equipment? First, we must determine the book value of property, plant, and equipment sold, as follows:

Property, plant, and equipment (net)

Beginning balance	+	Acquisitions	−	Amortization	−	Book value of assets sold	=	Ending balance
$219,000	+	$206,000	−	$18,000		−X	=	$353,000
						−X	=	$353,000 − $219,000 − $206,000 + $18,000
						X	=	$54,000

The sale proceeds are $62,000, determined as follows:

$$\text{Sale proceeds} = \text{Book value of assets sold} + \text{Gain} - \text{Loss}$$

$$= \$54,000 + \$8,000 - \$0$$

$$= \$62,000$$

Trace the sale proceeds of $62,000 to the cash flow statement in Exhibit 12-7. The Property, Plant, and Equipment T-account provides another look at the computation of the book value of the assets sold.

Property, Plant, and Equipment

Beginning balance	219,000	Amortization	18,000
Acquisitions	206,000	Book value of assets sold	54,000
Ending balance	353,000		

If the sale had resulted in a loss of $3,000, the sale proceeds would have been $51,000 ($54,000 − $3,000), and the statement would report $51,000 as a cash receipt from this investing activity.

Computing Acquisitions and Sales of Investments, and Loans and Collections. The cash amounts of investment transactions can be computed in the manner illustrated for property, plant, and equipment. Investments are easier because there is no amortization to account for, as shown in the following equation:

Investments (amounts assumed for illustration only)

Beginning balance	+	Purchases	−	Book value of investments sold	=	Ending balance
$100,000	+	$50,000		−X	=	$140,000
				−X	=	$140,000 − $100,000 − $50,000
				X	=	$10,000

The Investments T-account provides another look.

Investments

Beginning balance	100		
Purchases	50	Book value of investments sold	10
Ending balance	140		

Bradshaw Corporation has a long-term note receivable, and the cash flows from loan transactions on notes receivable can be determined as follows (data from Exhibit 12-4 and the general ledger):

Notes Receivable

Beginning balance	+	New loans made	−	Collections	=	Ending balance
$0	+	$X		−0	=	$11,000
		X			=	$11,000

Notes Receivable

Beginning balance	0		
New loans made	11	Collections	0
Ending balance	11		

Exhibit 12-8 summarizes the cash flows from investing activities, highlighted in colour.

Cash Flows from Financing Activities

Financing activities affect liabilities and shareholders' equity accounts, such as Notes Payable, Bonds Payable, Long-Term Debt, Common Shares, and Retained Earnings.

EXHIBIT 12-8 Computing Cash Flows from Investing Activities

Receipts

From sale of property, plant, and equipment	$\text{Beginning property, plant,} \atop \text{and equipment (net)} + {\text{Acquisition} \atop \text{cost}} - \text{Amortization} - {\text{Book value of} \atop \text{assets sold}} = \text{Ending property, plant, and equipment (net)}$

$$\text{Cash received} - {\text{Book value of} \atop \text{assets sold}} \underset{-}{\overset{+}{\text{or}}} {\text{Gain on sale} \atop \text{Loss on sale}}$$

From sale of investments	$\text{Beginning} \atop \text{investments} + {\text{Purchase cost} \atop \text{of investments}} - {\text{Cost of} \atop \text{investments sold}} = {\text{Ending} \atop \text{investments}}$

$$\text{Cash received} = {\text{Cost of} \atop \text{investments sold}} \underset{-}{\overset{+}{\text{or}}} {\text{Gain on sale} \atop \text{Loss on sale}}$$

From collection of notes receivable	$\text{Beginning} \atop \text{notes receivable} + \text{New loans made} - \text{Collections} = {\text{Ending notes} \atop \text{receivable}}$

Payments

For acquisition of property, plant, and equipment	$\text{Beginning property, plant,} \atop \text{and equipment (net)} + {\text{Acquisition} \atop \text{cost}} - \text{Amortization} - {\text{Book value of} \atop \text{assets sold}} = \text{Ending property, plant, and equipment (net)}$

For purchase of investments	$\text{Beginning} \atop \text{investments} + {\text{Purchase cost} \atop \text{of investments}} - {\text{Cost of} \atop \text{investments sold}} = {\text{Ending} \atop \text{investments}}$

For new loans made	$\text{Beginning} \atop \text{notes receivable} + \text{New loans made} - \text{Collections} = {\text{Ending notes} \atop \text{receivable}}$

Computing Issuances and Payments of Long-Term Debt. The beginning and ending balances of Long-Term Debt, Notes Payable, or Bonds Payable are taken from the balance sheet. If the amount of either the new issuances or the payments is known, the other amount can be computed. Bradshaw Corporation's new debt issuances total $94,000 (take this amount as given; Exhibit 12-7). Debt payments are computed from the Long-Term Debt account (see Exhibit 12-4).

Long-Term Debt (Notes Payable, Bonds Payable)

Beginning balance		Issuance of new debt		Payments of debt		Ending balance		
$77,000	+	$94,000	−	−X	=	$160,000		
				−X	=	$160,000	− $77,000	− $94,000
				X	=	$11,000		

Long-Term Debt

		Beginning balance	77,000
Payments	11,000	**Issuance of new debt**	94,000
		Ending balance	160,000

Computing Issuances of Shares and Repurchases of Shares. These cash flows can be determined from the share accounts. For example, cash received from issuing common shares or the cash paid for repurchase of common shares is determined from the Common Shares account. We use a single summary account for shares as we do for property, plant, and equipment. Using data from Exhibits 12-4 and 12-7, we have

Common Shares

Beginning balance		Issuance of new shares		Ending balance	
$258,000	+	$1,000	=	$259,000	

Common Shares

Beginning balance	258,000
Issuance of new shares	1,000
Ending	259,000

Apart from the Bradshaw Corporation example, cash flows affecting share repurchases can be computed as follows:

Common Shares (amounts assumed for illustration only)

Beginning balance	−	Repurchase of shares	=	Ending balance
$16,000	−	$3,000	=	$13,000

Common Shares

		Beginning balance	16,000
Repurchase of shares	3,000		
		Ending balance	13,000

Computing Dividend Payments. If dividend payments are not given elsewhere, they can be computed. Bradshaw Corporation's dividends declared are as follows:

Retained Earnings

Beginning balance	+	Net income	−	Dividends declared	=	Ending balance			
$86,000	+	$41,000		−X	=	$110,000			
				−X	=	$110,000	− $86,000	− $41,000	
				X	=	$17,000			

The T-accounts provide another view of the dividend declaration computation.

Retained Earnings

Dividend declarations	17,000	Beginning balance	86,000
		Net income	41,000
		Ending balance	110,000

The credit when a dividend is declared is to the current liability account Dividends Payable. If there is not a balance in the Dividends Payable account on the balance sheet, the dividends have been paid and there will be a financing cash outflow equip to the dividend declared calculated above and the dividend actually paid.

STOP & THINK

Classify each of the following as an operating activity, an investing activity, or a financing activity as reported on the cash flow statement prepared by the *indirect* method.

a. Issuance of shares
b. Borrowing
c. Sales revenue
d. Payment of dividends
e. Purchase of land
f. Repurchase of shares

g. Paying bonds payable
h. Interest expense
i. Sale of equipment
j. Cost of goods sold
k. Purchase of another company
l. Making a loan

Answers:

a. Financing	d. Financing	g. Financing	j. Operating
b. Financing	e. Investing	h. Operating	k. Investing
c. Operating	f. Financing	i. Investing	l. Investing

EXHIBIT 12-9	Computing Cash Flows from Financing Activities

Receipts

From borrowing—issuance of long-term debt	Beginning long-term debt (notes payable)	+	Cash received from issuance of long-term debt	− Payment of debt =	Ending long-term debt
From issuance of shares	Beginning shares +		Cash received from issuance of new shares = Ending shares		

Payments

Of long-term debt	Beginning long-term debt (notes payable)	+	Cash received from issuance of long-term debt	− Payment of debt =	Ending long-term debt
To repurchase shares	Beginning shares − Repurchase cost of shares = Ending shares				
Of dividends	Beginning retained earnings + Net income − Dividend declarations and payments =				Ending retained earnings

Exhibit 12-9 summarizes the computation of cash flows from financing activities, highlighted in colour.

Noncash Investing and Financing Activities

Companies make investments that do not require cash. They also obtain financing other than cash. Our examples have included none of these transactions. Now suppose that Bradshaw Corporation issued common shares valued at $320,000 to acquire a warehouse. Bradshaw would journalize this transaction as follows:

Warehouse Building	320,000	
Common Shares		320,000

This transaction would not be reported on the cash flow statement because Bradshaw paid no cash. But the investment in the warehouse and the issuance of shares are important. Noncash investing and financing activities like this transaction can be reported in a separate schedule that follows the cash flow statement or can be disclosed in a note. Exhibit 12-10 illustrates noncash investing and financing activities (all amounts are assumed).

Now let's apply what you have learned about the cash flow statement prepared by the indirect method.

EXHIBIT 12-10	Noncash Investing and Financing Activities (All Amounts Assumed)

	(Amounts in thousands)
Noncash Investing and Financing Activities:	
Acquisition of building by issuing common shares......................	$320
Acquisition of land by issuing note payable................................	70
Acquisition of equipment by issuing note payable......................	30
Total noncash investing and financing activities	$420

MyAccountingLab   # MID-CHAPTER SUMMARY PROBLEM

Gorska Corporation reported the following income statement and comparative balance sheet, along with transaction data for 2009:

Gorska Corporation
Income Statement
For the Year Ended December 31, 2009

Sales revenue		$662,000
Cost of goods sold		560,000
Gross margin		102,000
Operating expenses		
Salary expense	$46,000	
Amortization expense, equipment	7,000	
Amortization expense, patent	3,000	
Rent expense	2,000	
Total operating expenses		58,000
Income from operations		44,000
Other items:		
Loss on sale of equipment		(2,000)
Income before income tax		42,000
Income tax expense		16,000
Net income		$ 26,000

Gorska Corporation
Balance Sheet
December 31, 2009 and 2008

Assets	2009	2008	Liabilities and Shareholders' Equity	2009	2008
Current:			Current:		
Cash and equivalents	$ 19,000	$ 3,000	Accounts payable	$ 35,000	$ 26,000
Accounts receivable	22,000	23,000	Accrued liabilities	7,000	9,000
Inventories	34,000	31,000	Income tax payable	10,000	10,000
Prepaid expenses	1,000	3,000	Total current liabilities	52,000	45,000
Total current assets	76,000	60,000	Long-term note payable	44,000	—
Long-term investments	18,000	10,000	Bonds payable	40,000	53,000
Equipment, net	67,000	52,000			
Patent, net	44,000	10,000	Shareholders' Equity		
Total assets	$205,000	$132,000	Common shares	42,000	15,000
			Retained earnings	27,000	19,000
			Total liabilities and		
			shareholders' equity	$205,000	$132,000

Transaction Data for 2009:

Purchase of equipment	$98,000
Payment of cash dividends	18,000
Issuance of common shares to retire bonds payable	13,000
Purchase of long-term investment	8,000
Issuance of long-term note payable to purchase patent	37,000
Issuance of long-term note payable to borrow cash	7,000
Issuance of common shares for cash	19,000
Sale of equipment (book value, $76,000)	74,000
Repurchase of common shares	5,000

Required

Prepare Gorska Corporation's cash flow statement for the year ended December 31, 2009. Format operating cash flows by the indirect method. Follow the four steps outlined below. For Step 4, prepare a T-account to show the transaction activity in each long-term balance sheet account. For each capital asset, use a single account, net of accumulated amortization (for example: Equipment, net).

Name: Gorska Corporation
Fiscal Period: Year ended December 31, 2009

Requirement 1

STEP 1 Lay out the template of the cash flow statement.
STEP 2 From the comparative balance sheet, determine the increase in cash during the year, $16,000.
STEP 3 From the income statement, take net income, amortization, and the loss on sale of equipment, to the cash flow statement.
STEP 4 Complete the cash flow statement. Account for the year-to-year change in each balance sheet account.

Answer

Gorska Corporation **Cash Flow Statement** **For the Year Ended December 31, 2009**		

The title must include the name of the company, "Cash Flow Statement," and the specific period of time covered. There are three sections: Cash flows from operating, investing, and financing activities.

Cash flows from operating activities:		
Net income		$26,000
Adjustments to reconcile net income to net cash provided by operating activities:		
Amortization	$ 10,000	
Loss on sale of equipment	2,000	
Decrease in accounts receivable	1,000	
Increase in inventories	(3,000)	
Decrease in prepaid expenses	2,000	
Increase in accounts payable	9,000	
Decrease in accrued liabilities	(2,000)	19,000
Net cash provided by operating activities		45,000
Cash flows from investing activities:		
Purchase of equipment	(98,000)	
Sale of equipment	74,000	
Purchase of long-term investment	(8,000)	
Net cash used for investing activities		(32,000)
Cash flows from financing activities:		
Issuance of common shares	19,000	
Payment of cash dividends	(18,000)	
Issuance of long-term note payable	7,000	
Repurchase of common shares	(5,000)	
Net cash provided by financing activities		3,000
Net increase in cash		16,000
Cash balance, December 31, 2008		3,000
Cash balance, December 31, 2009		$19,000
Noncash investing and financing activities:		
Issuance of long-term note payable to purchase patent		$37,000
Issuance of common shares to retire bonds payable		13,000
Total noncash investing and financing activities		$50,000

Add back noncash items: amortization, and gains or losses

$2,000 = $76,000 − $74,000

Any changes in current assets and current liabilities are included in the operating activities section. Calculate as 2009 balance − 2008 balance from the balance sheets.

Any cash changes in the long-term assets are included in the investing activities section. Check "Transaction Data for 2009."

Any cash changes in the long-term liabilities and contributed capital accounts are included in the financing activities section. Check "Transaction Data for 2009."

This result should equal the Dec. 31, 2009 balance sheet Cash amount.

Check "Transaction Data for 2009."

Long-Term Investments		
Bal.	10,000	
	8,000	
Bal.	18,000	

Equipment, Net		
Bal.	52,000	
	98,000	76,000
		7,000
Bal.	67,000	

Patent, Net		
Bal.	10,000	
	37,000	3,000
Bal.	44,000	

Long-Term Note Payable		
	Bal.	0
		37,000
		7,000
	Bal.	44,000

Bonds Payable		
	Bal.	53,000
13,000		
	Bal.	40,000

Common Shares		
	Bal.	15,000
		13,000
5,000		19,000
	Bal.	42,000

Retained Earnings		
	Bal.	19,000
18,000		26,000
	Bal.	27,000

Use the 2008 and 2009 balance sheet amounts and the transaction data for 2009 to complete these T-accounts.

The amortization amount of $10,000 in the cash flow statement is the total of Equipment ($7,000) and Patent ($3,000) amortization.

Preparing the Cash Flow Statement: Direct Method

Objective

4 **Prepare** a cash flow statement by the direct method

The CICA's Accounting Standards Board, in the *CICA Handbook*, has expressed a preference for the direct method of reporting cash flows from operating activities, because it provides clearer information about the sources and uses of cash. Very few companies use this method because it requires more computations than the indirect method. Investing and financing cash flows are unaffected by the method of formatting operating cash flows.

To illustrate the cash flow statement, we use Bradshaw Corporation, a dealer in playground equipment. To prepare the cash flow statement by the direct method, proceed as follows:

STEP 1 Lay out the template of the cash flow statement by the direct method, as shown in Part 1 of Exhibit 12-11. Part 2 (p. 580) gives a visual picture of the statement.

STEP 2 Use the comparative balance sheet to determine the increase or decrease in cash during the period. The change in cash is the "check figure" for the cash flow statement. Bradshaw Corporation's comparative balance sheet indicates that Bradshaw's cash decreased by $20,000 during 2009 (Exhibit 12-4, p. 568). *Why* did Bradshaw's cash fall during 2009? The cash flow statement explains.

STEP 3 Use the available data to prepare the cash flow statement. Bradshaw's transaction data appear in Exhibit 12-12. These transactions affected both the income statement (Exhibit 12-5, p. 569) and the cash flow statement. Some transactions affect one statement and some, the other. For example, sales (item 1) are reported on the income statement. Cash collections (item 2) go on the cash flow statement. Other transactions, such as the cash receipt of dividend revenue (item 5), affect both statements. *The cash flow statement reports only those transactions with cash effects* (those with an asterisk in Exhibit 12-12). Exhibit 12-13 gives Bradshaw Corporation's cash flow statement for 2009.

| **EXHIBIT 12-11** | Part 1—Template of the Cash Flow Statement: Direct Method |

Bradshaw Corporation
Cash Flow Statement
For the Year Ended December 31, 2009

Cash flows from operating activities:
  Receipts:
    Collections from customers
    Interest received on notes receivable
    Dividends received on investments in shares
    Other operating receipts
      Total cash receipts
  Payments:
    To suppliers
    To employees
    For interest
    For income tax
    Other operating payments
      Total cash payments
  Net cash provided by operating activities
Cash flows from investing activities:
  Sales of long-term assets (investments, land, building, equipment, and so on)
  − Purchases of long-term assets
  + Collections of long-term receivables
  − Long-term loans to others
  Net cash provided by (used for) investing activities
Cash flows from financing activities:
  Issuance of shares
  − Repurchase of shares
  + Borrowing (issuance of notes or bonds payable)
  − Payment of notes or bonds payable
  − Payment of dividends
  Net cash provided by (used for) financing activities
Net increase (decrease) in cash during the year
  + Cash at December 31, 2008
  = Cash at December 31, 2009

Cash Flows from Operating Activities

Operating cash flows are listed first because they are the most important. Exhibit 12-13 (p. 581) shows that Bradshaw is sound; operating activities were the largest source of cash.

Cash Collections from Customers. Both cash sales and collections of accounts receivable are reported on the cash flow statement as "Collections from customers... $271,000" in Exhibit 12-13.

Cash Receipts of Interest. The income statement reports interest revenue. Only the cash receipts of interest appear on the cash flow statement—$10,000 in Exhibit 12-13.

Cash Receipts of Dividends. Dividends are earned on investments in shares. Dividend revenue is reported on the income statement, and only cash receipts are reported on the cash flow statement—$9,000 in Exhibit 12-13. (Dividends *received* are operating activities, but dividends *paid* are financing.)

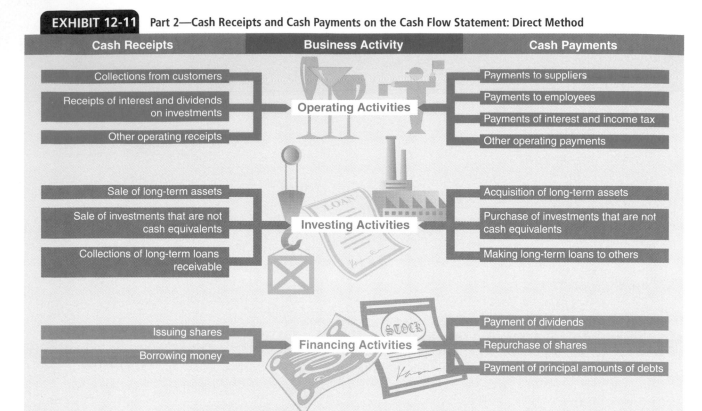

EXHIBIT 12-11 Part 2—Cash Receipts and Cash Payments on the Cash Flow Statement: Direct Method

---

EXHIBIT 12-12 Summary of Bradshaw Corporation's 2009 Transactions

Operating Activities
1. Sales on credit, $284,000
*2. Collections from customers, $271,000
3. Interest revenue on notes receivable, $12,000
*4. Collection of interest receivable, $10,000
*5. Cash receipt of dividend revenue on investments in shares, $9,000
6. Cost of goods sold, $150,000
7. Purchases of inventory on credit, $147,000
*8. Payments to suppliers, $133,000
9. Salary and wages expense, $56,000
*10. Payments of salary and wages, $58,000
11. Amortization expense, $18,000
12. Other operating expense, $17,000
*13. Interest expense and payments, $16,000
*14. Income tax expense and payments, $15,000

Investing Activities
*15. Cash payments to acquire property, plant, and equipment, $206,000
*16. Loan to another company, $11,000
*17. Proceeds from sale of property, plant, and equipment, $62,000, including $8,000 gain

Financing Activities
*18. Proceeds from issuance of common shares, $1,000
*19. Proceeds from issuance of long-term debt, $94,000
*20. Payment of long-term debt, $11,000
*21. Declaration and payment of cash dividends, $17,000

*Indicates a cash flow to be reported on the cash flow statement
Note: Income statement data are taken from Exhibit 12-16, page 584.

EXHIBIT 12-13 Cash Flow Statement—Direct Method

Bradshaw Corporation
Cash Flow Statement
For the Year Ended December 31, 2009

	(Amounts in thousands)	
Cash flows from operating activities:		
Receipts:		
Collections from customers	$ 271	
Interest received on notes receivable	10	
Dividends received on investments in shares	9	
Total cash receipts		$ 290
Payments:		
To suppliers	(133)	
To employees	(58)	
For interest	(16)	
For income tax	(15)	
Total cash payments		(222)
Net cash provided by operating activities		68
Cash flows from investing activities:		
Acquisition of property, plant, and equipment	(206)	
Loan to another company	(11)	
Proceeds from sale of property, plant, and equipment	62	
Net cash used for investing activities		(155)
Cash flows from financing activities:		
Proceeds from issuance of common shares	1	
Proceeds from issuance of long-term debt	94	
Payment of long-term debt	(11)	
Payment of dividends	(17)	
Net cash provided by financing activities		67
Net decrease in cash		(20)
Cash balance, December 31, 2008		42
Cash balance, December 31, 2009		$ 22

Payments to Suppliers. Payments to suppliers include all payments for inventory and operating expenses except employee compensation, interest, and income taxes. *Suppliers* are those entities that provide the business with its inventory and essential services. For example, a clothing store's suppliers may include Arrow Shirts, Gildan Activewear, and Levi Strauss. Other suppliers provide advertising, utilities, and various services that are operating expenses. Exhibit 12-13 shows that Bradshaw Corporation paid suppliers $133,000.

Payments to Employees. This category includes payments for salaries, wages, commissions, and other forms of employee compensation. Accrued amounts are excluded because they have not yet been paid. The cash flow statement in Exhibit 12-13 reports only the cash payments ($58,000).

Payments for Interest Expense and Income Tax Expense. Interest and income tax payments are reported separately. Bradshaw Corporation paid all its interest and income tax expenses in cash. Therefore, the same amount appears on the income statement and the cash flow statement. Interest payments are operating cash flows because the interest is an expense.

Amortization Expense. This expense is *not* listed on the cash flow statement in Exhibit 12-13 because it does not affect cash.

Cash Flows from Investing Activities

Investing is critical because a company's investments determine its future course. Large purchases of capital assets signal expansion. Low levels of investing over a period indicate that the business is not growing.

Purchases of Long-Term Assets; Purchasing Investments and Making Loans to Other Companies. These cash payments acquire long-term assets. Bradshaw Corporation's first investing activity in Exhibit 12-13 is the purchase of property, plant, and equipment ($206,000). Bradshaw also made an $11,000 loan and got a note receivable.

Proceeds from Selling Long-Term Assets and Investments and from Collecting Notes Receivable. These cash receipts are also investing activities. The sale of the property, plant, and equipment needs explanation. Bradshaw Corporation received $62,000 cash from the sale of property, plant, and equipment, and there was an $8,000 gain on this transaction. What is the appropriate amount to show on the cash flow statement? It is $62,000, the cash proceeds from the sale, not the $8,000 gain.

Investors are often critical of a company that sells large amounts of its property, plant, and equipment. That may signal an emergency. For example, budget cuts in the telecom industry required Nortel Networks Corporation to downsize significantly.

Cash Flows from Financing Activities

Cash flows from financing activities include the following:

Proceeds from Issuance of Shares and Debt. Issuing shares and borrowing money are two common ways to finance operations. In Exhibit 12-13, Bradshaw Corporation issued common shares and received cash of $1,000. Bradshaw also issued long-term debt (notes payable) to borrow $94,000.

Payment of Debt and Repurchases of the Company's Own Shares. The payment of debt (notes payable) decreases cash, which is the opposite effect of borrowing. Bradshaw Corporation reports long-term debt payments of $11,000. The repurchase of shares is another example.

Payment of Cash Dividends. The payment of cash dividends is a financing activity, as illustrated by Bradshaw's $17,000 payment in Exhibit 12-13. A *stock* dividend has no effect on Cash and is *not* reported on the cash flow statement.

Noncash Investing and Financing Activities

Companies make investments that do not require cash. They also obtain financing other than cash. Our examples thus far have included none of these transactions. Now suppose that Bradshaw Corporation issued common shares valued at $320,000 to acquire a warehouse. Bradshaw would journalize this transaction as follows:

Warehouse Building	320,000	
Common Shares		320,000

This transaction would not be reported on the cash flow statement because Bradshaw paid no cash. But the investment in the warehouse and the issuance of shares are important. Noncash investing and financing activities like this transaction

EXHIBIT 12-14	Noncash Investing and Financing Activities (All Amounts Assumed)	

	Thousands
Noncash Investing and Financing Activities:	
Acquisition of building by issuing common shares....................................	$320
Acquisition of land by issuing note payable	70
Acquisition of equipment by issuing short-term note payable	30
Total noncash investing and financing activities	$420

can be reported in a separate schedule that follows the cash flow statement or can be disclosed in a note. Exhibit 12-14 illustrates noncash investing and financing activities (all amounts are assumed).

STOP & THINK

Classify each of the following as an operating activity, an investing activity, or a financing activity. Also identify those items that are not reported on the cash flow statement prepared by the *direct* method.

a. Net income
b. Payment of dividends
c. Borrowing
d. Payment of cash to suppliers
e. Making a loan
f. Receipt of cash dividends
g. Amortization expense
h. Purchase of equipment

i. Issuance of shares
j. Purchase of another company
k. Payment of a note payable
l. Payment of income taxes
m. Collections from customers
n. Accrual of interest revenue
o. Expiration of prepaid expense

Answer:

a. Not reported	e. Investing	i. Financing	m. Operating
b. Financing	f. Operating	j. Investing	n. Not reported
c. Financing	g. Not reported	k. Financing	o. Not reported
d. Operating	h. Investing	l. Operating	

Now let's see how to compute the amounts of the operating cash flows by the direct method.

Computing Operating Cash Flows by the Direct Method

To compute operating cash flows by the direct method, we use the income statement and the *changes* in the related balance sheet accounts. Exhibit 12-15 diagrams the process. Exhibit 12-16 is Bradshaw Corporation's income statement and Exhibit 12-17 (page 585) is the comparative balance sheet.

Computing Cash Collections from Customers. Collections start with sales revenue (an accrual-basis amount). Bradshaw Corporation's income statement (Exhibit 12-16) reports sales of $284,000. Accounts Receivable increased from $80,000 at the beginning of the year to $93,000 at year-end, a $13,000 increase (Exhibit 12-17). Based on those amounts, Cash Collections equal $271,000. We must solve for cash collections (X).

Accounts Receivable

Beginning balance	+	Sales	−	Collections	=	Ending balance
$80,000	+	$284,000		−X	=	$93,000
				−X	=	$93,000 − $80,000 − $284,000
				X	=	$271,000

EXHIBIT 12-15 Direct Method of Computing Cash Flows from Operating Activities

RECEIPTS/PAYMENTS	From Income Statement Account	Change in Related Balance Sheet Account	
RECEIPTS:			
From customers	Sales Revenue	+ Decrease in Accounts Receivable − Increase in Accounts Receivable	
Of interest	Interest Revenue	+ Decrease in Interest Receivable − Increase in Interest Receivable	
PAYMENTS:			
To suppliers	Cost of Goods Sold	+ Increase in Inventory − Decrease in Inventory	+Decrease in Accounts Payable − Increase in Accounts Payable
	Operating Expense	+ Increase in Prepaids − Decrease in Prepaids	+ Decrease in Accrued Liabilities − Increase in Accrued Liabilities
To employees	Salary (Wages) Expense	+ Decrease in Salary (Wages) Payable − Increase in Salary (Wages) Payable	
For interest	Interest Expense	+ Decrease in Interest Payable − Increase in Interest Payable	
For income tax	Income Tax Expense	+ Decrease in Income Tax Payable − Increase in Income Tax Payable	

We thank Barbara Gerrity for suggesting this exhibit.

The T-account for Accounts Receivable provides another view of the same computation.

Accounts Receivable			
Beginning balance	80,000		
Sales	284,000	Collections	271,000
Ending balance	93,000		

Accounts Receivable increased, so collections must be less than sales.

All collections of receivables are computed in this way. Let's turn now to other cash receipts. In our example, Bradshaw Corporation earned interest revenue. Interest Receivable's balance increased by $2,000 (Exhibit 12-17). Cash receipts of interest were $10,000 (Interest Revenue of $12,000 minus the $2,000 increase in Interest Receivable). Exhibit 12-15 shows how to make this computation.

EXHIBIT 12-16 Income Statement for the Bradshaw Corporation

Bradshaw Corporation
Income Statement
For the Year Ended December 31, 2009

	(Amounts in thousands)	
Revenues and gains:		
Sales revenue	$284	
Interest revenue	12	
Dividend revenue	9	
Gain on sale of property, plant, and equipment	8	
Total revenues and gains		$313
Expenses:		
Cost of goods sold	150	
Salary and wages expense	56	
Amortization expense	18	
Other operating expense	17	
Interest expense	16	
Income tax expense	15	
Total expenses		272
Net income		$ 41

EXHIBIT 12-17 Comparative Balance Sheet for Bradshaw Corporation

Bradshaw Corporation
Comparative Balance Sheet
December 31, 2009 and 2008

(Amounts in thousands)	2009	2008	Increase (Decrease)	
Assets				
Current:				
Cash	$ 22	$ 42	$(20)	
Accounts receivable	93	80	13	⎫
Interest receivable	3	1	2	⎬ Changes in current assets—Operating
Inventory	135	138	(3)	⎪
Prepaid expenses	8	7	1	⎭
Long-term note receivable from another company	11	—	11	⎫ Changes in noncurrent assets—Investing
Capital assets, net of amortization	353	219	134	⎬
Total	$625	$487	$238	
Liabilities				
Current:				
Accounts payable	$ 91	$ 57	$ 34	⎫
Salary and wages payable	4	6	(2)	⎬ Changes in current liabilities—Operating
Accrued liabilities	1	3	(2)	⎭
Long-term debt	160	77	83	⎫ Changes in long-term liabilities and contributed capital accounts—Financing
Shareholders' Equity				
Common shares	259	258	1	⎬
Retained earnings	110	86	24	⎫ Change due to net income—Operating Change due to dividends—Financing
Total	$625	$487	$138	

Computing Payments to Suppliers. This computation includes two parts:

- Payments for inventory
- Payments for operating expenses (other than interest and income tax)

Payments for inventory are computed by converting cost of goods sold to the cash basis. We use Cost of Goods Sold, Inventory, and Accounts Payable. First, we must solve for purchases. All amounts come from Exhibits 12-16 and 12-17.

Cost of Goods Sold							
Beginning inventory	+	Purchases	−	Ending inventory	=	Cost of good sold	
$138,000	+	X		$135,000	=	$150,000	
		X			=	$150,000	− $138,000 + $135,000
		X			=	$147,000	

Now we can compute cash payments for inventory (Y), as follows:

Accounts Payable							
Beginning balance	+	Purchases	−	Payments for inventory	=	Ending balance	
$57,000	+	$147,000		−Y	=	$91,000	
				−Y	=	$91,000	− $57,000 − $147,000
				Y	=	$113,000	

The T-accounts show where the data come from: Start with Cost of Goods Sold.

Cost of Goods Sold			
Beg. inventory	138,000	End. inventory	135,000
Purchases	147,000		
Cost of goods sold	150,000		

Accounts Payable			
Payments for inventory	113,000	Beg. bal.	57,000
		Purchases	147,000
		End bal.	91,000

Accounts Payable increased, so payments are less than purchases.

Computing Payments for Operating Expenses. Payments for operating expenses other than interest and income tax can be computed from three accounts: Prepaid Expenses, Accrued Liabilities, and Other Operating Expenses. All Bradshaw Corporation data come from Exhibits 12-16 and 12-17.

Prepaid Expenses

Beginning balance	+	Payments	−	Expiration of prepaid expense	=	Ending balance			
$7,000	+	X	−	$7,000	=	$8,000			
		X			=	$8,000	− $7,000	+ $7,000	
		X			=	$8,000			

Accrued Liabilities

Beginning balance	+	Accrual of expense at year-end	−	Payments	=	Ending balance		
$3,000	+	$1,000		−X	=	$1,000		
				−X	=	$1,000	− $3,000	− $1,000
				X	=	$3,000		

Other Operating Expenses

Accrual of expense at year-end	+	Expiration of prepaid expense	+	Payments	=	Ending balance		
$1,000	+	$7,000	+	X	=	$17,000		
				X	=	$17,000	− $1,000	− $7,000
				X	=	$9,000		
		Total payments for operating expenses	=	$8,000	+	$3,000	+	$9,000
			=	$20,000				

The T-accounts give another picture of the same data.

Prepaid Expenses			
Beg. bal.	7,000	Expiration of prepaid expense	7,000
Payments	8,000		
End. bal.	8,000		

Accrued Liabilities			
Payment	3,000	Beg. bal.	3,000
		Accrual of expense at year-end	1,000
		End. bal.	1,000

Operating Expenses			
Accrual of expense at year-end	1,000		
Expiration of prepaid expense	7,000		
Payments	9,000		
End. bal.	17,000		

Computing Payments to Employees. It is convenient to combine all payments to employees into one account, Salary and Wages Expense. We then adjust the expense for the change in Salary and Wages Payable, as shown here.

Salary and Wages Payable

Beginning balance	+	Salary and wages expense	−	Payments	=	Ending balance			
$6,000	+	$56,000		−X	=	$4,000			
				−X	=	$4,000	− $6,000	−	$56,000
				X	=	$58,000			

The T-account gives another picture of the same data.

Salary and Wages Payable

	Beginning balance	6,000
Payments to employees 58,000	Salary and wages expense	56,000
	Ending balance	4,000

Computing Payments of Interest and Income Taxes. Bradshaw Corporation's expense and payment amounts are the same for interest and income tax so no analysis is required. If the expense and the payment differ, the payment can be computed as shown in Exhibit 12-15.

Computing Investing and Financing Cash Flows

Investing and financing cash flows are explained on pages 570–574. These computations are the same for both the direct and indirect methods.

STOP & THINK

Suncor Energy Inc., reported the following for 2007 and 2006 (adapted, in millions):

At December 31,	2007	2006
Receivables, net	$1,416	$1,050
Inventory	608	589
Accounts payable	1,341	897
Income taxes payable	244	—

For the Year Ended December 31, 2007	
Revenues	$17,933
Purchases of crude oil and products	5,935
Income tax expense	382

Based on these figures, how much cash did

- Suncor collect from customers during 2007?
- Suncor pay for purchases of crude oil and products during 2007?
- Suncor pay for income taxes during 2007?

Answers (in millions):

Collections from customers = $17,567

Beginning Receivables + Revenues − Collections = Ending Receivables

$1,050 + $17,933 − $17,567 = $1,416

Payments for purchases of crude oil and products = $5,510

Purchases of Crude Oil and Products + Increase in Inventory − Increase in Accounts Payable = Payments

$5,935 + ($608 − $589) − ($1,341 − $897) = $5,510

Payment of income taxes = $46

Beginning Income Taxes Payable + Income Tax Expense − Payment = Ending Income Taxes Payable

— + $382 − $138 = $244

Measuring Cash Adequacy: Free Cash Flow

Throughout this chapter, we have focused on cash flows from operating, investing, and financing activities. Some investors, creditors, and managers want to know how much cash a company can "free up" for new opportunities. The business world changes so quickly that new possibilities arise daily. The company with a significant free cash flow is better able to respond to new opportunities. **Free cash flow** is the amount of cash available from operations after paying for planned investments in property, plant, and equipment and other long-term assets. Free cash flow can be computed as follows:

$$\text{Free cash flow} = \frac{\text{Net cash flow provided by}}{\text{operating activities}} - \frac{\text{Cash outflow earmarked for investment}}{\text{in property, plant, and equipment}}$$
$$\text{and other long-term assets}$$

As an example, PepsiCo Inc. uses free cash flow to manage its operations. Suppose PepsiCo expects net cash inflow of $2.3 billion from operations. Assume PepsiCo plans to spend $1.9 billion to modernize its bottling facilities. In this case, PepsiCo's free cash flow would be $0.4 billion ($2.3 billion − $1.9 billion). If a good investment opportunity comes along, PepsiCo should have $0.4 billion to invest in that opportunity.

A large amount of free cash flow is preferable because it means that a lot of cash is available for new investments. High-tech companies, such as Research In Motion Ltd., depend on technological breakthroughs for a competitive edge. Investment opportunities may arise more quickly than those of older companies.

The Decision Guidelines feature shows some ways to use cash flow and income data for investment and credit analysis.

Decision Guidelines

INVESTORS' AND CREDITORS' USE OF CASH FLOW AND RELATED INFORMATION

Monique Brunet is a private investor. Through years of experience she has devised some guidelines for evaluating both share investments and bond investments. Brunet uses a combination of accrual accounting data and cash flow information. Here are her decision guidelines for both investors and creditors.

Investors

Question	Factors to Consider[*]	Financial Statement Predictor/Decision Model[*]
1. How much in dividends can I expect to receive from an investment in shares?	Expected future net income	Income from continuing operations[**]
	Expected future cash balance	Net cash flows from (in order): • Operating activities • Investing activities • Financing activities
	Future dividend policy	Current and past dividend policy
2. Is the share price likely to increase or decrease?	Expected future net income	Income from continuing operations[**]
	Expected future cash flows from operating activities	Income from continuing operations[**] Net cash flow from operating activities
3. What is the future share price likely to be?[*]	Expected future income from • continuing operations, *and* • net cash flow from operating activities	$\text{Expected future price of a share} = \dfrac{\text{Expected future earnings per share}^{**}}{\text{Investment capitalization rate}}$ or $\text{Expected future price of a share} = \dfrac{\text{Net cash flow from operations per share}}{\text{Investment capitalization rate}}$

[*]There are many other factors to consider in making these decisions. These are some of the most common.
[**]See Chapter 11.

Creditors

Question	Factors to Consider*	Financial Statement Predictor/Decision Model*
Can the company pay the interest and principal at the maturity of a loan?	Expected future net cash flow from operating activities	Income from continuing operations** Net cash flow from • Operating activities • Investing activities

END-OF-CHAPTER SUMMARY PROBLEM

Kapoor Products Inc. reported the following comparative balance sheet and income statement for 2009.

Kapoor Products Inc.
Balance Sheet
December 31, 2009 and 2008

	2009	2008
Cash	$ 19,000	$ 3,000
Accounts receivable	22,000	23,000
Inventories	34,000	31,000
Prepaid expenses	1,000	3,000
Equipment (net)	90,000	79,000
Intangible assets	9,000	9,000
	$175,000	$148,000
Accounts payable	$ 14,000	$ 9,000
Accrued liabilities	16,000	19,000
Income tax payable	14,000	12,000
Long-term debt	45,000	50,000
Common shares	22,000	18,000
Retained earnings	64,000	40,000
	$175,000	$148,000

Kapoor Products Inc.
Income Statement
For the Years Ended December 31, 2009 and 2008

	2009	2008
Sales revenue	$190,000	$165,000
Gain on sale of equipment	6,000	—
Total revenue and gains	196,000	165,000
Cost of goods sold	85,000	70,000
Amortization expense	19,000	17,000
Other operating expenses	36,000	33,000
Total expenses	140,000	120,000
Income before income tax	56,000	45,000
Income tax expense	18,000	15,000
Net income	$ 38,000	$ 30,000

Assume that you are an investment analyst for Canmore Investments Ltd. and have been tasked with analyzing Kapoor Products Inc. as Canmore is considering purchasing it. You determine that you need the following Kapoor cash flow data for 2009. There were no non-cash investing and financing activities.

a. Collections from customers
b. Cash payments for inventory
c. Cash payments for operating expenses
d. Cash payment for income tax
e. Cash received from the sale of equipment, with Kapoor Products Inc. paying $40,000 for new equipment during the year.
f. Issuance of common shares.
g. Issuance of long-term debt, with Kapoor Products Inc. paying off $20,000 of long-term debt during the year.
h. Cash dividends, with no stock dividends.

Name: Kapoor Products Inc.
Fiscal Period: Year ended December 31, 2009

Provide the analysts with the needed data. Show your work.

Answer

The change in Accounts Receivable of $1,000 ($22,000 − $23,000) is a result of sales and collections from customers.

a. Analyze Accounts Receivable (let X = Collections from customers):

Beginning	+	Sales	−	Collections	=	Ending
$23,000	+	$190,000	−	X	=	$22,000
				X	=	$191,000

First calculate the amount of purchases. Then calculate the change in Accounts Payable that relates to cash payments.

b. Analyze Inventory and Accounts Payable (let X = Purchases, and let Y = Payments for inventory):

Beginning inventory	+	Purchases	−	Ending inventory	=	Cost of Goods Sold
$31,000	+	X	−	$34,000	=	$85,000
		X			=	$88,000

Beginning Accounts Payable	+	Purchases	−	Payments	=	Ending Accounts Payable
$9,000	+	$88,000	−	Y	=	$14,000
				Y	=	$83,000

Cash payments for operating expenses must account for the changes that relate to prepaid expenses and accrued liabilities.

c. Start with Other Operating Expenses, and adjust for the changes in Prepaid Expenses and Accrued Liabilities:

Other Operating Expenses	+ Increase, or − Decrease in Prepaid Expenses	− Increase, or + Decrease in Accrued Liabilities	=	Payments for Operating Expenses
$36,000	− $2,000	+ 3,000	=	$37,000

The change in Income Tax Payable of $2,000 ($14,000 − $12,000) is a result of income tax expense and income tax payments made.

d. Analyze Income Tax Payable (let X = Payments of income tax):

		Income Tax				
Beginning	+	Expense	−	Payments	=	Ending
$12,000	+	$18,000	−	X	=	$14,000
				X	=	$16,000

e. Analyze Equipment (Net) (let X = Book value of equipment sold. Then combine with gain or loss on sale to compute cash received from sale.)

$$\overline{\text{Beginning} \; + \; \text{Acquisitions} \; - \; \text{Amortization} \; - \; \text{Book Value Sold}} \; = \; \text{Ending}$$
$$\$79{,}000 \; + \; \$40{,}000 \; - \; \$19{,}000 \; - \; \text{X} \qquad = \; \$90{,}000$$
$$\text{X} \qquad = \; \$10{,}000$$

$$\overline{\text{Cash received from sale} \; = \; \text{Book Value Sold} \; + \; \text{Gain, or} \; - \; \text{Loss on Sale}}$$
$$\$16{,}000 \qquad = \qquad \$10{,}000 \qquad + \; \$6{,}000$$

> Cash received from the sale of equipment is the book value of the equipment plus the gain or minus the loss on the sale. First determine the book value of the equipment sold.

f. Analyze Common Shares (let X = issuance):

$$\overline{\text{Beginning} + \text{Issuance} = \text{Ending}}$$
$$\$18{,}000 \; + \; \text{X} \; = \$22{,}000$$
$$\text{X} \; = \$4{,}000$$

> The change in Common Shares of $4,000 ($22,000 − $18,000) is a result of issuing shares.

g. Analyze Long-Term Debt (let X = issuance):

$$\overline{\text{Beginning} + \text{Issuance} - \text{Payment} = \text{Ending}}$$
$$\$50{,}000 \; + \; \text{X} \quad - \; \$20{,}000 = \$45{,}000$$
$$\text{X} \qquad\qquad = \$15{,}000$$

> Long-Term Debt declined by $5,000 ($45,000 − $50,000). However, since a $20,000 payment was made during the year, $15,000 of long-term debt must have been issued.

h. Analyze Retained Earnings (let X = dividends):

$$\overline{\text{Beginning} + \text{Net Income} - \text{Dividends} = \text{Ending}}$$
$$\$40{,}000 \; + \; \$38{,}000 \; - \quad \text{X} \quad = \; \$64{,}000$$
$$\text{X} \quad = \; \$14{,}000$$

> The change in Retained Earnings of $24,000 ($64,000 − $40,000) is a result of net income ($38,000 from the 2009 income statement) and the payment of cash dividends. The same information is shown on the statement of retained earnings.

REVIEW THE CASH FLOW STATEMENT

QUICK CHECK (Answers are given on page 619.)

1. All the following activities are reported on the cash flow statement except
   a. Operating activities   **c.** Financing activities
   b. Investing activities   **d.** Marketing activities

2. Activities that create long-term liabilities are usually
   a. Operating activities   **c.** Financing activities
   b. Investing activities   **d.** Noncash investing and financing activities

3. Activities affecting long-term assets are
   a. Operating activities   **c.** Financing activities
   b. Investing activities   **d.** Marketing activities

4. Hilltop Company borrowed $50,000, paid dividends of $12,000, issued 2,000 shares for $30 per share, purchased land for $24,000, and received dividends of $6,000. Net income was $80,000 and amortization for the year totalled $5,000. How much should be reported as net cash provided by financing activities?
   a. $85,000   **c.** $110,000
   b. $98,000   **d.** $104,000

5. Activities that obtain the cash needed to launch and sustain a company are
   a. Income activities   **c.** Financing activities
   b. Investing activities   **d.** Marketing activities

6. The exchange of shares for land would be reported as
   a. Exchanges are not reported on the cash flow statement.
   b. Noncash investing and financing activities
   c. Investing activities
   d. Financing activities

Use the following Baycraft Ltd. information for Questions 7 through 10.

Net Income	$47,000	Decrease in Inventories	$ 2,000
Amortization Expense	8,000	Increase in Accounts Payable	7,000
Payment of Dividends	2,000	Acquisition of Equipment	24,000
Increase in Accounts Receivable	4,000	Sale of Shares	3,000
Collection of Notes Receivable	6,000	Payment of Long-term Debt	9,000
Loss on Sale of Land	12,000	Proceeds from Sale of Land	36,000

7. Under the indirect method, net cash provided by operating activities would be
   a. $72,000   c. $83,000
   b. $76,000   d. $84,000

8. Net cash provided by (used for) investing activities would be
   a. $18,000   c. $(6,000)
   b. $(12,000)   d. $24,000

9. Net cash provided by (used for) financing activities would be
   a. $4,000   c. ($8,000)
   b. $2,000   d. ($11,000)

10. The cost of land must have been
    a. $30,000   c. $54,000
    b. $48,000   d. Cannot be determined from the data given.

11. Merryhill Industries began the year with $45,000 in accounts receivable and ended the year with $31,000 in accounts receivable. If sales for the year were $650,000, the cash collected from customers during the year amounted to
    a. $664,000   c. $733,000
    b. $672,000   d. $695,000

12. Mouton Cheese Ltée made sales of $690,000 and had cost of goods sold of $390,000. Inventory increased by $15,000, and accounts payable increased by $9,000. Operating expenses were $175,000. How much was Mouton's net income for the year?
    a. $110,000   c. $125,000
    b. $116,000   d. $300,000

13. Use the Mouton Cheese Ltée data from Question 12. How much cash did Mouton pay for inventory during the year?
    a. $374,000   c. $396,000
    b. $390,000   d. Some other amount ($fill in the blank)

ACCOUNTING VOCABULARY

cash equivalents Highly liquid short-term investments that can be converted into cash immediately.   (p. 564)

cash flows Cash receipts and cash payments (disbursements).   (p. 563)

direct method Format of the operating activities section of the cash flow statement; lists the major categories of operating cash receipts (collections from customers and receipts of interest and dividends) and cash disbursements (payments to suppliers, to employees, for interest and income taxes).   (p. 565)

free cash flow The amount of cash available from operations after paying for planned investments in plant, equipment, and other long-term assets.   (p. 588)

indirect method Format of the operating activities section of the cash flow statement; starts with net income and reconciles to net cash provided by activities.   (p. 565)

ASSESS YOUR PROGRESS

Make the grade with MyAccountingLab: The exercises and problems marked in red can be found on MyAccountingLab at www.myaccountinglab.com. You can practise them as often as you want, and they feature step by step guided solutions to help you find the right answer.

MyAccountingLab

SHORT EXERCISES

S12-1 State how the cash flow statement helps investors and creditors perform each of the following functions.
a. Predict future cash flows.
b. Evaluate management decisions.

Purposes of the cash flow statement
(Obj. 1)

S12-2 Examine the **Potash Corporation** cash flow statement on page 562. Suppose Potash's operating activities *used*, rather than *provided*, cash. Identify three things under the indirect method that could cause operating cash flows to be negative.

Evaluating operating cash flows—indirect method
(Obj. 2)

S12-3 Canada Wide Transportation (CWT) began 2009 with accounts receivable, inventory, and prepaid expenses totalling $65,000. At the end of the year, CWT had a total of $78,000 for these current assets. At the beginning of 2009, CWT owed current liabilities of $42,000, and at year-end current liabilities totalled $40,000.

Net income for the year was $80,000. Included in net income were a $4,000 gain on the sale of land and amortization expense of $9,000.

Show how CWT should report cash flows from operating activities for 2009. CWT uses the *indirect* method. Use Exhibit 12-6 (p. 569) as a guide.

Reporting cash flows from operating activities—indirect method
(Obj. 3)

S12-4 Bewell Clinic Inc. is preparing its cash flow statement (indirect method) for the year ended November 30, 2009. Consider the following items in preparing the company's cash flow statement. Identify each item as an operating activity—addition to net income (O+), or subtraction from net income (O–); an investing activity (I); a financing activity (F); or an activity that is not used to prepare the cash flow statement by the indirect method (N). Place the appropriate symbol in the blank space.

Identifying items for reporting cash flows from operations—indirect method
(Obj. 2)

___ a.	Loss on sale of land		___ h.	Increase in accounts payable
___ b.	Amortization expense		___ i.	Net income
___ c.	Increase in inventory		___ j.	Payment of dividends
___ d.	Decrease in prepaid expense		___ k.	Decrease in accrued liabilities
___ e.	Decrease in accounts receivable		___ l.	Issuance of common shares
___ f.	Purchase of equipment		___ m.	Gain on sale of building
___ g.	Collection of cash from customers		___ n.	Retained earnings

S12-5 (Short Exercise 12-6 is an alternate exercise.) Edwards Corporation Inc. accountants have assembled the following data for the year ended June 30, 2009.

Computing operating cash flows—indirect method
(Obj. 3)

Payment of dividends.....................	$ 6,000	Cost of goods sold.........................	$100,000
Proceeds from issuance of		Other operating expenses.............	35,000
common shares........................	20,000	Purchase of equipment................	40,000
Sales revenue...............................	224,000	Decrease in current liabilities	5,000
Increase in current assets		Payment of note payable	30,000
other than cash.........................	30,000	Proceeds from sale of land...........	60,000
Repurchase of common shares.......	5,000	Amortization expense...................	8,000

Prepare the *operating activities section* of Edwards' cash flow statement for the year ended June 30, 2009. Edwards uses the *indirect* method for operating cash flows.

Preparing a cash flow statement—indirect method
(Obj. 3)

S12-6 Use the data in Short Exercise 12-5 to prepare Edwards Corporation's cash flow statement for the year ended June 30, 2009. Edwards uses the *indirect* method for operating activities. Use Exhibit 12-7, page 571, as a guide, but you may stop after determining the net increase (or decrease) in cash.

Computing investing cash flows
(Obj. 3)

S12-7 Autos of Red Deer Inc. reported the following financial statements for 2009:

Autos of Red Deer Inc.
Income Statement
For the Year Ended December 31, 2009

(In thousands)	
Sales revenue	$710
Cost of goods sold	340
Salary expense	70
Amortization expense	20
Other expenses	130
Total expenses	560
Net income	$150

Autos of Red Deer Inc.
Comparative Balance Sheet
December 31, 2009 and 2008

(In thousands)					
Assets	**2009**	**2008**	**Liabilities**	**2009**	**2008**
Current:			Current:		
Cash	$ 19	$ 16	Accounts payable	$ 47	$ 42
Accounts receivable	59	48	Salary payable	23	21
Inventory	75	84	Accrued liabilities	8	11
Prepaid expenses	3	2	Long-term notes payable	68	58
Long-term investments	55	75	**Shareholders' Equity**		
Capital assets, net	225	185	Common shares	40	32
			Retained earnings	250	246
Total	$436	$410	Total	$436	$410

Compute the following investing cash flows.
a. Acquisitions of plant and equipment (all were for cash). Autos of Red Deer sold no plant and equipment.
b. Proceeds from the sale of investments. Autos of Red Deer purchased no investments.

Computing financing cash flows
(Obj. 3)

S12-8 Use the Autos of Red Deer data in Short Exercise 12-7 to compute:
a. New borrowing or payment of long-term notes payable. Autos of Red Deer had only one long-term note payable transaction during the year.
b. Issuance of common shares or repurchase of common shares. Autos of Red Deer had only one common share transaction during the year.
c. Payment of cash dividends (same as dividends declared).

Preparing a cash flow statement—direct method
(Obj. 4)

S12-9 Tally-Ho Horse Farm Inc. began 2009 with cash of $44,000. During the year, Tally-Ho earned service revenue of $500,000 and collected $510,000 from customers. Expenses for the year totalled $420,000, with $400,000 paid in cash to suppliers and employees. Tally-Ho also paid $100,000 to purchase equipment and a cash dividend of $50,000 to shareholders. During 2009, Tally-Ho borrowed $20,000 by issuing a note payable.

Prepare the company's cash flow statement for the year. Format operating activities by the direct method.

S12-10 (Short Exercise 12-11 is an alternate.) Maritime Fisheries Ltd. provides the following data for the year ended June 30, 2009.

Computing operating cash flows—direct method
(Obj. 4)

Cost of goods sold	$100,000	Payment of dividends	$ 6,000
Payments to suppliers	87,000	Proceeds from issuance of	
Purchase of equipment	40,000	common shares	20,000
Payments to employees	70,000	Sales revenue	210,000
Payment of note payable	30,000	Collections from customers	180,000
Proceeds from sale of land	60,000	Payment of income tax	10,000
Amortization expense	8,000	Repurchase of common shares	5,000

Prepare the *operating activities section* of Maritime Fisheries Ltd.'s cash flow statement for the year ended June 30, 2009. Maritime Fisheries uses the *direct* method for operating cash flows.

S12-11 Use the data in Short Exercise 12-10 to prepare Maritime Fisheries Ltd.'s cash flow statement for the year ended June 30, 2009. Maritime Fisheries uses the *direct* method for operating activities. Use Exhibit 12-13, page 581, as a guide, but you may stop after determining the net increase (or decrease) in cash.

Preparing a cash flow statement—direct method
(Obj. 4)

S12-12 Use the Autos of Red Deer data in Short Exercise 12-7 to compute the following:
a. Collections from customers
b. Payments for inventory

Computing operating cash flows—direct method
(Obj. 4)

S12-13 Use the Autos of Red Deer data in Short Exercise 12-7 to compute the following:
a. Payments to employees
b. Payments of other expenses

Computing operating cash flows—direct method
(Obj. 4)

EXERCISES

E12-14 B.C. Plating Inc. has experienced an unbroken string of 10 years of growth in net income. Nevertheless, the company is facing bankruptcy. Creditors are calling all B.C. Plating's loans for immediate payment, and the cash is simply not available. It is clear that the company's top managers overemphasized profits and gave too little attention to cash flow.

Identifying the purposes of the cash flow statement
(Obj. 1)

❙ Required

Write a brief memo, in your own words, to explain to the managers of B.C. Plating the purposes of the cash flow statement.

E12-15 Tyler-Bolton Investments specializes in low-risk government bonds. Identify each of Tyler-Bolton's transactions as operating (O), investing (I), financing (F), noncash investing and financing (NIF), or a transaction that is not reported on the cash flow statement (N). Indicate whether each item increases (+) or decreases (−) cash. The indirect method is used for operating activities.

Identifying activities for the cash flow statement—indirect method
(Obj. 2)

___ a.	Net income	___ k.	Acquisition of equipment by issuance
___ b.	Payment of cash dividend		of note payable
___ c.	Sale of long-term investment	___ l.	Payment of long-term debt
___ d.	Loss on sale of equipment	___ m.	Acquisition of building by cash payment
___ e.	Amortization of intangible assets	___ n.	Accrual of salary expense
___ f.	Issuance of long-term note payable	___ o.	Purchase of long-term investment
	to borrow cash	___ p.	Decrease in merchandise inventory
___ g.	Amortization of equipment	___ q.	Increase in prepaid expenses
___ h.	Repurchase of common shares	___ r.	Cash sale of land
___ i.	Issuance of common shares for cash	___ s.	Decrease in accrued liabilities
___ j.	Increase in accounts payable		

E12-16 Indicate whether each of the following transactions records an operating activity, an investing activity, a financing activity, or a noncash investing and financing activity. The cash flow statement is prepared by the *indirect* method.

a.	Equipment	18,000		h.	Cash	81,000	
	Cash		18,000		Common Shares		81,000
b.	Cash	7,200					
	Long-Term Investment		7,200	i.	Common Shares	13,000	
c.	Bonds Payable	45,000			Cash		13,000
	Cash		45,000	j.	Cash	60,000	
d.	Building	164,000			Accounts Receivable	10,000	
	Note Payable, Long-Term		164,000		Service Revenue		70,000
e.	Loss on Disposal of Equipment	1,400		k.	Salary Expense	22,000	
	Equipment, Net		1,400		Cash		22,000
f.	Dividends Payable	16,500		l.	Land	87,000	
	Cash		16,500		Cash		87,000
g.	Furniture and Fixtures	22,100		m.	Amortization Expense	9,000	
	Cash		22,100		Accumulated Amortization		9,000

E12-17 The accounting records of North Central Distributors Inc. reveal the following:

Net income	$35,000	Amortization	$18,000
Collection of dividend revenue	7,000	Decrease in current liabilities	20,000
Payment of interest	16,000	Increase in current assets other	
Sales revenue	9,000	than cash	27,000
Loss on sale of land	5,000	Payment of dividends	7,000
Acquisition of land	37,000	Payment of income tax	13,000

❚ Required

Compute cash flows from operating activities by the indirect method. Use the format of the operating activities section of Exhibit 12-6 (p. 569). Also evaluate the operating cash flow of North Central Distributors. Give the reason for your evaluation.

E12-18 The accounting records of Saskatoon Fur Traders Ltd. include these accounts:

Cash

Mar. 1	5,000		
Receipts	447,000	Payments	448,000
Mar. 31	4,000		

Accounts Receivable

Mar. 1	18,000		
Receipts	443,000	Collections	447,000
Mar. 31	14,000		

Inventory

Mar. 1	19,000		
Purchases	337,000	Cost of sales	335,000
Mar. 31	21,000		

Equipment

Mar. 1	93,000		
Acquisition	6,000		
Mar. 31	99,000		

Accumulated Amortization—Equipment

		Mar. 1	52,000
		Amortization	3,000
		Mar. 31	55,000

Accounts Payable

		Mar. 1	14,000
Payments	332,000	Purchases	337,000
		Mar. 31	19,000

Accrued Liabilities

		Mar. 1	9,000
Payments	14,000	Receipts	11,000
		Mar. 31	6,000

Retained Earnings

		Mar. 1	64,000
Quarterly dividend	18,000	Net income	41,000
		Mar. 31	87,000

Compute Saskatoon's net cash provided by (used for) operating activities during March. Use the indirect method. Does Saskatoon have trouble collecting receivables or selling inventory? How can you tell?

E12-19 The income statement and additional data of Noel Travel Products Inc. follow:

Preparing the cash flow statement—indirect method
(Obj. 3)

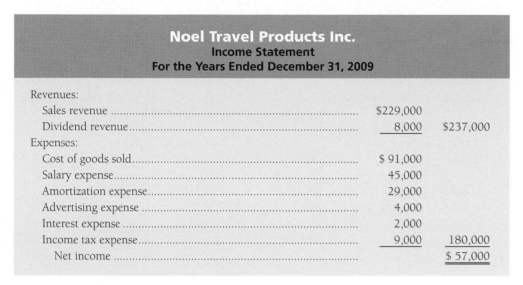

Noel Travel Products Inc.		
Income Statement		
For the Years Ended December 31, 2009		
Revenues:		
Sales revenue	$229,000	
Dividend revenue	8,000	$237,000
Expenses:		
Cost of goods sold	$ 91,000	
Salary expense	45,000	
Amortization expense	29,000	
Advertising expense	4,000	
Interest expense	2,000	
Income tax expense	9,000	180,000
Net income		$ 57,000

Additional data:
a. Acquisition of plant assets was $150,000. Of this amount, $100,000 was paid in cash and $50,000 by signing a note payable.
b. Proceeds from sale of land totalled $24,000.
c. Proceeds from issuance of common shares totalled $30,000.
d. Payment of long-term note payable was $15,000.
e. Payment of dividends was $11,000.
f. From the balance sheet:

	December 31,	
	2009	**2008**
Current Assets:		
Cash	$47,000	$20,000
Accounts receivable	43,000	58,000
Inventory	83,000	77,000
Prepaid expenses	9,000	8,000
Current Liabilities:		
Accounts payable	35,000	22,000
Accrued liabilities	13,000	21,000

❙ Required

1. Prepare Noel's cash flow statement for the year ended December 31, 2009, using the indirect method.
2. Evaluate Noel's cash flows for the year. In your evaluation, mention all three categories of cash flows and give the reason for your evaluation.

*Interpreting a cash flow
statement—indirect method*
(Obj. 3)

E12-20 Consider three independent cases for the cash flows of 827 Boulevard Shoes Ltd. For each case, identify from the cash flow statement how 827 Boulevard Shoes generated the cash to acquire new capital assets. Rank the three cases from the most financially healthy to the least healthy.

	Case A	Case B	Case C
Cash flows from operating activities:			
Net income...	$ 30,000	$ 30,000	$ 30,000
Amortization	11,000	11,000	11,000
Increase in current assets....................................	(1,000)	(19,000)	(7,000)
Decrease in current liabilities..............................	0	(6,000)	(8,000)
	$ 40,000	$ 16,000	$ 26,000
Cash flows from investing activities:			
Acquisition of capital assets................................	$(91,000)	$(91,000)	$ (91,000)
Sales of capital assets..	8,000	97,000	4,000
	$(83,000)	$ 6,000	$ (87,000)
Cash flows from financing activities:			
Issuance of common shares................................	$ 50,000	$ 16,000	$104,000
Payment of debt	(9,000)	(21,000)	(29,000)
	$ 41,000	$ (5,000)	$ 75,000
Net increase (decrease) in cash..............................	$ (2,000)	$ 17,000	$ 14,000

*Computing investing and
financing amounts for the cash
flow statement*
(Obj. 3)

E12-21 Compute the following items for the cash flow statement.
a. Beginning and ending Capital Assets, Net, are $103,000 and $107,000, respectively. Amortization for the period was $21,500, and purchases of new plant and equipment were $27,000. Capital assets were sold at a $1,000 loss. What were the cash proceeds of the sale?
b. Beginning and ending Retained Earnings are $45,000 and $73,000, respectively. Net income for the period was $47,000, and stock dividends were $8,000. How much were cash dividends?

*Identifying activities for the cash
flow statement—direct method*
(Obj. 4)

E12-22 Identify each of the following transactions as operating (O), investing (I), financing (F), noncash investing and financing (NIF), or not reported on the cash flow statement (N). Indicate whether each transaction increases (+) or decreases (−) cash. The *direct* method is used for operating activities.

___ a.	Repurchase of common shares		___ k.	Acquisition of equipment by
___ b.	Issuance of common shares for cash			issuance of note payable
___ c.	Payment of accounts payable		___ l.	Payment of long-term debt
___ d.	Issuance of preferred shares for cash		___ m.	Acquisition of building by payment
___ e.	Payment of cash dividend			of cash
___ f.	Sale of long-term investment		___ n.	Accrual of salary expense
___ g.	Amortization of patent		___ o.	Purchase of long-term investment
___ h.	Collection of accounts receivable		___ p.	Payment of wages to employees
___ i.	Issuance of long-term note payable		___ q.	Collection of cash interest
	to borrow cash		___ r.	Cash sale of land
___ j.	Amortization of equipment		___ s.	Distribution of stock dividend

*Classifying transactions for the
cash flow statement—direct
method*
(Obj. 4)

E12-23 Indicate where, if at all, each of the following transactions would be reported on a cash flow statement prepared by the *direct* method and the accompanying schedule of non-cash investing and financing activities.

a.	Equipment	18,000		h.	Retained Earnings	36,000		
	Cash		18,000		Common Shares		36,000	
b.	Cash	7,200		i.	Cash	2,000		
	Long-Term Investment		7,200		Interest Revenue		2,000	
c.	Bonds Payable	45,000		j.	Land	87,700		
	Cash		45,000		Cash		87,700	
d.	Building	164,000		k.	Accounts Payable	8,300		
	Cash		164,000		Cash		8,300	
e.	Cash	1,400		l.	Salary Expense	4,300		
	Accounts Receivable		1,400		Cash		4,300	
f.	Dividends Payable	16,500		m.	Cash	81,000		
	Cash		16,500		Common Shares		81,000	
g.	Furniture and Fixtures	22,100			Common Shares	13,000		
	Note Payable, Short-Term		22,100	n.	Cash		13,000	

E12-24 The accounting records of Jasmine Pharmaceuticals Inc. reveal the following:

Payment of salaries and wages	$34,000	Net income	$34,000
Amortization	22,000	Payment of income tax.................	13,000
Decrease in current liabilities..........	20,000	Collection of dividend revenue.....	7,000
Increase in current assets		Payment of interest......................	16,000
other than cash..........................	27,000	Cash sales....................................	38,000
Payment of dividends....................	12,000	Loss on sale of land	5,000
Collection of		Acquisition of land.......................	37,000
accounts receivable.....................	93,000	Payment of accounts payable........	54,000

Computing cash flows from operating activities—direct method
(Obj. 4)

❙ Required

Compute cash flows from operating activities by the *direct* method. Use the format of the operating activities section of Exhibit 12-13. Also evaluate Jasmine's operating cash flow. Give the reason for your evaluation.

E12-25 Selected accounts of Fishbowl Antiques Inc. show the following:

Identifying items for the cash flow statement—direct method
(Obj. 4)

Salary Payable

		Beginning balance	9,000
Payments	40,000	Salary expense	38,000
		Ending balance	7,000

Buildings

Beginning balance	90,000	Amortization	18,000
Acquisitions	145,000	Book value of building sold	109,000*
Ending balance	108,000		

   *Sale price was 140,000

Notes Payable

		Beginning balance	273,000
Payments	69,000	Issuance of note payable	
		for cash	83,000
		Ending balance	287,000

❙ Required

For each account, identify the item or items that should appear on a cash flow statement prepared by the *direct* method. State where to report the item.

E12-26 The income statement and additional data of Floral World Ltd. follow:

Floral World Ltd. Income Statement For the Year Ended June 30, 2009		
Revenues:		
Sales revenue	$229,000	
Dividend revenue	15,000	$244,000
Expenses:		
Cost of goods sold	103,000	
Salary expense	45,000	
Amortization expense	29,000	
Advertising expense	11,000	
Interest expense	2,000	
Income tax expense	9,000	199,000
Net income		$ 45,000

Additional data:

a. Collections from customers are $30,000 more than sales.
b. Payments to suppliers are $1,000 more than the sum of cost of goods sold plus advertising expense.
c. Payments to employees are $1,000 more than salary expense.
d. Dividend revenue, interest expense, and income tax expense equal their cash amounts.
e. Acquisition of plant and equipment is $150,000. Of this amount, $101,000 is paid in cash and $49,000 by signing a note payable.
f. Proceeds from sale of land total $24,000.
g. Proceeds from issuance of common shares total $30,000.
h. Payment of long-term note payable is $15,000.
i. Payment of dividends is $11,000.
j. Cash balance, June 30, 2008, was $20,000.

❙ *Required*

1. Prepare Floral World Ltd.'s cash flow statement and accompanying schedule of noncash investing and financing activities. Report operating activities by the *direct* method.
2. Evaluate Floral World's cash flows for the year. In your evaluation, mention all three categories of cash flows and give the reason for your evaluation.

E12-27 Compute the following items for the cash flow statement.

a. Beginning and ending Accounts Receivable are $22,000 and $32,000, respectively. Credit sales for the period total $60,000. How much are cash collections from customers?
b. Cost of goods sold is $111,000. Beginning Inventory was $25,000, and ending Inventory is $21,000. Beginning and ending Accounts Payable are $14,000 and $8,000, respectively. How much are cash payments for inventory?

CHALLENGE EXERCISES

E12-28 Morgan Industries Inc. reported the following in its financial statements for the year ended August 31, 2009 (in thousands):

Computing cash-flow amounts
(Obj. 3, 4)

	2009	2008
Income Statement		
Net sales	$24,623	$21,207
Cost of sales	18,048	15,466
Amortization	269	230
Other operating expenses	3,883	4,248
Income tax expense	537	486
Net income	$ 1,886	$ 777
Balance Sheet		
Cash and cash equivalents	$ 17	$ 13
Accounts receivable	601	615
Inventory	3,100	2,831
Property and equipment, net	4,345	3,428
Accounts payable	1,547	1,364
Accrued liabilities	938	631
Income tax payable	201	194
Long-term liabilities	478	464
Common shares	519	446
Retained earnings	4,380	3,788

Determine the following cash receipts and payments for Morgan Industries Inc. during 2009.

a. Collections from customers
b. Payments for inventory
c. Payments for other operating expenses
d. Payment of income tax
e. Proceeds from issuance of common shares
f. Payment of cash dividends

E12-29 Crown Specialties Ltd. reported the following at December 31, 2009 (in thousands):

Using the balance sheet and the cash flow statement together
(Obj. 3)

	2009	2008
From the comparative balance sheet:		
Property and equipment, net	$ 11,150	$9,590
Long-term notes payable	4,400	3,080
From the cash flow statement:		
Amortization	$ 1,920	
Capital expenditures	(4,130)	
Proceeds from sale of property and equipment	770	
Proceeds from issuance of long-term note payable	1,190	
Payment of long-term note payable	(110)	
Issuance of common shares	383	

Determine the following items for Crown Specialties during 2009:

1. Gain or loss on the sale of property and equipment
2. Amount of long-term debt issued for something other than cash

QUIZ

Test your understanding of the cash flow statement by answering the following questions. Select the best choice among the possible answers given.

Q12-30 Paying off bonds payable is reported on the cash flow statement under
a. Operating activities
b. Investing activities
c. Financing activities
d. Noncash investing and financing activities

Q12-31 The sale of inventory for cash is reported on the cash flow statement under
a. Operating activities
b. Investing activities
c. Financing activities
d. Noncash investing and financing activities

Q12-32 Selling equipment is reported on the cash flow statement under
a. Operating activities
b. Investing activities
c. Financing activities
d. Noncash investing and financing activities

Q12-33 Which of the following terms appears on a cash flow statement—indirect method?
a. Payments to suppliers
b. Amortization expense
c. Collections from customers
d. Cash receipt of interest revenue

Q12-34 On an indirect-method cash flow statement, an increase in prepaid insurance would be
a. Included in payments to suppliers
b. Added to net income
c. Added to increases in current assets
d. Deducted from net income

Q12-35 On an indirect-method cash flow statement, an increase in accounts payable would be
a. Reported in the investing activities section
b. Reported in the financing activities section
c. Added to net income in the operating activities section
d. Deducted from net income in the operating activities section

Q12-36 On an indirect-method cash flow statement, a gain on the sale of plant assets would be
a. Ignored, since the gain did not generate any cash
b. Reported in the investing activities section
c. Deducted from net income in the operating activities section
d. Added to net income in the operating activities section

Q12-37 Paying cash dividends is a/an _____ activity.
　　　　　Receiving cash dividends is a/an _____ activity.

Q12-38 Matlock Camera Co. sold equipment with a cost of $20,000 and accumulated amortization of $8,000 for an amount that resulted in a gain of $3,000. What amount should Matlock report on the cash flow statement as "proceeds from sale of plant and equipment"?
a. $9,000
b. $17,000
c. $15,000
d. Some other amount ($<u>fill in the blank</u>)

Questions 39 through 47 use the following data. Trudeau Corporation formats operating cash flows by the indirect method.

Trudeau Corporation
Income Statement for 2009

Sales revenue	$180,000	
Gain on sale of equipment	8,000	$188,000
Cost of goods sold	110,000	
Amortization	6,000	
Other operating expenses	25,000	141,000
Net income		$ 47,000

Trudeau Corporation
Comparative Balance Sheet at the End of 2009

Assets	2009	2008	Liabilities and Shareholders' Equity	2009	2008
Cash	$ 4,000	$ 1,000	Accounts payable	$ 6,000	$ 7,000
Accounts receivable	7,000	11,000	Accrued liabilities	7,000	3,000
Inventory	10,000	9,000	Common shares	20,000	10,000
Plant and equipment, net	93,000	69,000	Retained earnings	81,000	70,000
	$114,000	$90,000		$114,000	$90,000

Q12-39 How many items enter the computation of Trudeau's net cash provided by operating activities?

a. 2   c. 5
b. 3   d. 7

Q12-40 How do Trudeau's accrued liabilities affect the company's cash flow statement for 2009?
a. They don't because the accrued liabilities are not yet paid.
b. Increase in cash provided by operating activities
c. Increase in cash used by investing activities
d. Increase in cash used by financing activities

Q12-41 How do accounts receivable affect Trudeau's cash flows from operating activities for 2009?
a. Increase in cash provided by operating activities
b. Decrease in cash provided by operating activities
c. They don't because accounts receivable result from investing activities.
d. Decrease in cash used by investing activities

Q12-42 Trudeau's net cash provided by operating activities during 2009 was
a. $3,000   c. $51,000
b. $47,000   d. $58,000

Q12-43 How many items enter the computation of Trudeau's net cash flow investing activities for 2009?
a. 2   c. 5
b. 3   d. 7

Q12-44 The book value of equipment sold during 2009 was $20,000. Trudeau's net cash flow from investing activities for 2009 was
a. Net cash used of $22,000   c. Net cash used of $50,000
b. Net cash used of $28,000   d. Net cash provided of $28,000

Q12-45 How many items enter the computation of Trudeau's net cash flow from financing activities for 2009?

a. 2   c. 5
b. 3   d. 7

Q12-46 Trudeau's largest financing cash flow for 2009 resulted from

a. Sale of equipment   c. Issuance of common shares
b. Purchase of equipment   d. Payment of dividends

Q12-47 Trudeau's net cash flow from financing activities for 2009 was

a. Net cash used of $25,000   c. Net cash provided of $10,000
b. Net cash used of $20,000   d. Net cash used of $26,000

Q12-48 Sales totalled $800,000, accounts receivable increased by $40,000, and accounts payable decreased by $35,000. How much cash did the company collect from customers?

a. $760,000   c. $800,000
b. $795,000   d. $840,000

Q12-49 Income Tax Payable was $5,000 at the end of the year and $2,800 at the beginning. Income tax expense for the year totalled $59,100. What amount of cash did the company pay for income tax during the year?

a. $56,900   c. $61,300
b. $59,100   d. $61,900

PROBLEMS

(GROUP A)

Using cash flow data to evaluate performance
(Obj. 1, 2)

P12-50A Top managers of Relax Inns are reviewing company performance for 2009. The income statement reports a 20% increase in net income over 2008. However, most of the increase resulted from an extraordinary gain on insurance proceeds from fire damage to a building. The balance sheet shows a large increase in receivables. The statement of cash flow, in summarized form, reports the following:

Net cash used for operating activities	$(80,000)
Net cash provided by investing activities	40,000
Net cash provided by financing activities	50,000
Increase in cash during 2009	$ 10,000

❚ Required

Write a memo giving Relax Inns' managers your assessment of 2009 operations and your outlook for the future. Focus on the information content of the cash flow data.

Preparing an income statement, balance sheet, and cash flow statement—indirect method
(Obj. 2, 3)

P12-51A Vintage Automobiles of Orangeville Ltd. was formed on January 1, 2009, when Vintage issued common shares for $300,000. Early in January 2009, Vintage made the following cash payments:

a. $150,000 for equipment
b. $120,000 for inventory (4 cars at $30,000 each)
c. $20,000 for 2009 rent on a store building

In February 2009, Vintage purchased 6 cars for inventory on account. Cost of this inventory was $260,000 ($43,333.33 each). Before year-end, Vintage paid $208,000 of this debt. Vintage uses the FIFO method to account for inventory.

During 2009, Vintage sold 8 vintage autos for a total of $500,000. Before year-end, Vintage collected 80% of this amount.

The business employs 3 people. The combined annual payroll is $95,000, of which Vintage owes $4,000 at year-end. At the end of the year, Vintage paid income tax of $10,000.

Late in 2009, Vintage declared and paid cash dividends of $11,000.

For equipment, Vintage uses the straight-line amortization method over 5 years with zero residual value.

I Required

1. Prepare Vintage Automobiles of Orangeville Ltd.'s income statement for the year ended December 31, 2009. Use the single-step format, with all revenues listed together and all expenses listed together.
2. Prepare Vintage's balance sheet at December 31, 2009.
3. Prepare Vintage's cash flow statement for the year ended December 31, 2009. Format cash flows from operating activities by using the *indirect* method.
4. Comment on the business performance based on the cash flow statement.

P12-52A Primrose Software Inc. has assembled the following data for the year ended December 31, 2009.

Preparing the cash flow statement—indirect method
(Obj. 2, 3)

	December 31,	
	2009	2008
Current Accounts:		
Current assets:		
Cash and cash equivalents...	$38,700	$22,700
Accounts receivable..	69,700	64,200
Inventories..	88,600	83,000
Prepaid expenses...	5,300	4,100
Current liabilities:		
Accounts payable	57,200	55,800
Income tax payable	18,600	16,700
Accrued liabilities...	15,500	27,200

Transaction Data for 2009:			
Acquisition of land by issuing		Repurchase of common shares........	$14,300
long-term note payable	$ 95,000	Loss on sale of equipment..............	11,700
Stock dividends	31,800	Payment of cash dividends..............	18,300
Collection of loan...........................	8,700	Issuance of long-term note payable	
Amortization expense	27,100	to borrow cash...........................	34,400
Purchase of building	125,300	Net income...................................	45,100
Retirement of bonds payable by		Issuance of common shares	
issuing common shares	65,000	for cash.......................................	41,200
Purchase of long-term investment	31,600	Proceeds from sale of equipment	58,000

I Required

Prepare Primrose Software Inc.'s cash flow statement using the *indirect* method to report operating activities. Include an accompanying schedule of noncash investing and financing activities. How much of the cash used for investing activities was provided by operations?

P12-53A The comparative balance sheet of Northern Movie Theatre Company at March 31, 2009, reported the following:

Preparing the cash flow statement—indirect method
(Obj. 2, 3)

	March 31,	
	2009	2008
Current assets:		
Cash and cash equivalents..	$ 9,900	$14,000
Accounts receivable...	14,900	21,700
Inventories..	63,200	60,600
Prepaid expenses...	1,900	1,700
Current liabilities:		
Accounts payable	30,300	27,600
Accrued liabilities...	10,700	11,100
Income tax payable	8,000	4,700

Northern's transactions during the year ended March 31, 2009, included the following:

Acquisition of land by issuing note payable	$101,000	Sale of long-term investment	$13,700
Payment of cash dividend	30,000	Amortization expense	17,300
Cash purchase of equipment	78,700	Cash purchase of building	47,000
Issuance of long-term note payable to borrow cash	50,000	Net income	50,000
		Issuance of common shares for cash	11,000
		Stock dividend	18,000

▌ *Required*

1. Prepare Northern Movie Theatre Company's cash flow statement for the year ended March 31, 2009, using the *indirect* method to report cash flows from operating activities. Report non-cash investing and financing activities in an accompanying schedule.

2. Evaluate Northern's cash flows for the year. Mention all three categories of cash flows and give the reason for your evaluation.

Preparing the cash flow statement—indirect method
Obj. 2, 3)

P12-54A The 2009 comparative balance sheet and income statement of 4 Seasons Supply Corp. follow. 4 Seasons had no noncash investing and financing transactions during 2009. During the year, there were no sales of land or equipment, no issuance of notes payable, and no repurchase of shares transactions.

4 Seasons Supply Corp.
Comparative Balance Sheet

	December 31, 2009	December 31, 2008	Increase (Decrease)
Current assets:			
Cash and cash equivalents	$ 17,600	$ 5,300	$12,300
Accounts receivable	27,200	27,600	(400)
Inventories	83,600	87,200	(3,600)
Prepaid expenses	2,500	1,900	600
Capital assets:			
Land	89,000	60,000	29,000
Equipment, net	53,500	49,400	4,100
Total assets	$273,400	$231,400	$42,000
Current liabilities:			
Accounts payable	$ 35,800	$ 33,700	$ 2,100
Salary payable	3,100	6,600	(3,500)
Other accrued liabilities	22,600	23,700	(1,100)
Long-term liabilities:			
Notes payable	75,000	100,000	(25,000)
Shareholders' equity:			
Common shares	88,300	64,700	23,600
Retained earnings	48,600	2,700	45,900
Total liabilities and shareholders' equity	$273,400	$231,400	$42,000

4 Seasons Supply Corp. Income Statement for 2009		
Revenues:		
Sales revenue		$228,700
Expenses:		
Cost of goods sold	$70,600	
Salary expense	27,800	
Amortization expense	4,000	
Other operating expense	10,500	
Interest expense	11,600	
Income tax expense	29,100	
Total expenses		153,600
Net income		$ 75,100

I *Required*

1. Prepare the 2009 cash flow statement, formatting operating activities by using the *indirect* method.

2. How will what you learned in this problem help you evaluate an investment?

P12-55A World Mosaic Furniture Gallery Inc. provided the following data from the company's records for the year ended April 30, 2009:

Preparing the cash flow statement—direct method
(Obj. 2, 4)

a. Credit sales, $583,900
b. Loan to another company, $12,500
c. Cash payments to purchase property, plant, and equipment, $59,400
d. Cost of goods sold, $382,600
e. Proceeds from issuance of common shares, $8,000
f. Payment of cash dividends, $48,400
g. Collection of interest, $4,400
h. Acquisition of equipment by issuing short-term note payable, $16,400
i. Payments of salaries, $93,600
j. Proceeds from sale of property, plant, and equipment, $22,400, including $6,800 loss
k. Collections on accounts receivable, $428,600
l. Interest revenue, $3,800
m. Cash receipt of dividend revenue, $4,100
n. Payments to suppliers, $368,500

o. Cash sales, $171,900
p. Amortization expense, $59,900
q. Proceeds from issuance of note payable, $19,600
r. Payments of long-term notes payable, $50,000
s. Interest expense and payments, $13,300
t. Salary expense, $95,300
u. Loan collections, $12,800
v. Proceeds from sale of investments, $9,100, including $2,000 gain
w. Payment of short-term note payable by issuing long-term note payable, $63,000
x. Amortization expense, $2,900
y. Income tax expense and payments, $37,900
z. Cash balance: April 30, 2008, $39,300; April 30, 2009, $36,600

I *Required*

1. Prepare World Mosaic Furniture Gallery Inc.'s cash flow statement for the year ended April 30, 2009. Use the *direct* method for cash flows from operating activities. Follow the format of Exhibit 12-13 (p. 581), but do *not* show amounts in thousands. Include an accompanying schedule of noncash investing and financing activities.

2. Evaluate 2009 from a cash-flow standpoint. Give your reasons.

P12-56A Use the Vintage Automobiles of Orangeville Ltd. data from Problem 12-51A.

Preparing an income statement, balance sheet, and cash flow statement—direct method
(Obj. 2, 4)

I *Required*

1. Prepare Vintage's income statement for the year ended December 31, 2009. Use the single-step format, with all revenues listed together and all expenses listed together.

2. Prepare Vintage's balance sheet at December 31, 2009.

3. Prepare Vintage's cash flow statement for the year ended December 31, 2009. Format cash flows from operating activities by using the *direct* method.

Preparing the cash flow statement—direct method **(Obj. 2, 4)**

P12-57A Use the 4 Seasons Supply Corp. data from Problem 12-54A.

❙ Required

1. Prepare the 2009 cash flow statement by using the *direct* method.

2. How will what you learned in this problem help you evaluate an investment? (Challenge) Compare the cash from operations information with the Problem 12-54A solution.

Preparing the cash flow statement—direct and indirect methods **(Obj. 3, 4)**

P12-58A To prepare the cash flow statement, accountants for Franklin Electric Limited have summarized 2009 activity in two accounts as follows:

Cash				
Beginning balance	53,600	Payments on accounts payable	399,100
Sale of long-term investment	21,200	Payments of dividends	27,200
Collections from customers	661,700	Payments of salaries and wages	143,800
Issuance of common shares	47,300	Payments of interest	26,900
Receipts of dividends	17,100	Purchase of equipment	31,400
		Payments of operating expenses	34,300
		Payment of long-term note payable	41,300
		Repurchase of common shares	26,400
		Payment of income tax	18,900
Ending balance	51,600		

Common Shares			
Repurchase of common shares	26,400	Beginning balance	110,800
		Issuance for cash	47,300
		Issuance to acquire land	80,100
		Issuance to retire note payable	19,000
		Ending balance	230,800

❙ Required

1. Prepare the cash flow statement of Franklin Electric Limited for the year ended December 31, 2009, using the *direct* method to report operating activities. Also prepare the accompanying schedule of noncash investing and financing activities.

2. Use the following data from Franklin's 2009 income statement and balance sheet to prepare a supplementary schedule of cash flows from operating activities by using the *indirect* method.

Franklin Electric Limited
Income Statement
For the Year Ended December 31, 2009

Revenues:		
Sales revenue		$689,300
Dividend revenue		17,100
Total revenue		706,400
Expenses and losses:		
Cost of goods sold	$402,600	
Salary and wage expense	150,800	
Amortization expense	19,300	
Other operating expense	44,100	
Interest expense	28,800	
Income tax expense	16,200	
Loss on sale of investments	1,100	
Total expenses and losses		662,900
Net income		$ 43,500

Franklin Electric Limited
Selected Balance Sheet Data

	2009 Increase (Decrease)
Current assets:	
Cash and cash equivalents	$ (2,000)
Accounts receivable	27,600
Inventories	(11,800)
Prepaid expenses	600
Long-term investments	(22,300)
Equipment, net	12,100
Land	80,100
Current liabilities:	
Accounts payable	(8,300)
Interest payable	1,900
Salary payable	7,000
Other accrued liabilities	10,400
Income tax payable	(2,700)
Long-term note payable	(60,300)
Common shares	120,000
Retained earnings	16,300

P12-59A The comparative balance sheet of Graphic Design Studio Inc. at June 30, 2009, included these amounts.

Preparing the cash flow statement—indirect and direct methods
(Obj. 3, 4)

Graphic Design Studio Inc.
Balance Sheet
June 30, 2009 and 2008

	2009	2008	Increase (Decrease)
Current assets:			
Cash	$ 28,600	$ 8,600	$ 20,000
Accounts receivable	48,800	51,900	(3,100)
Inventories	68,600	60,200	8,400
Prepaid expenses	3,700	2,800	900
Long-term investment	10,100	5,200	4,900
Equipment, net	74,500	73,600	900
Land	42,400	96,000	(53,600)
	$276,700	$298,300	$(21,600)
Current liabilities:			
Notes payable, short-term	$ 13,400	$ 18,100	$ (4,700)
Accounts payable	42,400	40,300	2,100
Income tax payable	13,800	14,500	(700)
Accrued liabilities	8,200	9,700	(1,500)
Interest payable	3,700	2,900	800
Salary payable	900	2,600	(1,700)
Long-term note payable	47,400	94,100	(46,700)
Common shares	59,800	51,200	8,600
Retained earnings	87,100	64,900	22,200
	$276,700	$298,300	$(21,600)

Transaction data for the year ended June 30, 2009

a. Net income, $60,300
b. Amortization expense on equipment, $13,400
c. Purchased long-term investment, $4,900
d. Sold land for $46,900, including $6,700 loss
e. Acquired equipment by issuing long-term note payable, $14,300
f. Paid long-term note payable, $61,000
g. Received cash for issuance of common shares, $3,900
h. Paid cash dividends, $38,100
i. Paid short-term note payable by issuing common shares, $4,700

❚ Required

1. Prepare the cash flow statement of Graphic Design Studio Inc. for the year ended June 30, 2009, using the *indirect* method to report operating activities. Also prepare the accompanying schedule of noncash investing and financing activities. All current accounts except short-term notes payable result from operating transactions.

2. Prepare a supplementary schedule showing cash flows from operations by the *direct* method. The accounting records provide the following: collections from customers, $261,800; interest received, $1,300; payments to suppliers, $133,500; payments to employees, $40,500; payments for income tax, $10,600; and payment of interest $5,300.

(GROUP B)

Using cash-flow information to evaluate performance
(Obj. 1, 2)

P12-60B Top managers of Culinary Imports Limited are reviewing company performance for 2009. The income statement reports a 15% increase in net income, the fourth consecutive year showing an income increase above 10%. The income statement includes a nonrecurring loss without which net income would have increased by 16%. The balance sheet shows modest increases in assets, liabilities, and shareholders' equity. The assets posting the largest increases are plant and equipment because the company is halfway through a 5-year expansion program. No other asset and no liabilities are increasing dramatically. A summarized version of the cash flow statement reports the following:

Net cash provided by operating activities	$ 310,000
Net cash used for investing activities	(290,000)
Net cash provided by financing activities	50,000
Increase in cash during 2009	$ 70,000

❚ Required

Write a memo giving top managers of Culinary Imports Limited your assessment of 2009 operations and your outlook for the future. Focus on the net income and the cash flow data.

Preparing an income statement, balance sheet, and cash flow statement—indirect method
(Obj. 2, 3)

P12-61B Cruise Canada Motorhomes Inc. (CCM) was formed on January 1, 2009, when the company issued its common shares for $200,000. Early in January, CCM made the following cash payments:

a. For showroom fixtures, $50,000
b. For inventory, 2 motorhomes at $60,000 each, a total of $120,000
c. For rent on a store building, $12,000

In February, CCM purchased 3 motorhomes on account. Cost of this inventory was $160,000 ($53,333.33 each). Before year-end, CCM paid $140,000 of this debt. CCM uses the FIFO method to account for inventory.

During 2009, CCM sold 4 motorhomes for a total of $560,000. Before year-end, CCM collected 90% of this amount.

The store employs 3 people. The combined annual payroll is $90,000, of which CCM owes $3,000 at year-end. At the end of the year, CCM paid income tax of $64,000.

Late in 2009, CCM declared and paid cash dividends of $40,000.

For showroom fixtures, CCM uses the straight-line amortization method over 5 years with zero residual value.

I Required

1. Prepare CCM's income statement for the year ended December 31, 2009. Use the single-step format, with all revenues listed together and all expenses listed together.
2. Prepare CCM's balance sheet at December 31, 2009.
3. Prepare CCM's cash flow statement for the year ended December 31, 2009. Format cash flows from operating activities by the indirect method.
4. Comment on the business performance based on the cash flow statement.

P12-62B Accountants for Crowne Plaza Products Inc. have assembled the following data for the year ended December 31, 2009:

Preparing the cash flow statement—indirect method (Obj. 2, 3)

	December 31,	
	2009	2008
Current Accounts:		
Current assets:		
Cash and cash equivalents	$29,100	$34,800
Accounts receivable	70,100	73,700
Inventories	90,600	96,500
Prepaid expenses	3,200	2,100
Current liabilities:		
Accounts payable	71,600	67,500
Income tax payable	5,900	6,800
Accrued liabilities	28,300	23,200

Transaction Data for 2009:			
Payment of cash dividends	$48,300	Stock dividends	$ 12,600
Issuance of long-term note		Collection of loan	10,300
payable to borrow cash	71,000	Purchase of equipment	69,000
Net income	31,000	Payment of note payable by	
Issuance of preferred shares for cash	36,200	issuing common shares	89,400
Sale of long-term investment	12,200	Purchase of long-term investment	44,800
Amortization expense	30,300	Acquisition of building by issuing	
Payment of long-term note payable	47,800	long-term note payable	201,000
Gain on sale of investment	3,500		

I Required

Prepare Crowne Plaza Products' cash flow statement using the *indirect* method to report operating activities. Include an accompanying schedule of noncash investing and financing activities. How much of the cash used for investing activities was provided by operations?

P12-63B The comparative balance sheet of Crossbow Novelties Corp. at December 31, 2009, reported the following:

Preparing the cash flow statement—indirect method (Obj. 2, 3)

	December 31,	
	2009	2008
Current Assets:		
Cash and cash equivalents	$28,800	$12,500
Accounts receivable	28,600	29,300
Inventories	51,600	53,000
Prepaid expenses	4,200	3,700
Current Liabilities:		
Accounts payable	31,100	28,000
Accrued liabilities	14,300	16,800
Income tax payable	11,000	14,300

Crossbow's transactions during 2009 included the following:

Cash purchase of building.............	$124,000	Amortization expense....................	$17,800
Net income.....................................	52,000	Payment of cash dividends............	17,000
Issuance of common shares		Cash purchase of equipment.........	55,000
for cash......................................	105,600	Issuance of long-term note	
Stock dividend	13,000	payable to borrow cash..............	32,000
Sale of long-term investment.........	6,000	Retirement of note payable by	
		issuing common shares..............	30,000

❙ Required

1. Prepare the cash flow statement of Crossbow Novelties Corp. for the year ended December 31, 2009. Use the *indirect* method to report cash flows from operating activities. Report noncash investing and financing activities in an accompanying schedule.

2. Evaluate Crossbow's cash flows for the year. Mention all three categories of cash flows, and give the reason for your evaluation.

Preparing the cash flow statement—indirect method
(Obj. 2, 3)

P12-64B The 2009 comparative balance sheet and income statement of Riverbend Pools Inc. follow. Riverbend had no noncash investing and financing transactions during 2009. During the year, there were no sales of land or equipment, no issuances of notes payable, and no share repurchase transactions.

❙ Required

1. Prepare the cash flow statement of Riverbend Pools Inc. for the year ended December 31, 2009. Format operating activities by the indirect method.

2. How will what you learned in this problem help you evaluate an investment?

Riverbend Pools Inc.
Comparative Balance Sheet
December 31, 2009 and 2008

	2009	2008	Increase (Decrease)
Current assets:			
Cash and cash equivalents...	$ 28,700	$ 15,600	$13,100
Accounts receivable..	47,100	44,000	3,100
Inventories	94,300	89,900	4,400
Prepaid expenses...	1,700	2,200	(500)
Plant assets:			
Land..	35,100	10,000	25,100
Equipment, net	100,900	93,700	7,200
Total assets	$307,800	$255,400	$52,400
Current liabilities:			
Accounts payable	$ 22,700	$ 24,600	$(1,900)
Salary payable	2,100	1,400	700
Other accrued liabilities	24,400	22,500	1,900
Long-term liabilities:			
Notes payable..	55,000	65,000	(10,000)
Shareholders' equity:			
Common shares	131,100	122,300	8,800
Retained earnings..	72,500	19,600	52,900
Total liabilities and shareholders' equity	$307,800	$255,400	$52,400

Riverbend Pools Inc.		
Income Statement for 2009		
Revenues:		
Sales revenue	$438,000	
Interest revenue	11,700	
Total revenues	449,700	
Expenses:		
Cost of goods sold	$185,200	
Salary expense	76,400	
Amortization expense	15,300	
Other operating expense	49,700	
Interest expense	24,600	
Income tax expense	16,900	
Total expense		368,100
Net income		$ 81,600

P12-65B Rocco's Gourmet Foods Inc. provides the following data from the company's records for the year ended July 31, 2009:

a. Salary expense, $105,300
b. Cash payments to purchase property, plant, and equipment, $181,000
c. Proceeds from issuance of note payable, $44,100
d. Payments of long-term note payable, $18,800
e. Proceeds from sale of property, plant, and equipment, $59,700, including $10,600 gain
f. Interest revenue, $12,100
g. Cash receipt of dividend revenue on investments, $2,700
h. Payments to suppliers, $673,300
i. Interest expense and payments, $37,800
j. Cost of goods sold, $481,100
k. Collection of interest revenue, $11,700
l. Acquisition of equipment by issuing short-term note payable, $35,500
m. Payments of salaries, $104,000

n. Credit sales, $768,100
o. Loan to another company, $35,000
p. Income tax expense and payments, $56,400
q. Amortization expense, $27,700
r. Collections on accounts receivable, $741,100
s. Loan collections, $74,400
t. Proceeds from sale of investments, $34,700, including $3,800 loss
u. Payment of long-term note payable by issuing preferred shares, $107,300
v. Amortization expense, $23,900
w. Cash sales, $146,000
x. Proceeds from issuance of common shares, $50,000
y. Payment of cash dividends, $50,500
z. Cash balance: July 31, 2008—$23,800; July 31, 2009—$31,400

Preparing the cash flow statement—direct method
(Obj. 2, 4)

❙ Required

1. Prepare Rocco's Gourmet Foods Inc.'s cash flow statement for the year ended July 31, 2009. Use the *direct* method for cash flows from operating activities. Follow the format of Exhibit 12-13, but do *not* show amounts in thousands. Include an accompanying schedule of noncash investing and financing activities.
2. Evaluate 2009 in terms of cash flow. Give your reasons.

P12-66B Use the Cruise Canada Motorhomes Inc. (CCM) data from Problem 12-61B.

❙ Required

1. Prepare CCM's income statement for the year ended December 31, 2009. Use the single-step format, with all the revenues listed together and all expenses listed together.
2. Prepare CCM's balance sheet at December 31, 2009.
3. Prepare CCM's cash flow statement for the year ended December 31, 2009. Format cash flows from operating activities by using the *direct* method.

Preparing an income statement, balance sheet, and cash flow statement—direct method
(Obj. 2, 4)

Preparing the cash flow statement—direct method
(Obj. 2, 4)

P12-67B Use the Riverbend Pools Inc. data from Problem 12-64B.

❚ Required

1. Prepare the 2009 cash flow statement by using the *direct* method.

2. How will what you learned in this problem help you evaluate an investment? (Challenge) Compare the cash from operations information with the Problem 12-64B solution.

Preparing the cash flow statement—direct and indirect methods
(Obj. 3, 4)

P12-68B To prepare the cash flow statement, accountants for Powers Art Gallery Inc. have summarized 2009 activity in two accounts as follows:

Cash

Beginning balance	87,100	Payments of operating expenses	46,100
Issuance of common shares	60,800	Payment of long-term note payable	78,900
Receipts of dividends	1,900	Repurchase of common shares	10,400
Collection of loan	18,500	Payment of income tax	8,000
Sale of long-term investments	9,900	Payments on accounts payable	101,600
Receipts of interest	12,200	Payments of dividends	1,800
Collections from customers	308,100	Payments of salaries and wages	67,500
		Payments of interest	21,800
		Purchase of equipment	79,900
Ending balance	82,500		

Common Shares

Beginning balance	103,500
Issuance for cash	60,800
Issuance to acquire land	62,100
Issuance to retire long-term note payable	21,100
Ending balance	247,500

❚ Required

1. Prepare Powers' cash flow statement for the year ended December 31, 2009, using the *direct* method to report operating activities. Also prepare the accompanying schedule of noncash investing and financing activities. Powers' 2009 income statement and selected balance sheet data follow.

2. Prepare a supplementary schedule showing cash flows from operating activities by the *indirect* method.

Powers Art Gallery Inc.
Income Statement
For the Year Ended December 31, 2009

Revenues and gains:		
Sales revenue		$291,800
Interest revenue		12,200
Dividend revenue		1,900
Gain on sale of investments		700
Total revenues and gains		306,600
Expenses:		
Cost of goods sold	$103,600	
Salary and wage expense	66,800	
Amortization expense	20,900	
Other operating expense	44,700	
Interest expense	24,100	
Income tax expense	2,600	
Total expenses		262,700
Net income		$ 43,900

Power Art Gallery Inc.
Selected Balance Sheet Data

	2009 Increase (Decrease)
Current assets:	
Cash and cash equivalents	$ (4,600)
Accounts receivable	(16,300)
Inventories	5,700
Prepaid expenses	(1,900)
Loan receivable	(18,500)
Long-term investments	(9,200)
Equipment, net	59,000
Land	62,100
Current liabilities:	
Accounts payable	$ 7,700
Interest payable	2,300
Salary payable	(700)
Other accrued liabilities	(3,300)
Income tax payable	(5,400)
Long-term note payable	(100,000)
Common shares	133,600
Retained earnings	42,100

P12-69B Arts de France Ltée's comparative balance sheet at September 30, 2009, included the following balances:

Preparing the cash flow statement—indirect and direct method
(Obj. 3, 4)

Arts de France Ltée
Balance Sheet
September 30, 2009 and 2008

	2009	2008	Increase (Decrease)
Current assets:			
Cash	$ 21,700	$ 17,600	$ 4,100
Accounts receivable	46,000	46,800	(800)
Inventories	121,700	116,900	4,800
Prepaid expenses	8,600	9,300	(700)
Long-term investments	51,100	13,800	37,300
Equipment, net	131,900	92,100	39,800
Land	47,100	74,300	(27,200)
	$428,100	$370,800	$ 57,300
Current liabilities:			
Notes payable, short-term	$ 22,000	$ 0	$ 22,000
Accounts payable	88,100	98,100	(10,000)
Accrued liabilities	17,900	29,100	(11,200)
Salary payable	1,500	1,100	400
Long-term note payable	123,000	121,400	1,600
Common shares	113,900	62,000	51,900
Retained earnings	61,700	59,100	2,600
	$428,100	$370,800	$ 57,300

Transaction data for the year ended September 30, 2009:

a. Net income, $66,900
b. Amortization expense on equipment, $8,500
c. Purchased long-term investments, $37,300
d. Sold land for $38,100, including $10,900 gain
e. Acquired equipment by issuing long-term note payable, $26,300
f. Paid long-term note payable, $24,700
g. Received cash of $51,900 for issuance of common shares
h. Paid cash dividends, $64,300
i. Acquired equipment by issuing short-term note payable, $22,000

I Required

1. Prepare Arts de France's cash flow statement for the year ended September 30, 2009, using the *indirect* method to report operating activities. Also prepare the accompanying schedule of noncash investing and financing activities. All current accounts except short-term notes payable result from operating transactions.

2. Prepare a supplementary schedule showing cash flows from operations by using the *direct* method. The accounting records provide the following: collections from customers, $343,100; interest received, $8,600; payments to suppliers, $216,400; payments to employees, $63,000; payment of income tax, $21,200; payment of interest, $10,700.

APPLY YOUR KNOWLEDGE

DECISION CASES

Preparing and using the cash flow statement to evaluate operations
(Obj. 3)

Case 1. The 2009 income statement and the 2009 comparative balance sheet of T-Bar-M Camp Inc. have just been distributed at a meeting of the camp's board of directors. The directors raise a fundamental question: Why is the cash balance so low? This question is especially troublesome since 2009 showed record profits. As the controller of the company, you must answer the question.

T-Bar-M Camp Inc.
Income Statement
For the Year Ended December 31, 2009

	(In thousands)
Revenues:	
Sales revenue	$436
Expenses:	
Cost of goods sold	$221
Salary expense	48
Amortization expense	57
Interest expense	13
Total expenses	339
Net income	$ 97

T-Bar-M Camp Inc. **Comparative Balance Statement** **December 31, 2009 and 2008**		
(In thousands)	2009	2008
Assets		
Cash..	$ 17	$ 63
Accounts receivable, net..	72	61
Inventories...	194	181
Long-term investments	31	0
Property, plant, and equipment	369	259
Accumulated amortization	(244)	(198)
Patents	177	188
Totals..	$616	$554
Liabilities and Shareholders' Equity		
Accounts payable	$ 63	$ 56
Accrued liabilities...	12	17
Notes payable, long-term	179	264
Common shares	149	61
Retained earnings...	213	156
Totals..	$616	$554

❙ Required

1. Prepare a cash flow statement for 2009 in the format that best shows the relationship between net income and operating cash flow. The company sold no plant and equipment or long-term investments and issued no notes payable during 2009. There were *no* non-cash investing and financing transactions during the year. Show all amounts in thousands.

2. Answer the board members' question: Why is the cash balance so low? Point out the two largest cash payments during 2009.

3. Considering net income and the company's cash flows during 2009, was it a good year or a bad year? Give your reasons. Explain the format you chose for the cash flow statement.

Case 2. Applied Technology Inc. and Four-Star Catering Ltd. are asking you to recommend their shares to your clients. Because Applied and Four-Star earn about the same net income and have similar financial positions, your decision depends on their statements of cash flow summarized as follows:

Using cash-flow data to evaluate an investment
(Obj. 1, 2)

	Applied Technology Inc.		**Four-Star Catering Ltd.**	
Net cash provided by operating activities:......................		$ 30,000		$ 70,000
Cash provided by (used for) investing activities:				
Purchase of property, plant, and equipment...............	$(20,000)		$(100,000)	
Sale of property, plant, and equipment......................	40,000	20,000	10,000	(90,000)
Cash provided by (used for) financing activities:				
Issuance of common shares		—		30,000
Paying off long-term debt		(40,000)		—
Net increase in cash...		$ 10,000		$ 10,000

Based on their cash flows, which company looks better? Give your reasons.

ETHICAL ISSUE

Columbia Industries is having a bad year. Net income is only $37,000. Also, two important overseas customers are falling behind in their payments to Columbia, and Columbia's accounts receivable are ballooning. The company desperately needs a loan. The Columbia board of directors is considering ways to put the best face on the company's financial statements. Columbia's bank closely examines cash flow from operations. Daniel Peavey, Columbia's controller, suggests reclassifying the receivables from the slow-paying clients as long-term. He explains to the board that removing the $80,000 rise in accounts receivable from current assets will increase net cash provided by operations. This approach may help Columbia get the loan.

❘ *Required*

1. Using only the amounts given, compute net cash provided by operations, both without and with the reclassification of the receivables. Which reporting makes Columbia look better?

2. Under what condition would the reclassification of the receivables be ethical? Under what condition would it be unethical?

FOCUS ON FINANCIALS

Sun-Rype Products Ltd.

Using the cash flow statement
(Obj. 1, 2, 3, 4)

Use Sun-Rype Products Ltd.'s cash flow statement along with the company's other financial statements, all in Appendix A at the end of the book, to answer the following questions.

❘ *Required*

1. By which method does Sun-Rype report cash flows from *operating* activities? How can you tell?

2. Suppose Sun-Rype reported net cash flows from operating activities by using the direct method. Compute these amounts for the year ended December 31, 2007 (ignore the cash flow statement, and use only Sun-Rype's income statement and balance sheet).

   a. Collections from customers

   b. Payments to suppliers. Sun-Rype suppliers provide cost of sales, selling, and general and administrative expenses.

3. Prepare a T-account for Property, Plant, and Equipment, Net, and show all activity in this account for 2007. Use the amortization amount in the cash flow statement, and assume that Sun-Rype (a) disposed of property, plant, and equipment with book value of $1,252 thousand and (b) acquired $7,358 thousand of property, plant, and equipment as reported in the investing activity section of the cash flow statement.

4. Evaluate 2007 in terms of net income, total assets, shareholders' equity, cash flows from operating activities, and overall results. Be specific.

FOCUS ON ANALYSIS

Mullen Group Income Fund

Analyzing cash flows
(Obj. 1, 2, 3, 4)

Refer to the Mullen Group Income Fund financial statements in Appendix B at the end of this book. Focus on 2006.

1. What is Mullen Group's main source of cash? Is this good news or bad news to Mullen Group's managers, unitholders, and creditors? What is Mullen Group's main use of cash? Is this good news or bad news? Explain all answers in detail.

2. Explain in detail the three main reasons why net cash provided by operations differs from net income. Use Notes 5 and 6 to complete your answer.

3. Did Mullen Group buy or sell more property, plant, and equipment during 2007? How can you tell?

4. Identify the sale price, the book value, and the gain or loss from selling fixed assets during 2006. *Fixed assets* is another name for property, plant, and equipment.

5. How much cash in total did Mullen Group return to unitholders during 2007?

GROUP PROJECTS

Project 1. Each member of the group should obtain the annual report of a different company. Select companies in different industries. Evaluate each company's trend of cash flows for the most recent two years. In your evaluation of the companies' cash flows, you may use any other information that is publicly available—for example, the other financial statements (income statement, balance sheet, statement of shareholders' equity, and the related notes) and news stories from magazines and newspapers. Rank the companies' cash flows from best to worst and write a two-page report on your findings.

Project 2. Select a company and obtain its annual report, including all the financial statements. Focus on the cash flow statement and, in particular, the cash flows from operating activities. Specify whether the company uses the direct method or the indirect method to report operating cash flows. As necessary, use the other financial statements (income statement, balance sheet, and statement of shareholders' equity) and the notes to prepare the company's cash flows from operating activities by using the *other* method.

QUICK CHECK ANSWERS

1. *d*
2. *c*
3. *b*
4. *b* ($50,000 − $12,000 + $60,000 = $98,000)
5. *c*
6. *b*
7. *a* ($47,000 + $8,000 − $4,000 + $12,000 + $7,000 + $2,000 = $72,000)
8. *a* ($6,000 − $24,000 + $36,000 = $18,000)
9. *c* (−$2,000 + $3,000 − $9,000 = −$8,000)
10. *b* ($12,000 + $36,000 = $48,000)
11. *a* [$650,000 + ($45,000 − $31,000) = $664,000]
12. *c* ($690,000 − $390,000 − $175,000 = $125,000)
13. *d* ($390,000 − $15,000 + $9,000 = $384,000)

13 Financial Statement Analysis

Learning Objectives

1. **Perform** a horizontal analysis of comparative financial statements

2. **Perform** a vertical analysis of financial statements

3. **Prepare** common-size financial statements

4. **Use** the cash flow statement in decision making

5. **Compute** the standard financial ratios

6. **Use** ratios in decision making

7. **Measure** the economic value added by operations

SPOTLIGHT

This book began with the financial statements of Sun-Rype Products Ltd., the company that produces a wide range of popular fruit juices and fruit snacks. Throughout this book we have shown how to account for the operations, financial position, and cash flows of a variety of companies, such as Mullen Group Income Fund, Loblaw Companies Limited, EnCana Corporation, ATCO Ltd., and Bombardier Inc. Only one aspect of the course remains: the overall analysis of financial statements.

We have chosen Metro Inc., a leading Canadian grocery store chain, to illustrate different kinds of financial statement analysis. We begin with an analysis of Metro Inc.'s statement of earnings. In 2008, Metro had revenues of $10,725 million, and the company had net earnings of $293 million. These numbers look pretty good, but how good are they? We need to compare 2008 with prior years to see if Metro made progress during 2008. It could be that 2007 was a better year. We also need to compare Metro to its competitors.

Metro Inc.
▼ Consolidated Statements of Earnings (Adapted)
For the Years Ended September 27, 2008 and September 29, 2007

In millions of dollars	2008	2007
Sales	$ 10,725	$ 10,645
Cost of sales and operating expenses	(10,103)	(10,014)
Share of earnings in a public company subject to significant influence	17	25
Integration and rationalization costs	—	(30)
Earnings before interest, taxes, and amortization	639	626
Amortization	(176)	(166)
Operating income	463	460
Financial costs, net	(58)	(62)
Earnings before income taxes	405	398
Income taxes	(114)	(125)
Earnings before minority interest	291	273
Minority interest	2	4
Net earnings	$ 293	$ 277

This chapter covers the basic tools of financial analysis. The first part of the chapter shows how to evaluate Metro from year to year and also how to compare Metro to different companies. For this comparison we use two of Canada's leading grocery chains, Metro and Sobeys. The second part of the chapter discusses the most widely used financial ratios. You have seen many of these ratios in earlier chapters: the current ratio, days' sales in receivables, inventory turnover, return on assets, and return on equity.

By studying all these ratios together, you will do the following:

- Learn the basic tools of financial analysis.
- Enhance your business education.

Regardless of your chosen field—marketing, management, finance, entrepreneurship, or accounting—you will find these analytical tools useful as you move through your career.

DECISION How Does an Investor Evaluate a Company?

Investors and creditors cannot evaluate a company by examining only one year's data. This is why most financial statements cover at least two periods, like the Metro Inc. statement of earnings that begins this chapter. In fact, most financial analysis covers trends of three to five years. The goal of financial analysis is to predict the future.

The graphs in Exhibit 13-1 show Metro's three-year trend of sales and operating income. On one hand, Metro's sales declined in 2007 but increased in 2008, although not to the 2006 level. On the other hand, operating income increased in 2007 and 2008. These are good signs. How would you predict Metro's sales and operating income for 2009 and beyond? Based on the recent past, you would probably extend the sales line and the operating income line upward.

Let's examine some of the tools of financial analysis: we begin with horizontal analysis.

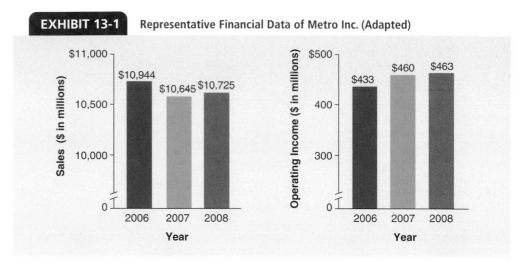

EXHIBIT 13-1 Representative Financial Data of Metro Inc. (Adapted)

Horizontal Analysis

Objective

① **Perform** a horizontal analysis of comparative financial statements

Many decisions hinge on the trend of the numbers in sales expenses, net income, and so on. Has the sales figure risen from last year? If so, by how much? Suppose that sales have increased by $200,000. Considered alone this fact is not very informative, but the *percentage change* in sales over time helps a lot. It is better to know that sales have increased by 20% than to know only that the increase is $200,000.

The study of percentage changes from year to year is called **horizontal analysis**. Computing a percentage change requires two steps:

1. Compute the dollar amount of the change from one period (the base period) to the next.

2. Divide the dollar amount of change by the base-period amount.

Illustration: Metro Inc.

Horizontal analysis is illustrated for Metro Inc. as follows (dollars in millions):

	2008	2007	Increase (Decrease) Amount	Percentage
Sales	$10,725	$10,645	$80	0.8%

Metro's sales increased by 0.8% during 2008, computed as follows:

STEP 1 Compute the dollar amount of change in sales from 2007 to 2008:

$$2008 - 2007 = \text{Increase}$$
$$\$10,725 - \$10,645 = \$80$$

STEP 2 Divide the dollar amount of change by the base-period amount. This computes the percentage change for the period:

$$\text{Percentage change} = \frac{\text{Dollar amount of change}}{\text{Base-year amount}}$$
$$= \frac{\$80}{\$10,645} = 0.8\%$$

Exhibits 13-2 and 13-3 are detailed for Metro Inc. The income statements show that sales increased by 0.8% during 2008.

STOP & THINK

Assume you are a financial analyst for an investment bank and have been charged with gathering information about Metro Inc. for a client. You have performed comparative analysis similar to Exhibit 13-2 of Metro's statements of earnings for 2008 and 2007. What do you think is the most important information for your analysis in Exhibit 13-2?

Answer:

Sales have increased by 0.8%, which may not seem a large increase but cost of sales and operating expenses have increased by only 0.9%. This information suggests that Metro is doing a good job of controlling expenses and that it is a well-run company.

Trend Percentages

Trend percentages are a form of horizontal analysis. Trends indicate the direction a business is taking. How have sales changed over a five-year period? What trend does income from continuing operations show? These questions can be answered by trend percentages over a representative period, such as the most recent five years.

Trend percentages are computed by selecting a base year whose amounts are set equal to 100%. The amount for each following year is expressed as a percentage of the base amount. To compute a trend percentage, divide an item for a later year by the base-year amount.

$$\text{Trend } \% = \frac{\text{Any year \$}}{\text{Base-year \$}}$$

EXHIBIT 13-2 Comparative Income Statement—Horizontal Analysis

Metro Inc.
Consolidated Statement of Earnings (Adapted)
For the Years Ended September 27, 2008 and September 29, 2007

(In millions of dollars)	2008	2007	Increase (Decrease) Amount	Increase (Decrease) Percentage
Sales	$10,725	$10,645	$80	0.8%
Cost of sales and operating expenses	(10,103)	(10,014)	(89)	(0.9)
Share of earnings in a public company subject to significant influence	17	25	(8)	(32.0)
Integration and rationalization costs	—	(30)	30	100.0
Earnings before interest, taxes, and amortization	639	626	13	2.1
Amortization	(176)	(166)	(10)	(6.0)
Operating income	463	460	3	0.7
Financial costs, net	(58)	(62)	4	6.5
Earnings before income taxes	405	398	7	1.8
Income taxes	(114)	(125)	11	8.8
Earnings before minority interest	291	273	18	6.6
Minority interest	2	4	(2)	(50.0)
Net earnings	$ 293	$ 277	$16	5.8

Note: Any increase from zero to a positive number is treated as an increase of 100%; any decrease to zero is treated as a decrease of 100%. Any decrease in a negative number is treated as an increase; any increase in a negative number is treated as a decrease.

EXHIBIT 13-3 Comparative Balance Sheet—Horizontal Analysis

Metro Inc.
Consolidated Balance Sheet (Adapted)
September 27, 2008, and September 29, 2007

(In millions of dollars)	2008	2007	Increase (Decrease) Amount	Percentage
ASSETS				
Current assets				
Cash and cash equivalents	$ 152	$ 100	$ 52	52.0%
Accounts receivable	310	328	(18)	(5.5)
Inventories	616	588	28	4.8
Prepaid expenses	7	12	(5)	(41.7)
Income taxes receivable	25	7	18	257.1
Future income taxes	38	29	9	31.0
	1,148	1,064	84	7.9
Investments and other assets	169	151	18	11.9
Fixed assets	1,232	1,203	29	2.4
Intangible assets	328	332	(4)	(1.2)
Goodwill	1,490	1,490	—	(0.0)
Future income taxes	3	4	(1)	(0.25)
Accrued benefit assets	41	33	8	24.2
	$4,411	$4,277	$134	3.1
LIABILITIES AND SHAREHOLDERS' EQUITY				
Current liabilities				
Bank loans	$ 1	$ —	$ 1	100.0%
Accounts payable	1,063	1,044	19	1.8
Income taxes payable	51	27	24	88.9
Future income taxes	6	—	6	100.0
Current portion of long-term debt	6	5	1	20.0
	1,127	1,076	51	4.7
Long-term debt	1,005	1,029	(24)	(2.3)
Accrued benefit obligations	51	55	(4)	(7.3)
Future income taxes	133	146	(13)	(8.9)
Other long-term liabilities	34	34	—	0.0
Minority interest	—	5	(5)	(100.0)
	2,350	2,345	5	0.2
Shareholders' equity				
Share capital	698	715	(17)	(2.4)
Contributed surplus	5	2	3	150.0
Retained earnings	1,359	1,214	145	11.9
Accumulated other comprehensive income	(1)	1	(2)	(200.0)
	2,061	1,932	129	6.7
	$4,411	$4,277	$134	3.1

IFRS

Metro Inc. showed operating income from continuing operations for the past five years as follows:

(In millions)	2008	2007	2006	2005	2004
Operating income	$463	$460	$433	$279	$248

We would like trend percentages for the four-year period 2005 to 2008. The base year is 2004. Trend percentages are computed by dividing each year's amount by the 2004 amount. The resulting trend percentages follow (2004 = 100%):

	2008	2007	2006	2005	2004
Operating income	187%	185%	175%	112%	100%

Operating income rose sharply in 2006 and rose steadily in 2007 and 2008.

You can perform a trend analysis on any item you consider important. Trend analysis is widely used for predicting the future.

Horizontal analysis highlights changes in an item over time. However, no single technique gives a complete picture of a business.

Vertical Analysis

Vertical analysis shows the relationship of a financial statement item to its base, which is the 100% figure. All items on the financial statement are reported as a percentage of that base. For the income statement, total revenue is usually the base. Suppose under normal conditions a company's net income is 8% of revenue. A drop to 6% may cause the company's share price to fall.

Objective

② **Perform** a vertical analysis of financial statements

Illustration: Metro Inc.

Exhibit 13-4 shows the vertical analysis of Metro's income statement as a percentage of sales. In this case,

$$\text{Vertical analysis \%} = \frac{\text{Each income statement item}}{\text{Sales}}$$

For Metro in 2008, the vertical-analysis percentage for operating income increased to 4.4% ($463 million/$10,725 million = 0.044) and as a result net income increased slightly to 2.7% in 2008 compared to 2.6% in 2007.

Exhibit 13-5 shows the vertical analysis of Metro's balance sheet. The base amount (100%) is total assets. The vertical analysis of Metro's balance sheet reveals several things about the company's financial position:

- Current assets make up a slightly larger percentage of total assets (26.0% in 2008 compared to 24.9% in 2007). Cash and cash equivalents increased from 2.3% in 2007 to 3.4% in 2008 while accounts receivable decreased from 7.7% in 2007 to 7.0% in 2008, which is a positive sign.

- Fixed assets (property, plant, and equipment) remain the second most significant asset. Metro is continuing to expand its capacity.

- Long-term debt decreased from 24.1% in 2007 to 22.8% in 2008.

DECISION **How Do We Compare One Company to Another?**

The percentages in Exhibits 13-4 and 13-5 can be presented as a separate statement that reports only percentages (no dollar amounts). Such a statement is called a **common-size statement**.

On a common-size income statement, each item is expressed as a percentage of the net sales amount. Net sales is the *common size* to which we relate the other amounts. In the balance sheet, the common size is total assets. A common-size statement eases the comparison of different companies because their amounts are stated in percentages.

Objective

③ **Prepare** common-size financial statements

| EXHIBIT 13-4 | Comparative Income Statement—Vertical Analysis Metro Inc. |

Metro Inc.
Consolidated Statement of Earnings (Adapted)
For the Years Ended September 27, 2008 and September 30, 2007

(In millions of dollars)	2008 Amount	2008 Percentage of Sales*	2007 Amount	2007 Percentage of Sales*
Sales	$10,725	100.0%	$10,645	100.0%
Cost of sales and operating expenses	(10,103)	(94.2)	(10,014)	(94.0)
Share of earnings in a public company subject to significant influence	17	0.2	25	0.2
Integration and rationalization costs	—	—	(30)	(0.3)
Earnings before interest, taxes, and amortization	639	6.0	626	5.9
Amortization	(176)	(1.6)	(166)	(1.6)
Operating income	463	4.4	460	4.3
Financial costs, net	(58)	(0.6)	(62)	(0.6)
Earnings before income taxes	405	3.8	398	3.7
Income taxes	(114)	(1.1)	(125)	(1.1)
Earnings before minority interest	291	2.7	273	2.6
Minority interest	2	0.0	4	0.0
Net earnings	$ 293	2.7%	$277	2.6%

*Some percentages may not be exact because of rounding.

STOP & THINK

Assume you are a financial analyst for an investment bank and have been charged with gathering information about K-M Inc. for a client. You have been provided with the following 2009 income statement by K-M and have decided to calculate the common-size percentages. Show your calculations.

Net sales	$150,000
Cost of goods sold	60,000
Gross margin	90,000
Operating expense	40,000
Operating income	50,000
Income tax expense	15,000
Net income	$ 35,000

Answer:

Net sales	100%	(= $150,000 ÷ $150,000)
Cost of goods sold	40	(= $60,000 ÷ $150,000)
Gross margin	60	(= $90,000 ÷ $150,000)
Operating expense	27	(= $40,000 ÷ $150,000)
Operating income	33	(= $50,000 ÷ $150,000)
Income tax expense	10	(= $15,000 ÷ $150,000)
Net income	23%	(= $35,000 ÷ $150,000)

Benchmarking

Benchmarking is the comparison of a company to a standard set by others. Suppose you are a financial analyst for ScotiaMcLeod. You are considering an investment in the shares of a grocery chain, and you are choosing between Metro Inc. and Sobeys Inc. A direct comparison of their financial statements in dollar amounts is not meaningful because the amounts are so different; however, you can convert the two companies' income statements to common size and compare the percentages. The comparison is meaningful, as we shall see.

EXHIBIT 13-5	Comparative Balance Sheet—Vertical Analysis

Metro Inc.
Consolidated Balance Sheet (Adapted)
September 27, 2008 and September 29, 2007

	2008		2007	
(In millions of dollars)	Amount	Percentage of Total*	Amount	Percentage of Total*
ASSETS				
Current assets				
Cash and cash equivalents	$ 152	3.4%	$ 100	2.3%
Accounts receivable	310	7.0	328	7.7
Inventories	616	14.0	588	13.7
Prepaid expenses	7	0.1	12	0.3
Income taxes receivable	25	0.6	7	0.2
Future income taxes	38	0.9	29	0.7
	1,148	26.0	1,064	24.9
Investments and other assets	169	3.8	151	3.5
Fixed assets	1,232	27.9	1,203	28.1
Intangible assets	328	7.4	332	7.8
Goodwill	1,490	33.8	1,490	34.8
Future income taxes	3	0.1	4	0.1
Accrued benefit assets...	41	1.0	33	0.8
	$4,411	100.0%	$4,277	100.0%
LIABILITIES AND SHAREHOLDERS' EQUITY				
Current liabilities				
Bank loans...	$ 1	—%	$ —	—%
Accounts payable..	1,063	24.1	1,044	24.4
Income taxes payable...	51	1.2	27	0.6
Future income taxes	6	0.1	—	—
Current portion of long-term debt	6	0.1	5	0.1
	1,127	25.5	1,076	25.1
Long-term debt..	1,005	22.8	1,029	24.1
Accrued benefit obligations	51	1.2	55	1.3
Future income taxes	133	3.0	146	3.4
Other long-term liabilities....................................	34	0.8	34	0.8
Minority interest...	—	—	5	0.1
	2,350	53.3	2,345	54.8
Shareholders' equity				
Share capital	698	15.8	715	16.7
Contributed surplus	5	0.1	2	—
Retained earnings...	1,359	30.8	1,214	28.5
Accumulated other comprehensive income...........	(1)	(—)	1	—
	2,061	46.7	1,932	45.2
	$4,411	100.0%	$4,277	100.0%

*Some percentages may not be exact because of rounding.

Benchmarking Against a Key Competitor

Exhibit 13-6 presents the common-size income statements of Metro Inc. and Sobeys Inc. Sobeys serves as an excellent benchmark because both are large, successful Canadian grocery chains. Although Sobeys is about a third bigger than Metro in terms of sales volume, the two companies are comparable in terms of operations.

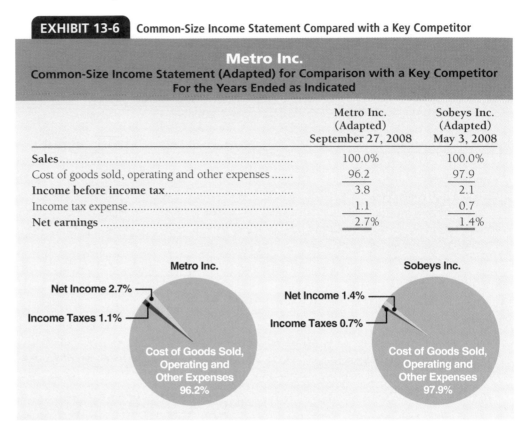

EXHIBIT 13-6 Common-Size Income Statement Compared with a Key Competitor

Metro Inc.
Common-Size Income Statement (Adapted) for Comparison with a Key Competitor
For the Years Ended as Indicated

	Metro Inc. (Adapted) September 27, 2008	Sobeys Inc. (Adapted) May 3, 2008
Sales	100.0%	100.0%
Cost of goods sold, operating and other expenses	96.2	97.9
Income before income tax	3.8	2.1
Income tax expense	1.1	0.7
Net earnings	2.7%	1.4%

Metro Inc.

Net Income 2.7%
Income Taxes 1.1%
Cost of Goods Sold, Operating and Other Expenses 96.2%

Sobeys Inc.

Net Income 1.4%
Income Taxes 0.7%
Cost of Goods Sold, Operating and Other Expenses 97.9%

DECISION Using the Cash Flow Statement

Objective

4 **Use** the cash flow statement in decision making

The chapter has focused on the income statement and balance sheet. To continue our discussion of its role in decision making, let's use Exhibit 13-7, the cash flow statement of SK Corporation.

Analysts find the cash flow statement more helpful for spotting weakness than for gauging success. Why? Because a *shortage* of cash can throw a company into bankruptcy, but lots of cash doesn't ensure success. The cash flow statement in Exhibit 13-7 reveals the following:

- SK Corporation's operations provide less cash than net income. Ordinarily, cash provided by operations exceeds net income because of the add-back of amortization. The increases in current assets and current liabilities should cancel out over time. For SK Corporation, current assets increased far more than current liabilities during the year. This may be harmless. But it may signal difficulty in collecting receivables or selling inventory. Either event may cause trouble.

- The sale of property, plant, and equipment is SK's major source of cash. This is okay if this is a one-time situation. SK may be shifting from one line of business to another, and it may be selling off old assets. But, if the sale of property, plant, and equipment is the major source of cash for several periods, SK will face a cash shortage. A company cannot continue to sell off its property, plant, and equipment forever. Soon, it will go out of business.

- The only strength shown by the cash flow statement is that SK paid off more long-term debt than it did new borrowing. This will improve the debt ratio and SK's credit standing.

Here are some cash flow signs of a healthy company:

- Operations are a major *source* of cash (not a *use* of cash).
- Investing activities include more purchases than sales of capital assets.
- Financing activities are not dominated by borrowing.

EXHIBIT 13-7 Cash Flow Statement

SK Corporation
Cash Flow Statement
For the Year Ended June 30, 2009

		Millions
Operating activities:		
Net income		$ 35,000
Adjustments for noncash items:		
Amortization	$ 14,000	
Net increase in current assets other than cash	(24,000)	
Net increase in current liabilities	8,000	(2,000)
Net cash provided by operating activities		33,000
Investing activities:		
Sale of property, plant, and equipment	91,000	
Net cash provided by investing activities		91,000
Financing activities:		
Borrowing	22,000	
Payment of long-term debt	(90,000)	
Repurchase of shares	(9,000)	
Payment of dividends	(23,000)	
Net cash used for financing activities		(100,000)
Increase (decrease) in cash		$ 24,000

MID-CHAPTER SUMMARY PROBLEM

MyAccountingLab

You, an employee at a bank lending office, are deciding whether to grant Jamate Corporation, which makes metal detectors, a large loan. You decide to perform a horizontal analysis and a vertical analysis of the comparative income statement of Jamate Corporation. State whether 2009 was a good year or a bad year and give your reasons.

Jamate Corporation
Comparative Income Statement
For the Years Ended December 31, 2009 and 2008

	2009	2008
Total revenues	$275,000	$225,000
Expenses:		
Cost of products sold	194,000	165,000
Engineering, selling, and administrative expenses	54,000	48,000
Interest expense	5,000	5,000
Income tax expense	9,000	3,000
Other expense (income)	1,000	(1,000)
Total expenses	263,000	220,000
Net earnings	$ 12,000	$ 5,000

Name: Jamate Corporation
Fiscal Period: Years ended December 31, 2009 and 2008

Answer

The horizontal analysis shows that total revenues increased 22.2%. This was greater than the 19.5% increase in total expenses, resulting in a 140% increase in net earnings.

Horizontal analysis compares 2009 with 2008 to determine the changes in each income statement item in dollar amounts and percent ($ and %). Large or unusual changes in $ or % should be investigated.

The net earnings increase of 140% occurred because the dollar amounts are quite small. Income tax expense increased 200%; this would be investigated.

Jamate Corporation
Horizontal Analysis of Comparative Income Statement
For the Years Ended December 31, 2009 and 2008

			Increase (Decrease)	
	2009	2008	Amount	Percent
Total revenues	$275,000	$225,000	$50,000	22.2%
Expenses:				
Cost of products sold..............................	194,000	165,000	29,000	17.6
Engineering, selling, and administrative expenses......................	54,000	48,000	6,000	12.5
Interest expense.......................	5,000	5,000	—	—
Income tax expense	9,000	3,000	6,000	200.0
Other expense (income)	1,000	(1,000)	2,000	—*
Total expenses	263,000	220,000	43,000	19.5
Net earnings..	$ 12,000	$ 5,000	$ 7,000	140.0%

*Percentage changes are typically not computed for shifts from a negative to a positive amount, and vice versa.

The vertical analysis shows decreases in the percentages of net sales consumed by the cost of products sold (from 73.3% to 70.5%) and by the engineering, selling, and administrative expenses (from 21.3% to 19.6%). Because these two items are Jamate's largest dollar expenses, their percentage decreases are quite important. The relative reduction in expenses raised 2009's net earnings to 4.4% of sales, compared with 2.2% the preceding year. The overall analysis indicates that 2009 was significantly better than 2008.

Vertical analysis expresses net earnings and expenses as a percentage of total revenues. The percentages for 2009 are compared with those of 2008. Any large or unexpected differences would be reviewed.

Jamate Corporation
Vertical Analysis of Comparative Income Statement
For the Years Ended December 31, 2009 and 2008

	2009		2008	
	Amount	Percent	Amount	Percent
Total revenues	$275,000	100.0%	$225,000	100.0%
Expenses:				
Cost of products sold..............................	194,000	70.5	165,000	73.3
Engineering, selling, and administrative expenses......................	54,000	19.6	48,000	21.3
Interest expense.......................	5,000	1.8	5,000	2.2
Income tax expense	9,000	3.3	3,000	1.4*
Other expense (income)	1,000	0.4	(1,000)	(0.4)
Total expenses	263,000	95.6	220,000	97.8
Net earnings..	$ 12,000	4.4%	$ 5,000	2.2%

*Number rounded up.

Using Ratios to Make Business Decisions

Ratios are a major tool of financial analysis. A ratio expresses the relationship of one number to another. Suppose your balance sheet shows current assets of $100,000 and current liabilities of $50,000, the ratio of current assets to current liabilities is $100,000 to $50,000. We can express this ratio as 2 to 1, or 2:1. The current ratio is 2.0.

Objective

(5) **Compute** the standard financial ratios

Many companies include ratios in a special section of their annual reports. RubberMate Corporation displays ratio data in the summary section of its annual report. Exhibit 13-8 shows data from that summary section. Investment services—such as Globe Interactive, with its online services, and the Financial Post—provide to subscribers data on public companies and industries in Canada. Credit agencies such as Dun & Bradstreet Canada (www.dnb.ca) offer industry averages as part of their financial services.

The ratios we discuss in this chapter may be classified as follows:

1. Ability to pay current liabilities
2. Ability to sell inventory and collect receivables
3. Ability to pay long-term debt
4. Profitability
5. Analysis of shares as an investment

How much can a computer help in analyzing financial statements for investment purposes? Time yourself as you perform one of the financial-ratio problems in this chapter. Multiply your efforts by 10 as though you were comparing 10 companies. Now rank these 10 companies on the basis of four or five ratios.

Online financial databases, such as SEDAR (www.sedar.com), offer complete information on all publicly filed data and reports by all Canadian public companies for the last several years. Assume that you want to compare companies' recent earnings histories. Use the database to compare several companies by doing vertical or horizontal analysis of their financial data or by computing the ratios discussed below for the companies in which you are interested. You might also review their press releases and other public statements. The investment services mentioned above are another source of information.

⚠ USER ALERT

Things May Not Always Be As They Seem

You will learn in the following pages that there are a number of ratios that managers and analysts, and other users of financial statements, use to assess the health and strength of a company. However, ratios can be and have been manipulated to present a picture of a business that is inaccurate and fraudulent.

The executives of WorldCom, one of the largest bankruptcies in history, manipulated both revenue and cost of sales in such a way that gross margin increased slightly every quarter to give the appearance of constant growth whereas, in fact, the gross margin was steadily declining. Such actions are a form of earnings management and are inappropriate. Earnings management is an important issue and one that you will cover in an advanced course.

Later in the chapter you will learn that it is important to consider all ratios over a period of years to get a more accurate picture of a company. Having said that, dishonest managers can and will, from time to time, present fraudulent information in an attempt to deceive users of that information.

EXHIBIT 13-8	Financial Summary of RubberMate Corporation (Dollar Amounts in Thousands Except Per-Share Amounts)		

Years Ended December 31	2009	2008	2007
Operating Results			
Net earnings	$ 218	$ 164	$ 163
Per common share	$1.32	$1.02	$1.02
Percent of sales	10.8%	9.1%	9.8%
Return on average shareholders' equity	20.0%	17.5%	19.7%
Financial Position			
Current assets	$570	$477	$419
Current liabilities	$359	$323	$345
Working capital	$211	$154	$ 74
Current ratio	1.59	1.48	1.21

Measuring Ability to Pay Current Liabilities

Working capital is defined as follows:

$$\text{Working capital} = \text{Current assets} - \text{Current liabilities}$$

Working capital measures the ability to meet short-term obligations with current assets. In general, the larger the working capital, the better the ability to pay debts. Recall that capital is total assets minus total liabilities. Working capital is like a "current" version of total capital. Consider two companies with equal working capital:

	Company A	Company B
Current assets	$100,000	$200,000
Current liabilities	50,000	150,000
Working capital	$ 50,000	$ 50,000

Both companies have working capital of $50,000, but Company A's working capital is as large as its current liabilities. Company B's working capital is only one-third as large as its current liabilities. Two decision-making tools based on working-capital data are the *current ratio* and the *acid-test ratio*.

Current Ratio. The most common ratio evaluating current assets and current liabilities is the *current ratio*, which is current assets divided by current liabilities. The current ratio measures the company's ability to pay current liabilities with current assets. Exhibit 13-9 gives the income statement and balance sheet of Meben Furniture Ltd.

The current ratios of Meben Furniture Ltd. at December 31, 2009 and 2008 follow, along with the average for the retail furniture industry:

		Meben's Current Ratio		Industry
	Formula	2009	2008	Average
Current ratio =	$\dfrac{\text{Current assets}}{\text{Current liabilities}}$	$\dfrac{\$262,000}{\$142,000} = 1.85$	$\dfrac{\$236,000}{\$126,000} = 1.87$	1.50

The current ratio was virtually unchanged during 2009. In general, a higher current ratio indicates a stronger financial position. The business has sufficient liquid assets to maintain its operations. Meben's current ratio of 1.85 compares favourably with the current ratios of some well-known companies:

EXHIBIT 13-9 Comparative Financial Statements

Meben Furniture Ltd.
Comparative Income Statement
For the Years Ended December 31, 2009 and 2008

	2009	2008
Net sales	$858,000	$803,000
Cost of goods sold	513,000	509,000
Gross margin	345,000	294,000
Operating expenses:		
Selling expenses	126,000	114,000
General expenses	118,000	123,000
Total operating expenses	244,000	237,000
Income from operations	101,000	57,000
Interest revenue	(4,000)	—
Interest expense	24,000	14,000
Income before income taxes	81,000	43,000
Income tax expense	33,000	17,000
Net income	$ 48,000	$ 26,000

Meben Furniture Ltd.
Comparative Balance Sheet
December 31, 2009 and 2008

	2009	2008
Assets		
Current assets:		
Cash	$ 29,000	$ 32,000
Accounts receivable, net	114,000	85,000
Inventories	113,000	111,000
Prepaid expenses	6,000	8,000
Total current assets	262,000	236,000
Long-term investments	18,000	9,000
Property, plant, and equipment, net	507,000	399,000
Total assets	$787,000	$644,000
Liabilities		
Current liabilities:		
Notes payable	$ 42,000	$ 27,000
Accounts payable	73,000	68,000
Accrued liabilities	27,000	31,000
Total current liabilities	142,000	126,000
Long-term debt	289,000	198,000
Total liabilities	431,000	324,000
Shareholders' Equity		
Common shares	186,000	186,000
Retained earnings	170,000	134,000
Total shareholders' equity	356,000	320,000
Total liabilities and shareholders' equity	$787,000	$644,000

Company	Current Ratio
Enbridge Inc. (Utility)	0.93
Research In Motion (Hi-tech company)	2.35
Loblaw Companies Limited (Grocery stores)	1.13

What is an acceptable current ratio? The answer depends on the industry. The norm for companies in most industries is around 1.50, as reported by the Risk Management Association. Meben's current ratio of 1.85 is better than average.

USER ALERT

The Limitations of Ratio Analysis

Business decisions are made in a world of uncertainty. As useful as ratios are, they aren't a cure-all. Consider a physician's use of a thermometer. A reading of 38.8° Celsius tells a doctor something is wrong with the patient, but doesn't indicate what the problem is or how to cure it.

In financial analysis, a sudden drop in the current ratio signals that something is wrong, but doesn't identify the problem. A user of financial information, such as a manager, an investor, a bank loan officer, or an analyst, must analyze the figures to learn what caused the ratio to fall. A drop in current assets may mean a cash shortage or that sales are slow. The user must evaluate all the ratios in the light of factors such as increased competition or a slowdown in the economy.

Legislation, international affairs, scandals, and other factors can turn profits into losses. To be useful, ratios should be analyzed over a period of years to consider all relevant factors. Any one year, or even any two years, may not represent the company's performance over the long term.

Acid-Test Ratio. The *acid-test* (or *quick*) *ratio* tells us whether the entity could pass the acid test of paying all its current liabilities if they came due immediately. The acid-test ratio uses a narrower base to measure liquidity than the current ratio does.

To compute the acid-test ratio, we add cash, short-term investments, and net current receivables (accounts and notes, net of allowances) and divide by current liabilities. Inventory and prepaid expenses are two current assets not included in the acid-test computations because they are less liquid. A business may not be able to convert inventory to cash immediately.

Meben Furniture Ltd.'s acid-test ratios for 2009 and 2008 follow:

	Formula	Meben's Acid-Test Ratio 2009	Meben's Acid-Test Ratio 2008	Industry Average
	Cash	$29,000	$32,000	
	+ Short-term investments	+ $0	+ $0	
Acid-test ratio =	+ Net current receivables / Current liabilities	+ $114,000 / $142,000 = 1.01	+ $85,000 / $126,000 = 0.93	0.40

The company's acid-test ratio improved during 2009 and is significantly better than the industry average. Compare Meben's acid-test ratio with the values of some well-known companies.

Company	Acid-Test Ratio
Enbridge Inc. (Utility)	0.72
Research In Motion (Hi-tech company)	1.89
Loblaw Companies Limited (Grocery stores)	0.51

An acid-test ratio of 0.90 to 1.00 is acceptable in most industries. How can a leading company, such as Loblaw Companies Limited with its 0.51 acid-test ratio, function with such a low ratio? Loblaw has almost no receivables. Its inventory is priced to turn over very quickly. This points us to the next two ratios.

STOP & THINK

Assume you are a financial analyst for an investment bank and have been charged with analyzing Meben's Furniture Ltd.'s financial statements. You calculate that Meben's current ratio is 1.85, which looks strong, whereas the company's acid-test ratio is 1.01, also strong. Suppose Meben's acid-test ratio were low, say 0.48. What would be the most likely reason for the discrepancy between a high current ratio and a weak acid-test ratio?

Answers:
In such a situation, it would appear that the company is having difficulty selling its inventory. The level of inventory must be relatively high, and the inventory is propping up the current ratio. The rate of inventory turnover may be low.

Measuring Ability to Sell Inventory and Collect Receivables

The ability to sell inventory and collect receivables is critical to business success. In this section, we discuss three ratios that measure this ability.

Inventory Turnover. Companies generally strive to sell their inventory as quickly as possible. The faster inventory sells, the sooner cash comes in.

Inventory turnover is a measure of the number of times a company sells its average level of inventory during a year. A fast turnover indicates ease in selling inventory; a low turnover indicates difficulty. A value of 6 means that the company's average level of inventory has been sold six times during the year, and that's better than a turnover of three times. But too high a value can mean that the business is not keeping enough inventory on hand, which can result in lost sales if the company cannot fill orders. Therefore, a business strives for the most *profitable* rate of inventory turnover, not necessarily the *highest* rate.

To compute the inventory turnover ratio, divide cost of goods sold by the average inventory for the period. We use the cost of goods sold—*not sales*—in the computation because both cost of goods sold and inventory are stated *at cost*. Meben Furniture Ltd.'s inventory turnover for 2009 is:

	Formula	Meben's Inventory Turnover	Industry Average
Inventory turnover =	$\dfrac{\text{Cost of goods sold}}{\text{Average inventory}}$	$\dfrac{\$513,000}{\$112,000} = 4.6$	3.4

Cost of goods sold comes from the income statement (Exhibit 13-9). Average inventory is calculated by averaging the beginning inventory ($111,000) and ending inventory ($113,000). (See the balance sheet, Exhibit 13-9.) If inventory levels vary greatly from month to month, compute the average by adding the 12 monthly balances and dividing the sum by 12.

Inventory turnover varies widely with the nature of the business. For example, most manufacturers of farm machinery have an inventory turnover close to three times a year. In contrast, companies that remove natural gas from the ground hold their inventory for a very short period of time and have an average turnover of 30. Meben's turnover of 4.6 times a year is high for its industry, which has an average turnover of 3.4. Meben's high inventory turnover results from its policy of keeping little inventory on hand. The company sells directly but also takes customer orders and has its suppliers ship directly to some customers.

To evaluate a company's inventory turnover fully, compare the ratio over time. A sharp decline in the rate of inventory turnover or a steady decline over a long period suggests the need for corrective action.

Accounts Receivable Turnover.

Accounts receivable turnover measures a company's ability to collect cash from credit customers. In general, the higher the ratio the better. However, a receivable turnover that is too high may indicate that credit is too tight, and that might cause you to lose sales to good customers.

To compute the accounts receivable turnover, divide net credit sales by average net accounts receivable. The ratio indicates how many times during the year the average level of receivables was turned into cash. Meben Furniture Ltd.'s accounts receivable turnover ratio for 2009 is:

	Formula	Meben's Accounts Receivable Turnover	Industry Average
Accounts receivable turnover	$= \dfrac{\text{Net credit sales}}{\text{Average net accounts receivable}}$	$\dfrac{\$858,000}{\$99,500} = 8.6$	51.0

Meben makes almost all sales on credit. It the company makes both cash and credit sales, this ratio is best computed by using only net credit sales. Average net accounts receivable is calculated by adding the beginning accounts receivable balance ($85,000) and the ending balance ($114,000), then dividing by 2. If the accounts receivable balances exhibit a seasonal pattern, compute the average by adding the 12 monthly balances and dividing the sum by 12.

Meben's receivable turnover of 8.6 times per year is much slower than the industry average. The explanation is simple: Meben is a hometown store that sells to local people who tend to pay their bills over a period of time. Many larger stores and chains of stores sell their receivables to other companies called *factors,* a practice that keeps receivables low and receivable turnover high. But companies that factor (sell) their receivables receive less than the face value of the receivables. Meben follows a different strategy.

Days' Sales in Receivables.

Businesses must convert accounts receivable to cash. All else being equal, the lower the receivable balance, the better the cash flow.

The *days'-sales-in-receivables* ratio tells us how many days' sales remain in Accounts Receivable. Compute the ratio by a two-step process:

1. Divide net sales by 365 days to calculate the average sales for one day.
2. Divide average net accounts receivable by average sales per day.

The data to compute this ratio for Meben Furniture Ltd. for 2009 are taken from the income statement and the balance sheet (Exhibit 13-9):

	Formula	Meben's Days' Sales in Accounts Receivable	Industry Average
Days' sales in *average* accounts receivable:			
1. One day's sales $=$	$\dfrac{\text{Net sales}}{365 \text{ days}}$	$\dfrac{\$858,000}{365 \text{ days}} = \$2,351$	
2. Days' sales in average accounts receivable $=$	$\dfrac{\text{Average net accounts receivable}}{\text{One day's sales}}$	$\dfrac{\$99,500}{\$2,351} = 42 \text{ days}$	7 days

Days' sales in average receivables can also be computed in a single step: $99,500/($858,000/365 \text{ days}) = 42$ days. Meben's collection period is much longer (worse) than the industry average because Meben collects its own receivables. As was noted above, most furniture stores sell their receivables and carry fewer days' sales in receivables.

Meben's ratio tells us that 42 average days' sales remain in accounts receivable and need to be collected. The company will increase its cash flow if it can decrease this ratio. To detect any changes over time in the firm's ability to collect its receivables, let's compute the days'-sales-in-receivables ratio at the beginning and the end of 2009:

Days' Sales in ENDING 2008 Accounts Receivable:

$$\text{One day's sales} = \frac{\$803,000}{365 \text{ days}} = \$2,200 \qquad \begin{array}{c}\text{Days' sales in}\\ \textit{ENDING 2008}\\ \text{accounts receivable}\end{array} = \frac{\$85,000}{\$2,200} = \begin{array}{c}39 \text{ days at the}\\ \text{beginning of 2009}\end{array}$$

Days' Sales in ENDING 2009 Accounts Receivable:

$$\text{One day's sales} = \frac{\$858,000}{365 \text{ days}} = \$2,351 \qquad \begin{array}{c}\text{Days' sales in}\\ \textit{ENDING 2009}\\ \text{accounts receivable}\end{array} = \frac{\$114,000}{\$2,351} = \begin{array}{c}48 \text{ days at the}\\ \text{end of 2009}\end{array}$$

This analysis shows a slowdown in Meben's collection of receivables; days' sales in accounts receivable have increased from 39 at the beginning of the year to 48 at year-end. The credit and collection department should strengthen its collection efforts. Otherwise, the company may experience a cash shortage in 2010 and beyond.

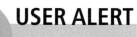 **USER ALERT**

Changes in Receivables Ratios

A company's days' sales in receivables might increase because the company loosens its credit terms (for example, from net 30 to net 45) in an effort to increase sales. Another reason might be that the company is doing a poor job of collecting its receivables. As is true of all the other ratios you study here, changes in the ratio are important but so is understanding why the ratio changed.

Measuring Ability to Pay Long-Term Debt

The ratios discussed so far relate to current assets and current liabilities. They measure the ability to sell inventory, collect receivables, and pay current liabilities. Most businesses also have long-term debt. Two indicators of the ability to pay total liabilities are the *debt ratio* and the *times-interest-earned ratio*.

Debt Ratio. Suppose you are a loan officer at a bank, and you have received $500,000 loan applications from two similar companies. The first firm already owes $600,000, and the second owes only $250,000. Other things being equal, which company gets the loan? Company 2 would, because it owes less.

This relationship between total liabilities and total assets is called the *debt ratio*. It tells us the proportion of the company's assets that it has financed with debt. A debt ratio of 1 reveals that debt has financed all the assets. A debt ratio of 0.50 means that debt financed half the assets. The higher the debt ratio, the greater the pressure to pay interest and principal. The lower the ratio, the lower the risk.

The debt ratios for Meben Furniture Ltd. follow:

		Meben's Debt Ratio		Industry
	Formula	2009	2008	Average
Debt ratio =	$\dfrac{\text{Total liabilities}}{\text{Total assets}}$	$\dfrac{\$431,000}{\$787,000} = 0.55$	$\dfrac{\$324,000}{\$644,000} = 0.50$	0.64

Risk Management Association reports that the average debt ratio for most companies ranges around 0.62, with relatively little variation from company to company. Meben's 0.55 debt ratio indicates a fairly low-risk debt position compared with the retail furniture industry average of 0.64.

Times-Interest-Earned Ratio. Analysts use a second ratio—the *times-interest-earned ratio*—to relate income to interest expense. To compute the times-interest-earned ratio, divide income from operations (operating income) by interest expense. This ratio measures the number of times that operating income can *cover* interest expense and is also called the *interest-coverage ratio*. A high ratio indicates ease in paying interest; a low value suggests difficulty.

Meben's times-interest-earned ratios are:

		Meben's Times-Interest-Earned Ratio		Industry
	Formula	2009	2008	Average
Times-interest-earned ratio =	$\dfrac{\text{Income from operations}}{\text{Interest expense}}$	$\dfrac{\$101,000}{\$24,000} = 4.21$	$\dfrac{\$57,000}{\$14,000} = 4.07$	2.80

The company's times-interest-earned ratio increased in 2009. This is a favourable sign.

Measuring Profitability

The fundamental goal of business is to earn a profit, and so the ratios that measure profitability are reported widely.

USER ALERT

Understanding Ratios That Measure Profitability

Suppose you are a personal financial planner who helps clients select share investments. Over the next few years, you might expect Metro Inc. to earn higher rates of return on a share investment than analysts are forecasting for Sobeys Inc. Which company's shares will you recommend? Perhaps Metro's—for reasons that you will better understand after studying four rate-of-return measurements.

Rate of Return on Sales. In business, *return* refers to profitability. Consider the **rate of return on net sales**, or simply *return on sales*. (The word *net* is usually omitted for convenience.) This ratio shows the percentage of each sales dollar earned as net income. The return-on-sales ratios for Meben Furniture Ltd. are:

		Meben's Rate of Return on Sales		Industry
	Formula	2009	2008	Average
Rate of return on net sales =	$\dfrac{\text{Net income}}{\text{Net sales}}$	$\dfrac{\$48,000}{\$858,000} = 0.056$	$\dfrac{\$26,000}{\$803,000} = 0.032$	0.008

Companies strive for a high rate of return. The higher the percentage, the more profit is being generated by sales dollars. Meben's return on sales is higher than the average furniture store. Compare Meben's rate of return on sales to the rates of some other companies:

Company	Rate of Return on Sales
Leon's Furniture Limited (Furniture stores).........................	0.092
Sobeys Inc. (Grocery stores)..	0.014
Tim Hortons Inc. (Quick-service restaurant chain)..............	0.142

Rate of Return on Total Assets. The *rate of return on total assets*, or simply *return on assets*, measures a company's success in using assets to earn a profit. Creditors have loaned money, and the interest they receive is their return on investment. Shareholders have bought the company's shares, and net income is their return. The sum of interest expense and net income is the return to the two groups that have financed the company. This sum is the numerator of the ratio. Average total assets is the denominator. The return-on-assets ratio for Meben Furniture Ltd. is:

Formula	Meben's 2009 Rate of Return on Total Assets	Industry Average
$\dfrac{\text{Rate of return}}{\text{on total assets}} = \dfrac{\text{Net income} + \text{Interest expense}}{\text{Average total assets}}$	$\dfrac{\$48,000 + \$24,000}{\$715,500} = 0.101$	0.078

To compute average total assets, add the beginning and ending balances and divide by 2. Compare Meben Furniture Ltd.'s rate of return on assets to the rates of these leading companies:

Company	Rate of Return on Assets
Gildan Activewear Inc. (Clothing manufacturer)..	0.154
RONA Inc. (Home improvement retailer and distributor).............................	0.094
Bombardier Inc. (Production of transportation equipment and services)........	0.037

Rate of Return on Common Shareholders' Equity. A popular measure of profitability is the *rate of return on common shareholders' equity*, often shortened to *return on equity*. This ratio shows the relationship between net income and common shareholders' investment in the company—how much income is earned for every $1 invested.

To compute this ratio, first subtract preferred dividends from net income to measure income available to the common shareholders. Then divide income available to common shareholders by the average common shareholders' equity during the year. Common shareholders' equity is total shareholders' equity minus preferred equity. The 2009 rate of return on common shareholders' equity for Meben Furniture Ltd. is:

Formula	Meben's 2009 Rate of Return on Common Shareholders' Equity	Industry Average
$\dfrac{\text{Rate of return on common shareholders' equity}}{} = \dfrac{\text{Net income} - \text{Preferred dividends}}{\text{Average common shareholders' equity}}$	$\dfrac{\$48,000 - 0}{\$338,000} = 0.142$	0.121

Average common shareholders' equity uses the beginning and ending balances [($356,000 + $320,000)/2 = $338,000].

Observe that Meben's return on equity (0.142) is higher than its return on assets (0.101). This is a good sign. This difference results from borrowing at one rate—say, 8%—and investing the funds to earn a higher rate, such as the firm's 14.2% return on equity. This practice is called using *leverage* or *trading on the equity*. The higher the debt ratio, the higher the leverage. Companies that finance operations with debt are said to *leverage* their positions.

For Meben Furniture Ltd., leverage increases profitability. This is not always the case because leverage can hurt profits. If revenues drop, debt and interest expense still must be paid. Therefore, leverage is a double-edged sword. It increases profits during good times but compounds losses during bad times.

Compare Meben Furniture Ltd.'s rate of return on common shareholders' equity with the rates of some leading companies:

Company	Rate of Return on Common Equity
Gildan Activewear Inc. (Clothing manufacturer)	0.196
RONA Inc. (Home improvement retailer and distributor)	0.151
Bombardier Inc. (Production of transportation equipment and services).......	0.120

Earnings per Share of Common Stock. *Earnings per share of common stock*, or simply *earnings per share (EPS)*, is the amount of net income earned for each share of outstanding *common* stock. EPS is the most widely quoted of all financial statistics. It is the only ratio that appears on the income statement.

Earnings per share is computed by dividing net income available to common shareholders by the number of common shares outstanding during the year. Preferred dividends are subtracted from net income because the preferred shareholders have a prior claim to their dividends. Meben Furniture Ltd. has no preferred shares outstanding and thus has no preferred dividends. The firm's EPS for 2009 and 2008 follows (Meben had 10,000 common shares outstanding):

	Formula	Meben's Earnings per Share 2009	Meben's Earnings per Share 2008
Earnings per share of common stock	$= \dfrac{\text{Net income} - \text{Preferred dividends}}{\text{Average number of common shares outstanding}}$	$\dfrac{\$48,000 - \$0}{10,000} = \$4.80$	$\dfrac{\$26,000 - \$0}{10,000} = \$2.60$

Meben Furniture Ltd.'s EPS increased 85%, which is good news. Its shareholders should not expect such a significant boost in EPS every year. Most companies strive to increase EPS by 10% to 15% annually.

Analyzing Share Investments

Investors purchase shares to earn a return on their investment. This return consists of two parts: (1) gains (or losses) from selling the shares, and (2) dividends.

Price/Earnings Ratio. The **price/earnings ratio** is the ratio of the market price of a common share to earnings per share. This ratio, abbreviated P/E, is available, for example, in *The Globe and Mail* stock listings and online at www.tsx.com. It shows the market price of $1 of earnings.

Calculations for the P/E ratios of Meben Furniture Ltd. follow. Meben is not a real company and is not listed on a stock exchange, but assume the market price of its common shares was $60 at the end of 2009 and $35 at the end of 2008. Share prices can be obtained from a financial publication, a stockbroker, the company's Internet site, or the Internet site of a stock exchange such as the Toronto Stock Exchange.

		Meben's Price/Earnings Ratio	
	Formula	2009	2008
P/E ratio $=$	$\dfrac{\text{Market price per common share}}{\text{Earnings per share}}$	$\dfrac{\$60.00}{\$4.80} = 12.5$	$\dfrac{\$35.00}{\$2.60} = 13.5$

Given Meben's 2009 P/E ratio of 12.5, we would say that the company's shares are selling at 12.5 times earnings. Each $1 of Meben's earnings is worth $12.50 to the stock market.

Dividend Yield. **Dividend yield** is the ratio of dividends per share to the share's market price. This ratio measures the percentage of a share's market value that is returned annually to the shareholders as dividends. *Preferred* shareholders pay special attention to this ratio because they invest primarily to receive dividends.

Meben Furniture Ltd. paid annual cash dividends of $1.20 per common share in 2009 and $1.00 in 2008. Assume the market prices of the company's common shares were $60 in 2009 and $35 in 2008. The firm's dividend yields on common shares are:

		Dividend Yield on Meben's Common Shares	
	Formula	2009	2008
Dividend yield on common share* $=$	$\dfrac{\text{Dividend per share of common stock}}{\text{Market price per share of common stock}}$	$\dfrac{\$1.20}{\$60.00} = 0.020$	$\dfrac{\$1.00}{\$35.00} = 0.029$

*Dividend yields may also be calculated for preferred shares.

An investor who buys Meben Furniture Ltd. common shares for $60 can expect to receive around 2% of the investment annually in the form of cash dividends. Dividend yields vary widely, from 3% to 9% for older, established firms (such as BCE and National Bank) down to the range of 0% to 3% for young, growth-oriented companies. Rogers Communications, for example, pays a cash dividend of $1.00 per share, for a dividend yield of 0.0298. Open Text and Research In Motion do not pay cash dividends.

Book Value per Share of Common Stock. *Book value per share of common stock* is simply common shareholders' equity divided by the number of shares outstanding. Common shareholders' equity equals total shareholders' equity less preferred equity. Meben Furniture Ltd. has no preferred shares outstanding. Calculations of its book-value-per-share-of-common-stock ratios follow. Recall that 10,000 common shares were outstanding at the end of years 2009 and 2008.

		Book Value per Share of Meben's Common Stock	
	Formula	2009	2008
Book value per share of common stock $=$	$\dfrac{\text{Total shareholders' equity} - \text{Preferred equity}}{\text{Number of shares of common stock outstanding}}$	$\dfrac{\$356,000 - \$0}{10,000} = \$35.60$	$\dfrac{\$320,000 - \$0}{10,000} = \$32.00$

Book value indicates the recorded accounting amount for each common share outstanding. Many experts believe that book value is not useful for investment analysis because it bears no relationship to market value and provides little information beyond shareholders' equity reported on the balance sheet. But some investors base their investment decisions on book value. For example, some investors rank shares on the basis of the ratio of market price to book value. The lower the ratio, the more attractive the shares. These investors are called "value" investors, as contrasted with "growth" investors, who focus more on trends in a company's net income.

Other Measures

Economic Value Added[1]

Objective

⑦ **Measure** the economic value added by operations

The top managers of Coca-Cola, Quaker Oats, and other leading companies use **economic value added (EVA®)** to evaluate a company's operating performance. EVA® combines the concepts of accounting income and corporate finance to measure whether the company's operations have increased shareholder wealth. EVA® can be computed as follows:

$$\text{EVA}^® = \text{Net income} + \text{Interest expense} - \text{Capital charge}$$

where

$$\text{Capital charge} = \left(\begin{array}{c} \text{Notes} \\ \text{payable}^* \end{array} + \begin{array}{c} \text{Current maturities} \\ \text{of long-term debt}^* \end{array} + \begin{array}{c} \text{Long-term} \\ \text{debt}^* \end{array} + \begin{array}{c} \text{Shareholders'} \\ \text{equity}^* \end{array} \right) \times \begin{array}{c} \text{Cost of} \\ \text{capital} \end{array}$$

*Using beginning amounts for the year

All amounts for the EVA® computation, except the cost of capital, come from the financial statements. The **cost of capital** is a weighted average of the returns demanded by the company's shareholders and lenders. Cost of capital varies with the company's level of risk. For example, shareholders would demand a higher return from a start-up computer software company than from Great-West Lifeco because the new company is untested and therefore more risky. Lenders would also charge the new company a higher interest rate because of this greater risk. Thus, the new company has a higher cost of capital than does Great-West Lifeco.

The cost of capital is a major topic in finance classes. In the following discussions, we assume a value for the cost of capital (such as 10%, 12%, or 15%) to illustrate the computation of EVA® and its use in decision making.

The idea behind EVA® is that the returns to the company's shareholders (net income) and to its creditors (interest expense) should exceed the company's capital charge. The **capital charge** is the amount that shareholders and lenders *charge* a company for the use of their money. A positive EVA® amount indicates an increase in shareholder wealth, and the company's shares should remain attractive to investors. If the EVA® measure is negative, shareholders will probably be unhappy with the company and sell its shares, resulting in a decrease in the share price. Different companies tailor the EVA® computation to meet their own needs.

Yum! Brands is the leading global developer of new restaurants. Recent activities include aggressive development in China. You are probably familiar with Yum!'s brands, which include KFC, Pizza Hut, Taco Bell, Long John Silver's, and A&W. Let's

---

[1] EVA® was popularized and trademarked by Stern, Steven & Co. in the United States. For more information see Armitage, Howard M., and Vijay Jog, "Economic Value Creation," *CMA Magazine*, October 1996, pp. 21–24. See also "A performance-measurement *takeover* bid?" *CA Magazine*, January–February 1998, p. 15.

apply EVA® to Yum! Brands. Yum!'s EVA® for 2006 can be computed as follows, assuming a 10% cost of capital for the company (dollar amounts in millions):

$$
\begin{array}{llllllllll}
\text{Yum!'s EVA}^{\circledR} = & \begin{array}{c}\text{Net}\\\text{income}\end{array} & + & \begin{array}{c}\text{Interest}\\\text{expense}\end{array} & - & \left(\begin{array}{c}\text{Short-term}\\\text{borrowings}\end{array}\right. & + & \begin{array}{c}\text{Long-term}\\\text{debt}\end{array} & + & \left.\begin{array}{c}\text{Shareholders'}\\\text{equity}\end{array}\right) \times \begin{array}{c}\text{Cost of}\\\text{capital}\end{array}
\end{array}
$$

$$= \quad \$824 \quad + \quad \$154 \quad - \quad [(\$74 \quad + \quad \$2,045 \quad + \quad \$1,437) \quad \times \quad 0.10]$$

$$= \quad \$978 \quad - \quad \$3,556 \quad \times \quad 0.10$$

$$= \quad \$978 \quad - \quad \$356$$

$$= \quad \$622$$

By this measure, Yum!'s operations during 2006 added $622 million of value to its shareholders' wealth after meeting the company's capital charge. This performance is very strong.

Red Flags in Financial Statement Analysis

Recent accounting scandals highlighted the importance of red flags in financial analysis. If the following conditions are present, the company may be too risky.

- **Earnings Problems.** Have income from continuing operations and net income decreased significantly for several years in a row? Has income turned into a loss? This may be okay for a company in a cyclical industry, such as an airline or a home builder, but most companies cannot survive consecutive loss years.
- **Decreased Cash Flow.** Cash flow validates earnings. Is cash flow from operations consistently lower than net income? Are the sales of capital assets a major source of cash? If so, the company may be facing a cash shortage.
- **Too Much Debt.** How does the company's debt ratio compare to that of major competitors and to the industry average? If the debt ratio is much higher than average, the company may be unable to pay debts during tough times.
- **Inability to Collect Receivables.** Are days' sales in receivables growing faster than for other companies in the industry? A cash shortage may be looming.
- **Buildup of Inventories.** Is inventory turnover slowing down? If so, the company may be unable to move products, or it may be overstating inventory. Recall from the cost-of-goods-sold model that one of the easiest ways to overstate net income is to overstate ending inventory.
- **Trends of Sales, Inventory, and Receivables.** Sales, receivables, and inventory generally move together. Increased sales lead to higher receivables and require more inventory to meet demand. Strange movements among these items may spell trouble.

Efficient Markets

An **efficient capital market** is one in which market prices fully reflect all information available to the public. Because share prices reflect all publicly accessible data, it can be argued that the stock market is efficient. Market efficiency has implications for management action and for investor decisions. It means that managers cannot fool the market with accounting gimmicks. If the information is available, the market as a whole can set a "fair" price for the company's shares.

Suppose you are the president of Kemble Corporation. Reported earnings per share are $4, and the share price is $40—so the P/E ratio is 10. You believe the corporation's shares are underpriced in comparison with other companies in the same industry. To correct this situation, you are considering changing your amortization method from accelerated to straight-line. The accounting change will increase earnings per share to $5. Will the share price then rise to $50? Probably not; the company's share price will probably remain at $40 because the market can understand the accounting change. After all, the company merely changed its method of computing amortization. There is no effect on the company's cash flows, and its economic position is unchanged. An efficient market interprets data in light of their true underlying meaning.

An appropriate investment strategy seeks to manage risk, diversify, and minimize transaction costs. Financial analysis consists mainly of identifying the risks of various shares to manage the risk.

The Decision Guidelines summarize the most widely used ratios.

DECISION GUIDELINES

USING RATIOS IN FINANCIAL STATEMENT ANALYSIS

Cynthia Li-chong and Raj Kumar operate a financial services firm. They manage other people's money and do most of their own financial-statement analysis. How do they measure companies' ability to pay bills, sell inventory, collect receivables, and so on? They use the standard ratios we have covered throughout this book.

Ratio	Computation	Information Provided
Measuring ability to pay current liabilities:		
1. Current ratio	$\dfrac{\text{Current assets}}{\text{Current liabilities}}$	Measures ability to pay current liabilities with current assets
2. Acid-test (quick) ratio	$\dfrac{\text{Cash} + \dfrac{\text{Short-term}}{\text{investments}} + \dfrac{\text{Net current}}{\text{receivables}}}{\text{Current liabilities}}$	Shows ability to pay all current liabilities if they come due immediately
Measuring ability to sell inventory and collect receivables:		
3. Inventory turnover	$\dfrac{\text{Cost of goods sold}}{\text{Average inventory}}$	Indicates saleability of inventory— the number of times a company sells its average inventory level during a year
4. Accounts receivable turnover	$\dfrac{\text{Net credit sales}}{\text{Average net accounts receivable}}$	Measures ability to collect cash from credit customers
5. Days' sales in receivables	$\dfrac{\text{Average net accounts receivable}}{\text{One day's sales}}$	Shows how many days' sales remain in Accounts Receivable—how many days it takes to collect the average level of receivables
Measuring ability to pay long-term debt:		
6. Debt ratio	$\dfrac{\text{Total liabilities}}{\text{Total assets}}$	Indicates percentage of assets financed with debt
7. Times-interest-earned ratio	$\dfrac{\text{Income from operations}}{\text{Interest expense}}$	Measures the number of times operating income can cover interest expense
Measuring profitability:		
8. Rate of return on net sales	$\dfrac{\text{Net income}}{\text{Net sales}}$	Shows the percentage of each sales dollar earned as net income
9. Rate of return on total assets	$\dfrac{\text{Net income} + \text{Interest expense}}{\text{Average total assets}}$	Measures how profitably a company uses its assets

10. Rate of return on common shareholders' equity

$$\frac{\text{Net income} - \text{Preferred dividends}}{\text{Average common shareholders' equity}}$$

Gauges how much income is earned with the money invested by common shareholders

11. Earnings per share of common stock

$$\frac{\text{Net income} - \text{Preferred dividends}}{\substack{\text{Average number of} \\ \text{common shares outstanding}}}$$

Gives the amount of net income earned for each share of the company's common stock

Analyzing shares as an investment:

12. Price/earnings ratio

$$\frac{\text{Market price per share of common stock}}{\text{Earnings per share}}$$

Indicates the market price of $1 of earnings

13. Dividend yield common stock

$$\frac{\substack{\text{Dividend per share of common} \\ \text{(or preferred) stock}}}{\substack{\text{Market price per share of} \\ \text{common (or preferred) stock}}}$$

Shows the percentage of a share's market value returned as dividends to shareholders each period

14. Book value per share of

$$\frac{\text{Total shareholders' equity} - \text{Preferred equity}}{\text{Number of common shares outstanding}}$$

Indicates the recorded accounting amount for each share of common stock outstanding

---

MyAccountingLab

END-OF-CHAPTER SUMMARY PROBLEM

The following financial data are adapted from the financial statements of Keppel Inc.

Keppel Inc.				
Four-Years' Selected Financial Data				
For the Years Ended June 30				
	2009**	2008	2007	2006
Operating Results*				
Sales	$6,550	$3,043	$4,048	$3,586
Cost of goods sold	4,913	2,344	3,107	2,761
Income from operations	254	208	260	225
Interest expense	42	12	25	16
Net income	179	133	164	140
Cash dividends	22	20	27	21
Financial Position				
Inventory	$ 904	$ 392	$ 491	$ 515
Total assets	$2,440	$1,344	$1,724	$1,662
Current ratio	1.90	2.01	1.88	2.02
Shareholders' equity	$1,080	$ 853	$1,020	$ 946
Average number of common shares outstanding (in thousands)	244	227	226	225

*Dollar amounts are in thousands.
**Keppel Inc. purchased all the shares of a competitor, Bognor Ltd., in November 2008.

Name: Keppel Inc.
Fiscal Period: Years ended June 30, 2006 to 2009.

Refer to the Decision Guidelines for the ratio formulas.

Required

Compute the following ratios for 2007 through 2009, and evaluate Keppel Inc.'s operating results. Are operating results strong or weak? Did they improve or deteriorate during the four-year period? Your analysis will reveal a clear trend.

1. Gross margin percentage[†]
2. Net income as a percentage of sales
3. Earnings per share

4. Inventory turnover
5. Times-interest-earned ratio
6. Rate of return on shareholders' equity

Remember to use the previous year's inventory balance when calculating average inventory in the inventory turnover ratio. Use the previous year's shareholders' equity when calculating average shareholders' equity in the rate of return on shareholders' equity.

	2009	2008	2007
1. Gross margin percentage	$\dfrac{\$6{,}550 - \$4{,}913}{\$6{,}550} = 25.0\%$	$\dfrac{\$3{,}043 - \$2{,}344}{\$3{,}043} = 23.0\%$	$\dfrac{\$4{,}048 - \$3{,}107}{\$4{,}048} = 23.2\%$
2. Net income as a percentage of sales	$\dfrac{\$179}{\$6{,}550} = 0.027$	$\dfrac{\$133}{\$3{,}043} = 0.044$	$\dfrac{\$164}{\$4{,}048} = 0.041$
3. Earnings per share	$\dfrac{\$179}{244} = \$0.73$	$\dfrac{\$133}{227} = \$0.59$	$\dfrac{\$164}{226} = \$0.73$
4. Inventory turnover	$\dfrac{\$4{,}913}{(\$904 + \$392)/2} = 7.58$ times	$\dfrac{\$2{,}344}{(\$392 + \$491)/2} = 5.31$ times	$\dfrac{\$3{,}107}{(\$491 + \$515)/2} = 6.18$ times
5. Times-interest-earned ratio	$\dfrac{\$254}{\$42} = 6.05$ times	$\dfrac{\$208}{\$12} = 17.33$ times	$\dfrac{\$260}{\$25} = 10.4$ times
6. Rate of return on shareholders' equity	$\dfrac{\$179}{(\$1{,}080 + \$853)/2} = 0.185$	$\dfrac{\$133}{(\$853 + \$1{,}020)/2} = 0.142$	$\dfrac{\$164}{(\$1{,}020 + \$946)/2} = 0.167$

Evaluation:

For the six ratios calculated, the higher the ratio, the better. Ratios that increase each year are a positive trend and indicate good news. Remember to evaluate all ratios along with other information about the company. One ratio will not tell the complete story.

The first thing to notice is that Keppel Inc.'s total assets and inventory almost doubled from 2008 to 2009. A review of Keppel's financial statements reveals that the purchase of Bognor Ltd. was for cash and that the financial statements of the competitor were consolidated with those of Keppel effective the date of acquisition. Keppel borrowed the funds to pay for the acquisition which resulted in a significant increase in interest expense.

The analysis shows that Keppel Inc. continues to perform well. Ratios 1 and 4 are relatively constant over the three years. Ratio 2 improved from 2007 to 2008 but declined in 2009 probably as a result of the consolidation. Ratio 3 improved to the 2007 level. Ratio 5 declined because of the increased debt taken on to finance the purchase. Ratio 6 improved from 2008 suggesting the acquisition of Bognor will provide enhanced value for shareholders in the future.

REVIEW FINANCIAL STATEMENT ANALYSIS

QUICK CHECK (Answers are given on page 675.)

Analyze the Donaldson Limited financial statements by answering the questions that follow. Donaldson owns a chain of restaurants.

Donaldson Limited Consolidated Statement of Income (Adapted) For the Years Ended December 31, 2009, 2008, and 2007			
In Millions, Except per Share Data	2009	2008	2007
Revenues			
Sales by company-operated restaurants................................	$12,795.4	$11,499.6	$11,040.7
Revenues from franchised and affiliated restaurants............	4,345.1	3,906.1	3,829.3
Total revenues...	17,140.5	15,405.7	14,870.0
Operating Expenses			
Company-operated restaurant expenses			
Food & paper (Cost of goods sold)................................	4,314.8	3,917.4	3,802.1
Payroll & employee benefits	3,411.4	3,078.2	2,901.2
Occupancy & other operating expenses........................	3,279.8	2,911.0	2,750.4
Franchised restaurants—occupancy expenses....................	937.7	840.1	800.2
Selling, general & administrative expenses	1,833.0	1,712.8	1,661.7
Other operating expense, net..	531.6	833.3	257.4
Total operating expenses..	14,308.3	13,292.8	12,173.0
Operating income	2,832.2	2,112.9	2,697.0
Interest expense...	388.0	374.1	452.4
Gain on sale of subsidiary..	—	—	(137.1)
Non-operating expense, net..	97.8	76.7	52.0
Income before income taxes and cumulative effect			
of accounting changes..	2,346.4	1,662.1	2,329.7
Income tax expense	838.2	670.0	693.1
Income before cumulative effect of accounting changes....	1,508.2	992.1	1,636.6
Cumulative effect of accounting changes,			
net of tax benefits of $9.4 and $17.6..............................	(36.8)	(98.6)	—
Net income...	$ 1,471.4	$ 893.5	$ 1,636.6
Per common share—basic:			
Income before cumulative effect of accounting changes......	$ 1.19	$ 0.78	$ 1.27
Cumulative effect of accounting changes..........................	(0.03)	(0.08)	
Net income...	$ 1.16	$ 0.70	$ 1.27
Dividends per common share..	$ 0.40	$ 0.24	$ 0.23

Donaldson Limited
Consolidated Balance Sheet
For the Years Ended December 31, 2009 and 2008

In Millions, Except per Share Data	2009	2008
Assets		
Current assets		
Cash and equivalents	$ 492.8	$ 330.4
Accounts and notes receivable	734.5	855.3
Inventories, at cost	129.4	111.7
Prepaid expenses and other current assets	528.7	418.0
Total current assets	1,885.4	1,715.4
Other assets		
Investments in affiliates	1,089.6	1,037.7
Goodwill, net	1,665.1	1,558.5
Miscellaneous	960.3	1,075.5
Total other assets	3,715.0	3,671.7
Property and equipment		
Property and equipment, at cost	28,740.2	26,218.6
Accumulated amortization	(8,815.5)	(7,635.2)
Net property and equipment	19,924.7	18,583.4
Total assets	$25,525.1	$23,970.5
Liabilities and Shareholders' Equity		
Current liabilities		
Accounts payable	$ 577.4	$ 635.8
Income taxes	71.5	16.3
Other taxes	222.0	191.8
Accrued interest	193.1	199.4
Accrued restructuring and restaurant closing costs	115.7	328.5
Accrued payroll and other liabilities	918.1	774.7
Current maturities of long-term debt	388.0	275.8
Total current liabilities	2,485.8	2,422.3
Long-term debt	9,342.5	9,703.6
Other long-term liabilities and minority interests	699.8	560.0
Deferred income taxes	1,015.1	1,003.7
Total liabilities	13,543.2	13,689.6
Shareholders' equity		
Preferred shares authorized—165.0 million shares; issued—none		
Common shares authorized—3.5 billion shares;		
issued—1,261.9 million shares	1,854.1	1,763.9
Retained earnings	10,763.3	10,118.3
Accumulated other comprehensive income (loss)	(635.5)	(1,601.3)
Total shareholders' equity	11,981.9	10,280.9
Total liabilities and shareholders' equity	$25,525.1	$23,970.5

1. Horizontal analysis of Donaldson's income statement for 2009 would show which of the following for Selling, general, & administrative expenses?
   - a. 1.14
   - b. 1.10
   - c. 1.07
   - d. None of the above (fill in the blank)

2. Vertical analysis of Donaldson's income statement for 2009 would show which of the following for Selling, general, & administrative expenses?
   - a. 1.144
   - b. 0.143
   - c. 0.107
   - d. None of the above (fill in the blank)

3. Which item on Donaldson's income statement has the most favourable trend during 2007–2009?

   a. Total revenues
   b. Net income

   c. Food & paper costs
   d. Payroll & employee benefits

4. On Donaldson's common-size balance sheet, Goodwill would appear as

   a. 0.065
   b. Up by 6.8%

   c. $1,665.1 million
   d. 9.7% of total revenues

5. A good benchmark for Donaldson Limited would be

   a. Whataburger
   b. Boeing

   c. Intel
   d. All of the above

6. Donaldson's inventory turnover for 2009 was

   a. 91 times
   b. 62 times

   c. 21 times
   d. 36 times

7. Donaldson's acid-test ratio at the end of 2009 was

   a. 1.49
   b. 0.49

   c. 0.30
   d. 0.20

8. Donaldson's average collection period for accounts and notes receivables is

   a. 1 day
   b. 2 days

   c. 30 days
   d. 17 days

9. Donaldson's total debt position looks

   a. Safe
   b. Middle-ground

   c. Risky
   d. Cannot tell from the financials

10. Donaldson's return on total revenues for 2009 was

    a. 13.2%
    b. $1.16

    c. 5.9%
    d. 8.6%

11. Donaldson's return on shareholders' equity for 2009 was

    a. 13.2%
    b. 8.6%

    c. 5.9%
    d. $1,471.4 million

12. On June 30, 2009, Donaldson's common shares sold for $26 per share. At that price, how much did investors say $1 of the company's net income was worth?

    a. $1.00
    b. $22.41

    c. $21.85
    d. $26.00

13. Use Donaldson's financial statements and the data in question 12 to compute Donaldson's dividend yield during 2009.

    a. 3.1%
    b. 2.4%

    c. 2.2%
    d. 1.5%

14. How much EVA® did Donaldson generate for investors during 2009? Assume the cost of capital was 8%.

    a. $973 million
    b. $1,471 million

    c. $239 million
    d. $1,859 million

ACCOUNTING VOCABULARY

benchmarking The comparison of a company to a standard set by other companies, with a view toward improvement. (p. 626)

capital charge The amount that shareholders and lenders charge a company for the use of their money. Calculated as (Notes payable + Current maturities of long-term debt + Long-term debt + Shareholders' equity) × Cost of capital. (p. 642)

common-size statement A financial statement that reports only percentages (no dollar amounts). (p. 625)

cost of capital A weighted average of the returns demanded by the company's shareholders and lenders. (p. 642)

dividend yield Ratio of dividends per share to the stock's market price per share. Tells the percentage of a share's market value that the company returns to shareholders as dividends. (p. 641)

economic value added (EVA®) Used to evaluate a company's operating performance. EVA® combines the concepts of accounting income and corporate finance to measure whether the company's operations have increased shareholder wealth.

EVA® = Net income + Interest expense − Capital charge. (p. 642)

efficient capital market A capital market in which market prices fully reflect all information available to the public. (p. 643)

horizontal analysis Study of percentage changes in comparative financial statements. (p. 622)

price/earnings ratio Ratio of the market price of a common share to the company's earnings per share. Measures the value that the stock market places on $1 of a company's earnings. (p. 640)

rate of return on net sales Ratio of net income to net sales. A measure of profitability. Also called *return on sales*. (p. 638)

return on equity Another name for *rate of return on common shareholders' equity*. (p. 639)

trend percentages A form of horizontal analysis that indicates the direction a business is taking. (p. 623)

vertical analysis Analysis of a financial statement that reveals the relationship of each statement item to a specified base, which is the 100% figure. (p. 625)

working capital Current assets minus current liabilities; measures a business's ability to meet its short-term obligations with its current assets. (p. 632)

ASSESS YOUR PROGRESS

MyAccountingLab Make the grade with MyAccountingLab: The exercises and problems marked in red can be found on MyAccountingLab at www.myaccountinglab.com. You can practise them as often as you want, and they feature step by step guided solutions to help you find the right answer.

SHORT EXERCISES

Horizontal analysis of revenues and net income
(Obj. 1)

S13-1 Cannes Corporation reported the following amounts on its 2009 comparative income statement.

(In thousands)	2009	2008	2007
Revenues	$10,889	$10,095	$9,777
Total expenses	5,985	5,604	5,194

Perform a horizontal analysis of revenues and net income—both in dollar amounts and in percentages—for 2009 and 2008.

Trend analysis of sales and net income
(Obj. 1)

S13-2 Zoobilee Inc. reported the following sales and net income amounts:

(In thousands)	2009	2008	2007	2006
Sales	$9,180	$8,990	$8,770	$8,550
Net income	520	500	460	400

Show Zoobilee's trend percentages for sales and net income. Use 2006 as the base year.

Vertical analysis to correct a cash shortage
(Obj. 2)

S13-3 Vision Software Limited reported the following amounts on its balance sheets at December 31, 2009, 2008, and 2007.

	2009	2008	2007
Cash	$ 6,000	$ 6,000	$ 5,000
Receivables, net	30,000	22,000	19,000
Inventory	148,000	106,000	74,000
Prepaid expenses	2,000	2,000	1,000
Property, plant, and equipment, net	96,000	88,000	87,000
Total assets	$282,000	$224,000	$186,000

Sales and profits are high. Nevertheless, Vision is experiencing a cash shortage. Perform a vertical analysis of Vision Software's assets at the end of years 2009, 2008, and 2007. Use the analysis to explain the reason for the cash shortage.

S13-4 Porterfield Inc. and Beasley Ltd. are competitors. Compare the two companies by converting their condensed income statements to common size.

Common-size income statements of two companies **(Obj. 3)**

(In millions)	Porterfield	Beasley
Net sales..	$9,489	$19,536
Cost of goods sold..	5,785	14,101
Selling and administrative expenses	2,690	3,846
Interest expense	59	16
Other expense..	34	38
Income tax expense..	331	597
Net income	$ 590	$ 938

Which company earned more net income? Which company's net income was a higher percentage of its net sales? Which company is more profitable? Explain your answer.

S13-5 Examine the financial data of RubberMate Corporation in Exhibit 13-8, page 632. Show how to compute RubberMate's current ratio for each year from 2007 through 2009. Is the company's ability to pay its current liabilities improving or deteriorating?

Evaluating the trend in a company's current ratio **(Obj. 5, 6)**

S13-6 Use the Metro Inc. balance sheet data in Exhibit 13-3, page 624.

Evaluating a company's acid-test ratio **(Obj. 5, 6)**

1. Compute Metro's acid-test ratio at September 27, 2008 and September 29, 2007.
2. Compare Metro's ratio values to those of Enbridge, Research In Motion, and Loblaw on page 634. Is Metro's acid-test ratio strong or weak? Explain.

S13-7 Use Metro Inc.'s 2008 income statement and balance sheet to compute the following:

Computing inventory turnover and days' sales in receivables **(Obj. 5)**

a. Metro's rate of inventory turnover for 2008. Assume 60% cost of sales.
b. Days' sales in average receivables during 2008. (Round dollar amounts to 1 decimal place.)
    Do these measures look strong or weak? Give the reason for your answer.

S13-8 Use the financial statements of Metro Inc.

Measuring ability to pay long-term debt **(Obj. 5, 6**

1. Compute the company's debt ratio at September 30, 2008. In which text exhibit does this ratio value appear?
2. Compute the company's times-interest-earned ratio for 2008. Financial costs represent interest expense.
3. Is Metro's ability to pay liabilities and interest expense strong or weak? Comment on the value of each ratio computed for requirements 1 and 2.

S13-9 Use the financial statements of Metro Inc. to locate or, if necessary, to compute these profitability measures for 2008. Show each computation.

Measuring profitability **(Obj. 5, 6)**

a. Rate of return on sales.
b. Rate of return on total assets
c. Rate of return on common shareholders' equity
    Are these rates of return strong or weak? Explain.

S13-10 The annual report of Classic Cars Inc. for the year ended December 31, 2009, included the following items (in thousands):

Computing EPS and the price/ earnings ratio **(Obj. 5)**

Preferred shares outstanding, $4, 5,000 issued	$500
Net income...	$990
Number of common shares outstanding	200

1. Compute earnings per share (EPS) and the price/earnings ratio for Classic Cars' common shares. Round to the nearest cent. The price of a common share of Classic Car is $77.60.
2. How much does the stock market say $1 of Classic Cars' net income is worth?

Using ratio data to reconstruct an income statement
(Obj. 5)

S13-11 A skeleton of Hill Country Florist Limited's income statement appears as follows (amounts in thousands):

Income Statement	
Net sales	$7,278
Cost of goods sold	(a)
Selling expenses	1,510
Administrative expenses	351
Interest expense	(b)
Other expenses	126
Income before taxes	1,042
Income tax expense	(c)
Net income	$ (d)

Use the following ratio data to complete Hill Country Florist's income statement:

a. Inventory turnover was 5 (beginning inventory was $775, ending inventory was $767).
b. Rate of return on sales is 0.12.

Using ratio data to reconstruct a balance sheet
(Obj. 5)

S13-12 A skeleton of Hill Country Florist Limited's balance sheet appears as follows (amounts in thousands):

Balance Sheet			
Cash	$ 253	Total current liabilities	$1,164
Receivables	(a)	Long-term debt	(e)
Inventories	555	Other long-term liabilities	826
Prepaid expenses	(b)		
Total current assets	(c)		
Property, plant, and		Common shares	185
equipment, net	(d)	Retained earnings	2,846
Other assets	1,150	Total liabilities and	
Total assets	$6,315	shareholders' equity	$ (f)

Use the following ratio data to complete Hill Country Florist's balance sheet:

a. Debt ratio is 0.52.
b. Current ratio is 1.20.
c. Acid-test ratio is 0.70.

Measuring economic value added
(Obj. 7)

S13-13 Compute economic value added (EVA®) for Hill Country Florist Inc. The company's cost of capital is 12%. Net income was $695 thousand, interest expense was $394 thousand, beginning long-term debt was $1,294 thousand, and beginning shareholders' equity was $3,031 thousand. Round all amounts to the nearest thousand dollars.

Should the company's shareholders be happy with the EVA®?

EXERCISES

Computing year-to-year changes in working capital
(Obj. 1)

E13-14 What were the dollar amount of change and the percentage of each change in Rocky Mountain Lodge Limited's working capital during 2009 and 2008? Is this trend favourable or unfavourable?

	2009	2008	2007
Total current assets	$326,000	$290,000	$280,000
Total current liabilities	170,000	167,000	150,000

E13-15 Prepare a horizontal analysis of the comparative income statement of Stamps Music Ltd. Round percentage changes to the nearest one-tenth percent (3 decimal places).

Horizontal analysis of an income statement
(Obj. 1)

Stamps Music Ltd.
Comparative Income Statement
For the Years Ended December 31, 2009 and 2008

	2009	2008
Total revenue	$403,000	$430,000
Expenses:		
Cost of goods sold	$188,000	$202,000
Selling and general expenses	93,000	90,000
Interest expense	4,000	10,000
Income tax expense	37,000	42,000
Total expenses	322,000	344,000
Net income	$ 81,000	$ 86,000

E13-16 Compute trend percentages for Carmel Valley Sales & Service Ltd. total revenue and net income for the following 5-year period, using year 0 as the base year. Round to the nearest full percent.

Computing trend percentages
(Obj. 1)

(In thousands)	Year 4	Year 3	Year 2	Year 1	Year 0
Total revenue	$1,418	$1,287	$1,106	$1,009	$1,043
Net income	125	104	93	81	85

Which grew faster during the period, total revenue or net income?

E13-17 Cobra Golf Limited has requested that you perform a vertical analysis of its balance sheet to determine the component percentages of its assets, liabilities, and shareholders' equity.

Vertical analysis of a balance sheet
(Obj. 2)

Cobra Golf Limited
Balance Sheet
December 31, 2009

Assets	
Total current assets	$ 92,000
Property, plant, and equipment, net	247,000
Other assets	35,000
Total assets	$374,000
Liabilities	
Total current liabilities	$ 48,000
Long-term debt	108,000
Total liabilities	156,000
Shareholders' Equity	
Total shareholders' equity	218,000
Total liabilities and shareholders' equity	$374,000

E13-18 Prepare a comparative common-size income statement for Stamps Music Ltd. using the 2009 and 2008 data of Exercise 13-15 and rounding percentages to one-tenth percent (3 decimal places).

Preparing a common-size income statement
(Obj. 3

E13-19 Identify any weaknesses revealed by the cash flow statement of Holland Marsh Farms Limited.

Holland Marsh Farms Limited
Cash Flow Statement
For the Current Year

Operating activities:		
Income from operations		$ 42,000
Add (subtract) noncash items:		
Amortization	$ 23,000	
Net increase in current assets other than cash	(45,000)	
Net decrease in current liabilities exclusive of short-term debt ...	(7,000)	(29,000)
Net cash provided by operating activities		13,000
Investing activities:		
Sale of property, plant, and equipment		101,000
Financing activities:		
Issuance of bonds payable	$ 102,000	
Payment of short-term debt	(159,000)	
Payment of long-term debt	(79,000)	
Payment of dividends	(42,000)	
Net cash used for financing activities		(178,000)
Increase (decrease) in cash		$ (64,000)

E13-20 The financial statements of National News Inc. include the following items:

	Current Year	Preceding Year
Balance Sheet:		
Cash	$ 17,000	$ 22,000
Short-term investments	11,000	26,000
Net receivables	64,000	73,000
Inventory	77,000	71,000
Prepaid expenses	16,000	8,000
Total current assets	$185,000	$200,000
Total current liabilities	$111,000	$ 91,000
Income Statement:		
Net credit sales	$654,000	
Cost of goods sold	327,000	

❚ Required

Compute the following ratios for the current year:

a. Current ratio
b. Acid-test ratio
c. Inventory turnover

d. Accounts receivable turnover
e. Days' sales in average receivables

E13-21 Patio Furniture Inc. has asked you to determine whether the company's ability to pay its current liabilities and long-term debts improved or deteriorated during 2009. To answer this question, compute the following ratios for 2009 and 2008.

a. Current ratio
b. Acid-test ratio

c. Debt ratio
d. Times-interest-earned ratio

Summarize the results of your analysis in a written report.

	2009	2008
Cash	$ 61,000	$ 47,000
Short-term investments	28,000	—
Net receivables	142,000	116,000
Inventory	286,000	263,000
Prepaid expenses	11,000	9,000
Total assets	643,000	489,000
Total current liabilities	255,000	221,000
Long-term debt	46,000	52,000
Income from operations	165,000	158,000
Interest expense	40,000	39,000

E13-22 Compute four ratios that measure ability to earn profits for PGI Decor Inc., whose comparative income statement follows:

Analyzing profitability
(Obj. 5, 6)

PGI Decor Inc.
Comparative Income Statement
For the Years Ended December 31, 2009 and 2008

Dollars in thousands	2009	2008
Net sales	$174,000	$158,000
Cost of goods sold	93,000	86,000
Gross profit	81,000	72,000
Selling and general expenses	46,000	41,000
Income from operations	35,000	31,000
Interest expense	9,000	10,000
Income before income tax	26,000	21,000
Income tax expense	9,000	8,000
Net income	$ 17,000	$ 13,000

Additional data:

	2009	2008	2007
Total assets	$204,000	$191,000	$171,000
Common shareholders' equity	$ 96,000	$ 89,000	$ 79,000
Preferred dividends	$ 3,000	$ 3,000	$ 0
Common shares outstanding during the year	21,000	20,000	18,000

Did the company's operating performance improve or deteriorate during 2009?

E13-23 Evaluate the common shares of Phillips Distributing Limited as an investment. Specifically, use the three share ratios to determine whether the common shares increased or decreased in attractiveness during the past year.

Evaluating shares as an investment
(Obj. 5, 6)

	2009	2008
Net income	$112,000	$ 96,000
Common share dividends	25,000	20,000
Total shareholders' equity at year-end (includes 80,000 common shares)	580,000	500,000
Preferred shares, $8, 1,000 shares issued	100,000	100,000
Market price per common share at year-end	$ 22.50	$ 16.75

Using economic value added to measure corporate performance
(Obj. 7)

E13-24 Two companies with different economic value added (EVA®) profiles are **Amazon.com** and **eBay**. Selected data from the two companies' financial statements are presented here (in millions):

	Amazon.com	eBay
Balance sheet data:		
Total assets	$ 4,363	$13,494
Interest-bearing debt	$ 1,247	$ 0
All other liabilities	2,685	2,589
Shareholders' equity	431	10,905
Total liabilities and equity	$ 4,363	$13,494
Income statement data:		
Total revenue	$10,711	$ 3,271
Interest expense	$ 78	$ 9
Net income	$ 190	$ 778

❙ *Required*

1. Before performing any calculations, which company do you think represents the better investment? Give your reasons.
2. Compute the EVA® for each company and then decide which company's shares you would rather hold as an investment. Assume both companies' cost of capital is 10%.

CHALLENGE EXERCISES

Using ratio data to reconstruct a company's balance sheet
(Obj. 2, 3, 5)

E13-25 The following data (dollar amounts in millions) are taken from the financial statements of Phase 1 Industries Inc.

Total liabilities	$11,800
Preferred shares	$ 0
Total current assets	$10,200
Accumulated amortization	$ 1,400
Debt ratio	59%
Current ratio	1.50

❙ *Required*

Complete the following condensed balance sheet. Report amounts to the nearest million dollars.

Current assets		$?
Property, plant, and equipment	$?	
Less Accumulated amortization	(?)	?
Total assets		$?
Current liabilities		$?
Long-term liabilities		?
Shareholders' equity		?
Total liabilities and shareholders' equity		$?

Using ratio data to reconstruct a company's income statement
(Obj. 2, 3, 5)

E13-26 The following data (dollar amounts in millions) are from the financial statements of Provincial Industry Limited.

Average shareholders' equity	$3,600
Interest expense	$ 400
Preferred shares	$ 0
Operating income as a percent of sales	25%
Rate of return on shareholders' equity	20%
Income tax rate	40%

I *Required*

Complete the following condensed income statement. Report amounts to the nearest million dollars.

Sales	$?
Operating expense	?
Operating income	?
Interest expense	?
Pretax income	?
Income tax expense	?
Net income	$?

QUIZ

Test your understanding of financial statement analysis by answering the following questions. Select the best choice from among the possible answers given. Use the Canada Technology Corporation (CTC) financial statements to answer the questions that follow.

Canada Technology Corporation
Consolidated Statements of Financial Position
(In millions)

	December 31, 2009	December 31, 2008
Assets		
Current assets:		
Cash and cash equivalents	$ 4,317	$ 4,232
Short-term investments	835	406
Accounts receivable, net	3,635	2,586
Inventories	327	306
Other	1,519	1,394
Total current assets	10,633	8,924
Property, plant, and equipment, net	1,517	913
Investments	6,770	5,267
Other noncurrent assets	391	366
Total assets	$19,311	$15,470
Liabilities and Shareholders' Equity		
Current liabilities:		
Accounts payable	$ 7,316	$ 5,989
Accrued and other	3,580	2,944
Total current liabilities	10,896	8,933
Long-term debt	505	506
Other noncurrent liabilities	1,630	1,158
Commitments and contingent liabilities	—	—
Total liabilities	13,031	10,597
Shareholders' equity:		
Preferred shares; shares issued: 0	—	—
Common shares; shares authorized: 7,000; shares issued;		
2,556 and 2,579 respectively	284	1,479
Retained earnings	6,131	3,486
Other comprehensive loss	(83)	(33)
Other	(52)	(59)
Total shareholders' equity	6,280	4,873
Total liabilities and shareholders' equity	$19,311	$15,470

Canada Technology Corporation
Consolidated Statements of Income
(In millions, except per share amounts)

	Years Ended December 31,		
	2009	2008	2007
Net revenue	$41,444	$35,404	$31,168
Cost of goods sold	33,892	29,055	25,661
Gross profit	7,552	6,349	5,507
Operating expenses:			
Selling, general, and administrative	3,544	3,050	2,784
Research, development, and engineering	464	455	452
Special charges	—	—	482
Total operating expenses	4,008	3,505	3,718
Operating income	3,544	2,844	1,789
Investment and other income (loss), net	180	183	(58)
Income before income taxes	3,724	3,027	1,731
Income tax expense	1,079	905	485
Net income	$ 2,645	$ 2,122	$ 1,246
Earnings per common share:			
Basic	$ 1.03	$ 0.82	$ 0.48

Q13-27 During 2009, CTC's total assets
a. Increased by $8,341 million
b. Increased by 24.8%
c. Both a and b
d. Increased by 19.9%

Q13-28 CTC's current ratio at year-end 2009 is closest to
a. 1.2
b. 1.1
c. 1.0
d. 0.8

Q13-29 CTC's acid-test ratio at year-end 2009 is closest to
a. 0.80
b. 0.65
c. 0.47
d. $8,787 million

Q13-30 What is the largest single item included in CTC's debt ratio at December 31, 2009?
a. Cash and cash equivalents
b. Accounts payable
c. Investments
d. Common shares

Q13-31 Using the earliest year available as the base year, the trend percentage for CTC's net revenue during 2009 was
a. 117%
b. Up by $10,276 million
c. Up by 17.1%
d. 133%

Q13-32 CTC's common-size income statement for 2009 would report cost of goods sold as
a. $33,892 million
b. Up by 16.6%
c. 81.8%
d. 132.1%

Q13-33 CTC's days' sales in average receivables during 2009 was
a. 22 days
b. 27 days
c. 32 days
d. 114 days

Q13-34 CTC's inventory turnover during fiscal year 2009 was
a. Very slow
b. 54 times
c. 107 times
d. 129 times

Q13-35 CTC's long-term debt bears interest at 6%. During the year ended December 31, 2009, CTC's times-interest-earned ratio was

a. 117 times　　　　　　　　　　c. 100 times

b. 110 times　　　　　　　　　　d. 125 times

Q13-36 CTC's trend of return on sales is

a. Improving　　　　　　　　　　c. Stuck at 6%

b. Declining　　　　　　　　　　d. Worrisome

Q13-37 How many common shares did CTC have outstanding, on average, during 2009? Hint: Use the earnings per share formula.

a. 2,721 million　　　　　　　　c. 2,645 million

b. 2,701 million　　　　　　　　d. 2,568 million

Q13-38 Book value per common share of CTC outstanding at December 31, 2009, was

a. $2.72　　　　　　　　　　　　c. $6,280

b. $4.37　　　　　　　　　　　　d. $2.46

PROBLEMS

(GROUP A)

P13-39A Net sales, net income, and total assets for Smart Pak Inc. for a 5-year period follow:

Trend percentages, return on sales, and comparison with the industry
(Obj. 1, 5, 6)

(In thousands)	2009	2008	2007	2006	2005
Net sales	$367	$313	$266	$281	$197
Net income	37	21	11	18	16
Total assets	286	254	209	197	185

❙ Required

1. Compute trend percentages for each item for 2006 through 2009. Use 2005 as the base year and round to the nearest percent.

2. Compute the rate of return on net sales for 2007 through 2009, rounding to 3 decimal places.

3. How does Smart Pak's return on net sales compare with that of the industry? In the packaging industry, rates above 8% are considered good, and rates above 10% are outstanding.

P13-40A Top managers of Medical Products Inc. have asked for your help in comparing the company's profit performance and financial position with the average for the industry. The accountant has given you the company's income statement and balance sheet and also the following data for the industry:

Evaluating a stock as an investment
(Obj. 5, 6)

Medical Products Inc. **Income Statement Compared with Industry Average** **For the Year Ended December 31, 2009**		
	Medical Products	**Industry Average**
Net sales	$957,000	100.0%
Cost of goods sold	652,000	55.9
Gross profit	305,000	44.1
Operating expenses	200,000	28.1
Operating income	105,000	16.0
Other expenses	3,000	2.4
Net income	$102,000	13.6%

Medical Products Inc.
Balance Sheet Compared with Industry Average
December 31, 2009

	Medical Products	Industry Average
Current assets..	$486,000	74.4%
Fixed assets, net	117,000	20.0
Intangible assets, net	24,000	0.6
Other assets...	3,000	5.0
Total...	$630,000	100.0%
Current liabilities...	$245,000	45.6%
Long-term liabilities	114,000	19.0
Shareholders' equity	271,000	35.4
Total...	$630,000	100.0%

I *Required*

1. Prepare a common-size income statement and balance sheet for Medical Products. The first column of each statement should present Medical Products' common-size statement, and the second column should show the industry averages.

2. For the profitability analysis, compute Medical Products' (a) ratio of gross profit to net sales, (b) ratio of operating income to net sales, and (c) ratio of net income to net sales. Compare these figures with the industry average. Is Medical Products' profit performance better or worse than the average for the industry?

3. For the analysis of financial position, compute Medical Products' (a) ratios of current assets and current liabilities to total assets and (b) ratio of shareholders' equity to total assets. Compare these ratios with the industry averages. Is Medical Products' financial position better or worse than the average for the industry?

Using the cash flow statement for decision making
(Obj. 4)

P13-41A You are evaluating two companies as possible investments. The two companies, similar in size, are commuter airlines that fly passengers up and down the West Coast. All other available information has been analyzed and your investment decision depends on the cash flow statement.

Commonwealth Airlines (Comair) Limited
Cash Flow Statement
For the Years Ended November 30, 2009 and 2008

	2009	2008
Operating activities:		
Net income (net loss)...	$(67,000)	$154,000
Adjustments for noncash items:		
Total	84,000	(23,000)
Net cash provided by operating activities...............	17,000	131,000
Investing activities:		
Purchase of property, plant, and equipment	$ (50,000)	$(91,000)
Sale of long-term investments	52,000	4,000
Net cash provided by (used for) investing activities...	2,000	(87,000)
Financing activities:		
Issuance of short-term notes payable	122,000	143,000
Payment of short-term notes payable	(179,000)	(134,000)
Payment of cash dividends.....................................	(45,000)	(64,000)
Net cash used for financing activities	(102,000)	(55,000)
Increase (decrease) in cash....................................	(83,000)	(11,000)
Cash balance at beginning of year...........................	92,000	103,000
Cash balance at the end of year.................................	$ 9,000	$ 92,000

	Jetway Inc.	
	Cash Flow Statement	
	For the Years Ended November 30, 2009 and 2008	

	2009	2008
Operating activities:		
Net income...	$184,000	$ 131,000
Adjustments for noncash items:		
Total	64,000	62,000
Net cash provided by operating activities	248,000	193,000
Investing activities:		
Purchase of property, plant, and equipment..... $(303,000)		$(453,000)
Sale of property, plant, and equipment 46,000		72,000
Net cash used for investing activities	(257,000)	(381,000)
Financing activities:		
Issuance of long-term notes payable 174,000		118,000
Payment of short-term notes payable............... (66,000)		(18,000)
Net cash provided by financing activities.........	108,000	100,000
Increase (decrease) in cash	99,000	(88,000)
Cash balance at beginning of year	116,000	204,000
Cash balance at end of year	$215,000	$ 116,000

❙ Required

Discuss the relative strengths and weaknesses of Comair and Jetway. Conclude your discussion by recommending one of the companies' shares as an investment.

P13-42A Financial statement data of Metro Engineering Limited include the following items:

Effects of business transactions on selected ratios
(Obj. 5, 6)

Cash..	$ 47,000	Accounts payable........................	$142,000
Short-term investments................	21,000	Accrued liabilities	50,000
Accounts receivable, net...............	102,000	Long-term notes payable.............	146,000
Inventories....................................	274,000	Other long-term liabilities...........	78,000
Prepaid expenses..........................	15,000	Net income	104,000
Total assets...................................	933,000	Number of common shares	
Short-term notes payable	72,000	outstanding.............................	22,000

❙ Required

1. Compute Metro's current ratio, debt ratio, and earnings per share. Use the following format for your answer. (Use dollar and share amounts in thousands except for EPS.)

Requirement 1		
Current ratio	**Debt ratio**	**Earnings per share**

2. Compute the three ratios after evaluating the effect of each transaction that follows. Consider each transaction *separately*.
   a. Borrowed $27,000 on a long-term note payable
   b. Issued 10,000 common shares, receiving cash of $108,000
   c. Paid short-term notes payable, $51,000
   d. Purchased merchandise of $48,000 on account, debiting Inventory
   e. Received cash on account, $6,000

Format your answer as follows:

Requirement 2 Transaction (letter)	Current ratio	Debt ratio	Earnings per share

Using ratios to evaluate a share investment
(Obj. 5, 6)

P13-43A Comparative financial statement data of Crest Optical Inc. follow:

Crest Optical Inc.
Comparative Income Statement
For the Years Ended December 31, 2009 and 2008

	2009	2008
Net sales	$667,000	$599,000
Cost of goods sold	378,000	313,000
Gross profit	289,000	286,000
Operating expenses	129,000	147,000
Income from operations	160,000	139,000
Interest expense	37,000	41,000
Income before income tax	123,000	98,000
Income tax expense	44,000	43,000
Net income	$ 79,000	$ 55,000

Crest Optical Inc.
Comparative Balance Sheet
December 31, 2009 and 2008

	2009	2008	2007*
Current assets:			
Cash	$ 37,000	$ 40,000	
Current receivables, net	208,000	151,000	$138,000
Inventories	152,000	186,000	144,000
Prepaid expenses	5,000	20,000	
Total current assets	402,000	397,000	
Property, plant, and equipment, net	287,000	256,000	
Total assets	$689,000	$653,000	607,000
Total current liabilities	$286,000	$217,000	
Long-term liabilities	145,000	185,000	
Total liabilities	431,000	402,000	
Preferred shareholders' equity, $4	50,000	50,000	
Common shareholders' equity	208,000	201,000	198,000
Total liabilities and shareholders' equity	$689,000	$653,000	

*Selected 2007 amounts.

Other information:

1. Market price of Crest common shares: $61 at December 31, 2009, and $45.50 at December 31, 2008.
2. Common shares outstanding: 15,000 during 2009 and 14,000 during 2008.
3. Preferred shares outstanding: 500 during 2009 and 2008.
4. All sales on credit.

❙ *Required*

1. Compute the following ratios for 2009 and 2008:

   a. Current ratio

   b. Inventory turnover

   c. Times-interest-earned ratio

   d. Return on assets

   e. Return on common shareholders' equity

   f. Earnings per share

   g. Price/earnings ratio

2. Decide (a) whether Crest's financial position improved or deteriorated during 2009 and (b) whether the investment attractiveness of Crest's common shares appears to have increased or decreased.

3. How will what you learned in this problem help you evaluate an investment?

P13-44A Assume that you are considering purchasing shares as an investment. You have narrowed the choice to two Internet firms, Video.com Inc. and On-Line Express Ltd., and have assembled the following data.

Using ratios to decide between two share investments; measuring economic value added
(Obj. 5, 6, 7)

Selected income statement data for current year:

	Video	Express
Net sales (all on credit)...	$603,000	$519,000
Cost of goods sold...	454,000	387,000
Income from operations	93,000	72,000
Interest expense	—	12,000
Net income	56,000	38,000

Selected balance sheet and market price data at *end* of current year:

	Video	Express
Current assets:		
Cash..	$ 25,000	$ 39,000
Short-term investments	6,000	13,000
Current receivables, net....................................	189,000	164,000
Inventories	211,000	183,000
Prepaid expenses..	19,000	15,000
Total current assets...	$450,000	$414,000
Total assets..	$974,000	$938,000
Total current liabilities	366,000	338,000
Total liabilities..	667,000*	691,000*
Preferred shares $4.00 (250 shares)............................		25,000
Common shares (150,000 shares)	150,000	
(20,000 shares)		100,000
Total shareholders' equity	307,000	247,000
Market price per common share..................................	$ 9	$ 47.50

*Includes Long-term debt; Video $-0-, and Express $350,000

Selected balance sheet data at *beginning* of current year:

	Video	Express
Current receivables, net...	$142,000	$193,000
Inventories	209,000	197,000
Total assets...	842,000	909,000
Long-term debt	—	303,000
Preferred shares, $4.00 (250 shares)........................		25,000
Common shares (150,000 shares)	150,000	
(20,000 shares)		100,000
Total shareholders' equity	263,000	215,000

Your strategy is to invest in companies that have low price/earnings ratios but appear to be in good shape financially. Assume that you have analyzed all other factors and that your decision depends on the results of ratio analysis.

❙ Required

1. Compute the following ratios for both companies for the current year and decide which company's shares better fit your investment strategy based on the

  a. Acid-test ratio

  b. Inventory turnover

  c. Days' sales in average receivables

  d. Debt ratio

  e. Times-interest-earned ratio

  f. Return on common shareholders' equity

  g. Earnings per share

  h. Price/earnings ratio

2. Compute each company's economic value added (EVA®) measure and determine whether the companies' EVA® measures confirm or alter your investment decision. Each company's cost of capital is 10%.

Analyzing a company based on its ratios
(Obj. 6)

P13-45A Take the role of an investment analyst at **Merrill Lynch**. It is your job to recommend investments for your client. The only information you have is the following ratio values for two companies in the direct mail industry.

Ratio	Fast Mail Ltd.	Message Direct Inc.
Days' sales in receivables	51	43
Inventory turnover	9	7
Gross profit percentage	62%	71%
Net income as a percent of sales	16%	14%
Times interest earned	12	18
Return on equity	29%	36%
Return on assets	19%	14%

Write a report to the Merrill Lynch investment committee. Recommend one company's shares over the other. State the reasons for your recommendation.

(GROUP B)

Trend percentages, return on common equity, and comparison with the industry
(Obj. 1, 5, 6)

P13-46B Net revenues, net income, and common shareholders' equity for Accenté Ltée for a 5-year period follow.

(In thousands)	2009	2008	2007	2006	2005
Net revenues	$781	$714	$681	$662	$581
Net income	41	35	32	28	20
Ending common shareholders' equity	386	354	330	296	263

❙ Required

1. Compute trend percentages for each item for 2006 through 2009. Use 2005 as the base year. Round to the nearest percent.

2. Compute the rate of return on common shareholders' equity for 2007 through 2009, rounding to 3 decimal places. Accenté has no preferred shares outstanding.

3. In this industry, rates of return on common shareholders' equity of 13% are average, rates above 16% are good, and rates above 20% are outstanding. How does Accenté's return on common shareholders' equity compare with the industry?

P13-47B Pathfinder Inc. has asked you to compare the company's profit performance and financial position with the industry average. The proprietor has given you the company's income statement and balance sheet as well as the industry average data for retailers.

Common-size statements, analysis of profitability, and comparison with the industry
(Obj. 2, 3, 5, 6)

Pathfinder Inc. Income Statement Compared with Industry Average For the Year Ended December 31, 2009		
	Pathfinder	Industry Average
Net sales..	$700,000	100.0%
Cost of goods sold..	497,000	65.8
Gross profit	203,000	34.2
Operating expenses..	163,000	19.7
Operating income	40,000	14.5
Other expenses	3,000	0.4
Net income	$ 37,000	14.1%

Pathfinder Inc. Balance Sheet Compared with Industry Average December 31, 2009		
	Pathfinder	Industry Average
Current assets	$300,000	70.9%
Fixed assets, net...	74,000	23.6
Intangible assets, net	4,000	0.8
Other assets	22,000	4.7
Total	$400,000	100.0%
Current liabilities	$206,000	48.1%
Long-term liabilities	64,000	16.6
Shareholders' equity..	130,000	35.3
Total	$400,000	100.0%

❙ Required

1. Prepare a common-size income statement and a balance sheet for Pathfinder. The first column of each statement should present Pathfinder's common-size statement, and the second column, the industry averages.

2. For the profitability analysis, compute Pathfinder's (a) ratio of gross profit to net sales, (b) ratio of operating income to net sales, and (c) ratio of net income to net sales. Compare these figures with the industry averages. Is Pathfinder's profit performance better or worse than the industry average?

3. For the analysis of financial position, compute Pathfinder's (a) ratio of current assets to total assets, and (b) ratio of shareholders' equity to total assets. Compare these ratios with the industry averages. Is Pathfinder's financial position better or worse than the industry averages?

P13-48B You have been asked to evaluate two companies as possible investments. The two companies, Norfolk Industries Inc. and Strafford Crystal Limited, are similar in size. Assume that all other available information has been analyzed, and the decision concerning which company's shares to purchase depends on their cash-flow data.

Using the cash flow statement for decision making
(Obj. 4)

❙ Required

Discuss the relative strengths and weaknesses of each company. Conclude your discussion by recommending one company's shares as an investment.

Norfolk Industries Inc.
Cash Flow Statement
For the Years Ended September 30, 2009 and 2008

	2009		2008
Operating activities:			
Net income		$ 17,000	$ 44,000
Adjustments for noncash items:			
Total		(14,000)	(4,000)
Net cash provided by operating activities		3,000	40,000
Investing activities:			
Purchase of property, plant, and equipment	$ (13,000)		$ (3,000)
Sale of property, plant, and equipment	86,000		79,000
Net cash provided by investing activities		73,000	76,000
Financing activities:			
Issuance of short-term notes payable	43,000		19,000
Payment of short-term notes payable	(101,000)		(108,000)
Net cash used for financing activities		(58,000)	(89,000)
Increase in cash		18,000	27,000
Cash balance at beginning of year		31,000	4,000
Cash balance at end of year		$ 49,000	$ 31,000

Strafford Crystal Limited
Cash Flow Statement
For the Years Ended September 30, 2009 and 2008

	2009		2008
Operating activities:			
Net income		$ 89,000	$ 71,000
Adjustments for noncash items:			
Total		19,000	—
Net cash provided by operating activities		108,000	71,000
Investing activities:			
Purchase of property, plant, and equipment	$(121,000)		$(91,000)
Net cash used for investing activities		(121,000)	(91,000)
Financing activities:			
Issuance of long-term notes payable	46,000		43,000
Payment of short-term notes payable	(15,000)		(40,000)
Payment of cash dividends	(12,000)		(9,000)
Net cash provided by (used for) financing activities		19,000	(6,000)
Increase (decrease) in cash		6,000	(26,000)
Cash balance at beginning of year		54,000	80,000
Cash balance at end of year		$ 60,000	$ 54,000

Effects of business transactions on selected ratios
(Obj. 5, 6)

P13-49B Financial statement data of HiFlite Electronics Limited include the following items (dollars in thousands):

Cash	$ 22,000
Short-term investments	39,000
Accounts receivable, net	83,000
Inventories	141,000
Prepaid expenses	8,000
Total assets	677,000
Short-term notes payable	49,000
Accounts payable	103,000
Accrued liabilities	38,000
Long-term notes payable	160,000
Other long-term liabilities	31,000
Net income	91,000
Number of common shares outstanding	40,000

▍Required

1. Compute HiFlite's current ratio, debt ratio, and earnings per share. Use the following format for your answer:

Requirement 1

Current ratio	Debt ratio	Earnings per share

2. Compute the three ratios after evaluating the effect of each transaction that follows. Consider each transaction *separately*.

   a. Purchased store supplies of $46,000 on account
   b. Borrowed $125,000 on a long-term note payable
   c. Issued 5,000 common shares, receiving cash of $120,000
   d. Paid short-term notes payable, $32,000
   e. Received cash on account, $19,000

   Format your answer as follows:

Requirement 2

Transaction (letter)	Current ratio	Debt ratio	Earnings per share

P13-50B Comparative financial statement data of Mira TV Sales Ltd. follow.

Using ratios to evaluate a share investment
(Obj. 5, 6)

Mira TV Sales Ltd.
Comparative Income Statement
For the Years Ended December 31, 2009 and 2008

	2009	2008
Net sales	$662,000	$527,000
Cost of goods sold	429,000	318,000
Gross profit	233,000	209,000
Operating expenses	136,000	134,000
Income from operations	97,000	75,000
Interest expense	9,000	8,000
Income before income tax	88,000	67,000
Income tax expense	30,000	27,000
Net income	$ 58,000	$ 40,000

Mira TV Sales Ltd. **Comparative Balance Sheet** **December 31, 2009 and 2008**			
	2009	2008	2007*
Current assets:			
Cash	$ 96,000	$ 97,000	
Current receivables, net	162,000	116,000	$103,000
Inventories	147,000	162,000	207,000
Prepaid expenses	16,000	7,000	
Total current assets	421,000	382,000	
Property, plant, and equipment, net	214,000	178,000	
Total assets	$635,000	$560,000	598,000
Total current liabilities	$206,000	$223,000	
Long-term liabilities	119,000	117,000	
Total liabilities	325,000	340,000	
Preferred shareholders' equity, $6.00 (1,000 shares outstanding)	100,000	100,000	
Common shareholders' equity	210,000	120,000	90,000
Total liabilities and shareholders' equity	$635,000	$560,000	

*Selected 2007 amounts.

Other information:

1. Market price of Mira's common shares: $83 at December 31, 2009, and $62.50 at December 31, 2008

2. Common shares outstanding: 10,000 during 2009 and 9,000 during 2008

3. All sales on credit

▌Required

1. Compute the following ratios for 2009 and 2008:

   a. Current ratio

   b. Inventory turnover

   c. Times-interest-earned ratio

   d. Return on common shareholders' equity

   e. Earnings per share

   f. Price/earnings ratio

2. Decide (a) whether Mira's financial position improved or deteriorated during 2009 and (b) whether the investment attractiveness of Mira's common shares appears to have increased or decreased.

3. How will what you learned in this problem help you evaluate an investment?

P13-51B Assume that you are purchasing an investment and have decided to invest in a company in the publishing business. You have narrowed the choice to Thrifty Nickel Corp. and The Village Cryer Limited and have assembled the following data.

Selected income statement data for the current year:

Using ratios to decide between two share investments; measuring economic value added
(Obj. 5, 6, 7)

	Thrifty Nickel	Village Cryer
Net sales (all on credit)	$371,000	$497,000
Cost of goods sold	209,000	258,000
Income from operations	79,000	138,000
Interest expense	—	19,000
Net income	48,000	72,000

Selected balance sheet data at *beginning* of the current year:

	Thrifty Nickel	Village Cryer
Current receivables, net...	$ 40,000	$ 48,000
Inventories	93,000	88,000
Total assets...	259,000	270,000
Long-term debt	—	86,000
Preferred shares: 5%, $200 issued	—	20,000
Common shares: (10,000 shares)	10,000	
(5,000 shares)		12,500
Total shareholders' equity	118,000	126,000

Selected balance sheet and market price data at *end* of the current year:

	Thrifty Nickel	Village Cryer
Current assets:		
Cash...	$ 22,000	$ 19,000
Short-term investments	20,000	18,000
Current receivables, net...	42,000	46,000
Inventories	87,000	100,000
Prepaid expenses...	2,000	3,000
Total current assets...	$173,000	$186,000
Total assets...	265,000	328,000
Total current liabilities	108,000	98,000
Total liabilities...	108,000*	131,000*
Preferred shares: $5.00 (200 shares)		20,000
Common shares: (10,000 shares)	10,000	
(5,000 shares)		12,500
Total shareholders' equity	157,000	197,000
Market price per share of common share............................	$51	$112

*Includes Long-term debt: Thrifty Nickel $-0- and Village Cryer $86,000

Your strategy is to invest in companies that have low price/earnings ratios but appear to be in good shape financially. Assume that you have analyzed all other factors and your decision depends on the results of ratio analysis.

I Required

1. Compute the following ratios for both companies for the current year, and decide which company's shares better fit your investment strategy.

   a. Acid-test ratio

   b. Inventory turnover

   c. Days' sales in average receivables

   d. Debt ratio

   e. Times-interest-earned ratio

   f. Return on common shareholders' equity

   g. Earnings per share

   h. Price/earnings ratio

2. Compute each company's economic value added (EVA®) measure, and determine whether the companies' EVA® measures confirm or alter your investment decision. Each company's cost of capital is 12%.

Analyzing a company based on its ratios
(Obj. 6)

P13-52B Take the role of an investment analyst at **RBC Dominion Securities**. It is your job to recommend investments for your clients. The only information you have is the following ratio values for two companies in the pharmaceuticals industry.

Ratio	Pain Free Ltd.	Remedy Inc.
Days' sales in receivables	36	42
Inventory turnover	6	8
Gross profit percentage	49%	51%
Net income as a percent of sales	7.2%	8.3%
Times interest earned	16	9
Return on equity	32.3%	21.5%
Return on assets	12.1%	16.4%

Write a report to your investment committee. Recommend one company's shares over the other's. State the reasons for your recommendation.

APPLY YOUR KNOWLEDGE

DECISION CASES

Assessing the effects of transactions on a company
(Obj. 5, 6)

Case 1. Assume a major Canadian company had a bad year in 2009, when it suffered a $4.9 billion net loss. The loss pushed most of the return measures into the negative column and the current ratio dropped below 1.0. The company's debt ratio is still only 0.27. Assume top management is pondering ways to improve the company's ratios. In particular, management is considering the following transactions:

1. Sell off a segment of the business for $30 million (receiving half in cash and half in the form of a long-term note receivable). Book value of the segment business is $27 million.

2. Borrow $100 million on long-term debt.

3. Repurchase common shares for $500 million cash.

4. Write off one-fourth of goodwill carried on the books at $128 million.

5. Sell advertising at the normal gross profit of 60%. The advertisements run immediately.

6. Purchase trademarks from a competitor, paying $20 million cash and signing a 1-year note payable for $80 million.

❚ *Required*

1. Top management wants to know the effects of these transactions (increase, decrease, or no effect) on the following ratios of the company:
   a. Current ratio
   b. Debt ratio
   c. Times-interest-earned ratio
   d. Return on equity
   e. Book value per common share

2. Some of these transactions have an immediately positive effect on the company's financial condition. Some are definitely negative. Others have an effect that cannot be judged as clearly positive or negative. Evaluate each transaction's effect as positive, negative, or unclear.

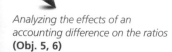

Analyzing the effects of an accounting difference on the ratios
(Obj. 5, 6)

Case 2. Company A uses the first-in, first-out (FIFO) method to account for its inventory, and Company B uses weighted-average cost. Analyze the effect of this difference in accounting methods on the two companies' ratio values. For each ratio discussed in this chapter, indicate which company will have the higher (and the lower) ratio value. Also identify those ratios that are unaffected by the inventory valuation difference. Ignore the effects of income taxes, and assume inventory costs are increasing. Then, based on your analysis of the ratios, summarize your conclusions as to which company looks better overall.

Case 3. Suppose you manage The Runner's Store Inc., a sporting goods store that lost money during the past year. To turn the business around, you must analyze the company and industry data for the current year to learn what is wrong. The company's and industry average data follow:

Identifying action to cut losses and establish profitability
(Obj. 2, 5, 6)

The Runner's Store Inc.
Common-Size Balance Sheet Data

	Runner's Store	Industry Average
Cash and short-term investments	3.0%	6.8%
Trade receivables, net	15.2	11.0
Inventory	64.2	60.5
Prepaid expenses	1.0	0.0
Total current assets	83.4	78.3
Fixed assets, net	12.6	15.2
Other assets	4.0	6.5
Total assets	100.0%	100.0%
Notes payable, short-term 12%	17.1%	14.0%
Accounts payable	21.1	25.1
Accrued liabilities	7.8	7.9
Total current liabilities	46.0	47.0
Long-term debt, 11%	19.7	16.4
Total liabilities	65.7	63.4
Common shareholders' equity	34.3	36.6
Total liabilities and shareholders' equity	100.0%	100.0%

The Runner's Store Inc.
Common-Size Income Statement Data

	Runner's Store	Industry Average
Net sales	100.0%	100.0%
Cost of sales	(68.2)	(64.8)
Gross profit	31.8	35.2
Operating expense	(37.1)	(32.3)
Operating income (loss)	(5.3)	2.9
Interest expense	(5.8)	(1.3)
Other revenue	1.1	0.3
Income (loss) before income tax	(10.0)	1.9
Income tax (expense) saving	4.4	(0.8)
Net income (loss)	(5.6)%	1.1%

❙ Required

On the basis of your analysis of these figures, suggest four courses of action The Runner's Store might take to reduce its losses and establish profitable operations. Give your reason for each suggestion.

ETHICAL ISSUE

Turnberry Golf Corporation's long-term debt agreements make certain demands on the business. For example, Turnberry may not repurchase common shares in excess of the balance of retained earnings. Also, long-term debt may not exceed shareholders' equity, and the current ratio may not fall below 1.50. If Turnberry fails to meet any of these requirements, the company's lenders have the authority to take over management of the company.

Changes in consumer demand have made it hard for Turnberry to attract customers. Current liabilities have mounted faster than current assets, causing the current ratio to fall to 1.47. Before releasing financial statements, Turnberry management is scrambling to improve the current ratio. The controller points out that an investment can be classified as either long-term or short-term, depending on management's intention. By deciding to convert an investment to cash within 1 year, Turnberry can classify the investment as short-term: a current asset. On the controller's recommendation, Turnberry's board of directors votes to reclassify long-term investments as short-term.

❚ *Required*

1. What effect will reclassifying the investments have on the current ratio? Is Turnberry's financial position stronger as a result of reclassifying the investments?

2. Shortly after the financial statements are released, sales improve; so, too, does the current ratio. As a result, Turnberry management decides not to sell the investments it had reclassified as short term. Accordingly, the company reclassifies the investments as long term. Has management behaved unethically? Give the reasoning underlying your answer.

FOCUS ON FINANCIALS

Measuring profitability and analyzing shares as an investment
(Obj. 1, 6)

Sun-Rype Products Ltd.

Use the 5-year summary of selected financial data for Sun-Rype Products to answer the following questions.

	2007	2006	2005	2004	2003
Net sales	$135,134	$130,622	$125,411	$115,214	$107,954
Gross profit	41,836	45,309	44,228	39,241	36,029
Net earnings	4,636	7,266	6,524	5,851	5,120
Cash flow from operating activities	10,266	5,739	14,354	5,750	9,220

❚ *Required*

1. Using 2003 as the base year, perform trend analysis of Sun-Rype's selected Financial Data for net sales, gross profit, net earnings, and net cash provided by operating activities for each year 2004 through 2007.

2. Evaluate Sun-Rype's operating performance during 2004 through 2007. Comment on each item computed. In your overall evaluation of performance, consider this information from the Management's Discussion and Analysis in the 2007 Annual Report.

OVERALL PERFORMANCE

Sun-Rype's net sales increased in 2007 by $4.5 million or 3.5% over 2006, to $135.1 million. The Company generated net earnings of $4.6 million in 2007, a decrease of $2.6 million, or 36.2%, over 2006.

The Company's results in the fourth quarter of 2007 were significantly impacted by the effects of a labour disruption that occurred over the last eight weeks of 2007. This labour disruption limited the Company's abilities to manufacture, distribute and promote its products.

Despite this setback, Sun-Rype's brands have evolved over time and are now making a greater connection with consumers through continued emphasis on the wholesome goodness of 100% fruit juices and 100% fruit snacks. This brand recognition coupled with continued product innovation has allowed Sun-Rype to expand sales once again in 2007.

Over the past three years, the Company has focused on the geographical expansion of its products. New markets have contributed positively to the current financial results.

FOCUS ON ANALYSIS

Mullen Group Income Fund

Use the Mullen Group financial statements in Appendix B at the end of this book to address the following questions:

Analyzing data
(Obj. 1, 6)

1. During 2007, Mullen Group had a loss before income taxes and earnings from equity investments. Prepare a common-size income statement for 2007 and 2006.

2. Discuss the results of Mullen Group based on the common-size income statement. Does the information in the cash flow statement support your conclusion?

3. In your opinion, what is the company's outlook for the future?

GROUP PROJECTS

Project 1. Select an industry in which you are interested, and use the leading company in that industry as the benchmark. Then select two other companies in the same industry. For each category of ratios in the Decision Guidelines feature on pages 644 and 645, compute at least two ratios for all three companies. Write a two-page report that compares the two companies with the benchmark company.

Project 2. Select a company and obtain its financial statements. Convert the income statement and the balance sheet to common size, and compare the company you selected to the industry average. **Risk Management Association's** *Annual Statement Studies,* **Dun & Bradstreet's** *Industry Norms & Key Business Ratios,* and **Prentice Hall's** *Almanac of Business and Industrial Financial Ratios* by Leo Troy publish common-size statements for most industries.

QUICK CHECK ANSWERS

1. *c ($1,833/$1,712.8 = 1.070)*

2. *c ($1,833/$17,140.5 = 0.107)*

3. *b (Net income: $1,471.4 − $893.5 = $577.9; $577.9/$893.5 = Increase of 64.7%)*

4. *a ($1,665.1/$25,525.1 = 0.065)*

5. *a*

6. $d\left[\dfrac{\$4,314.8}{(\$129.4 + \$111.7)/2}\right] = 35.8 \approx 36\ times$

7. *b [($492.8 + $734.5)/$2,485.8 = 0.49]*

8. $d\left[\dfrac{(\$734.5 + \$855.3)/2)}{\$17,140.5/365}\right] = 16.9 \approx 17\ days$

9. *a (Debt ratio is ($25,525.1 − $11,981.9)/$25,525.1 = 0.53. This debt ratio is lower than the average for most companies, given in the chapter as 0.62.)*

10. *d ($1,471.4/$17,140.5 = 0.086)*

11. $a \left[\dfrac{\$1,471.4}{(\$11,981.9 + \$10,280.9)/2} \right] = 0.132$

12. b ($\$26/\$1.16 = \$22.41$)

13. d ($\$0.40/\$26.00 = 0.015$)

14. c [$\$1,471.4 + \$388 - [(\$275.8 + \$9,703.6 + \$10,280.9) \times (0.08)] = \$238.6 \approx \$239$]

ANNUAL REPORT
**Financial Statements and Notes to the Financial Statements
for the Year Ended December 31, 2007**

Management is responsible for the preparation and integrity of the financial statements, including the maintenance of appropriate information systems, procedures and internal controls, and to ensure that information used internally or disclosed externally, including the financial statements and management's discussion and analysis, is complete and reliable.

Auditors' Report

To the Shareholders of Sun-Rype Products Ltd.

We have audited the balance sheets of Sun-Rype Products Ltd. as at December 31, 2007 and 2006 and the statements of operations and retained earnings and cash flows for the years then ended. These financial statements are the responsibility of the Company's management. Our responsibility is to express an opinion on these financial statements based on our audits.

We conducted our audits in accordance with Canadian generally accepted auditing standards. Those standards require that we plan and perform an audit to obtain reasonable assurance whether the financial statements are free of material misstatement. An audit includes examining, on a test basis, evidence supporting the amounts and disclosures in the financial statements. An audit also includes assessing the accounting principles used and significant estimates made by management, as well as evaluating the overall financial statement presentation.

In our opinion, these financial statements present fairly, in all material respects, the financial position of the Company as at December 31, 2007 and 2006 and the results of its operations and its cash flows for the years then ended in accordance with Canadian generally accepted accounting principles.

Deloitte & Touche LLP

Chartered Accountants
Vancouver, British Columbia
February 28, 2008

Sun-Rype Products Ltd.
Balance Sheets
As at December 31
(in thousands of dollars)

	2007	2006
Assets		
Current		
Cash and cash equivalents	$ 2,687	$ 1,534
Accounts receivable (note 4)	7,392	12,676
Income taxes receivable	818	-
Inventories (note 5)	17,304	18,708
Prepaid expenses	381	381
Future income taxes (note 6)	435	201
	29,017	33,500
Property, plant and equipment (note 7)	27,867	25,947
	$ 56,884	$ 59,447
Liabilities and Shareholders' Equity		
Current		
Promissory note payable (note 8)	$ 500	$ 600
Accounts payable and accrued liabilities	12,688	18,252
Unrealized foreign exchange loss	460	-
Income taxes payable	-	234
Current portion, long-term obligations (note 10)	321	211
	13,969	19,297
Long-term obligations (note 10)	744	918
Future income taxes (note 6)	1,148	1,224
	15,861	21,439
Shareholders' equity		
Share capital and contributed surplus (note 11)	18,698	18,698
Retained earnings	22,325	19,310
	41,023	38,008
	$ 56,884	$ 59,447

Commitments, guarantees and contingencies (note 13)

APPROVED BY THE BOARD OF DIRECTORS

_____   _____
D. Selman, Director   J. Alfonso, Director

See accompanying notes to these financial statements

- 14 -

Sun-Rype Products Ltd.
Statements of Operations and Retained Earnings
For the years ended December 31
(in thousands of dollars except per share amounts)

	2007	2006
Net sales (note 15)	$ 135,134	$ 130,622
Cost of sales	93,298	85,313
Gross profit	41,836	45,309
Expenses		
Selling, general, and administrative	28,538	30,476
Amortization	4,186	3,858
Interest	148	42
Loss on disposal of property, plant and equipment	213	135
Foreign exchange loss	1,977	106
	35,062	34,617
Earnings before income taxes	6,774	10,692
Income taxes (note 6)	2,138	3,426
Net earnings and comprehensive income	4,636	7,266
Retained earnings, beginning of year	19,310	29,585
Dividends paid	(1,621)	(17,541)
Retained earnings, end of year	$ 22,325	$ 19,310
Per share information		
Basic and diluted earnings per share	$ 0.43	$ 0.67
Dividends per share	$ 0.15	$ 1.62

See accompanying notes to these financial statements

- 15 -

Sun-Rype Products Ltd.
Statements of Cash Flows
For the years ended December 31
(in thousands of dollars)

	2007	2006
Cash provided by (used in):		
Operating activities		
Net earnings	$ 4,636	$ 7,266
Non-cash items:		
Deferred compensation	168	388
Amortization	4,186	3,858
Loss on disposal of property, plant and equipment	213	135
Unrealized foreign exchange loss	460	-
Future income taxes	(310)	(450)
	9,353	11,197
Changes in non-cash working capital items (note 12)	913	(5,458)
	10,266	5,739
Financing activities		
Dividends paid	(1,621)	(17,541)
Reduction of long-term obligations	(232)	-
	(1,853)	(17,541)
Investing activities		
Proceeds on disposal of property, plant and equipment	98	10
Payments for property, plant and equipment	(7,358)	(6,639)
	(7,260)	(6,629)
Increase (decrease) in cash position	1,153	(18,431)
Cash and cash equivalents, beginning of year	1,534	19,965
Cash and cash equivalents, end of year	$ 2,687	$ 1,534

Supplemental cash flow information (note 12)

See accompanying notes to these financial statements

Sun-Rype Products Ltd.
Notes to the Financial Statements
For the years ended December 31, 2007 and 2006

1. SIGNIFICANT ACCOUNTING POLICIES

(a) Basis of presentation

These financial statements have been prepared in accordance with Canadian generally accepted accounting principles ("Canadian GAAP").

(b) Measurement uncertainty

The presentation of financial statements in conformity with Canadian GAAP requires management to make estimates and assumptions that affect the reported amounts of assets and liabilities at the date of the financial statements and the reported amounts of revenues and expenses disclosed during reporting periods. Significant areas that involve estimates include provisions for uncollectible accounts receivable, the amortization rate and estimated useful life of property, plant and equipment, provisions for sales returns and allowances, and provisions for obsolete inventory. The actual amounts could differ from those estimates.

(c) Cash and cash equivalents

Cash and cash equivalents include cash and short-term deposits in high quality, low risk money market instruments, which are cashable on demand 90 days or less from the date of issue.

(d) Inventories

Raw materials, supplies and parts are recorded at the lower of cost, determined on a weighted average basis, and replacement cost.

Finished goods are recorded at the lower of cost and net realizable value. Finished goods include the cost of direct labour, direct materials and variable overhead related to production, applied at a standard rate, which approximates actual costs. Fixed overhead costs related to production are considered a period cost and, as such, are not included as a component of inventory but are expensed in the period they are incurred.

(e) Property, plant and equipment

Property, plant and equipment are recorded at cost, net of investment tax credits. The Company uses the straight-line method of recording amortization over the estimated useful lives of the property, plant and equipment as follows:

Buildings	10 - 20 years
Equipment - Processing	5 - 10 years
- Other	3 - 5 years

(f) Impairment of long-lived assets

The Company regularly compares the carrying value of long-lived assets to the estimated undiscounted future cash flows that may be generated from future use and eventual disposition of those assets. The Company records an impairment loss in the period when it is determined that the carrying amount of the asset exceeds the undiscounted estimate of future cash flows from the asset. The impairment loss is measured as the difference between the carrying amount and estimated fair value of the asset.

Sun-Rype Products Ltd.
Notes to the Financial Statements
For the years ended December 31, 2007 and 2006

1. SIGNIFICANT ACCOUNTING POLICIES *(continued)*

(g) *Asset retirement obligations*

The Company recognizes legal obligations associated with the retirement of property, plant and equipment that result from its acquisition, construction or normal operations. These obligations are recorded at fair value and subsequently adjusted for the accretion of discount and any changes in the underlying cash flows. The asset retirement cost is capitalized as part of the cost of the related asset, and amortized to earnings over the remaining life of the asset. Other than as described in Note 13, the Company has determined that it has no material asset retirement obligations at December 31, 2007.

(h) *Revenue recognition*

Sales are recognized upon the transfer of risk and title to finished goods to customers, which typically occurs upon shipment and when collectibility of proceeds is reasonably assured. The Company deducts from gross sales all payments to customers related to pricing discounts, returns and allowances, certain sales and marketing discounts, promotion funds, co-operative advertising, coupons and product listing fees.

(i) *Marketing and product launch costs*

The Company expenses new product marketing and launch costs as incurred.

(j) *Long term incentive plan*

The Company maintains a long-term incentive plan ("LTIP") that is more fully described in Note 10. A portion of the liability under this plan will vary with the market price of the Company's common shares.

The Company recognizes the LTIP compensation expense when earned and throughout the deferral period to the extent that the fair value of the performance units earned has changed. Should any amounts be forfeited due to future circumstances, these amounts will be accounted for in the period in which the forfeit is confirmed.

(k) *Research and development*

The Company incurs costs for activities that relate to research and development of new products. Research costs are expensed as they are incurred. Development costs are also expensed as incurred unless they meet all the criteria for deferral under Canadian GAAP and their recovery is reasonably assured. To date no amounts have been capitalized. Investment tax credits arising from research and development activities are deducted from the related costs and are accordingly included in the determination of earnings when there is reasonable assurance that the credits will be realized.

(l) *Income taxes*

The Company uses the liability method of accounting for income taxes. Under this method, temporary differences arising from the tax basis of an asset or liability and the corresponding carrying amount on the balance sheet are used to calculate future income tax assets or liabilities. Future income tax assets or liabilities are calculated using tax rates anticipated to be in effect in the periods that the temporary differences are expected to reverse. The effect of a change in income tax rates on future income tax assets and liabilities is recognized in income in the period the change is substantively enacted.

Sun-Rype Products Ltd.
Notes to the Financial Statements
For the years ended December 31, 2007 and 2006

1. **SIGNIFICANT ACCOUNTING POLICIES** *(continued)*

    (m) Foreign currency translation

    Transactions denominated in foreign currencies are translated into Canadian dollars at the exchange rate prevailing at the time of each transaction. At the balance sheet date, monetary assets and liabilities denominated in a foreign currency are translated at the period end rate of exchange. Exchange gains and losses arising on translation or settlement of foreign currency-denominated items are included in the determination of net income for the current period.

    (n) Foreign exchange forward contracts

    The Company periodically enters into foreign exchange forward contracts to manage foreign exchange risk associated with anticipated future purchases denominated in foreign currencies. Realized and unrealized gains and losses resulting from changes in the market value of these contracts are recorded as other investment income each period unless they meet specified criteria to qualify as hedging instruments under Canadian GAAP. If these contracts meet the criteria for hedging instruments, any unrealized gains or losses are deferred and recognized in earnings when the related hedged transaction is recognized in earnings.

    (o) Earnings per share

    Basic earnings per share is calculated by dividing the net earnings available to common shareholders by the weighted average number of common shares outstanding during the year. Diluted earnings per share is calculated using the treasury stock method, which assumes that any outstanding stock option grants are exercised, if dilutive, and the assumed proceeds are used to purchase the Company's common shares at the average market price during the year.

2. **CHANGE OF ACCOUNTING POLICIES**

    Financial instruments

    Effective January 1, 2007, the Company adopted the Canadian Institute of Chartered Accountants' new Handbook Section 1530 "Comprehensive Income", Section 3855 "Financial Instruments", and Section 3861 "Financial Instruments – Disclosure and Presentation". These accounting policy changes were adopted on a prospective basis with no restatement of prior year financial statements.

    (a) Other comprehensive income

    Section 1530 introduces new requirements for situations when certain gains and losses ("other comprehensive income", or "OCI") must be temporarily presented outside of net income. OCI is the change in shareholders' equity from non-owner sources. Cumulative changes in OCI are included in Accumulated Other Comprehensive Income ("AOCI"), which is presented as a new category of shareholders' equity on the balance sheet. The Company had no OCI transactions during the year ended December 31, 2007, and no opening nor closing balances for AOCI.

Sun-Rype Products Ltd.
Notes to the Financial Statements
For the years ended December 31, 2007 and 2006

2. CHANGE OF ACCOUNTING POLICIES *(continued)*

(b) *Financial instruments recognition, measurement, disclosure and presentation*

Under Section 3855, all financial instruments are classified into one of these five categories: held-for-trading, held-to-maturity investments, loans and receivables, available-for-sale financial assets or other financial liabilities. All financial instruments and derivatives are measured on the balance sheet at fair value upon initial recognition. Subsequent measurement depends on the initial classification of the instrument. Held-for-trading financial assets are measured at fair value, with changes in fair value recognized in net income. Available-for-sale financial instruments are measured at fair value, with changes in fair value recorded in OCI until the instrument is derecognized or impaired. Loans and receivables, held-to-maturity investments and other financial liabilities are measured at amortized cost. All derivative instruments, including embedded derivatives, are recorded in the balance sheets at fair value unless they qualify for the normal sales and purchases exemption. Changes in the fair value of derivatives that are not exempt are recorded in income.

Upon adoption of these new standards, the Company has designated its cash and cash equivalents as held-for-trading, which are measured at fair value. Additionally, the foreign exchange contracts and LTIP units are classified as held-for-trading instruments, and as such, any mark-to-market adjustments are included in the determination of income at the end of each reporting period. Accounts receivable are classified as loans and receivables, which are measured at amortized cost. Promissory note payable, accounts payable and accrued liabilities, and long-term obligations are classified as other liabilities, which are measured at amortized cost. At December 31, 2007, the Company had neither available-for-sale nor held-to-maturity financial instruments.

Section 3861 identifies and details information to be disclosed in the financial statements.

Future accounting and reporting changes

The Canadian Institute of Chartered Accountants issued new accounting standards which the Company will adopt, effective January 1, 2008: Section 1535 "Capital Disclosures"; Section 3862 "Financial Instruments – Disclosures"; Section 3863 "Financial Instruments – Presentation"; and Section 3031 "Inventories." The new requirements of Sections 1535, 3862 and 3863 are for disclosure purposes only and will not impact the financial results of the Company.

(i)   Section 1535 establishes guidelines for the disclosure of information on an entity's capital and how it is managed. This enhanced disclosure enables users to evaluate the entity's objectives, policies and processes for managing capital.

(ii) Sections 3862 and 3863 replace the existing Section 3861 "Financial Instruments – Disclosure and Presentation." Section 3862 requires enhanced disclosure on the nature and extent of financial instrument risks and how an entity manages those risks. Section 3863 carries forward the existing presentation requirements and provides additional guidance for the classification of financial instruments.

(iii) Section 3031 provides more guidance on the measurement and disclosure requirements for inventories. The Company does not expect to be materially affected by these recommendations upon adoption.   The effects on future periods are not determinable.

Sun-Rype Products Ltd.
Notes to the Financial Statements
For the years ended December 31, 2007 and 2006

3. BANK INDEBTEDNESS

The Company maintains a $15.0 million standby operating line of credit with a Canadian bank, which bears interest at the bank's prime lending rate (December 31, 2007 – 6.0%). This facility is secured by a general assignment of accounts receivable, inventories and demand debentures creating a fixed and floating charge over all Company assets. At December 31, 2007 and 2006, no balances were outstanding under this operating line of credit.

4. ACCOUNTS RECEIVABLE

(in thousands of dollars)	2007	2006
Trade	$ 6,876	$ 12,342
Other	516	334
	$ 7,392	$ 12,676

5. INVENTORIES

(in thousands of dollars)	2007	2006
Raw materials and supplies	$ 10,855	$ 9,581
Finished goods	4,301	7,222
Parts	2,148	1,905
	$ 17,304	$ 18,708

6. INCOME TAXES

The income tax provision differs from the amount that would be computed by applying the combined federal and provincial statutory income tax rates as a result of the following:

	2007	2006
Statutory income tax rates	33.8%	34.1%
(in thousands of dollars)		
Income tax provision at statutory rates	$ 2,292	$ 3,648
Effect on income taxes of:		
Non-deductible expenses	28	29
Tax rate reductions	(118)	(92)
Other	(64)	(159)
Effective income tax provision	$ 2,138	$ 3,426

The income tax provision consists of the following:

(in thousands of dollars)	2007	2006
Current income tax expense	$ 2,448	$ 3,876
Future income tax recovery	(310)	(450)
	$ 2,138	$ 3,426

Sun-Rype Products Ltd.
Notes to the Financial Statements
For the years ended December 31, 2007 and 2006

6.   **INCOME TAXES** *(continued)*

The net future income tax liability is reported as follows:

(in thousands of dollars)	2007	2006
Future income tax assets – current	$ 435	$ 201
Future income tax liabilities – long-term	(1,148)	(1,224)
Net future income tax liability	$ (713)	$ (1,023)

Significant components of future income tax assets and liabilities include:

(in thousands of dollars)	2007	2006
Accrued liabilities	$ 711	$ 508
Losses and other deductions	14	12
Future income tax assets	725	520
Property, plant and equipment	(1,360)	(1,524)
Other	(78)	(19)
Future income tax liabilities	(1,438)	(1,543)
Net future income tax liability	$ (713)	$ (1,023)

7.   **PROPERTY, PLANT AND EQUIPMENT**

(in thousands of dollars)	2007		
	Cost	Accumulated Amortization	Net Book Value
Land	$ 170	$ -	$ 170
Buildings	16,624	12,572	4,052
Processing equipment	50,384	28,560	21,824
Other equipment	7,775	5,954	1,821
	$ 74,953	$ 47,086	$ 27,867

	2006		
	Cost	Accumulated Amortization	Net Book Value
Land	$ 170	$ -	$ 170
Buildings	16,342	11,833	4,509
Processing equipment	45,091	26,186	18,905
Other equipment	8,175	5,812	2,363
	$ 69,778	$ 43,831	$ 25,947

Included in processing equipment at December 31, 2007, is construction in progress with a cost of $708,600 that has not been amortized (2006 - $5,073,600).

Sun-Rype Products Ltd.
Notes to the Financial Statements
For the years ended December 31, 2007 and 2006

11. SHARE CAPITAL AND CONTRIBUTED SURPLUS

Authorized

100,000,000 common shares fully participating and without par value

Issued and fully paid capital

(in thousands of dollars)	2007	2006
10,827,600 Common shares	$ 17,756	$ 17,756
Contributed surplus	942	942
	$ 18,698	$ 18,698

Earnings per share

The weighted average number of common shares outstanding in 2007 and 2006, on a basic and diluted basis, was 10,827,600.

Employee share purchase plan

The Company has an employee share purchase plan ("ESPP") enabling all permanent full- and part-time employees to acquire common shares through payroll deductions with financial assistance provided by the Company. Eligible employees may contribute monthly an amount, which shall not exceed 7% of salary, and the Company has agreed to contribute a further 35% of the amount contributed by each eligible employee. All funds and equity shares held by the administrator pursuant to the ESPP are held for the account of the individual eligible employee. The Company's contributions to the ESPP in the year totalled $228,000 (2006 - $241,000).

12. SUPPLEMENTAL CASH FLOW INFORMATION

(in thousands of dollars)	2007	2006
Changes in non-cash working capital items:		
Accounts receivable	$ 5,284	$ (808)
Inventories	1,404	(5,377)
Prepaid expenses	-	134
Promissory note payable	(100)	(75)
Accounts payable and accrued liabilities	(4,623)	1,353
Income taxes	(1,052)	(685)
	$ 913	$ (5,458)
Cash paid during the year for:		
Interest	$ 148	$ 42
Income taxes	$ 3,503	$ 4,533
Non-cash transactions:		
Additions to property, plant and equipment included in accounts payable and accrued liabilities	$ 58	$ 999

Sun-Rype Products Ltd.
Notes to the Financial Statements
For the years ended December 31, 2007 and 2006

11. SHARE CAPITAL AND CONTRIBUTED SURPLUS

Authorized

100,000,000 common shares fully participating and without par value

Issued and fully paid capital

(in thousands of dollars)	2007	2006
10,827,600 Common shares	$ 17,756	$ 17,756
Contributed surplus	942	942
	$ 18,698	$ 18,698

Earnings per share

The weighted average number of common shares outstanding in 2007 and 2006, on a basic and diluted basis, was 10,827,600.

Employee share purchase plan

The Company has an employee share purchase plan ("ESPP") enabling all permanent full- and part-time employees to acquire common shares through payroll deductions with financial assistance provided by the Company. Eligible employees may contribute monthly an amount, which shall not exceed 7% of salary, and the Company has agreed to contribute a further 35% of the amount contributed by each eligible employee. All funds and equity shares held by the administrator pursuant to the ESPP are held for the account of the individual eligible employee. The Company's contributions to the ESPP in the year totalled $228,000 (2006 - $241,000).

12. SUPPLEMENTAL CASH FLOW INFORMATION

(in thousands of dollars)	2007	2006
Changes in non-cash working capital items:		
Accounts receivable	$ 5,284	$ (808)
Inventories	1,404	(5,377)
Prepaid expenses	-	134
Promissory note payable	(100)	(75)
Accounts payable and accrued liabilities	(4,623)	1,353
Income taxes	(1,052)	(685)
	$ 913	$ (5,458)
Cash paid during the year for:		
Interest	$ 148	$ 42
Income taxes	$ 3,503	$ 4,533
Non-cash transactions:		
Additions to property, plant and equipment included in accounts payable and accrued liabilities	$ 58	$ 999

Sun-Rype Products Ltd.
Notes to the Financial Statements
For the years ended December 31, 2007 and 2006

13. COMMITMENTS, GUARANTEES AND CONTINGENCIES

(a) The Company has entered into operating lease and rental commitments for equipment and office space for the next five years as follows:

Year	Amount (in thousands of dollars)
2008	$ 144
2009	136
2010	120
2011	74
2012	57

(b) Under the terms of a processing and filling systems agreement, the Company is contingently liable until 2009 for annual rental payments of $775,000 should the Company's purchase of an annual volume of beverage packaging materials not meet a negotiated minimum threshold. Management estimates that penalties would only be payable in the event of a dramatic decline in market demand.

(c) In the normal course of business, the Company enters into commitments to purchase certain minimum quantities of raw materials, primarily in US dollars. At December 31, 2007, the Company had commitments to purchase approximately $2.6 million of these materials in 2008 and $2.7 million in 2009.

(d) The Company is subject to regulations that require the handling and disposal of asbestos that is contained in a certain property in a special manner if the property undergoes major renovations or demolition. Otherwise, the Company is not required to remove the asbestos from the property. The Company has determined that there is an indeterminate settlement date for this asset retirement obligation because the range of time over which the Company may settle the obligation cannot be estimated. Therefore, the Company cannot reasonably estimate the fair value of the liability. The Company will recognize a liability in the period in which sufficient information is available to reasonably estimate its fair value.

Sun-Rype Products Ltd.
Notes to the Financial Statements
For the years ended December 31, 2007 and 2006

14. FINANCIAL INSTRUMENTS AND CREDIT RISK

The Company's financial instruments include cash and cash equivalents, accounts receivable, promissory note payable, accounts payable and accrued liabilities and long-term obligations for which the carrying values approximate fair values. Other items are instruments that may be settled by the delivery of non-financial assets, such as a commodity futures contract.

Credit risk is the risk of loss from non-performance of suppliers, customers or financial counter parties to a contract. The Company maintains credit policies that include a review of a counter party's financial condition, measurement of credit exposure and monitoring of concentration of exposure to any one customer or counter party. At December 31, 2007, 81% of trade accounts receivable is attributable to ten customers (2006 - 86%).

The Company is exposed to foreign currency risk as certain of its raw material and packaging inputs are purchased in US dollars. In 2008, these purchases are estimated to be approximately USD$40.0 million.

The Company periodically enters into foreign exchange forward purchase contracts to manage foreign exchange risk associated with anticipated future purchases and contractual commitments denominated in foreign currencies. At December 31, 2007, the Company had currency contracts outstanding of USD$16 million (2006 – nil). These contracts allow the Company to purchase USD$16 million at an average exchange rate of 1.0529 should the spot rate be above the rate on the individual contracts, while requiring the Company to purchase US dollars at an average exchange rate of 1.0166 should the spot rate be below the rates on the individual contracts. At December 31, 2007, the Company has recorded an unrealized foreign exchange loss of $0.5 million to reflect the fair value of these currency contracts.

15. SEGMENTED INFORMATION

The Company operates in the food and beverage industry in Canada and has only one industry segment.

Details of net sales by significant product lines are as follows:

(*in thousands of dollars*)	2007	2006
Beverage products	$ 98,534	$ 95,793
Food products	36,600	34,829
	$ 135,134	$ 130,622

The Company's customers consist mainly of grocery stores, mass merchandisers and club stores across Canada. The Company's ten largest customers comprise 86% of net sales (2006 - 85%). Three of customers individually represent more than 10% of net sales, and in 2007 net sales to these customers totalled $71.2 million (2006 - $67.0 million).

Sun-Rype Products Ltd.
Notes to the Financial Statements
For the years ended December 31, 2007 and 2006

16. RELATED PARTIES

In the normal course of business, the Company sells products to a major food retailer in western Canada. Based on publicly available information, this retailer is controlled by an individual who also controls 34.6% of the Company's outstanding common shares (2006 – 31.0%). Sales to this retailer are less than 10% of the Company's total net sales in 2007 and 2006 and are recorded at the exchange amounts, which are the amounts agreed upon between the related parties.

17. COMPARATIVE FIGURES

Certain of the comparative figures have been reclassified in the financial statements to conform to the classifications used in 2007.

18. SUBSEQUENT EVENTS

On February 23, 2008, the Company's unionized employees, represented by the Teamsters Local Union No. 213, ratified a new four-year collective agreement which will expire August 31, 2010.

On February 28, 2008, the Company declared a quarterly dividend of $0.04 per common share, for a total of approximately $433,000, payable March 15, 2008, to shareholders of record at the close of business on March 10, 2008.

From time to time the Company enters into hedge arrangements to minimize the effect of fluctuations in currency rates on US dollar-denominated purchases. At February 28, 2008, the Company had hedge contracts outstanding of USD$13 million.

2007 CONSOLIDATED FINANCIAL STATEMENTS

AND

NOTES TO CONSOLIDATED FINANCIAL STATEMENTS

MANAGEMENT'S REPORT TO THE UNITHOLDERS

The accompanying consolidated financial statements of Mullen Group Income Fund (the "Fund") have been approved by the Board of Directors and have been prepared in accordance with Canadian generally accepted accounting principles. The financial information contained elsewhere in this report has been reviewed to ensure consistency with these consolidated financial statements. In preparing the report, the Fund undertakes steps to ensure the information presented is accurate and conforms to applicable laws and standards, including:

- The Board of Directors and management have established corporate governance practices that are consistent with guidelines set out in the report issued by The Toronto Stock Exchange Committee on Corporate Governance in Canada.

- Management maintains accounting control systems designed to provide reasonable assurance that assets are safeguarded, transactions are properly authorized, financial records are accurately maintained and statements are generated in a timely manner.

- The Board of Directors oversees the management of the business and the affairs for the Fund including ensuring management fulfills its responsibility for financial reporting, and is ultimately responsible for reviewing and approving the consolidated financial statements. The Board carries out this responsibility principally through its Audit Committee.

- The Audit Committee of the Board of Directors, comprised of four members considered to be "outside and unrelated" directors, has reviewed the consolidated financial statements with management and the external auditors.

- Management, with the participation of the Chief Executive Officer, Co-Chief Executive Officer and Chief Financial Officer, has evaluated the effectiveness of the Fund's disclosure controls and procedures (as defined in the rules of the Canadian Securities Administrators) and has concluded that such disclosure controls and procedures are effective.

- Management has evaluated the design and effectiveness of internal controls over financial reporting and has concluded the design is effective except for issues with the complexity of accounting and income tax issues and with control weaknesses related to segregation of duties.

- An independent firm of chartered accountants, appointed as external auditors by the unitholders, has audited the consolidated financial statements and its report is included below.

"SIGNED"   *"SIGNED"*

Murray K. Mullen   David E. Olson
Chairman, Chief Executive Officer and Director   Vice-President, Finance and Chief Financial
Officer

February 27, 2008

KPMG LLP
Chartered Accountants
2700 205 - 5th Avenue SW
Calgary AB T2P 4B9

Telephone   (403) 691-8000
Fax   (403) 691-8008
Internet   www.kpmg.ca

AUDITORS' REPORT TO THE UNITHOLDERS

We have audited the consolidated balance sheets of Mullen Group Income Fund as at December 31, 2007 and 2006 and the consolidated statements of income, retained earnings and cash flows for the years then ended.   These financial statements are the responsibility of the Fund's management. Our responsibility is to express an opinion on these financial statements based on our audit.

We conducted our audits in accordance with Canadian generally accepted auditing standards. Those standards require that we plan and perform an audit to obtain reasonable assurance whether the financial statements are free of material misstatement. An audit includes examining, on a test basis, evidence supporting the amounts and disclosures in the financial statements. An audit also includes assessing the accounting principles used and significant estimates made by management, as well as evaluating the overall financial statement presentation.

In our opinion, these consolidated financial statements present fairly, in all material respects, the financial position of the Fund as at December 31, 2007 and 2006 and the results of its operations and its cash flows for the years then ended in accordance with Canadian generally accepted accounting principles.

KPMG LLP

Chartered Accountants

Calgary, Canada

February 27, 2008

CONSOLIDATED BALANCE SHEETS

December 31, 2007 and 2006
($ thousands)

	2007	2006
Assets		
Current assets:		
Cash and cash equivalents	$ 79,155	$ 49,398
Accounts receivable	185,475	209,545
Income taxes recoverable	1,488	6,834
Prepaid expenses	27,715	27,675
	293,833	293,452
Investments (note 3)	9,884	1,825
Property, plant and equipment (note 4)	586,823	558,522
Goodwill (note 5)	794,448	1,041,827
Intangible assets (note 6)	82,674	116,284
Other assets (note 7)	2,828	9,335
	$ 1,770,490	$ 2,021,245
Liabilities and Unitholders' Equity		
Current liabilities:		
Accounts payable and accrued liabilities	$ 100,480	$ 107,423
Distributions payable (note 8)	12,112	12,291
Current portion of long-term debt (note 9)	3,817	21,734
	116,409	141,448
Long-term debt (note 9)	398,592	325,002
Future income taxes (note 10)	123,357	130,729
Unitholders' equity:		
Unitholders' capital (note 11)	1,185,340	1,201,677
Trust Units repurchased, pending cancellation (note 11)	(5,880)	—
Contributed surplus (note 12)	7,273	7,839
(Deficit) retained earnings	(54,601)	214,550
	1,132,132	1,424,066
Commitments and contingencies (note 14)		
	$ 1,770,490	$ 2,021,245

See accompanying notes to the consolidated financial statements.

Approved by the Board of Directors

"SIGNED"   *"SIGNED"*

Murray K. Mullen, Director   Dennis J. Hoffman, Director

CONSOLIDATED STATEMENTS OF INCOME AND (DEFICIT) RETAINED EARNINGS

Years ended December 31, 2007 and 2006 (*$ thousands, except per unit amounts*)	2007	2006
Revenue	$ 1,119,499	$ 1,003,287
Expenses:		
Direct operating	764,992	682,132
Selling and administrative	145,377	119,090
	209,130	202,065
Depreciation on property, plant and equipment	57,684	41,730
Amortization on intangible assets	16,761	10,905
Interest on long-term debt	20,970	13,410
Other interest	194	202
Unrealized (gain) loss on foreign exchange	(26,641)	7,500
Loss (gain) on sale of property, plant and equipment	725	(1,256)
Gain on sale of investments	(30)	(115)
Impairment of goodwill and intangible assets (notes 5 and 6)	275,000	—
(Loss) income before income taxes and earnings from equity investments	(135,533)	129,689
Provision for income taxes (note 10):		
Current (recovery)	(2,390)	(4,311)
Future (recovery)	(10,850)	6,866
	(13,240)	2,555
(Loss) income before earnings from equity investments	(122,293)	127,134
Earnings from equity investments	3,598	998
Net (loss) income	$ (118,695)	$ 128,132
Retained earnings, beginning of year	$ 214,550	$ 228,551
Split off of Horizon North Logistics Inc.	—	(18,096)
Distributions declared to unitholders	(146,804)	(124,037)
Repurchase of Trust Units (note 11)	(3,652)	—
(Deficit) retained earnings, end of year	$ (54,601)	$ 214,550
Earnings per unit (note 13):		
Basic	$ (1.45)	$ 1.86
Diluted	$ (1.45)	$ 1.86
Weighted average number of units outstanding:		
Basic	81,596	68,886
Diluted	81,596	68,886

See accompanying notes to the consolidated financial statements.

CONSOLIDATED STATEMENTS OF CASH FLOWS

Years ended December 31, 2007 and 2006
(in thousands of dollars)

	2007	2006
Cash provided by (used in):		
Operations:		
Net (loss) income	$ (118,695)	$ 128,132
Items not involving cash:		
Depreciation on property, plant and equipment	57,684	41,730
Amortization on intangible assets	16,761	10,905
Unit-based compensation	3,427	2,581
Unrealized (gain) loss on foreign exchange	(26,641)	7,500
Loss (gain) on sale of property, plant and equipment	725	(1,256)
Gain on sale of investments	(30)	(115)
Future income taxes (recovery)	(10,850)	6,866
Earnings from equity investments	(3,598)	(998)
Impairment of goodwill and intangible assets	275,000	—
	193,783	195,345
Changes in non-cash working capital items	18,611	(3,168)
	212,394	192,177
Financing activities:		
Change in bank indebtedness	—	(28,018)
Repayment of long-term debt	(23,664)	(162,393)
Proceeds of long-term debt	107,914	334,100
Net proceeds from Trust Unit issuances	1,247	97,036
Repurchase of Trust Units	(28,656)	—
Distributions paid	(146,983)	(118,124)
	(90,142)	122,601
Investing activities:		
Acquisitions (note 2)	(11,915)	(182,139)
Cash distribution from equity investment	3,123	—
Property, plant and equipment additions	(96,653)	(102,705)
Proceeds on sale of property, plant and equipment	16,450	17,408
Purchase of investments	(7,553)	—
Proceeds on sale of investments	46	141
Other assets	4,007	1,915
	(92,495)	(265,380)
Change in cash	29,757	49,398
Cash, beginning of year	49,398	—
Cash, end of year	$ 79,155	$ 49,398
Supplemental cash flow information:		
Interest paid	$ 21,808	$ 10,798
Income taxes paid (received)	$ (7,792)	$ 11,537

See accompanying notes to the consolidated financial statements

NOTES TO THE CONSOLIDATED FINANCIAL STATEMENTS
(Years ended December 31, 2007 and 2006)
(Tabular amounts in thousands, except per unit and unit amounts)

1. **Significant Accounting Policies**

These consolidated financial statements are prepared in accordance with Canadian generally accepted accounting principles ("GAAP"). Management is required to make estimates and assumptions that affect the reported amounts of assets and liabilities and disclosure of contingent assets and liabilities at the date of the consolidated financial statements and the reported amounts of revenues and expenses during the reported period. Actual results could differ from these estimates.

(a)   Basis of presentation

Mullen Group Income Fund ("Mullen" and/or the "Fund") is an unincorporated investment trust. The business of the Fund is held in indirectly owned subsidiaries and limited partnerships. The business of Mullen is a diversified transportation and oilfield services organization with its activities divided into two distinct business segments; Oilfield Services and Trucking/Logistics.

The Fund is an unincorporated open-ended investment trust governed by the laws of the Province of Alberta and created pursuant to a declaration of trust dated as of June 3, 2005. Pursuant to the provisions of section 193 of the Business Corporations Act (Alberta), Mullen Transportation Inc. ("MTI" and/or the "Company"), Mullen Acquisition Corp., certain subsidiaries of MTI and certain other corporations were amalgamated, effective as of July 1, 2005 to form MT Investments Inc. ("MT"). MT is wholly-owned by Mullen Co. Limited Partnership ("MCLP"). MCLP is approximately 75 percent owned by Mullen Holding Trust ("MHT") and the balance of MCLP is owned by other third parties. MHT is wholly-owned by the Fund. CIBC Mellon Trust Company is the Trustee under the Fund. The beneficiaries of the Fund are the holders of the trust units ("Trust Units") issued by the Fund ("unitholders"). The accompanying audited consolidated financial statements for the Fund have been prepared in accordance with GAAP for consolidated financial statements. Certain comparative figures have been reclassified to conform with the current consolidated financial statement presentation.

(b)   Changes in Accounting Policies

On January 1, 2007, the Fund adopted CICA Handbook Sections 1530, "Comprehensive Income", Section 3251 "Equity", Section 3855, "Financial Instruments - Recognition and Measurement", Section 3861, "Financial Instruments - Disclosure and Presentation" and Section 3865, "Hedges".

Section 1530 establishes standards for reporting and presenting comprehensive income, which is defined as the change in equity from transactions and other events from non-owner sources. Other comprehensive income refers to items recognized in comprehensive income that are excluded from net income calculated in accordance with GAAP.

Section 3861 establishes standards for presentation of financial instruments and non-financial derivatives, and identifies the information that should be disclosed about them. Under the new standards, policies followed for periods prior to the effective date generally are not reversed and therefore, the comparative figures have not been restated. Section 3865 describes when and how hedge accounting can be applied as well as the disclosure requirements. Hedge accounting enables the recording of gains, losses, revenues and expenses from derivative financial instruments in the same period as for those related to the hedged item.

NOTES TO THE CONSOLIDATED FINANCIAL STATEMENTS
(Years ended December 31, 2007 and 2006)
(Tabular amounts in thousands, except per unit and unit amounts)

1. **Significant Accounting Policies, (continued)**

Section 3855 prescribes when a financial asset, financial liability or non-financial derivative is to be recognized on the balance sheet and at what amount, requiring fair value or cost-based measures under different circumstances. Under Section 3855, financial instruments must be classified into one of these five categories: held-for-trading, held-to-maturity, loans and receivables, available-for-sale financial assets or other financial liabilities. All financial instruments, including derivatives, are measured in the balance sheet at fair value except for loans and receivables, held to maturity investments and other financial liabilities which are measured at amortized cost. Subsequent measurement and changes in fair value will depend on their initial classification, as follows: held-for-trading financial assets are measured at fair value and changes in fair value are recognized in net earnings; available-for-sale financial instruments are measured at fair value with changes in fair value recorded in other comprehensive income until the investment is de-recognized or impaired at which time the amounts would be recorded in net earnings.

Under adoption of these new standards, the Fund designated its accounts receivable as loans and receivables, which are measured at amortized cost. The Fund's bank indebtedness, accounts payable and accrued liabilities, long-term debt and capital lease obligations are classified as other financial liabilities, which are measured at amortized cost. The Fund's debt issuance costs have been netted against the related indebtedness and are amortized using the effective interest rate method. For the year ended December 31, 2007, $2.1 million of debt issuance costs were netted against the loan. As well, portfolio investments have been categorized as investments held for trading. Other than these changes the adoption of the standard had no material impact on the Fund's consolidated financial statements.

Any derivative instruments, including embedded derivatives, are to be recorded in the statement of income at fair value unless exempted from derivative treatment as a normal purchase and sale. All changes in their fair value are recorded in earnings unless cash flow hedge accounting is used, in which case changes in fair value are recorded in other comprehensive income. The Fund has elected to apply this accounting treatment for all embedded derivatives in host contracts entered into on or after January 1, 2003. The Fund has determined it currently has no derivative or embedded derivative instruments and as such is not impacted by the change in accounting policy.

New CICA Handbook Sections have been issued which will require additional disclosure in the Fund's consolidated financial statements commencing January 1, 2008. Sections 1535 "Capital Disclosures" requires the disclosure of qualitative and quantitative information about the Fund's objectives, policies and processes for managing capital. Sections 3862 "Financial Instruments – Disclosures" and 3863 "Financial Instruments – Presentation" will replace Section 3861 to prescribe the requirements for presentation and disclosure of financial instruments. Handbook section 3031 "Inventories", which prescribes the recognitions, measurement, disclosure and presentation issues related to inventories will become effective January 1, 2008. Section 3865 specifies the circumstances under which hedge accounting is permissible and how hedge accounting may be performed. The Fund believes that the adoption of these standards will not have a material impact on the consolidated financial statements.

(c)   Investments

Investments in affiliates over which the Fund has significant influence are accounted for using the equity method. Investments in which the Fund has no significant influence are carried at the fair value. If management determines there is a permanent decline in value in underlying assets and no expectation of future earnings, these investments are written down to net realizable value.

NOTES TO THE CONSOLIDATED FINANCIAL STATEMENTS
(Years ended December 31, 2007 and 2006)
(Tabular amounts in thousands, except per unit and unit amounts)

1. **Significant Accounting Policies, (continued)**

   (d) Property, plant and equipment and depreciation

   Property, plant and equipment are recorded at cost. Depreciation on additions and disposals is prorated from the month of purchase or disposal. Depreciation is provided annually over the estimated useful lives of the assets on the declining balance basis at the following rates:

Assets	Rate
Buildings	2.5 - 8%
Trucks and trailers	10 - 20%
Equipment, furniture and fixtures	20%
Automobiles, computer equipment and computer software	30 - 50%
Satellite communications equipment	20%

   Drilling rigs are depreciated by the unit-of-production method based on 1,500 operating days with a 20 percent residual value.

   (e) Intangible assets and amortization

   Intangible assets are mainly comprised of non-competition agreements and customer relationships and are amortized on a straight-line basis over five to ten years.

   Intangible assets are reviewed for impairment whenever events or changes in circumstances indicate that the carrying amount may not be recoverable. An impairment loss is recognized when the carrying amount of the asset is not recoverable and exceeds its estimated fair value.

   (f) Goodwill

   Goodwill is the residual amount that results when the purchase price of an acquired business exceeds the sum of the amounts allocated to the assets acquired less liabilities assumed, based on their fair values.

   Goodwill is not amortized, but is tested for permanent impairment annually in the fourth quarter, or more frequently if events or changes in circumstances indicate that the asset might be impaired. The impairment test is carried out in two steps. In the first step, the carrying amount of the reporting segment is compared with its fair value. When the fair value of a reporting segment exceeds its carrying amount, goodwill of the reporting segment is considered not to be impaired and the second step of the impairment test is unnecessary. The second step is carried out when the carrying amount of a reporting segment exceeds its fair value, in which case the implied fair value of the reporting segment's goodwill is compared with its carrying amount to measure the amount of the impairment loss, if any. The implied fair value of goodwill is determined in the same manner as the value of goodwill is determined in a business combination described in the preceding paragraph, using the fair value of the reporting segment as if it was the purchase price. When the carrying amount of a reporting segment's goodwill exceeds the implied fair value of the goodwill, an impairment loss is recognized in an amount equal to the excess.

NOTES TO THE CONSOLIDATED FINANCIAL STATEMENTS
(Years ended December 31, 2007 and 2006)
(Tabular amounts in thousands, except per unit and unit amounts)

1. **Significant Accounting Policies, (continued)**

    (g)   Revenue recognition

    The Fund's services are provided based upon orders and contracts with the customer that include fixed or determinable prices based upon daily, hourly or job rates. Contract terms do not include provision for post-service obligations. Revenue is recognized when services are rendered and when collectability is reasonably assured.

    (h)   Income taxes

    The Fund and its subsidiaries follow the liability method of accounting for future income taxes. Under the liability method, future income tax assets and liabilities are determined based on "temporary differences" (differences between the accounting basis and the tax basis of the assets and liabilities), and are measured using the currently enacted, or substantively enacted, tax rates and laws expected to apply when these differences reverse. The effect of a change in income tax rates on future tax liabilities and assets is recognized in income in the period in which the change occurs.

    On June 22, 2007, the Government of Canada enacted a new tax on distributions from specified investment flow-through ("SIFT") entities. This enactment has triggered the recognition of future income tax assets and liabilities expected to reverse after January 1, 2011. The effect of the income tax increase on the SIFT entity's future income tax balances in the Fund has been reflected as a future income tax expense in 2007.

    (i)   Unit-based compensation plan

    The Fund has a unit-based compensation plan, which is described in note 11. The Fund utilizes the fair value method to account for options. Under the fair value method, the fair value of options is calculated at the date of grant and that value is recorded as compensation expense over the vesting periods of those grants, with a corresponding increase to contributed surplus. When options are exercised, the proceeds received by the Fund, along with the amount in contributed surplus, will be credited to unitholders' capital.

    (j)   Per unit amounts

    Basic per unit amounts are calculated using the weighted average number of units outstanding during the year. Diluted per unit amounts are calculated based on the treasury stock method which assumes that any proceeds obtained on the exercise of options would be used to purchase Trust Units at the average market prices during the period. The weighted average number of units outstanding is then adjusted by the net change.

    (k)   Cash and cash equivalents

    Cash and cash equivalents are restricted to cash and highly liquid investments having an initial term of three months or less and are presented at cost which approximates fair value.

2. **Acquisitions and Dispositions**

    (a)   2007 Acquisitions

    On April 30, 2007, the Fund acquired all the outstanding shares of E.K. Inc. ("EK"), a specialized transportation carrier for $2.4 million. Based out of Aldersyde, Alberta, EK mainly specializes in transporting natural gas compressor units to the United States. EK's results from operations are included in the Trucking/Logistics segment.

NOTES TO THE CONSOLIDATED FINANCIAL STATEMENTS
(Years ended December 31, 2007 and 2006)
(Tabular amounts in thousands, except per unit and unit amounts)

2. **Acquisitions and Dispositions, (continued)**

On October 31, 2007, the Fund acquired all the outstanding shares of Pro North Well Management Ltd. and its wholly-owned subsidiary Pro North Oilfield Services Ltd. (collectively "Pro North") for $9.5 million. Pro North provides oilfield related fluid hauling services and is based out of Fort Nelson, British Columbia. Pro North's results from operations are included in the Oilfield Services segment.

The acquisitions in 2007 have been accounted for by the purchase method, and results of operations have been included in these consolidated financial statements from the date of acquisition. Details of the acquisitions are as follows:

2007		Total
Assets:		
Non-cash working capital items	$	234
Property, plant and equipment		6,507
Intangible assets		8,152
Goodwill		2,621
		17,514
Assumed liabilities:		
Long-term debt		2,800
Future income taxes		3,478
		6,278
Net assets before cash position		11,236
Cash position		679
Cash consideration	$	11,915

(b) 2006 Acquisitions
On January 12, 2006, the Fund acquired the remaining outstanding shares of Pe Ben Oilfield Services Ltd. ("Pe Ben"), a public transportation company for $56.0 million. The $56.0 million was comprised of $18.50 for each outstanding Pe Ben share and the original portfolio investment purchase of $1.4 million incurred prior to 2006. Results from Pe Ben's Canadian oilfield transportation and pipeline stringing operations are included in the Oilfield Services segment. Results from Pe Ben's liquid bulk transport operations ("Pe Ben Bulk") are included in the Trucking/Logistics segment.

On May 1, 2006, the Fund acquired all of the outstanding shares of Kleysen Investments Limited ("Kleysen") for consideration of $60.3 million and 154,875 trust units at a value of $5.0 million for a total of $65.3 million. Kleysen is a Winnipeg based transportation and logistics company offering four major integrated services including: bulk transportation, deck transportation, multi-commodity transload services and intermodal transportation services. Kleysen's results from operations are included in the Trucking/Logistics segment.

On June 1, 2006, the Fund completed a Plan of Arrangement (the "Arrangement") whereby it acquired all of the outstanding shares of Producers Oilfield Services Inc. ("Producers") by issuing 19.9 million Trust Units and 11.2 million B units at a combined value of $1.0 billion. Producers provides specialized oilfield transportation

NOTES TO THE CONSOLIDATED FINANCIAL STATEMENTS
(Years ended December 31, 2007 and 2006)
(Tabular amounts in thousands, except per unit and unit amounts)

2. **Acquisitions and Dispositions, (continued)**

solutions to its customers in the oil and gas industry in western Canada. The results from operations of Producers are included in the Oilfield Services segment.

On June 1, 2006, pursuant to the Arrangement, the Fund transferred its northern assets consisting of Beaufort Logistics Inc., Beaufort Oilfield Support Services Ltd., MacKenzie Delta Integrated Oilfield Services Ltd. and MacKenzie Valley Logistics Inc. into Horizon North Logistics Inc. ("Horizon"). The value of the assets transferred totaled $18.1 million which was distributed to unitholders by way of Horizon common shares and purchase warrants on closing of the Arrangement. As a result, the $18.1 million amount transferred has been included as a reduction to retained earnings in the second quarter of 2006.

On February 28, 2006 the Fund acquired all the outstanding shares of Spearing Service Ltd. ("Spearing"), Burnell Contractors Ltd. ("Burnell") and C. Steen Trucking Ltd. ("Steen"). On July 31, 2006, the Fund acquired all the outstanding shares of Canadian Dewatering Limited ("Canadian Dewatering"). On November 6, 2006, the Fund made its final acquisition of the year acquiring Carl Brady Trucking Ltd. and Brady Sand & Gravel Ltd. ("Brady"). Total consideration for these acquisitions was $65.0 million. Spearing's business, based out of Saskatchewan, involves the hauling of crude oil, produced water and other fluids associated with the production of crude oil. Burnell is a Calgary based company involved in providing specialized transportation services to the energy, pipeline, petrochemical and construction industries. The results from operations of Spearing and Burnell are included in the Oilfield Services segment. Steen is a flat deck carrier with operations based out of Edmonton. Steen's results from operations are included in the Trucking/Logistics segment. Canadian Dewatering is a British Columbia based company offering contract dewatering services and the rental and sale of pumps and support equipment. Canadian Dewatering's results from operations are included in the Oilfield Services Segment. Based out of Halbrite, Saskatchewan, Brady provides hauling services to the oil industry in the Midale and Weyburn fields located in southeastern Saskatchewan. The results from operations of Brady are included in the Oilfield Services segment.

These acquisitions have been accounted for by the purchase method, and results of operations have been included in these consolidated financial statements from the date of acquisition. Details of the acquisitions are as follows:

2006		Producers		Kleysen		Pe Ben		Other[1]		Total
Assets:	$	32,852	$	7,429	$	13,668	$	8,693	$	62,642
Non-cash working capital items										
Property, plant and equipment		172,331		51,114		36,389		35,508		295,342
Other assets		9,953		536		75		14		10,578
Intangible assets		88,150		9,800		3,180		17,259		118,389
Goodwill		842,082		34,099		18,108		16,194		910,483
		1,145,368		102,978		71,420		77,668		1,397,434
Assumed liabilities:										
Bank indebtedness		—		4,447		1,487		3,441		9,375
Due to shareholder		—		—		—		3,504		3,504
Long-term debt		76,485		20,468		11,941		7,101		115,995
Future income taxes		62,488		12,813		1,984		76		77,361
		138,973		37,728		15,412		14,122		206,235
Net assets before cash position		1,006,395		65,250		56,008		63,546		1,191,199
Cash position		1,789		—		—		1,435		3,224
Net assets		1,008,184		65,250		56,008		64,981		1,194,423
Consideration:										
Cash		900		60,250		56,008		64,981		182,139
Trust Units (20,045,110)		640,000		5,000		—		—		645,000
B Units (11,182,275)		359,808		—		—		—		359,808
Options issued (789,429)		7,476		—		—		—		7,476
	$	1,008,184	$	65,250	$	56,008	$	64,981	$	1,194,423

[1] *Other consists of Spearing, Burnell, Steen, Canadian Dewatering and Brady.*

NOTES TO THE CONSOLIDATED FINANCIAL STATEMENTS
(Years ended December 31, 2007 and 2006)
(Tabular amounts in thousands, except per unit and unit amounts)

3.   Investments

		2007		2006
Investments - held for trading	$	**7,584**	$	—
Investments accounted for by the equity method		**2,300**		1,825
	$	**9,884**	$	1,825

4.   Property, Plant and Equipment

2007		Cost		Accumulated depreciation		Net book value
Land	$	**66,189**	$	—	$	**66,189**
Buildings		**106,470**		**10,477**		**95,993**
Drilling equipment		**30,651**		**4,623**		**26,028**
Trucks and trailers		**423,764**		**116,286**		**307,478**
Equipment, furniture and fixtures		**117,669**		**40,485**		**77,184**
Automobiles, computer equipment and computer software		**28,805**		**18,394**		**10,411**
Satellite communications equipment		**8,116**		**4,576**		**3,540**
	$	**781,664**	$	**194,841**	$	**586,823**

2006		Cost		Accumulated depreciation		Net book value
Land	$	43,040	$	—	$	43,040
Buildings		93,463		8,525		84,938
Drilling equipment		31,678		3,734		27,944
Trucks and trailers		408,090		87,315		320,775
Equipment, furniture and fixtures		92,484		24,415		68,069
Automobiles, computer equipment and computer software		25,161		15,235		9,926
Satellite communications equipment		7,904		4,074		3,830
	$	701,820	$	143,298	$	558,522

Property, plant and equipment include equipment under capital leases which is recorded at cost, totaling $9.5 million (2006 - $9.6 million), less accumulated depreciation of $1.7 million (2006 - $0.7 million).

5.   Goodwill

Goodwill is the residual amount that results when the purchase price of an acquired business exceeds the sum of the amounts allocated to the assets acquired less liabilities assumed, based on their fair values. As at December 31, 2007, the Fund recorded an impairment of goodwill of $250.0 million. The impairment related to the goodwill acquired with the Producers acquisition, whose operating business units are Formula Powell, Swanberg and Withers which are in the Oilfield Services segment, where the carrying value of goodwill exceeded its fair value. The Fund's Trucking/Logistics segment had no impairment as the fair values of the segment exceeded their carrying values.

NOTES TO THE CONSOLIDATED FINANCIAL STATEMENTS
(Years ended December 31, 2007 and 2006)
(Tabular amounts in thousands, except per unit and unit amounts)

6. **Intangible Assets**

	2007	2006
Intangible assets - cost	$ **137,810**	$ 129,658
Less accumulated amortization	**55,136**	13,374
	$ **82,674**	$ 116,284

Intangible assets are mainly comprised of non-competition agreements and customer relationships and are amortized over their estimated life. As at December 31, 2007, the Fund recorded an impairment of intangible assets totalling $25.0 million. The impairment related to the intangible assets acquired with the Producers acquisition whose operating business units are Formula Powell, Swanberg and Withers, which are in the Oilfield Services segment, where the carrying value of intangible assets exceeded its fair value. There were no indications of impairment in the Fund's other business units as the fair values of those business units exceeded their carrying values.

7. **Other Assets**

Other assets are comprised of deferred compensation, amounts due from related parties and other as follows:

	2007	2006
Deferred compensation	$ **1,771**	$ 4,224
Deferred private debt cost	—	1,525
Due from related parties (note 16)		
Non-interest bearing, unsecured loan	—	540
Interest bearing, secured loan	248	667
	248	1,207
Other	809	2,379
	$ **2,828**	$ 9,335

The deferred compensation asset arose from the unearned stock-based compensation resulting from the exchange of stock options for Trust Unit options in the Producers acquisition.

8. **Distributions Payable**

The Fund declared distributions of $1.80 per unit during the year ended December 31, 2007. Total distributions paid were $147.0 million. Distributions payable is comprised of $12.1 million distributions declared of $0.15 per unit for holders of record on December 31, 2007.

NOTES TO THE CONSOLIDATED FINANCIAL STATEMENTS
(Years ended December 31, 2007 and 2006)
(Tabular amounts in thousands, except per unit and unit amounts)

9.   Long-term Debt

	2007	2006
Bank facility (a)	$ —	$ 18,600
Private placement (b) (c)	390,548	315,500
Term loan bearing interest at 6.3 percent. The loan is repayable in blended principal and interest payments of $57,732 and matures in February, 2014.	3,538	3,995
Various financing loans with no interest monthly principal payments not exceeding $1,238. These loans are secured by specific operating equipment.	30	211
Various financing loans with rates between 2.35 percent and 12.53 percent with monthly blended principal and interest payments not exceeding $23,258. These loans are secured by specific operating equipment.	7,153	6,952
Mortgage facility with a rate of 4.5 percent with blended principal and interest payments of $17,029. This mortgage is secured by specific land, building and operating equipment.	1,140	1,278
Vendor mortgage, non-interest bearing, secured by a general security agreement covering specific operating assets.	—	200
	402,409	346,736
Less current portion	3,817	21,734
	$ 398,592	$ 325,002

Aggregate principal repayments of long-term debt are as follows:	
2008	$ 3,817
2009	2,689
2010	1,916
2011	1,381
2012 and thereafter	392,606
	$ 402,409

(a)   The Fund has available a $150.0 million extendible revolving 364-day term facility convertible to a one year reducing facility.   Interest is payable monthly and is based on either the bank prime rate or bankers' acceptance rates plus a prime acceptance fee which varies from 0.85 percent to 2.0 percent per annum based upon achieving certain financial ratios.   At December 31, 2007, no amounts were drawn on this facility.

(b)   On September 5, 2007, the Fund issued Senior Guaranteed Unsecured Notes by way of private placement of U.S. $85.0 million of Series E Notes and CDN. $20.0 million of Series F Notes.   Both the Series E and Series F Notes mature on September 27, 2017.   The Series E and Series F Notes bear annual interest of 5.90 percent and 5.47 percent, respectively and interest is payable semi-annually.

(c)   On June 29, 2006, the Fund issued Senior Guaranteed Unsecured Notes by way of private placement of U.S. $100.0 million of Series A Notes, U.S. $50.0 million of Series B Notes, CDN. $70.0 million of Series C Notes and CDN. $70.0 million of Series D Notes.   The Series A and Series C Notes mature June 30, 2016 and the Series B and Series D Notes mature June 30, 2018.   The Series A, Series B, Series C, and Series D Notes bear interest of 6.29 percent, 6.39 percent, 5.60 percent and 5.76 percent per annum, respectively.   Interest is payable semi-annually.

(d)   The Fund has $1.8 million of Letters of Credit and Letters of Guarantee outstanding, which were issued to guarantee certain performance and payment obligations.   These Letters of Credit and Guarantee reduce the amount available under the bank credit facility.

(e)   The Fund's debt issuance costs of $2.1 million have been netted against the related indebtedness in accordance with changes in Accounting Policies.

NOTES TO THE CONSOLIDATED FINANCIAL STATEMENTS
(Years ended December 31, 2007 and 2006)
(Tabular amounts in thousands, except per unit and unit amounts)

10. Income Taxes

The provision for income taxes differs from the amounts which would be obtained by applying the expected Canadian statutory rates as follows:

	2007	2006
(Loss) income before income taxes and earnings from equity investments	$ **(135,533)**	$ 129,689
Income tax rate	**33%**	33%
Computed expected income tax expense (recovery)	**(44,726)**	42,797
Add (less):		
Impairment of goodwill	**84,050**	—
Amounts included in Trust income	**(46,934)**	(31,313)
Non-deductible unit-based compensation	**802**	700
Future tax adjustment on temporary differences in flow-through entities (a)	**3,072**	—
Reduction of future tax balances due to substantively enacted income tax rate changes (b)	**(12,562)**	(11,220)
Non-taxable portion of unrealized foreign exchange (gain) loss	**(4,367)**	1,239
Other	**7,425**	352
Provision for income taxes	$ **(13,240)**	$ 2,555

(a)   On June 22, 2007 the Government of Canada enacted a new tax on distributions from SIFT entities. This enactment has triggered the recognition of future income tax assets and liabilities expected to reverse after January 1, 2011. The effect of the income tax increase on the SIFT entity's future income tax balances in the Fund has been reflected as a future income tax expense in 2007.

Income earned directly by MCLP and its subsidiary limited partnerships are not subject to income taxes until January 1, 2011. Prior to January 1, 2011, the Fund is a taxable entity under the Income Tax Act (Canada) and income earned is taxable only to the extent it is not distributed or distributable to its unitholders.

(b)   In 2007, the Government of Canada enacted a Federal tax rate reduction of 1.0 percent in 2008, 1.0 percent in 2009, 1.0 percent in 2010, 2.0 percent in 2011 and 3.5 percent in 2012. The effect of the income tax rate reduction on the Corporation's future income tax balances in the Fund has been reflected as a reduction of future income tax expense in 2007.

The Fund owns eight businesses for which the operating results flow through to the Fund because such businesses are flow-through entities not owned by MT, the Fund's subsidiary. Current temporary income tax differences between the book value and the tax value of certain assets owned by these eight businesses do not result in future income taxes in the Fund's consolidated financial statements. These temporary differences amount to approximately $46.4 million at December 31, 2007 compared to $50.5 million in 2006. As a result of the legislation enacted on June 22, 2007, affecting tax on SIFT entities, the Fund recorded a future tax adjustment of $8.0 million reflecting anticipated differences of $27.8 million as of January 1, 2011.

NOTES TO THE CONSOLIDATED FINANCIAL STATEMENTS
(Years ended December 31, 2007 and 2006)
(Tabular amounts in thousands, except per unit and unit amounts)

10. Income Taxes, (continued)

The future income tax liability consists of the following:

	2007	2006
Liabilities:		
Property, plant and equipment	$ **71,261**	$ 71,614
Partnership income	**32,316**	42,276
Intangible assets and other	**20,687**	24,984
	124,264	138,874
Assets:		
Loss carryforwards	**(211)**	(7,152)
Financing fees	**(696)**	(993)
Future income tax liability	$ **123,357**	$ 130,729

11. Unitholders' Capital

Trust Units: **Authorized: Unlimited Number**	# of Trust Units	Amount
Balance at December 31, 2005	37,760,207	$ 82,792
Units issued for cash (net of unit issue costs of $5.6 million)	3,400,000	96,400
Units issued for Kleysen acquisition	154,875	5,000
Units issued for Producers acquisition	19,890,235	640,000
Issued on exercise of options	56,442	1,478
Issued on exchange of B Units	66,979	1,218
Balance at December 31, 2006	61,328,738	$ 826,888
Units issued on exercise of options	107,460	2,788
Units issued on exchange of B Units	438,983	6,444
Units repurchased	(1,703,700)	(25,005)
Units repurchased, pending cancellation	400,500	5,880
Balance at December 31, 2007	60,571,981	$ 816,995

Pursuant to the normal course issuer bid, the Fund repurchased 1,703,700 Trust Units for $28.7 million in 2007. Unitholders' capital has been reduced by $25.0 million, the stated value of the units. The excess of the amount paid over the stated value of the Trust Units of $3.7 million has been charged to the deficit.

NOTES TO THE CONSOLIDATED FINANCIAL STATEMENTS
(Years ended December 31, 2007 and 2006)
(Tabular amounts in thousands, except per unit and unit amounts)

11. Unitholders' Capital, (continued)

Of the 1,703,700 Trust Units repurchased, 400,500 Trust Units were pending cancellation at December 31, 2007. Accordingly, the stated value of the Trust Units pending cancellation has been recorded in unitholders' equity separate from unitholders' capital. The number of units has been shown as outstanding and has been excluded from per unit calculations.

MCLP B Units*:

Authorized: Unlimited Number	# of B Units		Amount
Balance at December 31, 2005	9,495,549	$	16,199
Units issued for Producers acquisition	11,182,275		359,808
Exchanged for Trust Units	(66,979)		(1,218)
Balance at December 31, 2006	20,610,845		374,789
Exchanged for Trust Units	(438,983)		(6,444)
Balance at December 31, 2007	20,171,862	$	368,345

*B Units are exchangeable for Trust Units on a one for one basis

Summary of Unitholders' Capital:	# of Units		Amount
Trust Units	60,571,981	$	816,995
B Units	20,171,862		368,345
Unitholders' capital at December 31, 2007	80,743,843	$	1,185,340

Unit-based compensation plan:	Options		Weighted average exercise price
Outstanding - December 31, 2005	2,550,000	$	20.66
Granted as part of Producers acquisition	789,429		16.26
Exercised	(56,442)		(11.26)
Cancelled	(103,954)		(18.57)
Outstanding December 31, 2006	3,179,033	$	19.28
Granted	5,000		21.82
Exercised	(107,460)		(11.61)
Cancelled	(162,510)		(19.09)
Outstanding - December 31, 2007	2,914,063	$	19.58
Exercisable - December 31, 2007	244,836	$	18.08

As at December 31, 2007 there are Trust Options outstanding to purchase 2,914,063 Trust Units with prices ranging from $1.59 to $25.50 per Trust Unit with expiry dates ranging from July 19, 2010 to September 9, 2010.

Under the Option Plan, the Fund may grant additional Trust Options to its employees and directors for 2,010,000 Trust Units which have been reserved for this purpose. Under the Option Plan, the exercise price of a Trust Option granted under the Option Plan shall be as determined by the Board of Directors when that Trust Option is granted subject to any limitations imposed by any relevant stock exchange or regulatory authority, and shall be an amount at least equal to the market value of the Trust Units.

NOTES TO THE CONSOLIDATED FINANCIAL STATEMENTS
(Years ended December 31, 2007 and 2006)
(Tabular amounts in thousands, except per unit and unit amounts)

11. Unitholders' Capital, (continued)

The range of exercise prices for options outstanding at December 31, 2007 are as follows:

| | Options Outstanding | | | Exercisable Options | |
Range of Exercise Prices	Number	Weighted Average Remaining Contractual life (years)	Weighted average exercise price	Number	Weighted average exercise price
$1.59 to 9.99	33,333	7.0	$ 8.34	7,408	$ 8.34
$10.00 to 19.99	2,763,519	3.1	19.64	169,284	17.45
$20.00 to 25.50	117,211	7.3	21.21	68,144	20.68
$1.59 to 25.50	2,914,063	3.3	$ 19.58	244,836	$ 18.08

Unit-Based Compensation

The following weighted average assumptions were used to determine the fair value of the options on date of grant:

Risk-free interest rate	3.63%
Expected life	5 - 9 years
Maximum life	10 years
Expected distribution	1.80 per Trust Unit
Expected Trust Unit price volatility	22.02

12. Contributed Surplus

The Fund records compensation expense using the fair value method. Fair values are determined using the Black-Scholes option pricing model. Compensation costs are recognized over the vesting period as an increase to compensation expense and contributed surplus. When options are exercised, the fair value amount in contributed surplus is credited to unitholders' capital.

	Amount
Balance at December 31, 2005	$ 330
Deferred compensation	4,224
Options vested upon Producers acquisition	1,546
Unit-based compensation expense	2,581
Unit options exercised	(842)
Balance at December 31, 2006	$ 7,839
Unit-based compensation expense	3,428
Unit-based compensation expense related to deferred compensation	(2,454)
Unit options exercised	(1,540)
Balance at December 31, 2007	$ 7,273

13. Per Unit Amounts

Basic per unit amounts have been calculated on the weighted average number of units outstanding during the year. The weighted average units outstanding for the year ended December 31, 2007 was 81,596,000 (2006 – 68,886,000).

NOTES TO THE CONSOLIDATED FINANCIAL STATEMENTS
(Years ended December 31, 2007 and 2006)
(Tabular amounts in thousands, except per unit and unit amounts)

13. Per Unit Amounts, (continued)

Diluted per unit amounts are calculated to reflect the dilutive effect of the exercise of options outstanding. The dilutive effect of the exercise of options for the year ended December 31, 2007 and December 31, 2006 was anti-dilutive, therefore, the diluted units for the year ended December 31, 2007 and December 31, 2006 was 81,596,000 and 68,886,000, respectively.

14. Commitments and Contingencies

(a) Commitments:

The Fund is committed to payments under operating leases for equipment and buildings to 2013 and thereafter. Annual minimum payments required subsequent to 2007 are as follows:

2008	$ 14,162
2009	10,483
2010	4,936
2011	1,420
2012	687
2013 and thereafter	641

(b) Contingencies:

The Fund is party to legal proceedings and claims that arise during the ordinary course of business. It is the opinion of management that the ultimate outcome of these matters will not have a material effect upon the Fund's financial position, results of operations or cash flows.

15. Segmented Information

The Fund conducts its business through indirectly owned subsidiaries and limited partnerships which are categorized into two business segments. The Oilfield Services segment provides transportation, drilling and other services to the oil and gas industry which includes exploration and development companies and production and gas transmission companies. The Trucking/Logistics segment provides both long-haul and local transportation services to customers in various industries.

				Intersegment eliminations		
Year ended December 31, 2007	Oilfield Services	Trucking/ Logistics	Corporate	Oilfield Services	Trucking/ Logistics	Total
Revenue	$ 685,384	$ 436,970	$ 2,652	$ (3,057)	$ (2,450)	$ 1,119,499
Revenue, less direct operating expenses, less selling and administrative expenses	151,257	64,311	(6,438)	—	—	209,130
Depreciation	45,964	8,828	2,892	—	—	57,684
Amortization	13,311	3,425	25	—	—	16,761
Total assets	1,424,753	270,482	75,255	—	—	1,770,490
Capital expenditures [(1)]	46,328	13,630	37,445	(586)	(164)	96,653
Goodwill	720,983	73,465	—	—	—	794,448

NOTES TO THE CONSOLIDATED FINANCIAL STATEMENTS
(Years ended December 31, 2007 and 2006)
(Tabular amounts in thousands, except per unit and unit amounts)

15. Segmented Information, (continued)

Year ended December 31, 2006	Oilfield Services	Trucking/ Logistics	Corporate	Intersegment eliminations Oilfield Services	Trucking/ Logistics	Total
Revenue	$ 604,270	$ 400,417	$ 2,279	$ (1,901)	$ (1,778)	$ 1,003,287
Revenue, less direct operating expenses, less selling and administrative expenses	141,587	60,751	(273)	—	—	202,065
Depreciation	32,792	7,421	1,517	—	—	41,730
Amortization	7,693	3,197	15	—	—	10,905
Total assets	1,642,976	253,197	125,072	—	—	2,021,245
Capital expenditures [1]	79,905	16,818	6,590	—	(608)	102,705
Goodwill	962,181	73,465	6,181	—	—	1,041,827

[1] *Excludes business acquisitions*

16. Related Party Transactions

All related party transactions are provided in the normal course of business under the same terms and conditions as transactions with unrelated companies.

Nature of transaction	Nature of relationship	Amount of the transaction 2007	2006
Revenue:			
Transportation services	a, b, c	$ **13,729**	$ 1,062
Management fees	a	**4,873**	—
Other revenue	a, b, c	**46**	49
Sale of property, plant and equipment	a, b, c	**3,798**	1,374
		$ **22,446**	$ 2,485
Expenses:			
Transportation services	a, b	$ **49**	$ 1,007
Other	a, b, c	**872**	857
Purchase of property, plant and equipment	a	**—**	119
		$ **921**	$ 1,983
Balances as at December 31:			
Accounts receivable		$ **1,000**	$ 1,062
Other assets (note 7)		**248**	1,207
Accounts payable		**7**	86

Nature of relationship:

		Equity Ownership
a	Related by equity investment:	
	Beaufort Oilfield Support Services Ltd. (until May 31, 2006)	49%
	Mackenzie Delta Integrated Oilfield Services Ltd. (until May 31, 2006)	39%
	Pe Ben USA Inc.	50%

b Related by common officer or director

c Private companies owned or controlled by an officer or director

NOTES TO THE CONSOLIDATED FINANCIAL STATEMENTS
(Years ended December 31, 2007 and 2006)
(Tabular amounts in thousands, except per unit and unit amounts)

17. **Financial Instruments**

(a) Fair values

The carrying values of cash and cash equivalents, accounts receivable, income taxes recoverable, prepaid expenses, accounts payable and accrued liabilities and distributions payable approximate their fair value due to their short terms to maturity. The fair value of investments and other assets included in the consolidated balance sheet do not materially differ from their carrying values. The fair value of the bank facility approximates its carrying value as it bears interest at floating rates. The carrying value of the private placement debt approximates the fair value as interest rates approximate current rates (see note 9).

(b) Credit risk

The Fund hauls a wide variety of freight for a broad customer base which spans numerous industries. Longer-term contracts are with large, well established customers. No customer accounted for more than 10 percent of the Fund's revenue in 2007 and 2006.

(c) Foreign exchange rate fluctuation

The Fund has U.S. $235.0 million in Senior Guaranteed Unsecured Notes which exposes the Fund to foreign currency fluctuations. The Fund also has U.S. activity in its operations which would partially offset the exposure.

(d) Interest rate risk

The Fund manages its interest rate risk through a combination of fixed and floating rate borrowings.

The Fund is exposed to fluctuations in floating interest rate terms in the bank facility (see note 9).

CORPORATE INFORMATION

DIRECTORS AND OFFICERS

Murray K. Mullen
Chairman, Chief Executive Officer and Director

Alan D. Archibald[1], [2]
Director

Greg Bay[1], [2]
Director

Dennis J. Hoffman, CA[1], [2]
Director

Stephen H. Lockwood, Q.C.
President, Co-Chief Executive Officer and
Director

Richard Peterson
Director

Patrick Powell
Director

Bruce W. Simpson[1], [2]
Director

David E. Olson
Vice President, Finance and Chief Financial
Officer

Bruce W. Mullen
Senior Vice President

Roberta A. Wheatcroft
Corporate Secretary

(1)   Member of the Audit Committee
(2)   Member of the Compensation, Nomination
       and Governance Committee

CORPORATE HEAD OFFICE

Mullen Group Inc.
P.O. Box 87
#1 Maple Leaf Road
Aldersyde, Alberta T0L 0A0
Telephone:(403) 652-8888
Canada/U.S.:   1-800-661-1469
Facsimile: (403) 601-8301
Internet: www.mullen-group.com
Email: IR@mullen-group.com

BANKER

The Royal Bank of Canada
Calgary, Alberta

LAWYERS

Burnet, Duckworth & Palmer LLP
Calgary, Alberta

AUDITORS

KPMG LLP
Calgary, Alberta

STOCK EXCHANGE

Toronto Stock Exchange
Trading Symbol: MTL.UN

TRANSFER AGENT AND REGISTRAR

CIBC Mellon Trust Company
Calgary, Alberta
Telephone: (403) 232-2400
North America: 1-800-387-0825
Outside North America: 1-416-643-5000
Internet: www.cibcmellon.com

Appendix C

Typical Charts of Accounts for Different Types of Businesses

A Simple Service Corporation

Assets	*Liabilities*	*Shareholders' Equity*
Cash	Accounts Payable	Common Shares
Accounts Receivable	Notes Payable, Short-Term	Retained Earnings
Allowance for Uncollectible Accounts	Salary Payable	Dividends
Notes Receivable, Short Term	Wages Payable	
Goods and Services Tax Receivable	Goods and Services Tax Payable	
Interest Receivable	Employee Withheld Income Tax Payable	
Supplies	Employment Insurance Payable	
Prepaid Rent	Canada (Quebec) Pension Plan Payable	*Revenues and Gains*
Prepaid Insurance	Employee Benefits Payable	
Notes Receivable, Long-Term	Interest Payable	Service Revenue
Land	Unearned Service Revenue	Interest Revenue
Furniture	Notes Payable, Long-Term	Gain on Sale of Land (Furniture, Equipment, or Building)
Accumulated Amortization—Furniture		
Equipment		*Expenses and Losses*
Accumulated Amortization—Equipment		
Building		Salary Expense
Accumulated Amortization—Building		Wages Expense
		Payroll Benefits Expense
		Insurance Expense for Employees
		Rent Expense
		Insurance Expense
		Supplies Expense
		Uncollectible Accounts Expense
		Amortization Expense—Furniture
		Amortization Expense—Equipment
		Amortization Expense—Building
		Property Tax Expense
		Interest Expense
		Miscellaneous Expense
		Loss on Sale (or Exchange) of Land (Furniture, Equipment, or Building)

Service Partnership

Same as service corporation, except for owners' equity

Owners' Equity

Partner 1, Capital
Partner 2, Capital
.
.
.
Partner N, Capital

Partner 1, Withdrawals
Partner 2, Withdrawals
.
.
.
Partner N, Withdrawals

A Complex Merchandising Corporation

Assets	Liabilities	Shareholders' Equity	

Assets	Liabilities	Shareholders' Equity
Cash	Accounts Payable	Preferred Shares
Short-Term Investments	Notes Payable, Short-Term	Common Shares
Accounts Receivable	Current Portion of Bonds	Contributed Surplus
Allowance for	Payable	Share Repurchase
Uncollectible Accounts	Salary Payable	Retained Earnings
Notes Receivable,	Wages Payable	Foreign Currency
Short-Term	Goods and Services Tax	Translation Adjustment
Goods and Services	Payable	Accumulated Other
Tax Receivable	Employee Withheld Income	Comprehensive Income
Interest Receivable	Tax Payable	
Inventory	Employment Insurance	
Supplies	Payable	
Prepaid Rent	Canada (Quebec) Pension	
Prepaid Insurance	Plan Payable	
Notes Receivable,	Employee Benefits Payable	
Long-Term	Interest Payable	
Investments in	Income Tax Payable	
Subsidiaries	Unearned Sales Revenue	
Long-term Investments	Notes Payable, Long-Term	
Other Receivables,	Bonds Payable	
Long-Term	Lease Liability	*Revenues and Gains*
Land	Minority Interest	Sales Revenue
Land Improvements		Interest Revenue
Furniture and Fixtures		Dividend Revenue
Accumulated		Equity-Method
Amortization—		Investment Revenue
Furniture and Fixtures		Gain on Sale of
Equipment		Investments
Accumulated		Gain on Sale of Land
Amortization—		(Furniture and Fixtures,
Equipment		Equipment, or
Buildings		Buildings)
Accumulated		Discontinued
Amortization—		Operations—Gain
Buildings		Extraordinary Gains
Organization Cost		Other Comprehensive Income
Franchises		
Patents		
Leaseholds		
Goodwill		

Expenses and Losses

Cost of Goods Sold
Salary Expense
Wages Expense
Commission Expense
Payroll Benefits Expense
Rent Expense
Insurance Expense
Supplies Expense
Uncollectible Accounts
  Expense
Amortization Expense—
  Land Improvements
Amortization Expense—
  Furniture and Fixtures
Amortization Expense—
  Equipment
Amortization Expense—
  Buildings
Amortization Expense—
  Franchises
Amortization Expense—
  Leaseholds
Amortization Expense—
  Goodwill
Incorporation Expense
Income Tax Expense
Loss on Sale of
  Investments
Loss on Sale (or Exchange)
  of Land (Furniture and
  Fixtures, Equipment,
  or Buildings)
Discontinued
  Operations—Loss
Extraordinary Losses

A Manufacturing Corporation

	Assets
Same as merchandising corporation, except for Assets	

Inventories:
  Materials Inventory
  Work-in-Process Inventory
  Finished Goods Inventory
Factory Wages
Factory Overhead

Appendix D

Time Value of Money: Future Value and Present Value

The following discussion of future value lays the foundation for our explanation of present value in Chapter 8 but is not essential. For the valuation of long-term liabilities, some instructors may wish to begin on page 718.

The term *time value of money* refers to the fact that money earns interest over time. *Interest* is the cost of using money. To borrowers, interest is the expense of renting money. To lenders, interest is the revenue earned from lending. We must always recognize the interest we receive or pay. Otherwise, we overlook an important part of the transaction. Suppose you invest $4,545 in corporate bonds that pay 10% interest each year. After one year, the value of your investment has grown to $5,000. The difference between your original investment ($4,545) and the future value of the investment ($5,000) is the amount of interest revenue you will earn during the year ($455). If you ignored the interest, you would fail to account for the interest revenue you have earned. Interest becomes more important as the time period lengthens because the amount of interest depends on the span of time the money is invested.

Let's consider a second example, this time from the borrower's perspective. Suppose you purchase a machine for your business. The cash price of the machine is $8,000, but you cannot pay cash now. To finance the purchase, you sign an $8,000 note payable. The note requires you to pay the $8,000 plus 10% interest one year from the date of purchase. Is your cost of the machine $8,000, or is it $8,800 [$8,000 plus interest of $800 ($8,000 × 0.10)]? The cost is $8,000. The additional $800 is interest expense and not part of the cost of the machine.

Future Value

The main application of future value is the accumulated balance of an investment at a future date. In our first example above, the investment earned 10% per year. After one year, $4,545 grew to $5,000, as shown in Exhibit D-1.

If the money were invested for five years, you would have to perform five such calculations. You would also have to consider the compound interest that your investment is earning. *Compound interest* is not only the interest you earn on your principal amount, but also the interest you receive on the interest you have already earned. Most business applications include compound interest. The following table shows the interest revenue earned on the original $4,545 investment each year for five years at 10%:

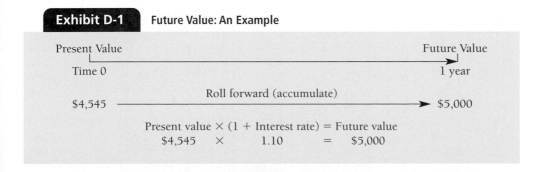

Exhibit D-1 Future Value: An Example

Present Value   Future Value

Time 0   1 year

Roll forward (accumulate)

$4,545 ————————————————————→ $5,000

Present value × (1 + Interest rate) = Future value
$4,545   ×   1.10   = $5,000

End of Year	Interest	Future Value
0	—	$4,545
1	$4,545 × 0.10 = $455	5,000
2	5,000 × 0.10 = 500	5,500
3	5,500 × 0.10 = 550	6,050
4	6,050 × 0.10 = 605	6,655
5	6,655 × 0.10 = 666	7,321

Earning 10%, a $4,545 investment grows to $5,000 at the end of one year, to $5,500 at the end of two years, and $7,321 at the end of five years. Throughout this appendix we round off to the nearest dollar.

Future-Value Tables

The process of computing a future value is called *accumulating* because the future value is *more* than the present value. Mathematical tables ease the computational burden. Exhibit D-2, Future Value of $1, gives the future value for a single sum (a present value), $1, invested to earn a particular interest rate for a specific number of periods. Future value depends on three factors: (1) the amount of the investment, (2) the length of time between investment and future accumulation, and (3) the interest rate. Future-value and present-value tables are based on $1 because unity (the value 1) is so easy to work with.

In business applications, interest rates are always stated for the annual period of one year unless specified otherwise. In fact, an interest rate can be stated for any period, such as 3% per quarter or 5% for a six-month period. The length of the period is arbitrary. For example, an investment may promise a return (income) of 3% per quarter for six months (two quarters). In that case, you would be working with 3% interest for two periods. It would be incorrect to use 6% for one period because the interest is 3% compounded quarterly, and that amount differs from 6% compounded semiannually. *Take care in studying future-value and present-value problems to align the interest rate with the appropriate number of periods.*

Let's see how a future-value table like the one in Exhibit D-2 is used. The future value of $1.00 invested at 8% for one year is $1.08 ($1.00 × 1.080, which appears at the

Exhibit D-2 Future Value of $1

				Future Value of $1						
Periods	4%	5%	6%	7%	8%	9%	10%	12%	14%	16%
1	1.040	1.050	1.060	1.070	1.080	1.090	1.100	1.120	1.140	1.160
2	1.082	1.103	1.124	1.145	1.166	1.188	1.210	1.254	1.300	1.346
3	1.125	1.158	1.191	1.225	1.260	1.295	1.331	1.405	1.482	1.561
4	1.170	1.216	1.262	1.311	1.360	1.412	1.464	1.574	1.689	1.811
5	1.217	1.276	1.338	1.403	1.469	1.539	1.611	1.762	1.925	2.100
6	1.265	1.340	1.419	1.501	1.587	1.677	1.772	1.974	2.195	2.436
7	1.316	1.407	1.504	1.606	1.714	1.828	1.949	2.211	2.502	2.826
8	1.369	1.477	1.594	1.718	1.851	1.993	2.144	2.476	2.853	3.278
9	1.423	1.551	1.689	1.838	1.999	2.172	2.358	2.773	3.252	3.803
10	1.480	1.629	1.791	1.967	2.159	2.367	2.594	3.106	3.707	4.411
11	1.539	1.710	1.898	2.105	2.332	2.580	2.853	3.479	4.226	5.117
12	1.601	1.796	2.012	2.252	2.518	2.813	3.138	3.896	4.818	5.936
13	1.665	1.886	2.133	2.410	2.720	3.066	3.452	4.363	5.492	6.886
14	1.732	1.980	2.261	2.579	2.937	3.342	3.798	4.887	6.261	7.988
15	1.801	2.079	2.397	2.759	3.172	3.642	4.177	5.474	7.138	9.266
16	1.873	2.183	2.540	2.952	3.426	3.970	4.595	6.130	8.137	10.748
17	1.948	2.292	2.693	3.159	3.700	4.328	5.054	6.866	9.276	12.468
18	2.026	2.407	2.854	3.380	3.996	4.717	5.560	7.690	10.575	14.463
19	2.107	2.527	3.026	3.617	4.316	5.142	6.116	8.613	12.056	16.777
20	2.191	2.653	3.207	3.870	4.661	5.604	6.728	9.646	13.743	19.461

junction of the 8% column and row 1 in the Periods column). The figure 1.080 includes both the principal (1.000) and the compound interest for one period (0.080).

Suppose you deposit $5,000 in a savings account that pays annual interest of 8%. The account balance at the end of one year will be $5,400. To compute the future value of $5,000 at 8% for one year, multiply $5,000 by 1.080 to get $5,400. Now suppose you invest in a 10-year, 8% guaranteed investment certificate (GIC). What will be the future value of the GIC at maturity? To compute the future value of $5,000 at 8% for 10 periods, multiply $5,000 by 2.159 (from Exhibit D-2) to get $10,795. This future value of $10,795 indicates that $5,000, earning 8% interest compounded annually, grows to $10,795 at the end of 10 years. Using Exhibit D-2, you can find any present amount's future value at a particular future date. Future value is especially helpful for computing the amount of cash you will have on hand for some purpose in the future.

Future Value of an Annuity

In the preceding example, we made an investment of a single amount. Other investments, called *annuities*, include multiple investments of an equal periodic amount at fixed intervals over the duration of the investment. Consider a family investing for a child's education. The Dietrichs can invest $4,000 annually to accumulate a college fund for 15-year-old Helen. The investment can earn 7% annually until Helen turns 18—a three-year investment. How much will be available for Helen on the date of the last investment? Exhibit D-3 shows the accumulation—a total future value of $12,860.

The first $4,000 invested by the Dietrichs grows to $4,580 over the investment period. The second amount grows to $4,280, and the third amount stays at $4,000 because it has no time to earn interest. The sum of the three future values ($4,580 + $4,280 + $4,000) is the future value of the annuity ($12,860), which can also be computed as follows:

End of Year	Annual Investment	Interest		Increase for the Year	Future Value of Annuity
0	—	—		—	0
1	$4,000	—		$4,000	$ 4,000
2	4,000	+ ($4,000 × 0.07 = $280)	=	4,280	8,280
3	4,000	+ ($8,280 × 0.07 = $580)	=	4,580	12,860

These computations are laborious. As with the Future Value of $1 (a lump sum), mathematical tables ease the strain of calculating annuities. Exhibit D-4, Future Value of Annuity of $1, gives the future value of a series of investments, each of equal amount, at regular intervals.

What is the future value of an annuity of three investments of $1 each that earn 7%? The answer, 3.215, can be found at the junction of the 7% column and row 3 in Exhibit D-4. This amount can be used to compute the future value of the investment for Helen's education, as follows:

Amount of each periodic investment	×	Future value of annuity of $1 (Exhibit D-4)	=	Future value of investment
$4,000	×	3.215	=	$12,860

Exhibit D-3   Future Value of an Annuity

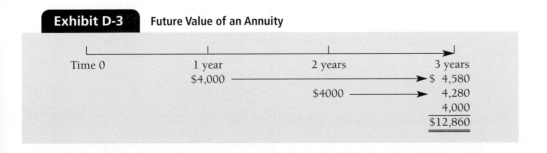

| Exhibit D-4 | Future Value of Annuity of $1 |

Future Value of Annuity of $1

Periods	4%	5%	6%	7%	8%	9%	10%	12%	14%	16%
1	1.000	1.000	1.000	1.000	1.000	1.000	1.000	1.000	1.000	1.000
2	2.040	2.050	2.060	2.070	2.080	2.090	2.100	2.120	2.140	2.160
3	3.122	3.153	3.184	3.215	3.246	3.278	3.310	3.374	3.440	3.506
4	4.246	4.310	4.375	4.440	4.506	4.573	4.641	4.779	4.921	5.066
5	5.416	5.526	5.637	5.751	5.867	5.985	6.105	6.353	6.610	6.877
6	6.633	6.802	6.975	7.153	7.336	7.523	7.716	8.115	8.536	8.977
7	7.898	8.142	8.394	8.654	8.923	9.200	9.487	10.089	10.730	11.414
8	9.214	9.549	9.897	10.260	10.637	11.028	11.436	12.300	13.233	14.240
9	10.583	11.027	11.491	11.978	12.488	13.021	13.579	14.776	16.085	17.519
10	12.006	12.578	13.181	13.816	14.487	15.193	15.937	17.549	19.337	21.321
11	13.486	14.207	14.972	15.784	16.645	17.560	18.531	20.655	23.045	25.733
12	15.026	15.917	16.870	17.888	18.977	20.141	21.384	24.133	27.271	30.850
13	16.627	17.713	18.882	20.141	21.495	22.953	24.523	28.029	32.089	36.786
14	18.292	19.599	21.015	22.550	24.215	26.019	27.975	32.393	37.581	43.672
15	20.024	21.579	23.276	25.129	27.152	29.361	31.772	37.280	43.842	51.660
16	21.825	23.657	25.673	27.888	30.324	33.003	35.950	42.753	50.980	60.925
17	23.698	25.840	28.213	30.840	33.750	36.974	40.545	48.884	59.118	71.673
18	25.645	28.132	30.906	33.999	37.450	41.301	45.599	55.750	68.394	84.141
19	27.671	30.539	33.760	37.379	41.446	46.018	51.159	63.440	78.969	98.603
20	29.778	33.066	36.786	40.995	45.762	51.160	57.275	72.052	91.025	115.380

This one-step calculation is much easier than computing the future value of each annual investment and then summing the individual future values. In this way, you can compute the future value of any investment consisting of equal periodic amounts at regular intervals. Businesses make periodic investments to accumulate funds for equipment replacement and other uses—an application of the future value of an annuity.

Present Value

Often a person knows a future amount and needs to know the related present value. Recall Exhibit D-1, in which present value and future value are on opposite ends of the same time line. Suppose an investment promises to pay you $5,000 at the *end* of one year. How much would you pay *now* to acquire this investment? You would be willing to pay the present value of the $5,000 future amount.

Like future value, present value depends on three factors: (1) the *amount of payment (or receipt)*, (2) the length of *time* between investment and future receipt (or *payment*), and (3) the *interest rate*. The process of computing a present value is called *discounting* because the present value is *less* than the future value.

In our investment example, the future receipt is $5,000. The investment period is one year. Assume that you demand an annual interest rate of 10% on your investment. With all three factors specified, you can compute the present value of $5,000 at 10% for one year:

$$\text{Present value} = \frac{\text{Future value}}{1 + \text{Interest rate}} = \frac{\$5,000}{1.10} = \$4,545$$

By turning the data around into a future-value problem, we can verify the present-value computation:

Amount invested (present value)..	$4,545
Expected earnings ($4,545 × 0.10)...	455
Amount to be received one year from now (future value).................................	$5,000

This example illustrates that present value and future value are based on the same equation:

$$\text{Future} = \text{Present value} \times (1 + \text{Interest rate})$$

$$\text{Present value} = \frac{\text{Future value}}{1 + \text{Interest rate}}$$

If the $5,000 is to be received two years from now, you will pay only $4,132 for the investment, as shown in Exhibit D-5. By turning the data around, we verify that $4,132 accumulates to $5,000 at 10% for two years:

Amount invested (present value)...	$4,132
Expected earnings for first year ($4,132 × 0.10)	413
Value of investment after one year..	4,545
Expected earnings for second year ($4,545 × 0.10)	455
Amount to be received two years from now (future value)	$5,000

You would pay $4,132—the present value of $5,000—to receive the $5,000 future amount at the end of two years at 10% per year. The $868 difference between the amount invested ($4,132) and the amount to be received ($5,000) is the return on the investment, the sum of the two interest receipts: $413 + $455 = $868.

Present-Value Tables

We have shown the simple formula for computing present value. However, calculating present value "by hand" for investments spanning many years is time-consuming and presents too many opportunities for arithmetic errors. Present-value tables ease our work. Let's reexamine our examples of present value by using Exhibit D-6: Present Value of $1 given at the top of the next page.

For the 10% investment for one year, we find the junction of the 10% column and row 1 in Exhibit D-6. The figure 0.909 is computed as follows: 1/1.10 = 0.909. This work has been done for us, and only the present values are given in the table. To calculate the present value for $5,000, we multiply 0.909 by $5,000. The result is $4,545, which matches the result we obtained by hand.

For the two-year investment, we read down the 10% column and across row 2. We multiply 0.826 (computed as 0.909/1.10 = 0.826) by $5,000 and get $4,130, which confirms our earlier computation of $4,132 (the difference is due to rounding in the present-value table). Using the table, we can compute the present value of any single future amount.

Present Value of an Annuity

Return to the investment example on page 757. That investment provided the investor with only a single future receipt ($5,000 at the end of two years). *Annuity investments* provide multiple receipts of an equal amount at fixed intervals over the investment's duration.

Consider an investment that promises *annual* cash receipts of $10,000 to be received at the end of each of three years. Assume that you demand a 12% return on your investment.

Exhibit D-5 Future Value: An Example

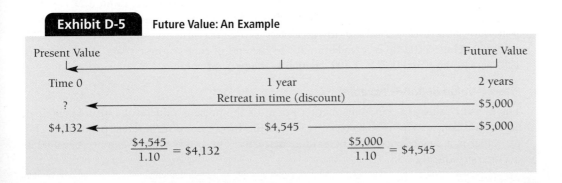

| Exhibit D-6 | Present Value of $1 |

Present Value of $1

Periods	4%	5%	6%	7%	8%	10%	12%	14%	16%
1	0.962	0.952	0.943	0.935	0.926	0.909	0.893	0.877	0.862
2	0.925	0.907	0.890	0.873	0.857	0.826	0.797	0.769	0.743
3	0.889	0.864	0.840	0.816	0.794	0.751	0.712	0.675	0.641
4	0.855	0.823	0.792	0.763	0.735	0.683	0.636	0.592	0.552
5	0.822	0.784	0.747	0.713	0.681	0.621	0.567	0.519	0.476
6	0.790	0.746	0.705	0.666	0.630	0.564	0.507	0.456	0.410
7	0.760	0.711	0.665	0.623	0.583	0.513	0.452	0.400	0.354
8	0.731	0.677	0.627	0.582	0.540	0.467	0.404	0.351	0.305
9	0.703	0.645	0.592	0.544	0.500	0.424	0.361	0.308	0.263
10	0.676	0.614	0.558	0.508	0.463	0.386	0.322	0.270	0.227
11	0.650	0.585	0.527	0.475	0.429	0.350	0.287	0.237	0.195
12	0.625	0.557	0.497	0.444	0.397	0.319	0.257	0.208	0.168
13	0.601	0.530	0.469	0.415	0.368	0.290	0.229	0.182	0.145
14	0.577	0.505	0.442	0.388	0.340	0.263	0.205	0.160	0.125
15	0.555	0.481	0.417	0.362	0.315	0.239	0.183	0.140	0.108
16	0.534	0.458	0.394	0.339	0.292	0.218	0.163	0.123	0.093
17	0.513	0.436	0.371	0.317	0.270	0.198	0.146	0.108	0.080
18	0.494	0.416	0.350	0.296	0.250	0.180	0.130	0.095	0.069
19	0.475	0.396	0.331	0.277	0.232	0.164	0.116	0.083	0.060
20	0.456	0.377	0.312	0.258	0.215	0.149	0.104	0.073	0.051

What is the investment's present value? That is, what would you pay today to acquire the investment? The investment spans three periods, and you would pay the sum of three present values. The computation is as follows:

Year	Annual Cash Receipt	Present Value of $1 at 12% (Exhibit D-6)	Present Value of Annual Cash Receipt
1	$10,000	0.893	$ 8,930
2	10,000	0.797	7,970
3	10,000	0.712	7,120
Total present value of investment			$24,020

The present value of this annuity is $24,020. By paying this amount today, you will receive $10,000 at the end of each of the three years while earning 12% on your investment.

This example illustrates repetitive computations of the three future amounts, a time-consuming process. One way to ease the computational burden is to add the three present values of $1 (0.893 + 0.797 + 0.712) and multiply their sum (2.402) by the annual cash receipt ($10,000) to obtain the present value of the annuity ($10,000 × 2.402 = $24,020).

An easier approach is to use a present value of an annuity table. Exhibit D-7 shows the present value of $1 to be received periodically for a given number of periods. The present value of a three-period annuity at 12% is 2.402 (the junction of row 3 and the 12% column). Thus, $10,000 received annually at the end of each of three years, discounted at 12%, is $24,020 ($10,000 × 2.402), which is the present value.

Present Value of Bonds Payable

The present value of a bond—its market price—is the present value of the future principal amount at maturity plus the present value of the future contract interest payments. The principal is a *single amount* to be paid at maturity. The interest is an *annuity* because it occurs periodically.

Exhibit D-6		Present Value of Annuity of $1							

				Present Value Annuity of $1					
Periods	4%	5%	6%	7%	8%	10%	12%	14%	16%
1	0.962	0.952	0.943	0.935	0.926	0.909	0.893	0.877	0.862
2	1.886	1.859	1.833	1.808	1.783	1.736	1.690	1.647	1.605
3	2.775	2.723	2.673	2.624	2.577	2.487	2.402	2.322	2.246
4	3.630	3.546	3.465	3.387	3.312	3.170	3.037	2.914	2.798
5	4.452	4.329	4.212	4.100	3.993	3.791	3.605	3.433	3.274
6	5.242	5.076	4.917	4.767	4.623	4.355	4.111	3.889	3.685
7	6.002	5.786	5.582	5.389	5.206	4.868	4.564	4.288	4.039
8	6.733	6.463	6.210	5.971	5.747	5.335	4.968	4.639	4.344
9	7.435	7.108	6.802	6.515	6.247	5.759	5.328	4.946	4.607
10	8.111	7.722	7.360	7.024	6.710	6.145	5.650	5.216	4.833
11	8.760	8.306	7.887	7.499	7.139	6.495	5.938	5.453	5.029
12	9.385	8.863	8.384	7.943	7.536	6.814	6.194	5.660	5.197
13	9.986	9.394	8.853	8.358	7.904	7.103	6.424	5.842	5.342
14	10.563	9.899	9.295	8.745	8.244	7.367	6.628	6.002	5.468
15	11.118	10.380	9.712	9.108	8.559	7.606	6.811	6.142	5.575
16	11.652	10.838	10.106	9.447	8.851	7.824	6.974	6.265	5.669
17	12.166	11.274	10.477	9.763	9.122	8.022	7.120	6.373	5.749
18	12.659	11.690	10.828	10.059	9.372	8.201	7.250	6.467	5.818
19	13.134	12.085	11.158	10.336	9.604	8.365	7.366	6.550	5.877
20	13.590	12.462	11.470	10.594	9.818	8.514	7.469	6.623	5.929

Let's compute the present value of the 9% five-year bonds of TELUS Communications Inc.[1] (discussed on page 381). The face value of the bonds is $100,000, and they pay $4^1/2\%$ contract (cash) interest semiannually (that is, twice a year).[2] At issuance, the market interest rate is expressed as 10% annually, but it is computed at 5% semiannually. Therefore, the effective interest rate for each of the 10 semiannual periods is 5%. We thus use 5% in computing the present value (PV) of the maturity and of the interest. The market price of these bonds is $96,149, as follows:

	Effective annual interest rate ÷ 2	*Number of semiannual interest payments*	
PV of principal:			
$100,000 × PV of single amount at 5%		for 10 periods	
$100,000 × 0.614 (Exhibit D-6)			$61,400
PV of contract (cash) interest:			
$100,000 × 0.045 × PV of annuity at 5%		for 10 periods	
$4,500 × 7.722 (Exhibit D-7)			34,749
PV (market price) of bonds			$96,149

The market price of the TELUS bonds shows a discount because the contract interest rate on the bonds (9%) is less than the market interest rate (10%).

---

[1]This issue of TELUS bonds is used for illustrative purposes and does represent actual bonds.

Let's consider a premium price for the 9% TELUS bonds. Assume that the market interest rate is 8% (rather than 10%) at issuance. The effective interest rate is thus 4% for each of the 10 semiannual periods:

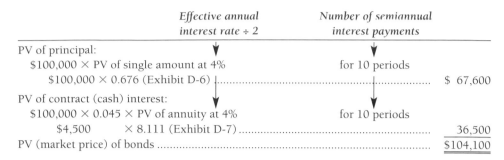

	Effective annual interest rate ÷ 2	Number of semiannual interest payments	
PV of principal:			
$100,000 × PV of single amount at 4%		for 10 periods	
$100,000 × 0.676 (Exhibit D-6)			$ 67,600
PV of contract (cash) interest:			
$100,000 × 0.045 × PV of annuity at 4%		for 10 periods	
$4,500 × 8.111 (Exhibit D-7)			36,500
PV (market price) of bonds			$104,100

We discuss accounting for these bonds on pages 386–387. It may be helpful for you to reread this section ("Present Value of Bonds Payable") after you've studied those pages.

Capital Leases

How does a lessee compute the cost of an asset acquired through a capital lease? (See page 424 for a definition of capital leases.) Consider that the lessee gets the use of the asset but does *not* pay for the leased asset in full at the beginning of the lease. A capital lease is therefore similar to an installment purchase of the leased asset. The lessee must record the leased asset at the present value of the lease liability. The time value of money must be weighed.

The cost of the asset to the lessee is the sum of any payment made at the beginning of the lease period plus the present value of the future lease payments. The lease payments are equal amounts occurring at regular intervals—that is, they are annuity payments.

Consider a 20-year building lease that requires 20 annual payments of $10,000 each, with the first payment due immediately. The interest rate in the lease is 10%, and the present value of the 19 future payments is $83,650 ($10,000 × PV of annuity at 10% for 19 periods, or 8.365 from Exhibit D-7). The lessee's cost of the building is $93,650 (the sum of the initial payment, $10,000, plus the present value of the future payments, $83,650). The lessee would base its accounting for the leased asset (and the related amortization) and for the lease liability (and the related interest expense) on the cost of the building that we have just computed.

Appendix Problems

PD-1 For each situation, compute the required amount.

a. Suppose **Enbridge Inc.** is budgeting for the acquisition of land over the next several years. Enbridge Inc. can invest $100,000 today at 9%. How much cash will Enbridge Inc. have for land acquisitions at the end of five years? At the end of six years?

b. Stedan Inc. is planning to invest $50,000 each year for five years. The company's investment adviser believes that Stedan Inc. can earn 6% interest without taking on too much risk. What will be the value of Stedan Inc.'s investment on the date of the last deposit if Stedan Inc. can earn 6%? If Stedan Inc. can earn 8%?

PD-2 For each situation, compute the required amount.

a. Suppose **Rogers Communications Inc.**'s operations are generating excess cash that will be invested in a special fund. During 2005, Rogers invests $5,643,341 in the fund for a planned advertising campaign on a new product to be released six years later, in 2011. If Rogers' investments can earn 10% each year, how much cash will the company have for the advertising campaign in 2011?

b. Rogers will need $10 million to advertise new software in 2011. How much must Rogers invest in 2005 to have the cash available for the advertising campaign? Rogers' investments can earn 10% annually.

c. Explain the relationship between your answers to *a* and *b*.

PD-3 Determine the present value of the following notes and bonds:

1. Ten-year bonds payable with maturity value of $500,000 and contract interest rate of 12%, paid semi-annually. The market rate of interest is 12% at issuance.
2. Same bonds payable as in number 1, but the market interest rate is 14%.
3. Same bonds payable as in number 1, but the market interest rate is 10%.

PD-4 On December 31, 2006, when the market interest rate is 8%, Circle 4 Corp. issues $400,000 of 10-year, 7.25% bonds payable. The bonds pay interest semiannually.

Required

1. Determine the present value of the bonds at issuance.
2. Assume that the bonds are issued at the price computed in Requirement 1. Prepare an effective-interest-method amortization table for the first two semiannual interest periods.
3. Using the amortization table prepared in Requirement 2, journalize issuance of the bonds and the first two interest payments and amortization of the bonds.

PD-5 St. Mere Eglise Children's Home needs a fleet of vans to transport the children to singing engagements throughout Normandy. Renault offers the vehicles for a single payment of €630,000 due at the end of four years. Peugeot prices a similar fleet of vans for four annual payments of €150,000 at the end of each year. The children's home could borrow the funds at 6%, so this is the appropriate interest rate. Which company should get the business, Renault or Peugeot? Base your decision on present value, and give your reason.

PD-6 Surrey Pre-School Inc. acquired equipment under a capital lease that requires six annual lease payments of $40,000. The first payment is due when the lease begins, on January 1, 2007. Future payments are due on January 1 of each year of the lease term. The interest rate in the lease is 16%.

Required

Compute the cost of the equipment to Surrey Pre-School Inc.

Appendix E

Summary of Generally Accepted Accounting Principles (GAAP)

Every technical area has professional associations and regulatory bodies that govern the practice of the profession. Accounting is no exception. In Canada, the Canadian Institute of Chartered Accountants (CICA) has the responsibility for issuing accounting standards that form the basis of generally accepted accounting principles (GAAP). The authority for setting GAAP was delegated to the CICA by the federal and provincial governments and the Canadian Securities Administrators in the 1970s.

The CICA's pronouncements, called *Recommendations*, are collected in Volume I of the *CICA Handbook*. The Recommendations specify how to account for particular business transactions and must be followed, except in those rare cases where a particular Recommendation or Recommendations would not lead to fair presentation. In those cases, the accountant should, using professional judgment, select the appropriate accounting principles. An accountant who determines that the *CICA Handbook* is not appropriate and selects some other basis of accounting must be prepared to defend that decision.

Each new Recommendation issued by the CICA becomes part of GAAP, the "accounting law of the land." In the same way that our laws draw authority from their acceptance by the people, GAAP depend on general acceptance by the business community. Throughout this book, we refer to GAAP as the proper way to do financial accounting.

The Objective of Financial Reporting

The basic objective of financial reporting is to provide information that is useful in making investment and lending decisions. Accounting information can be useful in decision making only if it is *understandable, relevant, reliable, comparable*, and *consistent*.

Accounting information must be *understandable* to users if they are to be able to use it. *Relevant* information is useful in making predictions and for evaluating past performance—that is, the information has feedback value. For example, Canadian Tire Corporation, Limited's disclosure of the profitability of each of its lines of business is relevant for investor evaluations of the company. To be relevant, information must be timely. *Reliable* information is free from significant error—that is, it has validity. Also, it is free from the bias of a particular viewpoint—that is, it is verifiable and neutral. *Comparable* and *consistent* information can be compared from period to period to help investors and creditors assess the entity's progress through time. These characteristics combine to shape the concepts and principles that comprise GAAP. Exhibit E-1 on page 727 summarizes the concepts and principles that accounting has developed to provide useful information for decision making.

EXHIBIT E-1	Summary of Important Accounting Concepts, Principles, and Financial Statements

Concepts, Principles and Financial Statements	Quick Summary	Text Reference
Concepts		
Entity concept	Accounting draws a boundary around each organization to be accounted for.	Chapter 1, page 10
Relevance characteristic	The information in financial statements must be appropriate to the decision a user wishes to make if the financial information is to be useful for the user.	Chapter 1, page 11
Understandability characteristic	Users must be able to understand the information in financial statements if the information is to be useful.	Chapter 1, page 12
Going-concern concept	Accountants assume the business will continue operating for the foreseeable future.	Chapter 1, page 12
Stable-monetary-unit concept	Accounting information is expressed primarily in monetary terms that ignore the effects of inflation.	Chapter 1, page 13
Time-period concept	Ensures that accounting information is reported at regular intervals.	Chapter 3, page 105
Conservatism concept	Accountants report items in the financial statements in a way that avoids overstating assets, owners' equity, and revenues, and avoids understating liabilities and expenses.	Chapter 6, page 265
Principles		
Reliability (objectivity) principle	Accounting records and statements are based on the most reliable data available.	Chapter 1, page 11
Cost principle	Assets and services, revenues and expenses are recorded at their actual historical cost.	Chapter 1, page 12
Revenue principle	Tells accountants when to record revenue (only after it has been earned) and the amount of revenue to record (the cash value of what has been received).	Chapter 3, page 106
Matching principle	Directs accountants to (1) identify and measure all expenses incurred during the period and (2) match the expenses against the revenues earned during the period. The goal is to measure net income.	Chapter 3, page 106
Consistency principle	Businesses should use the same accounting methods from period to period.	Chapter 6, page 265
Disclosure principle	A company's financial statements should report enough information for outsiders to make informed decisions about the company.	Chapter 6, page 265
Financial Statements		
Balance sheet	Assets = Liabilities + Owners' Equity at a point in time.	Chapter 1
Income statement	Revenues and gains − Expenses and losses = Net income or net loss for the periods.	Chapters 1 and 11
Cash flow statement	Cash receipts − Cash payments = Increase or decrease in cash during the period, grouped under operating, investing, and financing activities.	Chapters 1 and 12
Statement of retained earnings	Beginning retained earnings + Net income (or − Net loss) − Dividends = Ending retained earnings.	Chapters 1 and 11
Statement of shareholders' equity	Shows the reason for the change in each shareholders' equity account, including retained earnings.	Chapter 11
Financial statement notes	Provide information that cannot be reported conveniently on the face of the financial statements. The notes are an integral part of the statements.	Chapter 11

Appendix F

Check Figures*

Chapter 1

S1-1	NCF
S1-2	NCF
S1-3	NCF
S1-4	NCF
S1-5	NCF
S1-6	NCF
S1-7	NCF
S1-8	2004, 65.9%
S1-9	RE, end. $260
S1-10	Total assets $140,000
S1-11	Net cash provided by operations $80,000
S1-12	NCF
E1-13	NCF
E1-14	NCF
E1-15	NCF
E1-16	Telus Total assets $16,987 mil.
E1-17	2. $2,997.8 mil.
E1-18	1. No net loss 2. No net loss 3. Net loss of $1 mil.
E1-19	1. Total assets $840,000
E1-20	NCF
E1-21	2. Total assets $400 mil.
E1-22	1. Net inc. before tax $9 mil.
E1-23	Net cash provided by operations $360 thou.
E1-24	RE, July 31, 2009 $5,900
E1-25	Total assets $44,100
E1-26	Net cash provided by operations $11,100
E1-27	NCF
E1-28	NCF
Q1-29	a
Q1-30	a
Q1-31	c
Q1-32	a
Q1-33	b
Q1-34	d
Q1-35	b
Q1-36	b
Q1-37	d
Q1-38	b

Q1-39	a
Q1-40	c
Q1-41	c
Q1-42	a
Q1-43	c
P1-44A	1. Net inc. $28,000
P1-45A	Chain Inc.
P1-46A	1. Total assets $99,000
P1-47A	1. Total assets $160,000
P1-48A	2. RE, end. $116,000 3. Total assets $180,000
P1-49A	1. Net decrease in cash $41 mil.
P1-50A	1. b. $2.4 thou. g. $5,700 thou. m. $2,600 thou. s. $17,400 thou.
P1-51B	1. Net inc. $0.8 mil.
P1-52B	Groceries Inc. ending assets $3,389 mil.
P1-53B	1. Total assets $114,000
P1-54B	1. Total assets $199,000
P1-55B	2. RE, end. $90,000 3. Total assets $293,000
P1-56B	1. Net increase in cash $34
P1-57B	1. b. $5,850 thou. g. $15,400 thou. m. $3,670 thou. s. $43,490 thou.
DC1	NCF
DC2	2. Net inc. $0; Total assets $70,000
FOF	3. Amt. owed $638,358 thou.
FOA	2. Accounts receivable decrease of $12,676 thou.

Chapter 2

S2-1	NCF
S2-2	a. $12,000 b. $2,000
S2-3	Cash bal. $23,000
S2-4	NCF
S2-5	NCF
S2-6	2. A/P bal. $2,000
S2-7	3. Total assets $500
S2-8	T/B total $398 mil.
S2-9	1. $95,000 4. $38,500
S2-10	NCF
S2-11	NCF
S2-12	Total debits $160,000

E2-13	Total assets $270,000
E2-14	NCF
E2-15	NCF
E2-16	2. a. $68,300 d. $57,300
E2-17	NCF
E2-18	NCF
E2-19	2. T/B total $32,200 3. Total assets $30,700
E2-20	Cash bal. $10,700
E2-21	1. T/B total $71,200 2. Net inc. $14,300
E2-22	T/B total $94,200
E2-23	Cash bal. $4,200
E2-24	1. T/B total $27,500 2. Net income $8,500
E2-25	4. T/B total $14,400
E2-26	a. Cash paid $85,000
E2-27	1. T/B out of balance by $2,200 2. T/B total $118,200
E2-28	NCF
Q2-29	c
Q2-30	d
Q2-31	c
Q2-32	a
Q2-33	d
Q2-34	b
Q2-35	c
Q2-36	a
Q2-37	b
Q2-38	d
Q2-39	d
Q2-40	c
Q2-41	a
Q2-42	b
Q2-43	a
Q2-44	d
Q2-45	c
Q2-46	b
Q2-47	a
Q2-48	b
P2-49A	NCF
P2-50A	2. Net inc. $8,900 4. Total assets 23,700
P2-51A	3. Cash bal. $7,700; A/P bal. $5,000

---

*NCF = No check figure

P2-52A 2. Total assets $56,500

P2-53A 3. Cash bal. $10,800; Amt. owed $35,600

P2-54A 3. T/B total $35,000
4. Net inc. $2,205

P2-55A 3. T/B total $116,800
4. Net inc. $1,400

P2-56B NCF

P2-57B 2. Net inc. $16,400 4. Total assets $73,900

P2-58B 3. Cash bal. $32,500; A/P bal. $5,200

P2-59B 2. Total assets $56,400

P2-60B 3. Cash bal. $26,300; Amt. owed 30,000

P2-61B 3. T/B total $29,300
4. Net inc. $7,290

P2-62B 3. T/B total $174,600

DC1 3. T/B total $27,900
4. Net inc. $6,400

DC2 Net inc. $3,000; Total assets $21,000

FOF Cash $2.7 mil; A/R $7.4 mil.

FOA 3. Net sales increase $116,212,000

Chapter 3

S3-1 a. Net inc. $50 mil.

S3-2 NCF

S3-3 NCF

S3-4 1. Prepaid Rent bal. $2,000

S3-5 3. $20,000

S3-6 Income statement, $42,000,000; Balance sheet $2,000,000

S3-7 3. Interest Payable Dec. 31 bal. $1,500

S3-8 3. Interest Receivable Dec. 31 bal. $1,500

S3-9 NCF

S3-10 Prepaid Rent: a. $6,000 b. $0; Rent Expense: a. $0 b. $6,000.

S3-11 NCF

S3-12 Net inc. $3,500 thou.; Total assets $97,900 thou.

S3-13 Cumulative earnings $4,800 thou.

S3-14 a. 1.24, b. 0.69

S3-15 Trans. 1: Current ratio 1.42; Debt ratio 0.62; Trans. 2: Current ratio 1.29; Debt ratio 0.65

E3-16 NCF

E3-17 a. $10,000 b. $80,000

E3-18 NCF

E3-19 NCF

E3-20 NCF

E3-21 2. Net inc. overstated by $17,200

E3-22 NCF

E3-23 NCF

E3-24 NCF

E3-25 Net inc. $4,000 thou.; Total assets $22,200 thou.

E3-26 Sales rev. $20,900 mil.; Salary exp. $4,200 mil.

E3-27 Seaview B/S: Unearned service rev. 3,000

E3-28 1. B/S: Unearned service rev. $90 mil.

E3-29 Dec. 31, 2009, bal. of R/E $2,700 thou.

E3-30 NCF

E3-31 1. Total assets $39,100
2. Debt ratio Current Yr. 0.48

E3-32 b. Current ratio 1.50

E3-33 7. Net inc. $1,200, Total assets $12,800

E3-34 2008: 1.868; 2009: 2.174

E3-35 a. Net inc. $108,000
b. Total assets $158,000

Q3-36 b

Q3-37 b

Q3-38 a

Q3-39 b

Q3-40 d

Q3-41 d

Q3-42 c

Q3-43 c

Q3-44 c

Q3-45 d

Q3-46 b

Q3-47 c

Q3-48 a

Q3-49 d

Q3-50 c

P3-51A 1. $27 mil. 3. End. rec. $6 mil.

P3-52A 2. Cash basis—loss $700, Accrual basis—inc. $3,300

P3-53A NCF

P3-54A a. Insurance Exp. $3,100
d. Supplies Exp. $6,600

P3-55A 2. Net inc. $6,000, Total assets $54,000

P3-56A 2. Total assets $68,600, Net inc. $4,100

P3-57A 1. Net inc. $39,200, Total assets $47,000

P3-58A 2. March 31, 2009 bal. of RE 47,300

P3-59A 1. Total assets $83,300
2. Current ratio 2009 1.60

P3-60A 2. a. Current ratio 2.37, Debt ratio 0.37

P3-61B 1. $15; 3. End. rec. $5

P3-62B 2. Cash basis—loss $2,700, Accrual basis—inc. $1,100

P3-63B NCF

P3-64B c. Engineer. Supplies Exp. $11,400
f. Insurance Exp. $2,700

P3-65B 2. Net inc. $19,800, Total assets $61,600

P3-66B 2. Total assets $30,400, Net inc. $25,500

P3-67B 1. Net inc. $78,600, Total assets $109,000

P3-68B 2. Dec. 31, 2009 bal. of R/E $16,800

P3-69B 1. Total assets $55,100
2. Current ratio 2009 1.71

P3-70B 2. a. Current ratio 1.727, Debt ratio 0.614

DC1 1. $2,000 3. Current ratio 1.748

DC2 Net inc. $7,000, Total assets $32,000

DC3 1. $260,000 2. $148,000

FOF 5. 2007: Current ratio 2.08; Debt ratio 0.52

FOA 2. $57,684

Chapter 4

S4-1 NCF

S4-2 NCF

S4-3 NCF

S4-4 NCF

S4-5 Adj. bal. $3,005

S4-6 NCF

S4-7 NCF

S4-8 NCF

S4-9 NCF

S4-10 NCF

S4-11 Cash available $4 mil.

S4-12 NCF

E4-13 NCF

E4-14 NCF

E4-15 NCF

E4-16 NCF

E4-17 NCF

E4-18 NCF

E4-19 Adj. bal. $1,150

E4-20 Adj. bal. $1,780

E4-21 NCF

E4-22 NCF

E4-23 NCF

E4-24 New financing needed $(64) mil.

E4-25 NCF

E4-26 7.37%

E4-27 NCF

E4-28 1. Cash available $45 thou.
2. Current ratio 1.60; Debt ratio 0.50

Q4-29 c
Q4-30 b
Q4-31 a
Q4-32 d
Q4-33 d
Q4-34 a
Q4-35 b
Q4-36 c
Q4-37 d
Q4-38 a
Q4-39 d
Q4-40 c

P4-41A NCF
P4-42A NCF
P4-43A 1. Adj. bal. $6,090
P4-44A 1. Adj. bal. $2,242.16
P4-45A NCF
P4-46A 1. (New financing needed) $(3,700) thou.
P4-47A NCF
P4-48B NCF
P4-49B NCF
P4-50B 1. Adj. bal. $5,960
P4-51B 1. Adj. bal. $8,239.00
P4-52B NCF
P4-53B 1. (New financing needed) $(5,490)
P4-54B NCF

DC1 Bookkeeper stole $1,000
DC2 NCF
FOF 1. Adj. bal. $2,687,000
FOA NCF

Chapter 5

S5-1 NCF
S5-2 NCF
S5-3 Dr. Unrealized Loss $6,000
S5-4 NCF
S5-5 2. A/R, net $62,500
S5-6 Dr. Uncollect.-Acct. Exp. $15,000
S5-7 3. A/R, net $167,500
S5-8 d. Uncollect.-Acct. Exp. $12,000
S5-9 3. A/R, net $123,000
S5-10 b. Dr. Cash $93,600
S5-11 3. $102,667
S5-12 c. Dr. Cash $6,480
S5-13 c. Nothing to report d. Interest rev. $200

S5-14 1. 0.95 2. 24 days
S5-15 2. Net inc. $4,424 thou. 3. 1.60

E5-16 3. B/S: Short-term invest. $195,000 I/S: Unrealized gain $10,000
E5-17 I/S: Div. rev. $500; Unrealized (loss) $(500)
E5-18 Unrealized Gain on Invest. $5,000; Gain on Sale of Invest. $1,000
E5-19 NCF
E5-20 A/R, net $91,000
E5-21 3. A/R, net $50,500
E5-22 2. A/R, net $52,800
E5-23 3. A/R, net $224,850
E5-24 B/D Exp. $150; Write offs $148
E5-25 Dec. 31 Dr. Interest Rec. $1,326
E5-26 I/S: Interest rev. $750 for 2008 and $250 for 2009
E5-27 NCF
E5-28 a. 1.89 b. 53 days
E5-29 1. 10 days
E5-30 Expected net inc. w/bank cards $129,800
E5-31 a. $28 mil. b. $11,148 mil.

Q5-32 c
Q5-33 c
Q5-34 d
Q5-35 b
Q5-36 $201,000
Q5-37 d
Q5-38 b
Q5-39 $1,000
Q5-40 c
Q5-41 b
Q5-42 a
Q5-43 a
Q5-44 Dr. Cash $10,450
Q5-45 a
Q5-46 c
Q5-47 c

P5-48A 3. $7,500 4. Div. rev. $260; Unrealized (loss) on invest. $(1,500)
P5-49A NCF
P5-50A 5. I/S: Uncollect.-acct. exp. $380
P5-51A 3. A/R, net: 2009 $221,000; 2008 $207,800
P5-52A 2. Corrected ratios: Current 1.50; Acid-test 0.78 3. Net inc., corrected $82,000
P5-53A 2. 12/31/09 Note rec. $25,000; Interest rec. $82
P5-54A 1. 2009 ratios: a. 1.98 b. 1.14 c. 31 days

P5-55B 3. 40,000 4. Div rev. $1,250; Unrealized gain on invest. $2,500
P5-56B NCF
P5-57B 5. I/S: Uncollect.-acct. exp. $335 thou.
P5-58B 3. A/R, net: 2009 $109,200; 2008 $107,300
P5-59B 2. Corrected ratios: Current 1.39; Acid-test 0.85 3. Net inc., corrected $84,000
P5-60B 2. 12/31/09 Note rec. $20,000; Interest rec. $247
P5-61B 1. 2009 ratios: a. 1.87 b. 0.87 c. 35 days

DC1 Net inc. $223,000
DC2 2009: Days' sales in rec. 26 days; Cash collections $1,456 thou.
FOF 1. $1 2. Customers owed Sun-Rype $7,392 mil. (2007) and $12,676 mil. (2006) 3. Collected $139,067,000
FOA 1. Mullen expected to collect $185,475,000

Chapter 6

S6-1 NCF
S6-2 GP $160,000
S6-3 COGS: Weighted-Avg. $3,760; FIFO $3,740
S6-4 Net inc.: Weighted-Avg. $3,060; FIFO $3,100
S6-5 Inc. tax exp: Weighted-Avg. $551; FIFO $558
S6-6 NCF
S6-7 COGS $421,000
S6-8 GP% 0.32; Invy TO 3.0 times
S6-9 $100,000
S6-10 c. $1,190 mil. d. $510 mil.
S6-11 1. Correct GP $5.7 mil.
2. Correct GP $5.1 mil.
S6-12 NCF

E6-13 2. GP $1,100 thou.
E6-14 3. GP $3,790
E6-15 1. COGS: a. $1,730 b. $1,760 c. $1,710
E6-16 $12.50
E6-17 2. Net inc. $132
E6-18 1. GP: FIFO $0.2 mil.; Weighted-avg. cost $0.6 mil.
E6-19 NCF
E6-20 NCF
E6-21 GP $45,000
E6-22 a. $475 c. $56 f. $2 g. $3; Myers (net loss) $(136) mil.

E6-23 Myers GP% 0.125; Invy. TO 17.9 times

E6-24 GP $16.3 bil.; GP% 29.7; Invy. TO 5.3 times

E6-25 $1,272 mil.

E6-26 $33,000

E6-27 Net inc.: 2009 $65,000; 2008 $69,000

E6-28 NCF

E6-29 1. $150,410 2. $152,750

E6-30 2009 ratios: GP% 0.202, Invy. TO 3.7 times

Q6-31 b

Q6-32 b

Q6-33 d

Q6-34 d

Q6-35 c

Q6-36 a

Q6-37 c

Q6-38 b

Q6-39 a

Q6-40 d

Q6-41 a

Q6-42 d

Q6-43 d

Q6-44 c

Q6-45 a

Q6-46 c

Q6-47 c

P6-48A 3. Net inc. $561,125

P6-49A 2. GP $2,409 3. $2,437

P6-50A 1. COGS: Weighted-Avg. $7,299; FIFO $7,200 3. Net inc. $2,450

P6-51A 1. GP: Weighted-Avg. $60,286; FIFO $60,785

P6-52A NCF

P6-53A 1. Chocolate Treats: GP% 12.5%; Invy. TO 17.9 times

P6-54A 1. $476,500 2. GP $332,000

P6-55A 1. $771,000 2. Net inc. $160,000

P6-56A 1. Net inc. each yr. $2 mil.

P6-57B 3. Net inc. $1,403,436

P6-58B 2. GP $1,173 3. $340

P6-59B 1. COGS: Weighted-Avg. $40,937; FIFO $40,530 3. Net inc. $10,829

P6-60B 1. GP: Weighted-Avg. $291,571; FIFO $299,500

P6-61B NCF

P6-62B 1. 2007: Hewlett-Packard: GP% 24.7%; Invy. TO 8.0 times; Apple: GP% 33.8; Invy. TO 45.4 times

P6-63B 1. $2,442,000 2. GP $3,432,000

P6-64B 1. $802,000 2. $160,000

P6-65B 1. Net inc. (thou): 2009 $150; 2008 $320; 2007 $50

DC1 1. Net inc.: FIFO $370,300, Weighted-avg. $364,168

DC2 NCF

FOF 3. Purchases $91,894 thou.

Chapter 6 Appendix

S6A-1 NCF

S6A-2 2. $90,000 3. GP $50,000

E6A-3 COGS: Specific $2,890; Weighted-avg. $2,863; FIFO $2,800

E6A-4 4. $2,863

P6A-5 2. GP $2,843

P6A-6 2. GP $1,820 thou.

Chapter 7

S7-1 2. Book value $35,865 thou.

S7-2 NCF

S7-3 Building cost $56,000

S7-4 Net inc. overstated

S7-5 2. Book value: SL $21 mil.; DDB $15 mil.

S7-6 Amort.: UOP yr. 5 $2 mil.; DDB yr. 3 $3.6 mil.

S7-7 2. Save $787,500

S7-8 a. € = 1.25 mil. b. € = 3.5 mil. c. € = 2.857143 mil.

S7-9 Amort. Exp. $12,000

S7-10 1. $13,000

S7-11 3. Book value $2,863 mil.

S7-12 1. Goodwill $19.7 mil.

S7-13 1. Net inc. $2,100,000

S7-14 1. Net cash provided by investing $6 mil.

E7-15 Land $283,000 Building $3,820,000

E7-16 Machine 1 $25,000; 2 $41,700; 3 $33,300

E7-17 NCF

E7-18 2. Building, net $737,160

E7-19 NCF

E7-20 I/S: Amort. exp.-building $6,000; B/S: Bldg., net $192,000

E7-21 CCA saves $2,250

E7-22 Amort. yr. 12 $55,833

E7-23 Loss on sale $2,250

E7-24 Cost of new truck $290,800

E7-25 c. Amort. Exp $114,000

E7-26 2. Amort. yr. 3 $200,000

E7-27 NCF

E7-28 1. Cost of goodwill $17,000,000

E7-29 NCF

E7-30 NCF

E7-32 Sale price $20.2 mil.

E7-33 Expected net inc. for 2009 $21,426

E7-34 2012 Effects on: 2. Equip. $50,000 under; 3. Net inc. $50,000 over; 4. Equity $50,000 under

Q7-35 c

Q7-36 a

Q7-37 c

Q7-38 b

Q7-39 c

Q7-40 c

Q7-41 d

Q7-42 b

Q7-43 d

Q7-44 b

Q7-45 b

Q7-46 c

Q7-47 c

Q7-48 d

Q7-49 d

P7-50A 1. Land $296,600; Land Improve. $103,800; Sales Bldg. $1,241,000

P7-51A 2. A/Amort.-Bldg. $105,000; A/Amort.-Equip. $338,000

P7-52A Dec. 31 Amort. Exp.-Motor Carrier Equip. $58,667; Amort. Exp.-Bldgs. $1,050

P7-53A NCF

P7-54A 3. Cash-flow advantage of CCA $7,000

P7-55A 1. Book value $41,497 thou..

P7-56A Part 1. 2. Goodwill $1.2 mil. Part 2. 2. Net inc. $241,800

P7-57A 1. Loss on sale $0.1 mil. 2. Capital assets, net $0.7 mil.

P7-58B 1. Land $143,450; Land Improve. $86,000; Garage $654,000

P7-59B 2. A/Amort.–Bldg. $52,000; A/Amort.–Equip. $437,500

P7-60B Dec. 31 Amort. Exp.–Comm.; Equip. $4,000; Amort. Exp.–Televideo Equip. $1,333

P7-61B NCF

P7-62B 3. Cash-flow advantage of CCA $3,000

P7-63B 1. Book value $2,131 mil.

P7-64B Part 1. 2. Goodwill $5,500; Part 2. 2. Net inc. $930,000

P7-65B 1. Gain on sale $0.02 bil. 2. Capital assets, net $7.26 bil.

DC1 1. Net inc.: On call $142,125; Pagers $128,250

DC2 NCF

FOF	4. Proportion of capital assets used up in 2007 62.8%
FOA	2. Amortization expense $57,684 thou.

Chapter 8

S8-1	3/31/09 Debits include Interest Exp. $250
S8-2	2. Interest exp. $250
S8-3	2. Est. Warranty Pay. bal. $50,000
S8-4	NCF
S8-5	NCF
S8-6	a. $897,500 b. $551,875
S8-7	NCF
S8-8	12/31/09 Interest Exp. $312
S8-9	1. 7/31/10 Bond carry. amt. $88,302
S8-10	3. Interest exp. 2010 $3,934
S8-11	1. $9,400 4. $355.00
S8-12	b. Interest Exp. $375
S8-13	EPS: A $3.11; B $2.25
S8-14	Times-int.-earned ratio 1.81
S8-15	Total liab. $501,000
E8-16	2. Warranty exp. $9,000; Est. warranty pay. $7,600
E8-17	Unearned subscr. rev. $1,000
E8-18	P/R tax exp. $9,000; P/R tax pay. $2,200
E8-19	3. Interest exp. for 2008: $1,250; for 2009: $1,750
E8-20	Income tax pay. $130,000; Income tax exp. $180,000
E8-21	2. Debt ratio 0.76
E8-22	Est. Loss $2,000,000
F8-23	Total current liab. $149,625
E8-24	12/31 Interest Exp. $2,625
E8-25	3. and 4. $316,000
E8-26	1. 12/31/08 Bond carry. amt. $372,660
E8-27	1. 6/30/08 Bond carry. amt. $553,125
E8-28	12/31/11 Bond carry. amt. $300,000
E8-29	1. Carry. amt. $296,850
E8-30	Sobeys ratios: Current 1.00; Debt 0.51; Times-int.-earned 9.49
E8-31	1. EPS: A $6.86; B $3.55
E8-32	Pay off $1 bil.
E8-33	1. Gain on Retirement $37 mil. 3. Debt ratio after 0.68
E8-34	5. 3/15/11 Bond carry. amt. $97,632
Q8-35	a
Q8-36	d

Q8-37	b
Q8-38	b
Q8-39	a
Q8-40	c
Q8-41	a
Q8-42	d
Q8-43	f
Q8-44	a
Q8-45	c
Q8-46	d
Q8-47	Interest Exp. $7,650
Q8-48	Interest Exp. $2,550
Q8-49	e
Q8-50	d
Q8-51	a
Q8-52	c
Q8-53	c
P8-54A	e. Note pay. due in 1 yr. $20,000 Interest pay. $6,000
P8-55A	12/31/08 Warranty Exp. $3,800; 4/30/09 Interest Exp. $1,500
P8-56A	2. Interest pay. $2,917, Bonds pay. $500,000
P8-57A	4. Interest pay. $5,667, Bonds pay., net $194,250
P8-58A	2. $583,800 3. a. $24,900 b. $24,000
P8-59A	2. 12/31/12. 4 Bond carry. amt. $589,001
P8-60A	1. 12/31/10 Bond carry. amt. $474,920 3. Convert. bonds pay., net $284,952
P8-61A	NCF
P8-62A	1. Total current liab. $129,000, Total LT liab. $714,000 3. Times-int.-earned ratio 4.3
P8-63B	e. Note pay. due in 1 yr. $20,000; Interest pay. $2,083
P8-64B	12/31/08 Warranty Exp. $18,000 6/30/09 Interest Exp. $9,000
P8-65B	2. Interest pay. $20,000 Bonds pay. $1,000,000
P8-66B	4. Interest pay. $7,000 Bonds pay., net $289,000
P8-67B	2. $95,200 3. a. $4,600 b. $4,000
P8-68B	2. 12/31/12 Bond carry. amt. $483,439
P8-69B	1. 12/31/09 Bond carry. amt. $314,688 3. Convert. bonds pay., net $157,344
P8-70B	NCF
P8-71B	1. Total current liab. $53,900 Total LT liab. $512,000 3. Times-int.-earned ratio 2.7

DC1	1. Ratios after: Debt 0.93 Times-int.-earned 1.3
DC2	1. EPS: A $4.78 B $4.54; C $4.63
FOF	4. 0.279
FOA	1. Debt ratio 0.36 3. 6.05%

Chapter 9

S9-1	NCF
S9-2	NCF
S9-3	NCF
S9-4	NCF
S9-5	1. $1.80 3. 5,650
S9-6	NCF
S9-7	Total SE $1,246 thou.
S9-8	a. $585 thou. b. $3,011 thou. c. $4,257 thou.
S9-9	Overall, SE decreased $33 mil.
S9-10	RE increased $50,000
S9-11	1. $150,000 4. Pfd. $450,000
S9-12	No effect
S9-13	BV per share $61.60
S9-14	NCF
S9-15	ROA 1.5%; ROE 4.1%
S9-16	NCF
E9-17	NCF
E9-18	2. Total SE $92,500
E9-19	Total SE $143,000
E9-20	Total PIC $1,045,000
E9-21	NCF
E9-22	Overall increase in SE $19,700
E9-23	NCF
E9-24	Total SE $4,285 mil.
E9-25	3. 564 mil. shares 4. $136 mil. 5. $6.00, $1,430
E9-26	2009: Pfd. $24,000; Com. $26,000
E9-27	2. Total SE $8,134,000
E9-28	a. Decrease SE $80 mil.
E9-29	Total SE $2,755 mil.
E9-30	1. $10.40 2. $10.27
E9-31	ROA 0.116; ROE 0.183
E9-32	ROA 0.062; ROE 0.100
E9-33	NCF
E9-34	NCF
E9-35	NCF
E9-36	Div. $1,407 mil.
E9-37	12/31/09 Total equity $63 mil.
Q9-38	c
Q9-39	c
Q9-40	d
Q9-41	c

Q9-42 b

Q9-43 d

Q9-44 a

Q9-45 c

Q9-46 b

Q9-47 b

Q9-48 c

Q9-49 d

Q9-50 b

Q9-51 a

Q9-52 c

Q9-53 a

Q9-54 a

Q9-55 d

Q9-56 b

Q9-57 c

P9-58A NCF

P9-59A 2. Total SE $207,500

P9-60A Total SE $663,000

P9-61A NCF

P9-62A Total SE $7,580,000

P9-63A 4. $22,500

P9-64A 2. Total SE $92,800

P9-65A NCF

P9-66A 1. Total assets $439,000, Total SE $309,000 2. ROA 0.089; ROE 0.125

P9-67A NCF

P9-68B NCF

P9-69B 2. Total SE $323,800

P9-70B Total SE $540,000

P9-71B NCF

P9-72B Total SE $4,106,000

P9-73B 4. $183,700

P9-74B 2. Total SE $121,600

P9-75B NCF

P9-76B 1. Total assets $554,000, Total SE $290,000 2. ROA 0.090; ROE 0.107

DC1 3. Total SE: Plan 1 $220,000 Plan 2 $230,000

DC2 NCF

DC3 3. Debt ratio, adjusted 0.69

FOF 4. ROE 11.7%; ROA 8.2%

FOA NCF

Chapter 10

S10-1 1. Unrealized Loss on Invest. $500 2. LT avail.-for-sale invest. $7,000

S10-2 1. Gain on sale $300

S10-3 3. LT Invest. bal. $42.6 mil.

S10-4 (Loss) on sale $(7.3) mil.

S10-5 NCF

S10-6 NCF

S10-7 2. Cash interest $70,000 4. Interest rev. $68,175

S10-8 c. Dr. Interest Rev. $1,825

S10-9 Nov. 10 FC Transaction Gain $400

S10-10 Aug. 28 FC Transaction Gain $4,000

S10-11 NCF

S10-12 NCF

E10-13 d. Loss on Sale $4,000

E10-14 2. Unrealized Loss $63,560 3. LT investments $242,644

E10-15 Invest. end. bal. $1,055,000

E10-16 Gain on sale $1,645,000

E10-17 2. LT investment, at equity $525,000

E10-18 2. Consol. total SE $321,000

E10-19 3. Interest rec. $350, LT invest. in bonds $18,214

E10-20 1. 4/30 FC Transaction Loss $888

E10-21 FC translation adj. $23,000

E10-22 Net cash (used)-invest. $(11.8) mil.

E10-23 NCF

E10-24 3. c. LT invest., at equity $755,000

E10-25 3. Accum. other comp. (loss) $(40) mil.

Q10-26 a

Q10-27 d

Q10-28 Gain on Sale $8,000

Q10-29 b

Q10-30 c

Q10-31 a

Q10-32 d

Q10-33 b

Q10-34 a

Q10-35 b

Q10-36 d

Q10-37 c

P10-38A 2. B/S: LT invest. at equity $523,300; I/S: Equity-method invest. rev. $178,500; Div. rev. $240; Unrealized (loss) $(2,600)

P10-39A 2. LT Invest. in MSC bal. $659,000

P10-40A 3. Consol. debt ratio 0.898

P10-41A Consol. total assets $907,000

P10-42A 2. B/S: LT invest. in bonds $622,031, I/S: Interest rev. $25,031

P10-43A 1. I/S: FC transaction gain (loss), net $(1900)

P10-44A 1. FC translation adj. $46,000

P10-45A NCF

P10-46B 2. B/S: LT invest., at equity $526,300, I/S: Equity-method invest. rev. $87,500; Div. rev. $750; Unrealized (loss) $(3,300)

P10-47B 2. LT Invest. in Affil. bal. $535,000

P10-48B 3. Consol. debt ratio 0.901

P10-49B Consol. total assets $976,000

P10-50B 2. B/S: LT invest. in bonds $445,304, I/S: Interest rev. $35,304

P10-51B 1. I/S: FC transaction gain $1,500

P10-52B 1. FC translation adj. $230,000

P10-53B NCF

DC1 NCF

DC2 2. Gain on sale $4,200 3. Gain on sale $80,000

FOF NCF

FOA NCF

Chapter 11

S11-1 NCF

S11-2 NCF

S11-3 Net inc. $21,000 thou.

S11-4 EPS for net inc. $1.60

S11-5 Comp. inc. $24,000

S11-6 Est. value $38.00

S11-7 NCF

S11-8 2. Net inc. $82,500, Deferred tax liab. $5,000

S11-9 RE, 12/31/09 $201,000

S11-10 1. $92,000 3. $18,720

E11-11 Net inc. $1,790 thou.

E11-12 1. EPS for net inc. $4.59 2. $57.57

E11-13 NCF

E11-14 3.0%

E11-15 $4.78

E11-16 EPS for net inc. $0.74

E11-17 Net inc. $450,000, Future inc. tax liab. $12,500

E11-18 2. $62,500 3. $52,500

E11-19 RE, 12/31/09 $5=374 mil.

E11-20 Total SE 12/31/08 $2,010,000

E11-21 1. Total SE 12/31/09 $9,446 thou. 2. 44.3% 4. $10.00 per share

E11-22 NCF

Q11-23 b

Q11-24 b

Q11-25 d

Q11-26 a

Q11-27 b

Q11-28 c

Q11-29 c

Q11-30 d

Q11-31 a

Q11-32 b

Q11-33 d

Q11-34 c

P11-35A 1. Net inc. $43,000, EPS for net inc. $1.85

P11-36A RE, 12/31/09 $59,000

P11-37A Est. value $637,500; Current mkt. value $640,000

P11-38A 1. EPS for net inc. $1.41 2. Est. value at 6% $26.17

P11-39A Comp. inc. $101,870, EPS for net inc. $2.49

P11-40A 1. $120,000 2. Cr. Future Inc. Tax Liab. $3,300 3. Net inc. $87,100

P11-41A 1. $806 mil. 2. $5 per share 3. $10.00 per share 4. 7.8%

P11-42B 1. Net inc. $112,500, EPS for net inc. $4.27

P11-43B RE, 4/30/09 $191,500

P11-44B Est. value $1,108,333, Current mkt. value $1,200,000

P11-45B 1. EPS for net inc. $0.92 2. Est. value at 7% $15.71

P11-46B Comp. inc. $78,400, EPS for net inc. $1.37

P11-47B 1. $185,000 2. Cr. Future Inc. Tax Liab. $3,750 3. Net inc. $150,000

P11-48B 1. $537 mil. 2. $3 per share 3. $3.77 per share 4. 8%

DC1 Use $0.59

DC2 NCF

FOF 2. Est. value at 5% $8.60

FOA 3. Est. value at 6% $31.00

Chapter 12

S12-1 NCF

S12-2 NCF

S12-3 Net cash-oper. $70,000

S12-4 NCF

S12-5 Net cash-oper. $54,000

S12-6 Net cash-oper. $54,000; Net increase in cash $53,000

S12-7 a. $60,000 b. $20,000

S12-8 a. New borrowing $10,000 b. Issuance $8,000 c. Dividends $146,000

S12-9 Net cash-oper. $110,000; Net (decrease) in cash $(20,000)

S12-10 Net cash-oper. $13,000

S12-11 Net cash-oper. $13,000; Net increase in cash $12,000

S12-12 a. $699,000 b. $326,000

S12-13 a. $68,000 b. $134,000

E12-14 NCF

E12-15 NCF

E12-16 NCF

E12-17 Net cash-oper. $11,000

E12-18 Net cash-oper. $48,000

E12-19 1. Net cash-oper. $99,000, Net increase in cash $27,000, Noncash inv. and fin. $50,000

E12-20 NCF

E12-21 a. $500 b. $11,000

E12-22 NCF

E12-23 NCF

E12-24 Net cash-oper. $21,000

E12-25 NCF

E12-26 1. Net cash-oper. $102,000; Net increase in cash $29,000

E12-27 a. $50,000 b. $113,000

E12-28 (in thousands) a. $24,637 b. $18,134 c. $3,576 d. $530 e. $73 f. $1,294

E12-29 1. Gain $120 thou. 2. $240 thou.

Q12-30 c

Q12-31 a

Q12-32 b

Q12-33 b

Q12-34 d

Q12-35 c

Q12-36 c

Q12-37 financing; operating

Q12-38 c

Q12-39 d

Q12-40 b

Q12-41 a

Q12-42 c

Q12-43 a

Q12-44 a

Q12-45 a

Q12-46 d

Q12-47 d

Q12-48 a

Q12-49 a

P12-50A NCF

P12-51A 1. Net inc. $51,667 2. Total assets $396,667 3. Net cash-oper. $(49,000); Net increase in cash $90,000

P12-52A Net cash-oper. $63,200 Net increase in cash $16,000 Noncash inv. and fin. $160,000

P12-53A 1. Net cash-oper. $76,900 Net (decrease) in cash $(4,100); Noncash inv. and fin. $101,000

P12-54A 1. Net cash-oper. $80,000 Net increase in cash $12,300

P12-55A 1. Net cash-oper. $95,700 Net (decrease) in cash $(2,700) Noncash inv. and fin. $79,400

P12-56A 1. Net inc. $51,667 2. Total assets $396,667 3. Net cash-oper. $(49,000); Net increase in cash $90,000

P12-57A Net cash-oper. $80,000 Net increase in cash $12,300

P12-58A 1. Net cash-oper. $55,800 Net (decrease) in cash $(2,000) Noncash inv. and fin. $99,100

P12-59A 1. Net cash-oper. $73,200 Net increase in cash $20,000 Noncash inv. and fin. $19,000

P12-60B NCF

P12-61B 1. Net inc. $157,333 2. Total assets $340,333 3. Net cash-oper. $81,000; Net increase in cash $191,000

P12-62B Net cash-oper. $74,500 Net (decrease) in cash $(5,700) Noncash inv. and fin. $290,4000

P12-63B 1. Net cash-oper. $68,700 Net increase in cash $16,300 Noncash inv. and fin. $30,000

P12-64B 1. Net cash-oper. $90,600 Net increase in cash $13,100

P12-65B 1. Net cash-oper. $30,000 Net increase in cash $7,600 Noncash inv. and fin. $142,800

P12-66B 1. Net inc. $157,333 2. Total assets $340,333 3. Net cash-oper. $81,000; Net increase in cash $191,000

P12-67B 1. Net cash-oper. $90,600 Net increase in cash $13,100

P12-68B 1. Net cash-oper. $77,200 Net (decrease) in cash $(4,600) Noncash inv. and fin. $83,200

P12-69B 1. Net cash-oper. $40,400 Net increase in cash $4,100 Noncash inv. and fin. $48,300

DC1 (in thousands) 1. Net cash-oper. $132, Net (decrease) in cash $(46)

DC2 NCF

FOF 2. a. $140,600 thou. b. $125,996 thou.

FOA 4. BV sold $17,175 thou. 5. $175,639 thou.

Chapter 13

S13-1 2009 Net inc. (increase) 9.2%

S13-2 2009 Sales trend 107%

S13-3 2009 Cash 2.1%

S13-4 Net inc. % Porterfield 6.2%

S13-5 2007 Current ratio 1.21

S13-6 1. 2008: 0.41; 2007: 0.40

S13-7 a. 11 times b. 10.9 days

S13-8 1. 0.533 2. 8.0

S13-9 a. 2.7% b. 8.1% c. 14.7%

S13-10 1. EPS $4.85; P/E 16

S13-11 a. $3,855 thou. d. $873 thou.

S13-12 a. $562 thou. d. $3,768 thou.
e. $1,294 thou.

S13-13 $570 thou.

E13-14 2008 WC (decrease) (5.4)%

E13-15 Net inc. decreased 5.8%

E13-16 Yr. 4 Net inc. trend 147%

E13-17 Current assets 24.6%,
Total liab. 41.7%

E13-18 Net inc. 20% both years

E13-19 NCF

E13-20 a. 1.67 b. 0.83 c. 4.4 d. 9.5
e. 38 days

E13-21 2009 ratios: a. 2.07 b. 0.91
c. 0.47 d. 4.13

E13-22 2008 ratios: a. 0.098 b. 0.132
c. 0.151 d. $0.67

E13-23 2007 ratios: a. 17.3 b. 0.014
c. $6.00

E13-24 Amazon $100 mil.

E13-25 Total assets $20,000 mil. Current
liab. $6,800 mil.

E13-26 Sales $6,400 mil. Net inc. $720
mil.

Q13-27 b

Q13-28 c

Q13-29 a

Q13-30 b

Q13-31 d

Q13-32 c

Q13-33 b

Q13-34 c

Q13-35 a

Q13-36 a

Q13-37 d

Q13-38 d

P13-39A 1. 2009 trends: Net sales 186%;
Net inc. 231%; Total assets 155%
2. 2009 0.101

P13-40A 1. Net inc. 10.7%, Current assets
77.1%

P13-41A NCF

P13-42A 1. Current ratio before 1.74
2. a. Current ratio after 1.84

P13-43A 1. 2009 ratios: a. 1.41 b. 2.24
c. 4.32 d. 0.173 g. 11.9

P13-44A 1. Video: a. 060 b. 2.16 c. 100
d. 0.68 f. 0.196 2. Video $30,000

P13-45A NCF

P13-46B 1. 2009 trends: Net rev. 134%;
Net inc. 205%; SE 147%
2. 2009 0.111

P13-47B Net inc. 5.3%, Current assets
75.0%

P13-48B NCF

P13-49B 1. Current ratio before 1.54
2. a. Current ratio after 1.44

P13-50B 1. 2009 ratios a. 2.04 b. 2.78
c. 10.8 d. 0.315 f. 16

P13-51B 1. Thrifty Nickel: a. 0.78 b. 2.32
c. 40 d. 0.41 h. 10.6
2. Thrifty Nickel $34,000

P13-52B NCF

DC1 NCF

DC2 NCF

DC3 NCF

FOF 2007 trend: Total rev. 125%; Net
earnings 90%; Net cash-oper. 111%

FOA 2007 trend: Net (loss) (12)%

Glossary

Accelerated amortization method An amortization method that writes off a relatively larger amount of the asset's cost nearer the start of its useful life than the straight-line method does.

Account The detailed record of the changes that have occurred in a particular asset, liability, or shareholders' equity during a period. The basic summary device of accounting.

Account format A balance-sheet format that lists assets on the left, and liabilities and shareholders' equity on the right.

Account payable A liability for goods and services purchased on credit and backed by the general reputation and credit standing of the debtor.

Accounting The information system that measures business activities, processes that information into reports and financial statements, and communicates the results to decision makers.

Accounting equation The most basic tool of accounting: Assets = Liabilities + Owners' Equity.

Accounts receivable An asset, amounts due from customers to whom a business has sold goods or services.

Accounts receivable turnover Measures a company's ability to collect cash from credit customers. Net sales divided by average net accounts receivable.

Accrual An expense or a revenue that occurs before the business pays or receives cash. An accrual is the opposite of a deferral.

Accrual accounting Accounting that records the impact of a business event as it occurs, regardless of whether the transaction affected cash.

Accrued expense An expense incurred but not yet paid in cash.

Accrued liability A liability incurred but not yet paid by the company.

Accrued revenue A revenue that has been earned but not yet received in cash.

Accumulated amortization The cumulative sum of all amortization expense from the date of acquiring a capital asset.

Acid-test ratio Ratio of the sum of cash plus short-term investments plus net current receivables to total current liabilities. Tells whether the entity can pay all its current liabilities if they come due immediately. Also called the *quick ratio*.

Adjusted trial balance A list of all the ledger accounts with their adjusted balances.

Adverse opinion An audit opinion stating that the financial statements are unreliable.

Aging of accounts receivable A way to estimate bad debts by analyzing individual accounts receivable according to the length of time they have been receivable from the customer. Also called *balance-sheet approach* because it focuses on accounts receivable.

Allowance for Doubtful Accounts Also called *Allowance for Uncollectible Accounts*.

Allowance for Uncollectible Accounts A contra account, related to accounts receivable, that holds the estimated amount of collection losses. Another name for *Allowance for Doubtful Accounts*.

Allowance method A method of recording collection losses based on estimates of how much money the business will not collect from its customers.

Amortizable cost The cost of a capital asset minus its estimated residual value.

Amortization Allocation of the cost of a plant asset over its useful life.

Asset An economic resource that is expected to produce a benefit in the future.

Audit A periodic examination of a company's financial statements and the accounting systems, controls, and records that produce them.

Available-for-sale investment All investments held to earn dividend revenue and/or capital appreciation.

Bad-debt expense Another name for *uncollectible-account expense*.

Balance sheet List of an entity's assets, liabilities, and owners' equity as of a specific date. Also called the *statement of financial position*.

Bank collection Collection of money by the bank on behalf of a depositor.

Bank reconciliation A document explaining the reasons for the difference between a depositor's records and the bank's records about the depositor's bank account.

Bank statement Document showing the beginning and ending balances of a particular bank account and listing the month's transactions that affected the account.

Benchmarking The practice of comparing a company to a standard set by other companies, with a view toward improvement.

Board of directors Group elected by the shareholders to set policy for a corporation and to appoint its officers.

Bond market price The bond market price is the price investors are willing to pay for the bond. It is equal to the present value of the principal payment plus the present value of the interest payments.

Bonds payable Groups of notes payable (bonds) issued to multiple lenders called *bondholders*.

Book value (of a plant asset) The asset's cost minus accumulated amortization.

Book value (of a share) Amount of owners' equity on the company's books for each share of its stock.

Brand name A distinctive identification of a product or service. See *trademark* or *trade name*.

Budget A quantitative expression of a plan that helps managers coordinate the entity's activities.

Bylaws Constitution for governing a corporation.

Callable bonds Bonds that may be paid at a specified price whenever the issuer wants.

Capital Another name for the *owners' equity* of a business.

Capital asset Another name for *property, plant, and equipment*.

Capital charge The amount that shareholders and lenders charge a company for the use of their money. Calculated as (Notes payable + Current maturities of long-term debt + Long-term debt + Shareholders' equity) × Cost of capital.

Capital cost allowance (CCA) Amortization allowed for income tax purposes by Canada Revenue Agency; the rates allowed are called *capital cost allowance rates*.

Capital expenditure Expenditure that increases an asset's capacity or efficiency or extends its useful life. Capital expenditures are debited to an asset account. Also called *betterments*.

Capital lease Lease agreement that meets any one of four criteria: (1) The lease transfers title of the leased asset to the lessee at the end of the lease term. (2) The lease contains a bargain purchase option. (3) The lease term is 75% or more of the estimated useful life of the leased asset. (4) The present value of the lease payments is 90% or more of the market value of the leased asset.

Cash Money and any medium of exchange that a bank accepts at face value.

Cash equivalents Highly liquid short-term investments that can be converted into cash immediately.

Cash flow statement Reports cash receipts and cash payments classified according to the entity's major activities: operating, investing, and financing.

Cash flows Cash receipts and cash payments (disbursements).

Cash-basis accounting Accounting that records only transactions in which cash is received or paid.

Chairperson Elected by a corporation's board of directors, usually the most powerful person in the corporation.

Chart of accounts List of all of a company's accounts and their account numbers.

Cheque Document instructing a bank to pay the designated person or business the specified amount of money.

Classified balance sheet A balance sheet that shows current assets separate from long-term assets, and current liabilities separate from long-term liabilities.

Clean opinion An audit opinion stating that the financial statements are reliable. Also called an *unqualified opinion*.

Closing entries Entries that transfer the revenue, expense, and dividend balances from these respective accounts to the Retained Earnings account.

Closing the books The process of preparing the accounts to begin recording the next period's transactions. Closing the accounts consists of journalizing and posting the closing entries to set the balances of the revenue, expense, and dividends accounts to zero. Also called *closing the accounts*.

Common shares The most basic form of share capital. Common shareholders own a corporation.

Common-size statement A financial statement that reports only percentages (no dollar amounts).

Comprehensive income A company's change in total shareholders' equity from all sources other than from the owners of the business.

Conservatism The accounting concept by which the least favourable figures are presented in the financial statements.

Consistency principle A business must use the same accounting methods and procedures from period to period.

Consolidated statements Financial statements of the parent company plus those of majority-owned subsidiaries as if the combination were a single legal entity.

Contra account An account that always has a companion account and whose normal balance is opposite that of the companion account.

Contract interest rate Interest rate that determines the amount of cash interest the borrower pays and the investor receives each year. Also called *coupon interest rate* or *stated interest rate*.

Contributed capital The amount of shareholders' equity that shareholders have contributed to the corporation.

Controller The chief accounting officer of a business who accounts for cash.

Controlling interest Ownership of more than 50% of an investee company's voting shares.

Convertible bonds (or **notes**) Bonds (or notes) that may be converted into the issuing company's common shares at the investor's option.

Copyright Exclusive right to reproduce and sell a book, musical composition, film, other work of art, or computer program. Issued by the federal government, copyrights extend fifty years beyond the author's life.

Corporation A business owned by shareholders. A corporation is a legal entity,

an "artificial person" in the eyes of the law.

Cost of capital A weighted average of the returns demanded by the company's shareholders and lenders.

Cost of goods sold Cost of the inventory the business has sold to customers. Also called *cost of sales*.

Cost principle Principle that states that acquired assets and services should be recorded at their actual historical cost.

Cost-of-goods-sold model Brings together all the inventory data for the entire accounting period: Beginning inventory + Purchases = Goods available for sale. Then, Goods available for sale − Ending inventory = Cost of goods sold.

Credit The right side of an account.

Creditor The party to whom money is owed.

Cumulative preferred shares Preferred shares whose owners must receive all dividends in arrears before the corporation can pay dividends to the common shareholders.

Current asset An asset that is expected to be converted to cash, sold, or consumed during the next 12 months, or within the business's normal operating cycle if longer than a year.

Current installment of long-term debt The amount of the principal that is payable within one year. Also called *current portion of long-term debt*.

Current liability A debt due to be paid within one year or within the entity's operating cycle if the cycle is longer than a year.

Current ratio Current assets divided by current liabilities. Measures a company's ability to pay current liabilities with current assets.

Days' sales in receivables Ratio of average net accounts receivable to one day's sale. Indicates how many days' sales remain in Accounts Receivable awaiting collection. Also called the *collection period*.

Debentures Unsecured bonds—bonds backed only by the good faith of the borrower.

Debit The left side of an account.

Debt ratio Ratio of total liabilities to total assets. States the proportion of a company's assets that is financed with debt.

Debtor The party who owes money.

Deferral An adjustment for which the business paid or received cash in advance. Examples include prepaid rent, prepaid insurance, and supplies.

Deficit Debit balance in the Retained Earnings account.

Denial of opinion An audit opinion stating that the auditor was unable to reach a professional opinion regarding the quality of the financial statements.

Deposit in transit A deposit recorded by the company but not yet by its bank.

Direct method Format of the operating activities section of the cash flow statement; lists the major categories of operating cash receipts (collections from customers and receipts of interest and dividends) and cash disbursements (payments to suppliers, to employees, for interest, and income taxes).

Direct write-off method A method of accounting for bad debts in which the company waits until the credit department decides that a customer's account receivable is uncollectible and then debits Uncollectible-Account Expense and credits the customer's Account Receivable.

Disclosure principle A business's financial statements must report enough information for outsiders to make knowledgeable decisions about the business. The company should report relevant, reliable, and comparable information about its economic affairs.

Discount (on a bond) Excess of a bond's maturity (par value) over its issue price.

Dividend Distributions (usually cash) by a corporation to its shareholders.

Dividend yield Ratio of dividends per share to the share's market price per share. Tells the percentage of a share's market value that the company returns to shareholders as dividends.

Double taxation Corporations pay income taxes on corporate income. Then, the shareholders pay personal income tax on the cash dividends that they receive from corporations. Canada's tax laws attempt to minimize double taxation.

Double-declining-balance (DDB) method An accelerated amortization method that computes annual amortization by multiplying the asset's decreasing book value by a constant percentage, which is two times the straight-line rate.

Double-entry system An accounting system that uses debits and credits to record the dual effects of each business transaction.

Doubtful-account expense Another name for *uncollectible-account expense.*

Earnings per share (EPS) Amount of a company's net income per share of its outstanding common shares.

Economic value added (EVA) Used to evaluate a company's operating performance. EVA combines the concepts of accounting income and corporate finance to measure whether the company's operations have increased shareholder wealth. EVA = Net income + Interest expense − Capital charge.

Effective interest rate Another name for *market interest rate.*

Efficient capital market A capital market in which market prices fully reflect all information available to the public.

Electronic funds transfer (EFT) System that transfers cash by electronic communication rather than by paper documents.

Entity An organization or a section of an organization that, for accounting purposes, stands apart from other organizations or sections of an organization or individuals as a separate economic unit.

Equity method The method used to account for investments in which the investor has 20–50% of the investee's voting shares and can significantly influence the decisions of the investee.

Estimated residual value Expected cash value of an asset at the end of its useful life. Also called *scrap value* or *salvage value.*

Estimated useful life Length of a service that a business expects to get from an asset. May be expressed in years, units of output, kilometres, or other measures.

Expense Decrease in retained earnings that results from operations; the cost of doing business; opposite of revenues.

Extraordinary gains and losses Also called *extraordinary items,* these gains and losses are both unusual for the company and infrequent and are not determined by management.

Extraordinary item A gain or loss that is both unusual for the company and infrequent.

Face value of bond The principal amount payable by the issuer. Also called *maturity value.*

Fair value The amount that a business could sell an asset for, or the amount that a business could pay to settle a liability.

FIFO (first-in, first-out) method Inventory costing method by which the first costs into inventory are the first costs out to cost of goods sold. Ending inventory is based on the costs of the most recent purchases.

Financial accounting The branch of accounting that provides information to people outside the firm.

Financial statements Business documents that report financial information about a business entity to decision makers.

Financing activities Activities that obtain from investors and creditors the cash needed to launch and sustain the business; a section of the cash flow statement.

Fixed asset Another name for *property, plant, and equipment.*

Foreign-currency exchange rate The measure of one country's currency against another country's currency.

Foreign-currency translation adjustment The balancing figure that brings the dollar amount of the total liabilities and shareholders' equity of the foreign subsidiary into agreement with the dollar amount of its total assets.

Franchises and licences Privileges granted by a private business or a government to sell a product or service in accordance with specified conditions.

Free cash flow The amount of cash available from operations after paying for planned investments in plant, equipment, and other long-term assets.

Generally accepted accounting principles (GAAP) Accounting guidelines, formulated by the Canadian Institute of Chartered Accountants' (CICA) Accounting Standards Board, that govern how accountanting is practised.

Going-concern concept Holds that the entity will remain in operation for the foreseeable future.

Goodwill Excess of the cost of an acquired company over the sum of the market values of its net assets (assets minus liabilities).

Gross margin Sales revenue minus cost of goods sold.

Gross margin method A way to estimate inventory based on a rearrangement of the cost-of-goods-sold model: Beginning inventory + Net purchases = Goods available for sale − Cost of goods sold = Ending inventory.

Gross margin percentage Gross margin divided by net sales revenue.

Hedging To protect oneself from losing money in one transaction by engaging in a counterbalancing transaction.

Held-to-maturity investments Bonds and notes that an investor intends to hold until maturity.

Horizontal analysis Study of percentage changes over time comparative financial statements.

Imprest system A way to account for petty cash by maintaining a constant balance in the petty cash account, supported by the fund (cash plus payment slips) totalling the same amount.

Income statement A financial statement listing an entity's revenues, expenses, and net income or net loss for a specific period. Also called the *statement of operations* or the *statement of earnings*.

Indirect method Format of the operating activities section of the cash flow statement; starts with net income and reconciles to cash flows from operating activities. Also called the *reconciliation method*.

Intangible asset An asset with no physical form, a special right to current and expected future benefits.

Interest The borrower's cost of renting money from a lender. Interest is revenue for the lender, expense for the borrower.

Interest-coverage ratio Another name for the *times-interest-earned ratio*.

Internal control Organizational plan and all the related measures adopted by an entity to optimize the use of resources, prevent and detect error and fraud, safeguard assets and records, and ensure accurate and reliable accounting records.

Inventory The merchandise that a company sells; also includes raw materials for use in a manufacturing process.

Inventory turnover Ratio of cost of goods sold to average inventory. Indicates how rapidly inventory is sold.

Investing activities Activities that increase or decrease the long-term assets available to the business; a section of the cash flow statement.

Investment capitalization rate An earnings rate used to estimate the value of an investment in the share capital of another company.

Journal The chronological accounting record of an entity's transactions.

Lease Rental agreement in which the tenant (lessee) agrees to make rent payments to the property owner (lessor) in exchange for the use of the asset.

Ledger The book of accounts and their balances.

Lessee Tenant in a lease agreement.

Lessor Property owner in a lease agreement.

Leverage Earning more income on borrowed money than the related interest expense, thereby increasing the earnings for the owners of the business. Another name for *trading on the equity*.

Liability An economic obligation (a debt) payable to an individual or an organization outside the entity.

LIFO (last-in, first-out) method Inventory costing method by which the last costs into inventory are the first costs out to cost of goods sold. This method leaves the oldest costs—those of beginning inventory and the earliest purchases of the period—in ending inventory.

Limited liability No personal obligation of a shareholder for corporation debts. A shareholder can lose no more on an investment in a corporation's shares than the cost of the investment.

Liquidity Measure of how quickly an item can be converted to cash.

Long-term asset An asset that is not a current asset.

Long-term debt A liability that falls due beyond one year from the date of the financial statements.

Long-term investment Any investment that does not meet the criteria of a short-term investment; any investment that the investor expects to hold for longer than a year or that is not readily marketable.

Long-term liability A liability that is not a current liability.

Lower-of-cost-or-market (LCM) rule Requires that an asset be reported in the financial statements at whichever is lower—its historical cost or its market value (current replacement cost for inventory).

Majority interest Ownership of more than 50% of an investee company's voting shares.

Management accounting The branch of accounting that generates information for the internal decision makers of a business, such as top executives.

Marketable security Investment that a company plans to hold for one year or less. Also called *short-term investments*.

Market interest rate Interest rate that investors demand for loaning their money. Also called *effective interest rate*.

Market value (of a share) Price for which a person could buy or sell a share of stock.

Matching principle The basis for recording expenses. Directs accountants to identify all expenses incurred during the period, to measure the expenses, and to match them against the revenues earned during that same period.

Maturity date The date on which a debt instrument must be paid.

Maturity value The sum of principal and interest on a note.

Minority interest A subsidiary company's equity that is held by shareholders other than the parent company.

Multi-step income statement An income statement that contains subtotals to highlight important relationships between revenues and expenses.

Net assets Another name for *owners' equity*.

Net earnings Another name for *net income*.

Net income Excess of total revenues over total expenses. Also called *net earnings* or *net profit*.

Net loss Excess of total expenses over total revenues.

Net profit Another name for *net income*.

Nonsufficient funds (NSF) cheque A cheque for which the payer's bank account has insufficient money to pay the cheque. NSF cheques are cash receipts that turn out to be worthless.

No-stated-value shares Shares of stock that do not have a value assigned to them by the articles of incorporation.

Note payable A liability evidenced by a written promise to make a future payment.

Objectivity principle See *reliability principle*.

Operating activities Activity that creates revenue or expense in the entity's major line of business; a section of the cash flow statement. Operating activities affect the income statement.

Operating cycle Time span during which cash is paid for goods and services that are sold to customers and the business receives payment.

Operating lease Usually a short-term or cancellable rental agreement.

Outstanding cheque A cheque issued by the company and recorded on its books but not yet paid by its bank.

Outstanding shares Shares in the hands of shareholders.

Owners' equity The claim of the owners of a business to the assets of the business. Also called *capital* for proprietorships and partnerships and *shareholders' equity* for corporations. Sometimes called *net assets*.

Parent company An investor company that owns more than 50% of the voting shares of a subsidiary company.

Partnership An association of two or more persons who co-own a business.

Patent A federal government grant giving the holder the exclusive right for twenty years to produce and sell an invention.

Payroll Employee compensation, a major expense of many businesses.

Pension Employee compensation that will be received during retirement.

Percentage-of-sales method Computes uncollectible-account expense as a percentage of net sales. Also called the *income statement approach* because it focuses on the amount of expense to be reported on the income statement.

Periodic inventory system An inventory system in which the business does not keep a continuous record of the inventory on hand. Instead, at the end of the period, the business makes a physical count of the inventory on hand and applies the appropriate unit costs to determine the cost of the ending inventory.

Permanent account Assets, liabilities, and shareholders' equity.

Perpetual inventory system An inventory system in which the business keeps a continuous record for each inventory item to show the inventory on hand at all times.

Petty cash Fund containing a small amount of cash that is used to pay minor expenditures.

Plant assets Another name for *property, plant, and equipment*.

Posting Copying amounts from the journal to the ledger.

Preferred shares Shares that give their owners certain advantages, such as the priority to receive dividends before the common shareholders and the priority to receive assets before the

common shareholders if the corporation liquidates.

Premium (on a bond) Excess of a bond's issue price over its maturity (par) value.

Prepaid expense A category of miscellaneous assets that typically expire or get used up in the near future. Examples include prepaid rent, prepaid insurance, and supplies.

Present value Amount a person would invest now to receive a greater amount at a future date.

President Chief operating officer in charge of managing the day-to-day operations of a corporation.

Pretax accounting income Income before tax on the income statement.

Price/earnings ratio Ratio of the market price of a common share to the company's earnings per share. Measures the value that the stock market places on $1 of a company's earnings.

Principal The amount borrowed by a debtor and lent by a creditor.

Prior-period adjustment A correction to beginning balance of retained earnings for an error of an earlier period.

Private company Company that does not offer its securities for sale to the general public.

Property, plant, and equipment Long-lived assets, such as land, buildings, and equipment, used in the operation of the business. Also called *plant assets*, *fixed assets*, or *tangible capital assets*.

Proprietorship A business with a single owner.

Public company Company that offers its securities for sale to the general public.

Purchase allowance A decrease in the cost of purchases because the seller has granted the buyer a subtraction (an allowance) from the amount owed.

Purchase discount A decrease in the cost of purchases earned by making an early payment to the vendor.

Purchase return A decrease in the cost of purchases because the buyer returned the goods to the seller.

Qualified opinion An audit opinion stating that the financial statements are reliable, except for one or more items for which the opinion is said to be qualified.

Quick ratio Another name for the *acid-test ratio*.

Rate of return on common shareholders' equity Net income minus preferred dividends, divided by average common shareholders' equity. A measure of profitability. Also called *return on equity*.

Rate of return on net sales Ratio of net income to net sales. A measure of profitability. Also called *return on sales*.

Rate of return on total assets Net income plus interest expense, divided by average total assets. This ratio measures a company's success in using its assets to earn income for the persons who finance the business. Also called *return on assets*.

Receivables Monetary claims against a business or an individual, acquired mainly by selling goods and services, and by lending money.

Reliability principle The accounting principle that ensures that accounting records and statements are based on the most objective data available. Also called the *objectivity principle*.

Report format A balance-sheet format that lists assets at the top, followed by liabilities and shareholders' equity below.

Repurchased shares A corporation's own shares that it has issued and later reacquired.

Retained earnings The amount of shareholders' equity that the corporation has earned through profitable operation of the business and has not given back to shareholders.

Return on assets (ROA). See *rate of return on total assets*.

Return on equity (ROE). See *rate of return on common shareholders' equity*.

Revenue principle The basis for recording revenues; tells accountants when to record revenue and the amount of revenue to record.

Revenue Increase in retained earnings from delivering goods or services to customers or clients.

Segment of the business An identifiable division of a company.

Serial bonds Bonds that mature in installments over a period of time.

Shareholder A person who owns shares of stock in a corporation.

Shareholders' equity The shareholders' ownership interest in the assets of a corporation. Also called *owners' equity*.

Short-term investment Investment that a company plans to hold for one year or less. Also called *marketable securities.*

Short-term note payable Note payable due within one year.

Single-step income statement An income statement that lists all the revenues together under a heading such as Revenues, or Revenues and Gains. Expenses appear in a separate category called Expenses, or Expenses and Losses. There is only one step in arriving at net income.

Specific identification method See *specific-unit-cost method.*

Specific-unit-cost method Inventory cost method based on the specific cost of particular units of inventory. Also called the *specific identification method.*

Stable-monetary-unit concept The reason for ignoring the effect of inflation in the accounting records, based on the assumption that the dollar's purchasing power is relatively stable.

Stated interest rate Interest rate that determines the amount of cash interest the borrower pays and the investor receives each year. Another name for the *coupon rate* or *contract interest rate.*

Stated value Arbitrary amount assigned by a company to a share of its stock at the time of issue.

Statement of earnings Another name for the *income statement.*

Statement of financial position Another name for the *balance sheet.*

Statement of operations Another name for the *income statement.*

Statement of retained earnings Summary of the changes in the retained earnings of a corporation during a specific period.

Statement of shareholders' equity Reports the changes in all categories of shareholders' equity during the period.

Stock Shares into which the owners' equity of a corporation is divided.

Stock dividend A proportional distribution by a corporation of its own stock to its shareholders.

Stock split An increase in the number of authorized, issued, and outstanding shares of stock coupled with a proportionate reduction in the share's book value.

Straight-line (SL) method Amortization method in which an equal amount of amortization expense is assigned to each year (or period) of asset use.

Strong currency A currency whose exchange rate is rising relative to other nations' currencies.

Subsidiary company An investee company in which a parent company owns more than 50% of the voting shares.

Taxable income The basis for computing the amount of tax to pay the government.

Temporary account Revenues and expenses related to a limited period.

Term The length of time from inception to maturity.

Term bonds Bonds that all mature at the same time for a particular issue.

Time-period concept Ensures that accounting information is reported at regular intervals.

Times-interest-earned ratio Ratio of income from operations to interest expense. Measures the number of times that operating income can cover interest expense. Also called *interest-coverage ratio.*

Trademark, trade name A distinctive identification of a product or service. Also called a *brand name.*

Trading investment Share or bond investments that are to be sold in the near future with the intent of generating profits on the sale.

Trading on the equity Earning more income on borrowed money than the related interest expense, thereby increasing the earnings for the owners of the business. Also called *leverage.*

Transaction An event that has a financial impact on the business and can be measured reliably.

Treasurer In a large company, the person in charge of managing cash.

Trend percentages A form of horizontal analysis that indicates the direction a business is taking.

Trial balance A list of all the ledger accounts with their balances.

Uncollectible-account expense Cost to the seller of extending credit. Arises from the failure to collect from credit customers. Also called *doubtful-account expense* or *bad-debt expense.*

Underwriter Organization that purchases the bonds from an issuing company and resells them to its clients or sells the bonds for a commission, agreeing to buy all unsold bonds.

Unearned revenue An obligation arising from receiving cash before providing a service.

Units-of-production (UOP) method Amortization method by which a fixed amount of amortization is assigned to each unit of output produced by the plant asset.

Unqualified opinion Another name for *clean opinion.*

Vertical analysis Analysis of a financial statement that reveals the relationship of each statement item to a specified base, which is the 100% figure.

Weak currency A currency whose exchange rate is falling relative to other nations' currencies.

Weighted-average-cost method Inventory costing method based on the weighted average cost of inventory during the period. Weighted-average cost is determined by dividing the cost of goods available for sale by the number of units available. Also called the *average-cost method.*

Working capital Current assets minus current liabilities; measures a business's ability to meet its short-term obligations with its current assets.

Index